THE AMERICAN LANGUAGE

FOURTH EDITION *corrected, enlarged, and rewritten*

THE

American Language

AN INQUIRY
INTO THE DEVELOPMENT OF ENGLISH
IN THE UNITED STATES

BY

H. L. Mencken

1936

ALFRED A. KNOPF

NEW YORK

PUBLISHED *March*, 1919

REVISED EDITION *published December*, 1921

THIRD EDITION *again revised published February*, 1923

FOURTH EDITION *corrected, enlarged, and rewritten*

published April, 1936

MANUFACTURED IN THE UNITED STATES OF AMERICA

PREFACE

TO THE FOURTH EDITION

The first edition of this book, running to 374 pages, was published in March, 1919. It sold out very quickly, and so much new matter came in from readers that a revision was undertaken almost at once. This revision, however, collided with other enterprises, and was not finished and published until December, 1921. It ran to 492 pages. In its turn it attracted corrections and additions from many correspondents, and in February, 1923, I brought out a third edition, revised and enlarged. This third edition has been reprinted five times, and has had a large circulation, but for some years past its mounting deficiencies have been haunting me, and on my retirement from the editorship of the *American Mercury* at the end of 1933 I began to make plans for rewriting it. The task turned out to be so formidable as to be almost appalling. I found myself confronted by a really enormous accumulation of notes, including hundreds of letters from correspondents in all parts of the world and thousands of clippings from the periodical press of the British Empire, the United States and most of the countries of Continental Europe. Among the letters were many that reviewed my third edition page by page, and suggested multitudinous additions to the text, or changes in it. One of them was no less than 10,000 words long. The clippings embraced every discussion of the American language printed in the British Empire since the end of 1922 — at all events, every one that the singularly alert Durrant Press-Cutting Agency could discover. Furthermore, there were the growing files of *American Speech*, set up in October, 1925, and of *Dialect Notes*, and a large number of books and pamphlets, mostly in English but some also in German, French and other foreign languages, including even Japanese. It soon became plain that this immense mass of new material made a mere revision of the third edition out of the question. What was needed was a complete reworking, following to some extent the outlines of the earlier editions, but with many additions and a number of emendations and shortenings. That reworking has occupied me, with two or three intervals, since the beginning of 1934. The present book picks up bodily a few short passages from the third edition, but they are not many. In the main, it is a new work.

The reader familiar with my earlier editions will find that it not only presents a large amount of matter that was not available when they were written, but also modifies the thesis which they set forth. When I became interested in the subject and began writing about it (in the Baltimore *Evening Sun* in 1910), the American form of the English language was plainly departing from the parent stem, and it seemed at least likely that the differences between American and English would go on increasing. This was what I argued in my first three editions. But since 1923 the pull of American has become so powerful that it has begun to drag English with it, and in consequence some of the differences once visible have tended to disappear. The two forms of the language, of course, are still distinct in more ways than one, and when an Englishman and an American meet they continue to be conscious that each speaks a tongue that is far from identical with the tongue spoken by the other. But the Englishman, of late, has yielded so much to American example, in vocabulary, in idiom, in spelling and even in pronunciation, that what he speaks promises to become, on some not too remote tomorrow, a kind of dialect of American, just as the language spoken by the American was once a dialect of English. The English writers who note this change lay it to the influence of the American movies and talkies, but it seems to me that there is also something more, and something deeper. The American people now constitute by far the largest fraction of the English-speaking race, and since the World War they have shown an increasing inclination to throw off their old subservience to English precept and example. If only by the force of numbers, they are bound to exert a dominant influence upon the course of the common language hereafter. But all this I discuss at length, supported by the evidence now available, in the pages following.

At the risk of making my book of forbidding bulk I have sought to present a comprehensive conspectus of the whole matter, with references to all the pertinent literature. My experience with the three preceding editions convinces me that the persons who are really interested in American English are not daunted by bibliographical apparatus, but rather demand it. The letters that so many of them have been kind enough to send to me show that they delight in running down the by-ways of the subject, and I have tried to assist them by setting up as many guide-posts as possible, pointing into every alley as we pass along. Thus my references keep in step with the text, where they are most convenient and useful, and I have been able to dispense with the Bibliography which filled 32 pages of small type in my third edition. I have also omitted a few illustrative oddities appearing in that edition — for example, specimens of vulgar American by Ring W. Lardner and John V. A. Weaver, and my own translations of the Declaration of Independence and Lincoln's Gettysburg Address. The latter two, I am sorry to say, were mistaken by a number of outraged English critics for examples of Standard American, or of what I proposed that Standard American should be. Omitting them will get rid of that misapprehension and save some space, and those who want to consult them will know where to find them in my third edition.

I can't pretend that I have covered the whole field in the present volume, for that field has become very large in area. But I have at least tried to cover those parts of it of which I have any knowledge, and to indicate the main paths through the remainder. The Dictionary of American English on Historical Principles, now under way at the University of Chicago under the able editorship of Sir William Craigie, will deal with the vocabulary of Americanisms on a scale impossible here, and the Linguistic Atlas in preparation by Dr. Hans Kurath and his associates at Brown University will similarly cover the large and vexatious subject of regional differences in usage. In the same way, I hope, the work of Dr. W. Cabell Greet and his associates at Columbia will one day give us a really comprehensive account of American pronunciation. There are other inquiries in progress by other scholars, all of them unheard of at the time my third edition was published. But there are still some regions into which scholarship has hardly penetrated — for example, that of the vulgar grammar —, and therein I have had to disport as gracefully as possible, always sharply conscious of the odium which attaches justly to those amateurs who, "because they speak, fancy they can speak about speech." I am surely no philologian, and my inquiries and surmises will probably be of small value to the first successor who is, but until he appears I can only go on accumulating materials, and arranging them as plausibly as possible.

In the course of the chapters following I have noted my frequent debt to large numbers of volunteer aides, some of them learned in linguistic science but the majority lay brothers as I am. My contacts with them have brought me many pleasant acquaintanceships, and some friendships that I value greatly. In particular, I am indebted to Dr. Louise Pound, professor of English at the University of Nebraska and the first editor of *American Speech,* whose interest in this book has been lively and generous since its first appearance; to Mr. H. W. Seaman, of Norwich, England, whose herculean struggles with the chapter on "American and English Today" deserve a much greater reward than he will ever receive on this earth; to Dr. Kemp Malone, professor of English at the Johns Hopkins, who was kind enough to read the chapter on "The Common Speech"; to the late Dr. Robert Bridges, Poet Laureate of England and founder of the Society for Pure English, who was always lavish of his wise and stimulating counsel; to Professor Dr. Heinrich Spies of Berlin, who published a critical summary of my third edition in German, under the title of "Die amerikanische Sprache," in 1927; and to the late Dr. George Philip Krapp, professor of English at Columbia, who allowed me the use of the manuscript of his excellent "History of the English Language in America" in 1922, and was very obliging in other ways down to the time of his lamented death in 1934. Above all, I am indebted to my secretary, Mrs. Rosalind C. Lohrfinck, without whose indefatigable aid the present edition would have been quite impossible. The aforesaid friends of the philological faculty are not responsible, of course, for anything that appears herein. They have saved me from a great many errors, some of them of a large and astounding character, but others, I fear, remain. I shall be grateful, as in the past, for corrections and additions sent to me at 1524 Hollins street, Baltimore.

Baltimore, 1936   H. L. M.

Table of Contents

I. THE TWO STREAMS OF ENGLISH

1. The Earliest Alarms   3
2. The English Attack   12
3. American "Barbarisms"   23
4. The English Attitude Today   28
5. The Position of the Learned   49
6. The Views of Writing Men   67
7. The Political Front   79
8. Foreign Observers   85

II. THE MATERIALS OF THE INQUIRY

1. The Hallmarks of American   90
2. What is an Americanism?   97

III. THE BEGINNINGS OF AMERICAN

1. The First Loan-Words   104
2. New Words of English Material   113
3. Changed Meanings   121
4. Archaic English Words   124

IV. THE PERIOD OF GROWTH

1. A New Nation in the Making   130
2. The Expanding Vocabulary   140
3. Loan-Words and Non-English Influences   150

V. THE LANGUAGE TODAY

1. After the Civil War   164
2. The Making of New Nouns   168
3. Verbs   191
4. Other Parts of Speech   201
5. Foreign Influences Today   212

VI. AMERICAN AND ENGLISH

1. The Infiltration of English by Americanisms   223
2. Surviving Differences   232
3. English Difficulties with American   255
4. Briticisms in the United States   264
5. Honorifics   271
6. Euphemisms   284
7. Forbidden Words   300
8. Expletives   311

VII. THE PRONUNCIATION OF AMERICAN

1. Its General Characters   319
2. The Vowels   334
3. The Consonants   348
4. Dialects   354

VIII. AMERICAN SPELLING

1. The Influence of Noah Webster   379
2. The Advance of American Spelling   388
3. The Simplified Spelling Movement   397
4. The Treatment of Loan-Words   408
5. Punctuation, Capitalization, and Abbreviation   413

IX. THE COMMON SPEECH

1. Outlines of its Grammar   416
2. The Verb   427
3. The Pronoun   447
4. The Noun   461
5. The Adjective   463
6. The Adverb   464
7. The Double Negative   468
8. Other Syntactical Peculiarities   471

X. PROPER NAMES IN AMERICA

1. Surnames   474
2. Given-Names   505
3. Place-Names   525
4. Other Proper Names   544

XI. AMERICAN SLANG

1. The Nature of Slang   555
2. Cant and Argot   575

XII. THE FUTURE OF THE LANGUAGE

1. The Spread of English   590
2. English or American?   607

APPENDIX. NON–ENGLISH DIALECTS IN AMERICA

1. Germanic   616
   - *a.* German   616
   - *b.* Dutch   621
   - *c.* Swedish   624
   - *d.* Dano-Norwegian   627
   - *e.* Icelandic   631
   - *f.* Yiddish   633
2. Latin   636
   - *a.* French   636
   - *b.* Italian   640
   - *c.* Spanish   647
   - *d.* Portuguese   652
   - *e.* Rumanian   653
3. Slavic   655
   - *a.* Czech   655
   - *b.* Slovak   659
   - *c.* Russian   662
   - *d.* Ukrainian   663
   - *e.* Serbo-Croat   667
   - *f.* Lithuanian   669
   - *g.* Polish   673
4. Finno-Ugrian   675
   - *a.* Finnish   675
   - *b.* Hungarian   680
5. Celtic   682
   - *a.* Gaelic   682
6. Semitic   683
   - *a.* Arabic   683
7. Greek   685
   - *a.* Modern Greek   685
8. Asiatic   688
   - *a.* Chinese   688
   - *b.* Japanese   691
9. Miscellaneous   693
   - *a.* Armenian   693
   - *b.* Hawaiian   693
   - *c.* Gipsy   696

LIST OF WORDS AND PHRASES

INDEX

THE AMERICAN LANGUAGE

I

THE TWO STREAMS OF ENGLISH

1. THE EARLIEST ALARMS

The first American colonists had perforce to invent Americanisms, if only to describe the unfamiliar landscape and weather, flora and fauna confronting them. Half a dozen that are still in use are to be found in Captain John Smith's "Map of Virginia," published in 1612, and there are many more in the works of the New England annalists. As early as 1621 Alexander Gill was noting in his "Logonomia Anglica" that *maize* and *canoe* were making their way into English.[1] But it was reserved for one Francis Moore, who came out to Georgia with Oglethorpe in 1735, to raise the earliest alarm against this enrichment of English from the New World, and so set the tone that English criticism has maintained ever since. Thus he described Savannah, then a village only two years old:

> It stands upon the flat of a Hill; the Bank of the River (which they in barbarous English call a *bluff*) is steep, and about forty-five foot perpendicular.[2]

John Wesley arrived in Georgia the same year, and from his diary for December 2, 1737, comes the Oxford Dictionary's earliest example of the use of the word. But Moore was the first to notice it, and what is better to the point, the first to denounce it, and for that pioneering he must hold his honorable place in this history. In colonial times, of course, there was comparatively little incitement to hostility to Americanisms, for the stream of Englishmen coming to America to write books about their sufferings had barely begun to flow, and

[1] British Recognition of American Speech in the Eighteenth Century, by Allen Walker Read, *Dialect Notes*, Vol. VI, Pt. VI, 1933, p. 313.
[2] A Voyage to Georgia, Begun in the Year 1735; London, 1744, p. 24. Moore was something of an adventurer. He went to West Africa for the Royal Africa Company in 1730, and got into obscure difficulties on the river Gambia. But when he came to Georgia in 1735 it was in the prosaic character of storekeeper to the colony. He arrived late in the year and remained until July, 1736. In 1738 he was back, staying this time until 1743. His subsequent career is unknown.

the number of American books reaching London was very small. But by 1754 literary London was already sufficiently conscious of the new words arriving from the New World for Richard Owen Cambridge, author of "The Scribleriad," to be suggesting [1] that a glossary of them would soon be in order, and two years later the finicky and always anti-American Samuel Johnson was saying, in a notice of Lewis Evans's "Geographical, Historical, Political, Philosophical, and Mechanical Essays," [2] substantially what many English reviewers still say with dogged piety:

This treatise is written with such elegance as the subject admits, tho' not without some mixture of the American dialect, a tract [*i.e.*, trace] of corruption to which every language widely diffused must always be exposed.

As the Revolution drew on, the English discovered varieties of offensiveness on this side of the ocean that greatly transcended the philological, and I can find no record of any denunciation of Americanisms during the heat of the struggle itself. When, on July 20, 1778, a committee appointed by the Continental Congress to arrange for the "publick reception of the sieur Gerard, minister plenipotentiary of his most christian majesty," brought in a report recommending that "all replies or answers" to him should be "in the language of the United States," [3] no notice of the contumacy seems to have been taken in the Motherland. But a few months before Cornwallis was finally brought to heel at Yorktown the subject was resumed, and this time the attack came from a Briton living in America, and otherwise ardently pro-American. He was John Witherspoon (1723–94), a Scottish clergyman who had come out in 1769 to be president of Princeton *in partibus infidelium*.

Witherspoon took to politics when the war closed his college, and was elected a member of the New Jersey constitutional convention. In a little while he was promoted to the Continental Congress, and in it he sat for six years as its only member in holy orders. He

1 In the *World*, No. 102, Dec. 12, 1754. Quoted by Read.
2 The *Literary Magazine*, Sept.–Oct., 1756. Evans's book was published in Philadelphia in 1755 by Benjamin Franklin and D. Hall. It was accompanied by the author's General Map of the Middle British Colonies in America.
3 Secret Journals of the Continental Congress, Vol. II, p. 95. In the earlier editions of the present book I said that these instructions were issued to Franklin on his appointment as Minister to France. Where I picked up the error I don't recall. It was corrected by the late Fred Newton Scott in the *Saturday Review of Literature*, Oct. 11, 1924. The instructions to Franklin, dated Oct. 12, 1778, contained no mention of language.

signed both the Declaration of Independence and the Articles of Confederation, and was a member of the Board of War throughout the Revolution. But though his devotion to the American cause was thus beyond question, he was pained by the American language, and when, in 1781, he was invited to contribute a series of papers to the *Pennsylvania Journal and Weekly Advertiser* of Philadelphia, he seized the opportunity to denounce it, albeit in the politic terms proper to the time. Beginning with the disarming admission that " the vulgar in America speak much better than the vulgar in England, for a very obvious reason, *viz.*, that being much more unsettled, and moving frequently from place, they are not so liable to local peculiarities either in accent or phraseology," he proceeded to argue that Americans of education showed a lamentable looseness in their " public and solemn discourses."

I have heard in this country, in the senate, at the bar, and from the pulpit, and see daily in dissertations from the press, errors in grammar, improprieties and vulgarisms which hardly any person of the same class in point of rank and literature would have fallen into in Great Britain.

Witherspoon's mention of "the senate" was significant, for he must have referred to the Continental Congress, and it is fair to assume that at least some of the examples he cited to support his charge came from the sacred lips of the Fathers. He divided these " errors in grammar, improprieties and vulgarisms " into eight classes, as follows:

1. Americanisms, or ways of speaking peculiar to this country.
2. Vulgarisms in England and America.
3. Vulgarisms in America only.
4. Local phrases or terms.
5. Common blunders arising from ignorance.
6. Cant phrases.
7. Personal blunders.
8. Technical terms introduced into the language.[1]

By Americanisms, said Witherspoon,

I understand an use of phrases or terms, or a construction of sentences, even among people of rank and education, different from the use of the same terms

---

[1] Witherspoon's papers appeared under the heading of The Druid. This list and the foregoing quotation are from No. V, printed on May 9, 1781. The subject was continued in No. VI on May 16, and in No. VII (in two parts) on May 23 and 30. All the papers are reprinted in The Beginnings of American English, edited by M. M. Mathews; Chicago, 1931. They are also to be found in Witherspoon's Collected Works, edited by Ashbel Green, Vol. IV; New York, 1800–01.

or phrases, or the construction of similar sentences in Great Britain. It does not follow, from a man's using these, that he is ignorant, or his discourse upon the whole inelegant; nay, it does not follow in every case that the terms or phrases used are worse in themselves, but merely that they are of American and not of English growth. The word *Americanism*, which I have coined for the purpose, is exactly similar in its formation and significance to the word *Scotticism*.

Witherspoon listed twelve examples of Americanisms falling within his definition, and despite the polite assurance I have just quoted, he managed to deplore all of them. His first was the use of *either* to indicate more than two, as in "The United States, or *either* of them." This usage seems to have had some countenance in the England of the early Seventeenth Century, but it had gone out there by Witherspoon's day, and it has since been outlawed by the schoolmarm in the United States. His second caveat was laid against the American use of *to notify*, as in "The police *notified* the coroner." "In English," he said somewhat prissily, "we do not *notify* the person of the thing, but *notify* the thing to the person." But *to notify*, in the American sense, was simply an example of archaic English, preserved like so many other archaisms in America, and there was, and is, no plausible logical or grammatical objection to it.[1] Witherspoon's third Americanism was *fellow countrymen*, which he denounced as "an evident tautology," and his fourth was the omission of *to be* before the second verb in such constructions as "These things were ordered delivered to the army." His next three were similar omissions, and his remaining five were the use of *or* instead of *nor* following *neither*, the use of *certain* in "A *certain* Thomas Benson" (he argued that "A *certain person called* Thomas Benson" was correct), the use of *incident* in "Such bodies are *incident* to these evils," and the use of *clever* in the sense of worthy, and of *mad* in the sense of angry.

It is rather surprising that Witherspoon found so few Americanisms for his list. Certainly there were many others, current in his day, that deserved a purist's reprobation quite as much as those he singled out, and he must have been familiar with them. Among the verbs a large number of novelties had come into American usage since the middle of the century, some of them revivals of archaic

1 The Oxford Dictionary's first example is dated 1440. After 1652 all the examples cited are American, until 1843, when the usage reappears in England.

English verbs and others native inventions — *to belittle, to advocate, to progress, to notice, to table, to raise* (for *to grow*), *to deed, to locate, to ambition, to deputize, to compromit, to appreciate* (in the sense of increase in value), *to eventuate,* and so on. Benjamin Franklin, on his return to the United States in 1785, after nine years in France, was impressed so unpleasantly by *to advocate, to notice, to progress* and *to oppose* that on December 26, 1789 he wrote to Noah Webster to ask for help in putting them down, but they seem to have escaped Witherspoon. He also failed to note the changes of meaning in the American use of *creek, shoe, lumber, corn, barn, team, store, rock, cracker* and *partridge.* Nor did he have anything to say about American pronunciation, which had already begun to differ materially from that of Standard English.

Witherspoon's strictures, such as they were, fell upon deaf ears, at least in the new Republic. He was to get heavy support, in a little while, from the English reviews, which began to belabor everything American in the closing years of the century, but on this side of the ocean the tide was running the other way, and as the Revolution drew to its victorious close there was a widespread tendency to reject English precedent and authority altogether, in language no less than in government. In the case of the language, several logical considerations supported that disposition, though the chief force at the bottom of it, of course, was probably only national conceit. For one thing, it was apparent to the more astute politicians of the time that getting rid of English authority in speech, far from making for chaos, would encourage the emergence of home authority, and so help to establish national solidarity, then the great desideratum of desiderata. And for another thing, some of them were far-sighted enough to see that the United States, in the course of the years, would inevitably surpass the British Isles in population and wealth, and to realize that its cultural independence would grow at the same pace.

Something of the sort was plainly in the mind of John Adams when he wrote to the president of Congress from Amsterdam on September 5, 1780, suggesting that Congress set up an academy for " correcting, improving and ascertaining the English language." There were such academies, he said, in France, Spain and Italy, but the English had neglected to establish one, and the way was open for the United States. He went on:

It will have a happy effect upon the union of States to have a public standard for all persons in every part of the continent to appeal to, both for the
signification and pronunciation of the language. . . . English is destined to be
in the next and succeeding centuries more generally the language of the world
than Latin was in the last or French is in the present age. The reason of this
is obvious, because the increasing population in America, and their universal
connection and correspondence with all nations will, aided by the influence of
England in the world, whether great or small, force their language into general
use, in spite of all the obstacles that may be thrown in their way, if any such
there should be.[1]

Six years before this, in January, 1774, some anonymous writer,
perhaps also Adams, had printed a similar proposal in the *Royal
American Magazine*. That it got some attention is indicated by the
fact that Sir John Wentworth, the Loyalist Governor of New
Hampshire, thought it of sufficient importance to enclose a reprint
of it in a dispatch to the Earl of Dartmouth, Secretary of State for
the Colonies, dated April 24. I quote from it briefly:

The English language has been greatly improved in Britain within a century, but its highest perfection, with every other branch of human knowledge,
is perhaps reserved for this land of light and freedom. As the people through
this extensive country will speak English, their advantages for polishing their
language will be great, and vastly superior to what the people of England ever
enjoyed. I beg leave to propose a plan for perfecting the English language in
America, thro' every future period of its existence; *viz:* That a society for
this purpose should be formed, consisting of members in each university and
seminary, who shall be stiled *Fellows of the American Society of Language;*
That the society . . . annually publish some observations upon the language,
and from year to year correct, enrich and refine it, until perfection stops their
progress and ends their labor.[2]

Whether this article was Adams's or not, he kept on returning to
the charge, and in a second letter to the president of Congress, dated
September 30, 1780, he expressed the hope that, after an American
Academy had been set up, England would follow suit.

This I should admire. England will never more have any honor, excepting
now and then that of imitating the Americans. I assure you, Sir, I am not altogether in jest. I see a general inclination after English in France, Spain and
Holland, and it may extend throughout Europe. The population and commerce
of America will force their language into general use.[3]

1 The letter is reprinted in full in The
 Beginnings of American English,
 before cited, pp. 41–43.
2 The full text is in The Beginnings
 of American English, just cited.

3 For this letter I am indebted to
 George Philip Krapp: The English
 Language in America, Vol. I, p. 7.

In his first letter to the president of Congress Adams deplored the fact that " it is only very lately that a tolerable dictionary [of English] has been published, even by a private person,[1] and there is not yet a passable grammar enterprised by any individual." He did not know it, but at that very moment a young schoolmaster in the backwoods of New York was preparing to meet both lacks. He was Noah Webster. Three years later he returned to Hartford, his birthplace, and brought out his " Grammatical Institute of the English Language," and soon afterward he began the labors which finally bore fruit in his " *American* Dictionary of the English Language " in 1828.[2] Webster was a pedantic and rather choleric fellow — someone once called him " the critic and cockcomb-general of the United States " — , and his later years were filled with ill-natured debates over his proposals for reforming English spelling, and over the more fanciful etymologies in his dictionary. But though, in this enlightened age, he would scarcely pass as a philologian, he was extremely well read for his time, and if he fell into the blunder of deriving all languages from the Hebrew of the Ark, he was at least shrewd enough to notice the relationship between Greek, Latin and the Teutonic languages before it was generally recognized. He was always at great pains to ascertain actual usages, and in the course of his journeys from State to State to perfect his copyright on his first spelling-book[3] he accumulated a large amount of interesting and valuable material, especially in the field of pronunciation. Much of it he utilized in his " Dissertations on the English Language," published at Boston in 1789.

In the opening essay of this work he put himself squarely behind Adams. He foresaw that the new Republic would quickly outstrip England in population, and that virtually all its people would speak English. He proposed therefore that an American standard be set up, independent of the English standard, and that it be inculcated in the schools throughout the country. He argued that it should be determined, not by " the practise of any particular class of people," but by " the general practise of the nation," with due regard, in cases

---

1 His reference, of course, was to Johnson's Dictionary, first published in 1755.
2 His Compendious Dictionary of the English Language, a sort of trial balloon, was published in 1806. There

is a brief but good account of his dictionary-making in A Survey of English Dictionaries, by M. M. Mathews; London, 1933, pp. 37–45.
3 Published in 1783. There was no national copyright until 1790.

where there was no general practise, to "the principle of analogy." He went on:

> As an independent nation, our honor requires us to have a system of our own, in language as well as government. Great Britain, whose children we are, and whose language we speak, should no longer be *our* standard; for the taste of her writers is already corrupted,[1] and her language on the decline. But if it were not so, she is at too great a distance to be our model, and to instruct us in the principles of our own tongue. . . . Several circumstances render a future separation of the American tongue from the English necessary and unavoidable. . . . Numerous local causes, such as a new country, new associations of people, new combinations of ideas in arts and sciences, and some intercourse with tribes wholly unknown in Europe, will introduce new words into the American tongue. These causes will produce, in a course of time, a language in North America as different from the future language of England as the modern Dutch, Danish and Swedish are from the German, or from one another: like remote branches of a tree springing from the same stock, or rays of light shot from the same center, and diverging from each other in proportion to their distance from the point of separation. . . . We have therefore the fairest opportunity of establishing a national language and of giving it uniformity and perspicuity, in North America, that ever presented itself to mankind. Now is the time to begin the plan.[2]

What Witherspoon thought of all this is not recorded. Maybe he never saw Webster's book, for he was going blind in 1789, and lived only five years longer. Webster seems to have got little support for what he called his Federal English from the recognized illuminati of the time;[3] indeed, his proposals for a reform of American spelling,

1 Later on in the same essay Webster sought to support this doctrine by undertaking an examination of Johnson, Gibbon, Hume, Robertson, Home, Kaims and Blair. Of Johnson he said: "His style is a mixture of Latin and English; an intolerable composition of Latinity, affected smoothness, scholastic accuracy, and roundness of periods." And of Gibbon: "It is difficult to comprehend his meaning and the chain of his ideas, as fast as we naturally read. . . . The mind of the reader is constantly dazzled by a glare of ornament, or charmed from the subject by the music of the language."

2 The successive parts of the quotation are from pp. 20, 22, 22–3, and 36.

3 The members of the Philological Society of New York, organized in 1788, were for him, but they were young men of little influence, and their society lasted only a year or so. Webster became a member on March 17, 1788, but on Dec. 20 he left New York. The president was Josiah O. Hoffman and among the members were William Dunlap, the painter and dramatist, and Samuel L. Mitchell. On Aug. 27 Ebenezer Hazard, then Postmaster-General of the Confederation, wrote to a friend in Boston that Webster was "the monarch" of the society. In April, 1788 Webster printed in his *American Magazine* a notice saying that its purpose was that of "ascertaining and improving the American tongue." On July 4, 1788 the society passed a resolution approving the first part of his Grammatical Institute. See The Philological Society of New York, by Allen Walker Read, *American Speech*, April, 1934.

set forth in an appendix to his "Dissertations," were denounced roundly by some of them, and the rest were only lukewarm. He dedicated the "Dissertations" to Franklin, but Franklin delayed acknowledging the dedication until the last days of 1789, and then ventured upon no approbation of Webster's linguistic Declaration of Independence. On the contrary, he urged him to make war upon various Americanisms of recent growth, and perhaps with deliberate irony applauded his "zeal for preserving the purity of our language." A year before the "Dissertations" appeared, Dr. Benjamin Rush anticipated at least some of Webster's ideas in " A Plan of a Federal University," [1] and they seem to have made some impression on Thomas Jefferson, who was to ratify them formally in 1813; [2] but the rest of the contemporaneous sages held aloof, and in July, 1800, the *Monthly Magazine and American Review* of New York printed an anonymous denunciation, headed " On the Scheme of an American Language," of the notion that "grammars and dictionaries should be compiled by natives of the country, not of the British or English, but of the *American* tongue." The author of this tirade, who signed himself C, displayed a violent Anglomania. " The most suitable name for our country," he said, " would be that which is now appropriated only to a part of it: I mean New England." While admitting that a few Americanisms were logical and necessary — for example, *Congress, president* and *capitol* — , he dismissed all the rest as " manifest corruptions." A year later, a savant using the *nom de plume* of Aristarcus delivered a similar attack on Webster in a series of articles contributed to the *New England Palladium* and reprinted in the *Port Folio* of Philadelphia, the latter " a notoriously

1 Contributed to the *American Museum* for 1788. Under the heading of Philology he said: " Instruction in this branch of literature will become the more necessary in America as our intercourse must soon cease with the bar, the stage and the pulpit of Great Britain, from whence [*sic*] we received our knowledge of the pronunciation of the English language. Even modern English books should cease to be the models of style in the United States. The present is the age of simplicity of writing in America. The turgid style of Johnson, the purple glare of Gibbon, and even the studied and thick-set metaphors of Junius are all equally unnatural and should not be admitted into our country."

2 In a letter from Monticello, August 16, to John Waldo, author of Rudiments of English Grammar. On August 12, 1801 Jefferson wrote to James Madison: " I view Webster as a mere pedagogue, of very limited understanding and very strong prejudices and party passion," but this was with reference to a political matter. In his letter to Waldo, Jefferson adopted Webster's ideas categorically, and professed to believe that " an American dialect will be formed."

Federalistic and pro-British organ." " If the Connecticut lexicographer," he said, " considers the retaining of the English language as a badge of slavery, let him not give us a Babylonish dialect in its stead, but adopt, at once, the language of the aborigines." [1]

But if the illuminati were thus chilly, the plain people supported Webster's scheme for the emancipation of American English heartily enough, though very few of them could have heard of it. The period from the gathering of the Revolution to the turn of the century was one of immense activity in the concoction and launching of new Americanisms, and more of them came into the language than at any time between the earliest colonial days and the rush to the West. Webster himself lists some of these novelties in his " Dissertations," and a great many more are to be found in Richard H. Thornton's " American Glossary " [2] — for example, *black-eye* (in the sense of defeat), *block* (of houses), *bobolink, bookstore, bootee* (now obsolete), *breadstuffs, buckeye, buckwheat-cake, bull-snake, bundling* and *buttonwood*, to go no further than the *b's*. It was during this period, too, that the American meanings of such words as *shoe, corn, bug, bureau, mad, sick, creek, barn* and *lumber* were finally differentiated from the English meanings, and that American peculiarities in pronunciation began to make themselves felt. Despite the economic difficulties which followed the Revolution, the general feeling was that the new Republic was a success, and that it was destined to rise in the world as England declined. There was a widespread contempt for everything English, and that contempt extended to the canons of the mother-tongue.

2. THE ENGLISH ATTACK

But the Jay Treaty of 1794 gave notice that there was still some life left in the British lion, and during the following years the troubles of the Americans, both at home and abroad, mounted at so appalling a rate that their confidence and elation gradually oozed out of them. Simultaneously, their pretensions began to be attacked

1 See Towards a Historical Aspect of American Speech Consciousness, by Leon Howard, *American Speech*, April, 1930.
2 Published in two volumes; Phila-delphia and London, 1912. Thornton, who died in 1925, left a large amount of additional material, and its publication was begun in *Dialect Notes*, Vol. VI, Pt. III, 1931.

with pious vigor by patriotic Britishers, and in no field was the fervor of these brethren more marked than in those of literature and language. To be sure, there were Englishmen, then as now, who had a friendly and understanding interest in all things American, including even American books, and some of them took the trouble to show it, but they were not many. The general tone of English criticism, from the end of the Eighteenth Century to the present day, has been one of suspicion, and not infrequently it has been extremely hostile. The periods of remission, as often as not, have been no more than evidences of adroit politicking, as when Oxford, in 1907, helped along the graceful liquidation of the Venezuelan unpleasantness of 1895 by giving Mark Twain an honorary D.C.L. In England all branches of human endeavor are alike bent to the service of the state, and there is an alliance between society and politics, science and literature, that is unmatched anywhere else on earth. But though this alliance, on occasion, may find it profitable to be polite to the Yankee, and even to conciliate him, there remains an active aversion under the surface, born of the incurable rivalry between the two countries, and accentuated perhaps by their common tradition and their similar speech. Americanisms are forcing their way into English all the time, and of late they have been entering at a truly dizzy pace, but they seldom get anything properly describable as a welcome, save from small sects of iconoclasts, and every now and then the general protest against them rises to a roar. As for American literature, it is still regarded in England as somewhat barbaric and below the salt, and the famous sneer of Sydney Smith, though time has made it absurd in all other respects, is yet echoed complacently in many an English review of American books.[1]

There is an amusing compilation of some of the earlier diatribes

[1] "In the four quarters of the globe, who reads an American book? or goes to an American play? or looks at an American picture or statue? What does the world yet owe to American physicians or surgeons? What new substances have their chemists discovered? or what old ones have they analyzed? What new constellations have been discovered by the telescopes of Americans? What have they done in mathematics? Who drinks out of American glasses? or eats from American plates? or wears American coats or gowns? or sleeps in American blankets? Finally, under which of the old tyrannical governments of Europe is every sixth man a slave, whom his fellow-creatures may buy, and sell and torture." All this was a part of a review of Adam Seybert's Statistical Annals of the United States, *Edinburgh Review*, Jan.–May, 1820.

in William B. Cairns's "British Criticisms of American Writings, 1783–1815." [1] Cairns is not so much concerned with linguistic matters as with literary criticism, but he reprints a number of extracts from the pioneer denunciations of Americanisms, and they surely show a sufficient indignation. The attack began in 1787, when the *European Magazine and London Review* fell upon the English of Thomas Jefferson's "Notes on the State of Virginia," and especially upon his use of *to belittle*, which, according to Thornton, was his own coinage. "*Belittle!*" it roared. "What an expression! It may be an elegant one in Virginia, and even perfectly intelligible; but for our part, all we can do is to *guess* at its meaning. For shame, Mr. Jefferson! Why, after trampling upon the honour of our country, and representing it as little better than a land of barbarism — why, we say, perpetually trample also upon the very grammar of our language, and make that appear as Gothic as, from your description, our manners are rude? — Freely, good sir, will we forgive all your attacks, impotent as they are illiberal, upon our *national character;* but for the future spare — O spare, we beseech you, our mother-tongue! " The *Gentleman's Magazine* joined the charge in May, 1798, with sneers for the "uncouth . . . localities" [*sic*] in the "Yankey dialect" of Noah Webster's "Sentimental and Humorous Essays," and the *Edinburgh* followed in October, 1804, with a patronizing article upon John Quincy Adams's "Letters on Silesia." "The style of Mr. Adams," it said, "is in general very tolerable English; which, for an American composition, is no moderate praise." The usual American book of the time, it went on, was full of "affectations and corruptions of phrase," and they were even to be found in "the enlightened state papers of the two great Presidents." The *Edinburgh* predicted that a "spurious dialect" would prevail, "even at the Court and in the Senate of the United States," and that the Americans would thus "lose the only badge that is still worn of our consanguinity." The appearance of the five volumes of Chief Justice Marshall's "Life of George Washington," from 1804 to 1807, brought forth corrective articles from the *British Critic*, the *Critical Review*, the *Annual*, the *Monthly*, and the *Eclectic*. The *Edinburgh*, in 1808, declared that the Americans made " it

1 *University of Wisconsin Studies in Language and Literature*, No. 1; Madison, Wis., 1918.

a point of conscience to have no aristocratical distinctions — even in their vocabulary." They thought, it went on, "one word as good as another, provided its meaning be as clear." The *Monthly Mirror*, in March of the same year, denounced "the corruptions and barbarities which are hourly obtaining in the speech of our transatlantic colonies [*sic*]," and reprinted with approbation a parody by some anonymous Englishman of the American style of the day. Here is an extract from it, with the words that the author regarded as Americanisms in italics:

In America authors are to be found who make use of new or obsolete words which no good writer in this country would employ; and were it not for my *destitution* of leisure, which obliges me to hasten the *occlusion* of these pages, as I *progress* I should *bottom* my assertation on instances from authors of the first *grade;* but were I to render my sketch *lengthy* I should *illy* answer the purpose which I have in view.

The *British Critic*, in April, 1808, admitted somewhat despairingly that the damage was already done — that "the common speech of the United States has departed very considerably from the standard adopted in England." The others, however, sought to stay the flood by invective against Marshall, and, later, against his rival biographer, the Rev. Aaron Bancroft. The *Annual*, in 1808, pronounced its anathema upon "that torrent of barbarous phraseology" which was pouring across the Atlantic, and which threatened "to destroy the purity of the English language." In Bancroft's "Life of George Washington" (1808), according to the *British Critic*, there were "new words, or old words in a new sense," all of them inordinately offensive to Englishmen, "at almost every page," and in Joel Barlow's "The Columbiad" (1807; reprinted in England in 1809) the *Edinburgh* found "a great multitude of words which are radically and entirely new, and as utterly foreign as if they had been adopted from the Hebrew or Chinese," and "the perversion of a still greater number of English words from their proper use or signification, by employing nouns substantive for verbs, adjectives for substantives, &c." The *Edinburgh* continued:

We have often heard it reported that our transatlantic brethren were beginning to take it amiss that their language should still be called English; and truly we must say that Mr. Barlow has gone far to take away that ground of reproach. The groundwork of his speech, perhaps may be English, as that of the Italian is Latin; but the variations amount already to more than a change of dialect; and really make a glossary necessary for most untravelled readers.

Some of Barlow's novelties, it must be granted, were fantastic enough — for example, *to vagrate* and *to ameed* among the verbs, *imkeeled* and *homicidious* among the adjectives, and *coloniarch* among the nouns. But many of the rest were either obsolete words whose use was perfectly proper in heroic poetry, or nonce-words of obvious meaning and utility. Some of the terms complained of by the *Edinburgh* are in good usage at this moment — for example, *to utilize, to hill, to breeze, to spade* (the soil), *millenial, crass,* and *scow.*[1] But to the English reviewers of the time words so unfamiliar were not only deplorable on their own account; they were also proofs that the Americans were a sordid and ignoble people with no capacity for prose, or for any of the other elegances of life.[2] " When the vulgar and illiterate lose the force of their animal spirits," observed the *Quarterly* in 1814, reviewing J. K. Paulding's " Lay of the Scottish Fiddle " (1813), " they become mere clods. . . . The founders of American society brought to the composition of their nation few seeds of good taste, and no rudiments of liberal science." To which may be added Southey's judgment in a letter to Landor in 1812: " See what it is to have a nation to take its place among civilized states before it has either gentlemen or scholars! They have in the course of twenty years acquired a distinct national character for low and lying knavery; and so well do they deserve it that no man ever had any dealings with them without having proofs of its truth." Landor, it should be said, entered a protest against this, and on a somewhat surprising ground, considering the general view. " Americans," he said, " speak our language; they read ' Paradise Lost.' " But he hastened to add, " I detest the American character as much as you do."

The War of 1812 naturally exacerbated this animosity, though when the works of Irving and Cooper began to be known in England some of the English reviewers moderated their tone. Irving's " Knickerbocker " was not much read there until 1815, and not much talked about until " The Sketch-Book " followed it in 1819,

---

1 See A Historical Note on American English, by Leon Howard, *American Speech*, Sept., 1927.

2 Cairns says that the *Edinburgh*, the *Anti-Jacobin*, the *Quarterly*, and the *European Magazine and London Review* were especially virulent. He says that the *Monthly*, despite my quotations, was always " kindly toward America " and that the *Eclectic* was, " on the whole, fair." The *Literary Magazine and British Review* he describes as enthusiastically pro-American, but it lived only a short time.

but Scott had received a copy of it from Henry Brevoort in 1813, and liked it and said so. Byron mentioned it in a letter to his publisher, Murray, on August 7, 1821. We are told by Thomas Love Peacock that Shelley was " especially fond of the novels of Charles Brockden Brown, the American," but Cairns says there is no mention of the fact, if it be a fact, in any of Shelley's own writings, or in those of his other friends. " Knickerbocker " was published in 1809, the *North American Review* began in May, 1815, Bryant's " Thanatopsis " was printed in its pages in 1817, and Paulding's " The Backwoodsman," with an American theme and an American title, came out a year later, but Cooper's " Precaution " was still two years ahead, and American letters were yet in a somewhat feeble state. John Pickering, so late as 1816, said that " in this country we can hardly be said to have any authors by profession," and Justice Story, three years later, repeated the saying and sought to account for the fact. " So great," said Story, " is the call for talents of all sorts in the active use of professional and other business in America that few of our ablest men have leisure to devote exclusively to literature or the fine arts. . . . This obvious reason will explain why we have so few professional authors, and those not among our ablest men." In 1813 Jefferson, anticipating both Pickering and Story, had written to John Waldo:

We have no distinct class of literati in our country. Every man is engaged in some industrious pursuit, and science is but a secondary occupation, always subordinate to the main business of life. Few, therefore, of those who are qualified have leisure to write.

Difficulties of communication hampered the circulation of such native books as were written. " It is much to be regretted," wrote Dr. David Ramsay, of Charleston, S. C., to Noah Webster in 1806, " that there is so little intercourse in a literary way between the States. As soon as a book of general utility comes out in any State it should be for sale in all of them." Ramsay asked for little; the most he could imagine was a sale of 2,000 copies for an American work in America. But even that was apparently beyond the possibilities of the time. It would be a mistake, however, to assume that the Americans eschewed reading altogether; on the contrary, there is some evidence that they read many English books. In 1802 the *Scot's Magazine* reported that at a book-fair held shortly before in New York the sales ran to 520,000 volumes, and that a similar fair was projected for Philadelphia. Six years before this the London book-seller, Henry Lemoine, made a survey of the American book trade for the *Gentleman's Magazine*.[1] He found that very few books were being printed in the country, and ascribed the fact to the high cost of labor, but he encountered well-stocked bookstores in New York, Philadelphia and Baltimore, and plenty of customers for their importations. He went on:

> Their sales are very great, for it is scarcely possible to conceive the number of readers with which every little town abounds. The common people are on a footing, in point of literature, with the middle ranks in Europe; they all read and write, and understand arithmetic. Almost every little town now furnishes a small circulating-library. . . . Whatever is useful sells, but publications on subjects merely speculative, and rather curious than important, controversial divinity, and voluminous polemical pieces, as well as heavy works on the arts and sciences, lie upon the importer's hands. They have no ready money to spare for anything but what they find useful.

But other visitors were much less impressed by the literary gusto of the young Republic. Henry Wansey, who came out in 1794, reported in his " Excursion to the United States of North America " [2] that the American libraries were " scanty," that their collections were " almost entirely of modern books," and that they were deficient in " the means of tracing the history of questions, . . . a want which literary people felt very much, and which it will take some years to remedy." And Captain Thomas Hamilton, in his " Men and Manners in America," [3] said flatly that " there is . . . nothing in the United States worthy of the name of library. Not only is there an entire absence of learning, in the higher sense of the term, but an absolute want of the material from which alone learning can be extracted. At present an American might study every book within the limits of the Union, and still be regarded in many parts of Europe — especially in Germany — as a man comparatively ignorant. Why

1 November, 1796. I take what follows from Cairns.
2 Salisbury, 1796. Wansey stayed but two months, and his journey was confined to the region between Boston and Philadelphia.
3 Published in Edinburgh in 1833, and reprinted in Philadelphia the same year. The book did not bear Hamilton's name, but was ascribed on the title page to " the author of ' Cyril Thornton.' " Hamilton was a younger brother to Sir William Hamilton, the metaphysician, and a friend to Sir Walter Scott. He was himself a frequent contributor to *Blackwood's*. " Cyril Thornton," published in 1827, was a successful novel, and remained in favor for many years. Hamilton died in 1842. " Men and Manners in America " was translated into French and twice into German.

does a great nation thus voluntarily continue in a state of intellectual destitution so anomalous and humiliating? " According to Hamilton, all the books imported from Europe for public institutions during the fiscal year 1829–30 reached a value of but $10,829.

But whatever the fact here, there can be no doubt that the Americans were quickly aware of every British aspersion upon their culture, whether it appeared in a book or in one of the reviews. If nothing else was read, such things were certainly read, and they came with sufficient frequency, and were couched in terms of sufficient offensiveness, to keep the country in a state of indignation for years. The flood of books by English visitors began before the end of the Eighteenth Century, and though many of them were intended to be friendly, there was in even the friendliest of them enough of what Cairns calls " the British knack for saying gracious things in an ungracious way " to keep the pot of fury boiling. At the other extreme the thing went to fantastic lengths. The *Quarterly Review*, summing up in 1814, accused the Americans of a multitude of strange and hair-raising offenses — for example, employing naked colored women to wait upon them at table, kidnapping Scotsmen, Welshmen and Hollanders and selling them into slavery, and fighting one another incessantly under rules which made it " allowable to peel the skull, tear out the eyes, and smooth away the nose." In this holy war upon the primeval damyankee William Gifford, editor of the *Anti-Jacobin* in 1797–98, and after 1809 the first editor of the *Quarterly*, played an extravagant part,[1] but he was diligently seconded by Sydney Smith, Southey, Thomas Moore and many lesser lights. " If the [English] reviewers get hold of an American publication," said J. K. Paulding in " Letters From the South " in 1817, " it is made use of merely as a pretext to calumniate us in some way or other." There is an instructive account of the whole uproar in the fifth volume of John Bach McMaster's " History of the People of the United States From the Revolution to the Civil War." McMaster says that it

[1] Gifford was a killer in general practise, and his onslaughts on Wordsworth, Shelley and Keats are still remembered. He retired from the *Quarterly* in 1824 with a fortune of £25,000 — the first magazine editor in history to make it pay. On his death in 1826 he was solemnly buried in Westminster Abbey. The *Quarterly*, despite its anti-American ferocity, was regularly reprinted in Boston. But when its issue for July, 1823 appeared with an extraordinarily malignant review of William Faux's Memorable Days in America (London, 1823) the American publishers were warned that it contained a libel on "a distinguished individual at Washington," and accordingly withheld it.

was generally believed that the worst calumniators of the United States were subsidized by the British government, apparently in an effort to discourage emigration. He goes on:

The petty annoyances, the little inconveniences and unpleasant incidents met with in all journeys, were grossly exaggerated and cited as characteristic of daily life in the States. Men and women met with at the inns and taverns, in the stage-coaches and far-away country towns, were described not as so many types, but as the typical Americans. The abuse heaped on public men by partisan newspapers, the charges of corruption made by one faction against the other, the scandals of the day, were all cited as solemn truth.

Even the relatively mild and friendly Captain Hamilton condescended to such tactics. This is what he had to say of Thomas Jefferson:

The moral character of Jefferson was repulsive. Continually puling about liberty, equality, and the degrading curse of slavery, he brought his own children to the hammer, and made money of his debaucheries.[1]

Such violent assaults, in the long run, were bound to breed defiance, but while they were at their worst they produced a contrary effect. " The nervous interest of Americans in the impressions formed of them by visiting Europeans," says Allan Nevins,[2] " and their sensitiveness to British criticism in especial, were long regarded as constituting a salient national trait." The native authors became extremely self-conscious and diffident, and the educated classes, in general, were daunted by the torrent of abuse: they could not help finding in it an occasional reasonableness, an accidental true hit. The result was uncertainty and skepticism in native criticism. " The first step of an American entering upon a literary career," said Henry Cabot Lodge, writing of the first quarter of the century,[3] " was to

---

1 See also The Cambridge History of American Literature, Vol. I; New York, 1917, pp. 205-8; As Others See Us, by John Graham Brooks; New York, 1909, Ch. VII; James Kirke Paulding, by Amos L. Herold; New York, 1926, Ch. IV; American Social History as Recorded by British Travellers, by Allan Nevins; New York, 1923, pp. 3-26 and pp. 111-138; One Hundred Years of Peace, by Henry Cabot Lodge: New York, 1913, pp. 41-55; and The English Traveller in America, 1785-1835, by Jane Louise Mesick; New York, 1922, pp. 241-45. There is a brief but comprehensive view of the earlier period in British Recognition of American Speech in the Eighteenth Century, by Allen Walker Read, Dialect Notes, Vol. VI, Pt. VI, 1933. A bibliography of British books of American travel is in The Cambridge History of American Literature, Vol. I, pp. 468-90, and another, annotated, in Nevins, pp. 555-68.

2 American Social History as Recorded by British Travelers; New York, 1923, p. 3.

3 In his essay, Colonialism in America, in Studies in History; Boston, 1884.

pretend to be an Englishman in order that he might win the approval, not of Englishmen, but of his own countrymen." Cooper, in
his first novel, " Precaution," (1820) chose an English scene, imitated English models, and obviously hoped to placate the English
critics thereby. Irving, too, in his earliest work, showed a considerable discretion, and his " Knickerbocker" was first published
anonymously. But this puerile spirit did not last long. The English libels were altogether too vicious to be received lying down;
their very fury demanded that they be met with a united and courageous front. Cooper, in his second novel, " The Spy " (1821), boldly
chose an American setting and American characters, and though the
influence of his wife, who came of a Loyalist family, caused him to
avoid any direct attack upon the English, he attacked them indirectly, and with great effect, by opposing an immediate and honorable success to their derisions. " The Spy " ran through three editions in four months, and was followed by a long line of thoroughly
American novels. In 1828 Cooper undertook a detailed reply to the
more common English charges in " Notions of the Americans," but
he was still too cautious to sign his name to it: it appeared as " by a
Travelling Bachelor." By 1834, however, he was ready to apologize
formally to his countrymen for his early truancy in " Precaution."
Irving, who was even more politic, and suffered moreover from
Anglomania in a severe form, nevertheless edged himself gradually
into the patriot band, and by 1828 he was brave enough to refuse the
Quarterly's offer of a hundred guineas for an article on the ground
that it was " so persistently hostile to our country " that he could
not " draw a pen in its service."

The real counter-attack was carried on by lesser men — the elder
Timothy Dwight, John Neal, Edward Everett, Charles Jared Inger-
soll, J. K. Paulding, and Robert Walsh, Jr., among them. Neal went
to England, became secretary to Jeremy Bentham, forced his way
into the reviews, and so fought the English on their own ground.
Walsh set up the *American Review of History and Politics*, the first
American critical quarterly, in 1811, and eight years later published
" An Appeal From the Judgments of Great Britain Respecting the
United States of America." Everett performed chiefly in the *North
American Review* (founded in 1815), to which he contributed many
articles and of which he was editor from 1820 to 1824. Wirt pub-
lished his " Letters of a British Spy " in 1803, and Ingersoll followed

with "Inchiquin the Jesuit's Letters on American Literature and Politics" in 1811. In January, 1814 the *Quarterly* reviewed "Inchiquin" in a particularly violent manner, and a year later Dwight replied to the onslaught in "Remarks on the Review of Inchiquin's Letters Published in the *Quarterly Review*, Addressed to the Right Honorable George Canning, Esq." Dwight ascribed the *Quarterly* diatribe to Southey. He went on:

> Both the travelers and the literary journalists of [England] have, for reasons which it would be idle to inquire after and useless to allege, thought it proper to caricature the Americans. Their pens have been dipped in gall; and their representations have been, almost merely, a mixture of malevolence and falsehood.

Dwight rehearsed some of the counts in the *Quarterly's* indictment — that "the president of Yale College tells of a *conflagrative* brand," that Jefferson used *to belittle*, that *to guess* was on the tongues of all Americans, and so on. "You charge us," he said, "with making some words, and using others in a peculiar sense. . . . You accuse us of forming projects to get rid of the English language; 'not,' you say, 'merely by barbarizing it, but by abolishing it altogether, and substituting a new language of our own.'" His reply was to list, on the authority of Pegge's "Anecdotes of the English Language," 105 vulgarisms common in London — for example, *potecary* for apothecary, *chimly* for chimney, *saace* for sauce, *kiver* for cover, *nowheres* for nowhere, *scholard* for scholar, and *hisn* for his — to accuse "members of Parliament" of using *diddled* and *gullibility* [1] and to deride the English provincial dialects as "unintelligible gabble."

But in this battle across the ocean it was Paulding who got in the most licks, and the heaviest ones. In all he wrote five books dealing with the subject. The first, "The Diverting History of John Bull and Brother Jonathan" (1812) was satirical in tone, and made a considerable popular success. Three years later he followed it with a more serious work, "The United States and England," another reply to the *Quarterly* review of "Inchiquin." The before-mentioned "Letters From the South" came out in 1817, and in 1822

---

1 At that time both words were neologisms. The Oxford Dictionary's first example of *gullibility* is dated 1793. So late as 1818 it was denounced by the Rev. H. J. Todd, one of the improvers of Johnson's Dictionary, as "a low expression, sometimes used for *cullibility*." The Oxford's first example of *to diddle* is dated 1806.

Paulding resumed the attack with " A Sketch of Old England," a sort of *reductio ad absurdum* of the current English books of American travels. He had never been to England, and the inference was that many of the English travelers had never been to America. Finally, in 1825, he resorted to broad burlesque in " John Bull in America, or The New Munchausen." [1] Now and then some friendly aid came from the camp of the enemy. Cairns shows that, while the *Quarterly*, the *European Magazine* and the *Anti-Jacobin* were " strongly anti-American " and " deliberately and dirtily bitter," three or four of the lesser reviews displayed a fairer spirit, and even more or less American bias. After 1824, when the *North American Review* gave warning that if the campaign of abuse went on it would " turn into bitterness the last drops of good-will toward England that exist in the United States," even *Blackwood's* became somewhat conciliatory.

3. AMERICAN " BARBARISMS "

But this occasional tolerance for things American was never extended to the American language. Most of the English books of travel mentioned Americanisms only to revile them, and even when they were not reviled they were certainly not welcomed. The typical attitude was well set forth by Captain Hamilton in " Men and Manners in America," already referred to as denying that the United States of 1833 had any libraries. " The amount of bad grammar in circulation," he said, " is very great; that of barbarisms [*i.e.*, Americanisms] enormous. " Worse, these " barbarisms " were not confined to the ignorant, but came almost as copiously from the lips of the learned.

I do not now speak of the operative class, whose massacre of their mother-tongue, however inhuman, could excite no astonishment; but I allude to the great body of lawyers and traders; the men who crowd the exchange and the hotels; who are to be heard speaking in the courts, and are selected by their fellow-citizens to fill high and responsible offices. Even by this educated and respectable class, the commonest words are often so transmogrified as to be placed beyond recognition of an Englishman.

1 This book, like John Bull and Brother Jonathan, seems to have had readers for a generation or more. So late as 1867 the Scribners brought out a new edition of the two in a single volume, under the title of The Bulls and Jonathans, with a preface by William I. Paulding. It still makes amusing reading.

Hamilton then went on to describe some of the prevalent " barbarisms " :

> The word *does* is split into two syllables, and pronounced *do-es*. *Where*, for some incomprehensible reason, is converted into *whare*, *there* into *thare*; and I remember, on mentioning to an acquaintance that I had called on a gentleman of taste in the arts, he asked " whether he *shew* (showed) me his pictures." Such words as *oratory* and *dilatory* are pronounced with the penult syllable long and accented: *missionary* becomes *missionairy*, angel, *ângel*, danger, *dânger*, etc.
>
> But this is not all. The Americans have chosen arbitrarily to change the meaning of certain old and established English words, for reasons they cannot explain, and which I doubt much whether any European philologist could understand. The word *clever* affords a case in point. It has here no connexion with talent, and simply means pleasant or amiable. Thus a good-natured blockhead in the American vernacular is a *clever* man, and having had this drilled into me, I foolishly imagined that all trouble with regard to this word, at least, was at an end. It was not long, however, before I heard of a gentleman having moved into a *clever* house, of another succeeding to a *clever* sum of money, of a third embarking in a *clever* ship, and making a *clever* voyage, with a *clever* cargo; and of the sense attached to the word in these various combinations, I could gain nothing like a satisfactory explanation. . . .
>
> The privilege of barbarizing the King's English is assumed by all ranks and conditions of men. Such words as *slick, kedge* and *boss*, it is true, are rarely used by the better orders; but they assume unlimited liberty in the use of *expect, reckon, guess* and *calculate*, and perpetrate other conversational anomalies with remorseless impunity.

This Briton, as usual, was as full of moral horror as of grammatical disgust, and put his denunciation upon the loftiest of grounds. He concluded:

> I will not go on with this unpleasant subject, nor should I have alluded to it, but I feel it something of a duty to express the natural feeling of an Englishman at finding the language of Shakespeare and Milton thus gratuitously degraded. Unless the present progress of change be arrested by an increase of taste and judgment in the more educated classes, there can be no doubt that, in another century, the dialect of the Americans will become utterly unintelligible to an Englishman, and that the nation will be cut off from the advantages arising from their participation in British literature. If they contemplate such an event with complacency, let them go on and prosper; they have only to *progress* in their present course, and their grandchildren bid fair to speak a jargon as novel and peculiar as the most patriotic American linguist can desire.[1]

All the other English writers of travel books took the same line, and so did the stay-at-homes who hunted and abhorred Americanisms from afar. Mrs. Frances Trollope reported in her " Domestic

1 The quotations are from pp. 127-9.

Manners of the Americans " (1832) that during her whole stay in the Republic she had seldom " heard a sentence elegantly turned and correctly pronounced from the lips of an American " : there was " always something either in the expression or the accent " that jarred her feelings and shocked her taste. She concluded that " the want of refinement " was the great American curse. Captain Frederick Marryat, in " A Diary in America " (1839) observed that " it is remarkable how very debased the language has become in a short period in America," and then proceeded to specifications — for example, the use of *right away* for immediately, of *mean* for ashamed, of *clever* in the senses which stumped Captain Hamilton, of *bad* as a deprecant of general utility, of *admire* for like, of *how?* instead of *what?* as an interrogative, of *considerable* as an adverb, and of such immoral verbs as *to suspicion* and *to opinion*. Marryat was here during Van Buren's administration, when the riot of Americanisms was at its wildest, and he reported some really fantastic specimens. Once, he said, he heard " one of the first men in America " say, " Sir, if I had done so, I should not only have doubled and trebled, but I should have *fourbled* and *fivebled* my money." Unfortunately, it is hard to believe that an American who was so plainly alive to the difference between *shall* and *will*, *should* and *would*, would have been unaware of *quadrupled* and *quintupled*. No doubt there was humor in the country, then as now, and visiting Englishmen were sometimes taken for rides.

Captain Basil Hall, who was here in 1827 and 1828, and published his " Travels in North America " in 1829, was so upset by some of the novelties he encountered that he went to see Noah Webster, then seventy years old, to remonstrate. Webster upset him still further by arguing stoutly that " his countrymen had not only a right to adopt new words, but were obliged to modify the language to suit the novelty of the circumstances, geographical and political, in which they were placed." The lexicographer went on to observe judicially that " it is quite impossible to stop the progress of language — it is like the course of the Mississippi, the motion of which, at times, is scarcely perceptible; yet even then it possesses a momentum quite irresistible. Words and expressions will be forced into use, in spite of all the exertions of all the writers in the world."

" But surely," persisted Hall, " such innovations are to be deprecated? "

"I don't know that," replied Webster. "If a word becomes universally current in America, where English is spoken, why should it not take its station in the language?"

To this Hall made an honest British reply. "Because," he said, "there are words enough already."

Webster tried to mollify him by saying that "there were not fifty words in all which were used in America and not in England" — an underestimate of large proportions —, but Hall went away muttering.

Marryat, who toured the United States ten years after Hall, was chiefly impressed by the American verb *to fix*, which he described as "universal" and as meaning "to do anything." It also got attention from other English travelers, including Godfrey Thomas Vigne, whose "Six Months in America" was printed in 1832, and Charles Dickens, who came in 1842. Vigne said that it had "perhaps as many significations as any word in the Chinese language," and proceeded to list some of them — "to be done, made, mixed, mended, bespoken, hired, ordered, arranged, procured, finished, lent or given." Dickens thus dealt with it in one of his letters home to his family:

> I asked Mr. Q. on board a steamboat if breakfast be nearly ready, and he tells me yes, he should think so, for when he was last below the steward was *fixing* the tables — in other words, laying the cloth. When we have been writing and I beg him . . . to collect our papers, he answers that he'll *fix* 'em presently. So when a man's dressing he's *fixing* himself, and when you put yourself under a doctor he *fixes* you in no time. T'other night, before we came on board here, when I had ordered a bottle of mulled claret, and waited some time for it, it was put on the table with an apology from the landlord (a lieutenant-colonel) that he fear'd it wasn't properly *fixed*. And here, on Saturday morning, a Western man, handing his potatoes to Mr. Q. at breakfast, inquired if he wouldn't take some of "these *fixings*" with his meat.[1]

In another letter, written on an Ohio river steamboat on April 15, 1842, Dickens reported that "out of Boston and New York" a nasal drawl was universal, that the prevailing grammar was "more than doubtful," that the "oddest vulgarisms" were "received idioms," and that "all the women who have been bred in slave States speak more or less like Negroes." His observations on American speech

[1] The letter appears in John Forster's Life of Charles Dickens; London, 1872-74; Book III, Chapter V. It is reprinted in Allan Nevins's American Social History as Recorded by British Travelers; New York, 1923, p. 268. It was written on a canalboat nearing Pittsburgh, and dated March 28, 1842.

habits in his "American Notes" (1842) were so derisory that they drew the following from Emerson:

> No such conversations ever occur in this country in real life, as he relates. He has picked up and noted with eagerness each odd local phrase that he met with, and when he had a story to relate, has joined them together, so that the result is the broadest caricature.[1]

Almost every English traveler of the years between the War of 1812 and the Civil War was puzzled by the strange signs on American shops. Hall couldn't make out the meaning of *Leather and Finding Store*, though he found *Flour and Feed Store* and *Clothing Store* self-explanatory, albeit unfamiliar. Hamilton, who followed in 1833, failed to gather "the precise import" of *Dry-Goods Store*, and was baffled and somewhat shocked by *Coffin Warehouse* (it would now be *Casketeria!*) and *Hollow Ware, Spiders,* and *Fire-Dogs*. But all this was relatively mild stuff, and after 1850 the chief licks at the American dialect were delivered, not by English travelers, most of whom had begun by then to find it more amusing than indecent, but by English pedants who did not stir from their cloisters. The climax came in 1863, when the Very Rev. Henry Alford, D.D. dean of Canterbury, printed his "Plea for the Queen's English." [2] He said:

> Look at the process of deterioration which our Queen's English has undergone at the hands of the Americans. Look at those phrases which so amuse us in their speech and books; at their reckless exaggeration and contempt for congruity; and then compare the character and history of the nation — its blunted sense of moral obligation and duty to man; its open disregard of conventional right when aggrandisement is to be obtained; and I may now say, its reckless and fruitless maintenance of the most cruel and unprincipled war in the history of the world.

1 Journal, Nov. 25, 1842.

2 A second edition followed in 1864, and an eighth was reached by 1880. There was also an American edition. In October, 1864, an American resident in England, G. Washington Moon by name, brought out a counterblast, The Dean's English. This reached a seventh edition by 1884. Moon employed the ingenious device of turning Alford's pedantries upon him. He showed that the dean was a very loose and careless writer, and often violated his own rules. Another American, Edward S. Gould, bombarded him from the same ground in Good English, or Popular Errors in Language; New York, 1867. Alford was a favorite scholar of the time. He wrote Latin odes and a history of the Jews before he was ten years old, and in later life was the first editor of the *Contemporary Review* and brought out a monumental edition of the New Testament in Greek. He was born in 1810, served as dean of Canterbury from 1857 to 1871, and died in the latter year.

It will be noted that Alford here abandoned one of the chief counts in Sydney Smith's famous indictment, and substituted its exact opposite. Smith had denounced slavery, whereas Alford, by a tremendous feat of moral virtuosity, was now denouncing the war to put it down! But Samuel Taylor Coleridge had done almost as well in 1822. The usual English accusation at that time, as we have seen, was that the Americans had abandoned English altogether and set up a barbarous jargon in its place. Coleridge, speaking to his friend Thomas Allsop, took the directly contrary tack. "An American," he said, "by his boasting of the superiority of the Americans generally, but especially in their language, once provoked me to tell him that ' on that head the least said the better, as the Americans presented the extraordinary anomaly of a *people without a language*. [Allsop's italics] That they had mistaken the English language for baggage (which is called *plunder* in America), and had stolen it.' " And then the inevitable moral reflection: " Speaking of America, it is believed a fact verified beyond doubt that some years ago it was impossible to obtain a copy of the Newgate Calendar, as they had all been bought up by the Americans, whether to suppress the blazon of their forefathers, or to assist in their genealogical researches, I could never learn satisfactorily." [1]

4. THE ENGLISH ATTITUDE TODAY

Smith, Alford and Coleridge have plenty of heirs and assigns in the England of today. There is in the United States, as everyone knows, a formidable sect of Anglomaniacs, and its influence is often felt, not only in what passes here for society, but also in the domains of politics, finance, pedagogy and journalism, but the corresponding sect of British Americophils is small and feeble, though it shows a few respectable names. It is seldom that anything specifically American is praised in the English press, save, of course, some new manifestation of American Anglomania. The realm of Uncle Shylock remains, at bottom, the "brigand confederation" of the *Foreign Quarterly*, and on occasion it becomes again the " loathsome creature, . . . maimed and lame, full of sores and ulcers," of Dickens.

[1] Letters, Conversations and Recollections of S. T. Coleridge, edited by Thomas Allsop; London, 1836.

In the field of language an Americanism is generally regarded as obnoxious *ipso facto*, and when a new one of any pungency begins to force its way into English usage the guardians of the national linguistic chastity belabor it with great vehemence, and predict calamitous consequences if it is not put down. If, despite these alarms, it makes progress, they often switch to the doctrine that it is really old English, and search the Oxford Dictionary for examples of its use in Chaucer's time, or even in the Venerable Bede's; [1] but while it is coming in they give it no quarter. Here the unparalleled English talent for discovering moral obliquity comes into play, and what begins as an uproar over a word sometimes ends as a holy war to keep the knavish Yankee from undermining and ruining the English *Kultur* and overthrowing the British Empire. The crusade has abundant humors. Not infrequently a phrase denounced as an abominable Americanism really originated in the London music-halls, and is unknown in the United States. And almost as often the denunciation of it is sprinkled with genuine Americanisms, unconsciously picked up.

The English seldom differentiate between American slang and Americanisms of legitimate origin and in respectable use: both belong to what they often call the American slanguage.[2] It is most unusual for an American book to be reviewed in England without some reference to its strange and (so one gathers) generally unpleasant diction. The Literary Supplement of the London *Times* is especially alert in this matter. It discovers Americanisms in the writings of even the most decorous American authors, and when none can be found it notes the fact, half in patronizing approbation and half in incredulous surprise. Of the 240 lines it gave to the first two volumes of the Dictionary of American Biography, 31 were devoted to animadversions upon the language of the learned authors.[3] The Man-

---

1 "This dichotomy," says Allen Walker Read in British Recognition of American Speech in the Eighteenth Century, *Dialect Notes*, Vol. VI, Pt. VI, 1933, p. 331, "runs through most British writing on American speech . . . : on the one hand the Americans are denounced for introducing corruptions into the language, and on the other hand those very expressions are eagerly claimed as of British origin to show that the British deserve the credit for them."

2 According to *American Speech* (Feb. 1930, p. 250) this term was invented in 1925 or thereabout. At that time the English war debt to the United States was under acrimonious discussion, and Uncle Sam became Uncle Shylock.

3 Aug. 29, 1929. The passage is perhaps worth quoting in full: "The literary style of the articles is, in

chester *Guardian* and the weeklies of opinion follow dutifully. The *Guardian,* in a review of Dr. Harry Emerson Fosdick's " As I See Religion," began by praising his " telling speech," but ended by deploring sadly his use of the " full-blooded Americanisms which sometimes make even those who do not for a moment question America's right and power to contribute to the speech which we use in common wince as they read." [1] One learns from J. L. Hammond that the late C. P. Scott, for long the editor of the *Guardian,* had a keen nose for Americanisms, and was very alert to keep them out of his paper. Says Hammond:

> He would go bustling into a room, waving a cutting or a proof, in which was an obscure phrase, a preciosity, or an Americanism. " What does he mean by this? He talks about a *final showdown?* An Americanism, I suppose. What does it mean? Generally known? I don't know it. Taken from cards? I never heard of it." [2]

This war upon Americanisms is in progress all the time, but it naturally has its pitched battles and its rest-periods between. For

most instances, suitable to their purpose. Some of them afford obvious indications of their country of origin, as when we read that Bishop Asbury was at no time a *well man,* or that Chester A. Arthur's chief did not uphold the power of the Conkling *crowd,* or that Robert Bacon announced his *candidacy* for the Senate, or that Governor Altgeld *protested* the action of President Cleveland, or that Dr. W. Beaumont, when a doctor's apprentice, learned to *fill* prescriptions, or that J. G. Blaine *raised* a family of seven children, or that Prof. B. P. Bowne tested the progress of his pupils by a written *quiz.* The article on Blaine contains a curious illustration of the peculiar American use of the word *politician.* We read that ' however much Blaine was a politician, it seems to be the fact that from 1876 he was the choice of the majority, or of the largest faction, of Republicans.' One naturally wonders why it should be thought surprising for a politician to win popular support within his own party. The explanation is that *politician* is here very nearly a synonym for *wire-puller* or *intriguer,* and the point the writer wishes to make is that Blaine's influence was not wholly due to his adroit manipulation of the political machine." The following is from the *Times'* review of Hervey Allen's Toward the Flame (*Literary Supplement,* June 7, 1934): " Mr. Allen may or not feel complimented by the statement that, apart from military terms which appear strange to us, there is not an Americanism in his strong and supple prose; but the fact adds to an English reader's pleasure. Yet one would like to know what were the functions of the individual called the colonel's *striker.*" The English term for *striker,* as the reviewer might have discovered by consulting the Oxford Dictionary, is *batman.* Both signify a military servant.

1 Weekly edition, Aug. 26, 1932, p. 175.
2 C. P. Scott of the Manchester *Guardian;* London, 1934, p. 314.

months there may be relative quiet on the linguistic Western front, and then some alarmed picket fires a gun and there is what the German war *communiqués* used to call a sharpening of activity. As a general thing the English content themselves with artillery practise from their own lines, but now and then one of them boldly invades the enemy's country. This happened, for example, in 1908, when Charles Whibley contributed an extremely acidulous article on "The American Language" to the *Bookman* (New York) for January. "To the English traveler in America," he said, "the language which he hears spoken about him is at once a puzzle and a surprise. It is his own, yet not his own. It seems to him a caricature of English, a phantom speech, ghostly yet familiar, such as he might hear in a land of dreams." Mr. Whibley objected violently to many characteristic American terms, among them, *to locate, to operate, to antagonize, transportation, commutation* and *proposition.* "These words," he said, "if words they may be called, are hideous to the eye, offensive to the ear, meaningless to the brain." The onslaught provoked even so mild a man as Dr. Henry W. Boynton to action, and in the *Bookman* for March of the same year he published a spirited rejoinder. "It offends them [the English]," he said, "that we are not thoroughly ashamed of ourselves for not being like them." Mr. Whibley's article was reprinted with this counterblast, so that readers of the magazine might judge the issues fairly. The controversy quickly got into the newspapers, and was carried on for months, with American patriots on one side and Englishmen and Anglomaniacs on the other.

I myself once helped to loose such an uproar, though quite unintentionally. Happening to be in London in the Winter of 1929–30, I was asked by Mr. Ralph D. Blumenfeld, the American-born editor of the *Daily Express*, to do an article for his paper on the progress of Americanisms in England since my last visit in 1922. In that article I ventured to say:

The Englishman, whether he knows it or not, is talking and writing more and more American. He becomes so accustomed to it that he grows unconscious of it. Things that would have set his teeth on edge ten years ago, or even five years ago, are now integral parts of his daily speech. . . . In a few years it will probably be impossible for an Englishman to speak, or even to write, without using Americanisms, whether consciously or unconsciously. The influence of 125,000,000 people, practically all headed in one direction, is simply too great to be resisted by any minority, however resolute.

The question whether or not this was sound will be examined in Chapters VI and XII. For the present it is sufficient to note that my article was violently arraigned by various volunteer correspondents of the *Express* and by contributors to many other journals. One weekly opened its protest with " That silly little fellow, H. L. Mencken, is at it again " and headed it " The American Moron," and in various other quarters I was accused of a sinister conspiracy against the mother-tongue, probably political or commercial in origin, or maybe both. At this time the American talkie was making its first appearance in England, and so there was extraordinary interest in the subject, for it was obvious that the talkie would bring in far more Americanisms than the silent movie; moreover, it would also introduce the hated American accent. On February 4, 1930 Sir Alfred Knox, a Conservative M.P., demanded in the House of Commons that the Right Hon. William Graham, P.C., then president of the Board of Trade, take steps to " protect the English language by limiting the import of American talkie films." In a press interview he said:

> I don't go to the cinema often, but I had to be present at one a few days ago, when an American talkie film was shown. The words and accent were perfectly disgusting, and there can be no doubt that such films are an evil influence on our language. It is said that 30,000,000 [British] people visit the cinemas every week. What is the use of spending millions on education if our young people listen to falsified English spoken every night? [1]

There had been another such uproar in 1927, when an International Conference on English was held in London, under the presidency of the Earl of Balfour. This conference hardly got beyond polite futilities, but the fact that the call for it came from the American side [2] made it suspect from the start, and its deliberations

[1] According to the Associated Press, Mr. Graham pointed to the Cinematographic Act as designed to encourage British films, but added: " I'm not prepared to place direct restrictions on the importations of American talking films into this country."

[2] It was issued in March, 1922, and was signed by the late James W. Bright, then professor of English at the Johns Hopkins; Charles H. Grandgent of Harvard; Robert Underwood Johnson, secretary of the American Academy of Arts and Letters; John Livingston Lowes of Harvard; John M. Manly of the University of Chicago; Charles G. Osgood of Princeton, and the late Fred Newton Scott of the University of Michigan. A reply was received in October, 1922, from an English committee consisting of the Earl of Balfour, Dr. Robert Bridges and Sir Henry Newbolt, but it was not until five years later that the conference was actually held. It will be referred to again a bit later on.

met with unconcealed hostility. On June 25, 1927, the *New Statesman* let go with a heavy blast, rehearsing all the familiar English objections to Americanisms. It said:

It is extremely desirable, to say the least, that every necessary effort should be made to preserve some standard of pure idiomatic English. But from what quarter is the preservation of such a standard in any way threatened? The answer is "Solely from America." Yet we are asked to collaborate with the Americans on the problem; we are to make bargains about our own tongue; there is to be a system of give and take. . . . Why should we offer to discuss the subject at all with America? We do not want to interfere with their language; why should they seek to interfere with ours? That their huge hybrid population of which only a small minority are even racially Anglo-Saxons should use English as their chief medium of intercommunication is our misfortune, not our fault. They certainly threaten our language, but the only way in which we can effectively meet that threat is by assuming – in the words of the authors of "The King's English" [1] that "Americanisms are foreign words and should be so treated."

The proposal that a permanent Council of English be formed, with 50 American members and 50 from the British Empire, brought the *New Statesman* to the verge of hysterics. It admitted that such a council "might be very useful indeed," but argued that it " ought not to include more than one Scotsman and one Irishman, and should certainly not include even a single American." Thus it reasoned:

The American language is the American language, and the English language is the English language. In some respects the Americans may fairly claim superiority. *Sidewalk*, for example, is a better word than *pavement*, and *fall* an infinitely better word than *autumn*. If we do not adopt these better words it is simply because of their " American flavor "; and the instinct which makes us reject them, though unfortunate in certain cases, is profoundly right. The only way to preserve the purity of the English language is to present a steadily hostile resistance to every American innovation. From time to time we may adopt this word or that, or sometimes a whole vivid phrase. But for all serious lovers of the English tongue it is America that is the only dangerous enemy. She must develop her own language and allow us to develop ours.

The other English journals were rather less fierce in their denunciation of the council and its programme, but very few of them greeted either with anything approaching cordiality.[2] The *Times*,

[1] By H. W. and F. G. Fowler; Oxford, 1908.
[2] There is an account of their attitude, with quotations, by Dr. Kemp Malone of the Johns Hopkins, who was an American delegate to the conference, in *American Speech*, April, 1928, p. 261. The conference held two sessions, both at the quarters of the Royal Society of Literature. On the first day Lord Balfour presided, and on the second day Dr. Johnson. The speakers on the first day were Lord

obviously trying to be polite, observed that "without offense it may be said that no greater assaults are made on the common language than in America," and the *Spectator* ventured the view that in the United States English was departing definitely from the home standard, and was greatly "imposed upon and influenced by a host of immigrants from all the nations of Europe." This insistence that Americans are not, in any cultural sense, nor even in any plausible statistical sense, Anglo-Saxons is to be found in many English fulminations upon the subject. During the World War, especially after 1917, they were hailed as blood-brothers, but that lasted only until the first mention of war-debts. Ever since 1920 they have been mongrels again, as they were before 1917, and most discussions of Americanisms include the objection that yielding to them means yielding to a miscellaneous rabble of inferior tribes, some of them, by English standards, almost savage. There was a time when the American in the English menagerie of comic foreigners was Hiram Q. Simpkins or Ulysses X. Snodgrass, a Yankee of Puritan, and hence of vaguely English stock, but on some near tomorrow he will probably be Patrick Kraus, Rastus O'Brien, Ole Ginzberg, or some other such fantastic compound of races.

The complaint that Americanisms are inherently unintelligible to civilized Christians is often heard in England, though not as often as in the past. It is a fact that they frequently deal with objects and ideas that are not familiar to the English, and that sometimes they make use of metaphors rather too bold for the English imagination. In consequence, there has been a steady emission of glossaries since the earliest days, some of them on a large scale. The first seems to have been that of the Rev. Jonathan Boucher, which was probably drawn up before 1800, but was not published until 1832, when it

---

Balfour, Dr. Canby, George Bernard Shaw, Prof. Lloyd Jones of the British Broadcasting Corporation, Sir Israel Gollancz, Dr. Lowes, and Dr. Johnson. Those on the second day were Dr. Canby, Dr. Louise Pound of the University of Nebraska, Professor F. S. Boas, Dr. Lowes, Sir Henry Newbolt, and J. C. Squire. In addition to the speakers, those in attendance were Dr. Scott, Dr. George Philip Krapp, Prof. W. H. Wagstaff, Prof. J. Dover Wilson, Prof. A. Lloyd James, Dr. W. A. Craigie, and John Bailey. The conference was financed by the Commonwealth Fund, with some aid from Thomas W. Lamont. Later on the support of the Commonwealth Fund was withdrawn, and so the project to form a permanent Council of English fell through.

appeared in the second edition of his "Glossary of Archaic and Provincial Words." [1] It was followed by that of David Humphreys, one of the Hartford Wits, which was printed as an appendix to his play, "The Yankey in England," in 1815.[2] A year later came John Pickering's "Vocabulary or Collection of Words and Phrases Which Have Been Supposed to be Peculiar to the United States of America." Pickering got many of his words from the current English reviews of American books, and his purpose was the double, and rather contradictory, one of proving to the English reviewers that they were good English, and of dissuading Americans from using them.[3] Robley Dunglison's glossary followed in 1829–30, John

1 Boucher, who was born in England in 1737, came out to Virginia in 1759 as a private tutor. In 1762 he returned home to take holy orders, but was soon back in Virginia as rector of Hanover parish. He also conducted a school, and one of his pupils was young John Parke Custis, Washington's stepson. Boucher made the most of this connection. In 1770 he became rector at Annapolis, and soon afterward he married an heiress and bought a plantation on the Maryland side of the Potomac. His Loyalist sentiments got him into difficulties as the Revolution approached, and in 1775 he returned to England, where he died in 1804. In 1797 he published A View of the Causes and Consequences of the American Revolution, a series of thirteen sermons. After his death his friends began the publication of his Glossary of Archaic and Provincial Words, on which he had been engaged for thirty years. The first part, covering part of the letter A, came out in 1807. In 1832 the Rev. Joseph Hunter and Joseph Stevenson undertook to continue the work, but it got no further than Bl. Boucher's brief glossary of Americanisms appeared in the introduction to this second edition. It listed but 38 words. With it was printed Absence: a Pastoral; "drawn from the life, from the manners, customs and phraseology of planters (or, to speak more pas-

torally, of the rural swains) inhabiting the Banks of the Potomac, in Maryland." Boucher accused the Americans of "making all the haste they conveniently can to rid themselves of" the English language. "It is easy to foresee," he said, "that, in no very distant period, their language will become as independent of England as they themselves are, and altogether as unlike English as the Dutch or Flemish is unlike German, or the Norwegian unlike the Danish, or the Portuguese unlike Spanish." Absence is reprinted in *Dialect Notes*, Vol. VI, Pt. VII, 1933, with a commentary by Allen Walker Read.

2 It is reprinted in The Beginnings of American English, by M. M. Mathews; Chicago, 1931, pp. 56–63. About 280 terms are listed. They are mainly New England dialect forms, but one finds a few Americanisms that were in general use, and have survived, *e.g., breadstuffs, spook, nip* (a measure of drink), *to boost, to stump,* and *tarnation.*

3 Pickering's long introductory essay, but not his vocabulary, is reprinted in Mathews, pp. 65–76. On March 18, 1829, Dr. T. Romeyn Beck, a New York physician and antiquary, read a paper on the Pickering book before the Albany Institute. It was published in the *Transactions* of the Institute for 1830, and is reprinted by Mathews, pp. 78–85.

Mason Peck's in 1834,[1] J. O. Halliwell-Phillips's "Dictionary of Archaisms and Provincialisms, Containing Words Now Obsolete in England, All of Which Are Familiar and in Common Use in America" in 1850, John Russell Bartlett's "Glossary of Words and Phrases Usually Regarded as Peculiar to the United States" (about 3725 terms) in 1848, A. L. Elwin's "Glossary of Supposed Americanisms" (about 465 terms) in 1859, Maximilien Schele de Vere's "Americanisms" (about 4000 terms) in 1872, John S. Farmer's "Americanisms Old and New" (about 5000 terms) in 1889, Sylva Clapin's "New Dictionary of Americanisms" (about 5250 terms) in 1902, and Richard H. Thornton's "American Glossary" (about 3700 terms) in 1912. These were mainly the work of philological amateurs, and only Thornton's two volumes had any scientific value.

So long ago as 1913 Sir Sidney Low, who had lived in America and had a sound acquaintance with Americanisms, suggested ironically in an article in the *Westminster Gazette* that American be taught in the English schools. This was before the movie invasion, and he reported that the English business man was "puzzled by his ignorance of colloquial American" and "painfully hampered" thereby in his handling of American trade. He went on:

In the United States the study of the English tongue forms part of the educational scheme. . . . I think we should return the compliment. We ought to learn the American language in our schools and colleges. At present it is strangely neglected by the educational authorities. They pay attention to linguistic attainments of many other kinds, but not to this. How many thousands of youths are at this moment engaged in puzzling their brains over Latin and Greek grammar only Whitehall knows. Every well-conducted seminary has some instructor who is under the delusion that he is teaching English boys and girls to speak French with a good Parisian accent. We teach German, Italian, even Spanish, Russian, modern Greek, Arabic, Hindustani. For a moderate fee you can acquire a passing acquaintance with any of these tongues at the Berlitz Institute and the Gouin Schools. But even in these polyglot establishments there is nobody to teach you American. I have never

[1] Dunglison's glossary, dealing with about 190 terms, was published in three instalments in the *Virginia Literary Museum*. It was reprinted in *Dialect Notes*, Vol. V, Pt. X, 1927, with a commentary by Allen Walker Read. Peck's appeared in his Emigrant's Guide and Gazetteer of the State of Illinois, first published in 1834, and reissued with revisions in 1836 and 1837. See John

Mason Peck and the American Language, by Elrick B. Davis, *American Speech*, Oct., 1926. "An examination of the vocabulary of the 1837 edition," says Davis, "shows that out of 648 specific words used in strategic positions only 313 show a history in the Oxford Dictionary complete in Peck's use of them before 1789, the year of his birth."

seen a grammar of it or a dictionary. I have searched in vain at the book-sellers for "How to Learn American in Three Weeks" or some similar compendium. Nothing of the sort exists. The native speech of one hundred millions of civilized people is as grossly neglected by the publishers as it is by the schoolmasters. You can find means to learn Hausa or Swahili or Cape Dutch in London more easily than the expressive, if difficult, tongue which is spoken in the office, the barroom, the tramcar, from the snows of Alaska to the mouths of the Mississippi, and is enshrined in a literature that is growing in volume and favor every day.

Low quoted an extract from an American novel then appearing serially in an English magazine — an extract including such Americanisms as *side-stepper, saltwater-taffy, Prince-Albert* (coat), *boob, bartender* and *kidding,* and many characteristically American extravagances of metaphor. It might be well argued, he said, that this strange dialect was as near to "the tongue that Shakespeare spoke" as "the dialect of Bayswater or Brixton," but that philological fact did not help to its understanding. "You might almost as well expect him [the British business man] to converse freely with a Portuguese railway porter because he tried to stumble through Caesar when he was in the Upper Fourth at school."

At the time Low published his article the invasion of England by Americanisms was just beginning in earnest, and many words and phrases that have since become commonplaces there were still strange and disquieting. Writing in the London *Daily Mail* a year or so later W. G. Faulkner thought it necessary to explain the meanings of *hobo, hoodlum, bunco-steerer, dead-beat, flume, dub, rubber-neck, drummer, sucker, dive* (in the sense of a thieves' resort), *clean up, graft* and *to feature,* and another interpreter, closely following him, added definitions of *hold-up, quitter, rube, shack, bandwagon, road-agent, cinch, live-wire* and *scab.*[1] This was in the early days of the American-made movie, and Faulkner denounced its terminology as "generating and encouraging mental indiscipline." As Hollywood gradually conquered the English cinema palaces,[2]

[1] In Thornton's American Glossary *hobo* is traced to 1891, *hold-up* and *bunco* to 1887, *dive* to 1882, *deadbeat* to 1877, *hoodlum* to 1872, *road-agent* to 1866, *drummer* to 1836, and *flume* to 1792.

[2] The first American films reached England in 1907, but until 1915 they came in such small numbers that they were not separated, in the customs returns, from "optical supplies and equipment." In 1915 their total value was fixed at £47,486. But the next year it leaped to £349,919, and thereafter it mounted, with occasional recessions, to the peak of £880,240 in 1927. These values represented, of course, only the cost of the actual films, not that of the productions. In 1927 the Cinematograph Films Act was passed. It provided that all English exhibitors

such warnings became more frequent and more angry, and in 1920 the London *Daily News* began a formal agitation of the subject, with the usual pious editorials and irate letters from old subscribers. I quote a characteristic passage from one of the latter:

> I visited two picture theaters today for the express purpose of collecting slang phrases and of noticing the effect of the new language on the child as well as on the adult. What the villain said to the hero when the latter started to argue with him was, "*Cut out* that *dope*," and a hundred piping voices repeated the injunction. The comic man announced his marriage to the Bell of Lumbertown by saying, "I'm *hitched*."

On January 22, 1920 the London bureau of the Associated Press made this report:

> England is apprehensive lest the vocabularies of her youth become corrupted through incursions of American slang. Trans-Atlantic tourists in England note with interest the frequency with which resort is made to "Yankee talk" by British song and play writers seeking to enliven their productions. Bands and orchestras throughout the country when playing popular music play American selections almost exclusively. American songs monopolize the English music hall and musical comedy stage. But it is the subtitle of the American moving picture film which, it is feared, constitutes the most menacing threat to the vaunted English purity of speech.

When the American talkie began to reinforce the movie, in 1929 [1] there was fresh outburst of indignation, but this time it had a despairist undertone. Reinforced by the spoken word, Americanisms were now coming in much faster than they could be challenged and disposed of. "Within the past few years," said Thomas Anderson in the Manchester *Sunday Chronicle* for January 12, 1930, "we have

would have to show at least 5% of English-made films after Sept. 30, 1928, 7½% after the same date in 1930, 10% after 1931, 12½% after 1932, 15% after 1933, and 20% from Sept. 30, 1935 onward. The English duty is 1d. a foot on positives and 5d. on negatives. I am indebted for these figures and for those following to Mr. Lynn W. Meekins, American commercial attaché in London, and Mr. Henry E. Stebbins, assistant trade commissioner.

[1] After the introduction of the talkie the imports of American films showed a great decline in value. They dropped from £861,592 in 1929, to £506,477 in 1930, and to £130,847 in 1932. In part this was due to the operation of the Cinematograph Films Act, but in larger part it was produced by a change in trade practise. In the silent days many positives were sent to England, but since the talkie came in the film companies have been sending negatives and duplicating them in England. Thus the total annual footage is probably but little less than it was in 1929. Of the 476 imported films shown in England, Scotland and Wales in 1933, 330 were American, and according to Henry J. Gibbs, writing in the *Blackshirt*, "their value was 90 to 95% of the total."

gradually been adopting American habits of speech, American business methods, and the American outlook." To which Jameson Thomas added in the London *Daily Express* for January 21:

> One must admit that we write and speak Americanisms. So long as Yankeeisms came to us insiduously we absorbed them carelessly. They have been a valuable addition to the language, as nimble coppers are a valuable addition to purer currency. But the talkies have presented the American language in one giant meal, and we are revolted.

But this revolt, in so far as it was real at all, was apparently confined to the aged: the young of the British species continued to gobble down the neologisms of Hollywood and to imitate the Hollywood intonation. "Seldom do I hear a child speak," wrote a correspondent of the London *News Chronicle* on June 15, 1931, "who has not attached several Americanisms to his vocabulary, which are brought out with deliberation at every opportunity." During the next few years the English papers printed countless protests against this corruption of the speech of British youth, but apparently to no avail. Nor was there any halt when Col. F. W. D. Bendall, C.M.G., M.A., an inspector of the Board of Education, began stumping the country in an effort to further the dying cause of linguistic purity.[1] Nor when the chief constable — *i.e.*, chief of police — of Wallasey, a suburb of Liverpool, issued this solemn warning in his annual report:

> I cannot refrain from commenting adversely on the pernicious and growing habit of . . . youths to use Americanisms, with nasal accompaniment, in order to appear, in their own vernacular, *tough guys.* On one of

[1] The following is from the Denby *Herald's* report of an address by Col. Bendall before the Dudley Literary Society on January 31, 1931: "He suggested that though it was true that American had a remarkable capacity for growth, there was no need to suppose that it would eventually settle the form which English must take. Such a state of affairs would necessarily result either in a wider divergence between literary and spoken English or in literary English becoming affected. The former position would lead to a loss of subtlety in spoken English and to literature's becoming unintelligible to the masses, while to illustrate how deplorable the latter would be, the speaker read a part of Mr. Mencken's translation of the Declaration of Independence into modern American." The colonel's apparently grave acceptance of my burlesque as a serious specimen of "modern American" was matched by a sage calling himself John O'London in Is It Good English?; London, 1924, p. 92. After quoting the opening paragraph of my version, he said solemnly, "I hope 'these States' will suppress all such translations."

my officers going to search him, a young housebreaker told him to "*Lay off, cop*." *Oh-yeahs* are frequent in answer to charges, and we are promised *shoots up in the burg* [*sic*] and threatened to be *bumped off*.[1]

Parallel with this alarmed hostility to the jargon of the movies and the talkies, much of it borrowed from the American underworld, there has gone on in England a steady opposition to the more decorous varieties of American. I have already mentioned the *Times'* sneering review of the first two volumes of the Dictionary of American Biography. Back in 1919 H. N. Brailsford, the well-known English publicist, who has been in the United States many times and often contributes to American magazines, actually objected to the vocabulary of the extremely precious and Anglomaniacal Woodrow Wilson, then in action in Versailles. " The irruption of Mr. Wilson upon our scene," he wrote in the London *Daily Herald* on August 20, " threatens to modify our terminology. If one knew the American language (as I do not)," and so on.[2] A little while before this a leading English medical journal had been protesting against the Americanisms in an important surgical monograph.[3] Translations done in the United States are so often denounced that denouncing them has become a sort of convention. There was a storm of unusual violence, in 1925, over the plays of Luigi Pirandello. Their merit had been recognized in America earlier than in England — indeed, some of them had been forbidden, at least in English, by the English censor —, and in consequence the first translations were published in this country. What followed when they reached England was thus described by the London correspondent of the *Bookman* (New York) in its issue for September, 1925:

A strange situation has arisen over the Pirandello translations. These were made in America, and they contain phraseology which is peculiarly

1 Chief Constable's Report for the Year Ended 31st December, 1932; Wallasey, 1933, p. 13.
2 In the London *Times* for June 15, 1927, George Bernard Shaw was reported as saying: " When President Wilson came to this country he gave us a shock by using the word *obligate* instead of *oblige*. It showed that a man could become President in spite of that, and we asked ourselves if a man could become King of England if he used

the word *obligate*. We said at once that it could not be done."
3 Review in the *Medical Press*, Sept. 17, 1919, of an article by MacCarty and Connor in *Surgery, Gynecology and Obstetrics*. "In the study of the terminology of diseases of the breast," said the reviewer, " [the authors] suggest a scheme which seems simple, but unfortunately for British understanding, it is written in American."

American. As a consequence they have been generally condemned in the English press as being translations from one foreign tongue into another. . . . It will be understood that when an English reader is used to calling comfits *sweets* and finds them called *candies* he feels he is not getting an English equivalent of the Italian author's word.

This correspondence was signed Simon Pure; its actual author, I am informed, was Rebecca West. She expressed the opinion that English translations of foreign books were frequently offensive to Americans, and for like reasons. " It seems to me to be a pity," she continued, " that the habit should have grown up among Continental authors of selling ' world rights in the English language.' If the English translation does not satisfy the Americans, and the American translation does not please the English, it would surely be far better that there should be two translations." In a long reply to this, published in the *Saturday Review of Literature* (New York) for December 26, 1925, Ernest Boyd — himself a translator of wide experience, born in Ireland, educated there and in England, for seven years a member of the British consular service, and resident in New York since 1920 — denied that there was any hostility to English translations in this country. " English translators," he said, " are accepted at their own — or their publishers' — valuation in America," but American translators " are received with prejudice and criticized with severity " in England. The American edition of Pirandello's plays consisted of two volumes, one translated by Dr. Arthur Livingston of Columbia University, and the other by Edward Storer, an Englishman. Said Mr. Boyd:

Dr. Livingston, the American, is taken to task though his Italian scholarship is well authenticated and beyond dispute. Mr. Storer, on the contrary, is an Englishman, and his translations are so defective in places as to show a complete misunderstanding of the text, but no complaints have been raised on that score. . . . One might have thought that the proper claim would be that a competent person, and only a competent person, irrespective of nationality, should translate. But British nationality is more important than American scholarship, apparently.

The ensuing debate ran on for several years; in fact, it is still resumed from time to time, with the English champions holding stoutly to the doctrine that there can be but one form of English pure and undefiled, and that it must, shall and will be the Southern English variety. Thus Raymond Mortimer in the *Nation and Athenaeum* for July 28, 1928:

It is most unfortunate that American publishers should be able to buy the English as well as the American rights of foreign books. For the result usually is that these books remain permanently closed to the English reader.[1]

The English objection is not alone to the American vocabulary; it is also to the characteristic American style, which begins to differ appreciably from the normal English style. In every recent discussion of the matter the despairist note that I was mentioning a few paragraphs back is audible. There was a time when the English guardians of the mother-tongue tried to haul American into conformity by a kind of *force majeure*, but of late they seem to be resigned to its differentiation, and are concerned mainly about the possibility that Standard English may be considerably modified by its influence. As I have noted, H. W. and F. G. Fowler, in "The King's English," were deciding so long ago as 1906 that "Americanisms are foreign words, and should be so treated." They admitted that American had its points of superiority — "*Fall* is better on the merits than *autumn*, in every way; it is short, Saxon (like the other three season names), picturesque; it reveals its derivation to everyone who uses it, not to the scholar only, like *autumn*" —, but they protested against taking even the most impeccable Americanisms into English. "The English and the American language and literature," they argued, "are both good things, but they are better apart than mixed." In

1 Many more examples might be added, some of them not without their humors. Back in 1921 J. C. Squire (now Sir John) was protesting bitterly because an American translator of the Journal of the Goncourts "spoke of a *pavement* as a *sidewalk*." See the *Literary Review* of the New York *Evening Post*, July 23, 1921. In Dostoevsky: Letters and Reminiscences, translated from the Russian by S. S. Kotelinansky and J. Middleton Murry (New York, 1923; American binding of English sheets) there is this note, p. 282: "Saltykov, Mihail Efgrafovich (who used the pseudonym N. Schedrin), author of the Golovlevs, one of the greatest of Russian novels, which has been translated into French and American, but not yet into English." Such sneers are now answered by defiance as often as with humility.

When Dr. Edgar J. Goodspeed, professor of Biblical and patristic Greek at the University of Chicago, published his new version of the New Testament (Chicago, 1923) he boldly called it "an American translation," and in it he as boldly employed Americanisms in place of the English forms of the Authorized Version. Thus *corn*, meaning wheat in England but maize in America, was changed to *wheat* in Mark II, 23, Mark IV, 28, and Matthew XII, 1. Similarly, when Ezra Pound published Ta Hio: the Great Learning (*University of Washington Chapbooks*, No. 14; Seattle, 1928) he described it on the title-page as "newly rendered into the American language." See American and English translations of "The Oppermanns," by Edmund E. Miller, *American Speech*, Oct., 1935.

1910 the Encylopædia Britannica (Eleventh Edition) admitted that this falling apart had already gone so far that it was " not uncommon to meet with American newspaper articles of which an untravelled Englishman would hardly be able to understand a sentence." " The fact is," said the London *Times Literary Supplement* for January 21, 1926, in a review of G. P. Krapp's " The English Language in America," " that in spite of the greater frequency of intercourse the two idioms *have* drifted apart; farther apart than is, perhaps, generally recognized. . . . A British visitor in America, if he has any taste for the niceties of language, experiences something of the thrills of contact with a foreign idiom, for he hears and reads many things which are new to him and not a few which are unintelligible." " If the American temperament, despite its general docility, persists in its present attitude towards a standardized language," said Ernest Weekley in " Adjectives — and Other Words " (1930), " spoken American must eventually become as distinct from English as Yiddish is from classical Hebrew." Or, added Professor J. Y. T. Greig of Newcastle in " Breaking Priscian's Head " (1929), as " Spanish is from Portuguese."

This echo of Noah Webster is itself echoed frequently by other English publicists and philologians. There is, indeed, a school of English thought which holds that the United States is not only drifting away from the mother country linguistically, but is fundamentally differentiated from it on wider cultural grounds. " Those who have had to do with Americans," said Geoffrey Grigson in the London *Morning Post* for February 13, 1934, " will not mistake them for our intimate cousins, our near psychic relations." He continued:

> They are linked to us by many strands of sympathy, but they are a different people, or a number of different peoples. Their language, their real literature — witness Poe, Hawthorne, Melville, James, Ransom, Macleish, Hemingway — are different; and one might say even that the more they are English the more they are alien. The New Englander, for example, feels and thinks differently; his communal, political, and person " mythology " — to use a convenient word for those bodies of fiction and " belief " which unite each social entity — differentiates him completely from an Englishman. I am not sure, in fact, that we cannot more easily get to understand the soul of Frenchman, Italian, German, Spaniard even. After all, we belong geographically and spiritually to the European cultural *bloc*.

The late Cecil Chesterton was saying something to the same general effect in the London *New Witness* so long ago as 1915. "I do not believe," he wrote, " that nations ever quarrel merely because they feel that they do not understand each other. That attitude of mind of itself tends to produce a salutary humility on the one side and a pleasantly adventurous curiosity on the other. What really produces trouble between peoples is when one is quite certain that it understands the other — and in fact doesn't. And I am perfectly certain that that has been from the first one of the primary causes of trouble between England and America." [1] To which may be added the following from an article by Herbert Agar in the *New Statesman* for August 8, 1931:

> The English should try to cope with their philological ignorance. They should train themselves to realize that it is neither absurd nor vulgar that a language which was once the same should in the course of centuries develop differently in different parts of the world. If such were not the case, we should all still be speaking a sort of Ur-Sanskrit. Just as French and Italian may be described as divergent forms of modern Latin, so it would be helpful to think of the language of Oxford and the language of Harvard as divergent forms of modern English. It is perhaps a pity, from the point of view of international good feeling, that the two forms have not diverged a little further. At any rate, when the Englishman can learn to think of American as a language, and not merely as a ludicrously unsuccessful attempt to speak as he himself speaks, when he can learn to have for American only the normal intolerance of the provincial mind for all foreign tongues, then there will come a great improvement in Anglo-American relations. For even though Americans realise the absurdity of the English attitude toward their language, nevertheless they remain deeply annoyed by it. This is natural, for a man's language is his very soul. It is his thoughts and almost all his consciousness. Laugh at a man's language, and you have laughed at the man himself in the most inclusive sense.

But not all Englishmen, of course, indulge themselves in the derision that Mr. Agar denounces. The prevailing tone of English opinion remains loftily anti-American, in linguistic as in other matters, but there have arisen in late years two factions which take a more moderate position, the one contending that American speech is really not the barbaric jargon it is commonly thought to be, and the other arguing boldly that its peculiarities, though maybe somewhat uncouth, nevertheless have a merit of their own. A representative spokesman of the first faction is Sir Charles Strachey, M.C.M.G., a former official of the Foreign and Colonial Offices. On May 2, 1931, he wrote to the London *Times* to protest against the assumption that the argot of Chicago gunmen is the official language of the

[1] The article is summarized, with long extracts, in the *Literary Digest* for June 19, 1915, p. 1468.

United States. " American diplomatic correspondence," he said, " is always a model of correct English, and it would be a gross error to suppose that the United States Ambassador calls revenue the *dough* or the *berries*, and refers to his Italian colleagues as a *wop*." But this Strachey faction is not large, and as a general thing even the language of American diplomacy grates on English nerves, as I was lately noting in the case of H. N. Brailsford's objection to the style of Woodrow Wilson.

The revolutionary theory that the American language actually has some merit seems to have been launched by William Archer, a Scotsman, in an article entitled " American Today," printed somewhat prudently, not in England, but in *Scribner's Magazine* for February, 1899. " New words," he said, " are begotten by new conditions of life; and as American life is far more fertile of new conditions than ours, the tendency toward neologism cannot but be stronger in America than in England. American has enormously enriched the language, not only with new words, but (since the American mind is, on the whole, quicker and wittier than the English) with apt and luminous colloquial metaphors." Twenty years later Archer returned to the matter, this time on English soil, in an article written for the *Westminster Gazette*.[1] In it he protested vigorously against the English habit of " pulling a wry face over American expressions, not because they are inherently bad, but simply because they are American. The vague and unformulated idea behind all such petty cavillings," he continued, " is that the English language is in danger of being corrupted by the importation of Americanisms, and that it behooves us to establish a sort of quarantine in order to keep out the detrimental germs. This notion is simply one of the milder phases of the Greater Stupidity."

Two years before this, Frank Dilnot, an English journalist with American experience, had come out for American in a large way. " Show me the alert Englishman," he wrote,[2] " who will not find a stimulation in those nuggety word-groupings which are the commonplaces in good American conversation. They are like flashes of crystal. They come from all kinds of people — who are brilliantly innocent of enriching the language. . . . The American tongue, written or spoken with its alteration from the English of England,

1 Reprinted in the *Literary Review* of the New York *Evening Post*, July 23, 1921.   2 The New America; New York, 1919, Ch. III.

is a potent and penetrating instrument, rich in new vibrations, full of joy as well as shocks for the unsuspecting visitor." In May, 1920, Richard Aldington joined the American party in an article contributed to *Poetry* (Chicago). In it he made an eloquent plea for American linguistic independence, and praised the development of a characteristically American idiom by the American poets and novelists of the day. "Are Americans," he demanded,

> to write the language which they speak, which is slowly but inevitably separating itself from the language of England, or are they to write a devitalized idiom learned painfully from books or from a discreet frequentation of London literary cliques? . . . Englishmen of letters and literary journalists may publish these exhortations and practise their refinements: in vain — a vast and increasingly articulate part of the English-speaking and English-writing world will ignore them. Another century may see English broken into a number of dialects or even different languages, spoken in Canada, Australia, South Africa, the United States and England. The result may eventually be similar to the break-up of Latin.

This pro-American party is still small, but it can show some well-known names. The late Robert Bridges, Poet Laureate and founder of the Society for Pure English, was in sympathy with it,[1] and it has got support from Wyndham Lewis, Edward Shanks, Virginia

---

1 The Society was organized in 1913, but the intervention of the war suspended its proceedings until 1918. The first of its Tracts was issued in October, 1919. The original committee consisted of Dr. Bridges, Henry Bradley, Sir Walter Raleigh and L. Pearsall Smith, the last-named an American living in England. In Tract No. I one of its purposes was stated to be the encouragement of "those who possess the word-making faculty," and another was the enrichment of Standard English with dialectic and "democratic" forms and usages. In Tract No. XXIV, 1926, Dr. Bridges protested against an allegation that the Society was "working for uniformity and standardization against idiom and freedom. Our readers," he went on, "know that this is not what we intend or desire; indeed teachers, who as a class advocate standardization of speech as the necessary basis for general tuition, sometimes complain of us as mis-chief-makers because we do not support them more thoroughly." In 1922 Dr. Bridges wrote to Dr. H. S. Canby: "We desire as many American subscribers as possible, *in order to make our Society seem as much American as it is English.* [His italics.] There is a great and natural prejudice in America against English dictation in the matter of our language, and that followed, I think, as a protest against the insular contempt which the English felt a couple of generations ago for American forms of speech. We now in England feel very differently and the S.P.E. would certainly treat American usages and preferences with full respect" (*Literary Review*, May 20, 1922). "The S.P.E.," says J. Y. T. Greig in Breaking Priscian's Head (London, 1929), "despite its inauspicious name, has done a great deal of splendid work, but only because it happened to be founded by, and to have remained under, the control of men like Dr.

Woolf and Sir John Foster Fraser. "The Americans," said Mrs. Woolf in the *Saturday Review of Literature* on August 1, 1925, " are doing what the Elizabethans did — they are coining new words. They are instinctively making the language adapt itself to their needs." She continued:

> In England, save for the impetus given by the war, the word-coining power has lapsed; our writers vary the metres of their poetry, remodel the rhythms of prose, but one may search English fiction in vain for a single new word. It is significant that when we want to freshen our speech, we borrow from American — *poppycock, rambunctious, flip-flop, booster, good mixer*. All the expressive, ugly, vigorous slang which creeps into use among us, first in talk, later in writing, comes from across the Atlantic.

In February, 1925, H. E. Moore printed an elaborate defense of Americanisms in the *English Review*, then edited by Austin Harrison. He contrasted the tendency to academic tightness in Standard English with the greater naturalness of American, and gave high praise to some of the salient characters of the latter — its hospitality to neologisms, its fertility in effective metaphor, its " fluid " spelling. " As this divergence of English and American," he said, " has proceeded through strata of English derision and American defiance it has tended to become deliberate and constructive. England and academic America generally have asserted the old criteria. But they have been swept aside by America's egalitarian millions, and established changes have now made any acceptance of literary Southern English impossible." " I have never found it possible," said Mr. Shanks in the London *Evening Standard* in 1931,

> to understand why with so many people there should be an automatic objection to anything that can be called an Americanism. An Americanism is an expression adopted by those who speak our common language but who live in the United States. There are more of them than there are of us, and so one would suppose, on democratic principles, that their choice was entitled at least to our serious consideration. There are, in fact, more of them than of all the other English-speaking peoples put together, and a majority vote on the question to whom the language really belongs would certainly give a verdict against us. Yet, for many of us " Americanism " is simply a term of abuse. . . . The facts that we ought to realise and that we ignore when we talk loftily about " Americanisms " are that America is making a formidable contribution to the development of our language and that all our attempts to reject that contribution will in the long run be vain — quite apart from the other fact

---

Bridges, Mr. L. P. Smith, and Mr. H. W. Fowler. This was a fortunate and very rare accident. In wrong hands it would have long ago become a dreadful curse, a veritable Inquisition and Congregation of the Propaganda rolled into one."

that we ought to rejoice in this proof that the language is still alive and capable of learning from experience.

Writing a year later, Sir John Fraser[1] made a vigorous attack upon the dominant anti-American party, and accused it of trying absurdly to halt a process of inevitable change. He said:

> Quite respectable people, very refined, even literary gents and prelates, would faint were they not so angry at the Americanization of our ways, and particularly the degradation of our speech. Why? If we take up the position that because we are British we must be right there is no argument. But if the Anglicization of the world is good, why is the Americanization of England bad? . . . Is our language to remain staid and dignified like a piece of furniture made when good Victoria was Queen, or, as we live in swiftly shifting times, aeroplanes and record-smashing cars, is there something to be said for adapting our ways of speech to the newer generations? . . . Then there is the other school, which is called the Oxford manner, though mostly adopted by people who know nothing about Oxford. With their stuffy, roof-of-the-mouth inflections [*sic*] they have developed a speech of their own. . . . I prefer slangy American.

In *Life and Letters* for April, 1934, Wyndham Lewis argued at length that, even if it were rational, it was too late for the English to stem the advance of American. He said:

> While England was a uniquely powerful empire-state, ruled by an aristocratic caste, its influence upon the speech as upon the psychology of the American ex-colonies was overwhelming. But today that ascendancy has almost entirely vanished. The aristocratic caste is nothing but a shadow of itself, the cinema has brought the American scene and the American dialect nightly into the heart of England, and the Americanizing process is far advanced. . . . There has been no reciprocal movement of England into the United States; indeed, with the New American nationalism, England is deliberately kept out. . . . So the situation is this, as far as our common language is concerned: the destiny of England and the United States is more than ever one, but it is now the American influence that is paramount. The tables have effectively been turned in this respect.

Finally, I extract a few sentences of sage advice from a radio speech to his fellow-countrymen by Alistair Cooke, of the British Broadcasting Corporation:

> When you hear an expression that seems a little odd to you, don't assume it was invented by a music-hall comedian trying to be smart. It was probably spoken by Lincoln or Paul Jones. . . . And when you hear a strange pronunciation remember you are not hearing a chaotic speech that anyone has deliberately changed. . . . It is the cultivated speech of a New England gentleman of 1934, and it happens in essentials also to be the cultivated speech you would have heard in London over two hundred years ago.[2]

1 London *Sunday Graphic*, Jan. 3, 1932.

2 Printed as That Dreadful American, *Listener*, Jan. 30, 1935.

5. THE POSITION OF THE LEARNED

But these witnesses to the virtues and glories of the American language are not to be taken as representative of English opinion; nor even as spokesmen for any considerable part of it. In general, it remains almost as hostile to Americanisms as it was in the Golden Age of the critical reviews. Nor does its hostility go without support in the United States. On the contrary there has been, since the early Eighteenth Century, a party of Americans vowed to the strict policing of the national speech habits, usually with the English example in mind, and it has always had a formidable body of adherents. In 1724 Hugh Jones, professor of mathematics at William and Mary College, expressed the wish that a " Publick Standard were fix'd " to " direct Posterity, and prevent Irregularity, and confused Abuses and Corruptions in our Writings and Expressions." [1] In Section 1 of the present chapter I have mentioned John Adams's keen interest in a project to set up an American Academy to " correct, enrich and refine " the language, " until perfection stops their progress and ends their labor." In 1806 a bill to establish such an academy was actually introduced in the Senate by Senator George Logan of Pennsylvania and given a favorable report by a committee of which John Quincy Adams was a member, but some irreverent member moved that the word *national* be stricken out of the title, and when this motion was carried the enterprise died. Soon afterward an American Academy of Arts and Sciences was formed in Boston, and in 1820 an American Academy of Language and Belles Lettres followed in New York, with John Quincy Adams as president. The latter appointed a committee headed by the Rev. John M. Mason, provost of Columbia College and later president of Dickinson College, " to collect throughout the United States a list of words and phrases, whether acknowledged corruptions or words of doubtful authority, which are charged up as bad English, with a view to take the best practical course for promoting the purity and uni-

[1] An Accidence to the English Tongue; London, 1724. This was the first English grammar written in America. For the reference to it I am indebted to American Projects For an Academy to Regulate Speech, by Allen Walker Read, *Publications of the Modern Language Association*, 1935. For part of what follows I am also indebted to Mr. Read.

formity of our language." And the former received from one of its
members, John Pickering, that "Vocabulary or Collection of Words
and Phrases Which Have Been Supposed to be Peculiar to the
United States of America" (1816) which I have already noticed.

Pickering's professional career was made in the law, with occasional ventures into politics, but he passed for a scholar in his time,
he was offered the chair of Oriental languages at Harvard in 1806
and that of Greek in 1814, and he published a Greek-English lexicon
in 1826. The preface to his Vocabulary was largely devoted to a
defense of the English reviewers. "It cannot be denied," he said,
"that we have in several instances deviated from the standard of
the language, as *spoken and written in England at the present day.*
[His italics.] By this I do not mean that so great a deviation has
taken place as to have rendered any considerable part of our language unintelligible to Englishmen, but merely that so many corruptions have crept into *our English* as to have become the subject
of much animadversion and regret with the learned of Great Britain." Pickering then proceeded to argue that these animadversions
and regrets were well founded, and called upon his erring countrymen to "imitate the example of the learned and modest Campbell," [1]
who, though he had devoted a great part of a long life to the study
of the English language, "yet thought it no disgrace to make an
apology for his style," and to remember the similar diffidence of
Irenaeus, Bishop of Lugdunum (Lyons) in Gaul, who prefixed a
similar apology for his shaky provincial Latin to his "Adversus
Hæreses." Thus Pickering summed up:

> Upon an impartial consideration of the subject, therefore, it seems impos-
> sible to resist the conclusion that, although the language of the United States
> has perhaps changed less than might have been expected, when we consider
> how many years have elapsed since our ancestors brought it from England,
> yet it has in so many instances departed from the English standard that our
> scholars should lose no time in endeavoring to restore it to its purity, and to
> prevent further corruption. . . . As a general rule, we should undoubtedly
> avoid all those words which are noticed by English authors of reputation as
> expressions with which *they are unacquainted*, for although we might produce
> some English authority for such words, yet the very circumstance of their
> being thus noticed by well-educated *Englishmen* is a proof that they are not
> in use at this day in England, and, of course, ought not to be used elsewhere
> by those who would speak *correct English.*

1 George   Campbell   (1719–96), a   ever, for his Philosophy of Rhet-
Scottish theologian who published   oric, 1776. Pickering's reference
a New Translation of the Gospels   is to the preface to the Gospels.
in 1778. He is best known, how-

Again I follow Pickering's italization. His theory is still entertained by multitudes of American pedagogues. They believe as he did that the natural growth of the language is wild and wicked, and that it should be regulated according to rules formulated in England. To this end they undertake periodical crusades against "bad grammar," the American scheme of pronunciation, and the general body of Americanisms — in the classroom, by means of hortatory pamphlets and leaflets, and over the air. In 1915 the National Council of Teachers of English, following that hopeful American custom which gave the nation Mothers' Day, and Safety-First, Paint-Up-Clean-Up and Eat-More-Cheese Weeks, proposed to make the first seven days of November Better-Speech Week. Ten years later the General Federation of Women's Clubs joined the movement, and for some unknown reason the time was changed to the last week in February. For awhile Better-Speech Week was much discussed in the newspapers, and it is still observed, I believe, in parts of the country. Some of the schoolmarms, despairing of effecting a wholesale reform, concentrated their efforts upon various specific crimes against their canons, and among the subsidiary weeks thus launched were *Ain't*-less Week and Final-*G* Week. They also established a Tag Day, and hung derisory tags on youngsters guilty of such indecencies as "I have *got*" and "It's *me*."[1] This missionary effort was not confined to school-children. Efforts were also made to perfect the speech of their parents and of the public in general, and even the newspapers were besought to mend their linguistic ways. In 1925, a Los Angeles schoolmarm went about Southern California inducing women's clubs to pass the following resolution:

Whereas, we believe that if newspaper comic strips and jokes use English free from grammatical errors (except for decided character rôles) they will become more attractive to many readers, and

Whereas, we believe that this effort on the part of the newspapers will be of invaluable aid in raising the standard of American speech, therefore

Be it resolved, that we request editors of newspapers and comic writers to eliminate grammatical errors in the comic strips and jokes except for decided character rôles.[2]

The object of attack here, of course, was the grotesque slang that appears from nowhere, has its brief day, and then vanishes. But the

[1] The Baltimore *Evening Sun* reported that this was a new project in the Baltimore public-schools on Jan. 21, 1925.

[2] *American Speech*, Jan., 1926, p. 250.

American pedagogues, with few exceptions, seem to be opposed also to more decorous Americanisms, and many of them devote themselves to teaching a pronunciation that is quite foreign to the country, and to inculcating grammatical niceties that were concocted during the earnest but innocent days when English grammar was assumed to be a kind of Latin grammar — niceties that have been long since abandoned by the English themselves. The influence of Samuel Johnson is thus still more or less potent in the American public schools, though Noah Webster was denouncing it so long ago as 1789. On this melancholy theme I shall discourse at greater length in Chapter IX.

The higher varieties of gogues are somewhat less naïve, but they nevertheless show a considerable reluctance to deal with American as the living language of a numerous and puissant people, making its own rules as it goes along and well worthy of scientific study. Very few American philologians have specialized in it, and such study of it as has been undertaken has been carried on by amateurs quite as often as by professionals. It is rare for any discussion of it to appear in such journals as *Modern Language Notes*, *Modern Philology*, *Language*, the *American Philological Journal*, the *English Journal*, and the *Journal of English and Germanic Philology*, or for it to be undertaken seriously at the annual meetings of the philological associations.[1] *Dialect Notes*, the first journal to be devoted to it, was not set up until 1890, and *American Speech* did not follow until 1925. Both have had very meager support. *Dialect Notes* was launched by the American Dialect Society, which had been organized at Harvard

---

1 For example, in *Modern Language Notes*, Vol. XLVIII, 1933, there is but one reference to it and that is in a review of H. C. Wyld's Universal Dictionary, 1932, by Kemp Malone. In *Modern Philology*, Vol. XXXII, 1933–34, there is no mention of American. In *Publications of the Modern Language Association*, Vol. XLVIII, 1933, which runs to 1400 pages, there is only a brief note by Sir William Craigie, editor of the Dictionary of American English, calling on American philologians for aid. In the annual bibliography of philological papers for 1932, p. 1342 ff., 45 articles on American English are listed, but 31 of them appeared in *American Speech*, 6 in *Dialect Notes*, 6 in popular magazines, and only 2 in professional journals. The Modern Language Association has a Present-Day Speech Section, but it shows little effective activity. The association, which was founded in 1883, had 4,132 members in 1932. " Under the protection of our ægis," said Dr. A. H. Thorndike in his presidential address in 1927, " are gathering languages whose applications for membership not even the secretary can read." Perhaps American will one day be one of them.

University in 1889, with the late Professor Francis J. Child, the authority on English and Scottish ballads, as its first president.¹ It made very slow progress. Though there were, at that time, fully 5,000 teachers of English in the United States, including at least 500 in the colleges,² it started off with but 140 members, and the publication of the first volume of *Dialect Notes*, running to 497 pages, dragged through six years. When the second volume was completed, in 1904, the society had 310 members, but many of them failed to pay their dues, and by 1912 successive purges had reduced the roll to 219. The income was then less than $400 a year. By 1926 the membership had grown to 266 and by 1932 the income was $776.38. Neither membership nor income appears to have increased since, for *Dialect Notes* now comes out only at long intervals, and its average issue is very thin. Yet its files contain a very large amount of invaluable matter, as my frequent references to them will show, and it long offered the only outlet for the work of that small minority of American scholars who took the national language seriously, and gave it scientific study — among them, Drs. Percy W. Long, C. H. Grandgent and E. S. Sheldon of Harvard, E. H. Babbitt of Columbia, George Hempl of Michigan, George T. Flom of Iowa, E. H. Sturtevant of Yale, O. F. Emerson of Western Reserve, C. S. Northrup of Cornell, J. W. Carr of Maine, L. W. Payne, Jr., of Texas, William A. Read of Louisiana, Josiah Combs of Texas Christian, John M. Manly and Allen Walker Reed of Chicago, and Louise Pound of Nebraska.

The work of Dr. Pound has been especially productive, for whereas most of the other members of the Dialect Society have

---

1 The original members included C. H. Grandgent, E. S. Sheldon, George L. Kittredge and J. M. Manly of Harvard, James W. Bright and A. Marshall Elliott of the Johns Hopkins, Eugene H. Babbitt of Columbia, O. F. Emerson and Benjamin Ide Wheeler of Cornell, W. D. Whitney and W. R. Harper of Yale, and F. A. March of Lafayette. James Russell Lowell was also a member.

2 Just how many are in practise today I do not know, but it must be a very large number. L. J. O'Rourke, in Rebuilding the English-Usage Curriculum; Washington, 1934, p. 4, says that "more than 40,000 teachers of English" aided him in his inquiry — all of them, it appears, teaching in grade-schools. The Educational Lists Company of New York and Chicago, which supplies the names and addresses of teachers to advertisers, offers a list of 18,000 names of high-school teachers teaching "English language, literature, drama and public speaking," and one of 5,750 "English teachers" in the colleges and normal-schools. Some of these, of course, also teach other subjects.

confined their investigations to the regional dialects of American, she and her pupils have studied the general speechways of the country. She took her doctorate at Heidelberg under the distinguished Anglicist, Johannes Hoops, and soon afterward joined the English faculty of the University of Nebraska. Her first contribution to *Dialect Notes* was published in 1905; thereafter, for twenty years, she or her pupils were represented in almost every issue. In 1925, in association with Dr. Kemp Malone of the Johns Hopkins and Dr. Arthur G. Kennedy of Stanford, she founded *American Speech*, becoming its first editor. She continued in that capacity until 1933, when she was succeeded by Dr. William Cabell Greet of Barnard College, Columbia University. *American Speech*, even more than *Dialect Notes*, has encouraged the study of American: its files constitute a rich mine of instructive and often very amusing stuff. But it has got but little more support from American teachers of English than its predecessor. Though its first issues contained many articles addressed to them directly, they refused to be interested, and during its later years its pages have been supplied largely by lay students of the language. During its first five years its subscription list never reached 1500 names, and at the beginning of its sixth year it had but 329 subscribers. When Dr. Pound retired in 1933 it was taken over by the Columbia University Press. Today it continues to be published at a loss, though Dr. Greet and his associates make it a very useful journal.[1] Beginning as a monthly, it is now a quarterly.

This failure of support has greatly hampered the work of the American Dialect Society. It projected an American Dialect Dictionary immediately after its organization in 1889, and by 1930 its collection of materials embraced more than 30,000 words and phrases. But so far the lack of funds has prevented the completion of the work,[2] and it has had to give place to two more recent enter-

---

[1] This lack of academic interest in the American language was for many years matched by a lack of interest in American literature, but since the setting up of the quarterly, *American Literature*, at Duke University in 1929, partly as a result of the activities of the American Literature Group of the Modern Language Association, there has been something of an awakening. The old neglect of Whitman, Melville and Clemens will be recalled. The first professorship of American literature seems to have been established at the Pennsylvania State College in 1894, with Dr. Fred Lewis Pattee as the incumbent. The chair is still a rare one in the American colleges.

[2] Another enterprise of the Dialect Society that has suffered from inadequate support is its publication of the third volume of R. H. Thorn-

prises, both of which seem to be adequately financed, and promise to give the study of American English great encouragement, and to set it, in combination, upon a scientific foundation. The first is the Dictionary of American English on Historical Principles, now going forward at the University of Chicago under the direction of Sir William Craigie, one of the editors of the New English Dictionary (now called the Oxford English Dictionary); the other is the Linguistic Atlas of the United States, in charge of Dr. Hans Kurath of Brown University and sponsored by the American Council of Learned Societies. The first fascicle of the former appeared early in 1936, and the first map of the latter shortly afterward. Both will require years for their completion. Sir William and Dr. Kurath are alike of foreign birth, the former being a Scotsman and the latter an Austrian.[1]

ton's American Glossary. Before his death Thornton deposited his manuscript in the Widener Library, and in 1931 its publication was begun in *Dialect Notes* under the editorship of Percy W. Long. The first instalment ran to 112 pages, and it was hoped to complete the work by December, 1933. But the failure of expected aid caused such a slacking of pace that by that time only *J* had been reached. Thornton's first two volumes came out in England in 1912 in a modest edition of 2000 copies. Of these, 250 were imported by an American publisher. Selling them was slow work, and when they were exhausted at last no more were imported. In this connection it may be recalled that George Philip Krapp's The English Language in America; New York, 1925, a work of very high value, failed to find a commercial publisher, and had to be brought out "for the Modern Language Association of America" at the cost of the Carnegie Corporation. Thornton's somewhat pathetic account of his difficulties is to be found in *Dialect Notes*, Vol. V, Pt. II, 1919. "Early in 1917," he said, "I made an appeal to a large number of wealthy Americans — this was before we were in the war — to help

the venture financially. To their lasting infamy, they were uniformly too unappreciative to respond."

[1] On Oct. 18, 1924 the Chicago *Tribune* announced Sir William's appointment under these headlines:

MIDWAY SIGNS
LIMEY PROF. TO
DOPE YANK TALK

He was born at Dundee in 1867 and was educated at St. Andrews and at Oxford. He joined the staff of the New English Dictionary in 1897, and became joint editor in 1901. His specialty is Scandinavian, but he has also written on Anglo-Saxon, Gaelic, Scottish and modern English. He was knighted in 1928, but, rather curiously, this fact is not noted in Who's Who in America. Dr. Kurath was born in Austria in 1891 and came to America in 1907. He studied at the Universities of Wisconsin, Texas and Chicago, and took his Ph.D. at the last-named. His specialty is the comparative grammar of the Indo-European languages. He was assistant professor of German at Northwestern, 1920–27, and professor of German at Ohio State, 1927–32. In 1932 he became professor of German at Brown.

Sir William described the origin of the Dictionary of American English in the *English Journal* (Chicago) for January, 1926. The dictionaries hitherto published in the United States, he said,

have commonly noted the different usage of the two countries, in respect both of the words and of their pronunciation. In none of these dictionaries, however, has there been any attempt to make the language of the United States the sole, or even main, basis of the matter they contain. Even Webster, although he patriotically called for a " national language " as well as a national government, contented himself, when he published " An American Dictionary of the English Language," with having cited American authors as well as English. All subsequent dictionaries which have appeared in this country have adhered to the same principle – their American material is merely an addition (sometimes a very restricted addition) to that drawn from English or British sources. . . . So far as I am aware, this fact had not clearly presented itself to anyone until it occurred to me one day in the Summer of 1924, in Chicago, while I was reading some proofs of the Oxford English Dictionary. I observed that in the case of two or three words beginning with the prefix *un-* the older quotations (from the Seventeenth Century) were from English sources, while the later (of the Eighteenth Century) were all American. From the evidence it seemed probable that the use of the words had continued later in this country than at home. It then occurred to me that it would be interesting to know how far back the words could be traced in American use; and that thought immediately brought me up against the fact that we had no means of ascertaining this point, for the simple reason that no effort had yet been made to trace the whole vocabulary which had been in use on this side of the ocean from the Seventeenth Century to the present day. It was then a simple matter to draw the natural conclusion that what was required was a new dictionary.[1]

" As soon as the idea had presented itself to me," he continued, " I communicated it to Professor [John M.] Manly, [head of the department of English at Chicago], who at once took steps to interest the University of Chicago in the project." The upshot was that Sir William was made professor of English in the university, and provided with a competent staff of assistants at the cost of the General Education Board. Before sailing for the United States to

1 In an article in Tract No. XXVII of the Society for Pure English, 1927, Dr. Craigie noted that his idea had been anticipated, though not his plan. He said: " It is possible that this idea has occurred to more than one of those who have given their attention to the subject, but until very recently I have found it clearly expressed only in a review of a part of the Oxford Dictionary, written in 1913 by Dr. C. W. Ernst of Boston. ' The American bonanza,' he wrote, ' is in the hands of squatters; it is yet to be worked scientifically. That is impossible at Oxford; it must be done here, whether in Washington or the University of Texas is immaterial; only let it be done. It will take at least twenty-five years to gather the materials, and twenty-five years more to digest them properly. And neither dogma nor cash can help us; the thing needed is grace.' "

take up his work, in June, 1925, he said to the London correspondent
of the North American Newspaper Alliance:

> The United States is now at a period in the national development which
> corresponds closely to the Elizabethan age in England. It is a period of intel-
> lectual creativeness and invention. The extraordinary facility that you, as a
> people, exhibit in the coining of picturesque and expressive slang is only
> one of many manifestations of this. I thoroughly approve of American slang.
> It is often carried to an excess, but on the other hand many of your cur-
> rent colloquial phrases are extremely apt, and win the admiration of even
> the most strict purist. In America slang gets into general conversation much
> more widely than in England, and is therefore more likely to win a place in
> permanent usage. The real test of slang is its utility. If a slang phrase fills a
> long-felt want it will get into the language. There are some American expres-
> sions of comparatively recent vintage which have already been adopted
> wherever English is spoken, and they are so particularly apt and expressive
> that one wonders how the idea was expressed before they were invented.
> One instance of this is the phrase, *it's up to you.*

The Dictionary of American English is of course confined to the
written language. Its staff has been engaged since 1926 in a laborious
search of all available American records, whether printed or in
manuscript. While the staff of the Oxford English Dictionary was
similarly engaged, from 1859 to 1928, it had the aid of a large corps
of volunteer searchers, and some of its most valuable material came
from them, but Dr. Craigie and his collaborators, James Root Hulbert, George Watson, M. M. Mathews and Allen Walker Read,
have had relatively little such help. In order to keep the dictionary
within reasonable bounds its plan had to be made somewhat narrow.
According to Dr. Louise Pound,[1] it will deal with the following
classes of words only:

1. Those descriptive of the physical features of the country, as *backwoods,
bluff, canyon, prairie.*
2. Words connected with the material development of the country, as
frame-house, log-cabin, canoe, steamboat, turnpike, railroad.
3. Terms of administration, politics, religion, trade and other activities, as
Senate, caucus, Mormon, lumber, elevator.
4. Colloquialisms and slang, so far as they are specially American in origin
or in later use.

But the bounds of these classes will be elastic, and not only words
and phrases originating in this country will be included, but also,
as Sir William Craigie has explained, " every one which has a clear

1 The New Dictionary of American
English, *American Mercury,* July,
1933.

connection with the development of the country and its inhabitants. The most ordinary word may call for insertion on the latter ground, as having not only a real but often a vital connection with the life of the settlers and their descendants." No words will be included for which records before 1900 do not exist, and examples of the use of admitted words will not be carried beyond 1925. Slang and colloquialisms will be dealt with fully down to 1875, but after that date only terms that have come into literary use will be included. The work will be in no sense a dictionary of slang. Soon or late, said Dr. Craigie in 1927, it " must be supplemented by a dialect dictionary and a slang dictionary; otherwise the record will be either defective or ill balanced."

The Linguistic Atlas seems to have been first proposed by a committee of the Modern Language Association in 1924, but it owes its actual launching to Dr. E. H. Sturtevant of Yale, who interested the American Council of Learned Societies in the project in 1928. A conference of philologians was held at Yale on August 2 and 3, 1929, in connection with the Linguistic Institute of the Linguistic Society of America, and on its recommendation the Council appointed a committee to make definite plans. The chairman of this committee was Dr. Kurath, then of Ohio State University, who remains as director of the work, with his headquarters moved to Brown.[1] He has a staff of seven assistants, headed by Dr. Miles L. Hanley, secretary of the American Dialect Society,[2] and the collection of materials is being furthered by other members of the society and by a small number of outside volunteers. The project has received grants from the Carnegie Corporation, the General Education Board and the Rockefeller Foundation. It proposes eventually to publish maps covering the whole country, but so far it has concentrated most of its attention upon New England. The reasons for this are thus stated:

1. The dialects of New England are primary as compared with those of the more Western areas, such as the Ohio region. . . .

[1] The other members of the committee were Drs. Leonard Bloomfield of Chicago, C. H. Carruthers of McGill, C. H. Grandgent of Harvard, Miles L. Hanley of Wisconsin, Marcus L. Hansen of Illinois, John S. Kenyon of Hiram College, George P. Krapp of Columbia, Eduard Prokosch of Yale, and G. Oscar Russell of Ohio State.

Dr. Krapp, author of The English Language in America, died in 1934, and Dr. William A. Read of Louisiana has been added to the committee.

[2] It is perhaps worth noting that five of the seven bear non-English surnames — Hansen, Hultzén, Lowman, Bloch and Penzl.

2. New England has striking geographical dialects; the class dialects are perhaps more distinct than in any other part of the country; there are clear urban and rural dialects; there are large elements of the population that have been only recently assimilated or that are in part still unassimilated.

3. The fact that we possess more information regarding the present linguistic situation in New England than we have for any other area will shorten and simplify the important task of selecting the dialect features that are to be recorded in *all* the communities selected for study.

4. There is already available a considerable body of reliable information regarding the history of the population. . . . Thus a more scientific choice of representative communities is possible.

How many maps will be published in all is not yet determined, but the number will probably run to thousands. Each will show all the reported occurrences and permutations of a given locution, and in that way the dispersion of typical words and phrases, and of characteristic pronunciations, throughout the United States and Canada will be indicated. The Atlas will cover " all phases of the spoken language — pronunciation, accentuation (intonation and stress), the inflections, syntactical features, and vocabulary." The speech of all strata of society is being investigated, and an attempt is being made to differentiate between the vocabularies of the educated and the uneducated, the young and the old, men and women. In addition to the Atlas, the Council will publish a series of monographs showing " the influence on the spoken language of movements of population, of topography and arteries of communication, of the stratification of society and the rise of the lower classes to positions of importance in their communities, of political, religious, and racial particularism, of the schools, and of cultural centers." In particular, an effort will be made to find out to what extent the early immigrations to the West carried the speech habits of the older settlements with them. Finally, phonograph records are being collected, and copies of them will be available to persons interested.

These manifestations of a new interest in the scientific study of American English among American philologians are gratifying, but it would be a mistake to assume that that interest is widespread. It seems to be confined mainly, as collaboration in *Dialect Notes* and *American Speech* has always been confined, to a relatively small group of scholars, most of them either foreigners by birth or under foreign influences. The typical native teacher of English, now as in the past, fights shy of American, and can see in it only an unseemly corruption of English. Just as the elaborate obfuscations of Eight-

eenth Century law have been preserved in American law long after
their abandonment in England, so the tight rules of the Eighteenth
Century purists, with their absurd grammatical niceties, their fanciful etymologies and their silly spelling-pronunciations, tend to be
preserved. Noah Webster protested against this pedantry nearly a
century and a half ago, but it continues to be cherished among the
rank and file of American pedagogues, from the kindergarten up to
the graduate school. In the American colleges and high-schools
there is no faculty so weak as the English faculty. It is the common
catch-all for aspirants to the birch who are too lazy or too feeble in
intelligence to acquire any sort of exact knowledge, and the professional incompetence of its typical ornament is matched only by
his hollow cocksureness. Most of the American philologists, so-
called, of the early days — Witherspoon, Whitney, Worcester, Fowler, Cobb and their like — were uncompromising advocates of
conformity to English precept and example, and combated every
indication of a national independence in speech with the utmost
vigilance. One of their company, true enough, stood out against the
rest. He was George Perkins Marsh, and in his " Lectures on the English Language," [1] he argued that " in point of naked syntactical
accuracy, the English of America is not at all inferior to that of
England." But even Marsh expressed the hope that Americans would
not, " with malice prepense, go about to republicanize our orthography and our syntax, our grammars and our dictionaries, our nursery hymns [*sic*] and our Bibles " to the point of actual separation.
Moreover, he was a philologian only by courtesy; the regularly
ordained brethren were all against him. The fear voiced by William
C. Fowler, professor of rhetoric at Amherst, that Americans might
" break loose from the laws of the English language " [2] altogether,

1 They were delivered at Columbia
College during the Winter of 1858–
9, and were published in New York
in 1859. They had reached a fourth
edition by 1861. Marsh was educated for the law and went into
politics. He was successively a
member of the Vermont Legislature, a member of the Supreme
Executive Council of the State, a
Congressman, minister at Constantinople, special envoy to Greece,
railroad commissioner in Vermont,
and minister to Italy. Born in 1801,
he died at romantic Vallombrosa
in 1882. He was an amateur philologian of considerable repute in his
day, and in addition to his Lectures
published The Origin and History
of the English Language; New
York, 1862.
2 The English Language: New York,
1850; rev. ed., 1855. This was the
first American text-book of English
for use in colleges. Before its publication, according to Fowler himself (rev. ed., p. xi), the language
was studied only " superficially "

was echoed by the whole fraternity, and so the corrective bastinado was laid on.

It remained, however, for two sages of a later day to preach the doctrine that the independent growth of American was not only immoral, but a sheer illusion. They were Richard Grant White, for long the leading American writer upon language questions, at least in popular esteem, and Thomas R. Lounsbury, for thirty-five years professor of the English language and literature in the Sheffield Scientific School at Yale, and an indefatigable controversialist. Both men were of the utmost industry in research, and both had wide audiences. White's " Words and Their Uses," published in 1872, was a mine of more or less authentic erudition, and his " Everyday English," following eight years later, was another. True enough, Fitzedward Hall, the Anglo-Indian-American philologist, disposed of some of his etymologies and otherwise did execution upon him,[1] but in the main his contentions were accepted. Lounsbury was also an adept and favorite expositor. His attacks upon certain familiar follies of the grammarians were penetrating and effective, and his two books, " The Standard of Usage in English " and " The Standard of Pronunciation in English," not to mention his excellent " History of the English Language " and his numerous magazine articles, showed a sound knowledge of the early history of the language, and an admirable spirit of free inquiry. But both of these laborious scholars, when they turned from English proper to American English, displayed an unaccountable desire to deny its existence altogether, and to the support of that denial they brought a critical method that was anything but scientific. White devoted not less than eight long articles in the *Atlantic Monthly* [2] to a review of the fourth edition of John Russell Bartlett's " American Glossary " (1877) and when he came to the end he had disposed of nine-tenths of Bartlett's specimens and called into question the authenticity of at least half the remainder. And no wonder, for his method was simply that of erecting tests so difficult and so arbitrary that only the exceptional word or phrase could pass them, and then only by

and " in the primary schools." He goes on: " Afterward, when older in the academy, during their preparation for college, our pupils perhaps despised it, in comparison with the Latin and the Greek; and in the college they do not systemati-

cally study the language after they come to maturity."
1 In Recent Exemplifications of False Philology; London, 1872.
2 Americanisms, parts i-viii, April, May, July, Sept., Nov., 1878; Jan., March, May, 1879.

a sort of chance. "To stamp a word or a phrase as an Americanism," he said, "it is necessary to show that (1) it is of so-called 'American' origin — that is, that it first came into use in the United States of North America, or that (2) it has been adopted in those States from some language other than English, or has been kept in use there while it has *wholly* passed out of use in England." Going further, he argued that unless "the simple words in compound names" were used in America "in a sense different from that in which they are used in England" the compound itself could not be regarded as an Americanism. The absurdity of all this is apparent when it is remembered that one of his rules would bar out such obvious Americanisms as the use of *sick* in place of *ill*, of *molasses* for *treacle*, and of *fall* for *autumn*, for all these words, while archaic in England, are by no means wholly extinct; and that another would dispose of that vast category of compounds which includes such unmistakably characteristic Americanisms as *joy-ride*, *rake-off*, *show-down*, *up-lift*, *out-house*, *rubber-neck*, *chair-warmer*, *fire-eater* and *back-talk*.

Lounsbury went even further. In the course of a series of articles in *Harper's Magazine*, he laid down the dogma that "cultivated speech . . . affords the only legitimate basis of comparison between the language as used in England and in America," and then went on:

> In the only really proper sense of the term, an Americanism is a word or phrase naturally used by an educated American which under similar conditions would not be used by an educated Englishman. The emphasis, it will be seen, lies in the word "educated."

This curious criterion, fantastic as it must have seemed to European philologians, was presently reinforced, for in his fourth article Lounsbury announced that his discussion was "restricted to the *written* speech of educated men." The result, of course, was a wholesale slaughter of Americanisms. If it was not possible to reject a word, like White, on the ground that some stray English poet or other had once used it, it was almost always possible to reject it on the ground that it was not admitted into the vocabulary of a college professor when he sat down to compose formal book-English. What remained was a small company, indeed — and almost the whole field of American idiom and American grammar, so full of interest for the less austere explorer, was closed without even a peek into it.

Despite its absurdity, Lounsbury's position was taken by most of the American *Gelehrten* of his heyday. Their heirs and assigns have receded from it somewhat, but have yet to go to the length of abandoning it altogether. They admit, in despondent moments, that an American dialect of English really exists, but they still dream of bringing it into harmony with what they choose to regard as correct English. To the latter purpose the humorless omphalophysites of the American Academy of Arts and Letters address themselves periodically, and with great earnestness. Not many of them show any capacity for sound writing, whether in English or in American, but they nevertheless propose in all solemnity to convert themselves into a sort of American counterpart of the Académie Française, and to favor the country, from time to time, with authoritative judgments in matters of speech.[1] In 1916 the Academy was given $3,000 by Mrs. E. H. Blashfield to help it " determine its duty regarding both the preservation of the English language in its beauty and integrity, and its cautious enrichment by such terms as grow out of the modern conditions." The brethren laid out this money by paying one another honoraria for reading essays on the subject at plenary sessions, and in 1925 nine of these essays were printed in a book.[2] It begins with a declaration of fealty to England and ends with a furious assault upon Edgar Lee Masters, Amy Lowell and Carl Sandburg — and a grave bow to Don Marquis! The general theory under-

[1] The Académie itself pretends to no such omniscience. In the preface to the first edition of its dictionary (1694) it disclaimed any purpose " to make new words and to reject others at its pleasure." In the preface to the second edition (1718) it confessed that " ignorance and corruption often introduce manners of writing " and that " convenience establishes them." In the preface to the third edition (1740) it admitted that it was " forced to admit changes which the public has made," and so on. Says D. M. Robertson, in A History of the French Academy (London, 1910): " The Academy repudiates any assumption of authority over the language with which the public in its own practise has not first clothed it. So much, indeed, does it confine itself to an interpretation merely of the laws of language that its decisions are sometimes contrary to its own judgment of what is either desirable or expedient." But despite this, its natural leaning is toward tradition, and that leaning has greatly diminished its authority. Even some of its own members repudiate its judgments. " There are," says J. C. Tressler in the *English Journal*, College Ed., April, 1934, p. 296, " two French languages: the Academy's and the people's. In France, as in the United States, slang has flourished and has on the whole enriched, enlivened, and invigorated the language. In France, as in other countries, the language has evolved in its own way."

[2] Academy Papers: Addresses on Language Problems by Members of the American Academy of Arts and Letters; New York, 1925. The contributors were Paul Elmer More, William M. Sloane, William C. Brownell, Brander Matthews, Bliss Perry, Paul Shorey, Henry van Dyke, and Robert Underwood Johnson.

lying it seems to be divided into two halves. The first half is to the effect that the only sound models of English are to be found in the thunderous artificialities of Eighteenth Century England, and the second teaches that the only remedy for " entire abandonment to the loose-lipped lingo of the street " is "a little study of Latin, and translation of Cicero and Virgil." It should be added in fairness that some of the contributors dissent from this two-headed theory, but even so the book presents a sufficiently depressing proof of the stupidity of the learned.[1]

On June 13, 1923, there was a Conference of British and American Professors of English at Columbia University. Under the leadership of Henry van Dyke and Fred Newton Scott [2] its deliberations quickly resolved themselves into a violent assault upon every evidence of Americanism in the national speech. Dr. van Dyke, unconsciously echoing Witherspoon after 142 years, denounced "the slovenly way" in which the mother-tongue was spoken in this country, "not only in the streets, but also in the pulpit, on the stage, and even in the classroom." Such "lazy, unintelligible, syncopated speech," he continued, "is like a dirty face." Apparently as an answer to a possible accusation of Anglomania — for he had been one of the most vociferous of English propagandists during the World War —, he added that he had also " heard some folks talk in Lunnon

---

[1] An instructive account of some forerunners of the Academy, all of them dismal failures, is to be found in American Projects For an Academy to Regulate Speech, by Allen Walker Read, *Publications of the Modern Language Association*, 1935.

[2] Scott, who died in 1930, was one of the signers of the call for the International Conference on English held in London in 1927. He was, in his day, a great academic dignitary, and served as president of both the Modern Language Association and the National Council of Teachers of English. He was also a member of the American Association for the Advancement of Science and of the British Association. He wrote many books, including an English grammar, a treatise on literary criticism, and another on æsthetics. His Standards of American Speech, and Other Papers, published in 1925, offers a good gauge of his mentality. One of its chapters is devoted to proving that " of the 10,565 lines of 'Paradise Lost,' 670, or 6.3% contain each two or more accented alliterating vowels," and another to proving that in such doublets as *rough and ready* 68% put the monosyllable first. On January 2, 1925 he read a paper on British and American Idiom before the Committee on Philological Sciences of the American Association for the Advancement of Science. In 1926 he contributed a paper on American Slang to Tract No. XXIV of the Society for Pure English. In Tract No. XXVII, 1927, some of his definitions were disputed by an anonymous American.

who were hard to understand," but after this he returned to his muttons, and closed with the dictum that " the proposal to make a new American language to fit our enormous country may be regarded either as a specimen of American humor or as a serious enormity." Dr. Scott, going further, allowed that it was "for Americans not a matter of ridicule, but for the hair shirt and the lash, for tears of shame and self-abasement."

That Anglomania may have actually colored the views of both Dr. van Dyke and Dr. Scott is suggested by the case of their *Corpsbruder*, Dr. Brander Matthews. Before the war Matthews was a diligent collector of Americanisms, and often wrote about them with a show of liking them. But during the war he succumbed to a great upsurge of love for the Motherland, and took up a position almost identical with that of Lounsbury. Thus he once wrote in the intensely pro-English New York *Times*.

> We may rest assured that the superficial evidences of a tendency toward the differentiation of American-English and British-English are not so significant as they may appear to the unreflecting, and that the tendency itself will be powerless against the cohesive force of our common literature, the precious inheritance of both the English-speaking peoples. . . . So long as the novelists and the newspaper men on both sides of the ocean continue to eschew Briticisms and Americanisms, and so long as they indulge in these localisms only in quotation marks, there is no danger that English will ever halve itself into a British language and an American language.

After the war Matthews did some wobbling. He undoubtedly noticed that quotation marks were no longer being used to tag Americanisms, but so late as the time of his contribution to Academy Papers, *c.* 1923, he continued to believe that "the divergences of speech between the United States and Great Britain are not important, and are not more marked than those between . . . Boston and Wyoming." To this he added a sort of hurrah in the form of a solemn declaration, in his character of scholar, that " to the rest of the world German is still an uncouth tongue." But by 1926 he had so far returned to his first love that he was praising Logan Pearsall Smith, albeit somewhat cautiously, for speaking kindly of Americanisms in " Words and Idioms." I quote:

> I have called attention more particularly to Mr. Pearsall Smith's friendly attitude toward American words and phrases, usages and idioms, because I find here evidence of a change of heart in our kin across the sea. Time was when to stigmatize a verbal novelty as an Americanism was to condemn it

utterly. Most of those who took on themselves the duty of defending our common tongue did not doubt that the English language belonged exclusively to the British. They felt — and the feeling was natural enough — that the language was the exclusive possession of the inhabitants of the island where it had come into being. It is pleasant to see signs that this jealousy is now dying a natural death. It was pleasant indeed, to behold our right to our linguistic heritage cordially recognized in the review of Mr. Pearsall Smith's book in the Literary Supplement of the London *Times*.[1]

If any speaker arose at the Columbia Conference to defend American speechways, the fact did not appear in the published reports. Apparently, all the assembled "professors of English," whether actual Englishmen or only American colonials, were of like mind with Drs. Scott and van Dyke. On the lower levels of pedagogy there is the same general attitude. As I have noted, the National Council of Teachers of English, like the American Academy of Arts and Letters, frequently toys with the project of setting up machinery for "purifying" the language, and there are innumerable minor bands of schoolmarms, male and female, consecrated to the same end. But there is a party in the National Council, as in the American Academy, that dissents. One of its spokesmen is J. C. Tressler, head of the English department of the Richmond Hill High-School, New York City. Writing in the *English Journal*, College Edition, in April, 1934, he said:

> Although thousands of English teachers [*i.e.*, in the United States] with the blood of crusaders and martyrs in their veins have for decades fought heroically against the corruption and utter ruin of English, their warfare has had by and large slight effect on the language. . . . It's hardly wise for the National Council at this late date to attempt to confine it in a strait-jacket.

1 The *Literary Digest International Book Review*, March, 1926. Apparently, Matthews forgot here that Smith was not an Englishman. Actually he was born in Philadelphia, and did not migrate to England until after passing through Haverford and Harvard. His Words and Idioms was published in London in 1925. Matthews's war-time Anglomania was not taken seriously by the English. His belief that American novelists and newspaper men would "continue to eschew Americanisms" was derided by the London *Saturday Review*, a bit later on, as "obviously a war hope, like hanging the Kaiser." There is what may be called a blanket sneer at "Anglomaniac professors of English" in Breaking Priscian's Head, by J. Y. T. Greig, of Armstrong College, Newcastle (1929). "Some of them," says Professor Greig, "to judge by their *obiter dicta*, are as scholastically minded as the dismalest snob of a housemaster in an English public school."

6. THE VIEWS OF WRITING MEN

The great majority of American writers have always held out against the dominant pedagogical opinion, in this as in other matters. In every age, of course, there have been pedantic fellows who out-schoolmarmed the schoolmarms in their devotion to grammatical, syntactical and lexicographical niceties — Ambrose Bierce suggests himself as a good example [1] —, and in every age there have been Anglomaniacs of great earnestness — for example, Washington Irving and Henry James,[2] not to mention Matthews, van Dyke, and the other faithful colonials of the American Academy of Arts and Letters, already mentioned. But not many writers of the first distinction have belonged to either faction, and among the lesser ranks there has always been an active movement in the other direction. After the War of 1812, after the Civil War, and again after the World War there were deliberate efforts, among the literati as well as among the folk, to throw off English precept and example altogether, and among the authors concerned were such respectable figures as J. Fenimore Cooper, Walt Whitman, Mark Twain and Sinclair Lewis.

So long ago as 1820, in the twenty-seventh number of the *North American Review*, Edward Everett sought to turn the fire of the English reviews by arguing that the common language was not only spoken better in America than in England, but also better written. He said:

> We challenge any critic who shall maintain the corruption of the English language in America to assume whatever standard he shall choose of the English, the standard of dictionaries, or of good writers, or of good company; and whatever standard be taken, we engaged to detect in English writers of

1 Bierce was especially hostile to slang, but in 1909 he published a little book called "Write It Right," full of denunciations of common American idioms. His own writing, though cramped by his self-imposed rules, yet managed to be fluent, colorful and even melodious. It is possible that he was influenced by the fact that he spent nearly ten years of his early manhood in England.
2 In Afternoon Neighbors; New York, 1934, p. 43, Hamlin Garland reports that John S. Sargent once told him of James: "Henry became excessively English in his later years and resented all Americanisms in speech. I once heard him reproving his niece. She said: 'Uncle Henry, if you will tell me how you like your tea I will *fix* it for you.' To this James replied: 'Pray, my dear young lady, what will you *fix* it with and what will you *fix* it to?'"

respectable standing, and in respectable English society, more provincialisms, more good words in false acceptations, and more newly coined words, than can be found in an equal number of American writers, or in American society, of the same relative respectability. We think we should begin such a comparison with the number of the *Edinburgh Review* for March, 1817. . . . For in the *first article* of that number we fell upon forty-six words not authorized by the standards of our language. The English language corrupted in America! What are the Columbiads, or Webster's Dictionaries, or any other name of American innovation, compared with the lucubrations of Jeremy Bentham!

In the *North American* for July, 1821, in a review of an anti-American article in the *New London Monthly Magazine* for February of the same year, Everett returned to the subject, arguing that " on the whole, the English language is better spoken here than in England," and that " there is no part of America in which the corruption of the language has gone so far as in the heart of the English counties." He did not advocate a severance of American from English, but he insisted that, in the cases of many differences already noticeable, the American practise was better than the English. " We presume," he concluded somewhat loftily, " that the press set up by the American missionaries in the Sandwich Islands will furnish a good deal better English than Mr. Bentham's Church-of-Englandism."

Everett was supported by a number of other authors of the time, including, as I have already noted, Paulding, Timothy Dwight, and J. Fenimore Cooper, whose early Anglomania was by then only a memory. In the second volume of his " Notions of the Americans," printed anonymously in 1828, but quickly recognized as his and acknowledged by him, Cooper argued stoutly against the artificial English standards, mainly out of the Eighteenth Century, that the contemporary grammarians were trying to impose upon American, and contended that it should be left to its own devices, with due regard, of course, for reason, analogy, and any plausible indigenous authority that might develop. He went on:

This we are daily doing, and I think the consequence will be that in another generation or two far more reasonable English will be used in this country than exists here now. . . . I think it will be just as much the desire of England then to be in our fashion as it was our desire twenty years ago to be in hers.

In " The American Democrat," published in 1838, Cooper set himself up as the indigenous authority he had anticipated ten years before. By this time the American language was far gone upon the grand bust that had begun with the Jackson uprising, and there was a tremendous flow of neologisms from the West. The "common faults" of the popular speech, according to Cooper, were "an ambition of effect, a want of simplicity, and a turgid abuse of terms." He denounced the democratic substitution of *boss* for *master*, and of *help* for *servant*, and preached a smug sermon upon the true meaning of *lady* and *gentleman*. "To call a laborer, one who has neither education, manners, accomplishments, tastes, associations, nor any one of the ordinary requisites, a *gentleman*," he said, "is just as absurd as to call one who is thus qualified a *fellow*. . . . [A true gentleman] never calls his wife his *lady*, but his *wife*, and he is not afraid of lessening the dignity of the human race by styling the most elevated and refined of his fellow creatures *men* and *women*." Waspish words, but they at least avoided the pedantry of the pedagogues, and yielded no more than its just due to English precedent.

The first really full-length defense of American by an American appeared in a volume of "Cambridge Essays, Contributed by Members of the University," published in London in 1855. Its author was Charles Astor Bristed, a grandson of John Jacob Astor and one of the forgotten worthies of his era. He was graduated from Yale in 1839 and then went to Cambridge, where he took his degree in 1845. After that he devoted himself to literary endeavor, and during the next thirty years lived chiefly at Washington. There he gathered a small coterie of dilettanti about him, and became a sort of forerunner of Henry Adams. In 1852 he published "Five Years in an English University," and three years later he was asked to contribute to the aforesaid volume of "Cambridge Essays." His contribution bore the title of "The English Language in America"; it remains to this day, despite a few aberrations, the most intelligent brief discussion of the subject ever printed. He began by denouncing the notion, prevalent then as now, that the study of American was somehow undignified, and proceeded to argue that it was really worth any scholar's while "to investigate the course of a great living language, transplanted from its primitive seat, brought into contact and rivalry with other civilized tongues, and exposed to various influences, all having a *prima facie* tendency to modify it." He then proceeded to dispose of the familiar arguments against the existence of an American form of English, later to be reassembled and reinforced by Lounsbury —

(1) that most Americanisms "can be traced to an English source,"
(2) that "the number of actually new words invented in America is
very small," (3) that "the deviations from standard English which
occur in America are fewer and less gross than those which may be
found in England herself," and so on. Here is a specimen passage
from his caveat to the first two propositions, which he grouped together as embodying a single argument:

> We admit this argument to be true, *so far as it goes;* but it does not go
> so far, by any means, as its supporters imagine. They seem to forget that
> there is such a thing as applying a new *meaning* to existing words, and of
> this novelty the examples in America are sufficiently numerous. Thus *creek*
> is a perfectly legitimate English word, but its legitimate English meaning is
> "a small arm of the sea," whereas in America it is invariably used to desig-
> nate a small river, except when it happens to be used to designate a large
> one. *Draw* is an old-established English verb, but the Americans have further
> employed it as a noun, and made it do duty for *draw-bridge*.

The third proposition Bristed answered thus:

> This is the line of argument which sometimes develops itself into the
> amusingly paradoxical assertion that the Americans speak better English than
> the English themselves. But such reasoning is on a par with that of one who
> should consider himself to have demonstrated that the upper classes of
> America were richer than those of England by showing that the lower classes
> of England were poorer than those of America, or that the average wealth
> of the American population per head was greater than that of the English.
> There is no inconsistency in admitting that the worst English *patois* may be
> less intelligible than the worst American, and yet maintaining that the best
> currently spoken American contains appreciable deviations from the true
> English standard. The English provincialisms *keep their place;* they are con-
> fined to their own particular localities, and do not encroach on the metro-
> politan model. The American provincialisms are most equally distributed
> through all classes and localities, and though some of them may not rise
> above a certain level of society, others are heard everywhere. The senate
> or the boudoir is no more sacred from their intrusions than the farm-house
> or the tavern.

Bristed argued boldly that in many ways American usage was already superior to English. He defended, for example, the American
use of *sick*, and the American practise, borrowed from the Northern
British dialects, of sounding the *h* in such words as *which* and *wheel*.
In any case, he said, the Americans were perfectly free to modify
their language as they pleased, and no conceivable pressure could
dissuade them. Many American inventions had already "settled
down into and become established in the language. *Talented* is a
familiar example. It is of little use to inveigh against such words —

there they are in full possession, and cannot be turned out." In conclusion he thus philosophized:

Possibly, some of the American expressions are in themselves, abstractly and philosophically considered, better than the English; but this is not all that the *jus et norma loquendi* demands. Every language contains idioms and phrases philosophically reprehensible, as is clearly shown by the fact that the most ordinary phrases of one language become unmeaning or ludicrous absurdities when translated literally into another. All languages contain terms which have nothing but usage to plead in their favor. In English conversation, the panegyrical adjective of all-work is *nice*, in America it is *fine*. Both people often use their pet adjective inappropriately; perhaps the Americans do so in fewer cases than the English.

It was naturally the humorous writers who first began to turn Americanisms to literary uses, for many of the new locutions that came in between the War of 1812 and the Civil War showed a grotesque fancy. As Will D. Howe says in " The Cambridge History of American Literature," [1] there were two streams of American humor from the beginnings of the national letters — " the one following closely English models, especially Addison, Steele, Defoe, and Goldsmith in the Eighteenth Century, and Lamb, Hood, Jerrold, and Dickens in the Nineteenth Century; the other springing from American soil and the new conditions of American life, and assuming a character as new to the world as the country that produced it." To the first stream belonged the writings of Franklin, the Hartford Wits, Paulding, Irving and Holmes; to the second that of Seba Smith, Augustus Baldwin Longstreet, Joseph G. Bailey, Mrs. Frances M. Whicher, Charles G. Halpine, George H. Derby, Henry Wheeler Shaw, David R. Locke, Charles Farrar Browne, and Samuel L. Clemens (Mark Twain). The pioneers of a really indigenous humor were mainly dialect writers. Smith discovered the riches of the New England dialect ("The Life and Writings of Major Jack Downing ") in 1830; he was followed by Thomas C. Haliburton (" The Clockmaker, or The Sayings and Doings of Samuel Slick ") in 1837, and by James Russell Lowell (" The Biglow Papers ") in 1848. The Negro dialect, as we know it today, seems to have been formulated by the song-writers for minstrel shows; it did not appear in literature until the time of the Civil War; before that, as George Philip Krapp shows in " The English Language in America," [2] it was a vague and

1 Vol. II, p. 148.
2 New York, 1925; Vol. I, p. 246 *ff*.
  Krapp gives some curious examples
of early attempts at reducing
Negro American to writing. His
essay also deals with the Yankee,

artificial lingo which had little relation to the actual speech of the Southern blacks. The Civil War period also saw the rise of the Irish dialect, which seems to have been invented (or discovered) by Halpine, whose Miles O'Reilly sketches began to appear in 1862, and of the German dialect, which first took form in Charles Leland's "Hans Breitmann's Ballads" a year or two later. The dialect of the frontier was foreshadowed in Longstreet's "Georgia Scenes" in 1835, and in Baldwin's "Flush Times in Alabama and Mississippi" in 1853, but it did not displace the Yankee dialect as the typical American patois until Clemens published "The Jumping Frog" in 1867, and John Hay followed with "Pike County Ballads" in 1871.

These humorists, and their successors after them, were keenly conscious of the rich treasures lying in American speech, and whenever they discussed it seriously they argued for its autonomy. Clemens, who employed Americanisms with great freedom, even when he was attempting elegant writing, hailed "the vigorous new vernacular of the occidental plains and mountains" in "Roughing It" in 1872, and ten years later he printed an essay, "Concerning the American Language," in "The Stolen White Elephant," with a footnote describing it as "part of a chapter crowded out of 'A Tramp Abroad'" (1880). It is in the form of a dialogue with an Englishman met on a train. "The languages," says Mark, "were identical several generations ago, but our changed conditions and the spread of our people far to the South and far to the West have made many alterations in our pronunciation, and have introduced new words among us and changed the meaning of many old ones. . . . A nation's language is a very large matter. It is not simply a manner of speech obtaining among the educated handful; the manner obtaining among the vast uneducated multitude must be considered also. . . . I could pile up differences until I not only convinced you that English and American are separate languages, but that when I speak my native tongue in its utmost purity an Englishman can't understand me at all." Another American humorist, George Ade, came to

---

Southwestern, Hoosier, and Indian dialects. "The New England dialect as a literary form," he says, "is mainly popular or illiterate American English with a very occasional splash of genuine local color." Krapp reprints Lowell's seven rules for writing this dialect, as given in the introduction to Series I of The Biglow Papers, and C. Alphonso Smith's seven rules for writing "the Southern literary dialect." See also Notes on Negro Dialect in the American Novel to 1821, by Tremaine McDowell, *American Speech*, April, 1930.

the same conclusion a quarter of a century later. " The American," he said in his book of travel, " Pastures New," in 1906, " must go to England in order to learn for a dead certainty that he does not speak the English language. . . . This pitiful fact comes home to every American when he arrives in London — that there are two languages, the English and the American. One is correct; the other is incorrect. One is a pure and limpid stream; the other is a stagnant pool, swarming with bacilli."

Of the more serious American writers, the first to explore the literary possibilities of the national language was Walt Whitman. Once, in conversation with his *fidus Achates,* Horace Traubel, he described his " Leaves of Grass " as " only a language experiment — an attempt to give the spirit, the body, the man, new words, new potentialities of speech — an American . . . range of self-expression. The new world, the new times, the new peoples, the new vistas," he went on, " need a tongue according — yes, what is more, will have such a tongue — will not be satisfied until it is evolved." [1] During the early 50's, before the first publication of the " Leaves," Whitman began the preparation of a lecture entitled " An American Primer," the burden of which is indicated by an alternative title that he toyed with but finally rejected: " The Primer of Words, For American Young Men and Women, For Literati, Orators, Teachers, Musicians, Judges, Presidents, &c." This lecture was apparently never delivered, and the manuscript remained unpublished at Whitman's death in 1892. Twelve years later, in April, 1904, it was printed in the *Atlantic Monthly,* with a prefatory note by Traubel. It was an eloquent plea for national independence in language, and in particular for the development of an American style, firmly grounded upon the speech of everyday. " The Americans," said Whitman, " are going to be the most fluent and melodious voiced people in the world — and the most perfect users of words."

I see that the time is nigh when the etiquette of salons is to be discharged from that great thing, the renovated English speech in America. The occasions of the English speech in America are immense, profound — stretch over ten thousand vast cities, over through thousands of years, millions of miles of meadows, farms, mountains, men. The occasions of salons are for a coterie, a *bon soir* or two — involve waiters standing behind chairs, silent, obedient, with backs that can bend and must often bend. . . . Ten thousand native

1 The Fight of a Book for the World, by W. S. Kennedy; West Yarmouth, Mass., 1926, *pref.*

idiomatic words are growing, or are today already grown, out of which vast numbers could be used by American writers, with meaning and effect — words that would be welcomed by the nation, being of the national blood, — words that would give that taste of identity and locality which is so dear in literature.

Whitman ranged himself squarely against the pedagogues who, then as now, were trying to police American English, and bring it into accord with literary English. "Nobody ever actually talks," he said, "as books and plays talk." He argued that there should be a dictionary of the common speech, and that some attempt should be made to ascertain its grammar.

The Real Dictionary will give all the words that exist in use, the bad words as well as any. The Real Grammar will be that which declares itself a nucleus of the spirit of the laws, with liberty to all to carry out the spirit of the laws, even by violating them, if necessary. . . . These States are rapidly supplying themselves with new words, called for by new occasions, new facts, new politics, new combinations. Far plentier additions will be needed, and, of course, will be supplied. . . . Many of the slang words are our best; slang words among fighting men, gamblers, thieves, are powerful words. . . . The appetite of the people of These States, in popular speeches and writings, is for unhemmed latitude, coarseness, directness, live epithets, expletives, words of opprobrium, resistance. This I understand because I have the taste myself as large, as largely, as any one. I have pleasure in the use, on fit occasions, of — *traitor, coward, liar, shyster, skulk, doughface, trickster, mean cuss, backslider, thief, impotent, lickspittle*. . . . I like limber, lasting, fierce words. I like them applied to myself — and I like them in newspapers, courts, debates, Congress. Do you suppose the liberties and the brawn of These States have to do only with delicate lady-words? with gloved gentleman words? Bad Presidents, bad judges, bad clients, bad editors, owners of slaves, and the long ranks of Northern political suckers (robbers, traitors, suborned), monopolists, infidels, . . . shaved persons, supplejacks, eccle-siastics, men not fond of women, women not fond of men, cry down the use of strong, cutting, beautiful, rude words. To the manly instincts of the People they will be forever welcome.

At a time, says Louis Untermeyer, "when the rest of literary America was still indulging in the polite language of pulpits and the lifeless rhetoric of its libraries, Whitman not only sensed the richness and vigor of the casual word, the colloquial phrase — he champ-ioned the vitality of slang, and freshness of our quickly assimilated jargons, the indigenous beauty of vulgarisms. He even predicted that no future native literature could exist that neglected this racy speech, that the vernacular of people as opposed to the language of literati would form the living accents of the best poets to come. One has only to observe the contemporary works of Carl Sandburg,

Robert Frost, Edgar Lee Masters, Vachel Lindsay and a dozen others to see how his prophecy has been fulfilled. Words, especially the neglected words regarded as too crude and literal for literature, fascinated Whitman. The idea of an enriched language was scarcely ever out of his mind. . . . This interest . . . grew to great proportions; it became almost an obsession." [1] As everyone knows, Whitman was an assiduous word-coiner himself, and many of his inventions will be recalled — for example, the verbs *to promulge, to eclaircise, to diminute, to imperturbe, to effuse,* and *to inure,* the adjectives *ostent, omnigenous,* and *adamic,* the adverb *affetuoso,* and the nouns *presidentiad, deliveress, civilizee, literat, acceptress, yawp,* and *partiolist.* A large number of his coinages were in foreign, and especially in Romance metal; he believed that American should not be restricted to the materials of English, and he made frequent use of such French terms as *allons, feuillage, habitan, savant, ma femme, mon cher, militaire, rapport* and *éclaircissement,* and of such Spanish and pseudo-Spanish terms as *libertad, camerado, vaquero* and *Americano.* [2] I have heard it argued that he introduced *finale* into common American usage; the evidence is dubious, but certainly the word is much oftener employed in the United States than in England. Most of his coinages, alas, died with him, but *yawp* and *These States* have survived. Among his literary remains were many notes upon American speechways, and he often discussed the subject with Traubel. In November, 1885, he printed an article on "Slang in America" in the *North American Review,* and afterward included it in "November Boughs" (1888). [3]

Whitman got support in his time from James Russell Lowell and John Fiske, and a little later from William Dean Howells. Lowell undertook the defense of Americanisms in his preface to the first series of "The Biglow Papers" (1848). "The English," he said,

1 Whitman and the American Language, New York *Evening Post,* May 31, 1919. Mr. Untermeyer has himself made vigorous propaganda to the same end. Since 1932 or thereabout he has been delivering a lecture entitled A New Language For a New Generation which embodies a review of the gradual separation of American from English, and a valuable discussion of the present differences.

2 See Walt Whitman and the French Language, by Louise Pound, *American Speech,* May, 1926, and Walt Whitman's Neologisms, by the same, *American Mercury,* Feb., 1925.

3 See Walt Whitman and the American Language, by Leon Howard, *American Speech,* Aug., 1930.

" have complained of us for coining new words. Many of those so
stigmatized were old ones by them forgotten, and all make now an
unquestioned part of the currency, wherever English is spoken. Undoubtedly, we have a right to make new words as they are needed
by the fresh aspects under which life presents itself here in the New
World; and, indeed, wherever a language is alive, it grows. It might
be questioned whether we could not establish a stronger title to the
ownership of the English tongue than the mother-islanders themselves. Here, past all question, is to be its great home and center.
And not only is it already spoken here in greater numbers, but with
a far higher popular average of correctness than in Britain." Fiske,
writing home from England in 1873, reported that the English pronunciation grated upon his sensibilities. " The English," he said,
" talk just like Germans. So much guttural is very unpleasant, especially as half the time I can't understand them, and have to say, ' I
beg your pardon? ' Our American enunciation is much pleasanter to
the ear." [1]

Howells, in 1886, made a plea in *Harper's* for a concerted effort
to put American on its own legs. " If we bother ourselves," he said,
" to write what the critics imagine to be ' English,' we shall be prig-
gish and artificial, and still more so if we make our Americans talk
' English.' . . . It has always been supposed by grammarians and
purists that a language can be kept as they find it, but languages,
while they live, are perpetually changing. God apparently meant
them for the common people, . . . and the common people will use
them freely, as they use other gifts of God. On their lips our continental English will differ more and more from the insular English,
and we believe that this is not deplorable, but desirable. . . . We
have only to leave our studies, editorial or other, and go into the
shops and fields to find the ' spacious times of great Elizabeth '
again." In the same article Howells advised the young American
novelists of the day to give their ears to regional speechways, and
quoted what Alphonse Daudet once said of Turgenev: " What a
luxury it must be to have a big untrodden barbarian language to
wade into! " " We hope," he concluded, " that our inherited English may be constantly freshened and revived from the native sources
which literary decentralization will help to keep open." [2]

1 The Life and Letters of John Fiske,
by John Spencer Clark; Boston,
1917, Vol. I, p. 431.

2 The Editor's Study, *Harper's Magazine*, Jan., 1886.

The literature of the subject has taken on large proportions in recent years, and contributions to it have been made by authors as diverse as Vachel Lindsay and Rupert Hughes, Ernest Boyd and Richard Burton. For one article on Americanisms in the philological journals there are at least fifty in the popular magazines. Burton, with a long career as a teacher of English behind him, is convinced that the pedagogical effort to police the national speech will fail. " The pundit, the pedant, and the professor," he says, " who are fain to stem the turbid tide of the popular vernacular may suffer pain; but they can have little influence on the situation. Even college-bred folk revert to type and use people's speech — when they are from under the restraining, corrective monitions of academic haunts — in a way to shock, amuse, or encourage, according to the point of view." [1] Hughes has written on the subject more than once, and always with great vigor. " Could anyone imagine an English author," he says, " hesitating to use a word because of his concern as to the ability of American readers to understand it and approve it? . . . Why should he permit the survival of the curious notion that our language is a mere loan from England, like a copper kettle that we must keep scoured and return without a dent? "

Americans who try to write like Englishmen are not only committed to an unnatural pose, but doomed as well to failure, above all among the English; for the most likeable thing about the English is their contempt for the hyphenated imitation Englishmen from the States, who only emphasize their nativity by their apish antics. The Americans who have triumphed among them have been, almost without exception, peculiarly American. . . . Let us sign a Declaration of Literary Independence and formally begin to write, not British, but Unitedstatish. For there is such a language, a brilliant, growing, glowing, vivacious, elastic language for which we have no specific name. . . . Whatever we call it, let us cease to consider it a vulgar dialect of English, to be used only with deprecation. Let us study it in its splendid efflorescence, be proud of it, and true to it. Let us put off livery, cease to be the butlers of another people's language, and try to be the masters and the creators of our own.[2]

Lindsay, who gave the subtitle of " Rhymes in the American Language " to " The Golden Whales of California," published in 1920, had his say on the subject under the heading of " The Real American Language " in the *American Mercury* for March, 1928. He began by recounting " a few delusions in regard to the United States language." One of them, he said, " is that it came in with the

1 English As She is Spoken, *Book-man*, July, 1920.   2 Our Statish Language, *Harper's Magazine*, May, 1920.

ultra-flappers and the most saxophonish of the jazz, after Armistice Day." Another is that " the United States language is a New York novelty."

> It is really a new vocabulary arranged on an old British framework. It is true that the new vocabulary pours every day into our growing dictionaries, but this vocabulary is apt to mislead one. A smart phrase or new word is not the United States language. The very framework is as old as the writings of Captain John Smith of Virginia. . . . Wherever there is a touch of Virginia left, there is the United States language. The United States language is Virginia with the *r* put back into it. . . . When you reach the land of " Old Dan Tucker " and " Clementine " and the places where they sing the song, " Tell Me the Tale That I Once Held So Dear," you are getting into the region of the United States language in its essential fluency. . . . Mark Twain writes Virginian with the *r* put back into his alphabet when speaking in his own person.

The Irish brethren naturally range themselves on the side of autonomy for American English, and are firm believers in its merits: not many of them show any trace of Anglomania. Whenever the English reviews and newspapers begin one of their periodical denunciations of Americanisms, these Celts rush to the rescue. Thus Murray Godwin of Detroit sought the hospitality of the *Irish Statesman* in 1926 to flog and flay two English critics of American speechways, one writing in the *Quarterly Review* and the other in the Manchester *Guardian Weekly*. In the following burning words he paid his respects to the former:

> The author of this particular piece of refined skullduggery . . . quotes . . . a personal notice written by a Jewish clothing merchant, and containing some characteristic Yiddish English, to prove that grammar is no longer honored even in the written language of American business men. Of course we have come to expect such tactics on the part of our British step-cousins, whose reputation for fair play has been so firmly established by tradition that it has no longer any need to be supported by example. . . . Though I feel touched damn nigh to tears when I picture this noble Briton in the throes of molding and milling this length of literary leadpipe with which to bash the blinking Yank, I shall not pass up the chance to point out that his implication that English is a pure and integrated growth, while American is a nondescript tangle of underbrush, would seem to stem from a scholarly logic turned sour by contact with the viewpoint of an intestinally-constricted and malicious if unmuscular nitwit.[1]

To which may be added a few calmer reflections by Ernest Boyd:

> The time has passed when the English language could be claimed as the exclusive idiom of Britain, much less of any restricted area of England. Today

1 The American Slanguage, *Irish Statesman*, Oct. 9, 1926.

it is the tongue of millions who have no other language, but have also no other tie with the country from which English came. There is no authority which can enforce the recognition of a Standard English that does not exist, save in the imagination of a few people in London. When these people write or speak they betray their place of origin as definitely as a native of New York or Edinburgh. Their assumption that, while the latter are strange and provincial, they are standard and authoritative, is merely an illustration of self-complacent provincialism. It is an assumption which the great English-speaking world does not and cannot admit.[1]

7. THE POLITICAL FRONT

The American newspapers labor the subject constantly, but not often with much perspicacity. In general, they favor freedom for American from English-imposed rules, but there is a minority that pleads for conformity. Now and then politicians looking for popularity raise the banner of independence, and propose to give it reality by the characteristic American device of passing a law, but such plans seldom get beyond the stage of tall talk. They go back to the earliest days of the Republic. William Gifford, the bitterly anti-American editor of the *Quarterly Review,* is authority for the story that at the close of the Revolution certain members of Congress proposed that the use of English be formally prohibited in the United States, and Hebrew substituted for it.[2] Bristed, in his essay, "The English Language in America," makes the proposed tongue Greek, and reports that the change was rejected on the ground that "it would be more convenient for us to keep the language as it is, and make the English speak Greek." How a committee of the Continental Congress, in 1778, recommended that "the language of the United States" be used in all "replies or answers" to the French ambassador I have already noted. Seventy-six years later a similar order was issued by the celebrated William L. Marcy, author of the political maxim, "To the victor belong the spoils." After a long career in the Senate, Marcy became Secretary of War in the Cabinet of Polk and then Secretary of State in that of Pierce. While holding

1 Translations, *Saturday Review of Literature,* Dec. 26, 1925.
2 Gifford seems to have picked up this story from the Marquis François Jean de Chastellux, who made a tour of America in 1780–82, and printed Voyages dans l'Amérique septentrionale in 1786. (English translation in two volumes; London, 1787; New York, 1828). See The Philological Society of New York, 1788, by Allen Walker Read, *American Speech,* April, 1934, p. 131.

the latter post he issued a circular to all American diplomatic and consular officers, instructing them to employ only "the American language" in communicating with him. That was in 1854. After another septuagenarian interval, on May 9, 1927, Andrew W. Mellon, as Secretary of the Treasury, ordered that the redemption call for the Second Liberty Loan be advertised "in every daily paper printed in the American language throughout the United States."

In the *North American Review* for April, 1820, Edward Everett printed "a *jeu d'esprit* which has fallen in our way, under the name of 'Report of Resolutions to be proposed in the House of Representatives' . . . to return the compliment paid to us by the Marquis of Lansdowne, in the session [of Parliament] of 1819, in moving for an inquiry into the conduct of General Jackson." I can find no record that these resolutions were ever actually introduced in the House; indeed, they were probably written by Everett himself, or by one of his collaborators on the *North American*. But they fell in very well with the temper of the time, and if any member had dropped them into the basket it is certain that they would have received a large number of votes. They began with long satirical whereases directed at the English reviewers, and proceeded to deplore the corruption of the language in the Motherland, "to the degree that the various dialects which prevail, such as those in Yorkshire, Somersetshire and Cumberland, at the same time that they are in themselves utterly uncouth and hideous, are unintelligible to anyone but a person born and educated in these counties respectively." Then came this:

> The House farther regards, as still more pernicious, . . . that barbarity which from various causes is fast creeping into the language of the highest and best educated classes of society in England . . . ; an affectation, at one time, of forgotten old words, and at another of pedantic new ones, each equally unauthorized in a pure and chaste style of writing and of speaking; the perpetual recurrence of the plural number, instead of the singular, as *charities, sympathies, tendencies,* &c., a phraseology which tends in a high degree to weaken a language, by leading writers and speakers to place that emphasis in the grammatical plurality, which ought to reside in the term itself; an unwise attempt to ennoble such words as *clever, you know, vastly,* &c. which are pardonable only in colloquial use, and unworthy the dignity of grave and sustained discourse; an adoption by noblemen, gentlemen, and clergymen, of the terms of horse-jockeys, boxers and shooters, to the degree that a great number of vulgar and cant terms are heard in what are called the best circles; . . . and lastly, an alarming prevalence of profane and obscene language, . . . which, though it is unhappily a vice too common in

all countries, the House has unquestioned information prevails in England
to an unparalleled and odious extent, reaching into the societies which consider themselves the most polite and best bred.

Finally, after a sonorous declaration that in the United States the
language has been " preserved in a state of admirable purity " and
was, " by the blessing of God, quite untainted with most of the above
mentioned vulgarities prevalent in the highest English circles," the
resolutions concluded:

> *Resolved,* in consideration of these premises, that the nobility and gentry
> of England be courteously invited to send their elder sons, and such others
> as may be destined to appear as public speakers in church or state, to America,
> for their education; that the President of the United States be requested to
> concert measures with the presidents and heads of our colleges and schools
> for the prompt reception and gratuitous instruction of such young persons,
> and to furnish them, after the expiration of a term of —— years, certificates
> of their proficiency in the English tongue.

The Middle West has always been the chief center of linguistic
chauvinism, and so early as February 15, 1838, the Legislature of
Indiana, in an act established the State university at Bloomington,
provided that it should instruct the youth of the new Commonwealth (which had been admitted to the Union in 1816) "in
the American, learned and foreign languages . . . and literature."
Nearly a century later, in 1923, there was a violent upsurging of the
same patriotic spirit, and bills making the American language official
(but never clearly defining it) were introduced in the Legislatures
of Illinois, North Dakota, Minnesota and other States. At the same
time the Hon. Washington Jay McCormick, then a Republican
member of the House of Representatives from Montana, offered a
similar bill in Congress. It ran as follows:

A BILL

> To define the national and official language of the Government and people
> of the United States of America, including the Territories and dependencies
> thereof.
> *Be it enacted by the Senate and House of Representatives of the United
> States of America in Congress assembled,* That the national and official language
> of the Government and people of the United States of America, including
> Territories and dependencies thereof, is hereby defined as and declared to
> be the American language.
> Sec. 2. That all Acts and parts of Acts of Congress, including regulations
> of the departments of Government, wherein the speaking, reading, writing, or
> knowledge of the English language is set forth as a requirement for purposes
> of naturalization, immigration, official, legal, or other like use, shall be deemed

emended to the extent of substituting in the text for the word *English* the word *American*.

Sec. 3. That, until Congress shall make specific provision for the official and more particular standardization of the American language, words and phrases generally accepted as being in good use by the people of the United States of America shall constitute a part of the American language for all legal purposes.

Sec. 4. That this Act shall be in full force and effect six months after its passage and approval.

The Hon. Mr. McCormick thus explained the purposes behind his bill:

I might say I would supplement the political emancipation of '76 by the mental emancipation of '23. America has lost much in literature by not thinking its own thoughts and speaking them boldly in a language unadorned with gold braid. It was only when Cooper, Irving, Mark Twain, Whitman, and O. Henry dropped the Order of the Garter and began to write American that their wings of immortality sprouted. Had Noah Webster, instead of styling his monumental work the American Dictionary of the English Language, written a Dictionary of the American Language, he would have become a founder instead of a compiler. Let our writers drop their top-coats, spats, and swagger-sticks, and assume occasionally their buckskin, moccasins, and tomahawks.[1]

Despite this ringing appeal to the red-blooded Americanism of Congress, the Hon. Mr. McCormick was never able to rescue his bill from the dungeons of the Judiciary Committee, and there it died the *Heldentod* at the end of the session. The Hon. Frank Ryan, a member of the Illinois State Senate from Chicago, was more fortunate, for his bill " establishing the American language as the official language of the State of Illinois," introduced on January 10, 1923, became a law on June 19, albeit with certain discreet changes. In its original form it was as follows:

Whereas, Since the creation of the American Republic there have been certain Tory elements in our country who have never become reconciled to our republican institutions and have ever clung to the tradition of King and Empire; and

Whereas, The assumed dominance of this Tory element in the social, business and political life of America tends to force the other racial units, in self-defense, to organize on racial lines, thus creating nations without a nation and fostering those racial and religious differences which lead to disunion and disintegration; and

Whereas, The supreme problem of American statesmen, and supreme desire of American patriots, is to weld the racial units into a solid American nation in the sense that England, France and Germany are nations; and

Whereas, The name of the language of a country has a powerful influence in stimulating and preserving the national ideal; and

1 *Nation*, April 11, 1923.

Whereas, The languages of other countries bear the name of the countries to which they belong, the language of Germany being called German; of France, French; of England, English; and so on; and

Whereas, Our government, laws, customs and ideals as well as our language differ materially from those of England, now therefore;

Sec. 1. *Be it enacted by the People of the State of Illinois, represented in the General Assembly:* The official language of the State of Illinois shall be known hereafter as the "American" language, and not as the "English" language.

The newspapers of the time reported that only three of the Hon. Mr. Ryan's fellow Senators voted against his bill, but it seems to have had harder sledding in the lower House, despite the aid of Mayor Big Bill Thompson of Chicago, who was then in the midst of his campaign to keep the snout of King George V out of his bailiwick. At all events, it lost two of its whereases, suffered changes in two others, and gained two new ones. Those expunged were the second, third, and sixth. In place of the second and third, when the bill was finally passed and approved by the Governor, appeared the following:

Whereas, America has been a haven of liberty and place of opportunity for the common people of all nations; and

Whereas, These strangers within our gates who seek economic betterment, political freedom, larger opportunities for their children and citizenship for themselves, come to think of our institutions as American and our language as the American language.

In addition, the word *psychological* was inserted before *influence* in the fourth whereas, apparently in deference to the Freudian thought of the time, and the examples were stricken out of the fifth. The sixth disappeared without leaving a trace. This statute is still on the books of Illinois as Chapter 127, Section 178 of the Acts of 1923. But all the similar bills introduced in other Legislatures seem to have failed of passage. The one brought up in Minnesota (H.F. 993, March 8, 1923) was sponsored by two members of the House of Representatives, N. T. Moen and J. N. Jacobson, both of them apparently of Scandinavian origin. It was supported by two enthusiasts, John M. Leonard, president of "the American Foundation" of St. Paul, and A. J. Roberts, editor of the *American National Language Magazine,* published in the same city. But though the mighty Magnus Johnson also gave it some help, and it had a favorable report from the Committee on Education, it got no further. In 1908 the American-Language Legion was launched in New York " to secure popular use and statutory recognition of the name, the American language, as the exclusive designation of the official language of the United States and its dependencies." It issued a sticker bearing the word *American* in six sizes of type, and many times repeated. The idea was that " whenever friends of this movement encounter, in any of their books, any name sought to be relegated by the American-Language Legion, *American* in a corresponding size of type may be sheared from this sheet and pasted over, making it read: the American language." But this ingenious scheme seems to have come to nothing also.

Meanwhile, the plain people of England and the United States, whenever they come into contact, find it difficult to effect a fluent exchange of ideas. This was made distressingly apparent during the World War. When the American troops began to pour into France in 1917, fraternizing with the British was impeded, not so much because of hereditary animosities as because of the wide divergence in vocabulary and pronunciation between the doughboy and Tommy Atkins — a divergence interpreted by each as low mental visibility in the other. There was very little movement of slang from one camp to the other, and that little ran mainly from the American side to the British. The Y.M.C.A., always pathetically eager for the popularity that it could never gain, made a characteristic effort to turn the feeling of strangeness among the Americans to account. In the Chicago *Tribune's* Paris edition of July 7, 1917, I find a large advertisement inviting them to make use of the Y.M.C.A. clubhouse in the Avenue Montaigne, " where *American* is spoken." At about the same time an enterprising London tobacconist, Peters by name, affixed a sign bearing the legend " *American* spoken here " to the front of his shop, and soon he was imitated by hundreds of other London, Liverpool and Paris shopkeepers. Such signs are still familiar all over Europe, and they have begun to appear in Asia.[1]

---

1 Peters, it appears, had a remote forerunner in one Proctor, who was in practise as a teacher of English in Paris at the end of the Eighteenth Century. Mr. H. A. Larrabee of Cambridge, Mass., calls my attention to the following reference to him in John G. Alger's Paris in 1789–94: " In October, 1794, Proctor advertised that he taught the English and American languages — there had been no advertisements of lessons in foreign languages during the Terror — and he was still doing this in 1802." Apparently the strained relations between France and the United States in 1797–1800 did not force Proctor to suspend the teaching of American.

8. FOREIGN OBSERVERS

The continental awareness of the growing differences between English and American is demonstrated by the fact that some of the popular German *Sprachführer* now appear in separate editions, *Amerikanisch* and *Englisch*. This is true, for example, of the Metoula-Sprachführer and of the Polyglott Kuntze books.[1] The American edition of the latter starts off with the doctrine that "*Jeder, der nach Nord-Amerika oder Australien will, muss Englisch können*," but a great many of the words and phrases that appear in its examples would be unintelligible to many Englishmen — *e.g.*, *free-lunch, real-estate agent, buckwheat, corn* (for *maize*), *conductor* and *popcorn* — and a number of others would suggest false meanings or otherwise puzzle — *e.g.*, *saloon, wash-stand, water-pitcher* and *apple-pie*.[2] In the "Neokosmos Sprachführer durch England-Amerika"[3] there are many notes calling attention to differences between American and English usage, *e.g.*, *baggage-luggage, car-carriage, conductor-guard*. The authors are also forced to enter into explanations of the functions of the *boots* in an English hotel and of the *clerk* in an American hotel, and they devote a whole section to a discourse upon the nature and uses of such American beverages as *whiskey-sours, Martini-cocktails, silver-fizzes, John-Collinses*, and *ice-cream sodas*.[4] There are many special guides to the American language in German — for example, "The Little Yankee," by Alfred D. Schoch and R. Kron (Freiburg, 1912), "Uncle Sam and His English," by W. K. Pfeiler and Elisabeth Wittmann (Berlin,

1 Metoula-Sprachführer; Englisch von Karl Blattner; Ausgabe für Amerika; Berlin-Schöneberg. Polyglott Kuntze; Schnellste Erlernung jeder Sprache ohne Lehrer; Amerikanisch; Bonn a. Rh.

2 Like the English expositors of American Slang (See Chapter VI, Section 3), this German falls into several errors. For example, he gives *cock* for *rooster, boots* for *shoes, braces* for *suspenders* and *postman* for *letter-carrier*, and lists *iron-monger, joiner* and *linen-draper* as American terms. He also spells *wagon* in the English manner, with two *g's*, and translates *Schweine-*

füsse as pork-feet. But he spells such words as *color* in the American manner and gives the pronunciation of *clerk* as the American *klörk*, not as the English *klark*.

3 By Carlo di Domizio and Charles M. Smith; Munich, n.d.

4 Like the Metoula expositor, they make mistakes. Certainly no American bartender ever makes a *Hock*-cup; he makes a *Rhine-wine*-cup. They list several drinks that are certainly not familiar in America, *e.g.*, the *knickebein* and the *white-lion*. Yet worse, they convert *julep* into *jules*.

1932); and " Spoken American," by S. A. Nock and H. Mutschmann (Leipzig, 1930). It is also dealt with at length in various more general guides — for example, " Hauptfragen der Amerikakunde," by Walther Fischer (Bielefeld, 1928); " The American Wonderland," by S. A. Nock and G. Kamitsch (Leipzig, 1930); and " America of Today," by Frau Voight-Goldsmith and D. Borchard (Berlin, 1929). Nor is it overlooked by pedagogues. I have before me a circular of the Lessing Hochschule in Berlin, offering courses in both Amerikanisch and Englisch — two for *Anfänger*, one for *Vorgebildete*, and one for *Fortgeschrittene* — each of eight weeks, and at a fee of ten marks. The American language also gets attention in a number of French, Italian and Scandinavian guide-books for immigrants and travelers; in one of them [1] I find definitions of *butterine, cat-boat, clawhammer, co-ed, craps, dago, dumb-waiter, faker, freeze-out, gusher, hard-cider, hen-party, jitney, mortician, panhandle, patrolman, sample-room, shyster, sleuth, wet* (noun), *dry* (noun), *headcheese* and *overhead-expenses*. The standard guide-books for tourists always call attention to the differences between the English and American vocabularies. Baedeker's " United States " has a glossary for Englishmen likely to be daunted by such terms as *el, European-plan* and *sundae*, and in Muirhead's " London and Its Environs " there is a corresponding one for Americans, warning them that *bug* means only *bed-bug* in England, that a *clerk* there is never a shopman, and that *homely* means domestic, unpretending, homelike, never plain-looking, and giving them the meanings of *trunk-call, hoarding, goods-train, spanner* and *minerals*.

From the earliest days the peculiarities of American have attracted the attention of Continental philologians, and especially of the Germans. The first edition of Bartlett's Glossary (1848) brought forth a long review in the *Archiv für das Studium der neueren Sprachen und Literaturen* (Braunschweig) by Dr. Felix Flügel, and in 1866 Dr. Friedrich Köhler published a " Wörterbuch der Americanismen," based on it. In subsequent volumes of the *Archiv* and in the other German philological journals there have been frequent discussions of the subject by Ludwig Herrig, Karl Knortz, Johannes Hoops, Hermann U. Meysenberg, Ed. O. Paget, Paul Heyne, Georg Kartzke, Walther Fischer, Fritz Karpf, Martin Pawlik and H.

[1] De Forenede Stater, by Evald Kristensen; Omaha, Neb., 1921, Vol. I, pp. 207–219. For a translation of this chapter I am indebted to the kindness of Dr. A. Th. Dorf of Chicago.

Lüdeke. It has also been discussed at length in the German lay press, especially by C. A. Bratter, Friedrich Schönemann and Arnold Schöer. It is common in German for translations of American books to bear the words *aus dem Amerikanischen* on their title-pages, and the term is frequently in use otherwise.[1] Like his German colleagues, Dr. Otto Jespersen of Copenhagen, perhaps the first living authority on modern English, is greatly interested in Americanisms, and at one time contemplated doing a book on them. The third edition of the present work was translated into German with a commentary by Dr. Heinrich Spies of Berlin in 1927,[2] and the same scholar has lectured on the subject at Berlin, Greifswald and elsewhere. Various Dutch and Belgian philologians, among them Barentz, Keijzer, Aronstein, Zandvoort, Peeters, and van der Voort, have published studies of American, and so have various Frenchmen and Italians; and at the University of Paris, in 1921, Ray P. Bowen was appointed *lecteur d'américain*. At Tartu-Dorpat in Estonia Dr. Heinrich Mutschmann, professor of English in the university there, has printed an excellent Glossary of Americanisms (1931) — in fact, a much better one than any that has come out in America since Thornton's. Two other foreign scholars who show more interest in American English than is usually displayed at home are Professor Wincenty Lutoslawski, of the University of Wilna in Poland, and Professor Sanki Ichikawa, of the Imperial University at Tokyo. The early editions of the present work brought me into pleasant contact with these gentlemen, and I have received valuable suggestions from both. Says Dr. Ichikawa:

> It is a great question with us teachers of English in Japan whether we should teach American English or British English. We have more opportunities for coming into contact with Americans than for meeting Englishmen, but on the other hand books on phonetics are mostly done by English scholars. As to the vocabulary, we are teaching English and American indiscriminately — many of us, perhaps, without knowing which is which.

The literature on Americanisms in Japanese is already of some weight. It includes an excellent formal treatise, " English and Ameri-

---

1 For example, the following appears on the invitations to farewell dinners on Hamburg-Amerika Line ships (1935): "Einem geehrten Bordpublico kund und zu wissen: Dass das fröliche Bord-Glöcklin, so in *amerikanischen* Sprach *dinnerbell* geheisten ist," etc.

2 Die Amerikanische Sprache (Das Englisch der Vereinigten Staaten), von H. L. Mencken; Deutsch Bearbeitung von Heinrich Spies; Leipzig, 1917. Dr. Spies is also the author of Kultur und Sprach in neuen England; Leipzig, 1925.

can of Today," by G. Tomita (Tokyo, 1930), and a number
of smaller studies. Such monographs as "Japanized English" by
S. Aarkawa (Tokyo, 1930) and "English Influence on Japanese,"
by Dr. Ichikawa (Tokyo, 1928) give a great deal of attention to
American forms. The Russians are also conscious of the difference
between the two languages, and there is a party at Moscow which
holds that American should be taught in the schools, not English.
As yet this party does not seem to have prevailed, but so long ago
as March, 1930, it was bold enough to propose the following resolutions at a conference of teachers of language at Moscow:

1. Oxford English is an aristocratic tongue purposely fostered by the
highest British governing and land-holding classes in order to maintain their
icy and lofty exclusiveness.
2. It is not used by the majority of the residents in Great Britain and
certainly not by its intelligent working class elements.
3. It is not used by the majority of English-speaking peoples the world
over.
4. The aristocracy is introducing all sorts of affectations, such as the
chopping short of syllables and the swallowing of the terminations of words,
in order to make it all the more difficult for anyone else to speak the language in their manner.
5. The American language is more democratic, for the employing classes
speak no differently from their employés. It is more standard, due originally
to the settlement of the West by Easterners, and lately due to the radio and
talkies.
6. The American language is more alive and picturesque, tending more
to simplification both as to spelling and grammar.
7. Linguist "purity" is mere fiction for language does not grow out
of the air, but is determined by particular social conditions and in a measure
is a reflex of these conditions. Language purity at best reflects a pedantic
attitude and at worst an attitude either aristocratic or chauvinistic.
8. Since American engineers are preferred by the Soviet authorities to
the English, since the latest industrial technique finds its highest development
in the United States, good American English serves Soviet purposes best.[1]

The apparent feeling of so many American philologians that giving serious study to the common speech of their country would be
beneath their dignity is not shared by their European colleagues. In
England the local dialects have been investigated for many years,
and there is a formidable literature on slang, stretching back to the
Sixteenth Century and including a glossary in seven large volumes.
In France, as in Germany, Italy and Japan, a linguistic atlas has been

1 See The American Language   by Eli B. Jacobson, *American Mer-*
Fights for Recognition in Moscow,   *cury*, Jan., 1931.

published,[1] and the Société des Parlers de France makes diligent inquiries into changing forms; moreover, the Académie itself is endlessly concerned with the subject. There is, besides, a constant outpouring of books by private investigators, of which "Le Langage populaire," by Henry Banche, is a good example. In Germany, amid many other such works, there are admirable grammars of all the dialects. In Sweden there are several journals devoted to the study of the vulgate, and the government has granted a subvention of 7500 *kronor* a year to an organization of scholars called the Undersökningen av Svenska Folkmål, formed to investigate it systematically. In Norway there is a widespread movement to overthrow the official Dano-Norwegian, and substitute a national language based upon the speech of the peasants.[2] In Spain the Real Academia Española de la Lengua is constantly at work upon its great Diccionario, Ortografía and Gramática, and revises them at frequent intervals, taking in all new words as they appear and all new forms of old ones. And in Latin-America, to come nearer to our own case, the native philologists have produced a large literature on the matter closest at hand, and one finds in it excellent studies of the Portuguese dialect of Brazil, and the variations of Spanish in Mexico, the Argentine, Chili, Peru, Ecuador, Uruguay and even Honduras and Costa Rica.[3]

1 L'Atlas linguistique de la France, by J. Gillieron and E. Edmont; Paris, 1902–08. The German Sprachatlas des Deutschen Reiches was edited by Wenker and appeared ten years earlier. The Japanese atlas, Dai Nippon Hogen Chidzu, was prepared by M. Tojo.

2 This movement owes its start to Ivar Aasen (1813–96), who published a grammar of the *landsmaal*, or peasant speech, in 1848, and a dictionary in 1850. It won official recognition in 1885, when the Storthing passed the first of a series of acts designed to put the *landsmaal* on an equal footing with the official Dano-Norwegian. Four years later, after a campaign going back to 1874, provision was made for teaching it in the schools for the training of primary teachers. In 1899 a professorship of it was established in the University of Christiania. The school boards in the case of primary schools, and the pupils in the case of middle and high schools are now permitted to choose between the two languages, and the *landsmaal* has been given official status by the State Church. The chief impediment to its wider acceptance lies in the fact that it is not, as it stands, a natural language, but an artificial amalgamation of peasant dialects. See The Linguistic Development of Ivar Aasen's New Norse, by Einas Haugen, *Publications of the Modern Language Association*, Vol. XLVIII, Pt. 1, 1933.

3 There is a bibliography of this literature in the third edition of the present work; New York, 1923, pp. 460–61; and a better one in Estudios Sobre el Español de Nuevo Méjico, by Aurelio M. Espinosa; Buenos Aires, 1930, p. 24 *ff*.

II

THE MATERIALS OF INQUIRY

1. THE HALLMARKS OF AMERICAN

The characters chiefly noted in American English by all who have discussed it are, first, its general uniformity throughout the country; second, its impatient disregard for grammatical, syntactical and phonological rule and precedent; and third, its large capacity (distinctly greater than that of the English of present-day England) for taking in new words and phrases from outside sources, and for manufacturing them of its own materials.

The first of these characters has struck every observer, native and foreign. In place of the discordant local dialects of all the other major countries, including England, we have a general *Volkssprache* for the whole nation, and if it is conditioned at all it is only by minor differences in pronunciation and vocabulary, and by the linguistic struggles of various groups of newcomers. No other country can show such linguistic solidarity, nor any approach to it — not even Canada, for there a large minority of the population resists speaking English altogether. The Little Russian of the Ukraine is unintelligible to the citizen of Moscow; the Northern Italian can scarcely follow a conversation in Sicilian; the Low German from Hamburg is a foreigner in Munich; the Breton flounders in Gascony. Even in the United Kingdom there are wide divergences.[1] "When we remember," says the New International Encyclopedia, "that the dialects of the counties in England have marked differences — so marked, indeed, that it may be doubted whether a Lancashire miner and a Lincolnshire farmer could understand each other — we may well be proud that our vast country has, strictly speaking, only one language." There are some regional peculiarities in pronunciation and intonation, and they will be examined in some detail

1 W. W. Skeat distinguishes 9 principal dialects in Scotland, 3 in Ireland and 30 in England and Wales. See his English Dialects From the Eighth Century to the Present Day; Cambridge, 1911, p. 107 ff.

in Chapter VII, but when it comes to the words they habitually use and the way they use them all Americans, even the less tutored, follow pretty much the same line. A Boston taxi-driver could go to work in Chicago or San Francisco without running any risk of misunderstanding his new fares. Once he had flattened his *a*'s a bit and picked up a few dozen localisms, he would be, to all linguistic intents and purposes, fully naturalized.

Of the intrinsic differences that separate American from English the chief have their roots in the obvious disparity between the environment and traditions of the American people since the Seventeenth Century and those of the English. The latter have lived under a relatively stable social order, and it has impressed upon their souls their characteristic respect for what is customary and of good report. Until the World War brought chaos to most of their institutions, their whole lives were regulated, perhaps more than those of any other people save the Spaniards, by a regard for precedent. The Americans, though partly of the same blood, have felt no such restraint, and acquired no such habit of conformity. On the contrary, they have plunged to the other extreme, for the conditions of life in their country have put a high value upon the precisely opposite qualities of curiosity and daring, and so they have acquired that character of restlessness, that impatience of forms, that disdain of the dead hand, which now broadly marks them. From the first, says a literary historian, they have been " less phlegmatic, less conservative than the English. There were climatic influences, it may be; there was surely a spirit of intensity everywhere that made for short effort." [1] Thus, in the arts, and thus in business, in politics, in daily intercourse, in habits of mind and speech. The American is not, of course, lacking in a capacity for discipline; he has it highly developed; he submits to leadership readily, and even to tyranny. But, by a curious twist, it is not the leadership that is old and decorous that commonly fetches him, but the leadership that is new and extravagant. He will resist dictation out of the past, but he will follow a new messiah with almost Russian willingness, and into the wildest vagaries of economics, religion, morals and speech. A new fallacy in politics spreads faster in the United States than anywhere else on earth, and so does a new fashion in hats, or a new revelation

1 F. L. Pattee: A History of American Literature Since 1870; New York, 1916. See also The American Novel, by Carl Van Doren; New York, 1921.

of God, or a new means of killing time, or a new shibboleth, or metaphor, or piece of slang. Thus the American, on his linguistic side, likes to make his language as he goes along, and not all the hard work of the schoolmarm can hold the business back. A novelty loses nothing by the fact that it is a novelty; it rather gains something, and particularly if it meets the national fancy for the terse, the vivid, and, above all, the bold and imaginative. The characteristic American habit of reducing complex concepts to the starkest abbreviations was already noticeable in colonial times, and such highly typical Americanisms as *O.K.*, *N.G.*, and *P.D.Q.*, have been traced back to the early days of the Republic. Nor are the influences that shaped these tendencies invisible today, for institution-making is yet going on, and so is language-making. In so modest an operation as that which has evolved *bunco* from *buncombe* and *bunk* from *bunco* there is evidence of a phenomenon which the philologian recognizes as belonging to the most lusty stages of speech.

But of more importance than the sheer inventions, if only because much more numerous, are the extensions of the vocabulary, both absolutely and in ready workableness, by the devices of rhetoric. The American, from the beginning, has been the most ardent of recorded rhetoricians. His politics bristles with pungent epithets; his whole history has been bedizened with tall talk; his fundamental institutions rest far more upon brilliant phrases than upon logical ideas. And in small things as in large he exercises continually an incomparable capacity for projecting hidden and often fantastic relationships into arresting parts of speech. Such a term as *rubberneck* is almost a complete treatise on American psychology; it reveals the national habit of mind more clearly than any labored inquiry could ever reveal it. It has in it precisely the boldness and contempt for ordered forms that are so characteristically American, and it has too the grotesque humor of the country, and the delight in devastating opprobriums, and the acute feeling for the succinct and savory. The same qualities are in *rough-house, water-wagon, has-been, lame-duck, speed-cop* and a thousand other such racy substantives, and in all the great stock of native verbs and adjectives. There is indeed, but a shadowy boundary in these new coinages between the various parts of speech. *Corral*, borrowed from the Spanish, immediately becomes a verb and the father of an adjective. *Bust*, carved out of *burst*, erects itself into a noun. *Bum*, coming by way of an earlier *bummer* from the German, becomes noun, adjective, verb and adverb. Verbs are fashioned out of substantives by the simple process of prefixing the preposition: *to engineer, to stump, to hog, to style, to author.* Others grow out of an intermediate adjective, as *to boom.* Others are made by torturing nouns with harsh affixes, as *to burglarize* and *to itemize,* or by groping for the root, as *to resurrect* and *to jell.* Yet others are changed from intransitive to transitive; a sleeping-car *sleeps* thirty passengers. So with the adjectives. They are made of substantives unchanged: *codfish, jitney.* Or by bold combinations: *down-and-out, up-state, flat-footed.* Or by shading down suffixes to a barbaric simplicity: *scary, classy, tasty.* Or by working over adverbs until they tremble on the brink between adverb and adjective: *right, sure* and *near* are examples.

All these processes, of course, are also to be observed in the history of the English of England; at the time of its sturdiest growth they were in the most active possible being. They are, indeed, common to all tongues; " the essence of language," says Dr. Jespersen, " is activity." But if you will put the English of today beside the American of today you will see at once how much more forcibly they are in operation in the latter than in the former. The standard Southern dialect of English has been arrested in its growth by its purists and grammarians, and burdened with irrational affectations by fashionable pretension. It shows no living change since the reign of Samuel Johnson. Its tendency is to combat all that expansive gusto which made for its pliancy and resilience in the days of Shakespeare.[1] In place of the old loose-footedness there is set up a preciosity which, in one direction, takes the form of clumsy artificialities in the spoken

[1] Rather curiously, the two authorities who were most influential, during the Nineteenth Century, in keeping it to a rigid pattern were both Americans. They were Lindley Murray (1745–1826) and Joseph E. Worcester (1784–1865). Murray, a Pennsylvanian, went to England after the Revolution, and in 1795 published his Grammar of the English Language. It had an extraordinary sale in England, and was accepted as the court of last resort in usage down to quite recent times. Worcester's Universal and Critical Dictionary of the English Language, 1846, divided the honors of authority in England with B. H. Smart's Dictionary, published during the same year. It was extensively pirated. Thus, says Thomas R. Lounsbury (The Standard of Pronunciation in English; New York, 1904, p. 220), " the Londoner frequently got his pure London pronunciation from a citizen of this country who was never outside of New England for more than a few months of his life." Worcester was also accepted at Harvard and at the University of Virginia, but elsewhere in the United States Webster prevailed.

language, and in another shows itself in the even clumsier Johnsonese
of so much current English writing — the Jargon denounced by Sir
Arthur Quiller-Couch in his Cambridge lectures. This "infirmity
of speech" Quiller-Couch finds "in parliamentary debates and in
the newspapers; . . . it has become the medium through which
Boards of Government, County Councils, Syndicates, Committees,
Commercial Firms, express the processes as well as the conclusions
of their thought, and so voice the reason of their being." Distinct
from journalese, the two yet overlap, " and have a knack of assimilating each other's vices."[1]

American, despite the gallant efforts of the pedagogues, has so far
escaped any such suffocating formalization. We, too, of course, have
our occasional practitioners of the authentic English Jargon, but in
the main our faults lie in precisely the opposite direction. That is
to say, we incline toward a directness of statement which, at its
greatest, lacks restraint and urbanity altogether, and toward a hospitality which often admits novelties for the mere sake of their
novelty, and is quite uncritical of the difference between a genuine
improvement in succinctness and clarity, and mere extravagant raciness. "The tendency," says one English observer, "is . . . to consider the speech of any man, as any man himself, as good as any
other."[2] The Americans, adds a Scots professor, "are determined
to hack their way through the language, as their ancestors through
forests, regardless of the valuable growths that may be sacrificed in
blazing the trail."[3] But this Scot dismisses the English neologisms
of the day, when ranged beside the American stock, as "dwiny,
feeble stuff"; "it is to America," he admits, "that we must chiefly
look in future for the replenishment and freshening of our language." I quote one more Briton, this time an Englishman steeped
in the public school tradition:

The English of the United States is not merely different from ours; it
has a restless inventiveness which may well be founded in a sense of racial

1 See the chapter, Interlude on Jargon, in Quiller-Couch's On the Art
of Writing; New York, 1916. Ap-
propriately enough, large parts of
the learned critic's book are written
in the very Jargon he attacks. See
also Ch. VI of Growth and Structure of the English Language, by
O. Jespersen, 3rd ed., rev.; Leipzig,
1919, especially p. 143 ff. See also

Official English, in *English*, March,
1919, p. 7; April, p. 45, and Aug.,
p. 135, and The Decay of Syntax,
in the London *Times Literary Supplement*, May 8, 1919, p. 1.
2 Alexander Francis: Americans: An
Impression; New York, 1900.
3 Breaking Priscian's Head, by J. Y.
T. Greig; London, 1929.

discomfort, a lack of full accord between the temperament of the people and the constitution of their speech. The English are uncommunicative; the Americans are not. In its coolness and quiet withdrawal, in its prevailing sobriety, our language reflects the cautious economies and leisurely assurance of the average speaker. We say so little that we do not need to enliven our vocabulary and underline our sentences, or cry "Wolf!" when we wish to be heard. The more stimulating climate of the United States has produced a more eager, a more expansive, a more decisive people. The Americans apprehend their world in sharper outlines and aspire after a more salient rendering of it.[1]

This revolt against conventional bonds and restraints is most noticeable, of course, on the lower levels of American speech; in the regions above there still linger some vestiges of Eighteenth Century tightness. But even in those upper regions there are rebels a-plenty, and some of them are of such authority that it is impossible to dismiss them. I glance through the speeches of the late Dr. Woodrow Wilson, surely a conscientious purist and Anglomaniac if we have ever had one, and find, in a few moments, half a dozen locutions that an Englishman in like position would certainly hesitate to use, among them *we must get a move on,*[2] *to hog,*[3] *to gum-shoe,*[4] *onery* in place of *ordinary,*[5] and *that is going some.*[6] I turn to the letters of that most passionate of Anglomaniacs, Walter Hines Page, and find *to eat out of my hand, to lick to a frazzle, to cut no figure, to go gunning for, nothin' doin', for keeps,* and so on. I proceed to Dr. John Dewey, probably the country's most respectable metaphysician, and find him using *dope* for *opium.*[7] In recent years certain English magnificoes have shown signs of going the same route, but whenever they yield the corrective bastinado is laid on, and nine times out of ten they are accused, and rightly, of succumbing to American influence.

Let American confront a novel problem alongside English, and immediately its superior imaginativeness and resourcefulness become obvious. *Movie* is better than *cinema;* and the English begin to admit the fact by adopting the word; it is not only better American, it is better English. *Bill-board* is better than *hoarding. Office-holder* is

1 Pomona, or The Future of English, by Basil de Sélincourt; London, 1929.
2 Speech before the Chamber of Commerce Convention, Washington, Feb. 19, 1916.
3 Speech at a workingman's dinner, New York, Sept. 4, 1912.
4 Wit and Wisdom of Woodrow Wilson, comp. by Richard Linthicum; New York, 1916, p. 54.
5 Speech at Ridgewood, N. J., April 22, 1910.
6 Wit and Wisdom . . . p. 56.
7 *New Republic,* Dec. 24, 1919, p. 116, col. 1.

more honest, more picturesque, more thoroughly Anglo-Saxon than *public-servant*. *Stem-winder* somehow has more life in it, more fancy and vividness, than the literal *keyless-watch*. Turn to the terminology of *railroading* (itself, by the way, an Americanism): its creation fell upon the two peoples equally, but they tackled the job independently. The English, seeking a figure to denominate the wedge-shaped fender in front of a locomotive, called it a *plough;* the Americans, characteristically, gave it the far more pungent name of *cow-catcher*. So with the casting which guides the wheels from one rail to another. The English called it a *crossing-plate;* the Americans, more responsive to the suggestion in its shape, called it a *frog*. American is full of what Bret Harte called the "saber-cuts of Saxon"; it meets Montaigne's ideal of "a succulent and nervous speech, short and compact, not as much delicated and combed out as vehement and brusque, rather arbitrary than monotonous, not pedantic but soldierly, as Suetonius called Cæsar's Latin." One pictures the common materials of English dumped into a pot, exotic flavorings added, and the bubblings assiduously and expectantly skimmed. What is old and respected is already in decay the moment it comes into contact with what is new and vivid. "When we Americans are through with the English language," says Mr. Dooley, "it will look as if it had been run over by a musical comedy."

All this boldness of conceit, of course, makes for vulgarity. Unrestrained by any critical sense — and the critical sense of the pedagogues counts for little, for they cry wolf too often — it flowers in such barbaric inventions as *tasty, alright, go-getter, he-man, go-aheadativeness, tony, goof, semi-occasional,* and *to doxologize*. But vulgarity, after all, means no more than a yielding to natural impulses in the face of conventional inhibitions, and that yielding to natural impulses is at the heart of all healthy language-making. The history of English, like the history of American and of every other living tongue, is a history of vulgarisms that, by their accurate meeting of real needs, have forced their way into sound usage, and even into the lifeless catalogues of the grammarians. The purist performs a useful office in enforcing a certain logical regularity upon the process, and in our own case the omnipresent example of the greater conservatism of the English restrains, to some extent, our native tendency to go too fast, but the process itself is as inexorable in its workings as the precession of the equinoxes, and if we yield to it more eagerly than the English, it is only a proof, perhaps, that the future of what was once the Anglo-Saxon tongue lies on this side of the water. Standard English now has the brakes on, but American continues to leap in the dark, and the prodigality of its movement is all the indication that is needed of its intrinsic health, its capacity to meet the ever-changing needs of a restless and emotional people, inordinately mongrel, and disdainful of tradition. Language, says A. H. Sayce,

is not artificial product, contained in books and dictionaries and governed by the strict rules of impersonal grammarians. It is the living expression of the mind and spirit of a people, ever changing and shifting, whose sole standard of correctness is custom and the common usage of the community. . . . The first lesson to be learned is that there is no intrinsic right or wrong in the use of language, no fixed rules such as are the delight of the teacher of Latin prose. What is right now will be wrong hereafter; what language rejected yesterday she accepts today.[1]

2. WHAT IS AN AMERICANISM?

John Pickering was the first to attempt to draw up a schedule of Americanisms. In his " Vocabulary or Collection of Words and Phrases Which Have Been Supposed to be Peculiar to the United States of America " (1816) he divided them into three categories, as follows:

    1. "We have formed some new words."
    2. "To some old ones, that are still in use in England, we have affixed new significations."
    3. "Others, which have been long obsolete in England, are still retained in common use among us."

[1] Introduction to the Science of Language, 4th ed.; London, 1900, Vol. II, pp. 33–4. All this, of course, had been said long before Sayce. "Language," said Quintilian in his Institutiones Oratorias, I (*c.* 95), " is like money, which becomes current when it receives the public stamp." "Custom," said Ben Jonson in his Grammar (1640) " is the most certain mistress of language." "Language," said George Campbell in The Philosophy of Rhetoric, II (1776), " is purely a species of fashion, in which by the general, but tacit, consent of the people of a particular state or country, certain sounds come to be appropriated to certain things as their signs." "Established custom," said Hugh Blair in his Lectures on Rhetoric and Belles Lettres (1783), " is the standard to which we must at last resort for determining every controverted point in language." To which Noah Webster added in his Dissertations on the English Language (1789): "The general practise of a nation is the rule of propriety."

John Russell Bartlett, in the second edition of his "Glossary of Words and Phrases Usually Regarded as Peculiar to the United States" (1859), increased these three classes to nine:

1. Archaisms, *i.e.*, old English words, obsolete, or nearly so, in England, but retained in use in this country.
2. English words used in a different sense from what they are in England. "These include many names of natural objects differently applied."
3. Words which have retained their original meaning in the United States, though not in England.
4. English provincialisms adopted into general use in America.
5. New coined words, which owe their origin to the productions or to the circumstances of the country.
6. Words borrowed from European languages, especially the French, Spanish, Dutch and German.
7. Indian words.
8. Negroisms.
9. Peculiarities of pronunciation.

Some time before this, but after the publication of Bartlett's first edition in 1848, William C. Fowler, professor of rhetoric at Amherst, devoted a brief chapter to "American Dialects" in "The English Language" (1850) and in it one finds the following formidable classification:

1. Words borrowed from other languages.
   a. Indian, as *Kennebec, Ohio, Tombigbee, sagamore, quahaug, succotash.*
   b. Dutch, as *boss, kruller, stoop.*
   c. German, as *spuke* [?], *sauerkraut.*
   d. French, as *bayou, cache, chute, crevasse, levee.*
   e. Spanish, as *calaboose, chaparral, hacienda, rancho, ranchero.*
   f. Negro, as *buckra.*
2. Words "introduced from the necessity of our situation, in order to express new ideas."
   a. Words "connected with and flowing from our political institutions," as *selectman, presidential, congressional, caucus, mass-meeting, lynch-law, help* (for *servants*).
   b. Words "connected with our ecclesiastical institutions," as *associational, consociational, to fellowship, to missionate.*
   c. Words "connected with a new country," as *lot, diggings, betterments, squatter.*
3. Miscellaneous Americanisms.
   a. Words and phrases become obsolete in England, as *talented, offset* (for *set-off*), *back and forth* (for *backward and forward*).
   b. Old words and phrases "which are now merely provincial in England," as *hub, whap* [?], *to wilt.*
   c. Nouns formed from verbs by adding the French suffix *-ment*, as *publishment, releasement, requirement.*

d. Forms of words "which fill the gap or vacancy between two words which are approved," as *obligate* (between *oblige* and *obligation*) and *variate* (between *vary* and *variation*).

e. "Certain compound terms for which the English have different compounds," as *bank-bill* (*bank-note*), *book-store* (*bookseller's shop*), *bottom-land* (*interval-land*), *clapboard* (*pale*), *sea-board* (*sea-shore*), *side-hill* (*hill-side*).

f. "Certain colloquial phrases, apparently idiomatic, and very expressive," as *to cave in, to flare up, to flunk out, to fork over, to hold on, to let on, to stave off, to take on.*

g. Intensives, "often a matter of mere temporary fashion," as *dreadful, might, plaguy, powerful.*

h. "Certain verbs expressing one's state of mind, but partially or timidly," as *to allot upon* (for *to count upon*), *to calculate, to expect* (*to think* or *believe*), *to guess, to reckon.*

i. "Certain adjectives, expressing not only quality, but one's subjective feelings in regard to it," as *clever, grand, green, likely, smart, ugly.*

j. Abridgments, as *stage* (for *stage-coach*) *turnpike* (for *turnpike-road*), *spry* (for *sprightly*), *to conduct* (for *to conduct one's self*).

k. "Quaint or burlesque terms," as *to tote, to yank, humbug, loafer, muss, plunder* (for *baggage*), *rock* (for *stone*).

l. "Low expressions, mostly political," as *slang-whanger, loco foco, hunker, to get the hang of.*

m. "Ungrammatical expressions, disapproved by all," as *do don't, used to could, can't come it, Universal preacher* (for *Universalist*), *there's no two ways about it.*

Alfred L. Elwyn, in his "Glossary of Supposed Americanisms" (1859), attempted no classification. He confined his glossary to archaic English words surviving in America, and sought only to prove that they had come down "from our remotest ancestry" and were thus undeserving of the reviling lavished upon them by English critics. Schele de Vere, in his "Americanisms" (1872), followed Bartlett, and devoted himself largely to words borrowed from the Indian dialects, and from the French, Spanish and Dutch. But John S. Farmer, in his "Americanisms New and Old" (1889), ventured upon a new classification, prefacing it with the following definition:

An Americanism may be defined as a word or phrase, old or new, employed by general or respectable usage in America in a way not sanctioned by the best standards of the English language. As a matter of fact, however, the term has come to possess a wider meaning, and it is now applied not only to words and phrases which can be so described, but also to the new and legitimately born words adapted to the general needs and usages, to the survivals of an older form of English than that now current in the mother country, and to the racy, pungent vernacular of Western life.

He then proceeded to this classification:

1. Words and phrases of purely American derivation, embracing words originating in:
    a. Indian and aboriginal life.
    b. Pioneer and frontier life.
    c. The church.
    d. Politics.
    e. Trades of all kinds.
    f. Travel, afloat and ashore.
2. Words brought by colonists, including:
    a. The German element.
    b. The French.
    c. The Spanish.
    b. The Dutch.
    e. The Negro.
    f. The Chinese.
3. Names of American things, embracing:
    a. Natural products.
    b. Manufactured articles.
4. Perverted English words.
5. Obsolete English words still in good use in America.
6. English words, American by inflection and modification.
7. Odd and ignorant popular phrases, proverbs, vulgarisms, and colloquialisms, cant and slang.
8. Individualisms.
9. Doubtful and miscellaneous.

Sylva Clapin, in his " New Dictionary of Americanisms " (1902), reduced these categories to four:

1. Genuine English words, obsolete or provincial in England, and universally used in the United States.
2. English words conveying, in the United States, a different meaning from that attached to them in England.
3. Words introduced from other languages than the English: — French, Dutch, Spanish, German, Indian, etc.
4. Americanisms proper, *i.e.*, words coined in the country, either representing some new idea or peculiar product.

Richard H. Thornton, in his " American Glossary " (1912), substituted the following:

1. Forms of speech now obsolete or provincial in England, which survive in the United States, such as *allow, bureau, fall, gotten, guess, likely, professor, shoat.*
2. Words and phrases of distinctly American origin, such as *belittle, lengthy, lightning-rod, to darken one's doors, to bark up the wrong tree, to come out at the little end of the horn, blind tiger, cold snap, gay Quaker, gone coon, long sauce, pay dirt, small potatoes, some pumpkins.*
3. Nouns which indicate quadrupeds, birds, trees, articles of food, etc., that are distinctively American, such as *ground-hog, hang-bird, hominy, live-oak, locust, opossum, persimmon, pone, succotash, wampum, wigwam.*

4. Names of persons and classes of persons, and of places, such as *Buckeye, Cracker, Greaser, Hoosier, Old Hickory,* the *Little Giant, Dixie, Gotham,* the *Bay State,* the *Monumental City.*

5. Words which have assumed a new meaning, such as *card, clever, fork, help, penny, plunder, raise, rock, sack, ticket, windfall.*

In addition, Thornton added a provisional class of " words and phrases of which I have found earlier examples in American than in English writers; . . . with the *caveat* that further research may reverse the claim " — a class offering specimens in *alarmist, capitalize, eruptiveness, horse of another colour* [sic!], *the jig's up, nameable, omnibus bill, propaganda* and *whitewash.*

Gilbert M. Tucker, in his " American English " (1921) attempted to reduce all Americanisms to two grand divisions, as follows:

1. Words and phrases that originated in America and express something that the British have always expressed differently if they have mentioned it at all.

2. Words and phrases that would convey to a British ear a different meaning from that which they bear in this country.

To this he added seven categories of locution *not* to be regarded as Americanisms, despite their inclusion in various previous lists, as follows:

1. Words and phrases stated by the previous compiler himself to be of foreign (*i.e.,* chiefly of English) origin, like Farmer's *hand-me-downs.*

2. Names of things exclusively American, but known abroad under the same name, such as *moccasin.*

3. Names of things invented in the United States, like *drawing-room car.*

4. Words used in this country in a sense hardly distinguishable from that they bear in England, like *force* for a gang of laborers.

5. Nonce words, like Mark Twain's *cavalieress.*

6. Perfectly regular and self-explanatory compounds, like *office-holder, planing-machine, ink-slinger* and *fly-time.*

7. Purely technical terms, such as those employed in baseball.

Only a glance at these discordant classifications is needed to show that they hamper the inquiry by limiting its scope — not so much, to be sure, as the extravagant limitations of White and Lounsbury, noted in Chapter I, Section 5, but still very seriously. They leave out of account some of the most salient characters of a living language. Only Bartlett and Farmer establish a separate category of Americanisms produced by the shading of consonants and other such phonological changes, though even Thornton, of course, is obliged to take notice of such forms as *bust* and *bile,* and even Tucker lists *buster.* It must be obvious that many of the words and phrases excluded by his *Index Expurgatorius* are quite genuine Americanisms. Why should he bar out such a word as *moccasin* on the ground that it is also known in England? So is *caucus,* and yet he includes it. He is also far too hostile to such characteristic American compounds as *office-holder* and *fly-time.* True enough, their materials are good English, and they involve no change in the meaning of their component parts, but it must be plain that they were put together in the United States and that an Englishman always sees a certain strangeness in them. *Pay-dirt, panel-house, passage-way, patrolman, night-rider, low-down, know-nothing, hoe-cake* and *hog-wallow* are equally compounded of pure English metal, and yet he lists all of them. Again, he is too ready, it seems to me, to bar out archaisms, which constitute one of the most interesting and authentic of all the classes of Americanisms. It is idle to prove that Chaucer used *to guess.* The important thing is that the English abandoned it centuries ago, and that when they happen to use it today they are always conscious that it is an Americanism. *Baggage* is in Shakespeare, but it is not often in the London *Times.* Here Mr. Tucker allows his historical principles to run away with his judgment. His book represents the labor of nearly forty years and is full of shrewd observations and persuasive contentions, but it is sometimes excessively dogmatic.[1]

The most scientific and laborious of all these collections of Americanisms, until the Dictionary of American English got under way, was Thornton's. It presents an enormous mass of quotations, and they are all very carefully dated, and it corrects most of the more obvious errors in the work of earlier inquirers. But its very dependence upon quotations limits it chiefly to the written language, and so the enormously richer materials of the spoken language are passed over, and particularly the materials evolved during the past

[1] Tucker falls into a number of rather astonishing errors. *P.D.Q.* is defined as an abbreviation of "pretty *deuced* quick," which it certainly is not. *Passage* (of a bill in Congress) is listed as an Americanism; it is actually very good English and is used in England every day. *Standee* is defined as "standing place"; it really means one who stands. *Sundæ* (the soda-fountain mess) is misspelled *sunday;* it was precisely the strange spelling that gave the term vogue. *Mucker,* a brilliant Briticism, unknown in America save in college slang, is listed between *movie* and *muckraker.*

generation. In vain one searches the two fat volumes and their pedestrian appendix for such highly characteristic forms as *near-accident* and *buttinski*, the use of *sure* as an adverb, and the employment of *well* as a sort of general equivalent of the German *also*. These grammatical and syntactical tendencies lay beyond the scope of Thornton's investigation, and some of them lie outside the field of the American Dictionary, but it is plain that they must be prime concerns of any future student who essays to get at the inner spirit of the American language. Its difference from Standard English is not merely a difference in vocabulary, to be disposed of in an alphabetical list; it is also a difference in pronunciation, in intonation, in conjugation and declension, in metaphor and idiom, in the whole fashion of using words. Some of the aspects of that difference will be considered in the following pages. The vocabulary, of course, must be given first attention, for in it the earliest American divergences are embalmed and it tends to grow richer and freer year after year, but attention will also be paid to materials and ways of speech that are less obvious, and in particular to certain tendencies in vulgar American, the great reservoir of the language, and perhaps the forerunner of what it will be on higher levels, at least in one detail or another, in the years to come.

III

THE BEGINNINGS OF AMERICAN

1. THE FIRST LOAN-WORDS

The earliest Americanisms were probably words borrowed bodily from the Indian languages — words, in the main, indicating natural objects that had no counterparts in England. Thus, in Captain John Smith's " True Relation," published in 1608, one finds mention of a strange beast described variously as a *rahaugcum* and a *raugrough-cum*. Four years later, in William Strachey's " Historie of Trevaile Into Virginia Britannia " it became an *aracoune*, " much like a badger," and by 1624 Smith had made it a *rarowcun* in his " Virginia." It was not until 1672 that it emerged as the *raccoon* we know today. *Opossum* has had much the same history. It first appeared in 1610 as *apossoun*, and two years later Smith made it *opassom* in his " Map of Virginia," at the same time describing the animal as having " an head like a swine, a taile like a rat, and is of the bigness of a cat." The word finally became *opossom* toward the end of the Seventeenth Century, and by 1763 the third *o* had changed to *u*. In the common speech, as everyone knows, *raccoon* is almost always reduced to *coon*, and *opossum* to *possum*. Thornton traced the former to 1839 and the latter to 1705. *Moose* is another American primitive. It is derived from the Narragansett Indian word *moosu*, meaning " he trims or cuts smooth " — an allusion, according to the Oxford Dictionary, " to the animal's habit of stripping the lower branches and bark from trees when feeding." It had become *mus* by 1613, *mose* by 1637, and *moose* by 1672.

To the same category belong *skunk, hickory, squash, caribou, pecan, paw-paw, chinkapin, persimmon, terrapin, menhaden,* and *catalpa*. *Skunk* is from an Indian word variously reported to have been *segankw* or *segongw*, and on its first appearance in print, in William Wood's " New England's Prospect " (1643) it was spelled *squunck*, but it had got its present form by 1701. *Hickory*, in the form of *po-*

hickery, has been traced to 1653, and *persimmon*, in the form of *putchamin*, is in Captain John Smith's "Map of Virginia" (1612). In its early days the stress in *persimmon* was on the first or third syllables, not on the second, as now. |*Caribou* came into American from the French in Canada during the Eighteenth Century, but it is most probably of Indian origin. In the same way *pecan* came in through the Spanish: down to Jefferson's time it was spelled *paccan.*| *Paw-paw*, in the form of *papaios*, is to be found in Purchas's "Pilgrimage" (1613, a compilation of traveler's tales), and *terrapin*, in the form of *torope*, is in Whitaker's "Good Newes From Virginia" (1613). *Menhaden* seems to be derived from an Indian word, *munnawhattecug*, which appears as a verb, *munnohquahtean*, meaning to fertilize, in John Eliot's Indian Bible (completed 1638). The Indians used *menhaden* to manure their corn, and the fish is still used for fertilizer. *Catalpa* comes from one of the Indian languages of the South; it was adopted into American in the Eighteenth Century. Most such words, of course, were shortened like *munnawhattecug*, or otherwise modified, on being taken into colonial English. Thus, *chinkapin* was originally *checkinqumin*, and *squash* appears in early documents as *isquontersquash*, and *squantersquash*. But William Penn, in a letter dated August 16, 1683, used the latter in its present form. These variations show a familiar effort to bring a new and strange word into harmony with the language. By it the French *route de roi* has become *Rotten Row* in English, *écrevisse* has become *crayfish*, and the English *bowsprit* has become *beau pré* (beautiful meadow) in French. |*Woodchuck* originated in the same way. Its origin is to be sought, not in *wood* and *chuck*, but in the Cree word *otchock*, used by the Indians to designate the animal. |

| In addition to the names of natural objects, the early colonists, of course, took over a great many Indian place-names, and a number of words to designate Indian relations and artificial objects in Indian use. To the latter division belong *hominy*, *pone*, *toboggan*, *pemmican*, *mackinaw*, *moccasin*, *papoose*, *sachem*, *powwow*, *tomahawk*, *wigwam*, *succotash* and *squaw*, all of which were in common circulation by the middle of the Eighteenth Century.| Thornton has traced *hominy* to 1629, *pone* to 1634, *moccasin* to 1612, *moccasin-flower* to 1705, *moccasin-snake* to 1784, *powwow* to 1613, and *wigwam* to 1705. Finally, |new words were made during the period by translating Indian terms, whether real or imaginary — for example,

war-path, *war-paint*, *pale-face*, *big-chief*, *medicine-man*, *pipe-of-peace*, *fire-water*, and *to bury the hatchet* — , and by using the word *Indian*, as a prefix, as in *Indian-Summer*, *Indian-file* and *Indian-giver*. The total number of borrowings, direct and indirect, was larger than now appears, for with the recession of the Red Man from the popular consciousness the use of loan-words from his dialects has diminished. In our own time *papoose*, *sachem*, *tepee*, *samp*, *quahaug* and *wampum* have begun to drop out of everyday use; [1] at an earlier period the language sloughed off *ocelot*, *manitee*, *calumet*, *sagamore*, *supawn* and many others after their kind, or began to degrade them to the estate of provincialisms. [2] A curious phenomenon is presented by the case of *maize*, which came into the colonial speech from some West Indian dialect, apparently by way of the Spanish, went over into orthodox English, and from English into French, German and other Continental languages, and was then abandoned by the Americans, who substituted *corn*, which commonly means wheat in England. *Mugwump*, which is now obsolescent, is also an Indian loan-word, but its meaning has been narrowed. It was originally spelled *mugquomp*, and signified a chief. When the Rev. John Eliot translated the Old Testament into the Algonquian language, in 1663, he used it in place of the *duke* which appears so often in Genesis xxxvi in the Authorized Version. During the following century it began to work its way into American, and by the beginning of the Nineteenth Century it was in common use to designate a high and mighty fellow, and especially one whose pretensions were not generally con-

1 A number of such Indian words are preserved in the nomenclature of Tammany Hall and in that of the Improved Order of Red Men, an organization with more than 500,-000 members. The Red Men, borrowing from the Indians, thus name the months, in order: *Cold Moon, Snow, Worm, Plant, Flower, Hot, Buck, Sturgeon, Corn, Travelers', Beaver* and *Hunting*. They call their officers *incohonee*, *sachem*, *wampum-keeper*, etc. But such terms, of course, are not in general use.

2 Sylva Clapin lists 110 Indian loan-words in his New Dictionary of Americanisms; New York, c. 1902, and Alexander F. Chamberlain lists 132 in Algonquin Words in American English, *Journal of American Folk-Lore*, Vol. XV. But only 24 of Clapin's words would have any meaning to the average American today. The rest either survive only as proper names, *e.g.*, *tupelo*, *tuckhoe*, *tammany*, *michigouen*, *sing-sing*, *netop*, *catawba*, or are obsolete altogether. An elaborate dictionary of Indian loan-words, compiled by the late W. R. Gerard, is in the possession of the Smithsonian Institution, but it remains in manuscript. Parts of it are almost unintelligible, and there is little likelihood that it will ever be printed. The literature of the subject is rather meager. Probably the best discussion of it is in the first chapter of Schele de Vere's Americanisms; New York, 1872.

ceded. Its political use began in 1884, when James G. Blaine received the Republican nomination for the Presidency, and many influential Republicans, including Theodore Roosevelt, refused to support him. Most of these rebels were in what we now call the higher income-tax brackets, and so it was natural for the party journals to hint that they suffered from what we now call superiority complexes. Thus they came to be called *mugwumps*, and soon they were wearing the label proudly. " I am an independent — a *mugwump*," boasted William Everett in a speech at Quincy, Mass., on September 13, 1884. "I beg to state that *mugwump* is the best of American. It belongs to the language of the Delaware Indians; it occurs many times in Eliot's Indian Bible; and it means a great man." Until the end of the century any American who took an independent course in politics was a *mugwump*, but after that the word began to fade out, and we have developed nothing that quite takes its place.

Caucus is probably also an Indian loan-word. John Pickering, in his " Vocabulary or Collection of Words and Phrases Which Have Been Supposed to be Peculiar to the United States " (1816), hazarded the guess that it might be " a corruption of *caulkers'*, the word meetings being understood," but for this there was no ground save the fact that caulkers, like other workingmen, sometimes had meetings. In 1872 Dr. J. H. Trumbull, one of the earlier American specialists in Indian philology, suggested that the word was more probably derived from the Algonquian noun *caucauasu*, meaning one who advises, urges or encourages. *Caucauasu* is to be found in Captain John Smith's " General Historie of Virginia " (1624) in the formidable form of *cawcawaassough* — but Smith was notoriously weak at spelling, whether of English or of Indian words. Trumbull's suggestion is now generally accepted by etymologists, though with the prudent reservation that it has yet to be proved. *Caucauasu* is said to have given rise to another early American word, now obsolete. This was *cockarouse*, signifying a chief or other person of importance. *Caucus* apparently came in very early in the Eighteenth Century. The Rev. William Gordon, in his " History of the Rise and Independence of the United States " (London, 1788), said that " more than fifty years ago [that is, before 1738] Mr. Samuel Adams's father and twenty others, one or two from the north of the town where the ship business is carried on, used to meet, make a *caucus*, and lay their plans for introducing certain persons into places of trust and power." Down to 1763 a *caucus* seems to have been called a *caucus-club*, for it so appears in John Adams's diary for that year. " *Caucusing*," explained Gordon, " means electioneering."

→ From the very earliest days of English colonization the language of the settlers also received accretions from the languages of the other colonizing nations. The French word *portage*, for example, was already in use before the end of the Seventeenth Century, and soon after came *chowder, cache, voyageur*, and various words that, like the last-named, have since become localisms or disappeared altogether.[1] Before the Revolution *bureau*,[2] *batteau* and *prairie* were added, and soon afterward came *gopher, bogus* and *flume*. *Carry-all* is also French in origin, despite its English sound. It comes, by folk-etymology, from the French *carriole*. So is *brave*, in the sense of an Indian warrior. But the French themselves borrowed it from the Italian *bravo.* Other French terms came in after the Louisiana Purchase in 1803. They will be noticed in the next chapter.

→ The contributions of the New Amsterdam Dutch during the half century of their conflicts with the English included *cruller, cole-slaw*,[3] *cookey, stoop, sleigh, span* (of horses), *dope, spook, to snoop, pit* (as in *peach-pit*), *waffle, hook* (a point of land), *scow, patroon, boss, smearcase* and *Santa Claus.*[4] Schele de Vere credits them with *hay-barrack*, a corruption of *hooiberg*. That they established the use of *bush* as a designation for back-country is very probable; the word has also got into South African English and has been borrowed by Australian English from American. In American it has produced a number of familiar derivatives, *e.g., bush-whacker, bush-town, bush-league, busher, bush-ranger* and *bush-fighting*. Dutch may have also given us *boodle*, in the sense of loot. There is an old English

---

1 Clapin lists 131 loan-words from the French in his Dictionary, but not more than 20 of them would be generally recognized today. Most of the rest survive only along the Canadian border. A curious obsoletism is *movey-star*, from the French *mauvaises terres*. It is still used in the translated form of *bad-lands*, but *movey-star* went out many years ago.

2 (a) A chest of drawers, (b) a government office. In both senses the word is rare in England, though its use by the French is familiar. In the United States its use in (b) has been extended, *e.g.,* in *employment-bureau*.

3 *Cole-slaw* was quickly converted into *cold-slaw* by folk etymology. Thornton's first example of the latter is dated 1794, but it must have appeared earlier. Later on a *warm-slaw* was invented to keep *cold-slaw* company.

4 From *Sant Klaas* (Saint Nicholas). *Santa Claus* has also become familiar to the English, but the Oxford Dictionary still calls it an Americanism. It is always pronounced, of course, *Santy Claws*.

word, *buddle* or *boodle*, signifying a crowd or lot, and it remains familiar in the phrase, *whole kit and boodle* or *whole kit and caboodle*, but *boodle* in the opprobrious American sense is unknown in England save as an Americanism. It may have come from the Dutch *boedel*, meaning an estate or possession. Dutch also influenced Colonial American in indirect ways, *e.g.*, by giving reinforcement to the Scotch *dominie*, signifying a clergyman. It may have shared responsibility with the German of the so-called Pennsylvania Dutch for the introduction of *dumb* in the sense of stupid — *dom* in Dutch and *dumm* in German — a meaning almost unknown in England. Certain etymologists have also credited it with *statehouse* (from *stadhuis*) but Albert Matthews has demonstrated [1] that the word was in use in Virginia in 1638, fifteen years before a *stadhuis* was heard of in New Amsterdam. George Philip Krapp suggests in " The English Language in America " that the peculiar American use of *scout*, as in *good scout*, may have been suggested by the Dutch. He offers quotations from various authorities to show that in New Amsterdam the *schout* was a town officer who combined the duties of mayor, sheriff and district attorney. He was thus dreaded by the lower orders of the population, and "a good scout was notable chiefly because of his rarity." On this I attempt no judgment. Dutch, like German, French and Spanish, naturally had its largest influence in those areas where there were many settlers who spoke it as their native tongue. It was taught in the schools of New York until the end of the Dutch occupation in 1664, and it was used in the Dutch Reformed churches of the town for a century afterward. Up the Hudson it survived even longer, and Noah Webster heard Dutch sermons at Albany so late as 1786. Many Dutch terms are still to be found in the geographical nomenclature of the Hudson region, *e.g.*, *dorp*, *kill* and *hook*, and in isolated communities in the Catskills there is still a considerable admixture in the common speech, *e.g.*, *clove* (ravine), *killfish*, *pinkster* (a variety of azalea), *speck* (fat), *fly* (swamp), *blummie* (flower), *grilly* (chilly), *sluck* (a swallow of liquid), and *wust* (sausage).[2]

1 The Term *State-House, Dialect Notes*, Vol. II, Pt. IV, 1902.
2 Dutch Contributions to the Vocabulary of English in America, by William H. Carpenter, *Modern Philology*, July, 1908. Mr. Karl von Schlieder of Hackensack, N. J., sends me a list of curious forms encountered near Kingston, N. Y. It includes *pietje-kamaakal* (unreasonable), *surallikus* (so-so), *zwok* (soft, slippery), *connalyer* (crowd), *klainzaric* (untidy), *haidang* (nothing), *onnozel* (outland-

Perhaps the most notable of all the contributions of Knickerbocker Dutch to American is the word *Yankee*. The earlier etymologists, all of them amateurs, sought an Indian origin for it. Thomas Anbury, a British officer who served in the Revolution with Burgoyne, argued in his "Travels" (1789, Ch. II) that it came from a Cherokee word, *eankke*, meaning a coward or slave; Washington Irving, in "Knickerbocker's History of New York" (1809, Ch. VII) derived it (probably only humorously) from *yanokies*, "which in the Mais-Tschusaeg or Massachusetts language signifies silent men"; and the Rev. John Gottlieb Ernestus Heckewelder, a learned Moravian missionary who published "An Account of the History, Manners and Customs of the Indian Nations Who Once Inhabited Pennsylvania and the Neighboring States" in 1822, maintained therein that it was simply a product of the Indians' unhappy effort to pronounce the word *English*, which they converted, he said, into *Yengees*. Noah Webster accepted this guess, but other contemporary authorities held that the word the Indians were trying to pronounce was not *English* but the French *Anglais*. There were, however, difficulties in the way of all forms of this theory, for investigation showed that *Yankee* was apparently first applied, not to the English but to the Dutch. So early as 1683, it was discovered, *Yankey* was a common nickname among the buccaneers who then raged along the Spanish Main, and always the men who bore it were Dutchmen. Apparently it was derived either from *Janke*, a diminutive of the common Dutch given name *Jan*, or from *Jankees* (pronounced *Yoncase*), a blend of *Jan* and *Cornelis*, two Dutch names which often appear in combination. Analogues in support of the former hypothesis are to be found in the use of *dago* (*Diego*) to indicate any Spaniard (and now, by extension, any Italian), and of *Heinie* or *Fritz*, *Sandy* and *Pat* to indicate any German, Scotsman or Irishman, respectively;

ish), *poozly* (whining), *feaselick* (undesirable), *kanaapie* (child), *aislick* (no-account), *brigghity* (impudent), and *bahay* (confusion). That all of these are of Dutch origin is not certain, but some of them seem to be duplicated in the Jersey Dutch once spoken in Bergen and Passaic counties, New Jersey. See The Jersey Dutch Dialect, by J. Dyneley Prince, *Dialect Notes*, Vol. III, Pt. IV, 1910. Krapp

in The English Language in America, adds a few Long Island obsoletisms, *e.g.*, *scule*, from *fiskaal*, meaning a public prosecutor (Hempstead Records, 1675–84); *morgen*, a measure of land (do. 1658); *schepel*, a bushel (do. 1658); and *much*, from *mutsje*, a liquid measure (do. 1673). *Morgen* survived until 1869, and is to be found in the annual report of the Federal Commissioner of Agriculture for that year.

and for the latter there is reinforcement in such familiar back-formations as *Chinee* from *Chinese*, *Portugee* from *Portuguese*, *tactic* from
tactics, and *specie* from *species*. But how did this nickname for
Dutchmen ever come to be applied to Englishmen, and particularly
to the people of New England, male and female alike? To this day
no satisfactory answer has been made. All that may be said with any
certainty is that it was already in use by 1765 as a term of derision,
and that by 1775 the Yankees began to take pride in it. In the latter
year, in fact, John Turnbull spoke of it in his "McFingal" as
connoting "distinction." But he neglected to explain its transfer
from Dutch pirates to New England Puritans, and no one has done
so to this day. During the Civil War, as everyone knows, Yankee
became a term of disparagement again, applied by the people of the
South to all Northerners. But its evil significance began to wear off
after the turn of the century, and when in 1917 the English began
applying it to the men of the A.E.F., Southerners and Northerners alike, the former seem to have borne the affliction philosophically.
At that time a characteristic clipped form, *Yank*, came into popularity at home, launched by its use in George M. Cohan's war song,
"Over There." But *Yank* was not invented by Cohan, for it has been
traced back to 1778, and the Confederates often used it during the
Civil War. Incidentally, the verb *to yank*, in the sense of to jerk, is
also an Americanism, and its origin is almost as mysterious as that of
Yankee. That the two have any connection is doubtful. It seems
more probable that the verb comes from a Scottish noun, *yank*,
meaning a sharp, sudden blow.[1]

The Spanish contributions to the American vocabulary are far
more numerous than those of any other Continental language, but
most of them have come in since the Louisiana Purchase, and notices
of them will be deferred to the next chapter. There was relatively
little contact between the first English settlers and the Spaniards
to the southward; it remained for the great movement across the
plains, begun by Zebulon M. Pike's expedition in 1806, to make
Spanish the second language in a large part of the United States.
The first Spanish loan-words were mainly Spanish adaptations of

1 Of the 46 Dutch loan-words listed
by Clapin in his Dictionary only
a dozen or so remain in general use.
See also A Dictionary of the Low-
Dutch Element in the English Vocabulary, by J. F. Bense; Oxford,
1926; and The Dutch Influence on
the English Vocabulary, by G. N.
Clark, *S.P.E. Tracts*, No. XLIV,
1935.

Indian terms, picked up by the early adventurers in the West Indies. Of such sort were *tobacco, hammock, tomato, tapioca, chocolate, barbecue* and *canoe.* But with them also came some genuinely Spanish words, and of these *sarsaparilla* and *sassafras* have been traced to 1577, *alligator* to 1568, *creole* to 1604, *pickaninny* to 1657, *key* (islet) to 1697, and *quadroon* to the first years of the Eighteenth Century. A good many Spanish words, or Spanish adaptations of native words, went into English during the Sixteenth Century without any preliminary apprenticeship as Americanisms, for example, *mosquito, chocolate, banana* and *cannibal.* But *cockroach* (from the Spanish *cucaracha,* assimilated by folk etymology to *cock* and *roach*) is first heard of in Captain John Smith's " General Historie of Virginia " (1624), and most of the Oxford Dictionary's early examples of *mosquito* are American. *Mosquito* suffered some fantastic variations in spelling. The original Spanish was *mosquito,* a diminutive of *mosca,* a fly, but in Hakluyt's " Voyages " (*c.* 1583) it became *musketa,* in Whitbourne's " Newfoundland " (1623) *muskeito,* in Hughes's " American Physician " (1672) *muscato,* in Cotton Mather's " Magnalia " (finished in 1697 and published in 1702) *moscheto,* and at the hands of Benjamin Franklin (1747) *musqueto.* The *jerked* in *jerked-beef* was fashioned by folk-etymology out of a Spanish word which was in turn borrowed from one of the Peruvian dialects. The noun *barbecue* came from a Haitian word, *barbacoa,* signifying a frame set up to lift a bed off the ground. But it got the meaning of a frame used for roasting meat soon after it appeared in Spanish, and the derivative word has had its present sense in American since about 1660.

Before the Revolution a few German words worked their way into American, but not many. *Sauerkraut* has been traced by Thornton to 1789 and is probably much older; so are *noodle* and *pretzel.* But *lager, bockbeer, sangerfest, kindergarten, wienerwurst, ratskeller, zwieback, turnverein* and so on belong to the period after 1848, and will be noticed later. *Beer-soup* (probably from *biersuppe*) goes back to 1799, but *beer-garden* (from *biergarten*) has not been found before 1870. As I have suggested, German probably helped Dutch to put *dumb,* in the sense of stupid, into the American vocabulary. It also, I suppose, gave some help to *smearcase.* The native languages of the Negro slaves, rather curiously, seem to have left few marks upon American. *Buckra* is apparently of Negro origin, but it was never peculiar to America, and has long since gone out. *Gumbo* seems to be derived from an Angolan word, *'ngombo*, but it came into American relatively late, and may have been introduced by way of Louisiana French. *Okra*, which means the same thing, was first used in the West Indies, and may have had a Spanish transition form. *Yam* is not Negro, but apparently Spanish or Portuguese. *Banjo* is simply a Negro perversion of *bandore*, which was also of Latin origin. Whether *goober* and *juba* are Negro loan-words is unknown. Thornton's first example of the latter is dated 1834, Webster's New International (1934) ascribes the former, somewhat improbably, to a Congo source, *'nguba*, and it may have come from *jubilee. Voodoo* was borrowed from the Dahoman *tovôdoun*, still in use in West Africa, but it seems to have come in through the French. Its American corruption, *hoodoo*, probably owes nothing to the Negroes; moreover, the earliest use of it recorded by Thornton is dated 1889. The early slaves, of course, retained many words and phrases from their native languages, but they have all disappeared from the speech of their descendants today, save for a few surviving in the Gullah dialect of the South Carolina coast.[1]

2. NEW WORDS OF ENGLISH MATERIAL

Of far more importance than such small borrowings was the great stock of new words that the early colonists coined in English metal — words primarily demanded by the "new circumstances under which they were placed," but also indicative, in more than one case, of a delight in the business for its own sake. The American, even in the Seventeenth Century, already showed many of the characteristics that were to set him off from the Englishman later on — his bold and somewhat grotesque imagination, his contempt for digni-

[1] "The commonest there," says Reed Smith, in Gullah, *Bulletin of the University of South Carolina*, Nov. 1, 1926, "are the exclamation *ki* (or *kai*) to express wonder or to add emphasis to a statement, and *buckra* for white man. . . . To these may be added *nyam, oona, swanga* (or *swongger*), *du-du, goober, pinder, cooter, okra, gee-chy, cymbi, bakalingo* (obsoles-cent), *guffer, penepne, da, da-da. Malafee* for whiskey has been noted on St. Helena Island." How many of these are actually African I don't know. See also Gullah: a Negro Patois, by John Bennett, *South Atlantic Quarterly*, Oct., 1908, and Jan., 1909; and The Black Border, by Ambrose E. Gonzalez; Columbia, S. C., 1922. The latter contains a Gullah glossary.

fied authority, his lack of æsthetic sensitiveness, his extravagant humor. Among the first settlers there were a few men of education, culture and gentle birth, but they were soon swamped by hordes of the ignorant and illiterate, and the latter, cut off from the corrective influence of books, soon laid their hands upon the language. It is hard to imagine the austere Puritan divines of Massachusetts inventing such verbs as *to cowhide* and *to logroll,* or such adjectives as *no-account* and *stumped,* or such adverbs as *no-how* and *lickety-split,* or such substantives as *bull-frog, hog-wallow* and *hoe-cake;* but under their eyes there arose a contumacious proletariat which was quite capable of the business, and very eager for it. In Boston, so early as 1628, there was a definite class of blackguard roisterers, chiefly made up of sailors and artisans; in Virginia, nearly a decade earlier, John Pory, secretary to Sir George Yeardley, Deputy Governor, lamented that " in these five months of my continuance here there have come at one time or another eleven sails of ships into this river, but fraighted more with ignorance than with any other marchansize." In particular, the generation born in the New World was uncouth and iconoclastic; [1] the only world it knew was a rough world, and the virtues that environment engendered were not those of niceness, but those of enterprise and resourcefulness.

Upon men of this sort fell the task of bringing the wilderness to the ax and the plow, and with it went the task of inventing a vocabulary for the special needs of the great adventure. Out of their loutish ingenuity came a great number of picturesque names for natural objects, chiefly boldly descriptive compounds: *bull-frog, mud-hen, cat-bird, cat-fish, musk-rat, razor-back, garter-snake, ground-hog* and so on. And out of an inventiveness somewhat more urbane came such coinages as *live-oak, potato-bug, turkey-gobbler, sweet-potato, canvas-back, poke-weed, copper-head, eel-grass, reed-bird, egg-plant, blue-grass, katy-did, pea-nut, pitch-pine, cling-stone* (peach), *June-bug, lightning-bug,* and *butter-nut. Live-oak* appears in a document of 1610; *bull-frog* was familiar to Beverley in 1705; so was *James-town weed* (later reduced to *Jimson weed,* as the English *hurtleberry* or *whortleberry* was reduced to *huckleberry*). These early Americans were not botanists. They were often ignorant of the names of the plants that they encountered, even when those

1 See The Cambridge History of
American Literature, Vol. I, pp. 14
and 22.

plants already had English names, and so they exercised their fancy upon new ones. So arose *Johnny-jump-up* for the *Viola tricolor*, and *basswood* for the common European *linden* or *lime-tree* (*Tilia*), and *locust* for the *Robinia pseudacacia* and its allies. The *Jimson weed* itself was anything but a novelty, but the pioneers apparently did not recognize it as the *Datura stramonium*, and so we find Beverley reporting that " some Soldiers, eating it in a Salad, turn'd natural Fools upon it for several Days." The grosser features of the landscape got a lavish renaming, partly to distinguish new forms and partly out of an obvious desire to attain a more literal descriptiveness. I have mentioned *key* and *hook*, the one borrowed from the Spanish and the other from the Dutch. With them came *branch, fork, run* (stream), *bluff, cliff, neck, barrens, bottoms, watershed, foot-hill, hollow, water-gap, under-brush, bottom-land, clearing, notch, divide, knob, riffle, rolling-country* and *rapids*, and the extension of *pond* from artificial pools to small natural lakes, and of *creek* from small arms of the sea to shallow feeders of rivers. Such common English topographical terms as *down, weald, wold, fen, bog, fell, chase, combe, dell, tarn, common, heath* and *moor* disappeared from the colonial tongue, save as fossilized in a few localisms and proper names.[1] So did *bracken*.

With the new landscape came an entirely new mode of life — new foods, new forms of habitation, new methods of agriculture, new kinds of hunting. A great swarm of neologisms thus arose, and, as in the previous case, they were chiefly compounds. *Back-woods, back-street, back-lane, back-land, back-log, back-country, back-field, back-line* and *back-settler* were all in common use before the Revolution. *Back-log* was used by Increase Mather in 1684, and *back-street* has been traced to 1638.[2] *Log-house* appears in the Maryland Archives for 1669.[3] *Hoe-cake, Johnny-cake* (originally *Shawnee-cake* or *-bread*), *pan-fish, corn-dodger, roasting-ear, corn-crib,* and *pop-corn* all belong to the colonial period. So do *pine-knot, snow-plow, cold-snap, land-slide, ash-can, bob-sled, fox-grape, apple-*

1 For example, Chevy *Chase*, Boston *Common*, the Back Bay *Fens*, and *cranberry-bog*.
2 A long list of compounds based on *back*, from the collection of the editorial board of the Dictionary of American English, is to be found in *American Speech*, Oct., 1930. It runs to no less than 120 terms, all of them of American origin. In addition, there is a list of eleven peculiarly American uses of *back* as a verb, and five of its uses as an adjective.
3 *Log-cabin* came later. Thornton's first quotation is dated 1818. The *Log-Cabin* campaign was in 1840.

butter, salt-lick, prickly-heat, shell-road, worm-fence and *cane-brake.*
Shingle, in the American sense, was a novelty in 1705, but one S.
Symonds wrote to John Winthrop, of Ipswich, about a *clap-boarded*
house in 1637. *Frame-house* seems to have come in with *shingle.*
Selectman is first heard of in 1685, displacing the English *alderman.*
Mush had displaced *porridge* in general use by 1671. *Hired-man* is
to be found in the Plymouth town records of 1737, and *hired-girl*
followed soon after. So early as 1758, as we find in the diary of
Nathaniel Ames, the second-year students at Harvard were already
called *sophomores,* though for a while the spelling was often made
sophimores. Camp-meeting was later; it did not appear until 1799.
But *land-office* was familiar before 1700, and *side-walk, spelling-bee,*
bee-line, moss-back, crazy-quilt, stamping-ground and a hundred
and one other such compounds were in daily use before the Revolution. After that great upheaval the new money of the confederation brought in a number of new words. In 1782 Gouverneur Morris
proposed to the Continental Congress that the coins of the Republic
be called, in ascending order, *unit, penny-bill, dollar* and *crown.*
Later Morris invented the word *cent,* substituting it for the English
penny. In 1785 Jefferson, after playing with such terms as *pistarine*
and *piece-of-eight,* proposed *mill, cent, disme, dollar* and *eagle,* and
this nomenclature was made official by the Act Establishing a Mint,
approved April 2, 1792. Jefferson apparently derived *disme* from the
French word *dixième,* meaning a tenth, and the original pronunciation seems to have been *deem.* But *dime* soon supplanted it.[1]
    Various nautical terms peculiar to America, or taken into English
from American sources, came in during the Eighteenth Century,
among them, *schooner, cat-boat, mud-scow* and *pungy.* According
to an historian of the American merchant marine,[2] the first schooner
even seen was launched at Gloucester, Mass., in 1713. The word, it
appears, was originally spelled *scooner. To scoon* was a verb borrowed by the New Englanders from some Scotch dialect, and meant

1 I am indebted here to Mr. Maury
  Maverick, of San Antonio, Tex., a
  diligent searcher of the early laws
  of the Republic. A thorough investigation of them might yield materials of value to the philologian.
  Some of the early town-records
  were explored by George Philip
  Krapp (The English Language
  in America, Vol. II), but his

interest was in pronunciation rather
than in vocabulary. There are leads
to other material in E. G. Swem's
monumental Virginia Historical Index; Roanoke Va., 1934, which in-
dexes words as well as names.
2 Willian Brown Meloney: The
Heritage of Tyre, New York, 1916,
p. 15.

to skim or skip across the water like a flat stone. As the first schooner left the ways and glided out into Gloucester harbor, an enraptured spectator shouted: " Oh, see how she *scoons!* " " A *scooner* let her be! " replied Captain Andrew Robinson, her builder — and all boats of her peculiar and novel fore-and-aft rig took the name thereafter. The Scotch verb came from the Norse *skunna*, to hasten, and there are analogues in Icelandic, Anglo-Saxon and Old High German. The origin of *cat-boat*, *bug-eye* and *pungy* I have been unable to determine. Perhaps the last-named is related in some way to *pung*, a one-horse sled or wagon. *Pung* was once widely used in the United States, but later sank to the estate of a New England provincialism. Longfellow used it, and in 1857 a writer in the *Knickerbocker Magazine* reported that *pungs* filled Broadway, in New York, after a snow-storm.

The early Americans showed that spacious disregard for linguistic nicety which has characterized their descendants ever since. They reduced verb-phrases to simple verbs, turned verbs into nouns, nouns into verbs, and adjectives into either or both. Pickering, in his Vocabulary (1816) made a belated protest against the reduction of the English law-phrase, *to convey by deed*, to *to deed*, and argued solemnly that no self-respecting attorney would employ it, but American attorneys had actually been employing it for years, and they continue to do so to this day. So with *to table* for *to lay on the table*. *To tomahawk* appeared before 1650, and *to scalp* must have followed soon after. Within the next century and a half they were reinforced by many other such verbs, and by such adjectives made of nouns as *no-account* and *one-horse*, and such nouns made of verbs as *carry-all* and *goner*, and such adverbs as *no-how*. In particular, the manufacture of new verbs went on at a rapid pace. In his letter to Webster in 1789 Franklin deprecated *to advocate*, *to progress* and *to oppose* — a vain *caveat*, for all of them are now in perfectly good usage. *To advocate*, indeed, was used by Thomas Nashe in 1589, and by John Milton half a century later, but it seems to have been reinvented in America. In 1822 and again in 1838 Robert Southey, then Poet Laureate, led two belated attacks upon it, as a barbarous Americanism,[1] but its obvious usefulness preserved it, and it remains

---

1 Despite his implacable hostility to American innovations, Southey was himself a busy inventor of uncouth neologisms. In The Doctor (1834– 37), says George H. McKnight in Modern English in the Making, he used *agathokakological*, *cacodemonize*, *dendanthropology*, *gelastics*,

in good usage on both sides of the Atlantic today — one of the earliest of the English borrowings from America. In the end, indeed, even so ardent a purist as Richard Grant White adopted it, as he did *to placate.*

Webster, though he agreed with Franklin in opposing *to advocate,* gave his *imprimatur* to *to appreciate (i.e.,* to rise in value) and *to obligate* and is credited by Sir Charles Lyell [1] with having himself claimed the invention of *to demoralize.* In a letter to Thomas Dawes, dated August 5, 1809,[2] he said that he had also " enriched the vocabulary " with *absorbable, accompaniment, acidulous, achromatic, adhesiveness, adjutancy, admissibility, advisory, amendable, animalize, aneurismal, antithetical, appellor, appreciate, appreciation, arborescent, arborization, ascertainable, bailee, bailment, indorser, indorsee, prescriptive, imprescriptible, statement, insubordination, expenditure, subsidize,* " and other elegant and scientific terms, now used by the best writers in Great Britain and America." But most of these, though he could not find them in Samuel Johnson's Dictionary (1755), were already in English before he began to write dictionaries himself, and some were very old.[3] *To antagonize* seems to have been given currency by John Quincy Adams, *to immigrate* by John Marshall, *to eventuate* by Gouverneur Morris, and *to derange* by George Washington. Jefferson, as we saw in Chapter I, Section 2, used *to belittle* in his " Notes on Virginia," and Thornton thinks that he coined it. Many new verbs were made by the simple process of prefixing the preposition to common nouns, *e.g., to clerk, to dicker, to dump, to negative, to blow (i.e.,* to bluster or boast), *to cord (i.e.,* wood), *to stump, to room* and *to shin.* Others arose as metaphors, *e.g., to whitewash* (figuratively) and *to squat* (on unoccupied land). Others were made by hitching suffixes to nouns, or by groping for roots, *e.g., to deputize, to locate, to legislate, to infract, to com-*

---

kittenship, magnisonant and critikin, and even in the *Quarterly
Review,* the very G.H.Q. of anti-
American pedantry, he used *donivorous, humgig, frizzgig* and *evangelizationeer.*
1 In his Travels in North America in
the Years 1841–42; London, 1845;
New York, 1852, p. 53.
2 It is reprinted in The Beginnings
of American English, by M. M.
Mathews; Chicago, 1931, p. 48 *ff.*

3 The Oxford Dictionary traces
amendable to 1589, *antithetical* to
1583, *imprescriptible* to 1562, *bailment* to 1554, *bailee* to 1528 and *appellor* to *c.* 1400. The following
were also in use before Webster's
time: *absorbable,* 1779; *admissibility,* 1778; *statement,* 1775; *acidulous,*
1769; *achromatic,* 1766; *aneurismal,*
1757; *accompaniment,* 1756; *indorsee,* 1754; *animalize,* 1741; *arborescent,* 1675.

promit and *to happify*. Yet others seem to have been produced by onomatopœia, *e.g., to fizzle*, or to have arisen by some other such spontaneous process, so far unintelligible, *e.g., to tote*. With them came an endless series of verb-phrases, *e.g., to draw a bead, to face the music, to darken one's doors, to take to the woods, to fly off the handle, to go on the war-path* and *to saw wood* — all obvious products of pioneer life. Many coinages of the pre-Revolutionary era later disappeared. Jefferson used *to ambition*, but it dropped out nevertheless. So did *conflagrative*, though a president of Yale gave it his *imprimatur*. So did *to compromit* (*i.e.*, to compromise), *to homologize* and *to happify*.[1] Fierce battles raged round some of these words, and they were all violently derided in England. Even so useful a verb as *to locate*, now in quite respectable usage, was denounced in the third volume of the *North American Review*, and other purists of the times tried to put down *to legislate*.

The young and tender adjectives had quite as hard a row to hoe, particularly *lengthy*. The *British Critic* attacked it in November, 1793, and it also had enemies at home, but John Adams had used it in his diary in 1759 and the authority of Jefferson and Hamilton was behind it, and so it survived. By 1816, indeed, Jeremy Bentham was using it in England. Years later James Russell Lowell spoke of it as " the excellent adjective," [2] and boasted that American had given it to English. *Dutiable* also met with opposition, and moreover it had a rival, *customable;* but Marshall wrote it into his historic decisions, and thus it took root. The same anonymous watchman of the *North American Review* who protested against *to locate* pronounced his anathema upon " such barbarous terms as *presidential* and *congressional*," but the plain need for them kept them in the language. *Gubernatorial* had come in long before this, and is to be found in

---

1 Thornton's last example of the use of *to compromit* is dated 1842; of *to happify*, 1857, and of *to ambition*, 1861. So far as I know, no one has ever attempted to compile anything approaching a complete list of obsolete Americanisms, but a number are given in The English Language in America, by George Philip Krapp, Vol. I, Ch. II. They include *spong*, a strip of meadow; *bolts*, timber cut into lengths; *while* in the sense of until; *hole*, a synonym of *spong* (it survives in a few geographical names, *e.g.*, Woods *Hole*); *shruffe*, the undergrowth of a swamp; *cohoss*, a bend in a river; *folly*, a word of undetermined meaning, maybe from the Dutch *vallje*, a little valley; *seater*, a settler; and *crickthatch*, salt-water grass. Some of these were old English words that survived in America longer than in England.

2 The Biglow Papers, Series II, 1866, *pref.*

the New Jersey Archives of 1734. *Influential* was denounced by the Rev. Jonathan Boucher and by George Canning, who argued that *influent* was better,[1] but it was ardently defended by William Pinkney, of Maryland, and gradually made its way. *Handy, kinky, law-abiding, chunky, solid* (in the sense of well-to-do), *evincive, complected, judgmatical, underpinned, blooded* and *cute* were also already secure in revolutionary days. So with many nouns. Jefferson used *breadstuffs* in his Report of the Secretary of State on Commercial Restrictions, December 16, 1793. *Balance* in the sense of remainder, got into the debates of the First Congress. *Mileage* was used by Franklin in 1754, and is now sound English.[2] *Elevator*, in the sense of a storage house for grain, was used by Jefferson and by others before him. *Draw*, for *drawbridge*, comes down from revolutionary days. So does *slip*, in the sense of a berth for vessels. So does *addition*, in the sense of a suburb. So, finally, does *darky*.

The history of these Americanisms shows how vain is the effort of grammarians to combat the normal processes of language development. I have mentioned the opposition to *dutiable, influential, presidential, lengthy, to locate, to oppose, to advocate, to legislate* and *to progress*. *Bogus, reliable* and *standpoint* were attacked with the same academic ferocity. All of them are to be found in William Cullen Bryant's celebrated *Index Expurgatorius* (*c.* 1870),[3] and

1 In a letter to his sister Hannah, dated May 30, 1831, Macaulay told her of a visit to Holland House and a conversation with Lady Holland, who objected to various words, beginning with *constituency*, and going on to *influential, talented* and *gentlemanly*. Macaulay argued in favor of *talented*, saying that its root " first appeared in theological writing," and was taken from the Parable of the Talents. " She seemed surprised by this theory," he wrote to his sister, " never having, so far as I could judge, heard of the parable." *Talented* is sometimes listed as an Americanism, but it actually arose in England, *c.* 1825.
2 Franklin, incidentally, also invented the harmonica and its name. But his harmonica was not the mouth-organ that we know today, but a sort of improvement on the old

musical-glasses. Moreover, he called it the *armonica*, not the *harmonica*. This was in 1762. The term went over into English very quickly, and had ceased to be an Americanism before 1800. Later it seems to have become changed to *harmonicon*. But the prevalent present form is *harmonica*, and it now designates not only a mouth-organ, but also one of the organ-stops. The Oxford Dictionary's first example of *mouth-organ* is dated *c.* 1668. In Germany, where most mouth-organs come from, the instrument is called the *harmonika*. Whether the name was borrowed from Franklin or invented independently I do not know.
3 Reprinted in Helpful Hints in Writing and Reading, comp. by Grenville Kleiser; New York, 1911, pp. 15–17.

reliable was denounced by Bishop Coxe as "that abominable barbarism" so late as 1886.[1] Edward S. Gould, another uncompromising purist, said of *standpoint* that it was "the bright particular
star . . . of solemn philological blundering" and "the very counterpart of Dogberry's *non-com*."[2] Gould also protested against *to
jeopardize, leniency* and *to demean*, though the last named was very
old in English in the different sense of to conduct oneself, and
Richard Grant White joined him in an onslaught upon *to donate*.
But all these words are in good usage in the United States today, and
some of them have gone over into English.

3. CHANGED MEANINGS

The early Americans also made a great many new words by changing the meaning of old ones. The cases of *pond* and *creek* I have
already mentioned. *To squat,* in the sense of to crouch, had been
sound English for centuries, but they gave it the meaning of to settle
on land without the authority of the owner, and from it the noun
squatter quickly emanated. Of another familiar Americanism Krapp
says:

> The method of portioning out the common lands to the townsmen of the
> first New England communities has led to the general American use of *lot*
> to designate a limited section of land. . . . The town of Lunenburg (1721)
> paid for "Travil and Expenc When The *Lotts* Were Drawn at Concord," and
> the records contain a list of all the *lots* in the town with "the names of those
> That first Drew them.". . . In the Norwalk Records (1671) the agreement is
> recorded that "all those men that now draw *lots* with their neighbors shall
> stand to their *lots* that now they draw.". . . From this usage was derived also
> the popular saying, *to cut across lots*.[3]

1 A. Cleveland Coxe: Americanisms
in England, *Forum*, Oct., 1886.
2 Edward S. Gould: Good English,
or Popular Errors in Language;
New York, 1867, pp. 25–27. So
recently as 1918 an Anglophil reviewer denounced me for using it
in a book, and hinted that I had
borrowed it from the German
standpunkt.
3 The English Language in America
Vol. I, pp. 85–6. *Lott* appears in
the Connecticut Code of 1650. See
the edition of Andrus: Hartford,
1822. On page 35 is "their landes,

lotts and accommodations." On
page 46 is "meadow and home
lotts." American conveyancers, in
describing real property, still usually
speak of "all that *lot* or parcel of
land," though in the Southwest, so
I am told by Mr. Maury Maverick,
the more prosaic "the following described real estate" is coming in.
Lot has begotten a number of derivations, *e.g.*, *back-lots, building-
lot, front-lot, side-lot, pasture-lot,
garden-lot, house-lot* and *house and
lot*.

Other examples of the application of old words to new purposes are afforded by *freshet, barn* and *team*. A *freshet*, in Eighteenth Century English, meant any stream of fresh water; the colonists made it signify an inundation. A *barn* was a house or shed for storing crops; in the colonies the word came to mean a place for keeping cattle also. A *team*, in English, was a pair of draft horses; in the colonies it came to mean both horses and vehicle, though the former meaning, reinforced, survived in the tautological phrase, *double team*. The process is even more clearly shown in the history of such words as *corn* and *shoe*. *Corn*, in orthodox English, means grain for human consumption, and especially wheat, *e.g.,* the *Corn Laws*. The earliest settlers, following this usage, gave the name of *Indian corn* to what the Spaniards, following the Indians themselves, had called *maiz*. The term appears in Bradford's " History of Plimouth Plantation " (1647) and in Mourt's " Relation " (1622). But gradually the adjective fell off, and by the middle of the Eighteenth Century *maize* was called simply *corn* and grains in general were called *breadstuffs*. Thomas Hutchinson, discoursing to George III in 1774, used *corn* in this restricted sense, speaking of " rye and *corn* mixed." " What corn? " asked George. " *Indian* corn," explained Hutchinson, " or, as it is called in authors, *maize*." [1] So with *shoe*. In English it meant (and still means) a topless article of footwear, but the colonists extended its meaning to varieties covering the ankle, thus displacing the English *boot*, which they reserved for foot coverings reaching at least to the knee. To designate the English *shoe* they began to use the word *slipper*. This distinction between English and American usage still prevails, despite the fashion which has sought to revive *boot* in the United States, and with it its derivatives, *boot-shop* and *boot-maker*.

Store, shop, lumber, pie, dry-goods, cracker, rock and *partridge* among nouns and *to haul, to jew, to notify* and *to heft* among verbs

1 Hutchinson's Diary, Vol. I, p. 171; London, 1883–6. A great many derivatives go back to the same era, *e.g., corn-husk, corn-shuck, corn-crib, corn-stalk, corn-broom, corn-brake, corn-fritter, corn-fodder, corn-grater, corn-hook, corn-juice, corn-knife, corn-starch, pop-corn, corn-cob, corn-cake, corn-pone, corn-cutter, corn-dodger, corn-fed, corn-meal, corn-snake*. Some of these have since become obsolete. "The American colonists," says Allen Walker Read in The Comment of British Travelers on Early American Terms Relating to Agriculture, *Agricultural History*, July, 1933, " have never taken kindly to the word [*maize*]. . . . Even today [it] is wholly a book word in America."

offer further examples of changed meanings. Down to the middle of the Eighteenth Century *shop* continued to designate a small retail establishment in America, as it does in England to this day. *Store* was applied only to a large establishment — one showing, in some measure, the character of a warehouse. But in 1774 a Boston young man was advertising in the *Massachusetts Spy* for "a *place* as a *clerk* in a *store*" (three Americanisms in a row!). Soon afterward *shop* began to acquire its special American meaning of a factory, *e.g.*, *machine-shop*. Meanwhile *store* completely displaced *shop* in the English sense, and it remained for a late flowering of Anglomania, as in the case of *boot* and *shoe*, to restore, in a measure, the *status quo ante*. *Lumber*, in Eighteenth Century English, meant disused goods, and this is its common meaning in England today, as is shown by *lumber-room*. But the colonists early employed it to designate cut timber, and that use of it is now universal in America. Its familiar derivatives, *e.g.*, *lumber-yard*, *lumber-man*, *lumber-jack*, greatly reinforce this usage. *Dry-goods*, in England, means, "non-liquid goods, as corn" (*i.e.*, wheat); in the United States the term means "textile fabrics, cottons, woolens, linens, silks, laces, etc." [1] The difference had appeared before 1725. *Rock*, in English, always means a large mass; in America it may mean a small stone, as in *rock-pile* and *to throw a rock*. The Puritans were putting *rocks* into the foundations of their meeting houses so early as 1712.[2] *Cracker* began to be used for *biscuit* before the Revolution. *Tavern* displaced *inn* at the same time. In England *partridge* is applied only to the true *partridge* (*Perdix perdix*) and its nearly related varieties, but in the United States it is also often used to designate the ruffed grouse (*Bonasa umbellus*), the common quail (*Colinus virginianus*), and various other tetraonid birds. This confusion goes back to colonial times. So with *rabbit*. Zoölogically speaking, there are no native rabbits in the United States; they are all hares. But the early colonists, for some unknown reason, dropped the word *hare* out of their vocabulary, and it is rarely heard in American speech to this day. When it appears it is almost always applied to the so-called Belgian hare, which, curiously enough, is not a hare at all, but a

---

1 The definitions are from the Concise Oxford Dictionary of Current English (1914) and Webster's New International Dictionary (1934), respectively.

2 Samuel Sewall: Diary, April 14, 1712: "I lay'd a *Rock* in the Northeast corner of the Foundation of the Meeting-House."

true rabbit. *Bay* and *bayberry* early acquired special American meanings. In England *bay* is used to designate the bay-tree (*Laurus nobilis*); in America it designates a shrub, the wax myrtle (*Myrica cerifera*). Both the tree and the shrub have berries, and those of the latter are used to make the well-known *bayberry* candles. Other botanical and zoölogical terms to which the colonists gave new significances are *blackbird, beech, hemlock, lark, laurel, oriole, swallow* and *walnut*.

To haul, in English, means to move by force or violence; in the colonies it came to mean to transport in a vehicle, and this meaning survives in American. *To jew*, in English, means to cheat; the colonists made it mean to haggle, and devised *to jew down* to indicate an effort to work a reduction in price. *To heft*, in English, means to lift up; the early Americans made it mean to weigh by lifting, and kept the idea of weighing in its derivatives, *e.g., hefty*. Finally, there is the vulgar American misuse of *Miss* or *Mis'* (pro. *miz*) for *Mrs.* It was so widespread by 1790 that on November 17 of that year Webster denounced it as " a gross impropriety " in the *American Mercury*. The schoolmarm has made war on it ever since, but it survives unscathed in the speech of the common people.

4. ARCHAIC ENGLISH WORDS

Most of the colonists who lived along the American seaboard in 1750 were the descendants of immigrants who had come in fully a century before; after the first settlements there had been much less fresh immigration than many latter-day writers have assumed. According to Prescott F. Hall, " the population of New England . . . at the date of the Revolutionary War . . . was produced out of an immigration of about 20,000 persons who arrived *before* 1640," [1] and we have Franklin's authority for the statement

1 Immigration, 2nd ed.; New York, 1913, p. 4. Sir J. R. Seeley says, in The Expansion of England (2nd ed.; London, 1895, p. 84) that the emigration from England to New England, after the meeting of the Long Parliament (1640), was so slight for a full century that it barely balanced " the counter-movement of colonists quitting the colony." Richard Hildreth, in his History of the United States, Vol. I, p. 267, says that the departures actually exceeded the arrivals. See also The Founding of New England, by James Truslow Adams; Boston, 1921, p. 221 *ff*.

that the total population of the colonies in 1751, then about 1,000,-000, had been produced from an original immigration of less than 80,000. Even at that early day, indeed, the colonists had begun to feel that they were distinctly separated, in culture and customs, from the mother country, and there were signs of the rise of a new native aristocracy, entirely distinct from the older aristocracy of the royal governors' courts.[1] The enormous difficulties of communication with England helped to foster this sense of separation. The round trip across the ocean occupied the better part of a year, and was hazardous and expensive; a colonist who had made it was a marked man — as Hawthorne said, " the *petit maître* of the colonies." Nor was there any very extensive exchange of ideas, for though most of the books read in the colonies came from England, the great majority of the colonists, down to the middle of the century, seem to have read little save the Bible and biblical commentaries, and in the native literature of the time one seldom comes upon any reference to the English authors who were glorifying the period of the Restoration and the reign of Anne. " No allusion to Shakespeare," says Bliss Perry,[2] " has been discovered in the colonial literature of the Seventeenth Century, and scarcely an allusion to the Puritan poet Milton." Benjamin Franklin's brother, James, had a copy of Shakespeare at the *New England Courant* office in Boston, but Benjamin himself seems to have made little use of it, for there is not a single quotation from or mention of the bard in all his voluminous works.[3] " The Harvard College Library in 1723," says Perry, " had

1 Sydney George Fisher: The True Story of the American Revolution; Phila. and London, 1902, p. 27. See also John T. Morse's Life of Thomas Jefferson in the American Statesmen series (Boston and New York, 1898), p. 2. Morse points out that Washington, Jefferson and Madison belonged to this new aristocracy, not to the old one.
2 The American Spirit in Literature; New Haven, 1918, p. 61.
3 Since this statement appeared in my last edition Mr. Meyer Isenberg of Chicago has called my attention to what may be an echo of Shakespeare in Poor Richard's Almanac, 1735: " A ship under sail and a big-bellied woman are the handsomest things that can be seen in common." Mr.

Isenberg believes that this may have been suggested by Titania's speech in A Midsummer Night's Dream, Act II, Sc. 1, beginning " Set your heart at rest." But even if this be true, Franklin may have encountered the idea at second hand. He said in his Autobiography: " At the time I established myself in Philadelphia (1723) there was not a good bookseller's shop in any of the colonies to the southward of Boston. In New York and Philadelphia the printers were indeed stationers, but they sold only paper, almanacs, ballads, and a few common schoolbooks. Those who loved reading were obliged to send for their books to England."

nothing of Addison, Steele, Bolingbroke, Dryden, Pope and Swift, and had only recently obtained copies of Milton and Shakespeare. . . . Franklin reprinted 'Pamela' and his Library Company of Philadelphia had two copies of 'Paradise Lost' for circulation in 1741, but there had been no copy of that work in the great library of Cotton Mather." Moreover, after 1760, the eyes of the colonists were upon France rather than upon England, and Rousseau, Montesquieu, Voltaire and the Encyclopedists began to be familiar names to thousands who were scarcely aware of Addison and Steele, or even of the great Elizabethans.[1]

During the Seventeenth and Eighteenth Centuries England was wracked by a movement to standardize the language, alike in vocabulary, in pronunciation and in spelling, and it went far enough to set up artificial standards that still survive.[2] The great authority of Samuel Johnson gave heavy support to this movement, though he was wise enough in the preface to his Dictionary (1735) to admit somewhat sadly that "sounds are too volatile and subtile for legal restraints" and that "to enchain syllables, and to lash the winds, are equally the undertakings of pride, unwilling to measure its desires by its strength." But Johnson could never resist the temptation to pontificate, and so he thundered idiotically against *to wobble, to bamboozle, to swap, to budge, to coax, touchy, stingy, swimmingly, fib, banter, fop, row* (in the sense of a disturbance) and even *fun* and *chaperon*, all of them then somewhat novel.[3] He also permitted himself to read the death-warrants of many archaisms that were not really archaisms at all, for example, *glee, jeopardy* and *to smoulder*. The Americans, in the main, were cut off from this double policing, and in consequence they went on making new words freely and cherishing old ones that had come under the ban in England. A minority along the coast, to be sure, tried to keep up with the latest

1 See The Cambridge History of American Literature, Vol. I, p. 119. Francis Jeffrey, writing on Franklin in the *Edinburgh Review* for July, 1806, hailed him as a prodigy who had arisen "in a society where there was no relish and no encouragement for literature."

2 There is a detailed and excellent account of it in Modern English in the Making, by George H. McKnight; New York, 1928, Ch. XI ff.

3 See Adjectives — and Other Words, by Ernest Weekley; London, 1930, p. 37. Also, McKnight, pp. 372 and 412. McKnight says that among the other words "branded at one time or another by Eighteenth Century purists either as cant or as slang or as 'low'" were *banter, cocksure, dumbfounded, enthusiasm, extra, flimsy, flippant, flirtation, gambling, helter-skelter, humbug, jilt, mob, nervous, pell-mell, prig, quandary, shabby, sham, shuffle, topsy-turvy, touchy, turtle* and *twang.*

dictates of English fashion, but it was never large, and its speech habits had but small influence upon those of the majority. There was obviously only rhetoric in James Russell Lowell's saying that "our ancestors, unhappily, could bring over no English better than Shakespeare's," for relatively few of them had ever heard of Shakespeare, and to even fewer was he anything more than a vague name; [1] but it is nevertheless a fact that their way of using the language had something in it of his glorious freedom and spaciousness.[2] If they had any written guide it was the King James Bible (1611). Whenever an English reform or innovation percolated to them they were inclined to remain faithful to the sacred text, not only because of its pious authority but also because of the superior pull of its imminent and constant presence. Thus when fashionable prudery in English ordered the abandonment of the Anglo-Saxon *sick* for the later and more elegant *ill*, the colonists refused to follow, for *sick* was in both the Old Testament and the New; [3] and that refusal remains in force to this day.

A large number of words and phrases, many of them now ex-

1 Sir William Craigie discusses this matter in The Study of American English, *S.P.E. Tracts*, No. XXVII, 1927, p. 199 ff. "The colonists," he says, "were too few in number, and many of them too unlettered, to bring with them the whole of that marvellous language of which even Shakespeare could not exhaust the riches. It may safely be said that no colony ever carries with it the whole of its mother tongue, and this is all the more certain when that tongue has attained a high level of literary development. . . . It is necessary to draw a distinction between the potential and actual possession of the colonists and their immediate descendants. They had a heritage which was larger than they were able to occupy to the full."

2 McKnight, Ch. X, deals with Shakespeare's English at length. It was by no means untutored; in fact, the Bard was a consummate master of the rhetoric fashionable in the London of his time. But his genius was too vast to endure its bonds, and so he helped himself

to the riches of the common speech. "The effect produced" says McKnight, "is like that of the renewed metaphors to be heard in modern times in the speech of the frontier, where, free from the blighting influence of learning, forms of language are created afresh." All the characters that purists complain of in modern American are to be found in full flower in Elizabethan English — the bold interchange of parts of speech, the copious coinage of neologisms, the disregard of nice inflections, the free use of prepositions, and the liking for loan-words. "The general impression," says McKnight, "is that of a language little governed as yet by rules, but on account of its very irregularity, flexible, and, therefore, adaptable to the expression of varied meaning." See also Shakespeare's English, by George Gordon, *S.P.E. Tracts*, No. XXIX, 1928.

3 Examples of its use in the American sense are to be found in Gen. XLVIII, 1; II Kings VIII, 7; John XI, 1, and Acts IX, 37.

clusively American, are similar survivals from the English of the Seventeenth Century, long since obsolete or merely provincial in England. Among nouns Thornton notes *fox-fire, flap-jack, jeans, molasses, shoat, beef* (to designate the live animal), *chinch, cord-wood* and *home-spun;* Halliwell[1] adds *andiron, bay-window, cess-pool, clodhopper, cross-purposes, greenhorn, loop-hole, ragamuffin* and *trash;* and other authorities cite *stock* (for cattle), *fall* (for autumn), *offal, din, underpinning* and *adze. Bub*, used in addressing a boy, is very old English, but survives only in American. *Flap-jack* goes back to " Piers Plowman," but has been obsolete in England for two centuries. *Muss*, in the sense of a row, is also obsolete over there, but it is to be found in " Antony and Cleopatra." *Char*, as a noun, disappeared from Standard English long ago, save in the compound, *charwoman*, but it survives in American as *chore*. Among the verbs similarly preserved are *to whittle, to wilt* and *to approbate. To guess*, in the American sense of *to suppose*, is to be found in " Henry VI ":

> Not all together; better far, I *guess*,
> That we do make our entrance several ways.

In " Measure for Measure " Escalus says " I *guess* not " to Angelo. The Oxford Dictionary offers examples much older — from Chaucer, Wycliffe and Gower. *To loan*, in the American sense of to lend, is in 34 and 35 Henry VIII, but it dropped out of use in England early in the Eighteenth Century, and all the leading dictionaries, in both English and American, now call it an Americanism. *To fellowship*, once in good American use but now reduced to a provincialism, is in Chaucer. Even *to hustle*, it appears, is ancient. Among adjectives, *homely* was used in its American sense of plain-featured by both Shakespeare and Milton. Other such survivors are *burly, catty-conered, likely, deft, copious, scant* and *ornate*. Perhaps *clever* also belongs to this category, that is, in the American sense of amiable.

Most of the English archaisms surviving in American seem to be derived from the dialects of Eastern and Southern England, from which regions, in fact, a large percentage of the original English

1 J. O. Halliwell (Phillips): A Dictionary of Archaisms and Provincialisms, Containing Words Now Obsolete in England All of Which are Familiar and in Common Use in America, 2nd ed.; London, 1850. See also Gilbert M. Tucker's American English; New York, 1921, p. 39 *ff.*

settlers came. Sir William Craigie says [1] that in New England three areas are chiefly represented — Yorkshire and Lincolnshire, East Anglia, and the Southwestern counties. The Rev. Edward Gepp, of Colchester, who has made comparative studies of the Essex dialect and the common speech of the United States, says that the latter shows a "striking *absence* of words and forms characteristic of Scotland, and of the North and West of England." [2] Since the early colonial period there has been an accession of Northern forms, chiefly through the so-called Scotch-Irish influence, but the older archaisms are nearly all Southern or Eastern. Another English observer, the Rev. H. T. Armfield, has found many Essex place-names in New England, among them, Hedingham, Topsfield, Wethersfield, Braintree, Colchester, Haverhill and Billerica.[3] Among the vulgar forms now common in the United States which still survive in the Essex dialect Mr. Gepp notes *kilter, kiver, yarb, ary, nary, ellum, tonguey, pesky, snicker, bimeby, cowcumber, invite* (for *invitation*) and *hoss,* and the verbs *to argify, to slick up* and *to scrimp.* His word-lists also show a number of words that are now good American, *e.g., chump, given-name* and *heft.* But such archaisms are naturally most common on the lower levels of speech, and in remote and uncultured settlements. "It is a commonplace of the study of cultural history," says George Philip Krapp,[4] "that isolated communities tend to remain relatively stable. They retain their customs, their occupations, their speech, all their cultural traditions, very much as they were at the time when the members of the community seated themselves within the confines of the prison house which they call their home." Thus it is no wonder that the American spoken by the mountaineers of Appalachia shows an unusually large admixture of ancient forms, usually English but often Scottish, not only in its vocabulary, but also in its syntax and pronunciation. Archaic forms continue to flourish in such remote regions just as the Rheno-Franconian dialect of the Seventeenth Century survives among the more bucolic Germans of the lower counties of Pennsylvania. We shall encounter some of them in Chapter VII.

1 The Study of American English, *S.P.E. Tracts,* No. XXVII, 1927, p. 201.
2 A Contribution to an Essex Dialect Dictionary, Supplement III; Colchester, 1922.
3 Transactions of the Essex Archæological Society, Vol. IV, N.S., 1893.
4 Is American English Archaic?, *Southwest Review,* Summer, 1927, p. 296.

IV

THE PERIOD OF GROWTH

I. A NEW NATION IN THE MAKING

Sufficient evidence has been set forth, I take it, to show that the English of the United States had begun to be recognizably differentiated from the English of England by the opening of the Nineteenth Century. But as yet its free proliferation was impeded by two factors, the first being the lack of a national literature of any expanse and dignity and the second being an internal political disharmony which greatly conditioned and enfeebled the national solidarity. During the actual Revolution common aims and common dangers forced the Americans to show a more or less united front, but once they had achieved political independence they developed conflicting interests, and out of those conflicting interests came suspicions and hatreds which came near wrecking the new Confederation more than once. Politically, their worst weakness, perhaps, was an inability to detach themselves wholly from the struggle for domination then going on in Europe. The surviving Loyalists of the revolutionary era — estimated by some authorities to have constituted fully a third of the total population in 1776 — were ardently in favor of England, and such patriots as Jefferson were as ardently in favor of France. This engrossment in the rivalries of foreign nations was what Washington warned against in his Farewell Address. It was at the bottom of such bitter animosities as that between Jefferson and Hamilton. It inspired and perhaps excused the pessimism of such men as Burr. Its net effect was to make it difficult for the people of the new nation to think of themselves, politically and culturally, as Americans pure and simple.[1] Their

1 According to R. E. Spiller (The American in England During the First Half Century of Independence; New York, 1926), Benjamin Silliman's Journal of Travels in England, Holland, and Scotland, and of Two Passages Over the Atlantic, in the Years 1805 and 1806; New York, 1810, was "the first book of travels by an American which at-

state of mind, vacillating, uncertain, alternately timorous and pugnacious, has been well described by Henry Cabot Lodge in his essay on "Colonialism in America."[1] Soon after the Treaty of Paris was signed, someone referred to the late struggle, in Franklin's hearing, as the War for Independence. "Say, rather, the War of the Revolution," said Franklin. "The War for Independence is yet to be fought."

"That struggle," adds B. J. Lossing in "Our Country" (1873), "occurred, and that independence was won, by the Americans in the War of 1812." In the interval the New Republic had passed through a period of *Sturm und Drang* whose gigantic perils and passions we have begun to forget — a period in which disaster ever menaced, and the foes within were no less bold and pertinacious than the foes without. Jefferson, perhaps, carried his fear of "monocrats" to the point of monomania, but under it there was undoubtedly a body of sound fact. The poor debtor class (including probably a majority of the veterans of the Revolution) had been fired by the facile doctrines of the French Revolution to demands which threatened the country with bankruptcy and anarchy,[2] and the class of property-owners, in reaction, went far to the other extreme. On all sides, indeed, there flourished a strong British party, and particularly in New England, where the so-called codfish aristocracy (by no means extinct today) exhibited an undisguised Anglomania, and looked forward confidently to a *rapprochement* with the mother country.[3] This Anglomania showed itself, not only

---

tempted to describe and discuss England as though she were actually a foreign land."

[1] In Studies in History; Boston, 1884. Lodge says that Franklin, Hamilton and Noah Webster were brilliant exceptions. Franklin's autobiography, he says, was "American in feeling, without any taint of English colonialism." Hamilton's "intense eagerness for a strong national government made him the deadliest foe of the colonial spirit." As for Webster, he "went into open rebellion against British tradition. He was snubbed, laughed at, and abused. He was regarded as little better than a madman to dare to set himself up against Johnson and

his successors. But the hard-headed New Englander pressed on, and finally brought out his dictionary — a great work, which has fitly preserved his name."

[2] The best brief account of this uprising that I have encountered is not in any history book, but in Mr. Justice Sutherland's dissenting opinion in Home Building & Loan Ass'n *vs.* Blaisdell *et al*, 54 *Supreme Court Reporter*, p. 244 ff.

[3] The thing went, indeed, far beyond mere hope. In 1812 a conspiracy was unearthed to separate New England from the Republic and make it an English colony. The chief conspirator was one John Henry, who acted under the instructions of Sir

in ceaseless political agitation, but also in an elaborate imitation of English manners.

The first sign of the dawn of a new national order came with the election of Thomas Jefferson to the Presidency in 1800. The issue in the campaign was a highly complex one, but under it lay a plain conflict between democratic independence on the one hand and subservience to English precept and example on the other; and with the Alien and Sedition Laws about his neck, so vividly reminiscent of the issues of the Revolution itself, Adams went down to defeat. Jefferson was violently anti-British and pro-French; he saw all the schemes of his political opponents, indeed, as English plots; he was the man who introduced the bugaboo into American politics. His first acts after his inauguration were to abolish all ceremonial at the court of the Republic, and to abandon spoken discourses to Congress for written messages. That ceremonial, which grew up under Washington, was an imitation, he believed, of the formality of the abhorrent Court of St. James; as for the speeches to Congress, they were palpably modeled upon the speeches from the throne of the English kings. Both reforms met with wide approval; the exactions of the English, particularly on the high seas, were beginning to break up the British party. But confidence in the solidarity and security of the new nation was still anything but universal. The surviving doubts, indeed, were strong enough to delay the ratification of the Twelfth Amendment to the Constitution, providing for more direct elections of President and Vice-President, until the end of 1804, and even then three of the five New England States rejected it,[1] and have never ratified it, in fact, to this day. Democracy was still experimental, doubtful, full of gunpowder. In so far as it had actually come into being, it had come as a boon conferred from above. Jefferson, its protagonist, was the hero of the populace, but he was not a part of the populace himself, nor did he ever quite trust it.

It was reserved for Andrew Jackson, a man genuinely of the people, to lead the rise of the lower orders and give it dramatic effectiveness. Jackson was the archetype of the new American who appeared after 1814 — ignorant, pushful, impatient of restraint and precedent, an iconoclast, a Philistine, an Anglophobe in every fiber.

John Craig, Governor-General of Canada.

1 Maine was not separated from Massachusetts until 1820.

"He was," says his biographer, James Parton, "the most American of Americans — an embodied Declaration of Independence — the Fourth of July incarnate." He came from the extreme backwoods, and his youth was passed, like that of Abraham Lincoln after him, amid surroundings but little removed from savagery. Thousands of other young Americans of the same sort were growing up at the same time — youngsters filled with a vast impatience of all precedent and authority, revilers of all that had come down from an elder day, incorrigible libertarians. They swarmed across the mountains and down the great rivers, wrestling with the naked wilderness and set-ting up a casual, impromptu sort of civilization where the Indian still menaced. Schools were few and rudimentary; there was not the remotest approach to a cultivated society; any effort to mimic the amenities of the East, or of the mother country, in manner or even in speech, met with instant derision. It was in these surroundings and at this time that the thoroughgoing American of tradition was born; "blatant, illogical, elate," "greeting the embarrassed gods" uproariously, and matching "with Destiny for beers." Jackson was unmistakably of that company in every instinct and idea, and it was his fate to give a new and unshakable confidence to its aspiration at the Battle of New Orleans. Thereafter all doubts began to die out; the new Republic was turning out a success. And with success came a great increase in the national egoism. The hordes of pioneers rolled down the Western valleys and on to the great plains.[1] America began to stand for something quite new in the world — in government, in law, in public and private morals, in customs and habits of mind, in the minutiæ of social intercourse. And simultane-ously the voice of America began to take on its characteristic tone-colors, and the speech of America began to differentiate itself unmis-takably from the speech of England. The average Philadelphian or Bostonian of 1790 had not the slightest difficulty in making himself understood by a visiting Englishman. But the average Ohio boatman of 1810 or plainsman of 1815 was already speaking a dialect that the Englishman would have shrunk from as barbarous and unintelligible, and before long it began to leave its marks, at first only faintly but

1 Indiana and Illinois were erected into Territories during Jefferson's first term, and Michigan during his second. Kentucky was admitted to the Union in 1792, Tennessee in 1796, Ohio in 1803. Lewis and Clarke set out for the Pacific in 1804. The Louisiana Purchase was ratified in 1803, and Louisiana became a State in 1812.

in the end very clearly, upon a distinctively national literature. That literature, however, was very slow in coming to a dignified, confident and autonomous estate. Down to Jefferson's day it was predominantly and indeed almost wholly polemical, and hence lacking in anything properly describable as æsthetic value; he himself, an insatiable propagandist and controversialist, was one of its chief ornaments. " The novelists and the historians, the essayists and the poets, whose names come to mind when American literature is mentioned," said Barrett Wendell, " have all flourished since 1800." [1]

But when a beginning was made at last, it was made with what might almost be described as a whoop. The violent reviling of the English reviewers, described at length in Chapter I, had at last overshot its mark. Abashed and alarmed by it for years, the American literati were goaded, in the end, into meeting it with defiance, and that defiance both supported and got support from the rising national feeling. The same year, 1828, which saw the beginning of Jackson's first term also saw the publication of Noah Webster's " *American* Dictionary of the English Language," and a year later followed Samuel Lorenzo Knapp's " Lectures on American Literature," the first formal treatise on the national letters ever written. Knapp, by that time, had enough materials at hand to make a very creditable showing — for example, Bryant's " Thanatopsis " (published in the *North American Review* in 1817); Irving's " Knickerbocker " (1809), " The Sketch-Book " (1819), " Bracebridge Hall " (1822), " Tales of a Traveler " (1824) and "Columbus " (1828); Cooper's " The Spy " (1821), " The Pilot " (1823) and " The Prairie " (1826); Hawthorne's " Fanshaw " (1828); and Poe's " Tamerlane and Other Poems " (1827); not to mention Schoolcraft's " Through the Northwest " (1821) and "Travels in the Mississippi Valley " (1825), Kent's " Commentaries " (1826), Marshall's " Washington " (1804) and Audubon's " Birds of America " (1827). But Knapp was not content to put these new pearls in array; he must also deliver himself of Jacksonian exultations. Where in all England, he demanded, was there a " tuneful sister " comparable to Mrs. Lydia Sigourney, whose

strains of poetic thought are as pure and lovely as the adjacent wave [of the Connecticut river] touched by the sanctity of a Sabbath's morn? . . . What

1 A Literary History of America;
New York, 1900.

are the Tibers and Scamanders, measured by the Missouri and the Amazon? Or what the loveliness of Illyssus or Avon, by the Connecticut or the Potomack? The waters of these American rivers are as pure and sweet, and their names would be as poetical, were they as familiar to us in song as the others, which have been immortalized for ages. Whenever a nation wills it, prodigies are born. . . . In the smiles of publick favor poets will arise, yea, have already arisen, whose rays of mental fire will burn out the foul stain upon our reputation, given at first by irritated and neglected genius, and continued by envy and malice. . . . All things have become well settled upon true principles among us, and the agitation and bustle of their establishment having passed away, some of the first minds will gratify their ambition by literary distinction.

In brief, the national feeling, long delayed in appearing, leaped into being at last in truly amazing vigor. "One can get an idea of the strength of that feeling," says R. O. Williams,

by glancing at almost any book taken at random from the American publications of the period. Belief in the grand future of the United States is the keynote of everything said and done. All things American are to be grand – our territory, population, products, wealth, science, art – but especially our political institutions and literature. Unbounded confidence in the material development of the country . . . prevailed throughout the . . . Union during the first thirty years of the century; and over and above a belief in, and concern for, materialistic progress, there were enthusiastic anticipations of achievements in all the moral and intellectual fields of national greatness.[1]

Nor was that vast optimism wholly without warrant. An American literature was actually taking form, and with the memory of old wrongs still shutting them off from England, the new American writers turned to the Continent for inspiration and encouragement. Irving had already drunk at Spanish springs; Emerson and Bayard Taylor were to receive powerful impulses from Germany, following Ticknor, Bancroft and Everett before them; Bryant was destined to go back to the classics. Moreover, Irving, Cooper, John P. Kennedy and many another had shown the way to native sources of literary material, and Longfellow was making ready to follow them; novels in imitation of English models were no longer heard of; the ground was preparing for " Uncle Tom's Cabin." Finally, Webster himself, as Williams shows, worked better than he knew. His American Dictionary was not only thoroughly American: it was superior to any of the current dictionaries of the English, so much so that

1 Our Dictionaries and Other English Language Topics; New York, 1890, pp. 30–31. See also, for an excellent account of the spirit of the time, Localism in American Criticism, by Carey McWilliams, *Southwest Review*, July, 1934.

for a good many years it remained " a sort of mine for British lexicography to exploit."

Thus all hesitations disappeared, and there arose a national consciousness so soaring and so blatant that it began to dismiss every British usage and opinion as puerile and idiotic. The new Republic would not only produce a civilization and a literature of its own; it would show the way for all other civilizations and literatures. Rufus Wilmot Griswold, the enemy of Poe, rose in his decorous Baptist pulpit to protest that so much patriotism amounted to chauvinism and absurdity, but there seems to have been no one to second the motion. The debate upon the Oregon question gave a gaudy chance to the new breed of super-patriots, and they raged unchecked until the time of the Civil War. Thornton, in his Glossary, quotes a typical speech in Congress, the subject being the American eagle and the orator being the Hon. Samuel C. Pomeroy, of Kansas. I give a few strophes:

> The proudest bird upon the mountain is upon the American ensign, and not one feather shall fall from her plumage there. She is American in design, and an emblem of wildness and freedom. I say again, she has not perched herself upon American standards to die there. Our great Western valleys were never scooped out for her burial place. Nor were the everlasting, untrodden mountains piled for her monument. Niagara shall not pour her endless waters for her requiem; nor shall our ten thousand rivers weep to the ocean in eternal tears. No, sir, no! Unnumbered voices shall come up from river, plain, and mountain, echoing the songs of our triumphant deliverance, wild lights from a thousand hill-tops will betoken the rising of the sun of freedom.

This tall talk was by no means reserved for occasions of state; it decorated the everyday speech of the people, especially in the Jackson country to the southward and beyond the mountains. It ran, there, to grotesque metaphors and far-fetched exaggerations, and out of it came a great many Americanisms that still flourish. Thornton gives a specimen from a Florida newspaper, *c.* 1840, the speaker being a local fee-faw-fo-fum:

> This is *me*, and no mistake! Billy Earthquake, Esq., commonly called Little Billy, all the way from the No'th Fork of Muddy Run! . . . Whoop! won't *nobody* come out and fight me? Come out, some of you, and die decently, for I'm spiling for a fight. . . . I'm a poor man, it's a fact, and smell like a wet dog, but I can't be run over. . . . Maybe you never heard of the time the horse kicked me, and put both his hips out of jint — if it ain't true, cut me up for catfish bait! W-h-o-o-p! I'm the very infant that refused its milk before its eyes were open, and called out for a bottle of old rye. . . . Talk about grinning the bark off a tree — 'tain't nothing; one squint of mine at

a bull's heel would blister it. Oh, I'm one of your toughest sort — live forever, and then turn to a white-oak post. I'm the ginewine article, a real double-acting engine, and I can out-run, out-jump, out-swim, chaw more tobacco and spit less, and drink more whiskey and keep soberer than any man in these localities.

Another noble example comes from Mark Twain's " Life on the Mississippi," the time being *c.* 1852:

> Whoo-oop! I'm the old original iron-jawed, brass-mounted, copper-bellied corpse-maker from the wilds of Arkansaw! Look at me! I'm the man they call Sudden Death and General Desolation! Sired by a hurricane, dam'd by an earthquake, half-brother to the cholera, nearly related to the smallpox on the mother's side! Look at me! I take nineteen alligators and a bar'l of whiskey for breakfast when I'm in robust health, and a bushel of rattle-snakes and a dead body when I'm ailing. I split the everlasting rocks with my glance, and I squench the thunder when I speak! Whoo-oop! Stand back and give me room according to my strength! Blood's my natural drink, and the wails of the dying is music to my ear! Cast your eye on me, gentle-men, and lay low and hold your breath, for I'm 'bout to turn myself loose!

To which may be added the testimony of Dr. Thomas L. Nichols, an American who left the United States for England in 1861, and published " Forty Years of American Life " there in 1864:

> The language [of the West], like the country, has a certain breadth and magnificence. A Western man " sleeps so sound, it would take an earthquake to wake him " . . . "Stranger," he says, " in b'ar hunts I am numerous." . . . He tells of a person " as cross as a b'ar with two cubs and a sore tail." He "laughs like a hyena over a dead nigger." He "walks through a fence like a falling tree through a cobweb." He "goes the whole hog." . . . "Bust me wide open," he says, "if I didn't bulge into the creek in the twinkling of a bedpost, I was so thunderin' savagerous." [1]

This extravagance of metaphor, with its naïve bombast, had but little influence, of course, upon the more decorous native literati. It was borrowed eagerly by the humorous writers, and especially by those who performed regularly in the newspapers, and at the end of the period it was to leave its marks upon two literary artists of the highest quality, Whitman and Mark Twain, but the generality of American authors eschewed it very diligently. Most of them, in fact, looked back toward Addison, or, perhaps more accurately, toward Johnson. The dominant critics of the time — of whom the

[1] I borrow this example from Tall Talk in American Sixty Years Ago, by Mamie Meredith, *American Speech*, April, 1929. See also Big Talk, by Dorothy Dondore, *American Speech*, Oct., 1930; Frontier Tall Talk, by William F. Thompson, *American Speech*, Oct., 1934; and Tall Tales of the Southwest, 1830–60, by F. J. Meine; New York, 1930.

Baptist, Griswold, was a good example — followed Eighteenth Century models, and one searches their sonorous periods for even the slightest concession to colloquialism. The grand master of them all, Poe, achieved a style so rotund and ornate that many a contemporary English leader-writer must have envied it. Nor was there any visible yielding to the *sermo vulgus* in Emerson, Irving, Bryant, Cooper and Longfellow. " Whatever differences there may be," says Sir William Craigie,[1] " between the language of Longfellow and Tennyson, of Emerson and Ruskin, they are differences due to style and subject, to a personal choice or command of words, and not to any real divergence in the means of expression." But meanwhile, says Sir William, there was going on

a rise and rapid growth within the United States of new types of literature which would either give fuller scope to the native element by mingling it with the conventional, or would boldly adopt it as a standard in itself. . . . The runnels of popular speech, which had trickled underground for a century or more, come again to the light of day; they are joined by many more, which have sprung up in the same obscurity; and together they swell into a stream which at its highest flood may well seem to change and obliterate the old banks and landmarks of the language.

Henry James, in " The Question of Our Speech," had said much the same thing a quarter of a century before (1905):

Keep in sight the interesting historical truth that no language, so far back as our acquaintance with history goes, has known any such ordeal, any such stress and strain, as was to await the English in this huge new community it was so unsuspectingly to help, at first, to father and mother. It came *over*, as the phrase is, came over originally without fear and without guile — but to find itself transplanted to spaces it had never dreamed, in its comparative humility, of covering, to conditions it had never dreamed, in its comparative innocence, of meeting; to find itself grafted, in short, on a social and political order that was both without precedent and example and incalculably expansive.

Thus, on the levels below the Olympians, a wild and lawless development of the language went on, and many of the uncouth words and phrases that it brought to birth gradually forced themselves into more or less good usage. " The *jus et norma loquendi*," says W. R. Morfill, the English philologian, " do not depend upon scholars." Particularly in a country where scholarship is strange, cloistered and timorous, and the overwhelming majority of the people are engaged upon new and highly exhilarating tasks, far

1 The Study of American English,
S.P.E. Tracts, No. XXVII, 1927, p.
203.

away from schools and with a gigantic cockiness in their hearts. The old hegemony of the Tidewater gentry, North and South, had been shaken by the revolt of the frontier under Jackson, and what remained of an urbane habit of mind and utterance began to be confined to the narrowing feudal areas of the South and the still narrower refuge of the Boston Brahmins, who were presently recognized as a definite caste of *intelligentsia*, self-charged with carrying the torch of culture through a new Dark Age. The typical American, in Paulding's satirical phrase, became " a bundling, gouging, impious " fellow, without either " morals, literature, religion or refinement." Next to the savage struggle for land and dollars, party politics was the chief concern of the people, and with the disappearance of the old leaders and the entrance of pushing upstarts from the backwoods, political controversy sank to an incredibly low level. Bartlett, in the introduction to the second edition of his Glossary, described the effect upon the language. First the enfranchised mob, whether in the city wards or along the Western rivers, invented fantastic slang-words and turns of phrase; then they were " seized upon by stump-speakers at political meetings "; then they were heard in Congress; then they got into the newspapers; and finally they came into more or less good repute. Much contemporary evidence is to the same effect. W. C. Fowler, in listing " low expressions " in 1850, described them as " chiefly political." " The vernacular tongue of the country," said Daniel Webster, " has become greatly vitiated, depraved and corrupted by the style of the congressional debates." Thornton, in the appendix to his Glossary, gives some astounding specimens of congressional oratory between the 20's and 60's, and many more will reward the explorer who braves the files of the *Congressional Globe*. This flood of racy and unprecedented words and phrases beat upon and finally penetrated the austere retreat of the literati, but the dignity of speech cultivated there had little compensatory influence upon the vulgate. The newspaper was enthroned, and *belles lettres* were cultivated almost in private, and as a mystery. It is probable, indeed, that " Uncle Tom's Cabin " and " Ten Nights in a Bar-room," both published in the early 50's, were the first contemporary native books, after Cooper's day, that the American people, as a people, ever really read. Nor did the pulpit, now fast falling from its old high estate, lift a corrective voice. On the contrary, it joined the crowd, and

Bartlett denounced it specifically for its bad example, and cited, among its crimes against the language, such inventions as *to doxologize* and *to funeralize*. To these novelties, apparently without any thought of their uncouthness, Fowler, who was professor of rhetoric at Amherst, added *to missionate* and *consociational*.

This pressure from below eventually broke down the defenses of the purists, and forced the new national idiom upon them. Pen in hand, they might still achieve laborious imitations of the hated English reviewers, but their mouths began to betray them. "When it comes to *talking*," wrote Charles Astor Bristed for Englishmen in 1855, "the most refined and best educated American, who has habitually resided in his own country, the very man who would write, on some serious topic, volumes in which no peculiarity could be detected, will, in half a dozen sentences, use at least as many words that cannot fail to strike the inexperienced Englishman who hears them for the first time."

2. THE EXPANDING VOCABULARY

A glance at some of the characteristic coinages of the time, as they are revealed in the *Congressional Globe*, in contemporary newspapers and political tracts, and in that grotesque literature of humor which began with Thomas C. Haliburton's "Sam Slick" in 1835, is almost enough to make one sympathize with the pious horror of Dean Alford. *To citizenize* was used and explained by Senator Young, of Illinois, in the Senate on February 1, 1841, and he gave Noah Webster as authority for it. Bartlett quotes *to doxologize* from the *Christian Disciple*, a quite reputable religious paper of the 40's. *To funeralize* [1] and *to pastor*, along with the aforesaid *to missionate* and *consociational*, were other contributions of the evangelical pulpit; perhaps it also produced *hell-roaring* and *hellion*, the latter of which was a favorite of the Mormons and even got into a sermon by Henry Ward Beecher. *To deacon*, a verb of decent mien in

[1] The Oxford Dictionary quotes an example of its use in the sense of to render sad or melancholy from Thomas Browne's Urn Burial (1658). But in the sense of to conduct a funeral the verb seems to be American. It thus appears in the diary of Moses Waddel, president of the University of Georgia; 1825. See College Life in the Old South, by E. Merton Couleer; New York, 1928, p. 197.

colonial days, signifying to read a hymn line by line, responded to the rough humor of the time, and began to mean to swindle or adulterate, *e.g.*, to put the largest berries at the top of the box, to extend one's fences *sub rosa*, or to mix sand with sugar. A great rage for extending the vocabulary by the use of suffixes seized upon the corn-fed etymologists, and they produced a formidable new vocabulary, in *-ize, -ate, -ify, -acy, -ous* and *-ment*. Such inventions as *to concertize, to questionize, retiracy, savagerous, coatee* (a sort of diminutive for *coat*) and *citified* appeared in the popular vocabulary and even got into more or less respectable usage. Fowler, in 1850, cited *publishment* and *releasement* with no apparent thought that they were uncouth. And at the same time many verbs were made by the simple process of back formation, as, *to resurrect, to excurt, to resolute, to burgle*[1] and *to enthuse*.

Some of these inventions, after flourishing for a generation or more, were retired with blushes during the period of plush elegance following the Civil War, but a large number have survived to our own day. Not even the most meticulous purist would think of objecting to *to affiliate, to endorse, to collide, to jeopardize, to predicate, to itemize, to resurrect* or *to Americanize* today, and yet all of them gave grief to the judicious when they first appeared in the debates of Congress, brought there by statesmen from the backwoods. Nor to such simpler verbs of the period as *to corner* (*i.e.*, the market) and *to lynch*.[2] Nor perhaps to *to boom, to boost, to kick* (in the sense of to protest), *to coast* (on a sled), *to engineer, to chink* (*i.e.*, logs), *to feaze, to splurge, to bulldoze, to aggravate* (in

---

1 J. R. Ware, in Passing English of the Victorian Era; London, n.d., says that *to burgle* was introduced to London by W. S. Gilbert in The Pirates of Penzance, 1880. On Nov. 14, 1874 the London *Standard* was speaking of it as one of the " new words with which the American vocabulary has lately been enriched," but it probably goes back to the 40's or 50's.

2 The origin of *to lynch* was long in dispute, but it now appears to be established that it was derived from the name of Captain (or Colonel) Charles Lynch, of Pittsylvania county, Virginia, a primeval 100% American who devoted himself to

harassing Loyalists before and during the Revolution. He was a member of the House of Burgesses, but seems to have paid little heed to the statutes. In 1782 the Virginia Assembly purged him of charges that he had illegally imprisoned certain Loyalists in 1780. For an account of him, probably somewhat inaccurate in detail, see Rope and Faggott, by Walter White; New York, 1929, p. 83. See also the art. *Lynch law* in the Supplement to the Oxford Dictionary; London, 1933. A useful article on the subject was printed in the Lynchburg (Va.) *News*, July 30, 1922.

the sense of to anger), and *to crawfish*. These verbs have entered into the very fiber of the American language, and so have many nouns derived from them, *e.g., boomer, boom-town, bouncer, kicker, kick, lynching-bee, splurge, roller-coaster*. A few of them, *e.g., to collide* and *to feaze*, were archaic English terms brought to new birth; a few others, *e.g., to holler* [1] and *to muss*, were obviously mere corruptions. But a good many others, *e.g., to bulldoze, to canoodle, to honeyfogle, to hornswoggle* and *to scoot*, were genuine inventions, and redolent of the soil.

Along with these new verbs came a great swarm of verb-phrases, some of them short and pithy and others extraordinarily elaborate, but all showing the national talent for condensing a complex thought, and often a whole series of thoughts, into a vivid and arresting image. To the first class belong *to fill the bill, to fizzle out, to make tracks, to peter out, to plank down, to go back on, to keep tab, to light out* and *to back water*. Side by side with them we have inherited such common coins of speech as *to make the fur fly, to cut a swath, to know him like a book, to keep a stiff upper lip, to cap the climax, to handle without gloves, to freeze on to, to go it blind, to pull wool over his eyes, to have the floor, to know the ropes, to get solid with, to spread oneself, to run into the ground, to dodge the issue, to paint the town red, to take a back seat* and *to get ahead of*. These are so familiar that we use them and hear them without thought; they seem as authentically parts of the English idiom as *to be left at the post*. And yet, as the labors of Thornton have demonstrated, all of them appear to be of American nativity, and the circumstances surrounding the origin of some of them have been accurately determined. Many others are as certainly products of the great movement toward the West, for example, *to pan out, to strike it rich, to jump* or *enter a claim, to pull up stakes, to rope in, to die with one's boots on, to get the deadwood on, to get the drop, to back and fill, to do a land-office business* and *to get the bulge on*. And in many others the authentic American flavor is no less plain, for example, in *to kick the bucket, to put a bug in his ear, to see the elephant, to*

1 The spelling of this word shows large variations. The Oxford Dictionary gives *holow* (1542), *hollow* (1599), *holloe* (1642), *holo* (1654), *holloa* (1769), *holla* (1842), and *holler* (1883). In the United States the common pronunciation is *holler*, and this form has been accepted by the Public Printer. See the *Congressional Record*, May 12, 1917, p. 2309.

crack up, to do up brown, to bark up the wrong tree, to jump on with both feet, to go the whole hog, to make a kick, to buck the tiger, to let it slide and *to come out at the little end of the horn. To play possum* belongs to this list. To it Thornton adds *to knock into a cocked hat,* despite its English sound, and *to have an ax to grind. To go for,* both in the sense of belligerency and in that of partisanship, is also American, and so is *to go through* (*i.e.,* to plunder).

Of adjectives the list is scarcely less long. Among the coinages of the first half of the century that are still in use today are *non-committal, highfalutin, well-posted, down-town, two-fer, played-out, down-and-out, semi-occasional, under-the-weather, on-the-fence, flat-footed, whole-souled* and *true-blue.* The first appears in a Senate debate of 1841;[1] *highfalutin* in a political speech of 1848. Both are useful words; it is impossible, not employing them, to convey the ideas behind them without circumlocution. The use of *slim* in the sense of meager, as in *slim chance, slim attendance* and *slim support,* goes back still further. The English commonly use *small* in place of it. Other, and less respectable contributions of the time are *brash, brainy, peart, scary, beatingest, well-heeled, hardshell* (*e.g.,* Baptist), *low-flung, codfish* (to indicate opprobrium) and *go-to-meeting.* The use of *plumb* as an adverb, as in *plumb crazy,* is an English archaism that was revived in the United States in the early years of the century. In the more orthodox adverbial form of *plump* it still survives, for example, in " she fell *plump* into his arms." But this last is also good English. The characteristic American substitution of *mad* for *angry* appeared in the Eighteenth Century, and perhaps shows the survival of an English provincialism. Witherspoon noticed it and denounced it in 1781, and in 1816 Pickering called it " low " and said that it was not used " except in very familiar conversation." But it got into much better odor soon afterward, and by 1840 it was passing unchallenged. Its use is one of the peculiarities that Englishmen most quickly notice in American colloquial speech today. In formal written discourse it is less often encountered, probably because the English marking of it has so conspicuously singled it out. But it is constantly met with in the newspapers and in the *Congressional*

---

1 It quickly bred two nouns, *non-committal* and *non-committalism,* and the latter had the political significance of *straddling* in the 50's, but both seem to have gone out. An adverb, *non-committally,* has survived, and the Oxford Dictionary quotes it from W. D. Howell's The Rise of Silas Lapham, 1885.

Record. In the familiar simile, *as mad as a hornet,* it is used in the American sense, but *as mad as a March hare* is English, and connotes insanity, not mere anger. The English meaning of the word is pre-served in *mad-house* and *mad-dog,* but I have often noticed that American rustics, employing the latter term, derive from it a vague notion, not that the dog is demented, but that it is in a simple fury.

It was not, however, among the verbs and adjectives that the American word-coiners of the first half of the century achieved their gaudiest innovations, but among the substantives. Here they had temptation and excuse in plenty, for innumerable new objects and relations demanded names, and they exercised their fancy with-out restraint. As in the colonial and revolutionary periods, three main varieties of new nouns were thus produced. The first con-sisted of English words rescued from obsolescence or changed in meaning, the second of compounds manufactured of the common materials of the mother tongue, and the third of entirely new inven-tions. Of the first class, good specimens are *deck* (of cards), *gulch,* *gully* and *billion,* the first three old English words restored to usage in America and the last a sound English word changed in meaning. Of the second class, examples are offered by *gum-shoe, mortgage-shark, carpet-bagger, cut-off, mass-meeting, dead-beat, dug-out, shot-gun, stag-party, wheat-pit, horse-sense, chipped beef, oyster-supper, buzz-saw, chain-gang* and *hell-box.* And of the third there are instances in *buncombe, conniption, bloomer, campus, galoot, maverick, roustabout, bugaboo* and *blizzard.* Of these coinages per-haps those of the second class are most numerous and characteristic. In them American exhibits one of its most marked tendencies; a habit of achieving short cuts by bold combinations. Why describe a gigantic rain storm with the lame adjectives of everyday? Call it a *cloud-burst* and immediately a vivid picture of it is conjured up. *Rough-neck* is a capital word; it is more apposite and savory than any English equivalent, and it is unmistakably American.[1] The same instinct for the terse, the vivid and the picturesque appears in *boiled-shirt, blow-out, big-gun, claim-jumper, home-stretch, spread-eagle, come-down, back-number, bed-spread, claw-hammer* (coat), *bot-tom-dollar, poppycock,*[2] *cold-snap, back-talk, back-taxes, corn-belt,*

[1] *Rough-neck* often appears in lists of recent slang terms, but Thorn-ton shows that it was used in Texas so long ago as 1836.

[2] This innocent compound has given a great deal of concern to etymol-ogists. The Standard Dictionary (1893) derives it from the verb

calamity-howler, fire-bug, grab-bag, grip-sack, grub-stake, pay-dirt, tender-foot, stocking-feet, moss-back, crazy-quilt, ticket-scalper, store-clothes, small-potatoes, cake-walk, prairie-schooner, round-up, worm-fence, snake-fence, flat-boat and *jumping-off place.* Such compounds (there are thousands of them) have been largely responsible for giving the American vulgate its characteristic tang and color. *Bell-hop, square-meal* and *chair-warmer,* to name three charming specimens, are as distinctively American as jazz or the quick-lunch.

The spirit of the language also appears clearly in some of the coinages of the other classes. There are, for example, the English words that have been extended or restricted in meaning, *e.g., docket* (for court calendar), *betterment* (for improvement to property), *collateral* (for security), *crank* (for fanatic), *jumper* (for tunic), *backbone* (for moral courage), *tickler* (for memorandum or reminder),[1] *carnival* (in such phrases as *carnival of crime*), *scrape* (for fight or difficulty),[2] *flurry* (of snow, or in the market), *suspenders, diggings* (for habitation) and *range.* Again, there are the new workings of English materials, *e.g., doggery, rowdy, teetotaler, goatee, tony* and *cussedness.* Yet again, there are the purely artificial words, *e.g., sockdolager, hunkydory, scalawag, guyascutis, spondulix, slumgullion, rambunctious, scrumptious, to skedaddle, to absquatulate* and *to exfluncticate.*[3] In the use of the last-named coinages fashions change. In the 40's *to absquatulate* was in good usage, but it has since disappeared. Most of the other inventions of the time, however, have to some extent survived, and it would be difficult to find an American of today who did not know the meaning of *scalawag, rambunctious, to hornswoggle* and *to skedaddle,*[4] and

---

to *pop* and the noun *cock,* which seems very far-fetched. The Oxford Dictionary, attempting no etymology, dismisses it as " U. S. slang." Webster's New International (1934) derives it from " Colloq. D. *pappekak,* lit. soft dung," which seems silly.

1 This use goes back to 1839.
2 Thornton gives an example dated 1812.
3 See Terms of Approbation and Eulogy, by Elsie L. Warnock, *Dialect Notes,* Vol. IV, Pt. I, 1913. Among the curious recent coinages

cited by Miss Warnock are *scallywampus, supergobosnoptious, hyperfirmatious,* and *scrumdifferous.* See also Language and Nonce-Words, by Francis A. Wood, *Dialect Notes,* Vol. IV, Pt. I, 1913.

4 The origin of this noble word remains mysterious. Its first appearance in print seems to have been in 1861, but Ernest Weekley says in his Etymological Dictionary of Modern English that it " appeared earlier in a Northern English dialect in the sense of to spill," and Webster's New International fol-

did not occasionally use them. A whole series of artificial American words groups itself around the prefix *ker-*, for example, *ker-flop*, *ker-bim*, *ker-splash*, *ker-thump*, *ker-bang*, *ker-plunk*, *ker-swash*, *ker-swosh*, *ker-slap*, *ker-whut*, *ker-chunk*, *ker-souse*, *ker-slam* and *ker-flummux*. This prefix and its daughters have been borrowed by the English, but Thornton and Ware agree that it is American, and all of the Oxford Dictionary's examples down to 1875 are of American provenance. Several of my correspondents suggest that it may have been derived from the German prefix *ge-* — that it may represent a humorous attempt to make German verbs by analogy, *e.g.*, *geflop* and *gesplash*. Color is given to this theory by the fact that some of the Oxford Dictionary's earliest examples (Supplement, 1933) make the prefix *che-*, *ca-* or *co-*, which are all rather closer to *ge-* than *ker-* is. I offer these speculations for whatever they are worth. Certainly many *ge-* words must have been made by the early " Dutch " comedians in the United States, just as they are still made by college students.[1]

In Chapter II, Section 1, I mentioned the superior imaginativeness revealed by Americans in meeting linguistic emergencies, whereby, for example, in seeking names for new objects introduced by the building of railroads, they surpassed the English *plough* and *crossing-plate* with *cow-catcher* and *frog*. That was in the 30's. Already at that day the two languages were so differentiated that they produced wholly distinct railroad nomenclatures. Such commonplace American terms as *box-car*, *caboose* and *air-line* are still strangers in England. So are *freight-car*, *flagman*, *towerman*, *switch*, *switch-engine*, *switch-yard*, *switchman*, *track-walker*, *baggage-room*, *baggage-check*, *baggage-smasher*, *baggage-master*, *accommodation-train*, *conductor*, *express-car*, *flat-car*, *hand-car*, *gondola*, *way-bill*, *express-man*, *express-office*, *fast-freight*, *wrecking-crew*, *jerk-water*, *com-*

---

lows him. The Oxford Dictionary says that " there is some slight evidence " to that effect, but remains in doubt. It rejects the suggestion that the word is of Danish or Swedish genesis, made in the Webster of 1864. In 1927 the following appeared in the Dayton, O., *Daily News:* " [The word is] a corruption of *skedannumi*, a Greek word meaning to scatter: General Giles W. Shurtleff, a professor at Oberlin

College, commanded a regiment of Negroes [in the Civil War], and many of his subordinates were from Oberlin, where students knew their Greek. Corrupting the Greek word, officers and Negroes alike evolved *skedaddle*." (Reprinted in the Baltimore *Evening Sun*, Aug. 26, 1927).
1 See American Intensives in *Ka-*, *Ke-*, and *Ker-*, by Exha Akins Sadilek, *American Speech*, Dec., 1931.

mutation-ticket, commuter, round-trip, mileage-book, ticket-scalper, depot, limited, hot-box, iron-horse, stop-over, tie, fish-plate, run, train-boy, chair-car, club-car, bumpers, mail-clerk, passenger-coach, day-coach, railroad-man, ticket-office, truck and *right-of-way,* and the verbs *to flag, to express, to dead-head, to side-swipe, to stop-over, to fire (i.e.,* a locomotive), *to switch, to side-track, to railroad, to commute* and *to clear the track.* These terms are in constant use in America; their meaning is familiar to all Americans; many of them have given the language everyday figures of speech.[1] But the majority of them would puzzle an Englishman, just as the English *luggage-van, permanent-way, goods-waggon, guard, carrier, booking-office, railway-rug, tripper, line, points, shunt, metals* and *bogie* would puzzle the average untraveled American.[2]

In two other familiar fields very considerable differences between English and American are visible; in both fields they go back to the gaudy era before the Civil War. They are politics and that department of social intercourse which has to do with drinking. Many characteristic American political terms originated in revolutionary days and have passed over into English. Of such sort are *caucus* and *mileage.* But the majority of those in common use today were coined during the extraordinarily exciting campaigns following the defeat of Adams by Jefferson. Charles Ledyard Norton has devoted a whole book to their etymology and meaning;[3] the number is far too

---

1 *E.g., Single-track mind, to jump the rails, to collide head-on, broadgauge man, to walk the ties, blind-baggage, underground-railroad, tank-town.*

2 Some of the early American railroad terms are already obsolete. *Depot* is seldom used today; it has been displaced by *station* or *terminal.* The use of *cars* to designate a railroad train was universal down to the Civil War era, but today it survives only in the signs occasionally seen at grade-crossings; "Look Out for the *Cars,*" and in the verb-phrase, *to change cars.* The Pullman *palace-car* is now extinct, and the Pullman *Palace-Car* Company, incorporated in 1867, is now simply the Pullman Company. Even *parlor-car* has been elbowed out by *Pullman.* Incidentally, *tele-*

gram was suggested in the Albany *Evening Journal,* April 6, 1852, by E. Peshine Smith of Rochester, N. Y., and seems to have been his invention. It quickly ousted *telegraphic dispatch* and *telegraphic communication.*

3 *Political Americanisms;* New York, 1890. "In America," said Walt Whitman in An American Primer, *Atlantic Monthly,* April, 1904, " an immense number of new words are needed to embody the new political facts, the compact of the Declaration of Independence, and of the Constitution — the union of the States — the new States — the Congress — the modes of election — the stump speech — the ways of electioneering — addressing the people — stating all that is to be said in modes that fit the life and experi-

large for a list of them to be attempted here. But a few characteristic specimens may be recalled; for example, the simple compounds: *omnibus-bill, banner-state, favorite-son, anxious-bench, gag-rule, executive-session, spoils-system, mass-meeting, steering-committee, office-seeker* and *straight-ticket;* the humorous metaphors: *pork-barrel, pie-counter, land-slide, dark-horse, carpet-bagger, lame-duck* and *on-the-fence;* the old words put to new uses: *plank, pull, platform, ring, machine, wheel-horse, precinct, primary, floater, repeater, bolter, filibuster, regular* and *fences;* the new coinages: *gerrymander, buncombe, roorback, mugwump* and *bulldozing;* the new derivatives: *abolitionist, candidacy, boss-rule, per-diem* and *boodler;* and the almost innumerable verbs and verb-phrases: *to knife, to straddle, to crawfish, to split a ticket, to go up Salt River, to bolt, to lobby, to eat crow, to boodle, to divvy, to grab* and *to run.* An English candidate doesn't *run;* he *stands. To run,* according to Thornton, was already used in America in 1789; it was universal by 1820. *Platform* came in at the same time. *Machine* was first applied to a political organization by Aaron Burr. *Anxious-bench* (or *anxious-seat*) at first designated only the place occupied by the penitent at revivals, but was used in its present political sense in Congress so early as 1842. *Banner-state* appears in *Niles' Register* for December 5, 1840. *Favorite-son* appears in an ode addressed to Washington on his visit to Portsmouth, N. H., in 1789, but it did not acquire its present ironical sense until it was applied to Martin Van Buren. Thornton has traced *filibuster* to 1836, *roorback* to 1844, *split-ticket* to 1842, and *bolter* to 1812. *Regularity* was an issue in Tammany Hall in 1822. There were *primaries* in New York City in 1827, and hundreds of *repeaters* voted. In 1829 there were *lobby-agents* at Albany, and they soon became *lobbyists;* in 1832 *lobbying* had already extended to Washington. All of these terms are now as firmly imbedded in the American vocabulary as *election* or *congressman.*[1]

In the department of conviviality the imaginativeness of Americans was early shown both in the invention and in the naming of new and often highly complex beverages. So vast was the production of novelties during the Nineteenth Century that England borrowed many of them and their names with them. And not only England:

---

ence of the Indianian, the Michiganian, the Vermonter, the men of Maine."

1 See American Political Cant, by Lowry Charles Wimberly, *American Speech,* Dec., 1926.

one buys *cocktails* and *gin-fizzes* to this day in American bars that stretch from Paris to Yokohama. *Cocktail, stone-fence* and *sherry-cobbler* were mentioned by Washington Irving in " Knickerbocker " (1809);[1] by Thackeray's time they were already well-known in England. Thornton traces the *sling* to 1788, and the *stinkibus* and *anti-fogmatic*, both now extinct, to the same year. The origin of the *rickey, fizz, sour, cooler, skin, shrub* and *smash*, and of such curious American drinks as the *horse's neck, Mamie Taylor, Tom-and-Jerry, Tom Collins, John Collins, bishop, stone-wall, gin-fix, brandy-champarelle, golden-slipper, hari-kari, locomotive, whiskey-daisy, blue-blazer, black-stripe, white-plush* and *brandy-crusta* remains to be established; the historians of the booze arts, like the philologists, differ in their theories. But the essentially American character of most of them is obvious, despite the fact that a number have gone over into English. The English, in naming their own somewhat meager inventions, commonly display a far more limited imagination. Seeking a name, for example, for a mixture of whiskey and soda-water, the best they could achieve was *whiskey-and-soda*. The Americans, introduced to the same drink, at once gave it the far more original name of *high-ball*. So with *soda-water* and *pop*. So with *minerals* and *soft-drinks*. Other characteristic Americanisms (a few of them borrowed by the English) are *red-eye, corn-juice, eye-opener, forty-rod, squirrel-whiskey, phlegm-cutter, hard-cider, apple-jack* and *corpse-reviver*, and the auxiliary drinking terms, *boot-legger, sample-room, blind-pig, barrel-house, bouncer, bung-starter, dive, doggery, schooner, stick, duck, straight, hooch, saloon,*

---

1 The etymology of *cocktail* has long engaged the learned, but without persuasive result. It is thus set forth by William Henry Nugent in Cock Fighting Today, *American Mercury*, May, 1929, p. 80: " Feeding is an important thing in the process [of conditioning game-cocks]. The old-time English and Irish trainers made a specially prepared bread of flour and stale beer or ale. They also added white wine or sack, gin, whiskey or other spirits, and a whole *materia medica* of seeds, plants, roots, barks, and leaves. In sampling this concoction before pouring it into the dough they found it an appetizing tonic, not only for pit fowl, but also for man. They named it *cock-bread ale* or *cock ale*, and in the spelling of the time it became *cock ail*. Americans knew a variant of this beverage, as early as 1800, as the *cocktail*. Somehow a *t* had got into the mixture." Early in 1926 Marcel Boulenger printed an article in *Le Figaro Hebdomadaire* (Paris) arguing that *cocktail* was derived from *coquetel*, the name of a drink known for centuries in the vicinity of Bordeaux. See *Cocktail* French Invention, Baltimore *Evening Sun*, Feb. 11, 1926.

finger and *chaser*. Thornton shows that *jag, bust, bat* and *to crook the elbow* are also Americanisms. So are *bartender* and *saloon-keeper*.

It would be possible, too, to compile a formidable roster of theological and ecclesiastical Americanisms, *e.g., anxious bench,* or *seat* (first noted in 1839), *mourners' bench, amen corner, hard-shell* (1842), *camp-meeting* (1801), *circuit-rider* (1838), *come-outer* (1840), *deacon-seat* (1851), *desk,* for pulpit (1770), *blue-law* (1775), *book-concern* (1851), *go-to-meeting, hell-robber, experience-meeting, foot-wash, donation-party, pounding, pastorium,* and the verbs, *to pastor, to missionate, to get* (or *experience*) *religion, to fellowship* and *to shout.*

3. LOAN-WORDS AND NON-ENGLISH INFLUENCES

The Indians of the Far West, it would seem, had little to add to the contributions already made to the American vocabulary by the Algonquians of the Northeast. Most of the new loan-words that were picked up west of the Mississippi came in either through the Spanish, *e.g., coyote,* or through the Chinook trade-jargon of the Columbia river region,[1] *e.g., cayuse.*[2] There was also some translation of terms supposed to be in use among the Indians, *e.g., squaw-man, heap big chief, Great White Father, Father of Waters,* and *happy hunting-grounds,* but most of these, I suspect, owed more to the imagination of the pioneers than to the actual usage of the Indians. In the Oregon country Chinook is still understood by many Indians, and terms borrowed from it are heard as localisms, *e.g., tillicum* (friend), *cultus* (worthless, evil), *tumtum* (literally heart, used to signify belief, opinion, hunch), *potlatch* (feast, public meeting), *skookum* (strong, majestic, splendid), *nanitch* (a journey),

1 An amalgam of Chinook proper and various other Indian languages, *e.g.,* Nootka, Chehalis, Klickitat and Wasco, with contributions from French, English and probably also Russian. A good account of it, with a vocabulary, is in Gill's Dictionary of the Chinook Jargon, 15th ed.; Portland, Ore., 1909. It was in use all over the Northwest, from the Cascade Mountains to the coast. The Indian languages differed so greatly that they were mutually unintelligible. See also the Chinook Jargon, by Douglas Leechman, *American Speech,* July, 1926, and the Chinook Jargon, by E. H. Thomas, the same, June, 1927.

2 According to the Oxford Dictionary, *cayuse* is "said to be from the language of the Chinook Indians of Oregon," but Mr. H. L. Davis believes that it is from the French *cailloux* (pebbles).

and *kokshut* (used up, worn out, ruined).[1] It is possible that *hike* is derived from the Chinook *hyak* (to hurry), but this remains uncertain. In the Southwest many loan-words from the local Indian languages are similarly in more or less general use, *e.g.*, *hogan* (an Indian habitation), *kiva* (the central building of a pueblo), *sambuke* (a musical instrument), *tombé* (another), *katchina* (a spirit), *tiswin* (an intoxicant), and *tegua* (a sandal).[2]

Contact with the French in Louisiana and along the Northwestern border, and with the Spanish in Texas and farther West, brought in many new words. From the Canadian French, as we have seen in Chapter III, Section 1, *prairie, batteau, portage* and *rapids* had been borrowed during colonial days. To these French contributions *bayou, depot, picayune, levee, chute, butte, crevasse, lagniappe* and *coulee*[3] were now added, and probably also *shanty*[4] and *canuck*.[5] *Prairie* begat an enormous progeny during the great movement into the West. In 1828 Noah Webster omitted it altogether from his "American Dictionary of the English Language," but Thornton shows that its use to designate the Western steppes was already common before the Revolution, and that *prairie-hen* and *prairie-dog* had come in by 1805. By 1857, according to Sir William Craigie,[6] " at least thirty other combinations of the same type had been employed in the works of explorers and other writers." The Century Dictionary (1889–91) records thirty-four *prairie* combinations, the Oxford Dictionary (1909) sixty-three, and Webster's New International, Second Edition (1934), seventy-nine.

---

1 I am indebted here to Mr. H. L. Davis, author of Honey in the Horn, and to Mr. Lewis A. McArthur of Portland, secretary to the Oregon Geographic Board.
2 For a longer list, see The English Language in the Southwest, by T. M. Pearce, *New Mexico Historical Review*, July, 1932.
3 *Coulee*, from the French *coulée*, running or flowing, is applied to deep valleys or ravines. It is commonly debased to *coolly*, as in the title of Hamlin Garland's book, Rose of Dutchers Coolly (1895). Its use is confined to the Northwest.
4 *Shanty* is apparently derived from the French *chantier*, the camp of a

gang of loggers. A lumberman is often called a *shantyman*, and the word has spawned other derivatives, *e.g.*, Shanty Irish (title of a book by Jim Tully, 1928), *shanty-town* and *to shanty*. Shanty has been traced to 1820. Folk etymology has assimilated *chantey* to it, but the two words are distinct in derivation and meaning. *Chantey* is from the French *chantez*, the imperative of *chanter*, to sing, and is not American.
5 Thornton's first example of *canuck* is dated 1855.
6 The Study of American English, *S.P.E. Tracts* No. XXVII, 1927, p. 208.

From Spanish, once the Mississippi was crossed, and particularly during and after the Mexican War, there came a swarm of novelties, many of which have remained firmly imbedded in the language. Among them were numerous names of strange personages and objects: *rancho, alfalfa, mustang, sombrero, canyon, desperado, poncho, chaparral, corral, bronco, plaza, peon, alcalde, burro, mesa, tornado, presidio, patio, sierra* and *adobe.* To them, as soon as gold was discovered, were added *bonanza, eldorado, placer* and *vigilante.* Some of the borrowings of the time underwent phonetic change. The Spanish *cincho,* meaning a saddle girth, quickly became *cinch,* and in a little while took on a figurative significance that still clings to it. *Vamos,* the first person plural of the Spanish " let's go," became *vamose* or *vamoose* in American, and presently begat an American verb, *to mosey.* *Chigre,* which the English had borrowed from the Spanish in the Seventeenth Century, making it *chigoe* (the Oxford Dictionary still credits it to " the West Indies and South America "), was borrowed anew by the Western pioneers, and converted into the more American *chigger* or *jigger.* The Spanish *chinche,* which had been likewise borrowed by English in the Seventeenth Century but later abandoned, was reborrowed by American on the frontier, and became the still familiar *chinch,* a bedbug. *Estampida* was converted into *stampede, frijol* into *frijole* (pro. *free-holay*), *tamal* into *tamale, tortilla* into *tortillia,* and *vaquero* into *buckaroo.*[1] *Chile,* a pepper, came in with *frijole* and *tamale,* and at the same time the pioneers became acquainted with the Mexican beverages, *mescal,*[2] *pulque* and *tequila.* Such words as *señor, señorita, padre, siesta, sabe, poncho, pinto, yerba, hombre, casa* and *arroyo* began to bespatter their speech. They converted *calabozo* into *calaboose,* *(la)reata* into *lariat, lazo* into *lasso, rancho* into *ranch,* and *chaparejos* into *chaps,* made free use of such words and phrases as *poco, pronto* and *quien sabe?,* and outfitted many Spanish loan-words with derivatives, *e.g., ranchman, rancher, ranch-house, to ranch, to lasso, to corral, to cinch, hot-tomale, bronc, box-canyon, peonage, burro-load, -weed, -train* and *-trail, loco-weed* (Sp. *loco,*

1 *Vaquero* means cowboy, and is used in that sense in Argentina. In the American West it quickly acquired the special sense of a *Mexican* cowboy, and that sense it retains. *Buckaroo* seems to have dropped out. The American cowboy is always a *cow-puncher,* a *cow-hand,* or simply a *cowboy.*

2 *Mescal* like *chile, tamale, chocolate, coyote, mesquite, zarape, tobacco* and *tomato,* is of Indian origin, but like all of them it came into the language by way of the Spanish.

crazy), *locoed*, and so on. It is possible that they borrowed *coon*, in the sense of a Negro, from the Spanish *barracon* (commonly pronounced *barracoon* by the Americans), a rude shelter used by slaves. In the East *coon* was commonly applied to whites down to the Civil War, and especially to the adherents of Tyler in 1840. The precise history of its transfer to Negroes remains to be investigated.

Most of the terms that I have rehearsed came into the speech of the Western plainsmen and mountain-men before the Civil War, but some of them did not reach the East until the beginning of the movement to pacify and settle the Indian lands, toward the end of the 60's. Many others, in common use by the pioneers, have since sunk to the estate of Westernisms, or dropped out altogether. To the latter class belong *adelantado*, a military governor; *borracho*, a drunkard; *capitan*; *comisario*, a policeman; *ayuntamiento*, a city council; and *lepero*, a beggar. To the former belong *amigo*, a friend; *camino*, a road; *chico* and *chiquito*, small; *campo santo*, a cemetery; *hacienda*, a landed estate; *huero*, a blond; *jornada*, a desert; *mesa*, a tableland; *mocho*, bob-tailed; *mozo*, a servant; *pinto*, piebald; *zarape*, a cloak; *paseo*, a trip; and *sala*, a room. But the effect of Western fiction, of the movies and talkies, of the popularity of pseudo-Spanish bungalow architecture, and of the constant invasion of Southern California by transient visitors has been to keep a large number of Spanish loanwords alive in American speech. Thus most Americans know what a *patio* is, and a *pinto* pony, and a *hombre*. Such words are not often used save in the Southwest, but nevertheless they are understood almost everywhere.[1]

The period saw the beginning of the great immigrations, and the American people now came into contact, on a large scale, with peo-

[1] The best study of Spanish loanwords is to be found in A Dictionary of Spanish Terms in English, With Special Reference to the American Southwest, by Harold W. Bentley; New York, 1932. This admirable work discusses the Spanish influence upon American at length, and with historical insight, and presents a vocabulary of about 400 terms. In addition there is a list of Indian words that came in through the Spanish, and a long list of Spanish place-names in the United States. There is a brief bibliography. See also Geographical Terms in the Far West, by Edward E. Hale, *Dialect Notes*, Vol. VI, Pt. IV, 1932; A Contribution Towards a Vocabulary of Spanish and Mexican Words Used in Texas, by H. Tallichet, *Dialect Notes*, Pt. IV, 1892 (with addenda in Pt. V, 1893, and Pt. VII, 1894); Geographical Terms From the Spanish, by Mary Austin, *American Speech*, Oct., 1933; and The English Language in the Southwest, by T. M. Pearce, *New Mexico Historical Review*, July, 1932.

ples of divergent race, particularly Germans, Irish Catholics from the South of Ireland (the Irish of colonial days "were descendants of Cromwell's army, and came from the North of Ireland "),[1] and, on the Pacific Coast, Chinese. So early as the 20's the immigration to the United States reached 25,000 in a year; in 1824 the Legislature of New York, in alarm, passed a restrictive act.[2] The Know-Nothing movement of the 50's need not concern us here. It is enough to recall that the immigration of 1845 passed the 100,000 mark, and that that of 1854 came within sight of 500,000. These new Americans, most of them Germans and Irish, did not all remain in the East; a great many spread through the West and Southwest with the other pioneers. Their effect upon the language was a great deal more profound than most of us think. The Irish, speaking the English of Cromwell's time, greatly reinforced its usages in the United States, where it was beginning to yield to the schoolmarm. " The influence of Irish-English," writes an English correspondent, " is still plainly visible all over the United States. Some years ago, before I had seen America, a relative of mine came home after twelve years' farming in North Dakota, and I was struck by the resemblance between his speech and that of the Irish drovers who brought cattle to Norwich market." [3] The Germans also left indelible marks upon American, and particularly upon the spoken American of the common people. The everyday vocabulary shows many German words and turns of

1 Prescott F. Hall: Immigration; New York, 1913, p. 5. Even in colonial days there were more such non-Anglo-Saxon immigrants than is commonly assumed. Says Frederick J. Turner, in The Frontier in American History, pp. 22–23: " The Scotch-Irish and the Palatine Germans, or Pennsylvania Dutch, furnished the dominant element in the stock of the colonial frontier. . . . Such examples teach us to beware of misinterpreting the fact that there is a common English speech in America into the belief that the stock is also English."

2 Most of the provisions of this act, however, were later declared unconstitutional. Several subsequent acts met the same fate.

3 The same correspondent adds: " I find very little trace of Scotch on this continent. One might expect to find it in Toronto, the Presbyterian Lhassa, where slot-machines are removed from the streets on Sunday, but the speech of Toronto is actually not distinguishable from that of Buffalo. That is to say, it is quite Irish. The Scotch are not tenacious of their dialect, in spite of the fuss they make about it. It disappears in the second generation. I have met Prince Edward Islanders who speak Gælic and American, but not Scotch. The affinity between Scotch and French, by the way, is noticeable nowhere more than in the Province of Quebec, where I have met Macdonalds who couldn't speak English. The Scotch surrender their speech customs more readily than the English, and the Irish, it seems to me, are most tenacious of all."

phrase. *Sauerkraut* and *noodle*, as we have seen in Chapter III, Section 1, came in during the colonial period, apparently through the so-called Pennsylvania Dutch, *i.e.*, a mixture, somewhat debased, of the German dialects of Switzerland, Suabia and the Palatinate. The immigrants who came in after 1848 contributed *pumpernickel*, *hausfrau*, *beer-garden* (*biergarten*), *lager-beer*, *wienerwurst* (often reduced to *wiener* or *wienie*), *frankfurter*, *bock-beer*, *sauerbraten*, *schnitzel*, *leberwurst* (sometimes half translated as *liverwurst*), *blutwurst*, *dachshund*, *zwieback*, *stein* (drinking vessel), *rathskeller*, *schweizer* (cheese), *delicatessen*, *hamburger* (steak), *kindergarten* and *katzenjammer*.[1] Some of these words did not really lodge in the American vocabulary until after the second great German immigration began in 1870, but nevertheless they were heard before the Civil War. From the Germans, in all probability, there also came two very familiar Americanisms, *loafer* and *bum*. The etymology of the former is still to be worked out, but practically all authorities agree that it is of German origin. James Russell Lowell suggested that it was derived from the German *laufen* (in various dialects, *lofen*), meaning to run, but this seems improbable, and the Oxford

---

[1] The majority of these words, it will be noted, relate to eating and drinking. They mirror the profound effect of German immigration upon American drinking habits and the American cuisine. In July, 1921, despite the current prejudice against all things German, I found *sourbraten* on the bill-of-fare at Delmonico's in New York, and, more surprising still, "*braten* with potato-salad." The effort to substitute *liberty-cabbage* for *sauerkraut*, made by professional patriots in 1918, was a complete failure. It is a fact often observed that loan-words, at least on the level of the common speech, seldom represent the higher aspirations of the creditor nation. French and German mainly have borrowed from English such terms as *beefsteak, roastbeef, pudding, grog, jockey, tourist, sport, five-o'clock tea* and *sweepstakes*, and from American such terms as *tango, jazz, fox-trot, one-step, cocktail* and *canoe* (often *kanu*). "The contributions of England to European civilization, as tested by the English words in Continental languages," says L. P. Smith, "are not, generally, of a kind to cause much national self-congratulation." See The English Element in Foreign Language, by the same author, in *English*, March, 1919. Also, English and American Sport Terms in German, by Theodore McClintock, *American Speech*, Dec., 1933. But on higher levels a more decorous interchange goes on. From German, for example, both English and American have borrowed many scientific words, *e.g.*, *psychology, morphology, teleology, oceanography, ecology, spectroscope* and *statistics;* many medical and chemical words, *e.g.*, *morphine, laudanum, bacillus, bacterium, ether, creosote, pepsin, protozoa* and *aniline;* and a number of terms in everyday use, *e.g.*, *masterpiece, dollar, veneer, homesickness, taximeter, waltz* and *dahlia*. See The German Influence on the English Vocabulary, by Charles T. Carr, *S.P.E. Tracts*, No. XLII, 1934.

Dictionary rejects the derivation. A much more likely prototype is to be found in the German noun *landläufer*, meaning a tramp, and this etymology is favored by Ernest Weekley in his "Etymological Dictionary of Modern English" (1921). Thornton's first example is taken from the title of a sketch by Cornelius Matthews, "The Late Ben Smith, *Loafer*," printed in the *Knickerbocker Magazine*, for July, 1835. R. H. Dana, in "Two Years Before the Mast" (1840) spoke of *loafer* as "the newly invented Yankee word"; his book was an expansion of notes made in 1834–6. In 1855, in "Leaves of Grass," Whitman used *to loaf* in a phrase that seems destined to live: "I *loafe* [note the original spelling] and invite my soul." *Bum* was originally *bummer*, and apparently comes from the German word *bummler*.[1] Both *loafer* and *bummer* have provided numerous derivatives: *loaf* (noun), *to loaf, loafing-place, corner-loafer, common-loafer, town-loafer, to bum, bum* as an adjective (as in *bum steer* and *bum food*), *bum's-rush, bumming-place* and *bummery*, not to mention *to go* (or *be*) *on the bum. Loafer* has migrated to England, but *bum* is still unknown there in the American sense. In England an old English word, *bum*, dating from the Fourteenth Century, is used to designate the buttocks, and is thus not heard in polite discourse.

Another example of debased German is offered by the American *Kriss Kringle*. It is from *Christkindlein*, or *Christkind'l*, and properly designates, of course, not the patron saint of Christmas, but the child in the manger. A German friend tells me that the form *Kriss Kringle*, which is that given in "Webster's New International Dictionary," and the form *Krisking'l*, which is that most commonly used in the United States, are both unknown in Germany. Here,

---

[1] Thornton offers examples of *bummer* ranging from 1856 to 1892. Strangely enough, he does not list *bum*, which has now supplanted it. During the Civil War *bummer* acquired the special meaning of looter, and was applied by the Southerners to the men of Sherman's army of invasion. Here is a popular rhyme which survived until the early 90's:

Isidor, psht, psht!
Vatch de shtore, psht, psht!
Vile I ketch de *bummer*
Vhat shtole de suit of clothes!

Bummler has bred many derivatives in German, e.g., *bummelei*, meaning dawdling or laziness; *bummelig*, unpunctual, careless; *bummeln*, to waste time, to take it easy; *bummelleben*, a life of ease; *bummelzug*, a slow train. *Einen bummeln machen* means to take a leisurely stroll. Once, in Bremen, when my baggage came near missing a train, the portier of my hotel explained that a porter had *gebummelt* delivering it.

obviously, we have an example of a loan-word undergoing phonetic change. Whole phrases have gone through the same process, for example, *nix come erous*[1] (from *nichts kommt heraus*)[2] and *'rous mit 'im* (from *heraus mit ihm*). These phrases, like *wie geht's* and *ganz gut*, are familiar to practically all Americans, no matter how complete their ignorance of correct German. Most of them know, too, the meaning of *gesundheit, kümmel, seidel, spitzbub, gemütlich, männerchor, schützenfest, sängerfest, turnverein, hoch, yodel* and *zwei* (as in *zwei bier*). I once found *snitz* (Ger. *schnitz*) in the elegant pages of *Town Topics*.[3] *Prosit* is in all American dictionaries.[4] *Bower*, as used in cards, is an Americanism derived from the German *bauer* (peasant), meaning the jack. *Poker*, according to the Oxford Dictionary, is probably derived from *pochspiel*, " a similar bluffing card-game of considerable age, from *pochen*, to boast, brag, literally to knock, rap." From a correspondent I have a somewhat different account of this game. "Its name," he says, " is derived from the fact that at one stage of the play the players in turn declare the state of

1 Lincoln used *nix come erous* in a letter dated Nov. 11, 1854. It is quoted in Lincoln the Man, by Edgar Lee Masters; New York, 1931, p. 226.
2 Whether *nix* came into American direct from the German or by way of the English thieves' argot I do not know. The Oxford Dictionary's first example, dated 1789, is from George Parker's Life's Painter. "How they have brought a German word into cant," says Parker, "I know not, but *nicks* means *nothing* in the cant language." Bartlett, Farmer and Thornton fail to list it. A great many English criminals came to the United States between 1800 and the Civil War, and they brought some of their argot with them. Perhaps *nix* was included. Whatever the fact, the word bred a derivative, *nixie*, which seems to be peculiar to American. In the United States Official Postoffice Guide for 1885 *nixie* was defined as "a term used in the railway mail service to denote matter of domestic origin, chiefly of the second and first class, which is unmailable because addressed to places which are not postoffices, or to States, etc., in which there is no such postoffice as that indicated in the address." Its meaning has since been extended to include all mail "so incorrectly, illegibly, indefinitely or insufficiently addressed that it cannot be transmitted." (Sec. 1639, Postal Laws and Regulations.) The Postoffice informs me that it has no record showing when the word was introduced. *Nicht* is also at the bottom of *nit, aber nit, nixy* and *nitsky*, but most of them came in after the period under review. See Substitutes for *No*, by T. J. S., American Speech, Aug., 1927. In some of the German dialects *nicht* becomes *nöt* or *nit*, and *nichts* becomes *nix*.
3 Jan. 24, 1918, p. 4.
4 Nevertheless, when I once put it into a night-letter a Western Union office refused to accept it, the rules then requiring all night-letters to be in "plain English." Meanwhile, the English have borrowed it from American, and it is in the Oxford Dictionary. It comes originally from student Latin, but has been in German for centuries.

their hands by either passing or opening. Those who pass, signify it by saying 'Ich *poche*' or 'Ich *poch.*' This is sometimes indicated by knocking on the table with one's knuckles." But *poker* remains an enigma, and many other theories to account for the origin of the name have been advanced. In the Fourteenth Edition of the Encyclopædia Britannica (1929) R. F. Foster, author of several well-known card manuals, says that the game is of Persian origin, and reached the United States by way of New Orleans. Its Persian name is *as nas*, " but owing to its resemblance to the French game of *poque* and the German game of *pochen*, the French colonists called it *poque*, and this spelling was mispronounced by the English-speaking players as *po-que*, easily converted into *po-ker.*" Schele de Vere, in his " Americanisms " (1872) derived *poker* from the French *poche*, a pocket, but apparently on very shaky grounds.

The exclamation *ouch* is classed as an Americanism by Thornton, and he gives an example dated 1837. The Oxford Dictionary refers it to the German *autsch*, and Thornton says that " it may have come across with the Dunkers or the Mennonites." All of the Oxford's examples are American, for *ouch* is seldom used in English, save in the sense of a clasp or buckle set with precious stones (from the Old French *nouche*), and even in that sense it is archaic. *Shyster* may be German also; Thornton has traced it back to the 50's.[1] *Rum-dumb* is grounded upon the meaning of *dumb* borrowed from the Germans; it is not listed in the English slang dictionaries. Bristed says that the American meaning of *wagon*, which indicates almost any four-wheeled, horse-drawn vehicle in this country but only the very heaviest in England, was probably influenced by the German *wagen*. He also suggests that the American use of *hold on* for *stop* was influenced by the German *halt an*, and White says that the substitution of *standpoint* for *point of view*, long opposed by purists, was first made by an American professor who sought " an Anglicized form " of the German *standpunkt*. Other etymologists, professional and amateur, have discerned German influences in the peculiarly American use of *fresh* in the sense of saucy or impudent (Ger. *frech*); in *gee-whiz* (Ger. *gewiss* — but this is hardly convincing); in the American preference for *shoe* as against the English *boot*

1 Thornton's first example shows a variant spelling, *shuyster*. All subsequent examples show the present spelling. It is to be noted that the suffix *-ster* is not uncommon in English, and that it usually carries a deprecatory significance.

(Ger. *schuh*); in the common use of *Bladder* as a derisory title for a small and bad newspaper (Ger. *käseblatt*); in *stunt* (Ger. *stunde*, hour – another one hard to believe); in the American *bub*, once commonly used in addressing a boy (Ger. *bube*); in the American use of *check* instead of the English *bill* to designate a restaurant reckoning (Ger. *zeche*); and in such phrases as *it is to laugh*, and *five minutes of three* (instead of the English *to three*). German influence may also have something to do with the extraordinary facility with which American forms compound nouns. In most other modern languages the process is rare, and English itself lags far behind American. But in German it is almost unrestricted. " It is," says Logan Pearsall Smith, " a great step in advance toward that ideal language in which meaning is expressed, not by terminations, but by the simple method of word-position."

German, like Dutch, Spanish and French, has naturally left its most salient traces in those areas with the largest population of German-speaking immigrants. In the so-called Pennsylvania Dutch regions of Pennsylvania and in some of the Western States a great many Germanisms are in circulation. In the former, says W. H. Allen,[1] " many words and constructions are obviously of German origin. *That* equals *so that*, as in ' We like our mince-pie piping hot *that* it steams inside.' A *tut* or a *paper tut* is a paper bag. *Verdrübt* means sad. The *freinschaft* is the relationship. *All* is *all gone*, as in ' The butter is *all*.' *Look* means *be fitting*, as in ' It doesn't *look* for two girls to go there alone.' " Mr. Allen lists many other localisms, among them, *glick*, to come out right (Ger. *glück*); *siffer*, a heavy drinker (Ger. *säufer*); and *ritschi*, a frozen pond used for sliding (Ger. *rutschen*, to slide). Santa Claus, in such areas, is usually *Belsnickel*, as indeed he was among the Germans of Baltimore when I was a boy.[2] A. W. Meyer has assembled some curious examples from the Middle West,[3] for example, *brickstein* for *brick* (Ger. *backstein*), *heurack* for *hayrack* (Ger. *heu*, hay), and *büchershelf* for *bookshelf* (Ger. *bücher*, books). *Plunder* is still often used in

1 In *Dialect Notes*, Vol. IV, Pt. II, 1914, p. 157.
2 See also Linguistic Substrata in Pennsylvania and Elsewhere, by R. Whitney Tucker, *Language*, March, 1934. Dr. Tucker discusses the phonology of the American spoken in lower Pennsylvania. *Hex*, meaning a witch, is in common use there, and in 1930 the sensational trial of a York county *hex-doctor* made the term familiar throughout the United States.
3 Some German-Americanisms from the Middle West, *American Speech*, Dec., 1926.

that part of the country to designate baggage, a usage probably suggested by the identical German word, and going back to the first years of the Nineteenth Century. A peculiar intonation is remarked by visitors to the Pennsylvania German towns. " The voice," says Mr. Allen, " is raised at the beginning of a question and lowered at the end." Whether this is due to German influence I do not know, but it is also noticeable when the native speaker is using what passes locally for German. Mr. Allen goes on:

> Questions frequently contain an *ain't:* "You'll do that, *ain't* you will?." "You won't do that, *ain't* you won't?." "He's been gone a long time, *ain't* he has? " If one asks "Have you any good apples? " the answer is "I do." "Don't you think? " with a falling inflection is often added to questions. The most striking idiom is the use of *till* (and *until*) as a conjunction meaning *by the time,* and as a preposition meaning *at* or *on* (temporarily). "It will be raining *till* we get home." "We were tired *till* we were there." "We'll be back *till* (*at*) six." A sort of genitive of time is found in this sentence: "She came Saturdays and left Mondays." In each instance this means one particular day. An ethical dative is often heard: "Little Thomas ran away *for* his mother yesterday."

The immigrants from the South of Ireland, during the period between the War of 1812 and the Civil War, exerted an influence upon the language that was vastly greater than that of the Germans, both directly and indirectly, but their contributions to the actual vocabulary were probably less. They gave American, indeed, very few new words; perhaps *speakeasy, shillelah* and *smithereens* exhaust the list. *Lallapalooza* may also be an Irish loan-word, though it is not Gælic, nor even English. It apparently comes from *allay-foozee,* a Mayo provincialism, signifying a sturdy fellow. *Allay-foozee,* in its turn, comes from the French *allez-fusil,* meaning " Forward the muskets! " — a memory, according to P. W. Joyce,[1] of the French landing at Killala in 1798. Such phrases as *Erin go bragh* and such expletives as *begob* and *begorry* may perhaps be added: they have got into American understanding, though they are surely not distinctive Americanisms. But of far more importance, in the days of the great immigrations, than these few contributions to the vocabulary were certain speech habits that the Irish brought with them — habits of pronunciation, of syntax, and even of grammar. These habits were, in part, the fruit of efforts to translate the idioms of Gælic into English, and in part survivals from the English of the

1 English As We Speak It in Ireland,
2nd ed.; London, 1910, pp. 179–180.

age of James I. The latter, preserved by Irish conservatism in speech, came into contact in America with habits surviving, with more or less change, from the same time, and so gave those American habits an unmistakable reinforcement. The Yankees have lived down such Jacobean pronunciations as *tay* for *tea* and *desave* for *deceive,* and these forms, on Irish lips, strike them as uncouth and absurd, but they still cling, in their common speech, to such forms as *h'ist* for *hoist, bile* for *boil, chaw* for *chew, jine* for *join, sass* for *sauce, heighth* for *height, rench* for *rinse* and *lep* for *leaped,* and the employment of precisely the same forms by the thousands of Irish immigrants who spread through the country undoubtedly gave them support, and so protected them, in a measure, from the assault of the purists. And the same support was give to *drownded* for *drowned, oncet* for *once, ketch* for *catch, ag'in* for *against* and *onery* for *ordinary.* C. H. Grandgent shows in " Old and New " (1920) that the so-called Irish *oi-* sound in *jine* and *bile* was still regarded as correct in the United States so late as 1822, though certain New England grammarians, eager to establish the more recent English usage, had protested against it before the end of the Eighteenth Century. The Irish who came in in the 30's joined the populace in the war upon the reform, and to this day some of the old forms survive on the lower levels of the national speech.

Certain usages of Gælic, carried over into the English of Ireland, fell upon fertile soil in America. One was the employment of the definite article before nouns, as in French and German. An Irishman does not say " I am good at Latin," but " I am good at *the* Latin." In the same way an American does not say " I had measles," but " I had *the* measles." There is, again, the use of the prefix *a* before various continuing verbs, as in *a-going* and *a-riding.* This usage, of course, is native to English, but it is much more common in the Irish dialect, on account of the influence of the parallel Gælic form, and it is also much more common in American. There is, yet again, a use of intensifying prefixes and suffixes, often set down as characteristically American, which may have been borrowed from the Irish. Examples of such stretch-forms are *no-siree, yes-indeedy, teetotal.* The Irishman is almost incapable of saying plain *yes* or *no;* he must always add some extra and gratuitous asseveration.[1] The American

---

1 Amusing examples are to be found in Donlevy's Irish Catechism. To the question, " Is the Son God? " the answer is not simply " Yes," but

is in like case. His speech bristles with intensives, so the Irish extravagance of speech struck a responsive chord in the American heart, and American borrowed, not only occasional words, but whole phrases, and some of them have become thoroughly naturalized. Joyce shows the Irish origin of many locutions that are now often mistaken for native inventions, for example, *dead* as an intensive, not to mention many familiar similes and proverbs. Certain Irish pronunciations, Gaelic rather than archaic English, got into American during the early Nineteenth Century, often with humorous effect. Among them, one recalls *bhoy*, which entered our political slang in the middle 40's but has since passed out.

From other languages the borrowings during the period of growth were naturally less. Down to the last decades of the Nineteenth Century, the overwhelming majority of immigrants were either Germans or Irish; the Jews, Italians, Scandinavians and Slavs were yet to come. But the first Chinese appeared in 1848, and soon their speech began to contribute its inevitable loan-words. These words were first adopted by the argonauts of the Pacific Coast, and a great many of them have remained Western localisms. A number of others have got into the common speech of the whole country. Of such sort are the verbs *to yen* (meaning to desire strongly, as a Chinaman is supposed to desire opium), *to flop* (meaning to sleep or lie down), and *to kowtow*, and the nouns *joss, chow, yok-a-mi, fantan, chop-suey, chow-mein*[1] and *tong*. *Josshouse, flophouse, tong-war*, and *chopsuey-joint* are familiar derivatives. Contrary to what seems to be a popular opinion, *hop* is not Chinese. It is simply the common name of the *Humulus lupulus*, which, in English folklore, has long been held to have a soporific effect. *Hop-pillows* were brought to American by the first English colonists. Neither is *high-binder* a

---

"Yes, certainly He is." And to the question, "Will God reward the good and punish the wicked?" the answer is "Certainly; there is no doubt He will."

[1] The newspapers often report the discovery that neither *chop-suey* or *chow-mein* is a Chinese dish. This is probably true of the former. I have been told that it is a mixture of Chinese dishes, concocted for the American palate, and that the name, in Chinese, means slops. But according to Joe Lin, national secretary of the On Leong Chinese Merchants Association (quoted in the Minneapolis *Star*, April 19, 1929), *chow-mein* is actually Chinese, though it has been "a bit flavored up for Western palates." I am indebted here to Mr. R. S. Kelly, of the Honolulu *Star-Bulletin*.

translation from a Chinese term, as seems to be commonly believed. So long ago as 1840 Edgar Allan Poe wrote in his Marginalia:

As to *high-binder* which is so confidently quoted as modern ("not in use, *certainly*, before 1819,") I can refute all that is said by referring to a journal in my own possession — the *Weekly Inspector*, for Dec. 27, 1806 — published in New York:

"On Christmas Eve, a party of banditti, amounting, it is stated, to forty or fifty members of an association, calling themselves *high-binders*, assembled in front of St. Peter's Church, in Barclay-street, expecting that the Catholic ritual would be performed with a degree of pomp and splendor which has usually been omitted in this city. These ceremonies, however, not taking place, the *high-binders* manifested great displeasure."

In a subsequent number, the association are called *hide-binders*. They were Irish.

V

THE LANGUAGE TODAY

1. AFTER THE CIVIL WAR

The general characteristics of American English have been sufficiently described in the preceding chapters. It has maintained them unbrokenly since Jackson's day, though there was a formidable movement to bring it into greater accord with English precept and example during the years following the Civil War. This movement was led by such purists as Edward S. Gould, William D. Whitney and Richard Grant White, and seems to have got its chief support from schoolmarms, male and female, on the one hand, and from Anglomaniacs on the other.[1] Gould, in 1867, brought out his " Good English," the first of what was to be a long series of hortatory deskbooks, by himself and other sages.[2] He began by arguing that English, " within the last quarter of a century, through the agency of good writers, critics and lexicographers," had been " in many respects greatly improved," but lamented that there had also gone on a compensatory deterioration, and " in greater proportion." He said that he was not opposed, in principle, to " the fabrication of new words, and the new use of old words," but he maintained that such changes should be undertaken only by " educated men," each of

[1] Henry Cabot Lodge says in his essay, Colonialism in the United States, printed in his Studies in History (1884), that " the luxurious fancies which were born of increased wealth, and the intellectual tastes which were developed by the advances of the higher education . . . revived the dying spirit of colonialism." This spirit was confined largely to " young men who despised everything American and admired everything English." Such persons, says Lodge, " flatter themselves with being cosmopolitans, when in truth they are genuine colonists, petty and provincial to the last degree."

[2] Gould was born at Litchfield, Conn., in 1805, and died in New York in 1885. He lectured, contributed to the magazines, and wrote books and plays. In 1836 he published his Lectures Delivered Before the Mercantile Library Association, apparently as a counterblast to Samuel Lorenzo Knapp's Lectures on American Literature (1829). In this book he deplored the whooping up of American authors, and argued for the superiority of the British.

them capable of assuming "the burden of proof in support of his innovation." For the inventions of the "ignorant" he had only contempt and contumely, and in the forefront of the ignorant he put "the men generally who write for the newspapers." He then proceeded to denounce some of the familiar bugaboos of the English Americophobes, including *to jeopardize* (he agreed with Noah Webster that *to jeopard* was better), *controversialist* (though it had been used by Macaulay), *leniency* (though it had been used by Coleridge and even by the *Edinburgh Review*), *underhanded, to donate, standpoint, to demean, over his signature, to open up*, and *try and.*

White, like Gould, pretended to a broad tolerance, and even went to the length of admitting that "language is rarely corrupted, and is often enriched, by the simple, unpretending, ignorant man, who takes no thought of his parts of speech." More, he argued in the third chapter of his "Words and Their Uses" (1870) [1] that the English spoken and written in the United States was at least as good as that spoken and written in England. But at once it appeared that he was assuming that the Boston dialect was Standard American. "Next," he said, "to that tone of voice which, it would seem, is not to be acquired by any striving in adult years, and which indicates breeding rather than education, the full, free, unconscious utterance of the broad *ah* sound of *a* is the surest indication in speech of social culture which began at the cradle." He then proceeded to denounce most of the Americanisms in Gould's *Index Expurgatorius*, with the addition of *gubernatorial, presidential, reliable, balance* (remainder), *editorial, real-estate, railroad* (he preferred the English *railway*), *telegrapher* (he preferred *-ist*), *dirt* (as in *dirt-road:* he believed it should be restricted to its English sense of *filth*), *ice-water* (he preferred *iced*), and the verbs *to locate* ("a common Americanism, insufferable to ears at all sensitive"), *to enthuse, to aggravate*, and *to resurrect.* [2]

---

1 A book made up of articles contributed to the New York *Galaxy* in 1867, 1868 and 1869.

2 White was born in 1821 and died in 1885. He studied both medicine and law, but preferred journalism, and later had a political job in New York. He edited the Riverside Shakespeare, which is still in print.

He was extremely dogmatic, and a chronic controversialist. Perhaps his chief claim to fame is the fact that he was the father of Stanford White, the architect, whose assassination in 1906 made a famous sensation. His pedantic effort to limit the field of Americanisms has been described in Chapter I, Section 5.

Gould's pedantries were attacked by G. Washington Moon, the antagonist of Dean Alford, in "Bad English Exposed" (*c.* 1868; 4th ed., 1871; 8th ed., 1882), and with the same weapon that had proved so effective against the dean — that is, by showing that Gould himself wrote very shaky English, judged by his own standards. White was belabored by Fitzedward Hall in "Recent Exemplifications of False Philology" (1872) and again in "Modern English" (1873). Hall was a man of extraordinary learning and knew how to use it.[1] As one of the collaborators in the Oxford Dictionary he had access to its enormous store of historical material, then still unpublished, and that material he flung at White with great precision and effect. In particular, he brought heavy batteries to bear upon White's reverence for the broad *a* of Boston, and upon the doctrine, set forth in "Words and Their Uses," that "the authority of general usage, or even of the usage of great writers, is not absolute in language" — that "there is a misuse of words which can be justified by no authority, however great, by no usage, however general." He said:

> The critic neglects to furnish us with any criterion, or set of criteria, his own mandates and ordinances excepted, by which to decide when the misuse of a word becomes impossible of justification. His animadversions, where original, are, I believe, in almost every case, founded either on caprice, or defective information, or both. . . . We shall search in vain — for all the world as if he had been bred at Oxford — to find him conceding, as within the compass of the credible, the fallibility of his private judgments, or the inexhaustiveness of his meagre deductions.

Here, it will be noted by the judicious, Hall's righteous indignation ran away with his pen, and he wrote *inexhaustiveness* when he meant its opposite. His two books, with their close-packed and almost endless footnotes, presented a vast amount of philological

1 He was born at Troy, N. Y. in 1825, and educated at Harvard. He then went to India in search of a runaway brother. Settling there, he undertook the study of Sanskrit, and soon mastered it sufficiently to be made professor of it at Benares. He printed many learned editions of the Indian classics. In 1860 Oxford made him a D.C.L. and in 1862 he became professor of Sanskrit, Hindustani and Indian jurisprudence at King's College, London. In 1864 he became examiner in Hindustani for the British Civil Service Commission, and in 1880 he succeeded Max Müller as examiner in Sanskrit. He not only had an important hand in the Oxford Dictionary, but was also a collaborator in Joseph Wright's monumental English Dialect Dictionary (1896–1905). He died in 1901, much honored in England but hardly known in his own country.

knowledge, and should have been sufficient to destroy the baleful influence of White, whose learning was mainly only pretension. But, as George H. Knight says in " Modern English in the Making," Hall was undone by his very virtues. His scholarly approach and forbidding accumulation of facts repelled more readers than they attracted, and so he failed to prevail against his " amateurish rivals and opponents," though " the soundness of his methods has been generally recognized by the expert." Gould and White thus had it all their own way, and their pedantries were accented with complete gravity by the pedagogues of the 70's and 80's. White's " Words and Their Uses," in fact, is still in print and still enjoys a considerable esteem, and there are many latter-day imitations of it, most of them as cocksure as it is, and as dubious.

But the effort made by the authors of such works to police the language, though it has always had the ardent support of certain eminent American literati and of almost the whole body of pedagogues, has never really impeded the natural progress of American. It has gone on developing in spite of them, and in innocent accord with its native genius. The collections amassed for the " Dictionary of American English on Historical Principles " show that in the very heyday of White a large number of New Americanisms of characteristic vigor and vulgarity were coming in, and coming in to stay — among them, *wire-puller* and *to strike oil* in 1867, and *boom* and *to boom* a few years after. A glance through Thornton, Bartlett and the Oxford Dictionary and Supplement turns up many another of the same pungent sort — *claw-hammer* (coat, 1869), *mule-skinner* and *jack-rabbit* (1870), *tangle-foot* (whiskey, 1871), *cuss-word* (Mark Twain, 1872), *hoodlum* (1872), *dead-beat* (Petroleum V. Nasby, 1872), *jam* and *jig-saw* (1873), *sand* (courage, Bret Harte, 1875), *grub-stake* and *hold-up* (both *c.* 1875), *freeze-out* and *slate* (political, 1877), *heeler* (*c.* 1877), *stalwart* (political) and *crook* (1878), *set-back*, *joint* (a low den) and *spellbinder* (*c.* 1880). To them may be added the adverbs *to a frazzle* (General John B. Gordon to General Robert E. Lee, 1865) and *concededly* (1882), and the verbs *to itemize* (Webster, 1864), *to go through* (to plunder, 1867), *to go back on* (1868), *to suicide* (1871), *to guy* (1872), *to light out* (1878), *to side-track* (1880) and *to injunct* (1880). Many of these novelties were either invented or given currency by the emerging authors of the new American school — Walt Whitman,

Bret Harte, Mark Twain, W. D. Howells,[1] and the lesser humorists. Others popped up in the newspapers and in the debates in Congress. Some lasted for no more than a few brief months, or even weeks, and then joined the innumerable caravan of obsolete Americanisms; others got no higher in the vocabulary than the level of slang or argot, and linger there yet; still others gradually made their way into standard usage. It is, indeed, very difficult, dealing with neologisms, to know how to rate them. The most seemly, etymologically speaking, are often rejected in the long run, and the most grotesque are accepted. Many more go on dwelling in a twilight region, ordinarily disdained but summoned out for service on special occasions. In that twilight region are large numbers of the words that everyone who investigates the American language must discuss.

2. THE MAKING OF NEW NOUNS

All of the processes for the formation of new words that are distinguished by philologians have been in active operation in the United States since Jackson's time, and after the Civil War their workings took on a new impetus. It would take us beyond the range of the present work to attempt to trace those workings in any detail, but a few typical examples may be examined. Consider, for instance, the process called clipping, back-shortening, or back-formation — a sort of instinctive search for short roots in long words. This habit, in Restoration days, precipitated a quasi-English word, *mobile*, from

---

1 That Whitman, Howells and Mark Twain were acutely conscious of the changes that were occurring in American I have shown by quotations from them in Chapter I, Section 6. Howells, by an almost incredible paradox, was praised by White and denounced by Hall. White, in Words and Their Uses, spoke of his "unobtrusive and seemingly unconscious mastery of idiomatic English," but Hall, in Recent Exemplifications of False Philology, said that "among American writers of rising fame whose English is noticeably bad, Mr. Howells stands somewhat eminent." He then proceeded to belabor Howells's use of *to aggravate*, *on* the street, *to anecdote*, *muletress*, *mutual* friends, to *discommode*, to *experience*, *reliable* and *unrivaledest*. Some of these were obviously only nonce-words, used with humorous intent. Others were perfectly good American, and so remain. Hall's onslaught is hardly to be taken seriously; he was simply using Howells as a club to beat White. On p. 106 he belabored Howells for using *to experience* and *reliable*, but on p. 31 he defended the former vigorously against White, and on p. 100 he defended the latter. Such are the follies of the learned!

the Latin *mobile vulgus*, and in the days of William and Mary it went a step further by precipitating *mob* from *mobile*. *Mob* is now sound English, but in the Eighteenth Century it was violently attacked by the purists then in eruption,[1] and though it survived their onslaught they undoubtedly greatly impeded the formation and adoption of other words of the same category. There are, however, many more in Standard English, *e.g., patter* from *paternoster*, *van* from *caravan*, *spats* from *spatterdashes*, *wig* from *periwig*, *cab* from *cabriolet*, *gin* from *geneva*, *curio* from *curiosity*, and *pun* from *pundigrion*.[2] In Eighteenth Century America, save for a few feeble protests from Witherspoon and Boucher, they went unchallenged, and as a result they multiplied. *Rattler* for *rattlesnake*, *pike* for *turnpike*, *coon* for *raccoon*, *possum* for *opossum*, *cuss* for *customer*, *squash* for *askutasquash* — these American clipped forms are already antique; *Sabbaday* for *Sabbath-day* has actually reached the dignity of an archaism, as has the far later *chromo* for *chromolithograph*. They are still formed in great numbers, and scarcely a new substantive of more than two syllables comes in without bringing one in its wake. We have thus, in recent years, witnessed the genesis of *phone* for *telephone*, *gas* for *gasoline*, *photo* for *photograph*, *movie* for *moving picture*, and *auto* for *automobile*. Some of these newcomers linger below the salt, *e.g., pep* for *pepper*, *plute* for *plutocrat*, *pug* for *pugilist*, *vamp* for *vampire*, *pen* for *penitentiary*, *defi* for *defiance*, *ambish* for *ambition*, *pash* for *passion*, *beaut* for *beauty*, *steno* or *stenog* for *stenographer*, *loot* for *lieutenant*, *champ* for *champion*, *simp* for *simpleton*, *sap* for *saphead*, *mutt* for *muttonhead*[3] and *jit* for *jitney*, but many others, once viewed askance, are now in more or less decorous usage, *e.g., smoker* for *smoking-car*,

1 Among them, Jonathan Swift. In the *Tatler*, Sept. 28, 1710, he contended that "monosyllables are the disgrace of our land." "We cram one syllable," he continued, "and cut off the rest, as the owl fattened her mice after she had bit off their legs, to prevent them running away. If ours be the same reason for maiming our words, it will certainly answer the end; for I am sure no other nation will desire to borrow them."

2 There is an interesting discussion of such words in Otto Jespersen's Growth and Structure of the English Language, 3rd ed.; Leipzig, 1919, pp. 170–2. See also Stunts in Language, by Louise Pound, *English Journal*, Vol. IX, No. 2, Feb., 1920; Essays on English, by Brander Matthews; New York, 1921, p. 107 *ff*; Neuenglische Kurzformbildungen, by Leo Müller; Giessen, 1923; and Clipped Words: A Convenience and a Custom, in Do You Talk Like That?, by Richard Burton; Indianapolis, 1929, p. 213 *ff*.

3 This etymology for *mutt* is supported by Bud Fisher, creator of Mutt and Jeff. See the *Editor and Publisher*, April 17, 1919, p. 21.

diner for *dining-car*, *sleeper* for *sleeping-car*, *pa* for *papa*, *ma* for *mamma*, *flu* for *influenza*, *drapes* for *draperies*, *bronc* for *bronco*, *memo* for *memorandum*, *quotes* for *quotation-marks* and *knicker* for *knickerbocker*.[1] Back-formations often originate in college slang, e.g., *prof* for *professor*, *prom* for *promenade* (dance), *grad* for *graduate* (noun), *co-ed* from the adjective *co-educational*, *medic* for *medical-student*, *frat* for *fraternity*, *gym* for *gymnasium*, *dorm* for *dormitory*, *U* for *university*, *Y* for *Y.M.C.A.*, *plebe* for *plebeian*,[2] or in other varieties of slang, argot or dialect, e.g., *skeeter* or *skeet* for *mosquito*, *cap* for *captain*, *con* for *convict*, *coke* for *cocaine*, *doc* for *doctor*, *foots* for *footlights*, *hon* for *honey*, *pard* for *partner*, *rube* for *Reuben*, *sarge* for *sergeant*, *snap* for *snapshot*, *diff* for *difference*, *ham* for *hamfatter*, *pop* for *populist*, *spec* for *speculation*, *typo* for *typographer*, *secesh* for *secession* and *prelim* for *preliminary*.[3] *Ad* for *advertisement* is struggling hard for recognition; some of its compounds, e.g., *ad-writer*, *want-ad*, *display-ad*, *ad-rate* and *ad-man* are already accepted.[4] *Boob* for *booby* promises to become sound American in a few years; its synonyms are no more respectable than it is. At its heels are *bo* for *hobo*, and *bunk* for *buncombe*,[5] two altogether fit successors to *bum* for *bummer*. *Try*

1 In the Thorndike-Century Junior Dictionary; Chicago, 1935, edited by Dr. E. L. Thorndike, of Teachers College, Columbia, for the use of the young, the following are listed without any indication that they are not in good usage: *coon*, *pike*, *phone*, *gas*, *photo*, *movie*, *diner*, *sleeper*, *auto*, *smoker*, *bum*, *drape* and *knicker*. But *possum* is stated to be in use only " in common talk," and *cuss*, *draw*, *talkie*, *flu*, *pep* and *memo* are omitted altogether.

2 See College Words and Phrases, by E. H. Babbitt, *Dialect Notes*, Vol. II, Pt. I, 1900.

3 A long list of such forms is in Clipped Words, by Elisabeth Wittmann, *Dialect Notes*, Vol. IV, Pt. II, 1914.

4 In 1918 William C. D'Arcy, then president of a national association of advertising clubs, condemned the use of *ad* in high, astounding terms. " It is," he said, " the language of bootblacks, and is beneath the dig-

nity of men of the advertising profession." In 1925 Robert H. Cornell, executive secretary of an advertising men's convention held at Houston, Tex., " asked for the coöperation of the newspapers of Houston, the local advertisers, and all local organizations that have anything to do with the convention to avoid use of the abbreviation in all printed matter and letters going out in connection with the convention." See *Associated Advertising*, Jan., 1925. But *Associated Advertising* was forced to add that " many advertising clubs throughout the United States are commonly called *Ad-Clubs*, some of them even using the abbreviation on their letterheads, in their constitutions and by-laws, and in literature which they send out."

5 *Bunk* seems to have come in about 1910. It was first listed in the Addendum to Webster's New International Dictionary in 1918. The definite article often precedes it.

for *trial*, as in "He made a *try* at it," is also making progress, though only, so far, on the lower levels.

All the other historical processes of word-formation are to be observed among the new American nouns. There is, for example, a large stock of blends in the current vocabulary. A number of such words, of course, are in Standard English, *e.g.*, Lewis Carroll's *chortle* (from *chuckle* and *snort*), *squawk* (from *squeal* and *squall*), *dumbfound* (from *dumb* and *confound*) and *luncheon* (from *lunch* and *nuncheon*, the first going back to the Sixteenth Century and the second to the Fourteenth), but American began to make contributions at an early date, *e.g.*, *gerrymander* (from *Gerry* and *salamander*, *c.* 1812), and it has been supplying English with others ever since, *e.g.*, *cablegram* (from *cable* and *telegram*) and *electrolier* (*electric* and *chandelier*). A few additional examples will suffice: *boost* (*boom* and *hoist*, and maybe *boast*),[1] *Aframerican* (*African* and *American*), *Amerind* (*American* and *Indian*),[2] *hellenium* (*Hell* and *millennium*), *pulmotor* (*pulmonary* and *motor*) and *travelogue* (*travel* and *monologue*).[3] Many words of this class are trade names,

1 See *Boost*, by Klara H. Collitz, *American Speech*, Sept., 1926. Thornton traced *boost* to 1825 and *to boost* to 1826.

2 *Aframerican* was invented by Sir Harry Johnston, but remains a rarity in England. *Amerind*, which preceded it, was first used in the publications of the Bureau of American Ethnology, *c.* 1900. Dr. Robert H. Lowie tells me that he has heard that "it developed from merging the two abbreviations, *Amer.* and *Ind.*, which figured on the labels of specimens in the National Museum." Dr. Frank H. Vizetelly says in How to Use English; New York, 1932, p. 70, that it was coined by Major J. W. Powell of the Bureau of American Ethnology in 1899, first as *Amerindian* and then in the contracted form.

3 Burton Holmes, the lecturer, wrote to me as follows on Jan. 16, 1935: "In 1904 we planned an invasion of London with our *lectures* – a word that repels the ticket-buyer. My late manager, Louis Francis Brown, worried himself sick over the problem. When he came out of his pneumonia delirium he murmured weakly, 'Eureka! *Travelogue!*', and we proceeded to broadcast the word in our publicity. Later, the late Dr. [R. R.] Bowker [1848–1933] wrote us that he was the coiner of the word, and submitted circulars of an earlier date in which it was used thus: 'Each of Dr. Bowker's lectures is a complete *travelogue of* ——.' He had never used the word in any other way. We never saw it in print until he sent his circular. We were the first to give it any important publicity. Then everybody borrowed it, and we dropped it for *travel-revue*, *screen-journey*, and other inventions of our own. I have heard *pianologues*, *naturelogues* and other shockers." To these *organlog*, used in the movies, may be added. Mr. Holmes seems to have made an error of a year in the date of his début in London. The Supplement to the Oxford Dictionary gives the following from the London *Daily Chronicle* of April 16, 1903: "Mr.

made of initials or other parts of corporation names, *e.g.*, *socony* (*Standard Oil Company of New York*),[1] *ampico* (*American Piano Company*), *nabisco* (*National Biscuit Company*), or by other devices, *e.g.*, *bromo-seltzer* (*bromide* and *seltzer*) and *japalac* (*Japanese* and *lacquer*).[2] To the same class belong such blends as *Bancamerica* and *Bancorporation*. The American advertiser is also a very diligent manufacturer of wholly new terms, and many of his coinages, *e.g.*, *vaseline*,[3] *cellophane*, *carborundum*, *pianola*, *kotex*, *victrola*, *uneeda*, *listerine*,[4] *postum*, *lux*, and *kodak* [5] are quite as familiar

---

Burton Holmes, an American entertainer new to London, delivered last evening the first of a series of *travelogues*."

1 The oil men seem to be especially fond of such blends. See Trade Names in the Petroleum Industry, by Dora Lee Brauer, *American Speech*, April, 1935.

2 See Blends: Their Relation to English Word Formation, by Louise Pound; Heidelberg, 1914; Some New Portmanteau Words, by Robert Withington, *Philological Quarterly*, April, 1930; More Portmanteau Coinages, by the same, *American Speech*, Feb., 1932; Dickensian and Other Blends, by the same, *American Speech*, Oct., 1933; Blends, by Steven T. Byington, *American Speech*, Oct., 1927; Blend-Words in English, by Harold Wentworth; Ithaca, N. Y., 1933; Iteratives, Blends and Streckformen, by F. A. Wood, *Modern Philology*, Oct., 1911; Some English Blends, by the same, *Modern Language Notes*, June, 1912; On Blendings of Synonymous or Cognate Expressions in English, by G. A. Bergström, Lund (Sweden), 1906.

3 *Vaseline* was coined by Robert A. Chesebrough in 1870 or thereabout. It was made of the German *wasser*, meaning water, and the Greek *elaion*, meaning oil. Mr. Chesebrough was of the opinion that "petroleum is produced by the decomposition of water in the earth, and the union of the hydrogen thus evolved with the carbon of certain rocks, under the influence of heat

and pressure." (Private communication from Mr. T. J. Dobbins, secretary of the Chesebrough Manufacturing Company, March 15, 1935). *Vaseline* now appears in all the German and French dictionaries, but all rights to the name are still vested in the Chesebrough Company. Its original trade-mark was renewed on July 25, 1905, and upheld by a decree of the U. S. District Court for the Southern District of New York, May 26, 1933. It was similarly upheld in England by the Court of Appeal in 1902. *Vaseline* is now in most of the Continental languages.

4 *Listerine*, of course, is derived from the name of Lord Lister, the English surgeon who brought in aseptic surgery, but it was coined in the United States. Lord Lister objected to the use of his name, but in vain.

5 *Kodak* was coined by George Eastman, inventor of the camera, and he registered it as a trade-mark on Sept. 4, 1888. Its origin is described in George Eastman, by Carl W. Ackerman; New York, 1930. The *k* was suggested by the fact that it was the first letter of his mother's family name. *Kodak* has got into all the Continental languages. In October, 1917, the Verband Deutscher Amateurphotographen-Vereine was moved to issue the following warning: "Wer von einem *Kodak* spricht und nur allgemein eine photographische Kamera meint, bedenkt nicht, dass er mit der Weiterver-

to all Americans as *tractor* or *soda-mint,* and have come into general acceptance as common nouns. Dr. Louise Pound has made an interesting study of these artificial trade-names.[1] They fall, she finds, into a number of well-defined classes. There are those that are simply derivatives from proper names, *e.g., listerine, postum;* the blends, *e.g., jap-a-lac, locomobile, cuticura;* the extensions with common suffixes, *e.g., alabastine, protectograph, dictograph, orangeade, crispette, pearline;* the extensions with new or fanciful suffixes, *e.g., resinol, thermos, shinola, sapolio, lysol, neolin, crisco;* the diminutives, *e.g., cascaret, wheatlet, chiclet;* the simple compounds, *e.g., palmolive, spearmint, peptomint, autocar;* the blends made of proper names, *e.g., oldsmobile, hupmobile, valspar;* the blends made of parts of syllables or simple initials, *e.g., reo, nabisco;* the terms involving substitutions, *e.g., triscuit;* and the arbitrary formations, *e.g., kodak, tiz, kotex,*[2] *vivil.* Brander Matthews once published an Horatian ode, of unknown authorship, made up of such inventions:

> Chipeco thermos dioxygen, temco sonora tuxedo
> Resinol fiat bacardi, camera ansco wheatena;
> Antiskid pebeco calox, oleo tyco barometer
> Postum nabisco!
> Prestolite arco congoleum, karo aluminum kryptok,
> Crisco balopticon lysol, jello bellans, carborundum!
> Ampico clysmic swoboda, pantasote necco britannica
> Encyclopaedia?[3]

One of the words here used is not American, but Italian, *i.e., fiat,* a blend made of the initials of Fabbrica Italiano Automobili Torino,

breitung dieses Wortes die deutsche Industrie zugunsten der amerikanisch-englischen schädigt." Despite this warning, *kodak* is in all the more recent German (and French) dictionaries. In American there are a number of familiar derivatives, *e.g., to kodak, kodaker, kodak-fiend.*

1 Word-Coinage and Modern Trade Names, *Dialect Notes,* Vol. IV, Pt. I, 1913. See also Robots of Language, by Henry Bellamann, *Yale Review,* Sept., 1929.

2 In Trade-Name Suffixes, *American Speech,* July, 1927, Walter E. Myers calls attention to the popularity of *-ex* and *-tex.* He cites, among other familiar trade-terms, *cutex, pyrex, kleenex,* and *celotex.* He sur-

mises that *-tex* may owe something to *texture.* The etymology of some of these names is obvious, but others are somewhat puzzling. *Pyrex,* a name for glass ovenware, was not suggested by the Greek *pyra,* a hearth, but by the humble English word *pie.* The first baking-dish brought out was a pie-plate. For this I am indebted to Mr. William H. Curtiss, vice-president of the Corning Glass Works, Corning, N. Y.

3 The Advertiser's Artful Aid, *Bookman,* Feb., 1919. See also Word-Coinage, by Leon Mead; New York, n.d., and Burgess Unabridged, by Gelett Burgess; New York, 1914.

but most of the others are quite familiar to all Americans. Says
Matthews:

> Only a few of them would evoke recognition from an Englishman; and
> what a Frenchman or a German would make out of the eight lines is beyond
> human power even to guess. Corresponding words have been devised in
> France and in Germany, but only infrequently; and apparently the invention
> of trade-mark names is not a customary procedure on the part of foreign
> advertisers. The British, although less affluent in this respect than we are, seem
> to be a little more inclined to employ the device than their competitors on
> the Continent. Every American, traveling on the railways which converge
> upon London, must have experienced a difficulty in discovering whether the
> station at which his train has paused is Stoke Poges or Bovril, Chipping Norton
> or Mazzawattee. None the less it is safe to say that the concoction of a similar
> ode by the aid of the trade-mark words invented in the British Isles would
> be a task of great difficulty on account of the paucity of terms sufficiently
> artificial to bestow the exotic remoteness which is accountable for the aroma
> of the American " ode."

New words, of course, are no more produced by the folk than are
new ballads: they are the inventions of concrete individuals, some of
whom can be identified. The elder Roosevelt was responsible, either
as coiner or as propagator, for many compounds that promise to
survive, *e.g.*, *strenuous-life, nature-faker, pussy-footer, weasle-word,
100% American, hyphenated-American, Ananias-Club, big-stick* and
embalmed-beef. Scofflaw was coined simultaneously in 1924 by
Henry Irving Shaw, of Shawsheen Village, Mass., and Miss Kate L.
Butler, of Dorchester in the same State.[1] *Debunking,* and its verb,
to debunk, were launched by William E. Woodward in his book,
" Bunk," in 1923. Both have been taken over by the English, though
protests against them, often bitter in tone, still appear occasionally
in the English newspapers.[2] *Moron* was proposed by Dr. Henry H.
Goddard in 1910 to designate a feeble-minded person of a mental age

[1] Late in 1923 Delcevare King, a rich
Prohibitionist of Quincy, offered a
prize of $200 for the best word to
apply to "the lawless drinker to
stab awake his conscience." Mr.
King received more than 25,000
suggestions. The announcement
that *scofflaw,* suggested by both
Mr. Shaw and Miss Butler, had
won was made on Jan. 15, 1924.
The word came into immediate
currency, and survived until the
collapse of Prohibition.

[2] For example, A. E. Sullivan wrote

to the London *Daily Telegraph,*
March 2, 1935: " The origin of *to
debunk* is doubtless the same as
that of American jargon in general
— the inability of an ill-educated
and unintelligent democracy to assimilate long words. Its intrusion in
our own tongue is due partly to the
odious novelty of the word itself,
and partly to the prevailing fear
that to write exact English nowadays is to be put down as a pedant
and a prig."

of from eight to twelve years; it was formally adopted by the American Association for the Study of the Feeble-minded in May of that year, and immediately came into wide use. In Chicago, at the time of the Leopold-Loeb trial in 1924, the local newspapers began to misuse it in the sense of sexual pervert, and it has retained that meaning locally ever since.[1] Many new words, launched with impressive ceremony, have only short lives as nonce-words, or fail altogether. In his "Fifty Suggestions" (c. 1845) Edgar Allan Poe proposed that *suspectful* be used to differentiate between the two meanings of *suspicious,* one who suspects and one to be suspected, but though the word is in "Webster's New International" (1934) it is marked "now rare," and no one uses it. Most of Walt Whitman's inventions went the same way. On March 6, 1926, the Pennsylvania Society for the Prevention of Cruelty to Animals awarded a prize to Mrs. M. McIlvaine Bready, of Mickleton, N. J., for *pitilacker,* and tried to establish it in the sense of one cruel to animals, but it failed to make the success of *scofflaw.* In "The Mighty Medicine" (1929) the late Dr. Franklin H. Giddings proposed *taboobery* and *tomtomery,* but neither seized the public fancy. During the heyday of the I.W.W. (1912–1920) one of its chief propagandists was a writer calling himself T-Bone Slim; he wrote for most of the fugitive organs of the movement, but especially for the *Industrial Worker.* He invented many neologisms, and some of them were popular for a time, but only *brisbanality,* signifying a platitudinous utterance by Arthur Brisbane of the Hearst papers (or, at all events, one thought to be platitudinous by radicals), has survived. In February, 1927, the *Forum* issued a general call for new words, and during the months following many were proposed by its readers, but not one of them seems to have got into the American vocabulary.[2]

The formation of artificial words of the *scalawag, lallapaloosa* and *rambunctious* class goes on constantly. Some of them are blends: *grandificent* (from *grand* and *magnificent*) and *sodalicious* (from

1 *Moron* is the name of a character in Molière's La Princesse d'Elide, 1664. But Dr. Goddard got it from the Greek.
2 Some of them deserved a better fate, e.g., *sothers* (brothers and sisters), *megaphonia* (the habit of talking too loud), *hesh* (for he and she), and *radiorator.* In Nov., 1935 the readers of *Word Study* (published at Springfield, Mass., by the publishers of Webster's New International Dictionary, and edited by Max J. Herzberg of Newark, N. J.) were invited to send in invented words. Some of those received were *cacogen* (an anti-social person) *pajamboree,* and *Gersteinian* (from *Gertrude Stein*).

soda and *delicious*); others are made up of common roots and grotesque affixes: *whangdoodle, splendiferous* and *peacharino;* others are
arbitrary reversals, as *sockdolager* from *doxologer,* and yet others
are stretch-forms or mere extravagant inventions: *scallywampus,
dingus, doodad, supergobsloptious* and *floozy.*[1] Many of these are
devised by advertisement writers or college students and belong
properly to slang, but there is a steady movement of selected specimens into the common vocabulary. The words in *-doodle,* e.g.,
whangdoodle and *monkey-doodle,* hint at German influences, and
those in *-ino* may owe something to Italian or maybe to Spanish.
Such suffixes are sometimes worked heavily. The first to come into
fashion in the United States was apparently *-ery,* which appeared
in *printery* in 1638. When *beanery* followed it I do not know, but
it must have been before the end of the next century. *Grocery* (for
grocery-store) has been traced back to 1806, and *groggery* to 1822.
Bakery and *bindery* also seem to be American. In late years many
congeners have appeared, e.g., *boozery, bootery* and *breadery. Condensery* is used in the West to indicate a place where milk is con-
densed. *Creamery,* though it has now got into English, is listed in the
Oxford Dictionary as " first used in U. S." Dr. Louise Pound reports
hashery, drinkery and *drillery,* the last signifying a cramming-school
for the Civil Service, and E. S. Hills adds *cakery, car-washery, doughnutery, lunchery, mendery* (a place where clothes are mended), and
eatery.[2] In Three Rivers, Mich., so I am told by a correspondent,
there is a *shoe-fixery.* In Pasadena, Calif., there is a *hattery,* in South
Pasadena a *cyclery,* in Los Angeles a *nuttery* and a *chowmeinery,*
and near San Francisco a *squabery.*[3]

Cafeteria, as everyone knows, has produced an enormous progeny,
and some of its analogues are very curious. From the discussions of
the word that have appeared in *American Speech* since 1926 I cull
the following: *restauranteria, garmenteria, shaveteria* (a place where
shaving utensils are supplied to wayfarers), *shoeteria, resteteria* (a

---

1 See Some English Stretch-Forms,
by Louise Pound, *Dialect Notes,*
Vol. IV, Pt. I, 1913. Also, Terms of
Approbation and Eulogy in American Dialect Speech, by Elsie L.
Warnock, *Dialect Notes,* Vol. IV,
Pt. I, 1913, and Notes on the Vernacular, by Louise Pound, *American Mercury,* Oct., 1924, p. 236.

2 Vogue Affixes in Present-Day
Word Coinage, by Louise Pound,
Dialect Notes, Vol. V, Pt. I, 1918;
The Irradiation of Certain Suffixes,
by E. C. Hills, *American Speech,*
Oct., 1925.

3 *American Speech,* April, 1935, p.
154.

rest-room), *chocolateria, sodateria, fruiteria, radioteria, bobateria* (where hair is bobbed), *valeteria, marketeria, caketeria, candyteria, casketeria* (an undertaker's shop), *drugteria, basketeria, cleaneteria, groceteria* (with the variants *grocerteria* and *groceryteria*), *healtheteria, farmateria, mototeria* (a *grocereteria* on wheels), *cashateria, wrecketeria* (a bone-yard for old motor-cars), *luncheteria, haberteria, hatateria, kalfeteria* or *kafateria*,[1] *honeyteria, smoketeria,* and even *drygoodsteria*. A watchful correspondent, Dr. Harley K. Croessmann, reports a *millinteria* on Sheridan road in Chicago and a *scarfeteria* in Randolph street, and I myself, in 1928, encountered a *spaghetteria* in West 46th street, New York. *Cafeteria* is probably of Spanish origin, but when and where it got into American is still in dispute. Phillips Barry has found it in a dictionary of Cuban-Spanish published in 1862 [2] and other investigators point to analogues in Standard Spanish, in common use along the Mexican border, *e.g.,* *barberia* (barber-shop), *carniceria* (butcher-shop) and *panaderia* (baker-shop). In Cuban-Spanish the word means "a shop where coffee is sold." It did not get into any American dictionary until 1918, but it had been in general use in Southern California for at least ten years before. I have, however, received a caveat to the California claim to priory from a Chicago correspondent whose name I have unfortunately mislaid. "A Chicago man," he says, "was planning to open a new lunchroom in that city, with the new feature of the guests serving themselves. He wanted a new and appropriate name for it and applied to my cousin, who had lived in Buenos Aires. This cousin suggested *cafeteria*, which was adopted. It should be accented on the penultimate, but the patrons immediately moved the accent one place forward. This was about the year 1900." Another correspondent, Mr. Herbert Spencer Jackson, of Los Angeles, informs me that he remembers seeing a *cafeteria* in South LaSalle street, Chicago, "about 1895." There has been an extensive discussion of the word in *American Speech* and elsewhere, but some gaps in its history remain.[3]

1 At first glance I suspect that the *kalf-* and *kaf-* came from *kaif,* an interesting and instructive American form of *café*. But diligent inquiry revealed the fact that their origin was in *calf*. Both words indicate a shoe-store.

2 *Cafeteria, American Speech,* Oct.,

1927. The dictionary is E. Pichardo's Diccionario Provincial . . . de Vozes Cubanas, published at Havana.

3 See especially *Basketeria* and the Meaning of the Suffix *-teria,* by J. M. Steadman, Jr., *American Speech,* June, 1930. Mr. Steadman distin-

Other suffixes that have produced interesting forms are -*ette*, -*dom*, -*ster*, -*ite*, -*ist*, -*itis*, -*ician*, -*orium*, -*ogist* and -*or*.[1] *Cellarette* has been in English for more than a century, but *kitchenette* is American, and so are *farmerette, conductorette, officerette* and a number of other analogous words. Logan Pearsall Smith says in " The English Language " (1912) that -*dom* is being replaced in English by -*ness*, and that the effort made by Thomas Carlyle and others to revive it during the Nineteenth Century was so far a failure that only *boredom* (*c.* 1850) made any headway. But in the United States the affix retains a great deal of its old life, and has produced a long list of words, *e.g., sportdom, moviedom, flapperdom, dogdom, turfdom, newspaperdom, Elkdom, filmdom* and *crookdom*.[2] Now, as in the past, -*ster* has an opprobrious significance, and so its chief products are such words as *gangster, mobster, dopester, ringster, funster, shyster* and *speedster*. From -*ist* we have *monologuist, receptionist, columnist, trapezist, manicurist, electragist, behaviorist* and a number of others.[3] From -*ician* we have the lovely *mortician* and its

guishes three meanings for -*teria:* 1. A place where articles are sold on the self-service plan; 2. A place where certain articles are sold without the self-service feature; and 3. A place where certain services are rendered — by others, not by the customer himself. Other interesting notes on the word are in the Barry paper just quoted, and in The Pronunciation of *Cafeteria*, by E. C. Hills, *American Speech*, Nov., 1926; More *Cafeteria* Progeny, by Mamie Meredith, the same, Dec., 1927; *Barberia*, by Phillip Davis, the same, Aug., 1928; and The English Language in America, by George Philip Krapp, Vol. I; New York, 1925, p. 143.

1 Of these, -*ite* and -*ist* go back to the Sixteenth Century, and -*ette* to the Fifteenth. See English Words With Native Roots and With Greek, Latin, or Romance Suffixes, by George A. Nicholson, *University of Chicago Linguistic Studies in Germanic*, No. III, 1916.

2 In Three Hard-Worked Suffixes, *American Speech*, Feb., 1927, Josephine M. Burnham says that -*dom* has acquired four significances in

American. First, it means " realm or jurisdiction," as in *bookdom, playdom* and *traveldom*. Second, it means " state or condition," as in *pauperdom, stardom* and *gypsydom*. Third, it means " those of a certain type or character," as in *fandom, flapperdom* and *crookdom*. And fourth, it means " those interested in a given thing," as in *Shrinedom, flowerdom* and *puzzledom*.

3 *Receptionist* is used by English theologians to denote one who believes that " the bread and wine remain only bread and wine after consecration, but that, together with them, the faithful communicant really receives the body and blood of Christ." In the sense of one who receives the customers of a photographer or the patients of a physician or dentist it is American only. See the New York *Times*, Section 9, Oct. 5, 1924. *Manicurist* appeared in American in the 90's; it is still rare in England, where *manicure* is preferred. *Behaviorist* seems to have been invented by Dr. John B. Watson, 1913. *Electragist* is defined in Webster's New International (1934) as " one who installs

The Language Today

179

brothers,[1] *beautician, cosmetician* and *bootician,* to say nothing of *whooptician,* a college cheer-leader. In Hollywood they also speak of *dialogicians.* From *-itis* come *motoritis, golfitis, radioitis, Americanitis* and others after their kind.[2] From *-orium* we have *beautorium, healthatorium, preventorium, barberatorium, bobatorium* (apparently a more refined form of *bobateria*), *lubritorium* (a place where motor-cars are greased), *infantorium, hatatorium, motortorium, odditorium* (a side-show), *pantorium* or *pantatorium* (a pants-pressing parlor), *printorium, restatorium* or *restorium, shavatorium, suitatorium* and *pastorium.*[3] And from *-ogist* and *-or* come *boyologist* (a specialist in the training or entertainment of boys), *truckologist, mixologist* (a bartender), *clockologist* and *hygiologist,*[4] and *realtor, furnitor, chiropractor, avigator*[5] and *merchantor* (a member of the Merchants' Bureau of a Chamber of Commerce). In the case of *motorcade, autocade, camelcade* and *aerocade,* all sug-

---

electrical apparatus and sells electrical goods, and who is a member of the Association of Electragists International." It is thus a brother to *realtor,* noticed in Chapter VI, Section 6. See *American Speech,* April, 1928, p. 351, and March, 1926, p. 350. A recent novelty is *canitist,* apparently from the Latin *canities,* signifying grey hair. It is used by beauticians who specialize in "tinting hair for discriminating women." I owe its discovery and its etymology to Dr. Isaac Goldberg.

1 It is dealt with at length in Chapter VI, Section 6.
2 Josephine M. Burnham, in Three Hard-Worked Suffixes, above cited, gives some appalling specimens, e.g., *conventionitis, headlineitis, crosswordpuzzleitis, ain't-supposed-to-itis, let-George-do-it-itis,* and *Phi-Beta-Kappa-itis.*
3 *Pastorium* is widely used in the South, especially among the Baptists, in place of *parsonage.* According to Bernard M. Peebles (*Pastorium, American Speech,* Dec., 1926, p. 159) the word was invented, c. 1898, by the Rev. Morton Bryan Wharton, D.D., pastor of the Freemason Street Baptist Church, Nor-

folk, Va. "News reports on the invention," says Mr. Peebles, "brought forth editorial approval in several leading Baptist journals. One hardy brother attacked it in the Baltimore *Baptist,* only to be squelched by a 'scholarly article' from Professor Carroll, then of the Johns Hopkins." I am unable to identify Professor Carroll. In 1898 Dr. Wharton published a book of poems, "Pictures From A *Pastorium*," the first poem in which was called "The *Pastorium*." I quote one stanza:

The place where congregations meet
  We style an *auditorium;*
The place where pastors make their seat
  Should, then, be called *pastorium.*

See also Irradiations of Certain Suffixes, by E. C. Hills, *American Speech,* Oct., 1925.
4 For *boyology* see *American Speech,* Sept., 1927, p. 515. For *clockologist* see the same, June, 1927, p. 408.
5 For *avigator* see *American Speech,* Aug., 1928, p. 450. See also *Avigation,* by J. R. Killian, Jr., the same, Oct., 1928.

gested by *cavalcade*, a new suffix, *-cade*, seems to have come in.[1] Others have also begun to show themselves, *e.g.*, *-naper* (from *kidnaper*), as in *dognaper; -mobile* (from *automobile*), as in *health-mobile* (a motor-car driven about the country by health officers to instruct the yokelry in the elements of hygiene); *-iat*, as in *profes-soriat; -ee*, as in *donee*, *draftee* and *honoree;*[2] and *-thon* (from *marathon*), as in *walkathon, dancethon, reducathon* and *speedathon.*[3] The suffix *-ine* came in during the middle 80's, and seems to have been first hitched to *dude*, itself an American invention of 1883. But both *dude* and *dudine* are now obsolete save in the Far West, where they survive to designate the Easterners who come out to cavort on *dude-ranches* under the guidance of *dude-wranglers*. During the World War *patrioteer*, which had been in use in England at least as early as 1913, brought in various words in *-eer*, but only *fictioneer* shows any sign of surviving. About the same time *-ine* had a brief revival, producing *doctorine*, *actorine, chorine*, etc., but only the two last named are ever heard today.[4] Certain prefixes have come in for heavy service of late, *e.g.*, *anti-, super-, semi-* and *near-*. Words in *anti-* are numerous in English, but they seem to be even more numerous in American, especially in the field of politics. " If it were possible to collect the

1 It is denounced by R. S. G. in *American Speech*, Aug., 1930, p. 495. A letter by Garth Cate, printed in F. P. Adams's column in the New York *Herald Tribune*, June 29, 1931, ascribes the coining of *motorcade* to Lyle Abbott, automobile editor of the Phoenix (Ariz.) *Republican*, and fixes the date at 1912 or 1913. See The Earliest *Motorcade*, by W. L. Werner, *American Speech*, June, 1932, p. 388. Other notes on *motorcade* are in *American Speech*, Dec., 1930, p. 155; April, 1931, pp. 254 and 313, and Aug., 1931, p. 189; in *Modern Language Notes*, March, 1925, p. 189, and in *Notes and Queries*, April 19, 1924.
2 I am indebted here to Professor Atcheson L. Hench, of the University of Virginia, and to Vogue Affixes in Present-Day Word-Coinage, by Louise Pound, *Dialect Notes*, Vol. V, Pt. I, 1918.
3 The first use of *dance marathon* to

designate a long-distance dancing-match was in 1927. After a while the promoters introduced rest-periods, during which the dancers were free to walk about. In 1930 a promotor in Des Moines called such an ameliorated contest a *walkathon*, and the word quickly spread. I am indebted for this to Mr. Hal J. Ross of St. Louis, and to Mr. Don King, endurance-shows editor of the *Billboard* (Cincinnati). I have been informed by other authorities that the use of *walkathon* was encouraged by the passage of laws in some of the States forbidding dancing for more than eight hours on end. The cops, it appears, were easily persuaded that a *walkathon* was really a walking-match, which had no time limit.
4 See *Chorine*, by Louise Pound, *American Speech*, June, 1928, p. 368, and *Dudine*, by M. H. Dresen, the same, Aug., 1928.

material completely," says Allen Walker Read, "a 'History of Opposition Movements in America' could be written."[1] Read offers dozens of examples, beginning with *anti-Episcopalian* (1769) and *anti-Federalist* (1788) and running down to the present day. The list includes, of course, *anti-suffragist* (1886), which suffered the curious accident, in 1913 or thereabout, of losing its root and becoming simply *anti*. The numerous words in *near-* began to appear about 1900. George Horace Lorimer was writing of *near-seal* in "Letters of a Self-Made Merchant to His Son" in 1902, and soon thereafter the advertisements in the newspapers bristled with analogues, *e.g.*, *near-silk*, *near-antique*, *near-leather*, *near-mahogany*, *near-silver* and *near-porcelain*. A logical extension quickly produced *near-accident*, *near-champion*, *near-finish* and others after their kind, and in 1920 came *near-beer*, to flourish obscenely for thirteen long years and then sink into happy obsolescence. *Super-* has been very popular since 1920 or thereabout. It got a great lift when the movie press-agents began writing about *super-productions* and *super-films*, and various analogues have followed, *e.g.*, *super-highway*, *super-cabinet*, *super-criminal*, *super-gang* and *super-love*. The last signifies a kind of amour perfected by the virtuosi of Hollywood: it partakes of the characters of riot, delirium tremens and mayhem. Sometimes *super-* is employed to strengthen adjectives, as in *super-perfect* and *super-American*. H. W. Horwill, in his "Dictionary of Modern American Usage," says that *semi-* "is in much more frequent use in America than in England." He cites *semi-annual* (Eng. *half-yearly*), *semi-centennial* (Eng. *jubilee*), *semi-panic*, *semi-wild*, *semi-open-air*, *semi-national* and *semi-occasional*. There has been, of late, a heavy use of *air-*, as in the adjectives *air-cooled*, *air-conditioned*, *air-conscious* and *air-minded*, and the nouns *air-liner*, *air-rodeo* and *air-hostess*.[2] During the thirteen years of Prohibition *pre-Volstead* and *pre-war* threatened to bring in a flock of novelties in *pre-*, but the prefix seems to have died out of popularity.

All such neologisms, of course, find ready customers in the headline writers of the newspapers. But the exigencies of their arduous craft force them to give preference to the shorter ones, and they thus propagate back-formations more often than compounds. A veteran of the copy-desk has described their difficulties as follows:

1 The Scope of the American Dictionary, *American Speech*, Oct., 1933, p. 14.

2 Here I am again indebted to Professor Hench.

In writing the headline, the copy-reader must say what he has to say in a definite number of letters and spaces. If the headline has one or more lines — and this is the case at least 90% of the time — each line must balance so that it may be typographically pleasing to the reader's eye. The size of type and the width of column are also important considerations. Further, what is known as newspaper style may offer difficulties. Each newspaper has a set of rules peculiar to itself. On some papers each line of the head must end in a word of more than two letters and can never begin with a verb. No paper permits the splitting of a word from one line to another.[1]

The copy-reader accordingly makes heavy use of very short words, *e.g.*, *mob*, *probe*, *crash*, *pact*, *blast*, *chief* and *quiz*, and these words tend to be borrowed by the reporters who must submit to his whims and long for his authority and glory. Their way into the common speech thus comes easy. To most Americans, in fact, a legislative inquiry is no longer an *investigation* but a *probe*, and a *collision* is not a *collision* but a *crash*. So, again, any sort of contest or combat is a *clash* or *bout*, any reduction in receipts or expenditures is a *cut*, and all negotiations are *parleys* or *deals*. *Fiends* are so common in American criminology simply because the word itself is so short. English is naturally rich in very short nouns, but the copy-readers are not content with them as they stand: there are constant extensions of meaning. For example:

Ace. In the sense of expert or champion it came in during the World War. It has since been extended to mean any person who shows any ponderable proficiency in whatever he undertakes to do. I have encountered *ace* lawyers, *ace* radio-crooners and *ace* gynecologists in headlines.

Aid. Its military sense has been extended to include the whole field of human relations. Any subordinate is now an *aid*.

Balm. It now means any sort of indemnity or compensation. A derivative, *love-balm*, means damages paid to a deceived and deserted maiden.

Ban. All prohibitions are now *bans*.

Blast. It has quite displaced *explosion* in the headlines.

Boat. It now means any sort of craft, from the *Queen Mary* to a mud-scow.

Cache. This loan-word, one of the earliest borrowings of American from French, now signifies any sort of hidden store.

Car. It is rapidly displacing all the older synonyms for *automobile*, including even *auto*.

Chief. Any headman, whether political, pedagogical, industrial, military or ecclesiastical. I once encountered the headline *Church Chiefs Hold Parley* over a news item dealing with a meeting of the Sacred College.

Drive. Any concerted and public effort to achieve anything.

1 Headline Words, by Harold E. Rockwell, *American Speech*, Dec., 1926.

Edict. An almost universal synonym for *command, order, injunction* or *mandate.*

Envoy. It now signifies any sort of superior agent. *Ambassador* and *minister* are both too fat for the headlines.

Fete. Any celebration.

Gem. Any jewel.

Head. It means whatever *chief* means.

Hop. Any voyage by air.

Mecca. Any center of interest. *Mecca* has an *m* in it, and is thus troublesome to copy-readers, but it is still shorter than any other word signifying the same thing.

Plea. It means *request, petition, application, prayer, suit, demand* or *appeal.*

Row. Any sort of dispute.

Slate. Any programme, agenda, or list.

Snag. Any difficulty or impediment.

Solon. Any member of a law-making body.

Talk. Any discussion or conference.

In addition to these naturally short nouns many clipped forms are used constantly in headlines, *e.g., ad, confab, duo, exam, gas, isle, mart, photo* and *quake* (for *earthquake*). A *Japanese* is always a *Jap*, and the *Emperor of Japan* is very apt to shrink to *Jap Chief*. A *Russian* is often a *Russ*, and *Serb* commonly displaces *Serbian*. In the same way *Turk* displaces *Turkish*, *Norse* displaces *Norwegian*, and *Spaniard* becomes *don*. After Hitler's advent *Nazi* took the place of *German*. The popularity of *Hun* during the World War was no doubt largely due to its convenient brevity.[1] The shorter compounds are also used heavily, *e.g., clean-up, fire-bug, come-back* and *pre-war*.[2] Onomatopeia, of course, frequently enters into the

[1] It might be interesting to inquire how far the popularity of politicians and other public figures runs in proportion to the shortness of their names. I suspect that Mr. *Eden*, the English Foreign Secretary (1936), owes something to the fact that his name is not *Cholmondelay* or *Donoughmore*. The English newspapers have headlines more elastic than ours, but their contents-bills are just as crowded. In the case of politicians with long names abbreviations usually come into newspaper use, *e.g., T.R.* (the elder *Roosevelt*), *F.D.R.* (the younger), *C.B.* (Campbell Bannerman), and *L.G.* (Lloyd George). Sometimes nicknames take their place, *e.g., Cal* (Coolidge), *G.O.M.* (Grand Old Man, *i.e.,* Gladstone), and *Al* (Smith). Movie performers are commonly designated by their given names, or by abbreviations thereof, *e.g., Gloria* (Swanson), *Mary* (Pickford) and *Doug* (Fairbanks).

[2] More than 100 headline nouns are discussed in detail in Scribes Seek Snappy Synonyms, by Maurice Hicklin, *American Speech,* Dec., 1930. See also Newspaper English, by Francis F. Beirne, *American Speech,* Oct., 1926; The Art of the Copy-Reader, by Kittredge Wheeler, *American Mercury,* July, 1932; The Attributive Noun Becomes Cancerous, by Steven T. Byington, *American Speech,* Oct., 1926; and Newspaper Headlines, by George O. Curme, *American*

matter. "Hemmed in by many restrictions," says Mr. Rockwell, " and ever seeking a way out, the copy-reader, in addition to his constant use of short words, his peculiar phrasing, his bizarre syntax, and his lopping off of all unnecessary sentence members, has adopted, whenever possible, words which not only express the meaning which he wishes to convey but also connote the quality of sound. He believes that *crash* or *smash* will signify more to the reader than *accident*. So with *slash, blast, clash, flay, flit, fling, flee, hurtle, hurl, plunge, ram* and *spike*." This explosive headline terminology seems so natural today that we forget it is of recent growth. It did not come in, in fact, until the era of the Spanish-American War, and the memorable fight for circulation between Joseph Pulitzer and William R. Hearst. The American newspaper headline of the 70's and 80's was very decorous. The aim of its writer was to keep all its parts within the bounds of a single sentence, and inasmuch as it sometimes ran halfway down the column he was inevitably forced to resort to long words and a flowery style. That same flowery style appeared in the text of what was printed below it. Dean Alford's denunciation of the Newspaper English of 1870 [1] described Newspaper American also. "You never read," he said, " of a *man*, or a *woman*, or a *child*. A man is an *individual*, or a *person*, or a *party*; a woman is a *female*, or, if unmarried, a *young person*; a child is a *juvenile*, and children *en masse* are expressed by that most odious term, *the rising generation*." It was against such gaudy flowers of speech that William Cullen Bryant's famous *Index Expurgatorius* was mainly directed. We owe their disappearance, in part, to Charles A. Dana, of the New York *Sun*, who produced the first newspaper on earth that was decently written, but also, in part, to Pulitzer and Hearst, who not only brought in the fire-alarm headline-writer, but also the comic-strip artist. The latter has been a very diligent maker of terse and dramatic words. In his grim comments upon the horrible calamities which befall his characters he not only employs many ancients of English speech, *e.g.*, *slam, bang, quack, meeou, smash* and *bump*, but also invents novelties of his own, *e.g.*, *zowie, bam, socko, yurp, plop, wow, wam, glug, oof, ulk, whap, bing, flooie* and *grrr*. Similar

---

Speech, April, 1929. In Newspaper Headlines: A Study in Linguistic Methods, by Heinrich Straumann; London, 1935, the grammar of headline English is discussed with abysmal learning. Unfortunately, the author deals only with English headlines.

1 The Queen's English, 3rd ed., 1870.

onomatopeic forms of an older date are listed in the Supplement to the Oxford Dictionary as Americanisms, *e.g.*, *blah, wow, bust* and *flipflop.*[1] All these, and a great many like words, are familiar to every American schoolboy. Their influence, and that of the headline vocabulary, upon the general American vocabulary must be very potent, and no doubt they also have some influence upon American ways of thinking. Says a recent writer:

> I am morally certain that *probes* would not be so important a part of the activities of our government if the headline writers had not discovered that word. People generally do not become excited about a thing called an *investigation*, an *inquiry*, a *hearing*, or whatever other name such an interrogatory affair might be called by. But a *probe* is an interesting thing. The newspapers, which seek what is interesting, play up the *probe*, and the *prober* spends his time thinking up new *probes*, so that he can get into the headlines.[2]

" The headline," said the late E. P. Mitchell, for many years editor of the New York *Sun*, "is more influential than a hundred chairs of rhetoric in the shaping of future English [3] speech. There is no livelier perception than in the newspaper offices of the incalculable havoc being wreaked upon the language by the absurd circumstance that only so many millimeters of type can go into so many millimeters' width of column. Try it yourself and you will understand why the fraudulent use of so many compact but misused verbs, nouns and adjectives is being imposed on the coming generation. In its worst aspect, headline English is the yellow peril of the language." [4] " This," says G. K. Chesterton, " is one of the evils produced by that passion for compression and compact information which possesses so many ingenious minds in America. Everybody can see how an entirely new system of grammar, syntax, and even language has been invented to fit the brevity of headlines. Such brevity, so far from being the soul of wit, is even the death of meaning; and certainly the death of logic." [5]

The old American faculty for making picturesque compounds

1 See Exclamations in American Speech, by E. C. Hills, *Dialect Notes*, Vol. V, Pt. VII, 1924. This is an almost exhaustive and very valuable paper. See also The English of the Comic Cartoon, by Helen Trace Tysell, *American Speech*, Feb., 1935, especially p. 50.
2 Ex Libris, by The Bookman, Baltimore *Evening Sun*, June 16, 1923.

The Bookman is Hamilton Owens, editor of the paper.
3 He meant, of course, American.
4 Quoted by Brander Matthews in Newspaper English, 1920, reprinted in Essays on English; New York, 1921.
5 *G.K.'s Weekly* (London), May 2, 1931.

shows no sign of abating today. Many of them come in on the latitude of slang, *e.g., road-louse, glad-hand, hop-head, rahrah-boy, coffin-nail* (cigarette), *hot-spot, bug-house, hang-out* and *pin-head,* and never attain to polite usage, but others gradually make their way, *e.g., chair-warmer, canned-music, sob-sister, bell-hop, come-back, white-wings* and *rabble-rouser,* and yet others are taken into the language almost as soon as they appear, *e.g., college-widow* (1887), *sky-scraper* [1] and *rubber-neck* (*c.* 1890),[2] *loan-shark* (*c.* 1900), *high-brow* and *low-brow* (*c.* 1905),[3] *hot-dog* (*c.* 1905),[4] *joy-ride* (*c.* 1908), *love-nest* and *jay-walker* (*c.* 1920), and *brain-trust* (1932).[5] *Steam-roller,* in the political sense, was first used by Oswald F. Schuette, then Washington correspondent of the Chicago *Inter-Ocean,* to describe the rough methods used to procure the nomination of W. H. Taft as the Republican presidential candidate in 1908. *Spell-binder,* which came in during the 80's, is simply a derivative of an old English verb, *to spellbind. Fat-cat,* signifying a rich man

1 "*Sky-scraper*," says Charles White in a letter to the London *Morning Post,* Jan. 26, 1935, "was applied to Queen Anne's Mansions [an apartment-house in Queen Anne's Gate, London, near St. James's Park] in the early 80's, before American cities had any structures of their present variety." But this seems to have been a nonce-use, not generally imitated. The Oxford Dictionary's first quotation is from the Boston (Mass.) *Journal,* Nov., 1891. *Sky-scraper* had been used to designate a sky-sail (1794), a tall horse (1826), an exaggerated story (1841), and a tall man (1857).

2 *Rubber-neck* is described by Prof. J. Y. T. Greig, the Scottish philologian, in Breaking Priscian's Head; London, 1929, p. 83, as "one of the best words ever coined."

3 The date here is a guess. The first example in the Supplement to the Oxford Dictionary is dated 1908. *Low-brow* followed soon afterward. *Mezzo-brow* and *mizzen-brow* came later.

4 This is another guess. The inventor of the hot-dog was the late Harry Mozely Stevens, caterer at the New York Polo Grounds. The sale of

sausages in rolls was introduced in this country many years ago, but Stevens was the first to heat the roll and add various condiments. According to his obituary in the New York *Herald Tribune,* May 4, 1934, this was in 1900. But sausages in rolls were then called simply *wienies* or *frankfurters.* Stevens himself used to say that the late T. A. Dorgan (Tad), the sports cartoonist, coined *hot-dog,* but he was apparently uncertain about the date. The name was suggested, of course, by the folk-belief that *wienies* were made of dog-meat. In 1913 the Coney Island Chamber of Commerce passed a resolution forbidding the use of *hot-dog* on signs at Coney Island. See The *Hot-Dog* Mystery (editorial) in the New York *Herald Tribune,* June 2, 1931.

5 According to Henry F. Pringle (*New Yorker,* June 30, 1934) *brain-trust* "was invented by James M. Kiernan of the New York *Times* in the Summer of 1932 to describe the economists and other experts who were active in the [presidential] campaign" of Franklin D. Roosevelt.

willing to make a heavy contribution to a party campaign fund, appeared in 1920 or thereabout, and is still struggling for recognition. Many of the most popular of American compounds are terms of disparagement, e.g., *bone-head, clock-watcher, hash-slinger, four-flusher, rough-neck* (which goes back to David Crockett's time, and was used by him in "Colonel Crockett in Texas," 1836, but did not come into popularity until the beginning of the present century), *leather-neck, gospel-shark, back-number, cheap-skate, cow-college, stand-patter, lounge-lizard, do-gooder, kill-joy, lame-duck* and *chin-music*. Most of these linger below the salt, but now and then one of them edges its way into more or less decorous usage.[1]

The etymology and history of many common American nouns remain undetermined. *Phoney*, which is both a noun and an adjective, offers an example. Some of the earlier editions of Webster sought to relate it to *funny*, but in "Webster's New International" (1934) it is simply put down as "slang," without any attempt to guess at its origin. Again, its sources have been sought in *telephone*,[2] but this seems very far-fetched. The most probable etymology derives it from *Forney*, the name of a manufacturer of cheap jewelry. He made a specialty of supplying brass rings, in barrel lots, to street peddlers, and such rings, among the fraternity, came to be known as *Forney* rings. The extension of the designation to all cheap jewelry and its modification to *phoney* followed. Today, anything not genuine is *phoney* in the common American speech, and a person suspected of false pretenses is a *phoney*. The first example of *movie* in the Supplement to the Oxford Dictionary is dated 1913, but the word was already six or seven years old by that time. Who invented it no one knows. In those days, as now, the magnates of the movie industry disliked the word, and sought to find some more dignified substitute for it. In 1912 the Essanay Company offered a prize of $25 for such a substitute, and it was won by Edgar Strakosch with *photoplay*. But though *photoplay* became the title of a very successful fan magazine, it never displaced *movie*.[3] When the talking-pictures came in, in 1924, they were first called *speakies*, but *talkies*

---

1 See Terms of Disparagement, by Marie Gladys Hayden, *Dialect Notes*, Vol. IV, Pt. III, 1906.
2 "A statement is *phoney*," said an editorial in the Boston *Traveler*, Feb. 20, 1922, "if it is like the prac-

tical jokes and false impersonations that are so frequently perpetrated over the telephone."
3 See Movie Jargon, by Terry Ramsaye, *American Speech*, April, 1926.

quickly displaced it.[1] The early movie houses were usually called *parlors*, but in a little while *theatres* was substituted, and about 1920 the larger ones began to be designated *cathedrals*, or, by scoffers, *mosques*, *synagogues* or *filling-stations*.

There have been bitter etymological battles over a number of American nouns, some of them coming into good usage, e.g., *ballyhoo*, *hobo*, *hokum*, *jazz*, *jitney*, *maverick*, *sundae* and *wobbly*. The dictionaries try to connect *ballyhoo* with the name of *Ballyholly*, a village in County Cork, Ireland, and I did the same in my last edition, but no relationship has ever been demonstrated. George Milburn, who has spent much time in an investigation of circus words, tells me that old circus men say that it is a blend of *ballet* and *whoop*, but this also sounds somehow improbable. Another correspondent, Charles Wolverton, has it from an old-time carnival man, W. O. Taylor, that *ballyhoo* originated on the Midway of the Chicago World's Fair of 1893, and is an imitation of the cry of the dervishes in the Oriental Village, to wit, *b'Allah hoo*, meaning "Through God it is." "Webster's New International Dictionary" (1934) and Ernest Weekley in his "Etymological Dictionary of Modern English" (1921) say that the origin of *hobo* is unknown, and the Oxford Dictionary attempts no etymology. The Oxford's first example of its use is from an article by Josiah Flynt in the *Contemporary Review* for August, 1891. In that article Flynt simply said that "the tramp's name for himself and his fellows is *hobo*." The word was hardly new at that time; a verb, *to hobo*, followed soon afterward. In *American Speech* for June, 1929, Captain H. P. Wise, apparently an Army officer, suggested that it might be from an identical Japanese word, the plural of *ho* (side), and meaning, in the plural, all sides or everywhere. This suggestion is given some color by the fact that the term seems to have originated on the Pacific Coast, where there are many Japanese. If it is sound, then *hobo* is the one and only word that the Japanese immigrants have given to the American language. "Webster's New International" refers *hokum* to *hocus*, but without saying flatly that they are related, and the Oxford Supplement calls it "a blending of *hocus-pocus* and *bunkum*," but with a saving question-mark. Dr. Frank H. Vizetelly reports that "theorizing devotees in etymology" have

1 On Nov. 8, 1924 the New York *Evening Sun* reported that *speakies*   had recently appeared in *Film Fun*, a fan magazine.

sought to derive it from the Hebrew word *chakam* (a wise man), the Arabic and Hindustani *hakim* (of the same meaning), and the American Indian words *hoquiam*, *hokium* and *hoquium*, all of them proper names.[1] The late Walter J. Kingsley, an ardent amateur lexicographer, favored the theory that *hokum* originated in England. "Once upon a time," he said, "a retired Cockney sea-captain managed the Middlesex Music-Hall in London, and whenever a comedian lacked a consecutive routine or continuity, as they say in the movies, he informed him that there was a hole in his act, and that he should plug it up with 'a bit of oakum,' which he pronounced *hoakum*." [2] But Kingsley's etymologies were always far more ingenious than convincing. Dr. Vizetelly says that *hokum* came in about 1920. All the dictionaries report correctly that *maverick* comes from the name of Samuel A. Maverick (?–1870), a Texan who neglected to brand his calves, and so invited their bootleg branding by his neighbors. But when the word is discussed in the newspapers, which is not infrequently, it is sometimes stated that the thing ran the other way, and that Maverick himself did the stealthy branding. In November, 1889, one of his descendants, George M. Maverick of San Antonio, set the matter right in a letter to the St. Louis *Republic*, and some years later that letter, along with other documents in point, was reprinted as a pamphlet.[3] But old libels die hard. "Webster's New International" says that *jitney* may "possibly" come from the French *jeton* (a counter, or metal disk), from the verb *jeter* (to throw). The Oxford Supplement (1933) says that its origin is unknown, but quotes a statement in the *Nation* for Feb. 4, 1915, that the word "is the Jewish slang term for a nickel," and another from the same journal for March 18, 1915, that it means "the smallest coin in circulation in Russia." But nothing resembling *jitney* is to be found in any Yiddish word-book that I have access to, and I recall hearing it used to designate a five-cent piece long before there was any considerable immigration of Eastern Jews. It began to be used to designate a cheap automobile bus in 1914. "Webster's New International" says that *jazz* is a Creole word, and probably of African origin, but goes no further. The Oxford says that its origin is unknown, but that it is "generally said to be Negro."

1 *Hokum*, New York *World*, March 28, 1923. The same facts are given in The Lexicographer's Easy Chair, *Literary Digest*, May 5, 1923.

2 New York *World*, Oct. 21, 1925.
3 Ye *Maverick*; San Antonio, 1905.

Amateur etymologists have made almost countless efforts to run it down, or, more accurately, to guess at its history. The aforesaid Kingsley tried to connect it with *Jasper*, the name of a dancing slave on a plantation near New Orleans, *c*. 1825.[1] Vincent Lopez sought its origin in *Chaz*, the stable-name of Charles Washington, an eminent ragtime drummer of Vicksburg, Miss., *c*. 1895.[2] Other searchers produced even more improbable etymologies.[3] The effort to trace the word to Africa has failed, though it has been established that it was used by the Negroes in the Mississippi river towns long before it came into general use. But the meaning they attached to it was that of sexual intercourse. Its extension to the kind of music it now designates was perhaps not unnatural, but when, where and by whom that extension was made is not yet known.[4] *Sundae* remains almost as mysterious. All the dictionaries connect it with *Sunday*, but none of them ventures to trace the steps. The first use of the word cited by the Oxford Supplement was in the New York *Evening Post* for May 21, 1904, and it was there spelled *sundi*. A popular etymology runs thus: In 1902 or thereabout there was a sudden craze for enforcing the Blue Laws in Virginia (or some other Southern State), and selling ice-cream soda on Sunday became hazardous. An ingenious druggist, seeking to baffle the police, decided to give the beverage a new appearance and a new name, and so added a few berries to it and called it a *sundae*, in occult reference to the day.[5] I offer this for what it is worth, which is probably not much. The origin of *wobbly* is thus given by Mortimer Downing, a member of the I.W.W. in its heyday:

> In Vancouver, in 1911, we had a number of Chinese members, and one restaurant keeper would trust any member for meals. He could not pronounce the letter *w*, but called it *wobble*, and would ask: " You I. *Wobble Wobble?* " and when the card was shown credit was unlimited. Thereafter the laughing term among us was *I. Wobbly Wobbly*.[6]

1 New York *World*, Oct. 25, 1925. Kingsley had previously dealt with the matter in the New York *Sun* in 1917, and his lucubrations were reprinted in the *Literary Digest* for Aug. 25 of that year.
2 Where is Jazz Leading America? *Étude*, July, 1924.
3 Some of them are rehearsed in Jazz, by Henry Osborne Osgood, *American Speech*, July, 1926.
4 See a somewhat guarded discussion of its original meaning by

Clay Smith, *Étude*, Sept., 1924, p. 595.
5 This etymology is given in *Sundae*, by John Fairweather, London *Sunday Times*, Aug. 25, 1928, on the authority of " Miss Anna C. Mitchell, librarian to the Public Service Corporation of New Jersey, U. S. A."
6 Quoted in How *Wobbly* Originated, by Richard W. Hogue, *Nation*, Sept. 5, 1923, p. 242.

"Webster's New International" gives this etymology, but without formally accepting it. To me it seems unlikely. Perhaps the truth about the origin of *wobbly*, and with it the truth about the origins of *ballyhoo*, *hobo*, *hokum*, *jazz*, *jitney* and *sundae*, will be unearthed by the learned brethren now at work upon the "Dictionary of American English on Historical Principles." Maybe they will also solve some other vexing problems of American lexicography. For example, who was the first to use *graft* in its political sense, who was the first to make nouns of the adjectives *wet* and *dry*, and who was the first to make a noun of the verb *release*, signifying something to be published or otherwise made available on a given date? The latter is in wide use in movie, radio and newspaper circles, and has also spread afield. The history of baseball terms also deserves to be investigated, for many of them have entered the common speech of the country, *e.g.*, *fan*, *rooter*, *bleachers*, *circus-catch*, *home-run*, *homer*, *pinch-hitter*, *pennant-winner*, *batting-average*, *double-header*, *grandstand-play*, *charley-horse*, *gate-money*, *bush-leaguer* or *minor-leaguer*, and *three-strikes-and-out*, not to mention the verbs, *to strike out*, *to bunt*, *to knock out of the box*, *to put it* (or *one*) *across* (or *over*), *to root*, *to be shut out* and *to play ball*, and the adjectival phrases, *on the bench* and *on to his curves*. There are, too, the nouns borrowed from poker, *e.g.*, *kitty*, *cold-deck*, *full-house*, *jack-pot*, *four-flusher*, *ace-high*, *pot*, *show-down*, *penny-ante*, *divvy* and *three-of-a-kind*, along with the verbs and verb-phrases, *to call* (a bluff), *to ante up*, *to stand pat*, *to pony up*, *to hold out*, *to cash in*, *to chip in*, *to see* (a bet, or any other challenge), and *it's up to you*.

3. VERBS

The common verbs of vulgar American will be examined at length in Chapter IX, Section 2. On more decorous levels of speech they are notable chiefly for the facility with which new ones are made. Consider, for example, the process of back-formation. In Chapter III, Section 2, I have already described the appearance of such forms as *to locate* and *to legislate* in the earliest days of differentiation; in our own time many more have gradually attained to something resembling respectability, *e.g.*, *to auto*, *to jell*, *to phone*, *to taxi, to commute, to typewrite, to electrocute,*[1] and *to tiptoe* (for *to walk tiptoe*). Others are still on probation, *e.g., to reminisce, to insurge, to innovate, to vamp, to razz* (from *raspberry*), *to enthuse, to combust,*[2] *to divvy, to reune, to resolute, to housekeep, to peeve, to orate, to bach* (*i.e.,* to live in bachelor quarters), and *to emote;*[3] and yet others remain on the level of conscious humor, *e.g., to plumb* (from *plumber*), *to jan* (from *janitor*), *to barb* (from *barber*), *to chauf* (from *chauffeur*), *to crise* (from *crisis*), *to gondole* (from *gondola*), *to elocute, to burgle, to ush, to perc* (to make coffee in a *percolator*), *to sculp, to butch, to buttle* and *to boheme.* "There is a much greater percentage of humorous shortenings among verbs," says Miss Wittman, "than among other parts of speech. Especially is this true of verbs shortened from nouns and adjectives by subtracting what looks like a derivative suffix, *e.g., -er, -or, -ing, -ent* from nouns, or *y* from adjectives. Many clipped verbs have noun parallels, while some are simply clipped nouns used as verbs."[4] A great many new verbs are also made in the United States by other devices. Some of them are nouns unchanged, *e.g., to author, to service, to auto, to demagogue, to wassermann, to interview*[5] and *to debut;* others are formed by adding *-ize* to nouns

1 The first State to electrocute criminals was New York. The act substituting electrocution for hanging became effective Jan. 1, 1889, and the first criminal electrocuted was William Kemmler, on Aug. 6, 1890. *To electrocute,* at the start, had a rival in *to electrize,* but soon prevailed.

2 *To combust* seems to be an invention of dealers in heating apparatus, or, as they prefer to call themselves, *heating-engineers.* I find the following in an advertisement in the Chicago *Herald and Examiner,* Sept. 16, 1923: "There'd be no warning of exhausted coal deposits if fuel were properly *combusted.*"

3 I say these verbs are still on probation, but if their constant use in the debates of Congress gives them countenance they are quite sound American. My earliest example of *to enthuse* comes from a solemn war-time speech by the late Senator Lee S. Overman of North Carolina, made in the Senate on March 26,

1918. He used it not once, but over and over again. See the *Congressional Record* for that date, pp. 4376–7. *To resolute* was used by Senator L. Y. Sherman of Ohio on Jan. 14, 1918, and by Senator Thomas J. Walsh of Montana on May 16, 1921. *To peeve* was used by Mr. Borland of Missouri in the House Jan. 29, 1918, and has been used by other Representatives countless times since. So have *to reminisce, to orate* and *to insurge.*

4 Clipped Words, *Dialect Notes,* Vol. IV, Pt. II, 1914, p. 137.

5 There is an old English verb, *to interview,* meaning to meet, but it has been obsolete since the Seventeenth Century. The modern verb seems to have arisen in the United States soon after the Civil War, along with its noun. The latter has gone into French, and in 1923 the Académie Française voted to include it in the next edition of its Dictionary. On Dec. 31, 1884, in the course of a review of the year, the

or adjectives, *e.g.*, *to simonize, to slenderize, to winterize, to vaca-*
tionize, to hospitalize and *to picturize;* yet others by adding the old
English suffix *-en* to nouns, adjectives and even other verbs, *e.g.*, *to*
mistaken, to thinnen, to safen and *to loaden.*[1] Those of the last-
named class, of course, belong mainly to the vulgar speech, but
examples of the other classes are to be found on higher levels. Two
days after the first regulations of the Food Administration were
issued, in 1917, *to hooverize* appeared spontaneously in scores of
newspapers, and it retains sufficient repute to be in " Webster's New
International Dictionary " (1934). *To bryanize, to fletcherize* and *to*
oslerize came in just as promptly, the first in 1896, the second in
1904 or thereabout, and the third in 1905, following Dr. William
Osler's famous address at Baltimore.[2] I reach into my collection at
random and draw forth such monstrosities as *to backwardize, to*
fordize, to belgiumize, to respectablize, to scenarioize, to moronize,
to customize, to featurize, to expertize, to powerize, to sanitize, to
manhattanize and *to cohanize;* I suppose I could dredge up at least
a hundred more. Some of these, of course, are only nonce-words,
but certainly not all. *To expertize*, apparently suggested by the
French noun *expertise*, meaning a survey or valuation by experts,
is in universal use among American art and antique dealers, but it
does not appear to prevail in England (though the French noun
does), and the Oxford Dictionary's only example of it is taken from
Harper's Magazine for February, 1889. *To respectablize* I find in
a book review in the Portland *Oregonian:* " The Modern Library
has *respectablized* Casanova." *To backwardize* comes from the
Farm Journal, a very sedate periodical, for March, 1926; I have since
encountered it frequently in *Variety*. *To slenderize* is used by nearly
all the vendors of reducing-salts and other such quackeries. As for

---

Pall Mall Gazette (London) said
that " among the permanent gains
of the year the acclimatization of
the interview in English journalism
certainly should be mentioned."

1 See *Loadened*, by J. D., *American*
Speech, Aug., 1930. The author
calls attention to the fact that verbs
properly in *-en* sometimes take a
double past participle, *e.g.*, *awe-*
strickened and *ladened*. For *to safen*
see *American Speech*, April, 1931,
p. 305. It appears in the sentence:
" Let us *safen* your brakes."

2 *To oslerize* quickly acquired a
meaning that greatly embarrassed
Dr. Osler. What he said was:
" Study until twenty-five, investigation until forty, profession until
sixty, at which age I would have
him retired on a double allowance."
But *to oslerize* came to mean to
put a man to death as useless, and
the age recommended was commonly understood to be forty.

to sanitize, it was described by the Associated Press, on July 6, 1934, as the invention of Dr. Leon Henderson, one of the economic advisers to the NRA, and its meaning was given as "to put sanity and sanitation in[to] business."[1] The only prefix that seems to be commonly used for making verbs is *de-,* which has produced *to debunk, to delouse, to dewax, to dejelly, to debamboozle* and various other forms.

The list of American verbs made of simple nouns is almost endless. The process has been normal in English for a great many years, and at all periods it has produced forms that have survived, *e.g., to house* (Old English), *to shackle* (*c.* 1400) and *to waltz* (*c.* 1790). But it is carried on in the United States with a freedom which England has not seen since Elizabethan times, and though many of its products pass out almost as fast as they come in, others remain in the vocabulary, and rise slowly to respectable usage. A large number are succinct substitutes for verb phrases, and so give evidence of the American liking for short cuts in speech, *e.g., to service* for *to give service,*[2] *to intern* for *to serve as intern, to style* for *to cut in accord with the style, to biograph* for *to write the biography of,*[3] *to chamois* (or, perhaps more often, *to shammy*) for *to polish with chamois, to model* for *to act as a model, to taxpay* for *to pay taxes on,*[4] *to momentum* for *to give momentum to, to contact* for *to make*

1 I had hardly got this paragraph on paper when someone sent me a copy of the *Literary Supplement* of the London *Times* for June 7, 1934, with the ghastly verb *to obituarize* marked with a red circle. Worse, I discovered on investigation that it was in the Oxford Dictionary, credited to the London *Saturday Review* for Oct. 17, 1891. If I may intrude my private feelings into a learned work I venture to add that seeing a monster so suggestive of American barbarism in the *Times* affected me like seeing an archbishop wink at a loose woman.
2 *To service* was used by R. L. Stevenson in Catriona (1893), but it remained a nonce-word until American garages began *servicing* cars, *c.* 1910. It is now in almost universal use among the persons who keep machinery and fixtures in

repair. See *American Speech,* Nov., 1926, p. 112, and Jan., 1927, p. 214. Used by Mr. Justice Roberts, it appears in the decision of the U. S. Supreme Court in N. Y., N. H. & H. R. R. *vs.* Bezue, Jan. 25, 1932 (52 *Supreme Court Reporter,* 206).
3 Senator L. Y. Sherman of Illinois, *Congressional Record,* Jan. 4, 1918, p. 903.
4 After the passage of the War Revenue Act of 1917 cigar-boxes began to bear this inscription: "The contents of this box have been *taxed-paid* . . . as indicated by the Internal Revenue tax stamp affixed." A year or so later *taxed-paid* was changed to *taxpaid.* Prosecutions for the sale, transportation or possession of *untaxpaid* alcoholic beverages are now common in the Federal courts.

contact with,[1] *to ready* for *to make ready*, *to protest* for *to protest against*, *to vacation*, *to holiday* or *to week-end* for *to take a vacation or holiday* or *to go on a week-end trip*, and *to yes* for *to say yes to*.[2] There is another class of verbs that may be called " regular " substitutes for the forms that differ from the corresponding nouns or adjectives, *e.g.*, *to loan* for *to lend*,[3] *to author* for *to write*,[4] *to host* for *to entertain*, and *to signature* for *to sign*.[5] Of verbs made freely and fancifully of simple nouns, whether simple or compound, there is a huge stock and it is enough to cite a few, some of them only nonce-words but others in more or less good usage: *to gesture, to racketeer, to gavel, to reunion, to park*,[6] *to waste-basket, to lobby-display*,[7] *to press-agent, to clearance*,[8] *to railroad, to grand*

1 During the heyday of Babbittry (*c.* 1905–29) *to contact* was one of its counter-words. In 1931 Mr. F. W. Lienau, an official of the Western Union, forbade its use by employés of the company. " Somewhere," he said, " there cumbers this fair earth with his loathsome presence a man who, for the common good, should have been destroyed in early childhood. He is the originator of the hideous vulgarism of using *contact* as a verb. So long as we can meet, get in touch with, make the acquaintance of, be introduced to, call on, interview or talk to people, there can be no apology for *contact*." See the *Commonweal*, Dec. 9, 1931, p. 145. But Mr. Lienau's indignation had no effect, and *to contact* is still widely used.

2 *To yes* seems to have originated in Hollywood, where every movie personage is surrounded by a suite of sycophants. These sycophants are called *yes-men*.

3 *To loan* was once good English, and the Oxford Dictionary gives examples going back to *c.* 1200, but it has been supplanted in England by *to lend* and the Oxford calls it " now chiefly U. S." Here it rages almost unchallenged. It has even got into the text of laws. See *Congressional Record*, Dec. 19, 1921, p. 592, col. 2.

4 *To author*, I suspect, was first used

in *Variety*. But I have found it in the *Editor and Publisher* (Aug. 27, 1927, p. 7, col. 4).

5 *To signature* apparently has the imprimatur of the Postoffice. See Observations on the Duties of Contact Men As Applied to the Postoffice Department Organization, by John H. Bartlett, First Assistant Postmaster General; Cleveland (Postoffice Printing Department), 1924, p. 1.

6 *To park* is in Piers Plowman, C-Text, 143, *c.* 1390: " Among wives and widows I am wont to sit, *y-parked* in pews." But as Dr. Louise Pound points out in *American Speech*, May, 1927, it then meant to be enclosed, shut up, confined. In the sense of to arrange artillery or wagons in a park it came into English during the Napoleonic wars, apparently influenced by French example. Its modern vogue, and great extension of meaning, came in with the automobile. In the United States, as Dr. Pound says, one may now *park* a child with a neighbor, or a suitcase in a cloak-room, or jewelry in a vault.

7 Used in the theatre in the sense of to display photographs or lithographs in a theatre lobby.

8 Used by department-stores in the sense of to sell at a clearance sale. See *American Speech*, Dec., 1926, p. 163.

marshal,[1] *to New Thought,*[2] *to accession,*[3] *to demagogue, to belly-ache, to propaganda, to S.O.S., to steam-roller, to pan, to janitor,*[4] *to bible,*[5] *to census,*[6] and so on. Some of these, of course, belong to various argots, but practically all of them would be intelligible to any alert American, and it would scarcely shock him to see them in his newspaper.[7] The use of *to room* in the sense of to supply with a room is common, and it has brought in *to meal* and *to sleep.*[8] The movement toward simplicity is also responsible for the triumph of *to graduate* over *to be graduated* and of *to operate* over *to operate on.* The latter is denounced regularly by the *Journal of the American Medical Association* and other medical authorities, but it makes steady headway.[9] *To chiropract* is another sweet flower

1 New York *World-Telegram,* March 11, 1932, under the heading of Mayor Won't Ride Horse.

2 From *New Thought,* the name of a curious mixture of faith-healing, amateurish psychology and pseudo-oriental "philosophy," much patronized by persons moving either in or out of Christian Science. From its organ, the *Nautilus* for Jan., 1926, *American Speech* for April, 1926 quotes: "So I lost no time in trying *to New Thought* our way out of debt."

3 *To accession,* used by American librarians in the sense of to acquire a book, is said to have been invented by the late Melvil Dewey (1851–1931). See a letter signed J. W. R. on the editorial page of the New York *Times,* March 27, 1932.

4 Semi-Centennial Anniversary Book, University of Nebraska; Lincoln, Neb., 1919, p. 43. The verb seems to be making headway in competition with the more raffish *to janit* and *to jan.*

5 Used by the Gideon Society, an organization of pious traveling salesmen, to denote the act of outfitting a hotel with Bibles for the consolation of its guests.

6 I find the following in the New International Encyclopedia, 2nd ed., Vol. XIV, p. 674, col. 1, 1917: "The aboriginal tribes are chiefly Bhils, who are animists, though many have been *censused* as Hindus." The

editors of the second edition of the New International were Talcott Williams, dean of the School of Journalism at Columbia University, and the well-known essayist, Frank Moore Colby.

7 Mr. John S. Grover, of the Portland, Ore., *Journal,* sends in an addition that may be with us tomorrow. It is *to monoxide,* meaning to poison with carbon monoxide gas. In August, 1935, one Wells sued an automobile company in the Circuit Court for Multnomah county, Oregon, on the ground that he had been *monoxided* through its carelessness in repairing the heater on his car. Another likely candidate is *to stench,* meaning to empty a movie theatre by setting off stink-bombs. It is a device often employed by moving-picture operators on strike.

8 See *Mealed,* by Anne E. Perkins, *American Speech,* June, 1928, p. 434, and *Roomed,* by Willa Roberts, *American Speech,* Oct., 1927, p. 25. Another analogue, *to subsist,* meaning to provide provender, is to be found in Flying Boats and Sea-Planes, by Rear Admiral W. A. Moffett, U. S. N., *Liberty,* Aug. 18, 1928, p. 46.

9 See The Art and Practise of Medical Writing, by George H. Simmons, editor emeritus of the *Journal,* and Morris Fishbein, its present editor; Chicago, 1925, p. 43. The

of American speech [1] and to it, perhaps, *to goose* [2] should be added. When *to broadcast* began to be used widely, in 1925, there was a debate among American grammarians over its preterite. Should it be *broadcast* or *broadcasted?* The majority of them appear to have preferred *broadcasted,* as more regular, and they were supported by the English grammarian, H. W. Fowler,[3] but *broadcast* seems to have prevailed. It has bred the inevitable noun. Daily the newspapers announce that " His speech was *broadcast* last night " or that " A nation-wide *broadcast* has been arranged for tomorrow."

The common American tendency to overwork a favorite verb has been often noted by English observers. How those of an early day were affected by *to fix* I have reported in Chapter I, Section 3. In our own time *to get* has done the heaviest service. Says Ernest Weekley in " Adjectives — and Other Words " (1930):

> It has become a verb of motion, commonly used in the imperative, and a euphemism for kill, as when the gunman *gets* the sleuth or the sleuth *gets* the gunman. The successful yeggman makes his *getaway,* and the successful artist *gets away with it,* while comprehension of a speaker's meaning can be conveyed by the formula, " I *get* you, Steve."

Dr. Weekley might have added *to get going, to get it over, to get wise, to get off* (to publish or utter), *to get religion, to get back at, to get behind, to get there, to get together, it gets me, to get by, to get the bulge* (or *drop*) *on, to get ahead of, to get solid, to get sore,*

---

learned authors explain that *to operate* a patient really means *to work* him, and that the connotations thereof are embarrassing to the profession. But Marion L. Morse shows in The Verb *Operate,* *American Speech,* April, 1930, that they explain in vain. Miss Morse investigated the usage of nurses. Of those " doing their work out of hospitals for about five years or more," only 12% used *to operate;* the rest used *to operate on* or *upon.* But of those still in training, 50% used *to operate,* thus showing the trend of hospital usage. The medical brethren, in general, reveal a fondness for new verbs. Nearly all of them use *to intern* and *to special* (signifying service as a special nurse), *to wassermann* and *to cystoscope,* and many also use *to*

blood count and *to x-ray.* Drs. Simmons and Fishbein report the use of *to obstetricate,* and I have myself encountered *to diagnosticate.* (*Weekly Bulletin,* New York City Department of Health, May 22, 1926, p. 81.)

1 The Philadelphia *Evening Bulletin* for March 10, 1926 reports its use in court proceedings that day by District Attorney Charles Edwin Fox, and says that he thereby " coined a new word." But it was actually used before 1926. The proper chiropractic term is *to adjust.*

2 *To goose* does not appear in any of the dictionaries in its common American sense, which is known to every schoolboy.

3 In *S.P.E. Tracts,* No. XIX, 1925.

to make a get-away, to get on to, and scores of other verb-phrases, all of them in everyday American use. Most of them, it will be noted, are made by the simple device of adding a preposition or adverb to the verb. American, especially on the colloquial level, is very rich in such compounds,[1] and the differences in meaning between them and the verbs they come from are often great. Compare, for example, *to give* and *to give out, to go back* and *to go back on, to light* and *to light out, to bawl* and *to bawl out, to butt* and *to butt in, to turn* and *to turn down, to go*[2] and *to go big, to show* and *to show up, to put* and *to put over, to pass* and *to pass out, to call* and *to call down, to run* and *to run in, to wind* and *to wind up. To check* has bred a whole series, *e.g., to check up, to check in, to check out, to check with, to check against* and *to check over.* Sometimes, to be sure, the addition seems to be only rhetorical, and many of the resultant forms strike an Englishman as redundant. *Hurry up,* in the imperative, is common in England, but *to hurry up* in the indicative is used less than the simple *to hurry. Brush your hat off* would seem American there, and so would *to stop over, to open up, to beat up, to try out, to start off, to finish up, to average up, to lose out, to start in* (or *out*), and *to stay put.* But such forms are almost innumerable in this country, and most of them, if they lack the sanction of the *Yale Review,* at least have that of the *Congressional Record.*[3] Not a few of the characteristic American verb-phrases embody very bold and picturesque metaphors, *e.g., to go haywire, to muscle in, to turn up missing, to spill the beans, to shoot the chutes, to put the skids under, to do a tailspin, to eat crow, to chew the rag, to hit the ceiling, to play possum, to hand him a lemon, to kick in, to show a yellow streak, to saw wood, to throw a scare into,* and *to come out at the little end of the horn.* And some of the simple verbs show

1 They are common in English, too, and Samuel Johnson called attention to them in the preface to his Dictionary, but they are much more numerous in American. See Thought and Language, by P. B. Ballard; London, 1934, p. 167.
2 Mr. L. G. Lederer of Baltimore calls my attention to a rather curious transitive use of *to go,* noted in the Baltimore *Post* for Sept. 1, 1925: "Next Summer we'll probably see traffic cops stopping and *going* the entrants."

3 *To dope out:* Mr. Hamlin of Missouri in the House, Jan. 19, 1918, p. 1154. *To fall down:* Mr. Kirby of Arkansas in the Senate, Jan. 24, 1918, p. 1291, and Mr. Lewis of Illinois, in the Senate, June 6, 1918, p. 8024. *To jack up:* Mr. Weeks of Massachusetts in the Senate, Jan. 17, 1918, p. 988. *To come across:* Mr. Borland of Missouri in the House, May 4, 1917, p. 1853. *To butt in:* Mr. Snyder of New York in the House, Dec. 11, 1917.

equally bold and picturesque transfers of meaning, *e.g.*, *to fire* (in the sense of *to dismiss*), *to can* (in the same sense), *to star, to neck,* and so on.[1]

Verbs of the last-named class are heavily patronized by the headline writers, partly because they are pungent but mainly because most of them are very short. The favorite verbs of the newspaper copy-desk are those of three letters, *e.g.*, *to air* (which serves to indicate any form of disclosure), *to cut, to net, to set, to bar, to aid, to map, to nab, to hit, to rap, to vie* and *to ban.* It has revived an archaism, *to ire*, and has produced *to null* from *to nullify* by clipping. *Gassed* is always used in place of *asphyxiated.* *To admit* is used as a substitute for *to confess, to acknowledge, to concede, to acquiesce* and *to recognize.* *To cut* is a synonym for every verb signifying any sort of opposition to enhancement. *To back* is to give any sort of support or recognition, *to ban* indicates any sort of prohibition, and *to hit* connotes every variety of criticism. A few of the headline verbs are of five letters, *e.g.*, *to claim, to photo, to blame, to quash, to speed* and *to score*, and some are even of six letters, *e.g.*, *to attack, to debunk* and *to battle*, but that is only because the researches of the copy-desk Websters have not, as yet, discovered shorter synonyms. Their preference, after their three-letter favorites, runs to four letter verbs, *e.g.*, *to best, to cite, to curb, to flay, to loom, to lure, to name, to oust, to push, to quit, to rule, to spur* and *to void*, and among them, as among the nouns, their first choice is for those of onomatopeic tang.[2]

Writing in the late 60's of the last century, Richard Grant White said that "in New England . . . even the boys and girls playing on the commons" used the auxiliary verbs *will* and *shall* "correctly," which is to say, in accord with Southern English practice, and that "even in New York, New Jersey, and Ohio, in Virginia, Maryland, and South Carolina, fairly educated people of English stock" did the same.[3] But that was more than two generations ago, and the chances are that it wasn't actually true even then. Today the distinction between *will* and *shall* has become so muddled in all save

1 See Simile and Metaphor in American Speech, by B. Q. Morgan, *American Speech*, Feb., 1926.
2 See Scribes Seek Snappy Synonyms, by Maurice Hicklin, *American Speech*, Dec., 1930. Mr. Hicklin lists 70 headline verbs.

3 Words and Their Uses, new ed.; New York, 1876, p. 264. This book was made up of articles contributed to the New York *Galaxy* during 1867, '68 and '69.

the most painstaking and artificial varieties of American that it may almost be said to have ceased to exist.[1] Save for emphasis, *shall* and *should* are seldom used in the first person, and all of the confusions in other situations that are listed by H. W. Fowler in "Modern English Usage "[2] and by Fowler and his brother in "The King's English "[3] are encountered in the United States every day. No ordinary American, save after the most laborious reflection, would detect anything wrong in this sentence from the London *Times*, denounced as corrupt by the Fowlers: "We must reconcile what we would like to do with what we can do." Nor in this by W. B. Yeats: "The character who delights us may commit murder like Macbeth . . . and yet we will rejoice in every happiness that comes to him." When Leonard and Moffett submitted "Will you be at the Browns' this evening? " to a committee made up principally of American philologians, seven of them called it perfectly sound English, eighteen put it down as "cultivated informal English," and only four dismissed it as "uncultivated." Two thought it was American, not English, but the Fowlers' evidence shows that they were in error.[4] In "The King's English," the Fowlers admit that the idiomatic use of the two auxiliaries, "while it comes by nature to Southern Englishmen, . . . is so complicated that those who are not to the manner born can hardly acquire it." In Scotland and Ireland, as in the United States, the difference between them is largely disregarded, and no doubt Northern English example is at least partly responsible for American usage.[5] As Leonard once said,[6] "The whole mass of

1 In 1929 N. R. French, C. W. Carter, Jr., and Walter Koenig, Jr., of the staff of the American Telephone and Telegraph Company, undertook a statistical study of the words used in telephone conversations. Their material embraced 79,390 words used in 1900 conversations. They reported that *will* was used as an auxiliary 1,305 times in 402 conversations, but that *shall* was used but 6 times in 6 conversations. See a discussion of the matter in Grammar and Usage in Textbooks on English, by Robert C. Pooley; Madison, Wis., 1933, p. 60. The French-Carter-Koenig report has been published as The Words and Sounds of Telephone Conversa-

tions, *Bell System Technical Journal*, April, 1930.
2 Oxford, 1926, p. 526.
3 2nd ed., Oxford, 1908, pp. 133–154.
4 Current Definition of Levels in English Usage, by S. A. Leonard and H. Y. Moffett, *English Journal*, May, 1927.
5 P. W. Joyce says flatly in English As We Speak It in Ireland, 2nd ed.; London, 1910, p. 77, that, "like many another Irish idiom this is also found in American society chiefly through the influence of the Irish." At all events, the Irish example must have reinforced it. In Ireland " *Will* I light the fire, ma'am? " is colloquially sound.
6 *Shall* and *Will*, *American Speech*,

pronouncements about the matter in text-books is of very little importance now, since the future in English is most commonly expressed by neither *shall* nor *will*, but by the much commoner contraction *'ll*, and by the forms *is to go, about to go, is going to*, and the whole range of auxiliary verbs which mean both past and future."[1] More than two generations ago, impatient of the effort to fasten an arbitrary English distinction upon American, George P. Marsh attacked the differentiation of *shall* from *will* as of "no logical value or significance whatever," and predicted that "at no very distant day this verbal quibble will disappear, and one of the auxiliaries will be employed, with all persons of the nominative, exclusively as the sign of the future, and the other only as an expression of purpose or authority."[2] This prophecy has been substantially verified. *Will* is sound American "with all persons of the nominative," and *shall* is almost invariably an "expression of purpose or authority."

4. OTHER PARTS OF SPEECH

The schoolmarm, in fact, has virtually abandoned her old effort to differentiate between the two auxiliaries, but she continues the heroic task of trying to make her young charges grasp the difference between *who* and *whom*. Here, alas, the speechways of the American people seem to be again against her. The two forms of the pronoun are confused magnificently in the debates in Congress, and in most newspaper writing, and in ordinary discourse the great majority of Americans avoid *whom* diligently, as a word full of snares. When they employ it, it is often incorrectly, as in

---

Aug., 1929, p. 498. He quotes The Rules of Common School Grammars, by C. C. Fries, *Publications of the Modern Language Association*, March, 1927, to the effect that "the first statement that *will* is differently used in the first person and in the second and third is in a grammar of English written in Latin by Johannis Wallis and first published in 1653. From this book it was copied frequently by the imitative grammarians of the Eighteenth Century, and has been swallowed with eyes shut by most of the writers of common-school grammars, handbooks of correct English, and the like ever since."

1 In her Tendencies in Modern American Poetry; New York, 1917, Amy Lowell takes Carl Sandburg and Edgar Lee Masters to task for constantly using *will* for *shall*, and says that they share the habit "with many other modern American writers." See also Text, Type and Style, by George B. Ives; Boston, 1921, p. 289 *ff*.

2 Lectures on the English Language, 4th ed.; New York, 1870, p. 659.

" *Whom* is your father? " and " *Whom* spoke to me? " Noah Webster, always the pragmatic reformer, denounced it as usually useless so long ago as 1783. Common sense, he argued, was on the side of " *Who* did he marry? " Today such a form as " *Whom* are you talking to? " would seem very affected to most Americans; they might write it, but they would never speak it.[1] The use of *me* instead of *I* in " It's *me* " is also almost universal in the United States, but here it is the objective form that is prevailing, not the nominative, as in the case of *who* and *whom*. " It's *me* " will be discussed at length in Chapter IX, Section 3.

A shadowy line often separates what is currently coming into sound usage from what is still regarded as barbarous. No American of any pretensions, I assume, would defend *ain't* as a substitute for *isn't*, say in " He *ain't* the man," and yet *ain't* is already tolerably respectable in the first person, where English countenances the even more clumsy *aren't*. *Aren't* has never got a foothold in the American first person; when it is used at all, which is very rarely, it is always as a conscious Briticism. Facing the alternative of employing the unwieldy " *Am* I not in this? " the American turns boldly to " *Ain't* I in this? " It still grates a bit, perhaps, but *aren't* grates even more.[2] Here, as always, the popular speech is pulling the exacter speech along, and no one familiar with its successes in the past can have much doubt that it will succeed again, soon or late. In the same way it is breaking down the inflectional distinction between adverb and adjective, so that *in bad* begins to take on the dignity of a national idiom, and *sure, to go big* and *run slow*[3] become almost respectable. When, on the entrance of the United States into the World War, the Tank Corps chose " Treat 'em *rough* " as its motto, no one thought to raise a grammatical objection, and the clipped adverb was printed upon hundreds of thousands of posters and displayed in every town in the country, always with the imprimatur

1 Compare Matthew XVI, 13: " When Jesus came into the coasts of Cesarea Philippi, he asked his disciples, saying, *Whom* do men say that I, the Son of Man, am? " See also Modern English Usage, by H. W. Fowler, above cited, p. 723, and Chapters on English, by Otto Jespersen; London, 1918, p. 52.

2 For an interesting discussion of *aren't* see a letter by H. E. Boot in

English, June, 1920, p. 376, and one by Daniel Jones in the same periodical, Aug.–Sept., 1920, p. 399.

3 A common direction to drivers and locomotive engineers. The English form is *slow down*. I note, however, that " drive slow*ly* " is in the taxicab shed at the Pennsylvania Station, in New York. See also Chapter IX, Section 6.

of the national government. So again, American, in its spoken form, tends to obliterate the distinction between nearly related adjectives, e.g., *healthful* and *healthy*. And to challenge the somewhat absurd textbook prohibition of terminal prepositions, so that "Where are we *at?*" loses its old raciness. And to substitute *as though* for *as if*. And to split infinitives in a wholesale and completely innocent manner.[1] And to dally lavishly with a supererogatory *but*, as in " I have no doubt *but* that." The last occurs very frequently in the *Congressional Record*, and though it was denounced by Edward S. Gould so long ago as 1867 [2] it seems to be very firmly lodged in colloquial American, and even to have respectable standing in the standard speech. It was used often by the highly correct Henry Cabot Lodge,[3] and has been written into a decision of the Supreme Court of the United States by Charles Evans Hughes.[4] The *one-he* combination, so offensive to purists (among whom, in this case, I venture to include myself), is now so common in the United States that putting it down becomes quite hopeless. In 1921, when the late Warren Gamaliel Harding, LL.D., used it in his Inaugural Address, I mocked it in the *Nation*, but in vain, for most of the correspondents who wrote to me afterward argued for it. Of the twenty-nine philologians who voted on it in the Leonard-Moffett inquiry,[5] six called it good "literary or formal English " and sixteen thought it was "cultivated, informal English." It is, of course, not English at all, as Fowler observes in "Modern English Usage," though it is used by "a small minority of modern British writers." But in this

1 This splitting is defended eloquently by one of the most distinguished of American grammarians, George O. Curme, in The Split Infinitive, *American Speech*, May, 1927. He argues that it often helps to clarify the meaning. Thus " He failed completely to understand it " differs in meaning from " He failed to completely understand it." " Grammatical instruction in our schools," says Dr. Curme sagely, " might become a power and mighty interesting to students if it ceased to be a study of rules and became a study of the English language as something fashioned by the English people and still being shaped by the present generation. It will give a thrill to English-speaking students to discover that the English language does not belong to the school teacher but belongs to them and that its future destiny will soon rest entirely in their hands." See also Syntax, by Dr. Curme; Boston, 1931, p. 455 *ff*, and The Split Infinitive, by H. W. Fowler, *S.P.E. Tracts*, No. XV, 1923.

2 Good English, p. 59.

3 For example, see the *Congressional Record*, May 14, 1918, p. 6996.

4 Principality of Monaco *vs*. State of Mississippi, May 21, 1934. (54 *S. Ct. R.*, 748 note).

5 Current Definition of Levels in English Usage, cited in Section 3, above.

country its use is almost universal, and I have even found it in a serious treatise on the national letters by a former editor of the *Atlantic Monthly*, edited by a posse of Yale professors and published by the University Press.[1] The appearance of a redundant *s* at the end of such words as *downward, somewhere* and *forward* has been long marked in American. " In modern Standard English," says Logan Pearsall Smith,[2] " though not in the English of the United States, a distinction which we feel, but many of us could not define, is made between *forward* and *forwards; forwards* being used in definite contrast to any other direction, as ' If you move at all, you can only move *forwards*,' while *forward* is used where no such contrast is implied, as in the common phrase, ' to bring a matter *forward*.' " [3] This distinction, *pace* Smith, retains some force in the United States too, but in general our usage allows the *s* in cases where English usage would certainly be against it. Gould, in the 50's, noting its appearance at the end of such words as *somewhere* and *anyway*, denounced it as vulgar and illogical, and White, in the late 60's, was against it even in *towards*. But *towards*, according to Fowler, is now prevailing even in England. Thornton traced *anyways* back to 1842 and showed that it was an archaism, and to be found in the Book of Common Prayer (*c.* 1560); perhaps it has been preserved by analogy with *sideways*. Henry James attacked " such forms of impunity as *somewheres else* and *nowheres else, a good ways on* and *a good ways off* " as " vulgarisms with which a great deal of general credit for what we good-naturedly call ' refinement ' appears so able to coexist," [4] but his shrill complaint seems to have fallen upon sound-proofed ears. Perhaps he would have been even more upset, on his so unhappy American tour, if he had encountered *no place* and *some place*, which show some sign of dislodging *nowheres* and *somewheres*.

The general American liking for short cuts in speech, so plainly visible in the incessant multiplication of compounds and back-formations, is also shown in the popularity of abbreviations. They are employed in the United States, says John S. Farmer, " to an

1 The American Spirit in Literature, by Bliss Perry; New Haven, 1918, p. 117.
2 The English Language; New York, 1912, p. 79.
3 Common, that is, in England. An American would use " to take a matter up."
4 The Question of Our Speech; Boston, 1905, p. 30. See also *Dialect Notes*, Vol. IV, Pt. I, 1913, p. 48.

extent unknown in Europe. Life, they say, is short and the pace is quick; brevity, therefore, is not only the soul of wit, but the essence of business capacity as well. This trait of the American character is discernible in every department of the national life and thought — even slang being curtailed at times." [1] *O.K., C.O.D., N.G.* and *P.D.Q.* are American masterpieces; the first has been borrowed by all the languages of Western Europe and some of those of Asia, and in the days of the great immigrations the immigrants learned all four immediately after *hell* and *damn*. Thornton has traced *N.G.* to 1840, and *C.O.D.* and *P.D.Q.* are probably quite as old. The earliest use of *O.K.* that has been recorded in the dictionaries is dated 1840 also, and the story generally credited is that it originated in Champaign county, Ohio, during the presidential campaign of that year. The Whig candidate was William Henry Harrison, an Ohioan, and on September 15 there was a rally in his interest in a grove belonging to John A. Ward, father of J. Q. A. Ward the sculptor, at Urbana. In the parade preceding the speech-making there were 42 farm-wagons, each freighted with a small log-cabin. One of these wagons was driven by John Rock, a nearby farmer. It was drawn by 24 horses, and had 36 young women as passengers, all dressed in white. On it was a streamer bearing the words " The People is Oll Korrect," painted by Thomas Daniels, the local handy-man. The story is to the effect that Daniels's error was seized upon by Harrison's opponents, but that his friends, seeing the popular appeal in it, took it over themselves and made " The People is *O.K.*" their battle-cry. Unluckily, Mr. H. J. Carr, of the Urbana *Citizen*, has discovered that *O.K.* had appeared in Samuel Medary's *Ohio Statesman*, published at Columbus, on September 11, four days before the Urbana meeting.[2] More, it had been used in the Boston *Transcript* on April 15, five months before the meeting,[3] and again in the Boston *Atlas* on June 20.[4]

1 Americanisms Old and New; London, 1889, p. 1.
2 Mr. Carr published an account of his discovery in the Cleveland *Plain Dealer*, Nov. 20, 1934.
3 See *O.K.* at Ninety-Five, Boston *Transcript* (editorial), April 15, 1935. It occurred in a report of a Democratic meeting in New York, in the interest of Martin Van Buren's renomination for a second term. The *Transcript's* correspond-

ent said that " the tail of the Democratic party, the roarers, buttenders, ringtails, *O.K.*'s . . . and indomitables talked strong about Nullification and all that." " The allusion," says the *Transcript* editorial of 1935, " was probably to those who put their *O.K.* on the nomination of Van Buren."
4 In a report of a Whig convention held at Worcester on June 19. " The band of the delegation from

There are many rival etymologies for the abbreviation. One derives it from the initials of one Obediah Kelly, an early railway freight-agent, who signed them to bills of lading. Another derives it from *Keokuk*, the name of an Indian chief from whom the town of Keokuk, Iowa, was named. His admirers called him Old Keokuk, and usually added " He's all right! ", and so *Old Keokuk*, and finally the simple initials, came to mean the same thing.[1] A third etymology derives *O.K.* from *omnis korrecta*, supposed to have been once used by schoolmasters in marking examination-papers.[2] A fourth seeks its origin in *Aux Cayes*, the name of a port in what is now Haiti, whence the best rum came in the early days. A fifth holds that it was borrowed from the terminology of the early shipbuilders, who fashioned the timbers of their ships under cover, marked each one for identification, and then began the actual building by laying *O.K.* (*i.e.*, outer keel) *No. 1*.[3] A sixth contends that *O.K.* was invented by the early telegraphers, along with many other abbreviations, *e.g.*, *G.M.* (good morning), *G.A.* (go ahead) and *N.M.* (no more).[4] A seventh credits *O.K.* to the elder John Jacob Astor, "who marked it on bills presented to him for credit." [5] An eighth seeks its origin in the archaic English word *hoacky* or *horkey*, meaning the last load brought in from the fields at harvest.[6] A ninth derives it from a Choctaw word, *okeh*, signifying "it is so." "Webster's New International Dictionary" (1934) accepts this last, though adding a saving " probably," but the Supplement to the Oxford Dictionary

---

Barre," said the *Atlas*, "rode in a stage which had a barrel of hard-cider on the baggage-rack, marked with large letters *O.K.* – oll kor-rect."

1 I take this from the Louisville *Herald-Post*, Feb. 26, 1932.

2 This comes from a letter signed L. M., dated Calgary, March 4, 1935, and published in the Van-couver *Sun*. For it I am indebted to Mr. J. A. Macdonald, of the *Sun* staff.

3 For this I am indebted to Mr. John D. Forbes, of San Francisco.

4 See Topical Tittle-tattle, by Tatler, Sidmouth (England) *Observer*, March 27, 1935, and *O.K.* – Time Saver, by John Galt, New York *American*, March 22, 1935. Unfor-

tunately for this theory, there were no telegraph operators until 1844, and *O.K.*, as we have seen, had been used in 1840.

5 *O.K.* No Mystery, by Frank A. Kellman, New York *American*, March 20, 1935.

6 Derivation of *O.K.*, by Wilfrid White, London *Daily Telegraph*, March 7, 1935. Mr. White quotes an anonymous poem, Poor Robin, of 1676: " *Hoacky* is brought home with Hollwin" [Hollowe'en]. "There is also," he says, " a long poem by Herrick, entitled The *Hock* Cart, or Harvest Home. It seems but a short step from *hoacky*, signifying the satisfactory comple-tion of harvesting, to the snappy *O.K.* of today."

(1933) rejects it, saying that " it does not agree with the evidence." There is yet a tenth etymology, whereby *O.K.* is made to originate in a libel of Andrew Jackson by Seba Smith (Major Jack Downing), who is said to have alleged, *c.* 1832, that he saw Jackson's endorsement " *O.K.,* Amos," on the elegant pronunciamentoes drawn up for him by his literary secretary, Amos Kendall. Says a floating newspaper paragraph:

> Possibly the general did use this endorsement, and it may have been used by other people also. But James Parton has discovered in the records of the Nashville court of which Jackson was a judge, before he became President, numerous documents endorsed *O.R.,* meaning *Order Recorded.* He urges, therefore, that it was a record of that court with some belated business which Major Downing saw on the desk of the Presidential candidate.[1] However this may be, the Democrats, in lieu of denying the charge, adopted the letters *O.K.* as a sort of party cry and fastened them upon their banners.

This last theory, it seems to me, deserves more investigation than it has got. Certainly *O.K.* must have been in familiar use before 1840, and equally certainly it had some connection with Democrats. But Woodrow Wilson, himself the most eminent Democrat of his day, accepted the Choctaw etymology, and used *okeh* in approving official papers. His use of the form made it popular, and it became the name of a series of popular phonograph records, and of many shoe-shining parlors, lunch-rooms and hot-dog stands. An *Okey* Hosiery Company survives in New York along with an *Okay* Electric Company, an *Okay* Food Sales Company, an *Okay* Manufacturing Company, and an *Okay* Supply Company. *O.K.* has gone into English,[2] and also into all the Continental languages. Some years ago the British Privy Council decided solemnly that it was good English. Ba Maw, manager of a rice mill in Burma, had written *O.K.* on certain bills to indicate that they had been checked and found correct. The Privy Council agreed that his understanding of the meaning of the term was sound, and in doing so set aside a decree of the High Court of Rangoon, which had ruled that *O.K.* was not English. English or not, it has become the symbol for " we agree " in the code of the International Telecommunication Convention, signed by the dele-

---

1 *Presidential candidate* is probably an error for *President.* Jackson was elected for his first term in 1828. Smith did not begin to write his Letters of Major Downing until the early 30's.

2 " What has been my horror," wrote Mrs. Nicholas Murray Butler to the London *Daily Telegraph*, March 6, 1935, " to hear *O.K.* used in an English drawing-room, and, worse still, to find it in the Oxford Dictionary! "

gates to the International Radio Conference at Madrid, December
9, 1932. "It is estimated," says a recent newspaper writer, "that
O.K. is used [in the United States] not less than a million times a day,
even by the most high-hatted of auditors and certified public accountants. It is used in official business at Washington and in the
Army and Navy, in the Ford plant, on the railroads, and in the
American sections of London and Paris. Regardless of its possible
illegitimacy, it has a convincing and captivating ring, and it is undoubtedly the most popular of all American slang or idiom." [1] The
figure mentioned by this writer seems to be too modest. According
to James A. Bohannon, president of the Peerless Motor Car Corporation, "a half million *O.K.'s* are included in every motor-car built." [2]
A back-formation, *oke*, appeared about 1930.

Many other abbreviations are in common use in the United States.
I have mentioned *C.O.D.*, *N.G.* and *P.D.Q.* The first-named has
been borrowed by the English, but they always understand it to
mean *cash* on delivery, not *collect* on delivery. *G.O.P.* was formerly
popular as a designation for the Republican party (*Grand Old
Party*), and also, in the days of the horse-cars, as an abbreviation of
get out and push, but it seems to be fading. It was probably suggested
by the English *G.O.M.* for *Grand Old Man* (W. E. Gladstone,
1882). *A No. 1*, as in an *A No. 1* car, is also an Americanism of English parentage: it is borrowed from *A 1*, used in Lloyd's Register
to designate ships in first-class condition. Other familiar Americanisms are *G.B.* (grand bounce), *F.F.V.* (first families of Virginia),
F.O.B. (free on board), *G.A.R.* (Grand Army of the Republic),
S.A. (sex-appeal), *D. & D.* (drunk and disorderly), *on the Q.T.* (on
the quiet), *T.B.* (tuberculosis), *L* (elevated-railway), and *B.V.D.*,
the trade-name for a brand of men's underwear, but now in such
wide use that it is applied indiscriminately to the product of other
manufacturers. [3] Perhaps *Q-room* (*cue-room, i.e., billiard-room*),

1 Butte (Mont.) *Standard*, Oct. 11,
1929.
2 Cincinnati *Enquirer*, Oct. 6, 1929.
See also *Okeh: Legenden um ein
Modewort*, by A. J. Storfer, *Vossische Zeitung* (Berlin), Sept. 3,
1933. For the sake of the record I
add the following from the New
York *World-Telegram's* report of
the Hauptmann-Lindbergh trial,
Jan. 23, 1935: "Pincus Fisch, brother

of the late mysterious Isidor Fisch,
Hauptmann's tubercular friend, has
learned to say *okay*. It is now his
answer for everything."
3 Under date of March 29, 1935 I
received the following from Mr.
P. B. Merry of the B.V.D. Company, Inc.: "From the standpoint
of business psychology and because
of the great public curiosity as to
the meaning of our trademark, we

While-U-wait, and *Bar-B-Q* (*barbecue*), all of them familiar signs, should be added. There are many secret and semi-secret abbreviations, especially in college slang and other argots,[1] and nonce-forms often appear, e.g., *w.k.* (*well-known*). The World War brought in a great many novelties, headed by *A.E.F.* (*American Expeditionary Force*) and *a.w.o.l.* (*absent without leave*). There was a similar abundance of new forms in England: of them *D.O.R.A.* (*Defense of the Realm Act*) and *wren* (a member of the *Women's Royal Naval Service*) are examples. After the war the Russians contributed a large number, e.g., *cheka* (*Chrezvychainaya Komissiya, i.e., Extraordinary Commission*), *N.E.P.* (*New Economic Plan*), and *Gay-pay-oo* (*Gosundarstvennoe Politicheskoe Upravlenie, i.e., Government Political Administration*), which last somehow became *Ogpu* in the Western world. To these was presently added *Nazi* (*Nationalsozialistische*) from Germany. The effect was to encourage the invention of similar forms in America, and when the New Deal dawned, in 1933, scores began to appear, e.g., *N.R.A.* or *Nira* (*National Recovery Administration*), *T.V.A.* (*Tennessee Valley Authority*), *F.E.R.A.* (*Federal Emergency Relief Administration*), *C.C.C.* (*Civilian Conservation Corps*), *A.A.A.* (*Agricultural Adjustment Administration*), and so on — enough, in fact, to induce Alfred E. Smith to describe the government as submerged in a bowl of alphabetical soup.[2] The advertising brethren are fertile inventors of abbreviations. They seem to have produced *I.X.L.* many years ago, and of late they have added *XLent* (a brand of salmon), *E.Z.* (for easy: part of the name of a brand of shoes), *Fits-U* (a brand of eye-glasses), and many other combinations of *U*, e.g., *Uneeda*, *Uneedme* (a chair-pad), *U-Put-It-On* (a weather-strip), *U-Rub-It-In* (an ointment), *While-U-Wait*, and "*R.U.* interested in" —

would not care to have you publish any information regarding its origin, but for your personal use, if you request it, we will be glad to tell you the history of *B.V.D.*" I did not request it.

1 See Semi-Secret Abbreviations, by Percy W. Long, *Dialect Notes*, Vol. IV, Pt. III, 1915, and Vol. IV, Pt. V, 1916. Dr. Long lists, among others, *c. & s.* (Navy: *clean and sober*), *G.b.F.* (among teachers: *God bless Friday*), *c.o.p.* (department-stores: *customer's own prop-*

erty), *r.b.* (tailors: *round back*), *b.d.t.* (college: *back-door trot*), *g.p.* (medical men: *grateful patient*), *G.o.k.* (medical men: *God only knows*), *f.h.b.* (general: *family hold back*), and *b.s.* (college: euphemistically explained by Dr. Long as meaning *bovine excrescence*).

2 *Alphabetical soup* is itself an Americanism. It designates a noodle-soup in which the noodles are stamped out in the form of letters of the alphabet.

whatever happens to be for sale.[1] On the Pacific Coast the barbecues and hot-dog stands run to such signs as *Sit 'N Eat, Park 'N Dine* and so on.[2] In college slang the common abbreviation *W.C.* (water-closet) is sometimes expanded, ironically, to *Wesley chapel*. In a similar way sporting writers expand *K.O.* (knockout) to *kayo.*

One of the characteristics of slang, as we shall see in Chapter XI, Section 1, is that its novelties are sometimes worked so hard and in so many situations that they lose all definite meaning. This is also true of certain popular words on higher levels: philologians call them vogue- or counter-words. The common adjectives and adverbs of intensification offer examples *e.g., grand, dreadful, nice* and *awfully,* and we have seen another in the verb *to fix* (Chapter I, Section 3) and yet another in the verb *to get* (Chapter V, Section 3). The noun *proposition* began to take on wide and often preposterous significances in American during the 90's, and was soon in a lamentably swollen state. It meant a problem, proposal, person, parallel, premiss, postulate, parley, phenomenon, point, policy, philosophy, prospect, process, petition, paradox or possibility, to mention only a few of its meanings under its own first letter.[3] It went into English with the movies, and was denounced by H. W. Fowler in " Modern English Usage," but it remained distinctively American there, and is now fading out of both languages, at least in its character of counter-word. In 1910 or thereabout the more incompetent newspaper reporters of the United States began to use *angle* in the sense of any aspect of a person or an event,[4] and ten years later they adopted *alibi* as a synonym for any word signifying an explanation or excuse. Both wore out very quickly, but not, alas, quickly enough. Other counter-words that have flourished since the beginning of the century are *gesture, service, reaction, complex, analysis, plus* and *dingus,* the verbs *to function* and *to claim,*[5] and the adjectives *outstanding,*

1 See Notes on the Vernacular, by Louise Pound, *American Mercury,* Oct., 1924, p. 237.
2 See Showing Hollywood, by Cecelia Ager, *Variety,* July 23, 1930, p. 49.
3 In a speech in the Senate by Senator George W. Norris of Nebraska, on Feb. 21, 1921, it was used in five or six distinct senses. The speech may be found in the *Congressional Record* of the same date, p. 374 ff.
4 *Angle* got into English about 15 years later. For examples of its use there see The Supplement to the O.E.D., by George G. Loane, *Literary Supplement* to the London *Times,* March 8, 1934, p. 162.
5 In 1906, according to Enid C. Dauncey, *Living Age,* Dec. 15, *to claim* was "employed in the most inhuman fashion to do the work of a dozen healthy, willing substitutes," *e.g., to allege, assert, protest, profess, advance, propound, depose, avow.*

meticulous, exciting, conscious and *consistent.* Some of them began in the argot of a relatively small class, and then extended to the common tongue, *e.g., service,* which seems to have been launched by the visionaries of Rotary *c.* 1910. *Outstanding* began its career among the pedagogues, and they still overwork it cruelly,[1] but it is now also used by politicians, the rev. clergy, newspaper editorial writers, and other such virtuosi of bad writing. *Consistent* came in *c.* 1925 as an adjective designating every sort of harmony or continuity, and for a while drove out a whole flock of better words. *Exciting* apparently arose in the jargon of art criticism, but in 1933 it was borrowed by the writers of book reviews, and presently had a great run in publishers' advertising, especially on the slip-covers of books. *Plus* seems to have been the child of advertisement writers; it was noticed in *American Speech* for December, 1927, as in high favor among them. *Classic* followed a year or so later.[2] *Dingus* seems to have originated in the English of South Africa, but it has been in heavy use in the United States since the automobile and the radio brought in a host of novel contraptions, and with it have flourished a number of congeners, *e.g., jigger, gadget* and *doodad.*[3] *Complex,* of course, owed its vogue, *c.* 1915, to the popularity of the Freudian rumble-bumble. The use of *gesture* as a general indicator of any sort of action, movement, offer, threat or deed began in 1925 or thereabout. The late George Philip Krapp believed that it was suggested by the French *beau geste,* the title of a popular movie of the period.[4]

1 I find it used no less than five times on a single page of American Writers, by Edwin L. Miller, assistant superintendent of schools of Detroit; Philadelphia, 1934, p. 676. See Educational Lingo, by Olivia Pound, *American Speech,* March, 1926. Miss Pound makes some amusing comments upon the platitudinous and *cliché*-studded English of the gogues. When *outstanding* got to England it hatched an adverb, *outstandingly.* See *English,* Feb., 1920, p. 286, and Speech Degeneracy, by M. V. P. Yeaman, *American Speech,* Nov., 1925.

2 See *Classic,* by R. G. Lewis, *American Speech,* June, 1928, p. 433.
3 The Supplement to the Oxford Dictionary suggests that *dingus* is derived from the Dutch *ding* (a thing). The earliest quotation given is dated 1898. See American Indefinite Names, by Louise Pound, *American Mercury,* Oct., 1924, p. 236.
4 A Comprehensive Guide to Good English; Chicago, 1927, p. 269. See also *Beau Geste?,* by J. M. Steadman, Jr., *American Speech,* June, 1928.

5. FOREIGN INFLUENCES TODAY

The great flow of European immigration to the United States, perhaps the most significant event in human history since the close of the Middle Ages, began with the Irish potato famine of 1847 and the German political disturbances of the two years following. Between 1776 and 1846, a stretch of more than two generations, less than 1,600,000 immigrants from overseas had come into the country, though its population had increased nearly sevenfold, from 3,000,000 to 20,000,000. But after 1850 the movement began in earnest, and thereafter it continued for sixty-five years, with only two considerable interruptions, the first caused by the Civil War and the second by the Depression of 1893. In each of the years 1905, 1906, 1907, 1910, 1913 and 1914 more than a million immigrants were admitted, and by 1927 the total number arriving since 1820 reached 37,000,000. In 1930 there were 13,366,407 white persons in the United States who had been born in foreign countries, 16,999,221 whose parents were both foreign-born, and 8,361,965 of mixed parentage – a total of 38,727,593, or more than 35% of the whole white population. In addition, there were perhaps 200,000 Negroes, Chinese, Japanese, Filipinos, Hindus and Koreans who were either foreign-born or the children of foreign-born parents, and nearly 1,500,000 Mexicans.[1]

With the passage of the Immigration Act of 1921 the flow of immigration was considerably reduced, and when the Immigration Act of 1924 followed it was virtually halted. Both acts were qualitative as well as quantitative in purpose and effect. The first limited the annual immigration from each country to 3% of "the number of foreign-born persons of such nationality resident in the United States" in 1910, and the second reduced the quota to 2% and changed the year to 1890. The aim of the latter amendment was to diminish the relative number of immigrants from Eastern and South-

[1] The Census Bureau explains somewhat lamely (Fifteenth Census: Population, Vol. II; Washington, 1933, p. 27) that "by reason of its growing importance, the Mexican element was given a separate classification in 1930," though it had been " included for the most part with the white population at prior censuses." The instruction given to enumerators was that "all persons born in Mexico, or having parents born in Mexico, who are not definitely white, Negro, Indian, Chinese or Japanese, should be returned as Mexicans." Under this instruction, 1,422,533 Mexicans were returned in 1930, besides 65,968 "persons of Mexican birth or parentage returned as white."

ern Europe. Down to 1890 the overwhelming majority of entrants had come from Great Britain, Germany and the Scandinavian countries, but after that year those from Italy, Russia and the Austrian dominions had taken the lead. In 1914, for example, 383,738 came in from Italy, 255,660 from Russia and 278,152 from Austria-Hungary, whereas the arrivals from Germany were but 35,734, from Scandinavia 29,391, and from the United Kingdom and Ireland 73,417. It was generally felt that immigrants from Eastern and Southern Europe were harder to assimilate than those from the West and North, and that the country already had enough of them, and to spare. So the number of Italians admitted annually was reduced from 42,128 under the Act of 1921 to 3,845 under the Act of 1924, and the number of Poles from 30,977 to 5,977. A certain amount of anti-Semitism also got into the matter, for a large proportion of the immigrants from Eastern Europe were Jews. The two acts worked so well that by 1930 the year's immigration was reduced to 241,700, and by 1933 to 23,068. Indeed, since 1930 the number of immigrants coming in annually has been more than once surpassed by the number of former immigrants returning home, and from 1930 to 1935 the total excess amounted to 229,363.[1]

Of the 13,366,407 foreign-born whites in the country in 1930,[2] 13,216,928 were ten years old or older, and of this number only 3,907,021 spoke English as their native language. Nevertheless, all save 869,865 of the remainder managed to convince the census enumerators that they had acquired a workable command of the language. No doubt most of them spoke it badly, but at all events they tried to speak it, and their children were being taught it in the schools. The immigrants of the older immigrations had naturally made the most progress. The Scandinavians, about half of whom arrived before 1900, made the best showing, with hardly more than 2% of them unable to speak English, and less than 1% of the males. Next came the Germans: 58.3% of them arrived before 1900, and all save 2.9% (1.8% of males) could speak English. The Poles, Russians,

1 *Congressional Record*, Feb. 19, 1935, p. 2290.
2 Including Negroes, Mexicans and Asiatics, the total number was 14,-204,149. Of these, 7,919,536 were naturalized, 1,266,419 had taken out their first papers, 4,518,341 had made no move to be naturalized,

and 499,853 were of uncertain status. It was estimated in 1934 that the number of the unnaturalized had shrunk to 3,600,000. Very often the statement is made that there are also millions of unrecorded aliens in the country, but for this there is no evidence.

Italians, Greeks and Czechs, and the Baltic and Balkan peoples, most of whom came in between 1900 and 1914, fell much behind. Of the Poles, for example, 12.8% were still unable to speak English in 1930 (7.7% of males and 18.7% of females) and of the Italians 15.7% (8.9% and 25.1%). Here something more than mere duration of residence in the country seems to have had some influence, for though 12.7% of the Germans came in after 1925, only 2.9% were without English in 1930. These late-coming Germans were, on the whole, much better educated than the Eastern and Southern Europeans who arrived at the same time, and large numbers of them had probably received some instruction in English at home. Moreover, they dispersed themselves throughout the country, and did not collect in ghettoes, like a majority of the Italians, Slavs and Jews. Of the 1,808,289 Italians here in 1930 more than 1,500,000 were crowded into relatively few cities, and of the 1,222,658 Jews who reported Yiddish as their native language all save 19,000 were living in cities.[1]

This concentration of foreign-speaking people in limited areas has naturaly influenced the American of those areas, if only on its lower levels. Now that immigration has been virtually cut off, that influence will diminish, but how long it may be exerted is to be observed in the so-called Pennsylvania-Dutch region of Pennsylvania, where a dialect of German is still a living speech after more than 200 years of settlement, and the local dialect of English shows plain traces of it, both in vocabulary and in pronunciation. In the same way, the everyday speech of lower Louisiana is full of French terms not in use elsewhere, *e.g.*, *brioche, praline, lagniappe, armoir, kruxingiol (croquignole), pooldoo (poule d'eau), jambalaya, bogue, gris-gris* and *briqué.*[2]

---

1 These figures, it should be noted, do not show the total number of foreign-born Jews in the country. "Many Jews of foreign birth," says the Census Bureau (Fifteenth Census: Population, Vol. II; Washington, 1933, p. 342), "report German, Russian or other languages as their mother tongue."

2 See New Orleans Word-List, by E. Riedel, *Dialect Notes*, Vol. IV, Pt. IV, 1916; Louisiana, by James Routh, *Dialect Notes*, Vol. IV, Pt. V, 1916; and Terms From Louisiana, by James Routh and E. O.

Barker, *Dialect Notes*, Vol. IV, Pt. VI, 1917. Appended to the last-named is a long list of Louisiana names for birds and animals, many of them French, *e.g.*, *aigle tête blanche* (the bald eagle), *becassine* (a species of snipe), *biorque* (the bittern), *carencro* (vulture), *corbigeau* (plover), *dindon farouche* or *dindon sauvage* (wild turkey), *gros-bec* (heron), *paper bleu* (finch), and *bassaris* (civet cat). The word *ofay,* which may have come from the French *au fait* (signifying mastery), is in general

In Minnesota and the adjacent States many Swedish terms are in common use, e.g., *lutfisk* (a fish delicacy), *lingon* (a berry), *lefse* (a potato pancake), *fattigmand* (a pastry), *spruts* (another), *lag* (an association of Swedes from the same province), and *midsommarfest* (commonly Anglicized to *midsummer-feast*). There is also a considerable borrowing of Swedish idioms, as in *to cook coffee* (*koka kaffee*), *forth and back* (*fram och tillbaka*), and *to hold with* in place of *to agree with* (*håller med*). A recent observer collected the following among "English-speaking high-school and college graduates of Swedish descent" in Minnesota, Wisconsin and Illinois:

The Expression Heard	Standard English	The Swedish Original
She poured up the coffee	She poured the coffee	Hon *hällde upp* kaffet
The sour hen	The setting hen	Den *sura höna*
I cooked soup on that bone	I made soup with that bone	Jag *kokte soppa* på detta ben
I studied for him	I studied under him	Jag *studerade för honom*
They call him for a fool	They call him a fool	De kallade honom *för en narr*
I read for the minister	I studied with the minister	Jag *läste för prästen*
Ready till Christmas	Ready by Christmas	Färdigt *till* jul
I am freezing so	I am so cold	Jag *fryser* [1]

To this list a correspondent [2] adds the following:

The English of Swedish children often influences the English of their American playmates. A colleague who is a New Englander tells me that his Minnesota-born children used to say, "I want to go with" (*Jag vill gå med*). A Swedishism frequently heard is "It stands in the paper" (*Det står i tidningen*). "A couple, three dollars" apparently comes from *Ett par, tre dollar*.

---

use in the Negro press of the United States to designate a white person. It is possible that it originated in New Orleans. Its popularity, I suspect, is at least partly due to its brevity, which makes it a good headline word. Most of the more recent American borrowings from French have come in through English, e.g., *garage*, *gigolo* and *hangar*, or have entered the two languages simultaneously, but *rôtisserie*, with the accent omitted, seems to be an Americanism. It signifies an eating-house wherein chickens and butcher's meat are roasted at a charcoal-grill, usually in the show-window of the establishment. It has been in use in New York since 1900 or thereabout, but is encountered only infrequently elsewhere.

1 Twenty Idioms Illustrating the Influence of Swedish on English, by Thorvald E. Holter, *American Speech*, Feb., 1931.

2 Mr. Roy W. Swanson, of the editorial staff of the St. Paul *Dispatch*.

I once heard a second-generation university man use the sentence, "He will not live over it," meaning "He will not get over it." The Swedish is *Det kommer han inte att överleva.*

In the same way Czech words have got into American and Czech idioms have influenced usage in the regions wherein Bohemian immigrants are numerous. One of the former is listed in "Webster's New International Dictionary " (1934). It is *kolach*, and it is defined as " variety of kuchen made esp. by Bohemians." Why the German word *kuchen* is used in this definition I don't know. *Kolach* is the Czech *koláč*, with its accent lost in the melting-pot. Other Czech loan-words and phrases that are in local use are *rohlík* (a roll brushed with egg-yolk, salted, and sometimes sprinkled with caraway or poppy seeds), *povidla* (a prune marmalade), *buchta* (a coffee-cake), *počkij* (wait, hold on), *sokol* (literally, a falcon, but used to designate an athletic association), *na zdar* (good luck), and *to soc* (from the verb *sočiti*, meaning to scold or grumble). Another is *pantáta* (literally, *Mr. Father*, and signifying a father-in-law). This last was apparently in use in New York at the time of the Lexow investigation to designate a corrupt police-captain, but it has gone out.[1] In Bristol county, Massachusetts, where there are many Portuguese immigrants, a number of Portuguese loan-words are encountered, *e.g., cabeca* (head), *lingreese* (Port. *linguica*, a sausage), and *jick* or *jickie* (Englishman).[2] If *cuspidor* is actually an Americanism, which seems probable, then it most likely came from the Portuguese verb *cuspir* (to spit). The Oxford Dictionary's first example of its use (spelled *cuspadore*) is taken from Forrest's " Voyage to New Guinea," dated 1779, but after that there is no quotation until 1871, at which time an Englishman named Heath took out a patent for " an improvement in *cuspidores*." The word seems to have been in general use in the United States before 1870.[3] In New York City the high density of Eastern Jews in the population has made almost every New Yorker familiar with a long list of Yiddish words, *e.g., kosher, shadchan, matzoth, mazuma,*[4] *yom kippur, meshuggah* and

1 See Czech Influence Upon the American Vocabulary, by Monsignor J. B. Dudek, *Czecho-Slovak Student Life* (Lisle, Ill.), June, 1928.
2 I am indebted here to Mr. Charles J. Lovell. The prevalence of Dutch loan-words in the Hudson river region has been remarked in Chap-

ter III, Section 1, and of Spanish loan-words in the Southwest in Chapter IV, Section 3.
3 I am indebted here to Mr. Arthur R. Coelho.
4 According to H. Heshin (*American Speech*, May, 1926, p. 456) *mazuma* is derived from a Chal-

gefilte-fisch, and many non-Jewish New Yorkers have added others that are not generally familiar, e.g., *schul, bar-mitzva, blintzes, kaddish, trefa, dayyan, goy, dokus, schochet, schmus, schicker, schiksa, mohel, get, hesped, kishkes, kittl, meshummad* and *pesach*. The Yiddish exclamation, *oi-yoi*, is common New Yorkese, and the Yiddish greetings, *mazzaltov* and *scholom aleichim*, are pretty well known and understood. There is also some translation of Yiddish idioms, as in " That's something else again " and " Did I say no? " In 1915 or thereabout " I should worry " came into use in New York, and quickly spread throughout the country. It was said at the time to be a translation of a Yiddish phrase, *ish ka bibble*, but about this there is still some mystery. The common Yiddish saying is actually " *Es is mein daige* " (It is my worry).[1] There are not a few Yiddish loan-words in German, and some of them have probably been helped into American by that fact, e.g., *kosher, mazuma* (money), *matzoth, meshuggah* (crazy), and *dokus* (backside). I find *mazuma* in a word list from Kansas.[2] Contrariwise, there are many German words in Yiddish, and one of them, *kibitzer*, has come into American by the Yiddish route. In German *kiebitz* signifies the peewit or lapwing (*Vancellus cristallus*), and has long been in figurative use to designate a looker-on at cards, and especially one who offers unsolicited advice.[3] The word apparently acquired the agent suffix, *-er*, on coming into American. Yiddish has greatly enriched the vocabulary of those trades in which Jews are numerous. In the retail shoe business, " a customer who shops from store to store, trying on shoes but not buying, is known as a *schlepper*. In Yiddish the word means a mean fellow. Those who bargain in a one-price store are called *schnorrers*,

---

dean word, *m'zumon*, " meaning in literal translation the ready necessary." *Gefilte*, of course, is the German *gefüllte* (stuffed).

1 Here I am indebted to Mr. Albert Kaplan.

2 In the collectanea of Judge J. C. Ruppenthal, *Dialect Notes*, Vol. IV, Pt. V, 1916, p. 326.

3 The following is from a letter signed Philologist in the New York *Evening Post*, Feb. 15, 1929: " Any one who has ever visited drowsy little inns of the German countryside remembers the grotesque portrait of the chap with a topheavy,

huge and red nose, possibly behaired, on the tip of which a fat fly takes it easy. In order that the guests may not mistake it for a likeness of Cyrano, an invariable legend cautions energetically: ' *Kibitz*, halts maul! ' (Kibitzer, keep your mouth shut)." Another correspondent, Hermann Post, wrote on the same day: " The eggs of the peewit are very much sought after for their delicious taste. They are laid on the ground. The bird, to protect the eggs, flies frantically around the heads of people looking for them."

218 The American Language

from the Yiddish for a beggar. The most derogatory of all terms in shoe lingo is the word *momzer*, also derived from the Yiddish and meaning a bastard. A *momzer* is one who, after working the salesman to death, decides to buy in a store down the block."[1] The instalment furniture stores have also borrowed from the Yiddish. They are called by their salesmen *borax-houses*, and the *borax* apparently comes from the Yiddish *borg*, meaning credit. "When business is bad it's *shofle*, and a sucker is always a *schnookel*." When the credit department offers a customer such unfavorable terms that the sale is killed, it is said to be *schmiessed*.[2] In the garment trade Yiddish is probably used more than English, and such English as is employed is full of Yiddish terms.[3]

The largest body of loan-words in American is that from the Spanish, with that from the German following hard upon it. Both have been discussed in the last chapter. Since the Civil War the chief contribution of German has been the domestication of the suffix *-fest*. It came in with *sängerfest* and *turnfest* in the early 50's, but the manufacture of American analogues did not begin until 1900 or thereabout. I have encountered, among others, the following: *talkfest, swatfest* (a baseball game marked by many hits), *hoochfest, slugfest* (prizefight), *smokefest, walkfest, gabfest*,[4] *sobfest, egofest, spooffest, eatfest, stuntfest, ananiasfest, blarneyfest, smilefest, gossipfest, batfest* (baseball), *bloodfest* (war), *crabfest, gabblefest, jawfest, singfest, lovefest, bullfest, boozefest, bookfest* and *applefest*.[5] When,

1 Lingo of the Shoe Salesman, by David Geller, *American Speech*, Dec., 1934.
2 The Borax House, by Louise Conant, *American Mercury*, June, 1929.
3 I am indebted in Yiddish matters to Mr. B. H. Hartogensis of Baltimore, who has undertaken an extensive study of Loan-Words From the Hebrew in the American Language, not yet published.
4 A writer in the *Editor and Publisher* for Dec. 25, 1919, p. 30, credits the first use of *gabfest* to the late Joseph S. McCullagh, editor of the St. Louis *Globe-Democrat*. He says: "McCullagh coined the word while writing a comment upon an unusually prolonged and empty debate in Congress. No

other word in the dictionary or out of it seemed to fit the case so well, and as a great percentage of the readers of the *Globe-Democrat* throughout the Central West were of German birth or origin, *gabfest* was seized upon with hearty zest, and it is today very generally applied to any protracted and particularly loquacious gathering." In the Supplement to the Oxford Dictionary the first quoted use of the word is from the Grand Rapids (Mich.) *Evening Express*, July 30, 1904.
5 The "first annual *bookfest* and movie star rummage sale" of the League of American Penwomen was held at the Hotel Marion, Little Rock, Ark., Jan. 13–14, 1924. An *applefest* was held at the Mar-

on the repeal of Prohibition, American legislators began to search for euphemisms for *saloon,* one of the words they hit upon was the German *stube,* signifying, alone, simply a room, but often combined with *bier* (beer) or *wein* (wine) in *bierstube* or *weinstube.* According to Sir William Craigie, *beer-garden,* which came in about 1870, is "clearly from the German," *i.e.,* from *biergarten.*

The suffixes *-heimer* and *-bund* had brief vogues in 1900 or thereabout, but the former survives only in *wiseheimer* and the latter only in *plunderbund* and *moneybund,* the former of which is listed in "Webster's New International Dictionary" (1934). *Wanderlust* seems to have come in since 1900; it is also known in England, but is used much more frequently in the United States along with its derivatives, *wanderluster* (Eng. *rambler*), *wanderlusting* and *wanderlust-club* (Eng. *rambler-society*).[1] Like *sauerkraut,* it was under a patriotic ban during the World War, but recovered promptly. *Living-room* may have been suggested by the German *wohnzimmer.* The Oxford Dictionary cites a single use of it in England in 1825, but in the sense of "the room usually occupied during the day" it is called an Americanism in the Oxford Supplement, and assigned to 1867. *Blizzard* has been often listed among Americanisms of German origin, with that origin assigned variously to *blitzen* (lightning) or *blitzartig* (lightning-like), but the researches of Allen Walker Read reveal that it was in use to designate a violent blow (as with the fist) long before it came to mean a storm. It is probably onomatopeic.[2] *So-long,* the phrase of parting, has been credited similarly to the German *so lange* (and also to the Yiddish *sholom*), but it is actually of English origin, and does not appear to be an Americanism. In a letter from Bayard Taylor to Edmund Clarence Stedman, dated June 16, 1865, *and how* is laid to "the Germans,"[3]

---

ble Collegiate Church, New York City, in Dec., 1922. The North Side Community Choral Club, a Negro organization, held a *sangerfest* (without the umlaut) in Pittsburgh in April, 1927. (Pittsburgh *Courier,* April 9.) See Domestication of the Suffix *-fest,* by Louise Pound, *Dialect Notes,* Vol. IV, Pt. V, 1916.

1 *American Speech,* April, 1935, p. 155, reports a punning analogue, *squanderlust,* and ascribes it to

Louis Ludlow, a member of Congress from Indiana.

2 See The Word *Blizzard,* by Allen Walker Read, *American Speech,* Feb., 1928, and *Blizzard* Again, by the same, *American Speech,* Feb., 1930.

3 The letter is to be found in The Life and Letters of Bayard Taylor, by Marie Hansen Taylor; Boston, 1884. I am indebted for the reference to *And How,* by J. R. Schultz, *American Speech,* Dec., 1933, p. 80.

but no other evidence that it was borrowed seems to be available. On equally dubious evidence *rubber-neck* has been derived from a probably mythical German *gummihals*, and *it listens well*, a phrase of affirmation popular twenty years ago, has been linked with the Berlinese adage, *Et jinge woll, aber et jeht nicht. Junge* (from *klingen*) actually means to sound; the German verb for *to listen* is *horchen*. In all probability, *it listens well* was introduced by the German comedians who flourished before the World War. Like their Irish and Yiddish colleagues, they enriched the current slang with many fantastic locutions. The influence of Charles Godfrey Leland's " Hans Brietmann's Ballads " and other books also helped to familiarize Americans with many German and pseudo-German words and phrases.[1] *Phooey*, which plainly comes from the German (and Yiddish) *pfui*, seems to have been introduced by Walter Winchell, *c.* 1930. The barbecues which began to dot the country with the rise of the automobile soon offered *chickenburgers* as well as *hamburgers*, and there are even reports of *clamburgers*.[2] In 1930, for some reason to me unknown, Swift & Company, the Chicago packers, changed the name of their *frankfurters* to *frankfurts*, and introduced a substitute for *leberwurst* under the style of *livercheese*. The American *Gelehrten*, who began to resort to German universities in large number in the 80's, brought back *festschrift, seminar, semester, anlage* and *diener* and still cling to them, and it is possible that *outstanding*, the favorite counter-word of pedagogues lower in the scale, was suggested by *ausstehend*.[3]

The majority of the numerous Spanish loan-words in American came in before the Civil War, but the Spanish-American War added

1 See The Cambridge History of American Literature; New York, 1921; Ch. IX; p. 23 *ff.*
2 *New Yorker*, Feb. 16, 1935.
3 I am informed by the Rev. W. G. Polack, of Evansville, Ind., that certain Lutherans in the United States, following German usage, employ *vicar* to designate " a theological student, not yet ordained, who is doing temporary supply-work in a mission congregation." The verb *to vicar* means to occupy such a pulpit. Mr. Polack believes that *mission-festival*, common in the Middle West, comes from the German *missionsfest*. So with *agenda*, used by some of the Lutheran churches to designate their Book of Common Prayer. He says that it is not the English term, but the German *agende*. He notes also the use of *confirmand* to designate a candidate for confirmation; of *to announce* to indicate notifying a pastor of an intention to partake of communion (Ger. *sich anmelden*); and of *inner-mission* (Ger. *innere mission*) instead of the usual *home-mission*; and of *confessional-address* (*beichtrede*). All these terms are used by English-speaking Lutherans.

insurrecto, trocha, junta, ladrone, incommunicado, ley fuga, machete, manaña and *rurale,* some of which are already obsolete; and the popularity of Western movies and fiction has brought in a few more, e.g., *rodeo, hoosegow* (from *juzgado,* the past participle of *juzgar,* to judge) [1] and *wrangler* (from *caballerango,* a horse-groom), and greatly increased the use of others. *Chile con carne* did not enter into the general American dietary until after 1900. The suffix *-ista* came in during the troubles in Mexico, following the downfall of Porfirio Díaz in 1911. The case of *cafeteria* I have dealt with in Section 2 of this chapter. From the Indian languages the only recent acquisitions seem to be *chautauqua* and *hooch.* The latter goes back to the American occupation of Alaska in 1867. The first soldiers sent there were forbidden to have any spirituous liquors, so they set up stills and manufactured a supply of their own, of sugar and flour. The product was called *hoocheno* or *hoochino* by the natives, and it continued to bear that name until the Klondike gold-rush in 1897.[2] Then it was shortened to *hooch. Chautauqua* was borrowed from the name of the county and lake in Southwestern New York. The first *chautauqua* was opened on the shore of the lake on August 4, 1874, but the word did not come into general use until the end of the century. It was borrowed in the first place from the language of the Senecas, and it is reported, variously, to have meant the place of easy death, the place where one was lost, the foggy place, a place high up, two moccasins tied in the middle, and a pack tied in the middle. The French spelled it *tchadakoin,* and in early maps and books it appeared also as *tjadakoin, chataconit, chadakoin, chautauque, shatacoin, judaxque* and *jadaqua.* In 1859, by a resolution of the county

1 For the following I am indebted to Mr. Leon L. Kay, for six years a correspondent of the United Press in Latin America: " The lower classes always slur the consonant in the regular ending, *-ado,* of Spanish participles, and so do the upper classes in rapid speech or unguarded moments. Furthermore, the final *o* is sounded so lightly as to make a virtual diphthong of *ao,* equivalent to *ou* in *mouth.* Peons, never able to, are seldom asked to pay fines. To them, to be *juzgado* (sentenced) means simply to be jailed. When Felipe or José, after the usual week-end drunk, is missed and inquired after, the answer to ' Where is he? ' is ' *Juzgado.*' The first Americans, seeking missing ranch-hands, no doubt took this to be a Spanish word for jail, and so *hoosegow* was born. Apart from shifting the stress to the first from the penultimate syllable, the Southwesterners have achieved an almost perfect transliteration." The Spanish *j* is pronounced like our *h,* the Spanish *u* like our *oo,* and the Spanish *ado* like our *ou.*

2 Dearborn *Independent,* March 3, 1923: " It is said that one quart was sufficient to craze the brains of ten Indians."

board of supervisors, the present spelling was made official.[1] At the start *chautauqua* meant a Summer-school, permanently housed and of some pedagogical pretensions. But toward 1900 it began to signify a traveling show, often performing under canvas, and including vaudeville acts as well as lectures.

In the Concise Oxford Dictionary, which is on every literate Englishman's desk, *spaghetti* is italicized as a foreign word; in America it is familiar to every child. But not many other Italian loan-words have got into American, probably because the great majority of Italian immigrants have been poor folk, keeping much to themselves. I can think of *chianti* (more generally known as *dago-red*), *ravioli*, *minestrone*, *mafia* and *black-hand* (from *mano negra*), and that is about all.[2] Even the argot of roguery has been but little enriched by Italian words, though there have been many eminent Italian gunmen. It has been suggested that *and how* may owe something to the Italian *e come*, and that *sez you* may be a translation of *si dice*,[3] but there is no evidence in either case. It may be that *ambish* and its analogues were suggested by Italian difficulties with English, but that also is only a surmise. At the time of the Russian-Japanese War (1904–5) the suffix *-ski* or *-sky* had a popular vogue, and produced many words, e.g., *dunski*, *darnfoolski*, *smartski*, *devilinsky*, *allrightsky* and *buttinski*, but of these only *buttinski* seems to have survived.[4]

1 See *Chautauqua* Notes, by J. R. Schultz, *American Speech*, Oct., 1934, p. 232.
2 The word *policy*, which was used in the United States from about 1885 to 1915 to designate the form of gambling now called *numbers*, was from the Italian *polizza*. But it apparently came in by way of English, though with a change in meaning, and it is now virtually obsolete.
3 By M. H. Palmer in the London *Morning Post*, Feb. 9, 1935.
4 See the following notes by Louise Pound, all in *Dialect Notes*; Vol. IV, Pt. IV, 1916, p. 304; Vol. IV, Pt. V, 1916, p. 354; Vol. V, Pt. I, 1918, p. 11.

VI

AMERICAN AND ENGLISH

1. THE INFILTRATION OF ENGLISH BY AMERICANISMS

The English travelers and reviewers whose pious horror of Americanisms has been recorded in Chapters I and III were able, for a while, to shut off their flow into Standard English, but only for a while. The tide began to turn, according to Sir William Craigie,[1] in 1820, and soon thereafter a large number of Yankee neologisms that had been resisted with heroic dudgeon came into common use in England, e.g., *reliable, influential, talented* and *lengthy*. Charles Dickens was credited by Bishop Coxe[2] with responsibility for the final acceptance of all four words: he put them into his " American Notes " in 1842 and Coxe believed that he thus naturalized them. But as a matter of fact they had all come in before this. Coleridge used *reliable* in 1800 and *influential* in 1833, and though he was still denouncing *talented* as " that vile and barbarous vocable " in 1832, and it was dismissed as a word " proper to avoid " by Macaulay even in 1842,[3] it had been used by the critic and philologian, William Taylor, in 1830, by Sir William Herschel, the astronomer, in 1829, and by no less an Americophobe than Robert Southey in 1828. Southey, in his turn, sneered at *lengthy* in 1812 and again in 1834, but it was used by Jeremy Bentham so early as 1816, by Scott in 1827 (though still as a conscious Americanism), and by Dickens himself in " Pickwick " in 1837, five years before the publication of " American Notes." *Talented* had become so respectable by 1842 that it was accepted by E. B. Pusey, leader of the Oxford Movement,[4] and fifteen years later it received the imprimatur of Glad-

---

1 *S.P.E. Tracts*, No. XXVII, 1927, p. 208.
2 Americanisms in England, by A. Cleveland Coxe, *Forum*, Oct., 1886.
3 Letter to Macvey Napier, April 18, 1842, printed in The Life and Letters of Lord Macaulay, by G. Otto Trevelyan; New York, 1877, Vol. II, p. 100.
4 Here, as in so many other places, I am indebted to the Oxford Dictionary for its dated quotations.

stone. Along with *reliable, influential* and *lengthy* it now appears in the Concise Oxford Dictionary, published by the brothers Fowler in 1911, and of the four words, only *lengthy* is noted as " originally an Americanism." [1] All are listed in Cassell's Dictionary without remark. During the half century following 1820 many other Americanisms also made their way into English. Even *to belittle,* which had provoked an almost hysterical outburst from the *European Magazine and London Review* when Thomas Jefferson ventured to use it in 1787,[2] was so generally accepted by 1862 that Anthony Trollope admitted it to his chaste vocabulary.

John S. Farmer says [3] that the American humorists who flourished after the Civil War broke down most of the remaining barriers to Americanisms. The English purists continued to rage against them, as they do even to this day, but the success in England of such writers as Charles Godfrey Leland (Hans Breitmann), Charles Heber Clark (Max Adeler), Charles Farrar Browne (Artemus Ward), David R. Locke (Petroleum V. Nasby) and Samuel L. Clemens (Mark Twain) made the English public familiar with the pungent neologisms of the West, and many of them were taken into the language. George F. Whicher says that Leland and Clark " became better known in England than in the United States; " [4] as for Browne, he was so popular in London that he moved there in 1866, and died on English soil a year later. The influence of these men, according to Farmer, was still strong in the late 80's; they had popularized " American peculiarities of speech and diction to an extent which, a few years since, would have been deemed incredible." He continued:

Even our newspapers, hitherto regarded as models of correct literary style, are many of them following in their wake; and both in matter and phraseology are lending countenance to what at first sight appears a monstrously crude and almost imbecile jargon; while others, fearful of a direct plunge, modestly intro-

1 The Fowlers call *reliable* " an established word avoided by purists as of irregular formation." It has actually been in good usage in England since the 60's. In 1871, when the United States claimed a large sum from England as indemnity for the depredations of the Confederate cruiser *Alabama, Punch* suggested that the injury England had suffered through the introduction of the word was sufficient compensation.

2 See Chapter I, Section 2, for the text of its denunciation.

3 Americanisms Old and New; London, 1889, p. vii.

4 Cambridge History of American Literature; New York, 1921, Vol. III, p. 26.

duce the uncouth bantlings with a saving clause. The phrase, *as the Americans say*, might in some cases be ordered from the type-foundry as a logotype, so frequently does it do introduction duty.[1]

But before the great invasion of England by American movies, beginning in the first years of the World War, Americanisms commonly had to linger in a sort of linguistic Alsatia a long while before they were accepted, and even then they were sometimes changed in meaning. The cases of *caucus* and *buncombe* are perhaps typical. The former, as we have seen in Chapter III, Section 1, was borrowed from an Indian word so early as 1624, and was in general use in the American colonies before 1738, but in 1818 Sydney Smith was dismissing it as " the cant word of the Americans," and even in 1853 Bulwer-Lytton, using it in " My Novel," was conscious that it was a somewhat strange Americanism. It was not until 1878 that it came into general use in England, and then, in the words of the Oxford Dictionary, it was " grossly misapplied." In the United States it had the settled meaning of a meeting of some division, large or small, of a political or legislative body for the purpose of agreeing upon a united course of action in the main assembly, but in England it was applied to what we would call the *organization*. It was used by Benjamin Disraeli to designate the faction of Birmingham Liberals otherwise known as the Six Hundred, and in this sense was used thereafter by the *Times* and other English newspapers. It retains that meaning to this day; it signifies the managing committee of a party or faction — something corresponding to our national committees, our State committees, or to the half-forgotten congressional caucuses of the 1820's. It thus has a disparaging connotation, and the London *Saturday Review*, in 1888, denounced what it called a *caucuser* as " a machine politician." *Caucuser* is a derivative concocted in England; it is never used in the United States, and does not appear in " Webster's New International Dictionary " (1934). Nor does *caucusdom*, which appeared in England in 1885. *Buncombe* got into Standard English just as slowly as *caucus*, and suffered a change too, though it was of a different kind. The word has been in use in the United States since the beginning of the last century, and was spoken of as " old and common at Washington " by a writer

1 Americanisms Old and New, above
  cited, p. vii.

in *Niles's Register* on September 27, 1827, but it did not come into general use in England until the late 1850's, and then its spelling was changed to *bunkum*.

But when the American clipped form *bunk* arose toward the end of the World War it began to appear in England almost instantly, for it had the influence of the American movies behind it, and when the verb *to debunk* followed ten years later it got into use quite as quickly. Hundreds of other saucy Americanisms have followed it, often in successful competition with English neologisms. Thus, when the English police began to patrol the roads on motorcycles they were called, officially, *mobile police,* but in a little while an alternative name for them was *speed-cops,* borrowed from the American movies and talkies.[1] This invasion is resisted valiantly by swarms of volunteer guardians of the national linguistic chastity, and at irregular intervals they break out into violent crusades against this or that American novelty,[2] but many of the more colorful ones now get into circulation very rapidly. H. W. Horwill, in his " Dictionary of Modern American Usage," [3] notes a large number that have " become naturalized since the beginning of the present cen-

1 London letter in the *Boulevardier* (Paris) April, 1931. In July, 1932 (*News of the World,* July 24), the Assistant Bishop of Guildford, Dr. Cyril Golding-Bird, appeared before the Farnham (Surrey) magistrates on a charge of dangerous driving. The policeman who arrested him testified that, on being overhauled, he demanded " Are you a *speed-cop?* " His Lordship, evidently in fear that the use of an Americanism by one of his exalted station would prejudice the bench against him, stoutly declared that he " was not sufficiently colloquial " to have used it. But the magistrates, taking a serious view of the matter, fined him £10 and costs and suspended his driving license for three months.

2 In the Spring of 1935, for example, Major Brooke Heckstall-Smith, yachting correspondent to the London *Daily Telegraph,* raised a holy war against *to debunk* in the columns of his paper, and was presently joined by other viewers with alarm. One of them, A. E. Sullivan (March 2), ascribed its origin to " the inability of an ill-educated and unintelligent democracy to assimilate long words." But it was defended by Hubert Furst (March 2), author of a book entitled Art Debunked, and by Pearl Freeman (March 4), who called it " a fullblooded descriptive word." On March 2 *radio* was put at the head of a list of " bastard American expressions " by John C. Mellis (with *O.K., sez you, nerts, cute* and *bigfella* following), but on March 6 it was defended by Jan Stewer as " a beautiful coinage," and its English equivalent, *wireless,* denounced as " an abomination."

3 Oxford, 1935. Horwill excludes foreign loan-words in American, and words spelled differently in American and English, and his book naturally reveals a great many omissions; nevertheless, he manages to list nearly 3000 words and phrases that differ in the two languages.

tury," *e.g.*, the compounds *hot-air, bed-rock, come-back, filling-station, high-brow, jay-walker, round-up* and *foot-wear*, the simple nouns *crook* (a criminal), *boom, kick* (a powerful effect), *publicity* (advertising) and *conservatory* (musical), the verbs *to park* (automobile), *to rattle* and *to boom*, and the verb-phrases *to put across, to blow in* (to turn up), *to get away with, to make good, to get a move on, to put over* and *to turn down;* and an even larger number that are " apparently becoming naturalized," *e.g.*, the compounds *bargain-counter, bell-boy, schedule-time, speed-way, chafing-dish, carpet-bagger, come-down, joy-ride, hold-up, horse-sense, soap-box, frame-up dance-hall, key-man, close-up, close-call, rough-house, gold-brick, log-rolling* and *money-to-burn*, the simple nouns *rally, bromide, cub, cut* (in the sense of a reduction), *engineer* (locomotive), *fan* (enthusiast), *pep, machine* (political), *quitter, pull* (political), *pointer, mixer* and *cereal* (breakfast-food), the simple verbs *to ditch, to feature, to fire* (dismiss), *to pass* (a dividend) and *to hustle*, the verb-phrases *to bank on, to get busy, to come to stay, to crowd out, to fall down* (or *for*), *to try out, to pick on, to hand-pick, to iron out, to see the light, to deliver the goods, to soft-pedal, to sand-bag, to sit up and take notice, to snow under, to stay put, to side-step, to side-track, to stand for* and *to win out*, and the miscellaneous idioms *good and, on the side, up to* and *up against*. Many of these, of course, belong to slang but some of them are nevertheless making their way into relatively decorous circles. The late Dr. Paul Shorey, professor of Greek at the University of Chicago, used to amuse himself by collecting instances of the use of thumping Americanisms by English authors of dignified standing. He found *to make good* and *cold feet* in John Galsworthy, *rubber-neck* in Sir Arthur Quiller-Couch (King Edward VII professor of English literature at Cambridge!), *nothing doing* in Lowes Dickinson, *proposition* " as a word of all work " in Mrs. Humphrey Ward, *to cough up* in John Masefield, *the limit* in Archibald Marshall, and *up against a tough proposition* in William J. Locke.[1] Such *literati* seldom if ever adorn their discourse with the current slang of their own country, save of course in depicting low or careless characters. But they are fetched by the piquancy of Americanisms, and employ them for their pungent rhetorical effect. The same consideration influences

1 Academy Papers; New York, 1925,
  p. 150.

English politicians too, and " a veteran Parliamentarian " was lately saying:

> Every time the House [of Commons] meets things are said in a phraseology that would shock and baffle Mr. Gladstone. . . . Even Mr. Baldwin, one of the few authorities on the King's English in the House, used in his speech yesterday the expressions *backslider, best-seller* and *party dog-fight*. I have heard him use *to deliver the goods*. The House is undoubtedly Americanized in some of its phrases. I have heard *whoopee* and *debunked* in the debating chamber, and *oh, yeah* and *you're telling me* in the lobby. *To pass the buck* is a well-known House expression and it is often used.[1]

The argot of English politics has naturalized many Americanisms beside *caucus* and *buncombe*. *Graft*, wrote Harold Brighouse in 1929, " is acclimatized in England." [2] So is *gerrymander*. So are *platform, carpet-bagger, wire-puller, log-rolling, on the fence, campaign*,[3] *to stump*, and *to electioneer*.[4] In other fields there has been the same infiltration. The meaning of *bucket-shop* and *to water*, for example, is familiar to every London broker's clerk. English trains are now *telescoped* and carry *dead-heads*, there is an Associated Society of Locomotive *Engineers* and *Firemen*, and in 1913 a rival to the Amalgamated Order Of Railway *Servants* was organized under the name of the National Union of *Railway Men*. A movement against the use of the ignominious *servant* is visible in other directions, and the American *help* threatens to be substituted; at all events, *Help Wanted* advertisements are occasionally printed in English newspapers. The American *to phone* is now in general use over there, and " Hello " has displaced " Are you there? " as the standard telephone greeting. English journalists are ceasing to call themselves *pressmen*, and have begun to use the American *newspaper men*. They begin to write *editorials* instead of *leaders*. The English theaters continue to have *dress-circles* where ours have *balconies*, but there are *balconies* in the movie-houses. Since England began to grow sugar-beets the English *beet-root* has succumbed to the American (and earlier English) *beet*, and the American *can* seems to be ousting the English *tin*. *Sky-scraper, strap-hanger* and *fool-proof* were naturalized long ago,[5] and I have encountered *cafeteria, kitchen-cabinet, filing-cabinet, nut-sundae, soda-fountain, ice-*

1 Sunderland *Echo*, Oct. 31, 1934.
2 Manchester *Guardian*, April 5.
3 For example, Gladstone's *Midlothian campaign* of 1880.
4 The Study of American English,
by W. A. Craigie, *S.P.E. Tracts*, No. XXVII, 1927, p. 208.
5 See British English and American English, by Thomas G. Tucker, *Scribner's*, Dec., 1921.

cream-soda and *pop-corn* on shop signs in London, *chain-store* in a headline in a 100% British provincial newspaper,[1] *junk* in the London *Daily Telegraph* [2] and *sticker* instead of the English *sticky-back* or *tab* in another great London journal,[3] all within the space of a few days. On December 8, 1934, Miss Julia Hogan, of 245 Lord street, Southport, was advertising in the Southport *Visiter* [4] that she was a *beautician*, and a few months later J. A. Watson was reporting in the London *Daily Telegraph* [5] that " those truly loathsome transatlantic importations," *to help make, worth-while, nearby* and *colorful,* were " spreading like plague." No less a lexicographical dignitary than Dr. C. T. Onions, one of the editors of the Oxford Dictionary, is authority for the news that *to make good* " no longer gives the impression of being an alien idiom " in England, that " the American applications of the word *dope* have generally commended themselves and have obtained a wide currency," and that *yep* and *nope* " have penetrated even into the speech of the educated of the younger generation." [6] " Twenty years ago," said S. K. Ratcliffe in 1935,[7] " no one in England *started in, started out* or *checked up;* we did not *stand for* or *fall for,* as we do today. . . . We have learned from the American *to try out,* but not as yet *to curse out,* and when we *make out* we are still deciphering something, and not, as the American is, doing something fairly well." [8] Sometimes an Americanism that has long ceased to be a novelty in this country is suddenly taken up in England, and becomes popular almost overnight. Thus *shyster,* in use here since the 1850's, was introduced by Robert Louis Stevenson in " The Wrecker " in 1892; [9] *Indian-Summer* which goes back to Colonial days, was given a start by John Galsworthy's use of it in the title of " The *Indian Summer* of a Forsyte " (1918); and the Prince of Wales popularized the Rooseveltian *bully* by using it in a speech to Leicestershire huntsmen in 1930. *O.K.* has been known

1 Eastern *Evening News* (Norwich), March 27, 1935.
2 March 28, 1935.
3 *News-Chronicle,* March 21, 1935.
4 Note the archaic spelling here. Jane Austen used it in Pride and Prejudice, and in 1756 there was a newspaper in London called the *Universal Visiter.*
5 March 6, 1935.
6 Is English Becoming Too American?, London *Evening News,* Nov. 19, 1931. It is curious to note what

such bigwigs accept and reject. Dr. Onions, after accepting – or, at all events, condoning – *dope,* repudiates *witness-stand* and *to measure up to the standard.*
7 The American Language, *New Statesman and Nation,* July 27, p. 131.
8 See also American Prepositions, London *Times* (Weekly Ed.), Feb. 16, 1933.
9 Harold Brighouse in the Manchester *Guardian,* April 5, 1929.

and understood in England for at least thirty years, but it was not until 1932 that it came into general use.[1] The movies and talkies are now responsible for most such introductions, whether of new Americanisms or old ones, but they get active help from the radio, the stage and even the English newspapers. In 1933 Henry Hall broadcast from London a list of the songs most popular in Great Britain since 1919, estimated on the basis of the sales of sheet music and phonograph records. Of the sixteen he mentioned, all save five were American.[2] The English newspapers of wide circulation make a heavy use of Americanisms in their headlines and their more gossipy articles,[3] and in the popular magazines "a large number of the stories are set in American situations, or are at least written from an American viewpoint, in semi-American language."[4]

It is curious, reading the fulminations of American purists of the last generation, to note how many of the Americanisms they denounced have broken down all guards across the ocean. *To placate* and *to antagonize* are examples. The Concise Oxford and Cassell distinguished between the English and American meanings of the latter: in England a man may antagonize only another man, in America he may antagonize a mere idea or things. But, as the brothers Fowler show, even the English meaning is of American origin, and no doubt a few more years will see the verb completely naturalized in Britain. *To placate*, attacked vigorously by all native grammarians down to (but excepting) White, now has the authority of the *Spectator*, and is accepted by Cassell. Other old bugaboos

1 The London bureau of the United Press reported on April 28: "The American *O.K.* is rapidly displacing the British *righto* in everyday conversation in Great Britain, despite the opposition of educators. . . . One English columnist the other day made four telephone calls to different numbers and in each case the conversation ended with *O.K.* from the person at the other end."

2 The Most Popular Songs of a Decade, *World Almanac*, 1934, p. 800.

3 In Notes on the Way, *Time and Tide*, Dec. 8, 1934, Humbert Wolfe denounced this "baboon-jargon that we have proudly borrowed from across the Atlantic." The London *Daily Express* has lifted

the whole vocabulary of the American news-weekly, *Time*, and adopted even its eccentric syntax. (See, for example, These Names Make News, Aug. 28, 1935.) I once encountered *Bible Belt* in a headline in the London *Times*, but I have unfortunately forgotten the date. For the use of *but that* in a leading article in the *Times* I point sadly to Two More Days of Pilgrimage, July 13, 1934. Other lexicographical pathologists tell me they have found *high-brow* and *the limit* in the same great newspaper.

4 The Invasion From U. S. A., by Ellis Healey, Birmingham *Gazette*, April 11, 1932.

that have been embraced are *to donate, reliable, gubernatorial, presidential* and *standpoint*. White labored long and valiantly to convince Americans that the adjective derived from *president* should be without the *i* before its last syllable, following the example of *incidental, regimental, monumental, governmental, oriental, experimental* and so on; but in vain, for *presidential* is now perfectly good English. *To engineer, to collide,*[1] *to corner, to obligate,* and *to lynch* are in Cassell with no hint of their American origin, and so are *home-spun, out-house, cross-purposes, green-horn, blizzard, tornado, cyclone, hurricane, excursionist, wash-stand* and *wash-basin,* though *wash-hand-stand* and *wash-hand-basin* are also given. *Drug-store* is making its way in England; the firm known as Boots' the Chemists (formerly Boots Cash Chemists) uses the term to designate its branches. But it is not yet listed by either Cassell or the Concise Oxford, though both give *druggist*. *Tenderfoot* is in general use, though the English commonly mistake it for an Australianism; it is used by the English Boy Scouts just as our own Boy Scouts use it. *Scalawag* has got into English with an extra *l*, making it *scallawag* or *scallywag*. J. Y. T. Greig, in " Breaking Priscian's Head," [2] prints a long list of Americanisms that have become firmly lodged in English, and says that " few of us who have not taken the trouble to go into the matter are aware how many of our common expressions derive from the United States." His list includes, besides the words mentioned above, the compounds *back-woods, chewing-gum, cold-snap, dug-out, half-breed, hot-cake, mass-meeting, beach-comber, six-shooter, bee-line, indignation-meeting* and *pow-wow,* the simple nouns *blizzard, bluff, boodle, boss, caboodle, canyon, collateral* (in the Stock Exchange sense), *combine* (noun), *crank* (eccentric person), *cuss, dago, filibuster, fix* (in a *fix*), *floor* (in the sense of *to have, yield* or *hold the floor*), *flurry, goner, gulch, hustler, mileage, misstep, mugwump, paleface, persimmon, porterhouse* (steak), *ranch, rowdy, school-marm, scrap* (fight), *shack, shanty, shyster, snag* (in a river, and figuratively), *splurge, spook, squatter* and *stampede,* the adjectives *blue, bogus, colored* (Negro), *governmental, highfalutin, low-down, non-commital, pesky, pivotal, played-out, previous* (too *previous*), *rattled, slick* and *whole-souled,* the verbs *to bluff, to boost, to*

---

[1] *To collide* is barred by many English newspapers, which prefer *to come in collision*. But the aim here is simply to avoid any direct imputation of agency, and so head off possible libel suits.

[2] London, 1929, p. 79 ff.

bullyrag, to enthuse, to eventuate, to itemize, to jump (a claim), *to lobby, to locate, to lynch, to negative, to run* (for office), *to scoot, to splurge, to tote* and *to vamose*, the verb-phrases *to take the cake, to bury the hatchet, to cut no ice, to draw a bead on, to keep one's eye peeled, to fizzle out, to freeze out, to go back on, to go it blind, to go one better, to go the whole hog, to go under, to get the hang of, to hold up, to keep a stiff upper lip, to monkey with, to play possum, to pull up stakes, to put it through, to raise Cain, to shin up, to size up, to spread oneself, to go on the stump* and *to trade off*, the adverb *plumb*, and the phrases *best bib and tucker, not my funeral, true inwardness, for keeps, no flies on, no two ways about it, on time, no slouch* and *under the weather.* "It is difficult now," says Ernest Weekley,[1] "to imagine how we got on so long without the word *stunt*, how we expressed the characteristics so conveniently summed up in *dope-fiend* or *high-brow*, or any other possible way of describing that mixture of the cheap pathetic and the ludicrous which is now universally labelled *sob-stuff.*" "Every Englishman listening to me now," said Alistair Cooke in a radio broadcast from London,[2] "uses thirty or forty Americanisms a day." "We seem to offer less and less resistance," said Professor W. E. Collinson of the University of Liverpool,[3] "to the new importations."

2. SURVIVING DIFFERENCES

For each of the three earlier editions of this book I prepared a list of couplets showing variations between the everyday vocabularies of England and the United States, and in every instance that list had become archaic in some of its details before it could be got into print. The English reviewers had a great deal of sport demonstrating that a number of my Americanisms were really in wide use in England, but all they proved, save in a few cases of undeniable blundering, was that the exotic had at last become familiar. Others undertook to show that some term I had listed was not only accepted current English, but also discoverable in the works of Shakespeare, of Chaucer, or even of King Alfred, but as a rule the

1 Adjectives — and Other Words; London, 1930, p. 182.
2 Printed as English on Both Sides of the Atlantic, *Listener*, April, 1935.
3 Contemporary English: a Personal Speech Record; Leipzig, 1927, p. 114.

most they could actually prove was that it had been good English
once, but had fallen out of currency, and had then been taken back
from the United States, where it had survived all the while. From
those reviews I learned that opinions often differ as to whether a
given word or phrase is in general use. Sometimes, two reviewers
would differ sharply over a specimen, one arguing that every Englishman knew it and used it, and the other maintaining that it
was employed only by traitorous vulgarians under the spell of the
American movies.

Nevertheless, it is still possible to draw up an impressive roster of
common terms that remain different in England and the United
States, and so I attempt the business once more,[1] beginning with
some words from everyday home life:

American	English
alcohol-lamp	spirit lamp
apartment	flat
apartment-hotel	block of service-flats
apartment-house	block of flats
ash-can	dust-bin
ash-cart (or truck)	dust-cart
ashman	dustman [2]
atomiser	scent-spray
automobile	motor-car
baby-carriage	perambulator, or pram
baggage	luggage
bakery	bake-house, or baker's shop
bank-account	banking-account
bathing-suit	swim-suit
bathtub	bath
bedbug or chinch	bug
bill (money)	banknote, or note
billboard	hoarding
biscuit	scone, or tea-cake
boot	high-boot, or Wellington

1 I am indebted here to various English acquaintances, and to a number
of Americans resident in England,
but most of all to Mr. H. W. Seaman, of Norwich. Mr. Seaman is
an English journalist with ten years
of American experience behind
him, and so he is peculiarly alert
to differences in usage. Moreover,
he is greatly interested in linguis-
tics, and has done some valuable
writing upon the subject. My debt
to his friendly patience is enormous; he has willingly answered
scores of questions, some of them
difficult. But I hasten to add that
he is not to be held responsible for
anything that follows. The inevitable errors are my own.

2 Here, almost at the start of my
list, I must file a caveat against it
myself, for Mr. Seaman tells me
that *garbage*, in England as in the
United States, is coming to be applied to all sorts of refuse.

American	English
broiled (meat)	grilled
candy	sweets
candy-store	sweet-shop
can-opener	tin-opener, or key [1]
chain-store	multiple-shop
charged (goods bought)	put down
cheese-cloth	butter-muslin
chicken-yard	fowl-run
chores	odd jobs
cigarette-butt	cigarette-end
clothes-pin	clothes-peg
coal-oil	paraffin
collar-button	collar-stud
cook-book	cookery-book
cook-stove	cooking-stove
cookie	biscuit
corn	maize, or Indian corn
cornmeal	Indian meal
corn-starch	corn-flour
cotton (absorbent)	cotton-wool
cracker	biscuit (unsweetened)
custom-made (clothes)	bespoke, or made to measure
daylight time	Summer time
derby (hat)	bowler, or hard hat
dishpan	washing-up bowl
drawers (men's)	pants
druggist	chemist
drug-store	chemist's-shop [2]
drygoods-store	draper's-shop
elevator	lift
elevator-boy	liftman
fish-dealer	fishmonger
five-and-ten (store)	bazaar
floorwalker	shopwalker
frame-house	wooden-house
fruit-seller (or dealer)	fruiterer
fruit-store	fruiterer's
garbage-incinerator	destructor
garters (men's)	sock-suspenders
groceries	stores
hardware	ironmongery
huckster	coster, costermonger, or hawker

1 In the London *Daily Mail*, June 25, 1935, I found the heading: Key to the Can. It would have cost the job of any American copy-reader who wrote it. But in England it was a proper heading for a news story dealing with Treasury regulations for the importation of *can-openers* with *canned-goods*.

2 But *drug-store*, as we have seen in Section 1, is coming in. I am informed by an English correspondent, Mr. H. R. Rutter, that "the scientific chemists of England have for some time been agitating for the withdrawal of the designation *chemist* from the pharmacist, and the substitution of *druggist*."

American	English
instalment-plan	hire-purchase system, or hire system
janitor	caretaker, or porter
junk	rubbish, or odds and ends
kindergarten	infants'-school, or nursery-school
letter-box	pillar-box
letter-carrier	postman
living-room	sitting-room [1]
long-distance (telephone)	trunk
marriage-certificate	marriage-lines
molasses	black treacle
monkey-wrench	screw-spanner
mucilage	gum
necktie	tie
oatmeal (boiled)	porridge
package	parcel
phonograph	gramophone
pie (fruit)	tart
pitcher	jug
play-room	nursery
push-cart	barrow
raincoat	mackintosh, or mac
recess (school)	interval, or break
roast (of meat)	joint
roomer	lodger
rooster	cock, or cockerel
rubbers	overshoes, goloshes, or galoshes
run (in a stocking)	ladder
sack-suit (or business-suit)	lounge-suit
scarf-pin	tie-pin
second floor	first floor
sewerage (house)	drains
shoe	boot
shoestring	bootlace, or shoelace
sidewalk	footpath, or pavement
silverware	plate
sled	sledge
soda-biscuit (or cracker)	cream-cracker
spigot (or faucet)	tap
spool (of cotton)	reel
stairway	staircase, or stairs
stem-winder	keyless-watch
string-bean	French-bean
sugar-bowl	sugar-basin
suspenders (men's)	braces
syrup	treacle
taffy	toffee
taxes (municipal)	rates
taxpayer (local)	ratepayer

1 But *living-room* appears to be coming in.

American	English
tenderloin (of beef)	under-cut or fillet [1]
tinner	tinker, or tinsmith
transom (of door)	fanlight
undershirt	vest, or singlet
union-suit	combinations
wash-bowl	wash-basin
wash-rag	face-cloth
washstand	wash-hand stand
waste-basket	waste-paper basket
water-heater	geyser
window-shade	blind

Let us now turn to the field of sports and pastimes, and attempt another list of differences:

American	English
aisle (theatre)	gangway
bartender	barman, or potman
battery (automobile)	accumulator
beach	seaside
bouncer	chucker-out
bowling-alley	skittle-alley
bung-starter	beer-mallet
carom (billiards)	cannon
caroussel	runabout
checkers (game)	draughts
closed season (for game)	close season
deck (of cards)	pack
detour (road)	road diversion
fender (automobile)	wing, or mud-guard
gasoline, or gas	petrol
gear-shift (automobile)	gear-lever
generator (automobile)	dynamo
ground-wire (radio)	earth-wire
headliner (vaudeville)	topliner
highball	whiskey-and-soda
hood (automobile)	bonnet
hunting	shooting

1 There are many other differences between the names of cuts of meat in the two countries. I am indebted to Mr. H. Kendall Kidds of San Francisco, who is at work on a book on the butchering craft, for what follows. Our *porterhouse* steak is the *sirloin* in England, but *porterhouse* is coming in, with the prefix *Yankee*. Our *sirloin* is the *rump*, or *middle-rump*. The *bottom-round* is called the *silverside* in England, and the *top-round* is the *top-side*. The *rump* is known as the *H-bone piece* or *shellbone*. The part that contains the shoulder-blade is the *chuck*, as it is here. A leg of mutton or lamb cut with the hip-bone attached is called a *haunch* in England. If the hip-bone is left on the loin and cut into *chops*, they are known as *chump-bone* chops. What we call the *rib* chops are the *best end of the neck* or *best end*. Under the shoulder, which is raised in England, the chops are called the *middle-neck*, while the rest is the *scrag-end*.

American	English
intermission (at play or concert)	interval
lap-robe	carriage-rug
legal holiday	bank holiday
lobby (theatre)	foyer, or entrance-hall
low-gear (automobile)	first speed
movie-house	cinema, or picture-house
muffler (automobile)	silencer
oil-pan (automobile)	sump
orchestra (seats in a theatre)	stalls
pool-room	billiards-saloon
race-track	race-course
roadster (automobile)	two-seater
roller-coaster	switchback-railway
rumble-seat	dickey-seat
saloon	public-house, or pub
sedan (automobile)	saloon-car
shock-absorber (automobile)	anti-bounce clip
shot (athletics)	weight
sight-seeing-car or rubberneck-wagon	char-a-banc
soft-drinks	minerals
spark-plug	sparking-plug
sporting-goods	sports-requisites
ten-pins	nine-pins
stein (beer)	pint
top (automobile)	hood
vacation	holiday
vaudeville	variety [1]
vaudeville-theatre	music-hall
windshield (automobile)	windscreen [2]

Similar lists might be prepared to show differences in a great many other fields — business, finance, government, politics, education, ecclesiastical affairs, and most of the arts and sciences, including even cookery. Despite their steady gobbling of Americanisms, the English continue faithful to many words and phrases that are quite unknown in this country, and so the two languages remain recognizably different, especially in their more colloquial forms. An

[1] *Variety*, of course, is known and understood in the United States. Indeed, the chief theatrical paper of New York is called *Variety*. But in its columns it commonly refers to the thing itself as *vaudeville*, or *vaude*, or *vaud*. Some years ago a German movie, done into English, was called *Variety* here and *Vaudeville* in England. In both countries it thus carried an exotic flavor.

[2] See, for longer lists, Automobile

Nomenclature, *American Speech*, Sept., 1926, p. 686; The Automobile and American English, by Theodore Hornberger, the same, April, 1930; English Theatrical Terms and Their American Equivalents, by Henry J. Heck, the same, Aug., 1930; and British and American Fishing Terms, by Frederick White, *Outdoor Life*, Aug., 1934.

Englishman, walking into his house, does not enter upon the *first floor* as we do, but upon the *ground floor*. He may also call it the *first storey* (not forgetting the penultimate *e*), but when he speaks of the *first floor* he means what we call the *second floor*, and so on up to the roof, which is covered, not with *tin* or *shingles*, but with *tiles* or *leads*. He does not ask his servant, " Is there any *mail* for me? " but " Are there any *letters* for me? " for *mail*, in the American sense, is a word that he uses much less often than we do. There are *mail-trains* in his country, and they carry *mail-bags* (more often called *post-bags*) that are unloaded into *mail-vans* bearing signs reading " Royal *Mail*," but in general he reserves the word *mail* for letters going to or from foreign countries, and he knows nothing of the compounds so numerous in American, *e.g.*, *mail-car*, *-matter*, *-man*, *-box*, and *-carrier*. He uses *post* instead. The man who brings his *post* or *letters* is not a *letter-carrier* or *mailman*, but a *postman*. His outgoing letters are *posted*, not *mailed*, at a *pillar-box*, not at a *mail-box*. If they are urgent they are sent, not by *special delivery*, but by *express post*. Goods ordered by post on which the dealer pays the cost of transportation are said to arrive, not *postpaid* or *prepaid*, but *post-free* or *carriage-paid*. The American *mail-order*, however, seems to be coming in, though as yet the English have developed no mail-order firms comparable to Montgomery-Ward or Sears-Roebuck. To the list of railroad terms differing in the two countries, given in Chapter IV, Section 2, a number of additions might be made. The English have begun to use *freight* in our sense, though they prefer to restrict it to water-borne traffic, and they have borrowed *Pullman*, *ballast* and *track*, and begin to abandon *left-luggage room* for *cloak-room*, but they still get *in* or *out* of a train, not *on* or *off* it, and their only way of expressing what we mean by *commuter* is to say a *season-ticket-holder*.[1] They say a train is *up to* time, not *on* time, they designate what we call a station-agent by the more sonorous *station-master*, they call a ticket-agent a *booking-clerk*, a railway bill-of-lading a *consignment-note*, a bureau-of-information an *inquiry-office*, a bumper a *buffer*,[2] a caboose a *brake-van*, and the aisle of a Pullman its *corridor*, and they know nothing, according to Horwill, of *way-stations*, *flag-stops*, *box-cars*, *chair-cars*, *check-*

1 I am indebted here to suggestions by Messrs. H. F. Rutter, P. H. Muir and J. Dwight Francis of London, Dr. Ernest Wignall of the Rockefeller Institute, and Mr. George H. Mather of Moose Jaw, Canada.

2 But it is a *bumper* on a motor-car.

rooms, ticket-choppers, claim-agents, grade-crossings, classification-yards, flyers, long- and *short-hauls, trunk-lines* and *tie-ups.* An English *guard* (not *conductor*) [1] does not bellow " All aboard! " but " Take your seats, please! " *Railroad* itself is, to all intents and purposes, an Americanism; it has been little used in England for fifty years. In the United States the English *railway* is also used, but not as commonly as *railroad*. It has acquired the special sense of a line of rails for light traffic, as in *street-railway* (Eng. *tramway*), but it has been employed, too, to designate large railroad systems, and to differentiate between bankrupt railroad corporations and their more or less solvent heirs and assigns.[2] To return to the mails, the kind we call domestic is *inland* in England and the kind we call foreign is *overseas*. Our division of the mails into first, second, third and fourth classes is unknown there. The English internal revenue is the *inland revenue*.

An Englishman does not wear suspenders but *braces,* his undershirt is a *vest* or *singlet,* and his drawers are *pants.* He carries, not a billfold, but a *note-case.* His crazy-bone is his *funny-bone.* His watch-crystal is his *watch-glass,* though English jewelers, among themselves, sometimes use *crystal.* A stem-winder is a *keyless-watch,* a Derby hat is a *bowler,* an elevator is a *lift,* a fraternal-order is a *friendly-* or *mutual-society,* an insurance-adjuster is a *fire-assessor,* a lunch-counter is a *snack-bar,* a pen-point is a *nib,* the programme of a meeting is the *agenda,* a realtor is an *estate-agent,* the room-clerk in a hotel is the *reception-clerk,* a white-collar job is *black-coated,* a labor scab is a *blackleg,* a street-cleaner is a *road-sweeper,* a thumb-tack is a *drawing-pin,* a militia-armory is a *drill-hall,* a sham-battle is a *sham-fight,* what we call a belt (as in Cotton Belt, Corn Belt, Bible Belt) is a *zone,* a bid or proposal is always a tender (an Englishman *bids* only at auctions or cards), a traffic blockade is a *block,* a pay-roll is a *wage-sheet,* a weather-bureau is a *meteorological-office,* an eraser is usually an *india-rubber,* a newspaper clipping is a *cutting,* a grab-bag is a *lucky-dip,* hand-me-downs are *reach-me-downs,* a navy-yard is a *dock-yard* or *naval-yard,* a scratch-pad is a *scribbling-block,* a boy's sling-shot is a *catapult,* a laborer on the roads or railroads is a *navvy,* a steam-shovel is a *crane-navvy,* and instead of signs reading " Post No Bills " the English put up signs reading " *Stick* No Bills."

1 But the commander of an omnibus is a *conductor.*
2 See The Sins of the Railroad Period,
by F. Walker Pollock, *American Speech,* Feb., 1927, p. 248.

An Englishman, as we have seen, does not seek sustenance in a *tenderloin* but in an *undercut* or *fillet*. The wine on the table, if white and German, is not *Rhine wine*, but *Hock*. Yellow turnips, in England, are called *Swedes*, and are regarded as fit food for cattle only; when rations were short there, in 1916, the *Saturday Review* made a solemn effort to convince its readers that they were good enough to go upon the table. The English, of late, have become more or less aware of another vegetable formerly resigned to the lower fauna, to wit, American sweet corn. But they are still having some difficulty about its name, for plain corn, in England, means all the grains used by man. Some time ago, in the London *Sketch*, one C. J. Clive, a gentleman farmer of Worcestershire, was advertising *sweet corncobs* as the "most delicious of all vegetables," and offering to sell them at 6s.6d. a dozen, *carriage-paid*. By *chicken* the English can mean any fowl, however ancient. *Broilers* and *friers* are never heard of over there. The classes which, in America, eat *breakfast, dinner* and *supper* have *breakfast, dinner* and *tea* in England; *supper* always means a meal eaten late in the evening. The American use of *lunch* to designate any irregular meal, even at midnight, is strange in England. An Englishwoman's personal maid, if she has one, is not *Ethel* or *Maggie* but *Robinson*, and the nurse-maid who looks after her children is not *Lizzie* but *Nurse*. A general servant, however, is addressed by her given-name, or, as the English always say, by her *Christian* name. English babies do not use *choo-choo* to designate a locomotive, but *puff-puff;* a horse is a *gee-gee*. A nurse in a hospital is not addressed by her name, but as *Nurse*, and her full style is not *Miss Jones*, but *Nurse Jones* or *Sister*. The hospital itself, if it takes pay for entertaining the sick, is not a hospital at all, but a *nursing-home*, and its *trained* or *registered* nurses (as we would say) are plain *nurses*, or *hospital nurses*, or maybe *nursing sisters*. And the white-clad young gentlemen who make love to them are not *studying medicine* but *walking the hospitals*. Similarly, an English law student does not *study law* in his Inn of Court, but *reads the law*, though if he goes to a university to seek a doctorate in law he may be said to *study* it.

If an English boy goes to a *public school*, it is not a sign that he is getting his education free, but that his father is paying a good round sum for it and is accepted as a gentleman. A *public school* over there corresponds to the more swagger sort of American *prep school;* it is a place maintained chiefly by endowments, wherein boys of the upper classes are prepared for the universities. What we know as a *public school* is called a *council-school* in England, because it is in the hands of the education committee of the County Council; it used to be called a *board-school*, because before the Education Act of 1902 it was run by a school-board. The boys in a *public* (*i.e.*, private) *school* are divided, not into *classes*, or *grades*, but into *forms*, which are numbered, the highest usually being the *sixth*. The benches they sit on are also called *forms*. An English boy whose father is unable to pay for his education goes first into a *babies' class* in a *primary* or *infants' school*. He moves thence to *class one*, *class two*, *class three* and *class four*, and then into the *junior school*, where he enters the *first standard*. Until now boys and girls have sat together in class, but hereafter they are separated, the boy going to a boys' school and the girl to a girls'. The boy goes up a *standard* a year. At the *third* or *fourth standard*, for the first time, he is put under a male teacher. He reaches the *seventh standard*, if he is bright, at the age of twelve and then goes into what is known as the *ex-seventh*. If he stays at school after this he goes into the *ex-ex-seventh*. But some leave the *public elementary school* at the *ex-seventh* and go into the *secondary-school*, which, in this sense, is what Americans commonly call a *high-school*. But the *standard* system is being gradually replaced by a *form* system, imitating that of the more swagger schools. A *grammar-school*, in England, always means a place for the sons of the relatively rich. *Grade-schools* are unknown.

The principal of an English *public* (*i.e.*, private) *school* or *elementary-school* is a *head-master* or *head-mistress*, but in a *secondary-school* he or she may be a *principal*. Only girls' schools have *head-mistresses*. The lower pedagogues used to be *ushers*, but are now *masters* or *assistant masters* (or *mistresses*). The titular head of a university is a *chancellor*;[1] he is commonly a bigwig elected by the resident graduates for ornamental purposes only, and a *vice-chancellor* does the work.[2] Some of the universities also have *pro-chancellors*, who are bigwigs of smaller size; they have *deputy-pro-*

---

1 This title has been borrowed by some of the American universities, *e.g.*, Syracuse, but the usual title is *president*. On the Continent it is *rector*.

2 He serves for three years, and the heads of the various colleges take the office in rotation.

chancellors or *pro-vice-chancellors* to discharge their theoretical functions. Most English universities have *deans* of faculties much like our own, and some of them have lately laid in *deans of women,* and even *advisers to women students.* They have minor dignitaries of kinds unknown in the United States, *e.g., proctors, orators* and *high stewards.* In Scotland the universities also have *rectors,* who are chosen by election, and, like the chancellors, are mainly only ornaments.[1] The head of a mere college may be a *president, principal, master, warden, rector, dean* or *provost.* In the solitary case of the London School of Economics he is a *director.* The students are not divided into *freshmen, sophomores, juniors* and *seniors,* as with us, but are simply *first-year-men, second-year-men,* and so on, though a *first-year-man* is sometimes a *freshman* or *fresher.* Such distinctions, however, are not so important in England as in America; *undergraduates* (they are seldom called students) do not flock together according to seniority, and there is no regulation forbidding an upper classman, or even a graduate, to be polite to a student just entered. The American hierarchy of *assistant instructors, instructors, assistant professors, associate professors, adjunct professors* and *full professors* is unknown in the English universities; they have only *readers* or *lecturers* and *professors.* If his chair happens to have been endowed by royalty, a professor prefixes *regius* to his title. A student, though technically a *member* of the university, has few rights as such until he is graduated (or, in some cases, until he takes his M.A.); then he may vote in the election which chooses his university's representative (or representatives) in Parliament, and so enjoy double representation there. To hold this right he must pay dues to his college, which is a constituent part of the university, with rights and privileges of its own. The professors, lecturers and readers of a college or university do not constitute a *faculty,* but a *staff,*[2] and they are called collectively, its *dons,* though all teachers are not, necessarily, *dons* (*i.e.,* fellows). An English university student does not *study;* he *reads* — whether for a *pass-degree,* which is easy, or for *honours,* which give him seriously to think. He knows nothing of *frats, class-days, rushes, credits, points, majors, semesters, senior-proms* and other such things; save at Cambridge and Dublin he does not even speak of a *commencement;* elsewhere he calls it *degree-day*

1 See The Yearbook of the Universities of the Empire, edited by T. S. Sterling; London, annually.

2 But *faculty* is used to designate the staff of a special school, *e.g.,* of theology, medicine or law.

or *speech-day*. On the other hand his speech is full of terms unintelligible to an American student, *e.g.*, *wrangler, tripos, head, greats* and *mods*. If he is expelled he is said to be *sent down*. There are no college boys in England, but only *university-men*. Alumni are *graduates*, and the graduates of what we would call prep-schools are *old-boys*.

The upkeep of *council-schools* in England, save for some help from the Treasury, comes out of the *rates*, which are local taxes levied upon householders. For that reason an English municipal taxpayer is called a *rate-payer*. The functionaries who collect and spend the money are not *office-holders* or *job-holders*, but *public-servants*, or, if of high rank, *civil-servants*. The head of the local police is not a *chief of police*, but a *chief constable*. The fire department is the *fire-brigade*, and a fire-alarm box is a *fire-call*. A city ordinance is a *by-law*, and a member of a City Council is a *councillor*. The parish poorhouse is colloquially a *workhouse*, but officially a *poor-law institution*. A policeman is a *bobby* familiarly and a *constable* officially, though the American *cop* seems to be making progress. His club or espantoon is his *truncheon*. He is sometimes mentioned in the newspapers, not by his name, but as *P.C. 643 A* — *i.e.*, Police Constable No. 643 of the A Division. When he belongs to what we call the traffic division he is said to he *on point duty*. There are no police *lieutenants* or *captains;* the one rank between *sergeant* and *superintendent* is *inspector*. The blotter at a police-station is the *charge-sheet*. A counterfeiter is a *coiner*, a fire-bug is a *fire-raiser*, and a porch-climber is a *cat-burglar*. The warden of a prison is the *governor*, and his assistants are *warders*. There is no *third-degree* and no *strong-arm-squad*, though both have been made familiar in England by American movies. An English saloon-keeper is officially a *licensed victualler*. His saloon is a *public house*, or, colloquially, a *pub*. He does not sell beer by the *bucket, can, growler, shell, seidel, stein* or *schooner*, but by the *pint, half-pint* or *glass*. He and his brethren, taken together, are the *licensed trade*, or simply the *trade*. He may divide his establishment into a *public-bar*, a *saloon-bar* and a *private-bar*, the last being the toniest, or he may call his back room a *parlour, snug* or *tap-room*. If he has a few upholstered benches in his place he may call it a *lounge*. He employs no *bartenders*. *Barmaids* do the work, with maybe a *barman, potman* or *cellarman* to help. *Beer*, in most parts of Great Britain, means only the thinnest

and cheapest form of malt liquor; better stuff is commonly called
bitter. When an Englishman speaks of *booze* he means only ale or
beer; for our *hard liquor* (a term he never uses) he prefers *spirits*.
He uses *boozer* to indicate a drinking-place as well as a drinker.
What we call *hard* cider is *rough* cider to him. He never uses *rum*
in the generic sense that it has acquired in the United States, and
knows nothing of *rum-hounds, rum-dumbs, rum-dealers*, the *rum-
trade*, and the *rum-evil*, or of the *Demon Rum*. The American *bung-
starter* is a *beer-mallet* in England, and, as in this country, it is frequently used for assault and homicide.

In England *corporation* commonly designates a municipal or
university corporation, or some other such public body, *e.g.*, the
British Broadcasting *Corporation;* what we commonly think of
when we hear of the corporations is there called a *public company*
or *limited liability company*. But the use of the word in its American
sense seems to be gaining ground, and in 1920 Parliament passed an
act (10 & 11 Geo. V, Ch. 18) levying a *corporation-profits* tax. An
Englishman writes *Ltd.* after the name of a limited liability (what
we would call *incorporated*) bank or trading company, as we write
Inc. He calls its president its *chairman* if a part-timer, or its *managing director* if a full-timer.[1] Its stockholders are its *shareholders*, and
hold *shares* instead of *stock* in it. Its bonds are called *debentures*,
and the word is not limited in meaning, as in the United States, to
securities not protected by a mortgage. The place where such companies are floated and looted — the Wall Street of London — is called
the *City*, with a capital C. Bankers, stockjobbers, promoters, directors and other such leaders of its business are called *City* men. The
financial editor of a newspaper is its *City* editor. Government bonds
are *consols*, or *stocks*,[2] or the *funds*. *To have money in the stocks*
is to own such bonds. An Englishman hasn't a bank-account, but a
banking-account. His deposit-slip is a *paying-in-slip*, and the stubs
of his *cheque*-book (not *check*-book) are the *counterfoils*. He makes
a rigid distinction between a *broker* and a *stockbroker*. A *broker*
means, not only a dealer in securities, as in our *Wall Street broker*,
but also " a person licensed to sell or appraise distrained goods." *To
have the brokers* (or *bailiffs*) *in* means to be bankrupt, with one's

1 But the London, Midland and
Scottish Railway has a *president*.
2 This form survives in the American term *city-stock*, meaning the

bonds of a municipality. But State
and Federal securities are almost
always called *bonds*.

very household goods in the hands of one's creditors.[1] What we call a *grain-broker* is a *corn-factor*.

Tariff reform, in England, does not mean a movement toward free trade, but one toward protection. The word *Government*, meaning what we call *the administration*, is always capitalized and usually plural, *e.g.*, "The Government *are* considering the advisability, etc." *Vestry, committee, council, ministry* and even *company* are also plural, though sometimes not capitalized. A member of Parliament, if he be one who respects the integrity of his mother-tongue, does not *run* for office; he *stands*. But of late the American *to run* has been coming in, and not long ago an M.P. wrote to me: "If I think of my own *candidature* (*candidacy*), I say 'I *ran*,'" etc. An English candidate is not *nominated*, but *adopted*. If he *stands* successfully, he *sits* at Westminster, and is a *sitting member*. When it is said of a man that he is *nursing a constituency*, it means that he is attending fairs, subscribing to charities, and otherwise flattering and bribing the voters, in the hope of inducing them to *return* him. Once returned, he does not represent a *district*, but a *division* or *constituency*. At a political meeting (they are often rough in England) the ushers and bouncers are called *stewards;* the pre-war suffragettes used to delight in stabbing them with hatpins. An M.P. is not afflicted by most of the bugaboos that poison the dreams of an American Congressman. He has never heard, save as a report of far-off heresies, of *direct primaries*, the *recall*, or the *initiative and referendum*. A roll-call in Parliament is a *division*, and an appropriation is a *vote*. A member speaking is said to be *up* or *on his legs*. When the House adjourns it is said to *rise*. The word *politician* has no opprobrious significance in England; it is applied to themselves by statesmen of the first eminence. *Cabinet* is used as with us, but it has a synonym in *ministry*, and a member of it may be called a *minister*. A *contested* election, in England, is simply one in which there is more than one candidate; the adjective has no relation to charges of fraud.

The English keep up most of the old distinctions between physicians and surgeons, barristers and solicitors. A *barrister* is greatly superior to a *solicitor*. He alone can address the higher courts and the parliamentary committees; a solicitor must keep to office work

1 A Glossary of Colloquial Slang and Technical Terms in Use in the Stock Exchange and in the Money Market, by A. J. Wilson; London, 1895.

and the inferior courts. A man with a grievance goes first to his solicitor, who then *instructs* or *briefs* a barrister for him. If that barrister, in the course of the trial, wants certain evidence removed from the record, he moves that it be *struck out*, not *stricken out*, as an American lawyer would usually say. Only barristers may become judges. An English barrister, like his American brother, takes a *retainer* when he is engaged, but the rest of his fee does not wait upon the termination of the case: he expects and receives a *refresher* from time to time. A barrister is never *admitted* to the bar, but is always *called*. If he becomes a *King's Counsel*, or *K.C.* (a mainly honorary appointment though it carries some privileges, and usually brings higher fees), he is said to have *taken silk*. In the United States a lawyer *tries* a case and the judge either *tries* or *hears* it; in England it is the judge who *tries* it, and the barrister *pleads* it. The witness-stand is the *witness-box*. In the United States the court *hands down* a decision; in England the court hands it *out*. In the United States a lawyer *probates* a will; in England he *proves* it, or has it *admitted to probate*. The calendar of a court is a *cause-list*, and a lawyer's brief-case is an *attaché-case*. The *brief* in it is not a document to be filed in court, as with us, but a solicitor's instructions to a barrister. What we call a *brief* is called *pleadings*. A *corporation-lawyer*, of course, is a *company-lawyer*. *Ambulance-chasers* are unknown.

The common objects and phenomena of nature are often differently named in England and America. The Englishman knows the meaning of *sound* (*e.g.*, Long Island *Sound*), but he nearly always uses *channel* in place of it. Contrariwise, the American knows the meaning of the English *bog*, but rejects the English distinction between it and *swamp*, and almost always uses *swamp* or *marsh* (often elided to *ma'sh*). The Englishman, instead of saying that the temperature is 29 degrees (Fahrenheit) or that the thermometer or the mercury is at 29 degrees, sometimes says there are *three degrees of frost*. He never, of course, uses *down-East* or *up-State*, nor does he use *downtown* or *uptown*. Many of our names for common fauna and flora are unknown to him save as strange Americanisms heard in the talkies, *e.g.*, *terrapin*, *ground-hog*, *poison-ivy*, *persimmon*, *gumbo*, *eggplant*, *catnip*, *sweet-potato* and *yam*. He calls the *rutabaga* a *mangelwurzel*. He is familiar with many fish that we seldom see, *e.g.*, the *turbot*, and eats some that we reject, *e.g.*, the *ray*, which he calls the *skate*. He also knows the *hare*, which is seldom heard of in America. But he knows nothing of *devilled-crabs, crab-cocktails, club-sandwiches, clam-chowder* or *oyster-stews,* and he never goes to *oyster-suppers, sea-food* (or *shore*) *dinners, clam-bakes* or *barbecues,* or eats *boiled-dinners.*

An Englishman never lives *on* a street, but always *in* it, though he may live *on* an avenue or road. He never lives in a *block* of houses, but in a *row* of them or in a *block of flats* (not *apartments*); an *apartment,* to him, is a room. His home is never in a *section* of the city, but always in a *district.* The *business-blocks* that are so proudly exhibited in all small American towns are quite unknown to him. He often calls an office-building simply a *house, e.g., Lever House.* Going home from London by train he always takes the *down-train,* no matter whether he be proceeding southward to Wimbledon, westward to Shepherd's Bush, northward to Tottenham, or eastward to Noak's Hill. A train headed toward London is always an *up-train,* and the track it runs on (the left-hand track, not the right-hand one, as in the United States) is the *up-line.* Oxford men also speak of *up-* and *down-trains* to and from Oxford. In general, the Englishman seems to have a much less keen sense of the points of the compass than the American. He knows the *East End* and the *West End,* but the names of his streets are never preceded by *north, east, south* or *west,* and he never speaks of the *north-east corner* of two of them. But there are *eastbound* and *westbound* trains in the London tubes. English streets have no *sidewalks;* they are always called *pavements* or *foot-paths* or simply *paths. Sidewalk,* however, is used in Ireland. A *road,* in England, is always a road, and never a railway. A *car* means a tram-car or motor-car; never a railway-carriage. A telegraph-*blank* is a telegraph-*form.* The Englishman does not usually speak of having his shoes (or boots) *shined;* he has them *blacked.* He always calls russet, yellow or tan shoes *brown* shoes (or, if they cover the ankle, *boots*). He calls a pocketbook a *purse* or *wallet,* and gives the name of *pocketbook* or *pocket-diary* to what we call a *memorandum-book.* By *cord* he means something strong, almost what we call *twine;* a thin cord he always calls a *string;* his *twine* is the lightest sort of *string.* He uses *dessert,* not to indicate the whole last course at dinner, but to designate the fruit only; the rest is *the sweet.* If he inhabits bachelor quarters he commonly says that he lives in *chambers.* Flat-houses are often *mansions.* The janitor or superintendent thereof is a *care-taker* or *porter.*

The Englishman is naturally unfamiliar with baseball, and in consequence his language is bare of the countless phrases and metaphors that it has supplied to American. But he uses more racing terms and metaphors than we do, and he has got a good many phrases from other games, particularly cricket. The word *cricket* itself has a definite figurative meaning to him. It indicates, in general, good sportsmanship. To take unfair advantage of an opponent is not *cricket*. The sport of boating, once so popular on the Thames, has also given colloquial English some familiar terms, almost unknown in the United States, *e.g.*, *punt* and *weir*. The game known as *ten-pins* in America is called *nine-pins* in England, and once had that name over here. The Puritans forbade it, and its devotees changed its name in order to evade the prohibition.[1] *Bowls*, in England, means only the lawn game; the alley game is called *skittles*, and is played in a *skittle-alley*. The English vocabulary of racing differs somewhat from ours. When the odds are 2 to 1 in favor of a horse we say that its price is *1 to 2;* the Englishman says that it is *2 to 1 on*. We speak of backing a horse to *win, place* or *show;* the Englishman uses *each way* instead, meaning *win* or *place*, for *place*, in England, means both *second* and *third*. Though the English talk of racing, football, cricket and golf a great deal, they have developed nothing comparable to the sporting argot used by American sporting reporters. When, during the World War (which Englishmen always call the *Great War*), American soldier nines played baseball in England, some of the English newspapers employed visiting American reporters to report the games, and the resultant emission of technicalities interested English readers much more than the games themselves. One of the things that puzzled them was the word *inning*, as in *second inning;* in England it is always plural.

As a set-off to American sports-page jargon, the English have an ecclesiastical vocabulary with which we are almost unacquainted, and it is in daily use, for the church bulks much larger in public affairs over there than it does here. Such terms as *vicar, canon, verger, prebendary, primate, curate, nonconformist, dissenter, convocation, minster, chapter, crypt, living, presentation, glebe, benefice, locum tenens, suffragan, almoner, tithe, dean* and *pluralist* are to be met

1 "An act was passed to prohibit playing *nine-pins;* as soon as the law was put in force, it was notified everywhere, 'Ten-pins played here.'" — Capt. Frederick Marryat: A Diary in America; London, 1839, Vol. III, p. 195.

with in the English newspapers constantly, but on this side of the water they are seldom encountered. Nor do we hear much of *mattins* (which has two *t's* in England), *lauds, lay-readers, ritualism* and the *liturgy.* The English use of *holy orders* is also strange to us. They do not say that a young man aspiring to sacerdotal ease under the Establishment is *studying for the ministry*, but that he is *reading for holy orders*, though he may do the former if he is headed for the dissenting pulpit. Indeed, save he be a nonconformist, he is seldom called a *minister* at all, though the term appears in the Book of Common Prayer, and never a *pastor;* a clergyman of the Establishment is always either a *rector, vicar* or *curate*, or colloquially a *parson.* According to Horwill, the term *clergyman* is seldom applied to any other kind of preacher. In American *chapel* simply means a small church, usually the dependant of some larger one; in English it has acquired the special sense of a place of worship unconnected with the Establishment. Though three-fourths of the people of Ireland are Catholics (in Munster and Connaught, more than nine-tenths), and the Protestant Church of Ireland has been disestablished since 1871, a Catholic place of worship in that country is still legally a *chapel* and not a *church.*[1] So is a Methodist wailing-place in England, however large it may be, or any other dissenting house of worship. But here custom begins to war with the law, and in a current issue of the London *Times* I find notices of services in Presbyterian, Congregational, Baptist, Christian Science and even Catholic *churches.* *Chapel*, of course, is also used to designate a small house of worship of the Establishment when it is neither a parish church nor a cathedral, *e.g.*, St. George's *Chapel*, Windsor, and King's College *Chapel*, Cambridge. What the English call simply a *churchman* is an *Episcopalian* in the United States, what they call the *Church* (always capitalized) is the *Protestant Episcopal* Church, what they call a *Roman Catholic* is simply a *Catholic*, and what they call a *Jew* is usually softened to a *Hebrew.* The American language, of course, knows nothing of *nonconformists* or *dissenters.* Nor of such gladiators of dissent as the *Plymouth Brethren* and the *Methodist New Connexion*,

1 "The term *chapel*," says P. W. Joyce, in English as We Speak It in Ireland, 2nd ed.; London, 1910, "has so ingrained itself in my mind that to this hour the word instinctively springs to my lips when I am about to mention a Catholic place of worship; and I always feel some sort of hesitation or reluctance in substituting the word *church.* I positively could not bring myself to say, 'Come, it is time now to set out for *church.*' It must be either *mass* or *chapel.*"

nor of the *nonconformist conscience*, though the United States suffers from it even more damnably than England. The English, to make it even, get on without *holy-rollers, Dunkards, hard-shell Baptists, Seventh Day Adventists* and other such American alarmers of God, and they give a *mourners'-bench* the austere name of *penitent-seat* or *form*. The Salvation Army, which is of English origin uses *penitent-form* even in America.

In music the English cling to an archaic and unintelligible nomenclature, long since abandoned over here. Thus, they call a double whole note a *breve*, a whole note a *semibreve*, a half note a *minim*, a quarter note a *crotchet*, an eighth note a *quaver*, a sixteenth note a *semi-quaver*, a thirty-second note a *demisemiquaver*, a sixty-fourth note a *hemidemisemiquaver*, or *semidemisemiquaver*, and a hundred and twenty-eighth note a *quasihemidemisemiquaver*. This clumsy terminology goes back to the days of plain chant, with its *longa, brevis, semi-brevis, minima* and *semiminima*. The French and Italians cling to a system almost as confusing, but the Germans use *ganze, halbe, viertel, achtel*, etc. I have been unable to discover the beginnings of the American system, but it would seem to be borrowed from the German, for since the earliest times a great many of the music teachers in the United States have been Germans, and some of the rest have had German training. In the same way the English hold fast (though with a slacking of the grip of late) to a clumsy method of designating the sizes of printers' types. In America the point-system makes the business easy; a line of *14-point* type occupies exactly the vertical space of two lines of *7-point*. But the more old-fashioned English printers still indicate differences in size by such arbitrary and confusing names as *brilliant, diamond, small pearl, pearl, ruby, ruby-nonpareil, nonpareil, minion-nonpareil, emerald, minion, brevier, bourgeois, long primer, small pica, pica, English, great primer* and *double pica*. The English also cling to various archaic measures. Thus, an Englishman will commonly say that he weighs eleven *stone* instead of 154 *pounds*. A *stone*, in speaking of a man, is fourteen pounds, but in speaking of beef on the hoof it is only eight pounds. Instead of saying that his back-*yard* is fifty feet long, an Englishman will say that his back-*garden* is sixteen yards, two feet long. He employs such designations of time as *fortnight* and *twelve-month* a great deal more than we do. He says "a quarter *to* nine," not "a quarter *of* nine." He rarely says *fifteen minutes to* or *ten thirty;* nearly always he uses *quarter to* and *half past ten.* He never says *a quarter hour* or *a half hour;* he says *a quarter of an hour* or *half an hour.* To him, twenty-five minutes is often *five-and-twenty minutes.*

In Standard English usage *directly* is always used to signify *immediately;* " in the American language, generally speaking," as Mark Twain once explained, " the word signifies after a little." [1] In England, according to the Concise Oxford Dictionary, *quite* means " completely, wholly, entirely, altogether, to the utmost extent, nothing short of, in the fullest sense, positively, absolutely "; in America it is conditional, and means only nearly, approximately, substantially, as in " He sings *quite* well." An Englishman doesn't say, being ill, " I am *getting* on well," but " I am *going* on well." He never adds the pronoun in such locutions as " It hurts *me*," but says simply, " It hurts." He never " *catches up* with you " on the street; he " catches *you up*." He never *brushes off* his hat; he *brushes* it. He never says " Are you *through?* " but " Have you *finished?* " or " Are you *done?* " He never uses *gotten* as the perfect participle of *get;* he always uses plain *got,* and he is usually more careful than the American to insert it after *have.* Said Mark Twain to an Englishman encountered on a train in Germany:

You say, "I haven't *got* any stockings on," "I haven't *got* any memory," "I haven't *got* any money in my purse"; we usually say "I haven't any stockings on," "I haven't any memory," "I haven't any money in my purse." You say *out of window;* we always put in a *the.* If one asks "How old is that man? " the Briton answers, "He *will be* about forty"; in the American language we should say "He *is* about forty." [2]

In the United States *homely* always means ill-favored; in England it may also mean simple, friendly, home-loving, folksy. Drages, the furniture-dealer in Oxford street, London, advertises that his wares are for " nice, homely people." St. John Ervine reports that on his first visit to the Republic he got into trouble by praising a gracious female as *homely.* [3] *Sick* is in common use attributively in England, as in *sick-leave, sick-bed* and *sick-room,* but in the predicative situation it has acquired the special meaning of nauseated, and so *ill* is usually used in place of it. The English never apply *sick* to specific organs, as in the American *sick-nerves, sick-kidneys* and *sick-teeth.*

[1] Concerning the American Language, in The Stolen White Elephant; Hartford, 1882.

[2] Concerning the American Language, just cited.

[3] London *Observer*, Jan. 13, 1929.

When an Englishman *takes* a *bath* it is in a tub (or in the dishpan that he sometimes uses for a tub); when he goes for one in a swimming-pool, a river or the ocean it is a *bathe*. The use of *of* following *all*, as in " All *of* the time," still strikes him as American; he prefers " All the time." He prefers, again, *behind* to *in back of*. He seldom speaks of a *warm* day; he prefers to call it *hot*. The American use of *to jibe*, in the sense of to chime in with, is unknown to him, though he knows the word (as *gibe*) in the sense of to make game of. He seldom uses *to peek* in the sense of to peep, and the Oxford Dictionary marks *peek-a-boo* as " now chiefly U. S." The same mark is given to *to pry* in the sense of to raise or move by leverage; the Englishman always uses *to prize* or *to prise*. He knows the verb *to skimp*, but prefers *to scrimp*. He likewise knows *to slew*, but prefers *to swerve*, and is unacquainted with *slew-foot*. " The English newspapers," says H. W. Seaman,[1] " used to be very careful to avoid such Americanisms as *lifeboat* for *ship's-boat*, *life-preserver* for *lifebelt*, and *lifeguard* for the fellow on the beach who looks out for sharks, etc. Strictly, a *lifeboat* in England is a boat kept ready to go to the help of ships at sea, a *life-preserver* is a club or truncheon, and a *lifeguard* is a soldier in the Life Guards. In the last few years, however, this strictness has gone and the American usages have been generally adopted. We have only recently had *lifeguards* at beaches and pools, and since the idea came from America, we use the American name for them."

That an Englishman calls out "*I* say! " and not simply " Say! " when he desires to attract a friend's attention or register a protestation of incredulity — this perhaps is too familiar to need notice. The movies, however, have taught his children the American form. His *hear, hear!* and *oh, oh!* are also well known. He is much less prodigal with *good-bye* than the American; he uses *good-day* and *good-afternoon* far more often. Various very common American phrases are quite unknown to him, for example, *over his signature*. This he never uses, and he has no equivalent for it; an Englishman who issues a signed statement simply makes it *in writing*. His pet-name for a tiller of the soil is not *Rube* or *Cy*, but *Hodge*. When he goes gunning he does not call it *hunting*, but *shooting; hunting* is reserved for the chase of the fox, deer or otter. An intelligent Englishwoman,

1 In a private communication, April 26, 1935.

coming to America to live, once told me that the two things which
most impeded her first communications with untraveled Americans,
even above the differences between English and American pronunciation and intonation, were the complete absence of the general utility
adjective *jolly* from the American vocabulary, and the puzzling
omnipresence and versatility of the verb *to fix*. I marveled that she
did not also notice the extravagant American use of *just, right* and
good. In American *just* is almost equivalent to the English *quite*, as
in *just lovely*. Thornton shows that this use of it goes back to 1794.
The word is also used in place of *exactly* in other ways, as in *just in
time, just how many?* and *just what do you mean?* Thornton shows
that the use of *right* in *right away, right good* and *right now* was
already widespread in the United States early in the last century;
his first example is dated 1818. He believes that the locution was
"possibly imported from the Southwest of Ireland." Whatever its
origin, it quickly attracted the attention of English visitors. Dickens
noted *right away* as an almost universal Americanism during his
first American tour, in 1842, and poked fun at it in Chapter II of
"American Notes." *Right* is used as a synonym for *directly*, as in
right away, right off, right now and *right on time;* for *moderately*,
as in *right well, right smart, right good* and *right often*, and in place
of *precisely* or *certainly*, as in *right there* and "I'll get there *all right*."
More than a generation ago, in an article on Americanisms, an English critic called it "that most distinctively American word," and
concocted the following dialogue to instruct the English in its use:

> How do I get to ——?
> Go *right* along, and take the first turning on the *right*, and you are *right*
> there.
> *Right?*
> *Right.*
> *Right!* [1]

But this Englishman failed in his attempt to write correct American, despite his fine pedagogical passion. No American would ever
use *take the first turning;* he would use *turn at the first corner*. As
for *right away*, R. O. Williams argues that "so far as analogy can
make good English, it is as good as one could choose." [2] Nevertheless,
the Concise Oxford Dictionary admits it only as an Americanism,
and avoids all mention of the other American uses of *right*. *Good* is

1 I Speak United States, London
Saturday Review, Sept. 22, 1894.

2 Our Dictionaries; New York, 1890,
p. 86.

almost as protean. It is not only used as a general synonym for all adverbs connoting satisfaction, as in *to feel good, to be treated good, to sleep good*, but also as an adjectival reinforcement to adjectives, as in "I hit him *good* and hard" and "I am *good* and tired." The American use of *some* as an adjective indicating the superlative, as in "She is *some* girl," is now common in England, but its employment as an adverb to indicate either moderation or intensification, as in "I play golf *some*" and "That's lying *some*," is still looked upon as an Americanism there. The former usage has respectable English precedents, but the latter seems to be American in origin. Thornton has traced it to 1785. It enjoyed a revival during the World War, and produced a number of counter-phrases, *e.g.*, *going some*. In 1918 a writer in the *Atlantic Monthly* hailed *some* as "*some* word — a true super-word."[1] But a year later an Englishman writing in *English* (London) was denouncing it as "a pure vulgarism, which answers no real need."[2] The same word often has different meanings in the United States and England. Thus, a *davenport*, which is a couch here, is a desk or escritoire there; a *dumb-waiter*, which is an elevator here, is a revolving-table there; and a *bureau*, which is a chest of drawers here, is a desk or writing-table with drawers there. *Haberdashery*, in the United States, means men's wear (excluding shoes and outer clothes); in England it designates what we call *notions*. A *guy*, in England, is a ridiculous figure, and the word is thus opprobrious; in the United States the word is hardly more than an amiable synonym for *fellow*. The English *guy* owes its origin to the effigies of *Guy* Fawkes, leader of the Gunpowder Plot of 1605, which used to be burnt in public on November 5; the American word seems to be derived from the *guy-rope* of a circus tent, and first appeared in the complimentary form of *head-guy*. When G. K. Chesterton made his first visit to the United States he was much upset when an admiring reporter described him as a *regular guy*. But the English sense of the word is preserved in the American verb *to guy*. In this country *luggage* is coming to have the special meaning of the bags in which *baggage* is packed; in England it means their contents, though *baggage* is still used by military men. A *lobbyist*, in England, is not a legislative wire-puller, but a journalist who frequents the lobby of

<hr>

1 Should Language Be Abolished? by Harold Goddard, July, 1918, p. 63.   2 Words on Trial, by T. Michael Pope, Sept., 1919, p. 151.

the House of Commons, looking for news and gossip.[1] A *veteran* always means a soldier of long service; not, as with us, any ex-soldier. *Pussyfoot,* according to Horwill, means "a temperance propagandist" in England, obviously because of a misunderstanding of the nickname of William E. (*Pussyfoot*) Johnson, who set up shop in London in 1916 and proposed to convert the English to Prohibition. In the United States, of course, the word has a quite different meaning, and Johnson himself explains in "Who's Who in America" that it was applied to him "because of his catlike policies in pursuing law-breakers in the Indian Territory," 1906–7. The English use the same measures that we do, but in many cases their values differ. Their bushel, since 1826, has contained 2,218.192 cubic inches, whereas we retain the old Winchester bushel of 2,150.42 inches. Their peck, of course, follows suit. So with their gallon, quart, pint and gill, all of which are larger than ours. Their hundredweight is 112 pounds, whereas ours is 100 pounds. Of their *quarter* of wheat we know nothing, nor have we their *quartern-loaf* or their *quarter-days*. A billion, in England, is not 1,000,000,000, but 1,000,000,000,000; for the former the word is *milliard.* According to Alistair Cooke, it is these words of differing meaning in England and the United States that give a visiting Englishman most trouble. He says:

> If an Englishman reads "The floorwalker says to go to the *notion* counter," he knows at least one word he does not understand. If he reads a speech of President Roosevelt declaring that "our industries will have little doubt of *black-ink* operations in the last quarter of the year," he is at least aware of a foreign usage, and may be trusted to go off and discover it. But if I write "The *clerk* gave a *biscuit* to the *solicitor*," he will imagine something precise, if a little odd. The trouble is that, however lively his imagination, what he imagines may be precise but is bound to be wrong. For he is confronted with three nouns which mean different things in the United States and in England.[2]

3. ENGLISH DIFFICULTIES WITH AMERICAN

Very few English authors, even those who have made lengthy visits to the United States, ever manage to write American in a realistic manner. At the time the American movies were first terrorizing English purists the late W. L. George undertook a tour of this coun-

[1] In St. Bride's Church, Fleet Street, there is a tablet in memory of "Alfred Robbins, Kt., *Lobbyist* in the Palace of Westminster & Lon-don; Letter Writer in the Parish of St. Bride."

[2] *The American Language, Spectator*, Sept. 6, 1935.

256 *The American Language*

try, and on his return home wrote a paper dealing with his observations.[1] George was a very competent reporter, and he had no prejudice against Americanisms; on the contrary, he delighted in them. But despite his diligent effort to write them he dropped into many Briticisms, some almost as unintelligible to the average American reader as so many Gallicisms. On page after page of his paper they display the practical impossibility of the enterprise: *back-garden* for *back-yard*, *perambulator* for *baby-carriage*, *corn-market* for *grain-market*, *coal-owner* for *coal-operator*, *post* for *mail*, *petrol* for *gasoline*, and so on. And to top them there were English terms that had no American equivalents at all, for example, *kitchen-fender*. Every English author who attempts to render the speech of American characters makes the same mess of it. H. G. Wells's American in " Mr. Britling Sees It Through " is only matched by G. K. Chesterton's in " Man Alive." Even Kipling, who submitted the manuscript of " Captains Courageous " to American friends for criticism, yet managed to make an American in it say: " He's *by way of being* a fisherman now." [2] The late Frank M. Bicknell once amassed some amusing examples of this unanimous failing.[3] Sir Max Pemberton, in a short story dealing with an American girl's visit to England, made her say: " I'm right glad . . . You're as pale as spectres, I guess . . . Fancy that, now! . . . You are my guest, I reckon, . . . and here you are, my word! " C. J. Cutcliffe Hyne, in depicting a former American naval officer, made him speak of *saloon-corner men* (*corner-loafers?*). E. W. Hornung, in one of his " Raffles " stories, introduced an American prize-fighter who went to London and regaled the populace with such things as these: " Blamed if our Bowery boys ain't cock-angels to scum like this . . . By the holy tinker! . . . Blight and blister him! . . . I guess I'll punch his face into a jam pudding . . . Say, sonny, I like you a lot, but I sha'n't like you if you're not a good boy." The American use of *way* and *away* seems to have daunted many of the authors quoted by Mr. Bicknell; several of

1 Reprinted as Litany of the Novelist in his Literary Chapters; London, 1918.
2 On July 31, 1935 the Associated Press reported that the manuscript of an American movie version of Kipling's The Light That Failed was to be presented to the British Museum, and that it showed some corrections of Americanisms in the author's hand. Thus he struck out *to measure* up and inserted *to match*, as better English, and substituted *private* for *personal* in " He had some important *personal* business."
3 The Yankee in British Fiction, *Outlook*, Nov. 19, 1910.

them agree on forms that are certainly never heard in the United States. Thus H. B. Marriott Watson makes an American character say: " You ought to have done business with me *away* in Chicago," and Walter Frith makes another say: " He has gone *way* off to Holborn," " I stroll a block or two *way* down the Strand," " I'll drive him *way* down home by easy stages," and " He can pack his grip and be *way* off home." The American use of *gotten* also seems to present difficulties to English authors. For example, in " Staying with Relations " (1930), by Rose Macaulay, American characters are made to say " The kid's the only one who's *gotten* sense," " You've *gotten* but one small grip apiece," " That about uses up all the energy they've *gotten*," and " That's what's wrong with Mexico, they've *gotten* no public spirit." [1]

" No Englishman," says Bruce Bliven, " really understands our native tongue; interpreters are ever so much more needed than they are between French or Germans and ourselves. That is why British authors never put into the mouth of an American character anything other than weird gibberish — presumably deriving from a faint, incorrect memory of Bret Harte and George Ade, with a touch of erroneous Josh Billings." [2] The late John Galsworthy, who frequently visited the United States, never came within miles of writing sound American. His stock device for indicating American characters was to lard his dialogue with *I judge, gee, cats* (as an exclamation), *vurry* (for *very*), *dandy* and *cunning*. He almost invariably confused *have got* and *have gotten*, the latter of which is used by Americans only in the sense of *have acquired, received* or *become*, not in the sense of simple *have*. Rather curiously, he sometimes put good American phrases into the mouths of English characters, *e.g.*, *good egg* and *to say a mouthful*. [3] Arnold Bennett, like Galsworthy, was fond of making American he-men use *lovely* in such sentences as " It was a *lovely* party." Another shining offender was the late Edgar Wallace, and yet another was the late Sir Arthur Conan Doyle, whose American, Bill Scanlon, in " Maracot Deep " has been described as " one of the most extraordinary linguists ever known to fiction; the Bowery, Vermont, Whitechapel, Texas: all of these

1 See A British Misconception, by Stuart Robertson, *American Speech*, April, 1931, p. 314.
2 British Notes, *New Republic*, Feb. 24, 1926, p. 16.

3 American Speech According to Galsworthy, by Stuart Robertson, *American Speech*, April, 1932, p. 297.

tongues are his, not to mention a few fragments of Pennsylvania Dutch." [1] " Mannerisms of speech that to an American would identify the speaker as from the Middle West, South, Boston, or Philadelphia," says Miss Mildred Wasson,[2] " are mixed freely in the speeches of American characters as interpreted by English writers. Ridiculous uses of words, never to be heard from the tongue of an American man, are invariably ascribed to him." She continues:

> Granted that it is difficult for a stranger to understand our regional differences without years of residence in each part of this country, it is still more difficult for him to grasp that we have social lines of demarkation in speech as definite as those in England and France. There are horizontal lines which are not shown on the map. To sense those intangible lines, separating stratum from stratum in society and education, one must know America. To ignore them stamps a writer, to Americans at least, as being a bit off his ground. An American writing of an English lord and making him speak music-hall cockney would go just as far astray.

Miss Anna Branson Hillyard once offered publicly, in an article in the London *Athenæum*,[3] to undertake the revision of English manuscripts dealing with American people and speech for " fees carefully and inversely scaled by the consultant's importance." Miss Hillyard, in the same article, cited a curious misunderstanding of American by Rupert Brooke. When Brooke was in the United States he sent a letter to the *Westminster Gazette* containing the phrase " You bet your ——." The editor, unable to make anything of it, inserted the word *boots* in place of the dash. Brooke thereupon wrote a letter to a friend, Edward Marsh, complaining of this botching of his Americanism, and Marsh afterward printed it in his memoir of the poet. Miss Hillyard says that she was long puzzled by this alleged Americanism, and wondered where Brooke had picked it up. Finally, " light dawned by way of a comic cartoon. It was the classic phrase, *you betcha* (accent heavily on the *bet*) which Brooke was spelling conventionally! " And, as Miss Hillyard shows, incorrectly, as usual, for *you betcha* is not a collision form of *you bet your* but a collision form of *you bet you* — an imitative second person of *I bet you*, which in comic-cartoon circles is pronounced and spelled *I betcha*.[4]

1 If You Know What I Mean, by C. W. M., *Independent*, March 17, 1928.
2 Cockney American, *American Speech*, April, 1932.
3 American Written Here, Dec. 19, 1919, p. 1362.
4 To this Brooke anecdote a correspondent adds: " An Englishman, confronted by the puzzling American phrase, 'Where am I at?', interpreted it as a doubly barbarous form of 'Where *is me* 'at?'"

When they venture to deal with Americanisms humorously the British literati do even worse. The contributors to *Punch* often try their hands at the business, and with melancholy results. From their efforts an American pathologist of language has recovered the following:

He heard *foot noises* of quite a bunch.
I *reckon* to work through that programme twice a day, and I *garntee* them bears gets to know eighty *barrel* oil leaving Central daily under my *tabs*.
They *greased* for the trolley.
Young split, your lil jaunt soaks me twelve *dollar* seventy-five.[1]

Here, finally, is the effort of the advertising agent of the Morris motor-car to do an advertisement in the American manner:

Say, bud, jest haow do you calculate to buy an automobile? Do you act pensive *after* you've bought, or do you let a few facts form fours on your grey matter before you per-mit the local car agent to take a hack at your bank balance?
F'rinstance, what horse-power class do you aim to get into? Will your pocket bear a 20 h.p., and, if not, will a 10 h.p. bear your family? That's the first problem, and the best way to answer it is to think what old friend Solomon would have done and cut th' trouble in half by making your car an 11.9 — safe both ways up.
Wal, after you've laid out your cash an' folded its arms on its little chest, there are just two people who are liable to hold you up for ransom; the tax-collector and th' polisman. Per-sonally, I give a polisman just nuthin' and a tax-collector as little as George and Mary will let me. If I'm in the 11.9 h.p. class I can send the kids to school with th' tax balance. Get me? [2]

Colloquial English is just as unfathomable to most Americans as colloquial American is to Englishmen. Galsworthy not only puzzled his American readers with his bogus Americanisms; he also puzzled them with his attempts at English slang. When " The Silver Spoon "

1 If You Know What I Mean, by C. W. M., above cited. See also Speak the Speech, *Nation*, May 15, 1935, p. 562. The writer of the latter calls attention to the innocent way in which the brethren of *Punch* mix old and new American slang. A New York gangster, he says, is made to use *I swan* in the same sentence with *gun-moll* and *gat*. " He bets *dollars to doughnuts* and thinks that something *beats the Dutch* only a few seconds before he calls the object of his affection a *hot patootie* who refused to *middle-aisle* it with him because he

is a *palooka*. He also refers to a *fried* [*boiled?*] shirt, and speaks of someone as dead *from the hoofs up*, and of a *gazissey* [*sic*] with a dial like a painted doormat." The *Nation* writer says that when Berton Braley once protested to Sir Owen Seaman, editor of *Punch*, against such manhandling of American he got the reply: " In caricature it is more essential to give what our clientèle will recognize as a familiar likeness than to follow the very latest portrait from life."
2 *Autocar* (London), Feb. 4, 1922, p. 55.

was published in this country, in 1926, Harry Hansen was moved
to print the following caveat:

> When a character says, "I shall *break* for lunch now" we understand
> what he means, but how are we to know what is meant by *bees too bee busy,*
> and again, *bee weak-minded,* which apparently is not a typographical error.
> Mr. Galsworthy's characters *take a lunar,* and enjoy the prospect of getting
> *tonked.* They are hit on the *boko.* "It's not my business to *queer the pitch*
> of her money getting," says one, and of another the author writes: "What
> was his image of her but a *phlizz?*"[1]

The last word here, I suspect, was actually a typographical error
for *phiz.* But Galsworthy was too austere a man to write slang, and
Mr. H. W. Seaman tells me that he is also baffled by some of the
phrases that baffled Mr. Hansen. In the following passage from Mrs.
Joseph Conrad's cook-book (1923) there were no visible blunders,
yet to most American housewives it must have been almost unintelligible:

> We shall need several enameled *basins* of various sizes, a *fish-slice,* a
> *vegetable-slice,* a wire *salad-basket,* one or two wooden spoons, two large
> iron ones, a good toasting-fork, a small *Dutch* oven to hang in front of the
> fire.[2]

Nor would it be easy to find Americans able, without some
pondering, to comprehend such news items as the following:

> Lewis had driven the horse and *trap* laden with *milk-churns* to a *collect-
> ing-stage* on the main road, and to do so he had to cross Wood Green *level-
> crossing.* . . . He apparently failed to see a train approaching around a
> *bend.* . . . The *driver* of the train pulled up promptly. . . .[3]

Even ordinary business correspondence between Englishmen and
Americans is sometimes made difficult by differences in the two
vocabularies. In 1932 the publisher of the Decatur, Ill., *Review* wrote
to the London *Times,* asking what its practice was in the matter of
stereotyping half-tones. The reply of its chief engineer was not
downright unintelligible, but it contained so many strange words
and phrases that the *Review* was moved to print an editorial about

1 The First Reader, New York
World, July 9, 1926.
2 This cook-book was reviewed in
the Baltimore *Evening Sun,* April
14, by a writer who had recently
returned from a long sojourn in
England. "What we Americans
called *endive,*" he said, "the Kent-
ish gardener called *chicory. Chicory* was our *endive. Romaine* let-
tuce was *cos, string-beans* were

runner-beans, lima-beans were
broad-beans, and so on." "What
is here [in England], "known as a
hash," said Eugene Field in Sharps
and Flats; New York, 1900, p. 210,
"we should call a *stew,* and what
we call a *hash* is here known as a
mince." Field printed a list of about
30 terms differing in English and
American.
3 *News of the World,* Sept. 10, 1932.

them.[1] In England, it appeared, stereotypers' blankets were called *packing*, mat-rollers were *mangles*, mats (matrices) were *flongs*, and *to underlay a cut* was *to bump a block*. *To underlay* has since been adopted in England, but *cut* is seldom used. As we have seen in Chapter I, Section 4, the English often have difficulty understanding American books, and protest against their strange locutions with great bitterness. When my series of "Prejudices" began to be reprinted in London in 1921, many of the notices they received roundly denounced my Americanisms. But when, five years later, I translated the text from American into Standard English for a volume of selections, it was reviewed very amiably, and sold better than any of the books from which its contents were drawn.[2] At about the same time William Feather of Cleveland, the editor of a syndicated house-organ, sold the English rights thereto to Alfred Pemberton, a London advertising agent. Mr. Feather writes excellent English, as English is understood in this country, but for British consumption many of his articles had to be extensively revised. In *American Speech* he later printed two amusing papers listing some of the changes made.[3] I content myself with parallel passages from the American and English version of an article describing an ideal weekend in the country:

Feather's American

The interior essentials are several lamps, a large supply of logs, a blazing fire, and a table loaded with broiled Spring chicken, steaming Golden Bantam corn, young string-beans, a pitcher of fresh milk, a pot of black coffee, and perhaps a large peach shortcake, with whipped cream.

Pemberton's English

The interior essentials are several lamps, a large supply of logs, a blazing fire, and a table loaded with roast pheasant and bacon, steaming hot spinach, crisp potatoes, and bread sauce, a jug of cream, a pot of black coffee, and perhaps a large Stilton cheese and a jug of old ale.[4]

1 We Translate a Letter From London, April 17, 1932.
2 When Herman Melville's Moby Dick was brought out in England, c. 1885, many changes were made in the text in order to get rid of Americanisms and American spellings. "In Ch. XVI alone there are 106 variations." See Some Americanisms in Moby Dick, by William S. Ament, *American Speech*, June, 1932, and Bowdler and the Whale, by the same, *American Literature,* March, 1932.

3 Anglicizing Americanisms, Feb., 1926, and Anglicizings, Jan., 1927.
4 Claude de Crespigny, an Englishman resident in the United States, objected to some of Mr. Pemberton's Anglicizations in Peculiar Anglicizing, *American Speech*, July, 1926, and was answered by Mr. Pemberton in Anglicizing Americanisms, *American Speech*, Jan., 1927.

Similar changes are frequently made in American short stories reprinted in English magazines,[1] and American advertisements are commonly rewritten for English use.[2] In 1930 the Department of Commerce issued a business handbook of the United Kingdom [3] giving warning that the American " sales-promoter will have to use British English in his sales drive " in the British Isles. " While American exporters and advertisers doing business in Britain," it continued, " find it is of distinct advantage that English is the common language of the two countries, it is not by any means on as common a basis as it is widely assumed to be." There followed a list of trade-terms differing in England and the United States. In the early days of the movie invasion the titles in American films were commonly translated into English,[4] but as the flood mounted that effort had to be abandoned as hopeless, and today the talkies pour a constant stream of American neologisms into English. Not infrequently they are puzzling at first blush, and to the end that they may be understood, glossaries are often printed in the English newspapers.[5] Similar glos-

1 See Another Language, by Anna R. Baker, *Writer's Digest*, Sept., 1934. Miss Baker describes the revision of a story called Try to Forget Me, by Sewell Peaslee Wright, first published in the *Woman's Home Companion* for Feb., 1934. In the English reprint *to go over big* was changed *to be successful, sure* to *of course, sure-fire* to *popular, to boss around* to *to boss about, grip* to *control, all set* to *ready,* and so on. Altogether, Miss Baker notes 74 changes, including a few in spelling.

2 Addressing American advertisers in *Anglo-American Trade* (London), Jan., 1928, Paul E. Derrick, vice-president of the American Chamber of Commerce in London, said: " I strongly advise Americans who aim to cultivate the British market to have their American advertising translated into idiomatic English by trained English advertising writers. I know, from my long and wide experience, that the distributors and consumers in both Britain and America are distracted from concentration upon the message by every unfamiliar word and expression they encounter. . . . It is time

that both Britons and Americans came to know, and to accept the fact, that they do not speak in the same idiom."

3 The United Kingdom: an Industrial, Commercial and Financial Handbook (Trade Promotion Series No. 94). My quotations are from Ch. XXVI: Selling American Merchandise in the United Kingdom. I am indebted for the reference to Mr. R. M. Stephenson, chief of the European Section, Division of Regional Information, Department of Commerce.

4 Sometimes with sad results. In 1923 D. L. Blumenfeld wrote to the *Cinema* (London, June 5): " The other day I saw an American film in which one of the characters was made to say, in a rough-house scene, " 'Ere you — 'op it! " — which is tantamount to making an Englishman in similar circumstances say " G'wan, you big stiff — beat it! "

5 For example, American Without Tears, by Hamilton Eames, London *Times*, May 6, 1931. Mr. Eames undertook to define 118 terms, ranging from *alky-cooking* to *yen.*

saries are sometimes attached to American books, or inserted in the programmes of American plays. When James Gleason's " Is Zat So? " was presented in London in 1926, Hal O'Flaherty, the correspondent of the Chicago *Tribune*, cabled to his paper as follows:

> From the first act to the last the English section of the audience was forced to refer incessantly to a printed glossary of American slang words and phrases. Even then, when they learned that *to moyder a skoyt* meant to kill a girl, they found themselves three or four sentences behind the actors.

This glossary [1] included definitions of *goof, applesauce, to crab, to can* (to dismiss), *to frame, gorilla, hick, hooch, to lamp, pippin, to stall, sucker, wise-crack* and *to wise up*, most of which have since entered into the English slang vocabulary. When Carl Sandburg's "Collected Poems" were reprinted in London a similar word-list was given in the introduction, with definitions of *bunk-shooter, con-man, dock-walloper, honky-tonk, floozy, yen, cahoots, leatherneck, mazuma* and *flooey*, and when Sinclair Lewis's " Babbitt " was published there in 1922, there was added a glossary defining about 125 American terms, including *bellhop, booster, to bulldoze, burg, dingus, flivver, frame-house, getaway, hootch, jeans, kibosh, lounge-lizard, nut, once-over, pep, plute, room-mate, saphead, tinhorn, wisenheimer* and *yeggman*. Nearly all of these are now understood in England.[2] In 1927 the Oxford University Press brought out an American edition, revised by George Van Santvoord, a former Rhodes scholar, of the Pocket Oxford Dictionary of F. G. and H. W. Fowler. It gave American spellings and pronunciations, and listed a great many words not to be found in the original English edition, e.g., *jitney, goulash, chop-suey* and *drug-store*. In 1934 there followed a new edition of the Concise Oxford Dictionary, revised by H. G. LeMesurier and H. W. Fowler, with an appendix largely devoted to American terms, e.g., *alfalfa, attaboy, bad-lands, bingle, bohunk, boloney* (in the Al Smith sense), *boob, bourbon, burg, calaboose, campus, chaps, chiropractic, co-ed, cole-slaw, con-*

---

1 It was reprinted in *American Speech*, May, 1926, p. 462, and again in the same, Dec., 1927, p. 167.
2 The Lewis glossary was made by Montgomery Belgion, an English-man who once lived in New York. Despite his American experience, he made a number of errors. Thus he defined *to buck* as to cheat, *bum* as a rotter, *flipflop* as rot, *high-*

binder as an extravagant person, and *roustabout* as a revolutionary. The glossaries printed in the English newspapers are usually full of howlers. Even the otherwise accurate Hamilton Eames, whose contribution to the London *Times* has just been cited, defined *panhandler* as a swindler. It means, of course, a street beggar.

*niption, coon, craps, third-degree, crackerjack, to doll up, to dope
out, to fade out, to frame* and *to get away with.* " The cinema, now
vocal," says Mr. LeMesurier, " has made [the Englishman] familiar
with many Americanisms at the meaning of which he has often to
guess."

4. BRITICISMS IN THE UNITED STATES

" While England was a uniquely powerful empire-state, ruled by
an aristocratic caste," said Wyndham Lewis in 1934,[1] " its influence
upon the speech as upon the psychology of the American ex-colonies
was overwhelming. But today that ascendancy has almost entirely
vanished. The aristocratic caste is nothing but a shadow of itself, the
cinema has brought the American scene and the American dialect
nightly into the heart of England, and the Americanizing process is
far advanced. . . . There has been no reciprocal movement of
England into the United States; indeed, with the new American
nationalism, England is kept out." This is certainly true in the field
of language. It is most unusual for an English neologism to be taken
up in this country, and when it is, it is only by a small class, mainly
made up of conscious Anglomaniacs. To the common people everything English, whether an article of dress, a social custom or a word
or phrase has what James M. Cain has called " a somewhat pansy
cast." That is to say, it is regarded as affected, effeminate and ridiculous. The stage Englishman is never a hero, and in his rôle of
comedian he is laughed at with brutal scorn. To the average red-
blooded he-American his tea-drinking is evidence of racial decay,
and so are the cut of his clothes, his broad *a*, and his occasional use
of such highly un-American locutions as *jolly, awfully* and *ripping.*
The American soldiers who went to France in 1917 and 1918 did
not develop either admiration or liking for their English comrades;
indeed, they were better pleased with the French, and reserved their
greatest fondness for the Germans. As we shall see in Chapter XI,
Section 1, one of the evidences of their coolness toward Tommy
Atkins was that they borrowed very little of his slang. They found
him singing a number of American songs — for example, " Casey
Jones," " John Brown " and " We're Here Because We're Here " —

1 The Dumb Ox, *Life and Letters,*
  April, 1934, p. 42.

but they adopted only one of his own, to wit, " Mademoiselle from Armenteers." [1] In an elaborate vocabulary of American soldiers' slang compiled by E. A. Hecker and Edmund Wilson, Jr., [2] I can find very few words or phrases that seem to be of English origin. *To carry on* retains in American its old American meaning of to raise a pother, despite its widespread use among the English in the sense of to be (in American) *on the job*. Even *to wangle*, perhaps the best of the new verbs brought out of the war by the English, and *wowser* [3] an excellent noun, have never got a foothold in the United States, and would be unintelligible today to nine Americans out of ten. As for *blighty, cheerio* and *righto* they would strike most members of the American Legion as almost as unmanly as *tummy* or *pee-pee*. After the success of " What Price Glory? " by Laurence Stallings and Maxwell Anderson, in 1924, *what price* had a certain vogue, but it quickly passed out.

On higher and less earthly planes there is a greater hospitality to English example. Because the United States has failed to develop anything properly describable as a Court, or a native aristocracy of any settled position and authority, persons of social pretensions are thrown back upon English usage and opinion for guidance, and the vocabulary and pronunciation of the West End of London naturally flavor their speech. Until the beginning of the present century the word *shop*, in American, always meant a workshop, but in 1905 or thereabout the small stores along the Fifth avenues of the larger American cities began turning themselves into *shops*. Today the word has the special meaning of a store dealing in a limited range of merchandise, as opposed to a department-store; indeed, *shop* and

1 Eric Partridge, in his introduction to Songs and Slang of the British Soldier, 1914–1918; London, 1930, p. 6, says that it appeared in 1915, and (p. 48) that its tune was borrowed from the French music-halls.
2 I have had access to it through the courtesy of Mr. Wilson. Unfortunately, it remains unpublished.
3 *Wowser* is of Australian origin, and was in use in Australia at least as early as 1908, but it did not come into use in England until it was introduced by the Australian troops in 1915. Its etymology is uncertain. I am told by Mr. J. A. B. Foster, of Hobart, Tasmania, that it was invented by one John Norton, who defined it as " a fellow who is too niggardly of joy to allow the other fellow any time to do anything but pray." Mr. Roger C. Hackett, of Cristobal, C. Z., says he has heard that it represents the initials of a slogan employed by a reform organization in Australia (or New Zealand), *c.* 1900, viz.: " We only want social evils righted." I tried to introduce it in the United States after the World War, but without success. It was used by Dr. William Morton Wheeler in the *Scientific Monthly*, Feb., 1920, p. 116.

specialty-shop are used interchangeably. Every American town of any pretensions now has *gift-shops* (or *shoppes*),[1] *book-shops, hat-shops, tea-shops, luggage-shops* and *candy-shops*. But the plain people continue to call a *shop* a *store*, though they use *shopping* and *shopper*. The effort, made at the time *shop* came in, to substitute *boot* for *shoe* did not get very far, and there are not many *boot-shops* left, and even fewer *boot-makers*, save in the strict American sense. *Bootery* and *toggery* did not last long. But *tradesmen's-entrance* fared better, and so did *charwoman*, which has now pretty well supplanted *scrubwoman*, and, in the cities at least, caused Americans to forget their native modification of *char*, to wit, *chore*. *Hired-girls* began to vanish from the cities so long ago as the second Cleveland administration, and now they are all *maids*. *Drawing-room*, always used in the South, began to challenge the Northern *parlor* about 1895, but by the turn of the century both encountered stiff competition from *living-room*. *To Let* signs, once conscious affectations, are now almost as common, at least in the New York area, as *For Rent* signs, *postman* seems to be making some progress against *letter-carrier*, the tunnels under the Hudson are *tubes, flapper* is now good American, and *nursing-home* has got some lodgment. In August, 1917, signs appeared in the New York surface cars in which the conductors were referred to as *guards;* all of them are now *guards* on the elevated lines and in the subways save the forward men, who remain *conductors* officially. During the war even the government seemed inclined to substitute the English *hoarding* for the American *billboard*.[2] In the Federal Reserve Act (1913) it borrowed the English *governor* to designate the head of a bank,[3] and in 1926 the Weather Bureau formally adopted the English *smog* for a mixture of smoke and fog.[4] How and when the National *Biscuit* Company acquired its name I don't know. What it manufactures

1 Whether this form is English or American I don't know, but certainly it is much oftener encountered in the United States than in England. It is sometimes pronounced as spelled, *i.e., shoppy*. In 1934, in the town of Rabat, Morocco, I heard it so pronounced by a native guiding Americans through the bazaars. Sometimes it is combined with the archaic *ye*, as in "Ye Olde Tea Shoppe." In such cases *ye* is often pronounced as

spelled, though it is simply an abbreviation for *the*.
2 See p. 58 of The United States at War, a pamphlet issued by the Library of Congress, 1917. The compiler of this pamphlet was a savant bearing the fine old British name of Herman H. B. Meyer.
3 He is addressed as *Governor*, and is commonly referred to as *Hon*.
4 This was announced in an Associated Press dispatch from Washington, Feb. 7, 1926.

are *biscuits* in England, but *crackers* in the United States. Evacustes A. Phipson, an Englishman, says that *railway* came into American as "a concession to Anglomania,"¹ but about that I am uncertain. In any case, the number of such loans is small, and not many of them are of any significance. More interesting is the Briticism *penny*, which survives in American usage despite the fact that we have no coin bearing that name officially, and the further fact that the *cent* to which it is applied is worth only half an English penny. It occurs in many compounds, *e.g.*, *penny-bank* and *penny-in-the-slot*, and has even produced Americanisms, *e.g.*, *penny-ante* and *penny-arcade*. In 1928 the Legislature of South Carolina considered a bill providing that in certain prosecutions for criminal libel the culprit should " be fined a *penny* and the costs, and no more." ²

In the days when the theater bulked large in American life it supplied non-traveled Americans of Anglophil leanings with a steady supply of Briticisms, both in vocabulary and in pronunciation. Of plays dealing with fashionable life, most of those seen in the United States were of English origin, and many of them were played by English companies. Thus the social aspirants of provincial towns became familiar with the Standard English pronunciation of the moment and with the current English phrases. It was by this route, I suppose, that the use of *sorry* in place of the traditional American *excuse me* got in. The American actors, having no Court to imitate, contended themselves by imitating their English colleagues. Thus an American of fashionable pretensions, say in Altoona, Pa., or Athens, Ga., learned how to shake hands, eat soup, greet his friends, enter a drawing-room and pronounce the words *path, secretary, melancholy* and *necessarily* in a manner that was an imitation of some American actor's imitation of an English actor's imitation of what was done in Mayfair — in brief, an imitation in the fourth degree. The American actor did his best to mimic the pronunciation and intonation of the English, but inasmuch as his name, before he became Gerald Cecil, was probably Rudolph Goetz or Terence Googan, he frequently ran upon laryngeal difficulties. Since the decay of the theater this influence has vanished. The movie actors in Hollywood, with a few exceptions, make no effort to imitate the

1 *Dialect Notes,* Vol. I, Pt. IX, p. 432.
2 Freedom of the Press (editorial), Savannah *News,* Jan. 15, 1928.

English pronunciation, and the dialogue put into their mouths seldom contains recognizable Briticisms. To the English it sounds like a farrago of barbaric Americanisms, and on frequent occasions they arise to denounce it with pious indignation.

The Protestant Episcopal Church, on account of its affiliation with the Church of England and its generally fashionable character, is a distributing-station for Anglomania in the United States, but its influence upon the language seems to be very slight. Most of its clergy, in my experience, use sound American in their pulpits, and not long ago, at the funeral orgies of a friend, I heard one of the most Anglophil of them pronounce *amen* in the best Middle Western manner. The fashionable preparatory schools for boys, most of which are under Protestant Episcopal control, have introduced a number of Briticisms into the vocabulary of their art and mystery, *e.g.*, *head-master*, *chapel* (for the service as well as the building), *house-master*, *monitor*, *honors*, *prefect* and *form*. The late Dr. J. Milnor Coit, while rector of the fashionable St. Paul's School at Concord, N. H., diligently promoted this Anglicization. He encouraged the playing of cricket instead of baseball, and " introduced English schoolroom nomenclature to the American boy." But his successors suffered a relapse into Americanisms, and while " St. Paul's still has *forms*, the *removes*, *evensong* and *matins*, and even the cricket of Dr. Coit's time are now forgotten." [1] At Groton, the most swagger of all the American prep-schools, the boys are divided into *forms* and there are *prefects*, *masters* and a *headmaster*, but an examination of the catalogue shows few other imitations of English nomenclature. The *staff* is actually called the *faculty*, and the *headmaster*, a Protestant Episcopal clergyman, is listed as *Rev.*, without the *the*.

Occasionally some American patriot launches an attack upon the few Briticisms that seep in, but it is not done often, for there is seldom any excuse. Richard Grant White, in 1870,[2] warned his followers against the figurative use of *nasty* as a synonym for *dis-*

1 American Private Schools, by Porter E. Sargent; Boston, 1920. Mr. Sargent says that the young boys at St. Paul's sleep in " alcoves in the dormitories similar to the cubicles of many of the English public-schools." It is curious to note that Dr. Coit, for all his Anglomania, was born at Harrisburg, Pa., began life as the manager of a tube works at Cleveland, and retired to Munich on resigning the rectorate of St. Paul's.
2 Words and Their Uses; New York, p. 198.

agreeable. This use of the word was then relatively new in England, though, according to White, the *Saturday Review* and the *Spectator* had already succumbed. His objections to it were unavailing; *nasty* quickly got into American, and has been there ever since.[1] Gilbert M. Tucker, in 1883,[2] protested against *good-form, traffic* (in the sense of travel), *to bargain* and *to tub* as Briticisms that we might well do without, but all of them took root and are sound American today. The locutions that are more obviously merely fashionable slang have a harder time of it, and seldom get beyond a narrow circle. When certain advertisers in New York sought to appeal to snobs by using such Briticisms as *swagger* and *topping* in their advertisements, the town wits, led by the watchful Franklin P. Adams (though he then served the *Tribune,* which Clement K. Shorter once called " more English than we are English "), fell upon them, and quickly routed them. To the average American of the plain people, indeed, any word or phrase of an obviously English flavor has an offensive smack. To call him *old dear* would be almost as hazardous as to call him *Percy,* and *bah Jove* and *my word* somehow set his teeth on edge. But in consciously elegant circles there is less aversion to such forms, and even *fed-up, rotter, priceless, swank, top-hole, cheerio, tosh,* and *no-end* are tolerated. Fashionable mothers teach their children to call them *Mummy,* and fox-hunters call a leaper a *lepper.*[3]

The grotesque errors that English authors fall into every time they essay to write American, referred to a few pages back, are matched by the blunders of Americans who try to write colloquial English. Some years ago, St. John Ervine, the Anglo-Irish playwright and critic, discussed the matter at length in *Vanity Fair.*[4] He said:

> When I was in Chicago two years ago, I read in one of the newspapers of that city an account of a jewel theft. . . . A young Englishman, belonging to the aristocracy, had married an American girl, and while they were on their honeymoon, thieves stole some of her jewels. A reporter hurried from Chicago to get a story out of the affair. He interviewed the young husband who

1 But the meaning of the word now differs somewhat in the two countries. In America it connotes disgusting as well as mere unpleasant. Dean W. R. Inge called attention to this difference in The English Language, London *Evening Standard,* Nov. 24, 1921.

2 American English, *North American Review,* April.
3 Noah Webster denounced this last so long ago as 1789, in his Dissertations on the English Language, II.
4 English Dialect and American Ears, June, 1922, p. 53.

was reported to have said something like this: "Haw, haw, yaas, by Jove! Isn't it awf'lly jolly rotten, what? They stole the bally jewels, haw, haw! . . ." I cannot remember the exact words put into this young man's mouth by the reporter, but they were not less foolish than those I have set out. . . . The reporter had either decided before the interview that all Englishmen of aristocratic birth speak like congenital idiots, and therefore could not listen accurately to what was being said to him, or he was too lazy or incompetent to do his work properly, and trusted to conventional caricature to cover up his own deficiencies.

Mr. Ervine then proceeded to a detailed analysis of a book called "Full Up and Fed Up," by Whiting Williams, an American who lived as a workingman in England, Wales and Scotland during 1920, and sought to report the conversations of the native workingmen among whom he worked. He recorded the speech of an English laborer as follows:

> If Hi wuz you, Hi'd walk right in ter the fountain-'ead o' these steel works 'ere, and sye, "Hi wants ter see the manager!" — just like thot. With wot ye've done in Hamerica, ye'll get on fine 'ere.

And that of an English soldier thus:

> Hi never seen a ranker make a good hofficer yet — awnd Hi've 'ad 'em over me a lot — hadjutants and all. In the hexercises and heverywhere it's allus "Hi've been there meself, boys, and it cawn't be done. Hi'm too wise, boys." You know 'ow it is. No, sir, never one.

Said Mr. Ervine of these alleged specimens of Cockney English:

> I have lived in England for twenty-one years and I know the country, North and South, East and West, country and town, far better than Mr. Williams can ever hope to know it. I have lived among working-people in London, in provincial towns, and in villages, and I have never heard any Englishman speak in that style. I have been in the Army, as a private soldier and as an officer, and I tell Mr. Williams that if he imagines he heard a soldier saying *hexercises* and *heverywhere*, then he simply has not got the faculty of hearing. The dropped *h* is common, but the sounding of it where it ought not to be sounded has almost ceased. I have never heard it sounded in a city, and only on one occasion have I heard it sounded in the country, where an old-fashioned fisherman, with whom I used to go sailing, would sometimes say *haccident* when he meant *accident*. This man's younger brother never misplaced the *h* at all in this way, though he often elided it where it ought to have been sounded. The *h* is more likely to be dropped than sounded because of the natural laziness of most people over language. . . . A considerable effort is necessary in order to sound it in words where there is no such letter, and this fact, apart altogether from the results of compulsory education, makes it unlikely that Mr. Williams heard anyone in England saying *Hi* for *I* and *Hamerica* for *America*.

Mr. Ervine continued:

I imagine that most Americans form their impressions about English dialect from reading Dickens, and do not check these impressions with the facts of contemporary life. . . . A popular novel will fix a dialect in the careless mind, and people will continue to believe that men and women speak in that particular fashion long after they have ceased to do so. Until I went to America, I believed that all Negroes spoke like the characters in "Uncle Tom's Cabin." Mr. John Drinkwater clearly thought so, too, when he wrote "Abraham Lincoln." I expected to hear a Negro saying something like "Yaas, massa, dat am so! " when he meant, "Yes, sir, that is so! " I daresay there are many Negroes in America who do speak in that way; in fact, Mr. T. S. Stribling's notable story, "Birthright," makes this plain. But *all* Negroes do not do so, and perhaps the most correct English I heard during my short visit to the United States two years ago came from the mouth of a red-cap in Boston.

5. HONORIFICS

The honorifics in everyday use in England and the United States show some notable divergences. On the one hand the English are almost as diligent as the Germans in bestowing titles of honor upon their men of mark, but on the other hand they are very careful to withhold such titles from men who do not legally bear them. In America every practitioner of any branch of the healing art, even a chiropodist or an osteopath, is a doctor *ipso facto*,[1] but in England a good many surgeons lack the title and even physicians may not have it. It is customary there, however, to address a physician in the second person as *Doctor*, though his card may show that he is only *medicinæ baccalaureus*, a degree quite unknown in Amerca. Thus an Englishman, when he is ill, always consults a *doctor*, as we do. But a surgeon is usually plain *Mr.*,[2] and

1 On April 1, 1926 the New York *Times* printed a warning by Assistant District Attorney Michael A. Ford that practitioners of the following non-Euclidian healing schemes were calling themselves *doctor* in New York: ærotherapy, astral-healing, autothermy, bio-dynamo-chromatic-therapy, chromo-therapy, diet-therapy, electro-homeopathy, electro-napro-therapy, geo-therapy, irido-therapy, mechano-therapy, neuro-therapy, napra-pathy, photo-therapy, physic-therapy, quartz-therapy, sanitratorism, spondylotherapy, spectro-chrome-therapy, spectra-therapy, tropho-therapy, theomonism, telatherapy, vitopathy, zodiac-therapy, zonet-therapy and Zoroastrianism.

2 In the appendix to the Final Report of the Royal Commission on Venereal Diseases, London, 1916, p. iv, I find the following: "*Mr.* C. J. Symonds, F.R.C.S., M.D.; *Mr.* F. J. McCann, F.R.C.S., M.D.; *Mr.* A. F. Evans, F.R.C.S." *Mr.* Symonds is consulting surgeon to

prefers to be so called, though he may have *M.D.* on his card, along with *F.R.C.S.* (fellow of the Royal College of Surgeons). A physician (or surgeon), if he manages to cure the right patients, is not infrequently knighted, in which event he becomes *Sir Basil* and ceases to be either *Dr.* or *Mr.* If royalty patronizes him he may even become *Lord Bolus.* The Englishman uses the word *physician* less than we do; he prefers *medical man.* But with women doctors increasing in number, *medical man* becomes inconvenient, and *medical woman* would seem rather harsh to the English, whose natural tendency would be to say *medical lady*, a plain impossibility. The late Henry Bradley proposed to get round the difficulty by reviving the archaic word *leech*,[1] but it has never been adopted. An English dentist or druggist or veterinarian is never *Dr.* Nor is the title frequent among pedagogues, for the *Ph.D.* is an uncommon degree in England, and it is seldom if ever given to persons trained in the congeries of quackeries which passes, in the American universities, under the name of " education." According to William McAndrew, once superintendent of schools in Chicago and famous as the antagonist of Mayor Big Bill Thompson, every school principal in Boston and New York " has secured a general usage of getting himself called *doctor.*"[2]

Professor, like *doctor*, is worked much less hard in England than in the United States. In all save a few of our larger cities every male pedagogue is a professor, and so is every band leader, dancing master, and medical consultant. Two or three generations ago the title was given to horse-trainers, barbers, bartenders, phrenologists, caterers, patent-medicine vendors, acrobats, ventriloquists, and pedagogues and champions of all sorts.[3] Of late its excessive misuse has brought it into disrepute, and more often than not it is applied satirically.[4] The real professors try hard to get rid of it. In 1925 those at the University of Virginia organized a society " for the

Guy's Hospital, *Mr.* McCann is an eminent London gynecologist, and *Mr.* Evans is a general surgeon in large practice. All would be called *Doctor* in the United States.

1 The Skilful *Leech*, *S.P.E. Tracts*, No. IV, 1920, p. 33.

2 Speaking of This and That, Chicago *School Journal*, Sept., 1925, p. 1.

3 See *Professor* or *Professional*, by Mamie Meredith, *American Speech*, Feb., 1934, p. 71, and *Professor Again*, by C. D. P., *American Speech*, June, 1929, p. 422.

4 See The Title *Professor*, by N. R. L., *American Speech*, Oct., 1927, p. 27, and *Professor Again*, by Charles L. Hanson, *American Speech*, Feb., 1928, p. 256.

encouragement of the use of *Mister* as applied to all men, professional or otherwise." In England *professor* is used less lavishly, and is thus better esteemed. In referring to any man who holds a professorship in a university it is almost always employed. But when he acquires a secular title, that title takes precedence. Thus it was *Professor* Almroth Wright down to 1906, but *Sir* Almroth afterward. Huxley was always called *Professor* until he was appointed to the Privy Council. This appointment gave him the right to have *Right Honourable* put before his name, and thereafter it was customary to call him simply *Mr.* Huxley, with the *Right Honourable*, so to speak, floating in the air. The combination, to an Englishman, was more flattering than *Professor*, for the English always esteem political dignities more than the dignities of learning. This explains, perhaps, why their universities distribute so few honorary degrees. In the United States every respectable Protestant clergyman, save perhaps a few in the Protestant Episcopal Church, is a *D.D.*,[1] and it is almost impossible for a man to get into the papers as a figure in anything short of felony without becoming an *LL.D.*, but in England such honors are granted only grudgingly.[2] So with military titles. To promote a war veteran from sergeant to colonel by acclamation, as is often done in the United States, is unknown over there. The English have nothing equivalent to the gaudy tin soldiers of our Governors' staffs, nor to the bespangled colonels and generals of the Knights Templar and Patriarchs Militant, nor to the nondescript captains and majors of our country towns.[3] An English railroad conductor (*railway guard*) is never *Captain*, as he often is in the United States. Nor are military titles used by the police. Nor is it the custom to make every newspaper editor a colonel, as used

---

1 Canon law among the Baptists, who are numerous in the South, permits any congregation to confer the degree. It is often given to a pastor as a solatium when he is dismissed from his post. In both England and America every Catholic and Church of England bishop is made a *D.D.* on his elevation.

2 But in Scotland any clergyman over fifty, never caught red-handed in simony or adultery, is likely to be a *D.D.*

3 In late years the creation of colonels and generals by State Governors has diminished, but it continues in Kentucky, where Governor Ruby Laffoon (gloriously he, despite his given-name) made thousands between 1931 and 1935. Col. Patrick H. Callahan of Louisville who owes his title to a former Governor, argues that military rank is conducive, at least in Kentucky, to easy social intercourse. "*Colonel*," he says, "is not much more than a nickname, like *Tom*, *Dick* or *Harry*, and is used and appreciated mostly on that account."

to be done south of the Potomac.[1] Nor is an Attorney-General or
Postmaster-General or Consul-General called *General.* Nor are the
glories of public office, after they have officially come to an end,
embalmed in such clumsy quasi-titles as *ex-United States Senator,
ex-Judge of the Circuit Court of Appeals, ex-Federal Trade Commissioner* and *former Chief of the Fire Department.*[2] Nor does
every college swarm with *deans.* Nor is every magistrate a *judge.*
This American fondness for hollow titles goes back to colonial
days. An English traveler, Edward Kimber, wrote in 1746: " Where-
ever you travel in Maryland (as also in Virginia and Carolina) your
ears are constantly astonished at the number of colonels, majors and
captains that you hear mentioned: in short, the whole country seems
at first to you a retreat of heroes." Two years earlier the Scottish
physician, Alexander Hamilton, traveling along the Hudson, found
an immense number of colonels. " It is a common saying here," he
wrote, " that a man has no title to that dignity unless he has killed
a rattlesnake." After the Revolution many of the discharged soldiers
opened inns, and large numbers of them blossomed out as captains,
majors and colonels.[3] Every successive war brought in a swarm of
new military titles, and after the Civil War they were almost innumerable. During the Grant Era it also became common for wives
to borrow their husbands' titles in the German-Scandinavian fashion,
and the historian, Edward A. Freeman, who made a lecture tour
of the United States in 1881–82, reported when he got home that
he had seen *Mrs. Professor* on a woman's visiting card and had read
in a newspaper of *Mrs. ex-Senator.* A. Freeman was almost always
called either *Professor* or *Doctor* by the Americans he encountered.
" In some parts," he said, " a stranger is commonly addressed as
Colonel or *Judge.*" He called attention to an American peculiarity
that is still observable: the overuse of *Mister.* " I noticed," he said,
" that men who were thoroughly intimate with one another, men
who were old friends and colleagues, spoke of and to one another

1 " In Nebraska," according to Dr.
Louise Pound, *American Speech,*
April, 1935, p. 158, " auctioneers
customarily take to themselves the
title of *Colonel.*" They do so also
in Kansas, Oklahoma, Missouri and
parts of the South. See " Auctioneer
Colonels Again," by Dr. Pound,
American Speech, Oct., 1935.

2 The use of *former* in place of *ex-*
is an Americanism, and Horwill
says that it is unknown in England.

3 For these references I am indebted
to Words Indicating Social Status
in America in the Eighteenth Century, by Allen Walker Read,
American Speech, Oct., 1934.

with handles to their names, in a way which men in the same case would not do [in England]." [1] The leap in the United States is often directly from *Mister* to *Jack*. This use of the given-name was popularized by Rotary, the members of which so address one another, and no doubt was also fostered by the advent of the Hon. James A. Farley, whose greeting to all comers was " Call me Jim." [2]

But perhaps the greatest difference between English and American usage is presented by *the Honorable*. In the United States the title is applied loosely to all public officials of any apparent respectability, and with some show of official sanction to many of them, especially Congressmen, but it is questionable whether this application has any actual legal standing, save perhaps in the case of certain judges, who are referred to as *the Hon.* in their own court records. Even the President of the United States, by law, is not *the Honorable*, but simply *the President*. In the First Congress the matter of his title was exhaustively debated; some members wanted to call him *the Honorable* and others proposed *His Excellency* and even *His Highness*. But the two Houses finally decided that it was " not proper to annex any style or title other than that expressed by the Constitution." Congressmen themselves are not *Honorables*. True enough, the *Congressional Record*, in printing a set speech, calls it " Speech of *Hon.* John Jones " (without the *the* before the *Hon.* — a characteristic Americanism), but in reporting the ordinary remarks of a member it always calls him plain *Mr.* Nevertheless, a country Congressman would be offended if his partisans, in announcing his appearance on the stump, did not prefix *Hon.* to his name. So would a State Senator. So would a Mayor or Governor. I have seen the sergeant-at-arms of the United States Senate referred to as *Hon.* in the records of that body,[3] and the title is also accorded there to all former members of either House, to State Governors, to Ambassadors, to members of the Cabinet, past or present, and all their principal assistants, to all State officials of any dignity, and to a miscel-

---

1 Some Impressions of the United States; New York, 1888. The pertinent passages are reprinted in American Social History as Recorded by British Travelers, by Allan Nevins; New York, 1923, p. 481.
2 " Members of the United States Senate," says an editorial in the

Dayton (O.) *News*, Jan. 5, 1934, " largely address each other, in private at least, by their first names. The President of the United States, to hundreds of his friends, is simply *Frank*."
3 *Congressional Record*, May 16, 1918, p. 7147.

laneous rabble of other notables, including newspaper editors.[1] In February, 1935, an Interstate Assembly of various State officials was held at Washington. In the official report of it,[2] the following functionaries, among others, were set down as *Hons.*: State tax commissioners and assessors, State treasurers, comptrollers and auditors, the deputies and assistants of all these, and all members of State Legislatures.

In England the thing is more carefully ordered, and bogus *Hons.* are unknown. The prefix is applied to both sexes and belongs by law, *inter alia*, to all present or past maids of honor, to all justices of the High Court during their term of office, to the Scotch Lords of Session, to the sons and daughters of viscounts and barons, to the younger sons of earls, and to the members of the legislative and executive councils of the colonies. But *not* to members of Parliament, though each is, in debate, the *hon. member*, or the *hon. gentleman*. Even a member of the cabinet is not an *Hon.*, though he is a *Right Hon.* by virtue of membership in the Privy Council, of which the Cabinet is legally merely a committee. This last honorific be-

1 For the sake of the record I append a few examples. Clark Howell, editor of the Atlanta *Constitution* appears as *Hon.* in the *Record* for June 15 (all dates are 1935), p. 9811, and the chief editorial writer of another Southern paper on Sept. 10, p. 15335. Jeremiah T. Mahoney, president of the Athletic Union of the United States appears on Aug. 23, p. 14790; Norman Hapgood on May 23, p. 8405; Harry L. Hopkins on July 17, p. 11733; Rexford G. Tugwell on Sept. 10, p. 15253; Frederic A. Delano, President Roosevelt's uncle, Aug. 21, p. 14439; Leo T. Crowley, chairman of the Federal Deposit Insurance Corporation, on June 5, p. 9051; Chester C. Davis, administrator of the Agricultural Adjustment Act, on Aug. 14, p. 13618; Robert Fechner, director of Emergency Conservation Work, on Aug. 15, 13812; former Secretary of the Navy Charles Francis Adams on June 11, p. 9418; an ex-Assistant Postmaster-General on May 29, p. 8728; an Assistant Secretary of State on July 23, p. 12211; a former

Attorney-General of Massachusetts on Aug. 6, p. 13061; the Attorney-General of Indiana on Aug. 16, p. 13980; Knud Wefald, a member of the Minnesota Railroad and Warehouse Commission, on Aug. 23, p. 14778; a special assistant to the Postmaster-General on June 21, p. 10298; a resident commissioner from the Philippines on July 17, p. 11805; a Works Progress director for Idaho on July 17, p. 11733; the solicitor of the Postoffice on July 11, p. 11493; and Frank Delaney, general counsel of Investors and Policyholders, Inc., on Aug. 19, p. 14213. I sometimes receive letters from members of Congress. Almost invariably they make me *Hon.* on the envelope. Some time ago I received an invitation from a Senator who was giving a luncheon to another Senator. It was in the third person, and both the host and the guest of honor appeared as *the Hon.*

2 Printed in *State Government*, the organ of the American Legislators' Association, April, 1935, p. 89.

longs, not only to privy councillors, but also to all peers lower than marquesses (those above are *Most Hon.*), to Lord Mayors during their terms of office, to the Lord Advocate and to the Lord Provosts of Edinburgh and Glasgow. Moreover, a peeress whose husband is a *Right Hon.* is a *Right Hon.* herself.[1] The British colonies follow the jealous usage of the mother-country. Even in Canada the lawless American example is not imitated. I have before me a " Table of Titles to be Used in Canada," laid down by royal warrant, which lists those who are *Hons.* and those who are not *Hons.* in the utmost detail. Only privy councillors of Canada (not to be confused with imperial privy councillors) are permitted to retain the prefix after going out of office, though ancients who were legislative councillors at the time of the union, July 1, 1867, if any survive, may still use it by sort of courtesy, and former Speakers of the Dominion Senate and House of Commons and various retired judges may do so on application to the King, countersigned by the Governor-General. The following are lawfully *the Hon.*, but only during their tenure of office: the Solicitor-General, the Speaker of the House of Commons, the Presidents and Speakers of the provincial Legislatures, members of the executive councils of the Provinces, the Chief Justice, the judges of the Supreme Courts of Ontario, Nova Scotia, New Brunswick, British Columbia, Prince Edward Island, Saskatchewan and Alberta, the judges of the Courts of Appeal of Manitoba and British Columbia, the Chancery Court of Prince Edward Island, and the Circuit Court of Montreal — these, and no more. A Lieutenant-Governor of a Province is not *the Hon.*, but *His Honor.* The Governor-General is *His Excellency*, and his wife is *Her Excellency*, but in practise they usually have superior honorifics, and do not forget to demand their use. In Australia, it would seem, *the Hon.* is extended to members of the Federal Parliament; at least one of them, to my personal knowledge, has the title engraved upon his visiting-card.[2]

1 The proper use of titles in England is so complicated a matter that it has produced a large literature. Perhaps the best textbook is *Titles and Forms of Address* (anonymous); 2nd ed.; London, 1929.

2 In the Crown Colony of Hong Kong all members of the Legislative Council are *Hons.* and it is customary to add *Mr.* after the title, even when Christian names or initials follow. It is said to have been first inserted by order of Sir Matthew Nathan, a former Governor. See *Marriage at 6 A.M.*, by Tom Clarke; London, 1934. I am indebted here to Mr. F. H. Tyson of Hong Kong.

But though an Englishman, and, following him, a colonial, is thus very careful to restrict *the Hon.* to its legal uses, he always insists, when he serves without pay as an officer of any organization, upon indicating his volunteer character by writing *hon.* meaning *honorary*, before the name of his office. If he leaves it off it is a sign that he is a hireling. Thus, the agent of the New Zealand government in London, a paid officer, is simply the *agent*, but the agents at Brisbane and Adelaide, in Australia, who serve for the glory of it, are *hon. agents.* In writing to a Briton of condition one had better be careful to put *Esq.* behind his name, and not *Mr.* before it. The English have long made a distinction between the two forms. *Mr.*, on an envelope, indicates that the sender holds the receiver to be his inferior; one writes to *Mr.* John Jackson, one's green-grocer, but to James Thompson, *Esq.*, one's neighbor. But if one encloses an envelope for a reply, addressed to one's self, one's name on it must be preceded by *Mr.*, not followed by *Esq.* Any man who is entitled to the *Esq.* is a gentleman, by which an Englishman means a man of sound connections and what is regarded as dignified occupation — in brief, of ponderable social position. But in late years these distinctions have been losing force.[1] In colonial America *Esq.* seems to have been confined to justices of the peace, who acquired thereby the informal title of *Squire*, but inasmuch as every lawyer of any dignity became a justice almost automatically it was eventually applied to most members of the bar.[2] It is common to so apply it to this day. Lawyers, like judges, are often designated *Esq.* in court papers, and when one of them appears on a list of speakers at a political meeting he is usually distinguished from the general, especially in the South, by adding *Esq.* to his name.

The English in speaking or writing of public officials, avoid those long and clumsy combinations of title and name which figure so copiously in American newspapers. Such locutions as *Assistant Secretary of the Interior* Jones, *Fourth Assistant Postmaster-General* Brown, *Inspector of Boilers* Smith, *Judge of the Appeal Tax Court*

---

1 An English friend tells me that he might, "without grievous solecism," address his tailor as *Esq.* — on the ground that a tailor, like a lawyer, doctor or horse-dealer, renders his bill, not in pounds, but in guineas! In Etiquette, by Emily Post; New York, 1922, p. 459, we are told that "formal invitations are always addressed to *Mr.* Stanley Smith," but that "all other personal letters may be addressed to Stanley Smith, *Esq.*"

2 I am indebted here to Dr. S. E. Morison.

Robinson, *Chief Clerk of the Treasury* Williams and *Collaborating Epidemiologist* White [1] are quite unknown to him. When an Englishman mentions a high official, such as the Secretary for Foreign Affairs, he does not think it necessary to add the man's name; he simply says *the Secretary for Foreign Affairs* or *the Foreign Secretary*. And so with the Lord Chancellor, the Chief Justice, the Prime Minister, the Bishop of Carlisle, the Chief Rabbi, the First Lord (of the Admiralty), the Master of Pembroke (College), the Italian Ambassador, and so on. But certain ecclesiastical titles are sometimes coupled to surnames in the American manner, as in *Dean* Inge and *Canon* Wilberforce.

A lawyer appearing in court before a judge of the English higher courts addresses him as *My Lord*, and speaks of him in his presence as *His Lordship*. In the United States the form is *Your Honor*, which is also proper for county judges in England. A letter to an English high court judge is superscribed *The Hon. Mr. Justice —*. In America, in speaking to a judge outside his court, it is customary to say simply *Judge —*, or, if he is a member of the Supreme Court of the United States (or of one or two other courts) *Mr. Justice* without the surname, or *Mr. Chief Justice*. A justice of the peace in England is *His Worship*, and so is a Mayor, and the latter is *the Right Worshipful* on an envelope. In the United States a Mayor is sometimes called *His Honor*, but the form seems to have no warrant in law. The Governors of Massachusetts and New Hampshire are *Your Excellency* by statute. In England an Ambassador is *His Excellency*, and so are colonial Governors. But the intricacies of British titles are so vast that I can't go into them here.

I have spoken of the American custom of dropping the definite article before *Hon.* It extends to *Rev.* and the like, and has the authority of very respectable usage behind it. The opening sentence of the *Congressional Record* is always: " The Chaplain, *Rev. —*, D.D., offered the following prayer." When chaplains for the Army or Navy are confirmed by the Senate they always appear in the *Record* as *Revs.*, never as *the Revs.* I also find the honorific without the article in the New International Encyclopædia, in a widely-popular American grammar-book, and in the catalogue of Groton, the fashionable prep-school, whose headmaster must always be

1 I encountered this gem in *Public Health Reports*, a government publication, for April 26, 1918, p. 619.

a clergyman of the Protestant Episcopal Church.[1] So long ago as 1867, Edward S. Gould protested against this elision as barbarous and idiotic, and drew up the following *reductio ad absurdum:*

> At the last annual meeting of Black Book Society, honorable John Smith took the chair, assisted by reverend John Brown and venerable John White. The office of secretary would have been filled by late John Green, but for his decease, which rendered him ineligible. His place was supplied by inevitable John Black. In the course of the evening eulogiums were pronounced on distinguished John Gray and notorious Joseph Brown. Marked compliment was also paid to able historian Joseph White, discriminating philosopher Joseph Green, and learned professor Joseph Black. But conspicuous speech of the evening was witty Joseph Bray's apostrophe to eminent astronomer Jacob Brown, subtle logician Jacob White, etc., etc.[2]

This *reductio ad absurdum* (which sounds curiously like an extract from the *Time* of today) was ratified by Richard Grant White in "Words and Their Uses" (1870), and William Cullen Bryant included the omission of the article in his *Index Expurgatorius*, but their anathemas were as ineffective as Gould's irony. The Episcopalians in the United States, at least those of the High Church variety, usually insert the *the*, but the rest of the Protestants omit it, and so do the Catholics; as for the Jews, they get rid of it by calling their rabbis *Dr.* Now and then some evangelical purist tries to induce the Methodists and Baptists to adopt the *the*, but always in vain. Throughout rural America it is common to address an ecclesiastic *viva voce* as *Reverend.* This custom is also denounced by the more delicate clergy, but equally without effect upon the prevailing speech habit. Some years ago one of the suffering brethren was thus moved to protest in verse:

> Call me *Brother*, if you will;
> Call me *Parson* — better still.
> Or if, perchance, the Catholic frill
> Doth your heart with longing fill —
> Though plain *Mister* fills the bill,
> Then even *Father* brings no chill
> Of hurt or rancor or ill-will.

> To no D.D. do I pretend,
> Though *Doctor* doth some honor lend,
> *Preacher, Pastor, Rector, Friend,*
> Titles almost without end

---

1 For the *Record* see any issue. For the New International Encyclopædia see the article on Brotherhood of Andrew and Philip. The grammar-book is Longman's Briefer Grammar; New York, 1908, p. 160.
2 *Good English;* New York, 1867, p. 57.

Never grate and ne'er offend;
A loving ear to all I bend.
But how the man my heart doth rend,
Who blithely calls me *Reverend!* [1]

To which may be added a denunciation of *Reverend* in direct address which shows, incidentally, that the author, a Methodist bishop, does not object to the omission of the *the* in writing:

She was well dressed. Her manner was womanly. Her voice was gentle. She seemed intelligent and cultured. She approached me and said, " Is this Rev. Moore? " I was amazed at such a transgression against good usage. Anyone should know better than to say *Rev.* Moore or *Rev.* Smith. That word *Rev.* cannot be attached in speech or writing to a surname; it can be used only with the given name, or the initials, or with some title such as *Mister, Doctor, Professor* or *Bishop*. One may say *Rev. Mr.* Smith, or *Rev. Dr.* Smith, or *Rev. Prof.* Smith, or *Rev. G. W.* Smith, but never *Rev.* Smith. It is discreditable to transgress such usage.[2]

When it came into use in England, in the Seventeenth Century,[3] *Rev.* was commonly written without the article, and immediately preceding the surname. Thus, Bishop Joseph Hall (1574–1656) did not hesitate to write *Reverend Calvin*. But at the beginning of the Eighteenth Century *the* and the given-name began to be added, and by the end of the century that form was almost universal in England.

---

1 *Alabama Christian Advocate* (Birmingham), Nov. 7, 1929. The poem was clipped from the Richmond *Christian Advocate*, which had clipped it in turn from " an Atlanta church paper." Its author was said to be " an Episcopal rector."

2 Do You Speak English?, by Bishop John M. Moore, *Christian Index* (Jackson, Tenn.), Aug. 9, 1928. Dr. Moore is a Ph.D. of Yale, and also pursued ghostly studies at Leipzig and Heidelberg.

3 Dr. S. E. Morison tells me that the Mathers were probably the first American divines to call themselves *Rev.* Increase Mather seems to have picked up the title during his visit to England, 1688–92. Before that time American clergymen were simply *Mr.*, an abbreviation of *Master*. This was an indication that they were masters of arts. During the Middle Ages bachelors of arts were addressed as *Dominus*, which was Englished as *Sir*. That is why clergymen, in Shakespeare's time, were often called *Sir* — always with their surnames, not with their given names, which last form distinguished knights. The usage crossed the Atlantic, and persisted at Harvard and Yale down to 1800 or thereabout. It explains the belief of many Americans of today that their colonial ancestors were knights. There were relatively few *D.D.'s* in America before 1800, for the degree was seldom given by the American universities. But any clergyman who had published an edifying work could obtain it from one of the Scottish universities on payment of a fee, and in the middle of the Eighteenth Century it was not unusual for an admiring congregation to pass the hat to help its shepherd obtain the degree.

Here, as in many other cases, American usage is archaic.[1] It should be added that English practice, in late years, has been somewhat corrupted, maybe by American example. In the list of members printed in the first tract of the Society for Pure English (1919) *Rev.*, *Very Rev.*, *Hon.* and *Rt. Hon.* appeared without the *the*, and it is commonly omitted by the English Methodists and Baptists. In the United States there has arisen recently a habit of omitting it before the names of corporations. It is, in many cases, not a legal part thereof, and is thus properly omitted in bonds, stock certificates and other such documents, but its omission in other situations makes for a barbaric clumsiness. Among news-agents and advertising agents the article is likewise omitted before the names of magazines, and on Broadway it is omitted before the words *show business.*[2]

The use of the plural, *Revs.*, denounced by H. W. Fowler in his Dictionary of Modern English Usage (1926) is quite common in this country. A somewhat curious English custom, unknown here, is that of using *Messrs.* before single names designating firms. Thus, the *Literary Supplement* of the London *Times* often announces that *Messrs. Jonathan Cape* are about to publish this or that book.

In general, ecclesiastical titles are dealt with somewhat loosely in the United States. In England an archbishop of the Established Church is *the Most Rev.* and *His Grace*, and a bishop is *the Right Rev.* and *His Lordship*, but there are no archbishops in the American Protestant Episcopal Church and the bishops are seldom called *His Lordship*. The Methodists, in writing of their ordinaries, often omit *the Right*, contenting themselves with the simple *Rev.* Among the Catholics, by a decree of the Sacred Congregation of Rites, dated December 31, 1930,[3] an archbishop who is not a cardinal is now *the Most Rev.* and *His Excellency* (*Excellentia Reverendissima*), and so is a bishop. Formerly an archbishop was *the Most Rev.* and *His Grace*, and a bishop was *the Right Rev.* and *His Lordship*. A cardinal, of course, remains *His Eminence.* Before the decree it was the custom to address all monsignori as *the Right Rev.*, but now they are divided into two sections, those who are protonotaries apostolic

1 See The Use of the Abbreviation *Rev.* in Modern English, by Edward C. Ehrensperger, *American Speech*, Oct., 1931.
2 This last seems to have been introduced by *Variety*, which has a magnificent disdain for all the ordinary usages of the language. In 1926 Thyra Samter Winslow printed a volume of short stories called *Show Business*, without the article.
3 The text is in the *Acta Apostolicæ Sedis*, Jan. 15, 1931.

or domestic prelates remaining *the Right Rev.*[1] and those of inferior rank, *e.g.*, papal chamberlains, becoming *the Very Rev.* The American bishops and archbishops display a dubious Latinity by their assumption of *the Most Rev. Reverendissimus*, to be sure, is a superlative, but in the situation in which it is used Latin superlatives are understood only in the sense of *very*, *e.g.*, *altissimus mons* means a very high mountain, not the highest mountain. Moreover, if the bishops and archbishops are entitled to be called *the Most Rev.*, then so are the monsignori, for Rome applies *reverendissimus* to all of them alike. But the puissant brethren of the American hierarchy arrogate *the Most Rev.* to themselves, and the monsignori must be content with the lesser designations.[2]

In the Salvation Army honorifics follow a somewhat strange pattern. The ordinary member of the Army is called a *soldier*, and his status in his *post* is identical with that of a communicant in a church. He is forbidden to belong to any other church. He supports himself at whatever trade he knows, and pays a tenth of his income into the post funds. If he aspires to become an officer he is called a *candidate* and is sent to a training college, where he becomes a *cadet*. On his graduation he is made, if unmarried, a *probationary lieutenant*, or, if married, a *probationary captain*. He must serve a year in the field before he may hope for promotion to full rank. Above the captaincy the ranks are those of *adjutant, major, brigadier* (not *brigadier-general*), *lieutenant-colonel, colonel, lieutenant-commissioner, commissioner* and *general*. All ranks are open to women. A married woman always takes her husband's rank, and is known as *Mrs. Major, Mrs. Colonel,* and so on. If he dies, her own future promotions begin where his left off. No unmarried officer, whether male or female, may marry anyone save another officer without resigning from the corps of officers. Virtually every officer, after ten years' service, is promoted to *adjutant*. But this promotion, and others following it, may come sooner, and an exceptionally useful officer may be put in command of colleagues of higher rank.[3]

The use of *Madame* as a special title of honor for old women of

---

1 Abbots are also *Right Rev.* but in the United States they are not monsignors.
2 See *Right Reverend*, by Prelatus Domesticus, *Commonweal*, Oct. 18, 1935.

3 I am indebted here to Major Vincent Cunningham, editor of the *War Cry* (Southern edition).

good position survived in the United States until the 70's. It distinguished the dowager Mrs. Smith from the wife of her eldest son. After the Civil War *madame* became the designation of brothel-keepers, and so fell into bad repute. But it survives more or less among the colored folk, who often apply it to women singers of their race, and sometimes to the more pretentious sort of hairdressers, dressmakers and milliners. Mrs. Washington was commonly called *Lady* Washington during her life-time, but the title seems to have died with her. When women began to go into politics, after the proclamation of the Twenty-first Amendment in 1920, the widows of male politicians frequently became candidates for their dead husband's jobs. One of the first of these ambitious relicts, the Hon. Nellie Taylor Ross of Wyoming, made her campaign under the style of *Ma*, and the title was soon extended to others of her kind.[1] Mabel Walker Willebrandt, Assistant Attorney-General in charge of prosecutions under the Volstead Act, was generally know as *Ma* during her days in office, 1921–29. But the title now seems to be in decay.

6. EUPHEMISMS

The American, probably more than any other man, is prone to be apologetic about the trade he follows. He seldom believes that it is quite worthy of his virtues and talents; almost always he thinks that he would have adorned something far gaudier. Unfortunately, it is not always possible for him to escape, or even for him to dream plausibly of escaping, so he soothes himself by assuring himself that he belongs to a superior section of his craft, and very often he invents a sonorous name to set himself off from the herd. Here we glimpse the origin of a multitude of characteristic American euphemisms, *e.g.*, *mortician* for *undertaker*, *realtor* for *real-estate agent*, *electragist* for *electrical contractor*, *aisle manager* for *floor-walker*, *beautician* for *hairdresser*, *exterminating engineer* for *rat-catcher*, and so on. *Realtor* was devised by a high-toned

[1] La Ross's husband, the Hon. William B. Ross, died in office as Governor of Wyoming on Oct. 2, 1924, and she was elected his successor and went into office on Jan. 5, 1925. A few days before this another *Ma*, Ferguson by name, became Governor of Texas. Her husband, James E. Ferguson, had been impeached and removed from the governorship in 1917.

real-estate agent of Minneapolis, Charles N. Chadbourn by name. He thus describes its genesis:

It was in November, 1915, on my way to a meeting of the Minneapolis Real Estate Board, that I was annoyed by the strident peddling of a scandal sheet: "All About the Robbery of a Poor Widow by a Real Estate Man." The "real estate man" thus exposed turned out to be an obscure hombre with desk-room in a back office in a rookery, but the incident set me to thinking. "Every member of our board," I thought, "is besmirched by this scandal article. Anyone, however unworthy or disreputable, may call himself a real estate man. Why do not the members of our board deserve a distinctive title? Each member is vouched for by the board, subscribes to its Code of Ethics, and must behave himself or get out." So the idea incubated for three or four weeks, and was then sprung on the local brethren.[1]

As to the etymology of the term, Mr. Chadbourn says:

Real estate originally meant a royal grant. It is so connected with land in the public mind that *realtor* is easily understood, even at a first hearing. The suffix *-or* means a doer, one who performs an act, as in *grantor, executor, sponsor, administrator.*

The Minneapolis brethren were so pleased with their new name that Mr. Chadbourn was moved to dedicate it to the whole profession. In March, 1916, he went to the convention of the National Association of Real Estate Boards at New Orleans, and made a formal offer of it. It was accepted gratefully, and is now defined by the association as follows:

A person engaged in the real estate business who is an active member of a member board of the National Association of Real Estate Boards, and as such, an affiliated member of the National Association, who is subject to its rules and regulations, who observes its standards of conduct, and is entitled to its benefits.[2]

In 1920 the Minneapolis Real Estate Board and the National Association of Real Estate Boards applied to Judge Joseph W. Molyneaux of Minneapolis for an injunction restraining the Northwestern Telephone Exchange Company from using *realtor* to designate some of its hirelings, and on September 10 the learned judge duly granted this relief. Since then the National Association has obtained similar injunctions in Virginia, Utah and other States. Its general counsel is heard from every time *realtor* is taken in vain, and when, in 1922, Sinclair Lewis applied it to George F. Babbitt, there was an uproar. But when Mr. Chadbourn was appealed to he decided that Babbitt

[1] Private communication, Sept. 28, 1935.
[2] Realtor: Its Meaning and Use; Chicago (National Association of Real Estate Boards), 1925.

was "fairly well described," for he was "a prominent member of the local board and of the State association," and one could scarcely look for anything better in "a book written in the ironic vein of the author of ' Main Street.' " [1] Mr. Chadbourn believes that *realtor* should be capitalized, " like *Methodist* or *American*," [2] but so far it has not been generally done. In June, 1925, at a meeting of the National Association of Real Estate Boards in Detroit, the past presidents of the body presented him with a gold watch as a token of their gratitude for his contribution to the uplift of their profession. On May 30, 1934, the following letter from Nathan William MacChesney, general counsel of the National Association, appeared in the *New Republic*:

> [*Realtor*] is not a word, but a trade right, coined and protected by law by the National Association of Real Estate Boards, and the term is a part of the trade-mark as registered in some forty-four States and Canada. Something over $200,000 has been spent in its protection by the National Association of Real Estate Boards in attempting to confine its use to those real estate men who are members of the National Association of Real Estate Boards, subject to its code for ethics and to its discipline for violation. It has been a factor in making the standards of the business generally during the past twenty years, and the exclusive right of the National Association of Real Estate Boards has been sustained in a series of court decisions, a large number of injunctions having been issued, restraining its improper use.

In 1924 the *Realtors' Bulletin* of Baltimore reported that certain enemies of realtric science were trying to show that *realtor* was derived from the English word *real* and the Spanish word *tor*, a bull, and to argue that it thus meant *real bull*. But this obscenity apparently did not go far; probably a hint from the alert general counsel was enough to stop it. During the same year I was informed by Herbert U. Nelson, executive secretary of the National Association, that " the real-estate men of London, through the Institute of Estate Agents and Auctioneers, after studying our experience in this respect, are planning to coin the word *estator* and to protect it by legal steps." This plan, I believe, came to fruition, but *estator* never caught on, and I can't find it in the Supplement to the Oxford Dictionary. *Realtor*, however, is there — and the first illustrative quotation is from " Babbitt "! In March, 1927, J. Foster Hagan, of

---

1 Letter to W. A. Frisbie, editor of the Minneapolis *Daily News*. This was in 1922. The letter was subscribed " Yours *realtorially*." A

copy was sent to Mr. Lewis, who preserves it in his archives.
2 Private communication, Sept. 4, 1935.

Ballston, Va., reported to *American Speech* that he had encountered *realtress* on the window of a real-estate office there, but this charming derivative seems to have died a-bornin'. In 1925 or thereabout certain ambitious insurance solicitors, inflamed by *realtor*, began to call themselves *insurors*, but it, too, failed to make any progress.

Electragist, like *realtor*, seems to be the monopoly of the lofty technicians who affect it: "it is copyrighted by the Association of Electragists International, whose members alone may use it."[1] But *mortician* is in the public domain. It was proposed by a writer in the *Embalmers' Monthly* for February, 1895, but the undertakers, who were then *funeral-directors*, did not rise to it until twelve years later. On September 16, 1916, some of the more eminent of them met at Columbus, O., to form a national association, on the lines of the American College of Surgeons, the American Association of University Professors, and the Society of the Cincinnati, and a year later they decided upon National Selected *Morticians* as its designation.[2] To this day the association remains so exclusive that, of the 24,000 undertakers in the United States, only 200 belong to it. But any one of the remaining 23,800 is free to call himself a *mortician*, and to use all the other lovely words that the advance of human taxidermy has brought in. *Mortician*, of course, was suggested by *physician*, for undertakers naturally admire and like to pal with the resurrection men, and there was a time when some of them called themselves *embalming surgeons*. A *mortician* never handles a *corpse*; he *prepares* a *body* or *patient*. This business is carried on in a *preparation-room* or *operating-room*, and when it is achieved the patient is put into a *casket*[3] and stored in the *reposing-room* or *slumber-room* of a *funeral-home*. On the day of the funeral he is moved to the *chapel* therein for the last exorcism, and then hauled to the cemetery in a *funeral-car* or *casket-coach*.[4] The old-time shroud is now a *né-*

1 Electragist, by Corneil Ridderhof, *American Speech*, Aug., 1927, p. 477. It means, according to Mr. Ridderhof, "a combined electrical dealer and contractor."

2 I am indebted here to Mr. W. M. Krieger, executive secretary of the organization, the headquarters of which are in Chicago.

3 *Casket* seems to have come in during the Civil War period. In 1863 Nathaniel Hawthorne denounced it in *Our Old Home* as "a vile modern phrase, which compels a person . . . to shrink . . . from the idea of being buried at all." At the start it had a rival in *case*. The latter was used in the Richmond *Examiner's* report of the funeral of Gen. J. E. B. Stuart, May 13, 1864. But the *Examiner*, in the same report, used *corpse* and *hearse*.

4 Mortuary Nomenclature, *Hygeia*, Nov., 1925, p. 651.

gligé or *slumber-shirt* or *slumber-robe*, the mortician's work-truck
is an *ambulance*, and the cemetery is fast becoming a *memorial-
park*. In the West cemeteries are being supplanted by public mauso-
leums, which sometimes go under the names of *cloisters, burial-
abbeys*, etc.[1] To be laid away in one runs into money. The vehicle
that morticians use for their expectant hauling of the ill is no longer
an *ambulance*, but an *invalid-coach*. *Mortician* has been a favorite
butt of the national wits, but they seem to have made no impression
on it. In January, 1932, it was barred from the columns of the
Chicago *Tribune*. " This decree goes forth," announced the *Tribune*,
" not for lack of sympathy with the ambition of undertakers to be
well regarded, but because of it. If they haven't the sense to save
themselves from their own lexicographers, we shall not be guilty
of abetting them in their folly." [2] But *mortician* not only continues
to flourish; it also begets progeny, *e.g., beautician, cosmetician,
radiotrician* and *bootician*.[3] The barbers, so far, have not devised
a name for themselves in *-ician*, but they may be trusted to do so
anon. In my youth they were *tonsorial artists*, but in recent years
some of them have been calling themselves *chirotonsors*.[4] Practically
all American press-agents are now *public relations counsel, contact-
managers* or *publicists*, all tree-trimmers are *tree-surgeons*, all milk-
wagon and bakery-wagon drivers have become *salesmen*, nearly all
janitors are *superintendents*, many gardeners have become *landscape-
architects* (in England even the whales of the profession are simple
landscape-gardeners), cobblers are beginning to call themselves *shoe-
rebuilders*,[5] and the corn-doctors, after a generation as *chiropodists*,
have burst forth as *podiatrists*. The American fondness for such
sonorous appellations arrested the interest of W. L. George, the English novelist, when he visited the United States in 1920. He said:

1 The *Mortician*, by Elmer Davis,
American Mercury, May, 1927.
2 Editor and Publisher, Jan. 30, 1932.
3 I proposed the use of *bootician* to
designate a high-toned big-city
bootlegger in the *American Mercury*, April, 1925, p. 450. The term
met a crying need, and had considerable success. In March, 1927,
the San José *Mercury-Herald* said:
" Our bootleggers are now calling
themselves *booticians*. It seems that
bootlegger has some trace of odium
about it, while *bootician* has none."

(Reprinted in the Baltimore *Evening Sun*, April 4, 1927.) On July
23, 1931, according to the Associated Press, a man arrested in Chicago, on being asked his profession,
answered proudly that he was a
bootician.
4 In 1924 representatives of 3000 of
them met in Chicago, and voted for
chirotonsor. See the *Commonweal*,
Nov. 26, 1924, p. 58.
5 There is a *Shoe Rebuilders'* Association in Baltimore. See the Baltimore *Evening Sun*, Oct. 17, 1935.

Business titles are given in America more readily than in England. I know one *president* whose staff consists of two typists. Many firms have four *vice-presidents.* In the magazines you seldom find merely an *editor;* the others need their share of honor, so they are *associate* (not *assistant*) *editors.* A dentist is called a *doctor.* I wandered into a university, knowing nobody, and casually asked for the *dean.* I was asked, "Which *dean?*" In that building there were enough deans to stock all the English cathedrals. The master of a secret society is *royal supreme knight commander.* Perhaps I reached the extreme at a theatre in Boston, when I wanted something, I forgot what, and was told that I must apply to the *chief of the ushers.* He was a mild little man, who had something to do with people getting into their seats, rather a come-down from the pomp and circumstance of his title. Growing interested, I examined my programme, with the following result: It is not a large theatre, but it has a *press-representative,* a *treasurer* (box-office clerk), an *assistant treasurer* (box-office junior clerk), an *advertising-agent,* our old friend the *chief of the ushers,* a *stage-manager,* a *head-electrician,* a *master of properties* (in England called *props*), a *leader of the orchestra* (pity this — why not *president?*), and a *matron* (occupation unknown).[1]

George might have unearthed some even stranger magnificoes in other playhouses. I once knew an ancient bill-sticker, attached to a Baltimore theatre, who boasted the sonorous title of *chief lithographer.* Today, in all probability, he would be called a *lithographic-engineer.* For a number of years the *Engineering News-Record,* the organ of the legitimate engineers, used to devote a column every week to just such uninvited invaders of the craft, and some of the species it unearthed were so fantastic that it was constrained to reproduce their business cards photographically in order to convince its readers that it was not spoofing. One of its favorite exhibits was a bedding manufacturer who first became a *mattress-engineer* and then promoted himself to the lofty dignity of *sleep-engineer.* No doubt he would have called himself a *morphician* if he had thought of it. Another exhilarating specimen was a tractor-driver who advertised for a job as a *caterpillar-engineer.* A third was a beautician who burst out as an *appearance-engineer.* In an Atlanta department-store the *News-Record* found an *engineer of good taste* — a young woman employed to advise newly-married couples patronizing the furniture department, and elsewhere it unearthed *display-engineers* who had been lowly window-dressers until some visionary among them made the great leap, *demolition-engineers* who were once content to be house-wreckers, and *sanitary-engineers* who had an earlier incarnation as garbage-men. The *wedding-engineer* is a technician employed

1 Hail, Columbia!; New York, 1921, pp. 92–3.

by florists to dress churches for hymeneal orgies. The *commence-*
ment-e. arranges college and high-school commencements; he has
lists of clergymen who may be trusted to pray briefly, and some sort
of fire-alarm connection, I suppose, with the office of Dr. John H.
Finley, the champion commencement orator of this or any other
age. The *packing-e.* is a scientist who crates clocks, radios and china-
ware for shipment. The *correspondence-e.* writes selling-letters
guaranteed to pull. The *income-e.* is an insurance solicitor in a new
false-face. The *dwelling-e.* replaces lost keys, repairs leaky roofs, and
plugs up rat-holes in the cellar. The *vision-e.* supplies spectacles at
cut rates. The *dehorning-e.* attends to bulls who grow too frisky.
The *Engineering News-Record* also discovered a *printing-e.*, a *fur-*
niture-e., a *photographic-e.*, a *financial-e.* (a stock-market tipster),
a *paint-e.*, a *clothing-e.*, a *wrapping-e.* (a dealer in wrapping-paper),
a *matrimonial-e.* (a psychoanalyst specializing in advice to the love-
lorn), a *box-e.* (the *packing-e.* under another name), an *automotive-*
painting-e., a *blasting-e.*, a *dry-cleaning-e.*, a *container-e.*, a *furnish-*
ing-e., a *socio-religious-e.* (an uplifter), a *social-e.* (the same), a
feed-plant-e., a *milk-e.*, a *surface-protection-e.*, an *analyzation-e.*,
a *fiction-e.*, a *psychological-e.* (another kind of psychoanalyst), a
casement-window-e., a *shingle-e.*, a *fumigating-e.*, a *laminated-*
wood-e., a *package-e.* (the *packing-e.* again), a *horse-e.*, a *pediatric-e.*
(a corn-doctor), an *ice-e.*, a *recreation-e.*, a *tire-e.*, a *paint-mainte-*
nance-e., a *space-saving-e.*, a *film-e.* (or *filmgineer*), a *criminal-e.* (a
criminologist), a *diet-kitchen-e.*, a *patent-e.*, an *equipment-e.*, a *floor-*
covering-e., a *society-e.*, a *window-cleaning-e.*, a *dust-e.*, a *hospital-*
ization-e., a *baking-e.*, a *directory-e.*, an *advertising-e.*, a *golf-e.* (a
designer of golf-courses), a *human-e.* (another variety of psychoanalyst), an *amusement-e.*, an *electric-sign-e.*, a *household-e.*, a
pageant-e., an *idea-e.*, a *ballistics-e.*, a *lace-e.* and a *sign-e.*[1] Perhaps
the prize should go to the *dansant-e.* (an agent supplying dancers
and musicians to night-clubs), or to the *hot-dog-e.*[2] The *exterminat-*

[1] Many other varieties of engineers
have been unearthed by other fan-
ciers. On Oct. 19, 1935 the *New
Yorker* announced the discovery
of a *persuasion-e.* — "a man sent
somewhere by his company to try
and sell somebody an idea that
would be of advantage to the company." A few months before this
the *Professional Engineer* found a

pajama-e. in the *New Yorker's* advertising columns. For this last I
am indebted to Mr. M. E. McIver,
secretary of the American Association of Engineers. In *Popular Science*, Aug., 1935 a contributor
called himself a *coffee-e.*
[2] A curious anticipation of the
American misuse of *engineer*, by
an Englishman, is to be found in a

ing-engineers have a solemn national association and wear a distinguishing pin; whether or not they have tried to restrain non-member rat-catchers from calling themselves *engineers* I do not know. In 1923 the *Engineering News-Record* printed a final blast against all the pseudo-engineers then extant, and urged its engineer readers to boycott them. But this boycott apparently came to nothing, and soon thereafter it abated its indignation and resorted to laughter.[1] Next to *engineer*, *expert* seems to be the favorite talisman of Americans eager to augment their estate and dignity in this world. Very often it is hitched to an explanatory prefix, *e.g.*, *housing-*, *planning-*, *hog-*, *erosion-*, *marketing-*, *boll-weevil-*, or *sheep-dip-*, but sometimes the simple adjective *trained-* suffices. When the Brain Trust came into power in Washington, the town began to swarm with such quacks, most of them recent graduates of the far-flung colleges of the land. One day a humorous member of Congress printed an immense list of them in the *Congressional Record*, with their salaries and academic dignities. He found at least one whose expertness was acquired in a seminary for chiropractors. During the John Purroy Mitchel " reform " administration in New York City (1914–18) so many bogus *experts* were put upon the pay-roll that special desig-

---

memorandum submitted to Henry Dundas, first Viscount Melville, by Charles Stuart at the end of 1793. Dundas was Home Secretary from 1791 to 1794, and as such was in charge of the government's relations with the press. " I firmly believe, without any vanity," wrote Stuart, " that I know as much in the engineering of the press as any *press engineer* in Britain." See The History of the *Times;* London, 1925, p. 66. But Stuart's attempt to make the manipulation of the press a branch of engineering was not imitated, and there is no mention of pseudo-engineers in any of the English dictionaries.

1 See the issue for Jan. 15, 1925. Also, Some " Engineers " I Have Known, by a Civil Engineer, *Engineering News-Record*, April 19, 1923, p. 701. The engineers themselves have grossly misused the term designating them. In The Structure of the Engineering Profession, by

Theodore J. Hoover, dean of the School of Engineering at Stanford University, *Journal of Engineering Education*, Jan., 1935, appears an exhaustive report upon what the 10,542 listed in " Who's Who in Engineering " call themselves. Mr. Hoover finds 2518 different titles, including such absurdities as *sales-e., sales-promotion-e., promotion-e., application-e., college-e., social-e., technical-publicity-e., bank-management-e.,* and *export-e.* He advocates a complete reform of professional nomenclature, but when I last heard from him he didn't seem to have much hope. On Feb. 21, 1935 the Associated Press reported that the National Society of Professional Engineers was trying to induce the American railroads to call their locomotive-engineers *enginemen.* The New York Central and the Pennsylvania, it was said, were already doing so.

nations for them ran out, and in prodding through the Mitchel records later on Bird S. Coler discovered that a number had been carried on the books as *general experts.*

Euphemisms for things are almost as common in the United States as euphemisms for avocations. Dozens of forlorn little fresh-water colleges are called *universities,* and almost all *pawn-shops* are *loan-offices.* When *movie-cathedral* came in a few scoffers snickered, but by the generality of fans it was received gravely. *City,* in England, used to be confined to the seats of bishops, and even today it is applied only to considerable places, but in the United States it is commonly assumed by any town with paved streets, and in the statistical publications of the Federal government it is applied to all places of 8000 or more population. The American use of *store* for *shop,* like that of *help* for *servant,* is probably the product of an early effort at magnification. Before Prohibition saloons used to be *sample-rooms, buffets, exchanges, cafés* and *restaurants;* now they are *taverns, cocktail-rooms, taprooms, American-bars, stubes* and what not. Not long ago the *Furnished-Room Guide* undertook to substitute *hotelette* for *rooming-house,*[1] and in 1928 President E. L. Robins of the National *Fertilizer* Association proposed that the name of that organization be changed to the National Association of *Plant Food* Manufacturers or the American *Plant Food* Association.[2] In Pasadena the public garbage-wagons bear the legend: *Table-Waste Disposal Department.* The word *studio* is heavily overworked; there are *billiard-studios, tonsorial-studios, candy-studios,* and even *shoe-studios.*[3] Nor is this reaching out for sweet and disarming words confined to the lowly. Some time ago, in the *Survey,* the trade journal of the American uplifters, Dr. Thomas Dawes Eliot, associate professor of sociology in Northwestern University, printed a solemn argument in favor of abandoning all such harsh terms as *reformatory, house of refuge, reform school* and *jail.* "Each time a new phrase is developed," he said, "it seems to bring with it, or at least to be accompanied by, some measure of permanent gain, in standards or in viewpoint, even though much of the old may continue to masquerade as the new. The series, *alms, philanthropy, relief, rehabilitation, case work, family welfare,* shows such a progression from cruder to

---

1 See the *New Yorker,* Jan. 9, 1935, p. 74. The *New Yorker* expressed a waggish preference for *furnished-roomateria.*

2 United Press report, Nov. 13, 1928.
3 See *Studio,* by John T. Krumpelmann, *American Speech,* Dec., 1926, p. 158.

more refined levels of charity." Among the substitutions proposed by the learned professor were *habit-disease* for *vice, psycho-neurosis* for *sin, failure to compensate* for *disease, treatment* for *punishment, delinquent* for *criminal, unmarried mother* for *illegitimate mother, out of wedlock* for *bastard, behavior problem* for *prostitute, colony* for *penitentiary, school* for *reformatory, psychopathic hospital* for *insane asylum,* and *house of detention* for *jail.*[1] Many of these terms (or others like them) have been actually adopted. Practically all American insane asylums are now simple *hospitals,* many reformatories and houses of correction have been converted into *homes* or *schools,* all *almshouses* are now *infirmaries, county-farms* or *county-homes,* and most of the more advanced American penologists now speak of criminals as *psychopathic personalities.* By a law of New York it is provided that " in any local law, ordinance or resolution, or in any public or judicial proceeding, or in any process, notice, order, decree, judgment, record or other public document or paper, the term *bastard* or *illegitimate child* shall not be used, but the term *child born out of wedlock* shall be used in substitution therefor, and with the same force and effect."[2] Meanwhile, such harsh terms as *second-hand* and *ready-made* disappear from the American vocabulary. For the former the automobile dealers, who are ardent euphemists, have substituted *reconditioned, rebuilt, repossessed* and *used,* and for the latter department-stores offer *ready-tailored, ready-to-wear* and *ready-to-put-on.* For *shop-worn* two of the current euphemisms are *store-used* and *slightly-second.*

The English euphemism-of-all-work used to be *lady.* Back in the Seventeenth Century the court-poet Edmund Waller thought it quite proper to speak of actresses, then a novelty on the English stage, as *lady-actors,* and even today the English newspapers frequently refer to *lady-secretaries, lady-doctors, lady-inspectors, lady-golfers* and *lady-champions. Women's wear,* in most English shops, is *ladies' wear.* But this excessive use of lady seems to be going out, and I note *women's singles* and *women's ice hockey* on the sports pages of the London *Daily Telegraph.*[3] The *Times* inclines the same way, but I observe that it still uses *Ladies' International* to designate a golf tournament, *ladies' round* and *ladies' championship* (golf and

1 A Limbo for Cruel Words, *Survey,* June 15, 1922.
2 Laws of 1925, Ch. 515, in force April 9, 1925. I have to thank Mr.

Sylvan Baruch of the New York Bar for calling my attention to this statute.
3 March 29, 1935.

fencing).¹ In the United States *lady* is definitely out of favor. The *salesladies* of yesteryear are now all *saleswomen* or *salesgirls*, and the female superintendent of a hospital is not the *lady-superintendent*, but simply the *superintendent*. When women were first elected to Congress, the question as to how they should be referred to in debate engaged the leaders of the House of Representatives. For a while the phrase used was "the *lady* from So-and-so," but soon "the *gentlewoman*" was substituted, and this is now employed almost invariably. Its invention is commonly ascribed to the late Nicholas Longworth; if he actually proposed it, it was probably jocosely, for *gentlewoman* is clumsy, and in some cases, as clearly inaccurate as *lady*. The English get round the difficulty by using *the hon. member* in speaking of women M.P.'s, though sometimes *the hon. lady* is used.² A member who happens to be a military or naval officer is always, by the way, *the hon. and gallant member*, and a legal officer, say the Attorney-General or Solicitor-General, or a lawyer member in active practise, is *the hon. and learned member*. The English use *gentleman* much more carefully than we do, and much more carefully than they themselves use *lady*. *Gentleman-author* or *gentleman-clerk* would make them howl, but they commonly employ *gentleman-rider* and *gentleman-player* in place of our *amateur*, though *amateur* seems to be gaining favor. Here the man referred to is always actually a gentleman by their standards.

The English have relatively few aliens in their midst, and in consequence they have developed nothing comparable to our huge repertory of opprobrious names for them. They have borrowed our *dago* for Italian, and they have been calling Frenchmen *frogs* or *froggies* since the Napoleonic wars ³ but they quickly dropped the

---

1 April 12, 1935, p. 6.
2 I am indebted for the following to Mr. James Bone, London editor of the Manchester *Guardian:* "When a Minister answers a question in the House he says *Yes, sir* or *No, sir*, whether the question is asked by a man or a woman M.P. The reason is that he is supposed to be addressing the Speaker. There was some laughter among young members when a Minister replied *Yes, sir* to a question by Lady Astor, but elderly members wrote to the papers at once, rebuking them and

explaining the procedure." Some time ago I heard the trial of a case in one of the London Law Courts, with the Lord Chief Justice of England, Lord Hewart, on the bench. There were two women on the jury, but when they finished their labors he said "Thank you, *gentlemen*."
3 *Frog* was picked up by the American troops during the World War, and is occasionally heard in the United States. Its origin is uncertain. Farmer and Henley say that it comes from the French, and

war-time *hun* and *boche* for German, they have devised nothing more unpleasant to designate a Scotsman than *Sandy*, and their worst name for the damned Yankee is simply *Yankee*. To match these feeble efforts the American language offers:

For Canadian: *canuck*.[1]
For Chinese: *chink* and *yellow-belly*.
For Czech: *bohoe, bohick, bohee, bohunk, bootchkey* and *cheskey*.[2]
For Englishman: *lime-juicer* or *limey*.[3]
For Filipino: *gu-gu*.
For German: *dutchie, squarehead, heinie, kraut, pretzel* and *limberger*.
For Greek: *grease-ball*.
For Hungarian: *bohunk, hunk* and *hunkie*.
For Irishman: *mick, harp* and *turk*.[4]
For Italian: *dago, wop, guinea* and *ginzo*.[5]
For Japanese: *skibby*.[6]
For Jew: *kike, sheenie, arab, goose* and *yid*.[7]

---

formerly meant a Parisian, "the shield of whose city bore three toads, while the quaggy state of the streets gave point to a jest common at Versailles before 1791: Qu'en disent les grenouilles? *i.e.*, What do the *Frogs* (the people of Paris) say? " But this seems fanciful. In most Englishmen's minds, I believe, the term is connected with the fact that the French eat frogs, which are regarded as inedible in England, or, at all events, are not commonly eaten. The Oxford Dictionary shows that it was applied to Jesuits in 1626 and to Dutchmen in 1652, and Farmer and Henley that it was applied to policemen during the 80's of the last century.
1 Thornton's earliest example is dated 1855.
2 In The Čechs (Bohemians) in America; Boston, 1912, Thomas Čapek says that *bohoe* is obsolete. He calls *bohunk* a portmanteau word that originated in a confusion between Bohemians and Hungarians. *Cheskey* is simply the Czech adjective *český*, mistaken for a noun. *Bootchkey* is the Czech *počkej* (wait, hold on), a cry used by Czech boys at play. See also Czech Influence Upon the American Vocabulary, by Monsignor J. B. Dudek, *Czecho-Slovak Stu-*

dent Life (Lisle, Ill.) June, 1927, p. 16.
3 A term borrowed from Navy slang. It refers to the fact that, beginning in 1795, lime-juice was issued in the British Navy (and later in the merchant marine) as an anti-scorbutic.
4 See Some Current Substitutes for Irish, by W. A. McLaughlin, *Dialect Notes*, Vol. IV, Pt. II, 1914. Mr. McLaughlin discusses *harp, mick, Paddy, Turk* and *Tad*. *Turk* is commonly used among the Roman Catholic clergy in the United States to designate a priest or bishop of Irish blood, and especially one born in Ireland. The Irish are thought to be too adept at ecclesiastical politics, and to get an undue proportion of ecclesiastical promotions.
5 Gilbert Tucker says that *dago* goes back to 1832. It is probably a corruption of *Diego;* it was first applied to Mexicans. The etymologies of *wop* and *guinea* are uncertain, and frequently disputed.
6 This is used only on the Pacific Coast. It originally meant a Japanese loose woman, but is now applied to all persons of the race.
7 *Kike* is used to distinguish a Russian, Polish or other Eastern Jew from the German Jews. The origin

For Latin-American: *spiggoty* and *spick*.[1]

For Mexican: *greaser*.[2]

For Negro: *nigger, coon, shine, jigabo, jigaboo, spade, Zulu, skunk, jig, jit, buffalo, boogie, dinge, smoke, moke* and *snowball*.[3]

For Pole: *polack*.

For Scandinavian: *scowegian, scowoogian, scoovy, sowegian, scandihoovian, scandinoovian, squarehead, snooser* and *herring choker*.[4]

---

of the word is uncertain. J. H. A. Lacher, in *Kike, American Speech*, March, 1926, says it was suggested by the fact that the names of many of the early Eastern Jewish immigrants ended in *-ki* or *-ky*. The German Jews called them *kikis* and this gradually changed to *kike*. Webster's New International Dictionary (1934) hints that the word may have some relation to *keek*, a term used in the clothing trade to designate one employed to spy out the designs of rival manufacturers. *Keek* is an ancient English verb, now confined to Northern dialects, signifying to peep. Its past tense form appears in Chaucer's Miller's Tale (*c.* 1386) as *kiked*.

1 *Spiggoty*, of which *spick* is a variant, originated at Panama and now means a native of any Latin-American region under American protection, and in general any Latin-American. It is Navy slang, but has come into extensive civilian use. It is a derisive daughter of "No *spik* Ingles." The Marines in Nicaragua called the natives *gooks*. Those of Costa Rica are sometimes called *goo-goos*.

2 Thornton quotes from Ruxton's Life in the Far West, 1849: "The Mexicans are called . . . *greasers* from their greasy appearance."

3 The Oxford Dictionary's first example of *nigger* is dated 1786, but the word must be older. The American Negroes have many words of their own to designate shades of color, *e.g., brown-skin, high-brown* and *high-yellow*. As I have noted in Chapter V, Section 4, they use *ofay* to designate whites. But this usage is confined to the sophisticates. In 1919, Dr. P. P. Claxton, United States Com-

missioner of Education, devised a Code of Honorable Names to be subscribed to by the Boy Scouts, whereby they agreed to avoid all opprobrious terms for immigrants. But he omitted the Negroes, and the fact brought forth a protest from them. See Offensive Nicknames, by James W. Johnson, New York *Age*, Feb. 1, 1919.

4 The effects of race antagonism upon language are still to be investigated. The etymology of *slave* indicates that the inquiry might yield interesting results. The word *French*, in English, is largely used to suggest sexual perversion. In German anything *Russian* is barbarous, and *English* education hints at flaggellation. The French, for many years, called a certain contraband appliance a *capote Anglaise*, but after the *entente cordiale* they changed the name to *capote Allemande*. The common English name to this day is *French letter*. See The Criminal, by Havelock Ellis; London, 1910, p. 208. In France a *sharper* is called a *Greek*, *as drunk as a Pole* is a common phrase, and one of the mainstays of low comedy is *le truc du brésilien*. In most of the non-Prussian parts of Germany *cockroaches* are called *Preussen;* in Prussia they are *Franzosen;* in some places they are *Schwaben*. Finally, it will be recalled that Benvenuto Cellini, in his autobiography, says that he was accused in a French court of using one of his mistresses in "the *Italian* manner." See International Libels, by William Power, Glasgow (Scotland) *Record*, April 10, 1929, and Calling Names in Any Language, by Joachim Joesten, *American Mercury*, Dec., 1935.

The paucity of aliens in England also makes it unnecessary for the English to pay as much heed as we do to the susceptibilities of organized (and sometimes extremely self-assertive) foreign groups. Thus they are free to laugh at stage Irishmen without bringing down the dudgeon of the Knights of Columbus, and they continue to use the word *Jew* freely, and even retain the verb *to jew* in their vocabulary. In the United States, according to Richard Grant White, certain Jews petitioned the publishers of Webster's and Worcester's Dictionaries, so long ago as the early 70's, to omit their definitions of *to jew*, and the publishers of Worcester's complied. " Webster's New International " (1934) still includes the verb, but with the saving observation that it is " used opprobriously in allusion to practices imputed to the Jews by those who dislike them." *To jew down* is listed, but it is dismissed as slang. In the Standard Dictionary both *to jew* and *to jew down* are called slang. But in the Oxford Dictionary *to jew* gets the more respectable rank of a colloquialism. White says that there were also protests from Jews in the early 70's, both in England and in the United States, against the use of *Jew* as an adjective in reference to criminals. Both the New York *Times* and the London *Pall Mall Gazette*, he says, apologized for using it, and promised to sin no more. To this he objected, saying,

> The Jews are a peculiar people, who, in virtue of that strongly-marked and exclusive nationality which they so religiously cherish, have outlived the Pharaohs who oppressed them. . . . When they are mentioned as Jews no allusion is meant to their faith, but to their race. A parallel case to those complained of would be the saying that a *Frenchman* or a *Spaniard* had committed a crime, at which no offense is ever taken. A Jew is a Jew, whether he holds to the faith of his fathers or leaves it.[1]

But in the United States certain Jews carry on a continuous campaign against the use of *Jew*, and most American newspapers, in order to get rid of their clamor, commonly use *Hebrew* instead. Thus, one often encounters such forms as *Hebrew comedian*, *Hebrew holidays* and even *Hebrew rabbi*.[2] Some years ago a number

1 Words and Their Uses, new ed.; New York, 1876, p. 131.
2 Mr. Maximilian Hurwitz tells me that this movement originated among the so-called Reform Jews, most of whom were from Germany or Austria. Its leader was the Rev. Isaac M. Wise. In 1854 he established the *American Israelite*, in 1873 he organized the Union of American *Hebrew* Congregations, and in 1875 he founded the *Hebrew* Union College. The *Jews'* Hospital of New York changed its name to *Mount Sinai*, and in 1874, when a merger of Jewish eleemosynary institutions was effected, it took the name of the United *Hebrew* Chari-

of American Jews, alarmed by such incongruities, issued a "Note on the Word *Jew*" for the guidance of editors. From it I take the following:

1. The words *Jew* and *Jewish* can never be objectionable when applied to the whole body of Israel, or to whole classes within the body, as, for instance, *Jewish young men.*

2. There can be no objection to the use of the words *Jew* and *Jewish* when contrast is being made with other religions: "*Jews* observe Passover and Christians Easter."

3. The application of the word *Jew* or *Jewish* to any individual is to be avoided unless from the context it is necessary to call attention to his religion; in other words, unless the facts have some relation to his being a Jew or to his Jewishness. . . . Thus, if a Jew is convicted of a crime he should not be called a *Jewish criminal;* and on the other hand, if a Jew makes a great scientific discovery he should not be called an eminent *Jewish scientist.*

4. The word *Jew* is a noun, and should never be used as an adjective or verb. To speak of *Jew girls* or *Jew stores* is both objectionable and vulgar. *Jewish* is the adjective. The use of *Jew* as a verb, in *to jew down,* is a slang survival of the medieval term of opprobrium, and should be avoided altogether.

5. The word *Hebrew* should not be used instead of *Jew.* As a noun it connotes rather the Jewish people of the distant past, as *the ancient Hebrews.* As an adjective it has an historical rather than a religious connotation; one cannot say *the Hebrew religion,* but *the Jewish religion.*

Dr. Solomon Solis Cohen of Philadelphia calls my attention to the fact that the American Jews themselves are not consistent in their use of *Jew* and *Hebrew.* They have Young Men's *Hebrew* Associations all over the country, but they also have a Council of *Jewish* Women and many *Jewish* Community Centers. They have both a *Hebrew* Union College and a *Jewish* Theological Seminary. Their principal weekly is called the *American Hebrew and Jewish Tribune.* The distinction between the religious significance of *Jew* and the national significance of *Hebrew* is by no means always clear. Abraham, says Dr. Solis Cohen, was a *Hebrew* (*'Ibri*), but in the course of time his descendants divided into two moieties, the *Israelites* and the *Judeans*, and it is from *Judeans* that we get our word *Jew*. " When the Northern Kingdom was destroyed by Shalmaneser the

---

ties. The Eastern Jews, who began to flock in in the early 80's, objected to the abandonment of *Jew* and *Jewish* and began to call the German Jews *Yuhudi* in derision. They were influential enough by 1916 to cause a new amalgamation of Jewish charities to be called the Federation for the Support of *Jewish* Philanthropic Societies of New York. The theatrical weekly, *Variety*, which is owned and mainly staffed by Jews, takes a poke at *Hebrew* by reducing it to *Hebe*.

name *Israel*, as a territorial designation, disappeared except from poetry and prayer, until it was recently revived by the Zionists, who speak of all Palestine as *Erez Israel*." ¹ Dr. Solis Cohen suggests that the superior respectability of *Hebrew* in the United States may have been helped by the fact that it was a term of honor among the early Puritan divines, who studied the *Hebrew* language, and venerated the *Hebrew* scriptures. The word *Jew* has been given a dubious significance by " The Merchant of Venice," by the verb *to jew*, and by various other unpleasant associations. Whatever the fact, the sort of Jew who devotes himself to visiting editors seems to prefer *Hebrew*. Even in the advertisements of *kosher* hotels in the Jewish papers the old term, *Jewish cooking*, has been abandoned. But I have never observed the use of *Hebrew cooking* in its place: the popular term seems to be the somewhat incredible *Hungarian cuisine*. Jewish cookery is actually mainly German, with certain Russian and Polish fancies added. In New York the adjective *Jewish* seems to be regarded as less offensive than the noun *Jew*. Thus *Jewish boy* is often used as a sort of euphemism for *Jew*. The Jews listed in " Who's Who in America " sometimes write *Jewish religion* in their autobiographical sketches instead of *Jew*, but most of them omit all direct reference to their faith. Among the Cohens in the volume for 1934–35 I find one who describes himself as a *Hebrew*, one (only partly Jewish) who says he is an Episcopalian, one who puts down *Jewish religion*, and eight who are silent.

The Jews are not the only indignant visitors to American editorial offices. In Chicago, in the heyday of Al Capone and his assassins, the local Italians made such vociferous objection to the use of *Italian* in identifying gunmen that the newspapers began to use *Sicilian* instead. Apparently, the complaints had come chiefly from Northern Italians, and most of the gunmen were actually Sicilians or Neapolitans. But there were also thousands of Sicilians and Neapolitans in the Chicago region who were not gunmen, and why they did not protest in their turn I do not know. The Negroes everywhere carry on a double campaign — first, against the use of *nigger*, and secondly, for the capitalization of *Negro*. On March 7, 1930, when the New York *Times* announced that it would capitalize *Negro* thereafter, there was jubilation in the Negro press. The Association for the

¹ Private communication, April 10, 1925.

Advancement of Colored People had been advocating the change for a long while, but it was a letter from Major R. R. Moton, president of Tuskegee Institute, that moved the *Times*. It reported on March 9 that *Negro* was being used by most of the principal American magazines, and by a number of leading newspapers, including the Montgomery (Ala.) *Advertiser*, the Durham (N. C.) *Sun*, the Columbus (Ga.) *Ledger*, and the Raleigh (N. C.) *News* in the South. The rejoicing among the dark brethren was not shared by George S. Schuyler, the Negro iconoclast, who argued in the Pittsburgh *Courier*[1] that *Negro* meant a black man, and that but 20% of the Aframericans were actually black. " The truth is," he said, " that the American Negro is an amalgam of Caucasian, Amerindian and African. . . . Geographically, we are neither Ethiopians nor Africans, but Americans. Culturally, we are Anglo-Saxons." But the prevailing view in Aframerica was set forth three years later by the Negro poet and publicist, James Weldon Johnson, as follows:

Many white people, when they wish to be especially considerate, are in doubt about the term most acceptable to Negroes. There are indeed puzzlingly subtle distinctions, to which colored people are more or less sensitive. The adjective *colored* and the generic designations *Negroes, the Negro*, and *the Negro race* are always in order, but *a Negro man, a Negro woman*, etc. are somewhat distasteful. *Negress is considered unpardonable.*[2]

7. FORBIDDEN WORDS

The American people, once the most prudish on earth, took to a certain defiant looseness of speech during the World War, and when Prohibition produced its antinomian reaction they went even further. Today words and phrases are encountered everywhere — on the screen, in the theatres, in the comic papers, in the newspapers, on the floor of Congress, and even at the domestic hearth — that were reserved for use in saloons and bagnios a generation ago. A good example is *nerts*, in its sense of denial or disparagement. When it came in, in 1925, its etymology must have been apparent to everyone old enough to vote, yet it seems to have met with no opposition from guardians of the national morals, and in a little while it rivalled

1 March 15, 1930.
2 Along This Way; New York, 1933,
   p. 375.

American and English

wham and *wow* for popularity in the comic strips. My researches indicate that it was coined in Hollywood, that great fountain of American neologisms. There arose there, in the early 20's, a fashion for using openly the ancient four-letter words that had maintained an underground life since the Restoration. It was piquant, for a while, to hear them from the lovely lips of movie beauties, but presently the grand dames of Hollywood society prohibited them as a shade too raw, and they were succeeded by euphemistic forms, made by changing the vowel of each to *e* and inserting *r* after it. *Nuts* was not one of these venerable words, but it had connotations that made it seem somewhat raw too, so it was changed to *nerts*, and in that form swept the country. At the same time the college boys and girls launched *bushwah, hospice, horse's caboose* and a number of other such thinly disguised shockers, and there appeared a considerable amelioration of the old American antipathy to *bull, bitch, cock, stallion*, and so on. Even *pregnant* returned to good society.

Victoria was not crowned in England until 1838, but a Victorian movement against naughty words had been in full blast in this country since the beginning of the century. In 1830 or thereabout, as Mrs. Frances Trollope tells us, "a young German gentleman of perfectly good manners . . . offended one of the principal families . . . by having pronounced the word *corset* before the ladies of it." [1] James Flint, in his "Letters from America," [2] reported that *rooster* had been substituted for *cock* (the latter having acquired an indelicate anatomical significance) by 1821; indeed there is a quotation in Thornton's "American Glossary" which indicates that it may have come in by 1809. At the same time *haystack* began to supplant *haycock*, and *roach* to supplant *cockroach*, and a bit later a young man in Judge T. C. Haliburton's "Sam Slick" was telling a maiden that her brother had become a *rooster-swain* in the Navy. Bartlett, in his Glossary, says that this excessive delicacy was not most marked among the survivors of the New England Puritans, but in the West. He goes on (*c.* 1847):

> The essentially English word *bull* is refined beyond the mountains, and perhaps elsewhere, into *cow-creature, male-cow*, and even *gentleman-cow*. A friend who resided many years in the West has told me of an incident where a gray-headed man of sixty doffed his hat reverently and apologized to a clergy-

1 Domestic Manners of the Americans; London, 1832, Vol. I, p. 132.   2 Edinburgh, 1822.

man for having used inadvertently in his hearing the plain Saxon term. *Male-sheep, male-hog,* etc. are of a piece with the preceding, to which we may add *rooster, he-biddy, game-chicken,* etc.[1]

When Captain Frederick Marryat, the author of " Mr. Midshipman Easy," came to the United States in 1837, he got into trouble like Mrs. Trollope's German. Gazing upon the wonders of Niagara Falls with a young woman acquaintance, he was distressed to see her slip and bark her shin. As she limped home he asked, " Did you hurt your *leg* much? " She turned from him " evidently much shocked or much offended," but presently recovered her composure and told him gently that a *leg* was never mentioned before ladies: the proper word was *limb.*[2] Even chickens ceased to have *legs,* and another British traveler, W. F. Goodmane, was " not a little confused on being requested by a lady, at a public dinner-table, to furnish her with the *first and second joint.*"[3] In the same way *pantaloons* became *nether-garments* or *inexpressibles, stockings* yielded to *hose, antmire* was substituted for *pismire, breast* became *bosom, lady* took the place of the too frankly sexual *wife, bull* became not only *cow-creature* (more commonly, *cow-critter*) but also *seed-ox* and *Jonathan, shirt* was forbidden, *to go to bed* became *to retire,* servant girls ceased to be *seduced* and began to be *betrayed,* and *stomach,* then under the ban in England, was transformed, by some unfathomable magic, into a euphemism for the whole region from the nipples to the pelvic arch. The 30's and 40's saw the Golden Age of euphemism. *Bitch, ram, boar, stallion, buck* and *sow* virtually disappeared from the written language, and even *mare* was looked upon as rather racy. The biblical *ass,* because the prevailing American pronunciation made it identical with *arse,* was displaced by *jackass, jack* or *donkey,* and *to castrate* became *to change, to arrange* or *to alter,* even on the farm. *Chair* was abandoned for *seat,* which presently began to be used for *backside* too, and so became obscene itself. To use the word *shirt* in the presence of a woman was " an open insult."[4] The very

1 A Glossary of Words and Phrases Usually Regarded as Peculiar to the United States; New York, 1848, *intro.*
2 A Diary in America; Phila., 1839. The passage is reprinted in American Social History as Recorded by British Travellers, by Allan Nevins; New York, 1923, p. 245.

3 Seven Years in America; London, 1845, p. 16. I borrow this from Noah Webster as a Euphemist, by Allen Walker Read, *Dialect Notes,* Vol. VI, Pt. VIII, 1934.
4 John Graham Brooks: As Others See Us; New York, 1908, p. 11.

word *woman* became a term of reproach, comparable to the German *mensch*, and the uncouth *female* took its place.[1] But even *female*, after a while, acquired a bad name, and when Vassar was established in 1861, under the name of Vassar *Female* College, the redoubtable Mrs. Sarah Josepha Hale, editor of *Godey's Lady's Book*, protested loudly, and *female* was expunged.[2] Any hint of sex, in those delicate days, was forbidden. Even the word *decent*, if applied to a woman was indecent.[3] The Americans, according to Mrs. Trollope, rejected Shakespeare as obscene, and one of them said to her: "If we must have the abomination of stage plays, let them at least be marked by the refinement of the age in which we live."[4] When she mentioned Pope's "The Rape of the Lock" he muttered "The very title!" In 1833 Noah Webster actually undertook to bowdlerize the Bible. His version substituted *breast* for *teat*, *in embryo* for *in the belly*, *peculiar members* for *stones* (Leviticus XXI, 20), *smell* for *stink*, *to nurse* or *to nourish* for *to give suck*, *lewdness* for *fornication*, *lewd woman* or *prostitute* for *whore*, *to go astray* for *to go a-whoring*, and *impurities, idolatries* and *carnal connection* for *whoredom*. He got rid of *womb* by various circumlocutions, and expunged many verses altogether, as beyond the reach of effective bowdlerization.[5] This mania for the chaste afflicted even the terminology of the arts and sciences. For example, the name of the device in which the percussion-cap of a muzzle-loading gun was fixed and exploded was changed from *nipple* to *cone*. It so appeared in "The Prairie Traveler," by Randolph B. Macy (1859) — greatly to the indignation of Sir Richard Burton, who brought out an English edition of the book in 1863. "The American *cone*," he explained in a footnote, "is the English *nipple*. Beg pardon for the indelicacy! Our cousins, as we term them, so far

1 *Female*, of course, was epidemic in England too, but White says that it was "not a Briticism," and so early as 1839 the Legislature of Maryland expunged it from the title of a bill "to protect the reputation of unmarried *females*," substituting *women*, on the ground that *female* "was an Americanism in that application."
2 The Lady of *Godey's*, by Ruth E. Finley; Phila., 1931, p. 205.
3 See Squeamish Cant, in Words and

Their Uses, by Richard Grant White; new ed.; New York, 1876, p. 176 *ff*. Also, *Inexpressibles, Unmentionables, Unwhisperables*, and Other Verbal Delicacies of Mid-Nineteenth Century Americans, by Mamie Meredith, *American Speech*, April, 1930.
4 Domestic Manners of the Americans, quoted by Nevins, p. 162.
5 Noah Webster as a Euphemist, by Allen Walker Read, *Dialect Notes*, Vol. VI, Pt. VIII, 1934.

from calling a spade a spade, explain a *cock* by *rooster*, a *cockchafer* by *chafer*, and a *cockroach* by *roach*." [1]

After the Civil War there was a recurrence of delicacy, and many euphemisms that still adorn the American newspapers came into use, e.g., *interesting* (or *delicate*) *condition*, *criminal operation*, *house of ill* (or *questionable*) *repute*, *disorderly house*, *sporting house*, *statutory offense*, *fallen woman*, *felonious attack*, *serious charge* and *criminal assault*. Syphilis became transformed into *blood-poison*, *specific blood-poison* and *secret disease*, and it and *gonorrhea* into *social diseases*. Various French terms, *enceinte* and *accouchement* among them, were imported to conceal the fact that careless wives occasionally became pregnant and had lyings-in. Richard Grant White, between 1867 and 1870, launched several attacks upon these ludicrous gossamers of speech, and particularly upon *enceinte*, *limb* and *female*, but only *female* succumbed. The passage of the Comstock Postal Act, in 1873, greatly stimulated the search for euphemisms. Once that amazing law was upon the statute-book and Comstock himself was given the inquisitorial powers of a post-office inspector, it became positively dangerous to print certain ancient and essentially decent English words. To this day the effects of that old reign of terror are still visible. We yet use *toilet*, *retiring-room*, *washroom* and *public comfort station* in place of franker terms,[2] and such idiotic terms as *red-light district*, *statutory offense* and *criminal operation* are daily encountered. Now and then a really amusing curiosity turns up. I am informed by a correspondent that in 1933 the pious Los Angeles *Times* printed *sow-bosom* in lieu of *sow-belly*. In 1931 the Chattanooga police, on arresting a man for picking up a streetwalker on the street, announced that he was charged with " walking the streets accompanied by a woman," and it was so reported in the local papers.[3] In 1925 or thereabout the *Atlantic Monthly* gave a cruel blow to the moribund Puritan *Kultur* by printing the word

1 p. 109. I am indebted here to Mr. Bernard De Voto.
2 The French *pissoir* is still regarded as indecent in America, and is seldom used in England, but it has gone into most of the Continental languages, though the French themselves avoid it in print, and use the inane *Vespasien* in place of it. But all the Continental languages have their euphemisms. Most of them, for example, use *W.C.*, an abbreviation of the English *water-closet*, as a euphemism. The whole subject of national pruderies, in both act and speech, remains to be investigated.
3 Euphemism, Monroe (Mich.) *Evening News,* Nov. 21, 1931. See also A Note on Newspaper English, by Nelson Antrim Crawford, *Kansas Magazine* (an annual), 1935.

whore (as I recall it, in an article by Stuart Pratt Sherman), but when, in 1934, a play called "Within the Gates" was presented in New York, with one of its characters appearing simply as "The Young *Whore*," three of the local papers changed the designation, and another avoided it by omitting the cast. The *Sun* changed it to "The Young Prostitute," the *World-Telegram* to "The Young Harlot," and the *American* to "A Young Girl Who Has Gone Astray." It should be added that the *Times*, *Post* and *Telegraph* printed it boldly, and that the *Herald-Tribune*, which omitted the cast, gave the word in the third paragraph of its review.[1] Back in 1916 even *virgin* was a forbidden word, at least in Philadelphia. On February 26 of that year a one-act play of mine, "The Artist," was presented at the Little Theatre there, and the same day the *Public Ledger* printed specimens of the dialogue. One of the characters was called "A Virgin," but the *Ledger* preferred "A Young Girl."[2] In September, 1933, at the time of the Brain Trust's unfortunate effort to reduce the hog population of the Middle West, the Iowa Farmers' Union met at Des Moines and passed a resolution condemning "the scheme to raise livestock prices by slaughtering pigs and *enceinte* sows."[3] Hollywood, always under heavy pressure from official and volunteer censors, has its own *Index Expurgatorius*, augmented from time to time. It includes, as permanent fixtures, *broad* (for *woman*), *chippy, cocotte, courtesan, eunuch, fairy* (in the sense of homosexual), *floozy, harlot, hot mamma, huzzy, madam* (in the sense of brothel-keeper), *nance, pansy, slut, trollop, tart* and *wench*, and, of course, *whore*. *Sex* is also forbidden, as is the adjective *sexual*. *Jew* may be used only in complimentary connotations, and *kike, yid, dago* and *nigger* are prohibited altogether. *God* must be used circumspectly, and *Gawd* is under the ban. So are *Lord* ("when used profanely"), *Christ, guts, hell, hellcat, Jesus, Geez, son-of-a- ——, S.O.B.*,[4] *louse* and *punk*. *Traveling salesman* may

1 See The Theatre, by Robert Benchley, *New Yorker*, Nov. 3, 1934, reprinted in *American Speech*, Feb., 1935, p. 76.
2 Perhaps because of the Quaker influence, Philadelphia has always been one of the most Pecksniffian of American cities. Early in 1918, when a patriotic moving-picture entitled To Hell With the Kaiser was sent on tour under government

patronage, the word *hell* was carefully toned down, on the Philadelphia billboards, to *h——*.
3 Associated Press dispatch, Sept. 21. I have to thank Mr. Lewis Hawkins of the Atlanta *Constitution* for calling my attention to it.
4 This prohibition of two euphemistic forms of *son-of-a-bitch*, of course, includes the term itself.

not be used " where reference is made to a farmer's daughter," and *liar* is reserved for scenes " in a light comedy vein." Even the word *virtuous* is to be avoided, as is *bum*.¹ The radio is almost as prudish as Hollywood. Late in 1934 its syndics actually forbade the verb *to do* in songs, feeling that it was " a bit too suggestive." ²

Ever since the beginning of the Sex Hygiene movement, *c.* 1910, *syphilis* and *gonorrhea* have been struggling for recognition, but they work their way into the newspapers only slowly. At intervals vigorous protests against this prudery come from medical men. In 1918 the Army Medical Corps complained that the newspapers emasculated its bulletins regarding venereal disease in the Army by using euphemisms. One of the newspaper trade journals thereupon sought the opinions of editors upon the subject, and all of them save one declared against the use of the two words. One editor put the blame upon the Postoffice. Another reported that " at a recent conference of the Scripps Northwest League editors " it was decided that " the use of such terms as *gonorrhea*, *syphilis*, and even *venereal diseases* would not add to the tone of the papers, and that the term *vice diseases* can be readily substituted." ³ On April 29, 1919 the New York *Tribune* printed an article quoting with approbation a declaration by Major W. A. Wilson, of the Division of Venereal Control in the Merchant Marine, that " the only way to carry on the campaign [*i.e.*, against venereal disease] is to look the evil squarely in the face and fight it openly," and yet the word *venereal* was carefully avoided throughout the article, save in the place where Major Wilson's office was mentioned. Whereupon a medical journal made the following comment:

The words "the only way to carry on the campaign is to look the evil squarely in the face and fight it openly" are true, but how has the *Tribune* met the situation? Its subhead speaks of *preventable* disease; in the first paragraph *social diseases* are mentioned; elsewhere it alludes to *certain dangerous diseases*, *communicable diseases* and *diseases*, but nowhere in the entire article does it come out with the plain and precise designation of syphilis and gonorrhea as *venereal* diseases.⁴

1 See The Silver Screen, by Roger Whately, Jack O'Donnell and H. W. Hanemann; Los Angeles, 1935, p. 244. I suspect that the prohibition of *bum* is due to the fact that the word is obscene in England.
2 Rudy Vallee's Music Notebook, *Radioland*, March, 1935, p. 35. Mr. Vallee says that he was thus de-
prived of the use of one of his " greatest stage and radio vehicles, Let's Do It." He adds that Do It Again and You Do Something to Me were also prohibited.
3 *Pep*, July, 1918, p. 8.
4 *Social Hygiene Bulletin*, May, 1919, p. 7.

In 1933 the newspapers were full of articles about improvements in the use of malaria for treating tertiary syphilis, but few if any of them mentioned the name of the disease. According to the *Nation*,[1] the New York *Times* spoke of it " only as ' a dread form of insanity ' caused by ' a blood disease.' " The radio shares this prudery, and in 1934 it was belabored for it by Dr. Thomas Parran, Jr., health commissioner of New York State, who resigned from the public health committee of the National Advisory Council on Radio in Education as an earnest of his dudgeon. In the manuscript of an address that he had planned to deliver from Station CBS on November 19 the word *syphilis* was stricken out by the station Comstocks.[2] When the rejuvenation quackery began to engage the newspapers, in 1924 or thereabout, they found it necessary to invent a new set of euphemisms. So far as I have been able to discover, not one of them ever printed the word *testicles*. A few ventured upon *gonads*, but the majority preferred *glands* or *interstitial glands*, with *sex glands* as an occasional variation.[3] Even among medical men there is a faction which hesitates to violate the national canons of delicacy. Dr. Morris Fishbein, editor of the *Journal of the American Medical Association*, tells me that not a few of them, in communications to their colleagues, still state the fact that a patient has syphilis by saying that he has a *specific stomach* or a *specific ulcer*, and that the *Journal* once received a paper discussing the question, " Can a positive woman have a negative baby? " — *i.e.*, can a woman with a positive Wassermann, indicating syphilis, have a baby free from the disease? In all matters relating to the human body, of course, euphemisms are common and some of them are very old. The tendency to conceal the disagreeable under Latin names, which began with Chaucer's use of *hernia* for *rupture*, shows itself in our own time in the invention of such terms as *halitosis*. Sometimes French is used instead, as in the following advertisement in the New York *Times:*

"What can I wear that will make me flat enough for the new suits? " This question is most frequently asked by women who have large *derrières*. And we have a very specific answer for their problem. It takes a panelled corset with clever fashioning at the hips and waist to do the trick. To flatten the rear without making you look broad.[4]

1 May 31, 1933, p. 599.
2 *Variety*, Nov. 27, 1934, p. 37.
3 *Hygeia*, Feb., 1925, p. 107. *Interstitial glands*, of course, was used inaccurately.

4 Oct. 2, 1935. The advertiser was Bonwit Teller.

But outside the fields of anatomy, physiology and pathology, in which concepts of the disgusting may reinforce concepts of the indecent, the prudery once so universal in the United States has been abating since the World War. In speech, if not in writing, words and phrases are used freely that were formerly under a strict ban, even in bordelloes. I have given some examples in the first part of this section. Even the unutterable four-letter words, as I have shown, have begun to edge back in thin disguises. A learned and extremely interesting discussion of the most infamous of them, with sidelights on the others, by Allen Walker Read, of the staff of the "Dictionary of American English on Historical Principles," was published in *American Speech* in 1934.[1] To find the hyper-delicacy of the Grant Era in full flower one must resort to the remoter and more backward parts of the country — for example, the Ozark region. Mr. Vance Randolph reports that among the Ozarkians, *bull, boar, buck, ram, jack* and *stallion* are still taboo, and that even such harmless compounds as *bullfrog* and *buckshot* are regarded askance. So are all words involving *cock, e.g., cock-eyed, cock-sure* and even the proper names, *Cox* and *Hitchcock*. A cock, to the hillmen, is either a *rooster* or a *crower*. A stallion is a *stable-horse*, a bastard is a *woodscolt*, and a bull is a *cow-brute*. Certain everyday words are avoided whenever possible, *e.g., stone, maiden, virgin, piece, bed, decent, bag, leg, stocking, tail, breast:* for one reason or another they suggest blushful ideas. "Even *love*," says Mr. Randolph, "is considered more or less indecent, and the mountain people never use the term in its ordinary sense, but nearly always with some degrading or jocular connotation. If a hillman does admit that he *loved* a woman he means only that he caressed and embraced her — and he usually says that he *loved her up*." But

a woman who would be highly insulted if the word *bull* was used in her presence will employ *Gawd-a-mighty* and *Jesus Christ* freely as expletives; these words are not regarded as profane, and are used by the most staunch Christians

1 An Obscenity Symbol, Dec., 1934, p. 264 ff. Mr. Read is also the author of Lexical Evidence From Folk Epigraphy in Western North America; Paris, 1935, a sober and very interesting study of the written obscenity encountered on the walls of filling-station "rest-rooms" during "an extensive sight-seeing trip throughout the Western United States and Canada in the Summer of 1928." The four-letter words are treated very warily in the dictionaries. Even the great Oxford omits those of sexual significance, though it lists all those relating to excretions. Webster's New International admits *arse* and *piss* (the latter of which occurs seven times in the King James Bible), but bars all the rest.

in the backwoods districts. Women of the very best families *give tittie* to their babies in public, even in church, without the slightest embarrassment. Such inelegant terms as *spit* and *belch* are used freely by the hill women, and I have heard the wife of a prominent man tell her daughter to *git a rag an' snot thet young-un*, meaning to wipe the child's nose. . . . This same woman never uses *leg* and *breast* in the presence of strange men.[1]

Elsewhere in the Bible Belt the old taboos seem to be breaking down. In 1934 Dr. J. M. Steadman, Jr., of Emory University, Atlanta, Ga., undertook a study of the degree of prudery surviving among the students there incarcerated, most of them Georgians and probably a majority Methodists or Baptists. Altogether, 166 males and 195 females were examined, or 361 in all. Two of them proved their evangelical upbringing by listing the word *obscene* as itself " coarse or obscene," and five added *rotten*, but the remarkable thing about the inquiry was the high degree of tolerance that it revealed. Thus, of the 361, only 24 banned *whore* as coarse or obscene, though two others thought it " of a sinister or unpleasant suggestion." Some of the other votes were: against *ass*, 10; against *bull*, 5; against *knocked-up*, 2; against *pimp*, 2; against *garter*, 2; against *harlot*, 3; against *teat* or *tit*, 2. Rather curiously, the merely vulgar words got the highest adverse votes, *e.g.*, *belch*, 25; *sweat*, 33; *puke*, 51; *guts*, 59; *stink*, 69; *belly*, 87. Unfortunately, Dr. Steadman allowed his subjects to make up their own lists, and so the more delicate of them omitted the worst words altogether; moreover, he himself expunged a few words in his report. Nevertheless, it shows a considerable advance in antinomianism in the heart of the Gospel country. " The fear of using words of an indecent meaning or suggestion," he says, " is opposed, in different degrees for different students, by another powerful factor in the student's language consciousness, the fear of appearing affected or *sissy* by avoiding the blunt, direct word for even repulsive acts or ideas." [2] The inclusion of euphemisms in some of the lists was of considerable significance. Thus, *nerts* got six adverse votes, *halitosis* got five, *to pet* got two, *to neck* got eight, and *hussy* got fourteen. *To burp* and *to lay* do not seem to have been

1 Verbal Modesty in the Ozarks, *Dialect Notes*, Vol. VI, Pt. I, 1928. This paper is reprinted in Mr. Randolph's The Ozarks; New York, 1931, p. 78 *ff*.

2 A Study of Verbal Taboos, *American Speech*, April, 1935, and Language Taboos of American College Students, *English Studies*, June,

1935. See also the chapter on Euphemisms in Words and Their Ways in English Speech, by J. B. Greenough and G. L. Kittredge: New York, 1901, and the chapter on Euphemism and Hyperbole in English Words and Their Background, by George H. McKnight; New York, 1923.

included; maybe they had not yet reached Georgia. Euphemisms, says Dr. Leonard Bloomfield in " Language," [1] " may in time become too closely associated with the meaning, and in turn become taboo. Our word *whore*, cognate with the Latin *carus* (dear), must have been at one time a polite substitute for some word now lost."

An American visiting England discovers quickly that different words are under the ban on the two sides of the ocean. *Knocked-up*, which means pregnant in the United States and is avoided as vulgar even where *pregnant* itself would be tolerated, has only the harmless significance of exhausted in England. *Screw*, in England, means pay. But *bum* means the backside, and is thus taboo, though the English use *bum-bailiff*. An Englishman restricts the use of *bug* to the *Cimex lectularius*, or common *bedbug*, and hence the word has highly impolite connotations. All other crawling things he calls *insects*. An American of my acquaintance once greatly offended an English friend by using *bug* for *insect*. The two were playing billiards one Summer evening in the Englishman's house, and various flying things came through the window and alighted on the cloth. The American, essaying a shot, remarked that he had killed a *bug* with his cue. To the Englishman this seemed a slanderous reflection upon the cleanliness of his house.[2] Not so long ago *stomach* was in the English Index, and such euphemisms as *tummy* and *Little Mary* were used in its place, but of late it has recovered respectability. *Dirt*, to designate earth, and *closet*, in the sense of a cupboard, are seldom used by an Englishman. The former always suggests filth to him, and the latter has obtained the limited sense of *water-closet*. The more important English newspapers, compared to their American analogues, are very plain-spoken, but the popular sheets have a repertory of euphemisms to match those in use on this side of the ocean. The sheet of " Don'ts For Reporters and Sub-Editors " of the London *Daily Express*, for example, ordains that *was cited as corespondent* is to be used to avoid *adultery*, and that *betrayed* or *deceived* is to be used in place of *seduced*. Here are some other specimens, all dredged up from the *News of the World:*

1 New York, 1933, p. 401. I take this reference from Steadman.
2 On June 26, 1862, an Englishman named Joshua *Bug*, laboring under the odium attached to the name, advertised in the London *Times* that he had changed it to *Norfolk-*

Howard, a compound made up of the title and family name of the Dukes of Norfolk. The wits of London at once doubled his misery by adopting *Norfolk-Howard* as a Euphemism for *bedbug*.

For *prostitute: woman of a certain class.*
For *pregnant: in a certain condition.*
For *performing an abortion: producing a certain state.*
For *pandering: having, for purposes of gain, exercised influence over the movements of* the girl victim.
For *homosexuality: improper assault.*
For *rape: improper assault* or *to interfere with.*

Finally, there is the euphemistic address which begins every letter. In the United States, says Mrs. Emily Post,[1] " the most formal beginning of a social letter is *My dear Mrs. Smith,*" but " in England *Dear Mrs. Smith* is more formal." Archibald Marshall, the English novelist, says that when he first visited the United States *My dear* struck him " as effusive coming from strangers," and *Dear* " seemed slightly chilling from intimate friends," but that on reflection he concluded " that our usage must have precisely the same effect upon Americans." [2] But in this matter the rules are not rigid, and though the more conservative English seldom use the American forms, the English forms are not uncommonly encountered in this country.[3]

8. EXPLETIVES

Perhaps the most curious disparity between the vocabulary of the two tongues is presented by *bloody*. This word is entirely without improper significance in America, but in England it is regarded as indecent, with overtures of the blasphemous. The sensation produced in London when George Bernard Shaw put it into the mouth of the elegant Mrs. Patrick Campbell in his play, " Pygmalion," will be remembered. " The interest in the first English performance," said the New York *Times*,[4] " centered in the heroine's utterance of this banned word. It was waited for with trembling, heard shudderingly, and presumably, when the shock subsided, interest dwindled." But in New York, of course, it failed to cause any stir. Just why it is viewed so shudderingly by the English is one of the mysteries of the

---

1 Etiquette; New York, 1922, p. 455.
2 *Dear* and *My Dear*, London *Mercury*, Sept., 1922.
3 For the history of such forms in England since 1418 see A History of Modern Colloquial English, by H. C. Wyld; London, 1920, p. 379. This is a very interesting and valu-

able book. Unfortunately, using it is made a burden by the lack of an index.
4 April 14, 1914. In 1920 the English Licenser of Stage Plays ordered *bloody* expunged from a play dealing with labor. See *English*, Oct., 1920, p. 403.

language. It came in during the latter half of the Seventeenth Century, and remained innocuous for nearly a hundred years. Various amateur etymologists have sought to account for its present evil fame by giving it loathsome derivations, sometimes theological and sometimes catamenial, but the professional etymologists all agree that these derivations are invalid, though when it comes to providing a better one they unhappily disagree. Some hold that *bloody* was born of the rich young *bloods* who broke windows, upset sedan-chairs and beat up watchmen in the reign of Anne. Others argue that it goes back to the infancy of the Germanic languages, and is a brother to the German *blut*, often used in such combinations as *blutarm*, meaning bloody poor. And yet others think it is a degenerate form of either *'s blood* or *by 'r Lady*, both of them favorite oaths in Shakespeare's day, and then thought of as quite harmless. But none of these derivations justifies the present infamy of the word. Richard Henry Dana, who loved saline speech, put it into " Two Years Before the Mast " in 1840, but it failed to catch on in this country. In the Motherland, however, it has continued a lush life under cover, and the more it is denounced by the delicate, the more it is cherished by the vulgar. It is in constant use as a counterword, and has become a general intensive with no ponderable meaning – in Dean W. R. Inge's phrase, simply a sort of notice that a noun may be expected to follow.[1]

In England frequent efforts have been made to put down profanity, as distinct from obscenity. There was one so long ago as the first quarter of the Seventeenth Century, and B. A. P. Van Dam, in his study of the text of " Hamlet," shows that it even went to the length of bowdlerizing Shakespeare. The early versions of " Hamlet," published during the Bard's lifetime, were liberally besprinkled with the oaths of the time, but in the First Folio, printed seven years after his death, many of them were greatly toned down. Thus *God* was changed to *Heauen* (*i.e.*, Heaven), *'s wounds* (God's wounds) was changed to *come*, and *'s bloud* (God's blood) to *why*. *'S wounds* and *'s bloud* were regarded as innocuous when Shakespeare wrote them: like *bloody*, they had lost all literal significance. By 1623 both were under the ban. Later on *'s wounds* enjoyed a revival in the shape of *zounds*, to flourish for a century and a half and then disap-

1 See A Note on *Bloody*, by Robert Withington, *American Speech*, Oct., 1930, and Children of Linguistic Fashion, by the same author, *American Speech*, Dec., 1934.

pear. By 1823, according to an anonymous author of the time, quoted by George H. McKnight in " Modern English in the Making," [1] the only oath surviving in English circles having "any pretension to fashion " was *by Jove*. But on lower levels *bloody* was already making its way. In the United States, probably because of the decay of the legal concept of blasphemy, there has been little organized opposition to profanity. The New England Puritans attempted to punish it, but only half-heartedly; for, as one of the earliest English travelers in America, Ned Ward, reported in 1699, they were themselves, " notwithstanding their sanctity, . . . very prophane in their common dialect." In the more southerly colonies there must have been an even more lavish use of cuss-words. The Rev. Jonathan Boucher wrote home from Maryland on August 7, 1759, that visitors there were forced " to hear obscene conceits and broad expressions, and from this there are times w'n no sex, no rank, no conduct can exempt you," and on September 12, 1744, Dr. Alexander Hamilton, a Scottish physician then lodged in a New Jersey inn, recorded in his diary:

I was waked this morning before sunrise with a strange bawling and hollowing without doors. It was the landlord ordering his Negroes, with an imperious and exalted voice. In his orders the known term or epithet of *son-of-a-bitch* was often repeated.[2]

The Holy Name Society, which has flourished among American Catholics since the 1870's, has hardly done more than discourage the use of *Jesus* by its members; they appear to employ *hell* and *damn* for their daily occasions quite as freely as the admittedly damned. In this they follow the example of the Father of His Country, who was extremely skillful in the use of these expletives. In 1931, writing in *American Speech*, L. W. Merryweather observed that " *hell* fills so large a part in the American vulgate that it will probably be worn out in a few years more," and in anticipation of this catastrophe he suggested that the divines of the land be invited to propose a suitable successor to it.[3] But it continues in daily use, and there is every reason to believe that it will go on indefinitely. It is not

1 New York, 1928, p. 506.
2 For these references I am indebted to British Recognition of American Speech in the Eighteenth Century, by Allen Walker Read, *Dialect Notes*, Vol. VI, Pt. VI, July, 1933, p. 328.

3 *Hell* in American Speech, *American Speech*, Aug., 1931. See also a commentary on the foregoing by J. R. Schultz, *American Speech*, Feb., 1933, p. 81, and *Hellion*, by Willa Roberts, *American Speech*, Feb., 1932, p. 240.

only employed constantly in its naked form; it is also a part of almost countless combinations, many of them unknown to the English. Mr. Merryweather printed a long list of such combinations, and others have been published since by other philologians. *Hell-bent, hell-bender, hell-roaring, hell-raiser, hellion* — all these are Americanisms, and the English dictionaries know them not. The use of *hell* in such phrases as " He ran like *hell* " is apparently an English invention, but when *like hell* is put first, as in " *Like hell* you will," the form is American. So is " The *hell* you say." So is the use of *hell* as a verb, as in " *to hell* around." So is the adjective *hellishing*, as " He was in a *hellishing* hurry." So is the general use of *hell* as an intensive, without regard to its logical meaning, as in " It was colder than *hell*," " The pitcher was wilder than *hell*," " What in *hell* did you say? " and " *Hell*, yes." So is its use as a common indicator of inferiority or disagreeableness, as in " A *hell* of a drink," " A *hell* of a note," and " A *hell* of a Baptist." *Hell* also appears in many familiar American phrases — for example, " till *hell* freezes over," " from *hell* to breakfast," " *hell-bent* for election," " there was *hell* to pay," " *hell* and high water," " *hell* and red niggers," and " like a snowbird in *hell*." I turn to Farmer and Henley's monumental dictionary of English slang, and find only such flabby forms as *to give hell, hell-for-leather, to play* (or *kick up*) *hell*, and *hell and scissors* (this last, God save us all, credited falsely to the United States!). An American list would be much longer, and on it there would be a great many lovely specimens, most of them known to every American schoolboy.

Robert Graves, in his " Lars Porsena, or The Future of Swearing," published in 1927,[1] reported sadly that there was then " a notable decline of swearing and foul language " in England. The lower classes, he said, found *bloody* sufficient for all ordinary purposes, with *bastard* and three obscene auxiliaries to help out on great occasions. One of these auxiliaries resembles *bloody* in that it is not generally considered obscene in the United States. It is *bugger*. When I was a small boy my father used it often, as an affectionate term for any young male, and if it shows any flavor of impropriety today, the fact must be due to English influence. All three auxiliaries are discussed at length in " Songs and Slang of the British Soldier, 1914–1918," by John Brophy and Eric Partridge.[2] They say of one of them, a word of sexual significance:

1 London and New York.   2 London, 1930, p. 15 *ff*.

From being an intensive to express strong emotion it became a merely conventional excrescence. By adding *-ing* and *-ingwell* an adjective and an adverb were formed and thrown into every sentence. It became so common that an effective way for the soldier to express emotion was to omit this word. Thus, if a sergeant said, " Get your ——ing rifles! " it was understood as a matter of routine. But if he said " Get your rifles! " there was an immediate implication of urgency and danger.

All expletives tend to be similarly dephlogisticated by over-use. "Less than a generation ago, when I was at school," says H. W. Seaman, " *blast* was accounted a most corrosive blasphemy, and I once did a hundred lines for using it vainly. Today it is as innocent as *blow* or *bother*, and only a trifle stronger." [1] *Bloody* seems to be going the same way, though the English still profess to be shocked by it. There are many stories in point. One concerns two workmen who stopped before a poster set up in one of David Lloyd-George's pre-war campaigns. It read " One Man, One Vote." " What does that mean? " asked one workman of the other. " It means," said the other, " one *bloody* man, one *bloody* vote." The explanation somehow sufficed. The two *bloodys* were essentially meaningless, but they translated the sentiment into a familiar pattern, and so helped to its comprehension. There has been no revival of the old English oaths in England since Mr. Graves printed his plaint. In a former and more spacious day *Goddam* was used so freely by Englishmen that they were known as *Goddams* all over the Continent, but now the term is so rare among them that when it is heard the police take a serious view of it. It went out in Victorian days, and an English friend in the middle forties tells me that he was greatly shocked when, as a boy of ten, he heard his father use it. He says it seemed as quaint to him as *egad* or *odsblood*. The American custom of inserting *goddam* into other words, to give them forensic force, is generally believed by the learned to have been launched by the late Joseph Pulitzer, of the New York *World*, a great master of profanity in three languages. The story current is that he resorted to it in order to flabbergast the managing editor of the *World*, Foster Coates. " The trouble with you, Coates," he is said to have roared, " is that you are too inde*goddam*pendent! " Another version makes Coates the inventor. According to it, Pulitzer sent out an unwelcome order, and Coates replied to his catchpoll: " Tell Mr. Pulitzer that

1 Let's Stick To Our Own Bad Language, London *Sunday Chronicle*, Jan. 26, 1930. Mr. Seaman, in this article, discusses " the growing use of American swear-words by British swearers."

I'm under no obli*goddam*nation to do that, and I won't." [1] This ingenious device has been borrowed by the Australians, who are great admirers of the American language, but they use *bloody* instead of *goddam*, no doubt as a concession to Empire solidarity. Mr. David B. Dodge of San Francisco sends me this specimen: "It is imma-*bloody*material to me." It will be observed that the *ma* is duplicated, probably for the sake of euphony. The insertion of infixes into *Jesus Christ* also seems to be an American invention. The common form is *Jesus H. Christ,* but for special emphasis *Jesus H. Particular Christ* is sometimes used. *Holy jumping Jesus* is also heard.

Swearing, of course, is not the prerogative of all men. Many lack the natural gift for it, and others are too timorous. For such toters of inferiority complexes there is a repertory of what may be called denaturized profanity. For spoken discourse there are *darn, goldarn, doggone, jiminy, gosh, golly, gee-whiz, holy gee, son-of-a-gun* and their congeners, and for written discourse *damphool, damfino, helluva* and *s.o.b.,* by the Y.W.C.A. out of the tea-shoppe.[2] *All-fired* for *hell-fired, gee-whiz* for *Jesus,* tarnal for *eternal, tarnation* for *damnation, cuss* for *curse, holy gee* for *holy Jesus, goldarned* for *God-damned, by golly* for *by God, great Scott* for *great God,* and *what'ell* for *what the hell* are all Americanisms, but *by gosh* and *by gum* are English. Tornton has traced *all-fired* to 1835, *tarnation* to 1801 and *tarnal* to 1790; Tucker says that *blankety* is also American. *By golly* has been found in England so early as 1843, but it probably originated in America; down to the Civil War it was the characteristic oath of the Negro slaves — at all events in the literature of the time. The English have a number of euphemistic surrogates for *bloody* — among them, *bleeding, sanguinary* and *ruddy.* These, in their turn, have become somewhat raffish, and it would be a grave breach of etiquette to use any of them in a letter to the Archbishop of Canterbury. So long ago as 1887 W. S. Gilbert shocked the more

---

1 See Reporters Become of Age, by Isabelle Keating, *Harper's Magazine,* April, 1935, p. 601.
2 Both of the American telegraph companies have rules strictly forbidding the acceptance of telegrams containing profane words. Some time ago a telegram of mine containing the harmless adjective *damndest* was refused by both. I appealed to the higher authorities of the Western Union. After I had solemnly filed a brief in defense of the term, Mr. T. W. Carroll, general manager of the Eastern Division, as solemnly decided that the company "must take the position that, if there is any question or doubt on the subject, the safest plan is to request the sender to so modify his language as to make his message acceptable."

refined moiety of London theatre-goers by calling one of his operas "Ruddigore." *Darn* and *doggone* are both American inventions. They came into use during the first half of the last century. The late Professor George Philip Krapp gave over a long essay to proving, as he thought, that *darn* comes from *dierne*, an early English adjective signifying secret, dark, lamentable,[1] but Dr. Louise Pound has disposed of his case in a paper that is shorter but far more convincing.[2] She shows that the origin of the term is actually to be sought in *tarnal*, a corruption of *eternal* very common at the end of the Eighteenth Century. From *tarnal* arose *tarnation*, and presently *tarnation* was wedded to *damnation*, and the offspring of the union was *darned*, a virtuous sister to *damned*. Sometimes *darned* appears as *derned*. The English form used to be *demmed*, but it survives only historically, in *deminition bow-wows*. Used today, it would sound as archaic as *zounds*. *Doggone* seems to be a blend form of *dog on it;* in fact, it is still often used with *it* following. It is thus a brother to the old English phrase, "a pox upon it," but is considerably more decorous.

But *darn* and *doggone* are hardly more than proofs that profanity is not an American art. The chief national reliances are still *hell* and *damn*, both of them badly shop-worn. To support them we have nothing properly describable as a vocabulary of indecency. Our maid-of-all-work in that department is *son-of-a-bitch*, which seems as pale and ineffectual to a Slav or a Latin as *fudge* does to us. There is simply no lift in it, no shock, no sis-boom-ah. The dumbest policeman in Palermo thinks of a dozen better ones between breakfast and the noon whistle. The term, indeed, is so flat, stale and unprofitable that, when uttered with a wink or a dig in the ribs, it is actually a kind of endearment, and has been applied with every evidence of respect by one United States Senator to another. Put the second person pronoun and the adjective *old* in front of it, and scarcely enough bounce is left in it to shake up an archdeacon. Worse, it is frequently toned down to *s.o.b.*, or transmogrified into the childish *son-of-a-gun*. The latter is so lacking in punch that the Italians among us have borrowed it as a satirical name for an American: *la sanemagogna* is what they call him, and by it they indicate their contempt for his backwardness in the art that is one of their great

1 The English Language in America; New York, 1925, Vol. I, p. 118 ff. 2 The Etymology of an English Expletive, *Language*, June, 1927.

glories. In Standard Italian there are no less than forty congeners of *son-of-a-bitch*, and each and every one of them is more opprobrious, more brilliant, more effective. In the Neapolitan dialect there are thousands.[1]

1 For a long list of euphemistic substitutes for *God, Jesus, Christ, Lord, saints, devil, hell* and *damn* see Exclamations in American English, by E. C. Hills, *Dialect Notes*, Vol. V, Pt. VII, 1924.

VII

THE PRONUNCIATION
OF AMERICAN

1. ITS GENERAL CHARACTERS

"Language," said A. H. Sayce, in 1879, "does not consist of letters, but of sounds, and until this fact has been brought home to us our study of it will be little better than an exercise of memory."[1] The theory, at that time, was somewhat strange to English and American grammarians and etymologists; their labors were largely wasted upon deductions from the written word. But since then, chiefly under the influence of Continental philologians, they have turned from orthographical futilities to the actual sounds of the tongue, and a number of the more recent grammar-books are based upon the spoken language of educated persons — not, remember, of conscious purists, but of the general body of cultivated folk.[2] Unluckily, this new method also has its disadvantages. The men of a given race and time usually write a good deal alike, or, at all events, attempt to write alike, but in their oral speech there are wide variations. "No two persons," says a leading contemporary authority upon English phonetics,[3] "pronounce exactly alike." Moreover, "even the best speaker commonly uses more than one style." The result is that it is extremely difficult to determine the prevailing pronunciation of a given combination of letters at any time and place. The persons whose speech is studied pronounce it with minute shades of differences, and admit other differences according as they are conversing

1 Introduction to the Science of Language, 4th ed., London, 1900, Vol. II, p. 339.
2 For example, A Grammar of Spoken English, by H. E. Palmer; Cambridge, 1922. George O. Curme's College English Grammar; Richmond, Va., 1925, a popular text by a distinguished American philologian, is founded on "the English language as *spoken* and written today," p. iv.
3 Daniel Jones: The Pronunciation of English, 2nd ed.; Cambridge, 1914, p. 1. Jones is a professor of phonetics at University College, London.

319

naturally or endeavoring to exhibit their pronunciation. Worse, it is impossible to represent a great many of these shades in print. Sweet, trying to do it, found himself, in the end, with an alphabet of 125 letters. Prince L.-L. Bonaparte more than doubled this number, and A. J. Ellis brought it to 390.[1] During the late 80's of the last century the unwieldy Ellis alphabet was taken in hand by P. E. Passy, a French phonetician, and reduced to a workable compass. In its new form it was adopted by the Association Internationale Phonetique, which Passy had founded, and today, under the name of the International Phonetic Alphabet, or IPA, it is in general use. It suffices for recording most of the sounds commonly encountered in the Western European languages, but every time it is put to some new use defects in it are discovered, and when it was adopted by the Practical Phonetics Group of the Modern Language Association in 1927 a new character had to be added to represent the vowel in the American pronunciation of *hurt*. Unfortunately, its 50-odd characters include twenty or more that do not occur in any normal modern alphabet, and so it is readily interpreted only by phonologists, and the makers of dictionaries avoid it.[2] What Richard Grant White wrote in 1880, that " it is almost impossible for one person to express to another by signs the sound of any word," is still more or less true. He went on:

> Only the voice is capable of that; for the moment a sign is used the question arises, What is the value of that sign? The sounds of words are the most delicate, fleeting, and inapprehensible things in nature; far more so than the tones of music, whether made by the human voice or by instruments. Moreover, the question arises as to the capability to apprehend and distinguish sounds on the part of the person whose evidence is given.[3]

Some years ago certain German phonologists, despairing of the printed page, turned to the phonograph, and there is now a Deutsche

1 It is given in Ellis's Early English Pronunciation, p. 1293 *ff.*, and in Sayce's The Science of Language, Vol. I, p. 353 *ff.*

2 It is given on p. xxii of Webster's New International Dictionary, 1934, but a simpler if less scientific system of indicating pronunciations is used in the body of the work. See The International Phonetic Alphabet, by John S. Kenyon, *American Speech*, April, 1929, p. 324 *ff.*

3 Every-Day English; Boston, 1881, p. 29. The difficulty is discussed,

with examples, in Standards of Speech, by Elizabeth Avery, *American Speech*, April, 1926. One phonetic symbol is commonly used to represent the *e* in *met, led* and *sell*, yet the vowel differs in the three words. So with the *k* in *key, kaffir* and *kumquat*. " It is difficult if not impossible," says W. Cabell Greet in Southern Speech (in Culture in the South, Chapel Hill, N. C., 1934, p. 601) " to obtain an idea of speech from phonetic symbols."

Grammophon Gesellschaft in Berlin which offers to supply records of a great many languages and dialects, including English. The phonograph has also been adopted for teaching foreign languages by some of the American correspondence schools.[1] In 1924, at the request of the Present Day English Group of the Modern Language Association, Dr. Harry Morgan Ayres of Columbia University began to make phonograph records of American speech at the New York studios of the Columbia Phonograph Company. In 1927 he was joined by Dr. W. Cabell Greet, now editor of *American Speech*, and since then a machine for recording on aluminum disks has been installed at Columbia University, and under Dr. Greet's direction nearly 2500 records of about 3500 different speakers have been accumulated (1936). Approximately two thirds of them preserve recordings of a little story called "Arthur the Rat," so that minute comparisons are easily made. All parts of the country, save the Pacific Coast, are well represented. The same method has been employed by other phonologists, and it was used in accumulating material for the Linguistic Atlas. Transcriptions of Dr. Greet's records, in the IPA, have been printed in every issue of *American Speech* since February, 1933.[2] Of late efforts have been made to record speech by the oscillograph, which has already proved its usefulness in the investigation of the singing voice. It seems to be very likely that, in the near future, the study of oscillograph records on motion picture films will provide a means of distinguishing minute differences in pronunciation with great precision.[3] The lead in this work has been taken by Dr. E. W. Scripture, the American-born profes-

1 The first experiments were made in New York at the turn of the century. In 1901 the method was adopted by the International Correspondence Schools at Scranton, Pa. The director of their School of Languages, Mr. J. Navas, tells me that it is still in use, and has been a great success.

2 For an account of the early stages of the work of Drs. Ayres and Greet see their article, American Speech Records at Columbia University, *American Speech*, June, 1930.

3 The method employed is described by C. E. Parmenter and S. N. Treviño in The Length of the Sounds

of a Middle Westerner, *American Speech*, April, 1935. The subject's voice, picked up by a microphone, causes the oscillograph to vibrate, and the vibrations are photographed on a strip of film moving at the rate of two feet a second. Simultaneously, the vibrations of a 1000-cycle oscillator are recorded on the same film, to serve as a timer. In A Study of Dialect Differences, by H. E. Atherton and Darrell L. Gregg, *American Speech*, Feb., 1929, there is a comparison between Southern English and the pronunciation of North Carolina by a modification of this method.

sor of experimental phonetics at the University of Vienna; by Dr. S. N. Treviño of the University of Chicago; and by the acoustical engineers of the Bell Telephone System laboratories. The *x*-rays have also been employed, especially by Dr. G. Oscar Russell of Ohio State University.[1]

In view of the foregoing it would be hopeless to attempt to exhibit in print all the differences between English and American pronunciation, for many of them are extremely small and subtle, and only their aggregation makes them plain. According to Dr. R. J. Menner of Yale,[2] the most important of them do not lie in pronunciation at all, properly so called, but in intonation. It is in this direction, he says, that one must look for the true characters of "the English accent." Virtually all other observers agree. "What does an Englishman first notice on landing in America," asks Hilaire Belloc, "as the contrast between the two sides of the Atlantic so far as the *spoken* language is concerned?" The answer is: "The first thing which strikes him is the violent contrast in intonation."[3] "Though they use the same words," says John Erskine, "the Englishman and the American do not speak the same tune."[4] In general, the speech-tunes of the Englishman show wider melodic curves than those of the American, and also more rapid changes. The late Fred Newton Scott attempted to exhibit the difference by showing how the two speak the sentence, "The weather is rather warm to-day." The American, beginning at the tonic, "ascends gradually for about a major fourth to, and through the word *warm*, and then drops back

---

1 The method used is described by C. E. Parmenter and C. A. Bevans in Analysis of Speech Radiographs, *American Speech*, Oct., 1933. See also Speech and Voice, by Dr. Russell; New York, 1931.
2 The Pronunciation of English in America, *Atlantic Monthly*, March, 1915, p. 366.
3 A Note on Language, in The Contrast; New York, 1924, p. 219. Most of this chapter was printed in *Columbia*, Oct., 1924, under the title of The American Language.
4 Do Americans Speak English?, New York *Nation*, April 15, 1925, p. 410. "All speech, even the commonest speech," said Thomas Carlyle in Heroes and Hero-Worship,

"has something of song in it. . . . Accent is a kind of chanting." "If somebody asks you a question," says P. B. Ballard in Thought and Language; London, 1934, p. 70, "and you reply 'I don't know' you do not say the words at a dead level; you give them a tune. Sometimes, indeed, you give the tune without the words; you just hum them. And you are understood just the same." See Pitch Patterns in English, by Kemp Malone, *Studies in Philology*, July, 1926: Zur amerikanischen Intonation, by Fritz Karpf, *Die neuren Sprachen*, Sept., 1926, and English Intonation, by H. E. Palmer; Cambridge, England, 1922.

in the word *to-day* to the tonic." But the Englishman follows a much more complicated pattern. His voice drops below the tonic in enunciating *weather*, then rises sharply to the beginning of *warm*, then drops again, and finally turns upward on *-day*.[1] As a result of his use of such speech-patterns his talk sounds " abrupt, explosive and manneristic,"[2] to American ears, and shows what has been called " a somewhat pansy cast "[3] and " a mauve, Episcopalian ring."[4] His range of intonation, says Daniel Jones, " is very extensive. . . . It is not unusual for a man with a voice ♩ of ordinary pitch to have a range of over two octaves, rising to 𝄞 or even higher, and going down so low that the voice degenerates into a kind of growl which can hardly be regarded as a musical sound at all."[5] Such coloratura is surely not common among Americans. " Usually," says Scott, " their words will be spoken unemotionally, perhaps in a sort of recitative, with a rather dry, sharp articulation, especially if the speaker is from the Middle West." Erskine describes their speech as " horribly monotonous — it hasn't tune enough," and Krapp says that it sounds " hesitating, monotonous and indecisive " to an Englishman. Nevertheless, Krapp holds that " the American voice starts on a higher plane, is normally pitched higher than the British voice."[6] Here I incline to agree with Richard Grant White that the contrary is normally the case.[7] The nasal twang which Englishmen detect in *vox Americana*, though it has some high overtones, is itself not high pitched, but rather low pitched. The causes of that twang have long engaged phonologists, and there is respectable opinion in favor of the theory that our generally dry climate and rapid changes of temperature produce an actual change in the membranes concerned in the production of sound. Perhaps some such impediment to free and easy utterance is responsible both for the levelness of tone of American speech, and for the American tendency to pro-

1 The Standard of American Speech; Boston, 1926, p. 16.
2 George Philip Krapp in The Pronunciation of Standard English in America; New York, 1919, p. 50.
3 James M. Cain in Paradise, *American Mercury*, March, 1933, p. 269.
4 H. W. Seaman in The Awful English of England, *American Mercury*, Sept., 1933, p. 75.
5 The Pronunciation of English, above cited p. 60.

6 The Pronunciation of Standard English in America, above cited, p. 50.
7 " The pitch of the British Englishman's voice," he said in Words and Their Uses, new ed., New York, 1876, p. 57, " is higher and more penetrating than the American Englishman's." " His inflections are more varied than the other's," he added, " because they more frequently rise."

nounce the separate syllables of a word with much more care than an Englishman bestows upon them. The American, in giving *extraordinary* six careful and distinct syllables instead of the Englishman's grudging four, and two stresses instead of the Englishman's one, may be seeking to cover up a natural disability. George P. Marsh, in his " Lectures on the English Language," sought two other explanations of the fact. On the one hand, he pointed out that the Americans of his day read a great deal more than the English, and were thus much more prone to spelling pronunciations, and on the other hand he argued that " our flora shows that the climate of even our Northern States belongs . . . to a more Southern type than that of England," and " in Southern latitudes . . . articulation is generally much more distinct than in Northern regions." [1] In support of the latter proposition Marsh cited the pronunciation of Spanish, Italian and Turkish, as compared with that of English, Danish and German — rather unfortunate examples, for the pronunciation of German is at least as clear as that of Spanish. Swedish would have supported his case far better: the Swedes debase their vowels and slide over their consonants even more markedly than the English. Marsh believed that there was a tendency among Southern peoples to throw the accent toward the ends of words, and that this helped to bring out all the syllables. A superficial examination shows a number of examples of that movement of accent in American: *advertísement, primárily, telégrapher, temporárily*. The English accent all of these words on the first syllable except *advertisement*, which is accented on the second; Americans usually accent *primarily* and *telegrapher* on the second, and *temporarily* and *advertisement* [2] on the third. Again there are *frontier* and *harass*. The English accent

1 Lectures on the English Language, 4th ed.; New York, 1870, p. 671. Marsh had been anticipated here, though he probably didn't know it, by the Rev. Jonathan Boucher, who, in his glossary of Americanisms, printed in 1832, had said: " One striking peculiarity in American elocution is a slow, drawling unemphatic and unimpassioned manner; this, it is probable, is to be attributed, in general, to the heat of their climates, which is such as to paralyze all active exertion, even in speaking." Boucher did not say

directly that this languid style of speech made for clear utterance, but that inference may be fairly drawn from his other remarks on the English spoken in America.
2 Webster's New International Dictionary, 1934, prefers *advértisement*, but admits that *advertisement* is American. Old Noah himself argued for the latter on the analogy of *amusement, refinement* and so on. See his Dissertations on the English Language; Boston, 1789, p. 138.

the first syllables; we commonly accent the second. *Kilómeter* seems to be gaining ground in the United States, and on the level of the vulgar speech there are *theátre, defícit, mischíevous* and *exquísite.*[1] But when all such examples have been marshaled, the fact remains plain that there are just as many, and perhaps more, of an exactly contrary tendency. The chief movement in American, in truth, would seem to be toward throwing the accent upon the first syllable. I recall *mámma, pápa, ínquiry, céntenary, álly, récess, ídea, álloy* and *ádult;* I might add *défect, éxcess, áddress, súrvey, mágazine, mústache, résearch* and *rómance.* All these words are accented on the second syllable in the Concise Oxford Dictionary.[2] Perhaps the notion that American tends to throw the accent back has been propagated by the fact that it retains a secondary accent in many words that have lost it in English. Most of these end in *-ary, -ery* or *-ory, e.g., necessary, monastery* and *preparatory.* In American the secondary accent in *necessary,* falling upon *ar,* is clearly marked; in English only the primary accent on *nec* is heard, and so the word becomes *nécess'ry.* In *laboratory,* which the English accent on the second syllable, the secondary accent on the fourth, always heard in American, is likewise omitted, and the word becomes something like *labórat'ry.* The same difference in pronunciation is to be observed in certain words of the *-ative* and *-mony* classes, and in some of those of other classes. In American the secondary accent on *at* in *operative* is always heard, but seldom in English. So with the secondary accent on *mon* in *ceremony:* the third syllable is clearly enunciated in American, but in English everything after *cer* becomes a kind of *glissando.* So, finally, in *melancholy:* in English it sounds like *mélanc'ly.* Until relatively recently the English accented *adumbrate, compensate, concentrate, confiscate, demonstrate, illustrate, exculpate, objurgate,* and some of their congeners on the second syllable; indeed, *enervate* is still so accented by the Concise Oxford. But during the third quarter of the Nineteenth Century the accent

1 There is an interesting discussion of such vulgarisms in Our Agile American Accents, by John L. Haney, *American Speech,* April, 1926.
2 In a letter to the New York *Times,* Dec. 20, 1931, Charlton Andrews complained that the New York radio announcers were accenting

rebound, detour, cigarette, curator, narrator, acclimated, decoy, promulgate, recluse, respiratory, insane, inclement, entire and *tribunal* on the first syllable. The Concise Oxford accents the second syllable of all save *promulgate* and *respiratory.*

moved forward to the first syllable. This movement, I believe, began
in the United States earlier than in England.[1] Whether the colorless
and monotonous American manner of speech promoted the survival
of the secondary accent or the secondary accent helped to flatten
out the American speech-tune is a problem that has not been solved.
Krapp was inclined to choose the former hypothesis [2] but it may be
that the thing worked both ways.

Another factor which may have had something to do with the
retention of the secondary accent, and with the general precision
of American speech, is discussed at length by H. C. Wyld.[3] It has
operated in England too, but during the past century it has probably
exerted greater influence in this country. It may be described
briefly as the influence of a class but lately risen in the social scale
and hence a bit unsure of itself — a class intensely eager to avoid
giving away its vulgar origin by its speech habits. The great historical changes in Standard English, says Wyld, were synchronous
with the appearance of new " classes of the population in positions
of prominence and power in the state, and the consequent reduction
in the influence of the older governing classes." He lists some of the
events that produced such shifts in the balance of power: " the
break-up of the feudal system; the extinction of most of the ancient
baronial families in the War of the Roses; the disendowment of
the monasteries, and the enriching of the King's tools and agents;
the rise of the great merchants in the towns; the Parliamentary wars
and the social upheaval of the Protectorate; the rise of banking during the Eighteenth and early Nineteenth Centuries." These changes,
he said, brought forward an authority which ranged itself against
both " the mere frivolities of fashion, the careless and half-incoher-
ent babble of the fop " and " the lumbering and uncouth utterance
of the boor." Precision in speech thus became the hall-mark of
those who had but recently arrived. Obviously, the number of those
who have but recently arrived has always been greater in the
United States than in England, not only among the aristocracy of
wealth and fashion but also among the *intelligentsia*. The average
American schoolmarm, the chief guardian of linguistic niceness in

1 See American Pronunciation, by
J. S. Kenyon; Ann Arbor, Mich.,
1932, p. 159 ff, for a long list of
words pronounced differently in
England and the United States.

2 See his discussion of the matter in
The English Language in America;
New York, 1925, Vol. II, p. 14.
3 A History of Modern Colloquial
English; London, 1920, p. 18 ff.

the Republic, does not come from the class that has a tradition of culture behind it, but from the class of small farmers and city clerks and workmen. This is true, I believe, even of the average American college teacher. Such persons do not advocate and practise precision in speech on logical grounds alone; they are also moved, plainly enough, by the fact that it tends to conceal their own cultural insecurity. From them come most of the gratuitous rules and regulations that afflict schoolboys and harass the writers of the country. They are the chief discoverers and denouncers of "bad English" in the books of such men as Whitman, Mark Twain and Howells. But it would be a mistake to think of their influence as wholly, or even as predominantly evil. They have thrown themselves valiantly against the rise of dialects among us, and with such success that nothing so grossly unpleasant to the ear as the cockney whine or so lunatic as the cockney manhandling of the *h* is now prevalent anywhere in the United States. And they have policed the general speech to such effect that even on its most pretentious levels it is virtually free from the silly affectations which still mark Standard English. There was a time when they tried to saddle the Boston *a* upon the country, but that time is past. The Standard American that seems to be gathering form today is principally Western, and Dr. J. S. Kenyon, the author of the best existing textbook of American usage, did well to base it on "the cultivated pronunciation of his own locality — the Western Reserve of Ohio." [1]

In England the standard commonly recognized is, in the words of Daniel Jones, "the pronunciation which appears to be most usually employed by Southern English persons who have been educated at the great public boarding-schools." [2] Dr. Jones calls it Standard Pronunciation (StP) or Public School Pronunciation (PSP). H. C. Wyld prefers to call it Received Standard English (RS), but agrees that it owes its dominance to "the custom of sending youths from

---

1 American Pronunciation, above cited, p. iv. But Dr. Kenyon, of course, makes no claim that this Western American is better than any other kind. See his very wise discussion of the point in Correct Pronunciation, *American Speech*, Dec., 1928, p. 150. In Practical Phonetics of the American Language, by Ralph S. Boggs; San Juan, P. R., 1927, a text prepared for students at the University of Porto Rico, "the pronunciation of the well-educated people of the Middle West in normal conversation" is accepted as "the standard of American pronunciation."

2 The Pronunciation of English, above cited, p. 1.

certain social strata to the great public schools."¹ Wyld says that "it is not any more the English of London, as is sometimes mistakenly maintained, than it is that of York, or Exeter, or Cirencester, or Oxford, or Chester, or Leicester; . . . it is spoken everywhere, allowing for individual idiosyncrasies, to all intents and purposes, in precisely the same way." He believes that it is "the best kind of English," and in particular commends its vowels.² Nevertheless, there are plenty of Britons who dislike it heartily, and especially that form of it prevailing at Oxford. The late Robert Bridges delivered an onslaught upon it in Tract No. II of the Society for Pure English (1919) and drew up a formidable list of its absurdities and inconveniences, *e.g.*, the confusion, amounting to identification in pronunciation, of *lord* and *laud*, *maw* and *more*, *flaw* and *floor*, *alms* and *arms*, *source* and *sauce*, *ah* and *are*, *root* and *route*, *tray* and *trait*, *bean* and *been*. He also belabored such pronunciations as *ikstrodnry* for *extraordinary*, *intrist* for *interest*, and *pictsher* for *picture*. Dr. J. Y. T. Greig, in "Breaking Priscian's Head,"³ calls it "that silliest and dwabliest of all the English dialects," and argues that it is "artificial, slovenly to a degree, absurdly difficult for foreigners to acquire, and except to ears debased by listening to it, inharmonious." He continues:

It obliterates distinctions, tends to reduce all unstressed vowels to the same natural grunt, and then — as if by some obscure process of psychical compensation — diphthongizes and breaks up vowels that in other Standards are cleanly and simply articulated. . . . It needs to be taken out into the open air, and buffeted by trans-Atlantic winds.

Dr. Greig is a Scotsman, and his indignation may be discounted on that ground. But the following is by an Englishman born in East Anglia:

I speak for millions of Englishmen when I say that we are as sick and tired of this so-called English accent as you Americans are. It has far less right to be called Standard English than Yorkshire or any other country dialect has — or than any American dialect. It is as alien to us as it is to you. True, some of my neighbors have acquired it — for social and other reasons —, but then some of the Saxon peasants took pains to acquire Norman French, which was also imposed on them from above. The advantages to be gained from its acquisition, if not wholly imaginary, are of specious value. Boys from the great public schools, the cradles of snobbery, find that their speech is a passport to jobs in motor showrooms in Great Portland street

1 A History of Modern Colloquial English; London, 1920, p. 3.
2 The Superiority of Received Standard English, S.P.E. Tracts, No. XXXIX, 1934.
3 London, 1929.

and the Euston road, but even there its function is mainly decorative. As soon as the customer has been well slavered and purred over, he is passed on to a salesman who, whether he speaks broad Cockney or broad Northumbrian, knows something about cars.[1]

In 1925, when the announcers of the B.B.C., the government radio monopoly, began loosing this PSP over the air, there were many protests, and some of them were even leveled at the use of the broad *a* in *dance*, which most Americans think of as typically English. In consequence, the B.B.C. administration appointed an Advisory Committee on Spoken English, headed by Dr. Bridges and including Dr. Jones, Sir Johnston Forbes-Roberston, George Bernard Shaw and the American-born Logan Pearsall Smith, and handed over to it the difficult business of deciding disputes over pronunciation. This committee has been enlarged since, and now (1936) includes representatives of the British Academy, the Royal Society of Literature, the English Association, and the Royal Academy of Dramatic Art. In 1928 it issued a pamphlet for the guidance of announcers, dealing with 332 words; in 1932 there was a new edition, covering 503; and in 1935 there followed a third, covering 779.[2] This list, rather curiously, shows some concessions to American example, *e.g.*, the throwing forward of the accent in *adult*, but in general it follows the canons of PSP. George Bernard Shaw, a member of the advisory committee, has apparently dissented from most of its judgments. On January 25, 1934, he said in a letter to the London *Times:*

> An Oxford accent is considered by many graduates of that university to be the perfection of correct English; but unfortunately over large and densely populated districts of Great Britain it irritates some listeners to the point of switching off, and infuriates others so much that they smash their wireless sets because they cannot smash the Oxonian. The best English today is literally the King's English. Like his Royal grandmother before him, King

1 The Awful English of England, by H. W. Seaman, *American Mercury*, Sept., 1933, p. 73. Perhaps the testimony of a Briton of Welsh name should be added, to complete the circle. "English as spoken in America," said Wyndham Lewis, in The Dumb Ox, *Life and Letters*, April, 1934, p. 41, "is more vigorous and expressive than Oxford English, I think. It is easy to mistake a native from the wilds of Dorsetshire for an American, I have found: and were 'educated'

English used upon a strong reverberant Devonshire basis, for instance, it would be all to the good, it is my opinion. Raleigh, Drake, and the rest of them, must have talked rather like that."
2 Broadcast English. I. Recommendations to Announcers Regarding Certain Words of Doubtful Pronunciation, with an introduction by A. Lloyd James, professor of phonetics, School of Oriental Studies, London; London, 1935.

George is the best speaker in his realm; and his broadcasts are astonishingly effective in creating loyalty. If he delivered a single broadcast in an Oxford accent his people would rise up that very day and proclaim a republic.

But not many of the Britons who object to the PSP join Professor Greig and Mr. Lewis in commending American pronunciation. Its monotonous speech-tunes commonly seem unpleasantly drawling to their ears, and they are jarred by its frequent nasalization of vowels. As a Cockney once said after suffering an American talkie, " It ain't so much their bleedin' lengwidge; it's their blawsted neysal tweng." " The Englishman," says Philip R. Dillon, " squirms at the sounds of American English; they are strange to him, grate on him, offend his sense of harmony. The Dublin Irishman and the Edinburgh Scotsman also dislike and criticise American spoken English, but they have more humor than the Londoner, and refrain from being rude about it." [1] This adversion began to show itself soon after the War of 1812, and many of the English travelers of the decades following denounced the American accent as well as the American vocabulary. Thus Frances Trollope in her " Domestic Manners of the Americans " (1832):

I very seldom during my whole stay in the country heard a sentence elegantly turned and correctly pronounced from the lips of an American. There is always something either in the expression or the accent that jars the feelings and shocks the taste.

The patriots of the time met these sneers with claims that the American accent was not only quite as good as the English, but much better. Said J. Fenimore Cooper in " Notions of the Americans " (1828): [2]

The people of the United States, with the exception of a few of German or French descent, speak, as a body, incomparably better English than the people of the mother country. . . . In fine, we speak our language, as a nation, better than any other people speak their language. When one reflects on the immense surface of the country that we occupy, the general accuracy, in pronunciation and in the use of words, is quite astonishing. . . . The voices of the American females are particularly soft and silvery.[3]

1 English, Spoken and Written, Paris *Herald*, April 9, 1925.
2 " By a Travelling Bachelor," but later acknowledged by Cooper. It was published in London, in two volumes. The quotations are from Vol. II, Letter VII.
3 Many similar exultations might be quoted. Captain Frederick Marryat, in his Diary in America; Philadelphia, 1839, thus summed it up: " The Americans boldly assert that they speak English better than we do." He dissented, of course. " It is remarkable," he said piously, " how very debased the language has become in a short period in America."

Cooper's views are generally held by Americans today. Unconscious of the monotony of their speech-tunes, and of the nasalization which offends Englishmen, they believe that their way of using English is clearly better than the English way. In consequence, there is little imitation of English usage in this country. The relatively few Americans who have lived in England sometimes acquire the PSP accent, and it is mimicked by a small sect of Anglomaniacs, but the average American regards it as effeminate and absurd, and will thus have none of it. The broad *a* that the American schoolmarm formerly tried to propagate was not the English *a*, but the Boston *a*. What moved her to favor it was hardly a liking for English speech-habits, but rather a respect for the cultural preëminence of New England, and especially of Boston, now no more. This *a* survives in the more fashionable finishing-schools, but hardly anywhere else. There was a time when all American actors of any pretensions employed a dialect that was a heavy imitation of the dialect of the West End actors of London. It was taught in all the American dramatic schools, and at the beginning of the present century it was so prevalent on the American stage that a flat *a* had a melodramatic effect almost equal to that of *damn*. But the rise of the movies broke down this convention. They attracted actors from all parts of the world, to many of whom English was a foreign language, and when the talkies followed it was found that most of these newcomers had picked up ordinary American. Moreover, the native-born recruits were mainly without formal professional training, so the majority of them also spoke the vulgate. From time to time Hollywood has made some effort to model its speech on that of its English-born luminaries, but never with much success. Nor has the American Academy of Arts and Letters got far in the same direction, though it has given gold medals and other gauds to actors equipped with the PSP accent, *e.g.*, Edith Wynne Matthison, Julia Marlowe and George Arliss. The ideal of Broadway now seems to be what Kerry Conway has called a denationalized accent. It is, he explains, " clear, rounded speech, smacking neither of England nor of America, and free from the repugnant localisms of both countries. The late Holbrook Blinn achieved it. Walter Hampden and Arthur Byron employ it. It graces the utterance of the Canadian-born Margaret Anglin." [1]

1 God's Patience and the King's
English, New York *Herald Tribune*,
Sept. 8, 1929.

On April 26, 1931, it was reported by the Chicago *Radio Weekly* that the two big American radio chains, the Columbia and the N.B.C., were forcing their announcers to use "English as she is spoke in England." On inquiry I found that this was a canard. "What we try to get," I was told by Mr. Walter C. Stone of the N.B.C., "is decent American pronunciation, affected as little as possible by localisms." [1] Columbia, at the same time, announced that it had appointed Dr. Frank H. Vizetelly to advise its announcers in matters of pronunciation, and called attention to the fact that Dr. Vizetelly described himself as "a man ever ready to help in spreading the best traditions of American speech, which does not suppress its consonants, nor squeeze all the life out of its vowels." [2] Nevertheless, there are American announcers who affect what they think is English usage, and they have been belabored heartily for it by Dr. Josiah Combs.[3] As for the schoolmarms, they have been warned by Dr. Louise Pound. "My first caution," she says, "is, do not rely too far on British dictionaries, in these days. It is of interest to consult them, but they are no longer to be cited as authoritative for American English." [4] The extent to which this differentiation has gone is but little appreciated. In Palmer, Martin and Blandford's "Dictionary of English Pronunciation with American Variants" [5] no less than 28% of the words listed show differing pronunciations in England and the United States. The authors classify the major American variants in twelve categories, and add fourteen categories of minor ones.

The historical study of American pronunciation was put on a solid basis by the publication of the second volume of the late George Philip Krapp's "The English Language in America" in 1925. There had been scattering investigations on the subject before then, but Dr. Krapp was the first to undertake an exhaustive examination of the available material — the early dictionaries, grammars and spelling

1 In a letter dated May 26, 1931.
2 Letter from Jesse S. Butcher, director of public relations, May 22, 1931.
3 In Broadcasting and Pronunciation, *American Speech*, June, 1930, and again in The Radio and Pronunciation, the same, Dec., 1931.
4 Pronunciation in the Schools, *English Journal*, Oct., 1922. See also Dr. Pound's British and Ameri-

can Pronunciation, *School Review*, June, 1915, and The Pronunciation of English in America, by Robert J. Menner, *Atlantic Monthly*, March, 1915.
5 Cambridge (England), 1926; 2nd ed., 1935. Palmer is linguistic adviser to the Japanese Ministry of Education and a leading phonologist.

books, the attempts at devising phonetic alphabets, and the records of the Massachusetts, Connecticut and New York towns, many of them made by unlearned men and written phonetically. One of his conclusions was that most of the peculiarities of American pronunciation have historical precedents in England, and that many of them may be found to this day in the English dialects. Even the nasalization which Englishmen always mark in American speech " is by no means exclusively American." It was charged to the English Puritans by their critics, and is denounced in " Hudibras," Part I, Canto III. Dr. Krapp believed that " differences of practise among standard American speakers, that is, among members of good standing in the community, were formerly much more numerous than they are today," and that they " continue to show an increasing tendency to disappear in an all-embracing uniformity." He demonstrated that many forms now confined to isolated speech-islands, for example, in rural New England or the remoter parts of the South, were once almost universal. He showed that the type of American prevailing in the Boston area and in the tidewater regions of the South is closely related historically to the Southern type of English, and that Western America is derived, at least in large part, from Northern English.[1]

1 Other studies of interest and value are Early American Pronunciation and Syntax, by Henry Alexander, *American Speech*, Dec., 1925, which ante-dated the Krapp book, and Early New England Pronunciation, by Anders Orbeck; Ann Arbor, Mich., 1927, which Krapp saw in MS. A bibliography of American and English pronunciation to the end of 1922 will be found in Arthur G. Kennedy's Bibliography of Writings on the English Language; Cambridge, Mass., 1927. For the period since 1922 the bibliographies published in each issue of *American Speech* and annually in *Publications of the Modern Language Association* may be consulted. Alexander J. Ellis's On Early English Pronunciation, 4 vols.; London, 1869–89, is still invaluable, though in parts it has begun to date. Other useful works on the changes in spoken English are A History of English Sounds, by Henry Sweet; London, 1876; The Sounds of English, by the same; Oxford, 1908; The English Pronunciation at Shakespeare's Time, by R. E. Zachrisson; Upsala, Sweden, 1927; Pronunciation of English Vowels, 1400–1700, by the same; Göteborg, Sweden, 1913; Select Studies in Colloquial English of the Late Middle Ages, by Gösta Langenfelt; Lund, Sweden, 1933; English Pronunciation From the Fifteenth to the Eighteenth Century, by Constance Davies; London, 1934; and English Pronunciation as Described in Shorthand Systems of the Seventeenth and Eighteenth Centuries, by Helge Kökeritz, *Studia Neophilologica*, 1935. A history of Modern Colloquial English, by H. C. Wyld; London, 1920, gives an excellent account of the changes in English since 1450.

2. THE VOWELS

One of the most noticeable differences between Standard English and Standard American lies in the varying pronunciation of *a* in about 150 words in everyday use. The English, in general, prefer the broad *a* of *dark* before *f*, *ft*, *m*, *nch*, *nd*, *nt*, *sk*, *sp*, *ss*, *st* and *th*, as in *laugh*, *draft ca(l)m*, *branch*, *command*, *chant*, *ask*, *clasp*, *grass*, *last* and *path*, whereas most Americans use the flat *a* of *that*.[1] But these preferences are not invariable. There are many Englishmen, otherwise quite orthodox in their speech habits, who incline toward the flat *a* before *n* and *f* and before *s* followed by a consonant,[2] and nearly all of them use it in *fancy*, despite a general American belief, promoted by haw-haw types on the stage, that they always say *fahncy*. They also use it in *stamp*, though they cling to the broad *a* in *example*. Again, they prefer the flat *a* of *rack* in *amass*, *elastic*, *gas*, *lass*, *mass*, *massive*, *masticate* and *plastic*. Finally, they pronounce the verb *can* just as we do, though they sound the broad *a* in *can't*.[3] Contrariwise, most Americans use the broad *a* before *(l)m*, as in *palm*, and virtually all use it before *r*, or *r* and a consonant, as in *bar*, *cart*, *park*, *harm*, etc., and before *th* in *father*. Moreover, it is used in most of the English situations in the Boston area, though with a slight change in value, and in a number of words in the South, *e.g.*, *master*, *aunt*, *tomato*, *tassel*.[4]

It used to be believed that the broad *a* was historically the more respectable, and that the flat *a* had come into American and into some of the English dialects as a corruption, but the exhaustive researches of Krapp have disposed of that notion.[5] During most of the

1 This *a*, of course, is really two *a*'s, the first that of *that* and the other that of *ham*. They differ, however, only in length, and for the present purpose they may be regarded as substantially identical. For a discussion of the situations in which either the one or the other is used see The Pronunciation of Short *A* in American Standard English, by George L. Trager, *American Speech*, June, 1930.

2 The Pronunciation of English, by Daniel Jones; Cambridge, 1914, p. 38.

3 Pronunciation, a Practical Guide to American Standards, by Thorleif Larsen and Francis C. Walker; London, 1930, p. 23 *ff*.

4 J. S. Kenyon has calculated (Flat *A* and Broad *A*, *American Speech*, April, 1930, p. 324) that the number of situations in which the English and American *a*'s differ amounts to 14% of the total situations in which *a* occurs.

5 His conclusions are set forth at length in The English Language in America, Vol. II, p. 36 *ff*.

Eighteenth Century, in fact, a broad *a* was regarded in both England and America as a rusticism, and careful speakers commonly avoided it. When Thomas Sheridan published his "General Dictionary of the English Language" in London in 1780 he actually omitted it from his list of vowels. He had room for an *a* approximating *aw*, as in *hall*, but none for the *a* sounding like *ah*, as in *barn*. He gave the pronunciation of *papa* as if both its *a*'s were that of *pap*, and even ordained the same flat *a* before *r*, as in *car* and *far*. Benjamin Franklin, whose "Scheme for a New Alphabet and a Reformed Mode of Spelling" was published in Philadelphia in 1768, was in complete accord with Sheridan. He favored the flat *a*, not only in all the words which now carry it in American, but also in *calm, far, hardly* and even *what*, which last was thus made to rhyme with *hat*. Franklin's pronunciations were presumably those of the best circles in the London of his time, and it seems likely that they also prevailed in Philadelphia, then the center of American culture. But the broad *a* continued common in the folk-speech of New England, as it was in that of Old England, and in 1780 or thereabout it suddenly became fashionable in Standard London English. How and why this fashion arose is not known, nor is it known what influence it had upon the educated speech of New England. It may be that the New Englanders picked it up, as they picked up so many other English fashions, or it may be that they simply yielded to the folk-speech of their region. Whatever the fact, they were using the broad *a* in many words at the time Noah Webster published his "Dissertations on the English Language" at Boston in 1789. In it he gave *quality, quantity* and *quash* the sound of *a* in *hat*, but he gave *advance, after, ask, balm, clasp* and *grant* the *a* of *arm*. In subsequent editions of "The American Spelling Book" he favored the broad *a* before a final *r* or before *r* followed by a consonant, *e.g., bar, depart;* before (*l*)*m, e.g., embalm;* before a final *s* or *s* followed by a consonant, *e.g., pass, ask;* before *f, e.g., staff, half;* before *th, e.g., path;* before *lv, e.g., salve, calves;* before *n* followed by *ch, s* or *t, e.g., blanch, dance, ant;* in words spelled *au* before *s, e.g., sauce;* in words spelled *au* before *n* followed by *ch, d* or *t, e.g., staunch, jaundice, aunt;* and in a number of other words, *e.g., chamber, slander, gape.*[1] He even advocated the broad *a* in *bracelet*, though in his "Dictionary of the English Language Compiled for the Use of the Com-

---

1 I am indebted here to Krapp, p. 67.

mon Schools in the United States " (1807) he abandoned it for the flat *a*.

Webster's immense authority was sufficient to implant the broad *a* firmly in the speech of the Boston area. Between 1830 and 1850, according to C. H. Grandgent,[1] it ran riot, and was used even in such words as *handsome, matter, apple, caterpillar, pantry, hammer, practical, Saturday* and *satisfaction*. Oliver Wendell Holmes protested against it in " The Autocrat of the Breakfast Table " in 1857, but it survived his onslaught. It has been somewhat modified in sound with the passing of the years. Says Grandgent: " The broad *a* of New Englanders, Italianate though it be, is not so broad as that of Old England. . . . Our *grass* really lies between the *grahs* of a British lawn and the *grass* of the boundless prairies." In the New England cities, he adds, it has been " shaken by contact with the Irish," and is now restricted, in the main to

a few specific classes of words – especially those in which an *a* (sometimes an *au*) is followed by a final *r*, by an *r* that precedes another consonant, by an *m* written *lm*, or by the sound of *f*, *s*, or *th:* as *far, hard, balm, laugh, pass, rather, path*. In the first two categories, and in the word *father*, *ah* possesses nearly all the English-speaking territory; concerning the other classes there is a wide divergence, although flat *a* appears everywhere to be disappearing from words like *balm*. Yankeedom itself is divided over such combinations as *ant, can't, dance, example*, in which a nasal and another consonant follow the vowel; *aunt*, however, always has broad *a*.[2]

The imprimatur of the Yankee Johnson was not sufficient to establish the Boston *a* outside New England. His rival and bitter critic, Lyman Cobb, whose " Just Standard For Pronouncing the English Language " appeared in 1821, allowed it before *th* and *lv* and in words wherein it appeared as *au*, but ordained the flat *a* in *class, clasp, fast, ask, asp, branch, dance, chaff, raft* and their congeners. Webster's other great antagonist, Joseph E. Worcester, whose " Comprehensive Pronouncing and Explanatory Dictionary of the English Language " appeared in 1830, set up a distinction between the true British broad *a* and the modified New England *a* described above by Grandgent, and frowned upon the former. " His hesitation with respect to words like *ask, dance, chaff*, etc.," says Krapp, " was due not to the fear that the sound which he advocated might seem too near [the *a* of *hat*], but too near [the *a* of *bard*]. In

1 Fashion and the Broad *A* in Old and New; Cambridge, Mass., 1920, pp. 25–30.
2 This gradual decay of the Boston *a* is also discussed in Observations on the Broad *A*, by Miles L. Hanley, *Dialect Notes*, Vol. V, Pt. VIII, 1925.

other words, the vulgar extreme which was to be avoided was [the latter and not the former]." William Russell, who published a number of popular textbooks during the second quarter of the century, advocated the flat *a* in all words of the *glass, grasp, past, graft, grant, dance, branch, chant, rather* and *bland* classes. By 1850 it was dominant everywhere west of the Berkshires and south of New Haven, save for what Grandgent calls " a little *ah*-spot in Virginia," and its sound had even got into such proper names as *Alabama* and *Lafayette*.[1] " In the United States beyond the Hudson — perhaps beyond the Connecticut," says Grandgent, " the flat *a* prevails before *f, s, th*, and *n*." Nevertheless, the broad *a* has got into a few words, if not many. Those in which it is followed by *lm* I have mentioned. They were once pronounced to rhyme with *ram* and *jam*, but their pronunciation that way has begun to seem provincial and ignorant. Krapp says that the *a* has likewise broadened in *alms, salmon* and *almond*,[2] but it is my own observation that this is not yet generally true. The first syllable of *salmon*, true enough, does not quite rhyme with *ham*, but it is nevertheless still very far from *palm*. The broad *a*, by a fashionable affectation, has also appeared in *vase, drama, amen* and *tomato* — in the last case probably helped by the example of Southern speech. This intrusion has been vigorously denounced by an Englishman, Evacustes A. Phipson. He says:

> It is really distressing to a cultivated Briton visiting America to find people there who . . . follow what they suppose to be the latest London mannerism, regardless of accuracy. Thus we find one literary editress advocating the pedantic British pronunciation *tomahto* in lieu of the good English *tomato*, rhyming with *potato*, saying it sounds so much more " refined." I do not know whether she would be of the same opinion if she heard one of our costermongers bawling out " 'Ere's yer foine *termarters*, lyde, hownly tuppence a pahnd." Similarly, we sometimes hear Anglomaniac Americans saying *vahz* for *vase*. Why not *bahz*, and *cahz*?[3]

Amen, with the broad *a*, seems to be making progress. E. W. Howe tells a story of a little girl in Kansas whose mother, on acquiring social aspirations, entered the Protestant Episcopal Church from the Methodist Church. The father remaining behind, the little girl had

1 Richard Meade Bache denounced it in *Lafayette*, in his Vulgarisms and Other Errors of Speech, 2nd ed., Philadelphia, 1869, p. 65.
2 The Pronunciation of Standard English in America, above cited, p. 60.

3 New York *Nation*, Aug. 30, 1919, p. 290. See also *Vays, Vayz* or *Vahz*, by Janet R. Aiken, *North American Review*, Dec., 1929.

to learn to say *amen* with the *a* of *rake* when she went to church with her father and *amen* with the *a* of *car* when she went to church with her mother.[1] In Canada, despite the social influence of English usage, the flat *a* has conquered, and along the Canadian-New England border it is actually regarded as a Canadianism, especially in such words as *calm* and *aunt*. The broad *a*, when heard at all, is an affectation, and, as in Boston, is sometimes introduced into words, e.g., *stamp*, which actually have the flat *a* in England. In the United States, save in the Boston area, one never hears it in *gather*, *lather* and *blather*, and even in Boston it is often abandoned for the flat *a* by speakers who are very careful to avoid the latter in *palm*, *dance* and *aunt*. Krapp says that it is used in "some words of foreign origin," notably *lava*, *data*, *errata*, *bas-relief*, *spa*, *mirage* and *garage*, but this is certainly not true of the first three, all of which, save exceptionally, have the flat *a*. So has *piano*, though the Italian *i* is preserved, and *pyano* is now only a vulgarism. *Patent*, in American, always has the *a* of *cat*, but in English the *a* of *late* is often heard when the word is used in the sense of a license or monopoly. In England *mater*, a common synonym for *mother*, has the same *a*, but in the American *alma mater*, which is seldom used in England, the second and third *a*'s are that of *bard*, though the first is commonly that of *pal*. In English the second *a* of *apparatus* is always that of *late*, but in the United States it is often that of *cat*. The same difference is to be noted in the pronunciation of *data*, *gratis*, *status* and *strata*. In *phalanx* it runs the other way, with the English preferring, for the first syllable, the *a* of *rack*, and Americans that of *mate*. In *radio* the usual American pronunciation shows the *a* of *mate*, but the plain people of New York City apparently prefer the *a* of *rack*, and Alfred E. Smith's use of it in 1928 attracted nation-wide attention, and inspired some imitation. There were pundits at the time who argued that Al was right, and cited the analogy of *radical*. The English use a broad *a* in the final syllables of *charade* and *promenade*,

---

1 The Rev. W. G. Polack, of Evansville, Ind., who has made a valuable inquiry into ecclesiastical terminology in America, tells me that among the Lutherans of the Middle West, *amen* has the flat *a* when spoken and the broad *a* when sung. So with the first syllable of *hallelujah*, though the last *a* is always broad. The Baptists appear to follow the same plan. Their denominational papers print frequent notices that *amen* should have the long *a* in hymns but the short *a* in ordinary speech. See, for example, the *Baptist and Commoner* (Little Rock, Ark.), Jan. 2, 1928, and the *Western Recorder* (Louisville, Ky.), Oct. 2, 1924.

but most Americans prefer the *a* of *mate*. In the second syllable of *asphalt* the English always use the *a* of *rack*, but Americans sometimes use the *aw* of *bawl*. In England the *a* of *patriotism* is always the *a* of *rack*, but in the United States it is often that of *late*.[1] Larsen and Walker [2] say that the latter *a* is used by Americans in *ignoramus*, *tornado* and *ultimatum*, but I often hear the *a* of *dram* in *ignoramus*, and either that of *rack* or that of *bar* in *tornado* and *ultimatum*. In *radish* the *a* is sometimes that of *cab* and sometimes a sort of *e*, hard to distinguish from that of *red*. In such proper names as *Alabama*, *Alaska*, *Montana*, *Nevada* and *Colorado* the flat *a* of *has* is often heard, especially in the States themselves, but a broad *a* is certainly not unknown. The usual pronunciation of *again* and *against* gives them a second *a* indistinguishable from the *e* of *hen*, but there is also a spelling pronunciation employing the *a* of *lame*. In the years before the Civil War the plain people converted the *a* of *care* into the *a* of *car* in *bear*, *dare*, *hair* and *where*, into a short *i* in the verb *can*, into a short *e* in *catch*, and into a long *e* in *care*, *scarce* and *chair*, thus producing *bar*, *dar*, *har*, *whar*, *kin*, *ketch*, *keer*, *skeerce* and *cheer*. They flattened the long *a* of *marsh* and omitted the *r*, making the word rhyme with *lash*, and they reduced *sauce* to *sass*, *saucy* to *sassy* and *because* to *becuz* or *bacaze*. The *e* of *learn*, *serve*, *mercy*, *certain* and *eternal* became a broad *a*, producing *larn*, *sarve*, *marcy*, *sartin* and *tarnal;* the *a* of *caught* was flattened, producing *catcht* or *ketcht;* and the *a* of *drain* was turned into a long *e*, producing *dreen*. Some of these toyings with *a* survive, but not all. The rest have been exterminated by the schoolmarm, or forced into exile among the remoter dialects.[3]

There are some differences between the pronunciation of *e* in English and American, but not many. The English use a long *e*, like that of *bee*, in the first syllable of *evolution*, which is always short

1 In his Dissertations on the English Language, 1789, Webster said that the English then made the *a* of *patriotism* long and the Americans made it short. How the double reversal came about I don't know. "In all these cases, where the people are not uniform," said Webster, "I should prefer the short sound, for it appears to me the most analogous." He was probably thinking of *cat* and *rat*.

2 Pronunciation, above cited, p. 24.

3 A long list of the vulgarisms of the late 40's is in the introduction to J. R. Bartlett's Dictionary of Americanisms, 2nd ed.; Boston, 1859. Many of those of a somewhat earlier period are in the glossary attached to The Yankey in England, by David Humphreys; Hartford, 1815. This glossary is reprinted in The Beginnings of American English, edited by M. M. Mathews; Chicago, 1931.

in American. They also prefer a long *e* in *epoch*, but in the United States it is often short. Contrariwise, the English use a short *e* in *penalize, lever* and *egoist*, whereas most Americans prefer a long one. The English are always careful to make the first syllable of *seamstress sem* and that of *cleanly clen*, but Americans commonly stick to the *e* of the stems. In the United States a spelling pronunciation often appears in *pretty*, making the first syllable rhyme with *set;* it always rhymes with *sit* in English. The use of the long *e* in *deaf*, though historically very respectable and ardently advocated by Noah Webster,[1] has disappeared from cultivated American speech; it persists, however, in the vulgate. In the same way the *i*-sound, as in *sit*, has disappeared from *get, yet, general, steady, chest* and *instead;* Benjamin Franklin defended it, but now even the vulgate is losing it: This pronunciation, according to Menner,[2] was correct in Seventeenth Century England, and perhaps down to the middle of the next century. It is probable that the colonists clung to such disappearing usages longer than the English. The latter, according to Webster, were unduly responsive to illogical fashions set by the exquisites of the court and by popular actors. He blames Garrick, in particular, for many innovations, most of them not followed in the colonies. But Garrick was surely not responsible for the displacement of *mercy* by *marcy*, which Webster ascribed somewhat lamely to the fact that the letter *r* is called *ar:* he proposed to dispose of it by changing the *ar* to *er*. In his time the *a* of *lame* was generally heard in *egg, peg, leg* and so on, but it too is now confined to the vulgate, as is the *a* of *bag* in *keg*. As Krapp shows, the neutral *e* that has taken its place, and toward which all our vowels seem to be tending,[3] shows signs of itself disappearing. This is particularly

1 The following is from his Dissertations on the English Language, 1789, p. 128. "*Deaf* is generally pronounced *deef*. It is the universal practice in the Eastern States; and it is general in the Middle and Southern; though some have adopted the English pronunciation, *def*. The latter is evidently a corruption; for the word is in analogy with *leaf* and *sheaf*, and has been from time immemorial." Always his analogies!

2 The Pronunciation of English in America, *Atlantic Monthly*, March, 1915, p. 361.

3 This tendency is not confined to English. The same *e* is encountered in languages as widely differing otherwise as Arabic, French and Swedish. "Its existence," says Sayce, in The Science of Language, Vol. I, p. 259, "is a sign of age and decay; meaning has become more important than outward form, and the educated intelligence no longer demands a clear pronunciation in order to understand what is said."

noticeable, in American, in such words as *moral, quarrel* and *real,* which become *mor'l, quar'l* and *reel,* each a single syllable. In the vulgar speech this neutral *e* is also dropped from other words, notably *poem, diary, violet* and *diamond,* which become *pome, di'ry, vi'let* and *di'mond.* Even in Standard American it grows shadowy in the second syllables of *fertile, hostile, docile, servile, agile, reptile,* etc. In Standard English these words are pronounced with the second syllables rhyming with *vile,* but the English use a short *i* in *fragile* and *facile.* They also use it in *senile,* which commonly shows the long *i* in American. The long *e*-sound in *creek* and *creature* is maintained in Standard American, but changed to the short *i* of *sit* in the vulgate. *Sleek* has divided into two words, *slick* and *sleek,* the former signifying cunning and ingratiating, and the latter referring especially to appearance. Of late there has been a strong tendency to abandon the old *e*-sound in such terms as *bronchitis* and *appendicitis* for an *ai*-sound, as in *pie* and *buy;* this is a senseless affectation, but it seems to be making progress. A contrary movement to abandon the old *ai*-sound in *iodine, quinine,* etc., for an *e*-sound, as in *sleep,* has better support in etymology, but is apparently less popular. *Chlorine* and *vaccine* are always pronounced with the *e*-sound, but *iodine* continues to be *iodyne, strychnine* is still usually *strychnyne,* and *kin-een* for *quinine* still sounds strange. In two other familiar words the *ai*-sound has been supplanted in American: in *sliver* by the short *i* of *liver,* and in *farina* by an *e*-sound. Both have the *ai*-sound in Standard English. *Dynasty,* in American, has a first syllable like *dine,* but in English it is *din. Isolate* is always *eye-solate* in English, but sometimes it is *iss-solate* in American. *Tribunal* and *simultaneous* have the *y*-sound in American, the short *i* in English. *Misogynist* has the short *i* in American but the long one of *mice* in English. *Been,* in American, is almost always *bin* or *ben; bean* never appears save as a conscious affectation. But in England *bean* is preferred.

Webster, in his "Dissertations on the English Language," favored the pronunciation of *either* and *neither* as *ee-ther* and *nee-ther,* and so did most of the other authorities of the time, whether American or English. But the pronunciation of the words as *eye-ther* and *nye-ther* has been common in New England for a century or more, and at an earlier date they had been pronounced *ay-ther* and *nay-ther,* a usage still surviving in the English of Ireland. How the fashion for the *eye*-pronunciation arose is not known, but it was raging on both sides of the ocean by the middle of the Nineteenth Century, and is still in force. It was resisted stoutly by all the contemporary American virtuosi of language, including Edward S. Gould, W. D. Whitney and Richard Grant White. Said Gould in the middle 60's:

> A common reply, in the United States, to the question, "Why do you say *i-ther* and *ni-ther?*" is, "The words are so pronounced by the best educated people in England." But that reply is *not true*. That is to say, a majority of the best English usage is not on that side of the question. All that any man in the United States can *gain* by the pronunciation of *i-ther* and *ni-ther* is the credit, or the discredit, of affectation, or ostentation, — as who should say, "*I* know how they do it in England"; for assuredly, that pronunciation is not sanctioned by a majority of *our* best-educated men.[1]

Whitney, in 1867, admitted the *eye-ther* and *nye-ther* were spreading in the United States, but denounced them as "the deliberate choice of persons who fancy that there is something more *recherché*, more English " in them.[2] Seven years later he called the fashion for them " a relentless and senseless infection, which can only be condemned and ought to be stoutly opposed and put down," and said that those Americans who had succumbed to it " ought to realize with shame the folly of which they have been guilty, and reform." [3] White, who was ordinarily something of an Anglomaniac, and strongly favored the broad *a*, nevertheless declared in 1870 that there was " no authority, either of analogy or of the best speakers, for *eye-ther* and *nye-ther*," and called their use " an affectation, and in this country, a copy of a second-rate British affectation." [4] But they continued to make headway in both England and the United States. The Oxford Dictionary, in 1897, gave the preference to *ee-ther* and *nee-ther*, but admitted that *eye-ther* and *nye-ther* were " somewhat more prevalent in educated English speech." H. W. Fowler, in " A Dictionary of Modern English Usage " (1926), predicted that they would " probably prevail," though adding that they were " not more correct" than *ee-ther* and *nee-ther*. " Webster's New International " (1934) held out for the latter, but gave *eye-ther* and *nye-ther* as variants. It used to be believed that they came into use in

1 Good English; New York, 1867, pp. 42–43. This book was a reprint of articles contributed to the New York *Evening Post*, then edited by William Cullen Bryant.
2 Language and the Study of Language; New York, 1867, p. 43.
3 The Elements of English Pronunciation, in Oriental and Linguistic Studies; New York, 1874, p. 221.
4 Words and Their Uses; New York, 1876. My quotations are from the revised edition, 1876, pp. 263–4.

England on the accession of George I, who, speaking English badly, gave the diphthong its German value, but Dr. Louise Pound has demonstrated that this theory was nonsense.[1]

Hilaire Belloc has said that " every vowel sound without exception " has taken in the United States "some different value from what it has " in England.[2] This is an exaggeration, but there is sufficient truth in it to give it a certain plausibility. Even the *a* of such common words as *cab, back* and *hand* differs in the two countries: when Englishmen speak them rapidly they often sound, to American ears, like *keb, beck* and *hend*. In the United States, in keeping with our generally more precise habits of speech, they are pronounced more clearly. The differences between the English *o* in *rock* and the American *o* in the same word have long engaged phonologists. The former is described by Larsen and Walker[3] as " a lightly rounded vowel, not usually found in General American Speech, though it is close to the short form of the American *aw* heard in the opening syllables of *authentic* and *autocracy* "; the latter is " the shortened *ah*-sound usually heard in *what, not*, as pronounced in General American Speech." They go on:

> Cultivated English speakers do not recognize this *ah*-sound in the words commonly spelled in *o*, e.g., *not, rod, rock, fog, hop, rob, pomp, on, beyond, novel;* English phoneticians indeed condemn it as dialectal in these words, and recognize only the first sound described above. In American, on the other hand, both sounds are heard in all these words, the shortened *ah*-sound being preferred in all positions. Both sounds are heard in American speech also in the *wa* words, e.g., *wander, want, wash, watch, swamp, swan, quarrel, squander, squalid;* but here too the shortened *ah*-sound is preferred.

Yet a third sound is sometimes heard in these *wa* words — it is a downright *aw*. One encounters it in *water, wash, swamp, swan* and *squalid*, which become, roughly, *wawter, wawsh, swawmp, swawn* and *squawlid*. It also appears in *God*, which may be variously *God*

1 On the Pronunciation of *Either* and *Neither, American Speech,* June, 1932. A very informing and amusing paper. Dr. Pound quotes the following from The Lady Buyer, by Frances Anne Allen, *American Mercury,* Feb., 1928: " [The department-store lady buyer] may say *Eye-talian* even after having been sent abroad for her firm, she may write *formally* for *formerly* and *shamme* for *chamois,* and may unashamedly flaunt a dozen grammatical errors, but always standing her in good stead, and ready at the tip of her tongue, is her crystal-clear British pronunciation of *either.* . . . Nothing on earth could make her whisper *ee-ther* in the darkest corner of the stock-room."

2 The Contrast; New York, 1924, p. 225.

3 Pronunciation, above cited, p. 46.

(rhyming with *nod*), *Gahd* or *Gawd*. The first of the three, I believe, is commonly regarded as the most formal, and I have often noticed that a speaker who says *Gawd* in his ordinary discourse will switch to *God* (or maybe *Gahd*) when he wants to show reverence. Miss Sarah T. Barrows of the State Teachers College at San José, Calif., once determined the practice of 268 university students, all born in Iowa, in the pronunciation of *watch*, *water* and *wash*. She found that 156 preferred the *ah*-sound in *watch*, 96 the *aw*-sound and 16 the English *o*-sound. In *water* their preferences ran 128, 80 and 80, and in *wash* 165, 58 and 45.[1] In the Eighteenth Century, as Krapp's researches show,[2] it was not unheard of for the *a* of *care* to be used in such words. Thus, the poets of the time rhymed *war* not only with *care*, but also with *air*, *dare*, *glare*, *forbear*, *spare*, *share*, *blare*, *snare*, *despair*, *bear*, *bare* and *prepare*. But the rhymes of poets are not always to be trusted, and it is to be noted that those examined by Krapp also occasionally rhymed *war* with *car*, *mar*, *far*, *jar*, *scar* and *tar*. In any case, it began to be rhymed with *more* after the beginning of the Nineteenth Century. At the present time its *a* is substantially equivalent to the *o* of *story*, but *ah* is also heard. In words containing *au*, *aw* or *ou* the sound is usually *aw*, but in the vulgar speech a flat *a* like that of *land* gets into *haunt*, *jaundice* and sometimes *launch*. *Laundry* may be *lawndry*, *lahndry* or *londry*. *Aunt*, of course, is *ant* to the plain people everywhere, save in the Boston area and parts of the South.

Usage in the pronunciation of *u* still differs widely in the United States. Two sounds, that of *oo* in *goose* and that of *u* in *bush*, are used by different speakers in the same word. The *oo*-sound prevails in *aloof*, *boot*, *broom*, *food*, *groom*, *proof*, *roof*, *rood*, *room*, *rooster*, *root*, *soon*, *spook*, *spoon* and *woof*, and the *u*-sound in *butcher*, *cooper*, *hoof*, *hoop*, *nook*, *rook* and *soot*, but there are educated Americans who employ the *oo*-sound in *coop*, *hoof* and *hoop*. In *hooves* and *rooves* I have heard both sounds. *Rooves* seems to be extinct in the written speech as the plural of *roof*, but it certainly survives in spoken American. In words of the *com*-class, save *company*, Americans substitute *ah* for the *u* used by Englishmen; even *compass* often shows it. So do *constable* and *conjure*. The English are far more careful with the shadowy *y* preceding *u* in words of

1 *Watch, Water, Wash, American Speech*, April, 1929.   2 The English Language in America, Vol. II, p. 83.

the *duty* class than Americans. The latter retain it in the initial position and in the medial position when unstressed, but omit it in almost all other situations. *Nyew, nyude, dyuke, Tyuesday, enthyusiasm, styupid* and *syuit* would seem affectations in most parts of the United States.[1] The schoolmarm still battles valiantly for *dyuty*, but in vain. In 1912 the Department of Education of New York City warned all the municipal high-school teachers to combat the *oo*-sound [2] but it is doubtful that one pupil in a hundred was thereby induced to insert the *y* in *induced*. In *figure*, however, Americans retain the *y*-sound, whereas the English drop it. Noah Webster was violently against it in all situations. The English lexicographer, John Walker, had argued for it in his "Critical Pronouncing Dictionary and Expositor of the English Language," 1791, but Webster's prestige, while he lived, remained so high in some quarters that he carried the day, and the older professors at Yale, it is said, continued to use *natur* down to 1839. In the South a *y* is sometimes inserted before *a, i* or *o*, especially following *k*, e.g., in *cyard, Cyarter, kyind, cyow*. This intrusion of the *y* was formerly common in New England also, and as Krapp says, "is not yet wholly extinct." In *lieutenant* the Englishman pronounces the first syllable *lef* or *lev;* the American makes it *loo*. White says that the prevailing American pronunciation is relatively recent. "I never heard it," he reports, "in my boyhood." [3] He was born in New York in 1821. Nevertheless, it was advocated by Walker in 1793. The word was originally French, and *loo* comes closer to the original pronunciation than *lef* or *lev*. How the latter form arose is uncertain.[4]

In Middle English the diphthong *oi* was pronounced like the *oy* of *boy*, but during the early Modern English period the pronunciation became assimilated with that of *i* in *wine*, and this usage prevailed at the time of the settlement of America. The colonists thus brought it with them, and at the same time it lodged in Ireland, where it still prevails. But in England, during the late Eighteenth Century

1 A woman teacher of English, born in Tennessee, tells me that the *y*-sound is much more persistent in the South than in the North. "I have never," she says, "heard a native Southerner fail to retain the sound in *new*. The same is true of *duke, stew, due, duty* and *Tuesday*. But it is not true of *blue* and *true*."

2 High School Circular No. 17, June 19, 1912.
3 Every-Day English; Boston, 1881, p. 243.
4 There is an inconclusive discussion of the question in the Oxford Dictionary, under *lieutenant*.

this *i*-sound was displaced in many words by the original *oi*-sound, not by historical research but by deduction from the spelling, and that new pronunciation soon extended to the polite speech of America. In the common speech, however, the *i*-sound persisted, and down to the time of the Civil War it was constantly heard in such words as *boil, hoist, oil, join, spoil, joist, pennyroyal, poison* and *roil*, which thus became *bile, hist, ile, jine, spile, jist, pennyr'yal, pisen* and *rile*. Even *brile* for *broil* was sometimes noted. Since then the schoolmarm has combated the *i*-sound with such vigor that it has begun to disappear, and such forms as *pisen, bile* and *ile* are seldom heard. But in certain other words, perhaps supported by Irish influence, the *i*-sound still persists. Chief among them are *hoist* and *roil*. An unlearned American, wishing to say that he was enraged, never says that he was *roiled*, but always that he was *riled*. Desiring to examine the hoof of a horse, he never orders the animal to *hoist* but always to *hist*. In the form of *booze-hister*, the latter is almost in good usage. In the coal-mines of Southern Illinois *hoist* is pronounced correctly in *hoisting-engineer*, but he always *hists* the coal.[1] *Jine* as a verb has retired to certain dialects, but the noun *jiner*, signifying a man given to joining fraternal orders, is still in common use. Most of the other vowel changes in vulgar American are also to be encountered in the British dialects. A flat *a* displaces the long *e* in *rear* (*e.g.*, as a horse) and the short *e* of *thresh* and *wrestle*, producing *rare, thrash* and *wrassle*. In the days before the Civil War a short *i* displaced *o* in *cover* and *e* in *chest* and *kettle*, producing *kiver, chist* and *kittle*, but now only *kittle* is heard. *Jedge* for *judge* and *empire* for *umpire* survive more or less, but *jest* and *jist* for *just* are almost extinct. So are *leetle* for *little, fust* for *first, sech* for *such*, and *tech* for *touch*. But *shet* for *shut* is still in use and so is *gal* for *girl*. The substitution of *guardeen* and *champeen* for *guardian* and *champion* is very common. So is that of *snoot* for *snout*. So is that of *muss* for *mess*. In *jaundice* not only is the *a* flattened, but the final syllable becomes *-ers*. One *stamps* a letter but *stomps* with the foot. This last differentiation seems to have a number of parallels in English: the case of *strap* and (razor)-*strop* suggests itself at once. In vulgar American a horse *chomps* its bit, but *champ* remains a good shortened form of *champeen*. Similarly, a cow *tromps* her fodder,

1 I am indebted here to Dr. H. K. Croessmann, of Du Quoin, Ill.

but a vagrant remains a *tramp.* By assimilation *cartoon* (a drawing) has been substituted for *carton* (a cardboard package). The last syllables of *engine* and *genuine* often rhyme with *line.* Webster said in his " Dissertations on the English Language " (1789) that *mought* for *might* was then " heard in most of the States, but not frequently except in a few towns." It has now gone out, but the American Freemasons still use the archaic *mote* for *may* in their occult ceremonials.

I have spoken of the American pronunciation of a few foreign words, *e.g., piano, tornado, alma mater,* the medical terms in *-itis* and the chemical terms in *-ine.* George O. Curme, a distinguished authority, says that in the plural of Latin words in *-a* the final *-ae* is " pronounced as *e* in *react*"[1] but it is my observation that *-ay* is more often heard, and Larsen and Walker give it as a variant. Certainly *vertebray* is commoner than *vertebree,* and *alumnay* is at least as common as *alumnee.* On the level of refined discourse some effort is made in the United States to approximate the correct pronunciation of loan-words from living languages, and it would be unusual to hear an American medical man pronounce *röntgenogram* as if the first two syllables were *runtgen* — the pronunciation recommended to English radio announcers in " Broadcast English." Even among the plain people loan-words brought in by word of mouth are commonly pronounced more or less plausibly, *e.g., kosher, cabaret, buffet, chauffeur, chiffon, chef, négligé, frau, seidel, gesundheit, männerchor* and *café.* I have, however, heard *kaif* for *café,* and among the words first apprehended in print *brasseer* is common for *brassière, porteer* for *portière, jardeneer* for *jardinière, ratskiller* for *ratskeller, huffbrow* for *hofbräu, vawdvil* for *vaudeville, dash'und* for *dachshund, camoofladge* for *camouflage, shammy* for *chamois, fyancy* for *fiancée, massoor* for *masseur, de-bút* for *début, likkare* for *liqueur, nee* for *née, premeer* for *première, meenoo* for *menu, switeser* for *schweizer, ródeo* for *rodéo,* and *coop* for *coupé.* In the *Hinterwald* the musical terms brought it by wandering performers undergo a radical transformation. *Prélude* becomes *prelood, berceuse* becomes *bersoose, étude* becomes *ee-tude, scherzo* becomes *shirt-so,* and *träumerei* becomes *trowmerai.* Some years ago the word *protégé* had a brief vogue in fistic circles, and was often used by

1 Parts of Speech and Accidence;
Boston, 1935, p. 119.

announcers at prize-fights. They always pronounced it *proteege*. I once heard a burlesque show manager, in announcing a French dancing act, pronounce *M.* and *Mlle.* as *Em* and *Milly*. And who doesn't remember

> As I walked along the *Boys Boo-long*
> With an independent air

and

> Say *aw re-vore*,
> But not good-by!

Charles James Fox, it is said, called the red wine of France *Bordox* to the end of his days. He had an American heart; his great speeches for the revolting colonies were more than mere oratory. John Bright, another kind friend in troubled days, had one too. He always said *Bordox* and *Calass*.

3. THE CONSONANTS

The generally more distinct utterance of Americans preserves a number of consonants that have begun to decay in Standard English. The English have not only made a general slaughter of *r*; they also show a tendency to be careless about *l*, *d*, *g* and *t*, at least in certain situations, and even on the level of the best usage they drop a few *h*'s. An American always sounds the first *l* in *fulfill*; an Englishman commonly makes the first syllable *foo*. An American sounds the *d* in *kindness*; an Englishman doesn't. An American sounds the final *t* in *trait*, and usually the *t* in *often* also; an Englishman makes the first word homologous with *tray* and reduces the second to *off'n*. In the United States the final *g* in the *-ing* words is usually sounded clearly, at least by speakers of any education; in England it often disappears, and indeed its omission is fashionable, and a mark of social status.[1] Next after the use of the broad *a*, the elision of *r* before consonants and in the terminal position is the thing that Americans

---

1 " Why a dropped *g* should be considered to be good English," says St. John Ervine in The Curse of " Refanement," London *Daily Mail*, Aug. 30, 1926, " when a dropped *h* is considered to be a sign of ill-breeding I cannot imagine; but seemingly if those who drop their final *g*'s took to dropping their initial *h*'s, while those who drop their *h*'s took to dropping their *g*'s instead, *h*-dropping would be ' the best English ' and *g*-dropping would be damnable. The ' best people,' whoever they may be, have fashions of speech that are as vulgar as that of ' the worst people.' " Krapp shows that the change of *ng* to *n* was probably common in early American.

are always most conscious of in English speech. In 1913 the late Robert Bridges belabored the English clergy for saying "the *sawed* of the *Laud*" instead of "the *sword* of the *Lord*"[1] and six years later he drew up a list of homophones, showing that the following pairs and triplets were pronounced exactly alike by his countrymen: *alms-arms, aunt-aren't, balm-barm, board-bored-bawd, hoar-whore-haw, lorn-lawn, pore-paw, source-sauce, saw-soar-sore, stalk-stork, taut-taught-tort, father-farther, ah-are, bah-bar-baa, taw-tore, raw-roar, more-maw, floor-flaw.*[2] "The majority of educated Englishmen," says Robert J. Menner, "certainly do not pronounce the *r* before a consonant. Just as certainly the majority of educated Americans pronounce it distinctly."[3] John S. Kenyon estimates that two-thirds of all Americans do so.[4] The violent Anglophile, Henry James, revisiting the United States after many years in England, was so distressed by this clear sounding of *r* that he denounced it as "a morose grinding of the back teeth,"[5] and became so sensitive to it that he began to hear it where it was actually non-existent, save as an occasional barbarism, *e.g.*, in *Cuba-r, vanilla-r* and *California-r*. He put the blame for it, and for various other departures from the strict canon of Oxford English, upon "the American school, the American newspaper, and the American Dutchman and Dago," and went on piously:

> There are, you see, sounds of a mysterious intrinsic meanness, and there are sounds of a mysterious intrinsic frankness and sweetness; and I think the recurrent note I have indicated — *fatherr* and *motherr* and *otherr, waterr* and *matterr* and *scatterr, harrd* and *barrd, parrt, starrt,* and (dreadful to say) *arrt* (the repetition it is that drives home the ugliness), are signal specimens of what becomes of a custom of utterance out of which the principle of taste has dropped.

James's observations must have been made west of the Connecticut river and north of the Potomac, for in the Boston area and in all of the South save the mountain region *r* is elided in something

---

John Walker, in his Critical Pronouncing Dictionary and Expositor of the English Language; London, 1791, argued for dropping the g in the final syllables of participles of verbs ending in g, *e.g., singing* and *ringing.*

1 A Tract on the Present State of English Pronunciation; Oxford, 1913.

2 On English Homophones; Oxford, 1919.

3 The Pronunciation of English in America, *Atlantic Monthly*, March, 1915, p. 362.

4 Some Notes on American R, *American Speech*, March, 1926, p. 333.

5 The Question of Our Speech; Boston, 1905, p. 29.

resembling the English manner.[1] H. C. Wyld offers evidences [2] that
it was lost before consonants " at least as early as the Fifteenth Century," and especially before -*s* and -*sh*, as in *sca'cely* and *ma'sh*.
Krapp gives many examples from the early American town records,
and calls attention to the fact that there are survivals in vulgar
American, as in *cuss, bust, passel* (for *parcel*) and *hoss*.[3] Toward the
end of the Eighteenth Century it became fashionable in England to
omit the *r* and Samuel Johnson helped that fashion along by denouncing the "rough snarling letter." It is now omitted in the
middle of words before all consonants, and at the end of words unless the following word of the sentence begins with a vowel. It is
retained, says Wyld, " initially, and when preceded by another consonant, before vowels," as in *run* and *grass;* " in the middle of words
between vowels," as in *starry* and *hearing;* and usually, " at the end
of words when the next word begins with a vowel, and there is no
pause in the sentence between the words," as in *for ever, over all* and
her ear. But Wyld admits that even in the last-named situation " the
younger generation " denies it clear utterance. In the American
South it is boldly omitted. No Tidewater Virginian says *over all;* he
says *ovah all*. Krapp speculates somewhat inconclusively regarding
the preservation of the *r* in General American. He says that the emigration to the West was largely made up of New Englanders from
west of the Connecticut, and that in that region the *r* was always
sounded. He alludes, too, to the probable influence of Scottish and
Irish immigrants. " Perhaps also," he adds,

formal instruction in the schools and the habit of reading have not been without influence in the Western pronunciation of *r*. New England has also had
its schools and its readers, but students of language are frequently called upon
to observe that only in unsettling social circumstances, such as migration, do
forces which may long have been present exert their full power.[4]

1 In the New York dialect it is lost
between the neutral vowel and a
consonant, as in *thoid, boid, goil,*
etc., but that is only on the vulgar
level.
2 A History of Modern Colloquial
English; London, 1920, p. 298.
3 The English Language in America,
Vol. II, p. 220.
4 The English Language in America,
p. 231. There is a long and interesting discussion of the variations in
the American *r* in Some Notes on

American *R*, by John S. Kenyon,
American Speech, March, 1926. See
also The Dog's Letter, by C. H.
Grandgent, in Old and New;
Cambridge, Mass., 1920; Loss of *R*
in English Through Dissimilation,
by George Hempl, *Dialect Notes*,
Vol. I, Pt. VI, 1893, and The
Humorous *R*, by Louise Pound,
American Mercury, Oct., 1924,
p. 233 *ff*. Dr. Pound deals with
such forms as *dorg, purp, schoolmarm, orter* and *orf*. She shows

The majority of Americans seem to have early abandoned all effort to sound the *h* in such words as *when* and *where*. It is still supposed to be sounded in England, and its absence is often denounced as an American barbarism, but as a matter of fact few Englishmen actually sound it, save in the most formal discourse. Some time ago the English novelist, Archibald Marshall, published an article in a London newspaper arguing that it was a sheer physical impossibility to sound the *h* correctly. " You cannot pronounce *wh*," he said, " if you try. You have to turn it into *hw* to make it any different from *w*." Nevertheless, Mr. Marshall argued, with true English orthodoxy, that the effort should be made. " Most words of one syllable beginning with *wh*," he said, " and many of two syllables have a corresponding word, but of quite different meaning, beginning with *w* alone. *When-wen, whether-weather, while-wile, whither-wither, wheel-weal*. If there is a distinction ready to hand it is of advantage to make use of it." That is to say, to make use of *hwen, hwether, hwile, hwither* and *hweel*. The Americans do not sound the *h* in *heir, honest, honor, hour* and *humor* and their derivatives, and frequently omit it in *herb, humble* and *humility*. In the vulgar speech *herb* is often *yarb*. In Standard English *h* is openly omitted from *hostler*, even in spelling, and is seldom clearly sounded in *hotel* and *hospital*. Certain English words in which it is now sounded apparently betray its former silence by the fact that not *a* but *an* is commonly put before them. It is still good English usage to write *an hotel* and *an historical*.[1] The intrusion of *h* into words

that when a *r* is intruded in English humorous writing, as in *larf, gorn*, and *arnswer* it is not intended to be pronounced: it simply indicates that the preceding vowel is to have the sound of *a* in *father*.

[1] In Concerning the American Language, which Mark Twain included in The Stolen White Elephant; Hartford, 1882, and described as " part of a chapter crowded out of A Tramp Abroad," he represented himself as saying to an Englishman met on a train in Germany: " If the signs are to be trusted even your educated classes used to drop the *h*. They say *humble* now [with the clear *h*], and *heroic*, and *historic*, etc., but I judge that they used to drop those *h*'s because your

writers still keep up the fashion of putting an *an* before those words instead of an *a*. This is what Mr. Darwin might call a 'rudimentary' sign that *an* was justifiable once, and useful — when your educated classes used to say *'umble*, and *'eroic*, and *'istorical*. Correct writers of the American language do not put *an* before those words." But a correspondent sends me the following argument for the use of *an*: " My sense of euphony (and, I believe, the genius of the English language) requires something between the *a* and the *h*-sound in all such cases. Witness the absence of English words showing such a combination. I believe that all English words beginning with *a*, in which

where it doesn't belong, a familiar characteristic of Cockney English, is unknown in any of the American dialects. The authority of Webster was sufficient to establish the American pronunciation of *schedule*. In England the *sch* is always given the soft sound, but Webster decided for the hard sound as in *scheme*. The name of the last letter of the alphabet, which is always *zed* in England, is often made *zee* in the United States. Thornton shows that this Americanism arose in the Eighteenth Century. Americans give *nephew* (following a spelling pronunciation, historically incorrect) a clear *f*-sound instead of the clouded English *v*-sound. They show some tendency to abandon the *ph(f)*-sound in *diphtheria*, *diphthong* and *naphtha*, for a plain *p*-sound.[1] English usage prefers a clear *s*-sound in such words as *issue* and *sensual*, but in America the sound is commonly that of *sh*. English usage prefers a clear *tu*-sound in *actual*, *punctuate*, *virtue*, and their like, but in America the *tu* tends to become *choo*. On the vulgar level *amateur* is always *amachoor*, and *picture* is *pitchur* or *pitcher*. *Literature* is *literater* in elegant American and *litrachoor* among the general; in England it is *litrachua* or *litrichua*. The American plain people have some difficulty with *t* and *d*. They add a *t* to *close*, *wish* and *once*, and displace *d* with *t* in *hold*, which becomes *holt*. In *told* and *old* they abandon the *d* altogether, preferring *tole* and *ole*. *Didn't* is pronounced *di'n't*, and *find* becomes indistinguishable from *fine*. The same letter is often dropped before consonants, as in *bran(d)-new*, *goo(d)-sized* and *corne(d)-beef*. The old *ax* for *ask* is now confined to a few dialects; in the current vulgate *ast* is substituted for it. The *t* is dropped in *bankrup*, *kep*, *slep*, *crep*, *quanity* and *les* (*let's*). The *l* is omitted from *a'ready* and *gent'man*, and the first *g* from *reco'nize*. As in Standard English, there is a frequent dropping of *g* in the *-ing* words, but it is usually preserved in *anything* and *everything*.[2] The

---

a syllable beginning with *h* follows, are dissyllables. That is to say, the *h*-syllable is accented. Witness *ahead*, *ahoy*, *ahem*." See Text, Type and Style, by George B. Ives; Boston, 1921, p. 269, and A and An Before H and Certain Vowels, by Louis Feipel, *American Speech*, Aug., 1929.

1 See Some Variant Pronunciations in the New South, by William A.

Read, *Dialect Notes*, Vol. III, Pt. VII, 1911, p. 504 *ff.*

2 The late Ring Lardner once said: "I used, occasionally, to sit on the players' bench at baseball games, and it was there that I noted the exceptions made in favor of these two words. A player, returning to the bench after batting, would be asked, 'Has he got *anything* in there?' ('He – in there' always

substitution of *th* for *t* in *height,* like the addition of *t* to *once,* seems to be an heirloom from the English of two centuries ago, but the excrescent *b,* as in *chimbley* and *fambly,* is apparently native. There are many parallels for the English butchery of *extraordinary;* for example, *bound'ry, pro'bition, int'res', gover'ment, chrysanthe'um, Feb'uary, hist'ry, lib'ry* and *prob'ly. Ordinary* is commonly enunciated clearly, but it has bred a degenerated form, *onry* or *onery,* differentiated in meaning.[1] Consonants are misplaced by metathesis, as in *prespiration, hunderd, brethern, childern, interduce, calvary, govrenment,* and *modren. Ow* is changed to *er,* as in *piller, swaller, beller* and *holler,* or to *a,* as in *fella,* or to *i* as in *minni (minnow).* Words are given new syllables, as in *ellum, fillum, reality* (realty), *lozenger, athaletic, bronichal, blasphemious, mischievious, Cubéan, mountainious, tremendious, mayórality* and *municipial,* or new consonants, as in *overhall* and *larcensy.*[2] In *yes* the terminal consonant is often omitted, leaving the vowel, which is that of *desk,* unchanged. This form is sometimes represented in print by *yeah,* which suggests *yay* and is inaccurate. But there are many other forms of *yes,* and Dr. Louise Pound once gathered no less than 37 in a single group of students at the University of Nebraska.[3] St. John Ervine, the Anglo-Irish critic, who is ordinarily extremely hospitable to Americanisms, has carried on a crusade against these American *yeses,* and especially against the one which omits the *s* and the one usually represented by *yep,* which last, he says, " can sometimes be heard on English tongues." He has denounced both as " disgusting." [4] " These variations of a single English word," he says, " are inevitable in a country with a polyglot population. . . . When an American immigrant says *yah* or *yep* he is probably trying to say *yes,* just as a baby when it mispronounces a word is trying to pronounce it cor-

means the pitcher.) The answer would be ' He's got *everything.*' On the other hand, the player might return and (usually after striking out) say, ' He ain't got *nothin'.*' And the manager: ' Looks like he must have *somethin'.*' "
1 This word, when written, often appears as *ornery,* but it is almost always pronounced *on'ry,* with the first syllable rhyming with *don.*
2 Not infrequently such forms are used by the sophisticated, especially in the halls of learning, for humor-

ous effect. See Intentional Mispronunciations, by Margaret Reed, *American Speech,* Feb., 1932. But in a headline in the San Francisco *Chronicle,* June 29, 1931, *mayorality* was printed quite seriously, and in Baltimore there is an *Autogenius* Company which does autogenous welding.
3 Popular Variants of *Yes, American Speech,* Dec., 1926.
4 English – According to American *Skedule,* London *Evening Standard,* Sept. 23, 1929.

rectly." [1] He says that the *yes* without the *s* sounds as if the speaker "had started out to say *yes*, but had suddenly contracted a violent pain in his stomach and was unable to sound the sibilant." *No* sometimes picks up a terminal *p*, and becomes *nope*.

4. DIALECTS

All the early writers on the American language remarked its strange freedom from dialects. The first of them to deal with it at length, the Rev. John Witherspoon, thus sought to account for the fact:

> The vulgar in America speak much better than the vulgar in Great Britain for a very obvious reason, *viz.*, that being much more unsettled, and moving frequently from place to place, they are not so liable to local peculiarities either in accent or phraseology. There is a greater difference in dialect between one county and another in Britain than there is between one State and another in America.[2]

Timothy Dwight and John Pickering took the same line. "In the United States," said Dwight in 1815, "there is not, I presume, a descendant of English ancestors whose conversation is not easily and perfectly intelligible to every other." [3] "It is agreed," said Pickering a year later, "that there is a greater uniformity of dialect throughout the United States (in consequence of the frequent removals of people from one part of the country to another) than is to be found in England." [4] The Rev. Jonathan Boucher, whose glossary was published in 1832, was of the same mind. "There is, properly speaking," he said, "no dialect in America . . . unless some scanty remains of the croaking, guttural idioms of the Dutch, still observable in New York; the Scotch-Irish, as it used to be called, in some of the back settlers of the Middle States; and the whining, canting drawl brought by some republican, Oliverian and Puritan emigrants from the West of England, and still kept up by their un-

1 Quoted from the London *Spectator* in *American Speech*, June, 1927, p. 413.
2 The Druid, No. V, May 9, 1781, reprinted in The Beginnings of American English, by M. M. Mathews; Chicago, 1931, p. 16. For the testimony of other early observers see British Recognition of American Speech in the Eighteenth Century, by Allen Walker Read,

Dialect Notes, Vol. VI, Pt. VI, July, 1933.
3 Remarks on the Review of Inchiquin's Letters, Published in the *Quarterly Review*; Boston, 1815.
4 A Vocabulary or Collection of Words and Phrases Which Have Been Supposed to be Peculiar to the United States of America; Boston, 1816, prefatory essay. It is reprinted in Mathews, just cited.

regenerated descendants of New England — may be called dialects." [1]
J. Fenimore Cooper, already quoted in praise of American speech in
Section 1 of this chapter, agreed thoroughly with Witherspoon,
Pickering and Boucher. He said in 1828:

If the people of this country were like the people of any other country
on earth we should be speaking at this moment a great variety of nearly
unintelligible patois, but . . . there is not, probably, a man (of English descent) born in this country who would not be perfectly intelligible to all
whom he should meet in the streets of London, though a vast number of
those he met would be nearly unintelligible to him. . . . This resemblance in
speech can only be ascribed to the great diffusion of intelligence, and to
the inexhaustible activity of the people which, in a manner, destroys space.[2]

Cooper added that such meager dialects as were to be encountered
in the United States were fast wearing down to uniformity. The
differences between New England, New York and Pennsylvania
speech, he said, " were far greater twenty years ago than they are
now." A generation later George P. Marsh reported that this iron-
ing out had been arrested. " I think no Eastern man," he said, " can
hear a native of the Mississippi Valley use the *o* vocative, or observe
the Southern pronunciation of ejaculatory or other emphatic phrases,
without perceiving a very marked though often indescribable difference between their and our utterance of the same things." But
Marsh was still convinced that American was singularly uniform.
He said:

Not only is the *average* of English used here, both in speaking and writing, better than that of the great mass of the English people; but there are
fewer local peculiarities of form and articulation in our vast extent of
territory than on the comparatively narrow soil of Great Britain. In spite of
disturbing and distracting causes, English is more emphatically one in America
than in its native land.[3]

A great many other authorities might be quoted, all supporting
the same doctrine. I choose two, both from the year 1919. The first
is the anonymous Englishman who edited the monthly called *English*, now defunct.[4] In his issue for October he said:

The citizen of the United States can travel from the Atlantic seaboard to
the Pacific, from the Great Lakes to the Gulf of Mexico, without experiencing

1 A Supplement to Johnson's Dictionary of the English Language;
London, 1832–33.
2 Notions of the Americans; London,
1828, Vol. II, pp. 164–5.
3 Lectures on the English Language;

New York, 1860; 4th ed., 1870,
Lecture XXX, pp. 666–67 and
674–75.
4 It was set up in London in March,
1919, and ran for about two years.

any change in the pronunciation that can be taken as evidence of dialect; but in England one cannot go from one county to another, and in many cases not from the West to East end of a single town, without noticing a most marked difference in the pronunciation of words. Many a Londoner has been hopelessly baffled when for the first time he has asked a Liverpool policeman or a Glasgow newsboy to direct him, and if an Essex laborer were suddenly to find himself in the bar-parlor of a Dartmoor inn, or at a meeting of Yorkshire miners, he would be scarcely more able to follow the conversation than if he were in Petrograd.

The other authority is the late George Philip Krapp, professor of English at Columbia and the author of two standard works on American pronunciation.[1] He said:

Relatively few Americans spend all their lives in one locality, and even if they do, they cannot possibly escape coming into contact with Americans from other localities. . . . We can distinguish with some certainty Eastern and Western and Southern speech, but beyond this the author has little confidence in those confident experts who think they can tell infallibly, by the test of speech, a native of Hartford from a native of Providence, or a native of Philadelphia from a native of Atlanta, or even, if one insist on infallibility, a native of Chicago from a native of Boston.

Krapp was discussing Standard American, but on the plane of the vulgate the leveling is quite as apparent. That vast uniformity which marks the people of the United States, in political theory, in social habit, in general information, in reaction to new ideas, in deep-lying prejudices and enthusiasms, in the veriest details of domestic custom and dress, is nowhere more marked than in their speech habits. The incessant neologisms of the national dialect sweep the whole country almost instantly, and the iconoclastic changes which its popular spoken form is constantly undergoing show themselves from coast to coast.

Nevertheless, there *are* dialectical differences in spoken American, and they have been observed and recorded by a multitude of phonologists, both professional and lay. The organization of the American Dialect Society in 1889, the continuous, if somewhat infrequent, appearance of *Dialect Notes* ever since, and the preparation of a Linguistic Atlas of the country are sufficient evidences that American dialects really exist. Disregarding local peculiarities, there are three of them. The most important is that which a leading authority, Dr. Hans Kurath, calls Western American: it is the tongue that the over-

1 The Pronunciation of Standard English in America; New York, 1919, and The English Language in America; New York, 1925, the second volume of which is devoted almost wholly to pronunciation. The quotation is from the former, p. viii.

whelming majority of Americans speak, and the one that Englishmen always have in mind when they discuss American English. Its territory includes all of New England west of the Connecticut river, the whole of the Middle Atlantic area save the lower Eastern Shore of Maryland and lower Delaware, and all the region west of the Cotton Belts of Texas and Arkansas and north of Central Missouri. In Ohio, Indiana and Illinois it comes down close to the Ohio river, and in the South it includes parts of the mountain country. It is also spoken east of the Connecticut river, in parts of Rhode Island, New Hampshire and Maine, and by many persons in Boston. No other form of American is so widespread, and none other is still spreading. The so-called New England dialect, once spoken all over the territory east of the Hudson, is now pretty well confined to the Boston area, and even there it is decaying. The Southern form of American occupies the area south of the Potomac and west to the Mississippi river, with extensions into Texas, Arkansas, Missouri, parts of Delaware and the Eastern Shore of Maryland, and the lower counties of Illinois, Indiana and Ohio. Dr. Kurath believes that these divisions in American English were produced by the character of the immigration settling the different parts of the country, and in this theory most other authorities agree with him. The early settlers of Eastern New England and the Tidewater region of the South came chiefly from the Southern parts of England,[1] and they brought with them those characters of Southern English speech that are still marked today in Standard English and separate the dialects of the Boston area and of the South from the speech of the rest of the United States, *e.g.*, the use of the broad *a* and the elision of *r* before consonants and in the terminal position. But the western parts of New England and the uplands of the South were settled mainly by immigrants speaking Northern varieties of English — many of them the so-called Scotch-Irish — and so were New Jersey, Pennsylvania and Maryland. When the movement into the West began there were two streams. The one, starting from the Tidewater South, carried Southern English into the cotton lands of Georgia, Alabama and Mississippi, into parts of Texas, Arkansas and Missouri, and into all save the mountainous parts of Kentucky; the other, starting from Western New England and

---

1 Including not only the London area, but also East Anglia and the Southwestern counties of Devon, Dorset and Somerset — in short, the whole region south of a line drawn from the mouth of the Severn to the Wash, but excluding Cornwall.

the Middle Atlantic region, carried Northern English into New York State, the Appalachian region down to the North Carolina-Tennessee border, and virtually the whole of the Middle and Far West. Thus the dialect of the Boston area and that of the South are closely allied. Both are forms of Southern English. But there is much less apparent influence of Southern English in the Western American which now dominates the country. It is, in many ways, nearer related to Lowland Scotch.[1]

The chief characters of Western, or General American and of New England and Southern American have been indicated in the preceding sections of this chapter. All three show local variations, and in the midst of the areas of each of them there are islands of one or another of the other forms. The literature dealing with some of the regional forms is very extensive; indeed, it is almost as extensive as the literature dealing with American pronunciation in general. This is true, especially, of the dialect of Appalachia, which includes the area of the Ozarks. It is interesting because the people speaking it have been isolated for many years, and have thus preserved speech-forms that have become archaic elsewhere. They are also, in the main, of low economic status, and it is among the poor that ancient forms are least affected by pedagogy and fashion. The dialect of Appalachia is based primarily upon the Southern English of the late Seventeenth Century, but it has been considerably modified by the Northern English brought in by the Scotch-Irish. The mountain folk are fond of thinking of themselves as the only carriers of pure Anglo-Saxon blood in America, but as a matter of fact many of them are Celts, as an examination of their surnames quickly shows. Their dialect was put to extensive literary use [2] before it got much attention from philologians, but since an account of it by Dr. Josiah Combs appeared in 1916 [3] it has been investigated at

1 Dr. Kurath discusses all these points at length in American Pronunciation, *S.P.E. Tracts*, No. XXX, 1928, and The Origin of the Dialectical Differences in Spoken American English, *Modern Philology*, May, 1928. See also The English Language in America, by G. P. Krapp, above cited, Vol. II, pp. 29–30, and Scotland and Americanisms, by William Craigie, an address delivered before the Institute of Medicine, Chicago, Dec. 4, 1928.

2 For example, by Mary N. Murfree (Charles Egbert Craddock) (1850–1922) and John W. Fox (1863–1919). Miss Murfree's first book of mountain stories, In the Tennessee Mountains, was published in 1884. Mr. Fox's Hell For Sartain, 1897, was an immense success in its day.

3 Old Early and Elizabethan English in the Southern Mountains, *Dialect Notes*, Vol. IV, Pt. IV, 1916. Dr. Combs has also published Early English Slang Survivals in

some length. The Ozark form has been the special province of Vance Randolph, a native of the region where it is spoken, and he has published a number of valuable studies of it.[1]

In his book, " The Ozarks," he gives the following specimen:

> Lee Yancey allus was a right work-brickel feller, clever an' biddable as all git-out, but he aint got nary smidgin' o' mother-wit, an' he aint nothin' on'y a tie-whackin' sheer-crapper noways. I seed him an' his least chaps a-bustin' out middles down in ol' man Price's bottom t'other ev'nin', a-whoopin' an' a-blaggardin' an' a-spewin' ambeer all over each an' ever', whilst thet 'ar pore susy hippoed woman o' hisn was a-pickin' boogers out'n her yeller tags, an' a-scunchin' cheenches on th' puncheon with a antiganglin' noodle-hook. D'rectly Lee he come a-junin' in all narvish-like an' tetchous, an' rid th' pore ol' trollop a bug-huntin' — jes' plum bodacious hipped an' ruinated her. They never did have nothin' on'y jes' a heap o' poke salat an' a passel o' these hyar hawg-mollies, but he must a got hisse'f a bait o' vittles some'ers, 'cause come can'le-light he geared up his ol' piedy cribber an' lit as huck fer Gotham Holler. The danged ol' durgen — he should orter be bored fer th' simples'.

The pronunciation of this dialect, according to Mr. Randolph,[2] is very much like that of general vulgar American as noted in Sections 2 and 4 of the present chapter, but it preserves many early forms that have fallen out of use elsewhere, and reinforces and exaggerates most of those that remain. The short *a* is so much favored that it appears even in *balm* and *gargle*, but in *narrow* and *barrel* a broad *a* is substituted, so that they become *nahrr'* and *bahr'l*. In other situations the broad *a* is turned into a *u*, as in *whut*, *fur* and *ruther* for *what*, *far* and *rather*. In *have* and *gather* the *a* becomes *e*, making

the Mountains of Kentucky, *Dialect Notes*, Vol. V, Pt. IV, 1921, and The Language of the Southern Highlanders, *Publications of the Modern Language Association*, Dec., 1931. There is a criticism of some of Combs's conclusions by J. M. Steadman, Jr., in *Dialect Notes*, Vol. IV, Pt. V, 1916.

1 A summary of his observations is in The Ozark Dialect, in The Ozarks: an American Survival of Primitive Society; New York, 1931. He has also published A Word-List From the Ozarks, *Dialect Notes*, Vol. V, Pt. IX, 1926; The Ozark Dialect in Fiction, *American Speech*, March, 1927; More Words From the Ozarks, *Dialect Notes*, Vol. V, Pt. X, 1927; The Grammar of the Ozark Dia-

lect, *American Speech*, Oct., 1927; Pronunciation in the Ozark Dialect (with Anna A. Ingleman), the same, June, 1928; Literary Words in the Ozarks, the same, Oct., 1928; A Possible Source of Some Ozark Neologisms, the same, Dec., 1928; Is There an Ozark Dialect?, the same, Feb., 1929; A Third Ozark Word-List, the same, Oct., 1929; Dialectical Survivals in the Ozarks (with Patti Sankee), the same, Feb., April, and June, 1930; Recent Fiction and the Ozark Dialect, the same, Aug., 1931; and A Fourth Ozark Word-List, the same, Feb., 1933.

2 Pronunciation in the Ozark Dialect (with Anna A. Ingleman), *American Speech*, June, 1928.

hev and *gether*. A final unstressed *a* often becomes *y*, as in *Clary*, *alfalfy* and *pneumony*. *Certain* is nearly always *sartain*, and *celery* is *salery*. The *u* is seldom pronounced correctly. *Brush* is *bresh*, *such* is *sich*, *sure* is *shore*, *until* is *ontil*, *gum* is *goom* and *ewe* is *yo*. The *au*-sound is usually changed. *Saucy*, as in the general vulgate, becomes *sassy*, and *jaundice* is *janders*. In addition, *haunt* is *hant* and *aunt* is either *ant* or something like *ain't*. The difficulties that all untutored Americans have with *t* are multiplied. " Such nouns as *post* and *nest*," says Mr. Randolph, " drop the *t* in the singular, but in the plural the *t* is pronounced distinctly and an unaccented syllable added — *nestes* and *postes*. *T* replaces the final *d* in words like *salad*, *ballad*, *killed*, *errand*, *scared* and *held*, so that they are best rendered *salat*, *ballat*, *kilt*, *errant*, *skeert* and *helt*. Occasionally the final *t* is replaced by a *k*-sound, as when *vomit* is turned into *vomick*." An excrescent *t* is added to many words beside the familiar *once*, *wish* and *close;* thus *sudden* becomes *suddint*, *trough* is *trought*, *cliff* is *clift* and *chance* is *chanct*. An intrusive *y* appears in *hear* and *ear*, which become *hyar* and *yhar*. The *sk* of *muskrat* and *muskmelon* is changed to *sh*. " The *-ing* ending is always pronounced *in*, with the short *i*-sound very distinct. . . . The Ozarker says *sleepin'* — never *sleep'n'*. . . . Sometimes the *g* is dropped from the middle of a word also, as in *strength* and *length*, which are nearly always pronounced *stren'th* and *len'th*." In many words the accent is thrown forward; thus, *catarrh*, *guitar*, *insane*, *harangue*, *relapse*, *police* and *hurrah* are accented on the first syllable. The Ozarker borrows a cockneyism in *hit* for *it*, but he uses it " only at the beginning of a clause, or when unusual emphasis is desired." [1]

In most ways the pronunciation of the hillmen of the main Appalachian range is identical with Ozarkian usage, but it shows a stronger influence of Tidewater Southern. There are, of course, many local variations, due to the extreme isolation of the mountain communities. Maristan Chapman discerns three chief sub-dialects — the first spoken in the Cumberlands of Kentucky and Tennessee, the second in the Great Smokies, and the third in the Blue Ridge of Virginia and West

1 On the Ozark Pronunciation of *It*, by Vernon C. Allison, *American Speech*, Feb., 1929. Word-lists from the Ozark dialect are to be found in A List of Words From Northwest Arkansas, by J. W. Carr, *Dialect Notes*, Vol. II, Pt. VI, 1904; Vol. III, Pt. I, 1905; Pt. II, 1906; Pt. III, 1907; Pt. V, 1909; and in Snake County Talk [McDonald county, Mo.], by Jay L. B. Taylor, the same, Vol. V, Pt. VI, 1923.

Virginia.¹ Differences are to be found, not only in pronunciation, but also in vocabulary, and Mr. Chapman gives some curious examples. In the Cumberlands a small portion of anything is a *smidgen*, in the Great Smokies it is a *canch*, and in the Blue Ridge it is a *tiddy-bit*. In the Cumberlands a cow is a *cow-beast*, in the Great Smokies she is a *cow-brute*, and in the Blue Ridge she is a *she-cow*. In the Ozarks, it may be added, *cow-brute* is a euphemism for *bull*. But these differences are yielding to good roads and the automobile, and in another generation the mountain folk, for the most part, will probably be speaking the general vulgate.² The mountain type of speech is not confined to the actual mountains. It has been taken to the Piedmont by hill-folk going to work in the cotton-mills, and Dr. W. Cabell Greet says that it is " well fixed on the Southwestern plains and in cities like Fort Worth and Dallas," and has echoes on the Delmarva Peninsula and on the islands of Chesapeake Bay. He adds that " it is often slower than the speech of the lowlands, where rapid speech is more common than slow speech "; also, that it is " often nasal and high pitched." ³

The popular belief ascribes some of the characters of General Southern American — for example, the elision of the *r* before consonants and the intrusion of the *y* before certain vowels — to Negro influence. This belief is not of recent origin, for on April 15, 1842, Charles Dickens, who was then in the United States, wrote home to his wife: " All the women who have been bred in slave States speak

1 American Speech as Practised in the Southern Highlands, *Century*, March, 1929.
2 See Variation in the Southern Mountain Dialect, by Charles Carpenter, *American Speech*, Feb., 1933. Mr. Carpenter says that the dialect of Northern and Central West Virginia has been much modified by the opening of coal-mines. The literature down to the end of 1922 is listed in A Bibliography of Writings on the English language, by Arthur G. Kennedy, above cited, pp. 413–16. See also The Southern Mountaineer and His Homeland, by John C. Campbell; New York, 1921; Dialect Words and Phrases From West-Central West Virginia, by Carey Woofter, *American Speech*, May, 1927; West

Virginia Dialect by Lowry Axley, the same, Aug., 1928; Elizabethan America, by Charles M. Wilson, *Atlantic Monthly*, Aug., 1929; How the Wood Hicks Speak, by Paul E. Pendleton, *Dialect Notes*, Vol. VI, Pt. II, 1930; Folk Speech in the Kentucky Mountain Cycle of Percy Mackaye, by B. A. Botkin, *American Speech*, April, 1931; Folk Speech of the Cumberlands, by Bess Alice Owens, the same, Dec., 1931; Remnants of Archaic English in West Virginia, by Charles Carpenter, *West Virginia Review*, Dec., 1934; Southern Mountain Accent, by C. G., *American Speech*, Dec., 1934.
3 Southern Speech, in Culture in the South; Chapel Hill, N. C., 1934, p. 614.

more or less like Negroes, from having been constantly in their childhood with black nurses." But Dr. Greet, in a notable essay,[1] argues convincingly that the thing has really run the other way. " When the slaves were brought to America," he says, " they learned the accent of their masters. There is literally no pronunciation common among Negroes, with possible exceptions in Gullah, that does not occur generally in vulgar or old-fashioned American speech." In this judgment two other students of Negro speech agree completely. One is Cleanth Brooks, Jr., of Louisiana State University, who says:

> In almost every case, the specifically Negro forms turn out to be older English forms which the Negro must have taken originally from the white man, and which he has retained after the white man has begun to lose them.[2]

The other is the late George Philip Krapp, who wrote in " The English Language in America ":

> The Negroes omitted their *r*'s because they heard no *r*'s in the speech of their white superiors. Since they were entirely dependent upon hearing in learning the sounds of speech, their sounds could not be affected by the visual impressions of spelling, and for this reason their pronunciation of words with *r* final before consonants may seem broader, may seem fuller and franker, than that of educated white speakers. Even this difference, however, is likely to be an illusion on the part of the critical hearer, who is inclined to hear the speech of educated persons in terms of conventional spelling but of uneducated persons in terms of illiterate spelling.[3]

In another place [4] Dr. Krapp argued that the common belief that the voice of the Negro differs from that of the white man is also unsupported by the facts. There is a slight difference, he said, in speech tunes, but not much. Put a Negro and a white man, both from the same part of rural Georgia and both on the same economic

1 Southern Speech, just cited. It is the best general survey of Southern American so far published. Other papers that will be found useful are The Vowel System of the Southern United States, by William A. Read, *Englishe Studien*, Vol. XLI, 1910; The Southern *R*, by the same, *Louisiana State University Bulletin*, Feb., 1910; Some Variant Pronunciations in the New South, by the same, *Dialect Notes*, Vol. III, Pt. VII, 1911; Who Lost the Southern *R*? by H. P. Johnson, *American Speech*, June, 1928; Southern American Dialect, by C. M. Wise, the same, April, 1933; Southern Standards, by Katherine E. Wheatley, the same, Feb., 1934; Some Unrecorded Southern Vowels, by George P. Wilson, the same, Oct., 1934; Southern Long *I*, by Medford Evans, the same, Oct., 1935; and Another Note on the Southern Pronunciation of Long *I*, by William B. Edgerton, the same, Oct., 1935.

2 The Relation of the Alabama-Georgia Dialect to the Provincial Dialects of Great Britain, *Louisiana State University Studies*, No. XX, 1935.

3 Vol. I, p. 226.

4 The English of the Negro, *American Mercury*, June, 1924.

level, behind a screen and bid them speak the same words, and it will be difficult if not impossible to distinguish one from the other. Dr. Krapp was even indisposed to grant that the use of *I is* for *I am* among the lower orders of Negroes is a true Negroism: he tracked it down in Joseph Wright's English Dialect Dictionary, and found that it was common in England so long ago as the Thirteenth Century.[1] Nevertheless, there is a conventionalized Negro dialect, perhaps launched by the minstrel shows of the past generation, that all Americans recognize, and it plays a large part in American literature.[2] Perhaps the Negro himself has imitated this dialect: nature, as Oscar Wilde once said, always imitates art. Walt Whitman not only believed in its existence, but saw vast potentialities in it. " The nigger dialect," he said in " An American Primer," [3] " has hints of the future theory of the modification of all the words of the English language, for musical purposes, for a native grand opera in America, leaving the words just as they are for writing and speaking, but the same words so modified as to answer perfectly for musical purposes, on grand and simple principles." But it is not certain that Walt knew precisely what he was talking about here.[4]

Dr. Greet, in the essay above mentioned, says that there are " many

1 The prevailing conjugation, according to Bertram H. Brown (*American Mercury*, May, 1933, p. 116) is *I is, you is, he is; us is, you-all* (or *y'all*) *is, they is.* Mr. Brown says that *he am* is never heard.
2 Dr. Krapp traces its literary development in The English Language in America, above cited, Vol. I, p. 246 ff. See also Notes on Negro Dialect in the American Novel to 1821, by Tremaine McDowell, *American Speech*, April, 1930; The Use of Negro Dialect by Harriet Beecher Stowe, by the same, the same, June, 1931; and The Vocabulary of the American Negro as Set Forth in Contemporary Literature, by Nathan Van Patten, the same, Oct., 1931.
3 *Atlantic Monthly*, April, 1904.
4 Negro speech has been little investigated by philologians. Kennedy lists but nine discussions of it before 1922, and only three of them are of any interest. There are some intelligent remarks upon it in the

preface to The Book of American Negro Spirituals, by James Weldon Johnson; New York, 1925. See also The Study of the Alabama-Georgia dialect by Cleanth Brooks, Jr., above cited; The Negro Dialects along the Savannah River, by Elisha K. Kane, *Dialect Notes*, Vol. V, Pt. VIII, 1925; Negro Dialect, by C. M. Wise, *Quarterly Journal of Speech*, Nov., 1933; and Aesop in Negro Dialect, *American Speech*, June, 1926. Gullah, spoken in the Sea Islands and along the coast of Georgia and South Carolina, has been described by Reed Smith in Gullah, *Bulletin of the University of South Carolina*, Nov. 1, 1926, and there is a glossary of it in The Black Border, by Ambrose E. Gonzales; Columbia, S. C., 1922. See also Folk Culture on St. Helena Island, S. C., by Guy B. Johnson; Chapel Hill, N. C., 1930, pp. 3 ff, and The Old Types Pass, by Marcellus S. Whaley; Boston, 1925. The dialect of Hatteras Island was

varieties of speech in the South, all closely related to speech in other parts of the country." He distinguishes three main varieties: the Virginia Tidewater type, the General Southern lowland type, and the Southern hill type. The first named prevails along the coast from the Delmarva Peninsula to South Carolina, and has colonies in the northern Shenandoah region and in the vicinity of Charlottesville. Its territory includes Richmond. The General Southern lowland type prevails everywhere else save in the mountains. In the Virginia Piedmont it is modified by the Tidewater type. The latter is, in general, more "Southern" than the other two: it embodies most of the peculiarities that Northerners associate with sub-Potomac speech, e.g., the intrusion of a *y*-sound before *a* after *g* or *k*, as in *gyarden* and *cyar*. " Elsewhere in the South and Southwest, hill and plain," says Dr. Greet, "*y* often appears before [*i*, the short *e* of *get* and the flat *a* of *hat*], but never before [broad *a*]." Even in the Tidewater region the *y* is not often heard in "the speech of business and professional men, if we except Episcopal ministers," but " certain gentlemen of the old school, many ladies of the old families, débutantes who have attended Episcopal institutions, professional Virginians, and parvenues are fond of the sound." Before *a* as in *gate, a* as in *carry, e* as in *get* and *i* as in *gift*, however, it " has no social merit," and before *o* as in *cow* it is " a real *faux pas.*" But it is favored before the *ir* in *girls.* " I am sufficiently under the influence of the sentimental South and speech snobbery," says Dr. Greet, "to think that *gyirls* is a very fine pronunciation. Every man to his own choice." [1]

The New England variety of American is anything but a homo-

---

described by one signing himself Marcel in the *Nation*, 1865, pp. 744–5, and his observations were reprinted in Lectures on the Science of Language, by F. Max Müller, 6th ed.; London, 1871, Vol. I, p. 75 ff.

[1] There have been many studies of local pronunciation in the South, mainly divided (somewhat irrationally) by States. Most of them will be found in the files of *Dialect Notes.* The following are of special interest: *Georgia:* Provincialisms, in A Gazeteer of the State of Georgia, by Adiel Sherwood, 3rd ed.; Washington, 1837, reprinted in The Beginnings of American English,

by M. M. Mathews; Chicago, 1931; Tales of the Okefinokee, by Francis Harper, *American Speech*, May, 1926 (a study of the dialect of a remote corner of Georgia); *North Carolina:* Early English Survivals on Hatteras Island, by Collier Cobb, *University of North Carolina Magazine*, Feb., 1910; *South Carolina:* Charleston Provincialisms, by Sylvester Primer, *American Journal of Philology*, Vol. IX, 1888; The Huguenot Element in Charleston's Pronunciation, *Publications of the Modern Language Association*, Vol. IV, 1889; *Tennessee:* A Tennesseean's Pronunciation in 1841, by Rebecca W. Smith, *American Speech*,

geneous whole. In its coastal form, centering in Boston, it is very like the Standard English of Southern England, but as one moves westward it gradually loses itself in General American. The New England dialect that has been put to such heavy use in American literature since the close of the Eighteenth Century is the lingo of untutored yokels, and has many points in common with ordinary vulgar American. In other ways it suggests the dialect of the Appalachian hillmen. It made its first appearance in print, according to Krapp, in Royall Tyler's play, " The Contrast " (1787), and it probably reached its apogee in Lowell's " Biglow Papers " (1848, 1866). In an address " To the Indulgent Reader " prefixed to the First Series of the latter Lowell printed " general rules " for its compounding, as follows:

1. The genuine Yankee never gives the rough sound to the *r* when he can help it, and often displays considerable ingenuity in avoiding it even before a vowel.
2. He seldom sounds the final *g*, a piece of self-denial, if we consider his partiality for nasals. The same of the final *d*, as *han'* and *stan'* for *hand* and *stand*.
3. The *h* in such words as *while, when, where*, he omits altogether.
4. In regard to *a*, he shows some inconsistency, sometimes giving a close and obscure sound, as *hev* for *have, hendy* for *handy, ez* for *as, thet* for *that*, and again giving it the broad sound it has in *father*, as *hânsome* for *handsome*.
5. To *ou* he prefixes an *e* (hard to exemplify otherwise than orally).
6. *Au*, in such words as *daughter* and *slaughter*, he pronounces *ah*.
7. To the dish thus seasoned add a drawl *ad libitum*.

Krapp argues that, of these rules, only the fourth and sixth show any genuine differentiation from ordinary vulgar American.[1] Other experts have wrestled with the peculiarities of this somewhat formalized Yankee more successfully than Lowell; it is best described, per-

---

Dec., 1934; *Virginia:* Word-Book of Virginia Folk-Speech, by Bennett W. Green; Richmond, 1899; new ed., 1912; English Pronunciation in Virginia, by Edwin F. Shewmake; Charlottesville, Va., 1927; Philip Vickers Fithian's Observations on the Language of Virginia (1774), by Claude M. Newlin, *American Speech*, Dec., 1929; A Phonographic Expedition to Williamsburg, Va., by W. Cabell Greet, the same, Feb., 1931; Dialect Notes on Records of Folk-Songs From Virginia, by A. K. Davis, Jr. and A. A. Hill, the same, Dec., 1933. The literature down to the end of 1922 is listed in Kennedy's Bibliography, above cited. For the period since 1922 the bibliographies in *American Speech* are useful, though they are by no means complete. It is a pity that no one has ever investigated Tidewater Southern American historically, on the plan of Krapp's investigation of New England American. The way to some promising material is pointed in E. G. Swem's Virginia Historical Index; Roanoke, 1934.

1 The English Language in America, above cited, Vol. I, p. 233.

haps, by Grandgent in "New England Pronunciation."[1] An extensive literature deals with its local forms, and especially with differences in the vocabulary.[2] The appearance of the Linguistic Atlas, the first sheets of which deal with New England, will make most of this literature useless. On the history of the coastal dialect the most useful work is "Early New England Pronunciation," by Anders Orbeck, which is based upon an examination of the town records of Plymouth, Watertown, Dedham and Groton, Mass., for the period 1636–1707.[3] Dr. Orbeck discusses at length the probable sources of this coastal dialect. He finds that 73% of the early settlers of the region where it is used came from the Eastern counties of England, including London. He reviews at length the previous speculations of G. F. Hoar, T. W. Higginson, Joseph L. Chester, H. T. Nöel-Armfield and Edward Gepp, and exposes their errors.[4]

Various authorities have sought to include New York City and Long Island in the New England speech area, but this is hardly justified by the facts. In a study made forty years ago B. S. Monroe found that there was some dropping of the terminal *r* in New York City and Kings, Queens, Suffolk, Westchester and Rensselaer counties, but that it was by no means general and was not accompanied by any significant use of the broad *a* in *grass, path* and *laugh*.[5] The

1 A chapter in Old and New; Cambridge, Mass., 1920.

2 For publications down to the end of 1922 see Kennedy's Bibliography, above cited, pp. 413–16. Most of those of later date are to be found in either *Dialect Notes* or *American Speech*. The following are of special interest: New England Dialect, by Windsor P. Daggett, *Billboard*, March 3, 1928 (a guide for actors cast for Yankee parts); The Real Dialect of Northern New England, by George A. England, *Writer's Monthly*, March, 1926 (a guide for writers of fiction); Vanishing Expressions of the New England Coast, by Anne E. Perkins, *American Speech*, Dec., 1927; New England Words for the *Earthworm*, by Rachel S. Harris, the same, Dec., 1933; New England Expressions For Poached Eggs, by Herbert Penzl, the same, April, 1934.

3 Ann Arbor, Mich., 1927.

4 Other publications worth consulting are A Sidelight on Eighteenth Century American English, by Henry Alexander, *Queen's Quarterly* (Kingston, Ont.) Nov., 1923; Early American Pronunciation and Syntax, by the same, *American Speech*, Dec., 1925; A Comparison of the Dialect of The Biglow Papers with the Dialect of Four Yankee Plays, by Marie Killheffer, the same, Feb., 1928; The Language of the Salem Witchcraft Trials, by Henry Alexander, the same, June, 1928; Die Volkssprache im Nordosten der Vereinigten Staaten von Amerika dargestellt auf Grund der Biglow Papers von James Russell Lowell, by J. A. Heil; Breslau, 1927.

5 The Pronunciation of English in New York State, *Dialect Notes*, Vol. I, Pt. IX, 1896.

broad *a* actually heard in the metropolitan region is confined to a very small class of persons, chiefly of social pretensions, and among them it is not the Boston *a* that is used but the English one. In the rest of the State the flat *a* of General or Western American prevails, and the *r* is not elided.[1] The common people of New York City have a dialect of their own, first described scientifically by Dr. E. H. Babbitt of Columbia in 1896.[2] Its most notable peculiarity lies in the pronunciation of the *e*-sound before *r*, as in *bird, third, first, nerve, work, earnest, curve, girl, perfect* and *pearl*, which become something that is usually represented as *boid, thoid, foist, noive, woik, oinest, coive, goil, poifect* and *poil*. Contrariwise, the true *oi*-sound, as in *oyster, noise* and *Boyd*, gets a touch of the *r*, and in print these words are often given as *erster, nerz* and *Byrd*. Dr. Henry Alexander says that the true sound is the same in both cases, and lies between *oi* and *er*. To a person unfamiliar with it, it sounds like *oi* in the *er*-words and like *er* in the *oi*-words. Dr. Alexander thus explains the process:

> Given two familiar sounds, *a* and *b*, and one unfamiliar sound, *x*, which, acoustically and phonetically, is intermediate between *a* and *b*. If a speaker is in the habit of substituting *x* for both *a* and *b*, then an untrained hearer will interpret *x* as *b* in words in which he expects to hear *a*, and *x* as *a* in words in which he expects to hear *b*.[3]

At the time the New York vulgar dialect first appeared in literature, in the early 90's,[4] this confusion between *oi* and *er* was not stressed; instead, the salient mark of the dialect was thought to be substitution of *t* and *d* for the unvoiced and voiced forms of *th*, respectively, as in *wit* and *dat* for *with* and *that*. This substitution, said Dr. Babbitt in 1896, " does not take place in all words, nor in the speech of all persons, even of the lower classes; but the tendency exists beyond doubt." It is my observation that it has declined in late

1 See The Ithaca Dialect, by O. F. Emerson; Boston, 1891; Dialect of Northeastern New York, by Gerald Crowninshield, *American Speech*, April, 1933; Pronunciation in Upstate New York, by C. K. Thomas, the same, April and Oct., 1935. Word-lists have appeared in *Dialect Notes*, Vol. III, Pt. VI, 1910, and Pt. VIII, 1912, and there is a list of colloquial expressions from Madison county in *American Speech*, Dec., 1929.

2 The English of the Lower Classes in New York City and Vicinity, *Dialect Notes*, Vol. I, Pt. IX, 1896.
3 *Soiving* the *Ersters, American Speech*, Feb., 1926. See also Popular Phonetics, by Robert J. Menner, the same, June, 1929, and Standards of Pronunciation in New York City, by C. K. Thomas, *Quarterly Journal of Speech*, April, 1935.
4 For example, in the Chimmie Fadden stories of E. W. Townsend.

years, probably through the labors of the schoolmarm. But she has not been able to stamp out *foist* and *thoid*, if, indeed, she has been sufficiently conscious of them to make the attempt. Their use by Alfred E. Smith during his campaign for the Presidency in 1928 made the whole country conscious of the New York *oi*. I have frequently noted it in the speech of educated New Yorkers, and it is very common in that of the high-school graduates who make up the corps of New York stenographers. It extends into New Jersey and up Long Island Sound into Connecticut. The origin of the New York dialect has not yet been accounted for with any plausibility. Its current peculiarities seem to have been unobserved until toward the end of the last century. Perhaps it owes something to the influence of Yiddish-speaking immigrants. Its *oi*-sound is certainly heard in Yiddish, and since 1900 the Jews have constituted the largest racial *bloc* in the boroughs of Brooklyn and the Bronx, and probably also in that of Manhattan. At least one observer sees its genesis in a revolt of the submerged masses against their oppressors. He says:

> This New York dialect, like its prototype in London [*i.e.*, Cockney], represents a class-protest, largely unconscious, against a life of terrible sounds, sights, smells and contacts. These exploitees would be as their masters, but they can not. Resisting all instruction, they take on this speech, which is the precise opposite of the speech of their masters. " Look what you made us," they all seem to say, " but since you will not let us have what we want, we will pretend to glory in what we have, and will make ourselves as objectionable as possible to you in a way which you can not effectively penalize." [1]

This theory sounds so dubious to me that I marvel that it has not been embraced by the proletarian Aristotles of the *New Republic* and *New Masses*. Among those New Yorkers to whom Yiddish is native there are forms reported in use that have not got into the general vulgate of the town, *e.g.*, the interchange of *e* and flat *a*, as in *baker* for *beggar* and *kettle* for *cattle;* the interchange of *k* and *g*, as in *glass* for *class* and *locker* for *lager;* the interchange of *b* and *p*, as in *bowl* for *pole* and *mop* for *mob;* the interchange of long *e* and short *i*, as in *dip* for *deep* and *beeg* for *big;* the interchange of *t* and *d*, as in *lid* for *lit* and *lift* for *lived*. But these interchanges may be more apparent than real: perhaps what occurs in each case is a median sound, resembling that described by Dr. Alexander as lying between *oi* and *er*.[2]

[1] The Origin of a Dialect, by Howard K. Hollister, *Freeman*, June, 1923.

[2] The speech of the New York Jews is discussed in Jewish Dialect and the New York Dialect, by C. K.

In the other Middle Atlantic States, General or Western American prevails, save only for a small part of New Jersey adjacent to New York City, where the New York vulgate has some footing, and the lower part of the Delmarva Peninsula, where, as I have noted, something resembling Tidewater Southern is used. Most of the early observers of American speech-ways thought that the pronunciation of the Western Shore of Maryland was especially euphonious and correct. " When you get as far South as Maryland," said J. Fenimore Cooper in 1828,[1] "the softest, and perhaps as pure an English is spoken as is anywhere heard." Two years earlier Mrs. Anne Royall said that " the dialect of Washington, exclusive of the foreigners, is the most correct and pure of any part of the United States I have ever yet been in." [2] Noah Webster also liked the pronunciation of this region, though he added that a t was added to *once* and *twice* by " a class of very well educated people, particularly in Philadelphia and Baltimore." [3] In parts of Pennsylvania, as we have seen in Chapter IV, Section 3, the German influence has not only introduced a number of words that are not commonly heard elsewhere, but has also established some peculiar speech-tunes. The Pennsylvania voice, indeed, is recognized instantly in the adjacent States. In the sentence " Are you going now," for example, there is a sharp rise on *go* and a fall on *now*. For the rest, Pennsylvania speaks General or Western American. " The true Western Pennsylvanian," says E. K. Maxfield, " pronounces a decidedly flat a . . . and his r gives him especial

Thomas, *American Speech*, June, 1932; in Re Jewish Dialect and New York Dialect, by Robert Sonkin, the same, Feb., 1933, and More on New York Jewish Dialect, by C. K. Thomas, the same, Oct., 1933. " None of the Jews who supplied my data," says Mr. Thomas in the last article, " were immigrants; all were at least second generation, the children, in some cases the grandchildren, of immigrants; yet they retain the dialect. On the other hand, the second Gentile generation ordinarily has no trace of its fathers' foreign dialect." The Yiddo-American of New York has produced a considerable literature, the chief contributors to which have been Montague Glass, Milt Gross and Arthur Kober. Its peculiarities were amusingly exaggerated in various Notes For an East Side Dictionary, written for the *New Yorker* during 1934 and 1935 by John J. Holzinges over the signature of J. X. J. There was a time when it was heard often on the comic stage, but it has gone out of fashion there, along with the German, Irish and Scandinavian dialects. See Yiddish in American Fiction, by Alter Brody, *American Mercury*, Feb., 1926.

1 Notions of the Americans, Vol. II, p. 175.

2 Sketches of History, Life and Manners in the United States; New Haven, 1826, p. 58.

3 Dissertations on the English Language; Boston, 1789, II.

pride and a sense of superiority over both East and South." [1] This flat *a* and conspicuous *r* are also sounded in Philadelphia, save perhaps by a small faction of the élite.[2] The speech of New Jersey, save in the New York suburbs, is likewise General American, but the vocabulary of the State is rich in local terms.[3] General American itself hardly needs any description here; it is the speech with which the present volume mainly deals. It has, of course, many minor variations, but they have to do principally with its vocabulary. In regions where there are ponderable minorities speaking non-English languages many loan-words are taken in — Spanish in the Southwest, German in parts of Pennsylvania and Wisconsin, and Scandinavian in Minnesota and the adjacent States. Some of these local borrowings have been noted in Chapter IV, Section 3, and Chapter V, Section 5. They are of small importance, for in pronunciation and intonation, as in the major part of its vocabulary, General American is singularly uniform.[4]

1 The Speech of South-Western Pennsylvania, *American Speech*, Oct., 1931.

2 See also Provincialisms of the Dutch Districts of Pennsylvania, by Lee L. Grumbine, *Proceedings of the American Philological Association*, Vol. XVII, 1886; Dialectical Peculiarities in the Carlisle, Pa., Vernacular, by William Prettyman, *German-American Annals*, Vol. IX, 1907; Dialects of the Western Pennsylvania Frontier, by Claude M. Newlin, *American Speech*, Dec., 1928; The English of the Pennsylvania Germans, by George G. Struble, the same, Oct., 1935.

3 See Jerseyisms, by F. B. Lee, *Dialect Notes*, Vol. I, Pt. VII, 1894, and some notes correcting and enlarging the foregoing, the same, Pt. VIII, 1895.

4 The literature dealing with localisms, down to the end of 1922, is listed in Kennedy's Bibliography, above cited, pp. 414–16. Later publications worth consulting include the following: *Indiana*: Eggleston's Notes on Hoosier Dialect, by Margaret Bloom, *American Speech*, Dec., 1934 (a reprint of the short glossary published with the 1899 edition of The Hoosier Schoolmas-

ter, by Edward Eggleston); *Iowa*: Some Iowa Locutions, by Katherine Buxbaum, *American Speech*, April, 1929; *Kansas*: Jottings From Kansas, by J. C. Ruppenthal, *Dialect Notes*, Vol. V, Pt. VI, 1923; *Missouri*: "It's In St. Louis That Americanese is Spoken," New York *World*, Nov. 9, 1928; The Strategic Position of Missouri in Dialect Study, by Allen Walker Read, *Missouri Alumnus*, April, 1932; Folk-Speech in Missouri, by the same, *Arcadian Magazine*, June, 1932; *Nebraska*: Nebraska Sandhill Talk, by Melvin Van den Bark, *American Speech*, Dec., 1928; Expressions From Boyd County, Neb., by M. A. Burwell, the same, Feb., 1931; Nebraska Pioneer English, by Melvin Van den Bark, *American Speech*, April and Oct., 1931, Feb., 1932, and Dec., 1933; *Oregon*: Wallowa County, Ore., Expressions, by T. Josephine Hausen, the same, Feb., 1931. The following more general discussions are also of interest: Westernisms, by Kate Mullen, *American Speech*, Dec., 1925; Some Observations Upon Middle Western Speech, by Josephine M. Burnham, *Dialect Notes*, Vol. V, Pt. IX, 1926; The Eng-

In Canada it prevails everywhere west of Montreal, and even to the eastward, as we have seen in Section 2, the flat *a* is dominant along the American border. The so-called Bluenose dialect of " the whole of New Brunswick and the greater part of Nova Scotia outside Halifax "[1] has affinities with the common speech of rural New England, but the early settlers of Ontario came mainly from New York and Pennsylvania, and those of the western regions have been principally American Middle Westerners, with admixtures of Germans, Scandinavians, Finns and Russians. In Ontario, the broad *a* " is never heard in *aunt* and *rather*," but the flat *a* is occasionally heard even in *father*.[2] Throughout Canada, of course, the American vocabulary is dominant. Its neologisms are frequently denounced by patriotic Canadians with an eye on London, but even the statesmen of the Dominion now employ it in their deliberations. Said the Ottawa *Journal* in a recent editorial on the subject:

With the disappearance of Gladstonian haberdashery and frock coats, ponderosity of language could no longer be properly sustained, and now antiquarians can trace but the faintest vestiges in the Senate chamber. The stimulus of Burke's orations and classical English speech has given place to the stimulus of Hollywood and the air waves.[3]

In Bermuda, rather curiously, the General American flat *a* is used by the upper classes, and is a sign of social consequence, whereas the Negroes employ the broad English *a* and are looked down upon for doing so. Says Dr. Harry Morgan Ayres:

I am not prepared to draw with precision the line demarking socially the distribution of this sound. I can only say that my hostess used [the flat *a*] consistently, even in *calm*, and her Negro maid, aged nineteen, used [the broad

lish Language in the Southwest, *New Mexico Historical Review,* July, 1932; The Length of the Sounds of a Middle Westerner, by C. E. Parmenter and S. N. Treviño, *American Speech,* April, 1935.

1 Canadian English, by W. D. Lighthall, Toronto *Week,* Aug. 16, 1889.

2 Ontario Speech, by Evelyn R. Ahrend, *American Speech,* April, 1934. The first treatise on Canadian English was written by A. S. Geikie and appeared in the *Canadian Journal* so long ago as 1857. There have been few additions to the literature since. Those appearing down to the end of 1922 are

listed in Kennedy's Bibliography, above cited, p. 404. Among the later ones, all fragmentary, are Newfoundland Dialect Items, by George Allen England, *Dialect Notes,* Vol. V, Pt. VIII, 1925; Montreal English, by Helen C. Munroe, *American Speech,* Oct., 1929; A Note on Canadian English, by W. S. W. McLay, the same, April, 1930 (a correction of errors by Miss Munroe); Terms From the Labrador Coast, by Mary S. Evans, the same, Oct., 1930; More Labrador Survivals, by W. D. Strong, the same, April, 1931.

3 Parliament Goes Hollywood, April 7, 1934.

a] with a distribution historically absolutely accurate. How far up the social scale [the broad *a*] has penetrated I cannot say; I suspect it has gone further in St. George than elsewhere in the islands. In this respect Bermuda presents us with an exact picture of what it is necessary to suppose English of the Seventeenth and early Eighteenth Centuries to have been. It presumably represents the distribution of the sounds which the settlers brought with them, and which they only among English emigrant communities have preserved.[1]

The *r* is sounded in Bermuda before consonants and in the terminal position by all classes, save in a few words, *e.g.*, *shirker, stern, perfectly, first* and *further.* " It appears to be present in sufficient quantity," says Dr. Ayres, " to require belief that the English immigrants brought it with them, as they brought it likewise to the American Continent." In the West Indies, including the Bahamas, an exaggerated form of Southern English prevails among the blacks, with a very broad *a* dominant. Their white overlords speak Southern English too, but in a more restrained manner, and with touches, now and then, of Lowland Scotch.

In Hawaii there has arisen a dialect of American that is confined to the islands, and is full of interesting peculiarities. Its basis seems to be Beach-la-Mar, the common trade speech of the Western Pacific, in which, for many years past, there have been a number of terms of American origin, *e.g.*, *alligator, boss, pickaninny, schooner* and *tomahawk,*[2] but since English began to be taught in the Hawaiian schools in 1853, and especially since the American annexation of the islands in 1898, this crude jargon has moved in the direction of Standard American, and today it is very far from its humble beginnings. The original Beach-la-Mar, considerably changed by Chinese influence, still survives,[3] but it is spoken only by " the immigrant generation of Orientals and Latins, and some elderly native Hawaiians."[4] The other non-American inhabitants, whether Japanese, Chinese, Koreans, Portuguese, Porto Ricans, Filipinos or native Hawaiians, speak the dialect aforesaid, in varieties ranging from something rising but little above Beach-la-Mar to something hard to distinguish from the speech of native Americans.[5] It is used, in one

1 Bermudian English, *American Speech*, Feb., 1933.
2 See Beach-la-Mar, by William Churchill; Washington, 1911.
3 There is a good account of it in Pidgin English in Hawaii, by William C. Smith, *American Speech*, Feb., 1933.

4 The English Dialect of Hawaii, by John E. Reinecke and Aiko Tokimasa, *American Speech*, Feb., 1934, p. 50.
5 For what follows I am chiefly indebted to the paper by Mr. Reinecke and Miss Tokimasa, just cited. It appeared in *American*

form or other, by probably two-thirds of the people of the islands. It resembles vulgar American in its disregard of grammatical niceties, but its vocabulary differs considerably from the speech of the main-land. Many familiar words and phrases, *e.g., to pitchfork, small potatoes* and *to go the whole hog,* are omitted because the objects to which they refer are unfamiliar in Hawaii; other common expressions have been changed in meaning, *e.g., bogus* has come to mean boastful or a boaster, *meat* signifies only beef, and by a confusion between *laboratory* and *lavatory, lab* has come to mean the latter. There are, of course, many loan-words from Hawaiian and the non-English immigrant languages, *e.g., aloha* (farewell), *haole* (a white of Germanic blood), *kuleana* (a small land-holding) and *wikiwiki* (quickly) from the Hawaiian; *jabon* (the shaddock), *hekka* (a popular stew), and *mama-san* (an old Japanese woman) from the Japanese; *stay* (from *esta,* meaning *is*) from the Portuguese; *kaukau* (food) from the Chinese; and *bagoong* (a shrimpy sauce) from one of the Filipino languages. In addition, there are a number of survivals from Beach-la-Mar, still in wide use, *e.g.,* the use of *been* as "the common device to express past time of action," the use of *one* as the indefinite article, and the use of *humbug* in the sense of bother. The different races speaking the dialect have borrowed or invented various more or less opprobrious names for one another, *e.g., dog-eater* for Hawaiian, *baccaliaos* (codfish) for a Portuguese, *yabo* (from the Japanese) for a Korean. A recent Japanese immigrant is a *Japan jack,* and his brother from China is a *China jack.* The re-duplication of words for intensification has been taken over from Hawaiian, *e.g., talk-talk* and *fight-fight.* In a number of cases words of similar sound have been confused, with resulting change in the meaning of one or both. Thus *slide* is commonly pronounced *sly, to sly* is to slide, and as an adjective *sly* means slippery. Similarly, *to bob* has been related (not illogically) to *barber,* and transformed

Speech in two parts, Feb. and April, 1934. The two authors, who are husband and wife, are teachers in Hawaii. Mr. Reinecke, who is an American, went there in 1926. Miss Tokimasa, who is a Japanese, was educated at the Honolulu Normal School. I am also indebted to the Rev. Henry P. Judd, associate secretary of the Board of the Hawaiian Evangelical Association, who kindly answered a number of questions; to Mr. Frederick B. Withington, who gave me access to his paper, The Hawaiian Language: Its Modern History as a Means of Communication; and to Mr. N. B. Beck, assistant professor of English in the University of Hawaii.

into *to barb*. The parts of speech are often interchanged, *e.g.*, *taxi* signifies the driver as well as his vehicle, a stupid person is a *dumb*, *hungry* is used in place of *hunger*, and *politeness* serves as adjective instead of *polite*. Within the confines of any given part of speech there is a disregard of small shades of difference in meaning. Thus, " there was *much* people, but they had *few* money."

The tendency to reduce all the tenses of the verb to a sort of historical present, so marked in vulgar American, goes the full way in the Hawaiian dialect. The auxiliaries *been* and *stay*, taken over from Beach-la-Mar and borrowed from Portuguese respectively, serve in lieu of tense inflections, at least in the easier sorts of discourse. Thus, "I *been* eat " means "I have eaten," and " Us *stay* sweating" means " We are sweating" or " We were sweating," according to the context. The final *s* is commonly omitted from the third person singular in the present tense, there is a hopeless confusion between the preterite and perfect participle, and *to* is often dropped before the infinitive, as in "I like go." In the use of the pronoun all the confusions between case-forms that occur in vulgar American are encountered, and in addition two forms are sometimes joined, as in " *Me I* will go." There is also some confusion in number, as in " Take *these* flowers and put *it* in a vase." The noun, in the genitive, seldom shows the final *'s*. The common form is " They stayed at *Hirata*," not " at *Hirata's*." The noun also loses *s* in the plural. The article is frequently omitted altogether, and *one* is often used in place of *a*. Sometimes *a* is used in the plural. Among the prepositions there is chaos. Sometimes a preposition is omitted, as in " The horse stepped [*on*] him "; sometimes it is put where it doesn't belong, as in " I attend *to* school "; and sometimes the wrong one is used, as in " We walked *till* Haina." The adverbs also suffer severely. Both adverbs and adjectives are placed before the subject when emphasis is desired, and after the interrogatives *what* and *where* the verb also precedes the subject. Conjunctions are often omitted between two members of a series, and when a sentence closes with a preposition the preposition is sometimes forgotten. The articulation of those who speak this dialect is reasonably clear, but they have a habit of prolonging stressed vowels, and of clipping unstressed vowels and all consonants. " Sometimes it is difficult for an ear trained to Mainland American speech to catch words because of the comparative rapidity of utterance. There is little drawling, even where there is hesitation; the speed and pitch of utterance remind us more of the British norm than of the American." [1] But British influence upon the dialect, of course, is actually infinitesimal. It is a form of American English, and in the course of time it will probably come closer and closer to everyday vulgar American. Since 1896 all the public schools of the islands have been conducted in American English, and every other language currently in use, including Hawaiian, shows signs of dying out.

Those Filipinos who have acquired American English in the public schools of the archipelago do it less violence than the Hawaiians, but nevertheless they make changes in it. It is most unusual for one of them to speak it well. For one thing, they learn it mainly, not by hearing it, but out of books, and under the tutelage of teachers who have learned it in the same way.[2] For another thing, it is full of sounds that are strange to their lips, and are not easily mastered, e.g., those of *th*, *sh*, *f*, *v*, *j* and *z*. Thus they commonly convert *there* into *dare*, *thin* into *tin*, *she* into *see*, *flea* into *plea*, *verb* into *herb*, *jelly* into *chelly*, *zig-zag* into *sig-sog*, *is* into *iss*, and *has* into *hass*. They are unable to pronounce combinations of *s* with *t*, *p*, *l* or *k* without prefixing *e*, so that *student* becomes *estudent*, *space* becomes *espace*, *sleep* becomes *esleep*, and *skate* becomes *eskate*. The word *Filipino*, as they utter it, sounds much like *Pilipino*. The combination of *m* or *n* with *d* is also difficult for them, as is the combination of *l* and *d*, so they commonly omit the *d* in such words as *blamed*, *chained* and *failed*. The *r* is always heavily trilled. The vowels are easier for them, save the flat *a* of *am*, but they often confuse one with another, and in writing they give all the vowels Spanish values, so that *chick* becomes *cheek* and *shed* becomes *shade*.[3] According to Dr. H. Otley Beyer, professor of ethnology in the University of the Philippines, the Filipinos speak no less than 87 languages and dialects, but nearly all of them belong to the Tagala branch of the

1 Reinecke and Tokimasa, above cited, Art. II, p. 130.
2 During the first years of the American occupation a great many American teachers went to the islands, but by 1925 they had been reduced in number to 305 in a corps of 25,530. The survivors taught only in the high-schools. In the primary grades virtually all the teachers of English were na-

tives. See Bamboo English, by George G. Struble, *American Speech*, April, 1929, pp. 277–78.
3 I am indebted here and below to Struble, just cited, to The English Language in the Philippines, by Emma Sarepta Yule, *American Speech*, Nov., 1925, and to A Little Brown Language, by Jerome B. Barry, the same, Oct., 1927.

Malayo-Polynesian family, and show the same general characters. For example, they all put the accent on the penultimate syllable in many common words. Inasmuch as Spanish does the same the natives are inclined to carry that accent into English, and in consequence they often say *probábly*, *charácter* and *distribúting*. Even when they do not push the accent all the way, they move it a step, thus producing such forms as *dyséntery* and *vegétable*. They also carry many Tagala idioms into English. Thus, the answer to a negative question is an affirmative, *e.g.*, " Have you no bananas? " " Yes." The affirmative is also used in answering a question embodying alternatives, and applies to the one mentioned last, *e.g.*, the reply to " Do you prefer meat or fish " is " Yes," meaning " I prefer fish." This Filipino English will probably not long survive the American withdrawal from the islands. It is " essentially a bookish language, a language of learning, somewhat in the sense that Latin was the language of learning in the Middle Ages," and not many natives have ever got sufficient command of it to speak it voluntarily and naturally.[1] Article XIII, Section 3 of the Philippine Constitution provides that it is to be supplanted as soon as possible, along with Spanish, by " a common national language based on one of the existing native languages."

The American spoken by Americans in the Philippines shows a large admixture of Spanish and Tagala words and phrases, just as the American spoken in Hawaii is shot through with terms borrowed from Hawaiian. But in both cases it is pronounced according to the General American pattern, and there are no changes in its grammar and syntax. Here is a specimen from Manila:

Hola, amigo.
Komusta kayo.
Porque were you *hablaing* with *ese señorita?*
She wanted a job as *lavandera.*
Cuanto?
Ten cents, *conant*, a piece, so I told her *no kerry.*
Have you had *chow?* Well, *spera*, till I sign this *chit* and I'll take a *paseo* with you.[2]

In this brief dialogue there are eight loan-words from the Spanish (*hola, amigo, porque, ese, señorita, lavandera, cuanto* and *paseo*), two Spanish locutions in a debased form (*spera* for *espera* and *no*

1 Struble, above cited, p. 284.
2 This is borrowed from What Americans Talk in the Philippines,

by Maurice P. Dunlap, *Review of Reviews*, Aug., 1913.

kerry for *no quiero*), two loan-words from the Tagala (*komusta* and *kayo*),[1] two from the Pidgin English of the China coast (*chow* and *chit*), one Philippine-American localism (*conant*), and a Spanish verb with an English inflection (*hablaing*). The following is from an article on Hawaiian English in the Christian Science *Monitor:* [2]

"Are you *pau?* " asks the American housekeeper of her Japanese yard-man. " All *pau*," he responds.

The housekeeper has asked if the yard-man is through. He has replied that he is. *Pau* — pronounced *pow* — conveys just as much meaning to the Honolulan as the English [3] word *through*.

In Honolulu one does not say "the northwest corner of Fork and Hotel streets." One says "the *makai-ewa* corner." *Makai* means toward the sea. *Ewa* means toward the north or in the direction of the big Ewa plantation which lies toward the north of Honolulu. Thus the *makai-ewa* corner means that corner which is on the seaward side and toward Ewa. Instead of saying *east* or the direction in which the sun rises, Honolulans say *mauka*, which means toward the mountains. To designate south, they say *waikiki*, which means toward Diamond Head or Waikiki Beach.

One often hears a little boy say he has a *puka* in his stocking. The housekeeper directs the yard-man to put the rubbish in the *puka*. It is a Hawaiian word meaning hole. Another common word is *lanai*. In English it means porch or veranda. The two words *pahea oe* are used as a term of greeting. In the States they say, "How do you do? " " How are you? " or " Good Day." In Honolulu, " *Pahea oe?* " conveys the same meaning. The response is " *Maikai no*," or " Very good," or " All right."

At two other places under the American flag dialects of English flourish. One is Key West and the other is the Virgin Islands. The Key West dialect is Southern American showing the influence of Bahaman English and Cuban Spanish. The *i* is frequently given its Spanish sound, especially in proper names, so that *Olivia* becomes *Oleevia*. The *a*, before *g*, is transformed into a short *i*, so that *bag* becomes *big* and *rag* becomes *rig*. The *w* and *v* are exchanged, so that *west* becomes *vest*, and *visit* becomes *wisit*. The *h* is treated in the Cockney manner, so that horse becomes *orse* and the letter *l* is called *hell*. *Ain't* is often used in place of *won't* or *haven't*. The *-ed* ending is omitted from the past tense forms of the verbs. Many Spanish idioms are translated literally, *e.g.*, *Quantos años tiene?* which becomes " How many years you got? " There are many loan-

---

1 But here *komusta* may be borrowed from the Spanish *como está* (how are you?).

2 Unfortunately, I have mislaid my memorandum of the date and the author's name.

3 That is, American; *through*, in this sense, is seldom used by the English.

words from the Spanish, and the inhabitants have invented the usual opprobrious terms for one another, *e.g., conch* (a West Indian), and *saw* (a native of Nassau).[1] The Virgin Islands dialect, of course, is not American, but English. Basically, it is simply the English of the late Seventeenth Century, but there are many Spanish, Portuguese, French, Dutch and Danish loan-words, and some vestiges of the West Coast African dialects. The phonology shows Danish influence. Among the special characters are the omission of *s* before consonants, so that *stocking* becomes *tocking,* and the use of a collective pronoun, *a-wee,* corresponding to the Southern American *us-all.*[2] This jargon is spoken not only in the Virgin Islands, but also in the British Lesser Antilles, in Dutch Saba and in French St. Martin, of course with local variations. A somewhat analogous dialect, but much less like Standard English, is spoken in Dutch Guiana, on the South American mainland.[3]

1 I am indebted here to A Philologist's Paradise, by Thomas R. Reid, Jr., *Opportunity,* Jan., 1926.
2 For a specimen of the dialect see Negro Dialect of the Virgin Islands, by Henry S. Whitehead, *American Speech,* Feb., 1932.
3 See Surinam Negro-English, by John Dyneley Prince, *American Speech,* Oct., 1934, and Colonial Survivals in Bush-Negro Speech, by A. G. Barnett, the same, Aug., 1932. The dialects spoken in Australia, India and South Africa lie outside the bounds of the present inquiry, but some reference to the literature may be useful. All of it down to the end of 1922 is listed in Kennedy's Bibliography, above cited, pp. 404–5. The following, too late for Kennedy or overlooked by him, are also of interest: South African English Pronunciation, by David Hopwood; Cape Town, 1928; The Pronunciation of English in South Africa, by W. E. C. Clarke; Johannesburg, 1913; Cockney English and Kitchen Dutch, by C. M. Drennan; Johannesburg, 1920; Some Notes on Indian English, by R. C. Goffin, *S.P.E. Tracts,* No. XLI, 1934; The Australian Accent, *Triad* (Sydney, N. S. W.), Nov. 10, 1920; How English is Spoken Here, by B. Sc., Sydney *Evening News,* May 5, 1925; Words, Words, Words, by Guy Innes, Melbourne *Herald,* Nov. 11, 1933. Vulgar Australian-English shows the Cockney whine, and is altogether a dreadful dialect. The vocabulary is heavy with loans from American, but there are also some picturesque native inventions, *e.g., wowser* (a kill-joy), *bullsh* (a false report), *to go hostile* (to become angry), and *woop-woop* (a country district). There is a brief glossary of it in Slang Today and Yesterday, by Eric Partridge, 2nd ed.; London, 1935. The Australian dialect is uniform throughout the country. In New Zealand a form of Southern English free from Cockney vowels is spoken.

VIII

AMERICAN SPELLING

I. THE INFLUENCE OF NOAH WEBSTER

At the time of the first English settlements in America the rules of English orthography were beautifully vague, and so we find the early documents full of spellings that seem quite fantastic today. *Aetaernall,* for *eternal,* is in the Acts of the Massachusetts General Court for 1646, *adjoin* is spelled *adioyne* in the Dedham Records for 1637, *February* is *Ffebrewarie* in the Portsmouth, R. I. Records for 1639–97, and *general* is *jinerll* in the Hartford Town Votes for 1635–1716.[1] There had been attempts in England since the middle of the Sixteenth Century to put the spelling of the language upon a more or less rational basis,[2] but their effects were only slowly realized. It was not, indeed, until about 1630, nearly a quarter of a century after the landing at Jamestown, that English printers began to differentiate clearly between *u* and *v,* *i* and *j.* The two pairs were still confused in the First Folio of Shakespeare, printed in 1623, and Sir John Cheke, one of the first English spelling reformers, was quite content to write *mijn* for *mine* and *vnmixt* for *unmixed.* The redundant final *e,* usually a relic of a long-lost inflection, was much oftener encountered then than now, and a glance through almost any Seventeenth Century American public document will show *toune* for *town, halfe* for *half, smale* for *small,* and *yeare* for *year.*

There were no dictionaries in those days — or, at all events, none of any generally admitted authority — but as printing increased, a movement toward uniformity in spelling, if not toward rationality,

---

1 Dr. Miles L. Hanley of the University of Wisconsin, with the aid of various other scholars, has unearthed a large number of such forms from "forty diaries and ten sets of town and parish records, ... chiefly from Massachusetts and Connecticut." His list of them was mimeographed in June, 1935, and he has kindly placed a copy at my disposal.

2 They are described in George H. McKnight's Modern English in the Making; New York, 1928, especially pp. 119–20, 191–2, and 229.

began to show itself. By the beginning of the Eighteenth Century all the principal English authors were spelling pretty much alike, and by 1711, when the first number of the *Spectator* appeared, they were spelling substantially as we spell now. But it was not until the publication of Samuel Johnson's Dictionary, in 1755, that the English had a real guide to orthography, of universal acceptance. Johnson, in the presence of conflicting usages, always took the conservative side. He preferred what he called " Saxon " spellings for what he conceived to be old English words, and thus ordained that *music*, *critic* and even *prosaic* should have a final *k*, though all three were actually borrowings from the Latin through the French. He decided for the *-our* ending in words of the *honor* class, and it remains in vogue in England to this day. When there was doubt, he proceeded with " a scholar's reverence for antiquity," and gave his imprimatur to many spellings based upon false etymologies and pointless analogies. Naturally enough, he fell into a number of contradictions, and it was easy for Lindley Murray to point them out, *e.g.*, such pairs as *deceit* and *receipt*, *moveable* and *immovable*, *sliness* and *slyly*, *deign* and *disdain*. Even among the *-our* words he permitted *exterior* to slip in alongside *interiour*, and *posterior* alongside *anteriour*. He also undertook occasional reforms that failed to make their way, *e.g.*, the reduction of final *-ll* to *-l*, leading to such forms as *downhil*, *catcal*, *unrol* and *forestal*. But on the whole, his professed respect for " the genius of the language " showed a very keen feeling for it, and his decisions ratified what had become customary usage far oftener than they sought to change it. His influence was tremendous, both in England and in America.

There is no evidence that his mandates were ever challenged on this side of the water until the Revolution. In 1768, to be sure, the ever busy and iconoclastic Benjamin Franklin had published " A Scheme for a New Alphabet and a Reformed Mode of Spelling," and induced a Philadelphia type-founder to cut the six new characters that it demanded, but this project was too extravagant to be adopted anywhere, or to have any appreciable influence.[1] It was

1 The Scheme is reprinted in Franklin's Words, edited by John Bigelow; New York, 1887–8; Vol. IV, p. 198 *ff*. The six new characters were a modified *a* for the long *a* in *ball*, an *h* upside down for the *u* in *unto*, a combination of long *s* and *i* for the *sh* in *wish*, a *y* with a curled tail for *ng*, an *h* with a curled tail for the *th* in *think*, and a somewhat similar *h*, but with a wavy appendage at the top, for the *th* of *thy*. Franklin expunged *c*, *w*, *y* and *j* from the alphabet as un-

Noah Webster who finally achieved a divorce between English precept and example and American practice. In his " Grammatical Institute of the English Language," published in Hartford in 1783, he was content to follow and even to praise Johnson's spellings, *e.g.*, in the *-our* words, but soon thereafter he was launched upon his grandiose plan to establish an independent " Federal " language in the new Republic, and in 1786 he approached Franklin and Timothy Pickering [1] with a project for reducing its orthography " to perfect regularity, with as few new characters and alterations of the old ones as possible." Franklin was receptive, and Webster seems to have submitted his ideas to the other " distinguished characters " of the time, including Washington and Jefferson. During the succeeding three years he carried on his campaign with his usual pertinacity, but it does not appear that he made many converts. In 1789 he published his " Dissertations on the English Language," and in an appendix thereto he printed his proposals in some detail. They were as follows:

1. The omission of all superfluous or silent letters; as *a* in *bread*. Thus *bread, head, give, breast, built, meant, realm, friend* would be spelt *bred, hed, giv, brest, bilt, ment, relm, frend*. Would this alteration produce any inconvenience, any embarrassment or expense? By no means. On the other hand, it would lessen the trouble of writing, and much more, of learning the language; it would reduce the true pronunciation to a certainty; and while it would assist foreigners and our own children in acquiring the language, it would render the pronunciation uniform, in different parts of the country, and almost prevent the possibility of changes.

2. A substitution of a character that has a certain definite sound for one that is more vague and indeterminate. Thus by putting *ee* instead of *ea* or *ie*, the words *mean, near, speak, grieve, zeal* would become *meen, neer, speek, greev, zeel*. This alteration could not occasion a moment's trouble; at the same time it would prevent a doubt respecting the pronunciation; whereas the *ea* and *ie*, having different sounds, may give a learner much difficulty. Thus *greef* should be substituted for *grief*; *kee* for *key*; *beleev* for *believe*; *laf* for *laugh*; *dawter* for *daughter*; *plow* for *plough*; *tuf* for *tough*; *proov* for

necessary. He proposed that the vowels be differentiated by using one letter for the short ones and two for the long ones. He made trial of his new alphabet in a letter to Miss Stephenson of London, apparently a bluestocking of the time. She replied on Sept. 26, 1768, saying that she could *si meni inkanviiniensis* in it. He defended it in a letter from *Kreven striit*, London, Sept. 28.

1 For his letter to Pickering, dated May 12, see American Projects for an Academy to Regulate Speech, by Allen Walker Read, *Publications of the Modern Language Association*, 1936. He said: " The idea is well received in New York, and many of the most discerning gentlemen in Congress are its warmest advocates." Timothy Pickering (1745-1829) was the father of John Pickering.

prove; blud for *blood;* and *draft* for *draught.* In this manner *ch* in Greek derivatives should be changed into *k;* for the English *ch* has a soft sound, as in *cherish,* but *k* always a hard sound. Therefore *character, chorus, cholic, architecture,* should be written *karacter, korus, kolic, arkitecture;* and were they thus written, no person could mistake their true pronunciation. Thus *ch* in French derivatives should be changed into *sh; machine, chaise, chevalier* should be written *masheen, shaze, shevaleer;* and *pique, tour, oblique* should be written *peek, toor, obleek.*

3. A trifling alteration in a character, or the addition of a point, would distinguish different sounds, without the substitution of a new character. Thus a very small stroke across *th* would distinguish its two sounds. A point over a vowel, in this manner: *à,* or *ò,* or *ī,* might answer all the purposes of different letters. And for the diphthong *ow,* let the two letters be united by a small stroke, or both engraven on the same piece of metal, with the left hand line of the *w* united to the *o.*

These changes, said Webster, " with a few other inconsiderable alterations, would answer every purpose, and render the orthography sufficiently correct and regular." They would " diminish the number of letters about one sixteenth or eighteenth," they would tend to " render the pronunciation of the language as uniform as the spelling in books," and they would " facilitate the learning of the language." The greatest argument, however, was the patriotic one:

A capital advantage of this reform in these States would be that it would make a difference between the English orthography and the American. This will startle those who have not attended to the subject; but I am confident that such an event is an object of vast political consequence.

The alteration, however small, would encourage the publication of books in our own country. It would render it, in some measure, necessary that all books should be printed in America. The English would never copy our orthography for their own use; and consequently the same impressions of books would not answer for both countries. The inhabitants of the present generation would read the English impressions; but posterity, being taught a different spelling, would prefer the American orthography.

Besides this, a national language is a band of national union. Every engine should be employed to render the people of this country national; to call their attachments home to their own country; and to inspire them with the pride of national character. However they may boast of Independence, and the freedom of their government, yet their opinions are not sufficiently independent; an astonishing respect for the arts and literature of their parent country, and a blind imitation of its manners, are still prevalent among the Americans. Thus an habitual respect for another country, deserved indeed and once laudable, turns their attention from their own interests, and prevents their respecting themselves.

But, as Dr. George Philip Krapp points out in " The English Language in America," [1] Webster was " above all a practical, not a

1 New York, 1925, Vol. I, p. 332 *ff.*

theoretical reformer," and in consequence he was slow himself to adopt the reforms he advocated. When in 1783, he republished the first part of his " Grammatical Institute " as the first edition of his famous " American Spelling Book," he used the orthodox English spelling of the time, and not only gave the *-our* words their English ending, but even commended it. And so late as 1806, in the preface to his first Dictionary, he tried somewhat disingenuously to disassociate himself from Franklin's scheme to reform the alphabet. Indeed, in all the editions of the Spelling Book printed before 1806 he avoided noticeable novelties in spelling, though after 1798 he noted, in his preface, his conviction that " common sense and convenience " would soon or late substitute *public, favor, nabor, hed, proov, flem, hiz, giv, det, ruf* and *wel* for *publick, favour, neighbour, head, prove, phlegm, his, give, debt, rough* and *well.* But in his Dictionary of 1806, despite his coolness to Franklin's alphabet, he used Franklin's saying that " those people spell best who do not know how to spell " — *i.e.,* who spell phonetically — as a springboard for a wholesale assault upon the authority of Johnson. He made an almost complete sweep of whole classes of silent letters — the *u* in the *-our* words, the final *e* in *determine* and *requisite*, the silent *a* in *thread, feather* and *steady*, the silent *b* in *thumb*, the *s* in *island*, the *o* in *leopard*, and the redundant consonants in *traveler, wagon, jeweler*, etc. (Eng. *traveller, waggon, jeweller*). He lopped the final *k* from *frolick, physick* and their analogues, and transposed the *e* and the *r* in many words ending in *re*, such as *theatre, lustre, centre* and *calibre*. More, he changed the *c* in all words of the *defence* class to *s*. Yet more, he changed *ph* to *f* in words of the *phantom* class, *ou* to *oo* in words of the *group* class, *ow* to *ou* in *crowd, porpoise* to *porpess, acre* to *aker, sew* to *soe, woe* to *wo, soot* to *sut, gaol* to *jail* and *plough* to *plow.* Finally, he antedated the simplified spellers by inventing a long list of boldly phonetic spellings, ranging from *tung* for *tongue* to *wimmen* for *women*, and from *hainous* for *heinous* to *cag* for *keg.*

Some of these new spellings, of course, were not actually Webster's inventions. For example, the change from *-our* to *-or* in words of the *honor* class was a mere echo of an earlier English uncertainty. In the first three folios of Shakespeare, 1623, 1632 and 1663–6, *honor* and *honour* were used indiscriminately and in almost equal proportions; English spelling, as we have seen, was then still fluid, and the *-our*-form was not used consistently until the Fourth Folio of 1685.

Moreover, John Wesley, the founder of Methodism, is authority for the statement that the *-or*-form was " a fashionable impropriety " in England in 1791. But the great authority of Johnson stood against it, and Webster was surely not one to imitate fashionable improprieties. He deleted the *u* for purely etymological reasons, going back to the Latin *honor, favor* and *odor* without taking account of the intermediate French *honneur, faveur* and *odeur*. And where no etymological reasons presented themselves, he made his changes by analogy and for the sake of uniformity, or for euphony or simplicity, or because it pleased him, one guesses, to stir up the academic animals. Webster, in fact, delighted in controversy, and was anything but free from the national yearning to make a sensation.

Many of his innovations, of course, failed to take root, and in the course of time he abandoned some of them himself. Among them were the dropping of the silent letter in such words as *head, give, built* and *realm*, making them *hed, giv, bilt* and *relm;* the substitution of doubled vowels for apparent diphthongs in such words as *mean, zeal* and *near*, making them *meen, zeel* and *neer;* and the substitution of *sh* for *ch* in such French loan-words as *machine* and *chevalier*, making them *masheen* and *shevaleer*. He had once declared for *stile* in place of *style*, and for many other such changes, but now quietly abandoned them. The successive editions of his Dictionary show still further concessions. *Croud, fether, groop, gillotin, iland, insted, leperd, soe, sut, steddy, thret, thred, thum* and *wimmen* appear only in the 1806 edition. In his " *American* Dictionary of the English Language " (1828), the father of all the Websters of today, he went back to *crowd, feather, group, island, instead, leopard, sew, soot, steady, thread, threat, thumb* and *women*, and changed *gillotin* to *guillotin*, and in addition, he restored the final *e* in *determine, discipline, requisite, imagine*, etc. In 1838, revising the " American Dictionary," he abandoned a good many spellings that had appeared even in his 1828 edition, *e.g.*, *maiz* for *maize*, *suveran* [1] for *sovereign* and *guillotin* for *guillotine*, but he stuck manfully to a number that were quite as revolutionary — *e.g.*, *aker* for *acre*, *cag* for *keg*, *grotesk* for *grotesque*, *hainous* for *heinous*, *porpess* for *porpoise* and *tung* for *tongue* — and they did not begin to disappear until the edition of 1854, issued by other hands and eleven years after

1 I find *soveran* in the London *Times Literary Supplement* for Aug. 5, 1920, p. 1, *art.* Words for Music, but it seems to have no support elsewhere.

his death. Three of his favorites, *chimist* for *chemist*, *neger* for *negro* and *zeber* for *zebra*, are incidentally interesting as showing changes in American pronunciation. He abandoned *zeber* in 1828, but remained faithful to *chimist* and *neger* to the last.

But though he was thus forced to give occasional ground, and in more than one case held out in vain, Webster lived to see many of his reforms adopted by his countrymen. The influence of his Spelling Book was really stupendous. It took the place in the schools of Dilworth's "Aby-sel-pha," the favorite of the Revolutionary generation, and maintained its authority for nearly a century. Until Lyman Cobb entered the lists with his "New Spelling Book," its innumerable editions had no really formidable rivalry, and even then it held its own. I have a New York edition, dated 1848, which contains an advertisement stating that the annual sale at that time was more than a million copies, and that more than 30,000,000 copies had been sold since 1783. In the late 40's the publishers, George F. Cooledge & Bro., devoted the whole capacity of the fastest steam press in the United States to the printing of it. This press turned out 525 copies an hour, or 5,250 a day. It was "constructed expressly for printing Webster's 'Elementary Spelling Book' [the name had been changed in 1829] at an expense of $5,000." Down to 1865, 42,000,000 copies had been sold, and down to 1889, 62,000,-000. The appearance of Webster's first Dictionary, in 1806, greatly strengthened his influence. Four other dictionaries had been published in the United States since 1798 — Samuel Johnson, Jr.'s, John Elliott's, Caleb Alexander's and William Woodridge's — but Noah's quickly dominated the popular field, and in those days dictionaries were accepted even more gravely than they are today.[1] Thus he left

1 Their influence was described by Allen Walker Read in The Development of Faith in the Dictionary in America, a paper read before the Present Day English Section of the Modern Language Association at Philadelphia, Dec. 29, 1934. So late as 1851 the deputy superintendent of the common schools of Massachusetts reported after he had made a tour through the State: "In many towns the dictionary was the only authoritative judge and umpire in literary matters." Webster's and its rivals were sold very cheaply. The following is from a letter by Bemis and Ward, booksellers of Canandaigua, N. Y., Jan. 16, 1833: "We published Walker's until last year, but . . . the market was crowded with them at 20 to 25 cents. Our country merchants get their supplies of them in the cities, and we have sold our plates, not being able or willing to make the book *poor* enough to compete with *such* editions. We retail Webster's [School Dictionary] at 87 cents — Walker's at 50. The *poorer* editions are probably sold at 37½."

the ending in -*or* triumphant over the ending in -*our*, he shook the security of the ending in -*re*, he rid American spelling of a great many doubled consonants, he established the *s* in words of the *defense* group, and he gave currency to many characteristic American spellings, notably *jail, wagon, plow, mold* and *ax*. These spellings still survive, and are practically universal in the United States today; their use constitutes one of the most obvious differences between written English and written American. Moreover, they have founded a general tendency, the effects of which reach far beyond the field actually traversed by Webster himself. His reforms, of course, did not go unchallenged by the guardians of tradition. A glance at the literature of the first years of the Nineteenth Century shows that most of the more pretentious authors of the time ignored them, though they were quickly adopted by the newspapers. For example, the Rev. Aaron Bancroft's " Life of Washington " (1807) contains -*our* endings in all such words as *honor, ardor* and *favor*. Washington Irving, who began to publish in the same year, also inclined toward them, and so did William Cullen Bryant, whose " Thanatopsis " came out in 1817, and most of the other literary bigwigs of the era followed suit. After the appearance of the " American Dictionary " in 1828 a formal battle was joined, with Lyman Cobb and Joseph E. Worcester as the chief formal opponents of the reformer. His inconsistencies gave them a handy weapon for use against him — until it began to be noticed that the orthodox English spelling was quite as inconsistent. He sought to change *acre* to *aker*, but left *lucre* unchanged. He removed the final *f* from *bailiff, mastiff, plaintiff* and *pontiff*, but left it in *distaff*. He changed *c* to *s* in words of the *offense* class, but left the *c* in *fence*. He changed the *ck* in *frolick, physick*, etc., into a simple *c*, but restored it in such derivatives as *frolicksome*. He deleted the silent *u* in *mould*, but left it in *court*. These slips were made the most of by Cobb in a furious pamphlet in excessively fine print, printed in 1831.[1] He also detected Webster in the frequent *faux pas* of using spellings in his definitions and explanations that conflicted with the spellings he advocated. Various other purists joined in the attack, and it was carried on with great fury on the appearance of Worcester's Dictionary, in 1846, three years

[1] A Critical Review of the Orthography of Dr. Webster's Series of Books . . . ; New York, 1831. A modern and more moderate review of Webster's inconsistences is in A Linguistic Patriot, by Kemp Malone, *American Speech*, Oct., 1925.

after Webster's death. The partisans of conformity rallied round Worcester, and for a while the controversy took on all the rancor of a personal quarrel. According to McKnight,[1] Harvard University required candidates for matriculation to follow Worcester's spellings " as late as the last decade of the Nineteenth Century."

Both Cobb and Worcester, in the end, accepted the *-or* ending and so surrendered on what was really the main issue, but various other champions arose to carry on the war. Edward S. Gould, in a once famous essay,[2] denounced the whole Websterian orthography with the utmost fury, and Bryant, reprinting this philippic in the *Evening Post*, said that on account of Webster " the English language has been undergoing a process of corruption for the last quarter of a century," and offered to contribute to a fund to have Gould's denunciation " read twice a year in every school-house in the United States, until every trace of Websterian spelling disappears from the land." But Bryant was forced to admit that, even in 1856, the chief novelties of the Connecticut schoolmaster " who taught millions to read but not one to sin " were " adopted and propagated by the largest publishing house, through the columns of the most widely circulated monthly magazine, and through one of the ablest and most widely circulated newspapers in the United States " — which is to say, the *Tribune* under Greeley. The last academic attack was delivered by Bishop A. C. Coxe in 1886, and he contented himself with the resigned statement that " Webster has corrupted our spelling sadly." T. R. Lounsbury, with his active interest in spelling reform, ranged himself on the side of Webster, and effectively disposed of the controversy by showing that the great majority of his spellings were supported by precedents quite as respectable as those behind the fashionable English spellings. In Lounsbury's opinion, a great deal of the opposition to them was no more than a symptom of antipathy to all things American among certain Englishmen and of subservience to all things English among certain Americans.[3]

Thus Webster gradually conquered the country, and many, though certainly not most, of the reformed spellings he advocated

1 Modern English in the Making, p. 490.
2 *Democratic Review*, March, 1856. In Good English New York, 1867, p. 145 *ff*, Gould gloated over the fact that in the Webster's Dictionaries of 1854 and 1866, brought out after Webster's death, many of his spellings were withdrawn, or reduced to the estate of variants.
3 See his English Spelling and Spelling Reform; New York, 1909, p. 229.

at one time or another are the American standard today. Moreover, not a few of them have been adopted in England, and others seem to be making headway there. This invasion, of course, does not go without resistance, and every now and then there is an uproar in the English papers against American orthography, matching in virulence the perennial uproars against American slang. Back in 1892 Brander Matthews noted sadly " the force, fervor and frequency of the objurgations in the columns of the *Saturday Review* and of the *Athenæum*." [1] Those objurgations continue to be launched in the more finicky section of the English press to this day. Here is a specimen from a letter in the Literary Supplement of the London *Times*, the object of the assault being an edition of Walter Pater's " Marius the Epicurean " with certain somewhat gingery concessions to American usage:

Hardly a page but is blistered with hideous vulgarisms such as *offenses, skillful, fiber, theater, somber, traveling, moldering, marvelous, jeweler, worshiper, esthetic;* things which to Pater, one feels, would have been merely horrible. Nor is there even the grace of consistency in evil-doing; since we get *mouldering* on page 49, and *moldering* on page 143, *favour* on page 69 with *favor* four pages farther on, and *traveller* on dust-cover and title-page against *traveler* throughout the book.

The reason? Small doubt that these monstrous hybrids in " English " publications of " English " literature are bred by mass-production out of Copyright Law; making the best of both worlds by slipping into an English series-cover a book printed from stereo-plates made in U.S.A.

Surely the re-issue of English classics in the " nu speling " from " America " might be left to American publishers. And if it pays London to cater for U.S.A. readers, one might at least expect some warning for those who prefer the King's English undefiled: such as asterisks in the list against those volumes in which the " nu speling " is used, or the use of the " nu speling " itself in the covers, title-pages, and advertisements. [2]

2. THE ADVANCE OF AMERICAN SPELLING

But such uncompromising defenders of English spelling lead a forlorn hope. Not only is there a general movement toward American forms in the newspapers — including the *Times* itself —; there is also a general yielding by English " authorities." The Concise Oxford Dictionary of the Brothers Fowler, which came out in

1 Americanisms and Briticisms; New York, 1892, p. 37.   2 This Nu Speling, by C. R. Prance; London *Times*, April 24, 1930.

1914, offers plenty of examples. The authors say in their preface that they " stop short of recognizing forms that at present strike every reader as Americanisms," but they surely go far enough. In all the words ending in *-ise* and *-isation* the English *s* is changed to the American *z*. They prefer *leveler* to *leveller* and *riveted* to *rivetted*, though clinging sentimentally to *traveller*. They retain the first *e* in *judgement*, but omit it from *likeable*, and even go ahead of American usage by omitting it from *mileage*. They dismiss the *-or* ending as " entirely non-British," but concede that it is necessary in *horror* and *torpor*. Finally, they swap the English *y* for the American *i* in *tire*, *cider* and *siphon*, recognize *a* as a variant for *y* in *pyjama*, concede that *jail* is as good as *gaol*, prefer the American *asphalt* to the English *asphalte*, *toilet* to *toilette*, and *balk* to *baulk*, and admit *program*, *wagon*, *check* (on a bank) and *skeptic* without precisely endorsing them. The monumental Oxford Dictionary upon which the Concise Oxford is grounded shows many silent concessions, and quite as many open yieldings — for example, in the case of *ax*, which is admitted to be " better than *axe* on every ground." Moreover, many English lexicographers tend to march ahead of it, outstripping the liberalism of its editor, the late Sir James A. H. Murray. In 1914, for example, Sir James was still protesting against dropping the first *e* from *judgement*, but two years earlier the " Authors' and Printers' Dictionary," edited by Horace Hart,[1] Controller of the Oxford University Press, had dropped *judgement* altogether. " The Authors' and Printers' Dictionary " was, and is, an authority approved by the Master Printers' and Allied Trades' Association of London, the Edinburgh Master Printers' Association, the Belfast Printing Trades Employers' Association, and the executive committee of the London Association of Correctors of the Press, *i.e.*, proofreaders. Hart is now dead, but the seventh edition (1933), revised by some unnamed hand, continues to show a great many characteristic American spellings. For example, it recommends the use of *jail* and *jailer* in place of the English *gaol* and *gaoler*, drops the final *e* from *asphalte* and *stye*, changes the *y* to *i* in *cyder*, *cypher* and *syren*, and advocates the same change in *tyre*, drops the redundant *t* from *nett*, changes *burthen* to *burden*, spells *wagon* with one *g*, prefers *fuse* to *fuze*, and takes the *e* out of

1 Authors' & Printers' Dictionary . . . an attempt to codify the best typographical practices of the present day, by F. Howard Collins; 4th ed., revised by Horace Hart; London, 1912.

storey. "Rules for Compositors and Readers at the University Press, Oxford," also edited by Hart (with the advice of Sir James Murray and Dr. Henry Bradley) is another very influential English authority.[1] It gives its imprimatur to *bark* (a ship), *cipher, siren, jail, story, tire* and *wagon*, and even advocates *kilogram, tiro* and *omelet.* Cassell's New English Dictionary [2] goes quite as far. Like the "Authors' and Printers' Dictionary" and the Concise Oxford it clings to the *-our* and *-re* endings and to the redundant *a* in such words as *æsthete* and *anæsthesia*, but it prefers *jail* to *gaol, net* to *nett, story* to *storey, asphalt* to *asphalte, tire* to *tyre, wagon* to *waggon, vial* to *phial*, and *pygmy* to *pigmy.*

There is, however, much confusion among these authorities; the English are still unable to agree as to which American spellings they will adopt and which they will keep under the ban for a while longer. The Concise Oxford and the "Authors' and Printers' Dictionary" prefer *bark* to *barque* and the late Poet Laureate, Dr. Robert Bridges,[3] adopted it boldly, but Cassell still clings to *barque.* Cassell favors *baritone;* the Oxford and the A. and P. are for *barytone.* The Oxford is for *czar;* Cassell and the A. and P. for *tsar.* The Oxford admits *program;* Cassell and the A. and P. stick to *programme.* Cassell and the A. and P. adopt the American *scimitar;* the Oxford retains the English *scimetar.* All three have abandoned *enquire* for *inquire*, but they remain faithful to *encumbrance, endorse* and *enclose*, though the Oxford and Cassell list *indorsation* and the Oxford also gives *indorsee.* Both the Oxford and Cassell have abandoned *æther* for *ether*, but they cling to *æsthetic* and *ætiology.* Neither gives up *plough, cheque, connexion, mould, mollusc* or *kerb*, and Cassell even adorns the last-named with an astounding compound credited to "American slang," to wit, *kerbstone broker.* All the English authorities that I have consulted prefer the *-re* and *-our* endings; nevertheless, the London *Nation* adopted the *-or* ending in 1919,[4] and George Bernard Shaw had adopted it years before,[5] as had Walter Savage

1 Horace Hart: Rules for Compositors and Readers at the University Press, Oxford: 23rd ed.; London, 1914. I am informed by Mr. Humphrey Davy, of the London *Times*, that, with one or two minor exceptions, the *Times* observes the rules laid down in this book.
2 Edited by Dr. Ernest A. Baker; London, 1919.

3 On English Homophones; *S.P.E. Tracts*, No. II, 1919, p. 7.
4 This note appeared in *English*, May–June, 1919, p. 88: "By the way, the *Nation* now spell *labor, honor, favor.*" Note the plural verb.
5 Shaw is, in general, an advanced speller. He was spelling *program* without the final *-me* when it still

Landor before him. The British Board of Trade, in attempting to fix the spelling of various scientific terms, has often come to grief. Thus, it detaches the final *-me* from *gramme* in such compounds as *kilogram* and *milligram*, but insists upon *gramme* when the word stands alone. In American usage *gram* is now common, and scarcely challenged. A number of spellings, some of them American, are trembling on the brink of acceptance in both countries. Among them is *rime* (for *rhyme*). This spelling was correct in England until about 1530, but its recent revival was of American origin. It is accepted by the Concise Oxford, by the editors of the " Cambridge History of English Literature," and by many English periodicals, including *Notes and Queries*, but not by Cassell. *Grewsome* has got a footing in both countries, but the weight of English opinion is still against it. *Develop* (instead of *develope*) has gone further in both. So has *engulf*, for *engulph*. And most English newspapers have begun to drop the redundant *a* in *medieval*, *esophagus*, etc. But they still spell *bologna* (sausage) *balony*, thus rivaling but not imitating Al Smith's *baloney*.

There is not much movement of English spellings in this direction; the traffic, as in the case of neologisms, runs heavily the other way. At Bar Harbor, in Maine, a few of the more Anglophil Summer residents are at pains to put *harbour* instead of *harbor* on their stationery, but the local postmaster still continues to stamp all mail *Bar Harbor*, the legal name of the place.[1] In the same way American haberdashers of the more doggy sort sometimes advertise *pyjamas* instead of *pajamas*, just as they advertise *braces* instead of *suspenders*, and *boots* instead of *shoes*. But this benign folly does not go very far. Even the most fashionable jewelers in Fifth avenue still deal in *jewelry*, not *jewellery*. The English *ketchup* has made some progress against the American *catsup*, and *cheque* has come into use of late among American accountants, but only as a convenient means of distinguishing between a bank *check* (to which it is applied) and

seemed barbaric in England, and he also prefers *catalog, toilet* and *etiquet*. But he clings to *to shew* (as in The *Shewing* Up of Blanco Posnet), though it is going out, and the Authors' and Printers' Dictionary recommends *to show* "except in Sc. law, and Bib. and Prayer Book citations."

[1] In Christopher Morley's Thunder on the Left; New York, 1925, the name of Deep Harbor, a place supposedly near New York City, is spelled *Harbour*. This natural slip by a Rhodes scholar is rebuked by Clifford H. Bissell in Is It Pedantry?, *Saturday Review of Literature*, Aug. 13, 1927.

check in the sense of a verification. Sometimes an American book, intended also for circulation in England, is printed in what American printers call English spelling. This English spelling, at best, is a somewhat lame compromise, and seems to be passing out. As used at the Riverside Press,[1] it embraced until a few years ago, all the *-our* endings and the following further forms:

cheque	grey
chequered	inflexion
connexion	jewellery
dreamt	leapt
faggot	premiss (in logic)
forgather	waggon
forgo	

But in the latest edition of the Riverside Press's Handbook of Style [2] all save the *-our* endings have been omitted, and I am informed by Mr. Henry A. McLaughlin of the Press that English spellings are used " only when we are doing books by English authors, and the English author prefers to have us follow the English usage rather than our own." Another great American press, that of the J. S. Cushing Company, follows a list which includes both the *-our* endings and these words:

behove	gaiety	lacquey	shily
briar	gaol	moustache	slily
cheque	gipsy	nought	staunch
connexion	inflexion	pigmy	storey (floor)
drily	instal	postillion	verandah
enquire	judgment	reflexion	waggon [3]

This list, along with the *-our* endings, appears also in the style-book of the Macmillan Company, the largest of the English-American publishing firms.[4] It would seem to need revision, for, as we have seen, the English themselves have begun to abandon *gaol, storey, waggon, judgement* and *pigmy*, and are showing a considerable

1 Handbook of Style in Use at the Riverside Press, Cambridge, Mass.; Boston, 1913.
2 Boston, 1930.
3 Preparation of Manuscript, Proof Reading, and Office Style at J. S. Cushing Company's; Norwood, Mass., n.d. Under date of Sept. 19, 1935, Mr. Robert T. Barr, one of the directors of the company, writes: " In practically all of the new books that are now being pub-

lished we have been requested by the several publishers to follow the new Webster's International Dictionary (1934) in regard to spelling. With the few English books we have been doing lately our orders have been to follow copy."
4 The Authors' Book; New York, 1925. I am indebted here to Mr. H. S. Latham, vice-president of the Macmillan Co.

uncertainty about *enquire*. " The Authors' and Printers' Dictionary," indeed, now prefers the American *brier* to the English *briar, dryly* to *drily*, *install* to *instal*, *lackey* to *lacquey*, *naught* to *nought*, *postilion* to *postillion*, *shyly* to *shily* and *veranda* to *verandah*, and allows *reflection* for *reflexion*. Thus there is little of English spelling left save the *-our* and *-re* words and the charges of fraud. The Government Printing Office at Washington has followed "Webster's New International" since 1864, when the Superintendent of Public Printing (he became the Public Printer in 1895) was authorized by law to determine "the forms and style in which the printing . . . ordered by any of the departments shall be executed." He issued his first Style Manual in 1887 and it has been revised a number of times since. Down to 1929 it was edited by a board of employés of the Government Printing Office, but in that year representatives of the State, Commerce, Agriculture and Interior Departments and of the Smithsonian Institution were invited to participate. A copy of this work is in the proofroom of nearly every American magazine and newspaper. It favors American spelling in all cases, and its rules are generally observed. The *Atlantic Monthly*, alone among American magazines of wide circulation, is inclined to be more conservative, probably under the influence of Worcester. It uses the *-re* ending in words of the *center* class, retains the *u* in *mould*, *moult* and *moustache*, retains the redundant terminal letters in such words as *gramme*, *programme* and *quartette*, retains the final *e* in *axe* and *adze*, and clings to the double vowels in such words as *mediæval* and *anæsthesia*. In addition, it uses the English *plough*, *whiskey*, *clue* and *gruesome*, differentiates between the noun *practice* and the verb *to practise*, and makes separate words of *to ensure*, to make certain, and *to insure*, to protect or indemnify.[1]

But American spelling is plainly better than English spelling, and in the long run it seems sure to prevail. The superiority of *jail* to *gaol* is made manifest by the common mispronunciation of the latter by Americans who find it in print, making it rhyme with *coal*. Other changes also carry their own justification. *Hostler* is obviously better English, etymologically speaking, than *ostler*, and *cozy* is more nearly phonetic than *cosy*. *Curb* has analogues in *curtain*, *curdle*, *cur-*

1 Text, Type and Style: A Compendium of *Atlantic* usage, by George B. Ives; Boston, 1921.

few, curl, currant, curry, curve, curtesy, curse, currency, cursory, cur, curt and many other common words: *kerb* has very few, and of them only *kerchief* and *kernel* are in general use. Moreover, the English themselves use *curb* as a verb and in all noun sense save that shown in *kerbstone*. Such forms as *monolog* and *dialog* still offend the fastidious, but their merit is not to be gainsaid. Nor would it be easy to argue logically against *gram, toilet, mustache, ax, caliber, gayety, gray, anesthetic, draft* and *tire.* Something may be said, even, for *chlorid, brusk, lacrimal, gage, eolian, niter, sulfite* and *phenix,*[1] which still wait for general recognition. A number of anomalies remain. The American retention of *e* in *forego* and *whiskey* is not easily explained, nor the unphonetic substitution of *s* for *z* in *fuse,* nor the persistence of the *y* in *gypsy* and *pygmy,* nor the occasional survival of a foreign form, as in *cloture.*[2] Here we have plain vagaries, surviving in spite of attack by orthographers. Webster, in one of his earlier books, denounced the *k* in *skeptic* as a "mere pedantry," but later on he adopted it. In the same way *pygmy, gray* and *mollusk* have been attacked, but they still remain sound American. The English themselves have many more such illogical forms to account for. They have to write *offensive* and *defensive* (nouns), despite their fidelity to the *c* in *offence* and *defence.*[3] They hesitate to abandon *programme,* but never think of using *diagramme* or *telegramme.* Worst of all, they are inconsistent in their use of the *-our* ending, the chief glory of orthodox English orthography.[4] In American the *u* appears only in *Saviour* and then

1 This form is used by the Chatham and *Phenix* National Bank, in New York. But the *Phœnix* Insurance Company, of Hartford, Conn., retains the old spelling. About 100 corporations having the word in their names are listed in the New York telephone directory. A fifth of them use *phenix.*

2 The Fowlers in The King's English, 2nd ed.; London, 1908, p. 23, say that "when it was proposed to borrow from France what we [*i.e.,* the English] now know as the *closure,* it seemed certain for some time that with the thing we should borrow the name, *clôture;* a press campaign resulted in *closure.*" But in the *Congressional Record* it is

still *cloture,* though with the loss of the circumflex accent, and this form is generally retained by American newspapers — that is, when they do not use *gag.*

3 Webster's New International prefers *offense* and *defense.* In *license, advice, device, prophecy, practise,* etc. the English rule is that the nouns shall take *c* and the verbs *s.* But the American Medical Association Press "has always spelled *practice* with *c,* whether for noun or for verb." *Journal of the American Medical Association,* April 26, 1930, p. 1342.

4 Says H. W. Fowler in Modern English Usage; Oxford, 1926, p. 415: "The American abolition of

only when the word is used in the biblical sense. In England it is used in most words of that class, but omitted from agent nouns, *e.g.*, *ambassador*, *emperor* and *progenitor*, and also from various other words, *e.g.*, *horror* and *torpor*. It is commonly argued in defense of it over there that it serves to distinguish French loan-words from words derived directly from the Latin, but Gilbert Tucker shows [1] that this argument is quite nonsensical, even assuming that the distinction has any practical utility. *Ancestor, bachelor, error, exterior, governor, metaphor, mirror, senator, superior, successor* and *torpor* all came into English from the French, and yet British usage sanctions spelling them without the *u*. On the other hand it is used in *arbour, behaviour, clangour, flavour* and *neighbour*, " which are not French at all." Tucker goes on:

> Even in *ardour, armour, candour, endeavour, favour, honour, labour, odour, parlour, rigour, rumour, saviour, splendour, tumour* and *vapour*, where the *u* has some color of right to appear, it is doubtful whether its insertion has much value as suggesting French derivation, for in the case of twelve of these words the ordinary reader would be quite certain to have in mind only the modern spelling — *ardeur, armure, candeur, faveur, honneur, labeur, odeur, rigueur, rumeur, splendeur, tumeur* and *vapeur* — which have the *u* indeed but no *o* (and why should not one of these letters be dropped as well as the other?) — while *endeavour, parlour* and *saviour* come from old French words that are themselves without the *u* — *devoir, parleor* and *saveor*. The *u* in all these words is therefore either useless or positively misleading. And finally in the case of *colour, clamour, fervour, humour, rancour, valour* and *vigour*, it is to be remarked that the exact American orthography actually occurs in old French! "Finally," I said, but that is not quite the end of British absurdity with these *-our -or* words. Insistent as our transatlantic cousins are on writing *arbour, armour, clamour, clangour, colour, dolour, flavour, honour, humour, labour, odour, rancour, rigour, savour, valour, vapour* and *vigour*, and "most unpleasant" as they find the omission of the excrescent *u* in any of these words, they nevertheless make no scruple of writing the derivatives in the American way — *arboreal, armory, clamorous, clangorous, colorific, dolorous, flavorous, honorary, humorous, laborious, odorous, rancorous, rigorous, savory, valorous, vaporize* and *vigorous* — not inserting the *u* in the second syllable of any one

-our in such words as *honour* and *favour* has probably retarded rather than quickened English progress in the same direction. Our first notification that a book we are reading is not English but American is often, nowadays, the sight of an *-or*. 'Yankee' we say, and congratulate ourselves on spelling like gentlemen; we wisely decline to regard it as a matter for argument; the English way cannot but be better than the American way; that is enough. Most of us, therefore, do not come to the question with an open mind." "The Americans," says Basil de Sélincourt in Pomona, or The Future of English; London, 1928, p. 40, "have dropped a *u* out of *humour* and other words; possibly we should have done so, *if they had not*." My italics.

[1] American English; New York, 1921, p. 37.

of these words. The British practice is, in short and to speak plainly, a jumble of confusion, without rhyme or reason, logic or consistency; and if anybody finds the American simplification of the whole matter "unpleasant," it can be only because he is a victim of unreasoning prejudice against which no argument can avail.

If the *u* were dropped in *all* derivatives, the confusion would be less, but it is retained in many of them, for example, *colourable, favourite, misdemeanour, coloured* and *labourer*. The derivatives of *honour* exhibit clearly the difficulties of the American who essays to write correct English. *Honorary, honorarium* and *honorific* drop the *u*, but *honourable* retains it. Furthermore, the English make a distinction between two senses of *rigor*. When used in its pathological sense (not only in the Latin form of *rigor mortis*, but as an English word) it drops the *u*; in all other senses it retains the *u*.

In Canada the two orthographies, English and American, flourish side by side. By an Order-in-Council of 1890, official correspondence must show the English spelling, and in 1931 the Canadian Historical Association, the Canadian Geographical Society and the Royal Society of Canada joined in urging its use by every loyal Canadian.[1] But though it is ordained in all the -*our* words in "Preparation of Copy For the Printer," issued by the King's Printer at Ottawa,[2] there are, in that pamphlet, various other concessions to American usage. The English *aluminium*, for example, is to be used in scientific documents, but the American *aluminum* is permitted in commercial writing. *Cipher, dryly, jail, net, program* and *wagon* are to be spelt in the American manner, and even *alright* is authorized. Nearly all the Canadian newspapers use the American spelling and it is also taught in most of the public schools, which are under the jurisdiction, not of the Dominion government, but of the provincial ministers of education. In Australia the English spelling is official, but various American forms are making fast progress. According to the *Triad* (Sydney), "horrible American inaccuracies of spelling are coming into common use" in the newspapers out there; worse, the educational authorities of Victoria authorize the use of the American -*er* ending. This last infamy has been roundly denounced by Sir Adrian Knox, Chief Justice of the Commonwealth, and the *Triad* has displayed a good deal of colonial passion in supporting

1 Canada Won't Even Import American Spelling, Baltimore *Evening Sun*, Aug. 5, 1931.   2 5th ed., 1928.

him. " Unhappily," it says, " we have no English Academy to guard the purity and integrity of the language. Everything is left to the sense and loyalty of decently cultivated people." But even the *Triad* admits that American usage, in some instances, is " correct." It is, however, belligerently faithful to the *-our* ending. " If it is correct or tolerable in English," it argues somewhat lamely, " to write *labor* for *labour*, why not *boddy* for *body*, *steddy* for *steady*, and *yot* for *yacht?* " Meanwhile, as in Canada, the daily papers slide into the Yankee orbit.

3. THE SIMPLIFIED SPELLING MOVEMENT

Franklin's " Scheme For a New Alphabet and Reformed Mode of Spelling " was by no means the first attempt to revise and rationalize English orthography. So long ago as the beginning of the Thirteenth Century a monk named Ormin tried to reform the spelling of the Middle English of his time. The chief difficulty then encountered was in distinguishing between long vowels and short ones, and Ormin proposed to get rid of it by doubling the consonants following the latter. Thus he spelled *fire, fir*, and *fir, firr*. His proposal got no support, and the manuscript in which he made it lay in obscurity for six centuries, but when it was exhumed at last it turned out to be very useful to philologians, for it threw a great deal of light upon early Middle English pronunciation. Thus, the fact that Ormin spelled *God* as we do showed that the word was then rhymed with *load*, and the fact that he spelled *goddspell* (gospel) with two *d*'s showed that a shorter *o* was beginning to prevail in the derivative.

Ormin was followed after three and a half centuries by Sir John Cheke (1514–57), the first regius professor of Greek at Cambridge. Middle English had passed out by that time, and Modern English was in, but many survivals of the former were still encountered, including a host of now-useless final *e*'s. Sir John proposed to amputate all of them. He also proposed to differentiate between the short and long forms of the same vowels by doubling the latter. Finally, he proposed to get rid of all silent consonants, thus making *doubt*, for example, *dout*, and turning *fault* into *faut*, for it was so pronounced at that time.[1] Cheke was supported in his reforms by a

1 He was in favor of what he called a " clean and pure " English, and opposed the excessive use of loanwords, then very popular. In a

number of influential contemporaries, including Roger Ascham, but English went on its wild way. In 1568 another attempt to bring it to rule was made by Sir Thomas Smith, one of his friends and colleagues at Cambridge. Smith's proposals were published in a Latin work entitled " De Recta et Emendata Linguæ Anglicanæ Scriptione," and the chief of them was that the traditional alphabet be abandoned and a phonetic alphabet substituted. A century later the Rev. John Wilkins, then Dean of Ripon and later Bishop of Chester, came forward with another phonetic alphabet — this time of about 450 characters! But though Wilkins argued for it very learnedly on physiological grounds, printing many engravings to show the action of the tongue and palate, it seems to have made no impression on his contemporaries, and is now forgotten save by antiquarians. Nor was any greater success made by his numerous successors. They framed some very apt and pungent criticisms of English orthography and projected a number of quite reasonable reforms, but they had little hand in the determination of actual spelling practise. That was mainly the work of printers, and after 1650 their rules began to be accepted by English authors, and most of them remain in force to this day.[1] Since Franklin's time the literature of the subject has taken on large proportions, and contributions to it have been made by all sorts of persons, ranging from scientific philologians to fanatics of the sort who project new religions and new political economies.[2] In the last century the most noise was made by Sir Isaac Pitman, the inventor of the system of shorthand bearing his name. In the early 40's, in association with Alexander J. Ellis, he proposed a new phonetic alphabet of forty letters, and during the years following

translation of the Gospel of Mark, published in 1550, he substituted *hunderder* for *centurion*, and *crossed* for *crucified*.

1 A good account of the early reformers is in Every-Day English, by Richard Grant White; Boston, 1881, Ch. X. See also Introduction to the Science of Language, by A. H. Sayce, 4th ed.; London, 1900, p. 330 ff; Modern English in the Making, by George H. McKnight; New York, 1928, p. 117 ff and the various passages listed under Spelling in his index; The Development

of Modern English, by Stuart Robertson; New York, 1934, pp. 271–80; and Handbook of Simplified Spelling; New York, 1920, p. 5.

2 A partial list of the books on the subject printed in the United States between 1807 and 1860 is in The English Language in America, by George Philip Krapp; New York, 1925, Vol. I, p. 330. Most of those printed down to the end of 1922 are listed in Arthur G. Kennedy's Bibliography of Writings on the English Language; Cambridge (Mass.), 1927.

he made vigorous propaganda for it in his *Phonographic Journal*, and through the Phonetic Society, which he organized in 1843.

But the real father of the Simplified Spelling movement was probably Noah Webster. The controversy over his new spelling, described in the last section, aroused a great deal of public interest in the subject, and in the early 70's even the dons of the American Philological Association began to give it some attention. In 1875 they appointed a committee consisting of Professors Francis A. March of Lafayette College, W. D. Whitney and J. Hammond Trumbell of Yale, S. S. Haldeman of the University of Pennsylvania, and F. J. Child of Harvard to look into it, and in 1876 this committee reported that a revision of spelling was urgent and that something should be done about it. Specifically, they proposed that eleven new spellings be adopted at once, to wit, *ar, catalog, definit, gard, giv, hav, infinit, liv, tho, thru* and *wisht*. During the same year there was an International Convention for the Amendment of English Orthography at Philadelphia, with several delegates from England present, and out of it grew the Spelling Reform Association, which immediately endorsed the eleven new spellings of the five professors. Three years later a similar body was organized in England, with A. H. Sayce, deputy professor of comparative philology at Oxford as its president, and Charles Darwin, Alfred Tennyson, Sir Isaac Pitman, Sir John Lubbock, and such eminent philologians as J. A. H. Murray, W. W. Skeat and Henry Sweet among its vice-presidents. The Philological Society of England and the American Philological Association kept a friendly watch upon the progress of events. In 1880 the former issued a pamphlet advising various "partial corrections of English spellings," and in 1886 the latter followed with recommendations affecting about 3500 words, and falling under ten headings. Most of the new forms listed had been put forward years before by Webster, and some of them had entered into unquestioned American usage in the meantime, *e.g.*, the deletion of the *u* from the *-our* words, the substitution of *er* for *re* at the end of words, and the reduction of *traveller* to *traveler*.

The trouble with the others was that they were either too uncouth to be adopted without a long struggle or likely to cause errors in pronunciation. To the first class belonged *tung* for *tongue, ruf* for *rough, batl* for *battle* and *abuv* for *above,* and to the second such

forms as *cach* for *catch* and *troble* for *trouble*. The result was that
the whole reform received a setback: the public dismissed the
reformers as a pack of lunatics. Twelve years later the National
Education Association revived the movement with a proposal that
a beginning be made with a very short list of reformed spellings,
and nominated the following twelve changes by way of experiment:
*tho, altho, thru, thruout, thoro, thoroly, thorofare, program, prolog,
catalog, pedagog* and *decalog*. Then, in 1906, came the organization
of the Simplified Spelling Board, with a subsidy of $15,000 a year
from Andrew Carnegie (later increased to $25,000 a year), and a
formidable list of members and collaborators, including Henry Bradley, F. I. Furnivall, C. H. Grandgent, W. W. Skeat, T. R. Lounsbury and F. A. March. The board at once issued a list of 300 revised
spellings, new and old, and in August, 1906, President Theodore
Roosevelt ordered their adoption by the Government Printing
Office. But this effort to hasten matters aroused widespread opposition, and in a little while the spelling reform movement was the
sport of the national wits. The Government Printing Office resisted,
and so did most of the departments, and in the end the use of the
twelve new spellings was confined to the White House. Not many
American magazines or newspapers adopted them, and they were
seldom used in printing books. When, in 1919, Carnegie died, his
subsidy ceased,[1] and since then the Simplified Spelling Board has
moved from the glare of Madison avenue, New York, to the rural
retirement of Lake Placid, and there has been a serious decline in its
activities. During Carnegie's lifetime it issued a great many bulletins
and circulars, but since 1924 it has published nothing save a small
magazine called *Spelling* — three issues in 1925 and four in 1931.[2]
In its heyday the board claimed that 556 American newspapers and
other periodicals, with a combined circulation 18,000,000, were using
the twelve simplified spellings of the National Education Association's list and " most of the 300 simpler spellings " recommended by
its own first list, and that 460 universities, colleges and normal-

---

1 First and last, he is said to have
spent $283,000 on the movement.
2 In 1920 it organized a Simplified
Spelling Leag [*sic*] to raise funds.
Members were asked to contribute
$10 a year and associates $1. A fellow made a single payment of $100,
and a patron one of $1000. But ap-
parently not many customers came
to the cashier's desk, and the Leag
now seems to be moribund.

schools were either using most of these spellings " in their official publications and correspondence," or permitting " students to use them in their written work."[1] But not many of these publications or educational institutions were of much importance. The *Literary Digest* led the very short list of magazines of national circulation, and the Philadelphia *North American* led the newspapers. With regard to the colleges, the situation in Massachusetts was perhaps typical. Three institutions had adopted the new spelling — Clark College, Emerson College and the International Y.M.C.A. College. But Harvard was missing, and so were the Massachusetts Tech, Wellesley, Smith and Boston University.

The board issued various lists of reformed spellings from time to time, and in 1919 it brought out a Handbook of Simplified Spelling summarizing its successive recommendations. They were as follows:

1. When a word begins with or includes *æ* or *œ* substitute *e: esthetic, medieval, subpena*. But retain the dipthong at the end of a word: *alumnæ*
2. When *bt* is pronounced *t*, drop the silent *b: det, dettor, dout*.
3. When *ceed* is final spell it *cede: excede, procede, succede*.
4. When *ch* is pronounced like hard *c*, drop the silent *h* except before *e, i* and *y: caracter, clorid, corus, cronic, eco, epoc, mecanic, monarc, scolar, scool, stomac, tecnical*. But retain *architect, chemist, monarchy*.
5. When a double consonant appears before a final silent *e* drop the last two letters: *bizar, cigaret, creton, gavot, gazet, giraf, gram, program, quartet, vaudevil*.
6. When a word ends with a double consonant substitute a single consonant: *ad, bil, bluf, buz, clas, dol, dul, eg, glas, les, los, mes, mis, pas, pres, shal, tel, wil*. But retain *ll* after a long vowel: *all, roll*. And retain *ss* when the word has more than one syllable: *needless*.
7. Drop the final silent *e* after a consonant preceded by a short stressed vowel: *giv, hav, liv*.
8. Drop the final silent *e* in the common words *are, gone* and *were: ar, gon, wer*.
9. Drop the final silent *e* in the unstressed final short syllables, *ide, ile, ine, ise, ite* and *ive: activ, bromid, definit, determin, practis, hostil*.
10. Drop the silent *e* after *lv* and *rv: involv, twelv, carv, deserv*.
11. Drop the silent *e* after *v* or *z* when preceded by a digraph representing a long vowel or a diphthong: *achiev, freez, gauz, sneez*.
12. Drop the *e* in final *oe* when it is pronounced *o: fo, ho, ro, to, wo*. But retain it in inflections: *foes, hoed*.
13. When one of the letters in *ea* is silent drop it: *bred, brekfast, hed, hart, harth*.
14. When final *ed* is pronounced *d* drop the *e: cald, carrid, employd,*

1 *Reasons and Rules For Simplified Spelling*, April, 1919.

marrid, robd, sneezd, struggld, wrongd. But not when a wrong pronunciation will be suggested: *bribd, cand, fild* (for *filed*), etc.

15. When final *ed* is pronounced *t* substitute *t: addrest, shipt, helpt, indorst.* But not when a wrong pronunciation will be suggested: *bakt, fact* (for *faced*), etc.

16. When *ei* is pronounced like *ie* in *brief* substitute *ie: conciet, deciev, wierd.*

17. When a final *ey* is pronounced *y* drop the *e: barly, chimny, donky, mony, vally.*

18. When final *gh* is pronounced *f* substitute *f* and drop the silent letter of the preceding digraph: *enuf, laf, ruf, tuf.*

19. When *gh* is pronounced *g* drop the silent *h: agast, gastly, gost, goul.*

20. When *gm* is final drop the silent *g: apothem, diafram, flem.*

21. When *gue* is final after a consonant, a short vowel or a digraph representing a long vowel or a diphthong drop the silent *ue: tung, catalog, harang, leag, sinagog.* But not when a wrong pronunciation would be suggested: *rog* (for *rogue*), *vag* (for *vague*), etc.

22. When a final *ise* is pronounced *ize* substitute *ize: advertize, advize, franchize, rize, wize.*

23. When *mb* is final after a short vowel drop *b: bom, crum, dum, lam, lim, thum.* But not when a wrong pronunciation would be suggested: *com* (for *comb*), *tom* (for *tomb*), etc.

24. When *ou* before *l* is pronounced *o* drop *u: mold, sholder.* But not *sol* (for *soul*).

25. When *ough* is final spell *o, u, ock,* or *up,* according to the pronunciation: *altho, boro, donut, furlo, tho, thoro, thru, hock, hiccup.*

26. When *our* is final and *ou* is pronounced as a short vowel drop *u: color, honor, labor.*

27. When *ph* is pronounced *f* substitute *f: alfabet, emfasis, fantom, fonograf, fotograf, sulfur, telefone, telegraf.*

28. When *re* is final after any consonant save *c* substitute *er: center, fiber, meter, theater.* But not *lucer, mediocer.*

29. When *rh* is initial and the *h* is silent drop it: *retoric, reumatism, rime, rubarb, rithm.*

30. When *sc* is initial and the *c* is silent drop it: *senery, sented, septer, sience, sissors.*

31. When *u* is silent before a vowel drop it: *bild, condit, garantee, gard, ges, gide, gild.*

32. When *y* is between consonants substitute *i: analisis, fisic, gipsy, paralize, rime, silvan, tipe.*

Obviously, this list was too long to have much chance of being accepted quickly. Some of the spellings on it, to be sure, were already in good American usage, brought in by Webster, but others were uncouth and even ridiculous. Worse, there were many exceptions to the rules laid down — for example, in rules 1, 4, 6, 12, 14, 15 and 21. The board, as if despairing of making any headway with so many words, brought out simultaneously a much shorter list, and leaflets arguing for it were distributed in large numbers. It was as follows:

ad	insted
addrest	liv(d)
anser(d)	program
ar	reciet
askt	reviev(d)
bil(d)	shal
buro	shipt
catalog	tel
det	telefone
engin	(al)tho
enuf	thoro(ly, -fare, etc.)
fil(d)	thru(out)
fixt	twelv
giv	wil
hav	yu

On the reverse of this leaflet was the following:

When yu hav by practis familiarized yourself with the 30 WORDS, why not, for the sake of consistency, apply the principles exemplified by their spellings to other words? For instance, if yu write

addrest, anserd, askt, bild, fild, fixt, livd, recievd, shipt, why not write *advanst, announst, cald, carrid, delayd, doubld, examind, followd, indorst, invoist, pleasd, preferd, signd, traveld, troubld, wisht,* etc.?

telefone, why not write *telegraf, fotograf, fonograf, alfabet,* etc.?

ar, engin, giv, hav, liv, reciev, twelv, why not write *activ, comparativ, definit, determin, examin, favorit, genuin, hostil, imagin, infinit, nativ, opposit, positiv, practis, promis, textil, believ, curv, resolv, serv,* etc.?

ad, bil, fil, shal, wil, why not write *od, eg, bel, wel, mil, bluf, stuf, pur, dres, les, buz,* etc.?

catalog, why not write *prolog, sinagog,* etc.?

det, why not write *dout,* etc.?

insted, why not write *bred, brekfest, ded, hed, red, helth, plesure, wether,* etc.?

program, why not write *gram, cigaret, quartet, gazet, bagatel, quadril, vaudevil,* etc.?

reciev, why not write *deciev, conciet,* etc.?

thoro, why not write *boro, furlo,* etc.

enuf, why not write *ruf, tuf, laf, cof,* etc.?

But this list also failed to win any considerable public support. On the contrary, its clumsy novelties gave the whole spelling reform movement a black eye. In the Summer of 1921 the National Education Association, which had launched the campaign for reform in 1898, withdrew its endorsement, and during the years following most of the magazines and newspapers that had adopted its twelve new spellings went back to the orthodox forms. So long ago as 1909, when W. H. Taft succeeded Roosevelt as President, the New York

Sun announced the doom of the movement in an editorial of one word: *thru*. This was somewhat premature, for Carnegie's money was still paying for a vigorous propaganda, but his death ten years later, as I have said, put an end to large-scale crusading, and since then spelling reform has been promoted mainly by individuals, no two of whom agree. Some of their schemes are extremely simple — for example, that of William McDevitt, a San Francisco bookseller, who simply drops out all the neutral vowels and silent consonants. Thus, *the* becomes *th*, *writer* is *riter*, *because* is *becaus*, *would* is *woud*, and *after* is *aftr*. Other current proposals involve changes in the values of the alphabet, and are thus more complicated. Dr. H. Darcy Power, an English-born professor at the University of Freiburg in Germany, proposes that *x*, *c* and *q*, which are redundant, be given the new values of *th*, *ch* and *qw* respectively, and that the different values of the vowels be indicated by drawing lines either above or below them, *e.g.*, *ā* for the *a* in hate, *a̦* for that in *car*, and *a* without any mark for that in *bat*. In order to distinguish between the two sounds of *th* he proposes that *x* be used in *thy* and *x̄* in *thigh*. The neutral vowel he disposes of by either dropping it altogether or displacing it with an apostrophe. Here is a specimen of his *fonetic speling*, prepared by himself:

Sir C. P. Hunter [names are not as yet modified], spēking as a reprēzentativ biznes man, said he had long strongli objekted tu x wāst ov tīm and muni in our skuls and x sakrifīs ov praktikl and intelektūal efishensi dū tu x tīm spent and wāsted in lurning our unnesesarili difikult speling. Xat muni, and wot wos mor importnt, tīm, kud be put tu infinitli mor praktikl ūs if it wer devōted tu rēl edukāshn. Our irashunl and difikult speling wos a hindrns and a handikap tu x impruvment ov our trād and komers.[1]

It will be noted that Dr. Power, like most spelling reformers, is not quite faithful to his own system, for he spells *said*, not as *sed*, but in the orthodox manner. Another revolutionist, Frederick S. Wingfield of Chicago, proposes in his *fwnetik orthqgrafi* to employ the redundant *c*, *j*, *q*, *w* and *y* to represent the vowels in *at*, *eat*, *ah*, *oh* and *ooze* respectively, and to make various other changes in the values of the letters. Here is the Lord's Prayer according to his system:

Qur Fqdhr, hy qrt in hevn: hclwd bj dhqi neim. Dhqi kizdm kam, dhqui uil bj dan, on rth cz it iz in hevn. Giv as dhis dei qur deili bred, cnd forgiv

1 The English Alphabet: What It Is, What I Should Be — and What It Could Be; Freiburg i. B., 1930.

as qur dets cz uj forgivn qur detrz. Cdn ljd as nqt intu temteishn, bat djlivr as frqm jvl. For dhquin iz dhj kixdm, dhj pquar, cnd dhj glwri forevr. Eimen.[1]

A somewhat similar scheme is that of Dr. R. E. Zachrisson, professor of English in the University of Upsala, Sweden. He calls it Anglic, and it seems to be backed by enthusiasts with plenty of cash, for a monthly magazine in advocacy of it was launched at Upsala in 1930, an illustrated *fortnietly* followed in 1931, and there are textbooks and phonograph records. Its rules fill nine pages of the official textbook,[2] and seem to be somewhat complicated. The consonants, with few exceptions, have their ordinary values, but there are many changes in the vowels, some of which are doubled or provided with modifying vowels. This clustering of vowels tends to be confusing, so italics or bold-face type are used to distinguish stressed syllables, *e.g.*, in *kreaet* (*create*) the *ae* is so distinguished. Here is the first sentence of Lincoln's Gettysburg Address in Anglic:

> Forskor and sevn yeerz agoe our faadherz braut forth on this kontinent a nue naeshon, konseevd in liberty, and dedikaeted to the propozishon that aul men ar kre*a*eted eequal.[3]

In 1927 the late Dr. Robert Bridges, Poet Laureate of England and founder of the Society for Pure English, began publishing a series of prose pamphlets embodying some new spellings and a few new letters. One of the latter was a symbol for the sound represented by *i, ic, ie, ei, y, ye, ig, igh, eigh, uy, ay, ai, ey* and *eye* in the words *I, indictment, tie, eider, fly, dye, sign, sigh, height, buy, ay, aisle, eying* and *eye*. It was an *i* with a hook attached to its right side, making it a sort of *h* with a dot over it. Another was a symbol for the *ng* of *sing*. It was an *n* with a similar hook. Dr. Bridges also used a script *a* to distinguish the broad *a* of *father* from the flat *a* of *cat*, and a script *g* to distinguish the soft *g* of *gentle* from the hard *g* of *thing*. Further, he omitted the final mute *e* in most situations, though retaining it when it indicated a long preceding vowel, as in *finite*, and when it occurred at the end of a syllable " which has a long vowel, and can

---

1 Among Spelling Reformers, by Frederick S. Wingfield, *American Speech*, Oct., 1931. Mr. Wingfield also gives specimens of the spelling of other reformers.
2 Anglic: A New Agreed Simplified English Spelling, final rev. ed.; Upsala, 1931.
3 There is a brief but cogent criti-

cism of Anglic, and of all like systems, in a review of the Anglic textbook in *American Speech*, June, 1931, p. 378 *ff.* It is signed A. G. K. and is apparently by Dr. Arthur G. Kennedy. Another devastating criticism is in Or Shall We Go Anglic?, by Janet Rankin Aiken, *Bookman*, Feb., 1931.

be recognized only as a whole, as *love*." [1] These reforms got no support in England, and seem to have passed out with their distinguished author, who died in 1930.

On January 28, 1935, the Chicago *Tribune* announced out of a clear sky that it had adopted twenty-four simplified spellings and was preparing to add others from time to time. Its first list was rather cautious — *catalog* for *catalogue*, *cotilion* for *cotillion*, *controled* for *controlled*, *fantom* for *phantom*, *hocky* for *hockey*, *skilful* for *skillful*, *advertisment* for *advertisement*, *harken* for *hearken*, and so on. Many of these, in fact, were already in more or less general use. But when, in its second list, dated February 11, it added *agast* for *aghast*, *aile* for *aisle*, *bagatel* for *bagatelle*, *bailif* for *bailiff*, *burocracy* for *bureaucracy*, *crum* for *crumb* and *missil* for *missile*, it got into wilder waters, and when, in subsequent announcements, it proceeded to *genuinly* for *genuinely*, *hefer* for *heifer*, *herse* for *hearse*, *staf* for *staff*, *warant* for *warrant*, *doctrin* for *doctrine*, *iland* for *island*, *lether* for *leather*, *trafic* for *traffic* and *yern* for *yearn*, it was far out upon the orthographical deep. [2] Its innovations met with a mixed reception. Some of its readers applauded, but others protested, and in a little while it was constrained to abandon *iland*. Its list did not include such favorites of the Simplified Spelling Board as *thro*, *thru* and *filosofy*.

But despite the fact that the activities of the board, as its secretary, Dr. Godfrey Dewey, admits sadly, have " slowed down almost to the stopping point," [3] it has probably had some influence upon the course of American spelling. It failed to bring in *tho* and *thoro*, but it undoubtedly aided the general acceptance of *catalog*, *program* and their congeners. The late George Philip Krapp of Columbia, who was certainly no Anglophobe, believed that *fonetic*, *fonograf*, *fosfate*, *fotograf* and the like were " bound to be the spelling of the future " in this country. [4] Such forms as *burlesk*, *nabor*, *naborhood*, *nite*,[5] *foto*, *sox*, *hi*, *lite*, *holsum*, *biskit*, *ho-made*, *thanx* and *kreem*, though they

1 Collected Essays, Papers, Etc.; London, 1927, *pref.*
2 All of the articles announcing and arguing for these changes were written by James O'Donnell Bennett. The dates of two have been given. The others appeared on Feb. 25, March 4, March 18 and March 25.
3 In a letter from the Lake Placid

Hindenburg Line, dated " 14 Je 34."
4 Modern English; New York, 1910, p. 181.
5 *Nite*, says Blanche Jennings Thompson in Our Vanishing Vocabulary, *Catholic World*, Aug., 1934, " connotes speakeasies, gin, cheapness and vulgarity." *Night* " suggests quiet, rest and beauty."

still lack the imprimatur of any academic authority, are used freely by the advertising writers, and by such advance-agents of change as the contributors to *Variety*. The former try to get rid of the twelve ways of representing the *k*-sound by employing *k* itself whenever possible, *e.g.*, in *kar*, *klothes*, *klassy*, *kwality*, *kosy*, *kollege-kut*, *butter-krust*, *keen-kutter*, *kutlery*, *kleen*, *kake*, and so on.[1] They also introduce many other novelties, *e.g.*, *uneeda*, *trufit* (shoes), *wilcut* (knives), *veribest*, *dalite* (alarm clocks), *staylit* (matches), *az-nu* (second-hand), *shur-on* (eye-glasses), *slipova* (covers), *nota-seme* (hosiery), *kant-leek* (water-bottle), and the like. Most of these, of course, rise and fall with the commodities they designate, and thus have only the dignity of nonce-words, but in their very number there is some sign of a tendency. Meanwhile the advertisement writers and authors combine in an attempt to naturalize *alright*, a compound of *all* and *right*, made by analogy with *already* and *almost*. In my days as a magazine editor I found it in American manuscripts very often, and it not seldom gets into print.[2] So far no dictionary supports it, but in " Webster's New International " (1934) it is listed as " commonly found." It has already migrated to England and has the imprimatur of a noble lord.[3] Another vigorous newcomer is *sox* for *socks*. The *White Sox* are known to all Americans; the *White Socks* would seem strange, and the new plural has got into the *Congressional Record*.[4] Yet another is *slo*, as in *go slo*. And there are also *someway*, *someplace*, etc., *drive urself* (automobiles for hire),[5] *nuf sed*, and *naptha*.[6]

1 The Craze for *K*, by Louise Pound, *American Speech*, Oct., 1925; Spelling-Manipulation and Present-Day Advertising, by the same, *Dialect Notes*, Vol. V, Pt. VI, 1923; and Word-Coinage and Modern Trade-Names, by the same, *Dialect Notes*, Vol. IV, Pt. I, 1913, especially p. 35.
2 For example, in Teepee Neighbors, by Grace Coolidge; Boston, 1917, p. 220; Duty and Other Irish Comedies, by Seumas O'Brien; New York, 1916, p. 52; Salt by Charles G. Norris; New York, 1918, p. 135, and The Ideal Guest, by Wyndham Lewis, *Little Review*, May, 1918, p. 3. O'Brien is an Irishman and Lewis an Englishman, but the printer in each case was

American. I find *allright*, as one word but with two *l's*, in Diplomatic Correspondence with Belligerent Governments, etc. European War, No. 4; Washington, 1918, p. 214.
3 Viscount Harberton, in How to Lengthen Our Ears, London, 1917, p. 28.
4 May 16, 1921, p. 1478, col. 2.
5 In Why Not *U* for *You?*, *American Speech*, Oct., 1929, Donald M. Alexander of Ohio Wesleyan University argues seriously that this substitution should be made, just as *I* has been substituted for various earlier forms of the first person pronoun.
6 See The Spelling of *Naphtha*, by J. J. Jones, *American Speech*, Dec.,

4. THE TREATMENT OF LOAN-WORDS

In the treatment of loan-words English spelling is much more conservative than American. This conservatism, in fact, is so marked that it is frequently denounced by English critics of the national speech usages, and it stood first among the "tendencies of modern taste" attacked by the Society for Pure English in its original prospectus in 1913 – a prospectus prepared by Henry Bradley, Dr. Robert Bridges, Sir Walter Raleigh and L. Pearsall Smith,[1] and signed by many important men of letters, including Thomas Hardy, A. J. Balfour, Edmund Gosse, Austin Dobson, Maurice Hewlett, Gilbert Murray, George Saintsbury and the professors of English literature at Cambridge and London, Sir Arthur Quiller-Couch and W. P. Ker. I quote from this *caveat:*

> Literary taste at the present time, with regard to foreign words recently borrowed from abroad, is on wrong lines, the notions which govern it being scientifically incorrect, tending to impair the national character of our standard speech, and to adapt it to the habits of classical scholars. On account of these alien associations our borrowed terms are now spelt and pronounced, not as English, but as foreign words, instead of being assimilated, as they were in the past, and brought into conformity with the main structure of our speech. And as we more and more rarely assimilate our borrowings, so even words that were once naturalized are being now one by one made un-English, and driven out of the language back into their foreign forms; whence it comes that a paragraph of serious English prose may be sometimes seen as freely sprinkled with italicized French words as a passage of Cicero is often interlarded with Greek. The mere printing of such words in italics is an active force toward degeneration. The Society hopes to discredit this tendency, and it will endeavour to restore to English its old recreative energy; when a choice is possible we should wish to give an English pronunciation and spelling to useful foreign words, and we would attempt to restore to a good many words the old English forms which they once had, but which are now supplanted by the original foreign forms.[2]

1930, p. 154. Mr. Jones prints the following letter from Fels and Company of Philadelphia, manufacturers of Fels-*Naptha* soap: "Fels-*Naptha* has been manufactured for almost forty years, and since the very beginning, when we wedded the name *Fels* and the word *naptha* we recognized that the first *h* was superfluous, and we merely discarded it. Since that time our spelling of *naptha* has found favor and it is now listed in all large and up-to-date dictionaries." This last seems to have been an exaggeration. I can't find *naptha* in Webster's New International (1934). The decay of *ph* to *p* is discussed in Chapter VII, Section 3.

1 Smith is an expatriate American.

2 *S.P.E. Tracts,* No. 1, Preliminary Announcement and List of Members, Oct., 1919, p. 7. The *Literary Supplement* of the London

Since this was written, and probably at least partly because of it, there has been some change in England,[1] but the more pretentious English papers continue to accent, and often italicize, words that have been completely naturalized in this country, *e.g.*, *café*, *début*, *portière*, *éclat*, *naïveté*, *régime*, *rôle*, *soirée*, *protégé*, *élite*, *gemütlichkeit*, *mêleé*, *tête-a-tête*, *porte-cochère*, *divorcée*, *fiancée* and *dénouement*. Even loan-words long since naturalized are sometimes used in their foreign forms, *e.g.*, *répertoire* for *repertory*, *muslim* for *moslem*, *crêpe* for *crape*, and *légion d'honneur* for *legion of honor*. The dictionaries seldom omit the accents from recent foreign words. Cassell's leaves them off *régime* and *début*, but preserves them on practically all the other terms listed above; the Concise Oxford always uses them. In the United States usage is much looser. *Dépôt* became *depot* immediately it entered the language, and the same rapid naturalization has overtaken *employé*, *matinée*, *débutante*, *negligée*, *exposé*, *résumé*, *hofbräu*, and scores of other loan-words. *Café* is seldom seen with its accent, nor is *señor* or *divorcée* or *attaché*. Writing in the *Atlantic Monthly* twenty years ago, Charles Fitzhugh Talman said that " the omission of the diacritic is universal. Even the English press of French New Orleans ignores it." [2] Mr. Talman listed some rather astonishing barbarisms, among them, *standchen* for *ständchen* in *Littell's Living Age*, and gave an amusing account of the struggles of American newspapers with *thé dansant*, then a novelty. He said:

Put this through the hopper of the typesetting machine, and it comes forth, " the *the dansant* " — which even Oshkosh finds intolerable. The thing was, however, often attempted when *thés dansant* came into fashion, and with various results. Generally the proof-reader eliminates one of the *the*'s, making *dansant* a quasi-noun, and to this day one reads of people giving or attending

Times supported the Society in a leading article on Jan. 8, 1920. " Of old," it said, " we incorporated foreign words rapidly and altered their spelling ruthlessly. Today we take them in and go on spelling them and pronouncing them in a foreign way. *Rendezvous* is an example, *régime* is another. They have come to stay; the spelling of the first, and at least the pronunciation of the second, should be altered; and a powerful organization of schoolmasters and journalists could secure changes which the working classes are in process of securing with the words (more familiar to them) *garridge* and *shofer*." See also A Few Practical Suggestions, by Logan Pearsall Smith, *S.P.E. Tracts*, No. III, 1920, especially Sections I, II and III.

1 In later Tracts the Society printed lists of proposed new spellings. In No. XIII (1923) it advocated *rencounter* for *recontre*, *role* for *rôle*, *tamber* for *timbre*, *intransigent* for *intransigeant*, and *malease* for *malaise*.

2 Accents Wild, Dec., 1915, p. 807 *ff.*

dansants. Latterly the public taste seems to favor *dansante*, which doubtless has a Frenchier appearance, provided you are sufficiently ignorant of the Gallic tongue. Two other solutions of the difficulty may be noted:
   Among those present at the "*the dansant*";
   Among those present at the *the-dansant;* that is, either a hyphen or quotation marks set off the exotic phrase.

There has been some improvement in recent years, but not much. Even in the larger cities, the majority of American newspapers manage to get along without using foreign accents. They are even omitted from foreign proper names, so that *Bülow* becomes *Bulow* and *Poincaré* becomes *Poincare.* For a number of years the Baltimore *Evening Sun* was the only Eastern daily that, to my knowledge, had linotype mats for the common French and German accents. The New York *American* did not acquire a set until late in 1934, when they were laid in to print some short lexicographical articles that I was then writing for the paper. Even when they are in stock they are seldom used correctly, for American copy-readers take a high professional pride in their complete ignorance of foreign languages, as they do in their ignorance of the terminology of all the arts and sciences. For the former they have the example of Walt Whitman, who, according to Dr. Louise Pound, often omitted accents in " his manuscript notes and in early editions," and used them incorrectly in his later editions.[1] The *Congressional Record* avoids them as much as possible, and the State Department, ordinarily very conservative and English, has abandoned *visé* for *visa,* though it is faithful to *chargé.* With this iconoclasm the late Dr. Brander Matthews was in hearty sympathy. Writing in 1917, and dealing with *naïve* and *naïveté,* which he welcomed into the language because there were no English equivalents, he argued that they would "need to shed their accents and to adapt themselves somehow to the traditions of our orthography." He went on:

> After we have decided that the foreign word we find knocking at the doors of English [he really meant American, as the context shows] is likely to be useful, we must fit it for naturalization by insisting that it shall shed its accents, if it has any; that it shall change its spelling, if this is necessary; that it shall modify its pronunciation, if this is not easy for us to compass; and that it shall conform to all our speech-habits, especially in the formation of the plural.[2]

1 Walt Whitman and the French Language, *American Speech,* May, 1926, p. 423.
2 Why Not Speak Or Own Language?, *Delineator,* Nov., 1917, p. 12. See also his French Words in the English Language, *S.P.E. Tracts,* No. V, 1921.

This counsel is heeded by many patriotic Americans. So far as I can find, *bozart* (for *beaux-arts*) is not in any dictionary, but it is used as the name of "America's second-largest verse magazine," published at Box 67, Station E, Atlanta, Ga., as the name of a lead-pencil very popular in the South, and in the titles of a number of business firms, including one with quarters in Radio City, New York.[1] *Exposé* long since lost its accent and is now commonly pronounced to rhyme with *propose. Schmierkäse* has become *smearkase*, and the *sauer* in *sauer-kraut* and *sauer-braten* is often spelled *sour*.[2] *Coleslaw*, by folk-etymology, has become *cold-slaw. Führer* is *fuhrer, cañon* is *canyon*, and *vaudeville* is sometimes *vodvil*. I have even seen *jonteel*, in a trade name, for the French *gentil*, and *parfay* for *parfait*. In derivatives of the Greek *haima* it is the almost invariable American custom to spell the root syllable *hem*, but the more conservative English make it *hæm* – e.g., in *hæmorrhage* and *hæmophilia*. In an exhaustive list of diseases issued by the United States Public Health Service [3] the *hæm-* form does not appear once. In the same way American usage prefers *esophagus, diarrhea* and *etiology* to the English *œsophagus, diarrhœa* and *ætiology*. In the style-book of the *Journal of the American Medical Association* I find many other spellings that would shock an English medical author, among them *curet* for *curette, cocain* for *cocaine, gage* for *gauge, intern* for *interne, lacrimal* for *lachrymal*, and a whole group of words ending in -*er* instead of in -*re*.[4]

American newspapers seldom distinguish between the masculine and feminine forms of common loan-words. *Blond* and *blonde* are used indiscriminately. The majority of papers, apparently mistaking

1 To compensate for this a firm in Hollysburg, N. Y. calls itself *Beaux-Artes*, Inc., thus giving the plural of *art* a complimentary *e*.

2 It is to be found thus in the 1852 edition of Webster's American Dictionary, edited by his son-in-law, Chauncey A. Goodrich, and in Mark Twain's Innocents Abroad; New York, 1869, p. 94. But *sauer-kraut* is given in the Standard Dictionary (1906), and Webster's New International (1934).

3 Nomenclature of Diseases and Conditions, prepared by direction of the Surgeon General; Washington, 1916.

4 American Medical Association Style Book; Chicago, 1915. At the 1921 session of the American Medical Association in Boston an English gynecologist read a paper and it was printed in the *Journal*. When he received the proofs he objected to a great many of the spellings, e.g., *gonorrheal* for *gonorrhæal*, and *fallopian* for *Falloppian*. The *Journal* refused to agree to his English spellings, but when his paper was reprinted separately they were restored.

blond for a simplified form of *blonde,* use it to designate both sexes. So with *employée, divorcée, fiancée,* etc. Here the feminine form is preferred; no doubt it has been helped into use in the case of the -*ee* words by the analogy of *devotee.*[1] In all cases, of course, the accents are omitted. In the formation of the plural American adopts native forms much more quickly than English. All the English authorities that I have consulted advocate retaining the foreign plurals of most of the loan-words in daily use, e. g., *sanatoria, appendices, indices, virtuosi, formulæ, libretti, media, thés-dansants, monsignori.* But American usage favors plurals of native design, and sometimes they take quite fantastic forms. I have observed *delicatessens, monsignors, virtuosos, rathskellers, vereins, nucleuses* and *appendixes. Banditti,* in place of *bandits,* would seem an affectation to an American, and so would *soprani* for *sopranos* and *soli* for *solos.* Both English and American labor under the lack of native plurals for the two everyday titles, *Mister* and *Missus.* In the written speech, and in the more exact forms of the spoken speech, the French plurals, *Messieurs* and *Mesdames,* are used, but in the ordinary spoken speech, at least in America, they are avoided, whenever possible, by circumlocution. When *Messieurs* has to be spoken it is pronounced *messers,* and in the same way *Mesdames* becomes *mezdames,* with the first syllable rhyming with *sez* and the second, which bears the accent, with *games.* In place of *Mesdames* a more natural form, *Madames,* seems to be gaining ground in America. Thus, I have found *Dames du Sacré Coeur* translated as *Madames of the Sacred Heart* in a Catholic paper of wide circulation,[2] and the form is apparently used by American members of the community.

Dr. Louise Pound[3] notes that a number of Latin plurals tend to become singular nouns in colloquial American, notably *curricula, data, dicta, insignia* and *strata,* and with them a few Greek plurals, e.g., *criteria* and *phenomena.* She reports hearing the following uses of them: " The *curricula* of the institution is being changed," " This *data* is very significant," " The *dicta,* ' Go West,' is said to have come from Horace Greeley," " What is that *insignia* on his sleeve? ", " This may be called the Renaissance *strata* of loan-words," " That is no *criteria,*" and " What a strange *phenomena!* " — all by speakers

1 See Words From the French (-*é*, -*ée*), by Matthew Barnes, *S.P.E. Tracts,* No. XXX, 1928.
2 *Irish World,* June 26, 1918.
3 The Pluralization of Latin Loan-Words in Present-Day American Speech, *Classical Journal,* Dec., 1919.

presumed to be of some education. The error leads to the creation of double plurals, *e.g., curriculas, insignias, stratas, stimulis, alumnis, bacillis, narcissis.* The Latin names of plants lead to frequent blunders. *Cosmos* and *gladiolus* are felt to be plurals, and from them, by folk-etymology, come the false singulars, *cosma* and *gladiola.* Dr. Pound notes many other barbarous plurals, not mentioned above, *e.g., antennas, cerebras, alumnas, alumnuses, narcissuses, apparatuses, emporiums, opuses, criterions, amœbas, cactuses, phenomenons.*

5. PUNCTUATION, CAPITALIZATION, AND ABBREVIATION

In capitalization the English are much more conservative than we are. They invariably capitalize such terms as *Government, Prime Minister, Church* and *Society,* when used as proper nouns; they capitalize *Press, Pulpit, Bar,* etc., almost as often. Some of the English newspapers, in their leading articles (Am.: editorials), print all names of persons in capitals and small capitals, *e.g.,* MR. RAMSAY MACDONALD, and also such titles as the KING and the PRIME MINISTER. In the London *Times* this is also done in news articles. But in the United States only the New York *Times* appears to do so, and it confines the practise to its editorials. In the Eighteenth Century there was a fashion for reducing all capitals to small letters, and Lord Chesterfield thus denounced it in a letter to his son, April 13, 1752:

It offends my eyes to see *rome, france, caesar, henry the fourth,* etc. begin with small letters; and I do not conceive that there can be any reason for doing it half so strong as the reason of long usage to the contrary. This is an affectation below Voltaire.

But Thomas Jefferson thought otherwise, and in the first draft of the Declaration of Independence *nature* and *creator,* and even *god* are in lower case.[1] During the 20's and 30's of the succeeding century, probably as a result of French influence, the movement against the capitals went so far that the days of the week were often spelled with small initial letters, and even *Mr.* became *mr.* Curiously enough, the most striking exhibition of this tendency of late years is offered by an English work of the highest scholarship, the Cambridge History of English Literature. It uses the lower case for all

[1] A correspondent tells me that, in the manuscripts of Jefferson's let- ters, even sentences are begun with small letters.

titles, even *baron* and *colonel*, before proper names, and also avoids capitals in such words as *presbyterian, catholic* and *christian*, and in the second parts of such terms as Westminster *abbey* and Atlantic *ocean*.

There are also certain differences in punctuation. The English, as everyone knows, usually put a comma after the street number of a house, making it, for example, *34, St. James's Street*.[1] They insert a comma instead of a period after the hour when giving the time in figures, *e.g., 9,27,* and omit the *o* when indicating less than 10 minutes, *e.g., 8,7* instead of *8.07*. They do not use the period as the mark of the decimal, but employ a dot at the level of the upper dot of a colon, as in 3·1416. They commonly write *8th October* instead of *October 8th,* and when they write *8/10/35* they mean October 8, 1935, not August 10, 1935, as we should usually mean. They cling to the hyphen in *to-day, to-night* and *to-morrow;* it is fast disappearing in America.[2] They are far more careful than we are to retain the apostrophe in possessive forms of nouns used in combination, *e.g., St. Mary's Church, ladies' room*. In geographical names they sometimes use it and sometimes omit it; in the United States the Geographic Board endeavors to obliterate it, and most American newspapers do so. The English newspapers usually spell out *street, avenue,* etc., print them as separate words, and give them capital initials, but in the United States they are commonly abbreviated and printed in small letters, and sometimes they are hooked to the preceding proper names with hyphens. "Some of our papers," says the Scripps-Howard Style Book, "abbreviate streets and avenues thus: Prospect-*st.,* Euclid-*av.,* Bulkley-*blvd.,* Wanamaker-*pl.* Notwithstanding certain objections, we approve of this abbreviated style, for space reasons." Many papers abbreviate *county* and *company* in the same way, *e.g.,* Grady-*co.* and Pullman-*co.* The Chicago *Tribune* does not abbreviate such words, but it prints them in lower case, and treats even *hall, house, mansion, building, park* and *palace* likewise.[3]

---

1 This custom is sometimes imitated by American Anglophiles, but it is certainly not general in the United States.

2 Mr. David H. Dodge of San Francisco reminds me that the Western Union used to charge for each of these words as two words. But now it counts only one. It also counts *good-bye* as one, though Webster's New International gives it a hyphen. In England *good-bye* has a hyphen but *good night* is two words.

3 Many American newspapers and chains of newspapers print style books for the use of their staffs. That of the Scripps-Howard group I have just quoted. Among the most elaborate are The Style Book of the Detroit *News,* edited by

There remains a class of differences that may as well be noticed under spelling, though they are not strictly orthographical. *Specialty, aluminum* and *alarm* offer examples. In English they are *speciality, aluminium* and *alarum*, though *alarm* is also an alternative form. *Specialty,* in America, is always accented on the first syllable; *speciality,* in England, on the third. The result is two distinct words, though their meaning is identical. How *aluminium,* in America, lost its fourth syllable I have been unable to determine, but all American authorities now make it *aluminum* and all English authorities stick to *aluminium.* Perhaps the *boric-boracic* pair also belongs here. In American *boric* is now almost universally preferred, but it is also making progress in England. How the difference between the English *behove* and the American *behoove* arose I do not know.

A. L. Weeks; Detroit, 1918; Style Book of the New York *Herald Tribune;* New York, 1929; Rules of Composition For the Use of Editors, Copy Readers, Operators and Proof Readers (Chicago *Tribune*); Chicago, 1934; and General Style Book (New York *News*); New York, 1931. Such books are not for sale, though copies usually may be obtained by persons interested. There are discussions of capitalization and abbreviation in virtually all the current desk-books of "good" English. For English usage see Modern English Punctuation, by Reginald Skelton; London, 1933.

IX

THE COMMON SPEECH

1. OUTLINES OF ITS GRAMMAR

The American common speech, of course, is closely related grammatically to the vulgar dialects of the British Isles, and in many ways it is identical with them. In both one encounters the double negative, the use of the adjective as an adverb, the confusion of cases in the pronoun and of tenses in the verb, and various other violations of the polite canon. But these similarities are accompanied by important differences. For one thing, vulgar American is virtually uniform throughout the country, whereas the British dialects differ so greatly that some of them are mutually unintelligible. There are, as we have seen in Chapter VII, certain group and regional peculiarities in the United States, but virtually all of them have to do with pronunciation and vocabulary, and are thus of no importance to grammar. A Boston taxicab-driver who moved to San Francisco would find the everyday speech of his fellows, save for a few vowel sounds and a few localisms, very like his own, and he would encounter little more difficulty in communicating with them if he moved to Chicago, New Orleans or Denver. For another thing, vulgar American shows the same tendency to ready change that characterizes the standard language, and is thus given to taking in new forms and abandoning old ones more rapidly than any of the English dialects. I myself remember when the use of the present form of the verb for the preterite, as in *he give*, began to develop into a wholesale adoption of a sort of historical present, as in *he win a dollar, I say to him*, and so on. And various observers have noted the disappearance of forms that were common only a generation or two ago, or their descent to the dialects, e.g., *sot* (for *sat*), *riz, driv, clomb, see'd*, and *gin* (for *given*).[1] The English dialects have changed too, as one may

1 See The Verbs of the Vulgate, by Robert J. Menner, *American Speech*, Jan., 1926, p. 239, and The

Verbs of the Vulgate in Their Historical Relations, by Henry Alexander, the same, April, 1929.

discover by comparing the Cockney of Dickens with the Cockney of today, but they have apparently changed less than vulgar American, and the changes occurring in some of them have affected others hardly at all.

For many years the indefatigable schoolmarm has been trying to put down the American vulgate, but with very little success. At great pains she teaches her pupils the rules of what she conceives to be correct English, but the moment they get beyond reach of her constabulary ear they revert to the looser and more natural speech-habits of home and work-place. They acquire, after a fashion, a reading knowledge of her correct English, and can even make shift to speak it on occasion, or, at all events, something colorably resembling it, but for all ordinary purposes they prefer a tongue that is easier, if less elegant. The schoolmarm's heroic struggles to dissuade them have got little aid from her professional superiors. They have provided her with a multitude of textbooks, most of them hopelessly pedantic, though others are sensible enough,[1] and they have invented a wealth of teaching methods, mostly far more magical than scientific, but they have not thrown much light upon the psychological problem actually before her. In particular, they have failed to make an adequate investigation of the folk-speech she tries to combat, seeking to uncover its inner nature and account for its vitality. American philologians have printed admirable studies of many of the other languages spoken in the United States, including the most obscure Indian tongues,[2] but incredible as it may seem,

[1] An excellent account of the contents of these books is to be found in Grammar and Usage in Textbooks on English, by Robert C. Pooley; Madison, Wis., 1933. The bad ones recall a dictum of Noah Webster in his Dissertations on the English Language; Boston, 1789, *pref.*, p. vii: "Our modern grammars have done much more hurt than good. The authors have labored to prove, what is obviously absurd, *viz.*, that our language is not made right; and in pursuance of this idea, have tried to make it over again, and persuade the English to speak by Latin rules, or by arbitrary rules of their own. Hence they have rejected many phrases of pure English, and substituted those which are neither English nor sense."

[2] If there were a Pulitzer Prize for such works it would undoubtedly go to Dr. Morris Swadesh's monograph, The Phonetics of Chitimacha, *Language*, Dec., 1934, p. 345 *ff.* Chitimacha is an Indian tongue that is now spoken by but two people, and "they employ slightly different phonemic systems." Thus Dr. Swadesh was forced to deal with one form as the standard language, and the other as a dialect. His immensely patient and exhaustive inquiry was carried on during the Summers of 1932 and 1933 on a grant from the Com-

they have yet to produce a grammar of the daily speech of nearly 100,000,000 Americans. It was not until 1908, indeed, that any serious notice of it was taken in academic circles,[1] and not until 1914 that an investigation of it was undertaken on an adequate scale and by an inquirer of adequate equipment. That inquirer was Dr. W. W. Charters, then professor of the theory of teaching at the University of Missouri, and now (1936) director of the Bureau of Educational Research at Ohio State University. One of the problems he found himself engaged upon in 1914 was that of the teaching of the grammar of Standard English in the public elementary schools. In the course of his investigation he encountered the theory that such instruction should be confined to the rules habitually violated — that the one aim of teaching grammar was to correct the speech of the pupils, and that it was useless to harass them with principles which they already observed. Apparently inclining to this somewhat dubious notion, Dr. Charters applied to the School Board of Kansas City for permission to undertake an examination of the language actually used by the children in the elementary schools of that city, and that permission was granted.

The materials he gathered were of two classes. First, the teachers of grades III to VII inclusive in twelve Kansas City public schools were instructed to turn over to Dr. Charters all the written work of their pupils, " ordinarily done in the regular order of school work " during a period of four weeks. Secondly, the teachers of grades II to VII inclusive in all the city schools, together with the principals, were instructed to make note of " all oral errors in grammar made in the school-rooms and around the school-buildings " during the five school-days of one week, by children of any age, and to dispatch these notes to Dr. Charters also. The ages thus covered ran from nine or ten to fourteen or fifteen, and perhaps five-sixths of the material studied came from children above twelve. Its examination

---

mittee on Research in American Native Languages. His report occupies no less than eighteen pages in *Language.*

1 The pioneer study seems to have been a brief investigation of the oral errors made by public-school children in Connersville, Ind. It was undertaken by G. M. Wilson, and his observations were printed in the report of the Connersville School Board for 1908. Unluckily, I am informed by Mr. Edwin C. Dodson, superintendent of schools at Connersville, that a fire destroyed the board's copy of this report, and I have been unable to find one elsewhere. But in Dec., 1909, Mr. Wilson printed a paper on Errors in the Language of Grade-Pupils, based upon the Connersville material, in the *Educator-Journal.*

threw a brilliant light upon the speech actually employed by children near the end of their schooling in a typical American city, and *per corollary*, upon the speech employed by their parents and other older associates. If anything, the grammatical and syntactical habits revealed were a bit less loose than those of the authentic *Volkssprache*, for practically all of the written evidence was gathered under conditions which naturally caused the writers to try to write what they thought to be correct English, and even the oral evidence was conditioned by the admonitory presence of the teacher, by her probably frequent failure to note errors, and by her occasional incapacity to detect them. Moreover, it must be obvious that a child of the lower classes, during the period of its actual contact with pedagogy, probably speaks better English than at any time before or afterward, for it is only then that any positive pressure is exerted upon it to that end. But even so, the departures from standard usage that were unearthed were numerous and striking, and their tendency to accumulate in definite groups appeared to show the working of general laws.[1]

The materials accumulated by Dr. Charters were so large that a complete Virchovian autopsy upon them was impracticable, and in consequence he confined his examination to parts of them. He chose (*a*) the oral errors " reported by the teachers of grades III and VII and by the principals "; (*b*) the oral errors made by another group consisting of the children of grades VI and VII; and (*c*) the written errors made by children of the last-named in twelve schools. The children of grade III had had no formal instruction in grammar, but it was in the curricula of grades VI and VII. He classified the oral errors of his (*a*) group as follows:

Error	*Illustration*	*Percentage of the Total Errors*
1. Subject of verb not in nominative case.	*Us* girls went.	4
2. Predicate nominative not in nominative case.	They were John and *him*. It is *me*.	2
3. Object of verb or preposition not in objective case.	She gave it to Martha and *I*.	1
4. Wrong form of noun or pronoun.	*Sheeps; theirself*. The problem *what* is —	2

1 Dr. Charters's report appears as Vol. XVI, No. 2, *University of Missouri Bulletin,* Education Series No. 9, Jan., 1915. He was aided in his inquiry by Edith Miller, teacher of English in one of the St. Louis high-schools.

Error	Illustration	Percentage of the Total Errors
5. First personal pronoun standing first in a series.	*Me* and *him*.	2
6. Failure of the pronoun to agree with its noun in number, person and gender.	Nobody can do what *they* like.	0
7. Confusion of demonstrative adjective and personal pronoun.	*Them* things.	3
8. Failure of verb to agree with its subject in number and person.	There *is* six. You *was*.	14
9. Confusion of past and present tenses.	She *give* us four. He *ask* me.	2
10. Confusion of past tense and past participle.	I *seen*, I have *saw*.	24
11. Wrong tense form.	*Attackted; had ought*.	5
12. Wrong verb.	*Lay* for *lie; ain't got;* confusion of *can* and *may, shall* and *will*.	12
13. Incorrect use of mood.	If I *was* in your place.	0
14. Incorrect comparison of adjectives.	*Joyfulest; beautifuler; more better; worser*.	1
15. Confusion of comparatives and superlatives.	She is the *tallest* (of two).	0
16. Confusion of adjectives and adverbs.	He looked up *quick*. That *there* book.	4
17. Misplaced modifier.	He *only* went two miles.	0
18. Double negative.	He *isn't hardly* old enough.	11
19. Confusion of preposition and conjunction.	He talks *like* he is sick.	0
20. Syntactical redundance.	Mother *she* said so. Where is it *at?*	10
21. Wrong part of speech due to similarity of sound.	I would *of* known; *they* for *there*.	1

It will be noted that 57% of the total errors discovered involved the use of the verb, and that nearly half of these, or 24% of the total, involved a confusion between the preterite and the perfect participle. Difficulties with pronouns accounted for 14%, double negatives for 11% and the confusion of adjectives and adverbs for 4%. The (*b*) group, composed of children of grades VI and VII, in both of which grammar was studied, made almost the same errors, and in substantially the same proportions. Those in the use of the verb dropped from 57% to 52%, but those in the use of pronouns remained at 14%, and those involving the double negative remained at 11%. In the written work of the (*c*) group certain changes appeared, but they were hardly significant. The percentage of errors

in the use of verbs dropped to 50, and those involving the double
negative to 1, but those in the use of pronouns rose to 24.

Dr. Charters, of course, confined himself to a comparative study
of errors actually made and observed, and no attempt was made to
relate them statistically to instances of correct usage. Twelve years
later Dr. Robert J. Menner of Yale argued that this method was
"likely to produce an exaggerated impression of the frequency of
errors"[1] — obviously, a plausible contention. Since then several efforts have been made to investigate the material quantitatively, but
so far without results that meet every critical standard. The most
ambitious of these attempts was that of Dr. L. J. O'Rourke and his
associates in 1930–33. With the coöperation of 40,000 teachers they
sought to test the grammatical knowledge of 1,500,000 public-
school children, ranging from the third grade to the thirteenth, in
the forty-eight States of the Union, the District of Columbia,
Hawaii, Porto Rico and the Philippines. Their test-papers included
three categories of questions. The first had to do with such essentials
as Charters covered in his inquiry; their second concerned more
delicate matters, and their third included points properly belonging
to style rather than to grammar, *e.g.*, the use of *he* or *his* following
one as a pronoun. The percentages of children passing the tests of
the first category, in the grades from the seventh to the thirteenth,
were as follows:

7	34.7	9	52.8	11	69.5
8	44.7	10	61.5	12	74.3 [2]

These figures, if they are to be depended upon as reasonably accurate, show that the schoolmarm's efforts to inculcate "good grammar" have some effect, but they also show that more than half the
school-children of the country speak the vulgate at least up to the
first year of high-school. And what they speak, of course, is simply
what they hear at home.[3] Indeed, Dr. Menner's own inquiries indi-

1 The Verbs of the Vulgate, above
cited, p. 231.
2 The report of Dr. O'Rourke is
summarized in English Use and
Misuse, by Paul S. Schilles, New
York *Times*, July 10, 1934. A more
extensive account of the investigation is in Rebuilding the English-
Usage Curriculum to Insure Greater
Mastery of Essentials, by Dr.
O'Rourke himself; Washington,
1934. It was made on a grant from
the Psychological Corporation,
with aid from the Carnegie Corporation and the Carnegie Foundation for the Advancement of
Teaching, and among its sponsors
were Dr. Charles H. Judd of the
University of Chicago and Dr.
Edward L. Thorndike of Teachers
College, Columbia.
3 In O'Rourke and Leonard, by Janet

cate that many of the errors on Dr. O'Rourke's list are common among persons presumably educated. His observations were made on the speech of about forty men and women, divided into three classes, described by him as follows:

1. People trained in some special profession (usually with college degrees), but with little general culture, and little literary background.
2. The average product of American high-schools.
3. People with little education and no background.

He found that individuals of his second class sometimes used *begin, come, done, give, sit* and *run* as preterites, and *broke, drank, rode* and *threw* as perfect participles, and that even those of his first class, " trained in some special profession (usually with college degrees)," occasionally resorted to *begin, come, done* and *give, broke* and *drank*. " The most meticulous speakers," he said, " occasionally lapse into carelessness, just as the most illiterate sometimes attempt to speak elegantly." This tendency, naturally enough, is chiefly found among educated persons living in close association with uncultured groups. The " bad grammar " of the Southern whites was noted by the earliest travelers below the Potomac, and it is still observable there, even in the loftiest circles. All of us, on occasion, slip easily into the circumambient speech habits, if only to enjoy their pleasant looseness, just as an educated German sometimes slips into the *Mundart* of his province. And what is thus borrowed from below not infrequently finds more or less secure lodgment above, as the frequent appearance of *it's me, rile, broke* and *bust* in perfectly good American usage well demonstrates.[1]

Rankin Aiken, *American Speech*, Dec., 1934, Dr. O'Rourke is criticized sharply for assuming that the " bad grammar " he unearthed is really bad. " The more people make a given mistake," she says, " the less it should be corrected. This fundamental principle, recognized by lexicographers and the more liberal grammarians, must be the basis of our thinking on the subject. Unlike arithmetic, where the more frequent an error is, the more attention it needs, the linguist must insist that speech errors proved to be very frequent are thereby proved to be not errors at all." As an example, Dr. Aiken cites the use of *who* in " Do you know *who*

they were waiting for this morning? " See also the preface to George O. Curme's Syntax; Boston, 1931, p. vi.

1 Logan Pearsall Smith, in Words and Idioms; London, 1925, p. 149, points out that there are no less than four distinct varieties of Standard English. The first is " the language of colloquial talk, with its expletives, easy idioms, and a varying amount of slang." Second comes " the vernacular of good conversation, more correct, more dignified, and entirely, or almost entirely, free from slang." Then comes written prose, " which is richer in vocabulary and somewhat more old-fashioned in construction

Dr. Menner argues that any list of conjugations of the verbs of the vulgate should include a " liberal intersprinkling of normal principal parts, at least as alternatives." But it must be manifest that this intersprinkling would be of little significance unless it were accompanied by statistical evidence as to the prevalence of the varying forms in a typical section of the general population. That evidence is still lacking, but meanwhile one may certainly give some credit to the testimony of one's ears. The vulgar, to be sure, occasionally say *I saw*, but no one who has ever listened to their speech attentively can doubt that they usually say *I seen*, just as, at the other end of the scale the *illuminati* occasionally say *I done*,[1] but usually say *I did*. If the study of dialects had to include the investigation of all shadings up to the purest form of the standard speech, then the study of dialects would be vain, and indeed absurd. As Dr. Menner himself says, there are verbs which the people of his lowest class conjugate improperly " without exception," *e.g.*, *to come* and *to run*. These, at least, need not be outfitted with alternatives. In the case of other verbs, usage among the humble is not fixed, and both the standard preterites and perfect participles and their vulgar variants are heard. In yet other cases, all persons not downright illiterate reveal a distaste for certain forms, *e.g.*, *brung*, *fit* and *druv*, and seldom employ them save in conscious attempts at waggishness. But all these verbs, save only those of the third class, actually belong to the vulgate, though they may not be used invariably, and their grammatical and syntactical history and relations deserve a great deal more patient study than they have got so far. The same thing is true of the pronouns of the common speech, and of all its other contents. The theory that it is somehow *infra dig* to investigate them is one that American scholarship can hardly entertain much longer.[2]

than the spoken language," and finally there is the language of poetry. "If we examine this linguistic ladder," says Mr. Smith, " we will find that its lowest rung is fixed close to the soil of popular and vulgar speech." The vulgar speech has like varieties. Its written form differs considerably from its spoken form, and the latter ranges from an almost simian gabble to something closely approximating ordinary colloquial American.

1 Menner, p. 232.
2 A bibliography of the very meager literature of the subject from 1908 to 1930, running to but 33 items, is to be found in The Most Common Grammatical Errors, by Henry Harap, *English Journal*, June, 1930. Mr. Harap lists the errors usually observed, but makes no attempt to estimate either their relative or their absolute frequency. He avoids the question, he says, because " of the lack of uniformity in recording

Rather curiously, the *sermo vulgus* was for long as diligently neglected by the professional writers of the country as by the philologians. There are foreshadowings of it in "The Biglow Papers," in "Huckleberry Finn" and in some of the frontier humor of the years before the Civil War, but the enormous dialect literature of the later Nineteenth Century left it almost untouched. Localisms in vocabulary and pronunciation were explored at length, but the general folk-speech went virtually unobserved. It is not to be found in "Chimmie Fadden"; it is not in "David Harum"; it is not even in the fables of George Ade. It began to appear in the stories of Helen Green during the first years of the century, but the business of reporting it with complete accuracy had to wait for Ring Lardner, a Chicago newspaper reporter, who began experimenting with it in 1908 or thereabout. In his grotesque but searching tales of baseball-players, pugilists, movie queens, song-writers and other such dismal persons he set down common American with the utmost precision, and yet with enough imagination to make his work a contribution of genuine and permanent value to the national literature. In any story of his taken at random it is possible to unearth almost every grammatical peculiarity of the vulgar speech, and he always resisted very stoutly the temptation to lay on its humors too thickly. Here, for example, are a few typical sentences from "The Busher's Honeymoon": [1]

I and Florrie *was* married the day before yesterday just *like* I told you we *was* going to be. . . . You *was* to get married in Bedford, where *not nothing* is nearly half so dear. . . . The sum of what I have *wrote* down is $29.40. . . . Allen told me I *should ought* to give the priest $5. . . . I never *seen* him before. . . . I didn't used to eat *no* lunch in the playing season except when I *knowed* I was not going to work. . . . I guess the meals *has* cost me all together about $1.50, and I have *eat* very little myself. . . . I was willing to tell her all about *them* two poor girls. . . . *They* must not be *no* mistake about who is the boss in my house. Some men *lets* their *wife* run all over them. . . . Allen has *went* to a college foot-ball game. One of the reporters *give* him a pass. . . . He called up and said he *hadn't* only the one pass, but he was not hurting my feelings *none*. . . . The flat across the hall from this *here*

them by various investigators." Some later studies are summarized in A Critical Summary of Selective Research in Elementary School Composition, Language, and Grammar, by W. S. Guiler and E. A. Betts, *Elementary English Review*, March–June, 1934. Of these, the most interesting is Studies in the

Learning of English Expression; No. V: Grammar, by Percival M. Symonds and Eugene M. Hinton, *Teachers College Record*, Feb., 1932.

1 *Saturday Evening Post*, July 11, 1914. Reprinted in You Know Me, Al; Garden City, L. I., 1915.

one is for rent. . . . If we should *of boughten* furniture it would cost us in the neighborhood of $100, even without *no* piano. . . . I consider myself lucky to *of* found out about this before it was too late and somebody else had *of* gotten the tip. . . . It will always be *ourn*, even when we move away. . . . Maybe you could *of did* better if you had *of went* at it in a different way. . . . Both *her* and you *is* welcome at my house. . . . I never *seen* so much wine *drank* in my life. . . .

Here are specimens to fit into most of Charters's categories — verbs confused as to tense, pronouns confused as to case, double and even triple negatives, nouns and verbs disagreeing in number, *have* softened to *of*, *n* marking the possessive instead of *s*, *like* used in place of *as*, and so on. A study of the whole story would probably unearth all the remaining errors noted by Charters in Kansas City. Lardner's baseball player, though he has pen in hand and is on his guard, and is thus very careful to write *would not* instead of *wouldn't* and even *am not* instead of *ain't*, provides us with a comprehensive and highly instructive panorama of popular linguistic habits. To him the forms of the subjunctive mood in the verb have no existence, so that *shall* has almost disappeared from his vocabulary, and adjectives and adverbs are indistinguishable, and the objective case in the pronoun is indicated only by word order. He uses the word that is simplest, the grammatical pattern that is handiest. And so he moves toward the philological millennium dreamed of by George T. Lanigan, when " the singular verb shall lie down with the plural noun, and a little conjunction shall lead them." [1] This vulgar American is a very fluent and even garrulous fellow, and he com-

1 Lardner died on Sept. 25, 1933, at the early age of 48. My own debt to him was very large. The first edition of the present work, published in 1919, brought me into contact with him, and for the second edition, published in 1921, he prepared two amusing specimens of the common speech in action. At that time, and almost until his death, he made penetrating and valuable suggestions. His ear for the minor peculiarities of vulgar American was extraordinarily keen. Once, sitting with him, I used the word *feller*. " Where and when," he demanded, " did you ever hear anyone say *feller?* " I had to admit, on reflection, that the true form was *fella*, though it is almost always written *feller* by authors.

But never by Lardner. So far as I can make out, there is not a single error in the whole canon of his writings. His first book of stories, You Know Me, Al, was published in 1915. He had many imitators, notably Edward Streeter, author of Dere Mable; New York, 1918; H. C. Witwer, who published more than a dozen books between 1918 and his death in 1929; and Will Rogers, who contributed a daily dispatch to a syndicate of newspapers, written partly in Standard English but partly in the vulgate, from 1930 to 1935. He also provided inspiration for the writers of popular songs and of captions for comic-strips. See Stabilizing the Language Through Popular Songs, by Sigmund Spaeth, *New Yorker*,

monly pronounces his words distinctly, so that his grammatical felonies shine forth clearly. In the conversation of a London Cockney, a Yorkshire farm-laborer or a Scots hillman precisely similar *attentats* upon the canon are obscured by phonological muddiness, but the Americano gives his consonants their full values and is kind to his vowels. His vocabulary is much larger than his linguistic betters commonly assume. They labor under a tradition that the lowly manage to get through life with a few hundred or a few thousand words. That tradition, according to a recent writer on the subject,[1] " originated with two English clergymen, one of whom stated that ' some of the laborers in his parish had not three hundred words in their vocabulary,' while the other, Archdeacon Farrar, said he ' once listened for a long time together to the conversation of three peasants who were gathering apples among the boughs of an orchard, and as far as I could conjecture, the whole number of words they used did not exceed a hundred.' " The famous Max Müller gave imprudent support to this nonsense, and it was later propagated by Wilhelm Wundt, the psychologist, by Barrett Wendell, and by various other persons who should have known better. It has now been established by scientific inquiry that even children of five or six years have vocabularies of between 2000 and 3000 words, and that even the most stupid adults know at least 5000. The average American, indeed, probably knows nearly 5000 nouns. As for the educated, their vocabularies range from 30,000 words to maybe as many as 70,000.[2]

July 7, 1934, and The English of the Comic Cartoons, by Helen Trace Tysell, *American Speech*, Feb., 1935. But these disciples never attained to Lardner's virtuosity.

1 Margaret Morse Nice, in On the Size of Vocabularies, *American Speech*, Oct., 1926.

2 The results of various investigations are set forth in Mrs. Nice's article, just cited. See also Measuring the Vocabulary of High-School Pupils, by H. L. Neher, *School and Society*, Sept. 21, 1918; Says Average Man Uses 8,000 Words (an interview with Dr. Frank H. Vizetelly), New York *Times*, July 15, 1923; The Speech of Five Hundred College Women, by Sara M. Stinchfield, *Journal of Applied Psy-*

chology, June, 1925; Contemporary English, by W. E. Collinson; Leipzig, 1927 (an account of the growth of the author's vocabulary); A Vocabulary Study of Children in a Foreign Industrial Community, by Alice M. Jones, *Psychological Clinic*, March, 1928; Statistics of Vocabulary, by E. A. Condon, *Science*, March 16, 1928; Extent of Personal Vocabularies and Cultural Control, by J. M. Gillette, *Scientific Monthly*, Nov., 1929; and Vocabulary of Children's Letters Written in Life Outside School, by J. A. Fitzgerald, *Elementary School Journal*, Jan., 1934. I list only a few studies. The literature of the subject is very large.

2. THE VERB

The chief grammatical peculiarities of vulgar American lie, as Charters shows, among the verbs and pronouns. The nouns in common use, in the main, are quite sound in form. Very often, of course, they do not belong to the vocabulary of English, but they at least belong to the vocabulary of American: the proletariat, setting aside transient slang, calls things by their proper names, and pronounces those names more or less correctly. The adjectives, too, are treated rather politely, and the adverbs, though commonly transformed into the forms of their corresponding adjectives, are not further mutilated. But the verbs and pronouns undergo changes which set off the common speech very sharply from both correct English and correct American. This process, of course, is only natural, for it is among the verbs and pronouns that nearly all the remaining inflections in English are to be found, and so they must bear the chief pressure of the influences that have been warring upon every sort of inflection since the earliest days. The hypothetical Indo-European language is assumed to have had eight cases of the noun; in Old English they fell to four, with a moribund instrumental, identical in form with the dative, hanging in the air; in Middle English the dative and accusative began to decay; in Modern English they have disappeared altogether, save as ghosts to haunt grammarians. But we still have two plainly defined conjugations of the verb, and we still inflect it, in part at least, for number and person. And we yet retain an objective case of the pronoun, and inflect it for person, number and gender.

Following are paradigms showing the conjugation of some of the more interesting verbs of the vulgate, with notes on variants:

Present	Preterite	Perfect Participle
am [1]	was [2]	been [3]

[1] The subjunctive *be*, of course, is extinct. In the plural, *are* is commonly used correctly. The use of *is* in the second and third persons singular and in all persons of the plural is a Negroism, though it is also observed occasionally among the lowest classes of Southern whites. There is a familiar story illustrating its use. A customer goes into a store and asks, "You-all ain't got no aigs, *is* you?" The storekeeper replies, "I ain't said I ain't," whereupon the customer retorts in dudgeon, "I ain't axed you is you ain't; I axed you is you *is*. *Is* you?" In the negative, whether singular or plural, *ain't* is em-

Present	Preterite	Perfect Participle
attackt	attackted [1]	attackted
beat	beaten,[2] or beat	beat
become [3]	become	became
begin	begun [4]	began
bend	bent	bent
bet	bet	bet
bind	bound	bound

ployed almost universally; *am not, is not* and *are not* are used only for emphasis, and *aren't* is unknown.

2 The use of *were* in the first person singular occurs in certain English dialects, and was once not uncommon in vulgar American, but it has passed out. Today *was* is often used in the second and third persons plural. In the Eighteenth Century *you was* was used in the singular and *you were* in the plural. George Philip Krapp, in The English Language in America, Vol. II, p. 261, quotes " *Was* you fond of seeing," etc., from a letter of John Adams, 1759.

3 Usually pronounced *bin*, but sometimes *ben*, and often appearing without *have*, as in " I *bin* there myself." The English *bean* is never heard.

1 In The Druid, No. VI, May 16, 1781, the Rev. John Witherspoon listed *attackted* among his " vulgarisms in America only."

2 R. J. Menner, in The Verbs of the Vulgate, *American Speech*, Jan., 1926, argues that *beaten* and its analogues, *bitten, broken, forsaken, hidden, ridden, shaken, taken, fallen, forgotten* and *gotten*, are preterites only in certain regional dialects. He says: " *Taken* appears in lists of dialectical peculiarities from Tennessee, Southern Ohio, Missouri, Kansas, Arkansas, Alabama and Virginia, and often occurs in stories written in a Southern dialect. But it is not characteristic of New England, New York and Pennsylvania; if it occurs in the North, it occurs exceptionally, and cannot be considered a preterite of the vulgar speech." This was writ-

ten in 1926. Since then, I believe, the form has made progress, and Mr. Charles J. Lovell tells me that he has heard it very frequently in Bristol county, Mass. There is a discussion of it in The Grammar of the Ozark Dialect, by Vance Randolph, *American Speech*, Oct., 1927, p. 2.

3 *Become* is seldom heard in the present tense. *Getting* is usually substituted, as in " I am *getting* old." But *become* is often used as a preterite, as in " What *become* of him? "

4 In Old English, according to Menner, *began(n)* was the preterite singular and *begunnon* the preterite plural. When this distinction began to fade, both *began* and *begun* came into good usage, and both were recognized by Ben Jonson in his Grammar, 1640. Henry Alexander, in The Verbs of the Vulgate in Their Historical Relations, *American Speech*, April, 1929, gives examples of *begun* from Easton's Relation of the Indyan Warr, 1675, and Madam Knight's Journal, 1704. Noah Webster preferred it to *began* in his Grammar of the English Language, 1807. In 1928 or thereabout the National Council of Teachers of English submitted a long list of current usages to a committee consisting of authors, editors, linguists, teachers and business men, and asked their judgment. Only 5% of them approved *begun* as the preterite, but all of those who did so were persons specially trained in English philology. See Current English Usage, by Sterling Andrus Leonard; Chicago, 1932, p. 116.

Present	Preterite	Perfect Participle
bite	bitten [1]	bit
bleed	bled	bled
blow	blowed, or blew, or blown [2]	blowed, or blown
break	broke, or broken [3]	broken, or broke
bring	brought, brung or brang [4]	brought, or brung
build	built	built
burn	burnt [5]	burnt
bust [6]	busted, or bust [7]	busted
buy	bought, or boughten	bought, or boughten [8]
cast	casted	casted
catch	caught, or catched [9]	caught, or catched
choose	chose, or chosen	chosen, or chose [10]

1 See the note under *beaten*, above. I have even heard "He *bitten* off more than he could chew."

2 Here usage seems to be uncertain. I have heard "The whistle *blowed*," "He *blew* in his money," and "They *blown* into town."

3 Alexander quotes *brake* from Samuel Sewall's Diary, 1673. It was frequently used in those days, apparently under the influence of the King James Bible, in which it occurs 63 times. But it never got into the common speech. *Broke* is always used in the passive. One hears "I was *broke*" but never "I was *broken*." *Broke* was once in good usage as a participial adjective. The Oxford Dictionary gives examples running from *c.* 1230 to 1647.

4 Menner argues that *brung* belongs only to the lowest levels of the vulgate. He says: "Everyone knows that many a person who regularly says *I sung* or *I begun* would be horrified at the thought of saying *I brung*." He adds that "some speakers who habitually say *I have did* and *I have saw* regard *I brung* as merely childish or humorous." But he finds *brung* as a preterite in Artemus Ward, *c.* 1865, and in John Neal's The Down-Easters, 1833, and reports it used as a perfect participle in the last-named and in J. G. Holland's The Bay Path, 1857. It appears in a list of Appalachian Mountain words in *Dialect Notes*, Vol. V, Pt. X, 1927, p. 470.

5 *Burned*, with a distinct *d*-sound, is almost unknown to the vulgate.

6 *Burst* is seldom heard. In combinations, *e.g.*, on a bust, bust-head and trust-buster, *bust* is almost Standard American.

7 The use of *bust* as the preterite is probably promoted by the fashion for a crude historical present, mentioned in Section 1.

8 *Boughten* is in common use as a participial adjective, as in *boughten bread*.

9 *Catched*, which was good English in the Eighteenth Century, is in Lardner, and also in Huckleberry Finn, The Biglow Papers and Thomas C. Haliburton's The Clockmaker, 1837, but I incline to believe that it is now used relatively seldom. *Cotched* is heard only in the South, and mainly among Negroes. It appears in the vocabulary of provincialisms printed in Adiel Sherwood's Gazetteer of the State of Georgia, 3rd ed., 1837, and was condemned by Noah Webster in his Dissertations on the English Language; Boston, 1789, p. 111, as "frequent" and "barbarous." As we have seen in Chapter VII, Section 2, *catch* is usually pronounced *ketch*.

10 Alexander reports finding *chose* as the past participle in a military diary of 1774, and *choosen*, now

Present	Preterite	Perfect Participle
climb	clumb [1]	clumb
cling (to hold fast)	clung, or clang	clung
cling (to ring)	clang	clung, or clang
come	come [2]	come, or came
creep	crep, or crope	crope
crow	crew	crowed
cuss [3]	cussed	cussed
cut	cut	cut
dare	dared, or dast [4]	dared
deal	dole	dealt
dig	dug	dug
dive	dove [5]	dived
do	done [6]	done, or did
drag	drug	drug
draw	drawed	drawed, or drew
dream	drempt, or dremp [7]	drempt, or dremp
drink	drunk, or drank [8]	drank

obsolete, in the town records of Jamaica, L. I., 1695. He says that the former was used as the participle of *to choose* so early as the Fourteenth Century, and that it survived in good usage until the days of Southey. *Choosed* is in Sherwood's Georgia Vocabulary, 1837.

1 *Clumb* is in Lardner, and also in Huckleberry Finn and The Biglow Papers. *Clomb* was in good usage down to the end of the Seventeenth Century, and has survived as a poetical archaism.

2 *Come* as the preterite is very old, but *came* as the past participle is apparently recent.

3 *To curse* is used only when the act shows a certain formality and solemnity. "The blind man *cursed* the guy what robbed him" would be heard, but not "He *cursed* his wife." In the latter situation *to cuss* would be used, most often followed by *out*. Bartlett, in his Dictionary of Americanisms, 1848, listed *to cuss* as then "common to various parts of the Union."

4 *Dast* is more common in the negative, as in "He *das'n't* do it." It was originally a form of the present, and is sometimes still used.

5 *Dove* seems to be making its way into Standard American, apparently

supported by *drove*. It occurs in Theodore Roosevelt's Hunting the Grizzly; New York, 1905, p. 111, and in Amy Lowell's Legends; Boston, 1921, p. 4. The judges appointed by the National Council of Teachers of English decided against it, but there was apparent among them a trend toward accepting it. See Leonard, above cited, p. 117. In 1926 Leonard submitted it to a committee of 26 eminent academic authorities on English. Five of them approved it unreservedly, and 11 called it sound "cultivated, informal English." *Div* is reported from the Ozarks, in Snake County Talk, by Jay L. B. Taylor, *Dialect Notes*, Vol. V, Pt. VI, 1923, p. 205.

6 Menner reports hearing *done* used as the preterite by persons belonging to all three of his classes. But he heard *did* as the past participle only among "people with little education and no background."

7 Vance Randolph, in The Grammar of the Ozark Dialect, *American Speech*, Oct., 1927, says that *dremp* is the usual form in the Ozarks. But elsewhere, I believe, *drempt* is more common.

8 *Drinked* is in The Biglow Papers and in Artemus Ward, but it seems to have gone out, save maybe in

Present	Preterite	Perfect Participle
drive	drove [1]	drove
drown	drownded [2]	drownded
eat	et, or eat [3]	eat, ate, or et [4]
fall	fell, or fallen	fell
feed	fed	fed
feel	felt	felt
fetch [5]	fetched	fetched
fight	fought [6]	fought
find	found	found
fine	found [7]	found
fling	flung, or flang	flung

remote areas. The committee of judges appointed by the National Council of Teachers of English condemned the preterite use of *drunk*, but "linguists and members of the Modern Language Association, probably because of their awareness of the historical justification for the form, placed it higher than the other groups." See Leonard, above cited, p. 116. Menner reports the use of *drank* as the perfect participle by persons of all three of his categories.

[1] *Driv* and *druv* seem to survive only in humorous use, save maybe in the remoter rural parts. Both, as past participles, are in The Biglow Papers, and Bartlett, in his Dictionary of Americanisms, 1848, listed *druv* as a preterite then in common use. *Driv* was denounced as a New England provincialism by T. G. Fessenden in The Ladies' Monitor; Bellows Falls, Vt., 1818, p. 171.

[2] This in the active voice. In the passive, I think, *drowned* is more common. "This is so common," said the Rev. John Witherspoon in The Druid, No. VI, May 16, 1781, "that I have known a gentleman reading in a book to a company, though it was printed *drowned*, read *drownded*."

[3] *Ate*, in my observation, is seldom used as the preterite, though it appears in Lardner, and is reported by Menner. The use of *eat* as its own preterite was formerly sound in English, and still survives more or less on relatively decorous levels.

I find it in Of Human Bondage, by W. Somerset Maugham; New York, 1915, p. 24. It is encountered plentifully in Shakespeare. According to Leonard, above cited, p. 118, *et* as the preterite is "entirely correct in England, incorrect in the United States." It is so given in Broadcast English; London, 1935, and H. W. Fowler, in Modern English Usage; Oxford, 1926, actually condemns *ate* as "wrong."

[4] *Eaten* is seldom used. In The Vulgate in American Fiction, *American Mercury*, Dec., 1927, Wallace Rice says that *eat* was used as the perfect participle by Shakespeare, Fletcher, Fuller, Evelyn, Mary II, Purchas, J. Collins, Arbuthnot, Pope, Malmesbury, Johnson, Prior, Coleridge, Jane Austen, Marryat, Tennyson, Dickens and Thackeray. He says that the Imperial Dictionary; London, 1892, prefers *eat* to *eaten*, and that it has been approved by various American grammarians.

[5] *Fotch* seems to be mainly confined to the Appalachian mountain dialect, though I have heard Lowland Negroes use it. Noah Webster, in his Dissertations on the English Language; Boston, 1789, p. 111, says that it was then "very common in several States, but not among the better classes of people."

[6] *Fit* appears to have gone out. It is in Congreve's The Way of the World, 1700, and was apparently in good usage then. Thornton gives American examples running from 1825 to 1869.

[7] "He was *found* $2" is much more

Present	Preterite	Perfect Participle
flow	flew	flowed
fly	flew	flew
forbid	forbid	forbid
forget	forgot, or forgotten	forgotten
forsake	forsaken	forsook
freeze	frozen, or froze [1]	froze
get [2]	got, or gotten	gotten, [3] or got
give	give, or given [4]	give, or gave
glide	glode [5]	glode
go	went	went, or gone
grope	grope [6]	grope
grow	growed	growed
hang	hung [7]	hung
have	had	had, or hadden
hear	heerd, or hern	heerd, or hern
heat [8]	het, or heaten	het, or heaten
heave	hove	hove

common than " He was *fined.*" The pull of the preterite of *to find* is obvious.

1 *Friz* seems to be archaic. It occurs in The Biglow Papers.

2 There was a time when *get* was almost invariably pronounced *git*, but the standard pronunciation is now more common. In " Do you *get* me? " the *e* is never *i*. *Gotten* is rare in England, save in *ill-gotten*.

3 Leonard says, in Current English Usage, p. 118: " Both linguists and dictionaries testify that this form is acceptable in the United States, although it is nearly obsolete in England." In the late Eighteenth Century *gotten* was fashionable in both countries, and Noah Webster, in his Dissertations, 1789, listed it among the affectations of " young gentlemen who have gone through a course of academical studies, and received the usual honors of a university." *Got*, as everyone knows, is a verb of all work in the vulgate. Its excessive use was denounced by the editor of the *English Journal*, March, 1927. See *Get* and *Got*, by Wallace Rice, *American Speech*, April, 1932. Also, *Gotten*, by George O. Curme, the same, Sept., 1927.

4 *Gin* and *guv* are archaic. The former, marked rare, appears in a

Maine word-list compiled by E. K. Maxfield, *Dialect Notes*, Vol. V, Pt. IX, 1926, p. 387. It was in common use from about 1800 to the Civil War, and is listed in Fessenden's Georgia Vocabulary, and in the glossary printed with David Humphrey's The Yankey in England; Boston, 1815. Lardner uses both *give* and *gave* as the perfect participle. Menner reports that he found *give* in use as the preterite among all three of his classes, but that *give* and *gave* as the perfect participle were confined to " people with little education and no background." Henry Harap lists *give* as the preterite among The Most Common Grammatical Errors, *English Journal*, June, 1930, p. 441.

5 *Glode* once enjoyed a certain respectability in the United States, as in England. It is to be found in the *Knickerbocker Magazine* for April, 1856. It is also in Shelley's The Revolt of Islam, 1818.

6 Almost invariably followed by *around*.

7 The literary *hanged* is never heard. " The man was *hung*," not *hanged*.

8 *To heat* is seldom heard. The common form is *to heaten*. When *het* is used it is always followed by *up*. Webster favored it as the preterite, and Krapp says (The English Lan-

Present	Preterite	Perfect Participle
help	helped, or help	helped, or help
hide	hidden [1]	hid
hist [2]	histed	histed
hit	hit	hit
hold	helt	helt, or held
holler	hollered	hollered
hurt	hurt	hurt
keep	kep	kep, or kept
kneel	kneeled	kneeled, or knelt
know	knowed	knew, or knowed [3]
lay	laid, or lain	lain, or laid
lead	led	led
lean	lent	lent
leap	lep	lep
learn	lernt	lernt
lend [4]	loaned	loaned
let	left [5]	left
lie (to falsify)	lied	lied
lie (to recline) [6]	laid, or lain	lain, or laid
light	lit	lit
loosen [7]	loosened	loosened
lose	lost	lost
make	made	made
mean	ment	ment
meet	met	met
mow	mown	mowed
pay	paid	paid
plead	pled	pled
prove	proven, or proved	proven [8]
quit	quit	quit

guage in America, Vol. II, p. 258), that it "only just failed to be accepted into good general use."

1 See the note under *beat*, above.

2 *Hoist* is seldom heard.

3 Both forms appear in Lardner, and both are reported by Menner.

4 *To lend* is being displaced by *to loan*. The standard preterite, *lent*, is seldom heard save as noted below. Harap notes in The Most Common Grammatical Errors, *English Journal*, June, 1930, p. 442, that *to lend* has begun to displace *to borrow*. Certainly, "I *lent* a dollar from him," meaning "I borrowed a dollar," is now common.

5 *To let* is being supplanted by *to leave*, as in "*Leave* me be," but this substitution has probably gone furthest in the preterite. "He *let*

me have it" is seldom heard; the usual form is "He *left* me."

6 Seldom used; *lay* takes its place. *To lay* was condemned by 93% of the judges appointed by the National Council of Teachers of English, but one of them, a linguist, noted that it "was good in the Eighteenth Century." See Leonard, above cited, p. 113.

7 *To loose* is very seldom heard. Even *to loosen* seems to be going out. The popular form is *to unloosen*, which is conjugated like *to loosen*.

8 The linguists, authors and editors on the committee of the National Council of Teachers of English placed *proven* "among the disputable usages; the other groups of judges regarded it as estab-

Present	Preterite	Perfect Participle
raise	raised [1]	raised
recognize [2]	recognize	recognize
rench [3]	renched	renched
ride	ridden [4]	rode [5]
rile [6]	riled	riled
ring	rung	rang
rise	rose, or riz [7]	rose, or riz
run	run	ran
sass [8]	sassed, or sass	sassed, or sass
say	sez, said, or say	said
see	seen, see, or seed	saw, or see [9]
set [10]	set	sat
shake	shaken, or shuck	shook
shine (to polish)	shined	shined
shoe	shoed	shoed
show	shown	shown
shut [11]	shut	shut
sing	sung	sang
sink	sunk	sank
skin	skun, or skan	skun
sleep	slep	slep, or slept
slide	slid	slid
sling	slung, or slang	slang, or slang

lished." See Leonard, before cited, p. 119.

1 *Riz* as the preterite of *to raise* is now confined to the rural regions. Various contributors to *Dialect Notes* report it from States as far apart as Connecticut and Louisiana.

2 Pronounced *reconize* in all three situations.

3 Used in place of *rinse*. In New England *rench* is sometimes *rense*. See *Dialect Notes*, Part II, 1890, p. 63.

4 *Rid* is in Artemus Ward, but it is seldom heard today.

5 Menner reports that he has heard *rode* by persons who are " the average product of American highschools."

6 Always used in place of *roil*.

7 *Riz* seems to be going out as the preterite of *to rise*, though it is still heard. *To rise*, says Menner, " is a rare verb in the vulgate. *Get up* (of people) and *come up* (of the sun) are substituted for it." But bread still *rises*. In her Journal, 1704, Sarah Kemble Knight used *riss* as the preterite.

8 *To sass* is always used in place of *to sauce*, which would seem a schoolmarmish affectation to the vulgar Americano. The adjective is *sassy*.

9 Lardner gives *seen*, *see* and *seed* as the preterite, and *saw* and *see* as the perfect participle. *See* as the preterite is in the New Haven Records (1639), the Easthampton Records (1654), the Huntington Records (1681), and the Journal of Sarah Kemble Knight (1704). It is denounced by the Rev. John Witherspoon in The Druid, No. VI, May 16, 1781, and he says that it was then " common in both England and the United States."

10 Used almost always in place of *sit*. The preterite *sot*, once in wide use, is now rarely heard.

11 Bartlett, in his Dictionary of Americanisms, 1848, listed *shet* as then in common use. It is still heard, but *shut* seems to be prevailing. Sometimes *shutted* appears as the preterite, as in " You bet he *shutted up*."

Present	Preterite	Perfect Participle
smell	smelt	smelt
sneak	snuck	snuck
speak	spoke, or spoken	spoke [1]
speed	speeded	speeded
spell	spelt	spelt
spill	spilt	spilt
spin	span	span, or spun
spit	spit	spit
spoil	spoilt	spoilt
spring	sprung	sprang
steal	stole	stole
sting	stang	stung
stink	stank	stunk, or stank
strike	struck	struck
sweat	sweat [2]	sweat
sweep	swep	swep
swell	swole	swollen
swim	swum	swam
swing	swang	swung
take	taken, or tuck	took,[3] or tuck
teach [4]	taught	taught
tear	torn	tore
tell	tole [5]	tole
tend [6]	tended, tend, or tent	tended
think	thought [7]	thought
throw	throwed, or thrown	throwed, or threw [8]
wake	woke	woken

---

1 Alexander traces *spoke* back to Gower, 1390, and says that it was still accepted as the perfect participle of *to speak* as late as 1754.

2 Dr. Josiah Combs reports that in the Southern mountains "the ending *-ed* is usually dropped in the preterite in verbs whose infinitive ends in *-t*." (*Dialect Notes*, Vol. IV, Pt. IV, 1916, p. 292.) In the general vulgate, I believe, *sweat* is fast becoming an invariable verb. I have heard "He *sweat* and puffed" and "I have *sweat* over it all night."

3 *Have took* is in The Biglow Papers, and Menner finds it in other humorous works of the period. He reports hearing it from the lips of his "people with little education and little literary background," but his "people trained in some special profession (usually with college degrees)" seem to have been guilt-less of it. *Tuck* as the preterite is listed as in common use in 1848 by Bartlett in his Dictionary of Americanisms.

4 *To teach*, of course, is seldom heard. *To learn* is used in its place.

5 Bartlett, in his Dictionary of Americanisms, 1848, says that *tell'd* was then in common used as the preterite. It seems to have passed out.

6 Always used in place of *attend*. The preterite, it seems to me, sometimes takes a distinct *t*, as in "He *tent* to his business."

7 *Thunk* is never used seriously; it always shows humorous intent.

8 Menner reports hearing *thrung*, which he describes as an Irishism. I have never encountered it. There was a time when *trun* was often heard, both as preterite and as perfect participle, but it seems to have gone out.

Present	Preterite	Perfect Participle
wear	wore	wore
weep	wep	wep
wet	wet	wet
win	won, wan, or win [1]	won, or wan
wish [2]	wished	wished
wring	wrung, or wrang	wrang, or wrung
write	written	wrote [3]

A glance at these paradigms is enough to show several general tendencies, the most obvious of which is the transfer of verbs from the strong conjugation with vowel change to the weak without it, and *vice versa*. The former began before the Norman Conquest, and was marked during the Middle English period. Chaucer used *growed* for *grew* in the prologue to " The Wife of Bath's Tale," and *rised* for *rose* and *smited* for *smote* are in John Purvey's edition of the Bible, *c.* 1385. Many of these transformations were afterward abandoned, but a large number survived, for example, *climbed* for *clomb* as the preterite of *to climb*, and *melted* for *molt* as the preterite of *to melt*. Others showed themselves during the early part of the Modern English period. *Comed* as the perfect participle of *to come*, and *digged* as the preterite of *to dig* are both in Shakespeare, and the latter is also in Milton and in the Authorized Version of the Bible. This tendency went furthest, of course, in the vulgar speech, and it has been embalmed in the English dialects. *I seen* and *I knowed*, for example, are common to all of them. But during the Seventeenth Century, for some reason to me unknown, there arose a contrary tendency — that is, toward strong conjugations. The vulgar speech of Ireland, which preserves many Seventeenth Century forms, shows it plainly. *Ped* for *paid*, *gother* for *gathered*, and *ruz* for *raised* are still heard there, and P. W. Joyce says flatly that the Irish, " retaining the old English custom [*i.e.*, the custom of the period of Cromwell's invasion, *c.* 1650], have a leaning toward the strong inflection." [4] Certain forms of the early American national period, now reduced to the estate of localisms, were also survivors of the Seventeenth Century.

1 Lardner once told me that he believed *win* was supplanting both *won* and *wan*. *Winned* is also heard.

2 Usually converted into *wisht*, as in " I *wisht* he would go," the present tense being understood.

3 " *I have wrote* " was in good usage until the middle of the Eighteenth Century.

4 English As We Speak It In Ireland, 2nd ed.; London, 1910, p. 77.

"The three great causes of change in language," says A. H. Sayce, "may be briefly described as (1) imitation or analogy, (2) a wish to be clear and emphatic, and (3) laziness. Indeed, if we choose to go deep enough we might reduce all three causes to the general one of laziness, since it is easier to imitate than to say something new."[1] This tendency to take well-worn paths, paradoxically enough, seems to be responsible both for the transfer of verbs from the strong to the weak declension, and for the transfer of certain others from the weak to the strong. A verb in everyday use tends almost inevitably to pull less familiar verbs with it, whether it be strong or weak. Thus, *fed* as the preterite of *to feed* and *led* as the preterite of *to lead* eased the way in the American vulgate for *pled* as the preterite of *to plead;* and *rung* as plainly performed the same office for *brung,* and *drove* for *dove* and *hove,* and *stole* for *dole,* and *won* for *skun.* Contrariwise, the same combination of laziness and imitativeness worked toward the regularization of certain verbs that were historically irregular. One sees the antagonistic pull of the two influences in the case of verbs ending in *-ow.* The analogy of *knew* and *grew* suggests *snew* as the preterite of *to snow,* and it is sometimes encountered in the American vulgate. But meanwhile *knew* and *grew* have been themselves succumbing to the greater regularity of *knowed* and *growed.* So *snew,* losing support, grows rare and is in palpable decay, but *knowed* and *growed* show great vigor, as do many of their analogues. The substitution of *heerd* for *heard* also presents a case of logic and convenience supporting analogy. The form is suggested by *feared, cheered, cleared,* etc., but its main advantage lies in the fact that it gets rid of a vowel change, always an impediment to easy speech.

Some of the verbs of the vulgate show the end-products of other language movements that go back to a very early period. There is, for example, the disappearance of the final *t* in such words as *crep, slep, lep, swep* and *wep.* Most of these, in Old English, were strong verbs. The preterite of *to sleep* (*slǽpan*), for example, was *slep,* and of *to weep* was *weop.* But in the course of time both *to sleep* and *to weep* acquired weak preterite endings, the first becoming *slǽpte* and the second *wepte.* This weak conjugation, in most cases, was itself degenerated. Originally, the inflectional suffix had been *-de* or

1 Introduction to the Science of Language; London, 1900, Vol. I, p. 166.

-*ede* and in some cases -*ode*, and the vowels were always pronounced. The wearing-down process that set in in the Twelfth Century disposed of the final *e*, but in certain words the other vowel survived for a good while, and we still observe it in such archaisms as *learnéd* and *belovéd*. Finally, however, it became silent in other preterites, and *loved*, for example, began to be pronounced (and often written) as a word of one syllable: *lov'd*.[1] This final *d*-sound now fell upon difficulties of its own. After certain consonants it was hard to pronounce clearly, and so the sonant was changed into the easier surd, and such words as *pushed* and *clipped* became, in ordinary conversation, *pusht* and *clipt*. In other verbs, the -*t* (or -*te*) ending had come in long before, and when the final *e* was dropped only their stem vowels needed to be changed. Thus arose such forms as *slept*. In vulgar American another step is taken, and the suffix is dropped altogether. Thus, by a circuitous route, verbs originally strong, and for many centuries hovering between the two conjugations, have eventually become strong again.

The case of *helt* is probably an example of change by false analogy. During the Thirteenth Century, according to Sweet[2] " *d* was changed to *t* in the weak preterites of verbs [ending] in *rd, ld, nd*." Before that time the preterite of *sende* (*send*) had been *sende;* now it became *sente*. It survives in our modern *sent*, and the same process is also revealed in *built, girt, lent, rent* and *bent*. The popular speech, disregarding the fact that *to hold* is a strong verb, arrives at *helt* by imitation.[3] In the case of *tole*, which I almost always hear in place of *told*, there is a leaping of steps. The *d* is got rid of by assimilation with *l* and without any transitional use of *t*. So also, perhaps, in *swole*, which is fast displacing *swelled*. *Attackted* and *drownded* seem to be examples of an effort to dispose of harsh combinations by a contrary process. Both are old in English. *Boughten* and *dreampt* present greater difficulties. Lounsbury says that *boughten* probably originated in the Northern (*i.e.*, Lowland Scots) dialect of English,

---

1 The last stand of the distinct -*ed* was made in Addison's day. He was in favor of retaining it, and in the *Spectator* for Aug. 4, 1711, he protested against obliterating the syllable in the termination "of our præter perfect tense, as in these words, *drown'd, walk'd, arriv'd,* for *drowned, walked, arrived,*

which has very much disfigured the tongue, and turned a tenth part of our smoothest words into so many clusters of consonants."
2 A New English Grammar; Oxford, 1900, Part I, p. 380.
3 The noun is commonly made *holt*, as in, "I got a-*holt* of it."

"which . . . inclined to retain the full form of the past participle," and even to add its termination "to words to which it did not properly belong."[1] The *p*-sound in *drempt* follows a tendency that is also seen in such pronunciations as *warm(p)th*, *com(p)fort* and *some(p)thing*, and that has actually inserted a *p* in *Thompson* (*Tom's son*). The general movement toward regularization is well exhibited by the new verbs that come into the language constantly. Practically all of them show the weak conjugation, for example, *to broadcast*.[2] Even when a compound has as its last member a verb ordinarily strong, it is often weak itself. Thus the preterite of *to joy-ride* is not *joy-rode*, nor even *joy-ridden*, but, unless my ears fail me, *joy-rided*. And thus *bust*, from *burst*, is regular and its usual preterite is *busted*, though *burst* is irregular and its preterite is the verb itself unchanged. The same tendency toward regularity is shown by the verbs of the *kneel* class. They are irregular in English, but tend to become regular in colloquial American. Thus the preterite of *to kneel*, despite the example of *to sleep* and its analogues, is not *knel'*, nor even *knelt*, but *kneeled*. I have even heard *feeled* as the preterite of *to feel*, as in "I *feeled* my way," though here *felt* still persists. *To spread* also tends to become weak, as in "He *spreaded* a piece of bread." And *to peep* remains so, despite the example of *to leap*. The confusion between the inflections of *to lie* and *to lay* extends to the higher reaches of spoken American, and so does that between *lend* and *loan*. In the vulgate the proper inflections of *to lend* are often given to *to lean*, and so *leaned* becomes *lent*, as in "I *lent* on the counter." In the same way *to set* has almost completely superseded *to sit*, and the preterite of the former, *set*, is used in place of *sat*. But the perfect participle (which is also the disused preterite) of *to sit* has survived, as in "I have *sat* there." *To speed* and *to shoe* have become regular, not only because of the general tendency toward the weak conjugation, but also for logical reasons. The prevalence of speed contests of various sorts, always to the intense interest of the proletariat, has brought such words as *speeder*, *speeding*, *speed-mania*, *speed-maniac* and *speed-limit* into

1 History of the English Language; revised ed.; New York, 1894, p. 398.
2 The effort of purists to establish *broadcast* as the preterite has had some success on higher levels, but very little on lower. "Ed Wynn *broadcasted* last night" is what one commonly hears. The effort to justify *broadcast* by analogy with *cast* fails, for the preterite of *to cast*, in the vulgar speech, is not *cast* but *casted*.

daily use, and *speeded* harmonizes with them better than the irregular *sped*. The American's misuse of *to learn* for *to teach* is common to most of the English dialects. More peculiar to his speech is the use of *to leave* for *to let*. Charters records it in "Washington *left* them have it," and there are many examples of it in Lardner.

In studying the American verb, of course, it is necessary to remember always, as Menner reminds us, that it is in a state of transition, and that in many cases the manner of using it is not yet fixed. "The history of language," says Lounsbury, "when looked at from the purely grammatical point of view, is little else than the history of corruptions." What we have before us is a series of corruptions in active process, and while some of them have gone very far, others are just beginning. Thus it is not uncommon to find corrupt forms side by side with orthodox forms, or even two corrupt forms battling with each other. Lardner, in the case of *to throw*, hears " if he had *throwed*"; my own observation is that *threw* is more often used in that situation. Again, he uses "the rottenest I ever seen *gave* "; my own belief is that *give* is far more commonly used. The conjugation of *to give*, however, is yet very uncertain, and so Lardner may report accurately. I have heard "I *given* " and "I would of *gave*," but "I *give* " seems to be prevailing, and "I would of *give* " with it, thus reducing *to give* to one invariable form, like those of *to cut, to hit, to put, to cost, to hurt* and *to spit*. My table of verbs shows various other uncertainties and confusions. The preterite of *to blow* may be *blowed, blew* or *blown*, and that of *to drink* oscillates between *drank* and *drunk*, and that of *to fall* is still usually *fell*, though *fallen* has appeared, and that of *to shake* may be either *shaken* or *shuck*. The conjugation of *to win* is yet far from fixed. The correct English preterite, *won*, is still in use, but against it are arrayed *wan* and *winned*, and Lardner, as I have noted, believed that the plain form of the present would eventually oust all of them. *Wan* seems to show some kinship, by ignorant analogy, with *ran* and *began*. It is often used as the perfect participle, as in "I have *wan* $4." This uncertainty shows itself in many of the communications that I have received since my last edition was published. Practically every one of my conjugations has been questioned by at least one correspondent; nevertheless, the weight of observation has supported all save a few of them, and I have not made many changes.

The misuse of the perfect participle for the preterite, so common in vulgar American, is also common in many other dialects of English. It has been going on for a long time, and in American, the most vigorous and advanced of all the dialects of the language, it is particularly well marked. Menner believes that it originated, at least as to some of the verbs, in the decay of the auxiliary *have* in the present perfect. The omission of the auxiliary, he says,

is one of the most familiar phenomena of rapid or careless speech. *I've been, I've bought, I've found, I've done* easily degenerate into *I been, I bought, I found, I done.* . . . The process is a purely phonetic one. When " *I've been* there several times " and " *I've done* that since I was born " are contracted to "*I been,*" etc. and " *I done,*" etc. *been* and *done* have not become preterites; the meaning is still perfect, though the form is syncopated. . . . Thus it is not unlikely that *I seen* and *I done,* when they first appeared in the vulgate, were still perfect tenses with the auxiliary syncopated; that owing to the confusion of the two tenses in such cases as " *I ('ve) never seen* it " and " *I never saw* it," *I seen* came to be regarded as a real preterite and extended to all the functions of the past tense, as in " *I seen* it yesterday." This explanation receives some support, in the case of *seen,* from the fact that the majority of the earliest instances of *seen* for *saw* that I have found are of the somewhat ambiguous type " I (they) *never seen.*" If this be indeed the earlier usage, it may well indicate that the modern genuine preterite *seen* developed from the genuine perfect *('ve) seen* by means of the intermediate stage *seen,* as in " I *never seen,*" of doubtful interpretation.[1]

In the case of certain strong verbs, says Menner, the substitution of the perfect participle for the preterite originated in a confusion between the singular and plural forms of the preterite, which were once distinct. When this distinction began to disappear, the plural preterite, usually with *u* for its vowel, was sometimes substituted for the singular form in *a,* and so the preterite and the perfect participle coalesced, for the latter was usually also in *u.*[2] Menner offers *begun, clumb, rung, sung* and *swum* as examples. Two further considerations may be mentioned. The first is that the perfect form of the verb was also commonly its adjectival form, and so got some support in mere familiarity. The second is that it was usually the authentic preterite in the passive voice, and so got more.

The contrary substitution of the preterite for the perfect participle is old in English, and there was a time indeed when even the best writers were apparently unconscious of its inelegance. An examination of any play of Shakespeare's will show many such forms

1 The Verbs of the Vulgate, *American Speech,* Jan., 1926, pp. 238-9.
2 This, of course, was not the case invariably. More often the singular triumphed over the plural. See A History of Modern Colloquial English, by H. C. Wyld; London, 1920, p. 343.

as " I have *wrote*," " I am *mistook* " and " He has *rode*." In several cases this confusion has survived. " I have *stood*," for example, is now perfectly correct English, but before 1550 the proper form was " I have *stonden*." Menner's inquiries indicate, however, that two of the false perfects now familiar, *saw* and *did*, are relatively recent. He says:

Many writers employ *seen* as preterite from the 40's to the 60's, whereas *saw* as past participle is extremely rare. The earliest instance I have run across is in Artemus Ward's " Scenes Outside the Fair-Grounds ": " We have *saw* a entertainment as we never saw before," and Josh Billings seems to have been the first humorist to employ *saw* for *seen*, as well as *did* for *done*, extensively. Even as late as " Huckleberry Finn," where *seen* and *see* largely replace *saw* in the past tense, *saw* does not occur in the participle. The priority of the incorrect preterite over the incorrect participle is likewise plain in the verb *do*, though *done* had not attained so wide a popularity in the first half of the century as *seen*. The remarks of grammarians and commentators on the state of the language corroborate the practise of the humorists as an accurate reflection of the vulgar speech. Bartlett, whose dictionary of Americanisms was published in 1848, and Schele de Vere, whose similar book was published in 1872, record only the use of the participle for the preterite in these verbs. . . . The oldest commentary on Americanisms, John Witherspoon's essays, originally printed in . . . 1781, notes *he had fell, he had rose, he had threw, he had drew,* but not *he had saw* or *he had did*.[1]

The substitution of the preterite for the perfect participle seems to me to be increasing of late, and such striking examples as " How old of a cat have you ever *saw?* "[2] are surely not uncommon. But a sense of its uncouthness appears to linger at the back of the proletarian mind, and sometimes it is embellished with an *en* suffix, and so brought into greater harmony with more orthodox forms of the perfect. I find that *boughten*, just discussed, is used much oftener in the perfect than in the simple past tense; for the latter *bought* usually suffices. The quick ear of Lardner detects various other coinages of the same sort, among them *tooken*, as in " little Al might of *tooken* sick." *Hadden* is also met with, as in " I would of *hadden*." But the majority of preterites remain unchanged. Lardner's baseball player never writes " I have *written* " or " I have *wroten*," but always " I have *wrote*." And in the same way he always writes " I have *did, ate, went, drank, rode, ran, saw, sang, woke* and *stole*."

In the American vulgate, as Menner notes, the auxiliary *have* is under heavy pressure in all situations, and promises to disappear

1 In the paper just cited, pp. 236–7.	2 Supplied by Mr. B. A. Bergman.

from those in which it is still used. I have heard *was* used in place of
have, as in " before the Elks *was* come here." [1] Sometimes it is confused ignorantly with a distinct *of*, as in " she would *of* drove " and
" I would *of* gave." [2] More often it is shaded to a sort of particle attached to the verb as an inflection, as in " He *woulda* tole you,"
" Who *coulda* took it?," " He *musta* been there." In going through
this change it drags its surrogate, *of*, along with it, and so one encounters such forms as *kinda, sorta, coupla* and *outa*.[3] But that is
not all. Having degenerated to *of*, *have* is now employed as a sort of
auxiliary to itself, in the subjunctive, as in " If you had *of* went,"
" If it had *of* been hard " and " If I had *of* had." [4] I have encountered
some rather astonishing examples of this doubling of the auxiliary.
One appears in " I wouldn't *hadda* went "; another in " I'd 'a' *hadda*
saved more money." Here, however, the *a* may belong partly to *had*
and partly to the verb; such forms as *a-going* are very common in
American. But in the other cases, and in such forms as " I *hadda*
wanted," it clearly belongs to *had*. Meanwhile, *to have*, ceasing to
be an auxiliary, becomes a general verb indicating compulsion. Here
it promises to displace *must*. The American seldom says " I *must*
go "; he almost invariably says " I *have* to go " [5] or " I *have got* to
go," in which last case *got* is the auxiliary.

Some typical inflections of the verb for mode and voice are shown
in the following paradigm of *to bite:*

1 Remark of a policeman talking to another. What he actually said was " before the Elks was *c'm 'ere.*" *Come* and *here* were one word, approximately *cmear*. The context showed that he meant to use the past perfect tense. Dr. Kemp Malone reminds me that *was* was once the auxiliary of *come*, and still is in German.

2 The following curious example, sent to me by Dr. Morris Fishbein, editor of the *Journal of the American Medical Association*, is from a letter received by a California physician: " If I *had of* waited a day longer before I wrote to you I *would not of had* to write that letter to you." Wallace Rice, in The Vulgate in American Fiction, *American Mercury*, Dec., 1927,

protests against rendering the degenerated *have* as *of*. Even in Standard English, he argues, it is sometimes pronounced *uv*, and so should keep its proper spelling. To support this he brings forward many authorities. But the fact remains, as Lardner was quick to notice, that the plain people, when they seize pen in hand, often turn *have* into *of*.

3 There are many examples in The English of the Comic Cartoons, by Helen Trace Tysell, *American Speech*, Feb., 1935, p. 47.

4 These examples are from Lardner's story, A New Busher Breaks In, in You Know Me, Al, p. 122 *ff*.

5 Pronounced *hafta*, or, in the past tense, *hatta*. Sometimes the *d* is retained, and *had to* becomes *hadda*.

Active Voice
Indicative Mode

Present	I bite	*Past Perfect*	I hadda bit
Present Perfect	I have bit	*Future*	I will bite
Past	I have bitten	*Future Perfect*	(wanting)

Subjunctive Mode

Present	If I bite	*Past Perfect*	If I hadda bit
Past	If I bitten		

Potential Mode

Present	I can bite	*Past*	I coulda bite
Present Perfect	(wanting)	*Past Perfect*	I coulda bit

Imperative (or Optative) Mode

Future	I shall (or will) bite

Infinitive Mode

(wanting)

Passive Voice
Indicative Mode

Present	I am bit	*Past Perfect*	I had or (hadda) been bit
Present Perfect	I been bit	*Future*	I will be bit
Past	I was bit	*Future Perfect*	(wanting)

Subjunctive Mode

Present	If I am bit	*Past Perfect*	If I hadda been bit
Past	If I was bit		

Potential Mode

Present	I can be bit	*Past*	I could be bit
Present Perfect	(wanting)	*Past Perfect*	I coulda been bit

Imperative Mode

(wanting)

Infinitive Mode

(wanting)

The subjunctive, which is disappearing from Standard American,[1] is virtually extinct in the vulgar tongue. One never hears " if I *were*

1 See American Use of the Subjunctive, by Thyra Jane Bevier, *American Speech*, Feb., 1931. Miss Bevier says that the late Walter Hines Page was the only American author of his time who used the subjunctive correctly. Says George Philip Krapp, in Modern English; New York, 1910, pp. 289–90: "Practically, the only construction in Modern English in which the subjunctive is in living, natural use, is in the condition contrary to fact: If I *were* you, I *shouldn't* do it."

you," but always " if I *was* you." In the third person the -*s* is not dropped from the verb. One hears, not " if she *go*," but always " if she *goes*." " If he *be* the man " is never heard; it is always " if he *is*." Such a sentence as " Had I wished her, I had had her " would be unintelligible to most Americans; even " I had rather " is forgotten. In the same way the distinction between *will* and *shall*, preserved in Standard English but already breaking down in the most correct American, has been lost entirely. *Will* has displaced *shall* completely, save in the imperative. This preference extends to the inflections of both. *Sha'n't* is very seldom heard; almost always *won't* is used instead. As for *should*, it is displaced by *ought to* (degenerated to *oughter* or *oughta*), and in its negative form by *hadn't oughter*, as in " He *hadn't oughter* said that," reported by Charters. Lardner gives various redundant combinations of *should* and *ought*, as in " I don't feel as if I *should ought* to leave " and " They *should not ought to of* had." I have encountered the same form, but I don't think it is as common as the simple *oughta* forms.[1] In the main, *should* is avoided, sometimes at considerable pains. Often its place is taken by the more positive *don't*. Thus " I *don't* mind " is used instead of " I *shouldn't* mind." *Ain't* has displaced *is not, am not, isn't* and *aren't*, and even *have not* and *haven't*. One recalls a famous speech in a naval melodrama of a generation ago: " We *ain't* got no manners, but we can fight like hell." Such forms as " He *ain't* here," " I *ain't* the man," " *Ain't* it the truth? ", " You been there, *ain't* you? ", " You *ain't* drank much," " Them *ain't* what I want " and " I *ain't* heerd of it " are common. Charters adds the incomparable " It *ain't* right to say, ' He *ain't* here today.' "

In the negative a clear *not* is used only for special emphasis, as in " You will *not* do it." In almost all other situations it is reduced to *n't*, and sometimes this *n't*, in rapid utterance, shrinks to *n* or is dropped altogether. Says Dr. E. C. Hills of the University of California:

Usually before a consonant, and regularly before a dental, *not* becomes merely vocalic *n*, as in " I *didn'*(*t*) do it," " We *couldn'*(*t*) stop," and " He *hasn'*(*t*) gone." With *can*, in rapid fluent speech uttered without self-consciousness, *not* before a consonant tends to disappear completely, so that " I *c'n* do it " is affirmative, while the negative form is " I *can'*(*t*) do it." Some of my friends who are not trained phoneticians insist that they pronounce the

1 In the negative, *ought not* has de-   as in " You *oughtna* (or *oughten*)
generated to *oughtna* or *oughten*,   do that."

t in "I *can'*(*t*) do it," but when they are off their guard I do not hear the *t*. Moreover, when they say "I *can'*(*t*) do it," or even "I *can'*(*t*) go tonight," without pronouncing the *t*, my friends regularly understand the expression to be negative. If one pronounces the *can* with emphasis and followed perhaps by a slight pause, "I *can* go tonight" is affirmative. In combination with the *y* of *you*, *nt* becomes *nch* as in "*Haven't you* seen it?" "*Didn't you* do it?" This change, however, does not occur before the initial *y* of a verb, as in "He *didn'*(*t*) yell," in which the *t* is usually not pronounced at all.[1]

Dr. Hills, of course, is here discussing a colloquial American lying somewhere between the vulgate and the standard speech, but what he says applies to the vulgate. He should have added that when *can* is used in the negative it takes the *a* of its mother, *can't* (and also of *pan*, *stand*, etc.), not the shorter *a* of *ran*, etc. Thus there is a phonetic difference between affirmative *can* and negative *can*, though they must be written alike. The *nch*-sound that Dr. Hill mentions has attracted the attention of the begetters of comic-strips. They frequently use *can cha* for *can't you*. When *to do* is used in the negative, the form is almost invariably *don't*; *doesn't* is seldom heard. Among Southerners this use of the plural for the singular rises almost to the level of cultured speech. When, a few years ago, a fresh effort to police the national speech habits was begun at Columbia University, the editor of the Petersburg, Va., *Progress-Index* replied as follows:

One of the expressions listed in the indictment of the savants is *he don't*, a contraction, of course, of *he does not*. Here in Virginia many men of the highest education use the phrase habitually. Their ancestors have used it for many generations, and it might be argued with some reason that when the best blood and the best brains of Virginia use an expression for so long a time it becomes correct, regardless of the protests of the professional grammarians.[2]

According to Menner, the widespread use of the present for the preterite is relatively recent. "In almost all the comic writers of the first half of the [Nineteenth] Century," he says, *gin* and *give* are

1 *Not* in American English, *American Speech*, Sept., 1927.
2 Oct. 21, 1931. Mark Twain, whose speechways were Southern, often used *don't* in the singular. For example, in Innocents Abroad, 1869, p. 84: "Sometimes the patient gets well, but as a general thing he *don't*." Otto Jespersen, in A Modern English Grammar; Heidelberg,

1922, Vol. I, p. 228, says that the use of *don't* for *doesn't* "cannot be explained as a simple morphological substitution of one personal form of the verb for another, as *do* is not similarly substituted for *does* when *not* follows." He finds analogues for it in *ent* (*ain't*) for *isn't* and *wan't* for *wasn't*.

in rivalry as the preterites of *to give*, but in "Huckleberry Finn" *give* prevails. He suggests that its rise may be due to the fact that a number of common verbs showing the same vowel, *e.g.*, *hit, quit* and *spit*, are unchanged in the preterite. Certainly it is a fact that such verbs are apparently rather more often put into the new historical present in the vulgate than those of any other class. Examples are *begin, sit* and *win*. But the other verbs seem to be going the same way, and the vulgar preterite of one of them, *sez, i.e., says*, appears to be older than *give*. Charters's material offers many specimens, among them "We *help* distributed the fruit," "She *recognize, hug*, and *kiss* him" and "Her father *ask* her if she intended doing what he *ask*"; and Lardner has "If Weaver and them had not of *begin* kicking" and "They would of *knock* down the fence." I notice that *used*, in *used to be*, is almost always reduced to simple *use*, as in "It *use* to be the rule," with the *s* very much like that of *hiss*. One seldom, if ever, hears a clear *d* at the end.[1] Here, of course, the elision of the *d* is due primarily to assimilation with the *t* of *to* — an example of one form of decay aiding another.

3. THE PRONOUN

The following paradigm shows the usual inflections of the personal pronoun in the American vulgate:

First Person
Common Gender

		Singular	Plural
Nominative		I	we
Possessive	Conjoint	my	our
	Absolute	mine	ourn
Objective		me	us

Second Person
Common Gender

Nominative		you	yous
Possessive	Conjoint	your	your
	Absolute	yourn	yourn
Objective		you	yous

[1] This substitution of *use* for *used* is listed by Henry Harap among The Most Common Grammatical Errors, *English Journal*, June, 1930, p. 441.

Third Person
Masculine Gender

Nominative		he	they
Possessive	{ *Conjoint*	his	their
	{ *Absolute*	hisn	theirn
Objective		him	them

Feminine Gender

Nominative		she	they
Possessive	{ *Conjoint*	her	their
	{ *Absolute*	hern	theirn
Objective		her	them

Neuter Gender

Nominative		it	they
Possessive	{ *Conjoint*	its	their
	{ *Absolute*	its	theirn
Objective		it	them

These inflections are often disregarded in use, but nevertheless it may be profitable to glance at them as they stand. The only variations that they show from Standard English are the substitution of *n* for *s* as the distinguishing mark of the absolute form of the possessive, and the attempt to differentiate between the logical and the merely polite plurals in the second person by adding the usual sign of the plural to the former. The use of *n* in place of *s* is not an American innovation. It is found in many of the dialects of English, and is, in fact, historically quite as sound as the use of *s*. In John Wycliffe's translation of the Bible (*c.* 1380) the first sentence of the Sermon on the Mount (Mark v, 3) is made: " Blessed be the pore in spirit, for the kyngdam in hevenes is *heren*." And in his version of Luke xxiv, 24, is this: " And some of *ouren* wentin to the grave." Here *heren* (or *herun*) represents, of course, not the modern *hers*, but *theirs*. In Old English the word was *heora*, and down to Chaucer's day a modified form of it, *here*, was still used in the possessive plural in place of the modern *their*, though *they* had already displaced *hie* in the nominative.[1] But in John Purvey's revision of the Wycliffe Bible, made a few years later, *hern* actually occurs in II Kings vii, 6, thus: " Restore thou to hir alle things that ben *hern*." In Old Eng-

---

1 Henry Bradley, in The Making of English; New York, 1904, pp. 54–5: " In the parts of England which were largely inhabited by Danes the native pronouns (*i.e.*, *heo*, *hie*, *heom* and *heora*) were supplanted by the Scandinavian pronouns which are represented by the modern *she*, *they*, *them* and *their*." This substitution, at first dialectical, gradually spread to the whole language.

lish there had been no distinction between the conjoint and absolute forms of the possessive pronoun; the simple genitive sufficed for both uses. But with the decay of that language the surviving remnants of its grammar began to be put to service somewhat recklessly, and there arose a genitive inflection of this genitive – a true double inflection. In the Northern dialects of English that inflection was made by simply adding *s*, the sign of the possessive. In the Southern dialects the old *n*-declension was applied, and there appeared such forms as *minum* and *eowrum* (*mine* and *yours*), from *min* and *eower* (*my* and *your*).[1] Meanwhile, the original simple genitive, now become *youre*, also survived, and the literature of the Fourteenth Century shows the three forms flourishing side by side: *youre*, *youres* and *youren*. All of them are in Chaucer.

As for the addition of *s* to *you* in the nominative and objective of the second person plural, it exhibits no more than an effort to give clarity to the logical difference between the pure plural and the merely polite plural. Another device to the same end is the familiar dual, *you-two*, which also appears in the first and second persons, as in *we-two*, *us-two* and *them-two*.[2] Yet another, confined to the South, is *you-all* or *y'all*, which simply means *you-jointly* as opposed to the *you* that means *thou*.[3] The substitution of the plural

1 See A New English Grammar, by Henry Sweet; Oxford, 1900, Pt. I, p. 344.
2 There is also a triple, *you-three*, but beyond that the device begins to fade.
3 It is commonly believed in the North that Southerners use *you-all* in the singular, but this is true, if it is ever true at all, of only the most ignorant of them. The word may be addressed to individuals, but only when they are thought of as representatives of a group. "Have *you-all* any eggs?" spoken to a storekeeper, means have you and your associates, the store as a group entity, any eggs. This distinction was elucidated at length by the late C. Alphonso Smith in *You-All* As Used in the South, *Uncle Remus's Magazine* (Atlanta) July, 1907, reprinted in *Kit-Kat* (Columbus, O.), Jan., 1920. The literature of the subject is extensive and full of bitterness. See especially *You-All* and *We-All*, by Estelle Rees Morrison, *American Speech*, Dec., 1926; *You-All* and *We-All* Again, by Lowry Axley, the same, May, 1927; *You-All*, by G. B., the same, Aug., 1927; *You-All*, by W. Fischer, the same, Sept., 1927; *You-All* Again, by Estelle Rees Morrison, the same, Oct., 1928; *Y'All*, by Lowry Axley, the same, Dec., 1928; an anonymous note in the same, Dec., 1928, p. 158; One More Word on *You-All*, by Lowry Axley, the same, June, 1929; Mr. Axley and *You-All*, by Herbert B. Bernstein, the same, Dec., 1929; The Truth About *You-All*, by Bertram H. Brown, *American Mercury*, May, 1933, p. 116; *You-All* Again, by W. E. Nesom, *American Mercury*, June, 1933, p. 248; *You-All* Once Again, by Alba W. Duke, *American Mercury*, July, 1933, p. 377. The newspaper literature of

you for the singular *thou* began in England in the Thirteenth Century, and at the same time analogous substitutions occurred in the other Western European languages. In these languages the true singular survives alongside the debased plural, but English has dropped it entirely, save for poetical and liturgical uses and in a few dialects. It had passed out of ordinary polite speech by Elizabeth's day. By that time, indeed, its use had acquired an air of the offensive, such as it has today, save between intimates or to children, in Germany. Thus, at the trial of Sir Walter Raleigh in 1603, Sir Edward Coke, then Attorney-General, displayed his animosity to Raleigh by addressing him as *thou*, and finally burst into the contemptuous " I *thou* thee, *thou* traitor! " And in " Twelfth Night " Sir Toby Belch urges Sir Andrew Aguecheek to provoke the disguised Viola to combat by *thouing* her.[1] In our own time, with *thou* passed out en-

---

the subject is enormous; I content myself with citing three articles: *You-All* Again (editorial) Richmond *Times-Dispatch*, May 24, 1925; Just a Moment, by Loudon Kelly, Denver *Rocky Mountain News*, Jan. 23, 1933; *You-All*, by H. L. Mencken, New York *American*, July 16, 1934. *You-All* has been traced by various fanciful writers to the French *vous tout* and to a somewhat analogous Pennsylvania German form. But Dr. Smith showed that it has deep roots in English. Mark Antony's " You all did see upon the Lupercal " will be recalled. According to R. C. Goffin (*S.P.E. Tracts*, No. XLI, p. 26) *you-all* is also used by native speakers of English in India. He says that it is there a translation of a Hindustani idiom. In the South *who-all* and *what-all* are also common, and in the more remote mountain regions *you-uns* and *we-uns* dispute for place with *you-all* and *we-all*. See The Plural Forms of *You*, by E. C. Hills, *American Speech*, Dec., 1926, p. 133. In the Ozarks, says Vance Randolph in The Grammar of the Ozark Dialect, *American Speech*, Oct., 1927, p. 6, even *us-uns* is occasionally encountered.

1 *Thou* was adopted by the Quakers,

c. 1650, precisely because it had a connotation of humility. " This *thou* and *thee*," said George Fox in his Journal, 1661, " was a sore cut to proud flesh, and them that sought self-honor; who, though they would say it to God and Christ, would not endure to have it said to themselves. So that we were often beaten and abused and sometimes in danger of our lives for using those words to some proud men, who would say, ' What, you ill-bred clown, do you *thou* me? " How and when the Quakers came to substitute *thee* for *thou* in the nominative has not been established. In all probability the change was effected by the same process that has changed *you* to *y'* in *y'ought* and *y'all*. The more careful Quakers still use *thou* in written discourse. But both *thou* and *thee* are passing out; save in the Philadelphia area, the younger members of the Society of Friends commonly use *you*. See The Speech of Plain Friends, by Kate W. Tibbals, *American Speech*, Jan., 1926; Quaker *Thee* and Its History, by E. K. Maxfield, the same, Sept., 1926; Quaker *Thee* and *Thou*, by E. K. Maxfield, the same, June, 1929.

tirely, even as a pronoun of contempt, the confusion between *you* in the plural and *you* in the singular presents plain difficulties to a man of limited linguistic resources. He gets around them by setting up a distinction that is well supported by logic and analogy. "I seen *yous*" is clearly separated from "I seen *you*." And in the conjoint position "*yous* guys" is separated from "*you* liar."

Of demonstrative pronouns, there are but two in Standard English, *this* and *that*, with their plural forms, *these* and *those*. To them, vulgar American adds a third, *them*, which is also the personal pronoun of the third person, objective case.[1] In addition it has adopted certain adverbial pronouns, *this-here*, *these-here*, *that-there*, *those-there* and *them-there*, and set up inflections of the original demonstratives by analogy with *mine*, *hisn* and *yourn*, to wit, *thisn*, *thesen*, *thatn* and *thosen*. I present some examples of everyday use:

> *Them* are the kind I like.
> *Them* men all work here.
> Who is *this-here* Smith I hear about?
> *These-here* are mine.
> *That-there* medicine ain't no good.
> *Those-there* wops has all took to the woods.
> I wisht I had one of *them-there* Fords.
> I like *thesen* better'n *thosen*.

The demonstratives of the *thisn*-group seem to be composition forms of *this-one*, *that-one*, etc., just as *none* is a composition form of *no(t)-one*. In every case of their use that I have observed the simple demonstratives might have been set free and *one* actually substituted for the terminal *n*. But it must be equally obvious that they have been reinforced very greatly by the absolutes of the *hisn*-group, for in their relation to the original demonstratives they play the part of just such absolutes and are never used conjointly. Thus, one says, in American, "I take *thisn*" or "*Thisn* is mine," but one never says "I take *thisn* hat" or "*Thisn* dog is mine." In this con-

---

[1] It occurs, too, of course, in other dialects of English, though by no means in all. The Irish influence probably had something to do with its prosperity in vulgar American. At all events, the Irish use it in the American manner. Joyce, in English As We Speak It in Ireland, pp. 34–5, argues that this usage was suggested by Gaelic. In Gaelic the accusative pronouns, *e*, *i* and *iad* (*him*, *her* and *them*) are often used in place of the nominatives, *se*, *si* and *siad* (*he*, *she* and *they*), as in "Is *iad* sin na buachaillidhe" (*Them* are the boys). This is "good grammar" in Gaelic, and the Irish, when they began to learn English, translated the locution literally. The familiar Irish "John is dead and *him* always so hearty" shows the same influence.

joint situation plain *this* is always used, and the same rule applies to *these, those* and *that. Them,* being a newcomer among the demonstratives, has not yet acquired an inflection in the absolute. I have never heard *them'n,* and it will probably never come in, for it is forbiddingly clumsy. One says, in American, both " *Them* are mine " and " *Them* collars are mine."

This-here, these-here, that-there, those-there and *them-there* are plainly combinations of pronouns and adverbs, and their function is to support the distinction between proximity, as embodied in *this* and *these,* and remoteness, as embodied in *that, those* and *them.* " *This-here* coat is mine " simply means " This coat *here,* or this *present* coat is mine." [1] But the adverb promises to coalesce with the pronoun so completely as to obliterate all sense of its distinct existence, even as a false noun or adjective. As commonly pronounced, *this-here* becomes a single word, somewhat like *thish-yur,* and *these-here* becomes *these-yur,* and *that-there* and *them-there* become *that-ere* and *them-ere. Those-there,* if I observe accurately, is still pronounced more distinctly, but it, too, may succumb to composition in time. The adverb will then sink to the estate of a mere inflectional particle, as *one* has done in the absolutes of the *thisn*-group. *Them,* as a personal pronoun in the absolute, of course, is commonly pronounced *em,* as in " I seen *em,*" and sometimes its vowel is almost lost, but this is also the case in all save the most exact spoken English. Sweet and Lounsbury, following certain German grammarians, argue that this *em* is not really a debased form of *them,* but the offspring of *hem,* which survived as the regular plural of the third person in the objective case down to the beginning of the Fifteenth Century. But in American *them* is clearly pronounced as a demonstrative. I have never heard " *em* men " or " *Em* are the kind I like," but always " *them* men " and " *Them* are the kind I like." It is possible that *them,* in this situation, may be a descendant of the Old English *thaem* (those).

The relative pronouns are declined in the vulgate as follows:

Nominative	who	which	what	that
Possessive	{ whose / whosen	whose / whosen		
Objective	who	which	what	that

1 The Rev. John Witherspoon, in The Druid, No. VI, May 16, 1781, denounced " *This-here* report of *that-there* committee." He said: " Some merchants, whom I could name, in the English Parliament,

Two things will be noted in this paradigm. First there is the disappearance of *whom* as the objective form of *who,* and secondly there is the appearance of an inflected form of *whose* in the absolute, by analogy with *mine, hisn* and *hern. Whom* is fast vanishing from Standard American;[1] in the vulgar language it is virtually extinct. Not only is *who* used instead in situations where good usage has begun to tolerate it; it is also used in such constructions as " The man *who* I saw " and " Them *who* I trust in." George Philip Krapp explains this use of *who* on the ground that there is a " general feeling," due to the normal word-order in English, that " the word which precedes the verb is the subject word, or at least the subject form.[2] But this explanation is probably fanciful. Among the plain people no such " general feeling " for case exists. Their only " general feeling " is a prejudice against case inflections in any form whatsoever. They use *who* in place of *whom* simply because they can discern no logical difference between the significance of the one and the significance of the other.

" The relative *whose,*" says R. J. Menner, " is a rare word in popular speech. One may listen to conversations for weeks without hearing it."[3] Not infrequently *that* and a genitive pronoun are substituted for it, as in " He's a fellow *that* I don't know *his* name," and sometimes *that* is omitted, as in " He was a man I never trusted his word." But sometimes *whose* is used in place of the forbidding *whom,* especially when a genitive sense is apprehended, *e.g.,* " Bless those *whose* it's our duty to pray for." In the absolute *whosen* is sometimes used, as in " If it ain't hisn, then *whosen* is it? ", obviously under the influence of the other absolutes in *-n.* There is an analo-

---

whose wealth and not merit raised them to that dignity, use this vulgarism very freely, and expose themselves to abundance of ridicule by so doing."

1 S. A. Leonard, in Current English Usage, says that " *Who* are you looking for? " is " established." " The linguists," he says, " rated it higher than did any of the other groups of judges [appointed by the National Council of Teachers of English]; the other groups placed the expression among disputed usages. All the groups save the business men and authors gave

majorities for approval." J. Y. T. Greig, in Breaking Priscian's Head; London, 1929, denounces *whom* in this situation as " pedantry " and " schoolmarmery." " Every sensible English-speaker on both sides of the Atlantic," he declares, " says ' *Who* were you talking to? ' and the sooner we begin to write it the better. *Whom* is a relic of the bad old days when inflections were cherished for their own sake."

2 Modern English; New York, 1910, p. 300.

3 Troublesome Relatives, *American Speech,* June, 1931.

gous form of *which*, to wit, *whichn*, resting heavily on *which one*. Thus "*Whichn* do you like? " and " I didn't say *whichn* " are plainly variations of " *Which one* do you like? " and " I didn't say *which one*." *That*, as we have seen, has a like form, *thatn*, but never, of course, in the relative situation. " I like *thatn* " is familiar, but " The one *thatn* I like " is never heard. If *that*, as a relative, could be used absolutely, I have no doubt that it would change to *thatn*, as it does as a demonstrative. So with *what*. As things stand, *what* is sometimes substituted for *that*, as in " Them's the kind *what* I like." Joined to *but* it can also take the place of *that* in other situations, as in " I don't know *but what*."

The substitution of *who* for *whom* in the objective case, just noticed, is typical of a general movement toward breaking down all case distinctions among the pronouns, where they make their last stand in English and its dialects. This movement, of course, is not peculiar to vulgar American; nor is it of recent beginning. So long ago as the Fifteenth Century the old clear distinction between *ye*, nominative, and *you*, objective, disappeared, and today the latter is used in both cases. Sweet says that the phonetic similarity between *ye* and *thee*, the objective form of the true second singular, was responsible for this confusion.[1] In modern spoken English, indeed, *you* in the objective often has a sound far more like that of *ye* than like that of *you*, as, for example, in " How do *y'* do? " and in American its vowel takes the neutral form of the *e* in the definite article, and the word becomes a sort of shortened *yeh*. But whenever emphasis is laid upon it, *you* becomes quite distinct, even in American. In " I mean *you*," for example, there is never any chance of mistaking it for *ye*. In Shakespeare's time the other personal pronouns of the objective case threatened to follow *you* into the nominative, and there was a compensatory movement of the nominative pronouns toward the objective. The late T. R. Lounsbury collected many examples.[2] Marlowe used " Is it *him* you seek? ", " 'Tis *her* I esteem " and " Nor *thee* nor *them* shall want "; Fletcher used " 'Tis *her* I admire "; Shakespeare himself used " That's *me*." Contrariwise, Webster used " What difference is between the duke and *I?* " and Greene

---

1 A New English Grammar, Pt. I, p. 339.
2 History of the English Language, revised ed.; New York, 1894, p. 274-5. There is an elaborate historical account of the process in Case-Shiftings in the Pronouns, in Chapters on English, by Otto Jespersen; London, 1918.

used "Nor earth nor heaven shall part my love and *I*." Krapp unearthed many similar examples from the Restoration dramatists.[1] Etheredge used " 'Tis *them*," " It may be *him*," " Let you and *I* " and " Nor is it *me* "; Matthew Prior, in a famous couplet, achieved this:

> For thou art a girl as much brighter than *her*
> As he was a poet sublimer than *me*.

This free exchange, in fact, continued until the Eighteenth Century was well advanced; there are examples of it in Addison. Moreover, it survived, on the colloquial level, even the furious attack that was then made upon it by grammarians, and to this day *it's me* is in good usage, and most authorities of any sense, if they do not actually defend it, at least condone it.[2] On the level of the vulgate, it is firmly intrenched. The schoolmarm continues to inveigh against it, but her admonitions go unheeded. Similarly, " *us* fellas " is so far established that " *we* fellas " from the mouth of an iceman would seem almost an affectation. So, too, is " *Me* and *her* are friends." So, again, are " *Her* and *I* set down together," " *Him* and his wife " and " I knowed it was *her*." Here are some other characteristic examples of the use of the objective forms in the nominative from Charters, Lardner, Rogers and others:

1 Modern English, before cited, pp. 288-9.

2 These authorities include Sayce, Sweet, Ellis, Jespersen and the Fowlers, and in America, Whitney, Barrett Wendell, Lounsbury and Oliver F. Emerson. Their remarks on the subject are summarized by Wallace Rice in Who's There? — *Me*, *American Speech*, Oct., 1933. George H. McKnight, in Modern English in the Making; New York, 1928, pp. 532-33, cites many examples of *it's me* from modern English writers, including Laurence Housman, May Sinclair, Anne Douglas Sedgwick, Joseph Conrad and St. John Ervine. He also cites examples of *it's her* from J. Middleton Murry and A. A. Milne, of *it's him* from J. W. Croker, James Stephens and A. S. M. Hutchinson, and of *it's us* from Hutchinson. The committee of judges appointed in 1926 by the National Council of Teachers of English approved *it's me* by a vote of 130 to 91. Rather significantly, the business men on the committee turned out to be far more conservative than the authors, editors, linguists and teachers. They voted against it 18 to 5. In 1921 it was formally approved by the late Edward J. Tobin, then superintendent of schools of Cook county, Ill. (*i.e.*, of Chicago), and in 1926 it got the imprimatur of the College Entrance Examination Board. See *American Speech*, Dec., 1926, p. 163. The Tobin pronunciamento was discussed all over the country for weeks. The analogous French form, *c'est moi*, was denounced by Petrus Ramus in his French grammar, 1562. But in a later edition, 1572, he admitted it, saying, " To rob our language of such expressions would be like drawing a sword against all France." See McKnight, cited above, p. 222.

Me and *her* was both late.
His brother is taller than *him*.
That little boy was *me*.
Us girls went home.
They were John and *him*.
Her and little Al is to stay here.
She says she thinks *us* and the Allens.
If Weaver and *them* had not of begin kicking.
Us two'll walk, me and him.
But not *me*.
Him and his gang.
Him and I are friends.
Me and *them* are friends.

Here are some grotesque confusions, indeed. Perhaps the best way to get at the principles underlying them is to examine first, not the cases of their occurrence, but the cases of their non-occurrence. Let us begin with the transfer of the objective form to the nominative in the subject relation. " *Me* and *her* was both late " is obviously sound American; one hears it, or something like it, on the streets every day. But one never hears " *Me* was late " or " *Her* was late " or " *Us* was late " or " *Him* was late " or " *Them* was late." Again, one hears " *Us* girls was there " but never " *Us* was there." Yet again, one hears " *Her* and John was married " but never " *Her* was married." The distinction here set up should be immediately plain. It exactly parallels that between *her* and *hern,* *our* and *ourn,* *their* and *theirn:* the tendency, as Sweet says, is " to merge the distinction of nominative and objective in that of conjoint and absolute." [1] The nominative, in the subject relation, takes the usual nominative form only when it is in immediate contact with its verb. If it be separated from its verb by a conjunction or any other part of speech, even including another pronoun, it takes the objective form. Thus " *Me* went home " would strike even the most ignorant shopgirl as " bad grammar," but she would use " *me* and my friend went " or " *me* and *him* " or " *me* and *them* " without the slightest hesitation. What is more, if the separation be effected by a conjunction and another pronoun, the other pronoun also changes to the objective form, even though its contact with the verb may be immediate. Thus one hears " *Me* and *her* was there," not " *me* and *she* "; " *Her* and *him* kissed," not " *her* and *he*." Still more, this second pronoun commonly undergoes the same inflection even when the first member of the

1 A New English Grammar, Pt. I,
  p. 341.

group is not another pronoun, but a noun. Thus one hears " John and *her* was married," not " John and *she*." To this rule there is but one exception, and that is in the case of the first person pronoun, especially in the singular. " *Him* and *me* are friends " is heard often, but " *Him* and *I* are friends " is also heard. *I* seems to suggest the subject powerfully, and is the actual subject of perhaps a majority of the sentences uttered by an ignorant man. At all events, it resists the rule, at least partially, and may even do so when separated from the verb by another pronoun, itself in the objective form, as, for example, in " *I* and *him* were there."

In the predicate relation the pronouns respond to a more complex regulation. " I seen *he* " or " He kissed *she* " or " He struck *I* " would seem as ridiculous to an ignorant American as to the Archbishop of Canterbury, and his instinct for simplicity and regularity naturally tends to make him reduce all similar expressions, or what seem to him to be similar expressions, to coincidence with the more seemly " I seen *him*." I incline to think that it is some such subconscious logic, and not the analogy of " It is *he*," as Sweet argues, that has brought " It is *me* " to conversational respectability, even among rather careful speakers of English.[1] In compensation for this use of the objective form in the nominative position there occurs in vulgar American a use of the nominative form in the objective position, as in " She gave it to mother and *I*," " She took all of *we* children " and " Anything she has is O.K. for *I* and Florrie," all borrowed from Lardner.[2] What lies at the bottom of this seems to be a feeling somewhat resembling that which causes the use of the objective

[1] It may be worth noting that the archaic misuse of *me* for *my*, as in " I lit *me* pipe," is almost unknown in American, either standard or vulgar, though a correspondent in Philadelphia tells me that it is a localism in that city, and is sometimes used by elderly persons of Irish birth. Even " *me* own " is seldom heard. This survival of the Middle English pronunciation of *mi* (*my*) is very common in England.

[2] The writers of popular songs supply many examples. Sigmund Spaeth, in Stabilizing the Language Through Popular Songs, *New Yorker*, July 7, 1934, cites " Re-

member I was once a girl like *she*," " A sweet slice of Heaven for just you and *I*," and " 'Twas foolish for *we* two to fight." In 1924 one Gehring, running for Congress in New York City, circulated a card reading " He thinks like you and *I*." On June 25, 1925, the Los Angeles *Examiner* printed on its first page a head reading " Silva Says Killing Prompted By Insults at *He* and Buddy." Sometimes there is a double exchange in case-forms, as in a speech heard by a correspondent in Wyoming: " Between *I* and you, *him* and *her* drinks too much."

•

form before the verb, but exactly contrary in its effects. That is to say, the nominative form is used when the pronoun is separated from its governing verb, whether by a noun, a noun-phrase or another pronoun, as in " She gave it to mother and *I*," " She took all of *we* children " and " He paid her and *I*," respectively. But here usage is far from fixed, and one observes variations in both directions — that is, toward using the correct objective when the pronoun is detached from the verb, and toward using the nominative even when it directly follows the verb. " She gave it to mother and *me*," " She took all of *us* children " and " He paid her and *me* " would probably sound quite as correct, to a Knight of Pythias, as the forms just given. And at the other end Charters and Lardner report such forms as " I want you to meet *he* and *I* " and " It is going to cost me $6 a week for a room for *she* and the baby." I have noticed, however, that the use of the nominative is chiefly confined to the pronoun of the first person, and particularly to its singular. Here again we have an example of the powerful way in which *I* asserts itself. And superimposed upon that influence is a cause mentioned by Sweet in discussing " between you and *I*." [1] It is a sort of by-product of the pedagogical war upon " It is *me*." " As such expressions," he says, " are still denounced by the grammars, many people try to avoid them in speech as well as in writing. The result of this reaction is that the *me* in such constructions as ' between John and *me* ' and ' he saw John and *me* ' sounds vulgar and ungrammatical, and is consequently corrected into *I*." Here the schoolmarm, seeking to impose an inelastic and illogical grammar upon a living speech, succeeds only in corrupting it still more.

Following *than* and *as* the American uses the objective form of the pronoun, as in " He is taller than *me* " and " such as *her*." He also uses it following *like*, but not when, as often happens, he uses the word in place of *as* or *as if*. Thus he says " Do it like *him*," but " Do it like *he* does " and " She looks like *she* was sick." What appears here is apparently an instinctive feeling that these words, followed by a pronoun only, are not adverbs, but prepositions, and that they should have the same power to put the pronoun into an oblique case that other prepositions have. Just as " the taller of *we* " would sound absurd to all of us, so " taller than *he*," to the unschooled American,

1 A New English Grammar, Pt. I, p. 341.

sounds absurd. This feeling has a good deal of respectable support. "As *her*" was used by Swift, "than *me*" by Burke and "than *whom*" by Milton. The brothers Fowler show that, in some cases, "than *him*" is grammatically correct and logically necessary.[1] For example, compare "I love you more than *him*" and "I love you more than *he*." The first means "I love you more than (I love) *him*"; the second, "I love you more than *he* (loves you)." In the first *him* does not refer to *I*, which is nominative, but to *you*, which is objective, and so it is properly objective also. But the American, of course, uses *him* even when the preceding noun is in the nominative, save only when another verb follows the pronoun. Thus he says "I love you better than *him*," but "I love you better than *he* does."

In the matter of the reflexive pronouns the American vulgate exhibits forms which plainly show that it is the spirit of the language to regard *self*, not as an adjective, which it is historically, but as a noun. This confusion goes back to Old English days; it originated at a time when both the adjectives and the nouns were losing their old inflections. Such forms as *Petrussylf* (*Peter's self*), *Cristsylf* (*Christ's self*) and *Icsylf* (*I, self*) then came into use, and along with them came combinations of *self* and the genitive, still surviving in vulgar American in *hisself* and *theirselves* (or *theirself*). Down to the Sixteenth Century these forms remained in perfectly good usage. "Each for *hisself*," for example, was written by Sir Philip Sidney, and is to be found in the dramatists of the time, though modern editors always change it to *himself*. How the dative pronoun got itself fastened upon *self* in the third person masculine and neuter is one of the mysteries of language, but there it is, and so, against all logic, history and grammatical regularity, *himself*, *themselves* and *itself* (not *its-self*) are in favor today. But the American, as usual, inclines against these illogical exceptions to the rule set by *myself*. I constantly hear *hisself* and *theirselves*, as in "He done it *hisself*" and "They know *theirselves*." Also, the emphatic *own* is often inserted between the pronoun and the noun, as in "Let every man save their *own* self." In general the American vulgate makes very extensive use of the reflexive. It is constantly thrown in for good measure, as in "I overeat *myself*" and it is as constantly used singly, as in "*self* and wife."

---

1 The King's English, 2nd ed.; Oxford, 1908, p. 63.

The American pronoun does not necessarily agree with its noun in number. I find " I can tell each one what *they* make," " Each fellow put *their* foot on the line," " Nobody can do what *they* like " and " She was one of *these* kind [1] of people " in Charters, and " I am not the kind of man that is always thinking about *their* record " and " If he was to hit a man in the head . . . *they* would think *their* nose tickled " in Lardner. At the bottom of this error there is a real difficulty: the lack of a pronoun of the true common gender in English, corresponding to the French *soi* and *son*.[2] *His*, after a noun or pronoun connoting both sexes, often sounds inept, and *his-or-her* is intolerably clumsy. Thus the inaccurate plural is often substituted. The brothers Fowler have discovered " Anybody else who have only *themselves* in view " in Richardson, and " Everybody is discontented with *their* lot " in Disraeli, and Ruskin once wrote " If a customer wishes you to injure *their* foot." I find two examples in a single paragraph of an article by Associate Justice George B. Ethridge of the Supreme Court of Mississippi: " We should keep it possible for anyone to correct *their* errors " and " No person can be happy in life if *they* ";[3] and another in a war speech by Woodrow Wilson: " No man or woman can hesitate to give what *they* have." [4] In the lower reaches of the language the plural is used with complete inno-

1 Here, of course, *kind* is probably felt to be plural. *Those* is used in the same way, as in " *Those* are the kind."

2 In 1858 Charles Crozat Converse of Erie, Pa., proposed *thon* for *he-or-she* and *thon's* for *his-or-her*, but though both are listed in Webster's New International Dictionary, 1934, they have made no progress. See *English*, Jan., 1920, p. 262. *Thon* is an old Northern English word signifying yonder, now sunk into dialect. The late Ella Flagg Young, the first woman president of the National Education Association, favored *hiser* and *himer*, and tried to induce the association to approve them, *c.* 1910. Mr. James F. Morton of Paterson, N. J., has proposed *hesh* for *he-and-she*, and some one else has proposed *heer* for *him-and-her*. Mr. Lincoln King of Primghar, Iowa, advocates *ha*, *hez* and *hem* in the nominative, genitive and objective respectively. Another re-

former, this time anonymous (The Post Impressionist, Washington *Post*, Aug. 20, 1935) proposes *hes*, *hir* and *hem*. In Thought and Language; London, 1934, p. 7, P. B. Ballard tells of a female revolutionist in England who complained that " while the masculine personal pronoun had three distinct forms, *he*, *his* and *him*, for the separate cases of the singular, the feminine pronoun had only two, *she* and *her*," and " suggested as a remedy for this gross piece of injustice that the feminine pronoun should be declined *she*, *shis* and *shim*." English, of course, also suffers from the lack of a word corresponding to the German *geschwister*, meaning brothers and/or sisters. The biologists use *siblings*, but it has not come into general use.

3 *Congressional Record*, Feb. 27, 1935, p. 2784.

4 The speech was made in New York City, Sept. 27, 1918.

cence, and such forms as "Everybody knows *their* way," "Some-body has gotten *theirs*," "Nobody could help *themselves*" and "A person ought never take what ain't *theirn*" are common.

In demotic American the pedantry which preserves such forms as *someone's else* is always disregarded; *someone else's* is invariably used. "I have heard "Who *else's* wife was there? " and "If it ain't his'n, it ain't nobody here *else's*." I note, too, that *he's* seems to be assimilating with *his*. In such sentences as "I hear *he's* coming here to work," the sound of *he's* is already almost that of *his*. Finally, there is a curious substitution of the simple personal pronoun for the geni-tive among the Negroes of the South, noted by George O. Curme.[1] Examples are in "He roll *he* eyeballs" and "*Who* dog is it? " But this substitution is not encountered in the general vulgate.

4. THE NOUN

The only inflections of the noun remaining in English are those for number and for the genitive, and so it is in these two regions that the few variations to be noted in vulgar American occur. The rule that, in forming the plurals of compound nouns or noun-phrases, the -*s* shall be attached to the principal noun is commonly disre-garded, and it goes at the end. Thus, "I have two *sons-in-law*" is never heard among the plain people; one always hears "I have two *son-in-laws*." So with the genitive. I once overheard this: "That umbrella is the *young lady I go with's*." [2] Often a false singular is formed from a singular ending in *s*, the latter being mistaken for a plural. *Chinee*, *Portugee* and *Japanee* are familiar: I have also en-countered *trapee*, *specie*,[3] *tactic* [4] and *summon* (from *trapeze*, *species*, *tactics* and *summons*). A correspondent of *American Speech* once reported hearing *calv* and *hoov* as singulars in Nebraska,[5] and Dr. Louise Pound has encountered *corp* and *appendic* in the same great

1 Parts of Speech and Accidence; Boston, 1935, p. 47.
2 The history of such forms is re-counted in The English Group Genitive, by Otto Jespersen, printed in his Chapters On Eng-lish; London, 1918.
3 This occasionally gets into print. See South American Travels, by Henry Stephens; New York, 1915,

p. 114. It is also used by Ezra Pound in his translation of Remy de Gour-mont's The Natural Philosophy of Love; New York, 1922.
4 "The *tactic* in Japan has always been," etc. Law and Order in Japan, by Harry F. Ward, New York *Nation*, Sept. 9, 1925, p. 289.
5 Folk-Etymological Singulars, by Wilbur Gaffney, Dec., 1927, p. 130.

State.[1] In the mountains along the Tennessee-North Carolina border *chee* is the singular of *cheese*,[2] and in the Ozarks likewise *cheese* is treated as a plural, though it apparently has no singular. *Molasses*, too, according to Vance Randolph, is considered a plural in the Ozarks, and both there and in North Carolina *license* is its own plural.[3] Throughout the South the Primitive Baptists use *Baptist* (pronounced *Baptiz*) as both singular and plural.[4] On at least one occasion a Texas Congressman referred to a fellow member of the House as " a *Knights* of Columbus," [5] and I believe that this usage is not uncommon among the Catholic proletariat. I have also encountered *intelligentsia* in the singular,[6] but here, of course, we go beyond the bounds of the vulgate. Dr. Pound has called attention to the facility with which plural nouns are treated as singulars, *e.g., woods, grounds, stairs, stockyards*, as in " The party reached a picnic *grounds*" and " We passed a *stockyards*." *Incidence*, in my observation, is commonly misused for *incident*, as in " He told an *incidence*." Here *incidence* (or *incident*) seems to be regarded as a synonym, not for *happening*, but for *story*. The general disregard of number often shows itself when the noun is used as object. I have already quoted Lardner's " Some of the men has brung their *wife* along "; in a popular magazine I lately encountered " Those book ethnologists . . . can't see what is before their *nose*." The common indicators of quantity seldom add *s* for the plural in the vulgate. Especially when preceded by a numeral, such words as *mile, bushel, dozen, pound, pair, foot, inch, gallon* and *peck* retain their singular form.

1 Some Singular-Plural Forms, *Dialect Notes*, Vol. IV, Pt. I, 1913, p. 48.
2 *Dialect Notes*, Vol. I, Pt. VIII, 1895, p. 376.
3 For this headline from the Oxford *Public Ledger*, Jan. 15, 1934, I am indebted to Mrs. B. K. Hays of Oxford: " Hunting License Bring in $85,000." *License* appeared as a plural in a syndicated cartoon by J. N. Darling (Ding), Feb. 4, 1936.
4 The following admonition is from the *Baptist and Commoner* (Little Rock, Ark.), Jan. 2, 1928: " Will the brethren never learn that when more than one Baptist is meant they should say *Baptists*, not *Baptist*. Over and over again they write like this: ' The *Baptist* believe,' or ' The *Baptist* in these parts,' etc. Which one of the Baptists do you mean, brother, when you say the *Baptist?* You never hear any one saying the *Methodist* believe and the *Methodist* in these parts. When they mean more than one Methodist they say *Methodists*. Why, then, say *Baptist* when you mean *Baptists*, that is, more than one? "
5 Mr. Blanton, *Congressional Record*, April 3, 1935, p. 5103.
6 Her World, by Lucile, San Francisco *News*, April 1, 1924.

5. THE ADJECTIVE

The adjectives in English are inflected only for comparison, and the American commonly uses them correctly, with now and then a double comparative or superlative to ease his soul. *More better* is the commonest of these. It has a good deal of support in logic. A sick man is reported today to be *better*. Tomorrow he is further improved. Is he to be reported *better* again, or *best?* The standard language gets around the difficulty by using *still better*. The American vulgate boldly employs *more better*. In the case of *worse*, *worser* is used, as Charters shows. He also reports *baddest, more queerer* and *beautifullest*, and from the Ozarks Vance Randolph reports *most Almighty God*.[1] The American of the folk freely compares adjectives that are incapable of the inflection logically. Charters reports *most principal*, and I myself have heard *uniquer* and even *more uniquer*, as in " I have never saw nothing *more uniquer*." I have also heard *more ultra, more worse, idealer, liver* (that is, more energetic, more alive), *perfectest*, and *wellest*, as in " He was the *wellest* man you ever seen." [2] In general, the *-er* and *-est* terminations are used instead of the *more* and *most* prefixes, as in *beautiful, beautifuller, beautifullest*. The fact that the comparative relates to two and the superlative to more than two is almost always forgotten. I have never heard " the *better* of the two," in the popular speech, but always " the *best* of the two." Charters also reports " the *hardest* of the two " and " My brother and I measured and he was the *tallest*." " It ain't so *worse* " is in common use. Superlatives are sometimes made from present participles, *e.g., fightingest*. Vance Randolph reports *shootingest* and *dancingest* from the Ozarks, and Dr. Louise Pound has dredged *kissingest, leakingest, goingest, laughingest* and *high-steppingest* from the general speech.[3] She adds *onliest, orphanest, womanishest, lunatickest, spindliest, unjustest, outlandishest* and *allrightest*, and the comparative *pathetiker*.

Adjectives are made much less rapidly in American than either substantives or verbs. The only suffix that seems to be in general use

1 The Grammar of the Ozark Dialect, *American Speech*, Oct., 1927, p. 8.
2 To which, perhaps, may be added *furtherest*, which appeared in a

Chicago dispatch on the first page of the San Francisco *Chronicle*, Feb. 2, 1922.
3 Notes on the Vernacular, *American Mercury*, Oct., 1924, p. 235.

for that purpose is *-y*, as in *tony, classy, hefty, daffy, nutty, ritzy, dinky, snappy,*[1] *leery,* etc. The use of the adjectival prefix *super-* tends to be confined to the more sophisticated classes; the plain people seldom use it.[2] This relative paucity of adjectives appears to be common to the more primitive varieties of speech. E. C. Hills, in his elaborate study of the vocabulary of a child of two,[3] found that it contained but 23 descriptive adjectives, of which six were the names of colors, as against 59 verbs and 173 common nouns. Moreover, most of the 23 minus six were adjectives of all work, such as *nasty, funny* and *nice.* Colloquial American uses the same rubber-stamps of speech. *Funny* connotes the whole range of the unusual; *hard* indicates every shade of difficulty; *nice* is everything satisfactory; *wonderful* is a superlative of almost limitless scope. The decay of *one* to a vague *n*-sound, as in *this'n,* is matched by a decay of *than* after comparatives. *Earlier than* is seldom if ever heard; composition reduces the two words to *earlier'n.* So with *better'n, faster'n, hotter'n, deader'n,* etc. Once I overheard the following dialogue: " I like a belt *more looser'n* what this one is." " Well, then, why don't you *unloosen* it *more'n* you got it *unloosened?* " That decay of the *-ed* termination which has substituted *damn* for *damned* has also clipped many other adjectives, *e.g., high-toned.* I never hear " a *high-toned* man "; it is always *high-tone.*

6. THE ADVERB

All the adverbial endings in English, save *-ly,* have gradually fallen into decay; it is the only one that is ever used to form new adverbs. At earlier stages of the language various other endings were used, and some of them survive in a few old words, though they are no longer employed in making new ones. The Old English endings were *-e* and *-lice.* The latter was, at first, merely an *-e*-ending to

1 See *Nifty, Hefty, Natty, Snappy,* by Klara H. Collitz, *American Speech,* Dec., 1927, and Observations on *Nifty, Hefty, Natty, Snappy,* by Henry J. Heck, the same, Oct., 1928. Mrs. Collitz tries to determine the etymology of the words she discusses, and Mr. Heck shows how they are defined in

various dictionaries, including two German ones and one Italian one.
2 See Vogue Affixes in Present-Day Word-Coinage, by Louise Pound, *Dialect Notes,* Vol. V, Pt. I, 1918.
3 The Speech of a Child Two Years of Age, *Dialect Notes,* Vol. IV, Pt. II, 1914.

adjectives in *-lic*, but after a time it attained to independence and was attached to adjectives not ending in *-lic*. In Middle English this *-lice* changed to *-li* and *-ly*. Meanwhile, the *-e*-ending, following the *-e*-endings of the nouns, adjectives and verbs, ceased to be pronounced, and so it gradually fell away. Thus a good many adverbs came to be indistinguishable from their ancestral adjectives, for example, *hard* in *to pull hard*, *loud* in *to speak loud*, and *deep* in *to bury deep* (Old English, *deop-e*). Worse, not a few adverbs actually became adjectives, for example, *wide*, which was originally the Old English adjective *wid* (*wide*) with the adverbial *-e*-ending, and *late*, which was originally the Old English adjective *læt* (*slow*) with the same ending.

The result of this movement toward identity in form was a confusion between the two classes of words, and from the time of Chaucer down to the Eighteenth Century one finds innumerable instances of the use of the simple adjective as an adverb. " He will answer *trewe* " is in Sir Thomas More; " and *soft* unto himself he sayd " in Chaucer; " the singers sang *loud* " in the Authorized Version of the Bible (Nehemiah xii, 42), and " *indifferent* well " in Shakespeare. Even after the purists of the Eighteenth Century began their corrective work this confusion continued. Thus one finds " The people are *miserable* poor " in Hume, " How *unworthy* you treated mankind " in the *Spectator*, and " *wonderful* silly " in Joseph Butler. To this day the grammarians battle against the amalgamation, still without complete success; every new volume of rules and regulations for those who would speak by the book is full of warnings against it. Among the great masses of the plain people, it goes without saying, it flourishes unimpeded. The cautions of the schoolmarm, in a matter so subtle and so plainly lacking in logic or necessary, are forgotten as quickly as her prohibition of the double negative, and thereafter the adjective and the adverb tend more and more to coalesce in a part of speech which serves the purposes of both, and is simple and intelligible and satisfying.

Charters gives a number of characteristic examples of its use: " wounded very *bad*," " I *sure* was stiff," " drank out of a cup *easy*," " He looked up *quick*." Many more are in Lardner: " a chance to see me work *regular*," " I am glad I was lucky enough to marry *happy*," " I beat them *easy*," and so on. And others fall upon the ear every day: " He done it *proper*," " He done himself *proud*," " They landed *safe*," "She drove *careless*," "They didn't know no *different*," "She was dressed *neat*," "She was *awful* ugly," "The horse ran *O.K.*," "It *near* finished him," "It sells *quick*," "I like it *fine*," "He et *hoggish*," "Everyone will be treated *fair*," "She acted *mean*," "He loved her something *fierce*," "They keep company *steady*," not to forget "Don't take it *serious*," which appeared some years ago in a song crooned by the once celebrated Rudy Vallée. The bob-tailed adverb, indeed, enters into a large number of the commonest coins of speech, and in many situations is perfectly " correct," though pedants may denounce it.[1] On the level of the vulgate there is an almost incomplete incapacity to distinguish any useful difference between adverb and adjective, and beneath it, perhaps, lies the similar incapacity to distinguish between the grammatical effects and relations of the common verb of being and those of any other verb. If " It *is* bad " is correct, then why should " It *leaks* bad " be incorrect? It is just this disdain of purely grammatical reasons that is at the bottom of most of the phenomena visible in vulgar American, and the same impulse is observable in all other languages during periods of inflectional decay. During the highly inflected stage of a language the parts of speech are sharply distinct, but when inflections fall off they tend to disappear. The adverb, being at best the step-child of grammar — as the old Latin grammarians used to say, *Omnis pars orationis migrat in adverbium* — is one of the chief victims of this anarchy. John Horne Tooke, despairing of bringing it to any order, even in the most careful English, called it, in his " Diversions of Purley," " the common sink and repository of all heterogeneous and unknown corruptions."

Where an obvious logical or lexical distinction has grown up between an adverb and its primary adjective the unschooled American is very careful to give it its terminal *-ly*. For example, he seldom confuses *hard* and *hardly*, *scarce* and *scarcely*, *real* and *really*. These words convey different ideas. *Hard* means unyielding; *hardly* means barely. *Scarce* means present only in small numbers; *scarcely* is substantially synonymous with *hardly*. *Real* means genuine; *really* is an

1 The case for it is stated with great eloquence by Wallace Rice in Go Slow — Proceed *Slowly*, *American Speech*, Sept., 1927. He cites a number of impeccable authorities in support of it. They agree, he shows, that the shortened form is usually good idiom whenever the adverb is stressed. " He is dying *slowly* " is sound, but so too is " How *slow* he dies." Thus *go slow* is justified, and so is *get-rich-quick*. *Get-rich-quickly* would sound feeble and banal.

assurance of veracity. So, again, with *late* and *lately*. Thus, an American says " I don't know, *scarcely*," not " I don't know, *scarce* "; " He died *lately*," not " He died *late*." [1] But in nearly all such cases syntax is the preservative, not grammar. These adverbs seem to keep their tails largely because they are commonly put before and not after verbs, as in, for example, " I *hardly* (or *scarcely*) know," and " I *really* mean it." Many other adverbs that take that position habitually are saved as well, for example, *generally, usually, surely, certainly*. But when they follow verbs they often succumb, as in " I'll do it sure," and when they appear in front of adjectives they usually succumb, too, as in " It was *sure* hot " and " I will write *real* soon." [2] Practically all the adverbs made of verbs in *-y* lose the terminal *-ly* and thus become identical with their adjectives. I have never heard *mightily* used; it is always *mighty*, as in " He hit him *mighty* hard." So with *filthy, dirty, nasty, lowly, naughty* and their cognates. One hears " He acted *dirty*," " He spoke *nasty*," " The child behaved *naughty*," and so on. Here even Standard English has had to make concessions to euphony. *Cleanlily* is seldom used; *cleanly* nearly always takes its place. And the use of *illy* and *thusly* is confined to the half educated. [3]

Vulgar American, like all the higher forms of American and all save the most precise form of written English, has abandoned the old inflections of *here, there* and *where*, to wit, *hither* and *hence*,

---

1 I have, however, noted " here *late* " for " here *lately*." But it is obviously derived from " here *of late*." The use of *real*, as in *real nice, real smart, real good*, etc., is an exception. But the American Legionary distinguishes between *real nice* and *really true*. He never says, " I *real* seen him."

2 That there is logical and historical justification for this is demonstrated by Robert C. Pooley in *Real* and *Sure* as Adverbs, *American Speech*, Feb., 1933. " No one," says Mr. Pooley, " ever says ' I will write *really* soon.' We may say ' I will write soon, *really*,' or ' I will *really* write soon,' but never ' I will write *really* soon.' It simply isn't English, grammar and grammarians notwithstanding."

3 Dr. Josiah Combs reports that

in the Southern mountains *-ly* is sometimes added to adverbs which lack it in Standard English, e.g., *ever*, as in " It has *everly* been the custom." But he adds: " This usage is rare, and is confined usually to Primitive Baptist syntax, when the preacher strikes an attitude, and attempts to place his language on stilts." See *Dialect Notes*, Vol. IV, Pt. IV, 1916, p. 288. In another paper (Language of the Southern Highlands, *Publications of the Modern Language Association*, Dec., 1931), Combs reports the use of adverbs as adjectives, as in " I'm as *gaily* as a girl " and " He feels *weakly*." This, of course, is nothing new in English: *poorly* has been used as an adjective, according to the Oxford Dictionary, since the Sixteenth Century.

thither and *thence, whither* and *whence.* These fossil remains of
dead cases are fast disappearing from the language. In the case of
hither (*to here*) even the preposition has been abandoned. One says,
not "I came *to here,*" but simply "I came *here.*" In the case of
hence, however, *from here* is still used, and so with *from there* and
from where. Finally, it goes without saying that the common American tendency to add *s* to such adverbs as *towards* is carried to full
length in the vulgar language. One constantly hears, not only *somewheres* and *forwards,* but even *noways* and *anyways, where'bouts*
and *here'bouts.* Here we have but one more example of the movement toward uniformity and simplicity. *Anyways* is obviously fully
supported by *sideways* and *always.* As for the dropping of the *a* of
about in *here'bouts* and *where'bouts,* it is supported by the analogous dropping of the *al* in *almost,* when the word precedes *all,
anyone* or *everybody.* One seldom hears "*Almost anyone* can do
that"; the common form is "*most anyone.*"[1]

7. THE DOUBLE NEGATIVE

In Vulgar American the double negative is so freely used that the
simple negative appears to be almost abandoned. Such phrases as
"I see nobody," "I could hardly walk," "I know nothing about it"
are heard so seldom among the masses of the people that they appear
to be affectations when encountered; the well-nigh universal forms
are "I *don't* see nobody," "I *couldn't* hardly walk," and "I *don't*
know nothing about it." Charters lists some very typical examples,
among them, "He ain't *never* coming back *no* more," "You *don't*
care for nobody but yourself," "Couldn't be *no* more happier" and
"I *can't* see nothing." In Lardner there are innumerable others:
"They was *not* no team," "I have *not* never thought of that," "I
can't write *no* more," "*No* chance to get *no* money from *nowhere,*"
"We *can't* have *nothing* to do," and so on. Some of his specimens
show a considerable complexity, for example, "Matthewson was
not only going as far as the coast," meaning, as the context shows,
that he was going as far as the coast and no farther. Many other
curious specimens are in my collectanea, among them: "One swaller

1 See Grammar and Usage in Text-
books on English, by Robert C.
Pooley; Madison, Wis., 1933, p. 136.

don't make *no* Summer," "I *never* seen nothing I would of rather
saw," and "Once a child gets burnt once it *won't* never stick its
hand in *no* fire *no* more," and so on. The last embodies a triple negative. In "You *don't* know *nobody* what don't want *nobody* to do
nothing for 'em, do you? there is a quadruplet, and in "I *ain't never*
done *no* dirt of *no* kind to *nobody*," reported from the Ozarks by
Vance Randolph, there is a quintuplet.

Like most other examples of "bad grammar" encountered in
American, the compound negative is of great antiquity and was
once quite respectable. The student of Old English encounters it
constantly. In that language the negative of the verb was formed
by prefixing a particle, *ne*. Thus, *singan* (*to sing*) became *ne singan*
(*not to sing*). In case the verb began with a vowel the *ne* dropped
its *e* and was combined with the verb; in case it began with an *h* or
a *w* followed by a vowel, the *h* or *w* of the verb and the *e* of *ne*
were both dropped, as in *næfth* (*has not*), from *ne-hæfth* (*not has*),
and *nolde* (*would not*), from *ne-wolde*. Finally, in case the vowel
following a *w* was *i*, it changed to *y*, as in *nyste* (*knew not*), from
ne-wiste. But inasmuch as Old English was a fully inflected language the inflections for the negative did not stop with the verbs;
the indefinite article, the indefinite pronoun and even some of the
nouns were also inflected, and survivors of those forms appear to
this day in such words as *none* and *nothing*. Moreover, when an
actual inflection was impossible it was the practice to insert this *ne*
before a word, in the sense of our *no* or *not*. Still more, it came to
be the practice to reinforce *ne*, before a vowel, with *na* (*not*) or
naht (*nothing*), which later degenerated to *nat* and *not*. As a result,
there were fearful and wonderful combinations of negatives, some
of them fully matching the best efforts of Lardner's baseball players.
Sweet gives several curious examples.[1] "*Nan ne* dorste *nan* thing
ascian," translated literally, becomes "*No* one dares *not* ask *nothing*." "Thæt hus *na ne* feoll" becomes "The house did *not* fall *not*."
As for the Middle English "He *never* nadde *nothing*," it has too
modern and familiar a ring to need translating at all. Chaucer, at
the beginning of the period of transition to Modern English, used
the double negative with the utmost freedom. In the prologue to
"The Knight's Tale" is this:

[1] A New English Grammar, Pt. I,
pp. 437-8.

Ne *nevere* yet *no* vileynye *ne* sayde
In al his lyf unto *no* maner wight.

By the time of Shakespeare this license was already much restricted, but a good many double negatives are nevertheless to be
found in his plays, and he was particularly shaky in the use of *nor*.
In "Richard III" one finds "I never was *nor never* will be"; in
"Measure for Measure," "Harp not on that *nor* do *not* banish trea-
son"; and in "Romeo and Juliet," "I will not budge for *no* man's
pleasure." Most of these have been expunged by ticklish editors, but
the double negative continues to flourish, not only in the vulgar
speech but also on higher levels. I turn to the *Congressional Record*
and at once find "*without hardly* the batting of an eye."[1] Indeed,
even such careful writers of English as T. H. Huxley, Robert Louis
Stevenson and Leslie Stephen have occasionally succumbed.[2] The
double negative is perfectly allowable in the Romance languages,
and now and then some anarchistic English grammarian boldly defends and even advocates it. A long time ago a writer in the *London
Review*[3] argued that its abandonment had worked "great injury
to strength of expression." Obviously, "I *won't* take *nothing*" is
stronger than either "I *will* take *nothing*" or "I *won't* take *anything*." And equally without doubt there is a picturesque charm, if
not really any extra vigor in the vulgar American "He *ain't* only got
but one leg," "I *ain't* scarcely got practically *nothing*," "She *never*
goes hardly *nowhere*," "Time is what we *ain't* got *nothing but*"
and "*Ain't nobody* there," the last, of course, being understood to
mean "There is no one there." "I *wouldn't* be surprised if it *didn't*
rain" is almost Standard American. So is the somewhat equivocal
form represented by "I have *never* been able to find *but* a single
copy."[4] In the Southern mountains the double negative flourishes
lushly. Here are some specimens submitted to a candid world by Dr.
Josiah Combs:[5]

He *ain't* got *nary none.*
Fotch-on [*i.e.*, educated] preachers *ain't never* a-goin' to do *nothin' nohow.*
I *hain't never* seen *no* men-folks of *no* kind do *no* washin' [of clothes].

1 Mr. Withrow of Wisconsin, March
28, 1935, p. 4881.
2 For some examples see The King's
English, by H. W. and F. G. Fowler, 2nd ed.; Oxford, 1908, p. 321 *ff.*
3 Oct. 1, 1864.
4 I take this, not from the *Congres-*

sional Record, but from Noah
Webster's Dissertations on the
English Language; Boston, 1789,
Pt. II, p. 150.
5 Old, Early and Elizabethan English, *Dialect Notes*, Vol. IV, Pt. IV,
1916, p. 284.

To which may be added the title of a once-popular song: "I ain't *never* done *nothing* to *nobody no* time." And the following contribution by Will Rogers: "*Neither don't* put anybody to work."[1] And the inquiry of a storekeeper in Washington county, Virginia, supplied by Mr. Carl Zeisberg, of Glenside, Pa.: "There *wouldn't* be *nothing* I *couldn't* show you, you *don't* think?" Says Mr. Zeisberg: "I think I know the reason for these complex negatives: their genesis lies in an innate consideration for the customer's wishes, an excessive timidity."

8. OTHER SYNTACTICAL PECULIARITIES

"Language begins," says Sayce, "with sentences, not with single words." In a speech in process of rapid development, unrestrained by critical analysis, the tendency to sacrifice the integrity of words to the needs of the complete sentence is especially marked. One finds it clearly in vulgar American. Already we have examined various assimilation and composition forms: *that'n, use'to, woulda, them'ere,* and so on. Many others are observable. *Off'n* is a good example; it comes from *off of* or *off from* and shows a preposition decaying to the form of a mere inflectional particle. One constantly hears "I bought it *off'n* John." *Sorta, kinda, coupla, outa* and their like follow in the footsteps of *woulda. Usen't* follows the analogy of *don't* and *wouldn't,* as in "I didn't *usen't* to be." *Would've* and *should've* are widely used; Lardner commonly heard them as *would of* and *should of.* The neutral *a*-particle also appears in other situations, especially before *way,* as in *that-a way, this-a way* and *atta-boy.* It is found again in *a tall,* a liaison form of *at all.*[2] It most often represents *of* or *have,* but sometimes it represents *to,* as in *orta* and *gonta* (going to). There are philologians who believe that the appearance of such particles indicates that English, having shed most of its old inflections, is now entering upon a new inflected stage. "Form," says George O. Curme,[3] "is now playing a greater rôle than in early Modern English. The simplification of our English, our most precious heritage, was carried a little too far in older English, and

1 New York *Times,* Aug. 20, 1934.
2 *At all* is often displaced by *any* or *none,* as "He don't love her *any,*" and "It didn't hurt me *none.*"

3 Parts of Speech and Accidence; Boston, 1935, p. v.

it was later found necessary to add more forms, and in the present interesting period of development still more are being created." "The articulatory words of a purely positional language," adds George Kingsley Zipf,[1] "will tend in time to become agglutinized to the words they modify, and through agglutinization become inflectional affixes. . . . As they become more firmly agglutinized they become more formally inflections which modify the meaning of the word to which they are appended. The use of the affix is extended to other words to modify their meaning in the same direction. The language thus becomes more and more inflected." Dr. Zipf calls this "the grand cycle in linguistic development," and believes that English is now on the up-curve. A study of liaison in spoken American — for example, the use of *farzino* for *as far as I know*, noted by David Humphreys in his glossary so long ago as 1815 — should throw some light upon this process, but that study still lags.[2]

Many of the forms that the grammatical pedants rail against most vehemently — for example, the split infinitive, the use of *between*, *either* and *neither* with more than one, the use of *than* after *different*, the use of *like* for *as*, and so on — are so firmly established in the American vulgate that the schoolmarm's attempts to put them down are plainly hopeless. Most of them, in fact, have crept into more or less elegant usage, and such reformers as Robert C. Pooley and Janet Rankin Aiken argue boldly that the war upon them should be abandoned. So long ago as 1872, the peppery Fitzedward Hall demonstrated, in his "Recent Exemplifications of False Philology," that *different than* had been used by Addison, Steele, Defoe, Richardson, Miss Burney, Coleridge, De Quincey, Thackeray and Newman, yet most of the current textbooks of "correct" English continue to denounce it. In September, 1922, the novelist, Meredith Nicholson, joined in the *jehad* against it in a letter to the New York *Herald:*

Within a few years the abominable phrase *different than* has spread through the country like a pestilence. In my own Indiana, where the wells of English undefiled are jealously guarded, the infection has awakened general alarm.

1 The Psycho-Biology of Language; Boston, 1935.
2 My files show only one published article on the subject, and that one is by a layman. He is Hugh Mearns, and his article, Our Own, Our Native Speech, was published in *McClure's Magazine*, Oct., 1916. Some rather elaborate investigations of liaison have been made by Mr. Harry Gwynn Morehouse, but they remain, I believe, unpublished. It is, of course, discussed incidentally in many treatises on American.

To which the New York *Sun*, a few days later, replied sensibly:

> The excellent tribe of grammarians, the precisians and all others who strive to be correct and correctors, have as much power to prohibit a single word or phrase as a gray squirrel has to put out Orion with a flicker of its tail.

The error of Mr. Nicholson, and of all such unhappy viewers with alarm, is in assuming that there is enough magic in pedagogy to teach " correct " English to the plain people. There is, in fact, far too little; even the fearsome abracadabra of Teachers' College, Columbia, will never suffice for the purpose. The plain people, hereafter as in the past, will continue to make their own language, and the best that grammarians can do is to follow after it, haltingly, and not often with much insight into it. Their lives would be more comfortable if they ceased to repine over it, and instead gave it some hard study. It is very amusing, and not a little instructive.

X

PROPER NAMES IN AMERICA

1. SURNAMES

On October 20, 1919, Mr. Mondell of Wyoming, then the majority leader, arose in the House of Representatives and called the attention of the House to the presence in the gallery of a detachment of 27 soldiers, " popularly known by the appropriate title and designation of Americans All." A few moments later Mr. Wilson of Connecticut had the names of these soldiers spread upon the record for the day. Here they are:

Pedro Arez	Frank Kristopoulos
Sylvester Balchunas	Johannes Lenferink
Arezio Aurechio	Fidel Martin
Jules Boutin	Attilio Marzi
Oasge Christiansen	Gurt Mistrioty
Kusti Franti	Michael Myatowych
Odilian Gosselin	Francisco Pungi
Walter Hucko	Joseph Rossignol
Argele Intili	Ichae Semos
Henry Jurk	Joe Shestak
David King	George Strong
John Klok	Hendrix Svennigsen
Norman Kerman	Fritz Wold
Eugene Kristiansen	

This was no unusual group of Americans, though it was deliberately assembled to convince Congress of the existence of a " melting pot that really melts." I turn to the list of promotions in the Army, sent to the Senate on January 10, 1935, and find *Taulbee, Bamberger, Lecocq, Brandt, Thuis, Campanole, Mauborgne, Cocheu, Wuest, Boschen, Schudt, Andruss, Ahrends* and *Mueller* among the new colonels, and *Plassmeyer, Munnikhuysen, Eichelberger, Schillerstrom, Koenig, Van Deusen, Goetz, Bluemel, Mercader, Milam, Ramee, Shurtleff* and *Selleck* among the new lieutenant-colonels. I proceed to the roll of the Seventy-fourth Congress and find *Bachman, Bilbo, Borah, Bulow, Dieterich, La Follette, Norbeck, Schall,*

Schwellenbach, Steiwer, Vandenberg, Van Nuys and *Wagner* in the Senate, and *Arends, Bacharach, Beiter, Biermann, Binderup, Boehne, Boileau, Brunner, Bulwinkle, Cavicchia, Carlson, Celler, Christianson, Citron, DeRouen, Dickstein, Dietrich, Dirksen, Ditter, Dockweiler, Dondero, Doutrich, Eckert, Eichner, Ekwall, Ellenbogen, Engel, Engelbright, Fernandez, Focht, Gasque, Gearhart, Gehrmann, Hildebrandt, Hoeppel, Hoffman, Imhoff, Jacobsen, Kahn, Keller, Kinzer, Kleberg, Kloeb, Knutson, Kocialkowski, Kopplemann, Kramer, Kvale, Lamneck, Lehlbach, Lemke, Lesinski, Lundeen, Maas, Marcantonio, Montet, Moritz, Palmisano, Peyser, Pfeifer, Rabaut, Ramspeck, Romjue, Sabath, Sadowski, Sauthoff, Schaefer, Schneider, Schuetz, Schulte, Seger, Sirovich, Sutphin, Utterback, Wallgren, Werner, Wolfenden, Zimmerman* and *Zioncheck* in the House. I go on to the roster of the National Institute of Arts and Letters (1935) and find *Becker, Benét, Cortissoz, Ferber, Hagedorn, Keller, Lefevre, Repplier, Sandburg, Schelling* and *Wister* among the literati, *Beaux, Dielman, DuMond, Groll, Guerin, Johansen, Jennewein, Kroll, Laessle, La Farge, Lie, Marr, Niehaus, Patigian, Roth, Speicher, Sterner, Volk, Vonnoh* and *Weinman* among the painters and sculptors, and *Damrosch, Kroeger, Loeffler, Oldberg, Schelling, Stock* and *Stoessel* among the musicians. I conclude with a glance through "Who's Who in America" for 1934–35, confining myself to the A's, and quickly unearth *Aasgaard, Abbé, Abrams, Abt, Acher, Ackerman, Adami, Adler, Adolphe, Adoue, Affleck, Agar, Agassiz, Aggeler, Agger, Ahl, Ahrens, Aigler, Albaugh, Aldrin, Almstedt, Alsberg, Alschuler, Altaffer, Alter, Althoff, Althouse, Altschul, Amateis, Amberg, Ameli, Amerman, Amstutz, Amweg, Anceney, Anders, Andress, Andrus, Angeli, Angelliotti, Angier, Angstman, Ansorge, Anspach, Anspacher, Anstadt, App, Appenzellar, Appleget, Arant, Archambault, Arendt, Arensberg, Arentz, Argow, Armbruster, Armentrout, Arn, Arnstein, Artman, Ascher, Asplund, Auer, Auerbach, Auf der Heide, Ault, Auman, Auringer, Authier* and *Aydelotte* – all "notable living men and women of the United States," and all native-born. If I took in the foreign-born I might add *Abbate, Achi, Adamowski, Agersborg, Aguinaldo, Alencastre, Altglass, Altrocchi, Amateis, Angoff, Aronovici, Aronstam, Arrighi, Asakawa, Askenstedt, Avancena* and *Avinoff*.

Almost any other list of Americans, covering the whole country, would show as large a proportion of non-British surnames. Indeed, every American telephone directory offers evidence that, despite the continued cultural and political preponderance of the original English strain, the American people, as a London weekly was saying nearly a generation ago, have ceased to be " predominantly of British stock." [1] The blood in their arteries is inordinately various and inextricably mixed, but yet not mixed enough to run a clear stream. A touch of foreignness still lingers about millions of them, even in the country of their birth. They show their alien origin in their domestic customs, in their habits of mind, and in their very names. Just as the Scotch and the Welsh have invaded England, elbowing out the actual English to make room for themselves, so the Irish, the Germans, the Italians, the Scandinavians and the Jews of Eastern Europe, and in some areas, the French, the Slavs and the hybrid-Spaniards have elbowed out the descendants of the first colonists. It is no exaggeration, indeed, to say that wherever the old stock comes into direct and unrestrained conflict with one of these new stocks, it tends to succumb. The Irish, in the big cities of the East, attained to a political hegemony before the first native-born generation of them had grown up.[2] The Germans, following the limestone belt of the Allegheny foothills, preëmpted the best lands East of the mountains before the new Republic was born. And in our own time we have seen the Swedes and Norwegians shouldering the natives from the wheat lands of the Northwest, and the Italians driving the decadent New Englanders from their farms, and the Jews gobbling New York, and the Slavs getting a firm foothold in the mining regions and disputing with the Irish for Chicago, and the French Canadians penetrating New Hampshire and Vermont, and the Japanese and Portuguese menacing Hawaii. The birth-rate among all these foreign stocks, though it is falling, is still appreciably greater than among the older stock, and though the death-rate is also somewhat above the white average, the net increase remains considerable. Even with immigration cut off it is probable that they will continue to rise in numbers faster than the original English and so-called Scotch-Irish.

1 London *Nation,* March 12, 1912. In Ch. XII the census returns of the foreign-born and of persons of foreign or mixed parentage are given.
2 The great Irish famine, which launched the chief emigration to America, extended from 1845 to 1847. The Know Nothing movement, which was chiefly aimed at the Irish, extended from 1852 to 1860.

Smith remains the predominant surname in the United States, followed by *Johnson, Brown, Williams, Jones, Miller, Davis, Anderson, Wilson* and *Moore* in order, but five of these have been heavily reinforced by non-English names. " One in every eighty-eight Americans," says Howard F. Barker, research associate of the American Council of Learned Societies,[1] " is now a *Smith*, but only a little better than half could trace their ancestry to the British Isles." The rest are German *Schmidts*, Scandinavian *Smeds*, Czech *Kovárs*, Hungarian *Kovácses*, Syrian *Haddads* and Polish *Kowalczyks*, and Jews who have sought escape from German or Slavic names. " Many a *Johnson*," continues Mr. Barker, " who traces his ancestry will find himself an Irish *McShane*, a Swedish *Johansson*, or a Dutch or Danish *Jansen*. By reason of these conversions *Johnson* has become our second most popular surname and the only name beside *Smith* to be borne by over a million Americans." He goes on:

A large proportion of our *Millers* would be more exactly known as *Müller, Mühler* or *Möller*, and another substantial group as *Millar*. . . . *Moore*, starting with fair backing in England and Ireland, has proceeded to acquire most of the usage belonging to the English *Moor* and *More*, the Scotch *Muir*, and the German *Moor, Mohr* and *Möhr*.

In the same way *Anderson* has assimilated many non-British names of similar etymology and sound, *e.g.*, *Andresen, Andriessen, Andersohn, Andersson*, and so on. In St. Paul and Minneapolis it now ranks second among surnames, being preceded only by *Johnson*, with *Nelson* and *Peterson* following. *Johnson* also leads in Chicago, with *Smith, Anderson, Miller* and *Brown* following. In New York as a whole the leaders run: *Smith, Cohen, Miller, Brown, Schwartz*. Many of the *Browns*, of course, were originally *Brauns, Braunsteins*, and the like. In Boston *Smith* is followed by *Sullivan, Brown, Johnson* and *Murphy*. In New Orleans it is followed, rather inexplicably, by *Levy*, with *Miller* and *Williams* following. In Cincinnati *Meyer* is in third place. In Philadelphia *Miller* is in second place, and in

1 Surnames in the United States, *American Mercury*, June, 1932, p. 228. Mr. Barker's ingenious studies of American surnames have uncovered a great deal of new material, and are marked by wide knowledge and shrewd judgment. His principal work, National Stocks in the Population of the United States as Indicated by Surnames in the Census of 1790, is part of the Report of the Committee [of the American Council of Learned Societies] On Linguistic and National Stocks in the Population of the United States, printed by the Government Printing Office; Washington, 1932.

San Francisco it is in fourth.[1] There have been notable changes during the past quarter century. In 1913 *Cohen* was in eighth place in New York City; it has now moved to second.[2] In Boston *Murphy* was in third place in 1913; it has now been displaced by *Brown* and *Johnson*, which then followed it.[3]

In 1928 Mr. Barker estimated that there were then 66,250,000 persons in the country using English and Welsh names, and that of the number 41,550,000 had got them by ancient inheritance, 7,500,000 were Negroes whose forebears had assumed them, and 17,200,000 were whites who had adopted them themselves, or got them from fathers or grandfathers who had adopted them. At the same time he estimated that, of the 18,000,000 persons bearing Irish names, 15,750,000 had got them by inheritance, 1,300,000 were Negroes, and 950,000 were whites who had them by adoption, and that, of the 8,800,000 bearing Scottish names, 6,600,000 had them by inheritance, 1,200,000 were Negroes, and 1,000,000 had them by adoption.[4] Changes in surnames go on in all countries, and at all times. They are effected very largely by transliteration or translation. Thus the name of *Taaffe*, familiar in Austrian history, had an Irish prototype, probably *Taft*. General *Demikof*, one of the Russian commanders at the battle of Zorndorf, in 1758, was a Swede born *Themicoud*, and no doubt the founder of the house in Sweden was a Frenchman. Edvard *Grieg*, the Norwegian composer, had a Scotch forefather named *Craig*. Franz Maria von *Thugut*, the Austrian diplomatist, was a member of an Italian Tyrolese family named *Tunicotto*. This became *Thunichgut* (*do no good*) in Austria, and was changed to *Thugut* (*do good*) to bring it into greater accord with its possessor's deserts. In *Bonaparte* the Italian *buon(o)* became the French *bon*. The family is said to have come from

1 Our Leading Surnames, by Howard F. Barker, *American Speech*, June, 1926.
2 In the Borough of Brooklyn *Cohen* is actually in first place. See the New York *Times*, Feb. 28, 1933. The count was made on a grant from the Emergency Unemployment Relief Committee. *Miller* was in third place, followed by *Brown* and *Jones*. In the 200-card set of guide-cards sold for office use only *Smith*, *Brown* and *Cohen* have cards of their own. Herbert Asbury

says in All Around the Town; New York, 1934, p. 272, that the first New York City directory, published in 1786, showed the names of seven *Smiths*, one *Kelly*, and one *Brown*, but no *Cohen*.
3 For the 1913 ranking see the *World Almanac* for 1914, p. 668.
4 How We Got Our Surnames, by Howard F. Barker, *American Speech*, Oct., 1928, and How the American Changes His Name, by the same, *American Mercury*, Sept., 1935.

Southern Greece to Corsica, and to have been named *Kalomeris* originally. Of this, *Buonaparte* was simply an Italian translation. Many familiar English surnames are Anglicized forms of Norman-French names, for example, *Sidney* from *St. Denis, Divver* from *De Vere, Bridgewater* from *Burgh de Walter, Garnett* from *Guarinot,* and *Seymour* from *Saint-Maure.* A large number of so-called Irish names are similarly the products of rough-and-ready transliterations of Gaelic patronymics, for example, *Findlay* from *Fionnlagh, Dermott* from *Diarmuid,* and *McLane* from *Mac Illeathiain.* In the United States, with a language of peculiar vowel-sounds and even consonant-sounds struggling against a foreign invasion unmatched for strength and variety, such changes have been far more numerous than across the ocean, and the legal rule of *idem sonans* is of much wider utility than anywhere else in the world. If it were not for that rule there would be endless difficulties for the *Wises* whose grandfathers were *Weisses,* and the *Leonards* born *Leonhards, Leonhardts* or *Lehnerts,* and the *Manneys* who descend and inherit from *Le Maines.*

"What changes names most," says Mr. Barker, "is the abrasion of common speech." They tend almost inevitably to be assimilated with more familiar names of like, or nearly like sound, and folk etymology often helps along the process. Thus the *Thurgods,* in the course of years, have become *Thoroughgoods,* and the German *Todenackers* have become the Pennsylvania *Toothachers,* and the Jewish *Jonases* have joined the tribe of *Jones,* and the Dutch *Wittenachts* have become the Kentucky *Whitenecks.* In Pennsylvania, says Mr. Barker, "*Bachmann* was first 'improved' as *Baughman,* promptly misunderstood as *Boughman* (pronounced to rhyme with *ploughman*), and then more easily spelled *Bowman,* which made possible one more shift in pronunciation." The original *Herkimer* in New York was a *Herchheimer;* the original *Waldo* in New England was a German named *Waldow.* Edgar Allan *Poe,* it has been alleged, was a member of a family settled in Western Maryland, the founder being one *Poh* or *Pfau,* a native of the Palatinate. Major George *Armistead,* who defended Fort McHenry in 1814, when Francis Scott Key wrote "The Star-Spangled Banner," was the descendant of an *Armstädt* who came to Virginia from Hesse-Darmstadt. John *Morton,* one of the signers of the Declaration of Independence, had a Finnish grandfather named *Marttinen.* Harriet *Lane*

Johnson was the descendant of Pennsylvania Germans named *Lehn*. General George A. *Custer*, the Indian fighter, was the great-grandson of one *Küster*, a Hessian soldier paroled after Burgoyne's surrender. William *Wirt*, anti-Masonic candidate for the Presidency in 1832, was the son of a German named *Wörth*. General J. J. *Pershing* is the descendant of a German named Friedrich *Pfoersching*, who immigrated to Pennsylvania in 1749; the name was at first debased to *Pershin*, but in 1838 the final g was restored.[1] General W. S. *Rosecrans* was really *Rosenkrantz*. General James *Longstreet* was the descendant of one Dirck Stoffels *Langestraet* who came to New Amsterdam in 1657. Herbert C. *Hoover* was the great-great-great-grandson of Andreas *Huber*, a German who settled in Lancaster county, Pennsylvania, in 1740. "In colonial times," says Mr. Barker, "some of the *Hubers* remained as such, but most changed to *Hoover*, some to *Hover*, others to *Hoober, Hoeber* and even *Hoofer*." Joshua *Levering*, Prohibition candidate for the Presidency in 1896, was descended from Pennsylvania German *Lieberings*. Samuel W. *Pennypacker*, Governor of Pennsylvania (1903–07), was descended from a Dutch *Pannebacker* who reached Pennsylvania before 1700. Edmund Burke *Fairfield*, once chancellor of the University of Nebraska, had a French forefather named *Beauchamp*. Even the surname of Abraham *Lincoln*, according to some authorities, was an anglicized form of the German *Linkhorn*.[2]

1 See The Name *Pershing*, by J. H. A. Lacher, *American Speech*, Aug., 1926, and *Pershing* Again, by the same, *American Speech*, May, 1927. Mr. Lacher tells me that there is no reason to believe that this *Stammvater Pfoersching* was an Alsatian, as the general appears to think. He arrived on Oct. 2, 1749 on the ship *Jacob*, Captain Adolph de Grove, from Amsterdam via Shields, England. It brought 290 passengers, and they were described as "from Swabia, Wirtemberg and Darmstadt."

2 See The German Element in the United States, by A. B. Faust; New York, 1909, Vol. II, pp. 183–4. Now and then the story goes round that *Roosevelt* is a Jewish name, originally *Rossacampo*. The Rooseveltii, it is said, were expelled from Spain in 1620, and sought refuge in Holland, Germany and other Northern countries, where their surname was changed to *Rosenfeldt, Rosenbau, Rosenblum, Rosenvelt* and *Rosenthal*. In Holland it finally became *Roosevelt*, and all branches of the family save one were baptized. When this story was published in 1935, on the authority of Chase S. Osborn, former Governor of Michigan, the editor of the Detroit *Jewish Chronicle* applied to President Franklin D. Roosevelt for light. The President's reply, dated March 7, 1935, was as follows: "All I know about the origin of the Roosevelt family in this country is that all branches bearing the name are apparently descended from Claes Martenssen Van Roosevelt, who came from Holland sometime

Such changes have been almost innumerable in the United States; every work upon American genealogy is full of examples. The first foreign names to undergo the process were Dutch and French. When, in 1664, the English drove the Dutch out of New Amsterdam, their property and their surnames were both at the mercy of the invaders. Some of the wealthier and more resolute of them, dug in up the Hudson, resisted both forms of spoliation with great pertinacity, and in consequence a number of their names survive to this day, along with some of their money — for example, *Van Rensselaer*, *Stuyvesant*, *Ten Eyck* and *Schuyler*. But the lesser folk were helpless, and in a little while most of the *Kuipers* were *Coopers*, nearly all the *Haerlens* were *Harlands*, and many of the *Van Arsdales*, *Van de Veers* and *Reigers* were *Vannersdales*, *Vandivers* and *Rikers*.[1] Among the French in New England there were similar transmogrifications, and *Petit* changed to *Poteet*, *Caillé* to *Kyle*, *De La Haye* to *Dillehay*, *Dejean* to *Deshong*, *Guizot* to *Gossett*, *Soulé* to *Sewell*, *Gervaise* to *Jarvis*, *Bayle* to *Bailey*, *Fontaine* to *Fountain*, and *Denis* to *Denny*. " Frenchmen and French Canadians who came to New England," says Schele de Vere, " had to pay for such hospitality as they there received by the sacrifice of their names. The brave *Bon Cœur*, Captain Marryatt tells us in his Diary, became Mr. *Bunker*, and gave his name to Bunker's Hill.[2] *Pibaudière* was changed

---

before 1648 — even the year is uncertain. Where he came from in Holland I do not know, nor do I know who his parents were. There was a family of the same name on one of the Dutch islands and some of the same name living in Holland as lately as 30 or 40 years ago, but, frankly, I have never had either the time or the inclination to try to establish the line on the other side of the ocean before they came over here, nearly 300 years ago. In the dim distant past they may have been Jews or Catholics or Protestants — what I am more interested in is whether they were good citizens and believers in God — I hope they were both." See the *Congressional Record*, March 15, 1933, p. 3915.
1 Among the early New Amsterdam Dutch, surnames were in a state of flux. " They wavered," says Barker in Surnames in the United States, *American Mercury*, June, 1932, p. 226, " from patronym to descriptive, as from *Jansen*, *Cornielsen* and *Hendricksen* to *Blauvelt*, *Ten Eyck* or *Van Buren*, and back again, as well as from patronym to patronym. When twenty years of English rule had influenced them to adopt the English manner, they generally settled on the descriptive, but without any unanimity regarding spelling or the retention of the *van* if this was involved."
2 Here Marryatt and Schele de Vere seem to have slipped. Dr. S. E. Morison, whose authority in Massachusetts history is undisputed, tells me that the hill was really named after George *Bunker*, who came to Charlestown from England before 1635.

into *Peabody*, *Bon Pas* into *Bumpus*, and the haughty *de l'Hôtel* became a genuine Yankee under the guise of *Doolittle*."[1] But it was the German immigration, beginning in 1683, and rising largely after 1717, that provoked the first really wholesale slaughter. The captains of ships landing at Philadelphia were required to furnish the authorities with lists of their passengers, and after 1727 this order was usually complied with. In addition, every immigrant was required to subscribe to an oath of allegiance, and to another abjuring the Church of Rome. Thus three lists of names were produced, and in recent years they have been published.[2] But when the newcomers got to the Pennsylvania uplands their names were barbarously manhandled by the officials, usually Scotch-Irish, of the local courts and other offices of record. Almost every *Johannes Kuntz* of the ship lists thus became a *John Coons* in the interior, and every *Pfeffer* a *Pepper*, and every *Schmidt* a *Smith*. The names including the more characteristic German sounds, impossible to the British larynx — for example, the guttural in *ch* and *g* — were under especially heavy pressure. Thus, *Bloch* was changed to *Block* or *Black*, *Hoch* to *Hoke*, *Albrecht* to *Albert* or *Albright*, and *Steinweg* to *Steinway*, and the *Grundwort*, *bach*, was almost always turned into *baugh* or *paugh*, as in *Baughman* and *Fishpaugh* (or *Fishpaw*). The *ü* met the same fate: *Grün* was changed to *Green*, *Sänger* to *Sanger* or *Singer*, *Glück* to *Gluck*, *Wärner* to *Warner*, *Löwe* to *Lowe*, *Brühl* to *Brill*, *Stäheli* to *Staley*, *Düring* to *Deering*, and *Schnäbele* to *Snabely*, *Snavely* or *Snively*.[3] In many other cases there were changes in spelling to preserve vowel sounds differently represented in German and English. Thus, *Blum* was changed to *Bloom*, *Alt* to *Ault*, *Reuss* to *Royce*, *Koester* to

1 Americanisms; New York, 1872, p. 112. A few years ago Professor Atcheson L. Hench of the University of Virginia discovered Schele de Vere's own copy of this work in the university library, with annotations in his hand. He listed, apparently for a revised edition that never appeared, some other curious changes, *e.g.*, *Ainse* to *Hanks*, *St. Cyr* to *Sears*, *Monat* to *Miner*, *L'Auvergne* to *Lovern*, *Dudelant* to *Douglas*, *Henri Livernois d'Oligney* to *Hy Alden*, and *Jean Baptiste Sans Souci l'Evêque* to *John Lavake*. I am indebted to Professor Hench for this.

2 Pennsylvania German Pioneers: a Publication of the Original Lists of Arrivals in the Port of Philadelphia From 1727 to 1808, edited by W. J. Hinke; 3 vols.; Norristown, Pa., 1934.

3 The name of August *Lüchow*, founder of the famous German restaurant in Fourteenth street, New York, is almost invariably pronounced *Loo-chow* in the town. Ask a taxi-driver to take you to *Lüchow's*, and he will stare at you blankly. This change was promoted by the prudent dropping of the umlaut from the sign of the establishment in 1917.

Kester, Kuehle to Keeley, Schroeder to Schrader, Stehli to Staley, Weymann to Wayman, Klein to Kline or Cline, Friedmann to Freedman, Bauman to Bowman, Braun to Brown, and Lang (as the best compromise possible) to Long. The change of Oehm to Ames belongs to the same category; the addition of the final *s* represents a typical effort to substitute the nearest related Anglo-Saxon name, or name so sounding. Other examples of that effort are to be found in *Michaels* for *Michaelis*, *Bowers* for *Bauer*, *Johnson* for *Johannsen*, *Ford* for *Furth*, *Hines* for *Heintz*, *Kemp* for *Kempf*, *Foreman* for *Führmann*, *Kuhns* or *Coons* for *Kuntz*, *Grosscup* for *Grosskopf*, *Westfall* for *Westphal*, *Rockefeller* for *Roggenfelder*,[1] *Kerngood* for *Kerngut*, *Collenberg* for *Kaltenberg*, *Cronkhite* for *Krankheit*, *Betts* for *Betz*, *Crile* for *Kreil*, *Swope* for *Schwab*, *Hite* or *Hyde* for *Heid*, and *Young* for *Jung*.[2] The early German immigrants had no very definite ideas about the spelling of their own names. Many variant forms are to be found in the Pennsylvania records. " They were easily swayed," says Barker, " in the use of vowels, converting from one to another.[3] They also shifted from one consonant to another within limits, as from *p* or *b* to *f*, or from *d* to *t*, or vice versa." [4]

1 The researches of the late Stephen Kekulé von Stradonitz showed that the original American *Rockefeller* was a German *Roggenfelder* (ryefielder) from the lower Rhine.
2 Many more such transliterations and modifications are listed by A. B. Faust, in The German Element in the United States, above cited, particularly in his first volume. Others are in Pennsylvania Dutch, by S. S. Haldemann; London, 1872, p. 60, and in The Origin of Pennsylvania Surnames, by L. Oscar Kuhns, *Lippincott's Magazine*, March, 1897, p. 395. See also Studies in Pennsylvania German Family Names, by the last named (his list is reprinted in Report of the Committee [of the American Council of Learned Societies] on Linguistic and National Stocks in the Population of the United States; Washington, 1932, p. 312 *ff*); Deutsche Familiennamen unter fremden Völkern, by Stephan Kekulé von Stradonitz, *Mitteilungen der Aka-*

demie zur wissenschaftlichen Erforschung und zur Pflege des Deutschtums (Munich), April–May, 1928; and Deutsche Namen in Amerika, by the same, B.-Z. am *Mittag* (Berlin), Sept. 22, 1927.
3 For example, *Schultz* often appeared in the early Pennsylvania records as *Scholtz*, *Shiltz* and *Shoultz*.
4 In the records of St. Paul's Lutheran Church, Arcadia, Md., founded *c.* 1770 (Twenty-third Report of the Society For the History of the Germans in Maryland; Baltimore, 1929, pp. 27–28) there are some curious variants from the period 1790–1825. Thus a name which now appears as *Algire* was then *Allgeiger*, *Algeier*, *Allgeier*, *Allgeyer* and *Allgire*, an *Elsroad* of today was *Eltzroth*, *Elseroad*, *Elserote*, *Elserode* and *Elsrode*, and a *Loudenslager* of today was *Lautenschläger*, *Laudensläger*, *Laudenschläger*, *Lautenschleger* and *Laudenslager*. I once knew a *Lautenberger* whose name had shrunk to

Even when no accent betrays it, the foreign diphthong is under hard pressure. Thus the German *oe* disappears and *Loeb* is changed to *Lobe* or *Laib*, *Oehler* to *Ohler*, *Loeser* to *Leser*, *Schoen* to *Schon* or *Shane*, and *Mueller* to *Miller* or *Muller*, as in Whittier's "Maud Muller" (1866). The *k* in German words beginning with *kn* tends to disappear: they are assimilated with the old Devonshire surname, *Knapp*. Thus *Knoebel* is often pronounced *Noble*. In the same way the German *sch* shrinks to *s*, and *Schneider* becomes *Snyder*, *Schlegel* becomes *Slagel*, and *Schluter* becomes *Sluter*. If a German or other foreigner in America clings to the original spelling of his name he must usually expect to hear it mispronounced. *Roth*, in America, quickly becomes *Rawth*, *Ranft* is pronounced *Ranf*; *Frémont*, losing both accent and the French *e*, becomes *Fremont*; *Blum* begins to rhyme with *dumb*; *Mann* rhymes with *van*, and *Lang* with *hang*; *Krantz*, *Lantz* and their cognates with *chance*; *Kurtz* with *shirts*; the first syllable of *Gutmann* with *but*; the first of *Kahler* with *bay*; the first of *Werner* with *turn*; the first of *Wagner* with *nag*. *Uhler*, in America, is always *Youler*. *Berg* loses its German *e*-sound for an English *u*-sound, and its German hard *g* for an English *g*; it becomes identical with the *berg* of *iceberg*. The same change in the vowel occurs in *Erdmann*. In *König* the German diphthong succumbs to a long *o*, and the hard *g* becomes *k*; the common pronunciation is *Cone-ik*. Often, in *Berger*, the *g* becomes soft, and the name rhymes with *verger*. It becomes soft, too, in *Bittinger*. In *Anheuser* the *eu* changes to *ow* or *ei*. The final *e*, important in German, is nearly always silenced; *Dohme* rhymes with *foam*; *Kühne* becomes *Keen*. In the collectanea of Judge J. C. Ruppenthal, of Russell, Kansas, a very careful observer, are many curious specimens. He finds *Viereck* transformed into *Fearhake*, *Vogelgesang* into *Fogelsong*, *Pfannenstiel* into *Fanestil*, *Pfüger* into *Phlegar*, *Pfeil* into *Feil*, and *Steinmetz* into *Stimits*. I have myself encountered *Isennock* for *Eisenach*, and *Duttera*, *Dutterer*, *Dotterer* and *Dutrow* (all in one family!) for *Dötterer*.[1]

In addition to these transliterations there are constant translations of foreign proper names. "Many a Pennsylvania *Carpenter*," says Dr. S. Grant Oliphant, "bearing a surname that is English, from

Lauten, pro. *Lawton*. What is now *Upperco* in Maryland was once *Oberkugen, Opferkuchen, Oberkuchen*.

1 Westminster (Md.) *Democratic Advance*, Aug. 10, 1934.

the French, from the Latin, and there a Celtic loan-word in origin, is neither English, nor French, nor Latin, nor Celt, but an original German *Zimmermann*." [1] A great many other such translations are under everyday observation. *Pfund* becomes *Pound; Becker, Baker; Schumacher, Shoemaker; König, King; Koch, Cook;* [2] *Newmann, Newman; Schaefer, Shepherd* or *Sheppard; Meister, Master(s); Schwartz, Black; Weiss, White; Kurtz, Short; Weber, Weaver; Bucher, Booker; Vogelgesang, Birdsong; Sonntag, Sunday,* [3] and so on. It is not unusual for some members of a family to translate the patronymic while others leave it unchanged. Thus, in Pennsylvania (and no doubt elsewhere) there are *Carpenters* and *Zimmermans* of the same blood. Partial translations are also encountered, *e.g., Studebaker* from *Studebecker*, and *Reindollar* from *Rheinthaler*, and radical shortenings, *e.g., Swiler* from *Lebenschweiler, Kirk* from *Kirkeslager*, and *Castle* (somewhat fantastically) from *Katzenellenbogen*. The same processes show themselves in the changes undergone by the names of the newer immigrants. The Hollanders in Michigan often have to submit to translations of their surnames. Thus *Hoogsteen* becomes *Highstone; Roos, Rose; Veldhuis, Fieldhouse; Huisman, Houseman; Prins, Prince; Kuiper, Cooper; Zwartefoote, Blackfoot; Zilvernagel, Silvernail; Bredevelt, Brookfreed; Wagenaar, Wagner; Dÿkhuis, Dykehouse; Koning, King; Werkman, Workman; Nieuwhuis, Newhouse;* and *Christiaanse, Christians.* [4] Similarly the Greek *Triantafyllou* (signifying *rose*) is often turned into *Rose, Mylonas* becomes *Miller*, and *Giannopoulos* (the descendant of *Giannis*, or *Ioannis*) becomes *Johnson*. The Greek surnames are often very long, and in American they have to be shortened. Thus, " *Pappadakis, Pappachristides* and *Pappadimitracoupoulos*," says Mr. Sotirios S. Lontos, editor of *Atlantis*, the Greek daily of New York, " become *Pappas* by taking a portion of the front part of the name, while *Panagiotopoulos, Constantinopoulos* and *Gerasimopoulos* change into *Poulos* by adopting only the tail end. So the *Pappases*

1 Baltimore *Sun*, Dec. 2, 1906.
2 *Koch*, a common German name, has very hard sledding in America. Its correct pronunciation is almost impossible to Americans; at best it becomes *Coke* or *Koash*. Hence it is often changed, not only to *Cook*, but to *Cox, Coke* or even *Cockey*.
3 The father of the once notorious evangelist, William A. Sunday, was

a German named *Sonntag*, killed in the Civil War, 1863.
4 For these Dutch examples I am indebted to President John J. Hiemenga and Prof. Henry J. G. Van Andel, of Calvin College, Grand Rapids, Mich., to Prof. B. K. Kuiper of the same city, and to Dr. Paul de Kruif.

and *Pouloses* have naturally become the *Smiths* and *Browns* of American Greeks, although these names are fairly uncommon in their native land." [1] But *Pappas* itself is sometimes sacrificed, despite its general popularity. Thus *Pappageorgiou* is shaved down to *Georgious*, *Pappadimitracoupoulos* becomes *Jameson* (part clipping and part translation), and *Pappapolychronopoulos* becomes *Chronos*, with *Poulos* following *Pappas* into the discard.[2] Other Greek names are changed to bring them into harmony with American analogues. Thus *Christides* becomes *Christie*, *Nikolaou* becomes *Nicholas*, and *Georgiou* becomes *George*. John *Cameron*, a train-robber sentenced to Leavenworth for twenty-seven years on December 29, 1926, was born *Kamariotis*. On April 5, 1935, a Greek living in Pontiac, Mich., broke into the news by reason of his name. It was *Glasfkos Pappatheodorokomoundoronicolucopoulos*, and his eight children, it appeared, favored changing the surname to *Pappas*. "There are many *Pappases* and many *Copouloses*," he said to a Pontiac *Daily Press* reporter, "and I would like my children to keep the name as it really is. But," with an expressive shrug of the shoulders, "I guess I'll have a tough time making them do it." [3]

The Slav immigrants to America brought with them names even more difficult to American tongues than those of the Greeks, and they had to make changes following all the usual patterns. Among the Czechs these include more or less crude transliterations, *e.g.*, of *Zděný* into *Stenny*, *Hřebec* into *Hurbick*, and *Cerviček* into *Servisk*; translations, *e.g.*, of *Kovář* into *Smith*, *Holič* into *Barber*, *Mlynář* into *Miller*, *Vlk* into *Wolf*, and *Zelény* into *Green*; and efforts to bring untranslatable names into harmony with English names of similar sound, *e.g.*, *Macá* becomes *Macy*, *Mosnička* becomes *Mason*, *Kutiš* becomes *Curtis*, and *Vališ* becomes *Wallace*. Some of the Czech

1 American Greek, *American Speech*, March, 1926, p. 308.
2 I am indebted here to Mr. T. D. Curculakis of Athens. *Pappas* means priest, and Mr. Curculakis explains that its popularity is at least partly due to the fact that the Greek priests, during the long years of bondage to the Turks, were the chief guardians of the national spirit. It was a *pappas* who raised the flag of liberty at the Monastery of St. Laura on March 25, 1821. Mr. Curculakis, who lived in the

United States for a number of years, was constrained to change his surname while he was here to *Kriton*, picked from Plato's Phaedon. At the same time he shortened his given names, *Timoleon Dimitriu*, to *Timon Damon*, and commonly used only their initials. Now that he has returned to Athens he is once more *Timoleon Dimitriu Curculakis*.
3 I am indebted here to Mr. H. A. Fitzgerald, editor and manager of the *Daily Press*.

immigrants, put down as Austrians in the earlier immigration returns, settled among Germans, and in consequence not a few of them adopted German names, often by translation. Thus *Krejčí* (tailor) became *Schneider*, *Dvořák* (courtier) became *Hoffman*, and *Svec* (shoemaker) became *Schumacher*.[1] A family named *Matoušek* changed its name to *Matuscheck* to accommodate German spelling, then modified it to *Mathushek*, and finally translated it into the English *Matthews*. Some of the Czechs also changed their names to Irish forms. Thus *Prujín* became *Brian* and then *O'Brien*, and *Otřáska* became *O'Tracy*. " Among freak aliases," says Monsignor J. B. Dudek, the leading authority on the Czech language in America, " *O'Hare* for *Zajíc* (rabbit), *O'Shaunnessy* for *Očenášek* (dim. ' Our Father,' used as a common term for the Lord's Prayer), *McLoud* for *Mráček* (a small cloud), and *Casey*, for which a Mr. *Sýr* (cheese) let pass a contemplated German *Käse*, will about tie for second honors. The first prize goes without question to one *Záchod* (originally, a bypath; then euphemistically, and now exclusively, the *châlet* de *nécessité*), who fondly imagined that a German *Backhaus* would escape the American interpretation, *back-house*. It did not; and a rapid translation to *Bakehouse* failed utterly to remove certain first impressions." Public opinion among the older Czechs was violently opposed to this abandonment of Czech patronymics, but it had to yield to natural forces. Says Monsignor Dudek:

The farmers of a certain county refused to patronize a banker who had assumed *Newer* in place of *Novák*. (*Newman*, a better translation, is now more commonly substituted for this name.) A storm of protest arose when a Nebraska politician, *Lapáček*, announced himself a *La Pache*, and a *Votruba*

1 A similar translation of Slavic names has probably gone on in the German areas of Pennsylvania, though I can find no record of it. In Louisiana, in the Eighteenth Century, a small Germany colony was assimilated by the French, and there were many changes in the German names. Thus, *Schaf* became *Chauffe*, *Buchwalter* became *Bouchevaldre*, *Buerckel* became *Birquelle*, *Wagensbach* became *Waguespack*, and *Katzenberger* became *Casbergue*. During the Spanish occupation some of the German names became Spanish. Thus *Hans Peter Keller* became *Juan Pedro Cueller*, and *Jacob Wil-* *helm Nolte* became *Santiago Villenol*. See Settlement of the German Coast of Louisiana, by J. Hanno Deiler, *German American Annals* (Philadelphia), New Series, Vol. VIII, No. 4, July–Aug., 1909, p. 192 *ff.* In the Catskill region of New York there is a family named *Masten*, always thought of as of Dutch origin, whose actual progenitor was an Englishman named *Marston*. Miss Lillian D. Wald tells me that in the early days of the, great Jewish invasion of New York, many Eastern Jews with difficult Slavic or Hungarian names changed them to *Cohen* or *Goldberg*.

who translated his name to *Bran* was thereafter in disrepute. . . . In spite, however, of indignation meetings, lodge resolutions and the newspaper jibes and denunciations provoked by the turncoats, a voluntary de-Bohemianization was constantly in progress, to which the younger set of Czech-Americans, surreptitiously at least, lent hearty encouragement. Removal to another, especially a purely American, community, attainment of majority, engagement in a new occupation, entrance into connubial felicity, and the like were seized as occasions for shaking off cognominal impedimenta.[1]

Even when a Czech clings to the original form of his patronymic, he must bear with its mutilation at the hands of his neighbors. Such forms as *Hořčička, Ranhojič, Trpaslik* and *Uprchl*, says Monsignor Dudek, " are, while they last, the despair of rural editors and printers, of postmasters, small-town bankers, county clerks, justices of the peace and other officials, and simply through repeated misspelling, misreading and mispronunciation by these worthies, the first steps toward their de-Bohemianization are taken." The Czech accents disappear almost at once, and the values of the Czech letters are quickly changed.

Hanska, Kouba, Kuba, Macá, Suva and others ending in *a* continue to be so written, but the owners succumb readily enough to pronunciations affected by their American neighbors — *Kobey, Koobie, Cuby, Kewpie, Macey, Soovy,* and the like. Similarly, *Myška* (or *Myšička*) is known as *Mitchky*, and one, at least, wrote it *Mitschka; Jedlička* condescends to be known as *Jedlicker* or *Shedlicker, Skála* as *Scaler, Žaba* as *Jobber* or *Chopper*, and *Hobza*, wearying at length of being called *Hubsy*, adopts *Hobbs* or even *Hobbes* of his own accord.[2]

Among the Poles, as among the Czechs, the older immigrants regard abandonment of the native surnames with aversion, but it goes on wholesale, and in all the usual ways. By translation *Krawiec* becomes *Taylor, Kowalczyk* becomes *Smith, Tomaszewski* becomes *Thompson, Mielnik* becomes *Miller*, and *Kucharz* becomes *Cook;* by transliteration *Jaroscz* is converted into *Jerris*, and *Waitr* into *Waiter;* by shortening *Filipowicz* changes to *Philip* or *Phillips, Winiarecki* to *Winar*, and *Pietruszka* to *Pietrus;* and by various com-

1 Czech Surnames in America, *American Mercury*, Nov., 1925.
2 The Americanization of Czech Surnames, by J. B. Dudek, *American Speech*, Dec., 1925. See also Czech-American Names, by the same, *Czechoslovak Student Life*, April, 1928. One Czech-American who refuses resolutely to change his name is the most distinguished of them all. He is Dr. Aleš Hrdlička, curator of the Smithsonian Institution. His given-name and surname lose their accents in "Who's Who in America," but not in the more accurate English "Who's Who." He explains humorously that an American transliteration of his surname would have to be something akin to *hard-liquor*. Here I am indebted to Mr. William Absolon, of Providence, R. I.

binations of these devices *Siminowicz* changes to *Simmons, Bart-oszewicz* to *Barton,* and *Chmielewski* (*chmiel* = hops) to *Hopson* and then to *Hobson.*[1] Many a poor Pole, despairing of making anything feasible to Americans out of his surname, abandons it for some quite unrelated English name, or elevates a given name to its place. The example of *Josef Konrad Korzienowski* will be recalled; he became *Joseph Conrad* in England, and made the name one that will be long remembered. The Polish suffixes, *-ewski, -owicz* and so on, are fast succumbing to linguistic pressure in this country, and it seems likely that after a few generations most of them will be gone. The Russian, Bulgarian and Serbian names are subject to the same attrition. They suffer, in addition, from the fact that the transliteration of the Cyrillic alphabet presents difficulties that have yet to be solved. Does *-owski, -ovski* or *-offski* come nearest the Russian original? This is a problem that confronts many a Russian.[2] All of these Slavs follow the examples of the Czechs and Poles in changing their names in this country. Of the Yugo- or South-Slavs, Louis Adamic, the well-known Yugoslav-American writer and publicist, says:

> Often they choose Anglo-Saxon names, or what appear to them to be Anglo-Saxon names, whose sound or spelling or both resemble the original Yugoslav patronymics. Thus *Onlak* becomes *O'Black; Miklavec* or *Milavič, McClautz; Ogrin, O'Green; Crček, Church; Jakša* or *Jakšič, Jackson; Bizjak, Busyjack; Oven, Owens;* and *Stritar, Streeter.* Not infrequently they translate their names into literal or near-literal English equivalents; for instance, *Cerne* into *Black, Belko* or *Belič* into *White,* or *Podlesnik* into *Underwood.*[3]

All the Slavs differentiate between the masculine and feminine forms of surnames. Thus the son of the famous actress, Helena *Modjeska,* became Ralph *Modjeski,* and as such attained to fame of his own as an engineer.[4] But in this country the feminine form disappears.[5] Perhaps the American gypsies should be included among

1 For aid here I am indebted to Mr. Sergei Senykoff of Detroit.
2 See Slavonic-English Transliterations, by H. B. Wells, *American Speech,* Sept., 1927. Also, Sixth Report of the United States Geographic Board; Washington, 1933, p. 41.
3 The Yugoslav Speech in America, *American Mercury,* Nov., 1927.
4 The family name was originally *Modrzejewski* – a palpable impossibility in America.

5 I am indebted here to Mr. Emil Revyuk, editor of the Ukrainian daily, *Svoboda,* of Jersey City. Mr. Revyuk says that Ukrainian surnames undergo all the usual changes. For example, *Petryshyn* and *Petryshak* become *Peterson, Perey* becomes *Parry, Danylchuk, Danylchenko* and *Danylshyn* become *Danielson, Makohon* becomes *MacMahon, Zhinchak* becomes *Smith, Shevchynsky* becomes *Wagner, Macheyovsky* is contracted to

the Slavs, for many of them, though they are largely of Rumanian blood, bear Slav surnames. For example, Joe *Adams*, long celebrated as the King of the Gypsies, was really Ioano *Adamovič*. Most gypsies have two names — the *nav romanes*, which is used among themselves and is formed by adding the father's given-name to the given-name of the son or daughter, and the *nav gajikanes*, which is an American-sounding name for general use. The numerous *Mitchells* among them all descend from a patriarch named *MiXail*.[1]

The Scandinavians have had to make almost as many changes in their surnames as the Slavs, and for much the same reasons. This is especially true of the Swedes. " A number of characteristic Swedish sounds, particularly *ö* and *sj*," says Roy W. Swanson,[2] " are almost impossible to the Anglo-Saxon vocal organs. Thus *Sjörgren*, that common name in which these obstacles occur, is variously written *Shogren, Schugren, Segren* or *Seagren*." Mr. Swanson continues:

> The fate of the *ö* in America is decided in divers ways: the umlaut is omitted, which is the most usual change (*Grondahl, Stromberg, Lonnquist, Mork, Soderstrom*, etc.); or the name is translated (*Grön* becomes *Green*); or there is an attempt by the learned few to perpetuate the *ö*-sound by resorting to French phonetics (*Huerlin, Leuvenmark*). . . . With the other two umlauted vowels, *ä* and *å*, the attempts to preserve the original sound are more successful. Thus *å* is replaced by *o* or *oh*, so that names like *Åman* and *Åslund* become *Ohman* and *Ohslund, Spångberg* becomes *Spongberg, Åkerberg* becomes *Okerberg*, etc. . . . [and] the English *e* seems to replace very satisfactorily the Swedish *ä*, [so that] *Änberg* becomes *Engberg; Sällström, Sellstrom; Slättengren, Slettengren*, etc.

Certain combinations of letters in Swedish, *e.g.*, *bj, hj, ki* and *lilj*, quickly succumb to Americanization. Thus, one *Esbjörn* enrolled in the Federal Army during the Civil War as *Esbyorn* and was mustered out as *Osborn*. Says Mr. Swanson:

> The native American persists in giving the *hj* sound a *j* instead of a *y* pronunciation. The *Hjelms* seem to get round the difficulty by universally dropping the *j*, and becoming *Helms*. In Swedish it is the *h* which is silent. The *Hjorts* find an acceptable English translation in *Hart*. *Kilberg, Kindbloom, Kindlund, Kilström, Kindberg, Kjellstrand, Kjellman, Kilgren* receive phonetic changes in *Chilberg, Chindbloom, Chinlund, Cilstrom, Chinberg,*

Mack, and *Nyzovych* to *Nash.* Mr. Vladimir Geeza, editor of the *New Life*, of Olyphant, Pa., adds the following: *Daniliwsky* becomes *Daniels, Petrusiw* becomes *Peters, Silwerovitch* becomes *Silvers*, and *Wowk* (wolf) becomes *Wolf.*

Here I follow the transliteration of my correspondents.
1 Gypsy Fires in America, by Irving Brown; New York, 1924, pp. 20 and 38.
2 The Swedish Surname in America, *American Speech*, Aug., 1928.

Chilstrand, Challman, Chilgren and *Gillgren.* This change seems to be universal. In fact, the Minneapolis telephone directory has less than ten Swedish-American names in the original *ki-.* *Liljedahl, Liljegren, Liljeqvist* often translate the first part: *Lilydahl, Lilygren, Lilyquist,* or in some other way remove the embarrassment of the *lj* combination: *Liliecrona, Lillquist.*

In other cases *lj* is got rid of by bolder devices, as when *Ljung* (signifying heather) is turned into *Young, Ljungdahl* into *Youngdahl,* and so on. Other attempts at transliteration are numerous. Thus *-qvist* and *-kvist* become *-quist* or *-quest; -gren* (a bough) becomes *green* or *grain,* as in *Holmgrain* and *Youngreen; -blad* (a leaf) becomes *blade,* as in *Cedarblade;* and *bo-* (an inhabitant) is turned into *bow,* as in *Bowman* from *Boman.* Direct translations are also frequent, *e.g.,* of *Nygren* into *Newbranch, Sjöstrand* into *Seashore* and *Högfelt* into *Highfield.* Sometimes the spelling of a name is changed to preserve the Swedish pronunciation, as when *Ros* becomes *Roos, Strid* becomes *Streed,* and *Andrén* becomes *Andreen.* " The *-een* termination," says Mr. Swanson, " seems to be very popular among the Swedes in America, and is sometimes carried even into the *-son* names, *e.g., Olseen* for *Olson.*" Nearly all these changes are in what the Swedes call *borgerliganamn, i.e.,* names of the plain people. The *prästnamn* (priest-names), all of which end with either *-us* or *-ander,* are changed less often, partly because their bearers are very proud of them, and partly because they usually present less difficulty to Americans. The *adelsnamn* (aristocratic names) are cherished even more jealously, but they are naturally not numerous. When Archbishop Nathan Söderblom visited the Swedish marches of the Middle West in 1923 he made an eloquent plea for the preservation of Swedish patronymics, but it seems to have had little effect. Many well-known Swedish-Americans bear changed names. Thus Col. Charles A. *Lindbergh's* family name was originally *Månsson,*[1] and that of Professor C. H. *Seashore* of the University of Iowa was *Sjöstrand.* The orthodox Swedish spelling calls for two *s*'s in such names as *Svensson, Jonsson* and *Olsson,* but one of them is usually dropped in America. In the names ending in *-ander, e.g., Lekander, Kilander* and *Bolander,* the accent is shifted from the second syllable, where it lies in Sweden, to the first.[2] Many of the early Swedish immigrants really had no surnames, in our sense of the word. The son of Johan *Karlsson* was not Lars *Karlson* but Lars *Johansson,* and

1 Days in Sweden, by James W. Lane, *Commonweal,* Sept. 9, 1931.

2 I am indebted here to Mr. John A. Stahlberg, of Plentywood, Mont.

Lars's son Johan in his turn was simply the son of Karl. Says Dr.
George M. Stephenson of the University of Minnesota:

So it went from father to son. The very limited number of given names
resulted in an unusually large number of *Johanssons, Anderssons, Peterssons,
Olssons, Karlssons* and *Swenssons*. In the United States, of course, much
confusion resulted in the delivery of mail, in legal transactions, and so forth.
The similarity of names led to nicknaming to give distinction to individuals:
for instance, *John Johnson* in the employ of Mr. *Green* was called John *Green*
to distinguish him from another *John Johnson;* the *John* Carlson who had gone
with the gold rush to California was known as *California* Carlson. The portly
Albert Swanson was called Albert *Fat* Swanson, and the Peter Anderson whose
house was set back some distance from the road was designated *Pete-in-the-
Field*, whereas a man by the same name residing in the village was *Pete-in-the-
Street*. John G. *Princell*, the religious leader, was the son of Magnus Gudmund-
son, who changed his name to *Gummeson* in America. Princell took his name
from Princeton, Ill.[1]

The Norwegians and Danes have also made changes in their
names — for example, *Bakken* has been translated as *Hill, Leebakken*
has been shortened as *Lee*, and *Bruss, Knutson* and *Terjesen* have
been transliterated as *Bruce, Newton* and *Toycen* (pro. *Tyson*) [2] —
but on the whole those changes have been fewer than among the
Swedish names, for many Norwegian patronymics lie well within
the phonological patterns of American. Indeed, not a few of them are
of English or Scotch origin, and even more are of German (or Swiss)
or Dutch origin.[3] The names of the Finns need a more extensive
overhauling in this country. Some of them are translated, e.g., *Mäki*
into *Hill, Jarvi* into *Lake, Unsijärvi* into *Newlake, Joki* into *River(s)*,
Hahti into *Bay, Tuisku* into *Storm, Talvi* into *Winter(s)*, and *Metsä*
into *Forest* or *Forrest;* others are transliterated, so that *Laine, e.g.,*
becomes *Lane, Hämäläinen* becomes *Hamlin, Paatalo* becomes *Patlow*, and *Hartikainen* becomes *Hartman;* and others are abbreviated,
e.g., *Peijariniemi* to *Niemi, Hakomäki* to *Maki* or *Mackey; Saarikoski*
to *Koski*, and *Höyhtyä* to *Hoyt. Lähteenmäki* (spring hill) may be
abbreviated to *Mäki* and then translated into *Hill. Pitkäjärvi* (long

---

1 The Religious Aspects of Swedish
Immigration; Minneapolis, 1932, p.
427.
2 I am indebted here to Mr. Wallace
Lomoe, of the Milwaukee *Journal*.
He says that when several cadets
of the House of Toycen went into
the World War, their comrades
pronounced the name as spelled,
and that this pronunciation has been

retained. But the other Toycens
call themselves *Tyson*. Mr. Lomoe's
own name was originally *Lömoe*.
It is commonly pronounced *LaMoe*,
with the accent on the second syllable.
3 See Norwegian Surnames, by
George T. Flom *Scandinavian
Studies and Notes*, Vol. V. No. 4,
1918.

lake) may be abbreviated to *Järvi*, and then changed to *Jarvis* or translated into *Lake*. *Pulkka* and *Pulkkinen* are often changed to *Polk*. At least 20% of the Finns bear Swedish surnames, and not infrequently a Finn makes a surname for himself, in the ancient Swedish manner, by adding *-son* to his father's given name. Thus, the son of *Jaakko* becomes *Jackson* and the son of *Antti* becomes *Anderson*. The fact that the Finnish *p* has a sound somewhere between the English *b* and *p* and the Finnish *t* a sound somewhere between the English *t* and *d* is responsible for other changes. Thus, when a Finn named *Pelto* gives his name, it may be written down *Beldo*, and like the German *Schneiders* who became *Snyders* he may decide to retain the " American " form.[1]

The Italians, in the early days of their immigration to the United States, changed their names with some frequency, but with the advent of Mussolini and the rise of a new Italian national spirit this process was halted. The late *James E. March*, Republican leader of the Third Assembly District in New York, was originally *Antonio Maggio*. *Paul Kelly*, leader of the Longshoremen's Union, was *Paolo Vaccarelli*. *Jim Flynn*, the only man who ever knocked out Jack Dempsey, was *Andrea Chiariglione*. One *Alessandro Smiraglia* has become *Sandy Smash*, *Francesco Napoli* is *Frank Knapp*, *Francesco Tomasini* is *Frank Thomas*, and *Luigi Zampariello* is *Louis Smith*. *Henry Woodhouse*, a gentleman once prominent in aeronautical affairs, came to the United States from Italy as Mario Terenzio *Enrico Casalegno;* his new surname is simply a translation of his old one. Other such translations are fairly common, *e.g.*, *Little* for *Piccolo*, *White* for *Blanco*, *Whitehand* for *Blancamano* and *Pope* for *Pape*. Transliterations and clipped forms are also occasionally encountered, *e.g.*, *Shellat* for *Scellato*, *Rondy* for *Rondinone*, *Bellows* for *Bello*, *Marinace* for *Marinaccio*, *Lowery* for *Lauria*, *Lance* for *Lanza* and *Silvy* for *Silvig*. There is an Italian *Galloway* in New York whose name was originally *Gallo*. The early Italians ran to Irish names for two reasons. The first was that they came into contact with the Irish in the Catholic churches, and not infrequently married Irish girls. The other was that most of the politicians and prizefighters of their admiration were Irishmen. Moreover, those who entered the prize-ring themselves soon found, like the Jews, that

1 I am indebted here to Mr. Reino W. Suojanen, editor of *Walwoja*, Calumet, Mich., and to Mr. Ivar Vapaa, editor of *Industrialisti*, Duluth, Minn.

Irish names drew larger houses. The Italian surnames, in the main, are not as difficult to Americans as those of the Greeks and Slavs; thus they have been under rather less pressure. But the long ones seem doomed to succumb. There is no reason why *Vitolo, Muccia* or *Guerci* should not survive, but there is hard sledding ahead for *Pietroluongo, Cicognani* and *Guglielminetti.*[1] In many cases the pronunciation of Italian names is changed. In particular, those ending with *e* tend to lose it, just as the analogous German names lose it. Thus, the surname of the celebrated Al *Capone* is commonly pronounced so that it rhymes with *zone,* and its bearer, I am informed, prefers it so. As for the Italian *a,* it is quickly Americanized, so that the first syllable of *Sacco* rhymes with *back,* and the first of *Vanzetti* with *can.*

The commoner Spanish names, like the commoner Italian names, seem to be easy for Americans, and hence they have been little changed. *Gomez, Garcia, Gonzalez, Castro, Valdez, Ruiz, Lopez, Sanchez* and the like have been taken in without resistance, and are usually pronounced, especially in the Southwest, with some approximation to correctness. There have been few translations, and even fewer attempts at transliteration.[2] Changes in other Latin names are much more frequent. The long Rumanian patronymics are quickly shortened in this country, and many of the more difficult shorter ones are supplanted by translated or transliterated forms, *e.g., Miller* for *Morariu, Jones* for *Ionescu, Patterson* for *Patraşcu, Sage* for *Suciu,* and *Stanley* or *Stanton* for *Stănilă.*[3] In Bristol county, Mass., where Portuguese immigrants are numerous, they often change their names, but in most cases the changes are slight. Thus, *Luiz* becomes *Lewis, Pereira* becomes *Perry, Marques* becomes *Marks, Martins* becomes *Martin, Freitas* becomes *Frates, Correia* becomes *Corey* or *Curry, Jorge* becomes *George, Jordão* becomes *Jordan, Silva* becomes *Silver, Lourenço* becomes *Lawrence, Morais* becomes *Morris,* and *Terra* becomes *Terry.* Sometimes there is a translation, *e.g.,* from *Ferreira* to *Smith,* and now and then there is a curious transliteration,

1 For material and suggestions here I am indebted to Mr. Guiseppe Cautela of Brooklyn, N. Y., and Mr. J. H. A. Lacher of Waukesha, Wis.
2 Mr. Hugh Morrison of New York, who has a wide acquaintance among Mexican-Americans, says that he knows of but two who bear

" American " names. One of them, born *Pérez,* is now *Peters;* the other, a full-blooded Indian, is *Jim Anderson.*
3 I am indebted here to Mr. George Stanculescu, editor of the *American Roumanian News,* Cleveland.

e.g., from *Caranguejo* to *Crabtree* and from *Soares* to the German *Schwartz*.[1] It is not uncommon for the surviving Portuguese names to be pronounced in the American manner, *e.g.*, *Lopes* for *Lopez*, *Nunes* for *Nunez* and *Alves* for *Alvez*, and for their bearers to yield to the American pronunciation.[2] But of all the Latin surnames, the French seem to fare the worst. In the early part of this chapter I have given examples of the radical changes some of them underwent in colonial days. The invasion of New England by French-Canadians has produced many more —*White* for *Le Blanc*, *Woods* for *Dubois*, *Drinkwater* for *Boileau*, *Larch* for *L'Archevêque*, *Larraby* for *La-Rivière*, *Shampoo* for *Archambault*, and so on.[3] A small colony of Hollanders including Flemings of French name settled in Boyle county, Kentucky, in the Nineteenth Century, and in a little while all its *Badeaus* were *Beddows*, its *La Rues* were plain *Rues*, its *De Bons* were *Debauns*, and its *Des Champses* were *Scomps*.[4] There was another slaughter, this time at the hands of the Spaniards, in the late Eighteenth Century. They were in control of the Mississippi from 1763 to 1800 and kept the public records. Thus the names of many French traders and settlers, coming up from Louisiana or down from Canada, were changed to accord with Spanish notions. In this way *Chouteau* became *Chotau* and *Choto* (and was later transformed by the invading Americans into *Shoto*). " The fine disregard for spelling," says John Francis McDermott,[5] " may be illustrated by the name *Kiercereau*, which is also spelled *Kiercerau*, *Kiersereau*, *Kierserau*, *Kersereau*, *Kerserau*, *Kesserau*, *Kessereau*, *Kiergerau*, *Kiergereaux*, *Kiercereaux*, *Kiergero*, *Kergzo*, *Quircero*, *Guiercero* (this is probably an inaccuracy of copying), *Tiercero*, *Tiercerot*, *Tercero*." Mr. McDermott says that French nomenclature was also considerably upset by the prevalence of *dit* names, *i.e.*, inherited nicknames, and by the confusion between estate-names and true surnames among certain of the immigrants from Canada.

The Hungarians, Armenians, Syrians and other newcomers to the

1 I am indebted here to Mr. João R. Rocha, proprietor of *O Independente*, New Bedford, Mass., and to Mr. Peter L. C. Silveira, editor of the *Jornal Portugues*, Oakland, Calif.

2 I am indebted here to Mr. Charles J. Lovell, of Pasadena, Calif.

3 See La Langue française au Canada, by Louvigny de Montigny; Ottawa,

1916, p. 146, and Name Tragedies, by C. P. Mason, *American Speech*, April, 1929, p. 329.

4 A Tragedy of Surnames, by Fayette Dunlap, *Dialect Notes*, Vol. IV, Pt. II, 1913.

5 French Surnames in the Mississippi Valley, *American Speech*, Feb., 1934.

Republic have had to modify their more difficult patronymics like the rest. The first-named, who sometimes bear surnames analogous to the English *St. John,* often translate them, *e.g., Szentgyörgyi* becomes *Saint George* and *Szentpétery* becomes *Saint Peter.* Sometimes other names are translated, *e.g., Borbély* into *Barber, Papp* into *Priest, Péntek* into *Friday, Kovács* into *Smith, Mészáros* into *Butcher, Sebes* into *Speed, Kerekes* into *Wheeler,* and *Szabó* into *Taylor;* and sometimes they are transliterated, *e.g., Kállay* into *Kelly, Gyulay* into *July, Horvath* into *Howarth, Szüle* into *Sewell, Szemán* into *Seaman, Nyiri* into *Neary, Kayla* into *Kayler,* and *Makláry* into *McCleary.* When names are retained they are frequently changed in spelling. Thus *Bela* sometimes becomes *Behla, Köszegy* becomes *Koesegi, Köves* becomes *Koevesh,* and *Kiss* becomes *Kish.* The Hungarians, like the Chinese, always put the surname first, and this custom is kept up after their names have been Americanized. Thus, *Charley Braun* is always *Braun Charley,* and *Steve Takach* is *Takach Steve. Ilona Nagy,* wife of *Peter Kiss,* is either *Kiss Péterné Nagy Iolna* or *Kissné Nagy Ilona.*[1] A well-known Hungarian-American, Mr. L. Lázzló *Ecker-Rácz,* has got round the difficulty presented by *Rácz* by abbreviating his surname to *Ecker-R.*[2] The Syrians and Armenians frequently bear names that are even stranger to Americans than the Hungarian names, and so they have to make radical changes. Thus, the Syrian *Sham'un* is changed to *Shannon, Hurayz* to *Harris, Musallem* to *Abraham, Muqabba'a* to *McKaba,* and *Abbud* to *Abbott. Khouri,* a common Syrian name, becomes *Khoury, Coury, Courey, Khuri, Koorey* or *Corey.* The Syrian *Haddad,* though it presents no phonological difficulties, is commonly translated into *Smith,* and *Ashshi* into *Cook.* Says Dr. Philip K. Hitti of Princeton:

"Did you not receive any aid from American sources?" asked I of the Maronite priest in Detroit who was showing me his newly built church, and priding himself on its being one of the finest Syrian church buildings in the

1 I am indebted here to Dr. Nicholas M. Alter of Jersey City; to Mr. Hugo Kormos, editor of the *Magyar Herald* of New Brunswick, N. J.; to Mr. Henry Miller Madden, of Columbia University; to Dr. Joseph Remény, of Western Reserve University; and to Mr. Joseph Yartin of New York.

2 At this writing Mr. *Ecker-R* is at-

tached to the Federal Emergency Relief Administration at Washington. "The abbreviation," he tells me, "was adopted in consideration of others, and to protect myself from some interesting variations in spelling. The *R* does not, as the Washington *Star* is wont to interpret, stand for *Republican.*"

country. No sooner had his negative reply been made than my eyes caught *Edward A. Maynard* on the altar, and, asking for an explanation, the priest replied, "Oh, well, that is *Wadi' Mu'auwad.*"[1]

The Armenian names go the same route. Sometimes they are translated, *e.g.*, *Tertzagian* into *Taylor*, *Ohanesian* or *Hovanesian* into *Johnson*, and *Hatzakordzian* into *Baker;* sometimes they are crudely transliterated, *e.g.*, *Jamgotvhain* into *Jamison*, *Bedrosian* into *Peterson*, *Melkonian* into *Malcolm*, and *Heditzian* into *Hedison;* sometimes they are abbreviated, *e.g.*, *Bozoian* into *Bozo*, *Karageozian* into *Kara*, *Dermenjian* into *Dermen*, *Mooradian* into *Moore*, and *Hampartzoomian* into *Hampar;* and sometimes they are subjected to even more brutal processes, as when *Garabedian* becomes *Charleston*, *Kizirboghosian* becomes *Curzon*, and *Khachadoorian* becomes *Hatch*.[2]

But of all the immigrant peoples in the United States, the Jews seem to be the most willing to change their names. Once they have lost the faith of their fathers, a phenomenon almost inevitable in the first native-born generation, they shrink from all the disadvantages that go with their foreignness and their Jewishness,[3] and seek to conceal their origin, or, at all events, to avoid making it unnecessarily noticeable.[4] At the height of the immigration from Eastern Europe even the members of the first generation moved rapidly in that direction, though they commonly remained true to

1 The Syrians in America; New York, 1924, p. 101. I am indebted here to Dr. Hitti and to Mr. H. I. Katibah, editor of the *Syrian World* of New York.

2 I am indebted here to Mr. R. Darbinian, editor of *Hairenik*, Boston, and to Dr. K. A. Sarafian, of La Verne College, University of Southern California, Los Angeles.

3 This last, on occasion, is a heavy burden, for there is always more or less Anti-Semitism afloat. Its causes remain to be investigated. The reasons for it that Jews commonly accept are almost as dubious as those advanced by anti-Semites. The literature of the subject is very large, but virtually all of it is worthless.

4 See The Jews, by Maurice Fishberg; New York, 1911, especially p. 485 ff. Also, Reaction to Personal Names, by Dr. C. P. Oberndorf, *Psychoanalytic Review*, Vol. V, No. 1, January, 1918. This, so far as I know, is the only article in English which deals with the psychological effects of surnames upon their bearers. Abraham Silberer and other German psychoanalysts have made contributions to the subject. Dr. Oberndorf alludes, incidentally, to the positive social prestige which goes with an English air or a French air in America. He tells of an Italian who changed his patronymic of *Dipucci* into *de Pucci* to make it more "aristocratic." And of a German bearing the genuinely aristocratic name of *von Landsschaffshausen* who changed it to "a typically English name" because the latter seemed more distinguished to his neighbors.

the synagogue. How many of the Jews of New York now sport new names I don't know, but it certainly must be a very large proportion of the whole number, and it may run to a full half. They follow all the patterns in vogue among the other newcomers to the country, and have added one of their own, *i.e.*, the prettification of their traditional names, whereby *Cohen* becomes *Cohn, Coyne, Conn, Cowan*, and even *Cain, Solomon* becomes *Salomon, Solmson* and *Salmon*, the names in *Rosen-* become *Rose* or *Ross*, and *Levy* becomes *Lewy, Levitt, Levay, Levoy, Levie, LeVie, Levene, Levien, Levin, Levine, Levey, Levvy, Levie* and *Lee*.[1] Like the Germans whose names they so often bear, they also seek refuge in translations more or less literal. Thus, *Blumenthal* is changed to *Bloomingdale, Reichman* to *Richman*, and *Schlachtfeld* to *Warfield*. One *Lobenstine* (*i.e., Lobenstein*) had his name changed to *Preston* during the war, and announced that this was " the English version " of his patronymic. A *Wolfsohn* similarly became a *Wilson*, though without attempting any such fantastic philological justification for the change, and a *Bernheimer* became a *Burton. Fielder*, a common name among the Russian Jews, often becomes *Harper* in New York; so does *Pikler*, which is Yiddish for *drummer. Stolar*, which is a Yiddish word borrowed from the Russian, signifying *carpenter*, is changed to *Carpenter. Lichtman* and *Lichtenstein* become *Chandler. Meilach*, which is Hebrew for *king*, becomes *King*, and so does *Meilachson. Sher* is changed into *Sherman, Michel* into *Mitchell, Rogowsky* into *Rogers, Rabinovitch* into *Robbins, Davidovitch* into *Davis, Moiseyev* into *Macy* or *Mason*, and *Jacobson, Jacobovitch* and *Jacobovsky* into *Jackson*. This last change proceeds by way of a transient change to *Jake* or *Jack* as a nickname. *Jacob* is always abbreviated to one or the other among the Russian and Polish Jews. *Yankelevitch* also becomes *Jackson*, for *Yankel* is Yiddish for *Jacob*.[2]

It has thus become impossible in America to recognize Jews by their names. There are not only multitudes of *Smiths, Browns* and *Joneses* among them, but also many *Adamses, Lincolns, Grants, Lees, Jeffersons* and *Harrisons*, and even *Vanderbilts, Goulds, Schuylers, Cabots* [3] and *Lowells*. I turn to the roster of the Social Justice Com-

1 The English Jews, who pronounce *Levy lev-vy* not *lee-vy*, often change it to *Lewis*. They also change *Abraham* and *Abrahams* to *Braham* and *Bram*, and *Moses* to *Moss. Taylor* and *Gordon* are favorites among them. There are many London Jews with Scotch names, including even *MacGregor*.

2 For these observations I am indebted to Mr. Abraham Cahan.

3 In 1923 the Boston Cabots sought

mission of the Central Conference of American Rabbis (1931), and
find an *Ellis*, a *Fox* and a *Wise*. I proceed to a list of committees of
the Zeta Beta Tau fraternity, an organization of Jewish college men,
otherwise highly race-conscious, and find *Waller, Harwick, Rose,
Ferguson, Livingston, Howland, Newman, Harte, Cotton, Ney,
Morgan, Harris, Lewis, Richards, Gladstone, Eno, Rand* and *Butt*.[1]
I go to a roll of Boston Jews who have written books, and find
Taylor, Lyons, Millin, Curtiss (*geb. Kirstein?*), *Coleman, Davis,
White* and *Burroughs*.[2] The process which turned a *Braunstein* into
a *Trotsky* in Russia, and a *Finkelstein* into a *Litvinoff* has gone on
in this country on a truly gigantic scale. And even when the old
names have been retained, they have been modified, in many thousands of cases, in pronunciation. All the familiar name-endings —
-stein, -baum, -thau, -thal and so on — acquire new values. The
fashion for changing the pronunciation of *stein* from *stine* to *stean*
seems to have come in during the World War, and it spread very
quickly and is now almost universal. The single name *Stein* is still
usually pronounced *stine, Klein* is still *Kline* and *Weinberg* is still
Wineberg, but *Epstein, Bernstein, Hammerstein* and their congeners
are now *Epstean, Bernstean*,[3] *Hammerstean*, etc. The name of Anton
Rubinstein, the composer, is always pronounced *-stean* by American radio announcers. Even the last syllables of names in *-stine, e.g.,
Durstine*, are commonly made *-stean* in New York. In *Einstein* the
first syllable retains the sound of the German diphthong, but the
-stein becomes *-stean*. In the same way *Weil* is *Weel*. How and why
this affectation came into vogue I do not know, but probably it
owes something to anti-German feeling during the war. French example may have helped, for in French *Goldstein* comes close to
gollsteen. The diphthong *ei*, with its German value, is of course
very rare in English, but in *either* it seems to be driving out *ee*.[4]

a remedy in equity against a *Kabot-chnick* who had borrowed their name, but the courts decided against them.

1 *Zeta Beta Tau Quarterly*, April, 1931.

2 Long List of Books Written by Boston Jews, by Fanny Goldstein, Boston *Evening Globe*, May 23, 1934.

3 In New York, of course, *Bernstein* is *Boinsteen*, just as *Stern* is *Stoin*.

4 The German names containing *ei* sometimes retain the German value and sometimes do not. *Schleigh* is commonly pronounced *sly* and *Reiter* remains *ry-ter*, but *Reifschneider* and its variants, *Reifsnyder* and *Reifsnider* tend to become *reef*. *Weigand*(*t*) is commonly *Wee-gand*. Soon or late, I suppose, even *Reilly* will become *Reel-y*, at any rate in New York.

Since the war *Lehman* has ceased to to be *layman* and become *lee-man*,[1] *Morgenthau* has become *morgen-thaw*, and *Strauss* has begun to turn into *straws*. The first German *s* in the last-named, of course, loses its *sh*-sound. In most other situations the German diphthong *au* is likewise *aw*, so that *Blaustein* becomes *Blawsteen* and *Rosenbaum* becomes *Rosenbawm*. *Kühn* (usually spelled *Kuhn*), *Loeb* & Company is always *coon-lobe*. *Meier* is often *meer*, *Bache* is *baysh*, *Shapiro* is sometimes *shap-yro*, and *Baruch* is *ber-ook*, with the accent on the last syllable. In New York, of course, the last syllable of the *-berg* names is often *boig*. In the case of the *-thal* names a new consonant has been invented. It is the *th* of *thick*, but with a distinct *t*-sound preceding. The name often sounds like *Rosent-thal*, and the same *tth* is also heard in *Thalberg*, *Thalheimer*, etc. The spelling of Jewish names is frequently changed, even when their pronunciation is but little modified. In New York I have encountered a *Dalshheimer* turned *Dalsemer*, *Schlesingers* turned *Slessinger* or *Slazenger*, and *Schöns* turned *Shain*, *Shane* or *Shean*. Elsewhere I have heard of *Labovitzes* turned *Laborises*, *Labouisses* and even *La Borwits*. I was once told — by a witness, alas, not too reliable — of a *Ginzberg* who spelled his name *Guinness-Bourg*.[2] The spelling of the *-heimer* names is often changed to *-himer*, that of the *-heim* names to *-hym*, and that of the *-baum* names to *-bem* or even *-bum*.

Many of the changes in Jewish surnames are effected by degrees. Thus *Goldstein* first becomes *Goldstone*, then *Golston* and finally *Golson*. Samuel *Goldwyn*, the movie magnate, was born *Gelbfisch*, and passed as *Goldfish* in his pupal stage.[3] Sometimes these successive changes have method in them, as is indicated by the following tale from Dr. Pepys's Diary in the *Journal of the American Medical Association* written by Dr. Morris Fishbein, himself a Jew:

> Today in ye clinic a tale told of Dr. *Levy* who hath had his name changed to *Sullivan*. A month after he cometh again to ye court, this time wishing to

1 When Herbert H. *Lehman* became a candidate for Governor of New York in 1932 his banking firm announced that he pronounced his name *leeman*. New York *Times*, Oct. 5, 1932.

2 Which recalls the *Ginzberg* in Anita Loos's But Gentleman Marry Brunettes (1928) who, following the example of the *Battenbergs* (now *Mountbattens*), changed his

name to *Mountginz*. Another, according to Miles L. Hanley (*American Speech*, Oct., 1933, p. 78), became *Gainsborough*. Other variants are *Ginsburgh*, *Guinsburg*, *Guinzburg*, *Ginzbourg*, *Ginsbourgh*, *Ginsbern*, *Ginsbury* and *Gins*.

3 Question of Assumed Names Passed On In Goldwyn Suit, *Variety*, Oct. 25, 1923, p. 19.

become *Kilpatrick*. On request for ye reason, he telleth ye court that ye patients continually ask of him, "What was your name *before?*" If granted ye change he shall then tell them "*Sullivan*."

The Jews make these changes with extraordinary facility for two reasons. One of them I have mentioned — their desire to get rid of the two handicaps of foreignness and Jewishness at one clip. The other lies in the fact that they have borne their surnames, taking one with another, for less time than most Christians, and thus have less sentimental attachment to them. "Surnames became general among them," says Dr. H. Flesch,[1] "only toward the end of the Eighteenth or at the beginning of the Nineteenth Century. In the years 1782–83 the Jews in Austria were compelled by law to assume surnames. In Frankfort-on-the-Main the same rule was prescribed by the edict of September 30, 1809; in Prussia by order of Hardenburg, dated March 11, 1812; and in Bavaria by the law of 1813." "In Austria," says C. L'Estrange Ewen,[2] "the commissioners appointed to select the designations looked upon the occasion as a harvest, and, when insufficient financial consideration was forthcoming, bestowed most unpleasant appellatives." He gives, among others, these examples: *Bettelarm* (destitute), *Eselkopf* (ass's head), *Fresser* (glutton), *Galgenvogel* (gallows-bird), *Geldschrank* (money-chest), *Karfunkel* (carbuncle), *Küssemich* (kiss me), *Rindkopf* (cow-head), *Saumagen* (hog's pauch), *Schmetterling* (butterfly) and *Veilchenduft* (scent of violets). To these many of the *-stein* names might be added: *Goldstein* (goldstone), *Edelstein* (precious-stone), *Einstein* (one stone), and so on.[3] The Sephardic or Spanish Jews whose surnames are much older, seldom change them, even in America: the *Cardozos*, *daSilvas*, *Fonsecas*, *Abarbanels*, *deCassereses* and *Solis Cohens* are as

---

1 Place-Names and First-Names as Jewish Family-Names, *Jewish Forum*, April, 1925.
2 In A History of Surnames of the British Isles; New York, 1931, p. 213.
3 Ewen tells of two Jews who compared notes after visiting the police-office. One had drawn an excellent name, *Weisheit* (wisdom), but the other had been labelled *Schweiszhund* (bloodhound). "Why *Schweiszhund?*" demanded Weisheit. "Didn't you pay enough?" "Gott und die Welt," replied

Schweiszhund, "I have given half of my wealth to buy that *w* alone!" The Jews themselves have a vast repertory of such stories. I borrow another from the London *Jewish Daily Post*, June 27, 1935, where it is credited to George Sokolsky's We Jews: A Mrs. Selby was introduced to a Mrs. Levy at the bridge-table. "Are you related," asked Mrs. Levy, "to the Selbys of Sydney?" "No," answered Mrs. Selby, "the Sydney Selbys are Silverbergs, while we are Schneiders."

proud of their patronymics as the *Percys* or *Salm-Salms.*[1] But the Ashkenazim (German, Polish and Russian) Jews have no such reason for clinging to the names clapped on them. Says Dr. Solomon Solis Cohen: [2]

Suppose a man's name to be Israel *Weisberg* — why should he not become Israel *Whitehill?* And if it be Jacob *Wittkofsky,* why not Jacob *Witt?* Why should any Central European or Eastern Jew burden his children with a lot of useless and generally mispronounced syllables, that seem to flaunt a foreign flavor? There is nothing Hebrew, Jewish or Israelitish about these cognomens. They are German, Polish, Russian, Hungarian, etc. If not changed in spelling they will inevitably be changed in pronunciation. Why not a rational deliberate change?

The literature dealing with English, Scotch, Welsh and Irish surnames is enormous,[3] but there is little in print about their permutations in the United States, and that little offers only meager light. The relative infrequency of hyphenated names is obvious; they began to appear on the wave of Anglomania that followed the Civil War, but the ribaldry of the vulgar quickly discouraged them.[4] They survive, speaking generally, only among grass-widows and

1 Some years ago the *Solis Cohens* of Philadelphia, a family distinguished in medicine, took action against a Jewish dentist who sought to assume their name. During the first days of the immigration of Jews from Russia many of them, on arriving in this country, borrowed German-Jewish names. (Many others, of course, had them already). " At that time," says Jane Doe in Concerning Hebrew Names, *Reflex,* Nov., 1928, " the aristocrat was the German Jew." Some of the English Jews had surnames long before those of Germany and the Slav countries. See Name List of English Jews of the Twelth Century, in The Jews of Angevin England, by Joseph Jacobs; London, 1893, p. 345 *ff.* Not many English Jews ever came to the United States.

2 In a memorandum prepared for the author, April 25, 1925.

3 See A Bibliography of Writings on the English Language From the Beginning of Printing to the End of 1932, by Arthur G. Kennedy; Cambridge (Mass.), 1927, pp. 57 *ff,* 149–50, 187, and 332 *ff.* The best

work on the subject is A History of Surnames of the British Isles, by C. L'Estrange Ewen; New York, 1931.

4 They arose in England through the custom of requiring an heir by the female line to adopt the family name on inheriting the family property. Formerly the heir dropped his own surname. Thus, the ancestor of the present Duke of Northumberland, born *Smithson,* took the ancient name of *Percy* on succeeding to the underlying earldom in the Eighteenth Century. But about a hundred years ago heirs in like case began to join the two names by hyphenation, and such names are now very common in England. Thus, the surname of Lord Barrymore is *Smith-Barry,* that of Lord Vernon is *Venables-Vernon,* that of Lord Saye and Sele is *Twisleton-Wykeham-Fiennes,* and that of the Earl of Wharncliffe is *Montagu-Stuart-Wortley-Mackenzie.* The name of Vice-Admiral the Hon. Sir Reginald Aylmer Ranfurly *Plunkett-Ernle-Erle-Drax,* K.C.B., C.B., D.S.O., R.N., brother to Lord Dunsany, the

female singers and elocutionists. The former sometimes indicate that they have been liberated from their bonds by prefixing their maiden surnames to their late husbands' names, with or without hyphens. The latter, when they marry, frequently make similar amalgamations, and at the same time begin to call themselves *Madame*. A few of the older English surnames have undergone modification in America, *e.g.*, *Venables*, which has lost its final *s*. There has also been a tendency to abandon *Griffiths* for *Griffith*.[1] And where spellings have remained unchanged, pronunciations have been modified, especially in the South.[2] *Callowhill*, in Virginia, is sometimes pronounced *Carrol; Crenshawe* is *Granger; Hawthorne, Horton; Norsworthy, Nazary; Ironmonger, Munger; Farinholt, Fernall; Camp, Kemp; Drewry, Droit; Enroughty, Darby;*[3] and *Taliaferro, Tolliver*. Dr. David Starr Jordan, in " The Days of a Man " (1922), tells of a neighbor in Western New York (*c.* 1860) who spelled his name *Zurhorst* and pronounced it *Zirst*, and of others who made *Cassia* of *Kershaw*, *Shuard* of *Sherwood* and *Glasby* of *Gillespie*. To match such prodigies the English themselves have *Sillinger* for *St. Leger*, *Sinjin* for *St. John*, *Crippiny* for *Crespigny*, *Weems* for *Wemyss*, *Looson-Gor* for *Leveson-Gower*, *Kaduggan* for *Cadogen*, *Mawlbra* for *Marlborough*, *Askew* for *Ayscough*, *Marshbanks* for *Marjoribanks*, *Po-ell* for *Powell*, *Beecham* for *Beauchamp*, *Trample-sure* for *Trampleasure*,[4] *Barkly* for *Berkeley*, *Chumly* for *Cholmondeley*, *Kookno* for *Cogenhoe*, *Trosley* for *Trottterscliffe*, and *Darby* for *Derby*.[5] In general, there is a tendency in America to throw the accents back, *i.e.*, in such names as *Cassels, Gerard, Doran, Burnett* and *Maurice*. In England the first syllable is commonly accented; in the United States, the second.

Irish writer, would ruin him in the United States. So would that of Walter Thomas James *Scrymsoure-Steuart-Fothringham*, a Scotch magnate.
1 According to Howard F. Barker (Surnames in -*is*, *American Speech*, April, 1927, p. 318), " the defection from *Griffiths* dates far back." In *Who's Who* (London), 1935, there are 16 *Griffithses* to 27 *Griffiths*, whereas in *Who's Who in America*, 1934–35, the 21 *Griffiths* are matched by but 3 *Griffithses*.
2 See *Word-Book of Virginia Folk-*

Speech of B. W. Green; Richmond, 1899.
3 A correspondent writes in explanation of this amazing pronunciation: " The family, having rather unwillingly had to change their name to *Enroughty* to secure an inheritance, balanced up by continuing to *pronounce* their original name — *Darby*."
4 See The *Trampleasures*, *Time and Tide* (London), June 29, 1935.
5 A long list is in Titles and Forms of Address; 2nd ed.; London, 1929, p. 15 *ff*.

504   *The American Language*

This difference is often to be noted in Irish names. "An Irishman," says Ernest Boyd, the Irish critic, now living in New York, "says *Wáddell, Móran, Bérnard, Púrcell, Máhony*, etc., but Americans and Irish-Americans stress the last syllable, as in *Morán*, or the penult, as in *Mahóny*. Another sea-change in Irish names," adds Mr. Boyd, "is in the gutturals: *Coughlin* and *Gallagher*, instead of being pronounced *Cochlin* and *Gallacher*, become *Coglin* and *Gallager*, with the hard *g*." The Irish in America have not taken to the revived Gaelic name-forms which delight so many of their *Landsleute* at home. I have searched several American telephone directories without finding any *MacSuibhne (McSweeney), OMaolcathaigh (Mulcahy), OSuilleobhain (O'Sullivan), OTreasaigh (Tracy), OMurchadha (Murphy)* or *MacEochagain (Geoghan)*.[1] The Welsh custom of spelling certain names in *F* with two small *f*'s, *e.g.*, *ffinch*, *ffrench*, *ffarington* and *ffoulkes* has been imitated in England, but not in America: there is not a single example in either "Who's Who in America" or the Manhattan telephone directory.[2] Such forms as John *Smith of F* and John *Jones of William* are occasionally found in the United States; they offer a convenient way to distinguish between cousins of the same name. The territorial form seen in Charles *Carroll of Carrollton* and John *Randolph of Roanoke* has not taken root; the only recent example that I can think of is *Kohler of Kohler*. But this is the trade-mark of a corporation rather than the name of a man.[3]

Any list of American names is bound to show some extremely curious specimens — most of them clumsy adaptations of non-English names, but others apparently of Anglo-Saxon provenance. Frank Sullivan, an eager collector of such delicacies, gives the place of honor in his cabinet to the names of the Misses Dagmar *Sewer* and Mary Lou *Wham*. Some time ago one of the large life-insurance companies printed a list designed to show "the colorful variety of appellations which policy-holders bear." From it I take the following:

1 My thanks are due to Mr. Boyd for help here. He tells me that in Gaelic names the *O* is never separated by an apostrophe. It is always either written close up or separated clearly, as in Sean *O Murchadha*. In the latter case it is not followed by a period.

2 See Two Little *f*'s, by Trevor Davenport-ffoulkes, London *Sunday Times*, April 22, 1934.

3 The Kohler Company of Kohler, Wis., manufacturers of plumbing materials. The president of the company, Walter J. Kohler, was Governor of Wisconsin, 1929–30.

Willy *Twitty*	Sello *Bibo*	Christian *Girl*
Edward J. *Bible*	G. H. *Upthegrove*	Memory D. *Orange*
Julius A. *Suck*	Chintz *Royalty*	Oscar R. *Apathy*
Harry B. *Ill*	Barnum B. *Bobo*	Alphonse *Forgetto*
E. J. *Cheesewright*	John *Bilious*	Henry *Kicklighter*
Robert *Redheffer*	James A. *Masculine*	William *Dollarhide*
Julia C. *Barefoot*	Ansen B. *Outhouse*	Ernest *Sons*
Ralph St. *Cathill*	F. *Bulpitt*	Emil E. *Buttermilk*

To which may be added a few specimens from Nebraska, collected by two of Dr. Louise Pound's disciples: [1]

George *Pig*	Irma *Halfway*	Mary *Admire*
Eche *Rattles*	George *Goatleg*	Keith R. *Catchpole*

2. GIVEN-NAMES

The non-British American's willingness to anglicize his patronymic is far exceeded by his eagerness to give "American" baptismal names to his children. The favorite given-names of the old country almost disappear in the first native-born generation. The Irish immigrants who flocked in after the famine of 1845–47 bearing such names as *Patrick*, *Terence* and *Dennis* named their American-born sons *John*, *George*, *William* and *James*. The Germans, in the same way, abandoned *Otto*, *August*, *Hermann*, *Ludwig*, *Rudolph*, *Heinrich*, *Wolfgang*, *Wilhelm*, *Johann* and *Franz*. For many of these they substituted English equivalents: *Lewis*, *Henry*, *William*, *John*, *Frank*, and so on, including *Raymond* for *Raimund*.[2] In the room of others they began giving their offspring fanciful names: *Roy*,

[1] Curious Names, by Mamie Meredith and Ruth Schad Pike, *American Speech*, Feb., 1928.

[2] My own given-names may throw some light on the process. They are *Henry Louis*. I was named Henry after my father's brother. Their mother was Harriet McClellan, who came to Baltimore from Kingston, Jamaica. She was of North Irish stock and a member of the Church of England. *Henry* seems to have been borrowed from some member of her family. I was named *Louis* after my paternal grandfather, but his actual given-names were *Burkhardt Ludwig*. I gather that it was at first proposed to call me *Henry Burkhardt*, but that there was some objection to the *Burkhardt*, probably from my mother. So a compromise was made on *Ludwig*. Its harsh sound, whether pronounced in the correct German way or in the American way, caused further qualms, and it was decided to translate it. But the clergyman employed to baptize me wrote in *Louis* in his certificate, and so I acquired a French name. It was, of course, always pronounced *Lewis* in the family circle. I have often thought of changing it to something more plausible, but have somehow never got to the business.

Lester, Milton and the like. Later on they abjured that madness, and today, save for an occasional *Rudolph, Fritz* or *Otto*, their given-names are hardly distinguishable from the general.[1]

The first Jews to come to America in any number were of the Sephardic moiety; the favorite given-names among them were *Solomon, Benjamin, Daniel, David, Elias, Emmanuel, Nathan, Isaac, Nathaniel* and *Mendes*, and these are pretty well preserved among their descendants today. But the German Jews who came in after 1848 were considerably less faithful to the ancestral *Samuel, Jonas, Isaac, Moses, Isidor, Israel* and *Leon*, most of which have been gradually disappearing. In the first American-born generation there were some rather fantastic attempts at substitution, *e.g.*, *Morton* for *Moses, Leo* or *Lee* for *Leon*, and *Seymour* or *Sanders* for *Samuel*, but in the main the old names were simply abandoned, and American names adopted instead. The later-coming Polish and Russian Jews went much faster and much further. Even the most old-fashioned of them, says Abraham Cahan, changed *Yosel* to *Joseph, Yankel* to *Jacob, Liebel* to *Louis, Feivel* to *Philip, Itzik* to *Isaac, Ruven* to *Robert*, and *Moishe* or *Motel* to *Morris* as soon as they began to find their way about, and presently their sons burst forth as *Sidney, Irving, Milton, Stanley* and *Monroe*. Their grandsons are *John, Charles, Harold, James, Edward, Thomas*, and even *Mark, Luke* and *Matthew*, and their daughters are *Mary, Jane, Elizabeth, Alice* and *Edith*. In Baltimore, probably due to Southern influence, *Carol* and *Shirley* are favorite given-names for girls among the Polish Jews. In the Middle West, prompted by Scandinavian examples, there are Jewish *Huldas, Karens* and *Helgas*. In the New York telephone directory (Winter, 1934–5) I find Cohens male named *Allen, Archie, Arthur, Bert, Carl, Charles, Clarence, DeWitt, Edgar, Edward, Ed-*

1 *Carl* has been adopted by Americans of other stocks, and such combinations as *Carl* Gray (a railroad president born in Arkansas), *Carl* Williams (a farm-paper editor, born in Indiana), and *Carl* Murphy (the founder of the Baltimore *Afro-American*, a leading Negro newspaper) are common. A feminine variant, *Karle*, has appeared, and I suspect that *Carl* has helped to popularize *Carlyle* and *Carleton*. Simon Newton (see the *World Almanac* for 1921, p. 150) sought to determine the most popular American given-names by examining 100,000 names in biographical dictionaries, Army and Navy registers, Masonic rosters and the Detroit City Directory. He found that *John, William, James, George* and *Charles* were the most popular, in the order named, but that *Carl* was thirty-eighth, and ahead of *Ernest, Michael, Lewis* and *Hugh*, all of which would have been far above it on an English list.

win, Elliot, Ellis, Ernest, Felix, Frank, Frederick, George, Godfrey, Harry,[1] *Harvey, Henry, Herbert, Howard, Irving, Jack, Jacques, James, Jerome, Jules, Lawrence, Lee, Lester, Malcolm, Mark, Martin, Marvin, Mathias, Maximilian, Maxwell, Michael, Mitchell, Mortimer, Morton, Murray, Norman, Oscar, Paul, Philip, Ralph, Sidney, Theodore, Victor* and *William,* and Cohens female named *Amelia, Annabel, Annette, Bessie, Betty, Birdie, Charlotte, Dorothy, Elizabeth, Emily, Estelle, Ethel, Florence, Gertrude, Helen, Irene, Jennie, Josephine, Lucille, Mae, Mary, Myra, Rae, Renee, Rose, Sophia, Sue* and *Sylvia.* There are but three *Moses* Cohens, three *Moes* and one *Moise,* but there are seven *Lawrences,* eight *Herberts* and fifteen *Henrys.* Among the ladies there is not a single *Rachel, Miriam* or *Rebecca,* and the four surviving *Sarahs* are overborne by three *Sadies,* two *Saras* and one *Sally.*

Any other list of Jewish names would show a similar disappearance of the older forms. I turn to a history of Zeta Beta Tau, the Jewish college fraternity, published in its *Quarterly* for April, 1931, and find the following given-names among Jews who are otherwise extremely conscious of their Jewishness: *Vernon, Lawrence, Clarence, Kay, Randolph, Pierce, Seymour, Lionel, Ernest, Tracy, Willis, Mortimer, Jules, Deane, Allyn, Lazarre, Les* and *Bert,* not to mention *Frederick, Edward, George, William, Charles, Harold, Richard, Ralph, Walter, Theodore, Arnold* and *Alan.* In a list including the names of more than 275 members I find but one *Abraham* and one *Samuel,* and not a single *Moses* or *Isaac.* In another issue of the same magazine is a somewhat spoofish article on current Jewish given-names.[2] The authors divide them into three classes, the Biblical, the mercantile, and the baronial. " Examples of the first group," they say, "though not entirely extinct, have about lapsed into disuse." The mercantile names " are those of children who are bound to succeed in the world of affairs."

We find possessors of these names in operators of the cloak and suit industry, and in the smaller towns they are invariably the proprietors of the leading clothing shoppes. Generally, the bearer of a mercantile name, *viz.: Julius, Max,*

1 In Berlin, according to the Jewish Encyclopedia, Vol. IX, p. 157, *Harry* is now monopolized by the Jews, and so are *Jacques* and *James.* All, it will be noted, are non-German names. But two old German names, *Ludwig* and *Julius,* are also greatly in favor. See N. Pulvermacher: Berliner Vornamen; Berlin, 1902.

2 On Naming the Boy, by Earl L. and Samuel G. Winer, *Zeta Beta Tau Quarterly,* Dec., 1926, p. 7.

Emanuel, Gus or *Nathan*, is a representative constituent of our most conservative and substantial citizenry. His business continues successfully through two or more generations. He passes important motions at the B'nai B'rith Conventions and at the Conventions of the National Clothiers Association. Horatio Alger's Julius the Street Boy was probably of Jewish extraction, for his exploits exemplify a protagonist of this type.

The authors divide their baronial group into four subgroups — Anglo-Saxon family names, *e.g., Sydney, Melvin* and *Murray;* names taken from the map of England, *e.g., Chester, Ely* and *Hastings;* aromatic French names, *e.g., Lucien, Jacques* and *Armand;* and surnames of popular heroes, *e.g., Lincoln, Sherman* and *Lee.* "The eldest son," they say, "is *Abraham;* then in order follow *Hyman, Julius, Sydney, Leonard,* and finally the élite *Llewelyn.*" They close with a warning that Jewish given-names begin to grow so incongruous that they may do damage to their bearers.

The owner of the name becomes a misfit because of his styling, and finds it exceedingly difficult to acclimate the man to the name. Wherefore the parents of a child, in bestowing upon him his given designation, should first invoke the gods that be, and then exercise care and caution to give their eight-day-old scion a name that will please him when he reaches an age whereat he has an appreciation of phonetics and an understanding of the association of ideas.

Among the East Side Jews of New York (now mainly translated to the Bronx) any youth showing a talent for music is likely to abandon his original given-name for *Misha, Jasha* or *Sasha,* all of them Russian diminutives; and among the younger female *intelligentsia Sonia* is a prime favorite. But these are probably only passing fashions.

The Latin immigrants to the United States have had even less difficulty with their given-names than with their surnames, and have thus changed them more rarely than the Jews. The Spanish *Jorge, José, Juan, Jaimé, Francisco, Manuel, Ignacio, Pedro, Tomas* and *Antonio* have fared pretty well in this country, and in the regions where there is a relatively large Spanish-speaking population they are even pronounced more or less correctly. Occasionally, along the border, *Francisco* becomes *Frank, José* becomes *Joe, Pedro* becomes *Pete,* and *Santiago* (not *Jaimé*) becomes *Jim,* but *Juan* seldom if ever changes his name to *John,* and *Jesus* (*hay-soos,* with the accent on the second syllable) commonly sticks to his name, despite the fact that it seems half-ridiculous and half-scandalous to most Americans. *María* is a frequent given-name for men in Mexico, but it is seldom heard in the American Southwest. Sometimes it is changed to the more masculine *Mariano,* and sometimes it is quietly dropped for something else. *Manuel* and *Ignacio* are never changed.[1] *Manoel* is a favorite given-name among the Portuguese, and the first-born son almost always bears it, just as the first-born daughter is *Maria.* But in the New Bedford region the Portuguese immigrants commonly change *Manoel* to *Manuel,* and *Maria* to *Mary.* Other frequent changes are from *José* to *Joseph* or *Joe,* from *Francisco* to *Frank,* from *Lourenço* to *Lawrence,* from *João* to *John* or *Jack,* from *Rafael* to *Ralph,* from *Guilherme* to *William* or *Bill,* from *Pedro* to *Peter,* from *Margarida* to *Margaret* or *Maggie,* from *Ignês* to *Agnes,* from *Amélia* to *Emma,* from *Ana* to *Annie,* and from *Izabel* to *Lizzie, Betty* or *Elizabeth.*[2] Among the Rumanians, similarly, *Ioan* becomes *John, Marin* becomes *Martin* or *Marian, Dănilă* and *Dumitrue* become *Daniel* or *Dan, Mihai* becomes *Mike, Gheorghe* becomes *George, Florea* becomes *Frank, Floarea* becomes *Florence* or *Flora, Cataline* becomes *Katie, Maria* becomes *Mary,* and *Lina,* rather curiously, becomes *Helen.*[3] The Italian given-names fare pretty well in the United States. Most Americans call any strange Italian *Joe* or *John,* but it does not outrage them to discover that his real name is *Antonio, Andrea, Carlo, Bartolomeo, Uberto, Nicolo, Tomaso* or *Vincenzo. Giuseppe, Giacomo* and *Giovanni,* being harder for them, are commonly changed to *Joseph, Jack* and *John.* In the second generation almost every *Vincenzo* becomes a *Vincent,* every *Riccardo* a *Richard,* every *Giuseppe* a *Joseph* and every *Tomaso* a *Thomas,* but the influence of the priests keeps the Italians, like the Mexicans, from venturing into the gaudy nomenclature of the Jews. The charming Italian names for women, *e.g., Antonietta, Bianca, Carlotta, Costanza, Letizia* and *Giuliana,* show signs of surviving in America: they are sometimes, though still rarely, borrowed by Americans of the older stocks. The Scandinavian names, in the

1 I am indebted here to Mr. Hugh Morrison of New York, who lived long among Mexicans in the West. He says he knows one sensitive immigrant who changed his given-name of *Jesús,* to *José* "to escape smirks."

2 I am indebted here to Mr. Peter L. C. Silveira, editor of the *Jornal Portugues* of Oakland, Calif., to Mr. Charles J. Lovell, of Pasadena, and to Mr. João R. Rocha, proprietor of *O Independente,* New Bedford, Mass. Mr. Lovell's investigations show that among the *Sylvias,* a numerous Portuguese-American tribe, the four names, *Manuel, Joseph, John* and *Antone,* account for 47.3% of all males.

3 I am indebted here to Mr. George Stanculescu, editor of the *American Roumanian News,* Cleveland.

main, are likewise under only light pressure, *e.g.*, *Gustaf*, *Erik*, *Olof* (or *Olaf*), *Nils*, *Anders*, *Magnus*, *Gunnar*, *Axel*, *Holger*, *Knut*, *Jens*, *Harald* and *Henrik*. *Hjalmar* is sometimes changed to *Elmer* or *Henry*, and *Sven* to *Stephen*, but the rest appear likely to survive. So do some of the Scandinavian women's names, *e.g.*, *Hedvig*, *Sigrid*, *Helma*, *Magdalene*, *Ingeborg* and *Karen* (or *Karin*). But a great many of the Scandinavians born in this country, of course, bear " American" names. The present Governor of Minnesota (1935) is *Floyd B.* Olson, and his Secretary of State is *Mike* Holm. However, it should be noted that the *B* in Governor Olson's name stands for *Bjerstjerne*,[1] and that among the other Olsons and Olsens in " Who's Who in America" are a *Nils*, an *Ingerval*, a *Karl*, a *Carl*, an *Ernst*, two *Oscars* and two *Juliuses*. The Finns abandon their native given-names much more willingly. Most of the children born in this country are given " American" names, and even among their elders *Kalle* and *Kaarlo* are commonly changed to *Charley* or *Charles*, *Jussi* and *Juhana* to *John*, *Matti* to *Matthew*, *Jaakko* to *Jack*, *Taavetti* to *David*, *Yrgö* to *George*, *Antti* to *Andrew* or *Andy*, *Kerttu* to *Gertrude*, *Maija* to *Mary*, *Lilja* to *Lillian*, *Elly* to *Ellen* and *Aili* to *Aileen*. The ineffable *Elmer* often displaces *Ilmari* and *Raymond* takes the place of *Reino*. For *Väinö* the common substitute is *Wayne*. Sometimes a *Kalle*, on changing his name to *Charley*, finds the combination of sounds impossible, and must make shift with *Sali*. Similarly, a *Liisa*, Americanized to *Lizzie*, calls herself *Lisi*, for there is no z-sound in the Finnish phonology. But she writes it *Lizzie*.[2]

It is the Slavs whose given-names suffer most sadly in the Republic. Whatever his own wishes in the premisses may be, every Pole named *Stanislaw* must resign himself to being called *Stanley* by his neighbors, and every *Sztefan* must consent to become a *Steve*. In the same way *Czeslaw* is changed to *Chester*, *Vladislaw* to *Walter*, *Vatslaw* to *Wallace*, *Piotr* to *Pete*, *Grzegdrz* to *Harry*, and *Kazimierz* to *Casey*, and, among women's names, *Miechyslawa* to *Mildred* and *Bronislawa* to *Bertha*. So, too, the Russian *Michayil* becomes *Mike*, his brother *Andrey* becomes *Andy*, and his cousin *Grisha* joins

1 If he spelled it out it would probably cost him some votes. Years ago a Norwegian tramp-steamer, the *Björnstjerne Björnson*, named after the celebrated contemporary of Ibsen, used to trade to Baltimore. The stevedores, baffled by the name, reduced it to *Be-jesus Be-johnson*.
2 For aid here I am indebted to Mr. Ivar Vapaa, editor of *Industrialisti*, Duluth, Minn., and to Mr. Reino W. Soujanen, editor of *Walwoja*, Calumet, Mich.

the Polish *Grzegdrz* as *Harry*. All *Ivans*, of course, quickly become *Johns*. Among the Ukrainians nearly every *Wasil* (a popular name in the Ukraine) becomes *William*, though *Basil* would be a better equivalent. In the case of *Hryhory* (Gregory) transliteration beats translation, and it becomes *Harry*. Other common changes are from *Volodymyr* (the Russian *Vladimir*) to *Walter*, from *Andrey* (Andrew) to *Albert*, from *Bohdan* to *Daniel*, from *Myroslav* to *Myron*, from its feminine form, *Myroslava*, to *Marilyn*, and from the lovely *Nadia* to the banal *Hope*.[1] Monsignor J. B. Dudek has described at length the slaughter of Czech given-names. When they show any resemblance to "American" names, as in the cases, for example, of *Jan*, *Petr*, *Tomáš*, *Antonín* and *Marie*, they are quickly displaced by the "American" names. In other cases they are translated, as when *Vavřinec* becomes *Lawrence* and *Bohdanka* becomes *Dorothy*. In yet other cases there are arbitrary changes to quite unrelated "American" names, as when *Václav*, which means crowned with a wreath, becomes *James* or *William*, and *Vojtěch*, which means the leader of an army, becomes *William* or *Albert*. Says Monsignor Dudek:

> *Cenék*, an old name dating back to pagan times, is still in use among modern Czechs. It is a corruption of *Castoslav* (*častovati*, to treat, to show hospitality). For no apparent reason *Vincent* is sometimes taken instead. *Hynek* is a corruption of the German nickname *Heinz* (*Heinrich*), and, through resemblance to the Spanish *Hinigo*, is often incorrectly translated *Ignatius*, which exists in Bohemian as *Ignát* or *Ignač*. Both *Hynek* and *Ignát* sometimes become *Enoch* in this country. . . . Small boys christened *Václav* are frequently called *Wesley* until their Catholic parents become aware of the incongruity of putting their offspring under the patronage of a Methodist saint. Occasionally, however, *Wesley* remains, or is shortened to *Wes*. *Silvestr* (*Sylvester*) turns also into *Wes*. Both *Míchal* (*Michael*) and *Mikuláš* become *Mike*, though *Mikuláš* is the Czech form of *Nicholas*, and should therefore be rather *Nick*, which I have not heard among American Czechs.[2]

Monsignor Dudek reports some curious efforts to take American given-names into American-Czech. He says:

1 I am indebted here to Mr. Emil Revyuk, editor of *Svoboda*, the Ukrainian daily of Jersey City, and to Mr. Vladimir Geeza, editor of the *New Life*, of Olyphant, Pa.
2 The Americanization of Czech Given-Names, *American Speech*, Oct., 1925. A list of "American" equivalents of Czech given names, apparently for the use of readers desiring to make changes, is printed annually in the Cesko-Americký Kalendář issued by *Katolík*, the Czech semi-weekly published by the Benedictine Fathers in Chicago. It is full of unconscious humors. Thus it gives *Patricius* and *Paddy* for *Vlastimil* but not *Patrick*, *Bess*, *Betsy* and *Betty* for *Alžběta* but not *Elizabeth*, and *Nell* and *Nelly* for *Helena* but not *Helen*.

Džán and *Džim* have obtained recognition in print as Bohemian versions of *John* and *Jim;* there are also the diminutives, *Džaník* (*Johnnie*) and *Džimik* (*Jimmie*).¹ *Gladyška* is American-Bohemian for *Gladys*, which, as far as I know, does not exist in Czech proper.

Chauncey, says Monsignor Dudek, is one American given-name from which Czech-American boys are safe, for it suggests the Czech word *čunče*, a suckling pig. The girls are likewise protected against *Mabel*, for most Czechs know sufficient German to think of the German word *möbel*, which means furniture. "But fond Bohemian-American mammas," he concludes, "have tried everything from *Abalina* to *Zymole* on female infants, and *Kenneth, Chilson, Luther, Dewey, Woodrow, Calvin*, etc., have been bestowed upon the sons of families clinging to surnames like *Kubíček, Ševčík, Borecký, Pospíšil, Veverka* and *Vrba*." Mr. William Absolon sends me some curious examples: *Ellsworth* Kos, *La Verne Joan* Vodnaňová, *Wayne* Stodola, *Priscilla* Zeman, *Marylin* Kučera and *Virgil Forrest* Strachota. "It is," he says, "beyond the powers of a *hostinský* in Nové Město, Praha, to fathom the visitor who signs the hotel register *Courtney Roland* Cížek, ordering a *veprová*, or *Leslie Wells* Zástěrka, raising a litre of *Plzenský*."

The Greek given-names go the same route. They are not changed, says Mr. Sotirios S. Lontos, editor of the *Atlantis*, the Greek daily of New York, "in a haphazard way, but more or less in accordance with established standards." He goes on:

[If a Greek's] first name is *Panagiotis* he is advised that henceforth he will be called *Pete*. *Demetrios* becomes *Jim*, *Basil* is changed into *Bill*, *Haralampos* into *Harry*, *Stacros* into *Steve*, and *Christos* into *Crist*. If his name is *Constantine* he has the choice of either *Gus* or *Charles*, and as a rule he gives preference to the first as nearer in sound to his original name. If he is called *Athanasios* he can select either *Athan* or *Nathan*, or *Tom* for his new name. *Demosthenes* is usually abbreviated into *Demos*. That was too plebeian a name, however, for a certain proprietor of an aristocratic candy shop, who very effectively gave his name the noble form of *De Moss*. Finally, while anybody called *Michael* may retain this name for American usage, among his countrymen here he will be known as *Mackis*, which is the Greek version of *Mike*.²

Similar patterns of change are to be found among the Syrians. *Mikha'il* becomes *Michael* or *Mitchell*, *Jurjus* becomes *George*,

---

1 In the same way the Lithuanians in America have developed *Džióvas* for *Joe*. See Einiges aus der Sprache der Amerika-Litauer, by Alfred Senn, *Sudi Baltici* (Rome), Vol. II, 1932, p. 47.

2 American Greek, *American Speech*, March, 1926. I am also indebted to Mr. T. D. Curculakis, of Athens.

Dauud becomes *David*, *Butrus* becomes *Peter*, and *Hanna* becomes *John*. So far the Christian Syrians. Among the Moslems *Mahmoud* takes the strange form of *Mike*, and *Habib* becomes *Harry*.[1] The Irish in America seldom succumb to that fashion for Gaelic given-names which now prevails in the Irish Free State. An occasional Irish boy is named *Padraic* (*Patrick*), *Sean* (*John*) or *Seumas* (*James*), but when this is done a concession is commonly made to American speech habits by giving *Padraic* three syllables instead of the proper two, by making *Sean Seen* instead of *Shawn*, and by making *Seumas Seemas* or *Sumas* instead of *Shamus*.[2] Such forms as *Peadar* (*Peter*), *Caitlin* (*Cathleen*), *Marie* (*Mary*), *Sighle* (*Sheila*), *Eibhlin* (*Eileen*), *Seosmh* (*Joseph*), *Liam* (*William*) and *Stiobhan* (*Stephen*) are not often encountered. The Chinese seldom change their family-names, but nearly all of them adopt "American" given-names. In the days when Chinese laundrymen were numerous in the big cities the generic name for them was *John*, but they also called themselves *Frank, George, Charlie, Lee* (from *Li*), *Tom, Jim* and so on, and I once encountered one named *Emil*. On higher levels more pretentious names are taken. Thus a late Chinese ambassador to the United States, educated in this country, was Dr. Vi-Kyuin *Wellington* Koo, one of his successors was Dr. Sao-ke *Alfred* Sze. Most such Chinese use their original Chinese names at home; the "American" given-names are commonly for use abroad only. In a recent issue of the *Chinese Christian Student* I find the following somewhat bizarre combinations:

Wesley K. C. May	*Tennyson* Chang
Luther Shao	*Hunter* Hwang
Tarkington Tseng	*Herman* Chan-en Liu
Jennings Pinkwei Chu	*Mabel* Ping-Hua Lee
Quentin Pen	*Fisher* Yu
Ivan Wong	*Moses* Swen

The American Indians, as they take on the ways of the white man, commonly abandon their native names, at least outside the tribal circle. In a list of the graduates of the Carlisle Indian School[3] I find a Chippewa named *Francis Coleman*, a Seneca named *Mary J. Greene*, a Gros Ventre named *Jefferson Smith*, and a Sioux named

1 I am indebted here to Mr. H. I. Katibah, editor of the *Syrian World*.

2 Here I am indebted to Mr. Ernest Boyd.

3 Names of Graduates of the Carlisle Indian School, 1889–1913; Carlisle, Pa., 1914.

Inez Brown. Sometimes the tribal names are retained as surnames, either translated or not, *e.g.*, *Standing Bear, Bighorse, Blackbear, Yellow Robe, Sixkiller, Lone Wolf, White Thunder, Red Kettle, Owl Wahneeta, Wauskakamick, Beaver, Nauwagesic, Tatiyopa, Weshinawatok, Kenjockety, Standingdeer, Yukkanatche, Ironroad* and *Whitetree*, but such forms are greatly outnumbered by commonplace English names, *e.g.*, *Jackson, Simpson, Brown, Johnson, Stevens, Jones, Smith* and *Walker*, and by names borrowed from the Spanish, *e.g.*, *Martinez, Miguel, Rodriguez* and *Ruiz*, and from various white immigrant languages, *e.g.*, *Leider, Geisdorff, Haffner, Snyder, Volz, Petoskey, McDonald, Hogan, Peazzoni, Lundquist* and *DeGrasse*. On the reservations, the tribal names are in wider use, but even there they are often translated. Says Mr. H. L. Davis:

The Indian Bureau for some years made an effort to retain the Indians' names in their original languages, translations into English only being sanctioned when the native version was too long or too unpronounceable to admit of fast handling. However, almost all Indian names are ungodly long and almost totally unpronounceable, so translation has been pretty generally adopted everywhere. Sometimes the results are upsetting, especially when the Indians aren't sufficiently saddle-broke to understand what a name that sounds entirely all right in their own lingo may sound like when translated literally. Appellations such as *Dirty Face* and *Big Baby* are received with the utmost solemnity by the Cheyennes, the Sioux have *Bull Head* and *Stink Tail*, I have heard of a chief on the Northwest Coast who answered with the utmost simplicity and frankness to *Unable-to-Fornicate* (or words to that effect), and I once knew a Siletz who insisted with firm complacency that his name, no matter what anybody thought about it, was *Holy Catfish.*—

Native names in the native language have generally been retained among the Navajo and to a considerable extent among the White Mountain Apache. It is a kind of half-and-half business, for the Indian Bureau requires the patronymic to apply to all heirs of a man's body, which by itself upsets the whole Indian name-system wherever it is applied. Indians in a free state don't use patronymics at all. Among the White Mountain Apache the problem is attacked more sensibly; the Indians are permitted to take what names they please, and for registration purposes are given reference-letters and numbers, like automobiles.

The Paiute Indians of the Great Basin get round the patronymic requirement by keeping their native names only for religious and ceremonial purposes, and adopting for business use the surname of some white family — generally that of some rancher whom the Indian works for or bums from regularly. This will eventually result, of course, in the native names disappearing entirely, as it has done among the Cherokee and such tribes of the Eastern United States, and as doubtless it did among the Negroes of the South in the early stages of slave-importation.[1]

[1] Private communication. See also Indian Personal Names from the Nebraska and Dakota Regions, by Margaret Kennell, *American Speech*, Oct., 1935.

John remains the favorite given-name among native Americans today, as it has been among people of British stock since the Norman Conquest. Following it comes *William*, and following *William* come *James*, *Charles* and *George*.[1] The popularity of *John* and *William*, says a writer in the *Nation* (New York), "cannot be explained on the grounds that they are short, for *William* is not, or that they are Biblical, for so are the now happily extinct *Shadrach*, *Meshach* and *Abednego*, or that they are fine, strong names, for so are *Roger*, *Guy*, *Nicholas* and *Bartholomew*, which have hardly any currency." For a time *John's* and *William's* popularity was so great that it was necessary to qualify them. In 1545 the will of John Parnell de Gyrton ran thus:

Alice, my wife, and *Olde John*, my son, to occupy my farm together til *Olde John* marries; *Young John*, my son, shall have Brenlay's land.[2]

I once knew an American family, of German origin, in which it was an immemorial custom to name every son *John*. There were eight or ten in that generation: they were distinguished by their middle names, which ranged from *Adam* to *Thomas*. After the publication of the Genevan Bible, in 1570, children began to be given Biblical names in England, but the fashion lasted only long enough to be transplanted to the New World, where vestiges of it are still encountered. I find *Reuben*, *Zebulon* and *Josh* (apparently a clipped form of *Joshua*) on the roll of the Seventy-fourth Congress, and *Ezra*, *Hiram*, *Ezekiel*, *Zechariah*, *Elijah*, *Isaiah* and *Elihu* in "Who's Who in America." These names excite the derision of the English; an American comic character, in an English novel or play, usually bears one — that is, when he is not named *Jefferson* or *Washington*. The pious extravagances of the Puritan nomenclature belong to half-forgotten history, but they are recalled by certain surviving

1 Simon Newton's study, summarized in the *World* Almanac for 1921, shows that *John* occurs 8280 in every 100,000 individuals, *William* 7611 times, *James* 4259, *Charles* 4253, and *George* 4171. Following come *Thomas* 2710, *Henry* 2366, *Robert* 2303, *Joseph* 2266, *Edward* 1997, *Samuel* 1628, *Frank* 1570, *Harry* 1112, *Richard* 1027, *Francis* 1003, *Frederick* 1000, *Walter* 970, *David* 967, *Arthur* 904, *Albert* 862, *Benjamin* 833, *Alexander* 748, *Daniel* 690, *Louis* 658, *Harold* 531, *Paul* 512, *Fred* 509, *Edwin* 500 and *Andrew* 485. *Raymond* is in forty-ninth place, with 244 occurrences, *Elmer* is sixty-first with 174, *Chester* in seventy-third with 131, *Harvey* in seventy-ninth with 122, *Milton* in ninety-fifth with 96. Rather curiously, *Washington* and *Marshall* are below *Homer* and *Luther*.
2 In the Driftway, *Nation*, Feb. 7, 1923.

women's names, *e.g.*, *Mercy*, *Faith*, *Charity*, *Hope* and *Prudence*, and by occasional men's names, *e.g.*, *Peregrine* and *Preserved*. The more old-fashioned Mormons sometimes name their children after eminent characters in the demonology of their faith, *e.g.*, *Nephi*, *Lehi*, *Mahonri* and *Moroni*, all of which are to be found in the Salt Lake City telephone directory, along with many *Hebers*, *Jareds* and *Lamans*. But the younger generation leans toward more fanciful names, *e.g.*, *La Rue*, *Yerma*, *Tola* and *Lavar* for girls, *La Mar*, *Feramorz* and *Herald* for boys, and *La Verne* for both girls and boys. Among the Youngs of Salt Lake I find two *Brighams*, a *Percival*, a *Don Carlos*, a *Spencer*, a *Seymour* and a *Leslie*, but no *Nephi* or *Moroni*.[1] Some years ago a devout Norwegian Mormon in Salt Lake City named his twin sons *Cherubim* and *Seraphim*. The use of surnames as given-names is far more general in the United States than in England, or, indeed, than in any other country. Fully three out of four eldest sons, in American families of any pretensions, bear their mothers' surnames either as first names or as middle names. This use of surnames originated in England during the Seventeenth Century, and one of its fruits was the adoption of a number of distinguished names, *e.g.*, *Cecil*, *Howard*, *Douglas*, *Percy*, *Duncan* and *Stanley*, as common given-names.[2] But the English began a return to *John*, *Charles* and *William* during the century following, and now the use of surnames is distinctively American. Of the fourteen Presidents of the United States who have had middle names at all, nine have had family names, and of these three dropped their given-names and used these family names instead. Six other Presidents have had family names as given-names. This makes fifteen in all, or half the whole number since Washington. On the roll of the House of Representatives, Seventy-fourth Congress, I find Representatives christened *Graham*, *Prentiss*, *Bryant*, *Wilburn*, *Glover*, *Parker*, *Colgate*, *Braswell*, *Everett*, *Usher*, *Wall*, *Aubert*, *Hampton*, *Allard*, *Finly*, *Byron*, *Dow*, *Lister*, *Marvin*, *Maury*, *Tilman*, *Jennings*, *Compton* and *Hatton*, beside the usual *Randolphs*, *Chesters*, *Lloyds*, *Cliffords*, *Melvins*, *Schuylers*, *Wesleys*, *Miltons*, *Deweys*, *Clevelands*, *Bayards*, *Warrens*, *Chaunceys* and *Elmers*. *Chauncey* was the surname of the second president of Harvard (1654–72). It was bestowed upon their offspring by some of his graduates, and came into im-

---

1 I am indebted for part of this to Mr. Theodore Long, of Salt Lake City.

2 See Curiosities of Puritan Nomenclature, by Charles W. Bardsley; London, 1880, p. 205 *ff.*

mediate popularity, possibly on the ground that it had a vaguely Biblical smack. *Elmer* was the surname of two brothers of New Jersey who played active but forgotten parts in the Revolution.[1] *Washington, Jefferson, Jackson, Lincoln, Marshall, Columbus, Lee, Calvin, Luther, Wesley* and *Homer*, all familiar given-names in the United States, are quite unknown in England. It is common in this country for a woman, on marrying, to use her maiden surname as a middle name; thus, Miss *Mary Jones*, on becoming Mrs. *Brown*, signs herself *Mary Jones Brown*. It is also common, as I have noted in Section 1 of this chapter, for divorcées to use their maiden surnames in combination with their late husbands' names, either with or without hyphenization; thus, Mrs. *John Brown*, née *Jones*, on leaving John's bed and board, becomes either Mrs. *Jones-Brown* or Mrs. *Jones Brown*.

Many strange given-names are to be found in any American list of names. A former Chicago judge, once constantly in the newspapers, was baptized *Kenesaw Mountain*, after the scene of General W. T. Sherman's defeat on June 27, 1864.[2] The general himself had *Tecumseh* for his middle name — one of the very few cases of a white man bearing an Indian name in American history. He was called *Cump* by Mrs. Sherman. A late politico of New York, once a candidate for Governor, had the given-name of *D-Cady*, and a late American ethnologist, McGee, always insisted that his first name was simply *W J*, and that these letters were not initials and should not be followed by periods. A public accountant in Philadelphia is *Will-A.* Clader: he tells me that " the hyphen is the result of poor chirography " and that he adopted the style because people began using it in writing to him. In Connecticut, some years ago, there was a politician named K. N. Bill whose given-names were *Kansas Nebraska*, and he had a sister baptized *Missouri Compromise*.[3] The

---

1 In Defense of *Elmer*, New York *Herald-Tribune* (editorial) Jan. 18, 1935. In the Toronto *Saturday Night*, March 16, 1935, J. H. Simpson says that *Elmer* has now invaded Canada. Mr. Simpson also notes the popularity of *Earl* — a two-syllable word, like *fil-lum* — " in what might be termed the less sophisticated parts of the United States." In these parts, he continues, " a peculiar custom is to hold hus-band-calling contests. One has to hear a Kansas farmer's wife calling her *Earl* or *Elmer* to appreciate the depths to which a so-called Christian name can sink."

2 The Geographic Board has decided that *Kenesaw* should be *Kennesaw*, but the learned judge sticks to one *n*.

3 For this I have to thank Mr. William J. Foote, of the Hartford *Courant*.

chaplain of the United States Senate is the Rev. Ze Barney T. Phillips, D.D.: the Public Printer had to have a character specially cut to print the name.¹ A well-known American writer, of Spanish ancestry, is *Emjo* Basshe. His given names were originally *Emmanuel Jode Abarbanel.* " When I grew older," he says, " and realized that one could not carry around so many names without tripping I took *Em* from my first name and *Jo* from my second, and *Em Jo* came to life. Foolishly I did not join the two, and a lot of critics had a holiday with them. But I did later, and *Emjo* became my name, legally and otherwise." ² There was a Revolutionary patriot named *Daniel of St. Thomas* Jenifer, and he has a descendant of that name in Maryland today. Thornton reprints a paragraph from the *Congressional Globe* of June 15, 1854, alleging that in 1846, during the row over the Oregon boundary, when " Fifty-four forty or fight" was a political slogan, many " canal-boats, and even some of the babies . . . were christened *54° 40'.*"

In many minor ways there are differences in nomenclatural usage between England and the United States. The English, especially of the upper classes, frequently give a boy three or more given-names, but it is most unusual in the United States. *Michael* is now fashionable in England, but here it is bestowed only rarely.³ *Evelyn*, in England, is given to boys as well as girls, but not in this country, though *Florence* is sometimes encountered among Irishmen, and a late Governor of Kentucky, indubitably he, was the Hon. *Ruby* Laffoon. Many aristocratic English given-names, *e.g.*, *Reginald, Algernon, Percy, Wilfred, Cedric, Cyril, Cecil, Aubrey* and *Claude*, are commonly looked upon as sissified in the United States, and any boy who bears one of them is likely to have to defend it with his fists.⁴

1 Dr. Phillips tells me that his given-name is the surname of some of his father's relatives. His father also bore it. The Ze Barney family, once well-known in Chautauqua county, New York, is now extinct there. There is a tradition that the Ze is roughly equivalent to the Mac in Gaelic names, but of this nothing is known certainly. C. L'E. Ewen, in A History of the Surnames of the British Isles, says (p. 379) that *zeu* appears as an element in some Cornish names, signifying black. It has *deu, sew* and *sue* as variants.

2 Private communication, July 22, 1935. Mr. Basshe has since informed me that his first child has been named *Emjo* likewise.

3 It stands in forty-second place on the Newton list, with 314 occurrences to every 100,000 individuals.

4 In *Claude* and *Percy, American Speech*, April, 1928, Howard F. Barker quotes the following from an unidentified issue of the *Christian Science Monitor* (Boston): " Captain Claude S. Cochrane, commander of the *Bear* and associated with its later adventures, will leave his old ship and go North in

Only one *Percival*, so far as I know, has ever appeared in "Who's Who in America." It is very uncommon, in England, for diminutives to be bestowed at baptism, but in this country many girls are christened *Peggy, Flo, Mamie, Mollie* or *Beth*, and on the roll of the Seventy-fourth Congress I find a *Ben*, a *Phil*, a *Josh*, a *Bert*, a *Dan*, a *Tom*, an *Abe*, a *Nat*, a *Sol*, a *Hattie* (once the only lady Senator), a *Fritz*, two *Pats* (both in the Senate), two *Wills*, three *Joes*, five *Sams*, five *Harrys* and seven *Freds*. The Texas delegation alone, twenty-three head of he-men, shows a *Tom*, a *Sam*, a *Nat*, a *Joe* and a *Fritz*. The Newton study of American given-names puts *Harry* in thirteenth place, with 1112 occurrences in every 100,000 individuals, and *Fred* in twenty-seventh, with 509. The English *Hal* is seldom used in this country; here the usual diminutives for *Henry* are *Harry, Hank* and *Hen*. *Alf* is also uncommon in the United States, and *Jem* is unknown. *Ted*, in England, is the diminutive for *Edward;* here it is used for *Theodore*, especially in the form of *Teddy*. In the Southern highlands, says Dr. Josiah Combs,[1] diminutives are very widely used, and " any highlander is lucky if he escapes with his original first-name." The same might be said of most parts of the country. Dr. Combs gives some examples: *Ad* for *Adam*, *Cece* for *Cecil*, *Am* for *Ambrose*, *Clem* for *Clement*, *Hence* for *Henderson*, *Jace* for *Jason*, *Lom* for *Columbus*, *Newt* for *Newton*, *Gid* for *Gideon*, *Lige* for *Elijah*, *Rance* for *Ransom*, *Ves* for *Sylvester*, and *Zach* for *Zachariah*, and, among girls' names, *Barb* for *Barbara*, *Em* for *Emma*, *Marg* for *Margaret*, *Millie* for *Millicent*, *Mildred* and *Amelia*, *Phronie* for *Sophronia*, *Suke* or *Sukey* for *Susan*, *Tavia* for *Octavia*, *Marth* for *Martha*, *Tildy* for *Matilda*, and *Tish* for *Letitia*. He might have added a great many more, e.g., *Lafe* for *Lafayette*, *Wash* for *Washington*, *Jeff* for *Jefferson*, *Frank* for *Francis*, *Bill* for *William*, *Mollie* for *Mary*, *Mamie* or *Polly* for *Margaret*, *Lizzie* or *Betty* for *Elizabeth*, *Gussie* for *Augusta*, and so on. The common mountain name for any boy, he says, is *Bud*, for any male, *Baby*, and for any female, *Sug*.[2] A number of given-names are pronounced differently in Eng-

---

command of the Bering Sea patrol-force. . . . It is said by those who know that he is the only man afloat in the Coast Guard who could afford to admit the name of *Claude*."
1 Language of the Southern Highlanders, *Publications of the Modern*

Language Association, Vol. XLVI, No. 4, p. 1313.
2 It might profit some aspirant to the Ph.D. to investigate the nick-names prevailing among boys. John Brophy and Eric Partridge say in Songs and Slang of the British Soldier, 1914–1918; London, 1930,

land and America. *Evelyn*, in England, is given two syllables instead of three and the first is made to rhyme with *leave*. *Irene* is given three syllables, making it *Irene-y*. *Ralph* is sometimes pronounced *Rafe*, and *Jerome* is accented on the first syllable. Some years ago there was a fashion for changing the spelling of American girls' names, and the country bloomed with *Sharlots*, *Ysobels*, *Edythes*, *Kathryns*, *Goldyes*, *Sadyes* and *Maes*, but now only *Mae* appears to flourish. Despite the frequent bestowal of diminutives at baptism, I believe that their use is also declining. When I was a boy it was very rare, at least in the South, to hear such names as *William*, *Charles*, *Frederick*, *Elizabeth*, *Margaret* and *Lillian* uttered in full, but now it is common. Finally, the American custom of annexing the regal *II*, *III*, etc., to the surnames of boys bearing the given names of uncles, grandfathers or other relatives is quite unknown in the Motherland,[1] and so it is the custom, now happily passing, of addressing boys named after their fathers as *Junior*.

There are some regional differences in American given-names. In the South it is common for a girl to be given a surname as a given-name. Thus *Barnett* Snodgrass or *Powell* Smith may be female and lovely. Mrs. George E. Pickett, the second wife of the general, was baptized *La Salle* and called *Sally*. *Beverly* and *Shirley* are often encountered. Sometimes a girl is actually called *George*, *Frank* or *Charles*, after her father. It is also a custom down there to give a girl two names, and to call her by both. If she is christened *Eva Belle* she remains *Eva Belle* on all occasions, and is never merely *Eva* or *Belle*. Even the servants are always careful to call her *Miss Eva Belle*. These peculiarities are to be observed among the gentry; on

---

that every British soldier named *Taylor* was nicknamed *Buck*, and that the following were also almost universal: *Darky* or *Smudge* for *Smith*, *Nappy* for *Clark*, *Pedlar* for *Palmer*, *Tug* for *Wilson*, *Spud* for *Murphy*, *Dolly* for *Gray* and *Dusty* for *Miller*. When I was a boy in Baltimore, *c.* 1890, every youngster whose father was a physician was called *Doc*, and any boy whose father had any other title got it likewise. Every *Smith* was *Smitty*. Skinny boys were called *Slim*, fat ones were *Fats*, and short ones were *Shortie*. In my gang an

extraordinarily obese boy bore the majestic name of *Barrel*.

1 A distinction seems to be growing up between the use of Roman and Arabic numerals. The latter tend to be reserved for individuals in the direct line of descent. Thus, John Smith 3*rd* is the son of John Smith, *Jr.*, who was the son of John Smith. But John Smith *II* may be a nephew of either John Smith or John Smith, Jr. However, these lines are not yet clearly marked. In the Groton School Catalogue for 1934–35 there are, among 180 boys, 6 II's, 9 III's and 51 Jr.'s.

lower levels there is a prodigious efflorescence of curious feminine names. The aim of every mother is to find a name for her darling that will be both exquisite and unprecedented, and not infrequently a rich if somewhat untutored fancy enters into the process. In the Cumberland Mountains of Tennessee a recent inquirer unearthed *Olsie, Hassie, Coba, Bleba, Onza, Retha, Otella* and *Latrina.*[1] " One girl," he says, " was named *Vest* for no other reason than that her father wrapped her in his vest (English: *waistcoat*) when she was only a week old and carried her proudly across the hollow to display his first-born before admiring neighbors." Another girl was called *Delphia* " cause her Pa, he went to Philadelphia once." In the same vicinity lived a girl named *Trailing Arbutus Vines.* Another investigator, this time in the Blue Ridge of Virginia, found girls named *Needa, Zannis, Avaline* and *Weeda* (the last possibly a corruption of *Ouida*).[2] Bold combinations of common given-names are frequent, *e.g., Lucybelle, Floramay, Lilymary* and *Sallyrose.* Dr. Louise Pound has unearthed some curious examples, *e.g., Olouise* (from *Olive* and *Louise*), *Marjette* (*Marjorie + Henrietta*), *Maybeth* (*May + Elizabeth*), *Lunette* (*Luna + Nettie*), *Leilabeth* (*Leila + Elizabeth*), *Rosella* (*Rose + Bella*), *Adrielle* (*Adrienna + Belle*), *Birdene* (*Birdie + Pauline*), *Bethene* (*Elizabeth + Christine*), *Olabelle* (*Ola + Isabel*), and *Armina* (*Ardelia + Wilhelmina*).[3] Even surnames and men's given-names are employed in these feminine blends, as in *Romiette* (*Romeo + Juliette*), *Adnelle* (*Addison + Nellie*), *Adelloyd* (*Addie + Lloyd*), and *Charline* (*Charles + Pauline*). A woman professor in the Middle West has the given-name of *Eldarema,* coined from those of her grandparents, *Elkanah, Daniel, Rebecca* and *Mary.* The common feminine endings are often used to make entirely new names, some of them very florid in fancy. From Iowa Miss Katherine Buxbaum, of the State Teachers College at Cedar Falls, reports *Darlene, Ombra, Orba, Eneatha, Bashie, Arrazeta, Averill, Beatha, Berneita, Burtyce, Chalene, Clarene, Coelo, Colice, Denva, Garnette, Glenice, Glenola, Icel, Lavaun, La Una, Mirnada, Orvetta, Retha, Twila, Vella, Verlie, Vista, Vola, Waive*

---

1 Christian Names in the Cumberlands, by James A. Still, *American Speech,* April, 1930.
2 Christian Names in the Blue Ridge of Virginia, by Miriam M. Sizer, *American Speech,* April, 1933.

3 Stunts in Language, *English Journal,* Feb., 1920, p. 92; Blends, *Anglistische Forschungen,* heft 42, p. 16.

and *Wave*.[1] From Idaho come *Lejitta, Neuta, Navilla, Uarda, Dupriel, Jeneal, Onola, Oha, Dretha, Vilda, Verla, Utahna* and *Fava;* from Texas, *Estha, Edina, Blooma, Ardis, Iantha, Inabeth, Versey, Vivinne, DeRue, Leora, Ila, Gomeria, Swanell, Verla* and *Valaria;*[2] from Western Maryland, *Le Esta, Dolor, Philadelphia, Emavida* and *Uretha;* from Rhode Island, *Murdena, Seril, Besma, Varlow, Satyra, Ithamer, Zilpah* and *Mosetta;*[3] from Alabama, *Luda, Arrillah, Pet, Eusona, Leetha, Conola, Aklus, Metella, Homera* and *Mahala;*[4] and from the Pacific Coast, *Mauna Loa, Icy Victorious, Henriola, Mirrle, Euliel, Catalpa, Syringia, Wistaria* and *Eschscholtzia*.[5] These regions of onomatological new growth, of course, are predominantly Protestant; in the domains of Holy Church the priests insist upon saints' names, or at all events upon names that conceivable saints might conceivably bear. It would be a mistake, however, to assume that only the lowly patronize novel girls' names. A correspondent in New York has unearthed the following from the Social Register for 1933 and 1934: *Ambolena, Adgurtha, Anzonetta, Armella, Helentzi, Theotiste, Thusnelda, Berinthia, Belva Dula, Credilla, Chancie, Daisette, Estherina, Columbia Maypole, Melrose Abbey, Edelweiss, Yetive, Nopie, Velvalee, Lotawana, Isophene* and *Lamiza*.

The masculine given-names of the Bible Belt are not quite so fanciful as the feminine names, but nevertheless they often depart widely from the accepted standards of the cities. American statesmen named *Hoke, Ollie, Finis* and *Champ* (a shortening of *Beauchamp*, pro. to rhyme with *lamp*) will be recalled. Miss Buxbaum reports pupils baptized *Osey, Thorrel, Burl, Hadwen, Oriel, Lath, Zotas, Koith* and *Iloah* (pro. *I-lo*), and "two stalwart young men named *Merl* and *Verl*."[6] From the Cumberlands of Tennessee James A. Still reports *Oder, Creed, Waitzel, Esco, Oarly, Oral, Osie, Irby, Cam* and *Mord*. Sometimes the pet-names of infancy persist, as in

1 Christian Names, *American Speech,* Oct., 1933.
2 The Texas specimens are from a list of high-school students competing in interscholastic games and debates at the University of Texas, May 4, 5 and 6, 1922.
3 The Sideshow, Providence *Journal,* May 29, 1935.
4 List of Qualified Voters of Talladega County, Ala., Sylcauga *News,* April 25, 1935.

5 This last is the given-name of a lady professor in the University of California. Apparently her parents were fond of the California poppy (*Eschscholtzia californica*). I am indebted here to Mr. Henry Madden of Palo Alto, to Dr. H. E. Rollins of Cambridge, Mass., to Miss Esther Smith of Lonaconing, Md., and to Mr. H. L. Davis.
6 Christian Names, *American Speech,* Oct., 1933.

the cases of young men named *Pee Wee, Poke, Cap, Babe* and *Hoss.* Kentucky, which produced the himalayan *Ollie* James, now has a *Cap* R. Carden (b. 1866) in the House of Representatives (1935). Says Mr. Still:

Three brothers in the little settlement of Shawnee bear the names *Meek, Bent* and *Wild. Lem* and *Lum* are the names of twins. One young man carried the substantial name of *Anvil,* and another that of *Whetstone.* A small mountain boy has *Speed* as his Christian name.[1]

Excessive inbreeding among the mountain people may be responsible in part for this vogue for strange given-names. " When forty-seven persons in one hollow," says Miss Miriam M. Sizer, of Sperryville, Va.,[2] " possess identical surnames, the given-name becomes the common distinguishing factor." Many of the usual American given-names are in use, but sometimes the supply that is locally familiar seems to run out. Miss Sizer's novelties include *Nias, Bloomer, Tera, Malen, Lony, Geurdon, Brasby, Ather, Delmer, Rector, Doley, Elzie, Ivason* and *Elmer Catholic.* " A man who was a great admirer of the James brothers," she says, " named his boy *Jesse-James-and-Frank.* Another . . . named his boy *Christopher-Columbus-Who-Discovered-America.*" At Wetumka, Ala., near Montgomery, there is a tombstone to the memory of " *Henry Ritter Ema Ritter Dema Ritter Sweet Potatoe Creamatartar Caroline* Bostick, daughter of Bob and Suckey Catlen; born at Social Circle, 1843; died at Wetumka, 1852." Obviously, Bob and Suckey admired the whole Ritter family.

Among the Negroes there is naturally a considerable exaggeration of this reaching out for striking and unprecedented names. They have, rather curiously, inherited no given-names from their African ancestors. It is possible that *Cuffy,* which was a common Negro name in the Eighteenth Century, and became a generic name for Negroes later on, was of African origin, but it seems more likely that it was derived from the Dutch *koffie (coffee).* The early slaves were given such names as *Cato, Caesar, Hector, Pompey, Jupiter* and *Agamemnon.*[3] But when they began to assume their masters' sur-

---

1 Christian Names in the Cumberlands, *American Speech,* April, 1930.
2 Christian Names in the Blue Ridge of Virginia, *American Speech,* April, 1933.
3 The only inquiry into early Negro

names that I am aware of has been made by Miss Blanche Britt Armfield, of Concord, N. C., who has kindly placed her observations at my disposal. From Southern newspapers of the period from 1736 to the end of the Eighteenth Century

names they also took all the more usual American given-names, and today the nomenclature of the educated portion of them is indistinguishable from that of the whites. Here are the given-names of the clergy mentioned on the church page of a single issue of the Pittsburgh *Courier,* one of the principal Negro newspapers: *Frederick, John, Talmadge, James, Allen, Miles, Louis, Arthur, Wilbur, George, Claude.* Even in the South, according to Urban T. Holmes of the University of North Carolina,[1] Negro parents " have, for the most part, kept to standard names." But when they depart from the standard they sometimes go even further than their fellow Methodists and Baptists of the dominant race. In Rockingham county, North Carolina, Mr. Holmes unearthed *Agenora, Alferita, Artice, Audrivalus, Earvila, Eldeese, Julina, Katel, Limmer, Louvenia, Ludie, Mareda, Margorilla, Matoka, Orcellia, Princilla, Reada, Roanza, Venton Orlaydo* and *Vertie Ven,* and elsewhere in the total immersion country other Marco Polos have discovered *Clendolia, Deodolphus, Pernella, Delsey, Nazarene, Zion, Vashti, Sociamelia* and *Messiah.* Medical men making a malaria survey of Northampton county, North Carolina, staggered back to civilization with the news that they had found male Aframericans named *Handbag* Johnson, *Squirrel* Bowes, *Prophet* Ransom, *Bootjack* Webb and *Solicitor* Ransom, and females named *Alimenta, Iodine, Zooa, Negolia, Abolena, Arginta* and *Dozine.*[2] And from New Orleans, at about the same time, came news of two Negro babies who, born during a flood, were christened *Highwater* and *Overflow.*[3] A similar catastrophe produced *William McKinley Louisiana Levee Bust* Smith, reported by Miss Naomi C.

(chiefly notices of runaway slaves) she has unearthed *Annika, Boohum, Boomy, Bowzar, Cuffee, Cuffey, Cuffy, Habella, Kauchee, Mila, Minas, Monimea, Pamo, Qua, Quaco, Quamana, Quamina, Quash, Quod, Yonaha* and *Warrah,* and in the files of Catterall's Judicial Cases, running from 1672 to 1848, she has found *Ails, Ama, Anaca, Aphnah, Cato Sabo, Cavannah, Comba, Conder, Cotica, Cuffy, Cush, Dunke, Grizzy, Guela, Isom, Juba, Liceta, Limus, Matha, Mealy, Miley, Minda, Mingo, Mood, Moosa, Mozingo, Naneta, Paya, Quash, Quashey, Quay, Quico, Quomana, Sabany, Sambo, Sauny, Sawney, Seac, Silla,* *Syphax, Tamer, Temba* and *Tenah.* Some of these were probably Indian rather than Negro names. Others were of French or Spanish origin. *Mingo* was the name of an Indian tribe, and it survives as a place-name. *Juba* was the name of two Numidian kings who played parts in the contest between Pompey and Julius Caesar, but it is also the name of a river in Africa.

1 A Study in Negro Onomastics, *American Speech,* Aug., 1930.
2 See the *American Mercury,* March, 1927, p. 303.
3 See Name-Lore From New Orleans, by Marion E. Stanley, *American Speech,* June, 1927, p. 412.

Chappell, of Richmond, Va.[1] On Miss Chappell's list are also *Chesapeake & Ohio Railroad Harry Stringfellow* Johnson, *Charlotte County* Roberts, *Theophilus Otis Israbestis* Tott, *Claude St. Junius Eugene Leech Abraham Bonaparte Springer Hartsfield Love Gray* Nixon, and *Matthew Mark Luke John Acts-of-the-Apostles Son-of-Zebedee Garden-of-Gethsemane* Hill, this last the name of a colored pastor's son. But Miss Chappell's prize discovery is *Pism C.* Jackson — named by a devout mother after the Hundredth Psalm (*Psalm C*)! Other investigators of Afro-American onomatology have favored me, *inter alia*, with the following specimens: *Himself* Yubank, *Slaughter* Bugg, *Lingo D.* Graham, *Notre Dame* Richards, *Erie Canal* Jackson, *Lemon* Mitchell, *Munsing Underwear* Johnson, *Gentle Judge* McEachern, *King Solomon* Ray, *Nazro* Barefoot, *Magazine* Shaw, *Pictorial Review* Jackson (called *Torial* for short), *Tennessee Iron and Coal* Brown, *Earthly* Gaskin, *Hebrew* Hill, *Lutheran* Liggon, *Utensil Yvonne* Johnson, *Savannah* Satan, *Missouri* Soup and *Fate* Cutts.[2] Three of the sisters of Joe Louis the pugilist are *Eammarell, Eulalia* and *Vunies*.[3] The name of *Positive Wassermann* Johnson, reported from Evanston, Ill., probably represents the indelicate humor of a medical student. The young brethren who deliver colored mothers in the vicinity of the Johns Hopkins Hospital in Baltimore sometimes induce the mothers to give their babies grandiose physiological and pathological names, but these are commonly expunged later on by watchful social workers and colored pastors. *Placenta, Granuloma* and *Gonadia*, however, seem to have survived in a few cases.

3. PLACE-NAMES

"There is no part of the world," said Robert Louis Stevenson,[4] "where nomenclature is so rich, poetical, humorous and picturesque as the United States of America. All times, races and languages have brought their contribution. *Pekin* is in the same State with *Euclid*, with *Bellfontaine*, and with *Sandusky*. The names of the States themselves form a chorus of sweet and most romantic vocables: *Dela-*

1 Negro Names, *American Speech*, April, 1929.
2 I am especially indebted here to Miss Lenora Lund of Greensburg, Pa., Mr. Beverly Entzler of Goldsboro, N. C., Mr. George Macready of Wakefield, R. I., Mr. Donald Moffat of Brookline, Mass., and Dr. Henry H. Haines of Buffalo, N. Y.
3 Hartford *Courant*, Sept. 25, 1935
4 In Across the Plains; New York, 1892.

ware, Ohio, Indiana, Florida, Dakota, Iowa, Wyoming, Minnesota and the *Carolinas:* there are few poems with a nobler music for the ear: a songful, tuneful land." A glance at the latest United States Official Postal Guide[1] or report of the United States Geographic Board[2] quite bears out this encomium. The map of the country is besprinkled with place-names from at least half a hundred languages, living and dead, and among them one finds examples of the most daring and charming fancy. There are Spanish, French and Indian names as melodious and charming as running water; there are names out of the histories and mythologies of all the great races of man; there are names grotesque and names almost sublime. " *Mississippi!* " rhapsodized Walt Whitman; " the word winds with chutes — it rolls a stream three thousand miles long . . . *Monongahela!* it rolls with venison richness upon the palate." Nor was Whitman the first to note this loveliness: Washington Irving was writing about it in the *Knickerbocker Magazine* so long ago as 1839,[3] and in 1844 Henry R. Schoolcraft printed an appreciative treatise upon the Indian names in New York State.[4] Between the end of the Civil War and the end of the century about thirty studies of American place-names appeared, and since then the number has run to nearly a hundred. The majority of these works have been of small value, but Lewis H. McArthur's " Oregon Geographic Names "[5] is a treatise worthy of the highest praise, and since the appearance of Allen Walker Read's very judicious " Plans for the Study of Missouri Place-Names " in 1928[6]

1 Issued annually, with monthly supplements.
2 The sixth report, embracing decisions down to 1932, was issued in 1933, and pamphlet supplements come out frequently. The board is composed of representatives of the State, War, Treasury, Commerce, Interior, Navy, Postoffice and Agriculture Departments, and of the Government Printing Office, the Library of Congress, and the Smithsonian Institution. It was created by an executive order of President Harrison, Sept. 4, 1890, and its decisions as to spelling are binding on all Federal departments. In the sixth report more than 26,000 geographical names are listed, covering the whole world, but with the continental United States pre-

dominating. There is a valuable preface on the spelling of geographical names.
3 National Nomenclature, Vol. XIV, p. 158.
4 Aboriginal Names and Geographical Terminology of the State of New York, *Proceedings of the New York Historical Society*, 1844.
5 Portland, 1928. The material was first printed in the *Oregon Historical Quarterly*, beginning in Dec., 1925.
6 *Missouri Historical Review*, Jan. See also Introduction to a Survey of Missouri Place-Names, by Robert L. Ramsay, Allen Walker Read and Esther Gladys Leech; Columbia, Mo., 1934. Mr. Read's Observations of Iowa Place-Names, *American Speech*, Oct., 1929, is an

the investigation of the subject has been put upon a really scientific basis.[1]

The original English settlers, it would appear, displayed little imagination in naming the new settlements and natural features of the land that they came to. Their almost invariable tendency, at the start, was to make use of names familiar at home, or to invent banal compounds. *Plymouth Rock* at the North and *Jamestown* at the South are examples of their poverty of fancy; they filled the narrow tract along the coast with new *Bostons, Cambridges, Bristols* and *Londons*, and often used the adjective as a prefix. But this was only in the days of beginning. Once they had begun to move back from the coast and to come into contact with the aborigines and with the widely dispersed settlers of other races, they encountered rivers, mountains, lakes and even towns that bore far more engaging names, and these, after some resistance, they perforce adopted. The native names of such rivers as the *James*, the *York* and the *Charles* succumbed, but those of the *Potomac*, the *Patapsco*, the *Merrimac* and the *Penobscot* survived, and they were gradually reinforced as the country was penetrated. Most of these Indian names, in getting upon the early maps, suffered somewhat severe simplifications. *Potowanmeac* was reduced to *Potomack* and then to *Potomac; Unéaukara* became *Niagara; Reckawackes*, by folk etymology, was turned into *Rockaway*, and *Pentapang* into *Port Tobacco*.[2] But, despite such

---

excellent discussion of the subject: what he says about Iowa names might be applied to the place-names of any other State. In The Basis of Correctness in the Pronunciation of Place-Names, *American Speech*, Feb., 1933, he makes another valuable contribution to the subject.

1 A bibliography running down to 1922 will be found in A Bibliography of Writings on the English Language from the Beginning of Printing to the End of 1922, by Arthur G. Kennedy; Cambridge and New Haven, 1927, p. 349 ff. For the period since 1925 the bibliographies printed in each issue of *American Speech* may be consulted. Unfortunately, most of the published studies of American place-names are amateurish, and it is unusual for a philologian as competent as Mr. Read to be concerned with the subject. In England the English Place-Name Society has been carrying on an elaborate and well coördinated survey of English place-names since 1922. It has the coöperation of linguists, historians, paleographers, archeologists, topographers and other experts, and under the editorship of Dr. Allen Mawer, provost of University College, London, and Professor F. M. Stenton, of Reading University, it has already published a dozen valuable volumes. There is a statement of its plans and aims in the *Literary Supplement* of the London *Times*, May 3, 1923.

2 The authority here is River and Lake Names in the United States, by Edmund T. Ker; New York, 1911. Stephen G. Boyd, in Indian

elisions and transformations, the charm of thousands of them remained, and today they are responsible for much of the characteristic color of American geographical nomenclature. Such names as *Tallahassee, Susquehanna, Mississippi*,[1] *Allegheny, Chicago, Kennebec, Patuxent* and *Kalamazoo* give a barbaric brilliancy to the American map.

> Ye say they all have passed away,
>   That noble race and brave;
> That their light canoes have vanished
>   From off the crested wave;
> That mid the forests where they roamed
>   There rings no hunter's shout;
> But their name is on your waters;
>   Ye may not wash it out.[2]

The settlement of the continent, once the Eastern coast ranges were crossed, proceeded with unparalleled speed, and so the naming of the new rivers, lakes, peaks and valleys, and of the new towns and districts, strained the inventiveness of the pioneers. The result is the vast duplication of names that shows itself in the Postal Guide. No less than eighteen imitative *Bostons* and *New Bostons* still appear, and there are nineteen *Bristols*, twenty-eight *Newports*, and twenty-two *Londons* and *New Londons*. Argonauts starting out from an older settlement on the coast would take its name with them, and so we find *Philadelphias* in Illinois, Mississippi, Missouri and Tennessee, *Richmonds* in Iowa, Kansas and nine other Western States, and *Princetons* in fifteen. Even when a new name was hit upon it seems to have been hit upon simultaneously by scores of scattered bands of settlers; thus we find the whole land bespattered with

Local Names; York (Pa.), 1885, says that the original Indian name was *Pootuppag*.

1 The best discussion of *Mississippi* that I have found is in Louisiana Place Names of Indian Origin, by William A. Read; *Bulletin of the Louisiana State University*, Feb., 1927. The name comes from two Algonkian words, *misi*, great, and *sipi*, water. The early Spaniards and French called the river the *Rio Grande*, the *Buade*, the *Rivière de la Conception*, the *Colbert* and the *St. Louis*. "The first European to use the Indian name," says Dr. Read, "was Peñolosa, the Governor of

New Mexico, who in 1661 wrote it *Mischipi*. . . . The modern spelling occurs as early as 1718." The Southern Choctaws called the lower river the *Malbanchya*, meaning a place of foreign languages, a reference to the early European settlements.

2 The bard here is the ineffable Lydia Huntley Sigourney (1791–1865), the Amy Lowell and Edna St. Vincent Millay of a more seemly era. She wrote 40 books, and contributed 2000 poems to 300 periodicals. The lines I quote are from Indian Names, *c.* 1822.

Washingtons, Lafayettes, Jeffersons and Jacksons, and with names
suggested by common and obvious natural objects, e.g., Bear Creek,
Bald Knob and Buffalo. The Geographic Board, in its fourth report,
made a belated protest against this excessive duplication. " The
names Elk, Beaver, Cottonwood and Bald," it said, " are altogether too
numerous." Of postoffices alone there are fully a hundred embodying Elk; counting in rivers, lakes, creeks, mountains and valleys, the
map of the United States probably shows at least twice as many
such names.

A study of American place-names reveals eight general classes, as
follows: (a) those embodying personal names, chiefly the surnames
of pioneers or of national heroes; (b) those transferred from other
and older places, either in the Eastern States or in Europe; (c) Indian names; (d) Dutch, Spanish, French, German and Scandinavian
names; (e) Biblical and mythological names; (f) names descriptive
of localities; (g) names suggested by local flora, fauna or geology;
(h) purely fanciful names. The names of the first class are perhaps
the most numerous. Some consist of surnames standing alone, as
Washington, Cleveland, Bismarck, Lafayette, Taylor and Randolph;
others consist of surnames in combination with various old and new
Grundwörter, as Pittsburgh, Knoxville, Bailey's Switch, Hagerstown, Franklinton, Dodge City, Fort Riley, Wayne Junction and
McKeesport; and yet others are contrived of given-names, either
alone or in combination, as Louisville, St. Paul, Elizabeth, Johnstown,
Charlotte, Williamsburg and Marysville. All our great cities are surrounded by grotesque Bensonhursts, Bryn Joneses, Smithvales and
Krauswoods. The number of towns in the United States bearing
women's given-names is enormous. I find, for example, eleven postoffices called Charlotte, ten called Ada and no less than nineteen
called Alma. Most of these places are small, but there is an Elizabeth with nearly 125,000 population, an Elmira with 50,000, and an
Augusta with more than 60,000.

The names of the second class we have already briefly observed.
They are betrayed in many cases by the prefix New; more than 600
such postoffices are recorded, ranging from New Albany to New
Windsor. Others bear such prefixes as West, North and South,
or various distinguishing affixes, e.g., Bostonia, Pittsburgh Landing,
Yorktown and Hartford City. One often finds Eastern county names
applied to Western towns and Eastern town names applied to West-

ern rivers and mountains. Thus, *Cambria*, which is the name of a county but not of a postoffice in Pennsylvania, is a town in seven Western States; *Baltimore* is the name of a glacier in Alaska, and *Princeton* is the name of a peak in Colorado. In the same way the names of the more easterly States often reappear in the West, *e.g.*, in *Mount Ohio*, Colo., *Delaware*, Okla., and *Virginia City*, Nev. The tendency to name small American towns after the great capitals of antiquity has excited the derision of the English since the earliest days; there is scarcely an English book upon the States without some fling at it. Of late it has fallen into abeyance, though sixteen *Athenses* still remain, and there are yet many *Carthages, Uticas, Spartas, Syracuses, Romes, Alexandrias, Ninevehs* and *Troys*.[1] The third city of the nation, *Philadelphia*, got its name from the ancient stronghold of Philadelphus of Pergamon. To make up for the falling off of this old and flamboyant custom, the more recent immigrants brought with them the names of the capitals and other great cities of their fatherlands. Thus the American map now bristles with *Berlins, Bremens, Hamburgs, Warsaws* and *Leipzigs*, and also shows *Stockholms, Venices, Belgrades* and *Christianias*.[2]

The influence of Indian names upon American nomenclature is obvious. No fewer than twenty-six of the States have names borrowed from the aborigines,[3] and the same thing is true of large num-

1 See Classical Place-Names in America, by Evan T. Sage, *American Speech*, April, 1929. Mr. Sage says that Pennsylvania shows more classical place-names than any other State, with Ohio ranking second, New York third, Texas fourth, and Connecticut last. He calls attention to the pseudo-classical names: *Demopolis* (Ala.), *Cosmopolis* (Wash.), *Gallipolis* (O.), *Indianapolis* (Ind.), *Thermopolis* (Wyo.), *Coraopolis* (Pa.), and *Opolis* (Kans.). See also Origin of the Classical Place-Names of Central New York, by Charles Maar, *Quarterly Journal of the New York State Historical Association*, July, 1926.

2 See Amerikanska Ortnamn af Svenskt Ursprung, by V. Berger; New York, 1915. The Swedish names listed by Mr. Berger are chiefly to be found in Minnesota,

Iowa, Kansas, Nebraska and the Dakotas. See also Scandinavian Place-Names in the American Danelaw, by Roy W. Swanson, *Swedish-American Historical Bulletin* (St. Peter, Minn.), Aug., 1929.

3 In most of the States local antiquaries have investigated the State names. See, for example, The Origin and Meaning of the Name *California*, by George Davidson; San Francisco, 1910; *California*, the Name, by Ruth Putnam; Berkely, 1917; *Arizona*, Its Derivation and Origin, by Merrill P. Freeman; Tucson, 1913; *Ohio*, 1803–1903, by Maria Ewing Martin; New Straitsville, 1903; the Naming of *Indiana*, by Cyrus W. Hodgin; Richmond (Ind.), 1903; *Idaho*, Its Meaning, Origin and Application, by John E. Rees; Portland (Ore.), 1917. See also The Origin of American State Names, by F. W. Lawrence, *Na-*

bers of towns and counties. The second city of the country bears one, and so do the largest American river, and the greatest American water-fall, and four of the five Great Lakes, and the scene of the most important military decision ever reached on American soil. "In a list of 1,885 lakes and ponds of the United States," says Louis N. Feipel,[1] "285 are still found to have Indian names; and more than a thousand rivers and streams have names derived from Indian words." Walt Whitman was so earnestly in favor of these Indian names that he proposed substituting them for all other place-names, even the oldest and most hallowed. "California," he said in "An American Primer,"[2] "is sown thick with the names of all the little and big saints. Chase them away and substitute aboriginal names. . . . Among names to be revolutionized: that of the city of *Baltimore*. . . . The name of *Niagara* should be substituted for the *St. Lawrence*. Among places that stand in need of fresh, appropriate names are the great cities of *St. Louis, New Orleans, St. Paul*." But eloquent argument has also been offered on the other side, chiefly on the ground that Indian names are often hard to pronounce and even harder to spell. In 1863 R. H. Newell (Orpheus C. Kerr), a popular humorist of the time, satirized the more difficult of them in a poem called "The American Traveler," beginning:

> To Lake *Aghmoogenegamook*,
> All in the State of Maine,
> A man from *Wittequergaugaum* came
> One evening in the rain.[3]

I can find neither of these names in the latest report of the Geographic Board, but there are still towns in Maine called *Anasaguntiook, Mattawamkeag, Oquossoc* and *Wytopitlock*, and lakes called *Unsuntabunt* and *Mattagomonsis*. But many Indian names began to disappear in colonial days. Thus the early Virginians changed the name of the *Powhatan* to the *James*, and the first settlers in New

---

tional Geographic Magazine, Aug., 1920. The literature on the names of cities is rather meager. A model contribution to the subject is *Baltimore* — What Does the Name Mean?, by Hermann Collitz, *Johns Hopkins Alumni Magazine*, Jan., 1934. Baltimore, of course, gets its name from the title of the Barons Baltimore, Lords Proprietor of Maryland. Dr. Collitz shows that the name comes from the Irish *ball-ti-more*, signifying "the place of the great lord."

1 *American Place-Names*, *American Speech*, Nov., 1925, p. 79.
2 *Atlantic Monthly*, April, 1904, pp. 468–9.
3 It is reprinted in Local Discolor, by Mamie Meredith, *American Speech*, April, 1931.

York changed the name of *Horicon* to *Lake George*. In the same way the present name of the *White* Mountains displaced *Agiochook;* and *New Amsterdam* (1626), and later *New York* (1664), displaced *Manhattan*, which survived, however, as the name of the island, and was revived in 1898 as the name of a borough. In our own time *Mt. Rainier* has displaced *Tacoma* (or *Tahoma*).¹ By various linguistic devices changes have been made in other Indian names. Thus, *Mau-wauwaming* became *Wyoming*, *Maucwachoong* became *Mauch Chunk*, *Ouemessourit* became *Missouri*, *Nibthaska* became *Nebraska*, *Rarenawok* became *Roanoke*, *Asingsing* became *Sing-Sing*, and *Machihiganing* became *Michigan*.

The Dutch place-names of the United States are chiefly confined to the vicinity of New York, and a good many of them have become greatly corrupted. *Brooklyn, Wallabout* and *Gramercy* offer examples. The first-named was originally *Breuckelen*, the second was *Waale Bobht*, and the third was *De Kromme Zee*. *Hell-Gate* is a crude translation of the Dutch *Helle-Gat*. During the early part of the last century the more delicate New Yorkers transformed the term into *Hurlgate*, but the change was vigorously opposed by Washington Irving, and *Hell-Gate* was revived. The Dutch *hoek* was early translated into the English *hook*, and as such is found in various place-names, *e.g., Kinderhook*, Sandy *Hook*, Corlaers's *Hook* and *Hook* Mountain. The Dutch *kill*, meaning channel, is in *Kill* van Kull, *Peekskill, Catskill* and *Schuylkill*. *Dorp* (village) is in New *Dorp*.² *Kloof* (valley, ravine) survives, in the Catskills, in Kaatersill *Clove*, North *Clove* and *Clove* Valley. *Bosch* (corrupted to *bush*), *wijk* (corrupted to *wick*) and *vlei* (usually written *vly* or *fly*) are also occasionally encountered. The first means a wood, the second a district, and the third either a valley or a plain. Very familiar Dutch place-names are *Harlem, Staten, Flushing* (from *Vlissingen*), *Cort-*

1 This substitution, I am informed, was due to the jealousy of Seattle, the citizens of which objected to having the greatest American peak south of Alaska bear the name of the rival city of Tacoma. But it is still called *Tacoma* in Tacoma.
2 The name of Jamaica, L. I., was originally *Rustdorp* and that of Westchester was *Ostdorp*. To this day Schenectady is commonly called *The Dorp* locally, and its people pass as *Dorpians*. See Dialectical Evidence in the Place-Names of Eastern New York, by Edward E. Hale, *American Speech*, Dec., 1929. Mr. Hale's errors in Dutch are corrected by A. E. H. Swaen, in Dutch Place-Names in Eastern New York, *American Speech*, June, 1930.

landt, Nassau, Coenties, Spuyten Duyvel, Yonkers, Barnegat and
Bowery (from *bouwerij*, a farmstead). *Block* Island was originally
Blok, and Cape *May*, according to Schele de Vere, was *Mey*. The
French place-names have suffered even more severely than the
Dutch. Few persons would recognize *Smackover*, the name of a
small town in Arkansas, as French, and yet in its original form it was
Chemin Couvert. Schele de Vere, in 1871, recorded the degeneration
of the name to *Smack Cover;* the Postoffice, always eager to shorten
and simplify names, has since made one word of it and got rid of
the redundant *c*. In the same way *Bob Ruly*, a Michigan name, de-
scends from *Bois Brulé; Glazypool*, the name of an Arkansas mountain, from *Glaise à Paul; Low Freight*, the name of an Arkansas
river, from *L'Eau Frais; Loose* creek, in Missouri, from *L'Ours;*
Swashing creek from *San Joachim; Baraboo*, in Wisconsin, from
Baribault; Picketwire, in Arkansas, from *Purgatoire;* and *Funny*
Louis, in Louisiana, from *Funneleur*. A large number of French
place-names, *e.g.*, *Lac Supérieur*, were translated into English at an
early day, and nearly all the original *Bellevues* are now *Belleviews*
or *Bellviews*. *Belair*, La., represents the end-product of a process of
decay which began with *Belle Aire*, and then proceeded to *Bellaire*
and *Bellair*. All these forms are still to be found, together with *Bel*
Air and *Belle Ayr*. The Geographic Board's antipathy to names of
more than one word has converted *La Cygne* in Kansas, to *Lacygne*.
Lamoine, Labelle, Lagrange and *Lamonte* are among its other improvements, but *Lafayette* for *La Fayette*, long antedated the beginning of its labors.[1] Sheer ignorance has often been responsible for

---

[1] The Geographic Board of Canada
is naturally more tender with
French names, but some of them
are so long that it is forced to
shorten them. *Le Petit Journal* of
Montreal reported on Nov. 22, 1931
that there was a *Coeur-Très-Pur-
de-la-Bienheureuse-Vierge-Marie-
de-Plaisance* (commonly reduced to
Plaisance) in Quebec, and a *Ste.
Marie-Madeleine-du-Cap-de-la-
Madeleine* to keep it company.
The board also makes war on the
numerous *k*'s in Canadian Indian
names on the ground that *k* is not
a French letter. Examples: *Kapiki-*
kikakik, Kakekekwaki. In general,
the board opposes the abandonment of French names. Thus it has
decided for *Matissard* (lake) as
against *Horsetail*, and for *Laberge*
(creek) as against *Lizard*. Some of
the Canadian names show strange
combinations. When the French-
speaking rustics found a village
they commonly give it a saint's
name and then tack on the name
of the district. The result is such
marvels as *St. Evariste de Forsyth*,
St. Hippolyte de Kilkenny and *St.
Louis du Ha Ha*.

the debasement of French place-names. Consider, for example, the case of *Grande Ronde*. It is the name of a valley and a river in Eastern Oregon, and it used to be the name of a town in Yamhill county. But then a big lumber company came along, enlarged the town-site, put a mortgage on it, and issued bonds against it. On these bonds, as in the incorporation papers of the company, the name was spelled *Grand Ronde*. The Oregon Geographic Board protested, but when it was discovered that rectifying the blunder would cost many hundreds of dollars, the lumber company refused to move, and so the place is now *Grand Ronde* – in French, a sort of linguistic hermaphrodite.[1]

According to Harold W. Bentley [2] no less than 2000 American cities and towns have Spanish names, and thousands more are borne by rivers, mountains, valleys and other geographical entities. He says that there are more than 400 cities and towns of Spanish name in California alone. They are numerous all over the rest of the trans-Mississippi region, and, curiously enough, are even rather common in the East. The Mexican War was responsible for many of the Eastern examples, but others e.g., *Alhambra*, *Altamont* and *Eldorado*, seem to reveal nothing more than a fondness for mellifluous names. The map of California is studded with lovely specimens: *Santa Margarita, San Anselmo, Alamagordo, Terra Amarilla, Sabinoso, Las Palomas, Ensenada, San Patricio, Bernalillo*, and so on. Unfortunately, they are intermingled with horrifying Anglo-Saxon inventions, *e.g.*, *Oakhurst, Ben Hur, Drytown, Skidoo, Susanville, Uno* and *Ono*, including harsh bastard forms, *e.g.*, *Sierraville, Hermosa Beach, Point Loma* and *Casitas Springs*. Many names originally Spanish have been translated, *e.g.*, *Rio de los Santos Reyes* into *Kings* river, and *Rio de las Plumas* into *Feather* river, or mauled by crude attempts to turn them into something more "American," *e.g.*, *Elsinore* in place of *El Señor*, and *Monte Vista* in place of *Vista del Monte*. Probably a fifth of the Spanish place-names in California are the names of saints. The names of the Jewish patriarchs and those of the holy places of

---

1 I am indebted here to Mr. Lewis A. McArthur, secretary to the Oregon Geographic Board. He tells me also of the fate of *Psyche*, a town in Clallam county. The local residents, baffled by the name, called it *Pysht*, and in the end the Postoffice succumbed, and *Pysht* it is today.

2 A Dictionary of Spanish Terms in English; New York, 1932, p. 17.

Palestine are seldom, if ever, encountered: the Christianity of the early Spaniards seems to have concerned itself with the New Testament far more than with the Old, and with Catholic doctrine even more than with the New Testament. There are no *Canaans* or rivers *Jordan* in the Southwest, but *Concepcions, Sacramentos* and *Trinidads* are not hard to find.

The Americans who ousted the Spaniards were intimately familiar with both books of the Bible, and one finds copious proofs of it on the map of the United States. There are no less than eleven *Beulahs,* nine *Canaans,* eleven *Jordans* and twenty-one *Sharons. Adam* is sponsor for a town in West Virginia and an island in the Chesapeake, and *Eve* for a village in Kentucky. There are five postoffices named *Aaron,* two named *Abraham,* two named *Job,* and a town and a lake named *Moses.* Most of the *St. Pauls* and *St. Josephs* of the country were inherited from the French, but the two *St. Patricks* show a later influence. Eight *Wesleys* and *Wesleyvilles,* eight *Asburys* and twelve names embodying *Luther* indicate the general theological trend of the plain people. There is a village in Maryland, too small to have a postoffice, named *Gott,* and I find *Gotts Island* in Maine (in the French days, *Petite Plaisance*) and *Gottville* in California, but no doubt these were named after German settlers of that awful name, and not after the Lord God directly. There are four *Trinities,* to say nothing of the inherited *Trinidads.* And in Arkansas and New York there are *Sodoms.*

Names wholly or partly descriptive of localities are very numerous throughout the country, and among the *Grundwörter* embodied in them are terms highly characteristic of American and almost unknown to the English vocabulary. *Bald Knob* would puzzle an Englishman, but the name is so common in the United States that the Geographic Board has had to take measures against it. Others of that sort are *Council Bluffs, Patapsco Neck, Delaware Water Gap,*[1] *Walden Pond, Sandy Hook, Key West, Bull Run, Portage, French Lick, Jones Gulch, Watkins Gully, Cedar Bayou, Keams Canyon, Poker Flat, Parker Notch, Sucker Branch, Frazier's Bottom* and *Eagle Pass. Butte Creek,* in Montana, a small inland stream, bears a name made up of two Americanisms. There are thirty-five post-

[1] *Gap* occurs in England, but it is very rare. There is a Goring *Gap* between the Chiltern Hills and the Berkshire Downs, on the railway from London to Oxford.

offices whose names embody the word *prairie*, several of them, *e.g.*, *Prairie du Chien*, Wis., inherited from the French. There are seven *Divides*, eight *Buttes*, eight town-names embodying the word *burnt*, innumerable names embodying *grove*, *barren*, *plain*, *fork*, *cove* and *ferry*, and a great swarm of *Cold Springs*, *Coldwaters*, *Summits*, *Middletowns* and *Highlands*. The flora and fauna of the land are enormously represented. There are twenty-two *Buffalos* beside the city in New York, and scores of *Buffalo Creeks*, *Ridges*, *Springs* and *Wallows*. The *Elks*, in various forms, are still more numerous, and there are dozens of towns, mountains, lakes, creeks and country districts named after the *beaver*, *martin*, *coyote*, *moose* and *otter*, and as many more named after such characteristic flora as the *paw-paw*, the *sycamore*, the *cottonwood*, the *locust* and the *sunflower*. There is an *Alligator* in Mississippi, a *Crawfish* in Kentucky and a *Rat Lake* on the Canadian border of Minnesota. The endless search for mineral wealth has besprinkled the map with such names as *Bromide*, *Oil City*, *Anthracite*, *Chrome*, *Chloride*, *Coal Run*, *Goldfield*, *Telluride*, *Leadville* and *Cement*.

There was a time, particularly during the gold rush to California, when the rough humor of the country showed itself in the invention of extravagant and often highly felicitous place-names, but with the growth of population and the rise of civic spirit they have tended to be replaced by more seemly coinages. *Catfish* creek, in Wisconsin, is now the *Yakara* river; the *Bulldog* mountains, in Arizona, have become the *Harosomas*. As with natural features of the landscape, so with towns. Nearly all the old *Boozevilles*, *Jackass Flats*, *Three Fingers*, *Hell-For-Sartains*, *Undershirt Hills*, *Razzle-Dazzles*, *Cow-Tails*, *Yellow Dogs*, *Jim-Jamses*, *Jump-Offs*, *Poker Citys* and *Skunktowns* have yielded to the growth of delicacy, but *Tombstone* still stands in Arizona, *Goose Bill* remains a postoffice in Montana, and the Geographic Board gives its imprimatur to the *Horsethief* trail in Colorado, to *Burning Bear* in the same State, and to *Pig Eye* lake in Minnesota. Various other survivors of a more lively and innocent day linger on the map: *Blue Ball*, Pa., *Hot Coffee*, Miss., *Cowhide*, W. Va., *Dollarville*, Mich., *Oven Fork*, Ky., *Social Circle*, Ga., *Sleepy Eye*, Minn., *Bubble*, Ark., *Shy Beaver*, Pa., *Shin Pond*, Me., *Gizzard*, Tenn., *Rough-and-Ready*, Calif., *Non Intervention*, Va., *T.B.*, Md., *Noodle*, Tex., *Vinegar Bend*, Ala., *Matrimony*, N. C., *Wham*, La., *Number Four*, N. Y., *Oblong*, Ill., *Stock Yards*, Neb.,

Stout, Iowa, and so on.[1] West Virginia, the wildest of the Eastern States, is full of such place-names. Among them I find *Affinity, Annamoriah (Anna Maria?), Bee, Bias, Big Chimney, Bille, Blue Jay, Bulltown, Caress, Cinderella, Cyclone, Czar, Cornstalk, Duck, Halcyon, Jingo, Left Hand, Raven's Eye, Six, Skull Run, Three Churches, Uneeda, Wide Mouth, War Eagle* and *Stumptown.* The Postal Guide shows two *Ben Hurs,* five *St. Elmos* and ten *Ivanhoes,* but only one *Middlemarch.* There are seventeen *Roosevelts,* six *Codys* and six *Barnums,* but no *Shakespeare. Washington,* of course, is the most popular of American place-names. But among names of postoffices it is hard pushed by *Clinton, Centerville, Liberty, Canton, Marion* and *Madison,* and even by *Springfield, Warren* and *Bismarck.* A number of charming double names dot the American map, *e.g., Perth Amboy, Newport News, Front Royal, Wilkes-Barré, Princess Anne, Port Tobacco, The Dalles, Baton Rouge, Walla Walla, Winston-Salem.* In the older States they are supported by some even more charming names for regions and neighborhoods, *e.g., Dame's Quarter, My Lady's Manor* and *Soldiers' Delight* in Maryland.

Many American place-names are purely arbitrary coinages. Towns on the border between two States, or near the border, are often given names made of parts of the names of the two States, *e.g., Pen-Mar (Pennsylvania + Maryland), Del-Mar* and *Mar-Dela (Maryland + Delaware), Texarkana (Texas + Arkansas + Louisiana), Kanorado (Kansas + Colorado), Texhoma (Texas + Oklahoma), Dakoming (Dakota + Wyoming), Texico (Texas + New Mexico), Nosodak (North Dakota + South Dakota), Calexico (California + Mexico).*[2] *Norlina* is a telescope form of *North Carolina. Ohiowa* (Neb.) was named by settlers who came partly from Ohio and partly from Iowa. *Penn Yan* (N. Y.) was named by Pennsylvanians and New Englanders, *i.e.,* Yankees. *Colwich* (Kansas) is a telescopic form of the name of the Colorado and Wichita Railroad. There are

See Picturesque Town-Names in America, by Mamie Meredith, *American Speech,* Aug., 1931; American Towns Bear Odd Names, New York *Times,* Feb. 7, 1932; and Strangers in Mississippi Find *Hot Coffee* is Place, Baltimore *Evening Sun,* Oct. 21, 1932. During the Winter of 1934-5 the *Evening Sun* printed a series of lists of odd place-names on its editorial page. Some grotesque English names, almost fit to match the specimens above, are listed in Queer Names, *American Church Monthly,* Sept., 1931, p. 173, *e.g., Upper Swell, Little Snoring, Nether Peover, Appledram, Swaffham, Eye Over, Fetcham, Snailwell, High Easter, Wooton, Wawen, Mutford.*

2 In State Border Place-Names, by Henry J. Heck, *American Speech,* Feb., 1928, 51 such names are listed.

twelve *Delmars* in the United States. The name of one of them is a blend of *Delaware* and *Maryland;* the name of another (in Iowa) was "made by using the names (*i.e.*, the initials of the names) of six women who accompanied an excursion that opened the railroad from Clinton, Iowa." [1] The lower part of the peninsula separating Chesapeake Bay from the Atlantic is known locally as *Delmarva,* a blend of the first three syllables of *Delaware, Maryland* and *Virginia.* A part of the area is in each of these States.[2] *Benld* (Ill.) is a collision form of *Benjamin L. Dorsey,* the name of a local magnifico; *Cadams* (Neb.) is a collision form of *C. Adams; Wascott* (Wis.) derives from *W. A. Scott; Eleroy* (Ill.) from *E. Leroy; Bucoda* (Wash.) is a blend of *Buckley, Collier* and *Davis; Caldeno,* a waterfall of the Delaware Water Gap, got its name in 1851 from the names of three visitors, *C. L. Pascal, C. S. Ogden,* and *Joseph McLeod;* [3] *Pacoman* (N. C.) derives from the name of *E. H. Coapman,* a former vice-president of the Southern Railway; *Gilsum* (N. H.) is a blend of *Gilbert* and *Sumner; Paragould* (Ark.) is a blend of *W. J. Paramore* and *Jay Gould; Marenisco* (Mich.) is named after *Mary Relief Niles Scott; Miloma* (Minn.) derives its name from the first syllable of *Milwaukee,* in the name of the Milwaukee, Chicago, Minneapolis & St. Paul Railroad, and the first two syllables of *Omaha,* in the name of the Chicago, Minneapolis & Omaha Railroad; *Gerled* (Iowa) is a blend of *Germanic* and *Ledyard,* the names of two nearby townships; *Rolyat* (Ore.) is simply *Taylor* spelled backward; *Biltmore* (N. C.) is the last syllable of *Vanderbilt* plus the Gaelic *more,* signifying great.

The Geographic Board, in its laudable effort to simplify American nomenclature, has played ducks and drakes with some of the most picturesque names on the national map. Thus, I find it deciding against *Portage des Flacons* and in favor of *Burro canyon,* against *Cañons y Ylas de la Cruz* and in favor of the barbarous *Cruz island.* The name of the *De Grasse* river it has changed to *Grass. De Laux*

---

1 Louise Pound: Blends, *Anglistische Forschungen,* Heft XLII, p. 10. The origin of the names of the other *Delmars* I do not know. Mr. Donald L. Cherry of Watsonville, Calif., suggests that some of them may derive from the Spanish *del mar,* signifying of the sea.

2 The proposal that it be made a separate State is frequently made by local politicians and boosters. This proposal gets some support in Baltimore, where the Delmarvian *Kultur* is not greatly admired.

3 The Delaware Water Gap, by L. W. Brodhead; Phila., 1870, p. 274.

it has changed to the intolerable *D'Llo*. It has steadily amalgamated French and Spanish articles with their nouns, thus achieving such barbarous forms as *Duchesne, Degroff* and *Eldorado*. But here its policy is fortunately inconsistent, and so a number of fine old names have escaped. Thus, it has decided in favor of *Bon Secour* and against *Bonsecours*, and in favor of *De Sota, La Crosse* and *La Moure*, and against *Desoto, Lacrosse* and *Lamoure*. Its decisions are confused and often unintelligible. Why *Laporte*, Pa., and *La Porte*, Ind. and Iowa; *Lagrange*, Ind., and *La Grange*, Ky.? Here it would seem to be yielding a great deal to local usage.

The Board proceeds to the shortening and simplification of native names by various devices. It deletes such suffixes as *town, city, mills, junction, station, center, grove, crossroads* and *courthouse*.[1] It removes the apostrophe and often the genitive *s* from such names as *St. Mary's;* it shortens *burgh* to *burg* [2] and *borough* to *boro;* and it combines separate and often highly discrete words. The last habit often produces grotesque forms, *e.g., Newberlin, Fallentimber, Bluehill* and *Threetops*. It apparently cherishes a hope of eventually regularizing the spelling of *Allegany*. This is now *Allegany* for the Maryland county, the Pennsylvana township and the New York and Oregon towns, *Alleghany* for the Colorado town and the Virginia county and springs, and *Allegheny* for the mountains, the Pittsburgh borough and the Pennsylvania county, college and river. The Board inclines to *Allegheny* for all. Other Indian names give it constant concern. Its struggles to set up *Chemquasabamticook* as the name of a Maine lake in place of *Chemquasabamtic* and *Chemquassabamticook*, and *Chatahospee* as the name of an Alabama creek

1 The addition of *courthouse* to a place-name to indicate a county-seat (it is commonly abbreviated to C. H.) seems to be a Southernism. "The county-towns of Virginia," said John R. Bartlett in his Glossary (2nd ed., 1859) "are often called *courthouses* without regard to their proper names. Thus, *Providence*, the county-town of Fairfax, is unknown by that name, and passes as *Fairfax Court-House*, and *Culpepper Court-House* has superseded its proper name of *Fairfax*. The same practise has existed to some extent in Maryland. Thus, after the Battle of Bladensburg, and the dispersion of our forces, they were ordered to assemble at *Montgomery Court-House*." John S. Farmer, in his Americanisms Old and New (1889), said that the practise also extended to South Carolina. It survives in the names of a few Virginia county-towns, and of one town in Ohio, but is going out.

2 Now and then it encounters a stout local resistance. When it tried to shorten *Pittsburgh* to *Pittsburg* that resistance was sufficient to preserve *Pittsburgh*, which is now official.

in place of *Chattahospee, Hoolethlocco, Hoolethloces, Hoolethloco* and *Hootethlocco* are worthy of its learning and authority.

The American weakness for spelling pronunciations shows itself in the case of geographical names. Richard Grant White, in 1880,[1] recorded an increasing tendency to give full value to the syllables of such borrowed English names as *Worcester* and *Warwick*. In *Worcester* county, Maryland, the name is usually pronounced *Wooster*, but on the Western Shore of the State one hears *Worcest'r*. *Norwich* is another such name; one hears *Nor-witch* quite as often as *Norrich*. Another is *Delhi;* one often hears *Del-high*. Yet another is *Birmingham;* it is pronounced as spelled in the United States, and never in the clipped English manner. *Greenwich* as the name of a Connecticut town is pronounced *Grennidge* as in England, but as the name of a San Francisco street it is *Green-witch*. *Thames* as the name of a Connecticut river is pronounced as spelled, but is *Temz* in England. *Houston* as the name of the Texas city is *Hyewston*, but as the name of a New York City street it is *Howston*. White said that in his youth the name of the *Shawangunk* mountains, in New York, was pronounced *Shongo*, but that the custom of pronouncing it as spelled had arisen during his manhood.[2] So with *Winnipiseogee*, the name of a lake; once *Winipisuakie*, it gradually came to be pronounced as spelled. There is frequently a considerable difference between the pronunciation of a name by natives of a place and its pronunciation by those who are familiar with it only in print. *Baltimore* offers an example. The natives always drop the medial *i* and so reduce the name to two syllables; in addition, they substitute a neutral vowel, very short, for the *o*. The name thus be- becomes *Baltm'r*. *Maryland*, at home, is always *Mare-l'nd*. *Anne Arundel*, the name of a county in the State, is *Ann'ran'l*. *Calvert* county, also in Maryland, is given a broad *a*, but in *Calvert* street,

1 Every-Day English, p. 100. See also American English, by Gilbert Tucker; New York, 1921, p. 33, and American Pronunciation, by J. S. Kenyon; Ann Arbor, Mich., 1932, pp. 135–6.
2 This spelling-pronunciation seems to have disappeared. The local pronunciation today is *Shongum*. I have often noted that Americans, in speaking of the familiar *Worcestershire* sauce, commonly pro- nounce every syllable and enun- ciate *shire* distinctly. In England it is always *Woostersh'r*. The English have a great number of decayed pronunciations, e.g., *Maudlin* for *Magdelen, Sissiter* for *Cirencester, Merrybone* for *Marylebone*. Their geographical nomenclature shows many corruptions due to faulty pronunciation and folk etymology, e.g., *Leighton Buzzard* for the Nor- man *Leiton Beau Desart*.

Baltimore, it is flat. *Staunton*, Va., the birthplace of Woodrow Wilson, is *Stanton* to its people, but *Taunton*, Mass., has acquired an *r*-sound. *Arkansas*, as everyone knows, is pronounced *Arkansaw* by the Arkansans.[1] The local pronunciation of *Illinois* is *Illinoy*. *Missouri*, at home, is *Mizzoora*, though efforts have been made for many years by the local schoolmarms and other purists to unvoice the *z's* and to convert the final *a* into *y*.[2] In the early days the pronunciation of *Iowa* was always *Ioway*, but the schoolmarm has brought in *Iowuh*, with the accent on the first syllable. *St. Louis*, to the people of the city, is *St. Lewis*, but *Louisville*, to its denizens, is *Louie-ville*, with the first syllable French and the second American. *Des Moines*, locally, is *Day-moin*, but *Dee-moin* is also heard; the two *s's* are always silent. *Terre Haute* is *Terry-hut*. *Beaufort* is *Byu-furt* in South Carolina but *Bo-furt* in North Carolina. *New Orleans* is *New Oar-lins*, with a heavy accent on the first syllable, but when *New* is omitted and *Orleans* is used as an adjective modifying a following noun it becomes *Or-leens*, with the accent on the second syllable. In Baltimore *Orleans* street is always *Or-leens*. *Coeur d'Alene* is *Kur-da-lane*, with the accent on the *lane*, and the vowel of *kur* lying between that of *cur* and that of *poor*.[3] *Cairo*, Ill., is always *Care-o* locally, never *Ky-ro*. *Raleigh*, N. C., is *Rolly*, rhyming with *jolly*. *Honolulu*, in the original native speech, was *Ho-nolulu*, but now it is *Hon-olulu*. *San Antonio*, Tex., is *Santonyo*, though the second *an* is often inserted by the fastidious. The name of *Taos*, N. Mex., is pronounced to rhyme with *house*. *Albuquerque*, N. Mex., is *Al-bu-ker-ky*, with the accent on the first syllable, the *a* of which is American, not Spanish. *Laramie*, Wyo., is often reduced to two syllables locally, and pronounced *Lormie* or *Lahrmie*. *Beatrice*, Neb., is accented on the second syllable. *Wichita* is *Witch-*

---

1 The Legislature of the State, by an act approved March 15, 1881, decided that the name "should be pronounced in three syllables, with the final *s* silent, the *a* in every syllable with the Italian sound, and the accent on the first and last syllable." But the Italian *a* in the second syllable has been flattened. In Kansas the *Arkansas* river is called the *Arkansas*, with the last two syllables identical with *Kansas*. The people of *Arkansas City* in the same State use the same pronunciation. See The Basis of Correctness in the Pronunciation of Proper Names, by Allen Walker Read, *American Speech*, Feb., 1935.

2 Pronunciation of the Word *Missouri*, by Allen Walker Read, *American Speech*, Dec., 1933.

3 I am indebted here to Mr. Marshall Ballard, editor of the New Orleans *Item*, and to Mr. H. F. Kretchman, editor of the Coeur d'Alene *Press*.

i-taw. The first syllable of *Akron* rhymes with *jack,* not with *jake.* *Spokane* is *Spo-can,* not *Spo-cane. Bonne Terre,* an old town near St. Louis, is *Bonnie-tar. Portage,* Wis., is pronounced as an English word. *Lafayette,* a frequent town name, is *Laugh-y-et. Havre de Grace* is pronounced *Haver de Grass,* with two flat *a's. Versailles,* in Indiana, is *Versales.* In Northern Michigan the pronunciation of *Sault* in *Sault Ste. Marie* is commonly more or less correct; the Minneapolis, St. Paul & Sault Ste. Marie Railroad is called the *Soo,* and there is a *Soo* canal. This may be due to Canadian example, or to some confusion between *Sault* and *Sioux.* The *Rouge* in *Baton Rouge* gets its French value locally, but the *Baton* becomes *bat'n,* with the *bat* rhyming with *cat,* and the *o* reduced to a neutral vowel. The local pronunciation of *Tucson,* according to the Tucson Sunshine-Climate Club, is *Tu-sahn,* with the accent on the second syllable, but most Americans make it *Too-s'n,* with the accent on the first syllable. It is a great point in San Francisco to pronounce the name of *Geary* street *Gary,* that of *Kearny Karny,* and that of *Sutter* with the *u* of *put:* doing so proves that one is an old-timer.[1] The Spanish place-names of California offer difficulties to natives and strangers alike. For years the Los Angeles *Times* has printed a standing notice that the name of the city should be pronounced *Loce Ahng-hayl-ais,* but the resident boosters and Bible-searchers continue to say *Loss Angle-iss, Loss Anjell-iss, Loce-Angle-iss, Loce Angle-ez,* and even *Sang-lis.* The common local abbreviation is *L. A.; Los* is seldom heard.[2] The name of the Indian village that originally occupied the site of the city was *Yang-na;* the Spaniards, in 1769, changed this to *El Pueblo de Nuestra Señora la Reina de Los Angeles* (The Town of Our Lady, Queen of Angels). Many other California towns have shortened their Spanish names in the same way. What is now *Ventura* was formerly *San Buena Ventura, San José* was *San José de Guadalupe,* and *Santa Clara* was *Santa Clara de Asis. Santa Fe,* in New Mexico, was originally the *Villa Real de Santa Fé de San Francisco.* Some of the Spanish place-names

---

1 Private communication from Miss Miriam Allen de Ford of San Francisco.
2 So far as I can find, no one has ever investigated the local abbreviations for town-names. A few suggest themselves: *Jax* for *Jacksonville, Balto* for *Baltimore, Philly* for *Philadelphia,* K. C. for *Kansas City,* and *Chi* for *Chicago.* In the familiar ballad, Casey Jones, *Casey* was originally K. C.

in the Southwest have been shortened for daily use. *Frisco* for *San Francisco* is frowned upon locally, but is used elsewhere. *San Bernardino* is *San Berna'dino, San B'rdino, San B'rdoo,* or *B'rdoo, San Pedro* is *Pedro, Santa Monica* is *Santa Mon, San Jacinto* is *San Jack,* and *Sacramento* is *Sacto* or *Sac.*[1] In New Mexico and Arizona, where the Spanish-speaking population is relatively large, the Spanish pronunciation is preserved, but in the adjoining States it is fast succumbing to Americanization. The name of the *Raton* pass, separating New Mexico from Colorado, is pronounced *Rah-ton* in New Mexico but *Ra-toon* in Colorado. Similarly, *Costilla,* a border-town, is *Koastee-yah* in New Mexico and *Kos-til-la* in Colorado. *San Luis,* in Colorado, is *San Loo-is, Garcia* is *Gar-shah,* Saguache is *Sigh-watch, La Junta* is *La Hunta* instead of *La Hoonta, Buena* is *Bew-nah, Salida* is *Sa-lye-dah* and *Cerro* is *Sir-ro.*[2] Even the name of the State is often *Color-ray-do.* The Spanish *a,* says Joseph B. Vasché of the State Teachers College at San José, Calif.,[3] appears to be doomed, and the *o* and *i* are going with it. There are frequent pedagogical efforts to restore the old pronunciations, but Mr. Vasché believes that any return to them is impossible. The value of *ñ* has been preserved only by changing it to *ny,* as in *canyon.* Another change in spelling is the abandonment of the accent in such place-names as *San José* and *Santa Fé.* It does not appear on the letterhead of the San José State Teachers College, just mentioned, and the Geographic Board omits it from the name of the capital of New Mexico, though retaining it on the name of the city in Argentina. The accents in French and Scandinavian names are sloughed off in the same way. Every *Belvédère* of the early days is now a *Belvidere,* and every *Ste. Thérèse* has become a *St. Therese.* In Minnesota the Swedish *Skåne* has become *Skane,* and *Malmö* is *Malmo.*[4] If there were any considerable number of German place-names on the American map their umlauts would be sacrificed. The German *ch*-sound, when it

1 I am indebted here to Dr. Joseph M. Prendergast, of Burlingame, Calif.

2 Spanish Place-Names in Colorado, by Eleanor L. Ritchie, *American Speech,* April, 1935, and Some Spanish Place-Names of Colorado, by George L. Trager, the same, Oct., 1935. See also Arizona Place-Names, by W. C. Barnes; Tucson, 1935.

3 Trends in the Pronunciation of the Spanish Place-Names of California, *American Speech,* Aug., 1931, p. 461.

4 For a list of other changes see Scandinavian Place-Names in the American Danelaw, by Roy W. Swanson, *Swedish-American Historical Bulletin* (St. Peter, Minn.), Aug., 1929, p. 16.

appears in *Loch*, a Scottish word, is always converted into *ck*.[1] The *Holston* river in Tennessee was originally the *Holstein*.[2]

4. OTHER PROPER NAMES

"Such a locality as *at the corner of Avenue H and Twenty-third street*," says W. W. Crane, "is about as distinctly American as Algonkian and Iroquois names like *Mississippi* and *Saratoga*."[3] Rudyard Kipling, in his "American Notes,"[4] gave testimony to the strangeness with which the number-names, the phrase *the corner of*, the word *block*, and the custom of omitting *street* fell upon the ear of a Britisher of a generation or more ago. He quotes with amazement certain directions given to him on his arrival in San Francisco from India: "Go six *blocks* north to [the] *corner of Geary and Markey* [*Market*?]; then walk around till you strike [the] *corner of Sutter and Sixteenth*."[5] The English almost always add the word *street* (or *road* or *place* or *avenue*) when speaking of a thoroughfare: such a phrase as *Oxford and New Bond* would strike them as incongruous.[6] The American custom of numbering and lettering

1 The Pennsylvania Germans, in return, make a frightful hash of certain familiar "American" names. In an appendix to his Dictionary of the Non-English Words of the Pennsylvania-German Dialect; Lancaster, Pa., 1924, M. B. Lambert lists *Nei Jarrick* for *New York*, *Baerricks* for *Berks*, *Daerm* for *Durham*, *Iesdaun* for *Easton*, *Heio* for *Ohio*, *Lenggeschder* for *Lancaster*, *Phildelphi* for *Philadelphia*, *Redden* for *Redding*, and *Tschaertschi* for *Jersey*. In New York, according to Arthur Livingston (La Merica Sanemagogna, *Romanic Review*, Vol. IX, No. 2, April–June, 1918), the Italians convert *Jersey City* into *Gerseri*, *Hoboken* into *Obochino*, and *Flatbush* into *Flabussce*. In Canada, according to Adjutor Rivard (Études sur les Parlers de France au Canada; Quebec, 1914, p. 167) the French-Canadians change *Somerset* to *Saint-Morissette*, *Sutherland* to *Saint-Irlande*, and *Sandy Brook's Point* to *Saint-Abroussepoil*. In Cleveland, so I am told by Dr. Joseph Remény of Cleveland College, the Hungarians call the *Buckeye road* the *Bakrud*, which has a silly meaning in Hungarian, where *baka* is a soldier and *rud* is a pole.

2 A curious bastard form is *Anaheim*, the name of a town near Santa Ana. It was founded by a German winegrower in the 80's. In Pennsylvania such forms as *Schultzville* and *Schaefferstown* are common.

3 Our Street Names, *Lippincott's Magazine*, Aug., 1897, p. 264.

4 New York, 1891, Ch. I.

5 Here Kipling made two errors. The *the* would never be omitted before *corner*, and Sutter and Sixteenth streets do not meet.

6 But I am reminded by Mrs. Pieter Juiliter, of Scotia, N. Y., that "true Oxonians always speak of *the Broad, the High, the Turl* and *the Corn* instead of *Broad street*, *High street*, *Turl street*, and *Cornmarket street*." The article, however, is always used; it is never used in the United States.

Proper Names in America 545

streets is usually ascribed by English writers to sheer poverty of invention, but of late some of them have borne witness to its convenience. One such is C. K. Ogden, who says in "Basic English": [1]

[By] anyone who has driven around the suburbs [looking for] *The Laurels, 13a, Aspidistra Court Gardens*, peering from a taxi through the darkness at *No. 8*, at *Catspaw Mansions*, at *The Chestnuts*, at *No. 41*, and at a variety of indiscernibles, before finally turning the corner of an unsuspecting mews, also known locally as *Smith's Passage*, the advantages of living in *No. 123 West 456th street* will hardly be disputed.

Another is E. Stewart Fay, author of a learned work on London street-names.[2] He says:

It is a great pity that the Marquis of Westminster and Thomas Cubitt developed Belgravia before the new system had become general in America. . . . However much the present residents of *Eaton place* may protest at the idea of their street being called *Sixth avenue* or *E street*, it is certain that long before now London would have been accustomed to street-naming sanity and would value an address in *E street* as highly as one in *Eaton place*. . . . I have no wish to see *the Strand* rechristened *First avenue*. But I do claim that the jerry-builders of Middlesex, Essex, Kent and Surrey would be very much better advised to plan their names upon some useful basis than to go on senselessly perpetrating meaningless *Romeo streets* and futile *Snowdrop crescents*.

The English often give one street more than one name. Thus, *Oxford street*, in London, becomes the *Bayswater road, High street, Holland Park avenue, Goldhawk road* and finally the *Oxford road* to the westward, and *High Holborn, Holborn viaduct, Newgate street, Cheapside, the Poultry, Cornhill* and *Leadenhall street* to the eastward. The *Strand*, in the same way, becomes *Fleet street, Ludgate hill* and *Cannon street*. But the American system of numbering and lettering streets shows some signs of increasing acceptance. There is a *First avenue* in Queen's Park, London, and parallel to it are *Second, Third, Fourth, Fifth* and *Sixth* avenues — all small streets leading northward from the Harrow road, just east of Kensal Green cemetery. Mr. Fay reports a set of three numbered avenues at East Acton, and one or two at Mortlake. "At Plaistow," he says, "someone has endeavored to see the light, but unfortunately without bringing much intelligence to the task, for his three numbered avenues are arranged in the shape of a triangle!" There is also a *First street* in Chelsea — a very modest thoroughfare near Lennox gardens and not far from the Brompton Oratory.[3] The English custom

1 London, 1930, p. 25.
2 Why Piccadilly?; London, 1935.
3 See the Chapter on London Street-Names in Adjectives — and Other

Words, by Earnest Weekley; London, 1930. A brief bibliography is appended.

of giving grandiloquent names to small houses in the suburbs has never taken root in the United States, but Summer-camps are usually named, and not infrequently their titles show a gay and saucy spirit, *e.g.*, *Kamp Takitezy*, *U Kan Kom In*, *Hatetoleaveit*, *Viol-Inn*, *The Cat's Meeow* and *Iszatso*.[1] Tourist-camps often bear names of the same sort. There was a time when all American apartment-houses were elegantly labeled, but of late many of them have been given only street-numbers. There are even hotels without names — six of them in Manhattan. The names of American suburbs often engage the national wits. Those in *-hurst* are so numerous that they have produced a satirical type, *Lonesomehurst*. The garden city movement, launched by an Englishman, Sir Ebenezer Howard, in 1898, was quickly imitated in this country, and with it came a new popularity for names suggesting feudal estates, *e.g.*, *Cecil Manor*, *Bryn Jenkins* and *Smithdale*. The developers of suburbs in low, marshy places have a great liking for adding *heights* to their names.

The numbering and lettering of streets was apparently invented by Major Pierre-Charles L'Enfant in 1791, when he laid out the plan of Washington. In the older American cities the downtown streets still usually have names surviving from colonial days, and some of them were borrowed originally from London, *e.g.*, *Cheapside*, *Cornhill* and *Broadway*.[2] In the United States such pretentious designations as *avenue*, *boulevard*, *drive* and *speedway* are used much more freely than in England. *Boulevard*, in some American cities, has of late taken on the meaning of a highway for through traffic, on entering which all vehicles must first halt. In England such a highway is commonly called an *arterial road*. Every American town of any airs has a *Great White Way*; in the Middle West, in the Era of Optimism, rows of fine shade-trees were cut down to make room for them. *Avenue* is used in England, but according to Horwill, it is " usually reserved for a road bordered by trees." Professor Weekley says that the first *avenue* in London was *St. Bride's*, opened in 1825. In America the word was formerly used to designate a thoroughfare in the suburbs, not built up like a street, but laid out for future building, and hence not a road. In the Baltimore of my youth

---

1 Naming the Bungalow, by Ida M. Mellen, *American Speech*, March, 1927.

2 I am informed by Miss Miriam Allen de Ford that *Broadway street*

appears on some street signs in San Francisco, and also in San Diego. This suggests that *Broadway* is recent on the Pacific Coast.

Charles street became *Charles street avenue* at the old city boundary, and the *Charles street avenue road* a bit farther out. At Towanda, Pa., there is a *Plank road street*. Many American towns now have *plazas*, which are quite unknown in England, and nearly all have *City Hall parks, squares* or *places*. The principal street of a small town, in the United States, used to be *Main street*, but since the appearance of Sinclair Lewis's novel of that name, in 1920, the designation has taken on a derogatory implication, and is going out. In England, *Main street* is usually *the High street*, not forgetting the article; but in Scotland there are many *Main streets*. The newer suburbs of American towns are full of *lanes, roads* and *ways*, but the English *circus, crescent, terrace, walk, passage* and *garden* are seldom encountered. *Alley* survives in a few of the older cities, but *row, court* and *yard* are virtually extinct. These English names for thoroughfares, like the American *boulevard* and *avenue*, have lost most of their original significance. "*À Londres*," complains André Maurois (quoted by Professor Weekley), "*Cromwell place est une rue, Cromwell gardens n'est un jardin, et Hyde Park terrace n'est pas une terrasse.*"

The pronunciation of street-names in the United States shows the same freedom that marks the pronunciation of place-names. The old Dutch names of New York City are sadly mangled by the present inhabitants of the town, *e.g.*, *Desbrosses*, which was *de Broose* in Dutch, is now *Des-brossez*. Spanish names are often corrupted in the same way in the Southwest, and French names in the Great Lakes region and in Louisiana and thereabout. In New Orleans *Bourbon* has become *Bur-bun* or *Boi-bun*, *Dauphine* is *Daw-fin*, *Foucher* is *Foosh'r*, *Enghien* is *En-gine*, *Chartres* is *Charters*, and *Felicity* (originally *Félicité*) *is Fill-a-city*. The French, in their far-off day, bestowed the names of the Muses upon certain of the city streets. They are now pronounced *Cal-y-ope* or *Cal-yop, You-terp* or *You-toip, Mel-po-mean, Terp-si-core, Drieds*, and so on. *Bons Enfants*, apparently too difficult for the present inhabitants, has been translated into *Good Children*, and the *rue Royale* into *Royal street*. In Montgomery, Ala., the local Darktown, *Boguehomme* by name, is called *Boag-a-home-a*.[1]

As everyone knows, the right of *Americans* to be so called is

1 For aid here I am indebted to Mr. Maurice K. Weil of New Orleans.

frequently challenged, especially in Latin-America, but so far no plausible substitute has been devised, though many have been proposed, e.g., *Unisians, Unitedstatesians, Columbards,* etc. On October 28, 1928, the Paris *Figaro* opened a discussion of the subject, in which M. Dumont-Wilden, editor of the *Revue Bleue,* Gabriel Louis-Jaray, of the Comité France-Amérique, André Siegfried, author of "America Comes of Age," and various other ingenious Frenchmen participated, but nothing came of it. There are also frequent debates over the designation to be applied to the inhabitants of various States and cities. The people of Alabama commonly call themselves *Alabamians,* and those of Indiana call themselves *Indianians,* but in both States there are minorities which object to the redundant *i.*[1] In Oklahoma *Oklahoman* has the weight of enlightened opinion behind it, but *Oklahomian* is often heard outside the State. In Idaho the English faculty of the State university favors *Idahovan,* but *Idahoan* is heard much more often. In Atlanta some of the people call themselves *Atlantans* and others prefer *Atlantians:* the Atlanta *Constitution* uses the former and the *Journal* the latter. In New Orleans *Orleanian,* with the accent on the *an,* is preferred by the elegant, but the vast majority of citizens say *Orleenian,* with the accent on the *leen.*[2] Larousse's Grand Dictionnaire Universal prints (under *noms*) a list of the designations of persons living in all the principal towns of France, but so far as I know, no such compilation has ever been attempted for the United States. Nevertheless, George R. Stewart, Jr., of the University of California, has attempted to determine the principles underlying their formation. His conclusions may be roughly summarized as follows:

1. If the name of the town ends in *-ia,* the name of the citizen is formed by adding *n,* e.g., *Philadelphian.*
2. If it ends in *-on, -ian* is added, e.g., *Bostonian, Tucsonian.*
3. If it ends in *-i, -an* is added, e.g., *Miamian.*
4. If it ends in *-y,* the *y* is changed to *i* and *an* is added, e.g., *Albanian, Kansas Citian.*
5. If it ends in *-o, -an* is added, e.g., *Chicagoan, Elpasoan.*

1 See Dunn and *Indianan,* by Jacob P. Dunn, Indianapolis *News,* Aug. 11, 1922. Mr. Dunn, forgetting *Canadian,* argues that *Indianian* is just as absurd as *Texian* or *Cubian.* But Mr. Julian Hall, editor of the Dothan (Ala.) *Eagle,* prefers *Alabamian* on the ground of long usage. "If there is any merit," he says, "in the rule of spelling a proper name just as the possessor spells it, then we are *Alabamians.*"
2 In the Canal Zone the Americans commonly call the people of Panama *Panamanians,* with the first syllable showing a Latin *a,* but the third rhyming with *cane.*

6. If it ends in a sounded *-e*, or in *-ie* or *-ee*, *-an* is added, *e.g.*, *Muskogeean*, *Albuquerquean*, *Guthrian*, *Poughkeepsian*.

7. If it ends in *-a*, not preceded by *i*, the common rule is to add *-n*, *e.g.*, *Topekan*, *Tacoman*.

8. If it ends in *-olis*, the change is to *-olitan*, *e.g.*, *Annapolitan*.

9. If it ends with a consonant or with a silent *-e*, *-ite* or *-er* is added, *e.g.*, *Brooklynite*, *Boiseite*, *Wheelingite; New Yorker*, *Pittsburgher*, *Davenporter*.[1]

But there are frequent exceptions to these rules. In California the Spanish names ending in *o* do not take *an*, but change the *o* to *a* and add *n*, *e.g.*, *San Franciscan*, *San Diegan*, *Sacramentan*, *Palo Altan*, *San Matean* and *Los Gatan*. Even those not ending in *o* tend to take *an*, *e.g.*, *Santa Cruzan*, *Salinan*, *San Josean* and *Montereyan*. A Buffalo man is not a *Buffaloan*, but a *Buffalonian*, and by the same token a Toronto man is a *Torontonian*. A Quincy, Ill., man is not a *Quincian*, but a *Quincyan*. The hideous suffix *-ite* seems to be gaining on all others. A citizen of Akron, O., used to be an *Akronian*, but after the town began to boom he became an *Akronite*. For many years an Episcopal clergyman, Dr. Ringwalt, who wrote editorials for the Camden, N. J., *Post-Telegram*, tried to make his readers accept *Camdenian*, but they preferred *Camdenite*, and *Camdenite* it is today. In Moscow, Idaho, the *intelligentsia* of the State University prefer *Moscovite*, with *Moscovian* as second choice, but the Moscow *Star-Mirror* prefers *Moscowite*, and so do the people of the town.[2] A citizen of Raleigh, N. C. (pronounced *Rolly*), should be a *Raleighan* by Mr. Stewart's rule, but he is actually a *Raleighite*, though a citizen of Berkeley, Calif., remains a *Berkeleyan*, not a *Berkeleyite*. There is apparently a strong tendency for *-ite* to follow *d, f, g, l, m, n, r* and *s*, as in *Englewoodite*, *St. Josephite*, *Wheelingite*, *Seattleite*, *Durhamite*, *Brooklynite*, *Fall Riverite* and *Yonkersite*,[3] but there are some exceptions, *e.g.*, *Richmonder*,[4] *Winnipegger*, *Montrealer*, *Lynner*, *Rochesterian*, *Memphian*. The names ending in *k* and *t* usually take *er*, *e.g.*, *Yorker*, *Quebecer*, *Davenporter*, *Rocky Mounter*, but in Passaic, N. J., *Passaicite* is preferred, and in Frederick,

1 Names For Citizens, *American Speech*, Feb., 1934, p. 78.
2 *Moscowite* or *Moscovian?*, Moscow *Star-Mirror*, April 22, 1935. I am indebted here to Mr. Louis A. Boas, editor of the *Star-Mirror*.
3 "So far as we are aware," says Kenneth A. Fowler, in The Town Crier, Yonkers *Herald Statesman*, April 25, 1935, "there is no official designation. The most common word is probably *Yonkersite*, with *Yonkers man* another quite frequently used phrase. The more tony term of *Yonkersonian* is seldom if ever heard."
4 This is used in Richmond, Va. In Richmond, Ind., *Richmondite* is preferred.

Md., the proper form is not *Frederieker* but *Fredericktonian*. In the few American towns whose names end with the French *g, an* is added, *e.g., Baton Rougean*. Those in *-ville* drop the final *e* and add *-ian, e.g., Louisvillian*. In Los Angeles the correct form is *Angeleño* (pro. *An-juh-lee-no*), but it is not yet in universal use, and in print it always loses its tilde. The average denizen of Los Angeles, asked what he is, still responds that he is an *Iowan*, a *Kansan*, a *Texan*, or what not. In Taos, N. Mex., *Taoseño* is used, with *Taoseña* for a female, and the tilde is carefully preserved. I am told by Mr. Spud Johnson, editor of the Taos *Valley News*, that *Taosian* and *Taosite* are sometimes used by tourists and the indigenous vulgar, but "partly because there is a well-known woman's club called Las Taoseñas, which has made the name familiar, and partly because it is graceful and easy and the alternatives are somewhat clumsy, the Spanish form is used even by the Lions and the Chamber of Commerce." [1] The people of Cambridge, Mass., borrowing from those of the English university town, call themselves *Cantabrigians*, and those of Saugus, Mass., call themselves *Saugonians*. Those of Providence, R. I., remembering proudly that they live in what is officially the State of Rhode Island and Providence Plantations, simply call themselves *Rhode Islanders*. A citizen of Schenectady, N. Y., is ordinarily a *Schenectadian*, but often says that he is a *Dorpian*, from the ancient Dutch designation of the town — the *Dorp*, or the *Old Dorp*. Similarly, a citizen of Reading, Pa., uses *Berks County Dutchman* in preference to *Readingite*. A citizen of Poughkeepsie, N. Y., is ordinarily a *Poughkeepsian*, but sometimes he calls himself an *Apokeepsian*, and some years ago the local Rotarians tried to make *Apokeepsian* official. It is supposed to be more nearly in accord with the original Indian name of the town. A citizen of Cape Girardeau, Mo., is a *Girardean*, omitting the *Cape*. A man of Greensboro, N. C., may be either a *Greensburger* or a *Greensboroite*, according to his private taste. A man of Lancaster, Pa., is a *Lancastrian*. A man of Hagerstown, Md., is not a *Hagerstownite* but a *Hagerstowner* or (occasionally) *Hagerstonian*. A *Montrealer*, if French, is *un Montréalais*, and if female *une Montréalaise*. A *Quebecer*, if French, is a *Québecois*.[2] In the towns bearing classical or pseudo-classical names

1 Private Communication, June 15, 1935.
2 For help here I am indebted to Mrs. Jessie I. Miller of Cairo, Ill.; Miss Jean E. Riegel, of Bethlehem, Pa.; Miss Helen Merrill Bradley, of Toronto; Mrs. F. M. Hanes, of Durham, N. C.; Miss Katherine

the inhabitants wear extremely majestic labels, *e.g.*, *Trojan*, *Carthagenian* (Carthage, Mo.), *Phoenician* (Phoenix, Ariz.), *Florentine* (Florence, Ala.), *Roman*, *Athenian*, *Spartan*, but a citizen of Columbus, O., is a *Columbusite* not a *Columbian*.[1] The names of certain American towns are so refractory that no special designations for their citizens have ever arisen. Examples are La Crosse, Wis., Oshkosh, Wis.,[2] Little Rock, Ark., Independence, Mo., Rutland, Vt.,[3] and

Ferguson, of Cedar Rapids, Iowa; Miss Nan Strum, of Rocky Mount, N. C.; Mrs. Carolina Penna Hyman, of Los Altos, Calif.; Miss Mable E. Bontz, of Sacramento, Calif.; Mrs. Alicia L. Rooney, of San Antonio, Tex.; Messrs. Maury Maverick, of San Antonio, Tex.; Mahlon N. Haines, of York, Pa.; Harry Allard, of Cape Girardeau, Mo.; S. H. Abramson, of Montreal; J. S. Creegan, of Albuquerque, N. Mex.; Wilson O. Clough, of Laramie, Wyo.; E. L. Clark, of Providence, R. I.; Henry Broderick, of Seattle, Wash.; J. A. Macdonald, of Vancouver, B. C.; Rowland Thomas, of Little Rock, Ark.; Philip G. Quinn, of Fall River, Mass.; Herman Baradinsky, of New York; Alfred C. Booth, of East Orange, N. J.; Israel Bloch, of Lynn, Mass.; N. R. Callender, of Benton Harbor, Mich.; Harry Corry, of Davenport, Iowa; John William Cummins, of Wheeling, W. Va.; Henry Ware Allen, of Wichita, Kansas; Marshall Ballard, of New Orleans; James Doolittle, of Grand Rapids, Mich.; J. A. Coneys, of Englewood, N. J.; Carl J. Ruskowski, of Schenectady, N. Y.; Charles Stewart Lake, of Columbus, O.; Duncan Aikman, of Los Angeles, Calif.; Eugene Davidson, of New Haven, Conn.; J. G. Sims, Jr., of Fort Worth, Tex.; J. L. Meeks, of Florence, Ala.; Gerald W. Johnson, of Baltimore; Leigh Toland, of La Crosse, Wis.; A. C. Ross, of Rochester, N. Y.; Folger McKinsey, of Baltimore; Virginius Dabney, of Richmond, Va.; Irving C. Hess, of San Diego, Calif.; Morris Fletcher Atkins, of Montpelier, Vt.; Donald L. Cherry, of Watsonville, Calif.;

R. R. Peters, of Bucyrus, O.; L. M. Feeger, of Richmond, Ind.; Charles F. Eichenauer, of Quincy, Ill.; Otto Stabell, of Passaic, N. J.; J. W. Spear, of Phoenix, Ariz.; Torrey Fuller, of Poughkeepsie, N. Y.; Raymond Fields, of Guthrie, Okla.; James Q. Dealey, of Dallas, Tex.; Charles P. Manship, of Baton Rouge, La.; Paul R. Kelty, of Portland, Ore.; Edwin M. Shanklin, of Des Moines, Iowa; Julian Hall, of Dothan, Ala.; C. Oliver Power, of Carthage, Mo.; J. E. Barbey, of Reading, Pa.; Samuel Grafton, of New York, and Clyde K. Hyder, of Lawrence, Kansas; Col. Patrick H. Callahan, of Louisville; Lieut. Col. E. L. M. Burns, of Ottawa; Monsignor J. B. Dudek, of Oklahoma City, Okla.; Dr. J. A. Kostalek, of the University of Idaho, Moscow, Idaho; Dr. W. L. Frazier, of Boise, Idaho; Dr. H. K. Croessmann, of DuQuoin, Ill.; Dr. D. C. Alldredge, of Berkeley, Calif.; Dr. J. Christopher O'Day, of Honolulu; and Messrs. Theodore W. Noyes and Philander Johnson, of Washington, D. C.

1 In Columbus, Ind., *Columbusite* is used only rarely, but *Columbusonian* even more rarely. "I don't believe," says Mr. Melvin Lostutter, editor of the Columbus *Evening Republican*, "you would be accurate in applying a local designation to our citizenry."

2 Mr. L. K. Bronson, managing editor of the Oshkosh *Northwestern*, tells me that *Oshkoshian* has been used, but only rarely. "*Oshkosh man*," he says, "is the more common description."

3 Miss Harriet E. Matthison, of the Rutland *Herald*, says that there is

the New Jersey Oranges. Some of the States are in the same position, *e.g.*, Massachusetts and Connecticut. A resident of the District of Columbia always calls himself a *Washingtonian*. A citizen of Arkansas is an *Arkansawyer*, following the local pronunciation of the State name. A citizen of Michigan is a *Michigander*. A citizen of New Jersey is a *Jerseyman*.[1] A rough popular humor often supplies opprobrious forms. Thus the people of Chicago (or at least some of them) have been called *Chicagorillas*, those of Baltimore *Baltimorons*,[2] those of Omaha *Omahogs*, those of Louisville *Louisvillains*, those of Swampscott, Mass., *Swampskeeters*, and those of Cedar Rapids, Iowa, *Bunnies* (See der rabbits). All the States have nicknames, and some have more than one. A number of these are almost as well known as the actual State names, *e.g.*, *Hoosier* (Indiana), *Keystone* (Pennsylvania), *Empire* (New York), *Buckeye* (Ohio), *Old Dominion* (Virginia), *Show Me* (Missouri), *Palmetto* (South Carolina), *Lone Star* (Texas), *Tarheel* (North Carolina), and *Bay* (Massachusetts).[3] In some cases the inhabitants are known by the nicknames of their States, *e.g.*, *Hoosiers*, *Tarheels*, *Buckeyes*, *Crackers* (Georgia). In other cases separate nicknames have arisen, *e.g.*, *Jayhawks* (Kansas), *Colonels* (Kentucky), *Blue Hen's Chickens* (Delaware). In the early days most of the designations in vogue were ribald, *e.g.*, *Lizards* (Alabama), *Buzzards* (Georgia), *Pukes* (Missouri), *Web-feet* (Oregon), *Whelps* (Tennessee), *Beetheads* (Texas), *Leatherheads* (Pennsylvania), *Foxes* (Maine), *Toothpicks* (Arkansas), *Bug-eaters* (Nebraska), *Weasels* (South Carolina), *Tadpoles* (Mississippi), *Muskrats* (Delaware), *Clam-catchers* (New Jersey), *Crawthumpers* (Maryland). In his "Slang in America" (part of "November Boughs," 1888) Walt Whitman printed a list largely identical with the foregoing: apparently he borrowed it from an anonymous newspaper article reprinted in the *Broadway Journal*

"no recollection" in the *Herald* office "of hearing Rutland people called by any particular name." "The secretary of the Chamber of Commerce," she adds, "informs me that she would think *Rutlander* preferable to *Rutlandite*."
[1] See On the Difficulty of Indicating Nativity in the United States, by Miriam Allen de Ford, *American Speech*, April, 1927, and Comments,

by Miles L. Hanley, *American Speech*, Oct., 1933, p. 78.
[2] *Chicagorilla* is the invention of Walter Winchell. *Baltimoron* was coined by Harry C. Black, of the Baltimore *Evening Sun*, and first appeared in that paper, Feb. 15, 1922.
[3] A list of those currently in use is printed annually in the *World* Almanac.

for May 3, 1845.[1] The etymology of the State nicknames has engaged a large number of amateur philologians, but with inconclusive
results. The origin of *Hoosier*, for example, remains uncertain.[2]
Many cities also have generally recognized nicknames, *e.g.*, *the Hub*
(Boston), *the Windy City* (Chicago), *the Monumental City* (Baltimore), and *the Quaker City* (Philadelphia), and nearly every small
place of any pretensions has tried to launch one for itself, usually
embodying *Queen* or *Wonder*.

Another field that awaits scientific exploration is that of the joke-
towns — *Podunk*, *Squedunk*, *Hohokus*, *Goose Hill*, *Hard-Scrabble*,
and so on. Almost every large American city is provided with such
a neighbor, and mention of it on the local stage arouses instant mirth.
For many years *Hoboken* was the joke-town of New York, *Watt*
was that of Los Angeles, and *Highlandtown* was that of Baltimore,
but *Hoboken* won its way to metropolitan envy and respect during
Prohibition, *Watt* has been absorbed in Los Angeles, and *Highlandtown* is now a glorious part of Baltimore. " The humorous connotation of certain Indian names," said the late George Philip Krapp,
" has always been felt, and names like *Hohokus*, *Hoboken*, *Kalamazoo*,[3] *Keokuk*, *Oshkosh*, *Skaneateles*, names of real places, have
acquired more than local significance, as though they were grotesque
creations of fancy. There is, however, no postoffice named *Podunk*
in the United States Official Postal Guide. Just how this word came
to be used as a designation for any small, out-of-the-way place is
not known. It is an Indian word by origin, the name of a brook in
Connecticut and a pond in Massachusetts, occurring as early as 1687.
There is also a *Potunk* on Long Island." [4] Here Dr. Krapp seems to
have been in error, for an onomastic explorer, E. A. Plimpton, re-

1 See Nicknames of the States; a
Note on Walt Whitman, by John
Howard Birss, *American Speech*,
June, 1932, p. 389.
2 See The Origin of the Term
Hoosier, by O. D. Short, *Indiana
Magazine of History*, June, 1929.
See also *Tar Heels* (anonymous),
American Speech, March, 1926.
3 Kalamazoo, which was settled in
1829 and chartered as a city in
1884, remained a joke-town down
to the end of the century. A set of
derisive verses, credited to the Den-

ver *News*, circulated through the
newspapers about 1900. Its refrain
was:

O Kalamazozle — mazizzle —
    Mazazzle-mazeezle-mazoo!
That liquid, harmonious, easy, eu-
    phonious
    Name known as Kalamazoo!

It will be noted that *k* is prominent in the names of all the towns
cited by Dr. Krapp.
4 The English Language in America;
New York, 1925, p. 176.

ported in the Boston *Herald* for February 8, 1933, that he had dis-covered a veritable *Podunk* in Massachusetts, not far from Worces-ter.[1] Dr. Louise Pound says that *Skunk Center, Cottonwood Crossing* and *Hayseed Center* are favorite imaginary towns in Nebraska, and that *Sagebrush Center* reigns in Wyoming, *Rabbit Ridge* in Kansas, and *Pumpkin Hollow* in the State of Washington. For Missouri Charles E. Hess reports *Gobbler's Knob, Possum Hollow, Hog Heaven, Slabtown, Hog-Eye, Skintown, Bugtown and Puckey-Huddle*.[2] *Frogtown* is a common nickname for a Negro settlement in many parts of the United States.

1 See The Locus of *Podunk*, by Louise Pound, *American Speech*, Feb., 1934, p. 80.
2 For Dr. Pound see the paper just cited. Mr. Hess's paper, *Poduck* in Southeast Missouri, is in *American Speech*, Feb., 1935, p. 80.

XI

AMERICAN SLANG

I. THE NATURE OF SLANG

Slang is defined by the Oxford Dictionary as " language of a highly colloquial type, considered as below the level of standard educated speech, and consisting either of new words or of current words employed in some special sense." The origin of the word is unknown. Ernest Weekley, in his " Etymological Dictionary of Modern English," 1921, suggests that it may have some relation to the verb *to sling*, and cites two Norwegian dialect words, based upon the cognate verb *slenge* or *slengje*, that appear to be its brothers: *slengjeord*, a neologism, and *slengjenamn*, a nickname. But he is not sure, so he adds the note that " some regard it as an argotic perversion of the French *langue*, language." A German philologian, O. Ritter, believes that it may be derived, not from *langue*, but from *language* itself, most probably by a combination of blending and shortening, as in *thieve(s' lang)uage, beggar(s' lang)uage*, and so on.[1] " Webster's New International," 1934, follows somewhat haltingly after Weekley. The Oxford Dictionary, 1919, evades the question by dismissing *slang* as " a word of cant origin, the ultimate source of which is not apparent." When it first appeared in English, about the middle of the Eighteenth Century,[2] it was employed as a synonym of *cant*, and so designated " the special vocabulary used by any set of persons of a low or disreputable character "; and half a century later it began to be used interchangeably with *argot*, which means the vocabulary special to any group, trade or profession. But

1 *Archiv für das Studium der neueren Sprachen*, Vol. CXVI, 1906. I am indebted for the reference to Concerning the Etymology of *Slang*, by Fr. Klaeber, *American Speech*, April, 1926. The process is not unfamiliar in English: *tawdry*, from *Saint Audrey*, offers an example.

2 It has since appeared in German, French and Swedish, as is shown by the titles of Deutsches Slang, by Arnold Genthe; Strassburg, 1892; Le Slang, by J. Manchon; Paris, 1923; and Stockholmska Slang, by W. P. Uhrström; Stockholm, 1911.

during the past fifty years the three terms have tended to be more or less clearly distinguished. The jargon of criminals is both a kind of slang and a kind of argot, but it is best described as *cant*, a word derived from the Latin *cantus*, and going back, in its present sense, to *c.* 1540. One of the principal aims of cant is to make what is said unintelligible to persons outside the group, a purpose that is absent from most forms of argot and slang. Argot often includes slang, as when a circus man calls his patrons *suckers* and speaks of refunding money to one full of complaints as *squaring the beef*, but when he calls the circus grounds the *lot* and the manager's quarters the *white wagon*, he is simply using the special language of his trade, and it is quite as respectable as the argot of lawyers or diplomats. The essence of slang is that it is of general dispersion, but still stands outside the accepted canon of the language. It is, says George H. McKnight,[1] " a form of colloquial speech created in a spirit of defiance and aiming at freshness and novelty. . . . Its figures are consciously far-fetched and are intentionally drawn from the most ignoble of sources. Closely akin to profanity in its spirit, its aim is to shock." Among the impulses leading to its invention, adds Henry Bradley,[2] " the two more important seem to be the desire to secure increased vivacity and the desire to secure increased sense of intimacy in the use of language." " It seldom attempts," says the London *Times*, " to supply deficiencies in conventional language; its object is nearly always to provide a new and different way of saying what can be perfectly well said without it." [3] What chiefly lies behind it is simply

---

1 English Words and Their Background; New York, 1923, p. 43.
2 *Art*. Slang, Encyclopaedia Britannica, 14 ed.; New York, 1929.
3 American Slang (leading article), May 11, 1931. Many other definitions of *slang* are quoted in What is Slang? by H. F. Reves, *American Speech*, Jan., 1926. A few by literati may be added. " Slang," said Carl Sandburg, " is language that takes off its coat, spits on its hands, and gets to work." " Slang," said Victor Hugo, " is a dressing-room in which language, having an evil deed to prepare, puts on a disguise." " Slang," said Ambrose Bierce, " is the speech of him who robs the literary garbage-carts on

their way to the dumps." Emerson and Whitman were its partisans. " What can describe the folly and emptiness of scolding," asked the former (Journals, 1840), " like the word *jawing?* " " Slang," said Whitman, " is the wholesome fermentation or eructation of those processes eternally active in language, by which the froth and specks are thrown up, mostly to pass away, though occasionally to settle and permanently crystalize." (Slang in America, 1885.) And again: " These words ought to be collected — the bad words as well as the good. Many of these bad words are fine." (An American Primer, *c.* 1856.)

a kind of linguistic exuberance, an excess of word-making energy. It relates itself to the standard language a great deal as dancing relates itself to music. But there is also something else. The best slang is not only ingenious and amusing; it also embodies a kind of social criticism. It not only provides new names for a series of everyday concepts, some new and some old; it also says something about them. "Words which produce the slang effect," observes Frank K. Sechrist,[1] "arouse associations which are incongruous or incompatible with those of customary thinking."

Everyone, including even the metaphysician in his study and the eremite in his cell, has a large vocabulary of slang, but the vocabulary of the vulgar is likely to be larger than that of the cultured, and it is harder worked. Its content may be divided into two categories: (*a*) old words, whether used singly or in combination, that have been put to new uses, usually metaphorical, and (*b*) new words that have not yet been admitted to the standard vocabulary. Examples of the first type are *rubberneck*, for a gaping and prying person, and *iceberg*, for a cold woman; examples of the second are *hoosegow*, *flimflam*, *blurb*, *bazoo* and *blah*. There is a constant movement of slang terms into accepted usage. *Nice*, as an adjective of all work, signifying anything satisfactory, was once in slang use only, and the purists denounced it,[2] but today no one would question " a *nice* day," " a *nice* time," or " a *nice* hotel." The French word *tête* has been a sound name for the human head for many centuries, but its origin was in *testa*, meaning a pot, a favorite slang word of the soldiers of the decaying Roman Empire, exactly analogous to our *block*, *nut* and *bean*. The verb-phrase *to hold up* is now perfectly good Ameri-

1 The Psychology of Unconventional Language, *Pedagogical Seminary*, Dec., 1913, p. 443. "Our feeling and reactions to slang words," continues Sechrist, "may be due to the word as such, to the use it is put to, to the individual using it, to the group using it, to the thing tabooed to which it applies, or to the context in which it is found. . . . Unconventional language keeps close to the objective world of things. It keeps oriented to the sense of touch, contact, pressure, preferring a language material which is ultimately verifiable by the most realistic sense." This

last, I fear, is somewhat dubious. See also An Investigation of the Function and Use of Slang, by A. H. Melville, *Pedagogical Seminary*, March, 1912; and La Psychologie de l'argot, by Raoul de La Grasserie, *Revue Philosophique* (Paris), Vol. LX, 1905.

2 It came in about 1765. During the early Eighteenth Century *elegant* was commonly used, and in Shakespeare's day the favorite was *fine*. *Nice* has had many rivals, *e.g.*, *ripping* and *topping* in England, and *grand* and *swell* in America, but it hangs on.

can, but so recently as 1901 the late Brander Matthews was sneering at it as slang. In the same way many other verb-phrases, *e.g., to cave in, to fill the bill* and *to fly off the handle*, once viewed askance, have gradually worked their way to a relatively high level of the standard speech. On some indeterminate tomorrow *to stick up* and *to take for a ride* may follow them. " Even the greatest purist," says Robert Lynd, " does not object today to the inclusion of the word *bogus* in a literary English vocabulary, though a hundred years ago *bogus* was an American slang word meaning an apparatus for coining false money. *Carpetbagger* and *bunkum* are other American slang words that have naturalized themselves in English speech, and *mob* is an example of English slang that was once as vulgar as *incog* or *photo.*" [1] Sometimes a word comes in below the salt, gradually wins respectability, and then drops to the level of slang, and is worked to death. An example is offered by *strenuous*. It was first used by John Marston, the dramatist, in 1599, and apparently he invented it, as he invented *puffy, chilblained, spurious* and *clumsy*. As strange as it may seem to us today, all these words were frowned on by the purists of the time as uncouth and vulgar, and Ben Jonson attacked them with violence in his " Poetaster," written in 1601. In particular, Ben was upset by *strenuous*. But it made its way despite him, and during the next three centuries it was used by a multitude of impeccable authors, including Milton, Swift, Burke, Hazlitt, and Macaulay. And then Theodore Roosevelt invented and announced the Strenuous Life, the adjective struck the American fancy and passed into slang, and in a little while it was so horribly threadbare that all persons of careful speech sickened of it, and to this day it bears the ridiculous connotation that hangs about most slang, and is seldom used seriously.

All neologisms, of course, are not slang. At about the time the word *hoosegow*, derived from the Spanish, came into American slang use, the word *rodeo*, also Spanish, came into the standard vocabulary. The distinction between the two is not hard to make out. *Hoosegow* was really not needed. We had plenty of words to designate a jail, and they were old and good words. *Hoosegow* came in simply because there was something arresting and outlandish about it — and the users of slang have a great liking for pungent novelties.

1 The King's English and the Prince's American, *Living Age*, March 15, 1928.

Rodeo, on the other hand, designated something for which there was no other word in American — something, indeed, of which the generality of Americans had just become aware — and so it was accepted at once. Many neologisms have been the deliberate inventions of quite serious men, *e.g., gas, kodak, vaseline. Scientist* was concocted in 1840 by William Whewell, professor of moral theology and casuistical divinity at Cambridge. *Ampere* was proposed solemnly by the Electric Congress which met in Paris in 1881, and was taken into all civilized languages instantly. *Radio* was suggested for wireless telegrams by an international convention held in Berlin in 1906, and was extended to wireless broadcasts in the United States about 1920, though the English prefer *wireless* in the latter sense. But such words as these were never slang; they came into general and respectable use at once, along with *argon, x-ray, carburetor, stratosphere, bacillus,* and many another of the sort. These words were all sorely needed; it was impossible to convey the ideas behind them without them, save by clumsy circumlocutions. It is one of the functions of slang, also, to serve a short cut, but it is seldom if ever really necessary. Instead, as W. D. Whitney once said, it is only a wanton product of " the exuberance of mental activity, and the natural delight of language-making." [1] This mental activity, of course, is the function of a relatively small class. " The unconscious genius of the people," said Paul Shorey, " no more invents slang than it invents epics. It is coined in the sweat of their brow by smart writers who, as they would say, are *out for the coin.*" [2] Or, if not out for the coin, then at least out for notice, *kudos,* admiration, or maybe simply for satisfaction of the " natural delight of language-making." Some of the best slang emerges from the argot of college students, but everyone who has observed the process of its gestation knows that the general run of students have nothing to do with the matter, save maybe to provide an eager welcome for the novelties set before them. College slang is actually made by the campus wits, just as general slang is made by the wits of the newspapers and theaters. The

1 The Life and Growth of Language; New York, 1897, p. 113.
2 The American Language, in Academy Papers; New York, 1925, p. 149. Henry Bradley says (*Art.* Slang, Encyclopaedia Britannica, 14th ed.; 1929) that "slang develops most freely in groups with a strong realization of group activity and interest, and groups without this interest, *e.g.,* farmers, rarely invent slang terms." The real reason why farmers seldom invent them, of course, is that farmers, as a class, are extremely stupid. They never invent anything else.

idea of calling an engagement-ring a *handcuff* did not occur to the young gentlemen of Harvard by mass inspiration; it occurred to a certain definite one of them, probably after long and deliberate cogitation, and he gave it to the rest and to his country. Toward the end of 1933 W. J. Funk of the Funk and Wagnalls Company, publishers of the Standard Dictionary and the *Literary Digest*, undertook to supply the newspapers with the names of the ten most fecund makers of the American slang then current. He nominated T. A. (Tad) Dorgan, the cartoonist; Sime Silverman, editor of the theatrical weekly, *Variety;* Gene Buck, the song writer; Damon Runyon, the sports writer; Walter Winchell and Arthur (Bugs) Baer, newspaper columnists; George Ade, Ring Lardner and Gelett Burgess.[1] He should have added Jack Conway and Johnny O'Connor of the staff of *Variety;* James Gleason, author of " Is Zat So? "; Rube Goldberg, the cartoonist; Johnny Stanley and Johnny Lyman, Broadway figures; Wilson Mizner and Milt Gross. Conway, who died in 1928, is credited with the invention of *palooka* (a third-rater), *belly-laugh, Arab* (for Jew), *S.A.* (sex appeal), *high-hat, pushover, boloney* (for buncombe, later adopted by Alfred E. Smith), *headache* (wife), and the verbs *to scram, to click* (meaning to succeed), and *to laugh that off*.[2] Winchell, if he did not actually invent *whoopee*, at least gave it the popularity it enjoyed, *c.* 1930.[3]

1 Mr. Funk added my own name to the list, but this, apparently, was only a fraternal courtesy, for I have never devised anything properly describable as slang, save maybe *booboisie*. This was a deliberate invention. One evening in February, 1922, Ernest Boyd and I were the guests of Harry C. Black at his home in Baltimore. We fell to talking of the paucity of words to describe the victims of the Depression then current, and decided to remedy it. So we put together a list of about fifty terms, and on Feb. 15 I published it in the Baltimore *Evening Sun*. It included *boobariat, booberati, boobarian, boobomaniac, boobuli* and *booboisie*. Only *booboisie*, which happened to be one of my contributions, caught on. A bit later I added *Homo boobus*, and Boyd, who is learned in the tongues, corrected it to

Homo boobiens. This also had its day, but its use was confined to the *intelligentsia*, and it was hardly slang. Even *booboisie* lies rather outside the bounds.

2 Conway's coinages are listed by Walter Winchell in Your Broadway and Mine, New York *Graphic*, Oct. 4, 1928, and in A Primer of Broadway Slang, *Vanity Fair*, Nov., 1927. In December, 1926, under the title of Why I Write Slang, Winchell contributed a very shrewd article to *Variety*. In it he differentiated clearly between the cant of criminals, which is unintelligible to the general, and what he called Broadway slang. The latter differs from the former, he said, " as much as Bostonese from hog Latin."

3 Lexicographical explorers have found *whoopee* in a cowboy song published by John A. Lomax in 1910, in Kipling's Loot (Barrack-

He is also the father of *Chicagorilla, Joosh* (for Jewish), *pash* (for passion) and *shafts* (for legs), and he has devised a great many nonce words and phrases, some of them euphemistic and others far from it, e.g., for married: *welded, sealed, lohengrined, merged* and *middle-aisled;* for divorced: *Reno-vated;* for contemplating divorce: *telling it to a judge, soured, curdled, in husband trouble, this-and-that-way,* and *on the verge;* for in love: *on the merge, on fire, uh-huh, that way, cupiding, Adam-and-Eveing,* and *man-and-womaning it;* for expecting young: *infanticipating, baby-bound* and *storked.* I add a few other characteristic specimens of his art: *go-ghetto, debutramp, phffft, foofff* (a pest), *Wildeman* (a homosexual), *heheheh* (a mocking laugh), *Hard-Times Square* (Times Square), *blessed-event* (the birth of young), *the Hardened Artery* (Broadway), *radiodor* (a radio announcer), *moom-pitcher* (moving picture), *girl-mad, Park Rowgue* (a newspaper reporter) and *intelligentlemen.* Most of these, of course, had only their brief days, but a few promise to survive. Dorgan, who died in 1929, was the begetter of *apple-sauce, twenty-three, skiddoo,*[1] *ball-and-chain* (for wife), *cake-eater, dumb Dora, dumbell* (for stupid person), *nobody home,* and *you said it.* He also gave the world, "Yes, we have no bananas," though he did not write the song, and he seems to have originated *the cat's pajamas,* which was followed by a long series of similar superlatives.[2] The sports writers, of course, are all assiduous makers of slang, and many of

Room Ballads), 1892, and in Mark Twain's A Tramp Abroad, 1880. *Whoope* was common in the English literature of the Fifteenth, Sixteenth and Seventeenth Centuries, but it was probably only our *whoop* with a silent final *e.* Said Winchell in the New York *Mirror,* Jan. 17, 1935: "They contend *whoopee* is older than Shakespeare. Well, all right. I never claimed it, anyhow. But let 'em take *makin' whoopee* from me and look out!"

1 Dorgan's claims to both *twenty-three* and its brother *skiddoo* have been disputed. An editorial in the Louisville *Times,* May 9, 1929, credits Frank Parker Stockbridge with the theory that *twenty-three* was launched by The Only Way, a dramatization of Dickens's Tale of Two Cities, presented by Henry Miller in New York in 1899. In

the last act an old woman counted the victims of the guillotine, and Sydney Carton was the twenty-third. According to Stockbridge, her solemn "Twenty-three!" was borrowed by Broadway, and quickly became popular. He says that *skiddoo,* derived from *skedaddle,* was "added for the enlightenment of any who hadn't seen the play."

2 See Tad Dorgan is Dead, by W. L. Werner, *American Speech,* Aug., 1929. *The flea's eyebrows, the bee's knees, the snake's hips* and *the canary's tusks* will be recalled. A writer in *Liberty,* quoted in *American Speech,* Feb., 1927, p. 258, says that Dorgan also helped to popularize *hard-boiled,* the invention of Jack Doyle, keeper of a billiard academy in New York.

their inventions are taken into the general vocabulary. Thus, those who specialize in boxing have contributed, in recent years, *kayo, cauliflower-ear, prelim, shadow-boxing, slug-fest, title-holder, punch-drunk,*[1] *brother-act, punk, to side-step* and *to go the limit;*[2] those who cover baseball have made many additions to the list of baseball terms given in Chapter V;[3] and those who follow the golf tournaments have given currency to *birdie, fore, par, bunker, divot, fairway, to tee off, stance,* and *onesome, twosome, threesome* and so on — some of them received into the standard speech, but the majority lingering in the twilight of slang.[4]

George Philip Krapp attempts to distinguish between slang and sound idiom by setting up the doctrine that the former is " more

1 For a learned discourse on the pathological meaning of this term see *Punch Drunk,* by Harrison S. Martland, *Journal of the American Medical Association,* Oct. 13, 1928. In severe cases " there may develop a peculiar tilting of the head, a marked dragging of one or both legs, a staggering, propulsive gait with facial characteristics of the parkinsonian syndrome, or a backward swaying of the body, tremors, vertigo and deafness." Some of the synonyms are *cuckoo, goofy, cutting paper-dolls* and *slug-nutty.*

2 See Jargon of Fistiana, by Robert E. Creighton, *American Speech,* Oct., 1933, and Color Stuff, by Harold E. Rockwell, the same, Oct., 1927. William Henry Nugent, in The Sports Section, *American Mercury,* March, 1929, says that the father of them all was Pierce Egan, who established *Pierce Egan's Life in London and Sporting Guide* in 1824. A year earlier Egan printed a revised edition of Francis Grose's Classical Dictionary of the Vulgar Tongues, 1785. In it appeared *to stall off, cheese it, to trim* (in the sense of to swindle), *to pony up, squealer, sucker, yellow-belly,* and many other locutions still in use.

3 See Baseball Slang, by V. Samuels, *American Speech,* Feb., 1927, p. 255. Hugh Fullerton, one of the rev. elders of the fraternity, says that the first baseball reports to be adorned with neologisms, *e.g., south-paw, initial-sack, grass-cutter, shut-out* and *circus-play,* were written by Charlie Seymour of the Chicago *Inter-Ocean* and Lennie Washburn of the Chicago *Herald* during the 80's. Some years ago the Chicago *Record-Herald,* apparently alarmed by the extravagant fancy of its baseball reporters, asked its readers if they would prefer a return to plain English. Such of them as were literate enough to send in their votes were almost unanimously against a change. As one of them said, " One is nearer the park when Schulte *slams the pill* than when he merely *hits the ball.*" For the argot of baseball players, as opposed to the slang of sports writers, see Baseball Terminology, by Henry J. Heck, *American Speech,* April, 1930.

4 See Golf Gab, by Anne Angel, *American Speech,* Sept., 1926. In 1934 Willis Stork, a student of Dr. Louise Pound at the University of Nebraska, prepared a paper on The Jargon of the Sports Writers, mainly confined to an examination of the sports pages of two Lincoln, Neb., papers, the *State Journal* and the *Star* from July 1, 1933 to July 15, 1934. So far it has not been published. See also Our Golf Lingo Peeves the British, *Literary Digest,* April 11, 1931.

expressive than the situation demands." "It is," he says, "a kind of hyperesthesia in the use of language. *To laugh in your sleeve* is idiom because it arises out of a natural situation; it is a metaphor derived from the picture of one raising his sleeve to his face to hide a smile, a metaphor which arose naturally enough in early periods when sleeves were long and flowing; but *to talk through your hat* is slang, not only because it is new, but also because it is a grotesque exaggeration of the truth."[1] The theory, unluckily, is combated by many plain facts. *To hand it to him, to get away with it* and even *to hand him a lemon* are certainly not metaphors that transcend the practicable and probable, and yet all are undoubtedly slang. On the other hand, there is palpable exaggeration in such phrases as "he is not worth the powder it would take to kill him," in such adjectives as *breakbone* (fever), and in such compounds as *fire-eater*, and yet it would be absurd to dismiss them as slang. Between *blockhead* and *bonehead* there is little to choose, but the former is sound English, whereas the latter is American slang. So with many familiar similes, *e.g., like greased lightning, as scarce as hen's teeth:* they are grotesque hyperboles, but hardly slang.

The true distinction, in so far as any distinction exists at all, is that indicated by Whitney, Bradley, Sechrist and McKnight. Slang originates in the effort of ingenious individuals to make the language more pungent and picturesque — to increase the store of terse and striking words, to widen the boundaries of metaphor, and to provide a vocabulary for new shades of difference in meaning. As Dr. Otto Jespersen has pointed out,[2] this is also the aim of poets (as, indeed, it is of prose writers), but they are restrained by consideration of taste and decorum, and also, not infrequently, by historical or logical considerations. The maker of slang is under no such limitations: he is free to confect his neologism by any process that can be grasped by his customers, and out of any materials available, whether native or foreign. He may adopt any of the traditional devices of metaphor. Making an attribute do duty for the whole gives him *stiff* for corpse, *flat-foot* for policeman, *smoke-eater* for fireman, *skirt* for woman, *lunger* for consumptive, and *yes-man* for sycophant. Hidden resemblances give him *morgue* for a newspaper's file of clippings, *bean*

1 Modern English; New York, 1910, p. 211.
2 Language: Its Nature, Development and Origin; London, 1922, p. 300.

G. K. Chesterton said pretty much the same thing in The Defendant; London, 1901: "All slang is metaphor, and all metaphor is poetry."

for head, and *sinker* for a doughnut. The substitution of far-fetched figures for literal description gives him *glad-rags* for fine clothing, *bonehead* for ignoramus, *booze-foundry* for saloon, and *cart-wheel* for dollar, and the contrary resort to a brutal literalness gives him *kill-joy*, *low-life* and *hand-out*. He makes abbreviations with a free hand — *beaut* for beauty, *gas* for gasoline, and so on. He makes bold avail of composition, as in *attaboy* and *whatdyecallem*, and of ono-matopoeia, as in *biff*, *zowie*, *honky-tonk* and *wow*. He enriches the ancient counters of speech with picturesque synonyms, as in *guy*, *gink*, *duck*, *bird* and *bozo* for fellow. He transfers proper names to common usage, as in *ostermoor* for mattress, and then sometimes gives them remote figurative significances, as in *ostermoors* for whiskers. Above all, he enriches the vocabulary of action with many new verbs and verb-phrases, *e.g.*, *to burp*, *to neck*, *to gang*, *to frame up*, *to hit the pipe*, *to give him the works*, and so on. If, by the fortunes that condition language-making, his neologism acquires a special and lim-ited meaning, not served by any existing locution, it enters into sound idiom and is presently wholly legitimatized; if, on the contrary, it is adopted by the populace as a counter-word and employed with such banal imitativeness that it soon loses any definite significance whatever, then it remains slang and is avoided by the finical. An ex-ample of the former process is afforded by *tommy-rot*. It first ap-peared as English school-boy slang, but its obvious utility soon brought it into good usage. In one of Jerome K. Jerome's books, " Paul Kelver," there is the following dialogue:

" The wonderful songs that nobody ever sings, the wonderful pictures that nobody ever paints, and all the rest of it. It's *tommy-rot!* "

" I wish you wouldn't use slang."

" Well, you know what I mean. What is the proper word? Give it to me."

" I suppose you mean *cant*."

" No, I don't. *Cant* is something that you don't believe in yourself.[1] It's *tommy-rot*; there isn't any other word."

Nor were there any other words for *hubbub*, *fireworks*, *foppish*, *fretful*, *sportive*, *dog-weary*, *to bump* and *to dwindle* in Shake-speare's time; he adopted and dignified them because they met genu-ine needs.[2] Nor was there any other satisfactory word for *graft*

1 This sense of the word, of course, is to be differentiated sharply from the philological sense of a more or less secret jargon.

2 A long list of his contributions to the vocabulary, including a num-ber borrowed from the slang of his time, is to be found in Modern English in the Making, by George H. McKnight; New York, 1928, p. 188 ff.

when it came in, nor for *rowdy*, nor for *boom*, nor for *joy-ride*, nor for *slacker*, nor for *trust-buster*. Such words often retain a humorous quality; they are used satirically and hence appear but seldom in wholly serious discourse. But they have standing in the language nevertheless, and only a prig would hesitate to use them as George Saintsbury used *the best of the bunch* and *joke-smith*. So recently as 1929 the Encyclopaedia Britannica listed *bootlegger, speakeasy, dry, wet, crook, fake, fizzle, hike, hobo, poppycock, racketeer* and *O.K.* as American slang terms, but today most of them are in perfectly good usage. What would one call a racketeer if *racketeer* were actually forbidden? It would take a phrase of four or five words at least, and they would certainly not express the idea clearly.[1]

On the other hand, many an apt and ingenious neologism, by falling too quickly into the gaping maw of the proletariat, is spoiled forthwith and forever. Once it becomes, in Oliver Wendell Holmes's phrase, " a cheap generic term, a substitute for differentiated specific expressions," it quickly acquires such flatness that the fastidious flee it as a plague. The case of *strenuous* I have already mentioned. One recalls, too, many capital verb-phrases, thus ruined by unintelligent appreciation, *e.g., to freeze on to, to have the goods, to cut no ice, to fall for,* and *to get by;* and some excellent substantives, *e.g., dope* and *dub,* and compounds, *e.g., come-on* and *easy-mark,* and simple verbs, *e.g., to neck* and *to vamp.* These are all quite as sound in structure as the great majority of our most familiar words and phrases — *to cut no ice,* for example, is certainly as good as *to butter no parsnips* — , but their adoption by the ignorant and their endless use and misuse in all sorts of situations have left them tattered and obnoxious, and soon or late they will probably go the way, as Brander Matthews once said, of all the other " temporary phrases which spring up, one scarcely knows how, and flourish unaccountably for a few months,

1 In 1932–33 Dr. Walter Barnes of the New York University set four of his associates to canvassing 100 college, high-school and elementary teachers on the subject of slang. They were asked to scrutinize a list of 432 slang terms, and to estimate them as acceptable, trite and forceless, doubtful, or offensive. Those chosen as most acceptable were *pep, fake, stiff upper lip, double-cross* and *booster.* All these, in ordinary discourse, are nearly if not quite irreplaceable. Others high on the list were *speakeasy, bone-dry, broke, fan, go-getter, snappy, to make the grade, pull* (in the sense of influence), *come-back, frame-up, racket, give-away, cinch* and *to turn down.* The results of the inquiry were issued in mimeograph as Studies in Current Colloquial Usage; New York, 1933.

and then disappear forever, leaving no sign." Matthews was wrong in two particulars here. They do not arrive by any mysterious parthenogenesis, but come from sources which, in many cases, may be determined. And they last, alas, a good deal more than a month. *Shoo-fly* afflicted the American people for four or five years, and " I *don't* think," *aber nit, over the left, good night* and *oh yeah* were scarcely less long-lived.[1] There are, indeed, slang terms that have survived for centuries, never dropping quite out of use and yet never attaining to good usage. Among verbs, *to do* for to cheat has been traced to 1789, *to frisk* for to search to 1781, *to grease* for to bribe to 1557, and *to blow* for to boast to *c.* 1400.[2] Among nouns, *gas* for empty talk has been traced to 1847, *jug* for prison to 1834, *lip* for insolence to 1821, *sap* for fool to 1815, *murphy* for potato to 1811, *racket* to 1785, *bread-basket* for stomach to 1753, *hush-money* to 1709, *hick* to 1690, *gold-mine* for profitable venture to 1664, *grub* for food to 1659, *rot-gut* to 1597 and *bones* for dice to *c.* 1386. Among the adjectives, *lousy* in the sense of inferior goes back to 1690; when it burst into American slang in 1910 or thereabout it was already more than two centuries old. *Booze* has never got into Standard English, but it was known to slang in the first years of the Fourteenth Century. When *nuts* in the sense revealed by " Chicago was *nuts* for the Giants " came into popularity in the United States *c.* 1920, it was treated by most of the newspaper commentators on current slang as a neologism, but in truth it had been used in precisely the same sense by R. H. Dana, Jr., in " Two Years Before the Mast,"

---

1 The life of such a word or phrase seems to depend, at least to some extent, upon its logical content. When it is sheer silliness the populace quickly tires of it. Thus " Ah there, my size, I'll steal you," " Where did you get that hat? ", " How'd you like to be the ice-man? ", " Would you for fifty cents? ", " Let her go, Gallegher ", " So's your old man " and their congeners were all short-lived. Many such vacuities have a faintly obscene significance. It is their function to conceal the speaker's lack of a logical retort by raising a snicker. Those of rather more sense and appositeness, *e.g.,* " Tell your troubles to a policeman," " How did you get that way? ", " Where do you get that stuff? ", " I'll say so " and " You said a mouthful," seem to last longer. In 1932 a Bridgeport, Conn., high-school teacher, Miss Julia Farnam, told the Bridgeport *Post* on returning from a visit to England that she had met there " the daughter of an earl " who thought " You said a mouthful " " the cleverest expression she ever heard." (*Post*, Oct. 3.)

2 These and the following examples are taken from The Age of Slang, by J. Louis Kuethe, *Baltimore Evening Sun*, July 3, 1934.

1840, and by Mark Twain in "Following the Equator," 1897.[1] Sometimes an old slang word suddenly acquires a new meaning. An example is offered by *to chisel.* In the sense of to cheat, as in "He *chiseled* me out of $3," it goes back to the first years of the Nineteenth Century, but with the advent of the N.R.A., in the late Summer of 1933, it took on the new meaning of to evade compliance with the law by concealment or stealth. It has been credited to Franklin D. Roosevelt, but I believe that its true father was General Hugh S. Johnson, J.D.

With the possible exception of the French, the Americans now produce more slang than any other people, and put it to heavier use in their daily affairs. But they entered upon its concoction relatively late, and down to the second decade of the Nineteenth Century they were content to take their supply from England. American slang, says George Philip Krapp, "is the child of the new nationalism, the new spirit of joyous adventure that entered American life after the close of the War of 1812."[2] There was, during the colonial and early republican periods, a great production of neologisms, as we have seen in Chapter III, but very little of it was properly describable as slang. I find *to boost,* defined as to raise up, to lift up, to exalt, in the glossary appended to David Humphreys's "The Yankey in England," 1815,[3] but all the other slang terms listed, *e.g., duds* for clothes, *spunk* for courage, and *uppish,* are in Francis Grose's "Classical Dictionary of the Vulgar Tongue," published in London thirty years before. The Rev. John Witherspoon's denunciation of slang in "The Druid," 1781, is a denunciation of English slang, though he is discussing the speech habits of Americans. But with the great movement into the West, following the War of 1812, the American vulgate came into its own, and soon the men of the ever-receding frontier were pouring out a copious stream of neologisms, many of them showing the audacious fancy of true slang. When these novelties penetrated to the East they produced a sort of linguistic shock, and the finicky were as much upset by the "tall talk" in which they were embodied as English pedants are today by the slang of Holly-

---

1 For this I am indebted to Mr. James D. Hart of Cambridge, Mass.
2 Is American English Archaic? *Southwest Review,* Summer, 1927, p. 302.
3 The first example in the Supplement to the Oxford Dictionary is from John Neal's Brother Jonathan, 1825.

wood.[1] That some of them were extremely extravagant is a fact: I need point only to *blustiferous, clam-jamphrie, conbobberation, helliferocious, mollagausauger, peedoodles, ripsniptiously, slang-whanger, sockdolager, to exflunctify, to flummuck, to giraffe, to hornswoggle, to obflisticate* and *to puckerstopple.*[2] Most of these, of course, had their brief days and then disappeared, but there were others that got into the common vocabulary and still survive, *e.g., blizzard, to hornswoggle, sockdolager* and *rambunctious,* the last-named the final step in a process which began with *robustious* and ran through *rumbustious* and *rambustious* in England before Americans took a hand in it. With them came many verb-phrases, *e.g., to pick a crow with, to cut one's eye-teeth, to go the whole hog.* This " tall talk," despite the horror of the delicate, was a great success in the East, and its salient practitioners — for example, David Crockett — were popular heroes. Its example encouraged the production of like neologisms everywhere, and by 1840 the use of slang was very widespread. It is to those days before the Civil War that we owe many of the colorful American terms for strong drink, still current, *e.g., panther-sweat, nose-paint, red-eye, corn-juice, forty-rod, mountain-dew, coffin-varnish, bust-head, stagger-soup, tonsil-paint, squirrel-whiskey* and so on, and for drunk, *e.g., boiled, canned, cock-eyed, frazzled, fried, oiled, ossified, pifflicated, pie-eyed, plastered, snozzled, stewed, stuccoed, tanked, woozy.*[3] " Perhaps the most striking difference between British and American slang," says Krapp,[4] " is that the former is more largely merely a matter of the use of queer-sounding words, like *bally* and *swank,* whereas American slang suggests vivid images and pictures." This was hardly true in the heyday of " tall talk," but that it is true now is revealed by a comparison of current English and American college slang. The vocabulary of Oxford and Cambridge seems inordinately obvious and banal to an American undergraduate. At Oxford it is made up in large part of a series of childish perversions of common and proper nouns, effected by adding *-er* or inserting *gg.* Thus, breakfast becomes *brekker,* collection becomes *collecker,* the Queen Street

---

1 Specimens of this tall talk are given in Chapter IV, Section 1.
2 For these examples I am indebted to M. M. Mathews, who prints a longer list in The Beginnings of American English; Chicago, 1931, pp. 114–15.
3 For a much longer list see Slang Synonyms for *Drunk,* by Manuel Prenner, *American Speech,* Dec., 1928.
4 The English Language in America; New York, 1925, Vol. I, p. 114.

Cinema becomes the *Queener,* St. John's becomes *Jaggers* and the Prince of Wales becomes the *Pagger-Wagger.* The rest of the vocabulary is equally feeble. To match the magnificent American *lounge-lizard* the best the Oxonians can achieve is *a bit of a lad,* and in place of the multitudinous American synonyms for *girl*[1] there are only *bint* and a few other such flabby inventions.[2] All college slang, of course, borrows heavily from the general slang vocabulary. For example, *chicken,* which designated a young girl on most American campuses until 1921 or thereabout,[3] was used by Steele in 1711, and, in the form of *no chicken,* by Swift in 1720. It had acquired a disparaging significance in the United States by 1788, as the following lines show:

> From visiting bagnios, those seats of despair,
> Where *chickens* will call you *my duck* and *my dear*
> In hopes that your purse may fall to their share,
> Deliver me![4]

1 There is a list of them in English Words and Their Background, by George H. McKnight; New York, 1923, p. 61.

2 I am indebted here to Mr. Hiram D. Blauvelt. The literature dealing with American college slang begins with A Collection of College Words and Customs, by B. H. Hall; Cambridge, Mass., 1851. Its contents are summarized in College Slang of a Century Ago, by Joseph C. Smith, *Delta Kappa Epsilon Quarterly,* May, 1933. For the slang in vogue at the beginning of the present century see College Words and Phrases, by Eugene H. Babbitt, *Dialect Notes,* Vol. II, Pt. I, 1900, a very valuable compilation. For later periods see College Slang, by M. C. McPhee, *American Speech,* Dec., 1927, and College Abbreviations, by W. E. Schultz, the same, Feb., 1930. There are many monographs on the slang of definite colleges, for example: College Slang Words and Phrases From Bryn Mawr College, by Howard J. Savage, *Dialect Notes,* Vol. V, Pt. V, 1922; Colgate University Slang, by J. A. Russell, *American Speech,* Feb., 1930; A Babylonish Cruise [Girard College], by Carroll H. Frey, *Steel and Garnet,* Dec., 1922;

Johns Hopkins Jargon, by J. Louis Kuethe, *American Speech,* June, 1932; Kansas University Slang, by Carl Pingry and Vance Randolph, the same, Feb., 1928; Midshipman Jargon, by Mary B. Peterson, the same, Aug., 1928; Negro Slang in Lincoln University, by Hugh Sebastian, the same, Dec., 1934; University of Missouri Slang, by Virginia Carter, the same, Feb., 1931; Slang at Smith, by M. L. Farrand, *Delineator,* Oct., 1920; Stanford Expressions, by W. R. Morse, *American Speech,* March, 1927; Stanfordiana, by John A. Shidler and R. M. Clarke, Jr., the same, Feb., 1932; More Stanford Expressions, by John A. Shidler, the same, Aug., 1932; and College Slang Words and Phrases From Western Reserve University, *Dialect Notes,* Vol. IV, Pt. III, 1915.

3 I take the date from Slang Today and Yesterday, by Eric Partridge; 2nd ed.; London, 1935, p. 429. Partridge says that it was displaced, at least for a time, by the English *flapper.*

4 The Married Man's Litany, *New Hampshire Spy,* June 10. I am indebted for the quotation to Dr. James Truslow Adams.

Like the vulgar language in general, popular American slang has got very little sober study from the professional philologians. The only existing glossary of it by a native scholar — "A Dictionary of American Slang," by Maurice H. Weseen, associate professor of English at the University of Nebraska — is an extremely slipshod and even ridiculous work.[1] There are several collections by laymen, but most of them are still worse.[2] The best, and by far, is "Slang Today and Yesterday," by Eric Partridge,[3] which deals principally with English slang, but also has a valuable section on American slang. All the dictionaries of Americanisms, of course, include words reasonably describable as slang, but they appear only incidentally, and not in large numbers. Thornton, for example, bars out a great deal of interesting and amusing material by confining his researches to written records. In England the literature of the subject is far more extensive. It began in the Sixteenth Century with the publication of several vocabularies of thieves' argot, and has been enriched in recent years by a number of valuable works, notably the Partridge volume just cited, "Slang, Phrase and Idiom in Colloquial English and Their Use," by Thomas R. G. Lyell,[4] and the monumental "Slang and Its Analogues," by John S. Farmer and W. E. Henley.[5] Before the com-

---

1 New York, 1934. Dr. Weseen seems to be uncertain about the meaning of the word *slang*. He extends it to embrace trade and class argots, the technical vocabularies of various arts and mysteries, common mispronunciations, and the general body of nonce-words. On what theory does he hold that *A No. 1*, *boss*, and *close call* are slang? Or *chaw*, *snoot* and *coupla?* Or *cold snap*, *eternal triangle* and *dead as a doornail?* Or *moron*, *journalese* and *Hoosier?* Or such painful artificialities as *Emersonthusiast*, *mound mainstay* ("the chief pitcher for a baseball team"), and *powerphobe* ("a person who fears the political power of public companies"). Some of his definitions are howlers, as, for example, "an uncouth person" for *leatherneck* (Tell it to the Marines!), and "the home of a newly married couple" — just that, and nothing more — for *love-nest*.
2 For example, A Thesaurus of Slang, by Howard N. Rose; New York,

1934. Rose's aim is the lowly one of aiding writers of pulp fiction. The ordinary English words are listed alphabetically, and the equivalents in slang or argot follow them. Thus the fictioneer who yearns to give verisimilitude to his otherwise bald and unconvincing narrative may learn readily what college students call a library or a lavatory, and how hoboes distinguish between the professional levels of their trade.
3 2nd ed.; London, 1935. It contains a long and interesting history of modern slang, and separate chapters on various varieties of cant and argot.
4 Tokyo, 1931.
5 In seven volumes; London, 1890–1904. This huge work is mainly devoted to cant, but it also contains a great deal of English and American slang. About 15,000 terms are listed. In many cases there are dated quotations, but the dates are not always accurate. In his preface Farmer promised to include a bib-

pletion of the last-named, the chief authorities on English slang were "A Dictionary of Slang, Jargon and Cant," by Albert Barrère and Charles G. Leland,[1] and "A Dictionary of Modern Cant, Slang and Vulgar Words," by J. C. Hotten.[2] Relatively little attention is paid to slang in the philological journals, but it is frequently discussed in the magazines of general circulation and in the newspapers.[3] When the English papers denounce Americanisms, which is very often, it is commonly slang that arouses their most violent dudgeon. This dudgeon, of course, is grounded upon its very success: the American movies and talkies have implanted American slang in England even more copiously than they have implanted more decorous American neologisms. As the *Spectator* was saying lately, its influence " on the British Empire continues, ever more rapidly, to increase – a portent frequently mentioned and almost as frequently deplored."[4] Sometimes it is belabored as intolerably vulgar, indecent and against God, as when the *Christian World*[5] blamed it for the prevalence of " dishonest and debased thought " and ascribed its use to " a sneaking fear and dislike of calling beautiful things by their beautiful names and of calling ugly things by their ugly names "; sometimes it is sneered at as empty and puerile, signifying nothing, as when Allan Monkhouse[6] demanded piously " What is the good of all this? " and answered " Such words are the ghosts of old facetiousness, and the world would be better without them "; and sometimes efforts are made to dispose of it by proving that it is all stolen from England, as when Dr. C. T.

liography, a vocabulary of foreign slang, and a study of comparative slang, but this intention seems to have been abandoned. An abridgment in one volume by the same authors appeared in London in 1905. Farmer alone printed a Dictionary of Americanisms in London in 1889. It included relatively little slang.

1 In two volumes; London, 1889-90. It listed about 4800 terms, and like Slang and Its Analogues was privately printed. There was a second edition in 1897.
2 Usually called simply the Slang Dictionary. The first edition appeared in London in 1859. There were later editions in 1860, 1864, and 1874, and many reprints.
3 The more respectable literature,

running down to 1922, is listed in A Bibliography of Writings on the English Language, by Arthur G. Kennedy; Cambridge and New Haven, 1927, p. 419 *ff*. There is a briefer bibliography in the third edition of the present work; New York, 1928, p. 463 *ff*. For the period since 1922 the bibliographies printed in each issue of *American Speech* and annually in the *Publications of the Modern Language Association* are useful, though they are far from complete.
4 In a review of the Weseen Dictionary of American Slang, March 15, 1935.
5 May 14, 1931.
6 American Slang, Manchester *Guardian Weekly*, March 8, 1935.

Onions, one of the editors of the Oxford Dictionary, offered to show a London reporter that the dictionary listed any American slang term he could name.[1] Alas, for Dr. Onions, after making good with *to grill, fresh, to figure* (in the sense of to conclude), *bunkum* (he apparently forgot its clearly American origin) and *rake-off* (he had to fall back upon an American example), he came to grief with *boloney* and *nerts*. One of the favorite forms of this latter enterprise is a letter to the editor announcing the discovery that this or that locution, lately come into popularity by way of the talkies, is to be found in Shakespeare,[2] or the Authorized Version of the Bible, or maybe even in Piers Plowman. There are also the specialists who devote themselves to demonstrating that American slang is simply a series of borrowings from the Continental languages, particularly French — for example, that *and how* is a translation of *et comment*, that *you're telling me* is from *à qui le dites-vous*, and that *to get one's goat* is from *prendre sa chèvre*.[3] But not all Englishmen, of course, oppose and deride the American invasion, whether of slang or of novelties on high levels. Not a few agree with Horace Annesley Vachell that " American slanguage is not a tyranny, but a beneficent autocracy. . . . *Lounge-lizard*, for example, is excellent. . . . It is humiliating to reflect that English slang at its best has to curtsey to American

1 London *Evening News*, April 30, 1934.
2 The same quest is sometimes pursued by Americans. See, for example, Shakespeare and American Slang, by Frederic S. Marquardt, *American Speech*, Dec., 1928, and Slang From Shakespeare, by Anderson M. Baten; Hammond, Ind., 1931.
3 *Prendre sa chèvre* has been traced to Henri Estienne's Satires, *c.* 1585. It is to be found also in Montaigne and Molière, and was included in the 1776 edition of the Dictionnaire de l'Académie. Mr. Rowland M. Myers, to whom I am indebted here, suggests that Estienne may have picked it up in the course of his Greek studies. I have been told that the locution originated, in America, in the fact that the old-time horse-trainers, having a nervous horse to handle, put a goat in its stall to give it company. When the goat was taken away the horse yielded to the heebie-jeebies, and so was easily beaten on the track. A variant etymology was printed in the London *Morning Post*, Jan. 31, 1935. It was so precious that it deserves to be embalmed: " Among the Negroes in Harlem it is the custom for each household to keep a goat to act as general scavenger. Occasionally one man will steal another's goat, and the household debris then accumulates, to the general annoyance." The phrase " Let George do it," once so popular in the United States, is said by some to have been only a translation of " Laissez faire à Georges," which originated in France during the Fifteenth Century, and at the start had satirical reference to the multiform activities of Cardinal Georges d'Amboise, Prime Minister to Louis XII.

slang." To which " Jackdaw " adds in *John O'London's Weekly:*[1] "We do but pick up the crumbs that fall from Jonathan's table."

During the World War there was some compensatory borrowing of English army slang and argot by the American troops, but it did not go very far. Indeed, the list of loan-words that came into anything approaching general use in the A.E.F. was about limited to *ace, blimp, cootie, Frog, Jack Johnson, Jerry, over the top* and *whizz-bang.* Some of the favorites of the British soldiers, *e.g., fag, blighty, cheerio, to strafe, funk-hole* and *righto,* were seldom if ever used by the Americans. The greater part of the American vocabulary came from the Regular Army, and some of it was of very respectable antiquity, *e.g., hand-shaker, Holy Joe* (for chaplain), *slum* (stew), *corned willie* (corned beef hash), *outfit, belly-robber, dog-robber* (an officer's servant or orderly),[2] *doughboy, jawbone* (meaning credit, or anything spurious or dubious), *mud-splasher* (artilleryman), *buck-private, top-kick, gold-fish* (canned salmon), *gob, leatherneck, padre, chow, outfit* and *punk* (bread). A few novelties came in, *e.g., tin-hat* and *a.w.o.l.,* and there was some fashioning of counterwords and phrases from French materials, *e.g., boocoo* or *boocoop* (beaucoup), *toot sweet* (tout de suite) and *trez beans* (très bien), but neither class was numerous. Naturally enough, a large part of the daily conversation of the troops was obscene, or, at all events, excessively vulgar. Their common name for cavalryman, for example, could hardly be printed here. The English called the military police *red-caps,* but the American name was *M.P.'s.* The British used *O.C.* for Officer Commanding; the Americans used *C.O.* for Commanding Officer. The British were fond of a number of Americanisms, *e.g., blotto, cold-feet, kibosh, nix, pal* and *to chew the rag,* but whether they were borrowed from the A.E.F. or acquired by some less direct route I do not know.[3] About *gob, leatherneck* and *dough-*

1 The Way They Talk Over There, Dec. 10, 1927.
2 I am informed by Staff Sergeant J. R. Ulmer, U.S.A., that *dog-robber* is an enlisted man's term; the officers commonly use *striker.* In the same way, the enlisted men speak of *civvies* and the officers of *cits* (civilian clothes). Sergeant Ulmer says that the Regular Army makes little use of a number of terms that are commonly believed to be in its vocabulary, *e.g., rookie:* it prefers *John* or *dumb John.*
3 I am indebted here to Dr. H. K. Croessman and to Mr. Elrick B. Davis. See A.E.F. English, by Mary Paxton Keeley, *American Speech,* 1930, and Soldier Slang, by Capt. Elbridge Colby, U.S.A., eight articles, *Our Army,* Oct., 1929 – June, 1930. An anonymous

boy there have been bitter etymological wrangles. *Gob* has been traced variously to a Chinese word (*gobshite*), of unknown meaning and probably mythical; to *gobble*, an allusion to the somewhat earnest methods of feeding prevailing among sailors; and to *gob*, an archaic English dialect word signifying expectoration. The English coast-guardsmen, who are said to be free spitters, are often called *gobbies*. In May, 1928, Admiral H. A. Wiley, then commander-in-chief of the United States Fleet, forbade the use of *gob* in ship's newspapers, calling it "undignified and unworthy." But the gobs continue to cherish it. *Leatherneck*, I have been told, originated in the fact that the collar of the Marines used to be lined with leather. But the Navy prefers to believe that it has something to do with the fact that a sailor, when he washes, strips to the waist and renovates his whole upper works, whereas a Marine simply rolls up his sleeves and washes in the scantier manner of a civilian. It is the theory of all gobs that all Marines are dirty fellows. But the step from unwashed necks to leather seems to me to be somewhat long and perilous. The term *devil-dogs*, often applied to the Marines during the World War, was supposed to be a translation of the German *teufelhunde*. During the fighting around Chateau Thierry, in June and July, 1918, the Marines were heavily engaged, and the story went at the time that the Germans, finding them very formidable, called them *teufelhunde*. But I have been told by German officers who were in that

---

article in the *Stars and Stripes*, the newspaper of the A.E.F., for April 12, 1918, is also worth consulting. For British war slang see Songs and Slang of the British Soldier, 1914–18, by John Brophy and Eric Partridge; London, 1930; Soldier and Sailor Words and Phrases, by Edward Fraser and John Gibbons; and War Words, in Contemporary English, by W. E. Collinson; Leipzig, 1927, p. 91 *ff.* The book by Brophy and Partridge also includes American terms, but there are many omissions, and a few gross errors. Its vocabulary is amplified in Additions to a Volume on the Slang and the Idioms of the World War, by Eugene S. McCartney, *Papers of the Michigan Academy of Science, Arts and Letters*, Vol. X, 1928. See also Lin-

guistic Processes as Illustrated by War Slang, by the same, the same, Vol. III, 1923. (For the last two I am indebted to Dr. W. W. Bishop, librarian of the University of Michigan.) For French war slang see The Slang of the Poilu, by Eric Partridge, *Quarterly Review*, April, 1932; L'Argot de la guerre, by Albert Dauzet; Paris, 1918; L'Argot des poilus, by François Dechelette; Paris, 1918; Le Langage des poilus, by Claude Lambert; Bordeaux, 1915; L'Argot des tranchées, by Lazar Saineau; Paris, 1915; and Le Poilu tel qu'il se parle, by Gaston Esnault; Paris, 1919. For German, see Wie der Feldgraue spricht, by Karl Bergmann; Giessen, 1916, and Deutsche Soldatensprache, by O. Mausser; Strassburg, 1917.

fighting that no such word was known in the German army. *Dough-boy* is an old English navy term for dumpling. It was formerly applied to the infantry only, and its use is said to have originated in the fact that the infantrymen once pipe-clayed parts of their uniforms, with the result that they became covered with a doughy mass when it rained.[1]

2. CANT AND ARGOT

The cant of criminals is, in part, international. In its English form it includes a number of German words, and in all forms it includes Hebrew, Italian and gypsy words. The first vocabulary of it to be compiled was that of a German, Gerold Edilbach, *c.* 1420. This was followed in 1510 by the famous " Liber vagatorum," which passed through many editions, and in which Martin Luther had a hand. The earliest English references to the subject are in Robert Copland's " The Hye Waye to the Spyttel House," 1517, a dialogue in verse between the author and the porter at the door of St. Bartholomew's Hospital, London. A great many similar books followed during the Sixteenth Century, and toward the end of the succeeding century appeared the first formal glossary, " The Dictionary of the Canting Crew," by some unknown lexicographer signing himself B. E. This remained the standard work until the publication of the first edition of Captain Francis Grose's " Classical Dictionary of the Vulgar Tongue " in 1785, which contained about 3000 entries. There was a second edition in 1788, with 1000 more entries, and a third in 1796. Grose went on gathering materials until his death in 1791, and a fourth edition was brought out by Hewson Clarke in 1811. A fifth, edited by Pierce Egan, followed in 1823, and a sixth in 1868. In 1931 Eric Partridge published a seventh, based on Grose's third, with somewhat elaborate comments. Most of the dictionaries of slang also include thieves' cant; I have listed the more important of them in the preceding section.

1 There have been several studies of the use of slang by the authors of fiction, British and American, but rather curiously all of them are by foreigners, *e.g.*, Slang bei Sinclair Lewis, Hanes-Werner Wasmuth; Hamburg, 1935; Slang and Cant in Jerome K. Jerome's Works, by Olaf E. Bosson; Cambridge (England), 1911; Das Prinzip der Verwendung des Slang bei Dickens, by Karl Westendorff; Greifswald, 1923. Dickens himself printed an article on slang in *Household Words*, Sept. 24, 1853.

576 *The American Language*

Down to the Civil War the cant of American criminals seems to have been mainly borrowed from England. During the 30's a great many professional criminals were driven out of London by Sir Robert Peel's act constituting the Metropolitan Police (1829), and not a few of them immigrated to the United States. In the 50's they were reinforced by escaped convicts and ticket-of-leave men from Australia, many of whom settled in California.[1] The argot of these argonauts was not only borrowed by their native brethren; a good part of it also got into the common slang of the day, especially along the two coasts. Some of it still survives, *e.g.*, *skirt* for woman, *hick* for countryman, *moonshine* for illicit whiskey, *dip* for pickpocket, and *rat* for betrayer.[2] But by the opening of the Civil War the American underworld was beginning to fashion its own cant, and by 1870 it was actually making exports to England. One of the first words exported seems to have been *joint*, in the sense of an illicit or otherwise dubious resort. Many others followed, and since the rise of racketeering in this country the eastward tide has been heavy. "Until about 1880," says Eric Partridge, "English cant was essentially English, with a small proportion of words from French, Italian, Spanish, Dutch and Low German, plus an occasional borrowing from *lingua franca*, the mongrel Esperanto of the Mediterranean coast. Since that date, however, and especially since the war, it has received many guests from America."[3] Meanwhile, a number of terms borrowed from English cant have been changed in meaning in this country, *e.g.*, *conk*, which means the nose to English criminals but has come to mean the head in the United States. The present jargon of the American underworld, says Dr. Elisha K. Kane of the University of North Carolina, "embraces the slang of three general classes — criminals, tramps and prostitutes. But as all

1 See All Around the Town, by Herbert Asbury; New York, 1934, p. 215.
2 There is a discussion of these borrowings in The American Underworld and English Cant, by Eric Partridge, printed in American Tramp and Underworld Slang, edited by Godfrey Irwin; London, 1931, p. 255 ff.
3 A *Fence* Turns *Beef* Before a *Beak*, London *Evening News*, Nov. 21, 1933. In the third of a series of articles entitled London of the

Crooks, printed in the same newspaper during June and July, 1935, George Dilnot printed definitions of *wise-guy, sucker, approach, build-up, pay-off, in-and-in, come-on* and *easy-mark*, all of them apparently borrowings from the cant of American thieves. Like the general slang of the Republic it is much more pungent than its English congener. Consider, for example, the literal English *mouthpiece* and the synecdochical American *lip*, both meaning a lawyer.

classes meet, the cant of one is understood, to a degree, by all." [1]
Dr. Kane says that of the terms listed in "the English beggar books
and cony-catching pamphlets of the Sixteenth Century, not a dozen
words have survived" in this country, and that these are "mostly
verbs." He adds that the lingo of all English-speaking criminals, as
it has come down through the centuries, has gained in simplicity,
and that the cumbersome polysyllables that once marked it, *e.g.*,
*clapperdogeon, hankstelo, holmendods, jobbernoll, jockungage, nig-
menog, supernaculum* and *tickrum-juckrum*, have now disappeared.
That it is true is proved by an examination of his own glossary, or
of any of the others that have been printed.[2]

In general, criminal argot bears a close resemblance to ordinary
slang, and employs the same devices to extend its vocabulary. Making an attribute do duty for the whole produces *broad* for woman,
clatter for patrol-wagon, *apple-knocker* for farmer, *law* for policeman, *yip* for dog, *hard stuff* for metal money, *eye* for Pinkerton
detective, and *big-house* for prison. Hidden resemblances produce
ice for diamonds, *paper-hanger* for forger, and *third-degree* (borrowed from Freemasonry) for police examination. The substitution
of far-fetched figures for literal description gives the felon *altar* for
toilet-seat, *bull* for policeman, *bug* for alarm-bell, *bone-orchard* for
cemetery, *Fourth of July* for gun-fight, and *clown* for village constable, and the contrary resort to a brutal literalness gives him
croaker for doctor, and *body-snatcher* for kidnaper. He is fertile in
abbreviations, *e.g.*, *dinah* for dynamite, *dick* for detective, *poke* for
pocketbook, *poly* for politician, and *to gyp*, obviously from *gypsy*.
He invents many quite new words, *e.g.*, *goofy* and *zook* (an old
prostitute), and borrows others from foreign languages, *e.g.*, *spiel*,

1 The Jargon of the Underworld, *Dialect Notes*, Vol. V, Pt. X, 1927.
2 For example, Criminal Slang, by Louis E. Jackson and C. R. Hell-yer; Portland, Ore., 1914; It's Greek to You — but the Crooks Get It, by Howard McLellan, *Collier's*, Aug. 8, 1925; Criminalese, by James J. Finerty; Los Angeles, 1926; the Argot of the Under-world, by David W. Maurer, *American Speech*, Dec., 1931; The Language of the Underworld, by Ernest Booth, *American Mercury*, May, 1928; Crook Argot, by Maurice G. Smith, *American Speech*, Feb., 1928; The Chatter of Guns, by Charles G. Givens, *Saturday Eve-ning Post*, April 13, 1929. Joseph M. Sullivan, who printed a brief glos-sary under the title of Criminal Slang; Boston, 1908, returned to the subject in two articles under the same title, *New England Magazine*, July, 1910, and *American Law Re-view*, Nov.–Dec., 1918. A few of the terms in the argot of English criminals are listed in English Un-derworld Slang, *Variety*, April 8, 1931, reprinted in *American Speech*, June, 1931, p. 391 *ff.*

fin and *gelt* from German, and *ganov, kibitzer, kosher* and *yentzer* from Yiddish.[1] He makes common nouns of proper nouns, *e.g., Brodie* (from Steve Brodie), meaning a leap; *Valentino*, meaning a handsome young man who preys upon women; and *Pontius Pilate*, a judge. Finally, he devises many new verbs and verb-phrases or provides old ones with new meanings, *e.g., to belch* (to talk), *to bible* (to make oath), *to breeze* (to clear out), *to case* (to spy out), *to crash* (to enter forcibly), *to drill* (to shoot), *to fall* (to be convicted), *to finger* (to point out), *to h'ist* (to hold up), *to bump off, to hi-jack, to do the book* (to serve a life sentence), *to flatten out* (to lie low), *to give the once-over, to go gandering* (to look for something or someone), *to shake down, to wipe out.* Down to a few years ago, for some reason unknown, Cockney rhyming cant, supposed to have come in by way of Australia, was very popular among American thieves. It consists largely of a series of rhyming substitutions, *e.g., mince-pie* for eye, *lump o' lead* for head, *north and south* for mouth, *tit for tat* for hat, *twist and twirl* for girl, *storm* (or *trouble*) *and strife* for wife, and *babbling brook* for crook. It has now gone out of fashion, but a few of its locutions, *e.g., twist* for girl, remain in use. The idea behind such far-fetched forms is to conceal meaning from the uninitiated. This is an essential character-istic of cant, as opposed to slang. The criminal frequently has to communicate with his fellows in the presence of the enemy, and under circumstances which make a revelation of his plans hazardous to him. For the same reason he inclines toward the terseness that Dr. Kane has remarked. "Brevity, conciseness," says Ernest Booth, "is the essence of thieves' jargon. To be able to convey a warning and the nature of the danger in a single word or phrase is the test." [2]

1 *Fin*, obviously from *fünf*, means five. It is used impartially to desig-nate five dollars, a five-dollar bill and a five-year sentence. Sometimes *finif*, which is closer to *fünf*, is used in place of it. *Spiel*, for *spielen*, to play or perform, has got into ordinary American slang. *Gelt*, meaning money in general, needs no gloss. *Kosher*, in criminal argot, has come to mean reliable, trust-worthy. *Kibitzer* is employed, as in non-felonious American, to desig-nate an onlooker, and especially one who offers unsolicited advice.

Yentzer means a cheater. *Ganov*, a thief, survives in its original form, and has also produced derivatives. Thus: *gun*, from its first syllable, means any sort of criminal, but es-pecially a pickpocket; *gun-mob* means a gang, and *gun-moll* means a criminal's girl. *Gun* has bred *cannon*, of the same meaning.

2 The Language of the Underworld, *American Mercury*, May, 1928. Mr. Booth is himself a felon of long professional experience, and is at the moment undergoing incarcera-tion in Folsom Prison in California.

Mr. Booth describes a tense situation in which " two or more thieves must make immediate decision regarding their actions." " *Lam* [*i.e.*, run away]? " pants a waverer. " No — *stick* [*i.e.*, remain and shoot it out]," replies the leader — " and the battle is on."

As Dr. Kane says, the argots of criminals, of tramps and of prostitutes have a great deal in common and are mutually intelligible; nevertheless, there are some differences. The criminals themselves are divided into classes that tend to keep apart, and the tramps and prostitutes shade off into the general population. There are also regional differences, and a term still in vogue in the East may be *passé* in the Middle West or on the Pacific Coast, or vice versa. Thus the Western crooks sometimes call a forger a *bill-poster* and on the Pacific Coast he may be a *scratcher*, whereas he is usually a *paper-hanger*, which is the eldest term, in the East. Again, in the East a jewelry-store is a *slum-joint*, whereas in the West it is an *ice-house*. Whenever a new form of thieving is invented it quickly develops a sub-cant of its own. Thus the automobile thieves who had their heyday in 1928 or thereabout devised a series of terms of their own to designate cars of the various more popular makes and designs, *e.g.*, *breezer* for an open car, *shed* for a closed car, *front-room* for a sedan, *B.I.* for a Buick, *caddy* (or *golfer*) for a Cadillac, *ducker* for a Dodge, *Hudson-pup* for an Essex, *papa* for a Lincoln, *spider* for a Ford, *Studie* for a Studebaker, and so on.[1] In the same way the drug peddlers who began to flourish after the passage of the Harrison Act in 1915 were ready with neologisms to reinforce the terminology of drug addiction in the general cant of the underworld. Physicians who supplied addicts with drugs became *ice-tong doctors*, the addicts themselves became *junkers*, and the Federal agents who tried to put down the traffic became *whiskers*, *gazers* or *uncles*. A mixture of cocaine and morphine was called a *whizz-bang*, an occasional user of drugs was a *joy-rider*, and to simulate illness in the hope of getting drugs was to throw a *wing-ding*.[2] The racketeers who came in with Prohibition in 1920, and quickly arose to first place in the underworld, were lavish enrichers of its language. Some of their inventions, indeed, were adopted by the whole

---

1 I Wonder Who's Driving Her Now, by William G. Shepherd, *Journal of American Insurance*, Feb., 1929.
2 See Junker Lingo, by David W.

Maurer, *American Speech*, April, 1933, and Addenda to Junker Lingo, by V. F. Nelson, the same, Oct., 1933.

population, *e.g.*, *big shot*, *bathtub-gin*, *torpedo*, *trigger-man*, *gorilla* (the last three meaning assassin), *hide-out*, *pineapple* (a bomb), *heat* (trouble), *to needle*, *to cook* (to redistil denatured alcohol), *to cut* (to dilute), *to muscle in*, *to take for a ride*, *to put on the spot*. Their term for genuine liquor, *McCoy*,[1] promises to survive, at least until the last memory of Prohibition fades. They added two Yiddishisms to the common stock of all American rogues: *meshuggah* (crazy) and *goy* (a Christian). *Racket* itself, of course, was not a new word. It had been used by English criminals, in exactly its present sense, in the Eighteenth Century. *Racketeer* was a novelty, but I suspect that it was introduced, not by anyone deserving to be so called, but by some ingenious newspaper reporter.[2]

There is a special prison argot, grounded in large part, of course, on thieves' cant, but with some special terms of its own.[3] Naturally enough, most of the articles of the prison bill-of-fare have derisory names. In virtually all American prisons stew is *slum*, bread is *punk* or *dummy*, gravy is *skilley*, sugar is *sand* or *dirt*, eggs are *bombs*, roast beef is *young-horse*, sausages are *beagles* or *pups*, and coffee is *jamoca* (apparently from *Java* and *Mocha*). A prisoner lately *dressed in* is a *fish*, a sentence is a *bit*, the isolation cells are the *hole*, the *ice-box*, or the *cooler*, *good time* is the prisoner's allowance for good behavior, a guard is a *screw* or *hack*, a recidivist is a *two-time loser* (or *three-time* or *n-time*, as the case may be), visiting day is the *big day*, a prison visitor is a *hoosier*, hacksaw blades are *briars*, the prison itself is the *big house*, a reformatory is a *college* or *ref*,

1 It usually appears as *the real Mc-Coy*. Its origin is disputed. One current etymology connects it with Bill *McCoy*, an eminent rum-runner in the heyday of Rum Row. Another holds that it comes from the name of Kid *McCoy*, welterweight champion of the world, 1898–1900. The story runs that a drunk once picked a quarrel with McCoy and refused to believe that he was the prize-fighter. After McCoy's fist had done its work, the drunk picked himself up, saying "It's the real *McCoy*." See The Real *McCoy*, by P. R. Beath, *American Speech*, Feb., 1932, p. 239.

2 Vocabularies of the terms employed by racketeers during their Golden Age are to be found in The Argot of the Racketeers, by James P. Burke, *American Mercury*, Dec., 1930, and English As It Is Spoken Owes Debt to Racketeer, New York *World*, Nov. 17, 1929. For an account of the contribution of Prohibition to the general speech see Volstead English, by Achsah Hardin, *American Speech*, Dec., 1931.

3 See Table Talk, *San Quentin Bulletin*, Jan., 1931; Can Cant, by J. Louis Kuethe, Baltimore *Evening Sun*, Dec. 9, 1932; Prison Lingo, by Herbert Yenne, *American Speech*, March, 1927; Convicts' Jargon, by George Milburn, the same, Aug., 1931; A Prison Dictionary (Expurgated), the same, Oct., 1933, and Prison Parlance, by J. Louis Kuethe, the same, Feb., 1934.

a county workhouse is a *band-box*, and a police-station is a *can*. To smuggle a letter out of the place is *to fly a kite*. To escape is *to crash*, *to blow*, *to cop a mope*, or *to go over the wall*. To be released is *to spring* or *to hit the bricks*. To go crazy while in confinement is *to go stir-bug*. To report a prisoner for violating a rule is *to turn him in*. To be imprisoned for life is *to do the book* or *to do it all*. To have no hope of release is *to be buried*, *lagged* or *settled*. To be sentenced to death is *to get the works*. To be hanged is *to be topped* or *to dance*. To be electrocuted is *to burn*, *to fry* or *to squat*. The march to the electric-chair is the *last waltz*. The chair itself is the *hot-seat* or *hot-squat*, and the death-house is the *dance-hall*. Special argots are also in use in various lesser sorts of hoosegow, *e.g.*, reformatories and orphanages. The only report that I have been able to find on the vocabulary of incarcerated orphans [1] indicates that the young inmates speak a jargon made up of borrowings from both school slang and criminal cant. From the former come *bull-fest*, *collegiate*, *nifty* and *pash*, and from the latter *to scram*, *to gyp* and *screw* (a watchman or officer).

The argot of tramps and hoboes also coincides with that of criminals, for though some of them are far from felons they inhabit a section of the underworld, and are pursued almost as relentlessly as yeggmen by the constabulary. Tramps and hoboes are commonly lumped together, but in their own sight they are sharply differentiated. A *hobo* or *bo* is simply a migratory laborer; he may take some longish holidays, but soon or late he returns to work. A *tramp* never works if it can be avoided; he simply travels. Lower than either is the *bum*, who neither works nor travels, save when impelled to motion by the police. The *wobblies* (members of the I.W.W.) of the years following the war were hoboes but certainly not tramps or bums. But all three classes use substantially the same argot.[2] In

1 The Argot of an Orphans' Home, by L. W. Merryweather, *American Speech*, Aug., 1932.
2 The best vocabulary of it is probably that in American Tramp and Underworld Slang, by Godfrey Irwin; London, 1931. Mr. Irwin spent " more than twenty years as a tramp on the railroads and roads of the United States, Canada, Mexico and Central America, and on tramp steamers in Central American waters." Other useful articles are Hobo Cant, by F. H. Sidney, *Dialect Notes*, Vol. V, Pt. II, 1919; Hobo Lingo, by Nicholas Klein, *American Speech*, Sept., 1926; The Argot of the Vagabond, by Charlie Samolar, the same, June, 1927; More Hobo Lingo, by Howard F. Barker, the same, Sept., 1927; The Vocabulary of Bums, by Vernon W. Saul (alias K. C. Slim), the same, June, 1929; Junglese, by Robert E. Oliver, the same, June, 1932; How the Hobo Talks, by Charles

it a bed-roll is a *bindle* or *balloon*, and the man who carries one is a *bindle-stiff*. A blanket is a *soogan* and a suitcase is a *turkey*. The place where tramps and hoboes foregather is a *jungle* or *hang-out*, and one who frequents it unduly, hoping to cadge food from the more enterprising, is a *jungle-buzzard*. A beggar is a *panhandler* and an old one is a *dino*. A sneak-thief is a *prowler*, a dirty fellow (most tramps are relatively clean) is a *grease-ball*, a Texan is a *long-horn*, a Southerner is a *rebel*, a migratory worker is a *boomer*, an employment-agent is a *shark*, and a farmer or other poor simpleton is a *scissor-bill*. The tramp who carries a boy with him, to rustle food for him and serve him otherwise, is a *jocker* or *wolf*, and the boy is a *punk, gazooney, guntzel, lamb* or *prushun*.[1] To steal washing off the line is to *gooseberry* it. The discourse heard in mission-halls is *angel-food*, and the bum who listens to it is a *mission-stiff*. A Catholic priest is a *buck* or *Galway*, and the Salvation Army is *Sally Ann*. In the days before hitch-hiking, hoboes spent a great deal of their time stealing rides on the railroads, and their railroad vocabulary remains rich and racy. A locomotive is a *hog*, a coal-car is a *battle-wagon*, a caboose is a *crummy*, a freight-car is a *rattler*, a refrigerator-car is a *reefer*, a freight-train is a *drag*, a fast freight is a *manifest* or *red-ball*, an engineer is a *hoghead*, a conductor is a *con*, a brakeman is a *shack* or *brakie*, and a section-hand is a *gandy-dancer*. Most of the larger railroads of the country have names in the argot of the road. The Chicago & Alton is the *Carry-all*, the Chicago, Burlington & Quincy is the *Q*, the Baltimore and Ohio is the *Dope*, the Missouri Pacific is the *Mop*, the Southern Pacific is the *Soup Line*, and that part of it between Maricope, Ariz., and Yuma is the *Gila Monster Route*. In the old days a small town used to be a *tank* or a *jerkwater*, but now it is a *filling-station*. A tramp's professional name is his *moniker*, e.g., *Frisco Slim*. The favorite jungle delicacy is *mulligan* or *slum*, a stew made of meat and vegetables. Food in general is *chuck, garbage* or *scoffings*, a meal given out at a kitchen door is a *lump*, milk is *cow-juice*, butter is *salve* or *axle-grease*, soup is *shackles* or *Peoria*, beer is *slops*, coffee is *hot-stuff, mud* or *embalming-fluid*, pancakes are *flat-cars*, sausage is *gut*, a chicken is a *gump* or *two-step*, catsup is *red-lead*, eggs are *headlights*, corned beef and cabbage

---

Ashleigh, *Everyman* (London), May 21, 1931; Wobbly Talk, by Stewart H. Holbrook, *American Mercury*, Jan., 1926.

1 The etymology of this word is mysterious. It seems to suggest *Prussian*, but I have been unable to find any evidence of a connection.

is *Irish turkey*, pastry is *toppings*, and the meringue on a pie is *calf-slobber*.

A large part of the argot of the hoboes is borrowed from that of the railroad men. In both, for example, a locomotive is a *hog* and an engineer is a *hoghead*. But the railroad men also have many picturesque terms that their unwelcome guests have never picked up. To them a conductor is not a *con*, but *Captain*, a *grabber*, the *master*, the *skipper*, the *king-pin*, the *big-ox* or the *brains*. A passenger brakeman is a *baby-lifter*, a fireman is a *bell-ringer*, *tallow-pot*, *stoker*, *smoke*, *bakehead*, *fireboy* or *diamond-cracker*, a train-master is a *master-mind*, a master-mechanic is a *master-maniac*, a machinist is a *nut-splitter*, a telegraph-operator is a *brass-pounder*, a car-repairer is a *car-toad* or *carwhacker*, an air-brake repairman is an *air-monkey*, a switchman is a *cinder-cruncher*, *snake*, *goose* or *clown*, a yard-master is a *dinger*, *ringmaster* or the *general*, his assistant is a *jam-buster*, a train-dispatcher is a *detainer*, a yard-conductor is a *drummer*, a track-laborer is a *jerry* or *snipe*, the foreman of a track-gang is the *king snipe*, and a yard-clerk is a *mudhop*, *number-grabber* or *number-dummy*. They use *crummy* to designate a caboose, but they also use *buggy*, *hack*, *hearse*, *cage*, *clown-wagon*, *crib*, *dog-house*, *louse-cage*, *monkey-house*, *parlor*, *way-car*, *shanty* or *hut*. The last is sometimes also applied to the cab of a locomotive. A Pullman sleeper is a *snoozer*, a large locomotive is a *battleship*, a stock-car is a *cow-cage*, a passenger-car is a *cushion*, a cross-over is a *diamond*, a train-order is a *flimsy*, a freight-yard is a *garden*, a switch is a *gate*, a yard-engine is a *goat*, a signal torpedo is a *gun*, a go-ahead hand or lantern signal is a *high-ball*, a fast passenger-train is a *high-liner*, the tool-box under the caboose is a *possum-belly*, a helper locomotive for mountain use is a *pusher*, *roof-garden* or *sacred-ox*, the step at the front end of a yard-engine is a *scoop*, telegraph wires are *strings*, and a yard-office is a *bee-hive*. To cool a hot-box is *to freeze the hub*, to set the brakes is *to anchor her*, to set the emergency-brakes is *to wing her*, to jump from a car is *to hit the grit*, to boast is *to blow smoke*, to quit for the day is *to pin for home*, and to quit the service is *to pull the pin*. The old term *boomer*, designating a railroad man given to drifting from road to road, is now almost obsolete, for there are very few boomers left.[1] Another argot that

1 I am indebted here to Our Own Language, *Railroad Men's Magazine*, June, 1930, and to an Old Timers' Dictionary issued by the Central Vermont Railway, the latter kindly sent to me by Mr. J. H.

impinges upon the speech of hoboes is that of the circus and carnival
men. The carnival men, indeed, also borrow a great deal from
criminal cant, for in parts at least their business skirts the dim fron-
tiers of the law. They have effected some changes of meaning in
their borrowings. Thus *gonov*, which means a thief to thieves, means
a fool on the carnival lot, and the same meaning is given to *guntzel*,
which means, in the jungles, the boy companion of a tramp. To the
carnival men a stand outside a show is a *bally-stand*, concessions are
joints or *hooplas*, a seller of cheap novelties is a *gandy-dancer*, a
hamburger-stand is a *grab-joint*, a fortune-teller's tent is a *mit-joint*,
a photograph-gallery is a *mug-joint*, cheap prizes are *slum* or *crap*,
a snake-eater or other such freak is a *geek*, a gambling concession is a
flat-joint, and the man operating it is a *thief*.[1] The circus men have
a rather more seemly vocabulary.[2] To them the gaudy pictures in
front of the side-shows constitute the *banner-line*, the circus-pro-
gramme is the *Bible*, toy balloons are *bladders*, tickets are *dukets*,
the ringmaster is always the *equestrian-director*, the powder used
for making pink lemonade and other such drinks is *flookum*, the
manager of the circus is the *gaffer*, a hamburger-stand is a *grease-
joint*, the men who drive stakes are the *hammer gang*, a dressing-tent
is a *pad-room*, that for clowns is *Clown Alley*, posters are *paper*,
bouncers are *pretty boys*, the big tent is the *rag*, the men who load
and unload the show are *razorbacks*, clowns are *white-faces* or *Joeys*,
acrobats are *kinkers*, bareback riders are *rosinbacks*, and the tattooed
man is the *picture-gallery*. The patrons are always *suckers*. A man
who works animals is never a *tamer*, but always a *trainer*. Elephants,

Fountain. In 1925 the Pennsylvania Railroad printed a brief glossary on the bills-of-fare of its dining-cars. It was reprinted in *American Speech*, Jan., 1926, p. 250. See also Railroad Terms, by F. H. Sidney, *Dialect Notes*, Vol. IV, Pt. V, 1916; A Glossary of Pullman Service Terms, *Pullman News*, Sept., 1922; Railroad Lingo, by Grover Jones, *Bookman*, July, 1929; Railroad Slang, by Robert S. Harper, *Writer's Digest*, May, 1931; Railroad Lingo, by Russell V. Batie, *American Speech*, Feb., 1934. There is some interesting and unfamiliar matter in The Sign Language of Railroad Men, by Charles Car-

penter, *American Mercury*, Feb., 1932.

1 I am indebted here to Mysteries of the Carnival Language, by Charles Wolverton, *American Mercury*, June, 1935. See also Carnival Cant, by David W. Maurer, *American Speech*, June, 1931, and Carnival Slang, by E. P. Conkle, the same, Feb., 1928, p. 253.

2 The best available glossary is in Circus Words, by George Milburn, *American Mercury*, Nov., 1931. See also A Circus List, by Percy W. White, *American Speech*, Feb., 1926, and More About the Language of the Lot, by the same, the same, June, 1928.

whether male or female, are *bulls*, zebras are *convicts*, tigers are *stripes*, and camels are *humps*. *To slough* is to strike the tents preparatory to moving on, *to spot* is to lay out their situation on the next lot, *to kife* is to swindle, and *to three-sheet* is to boast. The *Monday-man*, who had an exclusive concession to raid clothes-lines in the vicinity of the lot, has succumbed to the accumulating virtue of circuses, and the *mud-show*, drawn from town to town by horses, has gone with him.[1]

The theater, which is one of the chief sources of popular slang, also has a florid argot, and in part it is almost esoteric enough to amount to a cant. "Shouted by a breathless dancer to her companions, bawled by a lusty stage-hand to his mates, mulled sagely back and forth by two spent animal-trainers," says Gretchen Lee, "it conveys nothing whatever to the casual ear. They might better be speaking Choctaw."[2] This lingo reached its most extravagant forms among vaudeville performers, who are now much less important and numerous than they used to be in *show business*. (Observe that the article is always omitted.) Some years ago Julius H. Marx printed the following specimen dialogue between two of them, met by chance on Broadway:

First Vaudevillian – How they comin', Big Boy?

Second V. – Not so hot, not so hot. I'm playin' a hit-and-run emporium over in East New York.

First V. – Gettin' much jack?

Second V. – Well, the storm and me is cuttin' up two and a half yards, but when the feed bill and gas for the boiler is marked off, they ain't much sugar left.

First V. – Why don't you air her and do a single?

Second V. – I guess I should; every one that's caught us says that the trick is a hundred per cent. me. I had 'em howling so forte last night the whole neighborhood was in a uproar. What are you doing these days?

First V. – I just closed with a turkey that went out to play forty weeks and folded up after ten days. Believe me, them WJZ and WEAF wise-crackers ain't doin' show business any good. In the West now they are even gettin' the rodeo by radio.

Second V. – Why don't you get yourself a partner and take a flyer?

First V. – Well, if I could get a mama that could do some hoofin' and tickle a uke, I think I would.

Second V. – Well, ta ta, I gotta go now and make comical for the bozos.

1 The chautauqua, now also virtually extinct, developed an argot much more decorous than that of the circus and carnival. It is embalmed for posterity in Chautauqua Talk, by J. R. Schultz, *American Speech*, Aug., 1932. Mr. Schultz printed a brief supplement in *American Speech*, Oct., 1934, p. 233.

2 Trouper Talk, *American Speech*, Oct., 1925.

If you get a chance come over and get a load of me, but remember, Capt. Kidd, lay off my wow gags.[1]

Most of this, of course, would be intelligible to any college student: there is far more slang in it than argot or cant. The stage-hands and box-office men have lingoes of their own,[2] and there is a considerable difference between the vocabulary of a high-toned Broadway actor and that of a *hoofer* (dancer) who *grinds, bumps* and *strips* (*i.e.*, rotates her hips, follows with a sharp, sensuous upheaval of her backside, and then sheds all her clothes save a G-string) [3] in burlesque. Rather curiously, there seems to be no comprehensive glossary of theatrical argot in print.[4] That of the movies has found its Webster in Mr. Glendon Allvine, whose glossary of "Studio Lingo" is printed as an appendix to "The Silver Streak," by Roger

1 This was printed in the Conning Tower in the New York *World*, but I have been unable to determine the date.
2 For the former, see American Stage-Hand Language, by J. Harris Gable, *American Speech*, Oct., 1928, and for the latter The Strange Vernacular of the Box-Office, New York *Times*, Oct. 30, 1925.
3 For this lovely phrase I am indebted to Mr. Harry Van Hoven.
4 An inadequate one is in Stage Terms, by Percy W. White, *American Speech*, May, 1926, and an even more scanty one is in Theatrical Lingo, by Ottilie Amend, the same, Oct., 1927. Neither of these lexicographers shows any sign of having had personal experience in the theater. Rather better ones are in The Language of the Theatre, by B. Sobel, *Bookman*, April, 1929, and A Primer of Broadway Slang, by Walter Winchell, *Vanity Fair*, Nov., 1927. The latter includes some attempts at etymologies. The peculiar vocabulary of the theatrical weekly, *Variety*, which has supplied Broadway with many neologisms, is described in The Language of Lobster Alley, by Hiram Motherwell, *Bookman*, Dec., 1930, and *Variety*, by Hugh Kent, *American Mercury*, Dec., 1926. *Variety* was edited until his death in 1933 by Sime Silverman. In an obituary of

him by Epes W. Sargent, printed in his paper on Sept. 26, 1933, it was stated that at the start *Variety* was "written in the English language," but that it "never really bit into the business until Sime changed his policy and wrote as a majority of the actors of that day spoke. . . . It was not that he could not write English, but that most variety actors of that day did not speak it." Here is a specimen heading from *Variety*, reprinted in the Manchester *Guardian*, Jan. 30, 1930:

Pash Flaps M. C.
Fan Clubs Rated
Worthless to Theatres
As B. O. Gag.

The *Guardian* explained to its English readers that the intention here was "to convey the assurance that impassioned young women (flaps, flappers) organized into clubs because of their admiration for the master of ceremonies (usually the leader of the orchestra), have been found useless as a device for increasing box-office receipts." Some recent specimens from *Variety*: *to air* (to go on the air), *crix* (pl. of critic), *outstander* (one who is outstanding), *builder-upper*, *juve* (juvenile), *to guest* (to appear as a guest), *to ready* (to make ready).

Whately, Jack O'Donnell and H. W. Hanemann.[1] Some of the terms listed are very amusing. A *breakaway* is a weapon made of yucca-wood, so light that it will do no harm when a comedian is clouted with it. A studio hospital is a *butcher-shop*. The divan in a manager's office is the *casting-couch*. A face without expression is a *dead pan*. The cancellation of a call for extras is a *death-knell*. The head property-man is the *first broom*. A performer's business agent is a *flesh-peddler*. A Western picture is a *horse-opera*. An actor who seizes the center of the stage is a *lens-hog*. An elderly actress, commonly playing weeping mothers, is a *tear-bucket*. Camera lenses are *bottles*. A complaining actor is a *bleater*. A spoiled film is a *buzzard*. Noises in the sound-recording system are *canaries*. The fogging produced by halation is a *ghost*. An electrician's helper is a *grunt*. An assistant cameraman is a *jockey*. Any performer not a Caucasian is a *zombie*.

Nearly every other trade has its argot, and some of them are quite as picturesque as that of the movie people. Vocabularies of many of them have been published.[2] Nor is there any lack of such jargons,

1 Los Angeles, 1935. A shorter word-list is in Movie Talk, by Albert Parry, *American Speech*, June, 1928. There is a very brief list of radio terms in Radio Slang, by Hilda Cole, *Radioland*, March, 1935. For the usage in England, which differs considerably from that in this country, see A Dictionary of Wireless Terms, by R. Stranger; London, 1933.

2 I must content myself with references to only a small part of the literature: *Auctioneers:* Jewelry Auction Jargon, by Fred Witman, *American Speech*, June, 1928. *Aviators:* Aviation Lingo, by P. R. Beath, *American Speech*, April, 1930; The Speech of the American Airmen, by Chalmers K. Stewart; Akron, O., 1933 (a master's dissertation, still in MS). *Beauticians:* Beauty Shoppe Jargon, by N. R. L., the same, April, 1928. *Cattlemen:* Cow Country Lingo, Chicago *Daily News*, Aug. 14, 1922; Nebraska Cow Talk, by Melvin Van Denbark, *American Speech*, Oct., 1929; The Idiom of the Sheep Range, by Charles Lindsay, the same, June, 1931; Ranch Diction of

the Texas Panhandle, by Mary Dale Buckner, the same, Feb., 1933. *Firemen:* Firemen Invent Their Own Slang, New York *Sun*, March 16, 1932; The Word *Potsy*, the same, March 26, 1932. *Fishermen:* Schoonerisms: Some Speech-Peculiarities of the North-Atlantic Fishermen, by David W. Maurer, *American Speech*, June, 1930. *Furniture salesmen:* Furniture Lingo, by Charles Miller, the same, Dec., 1930. *Lumbermen:* Logger Talk, by Guy Williams; Seattle, 1930; Logger Talk, by James Stevens, *American Speech*, Dec., 1925; Sawmill Talk, by Edward Herry, the same, Oct., 1927; Lumberjack Lingo, by J. W. Clark, the same, Oct., 1931; It Ain't English, But It's Hiyu Skookum, by Stewart H. Holbrook, Portland *Sunday Oregonian*, Nov. 11, 1934. *Lunch-wagon attendants:* Lunch-Wagon Slanguage, *World's Work*, Feb., 1932. *Miners:* The Lingo of the Mining Camp, *American Speech*, Nov., 1926; Mining Town Terms, by Joseph and Michael Lopushansky, the same, June, 1929; Mining Expressions Used in Colorado, by L. J. Davidson, the

some of them unintelligible enough to the general to be almost classed as cant, on higher levels. The pedagogues, for example, employ many strange terms in their professional writings, *e.g.*, *mind-set* and *stimulus-response-bonds*, and use others in strange ways, *e.g.*, *project*, *to socialize* and *outstanding*. Two of their favorites, *reaction* and *outstanding*, have come into the common speech as counter-words. *I.Q.*, which they apparently invented, was taken in at once. But they have been less successful in introducing their confusing way of spelling out figures beginning with hundreds, *e.g.*, *three hundred seventy-one*, with the usual *and* omitted. The social-workers, whose passion is the uplift, have developed a similar lingo, and some of its pearls, *e.g.*, *community-chest, child-welfare, mental-hygiene* and *survey*, are now in general use.[1] Nor are the librarians, hospital nurses, fire insurance "engineers" and other such slaves to the common weal much behind.[2] In part, of course, these lingoes

same, Dec., 1929; California Gold-Rush English, by Marian Hamilton, the same, Aug., 1932. *Musicians:* Radio Bandmen Speak a Strange Language at Their Labors, by Louise Reid, New York *American*, June 22, 1935; Hot Jazz Jargon, by E. J. Nichols and W. L. Werner, *Vanity Fair*, Nov., 1935; Jazzing Up Our Musical Terms, by A. C. E. Schonemann, *American Speech*, June, 1926. *Newspaper reporters:* Newspaper Nomenclature, by Dorothy Colburn, the same, Feb., 1927; Going to Press, the same, Dec., 1928. *Oilfield workers:* The Language of the Oil Wells, by Clark S. Northup, *Dialect Notes*, Vol. II, Pts. V and VI, 1903–4; Oil Field Diction, by A. R. McTee, *Publications of the Texas Folk-Lore Society*, No. IV, 1925; Language of the California Oil Fields, by F. R. Pond, *American Speech*, April, 1932. *Postoffice workers:* Speech in the Post Office, the same, April, 1932. *Sailors:* Navy Slang, by B. T. Harvey, *Dialect Notes*, Vol. IV, Pt. II, 1914; Navy Terms, *American Speech*, March, 1926; Sailor Words, by E. J. Croucher, *Word-Lore*, April, 1928; Fo'c'sle Lingo, by Jack Healy, *American Speech*, April, 1928; Elegy for a Dying

Tongue, by C. B. W. Richardson, *Scribner's*, Aug., 1935. *Shoe salesmen:* Lingo of the Shoe Salesman, the same, Dec., 1934. *Sugar-beet workers:* Sugar Beet Language, the same, Oct., 1930. *Taxi-Drivers:* The Taxi Talk, by George Milburn, *Folk-Say*, Vol. I, 1929. *Telegraphers and linemen:* Some Telegraphers' Terms, by Hervey Brackbill, *American Speech*, April, 1929; Lineman's English, by C. P. Loomis, the same, Sept., 1926. *Undertakers:* Mortuary Nomenclature, *Hygeia*, Nov., 1925. The general terminology of the American labor movement is dealt with in Bulletin No. 25, Bureau of Business Research, Graduate School of Business Administration, Harvard University, 1921.

1 For an extensive glossary see The Terminology of Social Workers, by LeRoy E. Bowman, *American Speech*, June, 1926.

2 For the librarians see Library Language, by Nellie Jane Compton, *American Speech*, Nov., 1926. For the nurses see Hospital Talk, by Dorothy Barkley, the same, April, 1927. For the fire insurance brethren see Fire Insurance Terminology, by H. B. Bernstein, the same, July, 1926.

consist of legitimate technicalities, but they also contain a great deal of loose speech that is more properly describable as either argot or slang. In the case of the nurses it even verges on cant, for one of its purposes is to conceal meanings from patients.[1]

1 For the benefit of students who wish to travel further down this lane I append a brief bibliography of oddities: Aquarium English, by Ida Mellen, *American Speech*, Aug., 1928; The Language of the Saints [*i.e.*, Mormons], by Dorothy N. Lindsay, the same, April, 1933; The Speech of Plain Friends [*i.e.*, Quakers], by Kate W. Tibbals, the same, Jan., 1926; Some Peculiarities of Quaker Speech, by Anne W. Comfort, the same, Feb., 1933; The Catholic Language, by Benjamin Musser, *Ecclesiastical Review*, Dec., 1926; The Book Reviewer's Vocabulary, by W. O. Clough, *American Speech*, Feb., 1931; Auto-Tourist Talk, by L. J. Davidson, the same, April, 1934; Legal Lingo, by Reuben Oppenheimer, the same, Dec., 1926; A Dictionary of American Politics, by Edward Conrad Smith; New York, 1924; Twisting the Dictionary to Pad Political Vocabulary, New York *Times*, Dec. 16, 1923; American Political Cant, by Lowry Charles Wimberly, *American Speech*, Dec., 1926; and More Political Lingo, by the same, the same, July, 1927.

XII

THE FUTURE OF THE LANGUAGE

I. THE SPREAD OF ENGLISH

The English tongue is of small reach, stretching no further than this island of ours, nay not there over all.

This was written in 1582. The writer was Richard Mulcaster, headmaster of the Merchant Taylors' School, teacher of prosody to Edmund Spenser, and one of the earliest of English grammarians. At the time he wrote, English was spoken by between four and five millions of people, and stood fifth among the European languages, with French, German, Italian and Spanish ahead of it in that order, and Russian following. Two hundred years later Italian had dropped behind but Russian had gone ahead, so that English was still in fifth place. But by the end of the Eighteenth Century it began to move forward, and by the middle of the Nineteenth it had forced its way into first place. Today it is so far in the lead that it is probably spoken by as many people as the next two European languages — Russian and German — combined.

It is not only the first — and, in large part, the only — language of both of the world's mightiest empires; it is also the second language of large and populous regions beyond their bounds. Its teaching is obligatory in the secondary schools of countries as diverse as Germany and Argentina, Turkey and Denmark, Portugal and Rumania, Estonia and Japan. Three-fourths of all the world's mail is now written in it, it is used in printing more than half the world's newspapers, and it is the language of three-fifths of the world's radio stations.[1] No ship captain can trade upon the oceans without some knowledge of it; it is the common tongue of all the great ports, and likewise of all the maritime Bad Lands, from the South Sea Islands and the China Coast to the West Coast of Africa and the Persian

---

1 See The Geography of Great Languages, by E. H. Babbitt, *World's Work*, Feb., 1908; and The System of Basic English, by C. K. Ogden; New York, 1934, p. 5.

Gulf.[1] Every language that still resists its advance outside Europe — for example, Spanish and Portuguese in Latin-America, Italian and French in the Levant, and Japanese, Chinese and Hindi in the Far East — holds out against it only by making large concessions to it. Spanish is under heavy assault from English, and especially from American, in Cuba, Puerto Rico, Mexico and the Isthmian region, and everywhere in South and Central America it has taken in many English and American words.[2] Japanese has gone even further. Professor Sanki Ichikawa, of the University of Tokyo, reports that in a few months' reading of Japanese newspapers and magazines he encountered 1400 English words,[3] and Dr. Sawbay Arakawa lists nearly 5000 in his " Japanized English." [4] " Of the various European languages which have left a mark on the Japanese vocabulary," says Professor Ichikawa, " English is by far the most important, and its future influence will probably be such that not only words and expressions will continue to be borrowed in greater numbers, but even the structure and grammar of the Japanese language will be considerably modified." Chinese, at least along the coast, seems destined to go the same way. According to Professor Tsung-tse Yeh, of Tsing Hua University, Peking,[5] its stock of English loan-words has been greatly reinforced since the revolution of 1911, and it is now fashionable for journalists and other vernacular writers to make a large show of them. Dr. Tsung-tse presents only a meager list, but in it I find four Americanisms — *p'u-k'e* for *poker, fan-shih-ling* for *vaseline, te-lu-feng* for *telephone,* and *ch'ueh-erh-ssu-teng* for *charleston* (dance). According to another Chinese, Dr. W. W. Yen,

1 Cosmopolitan Conversation, by Herbert Newhard Shenton; New York, 1933, p. 315. When Dr. Shenton asked the secretary of the International Shipping Conference, representing 17 countries, what language was used at its meetings, the reply was: " The Conference is perhaps more fortunate than other bodies in that it has from the start [1921] adopted the simple unwritten rule that English is the only language to be employed, and as practically all the members are expert in that language we have no difficulty."
2 See The American Language in Mexico, by H. E. McKinstry, *American Mercury*, March, 1930;

Sports Slang in Latin-America, by Richard F. O'Toole, the same, Nov., 1930; and Spain's Waning Cultural Influence Over Hispanic-America, by Earle K. James, *American Speech*, Sept., 1926.
3 English Influence on Japanese; Tokyo, 1928, p. 165. See also The Impact of English on Japanese, by Lionel Crocker, *English Journal*, April, 1928, and Anglicized Japanese, by Frederick W. Brown, *Quarterly Journal of Speech Education*, Feb., 1927.
4 4th ed.; Tokyo, 1930.
5 On Chinese Borrowings From English and French, in The Basic Vocabulary, by C. K. Ogden; London, 1930, pp. 86–95.

the study and employment of the English language by thousands of our students, many of whom adopt the literary and teaching professions, and the translation of books from English into Chinese, bound to retain some of the original mode of expression, have unconsciously and inevitably affected our modes of thought and the expression thereof, so that slowly but surely Chinese diction, grammar and style will adopt to a certain extent the English.[1]

How many people speak English today? It is hard to answer with any precision, but an approximation is nevertheless possible. First, let us list those to whom English is their native tongue. They run to about 112,000,000 in the continental United States, to 42,000,000 in the United Kingdom, to 6,000,000 in Canada, 6,000,000 in Australia, 3,000,000 in Ireland, 2,000,000 in South Africa, and probably 3,000,-000 in the remaining British colonies and in the possessions of the United States. All these figures are very conservative, but they foot up to 174,000,000. Now add the people who, though born to some other language, live in English-speaking communities and speak English themselves in their daily business, and whose children are being brought up to it — say 13,000,000 for the United States, 1,000,-000 for Canada, 1,000,000 for the United Kingdom and Ireland, and 2,000,000 for the rest of the world — and you have a grand total of 191,000,000. Obviously, no other language is the everyday tongue of so many people. Spanish, it has been claimed, is spoken by more than 100,000,000,[2] but that is little more than half the toll of English. Whether German or Russian comes next is in some doubt, but in any case it is certain that both lie below Spanish. The census of December 17, 1926, indicated that but 80,000,000 of the 150,000,000 citizens of the U.S.S.R. used Russian as their first language; the number has increased since, but probably by no more than 10,000,000.[3] German is spoken by 65,000,000 Germans in the *Reich*, by perhaps 7,000,000 in Austria, by a scant 3,000,000 in German Switzerland, by perhaps 5,000,000 in the lost German and Austrian territories, and by another 5,000,000 in the German-speaking colonies in Russia, the Balkan and Baltic states, and South America. This makes 85,-

1 A lecture before the Literary and Social Guild of Peiping, Jan. 13, 1931. I borrow the quotation from C. K. Ogden's Debabelization; London, 1931, p. 133.
2 *Hispania*, May, 1935. I am indebted here to Dr. William H. Shoemaker of Princeton University.
3 I am indebted for the 1926 figures to Mr. S. S. Shipman of the Am-

torg Trading Corporation, New York. During 1935 the newspapers reported from Moscow that the population of Russia was estimated to be 162,000,000, but Russian estimates are always likely to be optimistic. Outside the national boundaries, of course, Russian is spoken hardly at all, save by emigrants who are rapidly losing it.

000,000 altogether. Italian and Portuguese [1] are the runners-up, and the rest of the European languages are nowhere. Nor is there any rival to English in Asia, for though Chinese is ostensibly the native tongue of more than 300,000,000 people, it is split into so many mutually unintelligible dialects that it must be thought of less as a language than as a group of languages. The same may be said of Hindi.[2] As for Japanese, it is spoken by no more than 70,000,000 persons, and thus lags behind not only English, but also Spanish, Russian and German. As for Arabic, it probably falls below even Italian.[3]

Thus English is far ahead of any competitor. Moreover, it promises to increase its lead hereafter, for no other language is spreading so fast or into such remote areas. There was a time when French was the acknowledged second language of all Christendom, as Latin had been before it, and even to this day, according to Dr. Frank E. Vizetelly, the number of persons who have acquired it is larger than the number of those who have it by birth. But the advantages of knowing it tend to diminish as English conquers the world, and

1 The relative ranking of Italian and Portuguese is in dispute. Portugal itself, including Madeira and the Azores, had but 6,698,345 inhabitants in Dec., 1930, but Brazil was estimated officially, in 1935, to have 42,345,096. Unfortunately, it is impossible to determine accurately how many of the people of Brazil really speak Portuguese, and how many of the people of the Portuguese colonies. Senhor Edgard Schwery of São Paulo, Brazil, sent me, under date of May 28, 1935, an estimate that there was then 56,460,128 Portuguese-speaking persons in the world, and Senhora Edith del Junco, also of São Paulo, ventured upon 57,514,856 on June 5. The Italian census of April 21, 1932, showed 41,176,671 persons in Italy, but it did not include the inhabitants of the Italian colonies, or the large number of Italian-speaking persons in Algiers, Tunis, Egypt, Malta and other Mediterranean countries and islands.

2 The population of India was 351,-399,880 on Feb. 26, 1931. How many of its people speak some dialect of Hindi is not known precisely, but probably not more than half. Dr. George William Brown, in *Language*, Sept., 1935, p. 271, estimates the number at 100,000,000. The language, however, serves the commercial classes as a *lingua franca*, and efforts are under way, led by the Mahatma Gandhi, to make it universal. It is already either in use or optional in thirteen of the eighteen Indian universities.

3 In my third edition, 1923, p. 382 *ff*, I printed various estimates of the number of persons speaking the principal languages at different periods, ranging from 1801 to 1921. Others for earlier periods, going back to 1500, will be found in Growth and Structure of the English Language, by O. Jespersen, 3rd ed.; Leipzig, 1919. F. Max Müller's estimate, *c*. 1870, is in his On Spelling, p. 7. Other estimates are given in Debabelization, by C. K. Ogden; London, 1931, p. 41 *ff*, and by Frank H. Vizetelly in the *World* Almanac, 1935, p. 242.

it is now studied as an accomplishment far more often than as a utility. In Czarist Russia, according to a recent observer,[1] " the educated classes spoke chiefly two foreign languages, French and German. French was the language of diplomacy, society, and fashion; German was utilized in the more prosaic fields of business and commerce. However, with the staggering efforts now made at industrialization, at attempts, as Stalin puts it, 'to overreach and outstrip all capitalist countries,' including America, German is of first importance, with English running a very close second." In our own high-schools and colleges French is retained in the curriculum, but it is hardly likely that more than 5% of the students ever acquire any facility at speaking it, or even at reading it. In the schools of Germany, Scandinavia and Japan, however, English is taught with relentless earnestness, and a great deal of it sticks. Indeed, even the French begin to learn it.

How far it has thus gone as a second language I do not know, but a few facts and figures taken at random may throw some light on the question. In February, 1929, the Stockholm newspaper, *Nya Dagligt Allehanda*, undertook to find out what proportion of the population of Stockholm had acquired it. All sorts of persons were interviewed, from bankers and business men to taxi-drivers and policemen. It was discovered that every fourth person had enough of the language for all ordinary purposes. This inquiry also showed that 65% of all the foreign business of Sweden was carried on in English. In writing to German correspondents the Swedish firms used German, but for all other foreign correspondence they used English. At the same time the Public Library of Stockholm reported " an incredible inquiry " for English and American books — classical English and modern American. The place thus held by English was formerly held by German and French; the change has come since 1900. In Norway and Denmark there has been a similar movement and in Finland " suggestions have been made that English should replace Swedish as the second official language." In Estonia, since 1920, " English has been the second language taught to the native-born, and the third to those minorities (Germans, Swedes, Russians, Jews) who use their own tongue first and learn the native language

1 Eli B. Jacobson, professor of American literature and history at the Second Moscow University, 1929–30. The quotation is from his The

American Language Fights for Recognition in Moscow, *American Mercury*, Jan., 1931.

at school. . . . A hundred thousand boys and girls in Estonia want to learn English." [1] Its position in Portugal is the same, with no minorities to challenge it, and "a very large proportion of the educated inhabitants [already] have a working knowledge of it." [2] In Turkey, before 1923, the second language was French, but since the proclamation of the Republic "the tendency has entirely changed, . . . and almost everybody, . . . not only in Constantinople but throughout Anatolia, is learning English as hard as he can go. . . . The Ministry of Public Instruction has introduced English as a regular part of the school routine in all the secondary schools throughout the country. . . . On all sides, and every day, one hears such expressions as ' I want to learn English ' and ' How long will it take me to learn English? ' " All this on the authority of Herbert M. Thompson, professor of English at the Galata Saray Lycée, "the Eton of Turkey." [3] Mr. Thompson says that in the commercial section of the school, "where pupils have the option of learning either English or German," all save one chose English both in 1928 and in 1929. In the evening classes the number of pupils taking English averages 150–200 a year, whereas the number taking German is but six or eight.

But perhaps the largest advances of English have been made in Latin-America. Half a century ago English was little used in the lands and islands settled by the Spaniards and Portuguese; the second language in all of them, in so far as they had a second language, was French. But the impact of the Spanish-American War has forced French to share its hegemony, as the English occupation of Egypt has pitted English against it in that country, and indeed throughout the Levant. The Latin-Americans still prefer French on cultural counts, for they continue to regard France as the beacon-light of Latin civilization, but they turn to English for the hard reasons of every day. This movement is naturally most marked in the areas that have come under direct American influence – above all, in Puerto Rico, where about a fourth of the people now speak Eng-

1 The English Language for Estonia, London *Spectator*, July 6, 1929, p. 11. The anonymous author of this article says that German, which was formerly the second language of the country, would be displaced faster if it were not for the fact that German text-books are cheaper than English text-books.

2 English in Portugal, by J. Da Providéncia Costa and S. George West, London *Times Literary Supplement*, Feb. 28, 1935, p. 124.

3 English for the Turks, London *Nation and Athenaeum*, Nov. 16, 1929.

lish [1] — but it is also visible everywhere below the Rio Grande. In the Philippines a survey of tenant rice-farmers' families, made so long ago as 1921–22, showed that 34% of the children were literate in English, as against only 2% literate in Spanish. Among the older people twice as many were literate in English as in Spanish. English is now widely used in the courts, executive offices and Legislative Assembly of the islands, and is frequently employed by political orators.[2] Under the Constitution of the new Philippine Commonwealth, Art. XIII, Section 3, "the Legislative Assembly shall take steps toward the development and adoption of a common national language based on one of the existing native languages," but there is not much likelihood that any such artificial tongue will be perfected in the near future, or that it will be used by the generality of Filipinos when it is. Meanwhile, "until otherwise provided by law, English and Spanish shall continue as official languages" — with English, it will be observed, put first.

English is making steady inroads upon French as the language of diplomacy and of other international intercourse, and upon German as the language of science. In the former case, to be sure, French still offers a sturdy resistance. "There are certain respects," says Dr. Herbert Newhard Shenton in "Cosmopolitan Conversation," [3] "in which the international-conference movement is characteristically French. This does not apply to all classes of interests in the movement, but does apply to the movement as a whole. The favored rendezvous of conferences are in France or in French-speaking countries; more of the permanent headquarters are located in France than in any other country, and many others are located in French-speaking countries." Thus French "still remains the preferred official language of international conferences." But certainly not by the old wide margin. Of the 330 international organizations dealt with in Dr. Shenton's book, 282 have one or more official languages, and among these 78% include French and 58% English. A century ago, or even half a century ago, the percentages would have been nearer

1 For this I am indebted to Dr. José Padín, commissioner of education for Puerto Rico. He says: "On the whole, I should say that about 400,000 people out of a total population of 1,600,000 speak and read English and, in a lesser degree, write it." See also his English in Puerto Rico; San Juan, 1935.

2 The English Language in the Philippines, by Emma Sarepta Yule, *American Speech*, Nov., 1925.

3 New York, 1933. This is a large work. A brief statement of Dr. Shenton's findings, prepared by himself, is to be found in International Communication, edited by C. K. Ogden; London, 1931.

100% and 25%. Perhaps the turn of the tide came with the Versailles Conference. At that historic gathering the two representatives of the English-speaking countries, Wilson and Lloyd George, had no French, whereas the French spokesman, Clemenceau, spoke English fluently — incidentally, with a strong American accent.[1] Thus English became the language of negotiation, and it has been heard round council tables with increasing frequency ever since.

All over the Far East it has been a *lingua franca* since the Eighteenth Century, at first in the barbarous guise of Pidgin English, but of late in increasingly seemly forms, often with an American admixture. In Japan, according to the Belgian consul-general at Yokohama, it is now " indispensable for all Europeans. One can do without Japanese, but would be lost without English. It is the business language." [2] In China, according to Dr. Lim-boon Keng, president of Amoy University, " we have practically adopted English," and in India, though but 2,500,000 natives can read and write it, it not only competes with Hindi in business, but is fast becoming the language of politics. Those Indians who know it, says Sir John A. R. Marriott [3] " are the only persons who are politically conscious. Indian nationalism is almost entirely the product of English education; the medium of all political discussion is necessarily English." It is, adds R. C. Goffin,[4] " the readiest means of obtaining (*a*) employment under the government; (*b*) employment in commercial houses of any standing, whether Indian or foreign; (*c*) command of the real *lingua franca* of the country — for Hindustani is of very little use south of the Central Provinces; (*d*) knowledge of Western ideas, both ancient and modern. . . . English in other ways has

[1] The consequences of this situation, and of like situations elsewhere, are discussed by Dr. Otto Jespersen in An International Language; London, 1928, p. 15 *ff.* Clemenceau, says Dr. Jespersen, " gained an undue ascendancy because he was practically the only one who had complete command of both languages."

[2] *English*, Aug., 1919, p. 122. He adds: " Before the war German was widely spread among medical men, university professors, scientists, the army officers, and politicians. The political ideas of those who built modern Japan were inspired by German thought. . . . Apart from this, everything is English (British or American). The foreign language for the Navy, of course, is English. There is little use for the French language." At the first World's Congress of Engineering, held in Tokyo in 1929, all the sessions were conducted in English, and not a single one of the 900 papers, including 400 presented by Japanese delegates, was translated into Japanese.

[3] The English in India; London, 1932, p. 18.

[4] Some Notes on Indian English, *S.P.E. Tracts*, No. XLI, 1934, p. 22.

shown itself a useful instrument for a country setting out to learn the habits of democracy. It is most convenient for the politician, for example, to be able to employ a language with only one word (instead of three or even four) for *you*. . . . There is no country today where a foreign language has been so thoroughly domesticated as has English in India." [1]

Altogether, it is probable that English is now spoken as a second language by at least 20,000,000 persons throughout the world [2] — very often, to be sure, badly, but nevertheless understandably. It has become a platitude that one may go almost anywhere with no other linguistic equipment, and get along almost as well as in large areas of New York City. Here, for example, is the testimony of an English traveler:

> It was only on reaching Italy that I began to fully realize this wonderful thing, that for nearly six weeks, on a German ship, in a journey of nearly 10,000 miles, we had heard little of any language but English!
>
> In Japan most of the tradespeople spoke English. At Shanghai, at Hong Kong, at Singapore, at Penang, at Colombo, at Suez, at Port Said — all the way home to the Italian ports, the language of all the ship's traffic, the language of such discourse as the passengers held with natives, most of the language on board ship itself, was English.
>
> The German captain of our ship spoke English more often than German. All his officers spoke English.
>
> The Chinese man-o'-war's men who conveyed the Chinese prince on board at Shanghai received commands and exchanged commands with our German sailors in English. The Chinese mandarins in their conversations with the ships' officers invariably spoke English. They use the same ideographs in writing as the Japanese, but to talk to our Japanese passengers they had to speak English. Nay, coming as they did from various provinces of the Empire, where the language greatly differs, they found it most convenient in conversation among themselves to speak English! [3]

And here is that of an American:

> In Berlin, Hamburg, Dresden, Munich, Vienna, Paris, Amsterdam, Venice, Florence, Rome, Milan, nearly all of Switzerland, and in such resorts as Wiesbaden, Baden-Baden, Carlsbad, Deauville, Biarritz, Vichy, St.-Jean-de-Luz, Lake Como, and the entire Riviera, it is difficult to find a first-class hotel

1 For a more detailed account of the spread of English see Debabelization, by C. K. Ogden; London, 1931, p. 53 ff.

2 How many persons are studying it today it is not easy to determine. Dr. Janet Rankin Aiken (*American Mercury*, April, 1933, p. 426) puts the number at 80,000,000, counting in the children in the English-speaking countries, but this is probably an overestimate. Dr. Aiken says that 500,000,000 people, " or more than one-fourth of all on earth," now live under governments which use English.

3 Alexander M. Thompson: Japan For a Week; Britain Forever!; London, 1910.

where they are willing to permit you to hear the language of the country. One might think the employees were required to abjure their own tongue.[1]

My own experience may be added for whatever it is worth. I have visited, since the World War, sixteen countries in Europe, five in Africa, three in Asia and three in Latin-America, beside a large miscellany of islands, but I don't remember ever encountering a situation that English could not resolve. I have heard it spoken with reasonable fluency in a Moroccan bazaar, in an Albanian fishing-port, and on the streets of Istanbul. During the war the German army of occupation in Lithuania used it as a means of communicating with the local Jews, many of whom had been in America. In part, of course, its spread has been due to the extraordinary dispersion of the English-speaking peoples. They have been the greatest travelers of modern times, and the most adventurous merchants, and the most assiduous colonists. Moreover, they have been, on the whole, poor linguists, and so they have dragged their language with them, and forced it upon the human race. Wherever it has met with serious competition, as with French in Canada, with Spanish along our southwestern border, and with Dutch in South Africa, they have compromised with its local rival only reluctantly, and then sought every opportunity, whether fair or unfair, to break the pact. If English is the language of the sea, it is largely because there are more English ships on the sea than any other kind, and English ship-captains refuse to learn what they think of as the barbaric gibberishes of Hamburg, Rio and Marseilles.

But there is more to the matter than this. English, brought to close quarters with formidable rivals, has won very often, not by mere force of numbers and intransigence, but by the weight of its intrinsic merit. " In riches, good sense and terse convenience (*Reichtum, Vernunft und gedrängter Fuge*)," said the eminent Jakob Grimm nearly a century ago,[2] " no other of the living languages may be put beside it." To which the eminent Otto Jespersen adds: " It seems to me positively and expressively masculine. It is the language of a grown-up man, and has very little childish or feminine about it." [3] Dr. Jespersen then goes on to explain the origin and nature of

1 English as Europe's Esperanto, by Harold Callender, New York *Times Magazine*, Aug. 24, 1930.
2 Ueber den Ursprung der Sprache, a lecture delivered before the Berlin Academy of Sciences, Jan. 9,

1851. Reprinted in Auswahl aus den kleineren Schriften; Berlin, 1871.
3 Growth and Structure of the English Language, 3rd ed.; Leipzig, 1919, p. 2.

this "masculine" air: it is grounded chiefly upon clarity, directness and force. He says:

> The English consonants are well defined; voiced and voiceless consonants stand over against each other in neat symmetry, and they are, as a rule, clearly and precisely pronounced. You have none of those indistinct or half-slurred consonants that abound in Danish, for instance (such as those in ha*d*e, ha*g*e, li*v*lig), where you hardly know whether it is a consonant or a vowel-glide that meets the ear. The only thing that might be compared to this in English is the *r* when *not* followed by a vowel, but then this has really given up definitely all pretensions to the rank of a consonant, and is (in the pronunciation of the South of England) [1] either frankly a vowel (as in *here*) or else nothing at all (in *hart,* etc.). Each English consonant belongs distinctly to its own type, a *t* is a *t,* and a *k* is a *k,* and there is an end. There is much less modification of a consonant by the surrounding vowels than in some other languages; thus none of that palatalization of consonants which gives an insinuating grace to such languages as Russian. The vowel sounds, too, are comparatively independent of their surroundings; and in this respect the language now has deviated widely from the character of Old English, and has become more clear-cut and distinct in its phonetic structure, although, to be sure, the diphthongization of most long vowels (in *ale, whole, eel, who,* phonetically *eil, houl, ijl, huw*) counteracts in some degree this impression of neatness and evenness.

Dr. Jespersen then proceeds to consider certain peculiarities of English grammar and syntax, and to point out the simplicity and forcefulness of the everyday English vocabulary. The grammatical baldness of the language, he argues (against the old tradition in philology), is one of the chief sources of its vigor. He says:

> Where German has, for instance, *alle diejenigen wilden tiere, die dort leben,* so that the plural idea is expressed in each word separately (apart, of course, from the adverb), English has *all the wild animals that live there,* where *all,* the article, the adjective, and the relative pronoun are alike incapable of receiving any mark of the plural number; the sense is expressed with the greatest clearness imaginable, and all the unstressed endings -*e* and -*en,* which make most German sentences so drawling, are avoided.

The prevalence of very short words in English, and the syntactical law which enables it to dispense with the definite article in many constructions "where other languages think it indispensable, *e.g.,* ' life is short,' ' dinner is ready ' " — these are further marks of vigor and clarity, according to Dr. Jespersen. " ' First come, first served,' " he says, " is much more vigorous than the French ' Premier venu,

---

[1] But certainly not in that of the United States, save maybe in the Boston area and parts of the South.

premier moulu ' or ' Le premier venu engrène,' the German ' Wer zuerst kommt, mahlt zuerst,' and especially than the Danish ' Den der kommer først til mølle, far først malet.' " Again, there is the superior logical sense of English — the arrangement of words, not according to grammatical rules, but according to their meaning. " In English," says Dr. Jespersen, " an auxiliary verb does not stand far from its main verb, and a negative will be found in the immediate neighborhood of the word it negatives, generally the verb (auxiliary). An adjective nearly always stands before its noun; the only really important exception is where there are qualifications added to it which draw it after the noun so that the whole complex serves the purpose of a relative clause." In English, the subject almost invariably precedes the verb and the object follows after. Once Dr. Jespersen had his pupils determine the percentage of sentences in various authors in which this order was observed. They found that even in English poetry it was seldom violated; the percentage of observances in Tennyson's poetry ran to 88. But in the poetry of Holger Drachmann, the Dane, it fell to 61, in Anatole France's prose to 66, in Gabriele d'Annunzio to 49, and in the poetry of Goethe to 30. All these things make English clearer and more logical than other tongues. It is, says Dr. Jespersen, " a methodical, energetic, business-like and sober language, that does not care much for finery and elegance, but does care for logical consistency and is opposed to any attempt to narrow life by police regulations and strict rules either of grammar or of lexicon." In these judgments another distinguished Danish philologist, Prof. Thomsen, agrees fully.

Several years ago an American philologian, Dr. Walter Kirkconnell, undertook to count the number of syllables needed to translate the Gospel of Mark into forty Indo-European languages, ranging from Persian and Hindi to English and French.[1] He found that, of all of them, English was the most economical, for it took but 29,000 syllables to do the job, whereas the average for all the Teutonic languages was 32,650, that for the Slavic group 36,500, that for the Latin group 40,200, and that for the Indo-Iranian group (Bengali, Persian, Sanskrit, etc.) 43,100. It is commonly believed that French is a terse language, and compared to its cousins, Italian and Spanish, it actually is, but compared to English it is garrulous, for it takes

[1] Linguistic Laconism, *American Journal of Philology*, Vol. XLVIII, 1927, p. 34.

36,000 syllables to say what English says in 29,000.[1] Dr. Kirkconnell
did not undertake to determine the average size of the syllables he
counted, but I am confident that if he had done so he would have
found those of English shorter, taking one with another, than those
of most other languages. "If it had not been for the great number
of long foreign, especially Latin, words," says Dr. Jespersen, "English would have approached the state of such monosyllabic languages
as Chinese." "They are marvellous," says Salvador de Madariaga,[2]
"those English monosyllables. Their fidelity is so perfect that one is
tempted to think English words are the right and proper names
which acts are meant to have, and all other words are pitiable failures.[3] How could one improve upon *splash, smash, ooze, shriek,
slush, glide, squeak, coo?* Is not the word *sweet* a kiss in itself, and
what could suggest a more peremptory obstacle than *stop?*" "The
Spanish critic," says Dean Inge, "is quite right in calling attention to
the vigor of English monosyllables. No other European language has
so many."[4]

For these and other reasons English strikes most foreigners as an
extraordinarily succinct, straightforward and simple tongue — in
some of its aspects, in fact, almost as a kind of baby-talk. When they

1 When I printed a brief account of
Dr. Kirkconnell's research in The
Future of English, *Harper's Magazine,* April, 1935, a number of correspondents challenged his conclusion. One of these was Mr. Louis
Rittenberg, editor of the *American
Hebrew and Jewish Tribune,* who
put in a plea for Hungarian.
"Whenever," he said, "I am called
upon to estimate the length of a
Hungarian novel for translation
into English, there is invariably an
increase in wordage of between
20% and 25%, and this is so recognized by publishers for whom I
have performed such tasks at one
time or another." (Private communication, June 6, 1935.) Similar
caveats were filed in behalf of
French, Russian, Spanish, and even
German. I leave Dr. Kirkconnell
to fight it out with his critics.
2 Englishmen, Frenchmen, Spaniards;
London, 1928.
3 Mark Twain's comparison of Eng-

lish and German, in A Tramp
Abroad, Appendix D; Hartford,
1880, will be recalled: "Our descriptive words have a deep, strong,
resonant sound, while their German equivalents seem thin and
mild. *Boom, burst, crash, roar,
storm, bellow, blow, thunder, explosion:* they have a force and
magnitude of sound befitting the
things which they describe. But
their German equivalents would
be ever so nice to sing the children
to sleep with. Would any man
want to die in a battle called by so
tame a term as *schlacht?* Would
not a consumptive feel too much
bundled up in a shirt-collar and a
seal ring who was about to go out
into a storm which the bird-song
word *gewitter* was employed to describe? If a man were told in German to go *hölle,* could he rise to
the dignity of feeling insulted?"
4 W. R. Inge: More Lay Thoughts
of a Dean; London, 1932.

proceed from trying to speak it to trying to read and write it they are painfully undeceived, for its spelling is almost as irrational as that of French or Swedish, but so long as they are content to tackle it *viva voce* they find it loose and comfortable, and at the same time very precise. The Russian, coming into it burdened with his six cases, his three genders, his palatalized consonants and his complicated pronouns, luxuriates in a language which has only two cases, no grammatical gender, a set of consonants which (save only *r*) maintain their integrity in the face of any imaginable rush of vowels, and an outfit of pronouns so simple that one of them suffices to address the President of the United States or a child in arms, a lovely female creature *in camera* or the vast hordes of the radio. And the German, the Scandinavian, the Italian, and the Frenchman, though the change for them is measurably less sharp, nevertheless find it grateful, too. Only the Spaniard brings with him a language comparable to English for logical clarity, and even the Spaniard is afflicted with grammatic gender.

The huge English vocabulary is likely to make the foreigner uneasy, but he soon finds that nine-tenths of it lies safely buried in the dictionaries, and is never drawn upon for everyday use. On examining 400,000 words of writing by 2500 Americans Dr. Leonard P. Ayres found that the 50 commonest words accounted for more than half the total number of words used, that 250 more accounted for another 25%, and that 1000 accounted for 90%.[1] That the language may be spoken intelligibly with even less than 1000 words has been argued by Dr. C. K. Ogden, the English psychologist. Dr. Ogden believes that 850 are sufficient for all ordinary purposes and he has devised a form of simplified English, called by him Basic (from *British American Scientific International Commercial*), which uses no more. Of this number, 600 are nouns, 100 are adjectives, 100 are "adjectival opposites," 30 are verbs, and the rest are particles, etc. Two hundred of the nouns consist of the names of common objects, *e.g., bottle, brick, ear, potato* and *umbrella;* the rest are the names of familiar groups and concepts, *e.g., people, music, crime, loss* and *weather.* No noun is admitted (save for the names of a few common objects) " which can be defined in not more than ten other words." The reduction of verbs to 30 is effected by taking advantage of one of the prime characteristics of English (and especially of American)

1 The Measurement of Spelling Ability; New York, 1915.

— its capacity for getting an infinity of meanings out of a single verb by combining it with simple modifiers. Consider, for example, the difference (in American) between *to get, to get going, to get by, to get on, to get on to, to get off, to get ahead of, to get wise, to get religion* and *to get over*. Why should a foreigner be taught to say that he has *disembarked* from a ship? Isn't it sufficient for him to say that he *got off?* And why should he be taught to say that he has *recovered* from the flu, or *escaped* the police, or *ascended* a stairway, or *boarded* a train, or *obtained* a job? Isn't it enough to say that he has *got over* the first, *got away* from the second, *got up* the third, *got on* the fourth, and simply *got* the fifth? The fundamental verbs of Basic are ten in number — *come, go, put, take, give, get, make, keep, let* and *do*. "Every time," says Dr. Ogden (he is writing in Basic), "you put together the name of one of these ten simple acts (all of which are free to go in almost any direction) with the name of one of the twenty directions or positions in space, you are making a verb." In addition to its 850 words, of course, Basic is free to take in international words that are universally understood, *e.g., coffee, engineer, tobacco, police* and *biology,* and to add words specially pertinent to the matter in hand, *e.g., chloride* and *platinum* in a treatise on chemistry. It is interesting to note that of the fifty international words listed by Dr. Ogden, no less than seven are Americanisms, new or old, *viz., cocktail, jazz, radio, phonograph, telegram, telephone* and *tobacco,* and that one more, *check,* is listed in American spelling.[1]

Whether Basic will make any progress remains to be seen.[2] It has been criticized on various grounds. For one thing, its vocabulary shows some serious omissions — for example, the numerals — and for another, its dependence upon verb-phrases may confuse rather than help the foreigner, whose difficulties with prepositions are notorious.[3] There is also the matter of spelling, always a cruel

1 The literature of Basic is already extensive. The most comprehensive textbook is The System of Basic English, by C. K. Ogden; New York, 1934.
2 Among its most ardent partisans is Mr. Crombie Allen, one of the dignitaries of Rotary International. He printed its 850 words on the back of his New Year's card for 1935, and says under date of May 6,

1935: "Alighting from a plane on a 20,000-mile airplane tour of Rotary Clubs in Latin-America after flying across the Andes, I found the club at Mendoza (Argentina) studying Basic from my New Year's greeting."
3 The sharpest criticism is in A Critical Examination of Basic English, by M. P. West, E. Swenson and others; Toronto, 1934. The authors

difficulty to a foreigner tackling English. But Dr. Ogden waives this difficulty away. For one thing, he argues that his list of 850 words, being made up mainly of the commonest coins of speech, avoids most of them; for another thing, he believes that the very eccentricity of the spelling of some of the rest will help the foreigner to remember them. Every schoolboy, as we all know, seizes upon such bizarre forms as *through, straight* and *island* with fascinated eagerness, and not infrequently he masters them before he masters such phonetically spelled words as *first, tomorrow* and *engineer*. In my own youth, far away in the dark backward and abysm of time, the glory of every young American was *phthisic*, with the English proper name, *Cholmondeley*, a close second. Dr. Ogden proposes to let the foreigners attempting Basic share the joy of hunting down such basilisks. For the rest, he leaves the snarls of English spelling to the judgments of a just God, and the natural tendency of all things Anglo-Saxon to move toward an ultimate perfection. Unluckily, his Basic now has a number of competitors on its own ground,[1] and it must also meet the competition of the so-called universal languages, beginning with Volapük (1880) and Esperanto (1887) and running down to Idiom Neural (1898), Ido (1907), Interlingua (1908), and Novial, invented by Dr. Jespersen (1928).[2] Some of these languages, and notably Esperanto and Novial, show a great ingenuity, and all

---

argue that the vocabulary of Basic, when all the various forms and different meanings of its words are counted in, really runs to 3925 words. See also Thought and Language, by P. B. Ballard; London, 1934, p. 166 *ff*, and Basic and World English, by Janet Rankin Aiken, *American Mercury*, April, 1933. In A New Kind of English, *American Mercury*, April, 1933, Dr. Aiken takes what seems to be a rather more favorable view. The latter article is written in Basic.

[1] One is Swenson English, invented by Miss Elaine Swenson, chief of the Language Research Institute at New York University. Another is the invention of H. E. Palmer, educational adviser to the Japanese Department of Education and chief of the Institute for Research in English Teaching, Tokyo. The latter has been called Iret, after the initials of the institute. Both are examined critically in English as the International Language, by Janet Rankin Aiken, *American Speech*, April, 1934. Dr. Aiken has herself lately (1935) put forward a rival to Basic under the name of Little English. It has a vocabulary of 800 words, or 50 less than Basic.

[2] The latest is Panamane (1934), invented by Manuel E. Amador, P. O. Box 1055, Panama, R. P., son of the first President of Panama. It seems to be a mixture of English and Spanish. Here is the first sentence of Lincoln's *Gettisburgo Adress*, translated by Señor Amador himself: " Kat skori ed sept yaryen ahgeo, nos padri brenguuh foth aupan esty kontinente un noe nasione konsibo na libertya ed dediso am propossya ke tui manni son kreo egale."

of them have enthusiastic customers who believe that they are about to be adopted generally. There are also persons who hold that some such language is bound to come in soon or late, though remaining doubtful about all those proposed so far — for example, Dr. Shenton, who closes his " Cosmopolitan Conversation," by proposing that the proponents of Esperanto, Interlingua, Novial and the rest come together in a conference of their own, and devise " a neutral, synthetic, international auxiliary language " that will really conquer the world.

But this, I believe, is only a hope, and no man now born will ever see it realized. The trouble with all the " universal " languages is that the juices of life are simply not in them. They are the creations of scholars drowning in murky oceans of dead prefixes and suffixes, and so they fail to meet the needs of a highly human world. People do not yearn for a generalized articulateness; what they want is the capacity to communicate with definite other people.[1] To that end even Basic, for all its deficiencies, is better than any conceivable Esperanto, for it at least springs from a living speech, and behind that speech are nearly 200,000,000 men and women, many of them amusing and some of them wise. The larger the gang, the larger the numbers of both classes. English forges ahead of all its competitors, whether natural or unnatural, simply because it is already spoken by more than half of all the people in the world who may be said, with any plausibility, to be worth knowing. After the late war I went to Berlin full of a firm determination to improve my German, always extremely anæmic. I failed to get anywhere because virtually all the Germans who interested me spoke very good English. During the same time many other men were having the same experience — one of them being John Cournos, the English novelist. " Nothing annoyed me more," he said afterward,[2] " than the frequency with

[1] The most persuasive argument that I am aware of against the feasibility of setting up an artificial international language is to be found in Interlanguage, by T. C. Macaulay, *S.P.E. Tracts*, No. XXXIV, 1930. And the best argument for it is in An International Language, by Otto Jespersen; London, 1928, Pt. I. English as a World Language, by Michael West, *American Speech*, Oct., 1934, is a judicious discussion of the elements that must enter into any international language, whether purely artificial or an adaptation of English. See also English as the International Language, by Janet Rankin Aiken, above cited, and English as an International Language: A Selected List of References, by Lois Holladay; Chicago, 1926.

[2] English as Esperanto, *English*, Feb., 1921, p. 451.

which my inquiries of the man in the street for direction, made in atrocious German, elicited replies in perfect English." A few years later Dr. Knut Sanstedt, general secretary to the Northern Peace Union, sent a circular to a number of representative European publicists, asking them " what language, dead or living or artificial " they preferred for international communications. Not one of these publicists was a native or resident of the British Isles, yet out of fifty-nine who replied thirty voted for English. Of the six Swedes, all preferred it; of the seven Norwegians, five; of the five Hollanders, four. Among the whole fifty-nine, only one man voted for Esperanto.[1]

2. ENGLISH OR AMERICAN?

But as English spreads over the world, will it be able to maintain its present form? Probably not. But why should it? The notion that anything is gained by fixing a language in a groove is cherished only by pedants. Every successful effort at standardization, as Dr. Ernest Weekley has well said, results in nothing better than emasculation.[2] " Stability in language is synonymous with *rigor mortis*." It is the very anarchy of English, adds Claude de Crespigny, that has made it the dominant language of the world today.[3] In its early forms it was a highly inflected tongue — indeed, it was more inflected than modern German, and almost as much so as Russian. The West Saxon dialect, for example, in the days before the Norman Conquest, had grammatical gender, and in addition the noun was inflected for number and for case, and there were five cases in all. Moreover, there were two quite different declensions, the strong and the weak, so that the total number of inflections was immense. The same ending, of course, was commonly used more than once, but that fact only added to the difficulties of the language. The impact of the Conquest knocked this elaborate grammatical structure into a cocked hat. The upper classes spoke French, and so the populace had English at its mercy. It quickly wore down the vowels of the endings to a neutral *e*, reduced the importance of their consonants by moving the stress

1 Anglic: A New Agreed Simplified English Spelling, by R. E. Zachrisson; Upsala (Sweden), 1931, p. 7.
2 English As She Will be Spoke, *Atlantic Monthly*, May, 1932. The quotation following is from The English Language, by the same author; New York, 1929, p. 9.
3 Esperanto, *American Speech*, Sept., 1926.

forward to the root, and finally lopped off many inflections *in toto.*
By the time of Chaucer (1340?–1400) English was moving rapidly
toward its present form. It had already become a virtually analytical language, depending upon word position rather than upon inflection for expressing meanings, and meanwhile the influence of French,
which had been official from 1066 to 1362, had left it full of new
words, and made it a sort of hybrid of the Teutonic and Romance
stocks. It has remained such a hybrid to this day, and in some ways,
indeed, its likeness to French, Italian and Spanish is more marked
than its likeness to German. Once its East Midland dialect had been
given preëminence over all other dialects by Chaucer and his followers, it began to develop rapidly, and in the time of Shakespeare
it enjoyed an extraordinarily lush and vigorous growth. New words
were taken in from all the other languages of Europe and from many
of those of Africa and Asia, other new words in large number were
made of its own materials, and almost everything that remained of
the old inflections was sloughed off.[1] Thus it gradually took on a
singularly simple and flexible form, and passed ahead of the languages
that were more rigidly bound by rule.

I think I have offered sufficient evidence in the chapters preceding
that the American of today is much more honestly English, in any
sense that Shakespeare would have understood, than the so-called
Standard English of England. It still shows all the characters that
marked the common tongue in the days of Elizabeth, and it continues
to resist stoutly the policing that ironed out Standard English in the
Seventeenth and Eighteenth Centuries. Standard English must always strike an American as a bit stilted and precious. Its vocabulary
is patently less abundant than his own, it has lost to an appreciable
extent its old capacity for bold metaphor, and in pronunciation and
spelling it seems to him to be extremely uncomfortable and not a
little ridiculous. When he hears a speech in its Oxford (or Public-
School) form he must be a Bostonian to avoid open mirth. He be-

1 The process is described at length
in Modern English in the Making,
by George H. McKnight; New
York, 1928. See also Modern English, by George Philip Krapp; New
York, 1910, especially Ch. IV; and
A History of the English Language,
by T. R. Lounsbury; rev. ed.; New
York, 1894. "English," says Harold
Cox in English as a World Language, London *Spectator*, May 10,
1930, " has the great advantage that
it more or less represents an amalgam of languages. It is largely
Scandinavian in origin, but it also
embodies a vast number of words
directly derived from Latin, and
many others coming to us from
French and Italian, besides not a
few coming from German."

lieves, and on very plausible grounds, that American is better on all counts — clearer, more rational, and above all, more charming. And he holds not illogically that there is no reason under the sun why a dialect spoken almost uniformly by nearly 125,000,000 people should yield anything to the dialect of a small minority in a nation of 45,000,000. He sees that wherever American and this dialect come into fair competition — as in Canada, for example, or in the Far East — American tends to prevail,[1] and that even in England many of its reforms and innovations are making steady headway, so he concludes that it will probably prevail everywhere hereafter. " When two-thirds of the people who use a certain language," says one of his spokesmen,[2] " decide to call it a *freight-train* instead of a *goods-train* they are ' right '; and the first is correct English and the second a dialect."

Nor is the American, in entertaining such notions, without English support. The absurdities of Standard English are denounced by every English philologian, and by a great many other Englishmen. Those who accept it without cavil are simply persons who are unfamiliar with any other form of the language; the Irishman, the Scotsman, the Canadian, and the Australian laugh at it along with the American — and with the Englishman who has lived in the United States. As an example of the last-named class I point to Mr. H. W. Seaman, a Norwich man who had spent ten years on American and Canadian newspapers and was in practice, when he wrote, as a journalist in London. He says:

I speak for millions of Englishmen when I say that we are as sick and tired of this so-called English as you Americans are. It has far less right to be called Standard English speech than Yorkshire or any other country dialect has — or than any American dialect. It is as alien to us as it is to you. True, some of my neighbors have acquired it — for social or other reasons — but

1 Its influence upon the English of Australia and of South Africa is already marked. In a glossary of Australianisms appended by the Australian author, C. T. Dennis, to his Doreen and the Sentimental Bloke; New York, 1916, I find the familiar verbs and verb-phrases, *to beef, to biff, to bluff, to boss, to break away, to chase one's self, to chew the rag, to chip in, to fade away, to get it in the neck, to back and fill, to plug along, to get sore, to turn down* and *to get wise;* the substantives, *dope, boss, fake, creek, knockout-drops* and *push* (in the sense of *crowd*); the adjectives, *hitched* (in the sense of *married*) and *tough* (as before *luck*), and the adverbial phrases, *for keeps* and *going strong.* In South Africa many Americanisms have ousted corresponding English forms, even in the standard speech.

2 William McAlpine, *New Republic*, June 26, 1929.

then some of the Saxon peasants took pains to acquire Norman French, which also was imposed upon them from above.[1]

Mr. Seaman describes with humor his attempts as a schoolboy to shed his native Norwich English and to acquire the prissy fashionable dialect that passes as Standard. He managed to do so, and is thus able today to palaver on equal terms with " an English public-school boy, an Oxford man, a clergyman of the Establishment, an announcer of the British Broadcasting Company, or a West End actor," but he confesses that it still strikes him, as it strikes an American, as having " a mauve, Episcopalian and ephebian ring." And he quotes George Bernard Shaw as follows:

> The English have no respect for their language. . . . It is impossible for an Englishman to open his mouth without making some other Englishman hate or despise him. . . . An honest and natural slum dialect is more tolerable than the attempt of a phonetically untaught person to imitate the vulgar dialect of the golf club.

The views of Basil de Sélincourt, author of " Pomona, or The Future of English," and of J. Y. T. Greig, author of " Breaking Priscian's Head," I have quoted in previous chapters. Both cling to the hope that some form of English denizened in England may eventually become the universal form of the language, but both are plainly upset by fears that American will prevail. " Right and wrong in such a matter," says Mr. de Sélincourt, " can be decided only by the event. However it be, the United States, obviously, is now the scene of the severest ordeals, the vividest excitements of our language. . . . The contrasting and competitive use of their one language by the English and the Americans gives it a new occasion for the exercise of its old and noble faculty of compromise. In a period of promise and renewal, it was beginning to grow old; the Americans are young. . . . Its strong constitution will assimilate tonics as fast as friends can supply them, and take no serious harm. Changes are certainly in store for it." Mr. Greig is rather less sanguine about the prospects of compromise between English and American. " It is possible," he says gloomily, " that in fifty or a hundred years . . . American and not English will be the chief foreign language taught in the schools of Asia and the European Continent. Some Americans look forward to this without misgiving, nay, with exultation; and I

[1] The Awful English of England, *American Mercury*, Sept., 1933, p. 73.

for one would rather have it fall out than see perpetuated and extended that silliest and dwabliest of all the English dialects, Public-School Standard." To which I add an extract from an English review of Logan Pearsal Smith's "Words and Idioms" (1925), quoted by the late Brander Matthews: [1]

> It is chiefly in America — let us frankly recognize the fact — that the evolution of our language will now proceed. Our business here is to follow sympathetically what happens there, admitting once for all that our title to decide what English is is purely honorary. The more unmistakably we make the admission, the more influence we shall have; for in language it is the *fait accompli* that counts, and in the capacity for putting new words over, the Americans, if only because they have twice the population, are bound to win every time. [2]

The defects of English, whether in its American or its British form, are almost too obvious to need rehearsal. One of the worst of them lies in the very fact that the two great branches of the language differ, not only in vocabulary but also in pronunciation. Thus the foreigner must make his choice, and though in most cases he is probably unconscious of it, he nevertheless makes it. The East Indian, when he learns English at all, almost always learns something approximating Oxford English, but the Latin-American is very apt to learn American, and American is what the immigrant returning to Sweden or Jugoslavia, Poland or Syria, Italy or Finland certainly takes home with him. In Russia, as we saw in Chapter I, Section 8, American has begun to challenge English, and in Japan and elsewhere in the Far East the two dialects are in bitter competition, with American apparently prevailing. That competition, which has been going on in Europe since the World War, presents a serious problem to foreign teachers of the language. Says Dr. R. W. Zandvoort of The Hague:

> A generation ago, this problem had scarcely arisen. Most Continental language teachers, if interrogated on the subject, would probably have stated that they recognized one standard only, that set by educated usage in the South of England, and that, except perhaps for scientific purposes, local variants did not come within their purview. Nor was this surprising, con-

1 American Leadership in the English Idiom, *Literary Digest International Book Review*, March, 1926. See also Shall We All Speak American?, by Frank D. Long, *Passing Show* (London), July 13, 1935.

2 "It is amusing to note," added Matthews, "that in this last sentence the British reviewer used two Americanisms — *putting new words over* and *every time*; and apparently he used them quite unconscious of their transatlantic origin."

sidering the proximity of the Continent to England, the prestige enjoyed by Southern English within the British Isles, and the distance from that other center of Anglo-Saxon culture, the United States of America. Since the Great War, however, it has become increasingly difficult for European teachers and scholars to ignore the fact that different norms of English usage are being evolved in another hemisphere, and that these norms are beginning to encroach on territory where hitherto Standard Southern English has held undisputed sway. Not that they are greatly concerned about the sort of English spoken in Australia, New Zealand, or Canada; these areas as yet exert no appreciable cultural influence upon the rest of the civilized world, and as members of the British Commonwealth of Nations are more or less amenable to the linguistic authority of the mother country. So long, too, as the attitude of educated Americans towards their own form of speech was expressed in the words of Richard Grant White that " just in so far as it deviates from the language of the most cultivated society of England, it fails to be English," there was no need for Continental language teachers to take even American English seriously. But with its world-wide dissemination through business, literature, the talking film, the gramophone record, on one hand, and the growing determination of Americans to assert their independence in matters of language on the other, the situation is taking on a different aspect.[1]

Unluckily, neither of the great dialects of English may be described as anything approaching a perfect language. Within the limits of both there are still innumerable obscurities, contradictions and irrationalities, many of which have been noticed in the preceding chapters. Those in spelling are especially exasperating. " Eight long vowels," says Dr. Arthur G. Kennedy,[2] " are spelled in at least sixty-six different ways; hardly a letter in the alphabet could be named which does not represent from two to eight different sounds; at least six new vowel characters and five new consonant characters are needed; nearly a fifth of the words on a printed page contain silent letters; and the spelling of many words such as *colonel, one* and *choir* is utterly absurd." " But spelling," says Dr. George Philip Krapp,[3]

would be only a beginning of the general house-cleaning for which our precious heritage of English speech as we know it today provides a profitable opportunity. The language is burdened with quantities of useless lumber, which from the point of view of common sense and reason might just as well be burned on the rubbish heap. . . . Why should we permit an exceptional plural *feet* or *teeth* when we possess a perfectly good regular way of making

1 Standards of English in Europe, *American Speech*, Feb., 1934.
2 The Future of the English Language, *American Speech*, Dec., 1933.
3 The Future of English, in The Knowledge of English; New York, 1927, p. 537.

plurals by adding *s?* And why should verbs like *write* have two past forms, *wrote* and *written*, when most verbs of the language get along quite satisfactorily with only one?

There is yet another difficulty, and a very serious one. Of it Dr. Janet Rankin Aiken says:

This difficulty is idiom – idiom observable in a large part of what we say and write, but centering particularly in verb and preposition. It has been calculated [1] that including all phrase constructions there are well over a hundred different forms for even a simple, regular verb like *call*, besides extra or lacking forms for irregular verbs like *speak*, *be* and *set*. Each of these verb forms has several uses, some as high as a dozen or more, to express not only time but such other motions as possibility, doubt, habit, emphasis, permission, ability, interrogation, negation, generalization, expectation, duration, inception, and a bewildering number of other ideas. Native speakers of English have difficulty with verb constructions; how much more so the foreign student of the language! [2]

Finally, there are the snarls of sentence order – naturally numerous in an analytical language. Says Dr. Aiken:

Each of the sentence types – declarative, interrogative, imperative, and exclamatory – has its own normal order, but there are many exceptional orders as well. In certain constructions the verb may or must come before the subject, and frequently the complement comes before the subject, or the subject is embedded within the verb phrase. All these orders, both normal and exceptional, must somehow be mastered before the student can be said to use English properly.

I introduce a foreign-born witness of high intelligence to sum up. He is Dr. Enrique Blanco, of the department of Romance languages at the University of Wisconsin, a native of Spain who has acquired a perfect command of English and writes it with vigor and good taste. He says:

English is not easy to learn. It is a puzzling, bewildering language; and the ambitious foreigner who sets himself to the task of learning it soon discovers that it can not be acquired in a short time. As Mr. Mencken quotes in his book: "The vowel sounds in English are comparatively independent of their surroundings." [3] We would suggest that the word "comparatively" be changed to "absolutely." That's one of the greatest troubles in the English language; one never knows how to pronounce a vowel. The *a*, for instance,

1 By Dr. Rankin herself in A New Plan of English Grammar; New York, 1933, Ch. XIX.
2 English as the International Language, *American Speech*, April, 1934, p. 104.
3 The reference is to the third edition of the present work; New York, 1923. The quotation, and the one following, are from Otto Jespersen's Growth and Structure of the English Language, 3rd ed.; Leipzig, 1919.

The American Language

that apparently inoffensive first letter of the alphabet, soon assumes, for the student of English, most terrifying proportions; it has a different sound in nearly every word. Beginning with *meat* and going on through *awful, alas, mat, ate, tall, fail, cap, said,* and so forth, one can run across nearly every conceivable sound in human speech. As soon as the enterprising would-be American has learned to pronounce *door* nicely, he is politely informed that *boor* must be pronounced differently. *Arch* and *march* sound very logical, but one gets a frown if he pronounces *patriarch* in the same manner. If a man goes to church he may sit on a humble *chair,* but the word *choir* must be pronounced with a greater degree of respectfulness; coming out of the sacred precinct, a man may be *robbed,* or just simply *robed.* An *egg* can take a mate unto itself and be *eggs,* but if a child has a friend they are not *childs* but *children;* a pastor may refer to *brother* Jones, but he is careful to speak to his *brethren.* Quotes Mr. Mencken: "Each English consonant belongs distinctly to its own type, a *t* is a *t*, . . . and there is an end." Unfortunately, the end is far from being there, for the *t* in English is often not a *t* at all, but an *sh,* as in *intuition, constitution,* where the *t* has two different sounds in the same word, and *nation, obligation,* where the *t* is not a *t* but something else. Need I go on? Yet, this language is supposed to be " vastly easier " than any other.[1]

As we have seen in Chapter VIII, efforts to remedy the irrationalities of English spelling have been under way for many years, but so far without much success. The improvement of English in other respects must await a revolutionist who will do for it what Mark Twain tried to do for German in " The Awful German Language " — but with much less dependence upon logic. " If English is to be a continuously progressive creation," said Dr. Krapp,[2] " then it must escape from the tyranny of the reason and must regain some of the freedom of impulse and emotion which must have been present in the primitive creative origins of language. . . . Suppose the children of this generation and of the next were permitted to cultivate expressiveness instead of fineness of speech, were praised and promoted for doing something interesting, not for doing something correct and proper. If this should happen, as indeed it is already beginning to happen, the English language and literature would undergo such a renascence as they have never known." Meanwhile, despite its multitudinous defects, English goes on conquering the world. I began this chapter with the pessimistic realism of Richard Mulcaster, 1582. I close it with the florid vision of Samuel Daniel, only seventeen years later:

1 American as a World-Language, *Literary Digest International Book Review,* April, 1924, p. 342.

2 The Future of English, above cited, p. 543.

And who in time knows whither we may vent
  The treasure of our tongue? To what strange shores
This gain of our best glory shall be sent,
  T' enrich unknowing nations with our stores?
What worlds in th' yet unformed Occident
May come refin'd with th' accents that are ours? [1]

[1] Musophilus, 1599. Musophilus is a dialogue between a courtier and a poet, in which the latter defends the worldly value of literary learning.

APPENDIX

NON-ENGLISH DIALECTS IN AMERICAN

1. GERMANIC

a. German

The so-called Pennsylvania-Dutch area of Pennsylvania and Maryland covers about 17,500 square miles. It began to be invaded by Germans before the end of the Seventeenth Century, and by 1775 nearly 90,000 had come in. They came " almost exclusively from Southwestern Germany (the Palatinate, Baden, Alsace, Württemberg, Hesse), Saxony, Silesia and Switzerland," [1] with the Palatines predominating. Pennsylvania-Dutch is based mainly upon the Westricher dialect of the Palatinate, and in the course of two centuries has become extraordinarily homogeneous. In the heart of its homeland, in Lehigh, Berks and Lebanon counties, Pennsylvania, between 60% and 65% of the total inhabitants can speak it, and between 30% and 35% use it constantly.[2] The fact that it has survived the competition of English for so many years is due mainly to the extreme clannishness of the people speaking it — a clannishness based principally upon religious separatism. This theological prepossession has colored their somewhat scanty literature, and most of the books they have produced have been of pious tendency. They printed the Bible three times before ever it was printed in English in America.[3] Their language was called *Dutch* by their English and Scotch-Irish neighbors because the early immigrants themselves called it *Deitsch* (H. Ger. *Deutsch*), and not because they were mistaken for Hollanders. To this day their descendants frequently use

1 A Dictionary of the Non-English Words of the Pennsylvania-German Dialect, by M. B. Lambert; Lancaster, Pa., 1924, p. viii.

2 Lambert, just cited.

3 The Early Literature of the Pennsylvania-Germans, by Samuel W. Pennypacker, *Proceedings of the Pennsylvania-German Society,* Vol. II, 1893; reprinted 1907, p. 41.

Pennsylvania-Dutch instead of *-German* in speaking of it. It has been studied at length by competent native philologians.[1]

Like the English of the Appalachian highlands, it includes a large number of archaisms, both in vocabulary and in pronunciation. The old German short vowel is retained in many words which have a long vowel or a diphthong in modern German, *e.g., nemme* (neh-men), *giwwel* (giebel), *hiwwel* (hübel), *votter* (vater), *huddle* (hudeln). In other cases an earlier diphthong is substituted for a later one, *e.g., meis* (mäuse), *leit* (leute), *Moi* (Mai). In yet others a long vowel takes the place of a diphthong, *e.g., bees* (böse), *aach* (auch), *kleen* (klein), or a neutral *e* is substituted, *e.g., bem* (bäume). When consonants come together in German, one of them is often dropped, *e.g., kopp* (kopf), *kinner* (kinder). In loan-words from English *st* often takes the sound of the German *scht*, and there is confusion between *t* and *d*, *b* and *w*, *p* and *b*, *s* and *z*. But a number of the characters of the underlying Westricher dialect have disappeared. " Von dem Verwandeln des *d* und *t* in *r*," says the Rev. Heinrich Harbaugh,[2] " und dem Verschmelzen des *d* und *t* nach *l* in *ll*, wie *laden* in *lare, gewitter* in *gewirrer, halten* in *halle, mild* in *mill*, findet man im Pennsylvanisch-Deutschen kaum eine Spur." He also says that the final *-en* is seldom dropped, though its *n* may be reduced to " einen Nasenlaut." The percentage of English loan-words in use is estimated by Lambert to run from " *nil* to 12% or 15%, depending upon the writer or speaker and the subject." Harbaugh gives many examples, *e.g., affis* (office), *beseid* (beside), *bisness* (business), *boghie* (buggy), *bortsch* (porch), *bresent* (present), *cumpaunde* (compound), *diehlings* (dealings), *dschillt* (chilled),

---

1 Lambert's dictionary has been mentioned. It includes an account of Pennsylvania-German phonology. The best treatise on the dialect is The Pennsylvania-German Dialect, by M. D. Learned, *American Journal of Philology*, Vol. IX, 1888, and Vol. X, 1889, a series of four papers. Other informative works are Pennsylvania-Dutch, by S. S. Haldeman; Philadelphia, 1872; Pennsylvania-German Manual, by A. R. Horne, 3rd ed.; Allentown, Pa., 1905; Common Sense Pennsylvania-German Dictionary, by James C. Lins; Reading, Pa., 1895;

Pennsylvania-German, by Daniel Miller, 2 vols.; Reading, 1903–11; Pennsylvania-Dutch Handbook, by E. Rauch; Mauch Chunk, Pa., 1879. There are many papers on various aspects of the dialect in the *Proceedings of the Pennsylvania-German Society*, 1891 — , and in the *Pennsylvania-German*, 1900 — . Unfortunately, there is no agreement among the writers on the dialect about its representation in English print.
2 Harbaugh's Harfe, rev. ed.; Philadelphia, 1902, p. 112.

dschuryman (juryman), *ebaut* (about), *ennihau* (anyhow), *fäct* (fact), *fäschin* (fashion), *fens* (fence), *gut-bei* (good-bye), *heist* (hoist), *humbuk* (humbug), *käsch* (cash), *krick* (creek), *ledscher-buch* (ledger-book), *lohnsom* (lonesome), *lof-letter* (love-letter), *nau* (now), *rehs* (race), *schkippe* (skip), *schtärt* (start), *tornpeik* (turnpike), *wälli* (valley), *weri* (very) and *'xäktly* (exactly). The pronunciation of *creek* and *hoist* will be noted; in the same way *sleek* becomes *schlick*. Many English verbal adjectives are inflected in the German manner, *e.g.*, *gepliehst* (pleased), *g'rescht* (arrested), *gedscheest* (chased), *gebärrt* (barred), *vermisst* (missed) and *verschwapped* (swapped). An illuminating brief specimen of the language is to be found in the sub-title of E. H. Rauch's " Pennsylvania Dutch Hand-book ": [1] " En booch for inschtructa." Here we see the German indefinite article decayed to *en*, the vowel of *buch* made to conform to English usage, *für* abandoned for *for*, and a purely English word, *instruction*, boldly adopted and naturalized. Some astounding examples of Pennsylvania-German are to be found in the humorous literature of the dialect, *e.g.*, " Mein *stallion* hat über die *fenz geschumpt* und dem nachbar sein *whiet* abscheulich *gedämätscht* " and " Ick muss den gaul *anharnessen* und den *boghie greasen* befor wir ein *ride* nemmen." Such phrases as " Es giebt gar kein *use* " and " Ick kann es nicht *ständen* " are very common. But the dialect is also capable of more or less dignified literary use, and the Pastor Harbaugh before-mentioned (1817–67) printed many poems in it, some of them not a little charming. Here are the first and last stanzas of his most celebrated effort, " Das Alt Schulhaus an der Krick ":

> Heit is 's 'xäctly zwansig Johr,
>   Dass ich bin owwe naus;
> Nau bin ich widder lewig z'rick
> Und schteh am Schulhaus an d'r Krick,
>   Juscht neekscht an's Dady's Haus
>
> Oh horcht, ihr Leit, wu nooch mir lebt,
>   Ich schreib eich noch des Schtick:
> Ich warn eich, droh eich, gebt doch Acht,
> Un nemmt uf immer gut enacht,
>   Des Schulhaus an der Krick! [2]

1 Mauch Chunk, Pa., 1879.
2 Other strains from Harbaugh's harp are given in Pennsylvania-Dutch, by Maynard D. Follin, *American Speech*, 1929.

Of late, with improvements in communication, the dialect shows signs of gradually disappearing. So recently as the 80's of the last century, two hundred years after the coming of the first German settlers, there were thousands of their descendants in Pennsylvania who could not speak English at all, but now the younger Pennsylvania-Germans learn it in school, read English newspapers, and begin to forget their native patois. An interesting, but almost extinct variant of it, remaining much closer to the original Westricher dialect, is to be found in the Valley of Virginia, to which German immigrants penetrated before the Revolution. In this sub-dialect the cases of the nouns do not vary in form, adjectives are seldom inflected, and only two tenses of the verbs remain, the present and the perfect, *e.g.*, *ich geh* and *ich bin gange*. The indefinite article, *en* in Pennsylvania-German, is a simple '*n*. The definite article has been preserved, but *das* has changed to *des*. It is declined as follows:

Nom.	der	die	des-'s	die
Dat.	dem-'m	der	dem-'m	dene
Acc.	den-der	die	des-'s	die

The only persons still speaking this Valley German are a few remote country-folk. It was investigated nearly a generation ago by H. M. Hays,[1] from whom I borrow the following specimen:

'S war eimol ei Mätel, wu ihr Liebling fat in der Grieg is, un' is dot gmacht wure. Sie hut sich so arg gedrauert un' hut ksat: " O wann ich ihn just noch eimol sehne könnt! " Ei Ovet is sie an 'n Partie gange, aver es war ken Freud dat für sie. Sie hut gwünscht, ihre Lieve war dat au. Wie freundlich sie sei hätt könne! Sie is 'naus in den Garde gange, un' war allei im Monlicht khockt. Kschwind hut sie 'n Reiter höre komme. 'S war ihre Lieve ufm weisse Gaul. Er hut ken Wat ksat, aver hut sie uf den Gaul hinner sich gnomme, un' is fatgritte. . . .[2]

The Germans, since colonial days, have always constituted the largest body of people of non-British stock in the country. In 1930, despite the sharp decline in immigration, the Census Bureau found 2,188,006 foreign-born persons whose mother-tongue was German. How many persons of native birth used it as their first language was not determined, but certainly there must have been a great many,

1 On the German Dialect Spoken in the Valley of Virginia, *Dialect Notes*, Vol. III, Pt. IV, 1908.
2 I am informed by Mr. August Blum of Pasadena, Calif., who was born in the Western Palatinate near Otterberg, that this specimen of Valley German is virtually identical with the dialect still spoken in his native village. " A few unimportant changes," he says, " would complete the identity, *e.g.*, *emol* for *eimol*, *aa* for *au*, *kumme* for *komme*, *genumme* for *gnomme*."

especially in Pennsylvania and the Middle West. Outside the Pennsylvania-German area, as within it, the German spoken in the United States shows a disregard of the grammatical niceties of the Standard language and a huge accession of English loan-words. Its vagaries supply rich material for the German-American wits, and almost all of the seventeen German dailies [1] print humorous columns done in it. I offer a specimen from " Der Charlie," a feature of the New York *Staats-Zeitung:*

"Was machst du denn in Amerika? " fragt der alte Onkel.
Well, der Kuno war sehr onnest. " Ich bin e Stiefellegger," sagt er.
"Bist du verrückt geworden? " rohrt der Onkel. " Was ist denn das? "
"Das," sagt der Kuno, " is a Antivereinigtestaatenconstitutionsverbesserungs-spirituosenwarenhändler." [2]

The same ghastly dialect provides the substance of a series of popular comic verses by Kurt M. Stein, most of them contributed to the Chicago *Tribune* or *Evening Post.* A specimen:

> Wenn die Robins Loff tun mache',
> Wenn der Frontlawn leicht ergrünt,
> Wenn der Lilacbushes shprouteh,
> Peddlers in der Alley shouteh,
> Da wird bei uns hausgecleant.[3]

" Every English noun," says Dr. Albert W. Aron of the University of Illinois, " is a potential loan-word in colloquial American German. Naturally, the great mass of borrowed words belongs to the stock vocabulary of everyday speech, but situations are easily conceivable where any English noun understood by the speaker and the listener may be used. Accordingly, every English noun may find itself returned to its pristine state of being masculine, feminine or neuter." [4] But Dr. Aron's investigation discloses that there is a tendency to

1 There were more before 1914. But the German press, as a whole, had been declining since 1894. See The Immigrant Press and Its Control, by Robert E. Park; New York, 1922, p. 318 *ff.*, and especially the chart facing p. 318. The New York *Staats-Zeitung* and the St. Louis *Westliche Post*, the two leading dailies, go back to 1834, and the *Volksblatt* of Cincinnati, now merged in the *Freie Presse*, was founded in 1836.
2 March 28, 1935. I am indebted for this to Mr. George Weiss, Jr., of

Richmond Hills, N. Y. *Stiefelbeiner*, perhaps, would have been better. The author of " Der Charlie " is Mr. Heinrich Reinhold Hirsch, editor of the *Staats-Zeitung.*
3 Mr. Stein has printed the following collections of his lays: Die schönste Lengvitch; Chicago, 1925; Gemixte Pickles; Chicago, 1927; and Limburger Lyrics; New York, 1932.
4 The Gender of English Loan-Words in Colloquial American German, *Language Monographs*, No. VII, Dec., 1930.

make most of them feminine. This is due, he believes, to a number of causes, among them, the fact that the German *die* sounds very much like the English *the*, the fact that *die* is the general German plural and thus suggests itself before the plural nouns, *e.g.*, *wages*, *reins*, *pants* and *scissors*, that are so numerous in English, and the fact that in some of the German dialects spoken by German immigrants there is a tendency in the same direction. Dr. Aron's investigation was made in the Middle West. He found some local variations in usage, but not many. Not a few loan-words, of course, remain masculine or neuter, chiefly because of the influence of their German cognates or by rhyming or other analogy. Thus, nouns signifying living beings are " practically always masculine," in accord with "the general German principle of allowing a masculine to designate both male and female beings," and " any loan-word ending in *-ing* is neuter if the meaning is equivalent to that of an English gerund in *-ing*," since "all German infinitives are neuter." But the movement toward the feminine gender is unmistakable, and to it belong many large groups of words, including all ending in *-ence*, *-ance*, *-sion* or *-tion*, *-y*, *-sure* or *-ture*, *-ege*, *-age*, *-ship*, *-hood* and *-ness* and most in *-ment*. Sometimes there is vacillation between masculine and feminine, or neuter and feminine, but never between masculine and neuter. "This," says Dr. Aron, "is in consonance with the theory of the feminine tendency of these loan-words." [1]

b. Dutch

As in the case of American German, two main varieties of Dutch American are to be found in the United States. The first is a heritage from the days of the Dutch occupation of the Hudson and Delaware river regions, and the second is the speech of more recent immigrants, chiefly domiciled in Michigan, Iowa, Minnesota and the Dakotas. The former is now virtually extinct, but in 1910, while it was still spoken by about 200 persons, it was studied by Dr. J. Dyneley Prince, then professor of Semitic languages at Columbia, and now professor of Slavonic.[2] It was originally, he said,

[1] Save for the Pennsylvania-German form, American German, like American English, has been very little studied by philologians. It offers rich opportunities to industrious young *Dozenten*.
[2] The Jersey Dutch Dialect, *Dialect Notes*, Vol. III, Pt. VI, 1910.

the South Holland or Flemish language, which, in the course of centuries (*c.* 1630–1880), became mixed with and partially influenced by English, having borrowed also from the Mindi (Lenâpe-Delaware) Indian language a few animal and plant names. This Dutch has suffered little or nothing from modern Holland or Flemish immigration, although Paterson (the county seat of Passaic county) has at present [1910] a large Netherlands population. The old county people hold themselves strictly aloof from these foreigners, and say, when they are questioned as to the difference between the idioms: " Onze tal äz lex däuts en hoelliz äs Holläns; kwait dääfrent " (Our language is Low Dutch and theirs is Holland Dutch; quite different). An intelligent Fleming or South Hollander with a knowledge of English can make shift at following a conversation in this Americanized Dutch, but the converse is not true.

Contact with English wore off the original inflections, and the definite and indefinite articles, *de* and *en*, became uniform for all genders. The case-endings nearly all disappeared, in the comparison of adjectives the superlative affix decayed from -*st* to -*s*, the person-endings in the conjugation of verbs fell off, and the pronouns were much simplified. The vocabulary showed many signs of English influence. A large number of words in daily use were borrowed bodily, *e.g.*, *bottle, town, railroad, cider, smoke, potato, match, good-bye*. Others were borrowed with changes, *e.g.*, *säns* (*since*), *määm* (*ma'm*), *belange* (*belong*), *boddere* (*bother*), *bääznäs* (*business*), *orek* (*earache*). In still other cases the drag of English was apparent, as in *blaubääse*, a literal translation of *blueberry* (the standard Dutch word is *heidebes*), in *mep'lbom* (*mapletree;* D., *ahoornboom*), and in *njeuspapier* (*newspaper;* D., *nieuwsblad* or *courant*). A few English archaisms were preserved, *e.g.*, the use of *gentry*, strange in America, as a plural for *gentleman*. This interesting dialect now exists only in the memory of a few old persons, and in Dr. Prince's excellent monograph.

The Dutch spoken by the more recent immigrants from Holland in the Middle West has been very extensively modified by American influences, both in vocabulary and in grammar. As in Jersey Dutch and in Afrikaans, the Dutch dialect of South Africa,[1] there has been a decay of inflections, and the neuter article *het* has been absorbed

1 The Dutch settled in South Africa in 1652, but it was not until about 1860 that Afrikaans began to produce a literature. It is so far from Standard Dutch that it has been described as a dialect of Hottentot, but this is an exaggeration. See *Grammar of Afrikaans*, by M. C. Botha and J. F. Burger; Cape Town, 1921, *pref.*; *Afrikaans for English-Speaking Students*, by D. J. Potgieter and A. Geldenhuys; Cape Town, n.d.; and *Oor die Onstaan van Afrikaans*, by D. B. Bosman; Amsterdam, 1928. The last is a valuable historical survey.

by the masculine-feminine article *de*. Says Prof. Henry J. G. Van Andel, of the chair of Dutch history, literature and art in Calvin College at Grand Rapids: " Almost all the American names of common objects, *e.g.*, *stove, mail, carpet, bookcase, kitchen, store, post-office, hose, dress, pantry, porch, buggy, picture, newspaper, ad, road, headline*, particularly when they differ considerably from the Dutch terms, have been taken into the everyday vocabulary. This is also true of a great many verbs and adjectives, *e.g.*, *to move* (*moeven*), *to dig* (*diggen*), *to shop* (*shoppen*), *to drive* (*drijven*), *slow, fast, easy, pink*, etc. The religious language has remained pure, but even here purity has only a relative meaning, for the constructions employed are often English."[1] English loan-nouns are given Dutch plural endings, *e.g.*, *boxen* (boxes), *roaden* (roads) and *storen* (stores), English verbs go the same route, *e.g.*, *threshen* (to thresh), *raken* (to rake) and *graden* (to grade), and Dutch prefixes are used in the past tense, *e.g.*, *ge-cut* and *ge-mailed*.[2] Sometimes these borrowings cause a certain confusion, *e.g.*, *drijven* (to drive) means to float in Standard Dutch.[3] There is an extensive borrowing of English idioms, *e.g.*, " What is de *troebel?* "[4] A little book of sketches by Dirk Nieland, called " Yankee-Dutch "[5] contains some amusing examples, *e.g.*, *piezelmietje* (pleased to meet you), and there are more in his " 'N Fonnie Bisnis,"[6] *e.g.*, *aan de we* (on the way), *baaienbaai* (by and by), *evverwansinnewail* (every once in a while), *goedveurnotting* (good for nothing), and *of kos* (of course). Mr. Nieland is fond of Americanisms, and introduces them in all his sketches, *e.g.*, *bieviedies* (B.V.D.'s), *sokker* (sucker), *bokhous* (bug-house), *boonhed* (bonehead), *sonnie* (sundae), *domtom* (down-town), *draaigoeds* (dry-goods), *gesselien* (gasoline), *hoombroe* (home-brew), *jenneker* (janitor), *lemmen-paai* (lemon-pie), and *sannege* —— (son of a ——). In *baasie* (bossy) the American Dutch have borrowed an American adjective made from what was originally a Dutch noun.

In 1930 there were 133,142 persons in the United States whose mother-tongue was Dutch. Of these, 133,133 had been born in Hol-

1 Private communication, April 13, 1921.
2 I am indebted here to the Rev. B. D. Dykstra of Orange City, Iowa.
3 I am indebted here to Mr. Frank Hanson of Redlands, Calif.

4 Nederlanders in Amerika, by J. van Hinte; Amsterdam, 1928, Vol. II, p. 554.
5 Grand Rapids, Mich., 1919.
6 Grand Rapids, 1929.

land. In addition, there were 170,417 persons of Dutch parentage and 110,416 of partly Dutch parentage, or 413,966 in all. There are no Dutch daily newspapers in the country, but there are ten Dutch and two Flemish weeklies.[1]

c. Swedish

The early Swedish immigrants to the United States, says Dr. George M. Stephenson,[2] spoke a multitude of Swedish dialects, but they soon vanished in the melting-pot, and " everybody spoke a ludicrous combination of English and Swedish that neither an American nor a recent arrival from Sweden could understand." To the children of the first American-born generation Swedish " was almost a dead language; it had to be kept alive artificially. Instead of using the conversational forms of the personal pronouns, *mej* and *dej,* they said *mig* and *dig.* They were so proper that they were improper." [3] The resultant jargon has been investigated at length by various Swedish-Americans of philological leanings, and especially by Mr. V. Berger, of the *Nordstjernan* (*North Star*) of New York, and by Rektor Gustav Andreen, of Rock Island, Ill.,[4] and there have also been studies of it by philologians at home.[5] It shows all the changes that we have just seen in German and Dutch. It takes in a multitude of American English words bodily, *e.g., ajskrim* (ice-cream), *baggage, bartender, bissniss* (business), *blajnpigg* (blind-pig), *bockvete* (buckwheat), *dinner, dress, dude, frilunsch* (free-lunch), *fäs* (face), *good-bye, höraka* (hay-rake), *jabb* or *jobb* (job), *jäl* (jail), *klerk* (clerk), *ledi* (lady), *license, meeting, mister, nice,*

1 I am indebted for information and suggestions to Prof. B. K. Kuiper, Dr. Paul de Kruif, Mr. Dirk Nieland, Mr. M. J. Francken, Mr. J. L. Van Lancker, Mr. W. A. Nyland, Mme. Hortense Leplae, Dr. John J. Hiemenga, Mr. H. H. D. Langereis and Mr. D. J. Van Riemsdyck, in addition to those already mentioned.
2 The Religious Aspects of Swedish Immigration; Minneapolis, 1932, p. 407.
3 Stephenson, just cited, p. 429.
4 Mr. Berger's first report on it, Vårt Språk, was published by the Augustana Book Concern at Rock Island

in 1912. In 1934 he brought out an enlarged edition under the title of Svensk-amerikanska Språket. Dr. Andreen's Det Svenska Språket i Amerika appeared as No. 87 of the series called Studentföreningen Småskrifter; Stockholm, 1900. It contains a map marking the Swedish areas in the United States.
5 For example, Engelskans Inflytande på Svenska Språket i America, by E. A. Zetterstrand, *Ungdomsvännen* (Stockholm), June, July and Aug., 1904, and Svenskan in Amerika, by Ruben G:son Berg; Stockholm, 1904.

peanut, påcketbok (pocketbook), *saloon, supper, svetter* (sweater), *taul* (towel), *trunktject* (trunk-check), *trubbel* (trouble), *velis* (valise); it displaces many Swedish words with translations of analogous but not cognate English words, *e.g., bransoldat* (fireman) with *brandman, brefkort* (postcard) with *postkort, ekonomidirektör* (business-manager) with *affärsförståndare, hushållsgöromål* (housework) with *husarbete, husläkare* (family doctor) with *familjemedicin;* and it takes over a large number of English idioms, either by translation or by outright adoption, *e.g., bära i minne* (to bear in mind), *efter allt* (after all), *gå republikanskt* (to go Republican), *i familjen* (in the family), *Junibrud* (June bride), *kalla till ordning* (to call to order), *på tid* (on time). In forming the plurals of loan-nouns, it not infrequently adds the Swedish plural article to the English *s, e.g., träcksena* (the tracks) and *karsarne* (the cars). Sometimes the singular article is suffixed to plurals, *e.g., buggsen* (bugs) and *tingsen* (things). In other cases the English *s* is used alone, *e.g., ekers* (acres). *Kars* is used as a singular noun, *en kars* meaning one car. The suffixal singular articles, *-en* and *-et,* are, of course, often (but not always) added to loan-nouns in the singular, *e.g., trusten* (trust), *sutkäsen* (suitcase) and *homesteadet* (homestead), and the loan-verbs take the Swedish suffixes *a* or *ar, e.g., mixa* (to mix), *kicka* (to keep), *talkar* (to talk), *resa garden* (to raise a garden), and *påka funn* (to poke fun).[1] There are sometimes difficulties when loan-words resemble or are identical with Swedish words. Thus, *barn* means a child in Swedish; nevertheless, it is used, and Mr. Berger says that *barn-dance* is in common use also. *Grisa* (to grease) also offers embarrassments, for it means to give birth to pigs in Swedish. So does *fitta* (to fit), which, in Swedish, signifies the female pudenda. Loan-words borrowed by American from other languages go into American-Swedish with the native terms, *e.g., bas* (boss), which is of Dutch origin; *luffa* (to loaf), which is German;[2] and *vigilans* (vigilantes) which is Spanish. The Swedish-American puts his sentences together American fashion. At home he would say *Bröderna Anderson,* just as the German would say *Gebrüder Anderson,* but in America he says *Anderson Bröderna.* In Sweden *all over* is *öfverallt;* in America, following the American construction, it becomes *allt öfver. Min vän* (my friend) is Ameri-

1 Notes on Swedish-American, by Robert Beckman, *American Speech,* Aug., 1928, p. 448.

2 In Standard Swedish *luffa* means to jog, to scamper, to trot.

canized into *en vän af mina* (a friend of mine). The American verb *to take* drags ,its Swedish relative, *taga*, into strange places, as in *taga kallt* (to take cold), *taga nöje i* (to take pleasure in), *taga fördel af* (to take advantage of), and *taga tåget* (to take a train). The thoroughly American use of *right* is imitated by a similar use of its equivalent, *rätt*, as in *rätt av* (right off), *rätt i väg* (right away) and *rätt intill* (right next to), or by the bold adoption of *rite*. *All right*, *well* and other such American counter-words are used constantly, and so are *hell* and *damn*. The Swedish-American often exiles the preposition, imitating the American vulgate, to the end of the sentence. He uses the Swedish *af* precisely as if it were the English *of*, and *i* as if it were *in*. Some instructive specimens of his speech are in " Mister Colesons Sverigeressa," by Gabriel Carlson,[1] for example:

> Du *foolar* icke mej, sa jag.
> Har du nå'n *transferticket*, sa han?
> Det är inte nå'n af din *bissniss*, sa jag.

Mr. John A. Stahlberg, of Plentywood, Mont., tells me that he once overheard the following dialogue between a farmer's wife and her son:

> Edvard, *kom an*,[2] nu! (Edward, come on, now!)
> Men, Mamma, ja må *finischa* de' här; ja må *stäpla vajern* på den här *fensposten*. (But, Mamma, I must finish this-here; I must staple the wire on this-here fence-post).
> Edvard! Nu *näver* du *majndar!* Nu *kommer* du *an!* *Mäka* mej inte *mäd*, nu, Edvard! (Edward! Now never you mind! Now you come on! Don't make me mad, now, Edvard!)

There are phonetic changes in some of the loan-words taken into American-Swedish. *J* commonly becomes *y*, to accord with its pronunciation in Swedish, *e.g.*, *yust* (just), and *th* often becomes *d*, *e.g.*, *dat* (that). But these changes are common in the speech of many other kinds of immigrants. Perhaps more characteristic is the occasional change from *y* to *g*, *e.g.*, *funnig* (funny) and *kresig* (crazy). The common American belief that all Swedes, in trying to speak Engish, use *been* in place of *am*, *is*, *are*, *was*, *were*, *had been*, etc., and pronounce it *bane* is hardly justified by the observed facts. It may be done but it is certainly not common, even on the lower levels. " I can confidently say," says Robert Beckman, himself a Swedish-

---

1 Chicago, 1908.
2 *Kom*, of course, is good Swedish,
but *kom an* is a loan.

American, "that I have never heard one utter I *bane* in ordinary conversation. . . . Perhaps inaccurate linguistic observers — listeners, rather — thought they heard *bane* where a trained ear would have caught something entirely different, though what, I dare not venture to state." [1]

The Swedes began to come to the United States before the Civil War, and there were many thousands of them in the upper Middle West by 1880. In 1930 there were 1,562,703 persons of Swedish stock in the country — 595,250 born in Sweden, 676,523 born here of Swedish parentage, and 290,930 born here of partly Swedish parentage. Of the whole number 615,465 gave their mother-tongue as Swedish. They were thus the seventh largest foreign *bloc* in the country, being surpassed only by the immigrants from England, Ireland, Italy, Germany, Poland and Russia. They have no daily papers, but they support twenty-seven weeklies (1935).[2]

d. Dano-Norwegian

The pioneer study of the Dano-Norwegian spoken by Norwegian immigrants to the United States was published by Dr. Nils Flaten, of Northfield, Minn., in 1900.[3] Two years later Dr. George T. Flom, then of Iowa State University and now of the University of Illinois, followed with a study of the dialects spoken in the Koshkonong settlement in Southern Wisconsin,[4] and since then he has continued his investigation of the subject.[5] The immigration of Danes and

1 Swedish-American *I Bane, American Speech*, Aug., 1928.
2 I am indebted for aid to Prof. Walter Gustafson, of Upsala College, East Orange, N. J., and to Messrs. John A. Stahlberg, V. Berger, A. H. Anderson, John Goldstrom, Robert Beckman and Valdemar Viking.
3 Notes on American-Norwegian, With a Vocabulary, *Dialect Notes*, Vol. II, Pt. II, 1900.
4 English Elements in the Norse Dialects of Utica, Wis., *Dialect Notes*, Vol. II, Pt. IV, 1902.
5 His principal publications are A Grammar of the Sogn Dialect of Norwegian, *Dialect Notes*, Vol. III, Pt. I, 1905; English Loan-Words

in American-Norwegian, *American Speech*, July, 1926; On the Phonology of Loan-Words in the Norwegian Dialects of Koshkonong in Wisconsin, in Studier tilägnade Axel Kock; Lund (Sweden), 1926; Um det norske målet i Amerika, *Saerprent* (Bergen), 1931; and The Gender of English Loan-Nouns in Norse Dialects in America, *Journal of Germanic Philology*, Vol. V, 1903. The first-named article deals with the noun, pronoun, adjective and numerals in the Americanized form of the Sogn dialect. "The verb," says Dr. Flom, "will form the subject of a later paper." That later paper was completed during 1935, but it has not yet appeared.

Norwegians began more than a century ago, and has been heaviest into the farming areas of the upper Middle West, though there are also large settlements of both peoples in some of the big cities, especially Chicago and Brooklyn. In 1930 there were 347,852 natives of Norway in the country, 476, 663 persons of Norwegian parentage, and 275,583 of partly Norwegian parentage, or 1,100,098 in all. In the same year there were 179,474 natives of Denmark, 219,152 persons of Danish parentage and 130,516 of partly Danish parentage, or 529,142 in all. The Dano-Norwegian language, of course, shows considerable dialectical variations, but they are not important for the present purpose. About thirty-five periodicals in it are published in the United States, including one daily paper.

Dr. Flom's admirable studies deal mainly with the spoken language, and his examples of loan-words are given in a phonetic alphabet which often differs considerably from the alphabet used in Norwegian-American publications. When a word beginning with an unstressed initial vowel is borrowed, he says, the vowel is often lost. Thus, *account* becomes *kaunt*, *election* becomes *leckshen*, and *assessor* becomes *sessar*. "The dissyllabic noun *efekt* (effect) is an exception, as is also the word *aperashen* (operation)." The word *edzukashen* (education) likewise keeps its initial vowel, for the consonantal sound *dz* would be hardly admissible in Norwegian at the beginning of a word. The vowel in an unstressed initial syllable is commonly suppressed, even when it is not the first letter, as in *spraisparti* (surprise-party) and *stiffiket* (certificate). In the latter case a transition form, *settifiket*, has been lost. There is also some loss of vowels in medial syllables, as in *bufflo* (buffalo), *fektri* (factory), *lakris* (licorice) and *probishen* (prohibition). Consonants are lost less often, but there are examples in *paler* (parlor), *korna* (corner), *potret* (portrait) and *blaekbor* (blackboard). In the last case the final *-bor* is not the English *board* but the Norwegian *bord*, having the same meaning and pronounced *bor*. In *insurance* the last syllable is changed to *ings*. The sound of *h* often disappears in compounds, as in *brikkus* (brick-house), *fremus* (frame-house) and *purus* (poorhouse). In cases where consonants are duplicated they may be reduced to a single consonant, as in *fretren* (freight-train), or separated by a vowel, as in *fensestretcher* (fence-stretcher). Sometimes an inorganic consonant appears, as in *hikril* (hickory), *gofert* (gopher) and *brand* (bran). The sound of *th* commonly becomes *t*, as in *latt* (lath) and *timoti* (timothy); *rs* becomes *ss*, as in *hosspaur* (horsepower); and final *dz* becomes *s*, as in *launs* (lounge) and in the proper name *Kemris* (Cambridge).[1] Miss Anne Simley, in a report on Norwegian phonology in Minnesota,[2] says that the common impression that *y* is always substituted for *j* and *dj* is not well founded. " The error is most often made," she says, " by Norwegians who have learned to read English after learning to read Norwegian, in which language the letter *j* has the sound usually expressed in [English] writing by *y*." For the same reason *v* is substituted for *w*.

Dr. Flaten supplies the following examples of American-Norwegian, gathered near Northfield, Minn.: [3]

Mrs. Olsen va *aafel bisi* idag; hun maatte *béke kék*. (Mrs. Olsen was awfully busy today; she had to bake cake.)

Reilraaden ha *muva schappa* sine. (The railroad has moved its shops.)

Je kunde ikke faa *resa* saa mye *kaes* at je fik betalt *morgesen i farmen* min. (I couldn't raise enough cash to pay the mortgage on my farm.)

Det *meka* ingen *difrens*. (That makes no difference.)

Hos'n *fila* du? *Puddi gud*. (How do you feel? Pretty good.)

This dialect, says Dr. Flaten, is " utterly unintelligible to a Norseman recently from the old country. In the case of many words the younger generation cannot tell whether they are English or Norse. I was ten years old before I found that such words as *paatikkel* (particular), *staebel* (stable), *fens* (fence) were not Norse, but mutilated English. I had often wondered that *poleit, trubble, söpperéter* were so much like the English words *polite, trouble, separator*. So common is this practice of borrowing that no English word is refused admittance into this vocabulary provided it can stand the treatment it is apt to get. Some words, indeed, are used without any appreciable difference in pronunciation, but more generally the root, or stem, is taken and Norse inflections are added as required by the rules of the language." Sometimes the English loan-word and a corresponding Norwegian word exist side by side, but in such cases, according to Dr. Flom,[4] " there is a prevalent and growing tendency " to drop the latter, save in the event that it acquires a special

---

1 English Loan-Words in American Norwegian, above cited.

2 A Study of Norwegian Dialect in Minnesota, *Dialect Notes*, Aug., 1930.

3 Notes on American-Norwegian, above cited.

4 English Elements in the Norse Dialects of Utica, Wis., above cited.

meaning. "Very often in such cases," he continues, "the English word is shorter and easier to pronounce or the Norse equivalent is a purely literary word — that is, does not actually exist in the dialect of the settlers. . . . In the considerable number of cases where the loan-word has an exact equivalent in Norse dialect it is often very difficult to determine the reason for the loan, though it would be safe to say that it is frequently due simply to a desire on the part of the speaker to use English words, a thing that becomes very pronounced in the jargon that is sometimes heard."

Dr. Flom's vocabulary of loan-words includes 735 nouns, 235 verbs, 43 adjectives and 7 verbs, or 1025 words in all — a very substantial part of the total vocabulary of the Norwegian-Americans of rural Wisconsin. Dr. Flaten's earlier vocabulary runs to almost 550 words. The Dano-Norwegian *øl* is abandoned for the English *beer*, which becomes *bir*. *Tønde* succumbs to *baerel, barel* or *baril* (barrel), *frokost* to *brekkfaest* (breakfast), *skat* to *taex* (tax), and so on. The verbs yield in the same way: *vaeljuéte* (valuate), *titsche* (teach), *katte* (cut), *klém* (claim), *savére* (survey), *refjuse* (refuse). And the adjectives: *plén* (plain), *jelös* (jealous), *kjokfuldt* (chockfull), *krésé* (crazy), *aebel* (able), *klir* (clear), *pjur* (pure), *pur* (poor). And the adverbs and adverbial phrases: *isé* (easy), *reit evé* (right away), *aept to* (apt to), *allreit* (all right). Dr. Flaten lists some grotesque compound words, *e.g.*, *nekk-töi* (necktie),[1] *kjaens-bogg* (chinch-bug), *gitte long* (get along), *staets-praessen* (state's prison), *traevling-maen* (traveling-man), *uxe-jogg* (yoke of oxen). Pure Americanisms are not infrequent, *e.g.*, *bösta* (busted), *bésbaal* (baseball), *dipo* (depot), *jukre* (to euchre), *kaemp-mid'n* (camp-meeting), *kjors* (chores), *magis* (moccasin), *malasi* (molasses), *munke-rins* (monkey-wrench), *raad-bas* (road-boss), *sjante* (shanty), *strit-kar* (street-car), *tru trin* (through train). The decayed American adverb is boldly absorbed, as in *han file baed* (he feels bad). "That this lingo," says Dr. Flaten, "will ever become a dialect of like importance with the Pennsylvania-Dutch is hardly possible. . . . The Norwegians are among those of our foreign-born citizens most willing to part with their mother tongue." But meanwhile it is spoken by many thousands of them, and it will probably

---

1 Mr. Valdemar Viking tells me that the *töi* here is not a corruption of the English *tie*, but a good Dano-Norwegian word. *Halstöi* means anything that is draped around the neck, such as ties, collars, mufflers, etc.

linger in isolated farming regions of the upper Middle West for years.[1]

e. Icelandic

The only study of American Icelandic in English that I have been able to unearth is a paper on its loan-nouns, published more than thirty years ago by Vilhjálmar Stefánsson, the Arctic explorer, who was born in the Icelandic colony at Árnes, Manitoba, on Lake Winnipeg.[2] But there is considerable interest in the subject among the Icelanders, both at home and in this country, and Dr. Stefán Einarsson of the Johns Hopkins University, a native of Iceland, has been, for some years past, collecting materials relating to it, and has in contemplation a treatise on it. The dialect is called Vestur-íslenska, and shows many of the characters that we have found in American-Swedish and American-Dano-Norwegian. But, since it is a much more ancient language than the tongues of the Scandinavian mainland, it is more highly inflected, and its inflections are almost invariably fastened upon its borrowings from American English. " No word," says Mr. Stefánsson, " can be used in Icelandic without being assigned a gender-form distinguished by the post-positive article." Thus *river* becomes *rifurinn* (masculine), *road* becomes *rótin* (feminine) and *depot* becomes *dípóidh* [3] (neuter). In general, either formal or semantical similarities to Icelandic words determine the gender of the loan-words. The effect is sometimes curious. Thus the American *candy, ice-cream, saloon, sidewalk, township* and *cornstarch* are all neuter, but *beer, boss, cowboy* and *populist* are masculine, and *tie* (railroad), *prohibition* and *siding* are feminine. In the case of some words usage varies. Thus *caucus* has no fixed gender; different speakers make it masculine, feminine or neuter. *Cracker, automobile, field, telephone* and *turkey* are other such words. *Banjo* may be either feminine or neuter, *bicycle* may be either masculine or neuter, and *bronco* may be either masculine or feminine. The gender of loan-words tends to be logical, but it is not always so.

1 In addition to the gentlemen already mentioned, I am indebted for aid to Messrs. A. H. Anderson and Wallace Lomoe.

2 English Loan-Nouns Used in the Icelandic Colony of North Dakota, *Dialect Notes*, Vol. II, Pt. V, 1903.

3 In order to avoid two Icelandic characters that are unknown in modern English and might be confusing, I have adopted the equivalents approved by the Royal Geographical Society of England.

Farmer is always masculine and so is *engineer*, and *nurse* is always feminine, but *dressmaker* is given the masculine post-positive article, becoming *dressmakerinn*. However, when the pronoun is substituted, in speaking of a dressmaker, *hún*, which is feminine, is commonly used. Words ending in *l* or *ll* are usually considered neuter, *e.g.*, *baseball*, *corral*, *hotel*, *hall*. "A striking example," says Mr. Stefánsson, "is the term *constable*. The natural gender is evidently masculine and the Icelandic equivalent, *lögreglumathur*, is masculine; yet *constable* is usually employed as a neuter, though occasionally as a masculine." Words in *-er* fall under the influence of the Icelandic masculine nouns in *-ari*, denoting agency, and so usually become masculine, *e.g.*, *director*, *ginger*, *mower*, *parlor*, *peddler*, *reaper*, *separator*. *Republican* and *socialist* are masculine, but *democrat* is neuter. *Cash-book*, *clique*, *contract*, *election* and *grape* are feminine for the reasons stated on page 631. Of the 467 loan-nouns listed by Mr. Stefánsson, 176 are neuters and 137 are masculines. There are but 44 clear feminines, though 80 others are sometimes feminine. Here are some specimens of Vestur-íslenska in action:

> Eg baudh honum inn á *salún* og atladhi adh *tríta* hann á einum *bír*, en hann vildi *bae nó míns* adh eg *trítadhi*: heldur vildi hann adh vidh skyldum *raffla* fyrir drykk. (I invited him to a saloon and intended to treat him to a beer, but he would by no means let me treat him; he preferred that we should raffle [throw dice?] for a drink.)
>
> Hvernig *fílardhu?* (How do you feel?)
>
> *Rétt* eftir adh vidh höfdhum *krossadh rifurinn* komum vidh á *dípóidh* og fórum út úr *karinu*. (Right after we had crossed the river we came to the depot and left the car.)
>
> *Bae djísos*, thú ert *rangur*. (By Jesus, you are wrong.)
>
> Mig *vantar* ekki ad láta *fúla* mig sona. (I don't want to be fooled like that.)[1]

The Icelanders sometimes borrow the sense of English loan-words which resemble Icelandic words of quite different meaning. For example, in the phrase "adh ganga *brotinn* á *gemlingshús*" (to go broke in a gambling-house), *brotinn* is an Icelandic word which always means broken, not broke, and *gemlings* is the genitive of the Icelandic noun *gemlingur*, meaning a yearling sheep. Similarly, the English verb *to beat*, which has been generally taken in, collides with the Icelandic verb *bíta* (to bite). Dr. Einarsson tells me

---

[1] These are mainly from Frá Ameríka, a lecture by Jón Ólafsson, delivered at Reykjavík in 1897 and printed in *Sunnanfari*, Vol. VII, 1898, p. 1 *ff*. For the reference and the translations I am indebted to the great courtesy of Dr. Einarsson.

that there have been a number of discussions of Vestur-íslenska in *Heimskringla* and *Lögberg*, the Icelandic weeklies published at Winnipeg. It has also been put to literary use by the Icelandic American novelist, J. M. Bjarnason,[1] and by Kristján N. Júlíus, " the Icelandic Bobby Burns." [2] The first Icelanders to come to the United States settled in Utah in 1855. The Census of 1930 showed 7413 persons of Icelandic stock in the country — 2768 born in Iceland, 3177 born here of Icelandic parentage, and the rest born here of partly Icelandic parentage. There are many more across the Canadian border, especially in Manitoba. The American Icelanders print no periodicals, but at Winnipeg, in addition to the two weeklies that I have mentioned, there are various other publications.

f. Yiddish

Yiddish, though it is spoken by Jews, and shows a high admixture of Hebrew,[3] and is written in Hebrew characters, is basically a Middle High German dialect, greatly corrupted, not only by Hebrew, but also by Russian, Polish, Lithuanian, Hungarian, and, in the United States, English. At the Census of 1930, 1,222,658 Jews gave Yiddish as their mother-tongue; in all probability another million could then speak it, or, at all events, understand it. Since the cutting off of immigration from Eastern Europe it has been declining, and there are many Jews who view it hostilely as a barbaric jargon, and hope to see it extirpated altogether; nevertheless, there are still thirty-seven Yiddish periodicals in the country, including twelve daily newspapers, and one of the latter, the Jewish *Daily Forward* of New York, had a circulation of nearly 125,000 in 1935.

The impact of American-English upon Yiddish has been tre-

[1] Bess-bréf, *Heimskringla*, 1893–4.
[2] Kvidhlingar; Winnipeg, 1920.
[3] Isaac A. Millner, in *What is Yiddish?*, *East and West*, April 20, 1923, says that 20% of the Yiddish vocabulary is Hebrew. This part includes some very important elements, classified by Mr. Millner as follows: (*a*) words that refer to the Jewish religion, *e.g.*, *kosher*; (*b*) words that stand in some relation to it, *e.g.*, *chedar*; (*c*) words that have to do with elementary education, *e.g.*, *cheshbon* (arithmetic); (*d*) generic words, *e.g.*, *chaye* (living being); (*e*) words signifying phenomena that " are clothed by the popular consciousness with a superstitious glamour," *e.g.*, *kadoches* (fever); (*f*) words referring to birth, marriage and death, *e.g.*, *levaya* (funeral); and (*g*) terms of opprobrium or approbation, *e.g.*, *bal-zedoko* (charitable person).

mendous; in fact, it has been sufficient to create two Yiddishes. " The one," says Dr. Ch. Zhitlowsky, " is the wild-growing Yiddish-English jargon, the potato-chicken-kitchen language; the other is the cultivated language of Yiddish culture all over the world." [1] But though Dr. Zhitlowsky and his fellow Yiddishists may rail against that potato-chicken-kitchen language, it is the Yiddish of the overwhelming majority of American Jews. In it such typical Americanisms as *sky-scraper, loan-shark, graft, bluffer, faker, boodler, gangster, crook, guy, kike, piker, squealer, bum, cadet, boom, bunch, pants, vest, loafer, jumper, stoop, saleslady, ice-box* and *raise* are quite as good Yiddish as they are American. For all the objects and acts of everyday life the Jews commonly use English terms, e.g., *boy, chair, window, carpet, floor, dress, hat, watch, ceiling, consumption, property, trouble, bother, match, change, party, birthday, picture, paper* (only in the sense of newspaper), *gambler, show, hall, kitchen, store, bedroom, key, mantelpiece, closet, lounge, broom, table-cloth, paint, landlord, fellow, tenant, bargain, sale, haircut, razor, basket, school, scholar, teacher, baby, mustache, butcher, grocery, dinner, street* and *walk*. In the factories there is the same universal use of *shop, wages, foreman, boss, sleeve, collar, cuff, button, cotton, thimble, needle, machine, pocket, remnant, piece-work, sample*, etc. Many of these words have quite crowded out the corresponding Yiddish terms, so that the latter are seldom heard. For example, *ingle*, meaning *boy* (Ger. *jungel*, a diminutive of *junge*, a boy), has been wholly obliterated by the English word. A Yiddish-speaking Jew almost invariably refers to his son as his *boy*, though strangely enough he calls his daughter his *meidel*. " Die *boys* mit die *meidlach* haben a good time " is excellent American Yiddish. In the same way *fenster* has been completely displaced by *window*, though *tür* (door) has been left intact. *Tisch* (table) also remains, but *chair* is always used, probably because few of the Jews had chairs in the Old Country. There the *beinkel*, a bench without a back, was in use; chairs were only for the well-to-do. *Floor* has apparently prevailed because no invariable corresponding word was employed at home: in various parts of Russia and Poland a floor is a *dill*, a *podlogé*, or a *bricke*. So with *ceiling*. There were six different words for it.

1 Quoted by George Wolfe in Notes on American Yiddish, *American Mercury*, Aug., 1933, p. 478.

Yiddish inflections have been fastened upon most of these loan-words. Thus, " Er hat ihm *abgefaked* " is " He cheated him," *zubunt* is the American *gone to the bad, fix'n* is *to fix, usen* is *to use,* and so on. The feminine and diminutive suffix *-ké* is often added to nouns. Thus *bluffer* gives rise to *blufferké* (hypocrite), and one also notes *dresské, hatké, watchké* and *bummerké.* " Oi! is sie a *blufferké!* " is good American Yiddish for " Isn't she a hypocrite! " The suffix *-nick,* signifying agency, is also freely applied. *Allrightnick* means an upstart, an offensive boaster, one of whom his fellows would say " He is all right " with a sneer. Similarly, *consumptionick* means a victim of tuberculosis. Other suffixes are *-chick* and *-ige,* the first exemplified in *boychick,* a diminutive of *boy,* and the second in *next-doorige,* meaning the woman next door, an important person in Jewish social life. Some of the loan-words, of course, undergo changes on Yiddish-speaking lips. Thus *landlord* becomes *lendler, certificate* becomes *stiff-ticket, lounge* becomes *lunch, tenant* becomes *tenner,* and *whiskers* loses its final *s.* " Wie gefällt dir sein *whisker?* " (How do you like his beard?) is good Yiddish, ironically intended. *Fellow,* of course, changes to the American *fella,* as in " Rosie hat schon a *fella* " (Rosie has got a *fella, i.e.,* a sweetheart). *Show,* in the sense of *chance,* is used constantly, as in " Git ihm a *show* " (Give him a *chance*). *Bad boy* is adopted *bodily,* as in " Er is a *bad boy.*" *To shut up* is inflected as one word, as in " Er hat nit gewolt *shutup'n* " (He wouldn't shut up). *To catch* is used in the sense of to obtain, as in *catch'n a gmilath chesed* (to raise a loan). Here, by the way, *gmilath chesed* is excellent Biblical Hebrew. *To bluff,* unchanged in form, takes on the new meaning of to lie: a *bluffer* is a liar. Scores of American phrases are in constant use, among them, *all right, never mind, I bet you, no sir* and *I'll fix you.* It is curious to note that *sure Mike,* borrowed by the American vulgate from Irish-English, has also gone over into American-Yiddish. Finally, to make an end, here are two complete American-Yiddish sentences: " Sie wet *clean'n* die *rooms, scrub'n* dem *floor, wash'n* die *windows, dress'n* dem *boy* und gehn in *butcher-store* und in *grocery.* Dernoch vet sie machen *dinner* und gehn in *street* für a *walk.*" [1]

For some time past there has been a movement among the New York Jews for the purification of Yiddish, and it has resulted in the

[1] I am indebted throughout this section to Mr. Abraham Cahan, editor of the leading Yiddish daily in New York, and a distinguished writer in both Yiddish and English.

establishment of a number of Yiddish schools. Its adherents do not propose, of course, that English be abandoned, but simply that the two languages be kept separate, and that Jewish children be taught Yiddish as well as English. The Yiddishists insist that it is more dignified to say *a gooten tog* than *good-bye*, and *billet* instead of *ticket*. But the movement makes very poor progress. " The Americanisms absorbed by the Yiddish of this country," says Abraham Cahan, " have come to stay. To hear one say ' Ich hob a *billet* für heitige vorschtellung' would be as jarring to the average East Side woman, no matter how illiterate and ignorant she might be, as the intrusion of a bit of Chinese in her daily speech." Yiddish, as everyone knows, has produced a very extensive literature during the past two generations; it is, indeed, so large and so important that I can do no more than refer to it here.[1] Much of it has come from Jewish authors living in New York. In their work, and particularly their work for the stage, there is extensive and brilliant evidence of the extent to which American-English has influenced the language.[2]

2. LATIN

a. French

Ever since the close of the Eighteenth Century patriotic French-Canadians have been voicing fears that the French language would be obliterated from their country, soon or late, by the growth of English, but so far it has not happened. At the present moment probably 25% of all the Canadians continue to speak French and to think of it as their mother-tongue, though most of them, of course, also speak more or less English. But the French they speak is by no means that of Paris. Dr. E. C. Hills, who spent five Summers in a French-speaking community near Montreal, studying the local speechways, came away convinced that " a Parisian would not understand the common language of the district." [3] It differs considerably from place to place, but all over Canada it is heavily shot with English,

1 See the article on Yiddish, by Nathaniel Buchwald, in the Cambridge History of American Literature, Vol. IV, p. 598, and the bibliography following, p. 822 *ff*, and also Curiosities of Yiddish Literature, by A. A. Roback; New York, 1933.

2 See Notes on Yiddish, by H. B. Wells, *American Speech*, Oct., 1928, p. 63 *ff*.

3 *Language*, March, 1928, p. 43.

and especially with American. "The effect of English on the French," says A. Marshall Elliott,[1] "has been immeasurably greater than that of French on the English. . . . The French has made use of all the productive means — suffixes, prefixes — at its disposal to incorporate the English vocables in its word-supply . . . and to adapt them by a skilful use of the inflectional apparatus to all the requirements of a rigid grammatical system." On one page of N. E. Dionne's "Le Parler Populaire des Canadiens Français"[2] I find *barkeeper, bargaine, barroom, bullseye, buckwheat, buggy, buckboard, bugle, bully, bum, business* and *bus* — most of them, it will be observed, American rather than English, and one of them, *bum*, an American loan from the German. In Sylva Chapin's "Dictionnaire Canadien-Français"[3] are many more, *e.g., lager* (another German loan), *overalls, cracker, gerrymander, baseball, blizzard, blue-nose, bluff, boodle* (from the Dutch originally), *boss* (also from the Dutch), *brakeman, cocktail, C.O.D., cowboy, greenback, johnny-cake, peanut, sleigh* (a third Dutch loan), *squatter, teetotaler, township* and *trolley*. A larger number have been Gallicized, *e.g., boodlage* (boodle), *boodleur* (boodler), *conducteur, lyncher* (to lynch), *élévateur* and *engin* (locomotive), and some appear in two forms, *e.g., bum* and *bommeur*, which have produced the verb *bommer*, and *loafer* and *lôfeur*, which have produced the verb *lôfer*. Here are some quotations from current Canadian-French newspapers: "sur le *scrîne*" (screen), "les effets du *vacouomme-clîneaur*," "Le *typewriter* empêche d'embrouiller les textes," "Les Goglus sont *wise*" (a headline), and "*Hold-up* de M. Houde" (another).[4] Louvigny de Montigny, in "La Langue Française au Canada"[5] complains bitterly that American words and phrases are driving out French words and phrases, even when the latter are quite as clear and convenient. Thus, *un patron*, throughout French Canada, is now *un boss, petrole* is *l'huile de charbon* (coal-oil), *une bonne à tout faire* is *une servante générale*, and *un article d'occasion* is *un article de seconde main!* "*Vous regardez bien, Monsieur*," which means "Your eyesight is good," or "You look in the right direction" in Standard French, means "You are looking well"

1 Speech Mixture in French Canada, *American Journal of Philology*, Vol. X, No. 2, 1889, p. 143.
2 Quebec, 1909. This work is a lexicon running to 671 pp.
3 Montreal, 1894.
4 For these I am indebted to Lieut. Col. E. L. M. Burns of Ottawa.
5 Ottawa, 1916, p. 22.

in Canadian-French. The latter is full of French dialect words inherited from the early settlers, and unknown in Standard French, *e.g.*, the Norman verbs *chouler* (to tease a dog), *fafiner* (to hesitate) and *jaspiner* (to gossip). The influence of the dialects is also responsible for numerous differences in grammatical gender between the two languages, *e.g.*, *hôtel, examen, arc* and *éclair*, which are masculine in Standard French, are feminine in Canada, and *garantie* and *écritoire*, which are feminine in Standard French, are masculine. It has also produced some peculiarities in phonology, *e.g.*, *a* for *elle*, *i* for *il, ils, lui* and *y*, *ah* for *e*, *aw* for *ah*, and *dz* for *d*. The final *d, r, s* and *t* are often sounded where they are now mute in Standard French.[1]

" Two varieties of French, different yet closely related," says Dr. William A. Read of Louisiana State University, " are spoken in Louisiana. The first variety is represented by a dialect which is not far removed from Standard French in syntax, vocabulary and pronunciation. This is the speech of most Creoles and of many cultivated Acadians. Naturally, some new words are used and various old words have acquired senses unknown in Standard French." [2] The Acadians (Cajuns), who are descendants of the French colonists expelled from Nova Scotia by the English in 1755, speak a dialect brought from their former home and showing kinship with

1 Dominion French Discovered, New York *Sun*, June 30, 1927. The literature of Canadian French, by native philologians, is extensive. There is a bibliography of it, down to 1908, in A Study of an Acadian-French Dialect Spoken on the North Shore of the Baie-des-Chaleurs, by James Geddes, Jr., Halle, 1908, and there are many references to later writings in the appendix to Louvigny de Montigny's La langue française au Canada, above cited. A Société du Parler Français au Canada was founded at Quebec in 1902 under the auspices of Laval University, and on June 29, 1912 the first Congrés de la Langue Française au Canada was held at Quebec. Its proceedings were published the same year. See also Dialect Research in Canada, by A. F. Chamberlain, *Dialect Notes*, Vol. I, Pt. II, 1890, which contains a bibliog-

raphy running to 1890. The earliest American writer on the subject was the late Dr. A. Marshall Elliott (1844–1910), professor of Romance languages at the Johns Hopkins University, and founder of the Modern Language Association (1883) and *Modern Language Notes* (1886). His pioneer paper, Contributions to a History of the French Language in Canada appeared in the *American Journal of Philology*, Vol. VI, Pt. II, 1885. He followed it with four papers on Speech Mixture in French Canada in the same journal, Vol. VII, Pt. II, 1886; Vol. VIII, Pts. II and III, 1887; and Vol. X, Pt. II, 1889.
2 Louisiana-French, *Louisiana State University Studies*, No. 5, 1931. This is a work of 253 pages, and is full of valuable material, especially on loan-words.

the dialects of the North, West and Center of France. There is yet a third variety of Louisiana-French. It is the Nègre spoken by the Negroes, or, as they often call it, Congo or Gumbo — a vulgate based on the speech of the white Creoles, but much debased.[1] It is, says Dr. George S. Lane of the Catholic University, " the usual speech not only between Negroes, but also between white and Negro. In fact, few Negroes understand Standard French, hardly any speak it. Negro-French . . . is often the only type of French known to the children, especially to those under fifteen years of age." [2] It is composed, says Dr. Read, " of a highly corrupt French vocabulary, some native African words, and a syntax for the most part essentially African." He gives the following specimen of it:

> Lendenmain matin Médo di moin,
> Mo chien apé mégri.
> Dépi milat-là rentré dans la cou-là,
> Ye na pi des os pu chats.

There is a large literature of this Gumbo-French, chiefly in the form of songs, and readers of Lafcadio Hearn, George W. Cable, Kate Chopin and Grace Elizabeth King will recall it. The written literature of the educated Creoles, now fading out in the face of the advance of English, was wholly in Standard French. Rather curiously, most of it was produced, not during the days of French rule, but after the American occupation in 1803. " It was not until after the War of 1812," says a recent historian,[3] " that letters really flourished in French Louisiana. The contentment and prosperity that filled the forty years between 1820 and 1860 encouraged the growth of a vigorous and in some respects a native literature, comprising plays, novels, and poems." The chief dramatists of the period were Placide Canonge, A. Lussan, Oscar Dugué, Le Blanc de Filleneufve, P. Pérennes and Charles Testut; today all their works are dead, and they themselves are but names. Testut was also a poet and novelist; other novelists were Canonge, Alfred Mercier, Alexandre Barde, Adrien Rouquette, Jacques de Roquigny and Charles Lemaître. The principal poets were Dominique Rouquette, Tullius Saint-Céran, Constant Lepouzé, Felix de Courmont, Alexandre Latil, A. Lussan

1 An account of it is in Louisiana Gumbo, by Edward Laroque Tinker, *Yale Review*, Spring, 1932.
2 Notes on Louisiana-French, *Language*, Dec., 1934.
3 Edward J. Fortier, in the Cambridge History of American Literature; New York, 1921, Vol. IV, p. 591. A bibliography is appended, p. 820 *ff*.

and Armand Lanusse. But the most competent of all the Creole authors was Charles E. A. Gayerré (1805–95), who was at once historian, dramatist and novelist. Today the Creole literature is only a memory. " The time will inevitably come," says Dr. Read, " when French will no longer be spoken in Louisiana; for Creoles and Acadians alike are prone to discard their mother-tongue, largely because they are compelled in their youth to acquire English in the public-schools of the State." Even in St. Martinville, *le petit Paris*, says Dr. Lane, " most native residents between twenty-five and forty, while able to speak French, use it only among close associates or in addressing older people. Few under twenty-five make use of it at all, though they understand it readily and are able to speak it. Today, one hears ordinarily on the street either bad English or the Negro-French dialect spoken by white and black alike." [1]

b. Italian

Rémy de Gourmont, the French critic, was the first to call attention to the picturesque qualities of the Americanized Italian spoken by Italian immigrants to the United States. This was in 1899.[2] Nineteen years later Dr. Arthur Livingston, of the Italian department of Columbia University, published an instructive and amusing study of it, under the title of " La Merica Sanemagogna " (The American Son-of-a-Gun), in the *Romanic Review* (New York).[3] Since then it has attracted other scholars in the United States, and a growing literature deals with it; [4] in addition, it is not infrequently discussed in the books which Italian visitors write about their adventures and observations in this country.[5] Finally, it has produced some interest-

1 There is a bibliography of Louisiana-French in Dr. Read's monograph, above cited, and another in The Survival of French in the Old District of Sainte Genevieve [Missouri], by W. A. Dorrance, *University of Missouri Studies*, Vol. X, No. 2, 1935.

2 L'Esthétique de la langue Française; Paris, 1899.

3 Vol. IX, No. 2, April–June, 1918, p. 206 *ff.*

4 Of especial value are two articles on Italian Dialects in the United States, by Herbert H. Vaughn, professor of Italian at the University of California, *American Speech*, May and October, 1926; Piedmontese Dialects in the United States, by A. G. Zallio of Sacramento Junior College, *American Speech*, Sept., 1927; and The Speech of Little Italy, by Anthony M. Turano, an Italian-American lawyer of Reno, Nev., *American Mercury*, July, 1932.

5 For example, Un Italiano in America, by Adolfo Rossi; Treviso,

ing writing of its own, ranging from such eloquent pieces as Giovanni Pascoli's "Italy"[1] to the Rabelaisian buffooneries of Carlo Ferrazzano. Ferrazzano, who died in 1926, wrote many *macchiette coloniali* for the cheap Italian theaters of New York. The *macchietta coloniale* was an Americanized variety of the Neapolitan *macchietta*, which Dr. Livingston describes as "a character-sketch — etymologically, a character-' daub ' — most often constructed on rigorous canons of ' ingenuity ': there must be a literal meaning, accompanied by a double sense, which, in the nature of the tradition, inclines to be pornographic." The *macchietta* was brought to New York by Edoardo Migliaacio (Farfariello),[2] purged of its purely Neapolitan materials, and so adapted to the comprehension of Italians from other parts of Italy. For nearly a generation it was the delight of the Italians of New York, but in late years it has gradually succumbed to the decline in Italian immigration and the competition of the movies and talkies. Farfariello wrote fully five hundred *macchiette* and Ferrazzano probably as many more; some of the latter were printed. They were commonly in verse, with now and then a descent to prose. I take from Dr. Livingston's study a specimen of the latter:

Ne sera dentro na *barra* americana dove il patrone era americano, lo visco era americano, la birra era americana, ce steva na ghenga de *loffari* tutti americani; solo io non ero americano; quanno a tutto nu mumento me mettono mmezzo e me dicettono: *Alò spaghetti; iu mericano men?* No! no! *mi Italy men! lu blacco enze?* No, no! *lu laico chistu contri?* No, no! *Mi laìco mio contry! Mi laìco Italy!* A questa punto me chiavaieno lo primo *fait!* "Dice: *Orré for America!* " Io tuosto: *Orré for Italy!* Un ato *fait*. "Dice: *Orré for America!* " *Orré for Italy! N'ato fait e n' ato fait,* fino a che me facetteno addurmentare; ma però, *orré for America* nun o dicette!

Quanno me scietaie, me trovaie ncoppa lu marciepiedi cu nu *pulizio* vicino che diceva; *Ghiroppe bomma!* Io ancora stunato alluccaie: *America 'nun gudde! Orré for Italy!* Sapete li *pulizio* che facette? Mi arrestò!

Quanno fu la mattina, lu *giorge* mi dicette: *Wazzo maro laste naite?* Io

1907, and Incontro col Nord America, by Franco Ciarlantini; Milan, 1929. A translation of Signor Ciarlantini's chapter, The Italian Language in the United States, was published in *Atlantica* (New York), March, 1930, p. 15.

1 It is to be found in his Poesie, Vol. II; Bologna, 1897; 5th ed., 1912. There is an account of it in La Merica Sanemagogna, by Dr. Livingston, who says that it was inspired by Pascoli's "contact with Italian emigrants returning to the Tuscan hills." It is also described and discussed in Italienisch-Amerikanisches, by Walther Fischer, *Neuere Sprachen*, Sept., 1920, p. 164 ff.

2 Still alive in 1936, but long since retired.

risponette: *No tocche ngles!* "No? *Tenne dollari.*" E quello porco dello *giorge* nun scherzava, perchè le diece pezze se le pigliaie! . . .

The Americanisms here are obvious enough: *barra* for *bar*, *visco* for *whiskey*, *blacco enze* for *black-hand*, *laico* for *like*, *chistu* for *this*, *contri* for *country*, *fait* for *fight* (it is also used for *punch*, as in *chiaver nu fait*, give a punch, and *nato fait*, another punch), *loffari* for *loafers*, *ghiroppe* for *get up*, *bomma* for *bum*, *pulizio* for *police*, *nun gudde* for *no good*, *orré* for *hurray*, *giorge* for *judge*, *wazzo maro* for *what's the matter*, *laste* for *last*, *naite* for *night*, *toccho* for *talk*, *tenne* for *ten*, *dollari* for *dollars*. All of the surviving *macchiette coloniali* are heavy with such loan-words; one of them, Farfariello's " A lingua 'nglese," is devoted almost wholly to humorous attempts to represent English words and phrases as the more ignorant Italians of New York hear and employ them. There has also been some attempt to make use of American-Italian on higher literary levels. Pascoli's " Italy " I have mentioned. A satirical poem by Vincenzo Campora, entitled " Spaghetti House " and well known to most literate Italians in the United States, embodies *tomato sauce, luncheonette, drug-store* and other characteristic Americanisms.[1] Others appear in the following *sonetto* by Rosiña Vieni:

> Vennero i *bricchellieri* a cento a cento,
> tutta una *ghenga* coi calli alle mani
> per far la casa di quaranta piano (1)
> senza contare il *ruffo* e il *basamento*
>
> Adesso par che sfidi il firmamento
> a onore e gloria degli americani;
> ma chi pensa ai *grinoni*, ai paesani
> morti d'un colpo, senza sacramento?
> che val, se per disgrazia o per *mistecca*
> ti sfracelli la carne in fondo al *floro* —
> povero *ghinni*, disgraziato *dego?*
>
> Davanti a mezzo *ponte* di bistecca
> il *bosso* ghigna e mostra i denti d'oro:
> — chi è morto è morto . . . io vivo e me ne frego.[2]

Relatively few of the Italians who came to the United States during the great migration before the World War brought any genuine

1 It is to be found in *Columbus* (New York), March, 1935.
2 *Zarathustra* (New York), May 15, 1926, p. 24. To the text is appended a glossary, as follows: *bricchellieri corrisponde a bricklayers; ghenga,* gang; *ruffo,* roof; *basamento,* basements; *grinoni,* greenhorns; *mistecca,* mistake; *floro,* floor; *ghinni,* guinea; *dego,* dago; *ponte,* pound; *bosso,* boss.

command of Standard Italian with them. Those who had been to school at home had more or less acquaintance with it, but in the family circle and among their neighbors they spoke their local dialects, some of which were mutually unintelligible. In the main, the immigrants from a given section of Italy flocked together — New York, for example, got mostly Neapolitans and Sicilians, and the Pacific Coast a preponderance of Piedmontese and Genoese — but there was still a sufficient mixture to make intercommunication difficult. If all of the newcomers had been fluent in Standard Italian it would have served them, but not many had an adequate vocabulary of it, so resort was had to an amalgam of Standard Italian, the various Italian dialects, and the common English of the country, with the latter gradually prevailing. The result, says Mr. Anthony M. Turano, was " a jargon which may be called American-Italian, a dialect no less distinct from both English and Italian than any provincial dialect is distinct from the Italian language." [1] Mr. Turano believes that American loan-words now comprise " as much as one-fourth of the spoken language of Little Italy." He divides them into three categories, as follows:

1. "Words for which a true Italian equivalent is lacking or remote, because of the absence of absolute identity between the American thing or act and its Italian counterpart," *e.g., gliarda* (yard), *visco* (whiskey), *pichinicco* (picnic), *ais-crima* (ice-cream), *ghenga* (gang), *rodomastro* (road-master).
2. "Words whose Italian equivalents were generally unknown or unfamiliar to the immigrant before his arrival," *e.g., morgico* (mortgage), *lista* (lease), *bosso* (boss), *fensa* (fence).
3. "Words that win the honors of Italianization by the sheer force of their repetition by the American natives, despite the fact that the Italian language affords familiar and ample equivalents," *e.g., stritto* (street), *carro* (car), *gambolo* or *gambolino* (gambler), *loncio* (lunch), *cotto* (coat), *bucco* (book), *storo* (store), *checca* (cake), *loya* (lawyer), *trampo* (tramp).

Mr. Turano continues:

Once an American word has been borrowed, its transformation does not end with its first changes. It is drafted for full service and made to run through all the genders, tenses and declensions of Italian grammar, until it presents the very faintest image of its former self. Thus the word *fight*, which was first changed into *faiti*, can be seen in such unrecognizable forms as *faitare, faitato, faitava, faito, faitasse*, and many more.

Sometimes Italian and English words are combined in a grotesque manner. Thus, Dr. Livingston reports hearing *canabuldogga* in New

York, from the Italian *cane*, meaning a dog, and the English *bulldog*. A half-time barber, working only on Saturdays, is a *mezzo-barbiere*, a half-time bartender is a *mezzo-barritenne*, and presser's helpers are *sotto-pressatori*, *sotto* being the common Italian designation for inferiority. The Italians in New York use *andara a flabussce* as a verb meaning to die: it depends for its significance on the fact that the chief Italian cemetery is in Flatbush. Similarly, they have made a word, *temeniollo*, meaning a large glass of beer, out of *Tammany Hall*. Not infrequently a loan-word collides with a standard Italian word of quite different meaning. Thus, *cecca* (check) means magpie in Italian, *intrepido* (interpreter) means fearless, *beccharia* (bakery) means butcher-shop, *rendita* (rent) means income, *libreria* (library) means bookstore, *tronco* (trunk) means cut off, and *sciabola* (shovel) means saber.[1] " I was both puzzled and amused during my first week in America," says Mr. Turano, " when I heard a laborer say quite casually that his daily work involved the use of a *pico* and a *sciabola* — that is to say, a pick and a saber! " Among the Sicilians, *gaddina*, meaning a chicken, is a common euphemism for the borrowed *goddam*.[2] There are, of course, some differences in the loan-words in use in different parts of the United States. The Italians of the West are all familiar with *ranchio* (ranch) but it is seldom heard in the East; similarly, *livetta* (elevated) is hardly known in the West. Among the Neapolitans *d* and *t* in loan-words sometimes change to *r*, so that *city* becomes *siri*, *suri* or *zuri*, and *city hall* becomes *siriollo*. But the following forms, like most of the terms quoted above, are in general use: [3]

Nouns

abbordato (boarder)
ais-bocsa (ice-box)
apricotto, or abricotto (apricot)
auschieppe (housekeeper)
avvenuta (avenue)
baga (bag)
barna (barn)

barritenne, or barrista (bartender)
baschetta or baschetto (basket)
beca (baker)
billo (bill)
bisiniss, or besenisso (business)
blocco (block)
bloffo (bluff)

1 I take these from Un Italiano in America, by Adolfo Rossi; Treviso, 1907, pp. 85-88.
2 Italian and Its Dialects as Spoken in the United States, by Herbert H. Vaughan, *American Speech*, May, 1926, p. 433.
3 This list is based on one included in Mr. Vaughan's Italian and Its Dialects as Spoken in the United States, just cited, but there are additions from The Speech of Little Italy, by Mr. Turano, *American Mercury*, July, 1932, and Dr. Livingston's La Merica Sanemagogna. I have also made use of material kindly sent to me by Mr. Giuseppe Cautela.

bordo (board)
bocsa (box)
boncio (bunch)
boto, or bot (boat)
boya (boy)
briccoliere (bricklayer)
bucia, or buccia (butcher)
canna, or canno (can)
canneria (cannery)
carpentieri (carpenter)
carpeta, or carpetto (carpet)
cecca (check)
cestenotto (chestnut) [1]
cianza (chance)
colle (coal)
collettoro (collector)
conduttore (conductor)
coppo (cop)
costume (customer)
cupa, or cuppa (cup)
dicce, dic or indiccio (ditch)
docco, or doc (dock)
elevete, or alveto (elevator)
faitatore (prize-fighter)
falo (fellow)
farma (farm)
farmaioulo (farm-hand)
fattoria (factory)
ferri (ferry)
ferriboto (ferry-boat)
foremme (foreman)
fornitura (furniture)
frencofutte (frankfurter)
fruttistenne (fruitstand)
galone or gallone (gallon)
garrita (garret)
ghemma (game)
ghirla, or ghella (girl)
giobba (job)
gliarda, or jarda (yard)
globbo (club)

grignollo, or grignona (greenhorn)
grollo (grower)
grossiere (grocer)
grosseria, or grussaria (grocery)
guaffo, or guarfo (wharf)
gum, or gumma (chewing-gum)
kettola, or chettola (kettle)
licenza (license)
loffaro, or loffarone (loafer)
lotto (lot)
maccio (match)
marchetto (market)
mascina (machine)
moni (money)
morgico, or morgheggio (mortgage)
naffia (knife)
nursa, or nirsa (nurse)
olla (hall)
ovrecoto (overcoat)
pensila, or pensula (pencil)
penta (pint)
pepa (paper)
piccio (moving-picture)
pinotto (peanut)
pipa (pipe)
pipoli (people)
pondo, or ponte (pound)
pulizzimmo (policeman)
pullo (pull)
quarto (quart)
racchettiere (racketeer)
raida (ride)
riccemanne (rich man)
rivolvaro (revolver)
road (road)
saiduak (sidewalk)
saina (sign)
salone (saloon)
sanemagogna, or sanimagogna (son-of-a-gun) [2]
schira, or scurta (skirt)

[1] The plural is *cestenozzi*. That of *pinotto* (peanut) is *pinozzi*.

[2] Dr. Livingston borrows *sanemagogna* from a *macchietta* by Ferrazzone. Mr. Turano thinks that the form should be *sanimagogna*. He says: " The component parts of the word are obviously *s-animagogna*. The first is a contraction of *questa*, which becomes *sta* in frequent semi-standard usage, and *sa* or *ssa* in most of the Southern Italian dialects. The second part means soul, and the third designates an iron collar once worn by Italian criminals. The result is *this degraded soul, that villainous* or *criminal soul,* or something equally opprobrious. The same operation is applied to a stronger American

sciain (shine)
sciainatore (bootblack)
scio (show)
sciumecco (shoemaker)
sparagrassi (asparagus)
sprini, sprigni, or springi (springs)
stic, or stico (stick)
stima (steamer)
stimbotto (steamboat)
stim-sciabola (steam-shovel)
stocco (stock)
strappa (strap)

stringa (string)
sueta (sweater)
tacsa, tachise, or taxe (taxes)
tichetta (ticket)
ticia (teacher)
tonica (tonic)
tracca (track)
trobolo (trouble)
trocco (truck)
tub (tub)
uilbarro (wheelbarrow)

Adjectives

isi (easy)
ruffo, or roffo (rough)
sciur (sure)

sechenenze (second-hand)
smarto, or smatto (smart)
stinge (stingy)

Verbs

abbordare (to board)
draivare (to drive)
fixare, ficsare, or fichisare (to fix)

giumpare (to jump)
parcare (to park)
strappare (to strop a razor)

Phrases

aidonchea (I don't care)
aigatiu, or aigaccia (I got you)
airono (I don't know)
alrait, or orraite (all right)
bigu (be good)
dezzo (that's all)
godam (goddam)

gudbai (good-bye)
il forte gelato (the fourth of July)
lo cuntri (old country)
oke or oche (O.K.)
rongue, or roune (wrong way)
sciacchenze (shake hands)
uatsius (what's the use?)

Dr. Livingston says that the Italians in the United States resent *dago* and *wop*, but have become reconciled to *guinea*, which they spell *ghini* and use frequently in good-humored abuse, as in *grannissimo ghini*, a sort of euphemism for *fool*. He reports that a number of Americanisms have been taken back to Italy by returning immigrants, *e.g.*, *schidu* (skiddoo) and *bomma* (bum), " which have become Neapolitan ejaculations." *Briccoliere* (bricklayer) " circulates in Sicily." [1]

The Census of 1930 showed that there were 1,790,424 persons of Italian birth in the United States at that time, 2,306,015 who had been

phrase. The result is *sanimabiggia*, meaning this *gray-colored soul*. My father had a pet variant that he used in milder cases, to wit, *sanimapicciula*, meaning, in the Calabrian dialect, *this small soul*." (Private communication, Jan. 29, 1935.)

1 In addition to the authors and correspondents already mentioned, I am indebted to Miss Adelina Rinaldi, business manager of *Atlantica* (New York), and to Mr. Giovanni Schiavo, author of The Italians in America Before the Civil War.

born here of Italian parentage, and 450,438 who had been born here of partly Italian parentage, or, 4,546,877 in all. Save for the Germans, they constituted the largest racial *bloc* in the country, and they exceeded the Germans in the number of individuals actually born in their country of origin. Of them, 1,808,289 reported that Italian was their mother-tongue. The Italian periodicals published in the United States number 113, of which eight are daily newspapers.

c. Spanish

The changes undergone by Spanish in the New World have been studied at length by Spanish-American philologians, and their numerous monographs on Cubanisms, Mexicanisms, Argentinisms, Chileanisms, Honduranisms and so on put to shame the neglect of the American vulgate by their American colleagues. Even the Spanish spoken in the Southwestern United States has been investigated scientifically, chiefly by Dr. Aurelio M. Espinosa, of Leland Stanford University. Dr. Espinosa's papers on the subject have been printed in both English and Spanish. In English he published a series of " Studies in New Mexican Spanish " in the *Revue de Dialectologie Romane* from 1909 to 1914,[1] and in Spanish he has brought out an elaborate study of New Mexican phonology in the Biblioteca de Dialectología Hispanoamericana edited by the Instituto de Filología of the University of Buenos Aires,[2] and a number of smaller studies.[3]

The New Mexican speech area investigated by Dr. Espinosa runs from El Paso in the south to beyond Pueblo, Colo., in the north, and

[1] His first, devoted to phonology, appeared in 1909; his second, dealing with morphology, in 1911, 1912 and 1913; and his third, discussing the English elements in the dialect, in 1914.
[2] Buenos Aires, 1930.
[3] They include Cuentitos Populares Nuevmejicanos y su Transcripción Fonética, *Bulletin de Dialectologie Romane*, Dec., 1912; Nombres de Bautismo Nuevomejicanos, *Revue de Dialectologie Romane*, Dec., 1913; Palabras Españolas e Inglesas, *Hispania*, Oct., 1922; and Aountaciones para un Diccionario de Nuevomejicanismos, in Homenaje a Bonilla y San Martin, Vol. II; Madrid, 1930. His publications in English include The Spanish Language in New Mexico and Southern Colorado, *Publications of the Historical Society of New Mexico*, May, 1911; Speech-Mixture in New Mexico, in The Pacific Ocean in History, edited by H. M. Stephens and H. E. Botton; New York, 1917; Syllabic Consonants in New-Mexican Spanish, *Language*, Dec., 1925; The Language of the Cuentos Populares Españoles, *Language*, Sept., 1927, and June, 1928.

from near the Texas border in the east to beyond the Arizona border in the west. At the time he made his inquiry it had about 250,000 Spanish-speaking inhabitants — 175,000 in New Mexico, 50,000 in Colorado, and 25,000 in Arizona. Within this area the dialect spoken is generally uniform. In Southern Arizona, Southern California and the upper part of the Mexican State of Sonora there is another speech area, using a dialect somewhat closer to Standard Castilian than that of New Mexico. It has been studied by Dr. Anita C. Post, who took her doctorate at Stanford under Dr. Espinosa.[1] Both dialects show a great many resemblances to American-English. There is the same tendency toward the decay of grammatical niceties, the same hospitality to loan-words, the same leaning toward a picturesque vividness, and the same survival of words and phrases that have become archaic in the standard language. " It is a source of delight to the student of Spanish philology," says Dr. Espinosa in " Studies in New Mexican Spanish," " to hear daily from the mouths of New Mexicans such words as *agora, ansi, naidien, trujo, escrebir, adrede* " — all archaic Castilian forms, and corresponding exactly to the *fox-fire, homespun, andiron, ragamuffin, fall* (for autumn), *flapjack* and *cesspool* that are preserved in American. They are survivors, in the main, of the Castilian Spanish of the Fifteenth and Sixteenth Centuries, though some of them come from other Spanish dialects. Castilian itself has changed very much since that time, as Standard English has changed; it is probable, indeed, that a Castilian of the year 1525, coming back to life today, would understand a New Mexican far more readily than he would understand a Spaniard, just as an Englishman of 1630 would understand a Kentucky mountaineer more readily than he would understand a Londoner.

New Mexico has been in the possession of the United States since 1846, and so it is natural to find its Spanish corrupted by American influences, especially in the vocabulary. Of the 1400 words that Dr. Espinosa chooses for remark, 300 are English, 75 are Nahuatl, 10 come from the Indian languages of the Southwest, and 15 are of doubtful or unknown origin; the rest are pure Spanish, chiefly archaic. As in the case of the Pennsylvania Germans, the French Canadians and the Scandinavians of the Northwest, the Spanish-speaking people of New Mexico have borrowed the American names of all

1 Southern Arizona Spanish Phonology, *Bulletin of the University of Arizona*, Vol. V, No. 1, 1934.

objects of peculiarly American character, *e.g.*, *besbol* (baseball), *grimbaque* (greenback), *játqueque* (hot-cake), *sosa* (soda), *quiande* (candy), *fayaman* (fireman), *otemil* (oatmeal), *piquenic* (picnic), *lonchi* (lunch). Most of them have been modified to bring them into accord with Spanish speech-habits. For example, all explosive endings are toned down by suffixes, *e.g.*, *lonchi* for *lunch*. So with many *r*-endings, *e.g.*, *blofero* for *bluffer*. And sibilants at the beginning of words are shaded by prefixes, *e.g.*, *esteque* for *steak* and *espechi* for *speech*. Not only words have been taken in, but also many phrases, though most of the latter are converted into simple words, *e.g.*, *olraite* (all right), *jaitun* (hightoned), *jamachi* (how much), *sarape* (shut up), *enejau* (anyhow). This Southwestern Spanish, like Pennsylvania-German, Yankee-Dutch and Vestur-islanska, seems doomed to vanish soon or late. "For a generation at least," says Dr. Post, "the child of Spanish-American parentage has really been learning Spanish at school, rather than at home. The present generation is not saying *truje*, *vide*, *muncho*, as their grandparents did. The Spanish of the future may be more nearly correct, if it does not die out completely."

English, of course, has also influenced the Spanish of the Antilles and of the Canal Zone. "Porto Ricans are conscious of the fact," says Salvador Rovira,[1] " that their Spanish has been debased with English idiom, and that it is rapidly becoming mongrel." In the large Puerto Rican colony in New York a large number of American loan-words are in everyday use, *e.g.*, *champu* (shampoo), *dresin* (dressing), *chopas* (chops), *cornfleques* (cornflakes), *ribsteque* (rib-steak), *chainaría* (shoe-shining stand), *corna* (corner of a street), *cuora* (quarter of a dollar), *fanfurria* (frankfurter), *bildin* (building), *cuilto* (quilt), *ticha* (teacher), *estor* (store), *marqueta* (market), *caucho* (couch), *lanlor* (landlord), *lanlora* (landlady), *boso* (boss), *meibi* (maybe).[2] From Panama comes news of *nacao* (knockout), *estrei* (straight), *managual* (man o' war), *guachiman* (watchman).[3] The people of each and every one of the Latin-American countries pride themselves on the purity of their Spanish, but the truth is, of course, that all of them speak dialects more or less marked, and use large numbers of words unknown to Standard Castilian.[4] The late

1 Bilingual Porto Rico, *Fleur de Lis* (St. Louis University), Dec., 1931.
2 I am indebted here to Mr. Hugh Morrison.
3 Tradiciones y Cantares de Panamá, by Narcisco Garay; Brussels, 1933.
4 I have mentioned the numerous studies of these dialects by native

Dr. A. Z. López-Penha, the Colombian poet and critic, once made up for me (1922) a list of American loans in common use in the Latin-American seaports: it included *cocktail, dinner-dance, fox-trot, sweater, kimono, high-ball, sundae, bombo* (boom), *plataforma* (platform, political), *mitin* (meeting), *alarmista, big-stick* and various forms of *bluff* (usually *blofero,* but *blofista* in Cuba). The American *auto* has been naturalized, and so has *ice-cream,* but in the form of *milk-cream,* pronounced *milclee* by the lower orders. The boss of a train is the *conductor del tren;* a commuter is a *commutador; switch* is used both in its American railroad sense and to indicate the electrical device; *slip, dock* and *wharf* (*guáfay*) are in daily use; so is *socket* (electrical), though it is pronounced *sokáytay;* so are *poker* and many of the terms appertaining to the game. The South Americans often use *just* in the American way, as in *justamente a* (or *en*) *tiempo* (just in time). They are very fond of *good-bye, dam-fool* and *go to hell.* They have translated the verb phrase, *to water stocks,* into *aguar las acciones.* In Cuba the *watermelon* (*patilla* or *sandía,* in Spanish) is the *mélon-de-agua.* Just as French-Canadian has borrowed Americanisms that are loan-words from other immigrant tongues, *e.g., bum* and *loafer* from the German, so some of the South American dialects have borrowed *rapidas* (rapids) and *kimono,* the first brought into American from the French and the second from the Japanese. The Spanish borrowings from American are naturally most numerous just south of the Rio Grande, just as the American borrowings from Spanish are most numerous along its north bank. Says a recent explorer: [1]

> When a border Mexican goes out *chopeando* (shopping), and meets a friend on the street, he cordially shouts: " *Como le* how do you *dea?,*" to be reassured by the reply: " Oh, very-well-*eando, gracias a dios.*" Pausing, as is his

philologians. Some of them are listed in my 3rd ed., 1923, pp. 460–61. Others are listed in Espinosa's Estudios Sobre el Español de Neuvo Méjico; Buenos Aires, 1930, p. 24 ff. When Spanish talkies for the Latin-American trade were first made in Hollywood, the movie magnates employed a Spanish actor to supervise their diction, and he ordained that the precise Castilian of the Madrid stage be used. This brought a protest from the Mexican actors, who argued that their own Spanish was the purest on earth. The matter was finally left to the Spanish Royal Academy, and there ensued a row at Madrid, with the result that the actors and authors of fourteen Latin-American countries renounced the Academy's authority. See Those Sensitive Latin-Americans, by Arthur Constantine, New York *World,* July 13, 1930.

1 H. E. McKinstry, in The American Language in Mexico, *American Mercury,* March, 1930.

custom, to pass the time of day, he will borrow a *mecha* (the Spanish word for wick or fuse sounds like *match*, so why not use it?) to light his cigarette, and since he has just received his *time-check* will ask if there is a *chanza* to get a *chamba* (job).[1]

The Latin-Americans have taken over the vocabulary of American sport along with the games. " If you read *El Universal*, the *soi-disant* great daily of Mexico," says the explorer just quoted, " you will be apprised that at a *match de box* a gentleman named, as like as not, Battling Martinez, has received from one Kid Sanchez *un K.O.* as the result of an *upper cut* (pro. *ooper coot*) or a *left hook* ('*ook*). . . . Next morning you can play *tenis* and keep score in English terms provided you have learned to give them the correct Spanish accent; and if you watch a game of *beisbol* or *futbol* or *basket* you virtuously call a foul a *foul*. In the afternoon you may shoot a few rounds of *golfo*." " Of a Monday morning," says another observer,[2] " when all the Latin-American journals are heavy with week-end sporting news, one's eye is apt to be arrested by *el score* at *los links* of *el country club*. Some local cup-collector may be featured at some length. *Su pivot*, one learns, leaves nothing to be desired; he is *un swinger rapído*, too, and always makes *un espléndido drive*. With such a reputation, one can hardly feel surprised to read that he won yesterday's match *por walkover*."

The number of Spanish-speaking persons in the United States at the moment (1936) is hard to estimate. There were 1,422,533 Mexicans in 1930, of whom 805,535 had been born in this country and 616,998 in Mexico, but many of the latter have since returned home. At the same time the enumerators unearthed 58,302 natives of Spain, 52,774 of Puerto Rico, 47,699 of the Philippines and 2,834 of the Canal Zone. The natives of Cuba and Central and South America do not seem to have been listed. The Puerto Ricans were nearly all concentrated in New York, which had 45,973 of them, and the Filipinos in California. The Cubans live mainly in New York and Florida. There are Spanish daily newspapers in Tampa (2), New York (2), El Paso (2), Los Angeles, Laredo, Tex., and San Antonio.

1 See also A Dictionary of Spanish Terms in English, by Harold W. Bentley; New York, 1932, p. 5.

2 Richard F. O'Toole, in Sports Slang in Latin America, *American Mercury*, Nov., 1930.

d. Portuguese

So far as I have been able to discover, there is no discussion in print of the Portuguese spoken in the United States. I am informed, however, by Mr. João R. Rocha, editor of *O Independente* of New Bedford, Mass., the oldest Portuguese weekly in the country, and Mr. Peter L. C. Silveira, editor of the *Jornal Portugues* of Oakland, Calif., that it has been markedly modified by American influence. The grammatical changes are few, but there is a heavy borrowing of English words and not a few Portuguese words have been changed in meaning. Thus, the word *frizado*, which means curled up in Standard Portuguese, has come to mean frozen in America, and the word *cigarro*, which means a cigarette in Standard Portuguese, means a cigar here. Again, the Portuguese immigrants have abandoned *remédios*, the Standard Portuguese word for medicines, in favor of *medicinas*, and have changed the meaning of *colégio* from a private grammar or secondary school to what we call a college.[1] In the case of *high-school*, they have produced a translated form, *escola alta*. From the phrase *to park a car* they have derived a verb, *parcar*, and use it in place of the Standard Portuguese *arrumar* or *estacionar*. Virtually all of the other verbs that they have borrowed have been given the Portuguese verbal termination *-ar*, *e.g.*, *drivar* (to drive), *feeda* (to feed), *treatar* (to treat), *ablievar* (to believe), *tirear* (to ride), *pinchar* (to pitch), *savar* (to save), *crackar* (to crack), *pumpear* (to pump). A number of nouns are also given Portuguese terminations, *e.g.*, *feeda* (feed), *mecha* (match), *rancho* (ranch, thus showing a return to the original Spanish form), *raça* (race), *pana* (pan), *córa* (quarter of a dollar), and *passe-presidente* (past-president). But loan-nouns are often used unchanged, as in " Vou falar com a meu *lawyer* por causa do *case* que tenho na *court* ". (I am going to talk with my lawyer about the case I have in court). In the case of nouns that are identical in Portuguese and English, *e.g.*, *conductor* and *inspector*, the Portuguese pronunciation is abandoned for the English. In the use of loan-words English idioms are often borrowed, *e.g.*, *não e das suas business* (none of your business), *fazar um speech* (to make a speech), *isso faz o spoil* (that spoils it), *está*

1 These notes were kindly made by Mr. A. S. Branco, secretary-general of the União Portuguesa Conti- nental dos Estados Unidos da America, and forwarded to me through Mr. Rocha.

alright (it's all right), *é fine* (it's fine). The Portuguese spoken in Brazil is also full of loans from English, *e.g.*, *aristú* (Irish stew), *buldogue* (bulldog), *sulipa* (slipper, and also sleeper, a railroad tie), *arceboque* (a boxcar for horses), *liderança* (leader), *araruta* (arrow-root). The Brazilians of the nether classes use *godeme* (God-damn) to signify a blow; they confused the exclamations of the fighting English sailors on the docks with their actual wallops. They use *bonde* to signify a street-car, for when the first line was established at Rio de Janeiro it was financed by the sale of bonds, and the operating company came to be known as the *companhia dos bonds*. In Portugal a street-car is called an *americano*.[1]

The Census of 1930 revealed 167,891 persons of Portuguese blood in the United States — 69,974 foreign-born and the rest born here of Portuguese or mixed parentage. Of this number, 110,197 gave Portuguese as their mother-tongue. There are thirteen Portuguese publications in the country, including a daily, the *Diario de Noricias*, at New Bedford, Mass., where the largest Portuguese colony is located.

e. Rumanian

The Rumanians constitute one of the smaller ethnic stocks in the United States. In 1930 the number of persons so classified by the Census Bureau was 293,453, of whom 146,393 had been born in Rumania, 125,479 had been born here of Rumanian parents, and 21,581 had been born here of mixed parentage. But of the 146,393 of Rumanian birth, but 53,452 reported that Rumanian was their mother-tongue. The rest spoke Yiddish (49,508), German (28,640), Hungarian (8,830) or some other language (5,963). The Rumanians proper have three periodicals in this country, of which one, the *America, Roumanian*[2] *News* of Cleveland, formerly a daily, now appears three times a week. Its former editor, Mr. George Stanculescu, informs me that American-Rumanian shows the characters of all the other immigrant languages. It has borrowed a large number of common nouns, especially those representing objects and concepts

1 I am indebted here to Mr. Arthur R. Coelho of New York, a native of Brazil.
2 I have followed the United States Geographic Board in omitting the *o* in Rumania, but the *America,* *Roumanian News* retains it. (The name of the journal is as I give it.) The Rumanians pronounce *Rumania* with the first syllable rhyming with *home*. They spell it *Romănia*.

unknown in Rumania, *e.g.*, *baseball-score*, *strike-breaker*, *lockout*, *picketing*, *golf-links*, *surprise-party*, *football-match*, *shower-party*. Sometimes they are taken in unchanged, but more often they are brought into harmony with Rumanian analogues, *e.g.*, *convenţie* (convention), *vilbără* (wheelbarrow), *grocerie* (grocery), *butcherie* (butcher-shop), *bort* (boarding-house), *saloner* (saloon-keeper), *platformă* (platform in the political sense), *poipuri* (pipes), *matchuri* (matches). The loan-verbs are inflected in the Rumanian manner, *e.g.*, *Te fixuluesc* (I'll fix you), *Am betuit* (I have made a bet), *Se resăluesc* (They are wrestling), *se matchue* (things matching one another), *L'au kidnăpuit* (They have kidnaped him), *Vrea să mă foolooe* (He wants to fool me), *Nu mă bădărui* (Don't bother me). There is a strong tendency to abandon Rumanian idioms for translated English idioms. Says Mr. Stanculescu:

A correct translation of the English sentence, " You look well in that hat " would be " Iţi stă bine cu pălăria acesta." But very often a Roumanian-American borrows the English word *look* and substitutes *în* (*in*) for *cu* (*with*), making the sentence " Arăţi bine în pălăria-acesta." Similarly " Pari obosit " (You look tired) is translated as " Arăţi obosit." The English word *for* is *pentru* in Roumanian, but it cannot be so used in all sentence constructions. Thus *Books for sale* should be *Cărţi de vânzare*. But the Americanized expression is *Cărţi pentru vânzare*, obviously under the influence of the English *for*.

In Roumanian any reflective action concerning one's bodily organs is done upon the agent. Thus, *I wash my hands, my face*, etc., should be expressed as *Mă spăl pe mâni, pe faţă*, etc. (literally, *I wash myself the hands, the face*, etc.). But the construction in America, following English example, is *Îmi spăl mânile, fata*, etc. *Mă tund* is the Roumanian for *I cut my hair*, but in America one says *Îmi tai părul*. *Mă piepten* is the correct Roumanian for *I comb my hair*, but the Americanized form is *Îmi piepten părul*.

The Roumanian dative is on its way to extinction in America. For " Give this letter to my brother " one should say " Dă scrisoarea această fratelui meu," but in most cases the Roumanian-Americans make it " Dă această scrisoare la fratele meu." Besides changing the word order by placing *această* (this) before the noun *scrisoare* (letter), they also adhere to the English preposition *to* (la), which in Roumanian denotes a movement toward the brother without ever touching him.

The Rumanian in the United States, especially if he be of small education, finds English very difficult, for there are usages in English which have no parallel in Rumanian. The latter, for example, makes no distinction between *may* and *can* or *will* and *shall*. *There is* and *there are* at the beginnings of sentences offer another difficulty, for there are no equivalents in Rumanian. There is also confusion in gender, for Rumanian has grammatical gender, and no *it* is in its vocabulary. As in many other languages, an action begun in the past but continued in the present is expressed by a verb in the present tense. Thus, the Rumanian immigrant commonly says *"I am in America ten years* instead of I *have been* in America ten years. He finds the sounds of *th, sh, ch, ph* and *gh* very strange, and often mispronounces them. Thus one hears *tis* for *this, tot* for *that, wort* for *worth, troot* for *truth, skarp* for *sharp, skort* for *short, Kicago* for *Chicago, pkarmachy* for *pharmacy* and *enugkh* for *enough.*

3. SLAVIC

a. Czech

The Right Rev. J. B. Dudek, chancellor of the Catholic diocese of Oklahoma City and Tulsa, who was born in this country of Czech parents, has written an exhaustive study of the changes undergone by the Czech language in the United States, but unfortunately only parts of it have been published.[1] Through the courtesy of Monsignor Dudek, however, I have had access to his complete manuscript, and present herewith a brief summary of his observations.

The first American loan-words, he says, were taken into American Czech by journalists and lecturers " whose chief claim to intellectual superiority seemed to rest, like that of some American Negroes, upon a propensity to employ a terminology unintelligible to the ordinary person." But the masses of immigrant Czechs soon took to imitating these pretenders, and in a little while the common vocabulary was largely English. " A volume half the size of Webster's International," says Monsignor Dudek, " would be required to list the words taken over in this popular manner." Most of them, of course, are nouns or verbs. All of the former are fully inflected " according to the declension, determined by the terminal letter or syllable, into which they would fall if written phonetically in Czech characters." Monsignor Dudek continues:

1 The Bohemian Language in America, Part I, *American Speech*, April, 1927; Part II, August, 1927; The Czech Language in America, *American Mercury*, June, 1925; Czech Surnames in America, *American Mercury*, Nov., 1925; The Americanization of Czech Surnames, *American Speech*, Dec., 1925; Czech-American Names, *Czechoslovak Student Life*, April, 1928; The Americanization of Czech Given-Names, *American Speech*, Oct., 1925.

The animate or inanimate nature of the object, as well as its gender, plays a part in deciding which of a dozen principal paradigms is to be followed. Thus, *bučerák*, of one masculine declension, means a *butcher;* of another, a *butcher-knife*. The gender of the Czech noun denoting the same object sometimes influences the declension of the loan-noun; hence a *barn*, for which the Czech word is feminine, is not *barn*, but *barna*. *Corn*, for the same reason, is *korna; street-car, strit-kára; pants, pence* (plural), and *whiskey, viska*. *Džurí* is declined after a neuter formula, but there being two Czech words translatable by *jury*, one masculine, the other feminine, the borrowed word takes modifiers of either gender. . . . *Melas*, molasses; *šuky* or *šůze* (plural only), a pair of shoes; *sodovka*, soda-water; *kornkabka*, a cob-pipe; *indyáynče*, an Indian child; *nygrlaté*, a pickaninny; *bínze*, a bean; *bejkbínze* (plural), baked beans; *můlák*, mule; *pičes*, peach; *medes*, tomato; *kal*, a gallon jar; *hempsenvič*, ham sandwich; *eprikoc*, apricot; *makinchprc*, mocking-bird; *recna*, rat, and *hefr* (masculine!) heifer, are only a few out of many curiosities for whose appreciation a detailed explanation of Czech phonetics, orthography and grammar is necessary.[1]

Nouns ending in a long *o*, in any *u*, or in a diphthong are generally avoided, for they cannot be readily inflected according to any of the twelve Czech declensions. Sometimes the plural *boys* is used instead of *boy*, becoming *bojse* in American-Czech. Words containing the sounds *qu, w, th* and *wh*, especially at their beginnings, are also avoided, for those sounds are difficult to the Czech, as is that of *h* in certain combinations. Sometimes a word is possible in one case, but not in all. Thus, *homebrew* is seldom attempted in the nominative, but in the instrumental it is used, *e.g.*, in *Otrávil se houmbruen* (He poisoned himself with homebrew), and there is a popular verb, *houmbrůovati*, to homebrew. In the same way, while *glue* is not used as a noun, the verb *zglůuju*, to glue, is in common use. The sound of *ng* is also avoided as much as possible, and words containing it are often changed. Thus *loving* becomes *lavování*. The simple *g*, on Czech lips, assimilates to *k*, so that *pig* and *pick* are homonyms. The agent-nouns are given Czech terminations — *-ák, -ař, -ník, -ista*, and the like. Thus, a drayman is an *ekspresak*, a station(depot)-agent is a *dýpař*, a street-railway employé is a *kárník*, and a lecturer is a *lekčrista*. To indicate a female the suffix *-ka* is used, or the masculine ending of the word is changed to a feminine form. Thus, a woman nurse is a *nrska*, and a woman Prohibitionist (*prohibičník*) is a *prohibičnice*. Sometimes a Czech feminine ending is added to an English one, as in *vejtreska* (waitress) and *čejmbrmejdka* (chamber-

1 The Czech Language in America,
American Mercury, June, 1925,
pp. 205–6.

maid). Loan-nouns beginning with *a* often lose it, *e.g.*, *knalidžmnt* (acknowledgment). Its loss is encouraged by the fact that in Czech the accent is always on the first syllable.

Verbs lose it for the same reason, *e.g.*, *kjuzovati* (to accuse), *dmitovati* (to admit). In sentences, the *a* (often changed to the neutral *e*) is commonly restored, usually by being added to the preceding word, but it is omitted when the word to which it belongs stands alone. There is an exception in the case of loan-words in *a* that have the accent on the first syllable, *e.g.*, *to agitate*, which becomes *édžitejtovati*, and *to amputate*, which becomes *empjutejtovati*. Monsignor Dudek says that practically all the English verbs in everyday use have been taken into American-Czech. They are put into the sixth conjugation " by the simple process of adding to the loan-words, as spoken, the Czech infinitive termination." Nouns are turned into verbs very facilely, *e.g.*, *brglařiti* (to burgle), *hauskípovati* (to housekeep), *kuklaksovati* (to Ku Klux), *gademovati* (to God-damn) and *sanamabičovati* (to son-of-a-bitch). There is also an immense borrowing of adjectives. Some of them, *e.g.*, *akorat* (accurate) and *olrajt* (all right) are taken in unchanged, but in the great majority of cases they are regularly declined. Almost any noun may become an adjective by adding one of the adjectival terminations to it. And adjectives may be turned into adverbs just as readily by changing their terminal vowels to *ě*. Monsignor Dudek thus describes the proliferation of American-Czech terms in one field, that of automobiling:

Besides the noun *automobil*, there are *automobilista*, an automobilist; its feminine, *automobilistka;* the verb *automobilovati*, to automobile; and the adjective *automobilový*. These are the printed forms, but one often hears *otomobil, otomobilista*, etc. *Mašina* and *kára* became synonymous with *automobil* as soon as *machine* and *car* did in American. *Autobus* or *otobus, autotrack* or *ototrak* (autotruck, not -track), *garáž* (garage), *garažník* (garage-man), *šofér, šofr* or *šoufr* (chauffeur), *tájr* (tire), *karburejtr* or *karbrejtr* (carburetor), *hajgír* and *lougír* (high-gear and low-gear), *hedlajt* (headlight), *dymr* (dimmer), and the like quickly followed. *Cylindr*, by which most Czechs formerly understood only a silk hat, has become the *silindr* of the automobile, which, in the adjective *silindrový*, is compounded with Czech numerals to describe a car of so many cylinders. *Džojraj* and *džojrajtovati* came into use as soon as Americans began joy-riding. The Ford is usually *fordka*, but both in speech and print it appears also as *fordovka*, of the same declension, or *ford*, with the diminutive *fordík. Flivr* is a flivver, and to ride in one is *flivrovati*. The adjectives *fordový* and *flivrový* follow as a matter of course. *Plechová* (tin) *lizí* competes with *dim lizínka*.[1]

[1] From Monsignor Dudek's MS.

The divagations of a single loan-word are often very interesting. Consider, for example, *bečlář* (bachelor), pronounced *batchelartch*. It also appears as *bečlák,* apparently under the influence of the notion that *-or* is an agent termination, and there is a feminine form, *bečlárka.* When used as an adjective it becomes *bečlácký* or *bečlář-ský,* and as a verb, meaning to cook for oneself (analogous to *to batch*), it is *béčovati.* But there are two other verbs, the first, *bečlovati* or *bečlařiti,* signifying to be a bachelor, and the second, *zbečlařiti,* signifying to be made a bachelor. The latter has produced a compound noun, *zbečlařeny muž,* meaning a man whose wife is away from home, and, by extension, a divorced man. *Butlegář* and *butlegr* (both forms of bootlegger) have been almost as productive. There is the noun *butleg* (bootleg), produced by back-formation, and there are the verbs *butlegovati* (to bootleg) and *butlegariti* (to be a bootlegger), the gerunds *butlegování* (bootlegging) and *but-legařeni* (literally, bootleggering), and the compound *butlegářství* (the bootlegging trade). A Czech at home naturally finds this vocabulary puzzling. When a Czech version of a movie called "Man With Courage," dealing with the life of the late Mayor Anton J. Čermak of Chicago and done by Czech-American actors in Hollywood, was exhibited in Prague, a large part of the dialogue baffled the Czech audiences, and a new recording had to be made in proper Czech.[1]

The Czechs at home also find it hard to understand the numerous translations of American phrases and idioms. They can make nothing of *bílý mezek* (white mule), *slepé prasátko* (blind pig), *filmová hvězda* (film star), *velký klacek* (big stick), *ohrivá voda* (firewater), *bledá tvář* (paleface) and *bílý otrokář* (white-slaver). The phrases that include loan-words puzzle them even more, *e.g., progresivní republikán* (Progressive Republican), *politický fence* (political fences), *strýc Sam* (Uncle Sam), *trafiční kop* (traffic cop), *kampánní komise* (campaign committee), *instruovaná delegace* (instructed delegation), and *běžeti pro ofis* (to run for office). Many loan-words conflict in meaning with Czech words substantially identical. Thus *konvikt,* in Czech, is the house of a religious community, but in American-Czech it has the meaning of a *convict.* Similarly, *detailní* means *retail* in Czech, but *detailed* in American-Czech, and

1 Hollywood's Czech Language Puzzles the Czechs, Baltimore *Evening Sun,* April 15, 1935.

kolej means *rut* or *track* in Czech but *college* in Czech-American. The borrowings of most of the other immigrant languages are principally confined to the names of objects and acts unknown in the Old Country, and to current slang. But American-Czech, through the influence of the journalists and lecturers mentioned by Monsignor Dudek, has also taken in many somewhat pretentious words, *e.g.*, *bakalářství* (baccalaureate), *bakalář* (bachelor of arts), *šaráda* (charade), *komercni* (commercial traveler), *kooperace* (coöperation), *decentralisace* (decentralization), and *delikt* (delinquency).

In 1930 there were 491,638 persons of Czech birth in the United States, 707,384 born in this country of Czech parentage, and 183,057 born here of partly Czech parentage, or 1,382,079 in all. Of those of Czech birth, 201,138 reported that their mother-tongue was Czech, and 240,196 that it was Slovak. The two languages are mutually intelligible, but they nevertheless differ considerably. The Czechs, says Monsignor Dudek, are scattered through virtually all the States of the Union. The largest colonies are in Illinois and Pennsylvania, with about 65,000 each. In Chicago alone there are 50,000 Czechs, and in 1931 one of them was elected mayor. They have nearly fifty publications in the United States, including six daily newspapers.[1]

b. Slovak

As I have just noted, Czech and Slovak are mutually intelligible, though by no means identical. Indeed, all the Slavonic languages are very closely allied, and the marked differences which, in Western Europe, separate English from German and French from Spanish are not encountered. It has been said that " a peasant from Slovakia, which enjoys the benefit of a central position in the Slavonic territory, is understood by a Slav from any other country." [2] So far as I am aware, there is no printed study of the mutations of Slovak in

1 I am also indebted to Miss Rose Zettel, of Cincinnati, and to the editors of the *Daily Svornost*, Chicago. The best recent treatise on the Czech language is Jazyk, edited by Oldrich Hujer; Prague; 1935. It is an exhaustive work to which all the leading Czech philologians have contributed, and it includes chapters on the changes undergone by German, Hungarian, Ruthenian and other languages in Czechoslovakia.

2 N. B. Jopson, reader in comparative Slavonic philology, University of London, in the Encyclopaedia Britannica, 14th ed.; Vol. XX, p. 788.

this country, but Mr. James R. Istochin of Omaha, Neb., has kindly supplied me with the following notes:

> As in Czech, loan-words from English are usually given Slovak inflections. A Slovak workman speaks of getting a *džab v šape* (job in the shop), *vo majne* (in the mine), or *v koksárni* (in the coke-yard), where he is super-vised by a *fórman* (foreman) while working *na mašine* (on a machine), *s píkom a šuflou* (with pick and shovel), or *s virbárom* (with a wheel-barrow). If all is well, every two weeks comes *peda* (pay-day). Then he goes to the bank *zkešovat ček* (to cash the check). Afterward he proceeds *do salony na konery bloku* (to the saloon on the corner of the block) to get a glass or two of *visky* (whiskey), but, while he may accept the American *páp* (pop) as a chaser, when he wants beer he asks for the Slovakian *pivo*. Some-times he has a *kejs* (case) or a *kek* (keg) delivered for home consumption. In Prohibition days he made his *hómbru* (home-brew) or bought *munšajn* (moonshine) from a *butleger* (bootlegger). However, not much of his money is spent for drink. After the necessary amounts for food, shelter, and clothing are deducted, most of his pay stays in the bank. His wife goes *do štóru* (to the store) to buy the household supplies. She asks for many staple items by their Slovakian names, but the *grocerista* (grocer) often has to supply such items as: *boksu pičesi* (box of peaches), *kenu korny* (a can of corn), *bonč binenes* (a bunch of bananas), *paje* (pies), *kendy* (candy) and *keksy* (cakes). It is interesting to note that *binenes* is used as both singular or plural, but that *pičesa, kenda,* and either the masculine *keks* or the feminine *keksa* are singular. Although this Slovak housewife asks for milk by its correct Slovak name, *mlieko,* her units of liquid measure are the *pajnta* (pint), *kvarta* (quart), and *galón* (gallon). She buys her meats *od bučera* (from the butcher) or *v bučerni* (in the butcher-shop). Most articles of apparel are called by their Slovakian names, but I have heard shoppers ask for *pence* (pants), *šusi* (shoes), *búce* (boots), *zút* (a suit), *dres* (a dress), *sveder* (a sweater), *over-hozy* (overalls), and even *stakince* (stockings). In waiting on them I have been guilty of asking *Jaký sajz?* (What size?) or *Jaké numero?* (What num-ber?). They in turn have asked the *prajs* (price) and the quality of the *štof* (stuff — material).

The Slovaks are very thrifty folk, and whenever there is enough money in hand the immigrant proceeds to build a *haus*. If the con-tractor is also a Slovak, the negotiations will be carried on mainly in correct Slovakian terms, but nevertheless, says Mr. Istochin,

> there will be talk of *flór* (floor), *štepse* (stairs), *slejt* or *šingl rúf* (slate or shingle roof), *fens* (fence), *penta* (paint), *bilding permit* (building permit), *inšurens* (insurance), *dýd* (deed), and *morgič* (mortgage). In the Summer there is always a *piknik* (picnic) or two. Sometimes it is some distance from home, necessitating the purchase of *tikety* (tickets) to ride on the *trén* (train). Of course, one may drive one's *automobil* — my grandfather used to call it *antonobil* —, which requires a quantity *gazolínu* (gasoline). Most often the *bojs* (boy, son) is the chauffeur. Some of the seasonal outdoor sports are *bejsbal* (baseball), *futbal* (football), and *skejtovanie* (skating). The Slovaks have not been much attracted by golf and tennis.

Once a month the Slovak-American attends a *míting* (meeting) of the local branch of the nationalistic society to which he always belongs. The largest of them are the First Catholic Slovak Union and the National Slovak Society, each of which prints a weekly organ. These papers, like the Czech journals, run to a somewhat florid vocabulary. Says Mr. Istochin:

In a recent editorial in *Jednota* (Middletown, Pa.) published by the F. C. S. U., I find *kooperácia* (coöperation), *konvencia* (convention), *direktne* (directly), *systém* (system), and *organizácia* (organization). The same editorial contains *čens* (chance, opportunity), although the word is enclosed in quotation marks and is followed by a good Slovakian word in parentheses. Another loan-word is *overcrowded.* This is also set off by quotation marks, but is not followed by a Slovakian equivalent. In the same issue of *Jednota* a column of personal observations written in a lighter vein contains such borrowings as *fulovat'* (to fool), *okej* (O.K.), and *džungle* (jungle), as well as the expletives *well* and *šúr* (sure).

A search through the advertising columns of the Slovak papers reveals even more Americanisms than are to be found in the editorial columns. In a list of the body types of a certain make of automobile advertised in *Národné Noviny* (Pittsburgh), published by the N. S. S., are: *športový roadster so zadným sediskom* (sport roadster with back — *i.e.*, rumble-seat), *päť-pasažiorový coupe* (five-passenger coupé), and *zmeniteľny cabriolet* (convertible cabriolet). When used as a substantive the name of the car may appear as *Chevroletka* or *Fordka.* A comparison of the translations of an identical advertisement reveals that while *Jednota* uses *produkty, originálny,* and *broadcasting* for products, original, and broadcasting, *Národné Noviny* uses *výrobky, pôvodný,* and *rozhlasovacíí.*

Many loan-words appear in the vocabularies and specimen sentences printed in the Rev. S. Morávek's "Slovak Self-Taught,"[1] *e.g., mlyne* (mill), *majner* (miner), *strajke* (strike), *prémia* (premium), *policu* (policy), *titul* (title), *bond* (bond), *muf* (muff) and *sveder* (sweater). Returning immigrants have taken loan-words back to Czechoslovakia, *e.g., sex-appeal, henna, kontrast, kapún* (capon) and *kúrio,* all of which, according to a comment in *Furdek,* the organ of the Catholic Slovak Students' Fraternity of America, appeared in one story in *Slovenské Pohľady,* a literary magazine published in Slovakia. The Slovaks print about twenty-five publications in this country, including five daily newspapers.

1 2nd ed.; Wilkes-Barre, Pa., 1924.

c. Russian

The only study of American-Russian that I have been able to find in print is a paper by Mr. H. B. Wells.[1] The barrier of a different alphabet, he says, discourages the free adoption of loan-words by the Russian periodicals published in this country, but nevertheless a great many seep in. Verbs of Latin derivation, so numerous in English, " are used with far greater frequency than in Russia, and sometimes practically displace the synonymous words of purely Slavic antecedents."

Thus, *importirovat'* and *eksportirovat'* contend with *vvozit'* and *vyvozit'* for the privilege of representing to import and to export; *annonsirovat'* and *objavljat'* represent to announce, and *registrirovat'* and *zapissat'sja* represent to sign up, to register one's self. Such a combination as *annulirovat' naturaliza- tsionnye sertifikaty* (to annul naturalization certificates) would be rare, to say the least, in Russia, though the writer has here obviously struggled for cor- rectness; otherwise he would have written *sertifikejty* instead of *sertifikaty*.[2]

In ordinary conversation the Russians in America use loan-words very freely. Says Mr. Wells:

The Russian-American New Yorker lives *v optaune* (in the uptown). . . . His apartment is in a *desjatifamil'nyi dom* (ten-family house) at *67 Vest 123 strit, ist of Brodvej*. There is an *élevator* in the building. The apartment is very *ap tu dejt* (up to date); it is furnished with *rejdiejtory* (radiators) and a *refridzherejtor* (refrigerator). Several of the rooms have *okna na front* (win- dows on the front); these he calls *frontovye komnaty* (front-rooms). In the living-room there is a *vik* or *viktrola*, and in the kitchen a *garbich kén*. . . . [His] wife is also quite *ap tu dejt*. When she wants to *imet' ljonch* or *ljonche- vat'* (have lunch), she calls up another *lédi* (lady) and they go to the *drogstor* and consume *séndvichi* (sandwiches), *kejk* (cake), and *ajskrim* (ice-cream), smoking *sigarety* furiously the while and discussing the cost of *potejta* (pota- toes), and whether to *mufovat'* in view of the unsuitability of the neighbor- hood. She boasts of her *boj* (boy) in *khaj-skul* (high-school), who plays foot- ball and made a *tochdaun* (touchdown) last Thanksgiving Day, but who is

1 The Russian Language in the United States, *American Mercury*, April, 1932. Mr. Wells is a native of New Jersey and a Harvard graduate. He is interested in Slavic languages, and studied at the Caro- line University of Prague, 1929–30.
2 I have adopted Mr. Wells's system of transliteration, which he explains in a footnote to his paper. The busi- ness of rendering Russian in the English alphabet is full of difficul-

ties. The system adopted by the United States Geographic Board is described and discussed in First Report on Foreign Geographic Names; Washington, 1932, and that of the Permanent Committee on Geographical Names For British Official Use is set forth in Alpha- bets of Foreign Languages, by Lord Edward Gleichen and John H. Reynolds; London, 1933.

nevertheless distraught because he had a *fajt* (fight) with his *gjorla* (girl). The *gjorla* is *ku-ku* (cuckoo) anyway, and the mother thinks of advising her son not to mix himself up in any *monki bisnes* (monkey business). . . . In the evening the Russian comes home to his *flét* (flat). . . . He has a *kara* (car) and the way it eats up *gazolin* and *ojl* is frightful. . . . A dark interlude in his life was the time he had a run-in with a *kop;* he was driving through a *uan-vej strit* (one-way street), and was exceeding the *spidlimit.* Moreover, he had left his *lajsens* at home on the piano, and the *kop* gave him a *tiket.*

The plurals of loan-nouns are formed either by adding the regular Russian suffixes, or by inserting the English *s* before the most frequent of them, *-y.* Thus one hears both *chil'dreny* and *chil'drensy.* The *h* in loan-words often becomes *kh* or *g. All right* has been taken in as *o right. Never mind* has become one word, *nevermine.* Such words as *teacher,* which have been adopted bodily, take a final *-ka* in the feminine, and the same particle is sometimes used to indicate the diminutive, as in *matchka* (little match).[1] The number of Russians in the United States is hard to determine. In 1930, 315,721 persons reported that Russian was their mother-tongue, but many of them were probably Jews. There are seventeen Russian publications in the country, including four daily newspapers.

d. Ukrainian

Ukrainian, or Little Russian, differs enough from Great Russian for a speaker of the one to find the other very difficult. In 1930 but 58,685 persons reported to the Census enumerators that Ukrainian was their mother-tongue; to the number should be added 9800 who gave Ruthenian, the name commonly applied to Ukrainian in the former Austrian Empire. Both figures suggest incomplete returns. In Canada the Ukrainians " form the fourth largest racial constituent in the polyglot population," [2] and in the prairie provinces of the West they number about 250,000. They publish eight periodicals at Winnipeg and two more at Edmonton, but in the whole United States they have but twelve, seven of which are published in Pennsyl-

1 I am indebted for material and suggestions to Mr. Peter Stephanovsky of Chicago, to Miss Helen P. Kirkpatrick, executive secretary of the American Russian Institute, New York, to Mr. Mark Weinbaum, editor of the *Novoye Russkaye*

Slovo of New York and to Messrs. E. Moravesky of Chicago and Sergei Senykoff of Detroit.
2 Ukrainian Poetry in Canada, by Watson Kirkconnell, *Slavonic Review,* July, 1934.

vania. There is a Ukrainian daily in Jersey City, the *Svoboda*, and another in New York, the *Ukrainian Daily News*. To the editor of the
former, Mr. Emil Revyuk, I am indebted for the following:

The Ukrainian in America makes a copious use of English loan-words.
Some of them are the names of things with which he was unfamiliar at home,
and others are words that he must use in his daily traffic with Americans.
Usually, he tries to bring these loans into harmony with the Ukrainian inflectional system. Thus, he forces most loan-nouns to take on grammatical
gender. Those that he feels to be feminine he outfits with the Ukrainian feminine ending, *-a*, e.g., *dreska* (dress), *vinda* (window), *hala* (hall), *grocernya*
(grocery store), *buchernya* (butcher's store), *strita* (street), *pikcha* (picture).
Mechka is the match which makes a fire but match in the meaning of contest
of skill is a masculine noun *mech*. Some nouns are felt to be plural and are
outfitted with plural endings. Thus *furniture* becomes *fornichi*, which is equivalent to "pieces of furniture," *pinatsy* is a Ukrainian adaptation of *peanuts*,
and *shusy* of *shoes*, and *Shkrenty* is the plural form of the name of the city
of Scranton. *Kendi* (candy), is declined like a plural noun because its ending
is the typical plural ending of Ukrainian nouns, and it reminds the Ukrainian
of his name for *candy*, the plural *tsukorky*. *Blubery* (blueberries), is also plural.

The adjective must be recast also to denote by its ending the number and
gender. For this reason the Ukrainian does not use many English adjectives,
for they do not lend themselves easily to such changes. He has adopted, however, the following: *faytersky* (of fighting character), *bomersky* (of the character of a bum), *gengstersky* (like a gangster), *sylkovy* (made of silk), *volna-
tovy* (made of walnut), *bosuyuchy* or *bosivsky* (bossing, domineering).
Adopted verbs, too, require a great deal of dressing up to fit them for use in
the Ukrainian language, e.g., *bosuvaty* (to boss), *klinuvaty* (to clean), *pon-
chuvaty* (to punch), *laykuvaty* (to like), *trubluvaty* (to trouble), *baderuvaty*
(to bother), *bostuvaty* (to bust), *shapuvaty* (to shop), *stykuvaty* (to stick),
faytuvatysya (to fight with), *ringuvaty* (to ring), *swimuvaty* (to swim),
peyntuvaty (to paint), *bonduvaty* (to bond), *bayluvaty* (to bail) and *djompaty*
(to jump). *Parkuvaty karu* is the common American Ukrainian for to park
the car.

Diminutives are formed by adding *-chyk* or *-syk*, e.g., *boysyk* (a
little boy), and augmentatives by adding *-ysche*, e.g., *boysysche*
(a big boy). The Ukrainian prefers to make his own logical feminines. He does not use *waitress* but has concocted *veyterka* from
veyter (waiter). In the same way he uses *tenerka*, *bucherka*, *jani-
torka*, *borderka*, *hauskiperka*, *svindlerka*, *ticherka*, *bomerka* (a female
tenant, butcher, janitor, boarder, housekeeper, swindler, teacher,
bum). He makes abstract nouns by adding *-stvo*, e.g., *farmerstvo*
(farming), *pedlerstvo* and *plomberstvo* (plumbing). He also makes
infinitives denoting finish or iterative action, e.g., *zbostuvaty* (to
have busted), *pofiksuvaty* (to fix completely), *popeyntuvaty* (to
paint all over) and *jompuvaty* (to be jumping). Says Mr. Revyuk:

Sometimes a Ukrainian word is changed under the influence of an American word, *e.g., lezhukh* (loafer), from *lezhaty* (to lie resting) becomes *leyzukh,* to emphasize its kinship with *lazy.* Some loan-words, in spite of all efforts, refuse to be changed. This is true of those that have endings strange to the Ukrainian, *e.g.,* those ending in *-y: city, lobby, party, lady, country,* etc., which by their ending suggest to a Ukrainian either a masculine adjective or a plural noun, but evidently are neither one nor the other. Hence the Ukrainian feels reluctant to inflect *Chicago, cemetery* and *Yankee.* He experiences still greater uneasiness with composite words: *jitney-boss, city-hall, Kansas City, Jersey City, Niagara Falls, cream-cheese* (pot-cheese, which he knows, he will call by the Ukrainian word, *syr*), *piece-work, Tammany Hall, hold-up, card-party, bridge-party, rocking-chair, bathing-suit, ice-cream, high-school, Sing Sing, lolly-pop, knickerbockers, ginger-ale, saleslady.* Some adjectives, too, balk at inflection, *e.g., jealous (vin tak jeles, vona taka jeles), easy, crazy.* Some words lead a double life. *Engine,* for instance, now passes as a male, assuming the form *injay,* and now as a female, *injaya.*

Not infrequently the American cuckoo accepted into the Ukrainian nest ejects some other cuckoo, hatched out of an egg deposited by the German, French, or Italian. Thus, in American-Ukrainian, *parasola* is replaced by *ambrela, kelner* by *veyter* (waiter), *buchhalter* by *bookkeeper, fryzier* by *barber, bilet* by *tyket* (ticket), *umbra* by *sheyd* (shade, especially lamp-shade), and *velotsyped* (velocipede) by *bysykel, bitsykel,* or even *bike.* Under the influence of American many Ukrainian words of foreign origin acquire additional meanings. Thus *kontrola,* which in the Old Country meant auditing, examination of accounts, assumes in America also the meaning of directing, regulating, and still later that of checking, as in the phrase *kontrola budyakiv* (weed control). *Konventsya,* which in Ukrainian means an agreement between nations, in American acquires the meaning of a gathering of a party, etc. *Mashynist* loses the Ukrainian meaning of locomotive engineer, and *operator* the meaning of surgeon. Each of them acquires the meanings of those words in America. *Kompania* in the Old Country means associates, a company of soldiers; in America the word comes to mean also a corporation. Likewise, the adjective *seriozny,* under the influence of American, comes to be used not only in reference to people, meaning serious, but also of conditions, meaning grave. Even original Ukrainian words become affected by this process, *e.g.,* the old Ukrainian word *vartuvaty* (to be worth), acquires the American idiomatic meaning of to have property of value.

Once the Ukrainian adopts an American word and then uses that word in a phrase which reminds him of some standard American phrase, the whole phrase rushes into his speech. Thus, having adopted *train,* he cannot refuse the phrases, *to get a train, to catch a train,* and so he translates them: *braty tren, zlovyty tren,* which to a person versed in Ukrainian can mean only to get hold of a train, and to overtake the train, respectively. Having borrowed *picture* and dressed it in Ukrainian costume as *pikcha,* he cannot shut the door in the face of the phrase *to take a picture,* and so he has *braty pikchu,* and also *braty dobru pikchu* (to take a good picture). Thus he has admitted such phrases as *sluzhyty na jury* (to serve on a jury), *distaty herkot* (to get a hair-cut), *pity na relief* (to go on relief), *dopustyty do bary* (to admit to the bar).

Many American phrases are translated bodily into Ukrainian, often against the well-established rules of the language. The Ukrainian who knows English is likely to say *kozdy odyn*, when *kozdy* is sufficient and correct, evidently translating the English *every one*. He replaces *rozsmishyty koho* with *robyty koho smiaty*, which is a word-for-word translation of the phrase *to make one laugh*, but a horror in Ukrainian. He contracts the sentence "Ya bachyv jak vin ishov" into "Ya bachyv yeho ity," which is an apish imitation of the English phrase, "I saw him go." He translates the phrase, "I cannot help it" into "Ya ne mozhu pomohty," as if the word *help* here meant to render assistance. He says, "Ya ne mozhlyvy preyty," which is a literal translation of "I am unable to come." "My maly dobry chas" follows word by word "We had a good time," and would be unintelligible in the Old Country. "Ya rad vas bachyty nazad" follows word for word the greeting, "I am glad to see you back." "Bery svey chas!" is a similar translation of "Take your time!" and "Trymayte drit!" of "Hold the wire."

The American-Ukrainian changes many Ukrainian idioms. Under the American influence he forgets the phrase, *robyty oko do koho* and uses *robyty ochy do koho* (to make eyes to one). The Ukrainian phrase is to make an eye to one. The Ukrainian phrase, *ne spuskaty ochey z koho* (not to close one's eyes to) becomes *derzhaty oko na kim* (to keep one's eye on). The idiomatic expression *spushcheny nis* (the drooping nose) is displaced by the American *long face* (*dovhe lytse*). Speaking of his son's age, the American-Ukrainian translates the American idiomatic sentence, "He is six years old," by "Vin ye shist lit stary," though no Ukrainian at home would refer to a child of six as *old*. His idiomatic phrase speaks of *having . . . years*.

The American-Ukrainian begins to add possessive pronouns in phrases which do not require them in Standard Ukrainian, often with a humorous effect for those who are still not initiated into the mysteries of the American-Ukrainian language. To use, for instance, the possessive *svoyu* in the sentence "Vin kuryt svoyu lulku" (He is smoking his pipe), may suggest a question, "Whose pipe do you expect him to smoke if not his own?" The Ukrainian in the Old Country would not use the possessive pronoun in the phrase *zatyraty svoyi ruky* (to rub one's hands); could you rub anybody else's hands but your own? Again, the possessive pronouns in the sentence, "Win derzhyt svoi ruky v svoiy kysheni" (He is holding *his* hands in *his* pocket), may suggest the suspicion that habitually he is holding in his pocket somebody's else's hands or has his hands in somebody else's pockets.

There is noticeable in American-Ukrainian a certain decay of synonyms. Fine distinctions between them are obliterated. *Divka*, which corresponds more or less to *maid*, is used also for *girl*, *daughter* and *sweetheart*. "Ya lublu vashu divku" (I love your maid), is rather a rude way of saying, "I love your daughter." Further degeneration of the language is noticeable in the loss of distinction between the verbs of duration, iteration, and conclusion, *e.g.*, *ity*, *pity* and *khodyty* (to be going, to be gone, to go); *zhynuty* and *zahynuty* (to die and to disappear). Decay is also promoted by the fact that English loan-adjectives cannot be inflected. After a certain time even the Ukrainian-born American will fail to inflect the adjective made of a proper noun but will follow the simple English device of placing it before another noun and letting it serve thus as adjective; in Standard Ukrainian *na rozi Napoleon ulytsi, do Notr Deym shpytalu, z Dubyuk universytetu, Richelieu vyshyvky* would all have to change the first noun into an adjective form or place it after the other noun in the genitive case.

The influence of English is also felt in the acquisition by the American-

Ukrainian of the feeling of the need of the article. He begins to punctuate his language with *toy, ta, to, ti* in all those passages where in English he would use the definite article. Also, he begins to roll his *r*'s after the American fashion even when speaking Ukrainian. Those who were born here find it difficult to enunciate certain typically Ukrainian sounds, such as guttural *kh.* Thus *mukha* (the fly), degenerates into *muha, khochu* into *hochu, tykho* into *tyho,* and even *khata* into *hata,* though *hata* in Ukrainian means a dam and *khata* a hut.[1]

e. Serbo-Croat

In 1930, 30,121 persons living in the United States reported to the Census enumerators that Serbian was their mother-tongue, 79,802 reported that it was Croat, and 77,671 that it was Slovene. Serbian and Croat are identical, though the former is written in the Cyrillic or Russian alphabet and the latter in the Latin, and Slovene differs from the two, according to Louis Adamic,[2] hardly more than the German of Vienna differs from that of Hamburg. There are twenty-two Serbo-Croatian-Slovene publications in the United States and Canada, including no less than seven daily newspapers. Mr. Adamic is the author of the only study of the changes undergone by Serbo-Croat in America that I have been able to find.[3] He says that, as it is printed in the vernacular press, it remains virtually Standard Serbian. "So far," he says, "I have noticed but a dozen or so of [loan-words] in the news and editorial colunms, *e.g.*, *majnar* and *majna, farmar* and *farma, štrajk* and *štrajkar, štor, viska* and *lota* (lot). There are one or two humorous columnists who go further in this direction, but they are exceptions." In the everyday speech of the immigrants, however, there is a much larger admixture of Americanisms. Says Mr. Adamic:

> The American Yugoslav is not likely to say *Združene* or *Zjedinjene države,* which are literal Slovene and Serbo-Croat translations of United States, but rather *Unajne štec,* or *Jus* (U. S.) for short. The holiday commemorating the birth of the nation becomes *Džulajevo* (July Day), after the manner of naming certain holidays in the Old Country. A house to him is *hauz* or *gauz;* a kitchen, *kična;* a bucket, *boket;* a stove, *štof;* a plate, *plet;* a pitcher and pic-

1 I am indebted also to Mr. Vladimir Geeza, editor of the *New Life* of Olyphant, Pa.
2 The Yugoslav Speech in America, *American Mercury,* Nov., 1927. Mr. Adamic is a native of Carniola in what was Austrian territory at the time of his birth but is now part of Jugoslavia. He came to this country at the age of fourteen, and has become well known as a writer in English.
3 It has just been cited.

ture, *pičer;* a shovel, *safla;* a spoon, *špuna;* a fork, *forka* or *forkla;* a basket, *bosket;* a bowl, *bol;* a garden-gate, *garten-gec;* upstairs and downstairs, *abštez* and *daštez;* a bed, *bet;* a needle, *nitl,* and a car, *kara.* Shoes are *suhi;* house-slippers, *hauz-* or *gauz-šlipari;* bloomers, *brumars;* rubberboots, *robarbuce;* overalls, *obergoz;* a sweater, *švidar,* and a blouse, *bluza.*

In the morning he *brekfešta* (breakfasts), picks up his *lonč-boket* (lunch-bucket), goes to the *majna* (mine), finds his *partnar* (partner), and then spends the rest of the day *vurkati* (working). In the mine there are all sorts of *basi* (bosses) who *basirajo* (boss) him. Every so often there is *peda* (payday) and he gets just enough *moni* to pay his *bord* (board), get a *šat* of *viska* (shot of whiskey), maybe go to a *tenc* (dance), and possibly put a few *toleri* (dollars) aside for a *reni tej* (rainy day) or the forthcoming *štrajk* (strike). In this *kontri* (country) a man must *roslat* (rustle) to make both ends meet.

Should one accompany an American-Yugoslav housewife who, besides taking care of her *hosban* (husband) and having a new *bebi* (baby) once a year, keeps half a dozen *bordarjev* (boarders), on her daily trip to the *market* or *štor* (store), one will see her purchase *potetus, redič, onjenc, keruc, epuls, pičus, kebič, kreps, vodamalone,* and *seleri* (potatoes, radishes, onions, carrots, apples, peaches, cabbage, grapes, watermelons, and celery). On the way to the butcher's she will probably remark that things are terribly *spensif* (expensive); that one had better watch these *štorkiparje,* for they are *krukani* (crooked) as a snake, always trying to slip one *štuf* that is *bum* or *enži* (n. g.), whereas she *lajka* to give her *bordarjem gut štuf* (likes to give her boarders good stuff). And at the butcher's she gets some *porčops* (pork-chops), *šteks* (steaks), maybe a few *rebec* (rabbits) or a young *luštar* (rooster) or two, and a little *ketsmit* (cat-meat). At the *društor* (drug-store) she buys a *fizik* (physic) for the *bebi* and is half tempted to blow herself to an *ajskrem soda* (ice cream soda).

Arriving home, she orders the wailing *bebi* to *šerap* (shut up), and tells two of her older children to cease their *fajtanje* (fighting) and *garjep* (hurry up) to the *rejrod jards* (railroad yards) with the biggest *bosket* in the house and see if they can't pick up some *kol* (coal). And so on; there is, indeed, hardly an everyday word that is not thus taken from the English language and refashioned to fit the Yugoslav tongue.

In *gauz* (house), *obergoz* (over(h)alls) and *garjep* (hurry up) the commonly Slavonic tendency to turn *h* into *g* is visible. Other nouns in common use are *džez* (jazz), *salun* (saloon), *bara* (bar), *džhumper* (jumper), *vikend* (week-end), *boom* (bum), *boj* or *poj* (boy), *ledi* (lady), *štrita* (street), *karpet* (carpet), *park* (park), *vošinmašina* (washing-machine), *redietor* (radiator), *penta* (paint), *livirum* (living-room), *lampa* (lamp), *šo* (show), *pajpa* (pipe), *štrickara* (street-car), *pence* (pants), *tutbroš* (tooth-brush), *rog* (rug), *papir* (writing-paper or newspaper), *pauder* (powder), *fekteria* (factory), *mila* (mill), *sajdvok* (sidewalk), *štepce* (steps), *porč* (porch), *redio* (radio), *polisman* (policeman), *major* (mayor), *kort* (court), *taksa* or *teks* (tax), *džuž* (judge), *džail* (jail), *tičar* (teacher), *pokbuk* (pocketbook), *džuri* (jury), *pučer* (butcher), *stejž* (stage), *noors* (nurse), *senvič* or *senič* (sandwich), *štajl* (style) and *sajn* (sign),[1] and, among the Croats, *unij* (union), *masina* (machine), *boykotirat* (boycott), *raketir* (racketeer), *situaciya* (situation) and *garaž* (garage).[2] Most loan-nouns are given grammatical gender and declined according to the Serbo-Croatian system, but some, *e.g.*, *karpet* and *park*, are taken in unchanged and not so declined. These last are commonly thought of as masculine. Very few adjectives have been incorporated, and not many verbs. A number of phrases and idioms have been adopted, *e.g.*, *majgundeš* (my goodness), *gerarehir* (get out of here), and the expletives *dži* (gee) and *džizakrajst* (Jesus Christ). *Yes* has displaced the Slavic *da*, and often appears as *yah* or *yeah*. A number of Americanisms have returned to the Old Country and are in common use there, *e.g.*, *džež* (jazz), *salun* (saloon), *bos* (boss), *nigr* (nigger) and *probišn* (prohibition).

f. Lithuanian

The only study so far undertaken of the changes undergone by the Lithuanian language in the United States is that of Dr. Alfred Senn of the University of Wisconsin, made on a Sterling research fellowship from Yale. Dr. Senn is a Swiss and his monograph was written in German and printed in Rome [3] — a combination that bears striking witness to the opportunities overlooked by American scholarship. His investigation was chiefly made in Connecticut, where there are several Lithuanian colonies, but he also extended it to New York City and Chicago. The first Lithuanians came to the United States before the middle of the last century, but there was no considerable immigration until 1863, when an unsuccessful rebellion against Russian rule drove many thousands into exile. It has been estimated that fully a third of all the patriots who survived the rebellion came to this country, and that there are 1,000,000 persons of Lithuanian blood, either pure or mixed, in the population today. The Census of 1930 unearthed less than half that number (193,606 born in Lithuania, 221,472 born in this country of Lithuanian parents,

---

1 I am indebted here to Miss Louise S. Ivey, of Wanwatosa, Wis., and to Mr. Stephen Stephanchev, of Chicago, whose interest was enlisted by Mr. Adamic.

2 I am indebted here to Dr. J. W. Mally, of Cleveland, O.

3 Einiges aus der Sprache der Amerika-Litauer, *Studi Baltici*, Vol. II, 1932, p. 35 *ff*.

and 24,117 born here of partly Lithuanian parentage, or 439,395 in all), but it is possible that the returns credited many Lithuanians to Russia or to Poland. In Chicago, says Dr. Senn, the Lithuanian colony numbers at least 80,000. In Waterbury, Conn., there is another of 15,000, and yet others are in New Jersey, New York, Pennsylvania, Massachusetts and Maryland. The Lithuanians in the United States support fourteen newspapers, of which four are dailies — three in Chicago and one in Brooklyn.

From 1864 to 1904 the Russian government made violent efforts to Russify the Lithuanians remaining in Lithuania. Their schools were closed and the printing of books in their native tongue was forbidden. Thus the colonies of exiles became centers of Lithuanian culture, and publishing houses were set up in Chicago, Boston, Shenandoah, Pa., and other American towns. In 1904 the interdict on Lithuanian books was removed by the Russians, and there began a great cultural revival in Lithuania. One of its fruits was an effort to purge the language of the Polish and Russian elements that had invaded it. This movement gathered fresh impetus after the World War, and so effective has it been that a young Lithuanian of today finds it difficult, on coming to the United States, to understand the speech of his compatriots here, which still retains most of the old loan-words. Even the names of the days of the week differ in the two forms of the language. In addition, American-Lithuanian has taken in a large number of American words and phrases, so the difficulty of intercommunication is really formidable. Meanwhile, the various Lithuanian dialects tend to disappear in this country, and all Lithuanians move toward a common speech. It consists, says Dr. Senn, of " a disorderly mixture of dialects, old Slavic loan-words brought from home, and new English loan-words picked up in America. It is a Pidgin-Lithuanian."

But this American-Lithuanian, though it may sound barbaric to a Lithuanian scholar, yet preserves most of the forms of the mother-tongue. The loan-noun, for example, is inflected precisely as if it were a native word. Thus *bòmas* (from the American bum) takes the masculine gender, is put into the second accent class, and undergoes the following changes for case and number:

	Singular	Plural	Dual
Nominative	bòmas	bòmai	dù bomù
Vocative	bòme	bòmai	

	Singular	Plural	Dual
Genitive	bòmo	bòmų	
Dative	bòmui	bòmams	dvíem bòmam
Accusative	bòmą	bomùs	dù bomù
Instrumental	bomù	bòmais	dviēm bòmam
Locative	bomè	bòmuose	

Save it be feminine logically, an American loan-noun usually takes the masculine gender, which may show any one of five endings in the nominative singular — -*as*, -*ỹs*, -*is*, -*us* or -*uo*. The ending attached is determined to some extent by the meaning, and by the form in English. Most names of inanimate objects seem to be given the -*as* ending, *e.g.*, *Amèrikas* (America), *háuzas* or *áuzas* (house), *bàksas* (box), *bólas* (ball), *divòrsas* (divorce), *fréntas* (friend), *fòrnisas* (furnace), *kãras* (car), *káutas* or *kótas* (coat), *kìsas* (kiss), *krýmas* (cream), *lãtas* (lot), *mùnšainas* (moonshine), *òfisas* (office), *pòketbukas* (pocketbook), *rèkordas* (phonograph-record), *saliúnas* (saloon), *sáidvokus* (sidewalk) and *štòras* (store). But agent-nouns in -*er* take the -*is* ending, *e.g.*, *békeris* (baker), *gròseris* (grocer), *blòferis* (bluffer), *bùtlegeris* (bootlegger) and *làbsteris* (lobster in the opprobrious sense), and so, by analogy, do most other nouns in -*er*, *e.g.*, *bòmperis* (bumper) and *fénderis* (fender). So, also, do nouns whose ending suggests -*er* to the Lithuanian ear, *e.g.*, *dóleris* (dollar) and *mūvingpìkčeris* (moving-picture). So, finally, do nouns in -*le*, *e.g.*, *báisikelis* (bicycle) and *tròbelis* (trouble). One English noun, *business*, seems to the Lithuanian to have an -*is* ending readymade, so he leaves it *bìznis*. When the last part of a compound word has already come into American-Lithuanian with an -*as* ending, *e.g.*, *štòras* (store), the compound itself sometimes takes the -*is* ending, *e.g.*, *drùgštoris* (drug-store). A few American loan-words take the -(*i*)*us* ending, chiefly by analogy. Thus *redietorius* (radiator) is suggested by the Lithuanian word *dirèktorius* (director). When the singular form of a loan-noun can't be fitted into the Lithuanian system of declensions, the plural is used as a singular, *e.g.*, *bòisas* (boy) and *šúsas* (shoe). The relatively few loan-words that take the feminine endings, -*a* and -*e*, not being themselves feminine in significance, usually do so because their English forms show those endings, or something approximating to them, *e.g.*, *ambrèla* (umbrella), *pãre* (party), *balióne* (bologna) and *pédė* (pay-day). *Sìnka* (sink), *krèkė* (cracker), *bètspredė* (bedspread) and *hèmė* (ham) are probably made feminine because they suggest the *Frau-*

enzimmer, and Dr. Senn says that *šapà* (shop) may be influenced by *shoppe*. The nouns *lòkė* (luck) and *fònė* (fun) were plainly suggested by the adjectives *lucky* and *funny* rather than by the corresponding English nouns. Even proper names are given Lithuanian endings, and regularly inflected. Thus *New York*, in the nominative singular, becomes *Nãjorkas*, *New Haven* becomes *Najévenas*, *Waterbury* (Conn.) becomes *Vòlberis*, *Vòrberis*, *Vòrbelis* or *Vòterburis*, and *Grand avenue*, a street in the last-named, becomes *Grináunė*.

But some of the commonest coins of American speech, *e.g.*, *yes*, *no*, *well*, *sure* and *O.K.*, are taken into Lithuanian bodily and without substantial change, and this is true also of most adjectives, *e.g.*, *busy* (*bìzi*), *particular* (*partìkli*), *nice* (*nais*), *ready* (*rèdi*), *big* (*big*), *crazy* (*kréize*), *good* (*gud*). Dr. Senn says he knows of but two loan-adjectives that are regularly declined, to wit, *dòrtinas* (dirty) and *fòniškas* (funny). Lithuanian is extraordinarily rich in diminutives; the word *brother* alone has fifteen.[1] Some of these are attached to loan-words; thus, *lady* has produced *leidùke*, and *miss* has produced *misēle*. A few masculine loan-nouns have feminine forms, *e.g.*, *bùtlegeris-bùtlegere* (bootlegger-ess) and *týčeris-týčerka* (teacher-ess). When English combinations of sounds happen to be difficult to Lithuanian lips they are sometimes changed. Thus *picnic* becomes *pìtnikas*, *order* becomes *òrdelis*, and *dollar* is often *dórelis* instead of *dóleria*. Loan-verbs, avoiding the complicated conjugations of correct Lithuanian, are all conjugated like *jùdinu* (to move). Among those in most frequent use are *álpinu* (to help), *dòrtinu* (to dirty), *dráivinu* (to drive), *júzinu* (to use), *láikunu* (to like), *mùvinu* (to move), *pùšinu* (to push) and *tròstinu* (to trust). But *to fix* becomes *fìksyt*, and *to spend* is *spéndyt*. When an English verb ends in a vowel it presents difficulties. Sometimes it is fitted with the *-inu* ending notwithstanding, *e.g.*, *trãjinu* (to try); at other times it is given a final *n* and some other ending, *e.g.*, *pléinina* (to play) and *mònkina* (to monkey). The verb *lúzinu* (to lose) becomes *lòstinu* in the past tense, obviously under the influence of *lost*. A few loan-verbs take the *-uoti* ending, *e.g.*, *bãderiuoti* (to bother), *čenčiúoti* (to change) and *faitúotis* (to fight). American-Lithuanian has borrowed many English and American idioms, *e.g.*, *to catch cold*, *half past six*, and *I have got*, and they are translated literally. Other

1 See The Daina: an Anthology of Lithuanian and Latvian Folk-Songs, by Uriah Katzenelenbogen; Chicago, 1931, p. 38.

phrases are taken over bodily. Thus *gudtaim* is *good time, big sur-praiz* is *big surprise,* and *kréizauze* is *crazy-house, i.e., lunatic asylum.*[1]

g. Polish

In September, 1933, at a meeting of the Syndykatu Dziennikarzy Polskich w Ameryce (Society of Polish-American Journalists) at Chicago, Mr. Ernest Lilien read a paper on " The Polish Language and Polish-American Writers." It was devoted mainly to the sins of the speaker's fellow-journalists, and was full of amusing stories. There was the one, for example, about the Polish-American tele-graph-editor who received a press dispatch one night (in English, of course) about a storm that had knocked over fifty telegraph-poles, and who translated *poles* as *Polacks,* to the consternation of his Polish readers. And there was the one about the other Polish-American editor who, trusting the dictionary too much, translated *sewer* as *szwacska* (seamstress, *i.e., sew-er*). Mr. Lilien handled these brethren somewhat roughly, but his very exposure of their crimes also revealed their defense. For they have to work at high pressure translating the words and idioms of American-English into a quite unrelated and far more formal language, and it is no wonder that they occasionally perpetrate astonishing howlers, and deface Polish with fantastic new growths. All the foreign-language editors of the United States labor under the same difficulty, and fall into the same snares. They try to follow the canons of the language they are writ-ing, but only too often it is impossible, and in consequence they promote the development of a bilingual jargon.

The Polish-American journalists are rather more careful than most, but, as Mr. Lilien showed in his paper, their writings are full of Americanisms, in both word and idiom. Instead of writing *obchód* or *święcenie* they turn the English *celebration* (a term they have to use incessantly) into the facile *celebracja,* instead of *zderzenie* (col-lision) they write *kolizja,* and instead of *wypytywać* or *przesłuchi-*

---

1 This account of American-Lithu-anian is based upon Dr. Senn's monograph, before mentioned. I am indebted, too, to his Kleine lit-auische Sprachlehre; Heidelberg, 1929, and to his great kindness in answering questions. He is, of course, not responsible for anything I have here written. I am also in debt to Mr. Pius Grigaitis, editor of *Naujienos,* the Lithuanian daily of Chicago.

wać (to question) they make it *kwestjonować*. In Polish the word for street (*ulica*) should precede the proper name, *e.g.*, *Ulica Kościuszkowska* or *Ulica Kościuszki*, but in American-Polish it is usually *Kosciuszko ulica* (or *sztryta*), and that is what it promises to remain. The American-Polish housewife, on setting out for the grocery-store, never says " Idę do *sklepu korzennego* (or *kolonialnego*)," which is Standard Polish; she says "Idę do *groserni*," with *groscernia* correctly inflected for case. Other nouns that have thus come into the language, displacing Polish terms, are *szapa* (shop), *sztor* (store), *buczernia* (butcher), *salun* (saloon), *salwak* or *sajdwok* (sidewalk), *pajpa* (pipe), *kołt* (coat), *owerholce* (overalls), *pajnt* (paint), *strytkara* (street-car), *wiska* (whiskey), *trok* (truck) and *piciosy* (peaches).[1] In *skład-departamentowy* the first half is good Polish for a large store, but the second half is the English *department*, outfitted with a Polish tail. To Mr. Adam Bartosz, editor of *Jednosc-Polonia* (Baltimore), I am indebted for the following account of a Polish immigrant's rapid introduction to American-Polish:

> When he arrived in this country he had little money and his clothes were old and out of the American fashion, but he brought with him a pair of strong shoulders and a willingness to work. So after a day or two of rest he went out to look for a *dziab* (job). They told him he must go to the *fekterja* (factory) and see the *forman* or *boss*. He got the *dziab* and worked hard, thinking of his first *pejda* (pay-day) on Saturday. Out of his first pay he had to pay for his *bord* and *rum* (room), and buy himself new *siusy* (shoes), for he would not dare to go to church in his Polish boots. When Sunday came his first duty was there. He wondered why he had to pay at the entrance, but some friend explained that it was for the *zytz* (seat). Then he wondered why they had a *kolekta* in the church, and the same friend explained that it was different here than in the Old Country. There the people paid *teksy* (taxes) and the priests were paid by the government, but here the priests got nothing from the government, so they had to have *kolekta*.
>
> After Mass the newcomer went home to enjoy his *rokinch* (rocking-chair), or perhaps he would get acquainted with some *bojsy* (boys) and go with them *na rajda* (for a ride), or to a *piknik*. He would come home all tired, and go to his *bedrum* to get a good night's sleep — providing his *matras* was free of *bedbogi*. With time, if he happened to be a young man, he would find himself a *sweetheartke*, take her to *muwing-pikciesy* (moving-pictures) and buy her *ajskrym* (ice-cream). Some time later he would go to a photographer and send a *pikciur* to the old folks at home.
>
> Thus the English words crowd out the Polish in the immigrant's vocabulary. They are changed so much that sometimes one hardly suspects them of English origin. Every Polish housewife in Baltimore, for instance, buys

1 I am indebted here to Mr. A. E.
Ruszkiewicz of the *Dziennik Dla
Wszystkich*, Buffalo.

oszezechy in season – and whether you hear the word spoken or see it written you are surprised to learn that it is the English *oyster* adopted into Polish-American. The same fate befell *tomato*, which is *merdysy*. Only the *intelligentsia* call crabs *raki;* the common folk use *krebsy*. Also, they use *steksy* and *ciapsy* for steaks and chops, *sasyćki* for sausages, *leberka* for liver pudding, *paje* for pies, *kieksy* for cakes, and *kiendy* for candies.

In 1930 there were 3,342,198 persons of Polish origin in the United States – 1,268,583 born in the territories now included in Poland, 1,781,280 born here of Polish-born parents, and 292,335 born here of mixed parentage. All these, of course, were not Poles; many, and perhaps a good half, were Polish Jews. But the Polish element in the population is still very large. The Polish National Alliance has 350,000 members and assets of $28,000,000, and the Polish Roman Catholic Union has 250,000 members and assets of $13,000,000. There are large Polish colonies in Chicago, Buffalo, Cleveland and Detroit, and in the last-named the population of the enclave of Hamtramck is said to be 80% Polish. In Buffalo the Poles are so thick on the East Side that less than ½ of 1% of the population is non-Polish. The early Polish immigrants set up parochial schools for the purpose of preserving the language as well as the faith, but of late the Catholic bishops have been Americanizing them. The Polish National Church, which separated from the Catholic Church thirty years ago, conducts its services in Polish and teaches the language in its schools. There are seventy-five Polish periodicals in the country, of which fifteen are daily newspapers.[1]

4. FINNO-UGRIAN

a. Finnish

In 1930, according to the census of that year, there were 142,478 persons of Finnish birth in the United States, 148,532 who had been born here of Finnish parents, and 29,526 of partly Finnish parentage – a total of 320,536. Of these, 124,994 reported that Finnish was their mother-tongue. The Finns are scattered through the country from Massachusetts to the Pacific Coast, with their largest colonies in Michigan and Minnesota. They support twenty-one publications

1 I am indebted also to Mr. Paul Klimowicz, of *Gwiazda Polarna*, Stevens Point, Wis.; to Dr. C. H. Wachtel, formerly editor of *Dziennik Chicagoski*, and to Mr. Ernest Lilien, of Stevens Point, Wis.

in their ancestral language, including five dailies. That language has been so greatly modified in the United States that Professor Nisonen, of Suomi College, Hancock, Mich., has proposed that it be called Finglish. Says Mr. John E. Rantamaki, editor of the *Amerikan Suometar*, a tri-weekly published at Hancock:

Many Finns who don't actually mix English words into their Finnish speech use forms that are idiomatically more English than Finnish. For example, consider the sentence " Take care of the boy." In correct Finnish the verb is *pidä*, but most American Finns use *ota*, which is a literal translation of take.[1]

Finnish belongs to the Finno-Ugrian group of languages, along with Hungarian, Lapp, Estonian and a number of minor dialects. It appears to be more closely related to Turkish and Mongolian than to the prevailing languages of Europe. It has fifteen cases, and all of them save the nominative are indicated by adding postpositions to the root. The root itself must always end in a vowel or diphthong. A loan-word, if it ends in a consonant, has a vowel-ending attached to it. Thus *house*, in the nominative, becomes *haussi*, *from the house* (elative) is *haussista*, and *into the house* (translative) is *haussiksi*. Proper names are subjected to the same inflections. Thus, *to Kenton* is *Kentoniin*, and *from Kenton* is *Kentonista*. The Finnish papers in the United States are full of such curious forms as *Ann Arborissa*, *Kalamazoon* and *New York Mills'ista*. Here is the paradigm of *haussi* (house), which has generally displaced the correct Finnish *talo*:

Case	Finglish	English
Nominative	haussi	house
Genitive	haussin	of the house
Accusative	haussi, haussin	house
Essive	haussina	as a house
Partitive	haussia	some of the house
Translative	haussiksi	into the house
Inessive	haussissa	in the house
Elative	haussista	from the house
Illative	haussiin	into the house
Adessive	haussilla	at the house
Ablative	haussilta	away from the house
Allative	haussille	toward the house
Abessive	haussitta	without a house
Comitative	haussineen (-nensa)	with a house
Instructive	haussein	with houses [2]

1 Private communicaton, April 18, 1935.
2 I am indebted here, and for much of what follows, to Mr. Reino W. Suojanen, editor of *Walwoja*, Calumet, Mich.

Appendix

677

Under the influence of English there is some decay of these case-endings, especially in the genitive and the accusative. Even perfectly good Finnish words tend to lose some of their inflections. Here, for example, is the way *kirja* (book) changes for person, in the genitive case, in Finnish and Finglish:

Finglish	*English*	*Finnish*
minun kirja	my book	minun kirjani
sinun kirja	your book	sinun kirjasi
hänen kirja	his book	hänen kirjansa
meidän kirja	our book	meidän kirjamme
teidän kirja	your book	teidän kirjanne
heidän kirja	their book	heidän kirjansa

It will be noted that in Finglish the noun remains invariable: the pronoun alone is felt to be a sufficient indicator of person, as it is in English. The conjugation of the verb is very complicated, involving a great many different endings. Here, for example, is the conjugation, in the indicative mood, of the loan-verb *kliinaan* (to clean), following precisely that of the proper Finnish verb, *puhdistan:*

English	*Finglish*
Present	
I clean	kliinaan
you clean	kliinaat
he (she) cleans	hän [1] kliinaa
we clean	kliinaamme
you clean	kliinaatte
they clean	kliinaavat
Past	
I cleaned	kliinasin
you cleaned	kliinasit
he (she) cleaned	kliinasi
we cleaned	kliinasimme
you cleaned	kliinasitte
they cleaned	kliinasivat
Future	
I shall clean	kliinaamme
you will clean	kliinaat
he will clean	kliinaavat
Present Perfect	
I have cleaned	olen kliinannut
you have cleaned	olet kliinannut
he has cleaned	on kliinannut

[1] The omission of *hän* would put the verb into the imperative mood.

English	Finglish
we have cleaned	olemme kliinannee
you have cleaned	olette kliinanneet
they have cleaned	ovat kliinanneet

Past Perfect

I had cleaned	olin kliinannut
you had cleaned	olit kliinannut
he had cleaned	oli kliinannut
we had cleaned	olimme kliinanneet
you had cleaned	olitte kliinanneet
they had cleaned	olivat kliinanneet

Future Perfect

I shall have cleaned	olen kliinannut vast'edes'
you shall have cleaned	olet kliinannut vast'edes'
he shall have cleaned	on kliinannut vast'edes'
we shall have cleaned	olemme kliinannut vast'edes'
you shall have cleaned	olette kliinanneet vast'edes'
they shall have cleaned	ovat kliinanneet vast'edes'

I Conditional

English	Finglish
I should clean	kliinaisin
you should clean	kliinaisit
he should clean	kliinaisi
we should clean	kliinaisimme
you should clean	kliinaisitte
they should clean	kliinaisivat

II Conditional

I should have cleaned	olisin kliinannut
you should have cleaned	olisit kliinannut
he should have cleaned	olisi kliinannut
we should have cleaned	olisimme kliinanneet
you should have cleaned	olisitte kliinanneet
they should have cleaned	olisivat kliinanneet

Nouns naturally constitute the majority of the English and American loan-words in Finglish. Finnish has a word of its own for *boot-legger*, to wit, *trokari*, but the Finns in the United States prefer *puutlekkeri*. Similarly, they prefer *pisnes* (business) to the correct *liiketoiminta*, *kaara* (car) to *vaunu*, *paarti* (party) to *kekkeri*, and *saitvookki* (sidewalk) to *jalkakäytävä*. Their common term for *housemaid* is *tiskari*, which comes from *dishwater;* the Finnish term is *palvelijatar*. There is a sentence, often heard, which contains only Finglish words, *viz: Pussaa peipipoki kitsistä petiruumaan* (Push the baby-buggy from the kitchen into the bedroom). In Finnish *pussaa* is a slang term for *kiss*. Here are some other loan-nouns, with the Finnish equivalents:

English	Finglish	Finnish
baby	peipi	vauva
bed	peti	sänky, or vuode
book	puuka	kirja
business	pisnes	liiketoiminta
coal	koli	kivihiili
clerk	klärkki	kirjuri, or liikeapulainen
fender	fenteri	likasuoja
grocer	krosseri	ruokatavarakauppa
linotype	lainotaippi	latomakone
orange	orenssi	appelsiini
room	ruuma	huone
sale	seili	myynti
shovel	saveli	lapio
store	stoori	kauppapuoti
street	striitti	katu
teacher	titseri	opettaja
tire	taieri	kumirengas

Most Finnish words end in vowels, so it is usual for the Finnish-Americans to add a vowel to every loan-word which lacks one. No Finnish word ever begins with two consonants, so loan-words which show them are frequently changed, especially by the more recent immigrants. Thus *steak* becomes either *steeki* or *teeki, truck* is either *troki* or *roki, stump* is either *stumppi* or *tumppi,* and *street* may be *striitti, triiti* or *riiti.* Since there is no *c* in the Finnish alphabet *crossing* becomes *kroosinki* or *roosinki.* Since there is no *f, drift* (mining) may become *drifti, rifti* or *rihti.* The differences in sound between the English *b* and *d* and the Finnish *p* and *t,* respectively, are very slight, so *bed* becomes *peti.* The hardest English sound for Finns is that of *th,* but its difficulties are as nothing compared to those presented by the English articles and prepositions, which have no equivalents in Finnish. The newcomer tends to use them when they are not called for, and to omit them when they are. Adjectives are taken into Finglish less often than nouns, but a few have been borrowed for daily use, *e.g., pisi* (busy) and *smartti* (smart). The correct Finnish equivalents are *touhukas* (or *kiire*) and *älykäs,* respectively. Among the loan-verbs in everyday use are *runnata* (to run, in the political sense), *pläännätä* (to plan), *skiimate* (to scheme), *titsata* (to teach) and *juusata* (to use). In the Finnish papers in the

United States the advertisements are commonly translated into Finglish rather than into Finnish. Done into the latter, a grocery or automobile advertisement would be unintelligible to a great many readers.[1]

b. Hungarian

Hungarian, like Finnish, belongs to the Finno-Ugrian group of languages, and in its structure differs very widely from English. In 1930 there were 274,450 persons of Hungarian birth in the United States, and of them 250,393 gave Hungarian as their mother-tongue. In addition there were 272,704 persons of Hungarian parentage and 43,614 of mixed parentage, making 590,768 in all. The Hungarians are mainly concentrated in the Middle Atlantic and East North Central States, and support thirty-three periodicals, of which four are dailies.

American-Hungarian takes in loan-words in large number, and inflects them according to the pattern of the mother-tongue. Thus the verb is commonly outfitted with the usual Hungarian suffix, *-ol* or *-el*, and so to move becomes *muffol*, to catch *kecsol*, to stop *sztoppol*, to drive *drájvol*, to bum *bomol*, to treat *tretel*, to cash *kesel* or *bekesel*, to lunch *luncsol*, to finish *finishel*, and so on. The Hungarian suffixes for case are attached to all nouns, so that into the room becomes *room-ba* and from the room, *room-bol*. Verbs are outfitted in the same manner, *e.g.*, *fixolni* (to fix), *muvolni* (to move), *shoppingolni* (to shop). The purest form of the infinitive suffix is *-ni*, *e.g.*, *irni* (to write), but there are variations expressive of repetitions, abilities, etc. Hungarian is extraordinarily rich in inflectional forms, and ideas that would take a sentence in English are expressed by one word, *e.g.*, *megfixolni* (to fix it), *megfixoltatni* (to get it fixed), *megfixoltathatni* (to be able to get it fixed), *megfixoltathatnánk* (we could get it fixed). In making agent-nouns the agent-suffix, *-os* or *-es*, is usually added either to the borrowed word or to its stem, *e.g.*, *burdos* (boarder), *groszeros* (grocer), *storos* (storekeeper), *bucseros* (butcher) and *szalónos* (saloon-

---

1 In addition to the two Finnish-American editors already mentioned, I am greatly indebted to

Mr. Ivar Vapaa, editor of *Indus-trialisti*, Duluth, Minn.

keeper), but sometimes it is omitted, as in *tícser* (teacher), *pénter* (painter), *feker* (faker), *koszcimer* (customer), *polisz* (policeman), *farmer* (farmer) and *oppretor* (operator). Other nouns are modified in other ways to accord with Hungarian analogues, *e.g.*, *bokszi* (box), *farma* (farm), *majna* (mine), *kéki* (cake), *báré* (bar), *trubli* (trouble); yet others are little changed save in spelling, *e.g.*, *groszeri* (grocery), *londri* (laundry), *dzsél* (jail), *ofisz* (office), *pádé* (party), *csenc* or *csensz* (chance), *szalon* (saloon), *ápsztész* (upstairs), *szvithárt* (sweetheart), *pikcser* (moving-picture), *szuer* (sewer), *piknik* (picnic), *aker* (acre), *bél* (bail), *bézment* (basement), *pléz* (place), *frend* (friend), *só* (show), *baket* (bucket), *páler* (parlor), *bajler* (boiler), *kontri* (country), *kvóder* (quarter), *biznesz* (business), *sztór* (store), *sop* (shop), *rum* (room), *kár* (car), *fíld* (field), *bász* (boss), *peda* (payday), *burdingház* or *burosház* (boarding-house), *fórman* (foreman), *bébi* (baby), *dáli* (dolly), *kendi* (candy).

Many of the common coins of idiom are adopted bodily, *e.g.*, *súr* (sure)¸, *radovéba* (right away), *vatsemetre?* (what's the matter?), *ó kontri* (old country), *ne vorrizz* (don't worry), *nevermajnd* (never mind), *ai donker* (I don't care), *ne baderolj* (don't bother me), *olrajt* (all right), *daczolrajt* (that's all right). At other times the idioms are translated, *e.g.*, *óhaza* (old country) and *vegye a venatot* (to take the train). Here is a sample conversation in American-Hungarian:

A. *Megfixolta* a *ploma* a *sinket?* És *olrajt* csinálta? (Did the plumber fix the sink? Did he do it all right?).

B. *Sure*, de *nevermajnd*, mert az a *landlord biznisze* (Sure, but never mind, that's the landlord's business).

A. *Daczolrajt!* miért *rézelte* a *rentet?* (That's all right! Why did he raise the rent?).

And here are some other specimens:

Fiam a *hájszkulba* jár, az elsó osztályt *finiseli*, a lányon *kifiniselte* a *hájszkult* és most *ofiszba* jár. (My son goes to high-school, and is finishing the first class; my daughter has finished high-school and goes to an office.)

Minden munkába jaró embernek van *kárja* és maga *drájvolja*. A fiam is maga *drájvolja* a *kárt*, miker kimegy a *fíldre*. (Every workingman has a car and drives it himself. My son himself drives a car when he goes to the field.)

Az uccán nagy a *trafik*, csak akker lehet átmenni a másik eldalra, ha *sztoppolták* a *trafikot*. (There is much traffic on the streets, and you can pass over only when the traffic is stopped.)

Kinyitok egy *kannát*, megmelegitem és veszek *kekit* meg *kendit*. (I open a can, warm it, and buy cakes and candy.) [1]

5. CELTIC

a. Gaelic

The Irish in America have made little progress in reacquiring the Goidelic Celtic which passes under the name of Gaelic in Ireland, and is now so busily inculcated by the Free State politicians. Some of the older folk among them make shift to speak it, but certainly not many. A column or so in it is sometimes printed in the Irish weeklies, but few can read it. The Welsh cling more resolutely to their national speech, which belongs to the Brythonic branch of Celtic, and there are two periodicals devoted to it — a monthly called *Cyfaill* and a weekly called *Y Drych*, both published at Utica, N. Y. The circulations of these journals seem to be small, and they contain much English matter. The 1931 Census showed 32,000 Gaelic-speaking persons in Canada, most of them Highland Scots. Of this number, 29,000 had been born west of the Atlantic, and 24,000 lived in Nova Scotia, mostly in Cape Breton. In the counties of Inverness and Victoria 75% of the population is Gaelic-speaking. On the Nova Scotian mainland there are about 2000 in the county of Antigonish who know the language, and perhaps 500 elsewhere. There are also 500 or more on Prince Edward Island.

The only study of this American-Gaelic that I know of has been made by Mr. J. L. Campbell,[2] to whom I am indebted for what follows. He remarks that it differs from the French of Quebec and the German of Pennsylvania in that it has had no support, for years past, from a parent-tongue in full vigor at home. Gaelic has been

1 I am indebted to Dr. József Balassa of Budapest; Dr. Nicholas M. Alter, of Jersey City, N. J.; Mr. A. Dessewffy, editor of *Otthon* (At Home), Chicago; Mr. Paul Nadanyi, managing editor of *Americanai Magyar Népszava*, New York; Mr. Joseph Yartin, of New York; Mr. Hugo Kormor, editor of the *Magyar Herald*, New Brunswick, N. J.; Dr. Joseph Reményi, of Western Reserve University; Mr. John Bencze, supreme secretary of the Verhovay Segély Egylet, Pittsburgh; Mr. George Kemeny, of Detroit; Dr. E. H. Bolgar, of Cleveland; and Mr. Anthony J. Orosz, editor of *Függetlenség*, Trenton, N. J.

2 Scottish Gaelic in Canada, Edinburgh *Scotsman*, Jan. 30, 1933. Mr. Campbell has also written a more elaborate paper, Scottish Gaelic in Canada: it is still unpublished, but he has courteously given me access to it.

under official disapproval in Scotland for 400 years, and it was supplanted by English in the schools of Nova Scotia in 1870. In 1918 provision was made for teaching it, but only as a second language, and it has made little if any progress. It is full of English loan-words, most of which it uses unchanged. But others have been Gaelicized, *e.g.*, *factoraidh* (factory), *càball* (cable), *copar* (copper), *dama* (dam), *stòbh* (stove), *fineadh* (fine), *Geancach* (Yankee), *post-mhaighstir* (postmaster), *bangaid* (banquet), *smuglair* (smuggler), *buiseal* (bushel), *bruis* (brush), *feansa* (fence), *mogais* or *mogaisean* (moccasin), *spruis* (spruce), *seudair* (cedar), *squa* (squaw), *staibh* (stave). The plurals are often formed in the Gaelic manner, *e.g.*, *factoraidhean* (factories), *tréineachan* (trains), *càrachean-sràide* (street-cars), *maidseachan* (matches), *sentaichean* (cents), *clirichean* (clearings), *logaichean* (logs). Mixed sentences are very frequent, *e.g.*, " Air son càradh *bhicycles* tha sinn làn-uidheamaichte air son *enamelling, brazing* agus *vulcanizing* a dheanamh " (For repairing bicycles we are fully equipped, and for doing enameling, brazing and vulcanizing). The softening of consonants is common, *e.g.*, *char* (car), *bheat* (beat), *pharty* (party). Loan-verbs are inflected for tense and mood, *e.g.*, gu 'n *callar* (until he is called), ma *phullas* (if we pull). In place of the English *-ing*, *-adh* is sometimes used, *e.g.*, *driveadh* (driving), *startadh* (starting), *smashadh* (smashing).

6. SEMITIC

a. Arabic

The chief speakers of Arabic in the United States are the Syrians, most of them Christians from the Lebanon. There are also some Moslems and Druzes, but not many. These Syrians used to be classified in the Census returns as Turks, but they are now properly segregated. In 1930 the Census Bureau found 137,576 of them in the country — 52,227 who had been born in Syria, 69,034 born here of Syrian parents, and 11,315 born here of mixed parentage. But the leaders of the Syrian colonies believe that these figures were too low. They estimate that there are from 250,000 to 350,000 persons of Syrian blood in the country. The largest colony is in New York City, but there are others from coast to coast. Indeed, the Syrian-Americans,

who are mainly merchants, are so widely dispersed that their historian, Dr. Philip K. Hitti of Princeton University, says that "there
is not a State in the Union, and hardly a town of 5000 population or
over, in which they are not represented."[1] They support many
periodicals in Arabic, and also have several daily newspapers. There
is also an English weekly in New York, the *Syrian World*, devoted
to their interests. I am indebted to its amiable editor, Mr. H. I.
Katibah, for notes which I summarize as follows:

Perhaps the first verb to be borrowed from English by the Syrian immigrants to the United States was *sannas* (to make a cent). It appears in the
sentence, "L'yom ma *sannasna*" (We haven't made a cent today). Another
early loan-verb was *shannaj* (to make change, whether of money or of situation). Examples "*Shannijli* ha-r-rval" (Change this dollar for me) and "Wayn
bi-n-*shannij?*" (Where do we change?). *Sharraj* (to charge) is also of some
antiquity. Here are some other verbs:
    bardan (to board). The form here is the past tense singular, masculine
gender.
    darrav (to drive).
    narvas (to become nervous or agitated). *Narvasu* might well represent "He
got his goat."
    layyat (to be late). Example: "L'train *mlayyit*" (The train is late).
    bather (to bother). Examples: "La *tbathirni*" (Don't bother me), and
"Haji *tbathru*" (Stop bothering him).
    bartak (to park).
    sammak (to smoke).
    anshar (to take out insurance).
    bunnab (to pump). There is no *p* in Arabic.
    karrak (to crank). A Syrian was heard to say "*Karrakna* l-car w'kakkna"
(We cranked the car and it kicked us).
    faxan (to fix). Example: "Hada mush *mfaxan*" (This is not fixed).
    fabrak (to manufacture). This verb is also heard in Syria.
    haldab (to hold up). A recent borrowing.
    sayyan (to sign, as a check).
    mass (to miss, as a train).
    farraz (to freeze).
    t'amrak (to become an American). This has an analogue in Standard Arabic,
to wit, *tfarnaj* (to become an *Ifranji*, or *Frank*, i.e., a European).
    Arabic has a large capacity for coining verbs which convey the meaning
of whole sentences in English. When a Syrian related a hard-luck story to a
Syrian friend a third Syrian present said *Fartinlu*, meaning "Tell him it is
unfortunate." *Kaddam* is a verb signifying to say God damn. Inflectional variants are *kaddimlu* (Tell him God damn) and *kaddamlu* (He told him God
damn). Sometimes a recent immigrant mistakes English suffixes, *e.g.*, *-ing*, for
Arabic case endings, with curious results. An old Syrian woman once said:

1 The Syrians in America; New
    York, 1924, p. 67. Dr. Hitti is asso-
    ciate professor of Oriental lan-
guages at Princeton. I am much indebted to him for his courteous aid.

Appendix

"Everytin you buy-it-in, in the house-in-it you make-it-in" ("Everything you buy, you can make in the house).

Loan-nouns are given Arabic pronominal suffixes. Thus *your business* is *bizinsak* and *my business* is *bizinsi*. Plurals are commonly formed by adding the Arabic *-at*, as in *house-at* (houses), *star-at* (stores), *baz-at* (bosses), *shoes-at* (shoes) and *lattat* (lots). It will be noted that *shoes-at* is a double plural. The doubling of the first *t* in *lattat* indicates what is known to Arabic grammarians as *tashdid*, or intensification: the word is pronounced *lat-tat*.[1]

American proper names offer some difficulty to the Syrian who has not mastered English. He commonly converts them into nearly related Arabic words, and sometimes the meaning of the latter is amusingly incongruous. Dr. Hitti tells, for example, of an old Syrian in New York who wrote down his own telephone exchange, Adirondack, as *al-qadi 'indak* (the judge is with you).

7. GREEK

a. Modern Greek

Classical Greek never begat children which devoured it, as classical Latin begat the Romance languages; nevertheless, it suffered serious injuries as the Hellenic world disintegrated. On the Greek mainland it now has two forms. The first, cultivated by the educated class, is called the *katharevousa*, and is a somewhat artificial imitation of the classical language; the second, called the *demoteke* and spoken by the masses of the people, is a Greek with changed vowels, new stresses, a vocabulary heavy with loan-words (from Latin, Romance, Slavic, Turkish and Arabic sources), and a greatly decayed grammar. In the other regions inhabited by Greeks (for example, the Ægean islands and the Asia Minor littoral) the popular language has proceeded in the same general direction but by different paths, so that some of its dialects are mutually unintelligible. There is a well-known comedy by D. K. Byrantios, "Babylonia" by title, which depicts a group of Greeks from all over the Near East trying in vain to make themselves comprehensible to one another and to "an Athenian scholar who speaks in the language of Plato and Xenophon." I quote from an article by Mr. Sotirios S. Lontos, editor of *Atlantis*, the Greek daily published in New York.[2] "It has often

---

1 I am indebted also to Mr. S. Baddour, editor of *Al-Bayan*, New York.

2 American Greek, *American Speech*, March, 1926, p. 307.

occurred to me," adds Mr. Lontos, "that had this play been written today, the author would surely have included among his *dramatis personæ* a Greek from America, who, speaking the Greek lingo he had acquired during his stay in the United States, would have the experience of his lifetime trying to make himself intelligible to his fellow countrymen in Greece."

This American-Greek is avoided as much as possible by the contributors to *Atlantis*, but it is used freely by the paper's advertisers and by its readers. Like all the other immigrant languages, it has taken in a great many American words, and more are added constantly. Most of them are given Greek suffixes and respond to such inflections as survive in the popular Greek of the homeland. Others suffer changes in their vowels or consonants, or both. Here are some examples from Mr. Lontos's list:

American	*American-Greek*
automobile	atmobilly
bank	panga
bar	barra
barber	barberis
basket	basketta
beef-stew	beefestoo
bill-of-fare	billoferry
boss	bossis
box	boxy
bum	bummis
car	carro
chef	seffis
city-hall	sityholly
coalmine	colmina
corporation	coporessio
cream	creamy
depot	typos
elevator	eleveta
fan (sporting)	fenna
farm	farma
floor	florry
ginger-ale	gingerella
greenhorn	grihonnis
hot-cakes	hati-kaekia
hotel	otelly
license	lasintza
lunch	launtzi
market	marketta
meat	mete
note	nota

American	American-Greek
parade	parata [1]
parking	parkin
peanut	pinotsi
picnic	picniki
pies (pl.)	paia
policeman	policemanos
postoffice	postoffy, or postoffeon
sheriff	sherrifis
shine (noun)	saina
showcase	sokessa
sidewalk	sadeveki
sport	sportis
stand	standtza
station (police)	stessio
steak	stecky
steward	stooars
taxes	texas
ticket	ticketto
train	traino
young man	youngmanos
young woman	youngwomana [2]

Many other words are used without any change, *e.g.*, *flat* and *street*. The Greeks have difficulty with our *ch* and *sh* sounds, and so have to modify words containing them. The sound of *d* becomes *th* or *t* in Modern Greek. Thus *depot* is converted into *typos*. Inasmuch as *typos* is a perfectly good Greek word, signifying printing-office, the latter change offers some inconvenience. In the same way newcomers from Greece are puzzled by *mappa*, which means both *map* and *mop* in American-Greek, but signifies cabbage at home. *Saina*, which is American-Greek for shine, also serves for sign. The American-Greeks, like all the other immigrants, quickly annex the common American expletives and terms of opprobrium. *God damn it*, at their hands, becomes *godamiti*, and *son-of-a-bitch* becomes *sonababitsi*. Even within the bounds of the Greek vocabulary they fall into new usages in this country. Thus, their common word for fire is *photia*, whereas *per* is more often used at home, and they prefer *xenodocheon* to *estiatorion* for restaurant. The numbered streets in America give them some difficulty. They do not translate *Twenty-fifth street* directly, but change the ordinal number to the cardinal, and make *street* plural, thus coming to

[1] The Greek is *parataxis.*
[2] To Mr. Lontos's list I have added some examples supplied by Mr.

T. D. Curculakis of Athens, to whom I am greatly indebted.

Twenty-five streets. In Greek, proper names take the article, which varies with the gender. Thus the name of every American city, in American-Greek, has its gender. *San Francisco* and *St. Louis* are masculine, *New York* is feminine, and *Chicago* is neuter. "*Boston and Milwaukee,*" says Mr. Lontos, "take the feminine article when used in good Greek, but in ordinary American-Greek are neuters." The Greeks suffer linguistic confusion immediately they attempt English, for in Modern Greek *nay* (spelled *nai*) means *yes*, *P.M.* indicates the hours *before* noon, and the letter *N* stands for *South*. To make things even worse, the Greek *papoose* means grandfather and *mammie* means grandmother.

The Census of 1930 revealed 174,526 persons of Greek birth in the United States, 101,668 persons born here of Greek parents, and 27,557 born here of parentage partly Greek, or 303,751 in all. Of these, 189,066 reported that Greek was their mother-tongue. The Greek-Americans are served by fifteen periodicals in Greek, of which four are daily newspapers.

8. ASIATIC

a. Chinese

As we have seen in Chapter XII, Section 1, the influence of English on Chinese, even in China, is already very considerable. Not only does Chinese absorb a great many English and American loan-words; it also tends toward grammatical and syntactical accord with English. In the United States these tendencies are naturally very noticeable, not only among the rank and file of Chinese-speaking immigrants, but also among the Chinese students who frequent American universities. Says Dr. Arthur W. Hummel, chief of the Division of Orientalia in the Library of Congress:

Dr. Hu Shih, leader of the current literary revolution in China, has told me, what I had myself previously observed, that his Chinese word-order is very much like that of English. He says that whereas, before he came to America to study, he could not get good English by keeping to the Chinese word-order, he now finds that he can translate his Chinese writings almost word for word. This is, perhaps, more true of Hu Shih's writings than of others; nevertheless, it represents a rather wide-spread tendency, due to the fact that all Chinese youths who go to school at all must spend some time on English.[1]

1 Private communication, July 11, 1934.

There are, of course, difficulties in the way of English loan-words, for on the one hand some of their sounds are absent from Chinese, and on the other hand the lack of an alphabet in Chinese makes it necessary, in writing, to find whole syllables approximating their sounds, and sometimes that leads to absurdity, or, indeed, is downright impossible. Consider, for example, the Chinese handling of the word *America*, which is first encountered in writings of the Ming Dynasty (1368–1644). It is represented by hooking together the ideograph for *ya*, a common prefix to proper names, with those for *mei* (beautiful, admirable), *li* (clever, or interest on money), *chia* (a suffix), and *chou* (region, country). The result is *Ya-mei-li-chia-chou*, meaning the beautiful and clever (or interest-collecting) land. In everyday use this is abbreviated to *Mei-kuo* (beautiful land). *American* is similarly reduced to *Mei-kuo-jên* (beautiful-country man). Sometimes the effect is amusing, as when *New York* becomes *Niu* (to grasp, to seize) *-yo* (important, compendious), *i.e.*, the grasping, important city, or *Roosevelt* becomes *Lo* (a net) *-s-fu* (a blessing), or *-fou* (to revive). Many common English words have been taken into Chinese by the same process. The Southern Chinese (who are most numerous in the United States) find our *r* difficult, so they sometimes change it to *l* or *h*, but the Northern Chinese under Manchu influence, make a guttural of it. In both cases, loans often have to be changed radically in order to represent them in Chinese ideographs, which are extremely numerous (about 10,000 are in use) but still fall short of being innumerable. The following examples are listed by Professor Tsung-tse Yeh of Tsing Hua University, Peiping: [1] *k'a fei* (coffee), *sha-fa* (sofa), *sai-yin-ssŭ* (science), *fan-shih-ling* (vaseline), *fan-o-ling* (violin), *hu-lieh-la* (cholera), *wei-shih-chi* (whiskey), *nik-ko-lo* (negro), *mo-t'o* (motor), *t'o-la-ssŭ* (trust), *p'u-k'ê* (poker), *shui-mên-ting* (cement), *wa-ssŭ* (gas), *tê-lü-fêng* (telephone), *hsüeh-ch'ieh* (cigar), *p'u-ou* (boy), *san-wei-chih* (sandwich), *su-ta* (soda), *ting* (tin), *ch'a-ssŭ-ta-ssŭ* (justice), *pi-k'o-ni-k'o* (picnic). In many cases, of course, translation takes the place of this onerous attempt at transliteration. Thus, *fork* becomes *ch'a-tzŭ*, from *ch'a*, a prong, with *tzŭ*, a common suffix, added, and *telephone* becomes *tien-hua*, literally, electricity talk. Other examples are:

[1] On Chinese Borrowings From English and French, in The Basic Vocabulary, by C. K. Ogden; London, 1930, p. 92 *ff.*

cigarette: *chih-yen* (paper smoke).
safety-razor: *t'ui-tzu* (gentleman instrument).
tooth-paste: *ya-kao* (tooth-grease).
elevator: *tien-t'i* (electricity, or lightning, ladder).
life-insurance: *jên-shou-pao-hsien* (man old-age guarantee to feel at ease).
locomotive: *huo-ch'e-t'ou* (fire wagon).
motor-car: *ch'i-ch'e* (vapor wagon).
moving-picture theatre: *tien-ying-yüan* (electricity shadow hall).
soda-water: *ch'i shui* (vapor water).[1]

Sometimes there is a combination of translation and transliteration, e.g., *yah-mee* (yard), in which the second syllable means rear in Chinese, and *ping-chi-ling* (ice-cream), in which the first syllable means ice. Many loans, of course, are taken in unchanged or almost so, e.g., *hello, kid, guy, nuts* and the universal *O.K.* The Americanized Chinese, even if he be a Cantonese, often masters the *r*, and is thus able to use such terms as *all right, girl, good-morning* and *dutch-treat*. In writing, they are represented, not by syllables of the same general sound, but by corresponding Chinese words. Thus, *all right* is represented by *shih* (yes), autumn by *chin* (autumn), and graft by *weila* (bribery). The third person pronoun *ta* is the same in Chinese in all genders, but under the influence of Western education the Chinese have begun to use slightly different ideographs to represent *he, she* and *it*, though all of them continue to be pronounced *ta*. There is a considerable difference of opinion as to the proper representation, in Chinese, of *God*. About a century ago the Catholic missionaries in China were ordered by a papal decree to use *T'ien-Chu* (Lord of Heaven), but most of the Protestant brethren use *Shang-Ti* (Emperor Above), with a minority preferring *Shên* (Spirit). The Chinese journalists of the United States incline toward purism in their writing, but their colleagues in China, following Liang Chi-chao (1869–1928), founder of Peiping's first daily newspaper, are extremely hospitable to neologisms. At the time of the Revolution of 1911 such reformers as Liang Chi-chao, K'ang Yu-wei, and Chang Shih-chao brought in a great many novel political terms from English, and they promise to stick, e.g., *teh-moh-ka-la-si* (democracy), *p'u-lo-lieh-t'a-li-ya* (proletariat) and *pao-êrh-hsi-wei-k'ê* (bolshevik). The English honorifics, *Mr., Mrs.* and *Miss,* are in common use both in China and among Chinese in this country,

1 I am indebted here to Dr. Verne
Dyson, director of the Institute of
Chinese Studies, New York.

albeit they usually take the forms of *Mi-tse-te*, *Mi-hsi-tse* and *Mi-tse*. Their use is opposed by a faction of Chinese, led by Dr. Liu Fu, president of the Women's College of Peiping, who ordained in 1931 that his charges should be called *Kuniang*, not *Miss*.[1] The transliteration of Chinese words into English presents difficulties. The system ordinarily used is that devised by Sir Thomas Wade half a century ago, but of late it has a rival in a scheme for the complete romanization of Chinese writing proposed by Dr. Chao Yüan-jên.[2]

The Census of 1930 disclosed 74,954 Chinese in the United States, of whom 30,868 had been born here. There are 27,179 in Hawaii. There were more in the Continental United States at earlier periods, but of late, because of the Chinese Immigration Act of 1882 and its successors, the flow of immigrants has been toward South America and the Malay Archipelago, not toward the United States. There are now twenty Chinese periodicals in the country, of which eight are daily newspapers.

b. Japanese

Standard Japanese, even more than Chinese, has been hospitable to English loan-words, and in Chapter XII, Section 1, I have described some of their effects upon the language. The Japanese spoken in this country, of course, is full of them. On account of the differences between the Japanese phonetic system and that of English many have to be changed materially. Every Japanese word ends either in a vowel or in *n*. Thus, Japanization produces such forms as the following: *aisukurimu* (ice-cream), *bata* (butter), *bazarin* (violin), *bifuteki* or *bisuteki* (beefsteak), *biru* (beer), *bisuketto* (biscuit), *bi-*

---

1 The Little Critic, by Lin Yutang, *China Critic* (Shanghai), April 2, 1931.

2 I am indebted to Mr. Arthur A. Young, editor of the *Chinese Christian Student*, New York; Mr. Y. E. Hsiao, general secretary of the Chinese Students' Christian Association in North America; Mrs. Elsie Clark Krug, of Baltimore; Mr. Su Chen Ho, of the Brooklyn Museum; Dr. W. W. Pettus, president of the College of Chinese Studies of California College in China, Peiping; Dr. James Stinch-comb, of the University of Pittsburgh; Mr. S. H. Abramson, of Montreal; Dr. A. Kaiming Chin, of the Chinese-Japanese Library, Harvard University; Mr. John E. Reinecke of Honokaa, Hawaii; Miss Rosalie Yee Quil, of the Pittsburgh Carnegie Library; Miss Grace Yee Quil, of Pittsburgh; Dr. Nancy Lee Swann, curator of the Gest Chinese Research Library, McGill University, Montreal; Mr. Ben Robertson, of the Associated Press, and Mr. Harold Coffin, of the Hawaii Tourist Bureau.

yahoru (beer-hall), *botan* (button), *chokoretto* (chocolate), *daiamondo* (diamond), *dansu* (dance), *dainamaito* (dynamite), *ereki* (electricity), *gasu* (gas), *hankachi* or *hankechi* (handkerchief), *katsuretsu* (cutlet), *kakuteiru* (cocktail), *kohi* (coffee), *kosumechikku* (cosmetics), *kyabetsu* (cabbage), *naifu* (knife), *penki* (paint), *ranpu* (lamp), *renkoto* (raincoat), *resu* (lace), *renzu* (lens), *risurin* (glycerin), *seruroido* (celluloid), *shatsu* (shirt), *sosu* (sauce), *suponji* (sponge), *taouru* (towel) and *toranpu* (tramp).[1] There are many substitutions of one vowel for another. The *ah* of *father* is commonly substituted for the *er* of *river*, the *ure* of *measure*, the *ir* of *girl* and the *or* of *labor*. An *i* like that of *police* is added to many words, e.g., *match*, *edge*, and the *oo* (or *u*) of *book* is added to others, e.g., *block*, *club*, *crab*, *map*. An *ee*-sound is substituted for the short *i* in *sit*, *it*, *miss*, *ship*, and for the *ai*-sound in *crime* and *guide*. The *g* is commonly nasalized, so that *Chicago* becomes *Chicango*, and *cigar* is *cingah*. Before *i*, *s* changes to *sh* and *z* to *dzh*, and before *i* and *u*, *t* and *d* become *ch* (*tsh*) and *j* (*dzh*). In words beginning with *hi* there is often a change to *shi*. There is a considerable confusion between *r* and *l*, and most Japanese find it hard to distinguish between such pairs as *grow-glow*, *broom-bloom*, *royal-loyal*. After *f* an *h* is often inserted, as in *fhence* (fence), and *o* frequently appears in compounds, e.g., *good-o-morningu*, *good-o-bye*. The sounds of *th* (both as in *the* and as in *thin*), *pl*, *bl* and *ks* are almost impossible to a Japanese.[2] There are two systems of transcribing Japanese into English, the Hepburn system and that of the Nippon Romazikwai (Roman Letter Association of Japan), which proposes to abolish the ancient Japanese use of modified Chinese ideographs. The Japanese government appears to be unable to decide between the two.

There were 138,834 Japanese in the Continental United States in 1930, of whom 68,357 had been born either in the United States or in its possessions. In addition, there were 139,631 in Hawaii. There are fourteen Japanese periodicals in the United States and eleven in

1 All these are from Japanese Borrowings of English Words, by H. Sato, *Notes and Queries*, May 25, 1929.
2 I am indebted here to Anglicized Japanese, by Frederick W. Brown, *Quarterly Journal of Speech Education*, Feb., 1927. See also The

Pronunciation of Japanese, by Masatoshi Gensen Mori; Tokyo, 1929, Japanized English, by Sawbay Arakawa, 4th ed.; Tokyo, 1930, and English Influence on Japanese, by Sanki Ichikawa, *Studies in English Literature* (Tokyo), April, 1928. The last lists 1397 words.

Hawaii, including nine daily newspapers in the former and three in the latter.[1]

9. MISCELLANEOUS

a. Armenian

Armenian is an independent Indo-European language lying between the Indo-Iranian group and Greek. In 1930 there were 51,741 persons in the United States who gave it as their mother-tongue. There are ten Armenian periodicals in the country, of which two are daily newspapers, both published in Boston. I can find no published study of the American dialect of the language. For the following brief note I am indebted to Mr. R. Darbinian, editor of *Hairenik*, the elder of the two Boston dailies:

A conversation carried on in half English and half Armenian is very common. One frequently hears " *Good time* me ounetza " (I had a good time), and sentences like the following:

Bossus z is *fire* erav (My boss fired me).

Lawyer in katzi *business* hamar (I went to the lawyer on business).

Aman, *nervous* gellam gor (Oh my, I am getting nervous).

Ays *pointé* goozem tzouytz dal (I want to show this point, or, I want to point out this).

Yete *wholesale house* me *special* oonena yerek chors *item cost price* garnes (If a wholesale house should have a special, you can get three or four items at cost price).

Yes garachargem *temporary board* me gazmel, yev togh *directornere investigate* enen (I move that we organize a temporary board, and let the directors investigate the matter).

Many words and phrases for which there is no equivalent in Armenian are often used, *e.g., all right, O.K., good time, jazz.* Others that have Armenian equivalents displace them, *e.g., yes, no, show, movies, radio, phone, hello, uncle, aunt, nurse, chauffeur, lunch, butcher, grocer, laundry, drug-store.*

b. Hawaiian

Hawaiian, which belongs to the Polynesian family of languages and is closely related to Samoan, Maori, Tahitian and Tongan, is the dying tongue of a dying people. The Census of 1930 discovered

1 For the statistics of publications throughout this Appendix I am indebted to N. W. Ayer & Sons Directory of Newspapers and Periodicals; Philadelphia, annually. The population figures are from Fifteenth Census of the United States, 1930: Population, Vol. II; Washington, 1933.

but 22,636 pure-blood Hawaiians in the archipelago, and even the addition of 28,224 persons of mixed blood left them greatly out- numbered by the Caucasians, the Filipinos and the Japanese. The Territorial Legislature, in 1923, passed an act providing for " the preparation and publication of a school text-book in the Hawaiian language," and seven years later a slim volume prepared by Mrs. Mary H. Atcherley was brought out under the imprint of the Hawaiian Board of Missions,[1] but English has been taught in the schools since 1853, and since 1896 it has been obligatory. Writing more than a generation ago, William M. Langdon said in an editorial in the *Paradise of the Pacific:*[2]

> By the end of this century the Hawaiian speech will have as little usage as Gaelic or Irish has now, and it will not be many years hence when there will be but small demand for Hawaiian-English interpreters. The native chil- dren in the public and private schools are getting a good knowledge of Eng- lish speech. Hawaiians who speak only their native tongue find it difficult to obtain employment. Time was, thirty years or so ago, when it was necessary for every foreigner to learn Hawaiian; now it becomes necessary for the Hawaiian to learn English.
>
> Since the time of Kamehameha the Great the Hawaiian tongue has been almost revolutionized, so many idioms have crept in and so many English ex- pressions with Hawaiian spelling and pronunciation have been adopted. The children now in school will retain, as long as they live, a comprehension of their mother-tongue and an affection for it too, but it is doubtful if the same can be said of *their* children.

" When Mr. Langdon wrote this," says Frederick B. Withington,[3] " there was considerable Hawaiian spoken throughout the Islands. Most of the important firms had . . . signs with their names in the native tongue. For instance, the law firm of Castle and Withington was known to the Hawaiians as *Kakela e Wilkinokona.* An under- standing of Hawaiian was often necessary in the law courts, and many documents were written or printed in both English and Hawaiian. Today little or none of this bilingual use is necessary." The decay of Hawaiian Mr. Withington ascribes to eight causes, as follows:

> (a) Its inadequacy. Hawaiian was a primitive language and was unable to satisfy the needs of a modern world.
> (b) The influx of foreign terms. As the Hawaiian became conscious of the

---

1 The First Book in Hawaiian; Honolulu, 1930.
2 November, 1903.
3 In The Hawaiian Language: Its

Modern History as a Means of
Communication, kindly placed at
my disposal by the author.

need of new terms he adopted them from the foreigner. Many of these came from uncultured traders and sailors and thus were crude.

(c) The tendency to vulgarity. The better classes used English and left the Hawaiian to the less cultured. The result was that the language tended toward the vulgar.

(d) The decrease of the Hawaiian population. If Captain Cook was correct in his estimate of the population, then the Hawaiian population has gone from over 400,000 to about 50,000 in three quarters of a century.

(e) The desire for English-conducted schools by the Hawaiians themselves.

(f) The paucity of a literature. There was no literature among the Hawaiians until the missionaries came and helped them to write it.

(g) The growing relations with the outside world. As the natives increased their trade they made more and more use of one of the great modern languages.

(h) The Islands become part of the United States. As Hawaii became an integral part of the United States, English became the official language.

Hawaiian has the shortest alphabet ever heard of — the five vowels and *h, k, l, m, n, p* and *w*, or twelve letters in all. It is thus constrained to make radical changes in many loan-words, *e.g., kapiki* (cabbage), *kala* (dollar), *keleponi* (telephone), *loke* (rose) and *Kelemania* (Germany). All the vowels are used as words, and all have multiple meanings, *e.g., a* is a verb in the perfect meaning lit, a noun meaning a small rock, an adjective meaning rocky, an adverb meaning to or until, and a preposition meaning to or of. Other words are formed by combining two vowels, *e.g., aa* (dwarf), *ia* (he, she or it), *ua* (rain), or a consonant and vowel, *e.g., ko* (sugar), *nu* (roar), *wa* (time), *hi* (cholera). Not only must every word end with a vowel, but also every syllable. Two consonants may never come together. The effect on loan-words is shown in *aila* (oil), *alemanaka* (almanac), *amene* (amen), *baka* (tobacco), *bele* (bell), *berena* (bread), *bipi* (beef cattle), *buke* (book), *eka* (acre), *galani* (gallon), *kanapi* (centipede), *kapena* (captain), *keneta* (cent), *paona* (pound), *pena* (paint), *peni* (pen), *penikala* (pencil), *pepa* (paper), *Sabati* (Sabbath), *sekona* (second), *silika* (silk), *talena* (talent). Here are some specimen sentences showing the use of loan-words:

Ke kamailio nei oia ma ka olelo *Beretania* (He speaks in British, *i.e.,* English).

Ua kuai lilo mai la au i elima mau *galani* (I bought five gallons).

Eia wau ke hoouna aku nei ia oe i umi mau *keneta* (I am sending you ten cents).

Ke kani nei ke kanaka i ka *bele* (The man is ringing the bell).[1]

1 For the loan-words and the sentences I am indebted to the Rev. Henry P. Judd, associate secretary of the Board of the Hawaiian Evangelical Association. I also owe thanks to Professor N. B. Beck, of the University of Hawaii, and to Mr. Carl S. Carlsmith, of Hilo.

The surviving Hawaiian periodical literature seems to consist only of a weekly published at Hilo and a Sunday-school monthly, in Hawaiian and English, at Honolulu.

c. Gipsy

The language of the Gypsies is a dialect related to those of the northwestern frontier of India, and their Indian ancestors seem to have wandered through Kabulistan into Persia and Syria in the Thirteenth Century. One section then struck southward into Egypt, and the other proceeded into Europe. They are now scattered over all of Europe, and most of northern Africa and North America. In every country where they have settled they have picked up many loan-words from the local language, but Romany or Romanes is still a distinct tongue, with a grammatical system of its own and a vocabulary understood by the Gypsies of widely separated countries.[1] Most Gypsies speak this Romanes more or less, but in the United States they commonly use English in their everyday business, with a copious admixture of Romanes words. An example: " *Once* apré *a* chairus *a* Romany chal chored *a* rāni chillico, *and then* jälled atút *a* prastraméngro 'pré *the* drum " (Once upon a time a Gypsy stole a turkey, and then met a policeman on the road).[2] There is a masculine definite article, *o*, in Romanes, and a feminine article, *i*, but the American Gypsies always use the English *the*. The indefinite article is also borrowed, but sometimes it is omitted altogether, as in " Dikóva gáiro " (I see a man). Many of the nouns have suffixes indicating gender, to wit, -*o* for the masculine, and -*i* for the feminine. There are some traces of grammatical gender, but in the main these suffixes are used logically. Thus, *chávo* is boy and *chavi* or *chai* is girl, *gáiro* is man and *gáiri* is woman. The plural is formed by adding -*e*, -*aw* or -*yaw*, e.g., *peéro* (foot), *peere* (feet); *grei* (horse), *gréiaw* (horses). But in many, and perhaps most cases the English -*s* is used. In Pennsylvania there are a few small groups of German Gypsies, known locally as *Shekener* or *Chikener* (Ger. *Zigeuner*). They immigrated from the Rhineland during the Eighteenth Century. Their

1 The best account of it is to be found in The Dialect of the English Gypsies, by B. C. Smart and H. T. Crofton, 2nd ed.; London, 1875.

2 I take this from The English Gypsies and Their Language, by Charles G. Leland, 4th ed.; London, 1893, p. 208.

dialect shows a great many loans from Pennsylvania-German, *e.g.,*
kotz (cat), *haws* (rabbit), *hausleira* (peddler), *bawm* (tree), *goul*
(horse), *schlong* (snake).[1] The number of Gypsies surviving in the
United States is unknown, for the Census Bureau is unaware of them.
The tribes that once roved the country have been much depleted by
disease, intermarriage and the hustling of the police. Most of them
are now located in large cities, where the women practise fortune-
telling and the men work at ordinary trades.

1 The Language of the Pennsylvania German Gypsies, by Henry W. Shoemaker, *American Speech*, Aug., 1926.

LIST OF WORDS AND PHRASES

Because they are so seldom encountered in publications in English, the non-English terms listed in the Appendix are here omitted. But non-English proper names are included. Verbs are indicated by the preposition of the infinitive. In virtually every other case the character of the word is obvious.

a, 329, 334, 335, 336, 337, 338, 339, 340, 343, 344, 346, 348, 351, 359, 366, 367, 368, 369, 371, 377, 381, 383, 389, 390, 391, 402, 404, 405, 441, 446, 468, 471, 613; -a, 347, 549; a-, 161; ä, 490; à, 382; å, 490
A 1, 208
A.A.A., 209
Aaron, 535
Abalina, 512
Abarbanel, 501
Abbott, 496
Abbud, 496
Abe, 519
Abednego, 515
aber nit, 157, 566
Abolena, 524
abolitionist, 148
about, 468
about to go, 201
above, 399
Abraham, 496, 507, 508, 535
absorbable, 118
absquatulate, to, 145
abuv, 399
acceptress, 75
accession, to, 196
acclimated, 325
accommodation-train, 146
accompaniment, 118
accouchement, 304
accumulator, 236
ace, 182, 573; -high, 191
achiev, 401
acromatic, 118

achtel, 250
acidulous, 118
acre, 383, 384, 386
activ, 401, 403
actorine, 180
actual, 352
Ad, 519
ad, 170, 183, 401, 403
Ada, 529
Adam, 515, 519, 535
Adam-and-Eve, to, 561
adamic, 75
Adamovič, 490
Adams, 490, 498
ad-club, 170; -man, 170; -rate, 170; -writer, 170
addition, 120
address, 325
addrest, 402, 403
adelantado, 153
Adelloyd, 521
Adgurtha, 522
adhesiveness, 118
adioyne, 379
adjoin, 379
adjunct professor, 242
adjutancy, 118
adjutant, 283
administration, 245
Admire, 505
admire, to, 25
admissibility, 118
admit, to, 199
admitted to the bar, to be, 246
Adnelle, 521
adobe, 152
adopted, 245
Adrielle, 521

adult, 325, 329
adultery, 310
adumbrate, 325
advance, 335
advanst, 403
advertisement, 324, 406
advertising-engineer, 290; -engineer, 289
advertize, 402
advice, 394
adviser, to women students, 242
advisory, 118
advize, 402
advocate, to, 7, 117, 118, 120
adze, 128, 393
ae, 405; -ae, 347; æ, 401
A.E.F., 209
aerocade, 179
æsthete, 390
æsthetic, 390
aetaernall, 379
æther, 390
ætiology, 390, 411
affetuoso, 75
affiliate, to, 141
Affinity, 537
Aframerican, 171
after, 335
aftr, 404
again, 339
against, 339
Agamemnon, 523
agast, 402, 406
agathokakological, 117
agenda, 220, 239
Agenora, 524
agent, 278

aggravate, to, 141, 165, 168
aghast, 406
agile, 341
ag'in, 161
Agiochook, 532
Agnes, 509
a-going, 443
agree with, to, 215
ah, 328, 335, 337, 343, 344, 349, 404
ahead, 352
ahem, 352
a-holt, 438
ahoy, 352
Ah there, my size, I'll steal you, 566
ai, 341
aid, 182, 199
aigle, 214
aile, 406
Aileen, 510
Aili, 510
Ails, 524
Ainse, 482
ain't, 51, 160, 202, 360, 377, 425, 445, 470
ain't got, 420
ain't-supposed-to-itis, 179
air, to, 199, 586
air, 181; -conditioned, 181; conscious, 181; -cooled, 181; -hostess, 181; -line, 146; -liner, 181; -minded, 181; -monkey, 583; -rodeo, 181
aisle, 236, 406; -manager, 284
aislick, 110
aker, 383, 384, 386
Åkerberg, 490
Aklus, 522
Akron, 542; -ian, 549; -ite, 549
Al, 183
al, 468
Alabama, 337, 339
Alabamian, 548
alabastine, 173
Alamagordo, 534
Alan, 507
alarm, 415
alarmist, 101
alarum, 415
alas, 614

Alaska, 339
Albanian, 548
Albert, 482, 511, 515
Albrecht, 482
Albright, 482
Albuquerque, 541; -an, 549
alcalde, 152
alcohol-lamp, 233
alderman, 116
ale, 600
Alexander, 515
Alexandria, 530
Alf, 519
alfabet, 402, 403
alfalfa, 152, 263
alfalfy, 360
Alferita, 524
Alfred, 513
Algeier, 483
Algernon, 518
Algire, 483
Alhambra, 534
alibi, 210
Alice, 506
Alimenta, 524
all, 159, 401
all aboard, 239
Allard, 516
allay-foozee, 160
Allegany, 539
Alleghany, 539
Allegheny, 528, 539
allemande, 296
Allen, 506, 524
all-fired, 316
Allgeier, 483
Allgeiger, 483
Allgeyer, 483
Allgire, 483
Alligator, 536
alligator, 112, 372
all of, 252
allons, 75
allot upon, to, 99
allow, to, 100
alloy, 325
all right, 253
allrightest, 463
allrightsky, 222
all set, 262
allus, 359
ally, 325
Allyn, 507
Alma, 529
alma mater, 338, 347

almond, 337
almoner, 248
almost, 468
alms, 292, 328, 337, 349
aloha, 373
aloof, 344
alphabetical soup, 209
alright, 96, 396, 407
Alt, 482
Altamont, 534
altar, 577
alter, to, 302
altho, 400, 402, 403
aluminium, 396, 415
aluminum, 396, 415
alumnae, 347, 401
alumnas, 413
alumni, 243
alumnis, 413
alumnuses, 413
Alves, 495
Alvez, 495
always, 468
Alžběta, 511
Am, 519
am, 427
Ama, 524
Āman, 490
amass, 334
amateur, 294, 352
ambassador, 395
ambish, 169, 222
ambition, to, 7, 119
Ambolena, 522
Ambrose, 519
ambulance, 288; -chaser, 246
ameed, to, 16
Amelia, 507, 519
Amélia, 509
amen, 268, 337, 338; -corner, 150
amendable, 118
American-bar, 292
Americanism, 6
Americanitis, 179
Americanize, to, 141
Americano, 75
Amerind, 171
Ames, 483
amigo, 153, 376
am not, 445
amœbas, 413
ampere, 559
ampico, 172
amusement-engineer, 290

an, 351; -an, 548, 549
Ana, 509
Anaca, 524
anæsthesia, 390, 393
analisis, 402
analysis, 210
analyzation-engineer, 290
Ananias-club, 174; -fest, 218
Anasagunticook, 531
Änberg, 490
ancestor, 395
anchor her, to, 583
-ander, 491
Anders, 510
Andersohn, 477
Anderson, 477, 493, 494
Andersson, 477, 492
and how, 219, 222, 572
andiron, 128
Andrea, 509
Andreen, 491
Andrén, 491
Andresen, 477
Andrew, 510, 511, 515
Andrey, 510, 511
Andriessen, 477
Andy, 510
anecdote, to, 168
anesthetic, 394
aneurismal, 118
angel, 24; -food, 582
Angeleño, 550
Anglais, 110
angle, 210
angry, 143
Anheuser, 484
aniline, 155
animalize, 118
anlage, 220
Annabel, 507
Annamoriah, 537
Annapolitan, 549
Anne Arundel, 540
Annette, 507
Annie, 509
Annika, 524
announce, to, 220
announst, 403
A No. 1, 208, 570
anser, 403
anserd, 403
ant, 335, 336, 360
antagonize, to, 31, 118, 230
antennas, 413

anteriour, 380
ante up, to, 191
Anthracite, 536
anti-, 180; -bounce-clip, 237; Episcopalian, 181; -Federalist, 181; -fog-matic, 149; -suffragist, 181
Antiskid, 173
antithetical, 118
antmire, 302
Antone, 509
Antonietta, 509
Antonin, 511
Antonio, 508, 509
Antti, 493, 510
Anvil, 523
anxious-bench, 148, 150; -seat, 148, 150
any, 471
anything, 352
anyways, 204, 468
Anzonetta, 522
apartment, 233, 247
apartment-hotel, 233; -house, 233
Apathy, 505
Aphnah, 524
Apokeepsian, 550
apothem, 402
apparatus, 338
apparatuses, 413
appearance-engineer, 289
appellor, 118
appendic, 461
appendices, 412
appendictis, 341
appendixes, 412
apple, 336; -butter, 115; -fest, 218; -jack, 149; -knocker, 577; -pie, 85; -sauce, 263, 561
application-engineer, 291
appreciate, to, 7, 118
appreciation, 118
approach, 576
approbate, to, 128
ar, 399, 401, 403
Arab, 295, 560
aracoune, 104
arboreal, 395
arborescent, 118
arborization, 118
arbour, 395
arch, 614
Archambault, 495

Archie, 506
architect, 401
architecture, 382
Ardis, 522
ardor, 386
ardour, 395
are, 328, 349, 401, 427
a'ready, 352
are not, 428
aren't, 202, 349, 428, 445
argify, to, 129
Arginta, 524
argon, 559
Arillah, 522
Arkansas, 541
Arkansawyer, 552
arkitecture, 382
Armand, 508
Armella, 522
Armina, 521
Armistead, 479
armoir, 214
armonica, 120
armory, 395
armour, 395
arms, 328, 349
Armstädt, 479
Arnold, 507
arnswer, 351
arrange, to, 302
Arrazeta, 521
arriv'd, 438
arroyo, 152
arse, 302, 308
art, 349
arterial road, 546
Arthur, 506, 515, 524
Artice, 524
ary, 129; -ary, 325
as, 458, 472
Asbury, 535
ascended, 604
ascertainable, 118
as cross as a b'ar with two cubs and a sore tail, 137
as drunk as a Pole, 296
ash-can, 115, 233; -cart, 233; -man, 233; -truck, 233
Ashshi, 496
as if, 203, 458
ask, 334, 335, 336, 352
Askew, 503
askt, 403
Åslund, 490
asp, 336

asphalt, 339, 389, 390
asphalte, 389, 390
ass, 302, 309
as scarce as hen's teeth, 563
assistant-instructor, 242; -master, 241; -profes- 242; -treasurer, 289
associate-editor, 289; -professor, 242
associational, 98
ast, 352
as though, 203
at, 404
a tall, 471
at all, 471
ate, 431, 442, 614
athaletic, 353
Athan, 512
Athanasios, 512
Athenian, 551
Ather, 523
-ative, 325
Atlantans, 548
atomiser, 233
atta-boy, 263, 471, 564
attaché, 409; -case, 246
attack, to, 199
attackt, 428
attackted, 420, 428, 438
attend, to, 435
au, 335, 336, 360
Aubert, 516
Aubrey, 518
Audrivalus, 524
August, 505, 519
Augusta, 529
Ault, 482
aunt, 334, 335, 336, 338, 344, 349, 371
au revoir, 348
authentic, 343
author, to, 93, 192, 195
auto, 169, 170
auto, to, 191, 192
autocade, 179
autocar, 173
autocracy, 343
autogenius, 353
automobile, 233
automotive-engineer, 290
autsch, 158
autumn, 33, 42, 62, 128
Avaline, 521
avenue, 546, 547
average up, to, 198

Averill, 521
avigator, 179
aw, 335, 339, 343, 344
away, 256
a-wee, 378
awe-strickened, 193
awful, 466, 614
awfully, 210, 264
a.w.o.l., 209, 573
ax, 352, 386, 389, 394
axe, 389, 393
Axel, 510
axle-grease, 582
-ay, 347
Ayscough, 503
ayuntamiento, 153
az-nu, 407
b, 353, 368, 401, 402
baa, 349
babbling brook, 578
Babe, 523
babies' class, 241
Baby, 519
baby-bound, 561
baby-carriage, 233, 256
baby-lifter, 583
bacardi, 173
bacaze, 339
baccaliaos, 373
bach, 482
bach, to, 192
Bache, 500
bachelor, 395
Bachmann, 479
bacillis, 413
bacillus, 155, 559
back, 115, 343; -country, 115; -field, 115; -gar- den, 250, 256; -land, 115; -lane, 115; -line, 115; -log, 115; -lots, 115; -number, 144, 187; settler, 115; -street, 115; -talk, 62, 144; -taxes, 144; -woods, 57, 115, 231; -yard, 250, 256
back, to, 199
back and fill, to, 142, 609
back and forth, 98
Back Bay Fens, 115
backbone, 145
Backhaus, 487
backside, 302
backslider, 74
backwardize, to, 193
back water, to, 142

bacterium, 155
bad, 25, 465
baddest, 463
Badeau, 495
bad-lands, 108, 263
bag, 308, 377
bagatel, 403, 406
bagatelle, 406
baggage, 85, 99, 102, 233, 254; -check, 146; -mas- ter, 146; -room, 146; -smasher, 146
bagoong, 373
bah, 349
bahay, 110
bah Jove, 269
bailee, 118
Bailey, 481
Bailey's Switch, 529
bailif, 406
bailiff, 386, 406
bailment, 118
bakalingo, 113
bakehead, 583
Bakehouse, 487
bake-house, 233
Baker, 485, 497
baker, 368
baker's shop, 233
bakery, 176, 233
baking-engineer, 290
Bakken, 492
bakt, 414
balance, 120, 165
balcony, 228
Bald, 529
Bald Knob, 529
balk, 389
ball-and-chain, 561
ballast, 238
ballat, 360
ballistics-engineer, 290
balloon, 582
bally, 270, 568
ballyhoo, 188, 191
bally-stand, 584
balm, 182, 335, 336, 349, 359
bologna, see boloney
baloney, see boloney
balony, see boloney
Baltimore, 530, 531, 540
Baltimoron, 552
bam, 184
bamboozle, to, 126
ban, 182

ban, to, 199
banana, 112
Bancamerica, 172
Bancorporation, 172
band-box, 581
bandits, 412
banditti, 412
bandwagon, 37
bang, 184
banjo, 113
bank-account, 244; -bill, 99; -holiday, 237; -note, 99, 233
banking-account, 233, 244
bank-management-engineer, 291
bank on, to, 227
bankrup, 352
banner-line, 584; -state, 148
banter, 126
Baptist, 462
bar, 334, 335, 339, 349
bar, to, 199
Baraboo, 533
Barb, 519
barb, to, 192, 374
Barbara, 519
barbaratorium, 179
barbecue, 112, 247
Barber, 486, 496
barber, 373
barberia, 177
Bar–B–Q, 209
bard, 349
Barefoot, 505
bargain, to, 269
bargain-counter, 227
Bar Harbor, 391
baritone, 390
bark, 390
Barkly, 503
bark up the wrong tree, to, 100, 143
barly, 402
barm, 349
barmaid, 243
barman, 236, 243
bar-mitzva, 217
barn, 7, 12, 122
Barnegat, 533
Barnum, 537
barque, 390
barracon, 153
barrel, 359; -house, 149

barren, 536
barrens, 115
barrister, 245
barrow, 235
bartender, 37, 150, 236, 243
Bartholomew, 515
Bartolomeo, 509
Barton, 489
Bartoszewicz, 489
Baruch, 500
barytone, 390
Bashie, 521
Basil, 511, 512
basin, 260
basketeria, 177
bas-relief, 338
bassaris, 214
basswood, 115
bastard, 293, 314
bat, 150
batfest, 218
bath, 233
bathe, 252
bathing-suit, 233
bathtub, 233
bathtub-gin, 580
batl, 399
batman, 30
Baton Rouge, 537, 542; -an, 550
batteau, 108, 151
Battenberg, 500
battery, 236
batting-average, 191
battle, 399
battle, to, 199
battleship, 583
battle-wagon, 582
Bauer, 483
bauer, 157
baugh, 482
Baughman, 479, 482
baulk, 389
Bauman, 483
bawd, 349
bawl, to, 198
bawl out, to, 198
Bay, 492, 552
bay, 124
Bayard, 516
bayberry, 124
Bayle, 481
bayou, 98, 151
Bay State, 101
bay-window, 128

bazaar, 234
bazoo, 557
b.d.t., 209
be, to, 427, 445, 613
beach, 236; -comber, 231
beagle, 580
bean, 328, 341, 428, 557, 563
beanery, 176
Bear Creek, 529
beat, to, 428
beaten, 428
Beatha, 521
beatingest, 143
Beatrice, 541
beat the Dutch, to, 259
beat up, to, 198
Beauchamp, 480, 503, 522
Beaufort, 541
beau pré, 105
beaut, 169, 564
beautician, 179, 229, 284, 288
beautiful, 463
beautifuler, 420
beautifuller, 463
beautifullest, 463
beautorium, 179
beaux-arts, 411
Beaver, 514, 529
beaver, 536
Beaver moon, 106
became, 428
becassine, 214
becaus, 404
because, 339
Becker, 485
become, to, 428
becuz, 339
bed, 308
bed-bug, 86, 233, 310
Beddow, 495
bed-rock, 227
Bedrosian, 497
bed-spread, 144
Bee, 537
beech, 124
Beecham, 503
beef, 128
beef, to, 609
beefsteak, 155
beeg, 368
bee-hive, 583
bee-line, 116, 231
been, 328, 341, 373, 374, 427, 441

beer, 243; -garden, 112, 155, 219; -mallet, 236, 244; -sort, 112
bee's knees, 561
bees too bee busy, 260
Beethead, 552
beet, 228; -root, 228
began, 428, 440
began(n), 428
beggar, 368
begin, to, 422, 428, 447
begob, 160
begorry, 160
begun, 428, 441
begunnon, 428
behavior problem, 293
behaviorist, 178
behaviour, 395
behind, 252
Behla, 496
behoove, to, 415
behove, 392
behove, to, 415
Be-jesus Be-johnson, 510
bel, 403
Bela, 496
Belair, 533
Bel Air, 533
belch, 309
belch, to, 578
Beldo, 493
beleev, 381
belgiumize, to, 193
Belgrade, 530
Belič, 489
believ, 403
belittle, to, 7, 14, 22, 100, 118, 224
Belko, 489
Bellair, 533
Bellaire, 533
bell-boy, 227
Belle Aire, 533
Belle Ayr, 533
beller, 353
Bellevue, 533
Bellfontaine, 525
bell-hop, 145, 186, 263
Bello, 493
bellow, 602
Bellows, 493
bell-ringer, 583
belly, 309
bellyache, to, 196
belly-laugh, 560
belly-robber, 573

belovéd, 438
Belsnickel, 159
belt, 239
Belva Dula, 522
Belvidere, 543
Ben, 519
ben, 341, 428
bend, 260
bend, to, 428
benefice, 248
Ben Hur, 534, 537
Benjamin, 506, 515
Benld, 538
Bensonhurst, 529
Bent, 523
bent, 528, 538
berceuse, 347
-berg, 500
Berg, 484
Berger, 484
Berinthia, 522
Berkeley, 503
Berkeleyan, 549
Berks County Dutchman, 550
Berlin, 530
Bernalilo, 534
Bérnard, 504
Berneita, 521
Bernheimer, 498
Bernstein, 499
berries, 45
Bert, 506, 507, 519
Bertha, 510
Besma, 522
bespoke, 234
Bess, 511
Bessie, 507
best, 463
best, to, 199
best bib and tucker, 232
best end, 236
best end of the neck, 236
best of the bunch, 565
bet, to, 428
betcha, 258
Beth, 519
Bethene, 521
betrayed, 302, 310
Betsy, 511
Bettelarm, 501
better, 463
betterment, 145
betterments, 98
better'n, 464
Betts, 483

Betty, 507, 509, 511, 519
between, 472
Betz, 483
Beulah, 535
Beverly, 520
beyond, 343
bhoy, 162
B.I., 579
Bianca, 509
Bias, 537
Bible, 505, 584
bible, to, 196, 578
Bible Belt, 230, 239
bid, 239
biergarten, 112
bierstube, 219
biff, 564
biff, to, 609
big, 368, 377; -chief, 106; -day, 580; -fella, 226; -gun, 144; -horse, 577, 580; -ox, 583; -shot, 580; -stick, 174
Big Baby, 514
Big Chimney, 537
Bighorse, 514
bil, 401, 403
Bilbo, 505
bild, 402, 403
bile, 102, 161, 346
Bilious, 505
Bill, 509, 512, 519
bill, 159, 233; -board, 95, 233, 266; -fold, 239; -of-lading, 238; -poster, 579
Bille, 537
billiards-saloon, 237
billiard-studio, 292
billion, 144, 255
bilt, 381, 384
Biltmore, 538
bimeby, 129
bin, 341, 428
bind, to, 428
bindery, 176
bindle, 582
bindle-stiff, 582
bing, 184
bingle, 263
bint, 569
biograph, to, 194
biology, 604
biorque, 214
bird, 367, 564
Birdene, 521

Birdie, 507
birdie, 562
Birdsong, 485
Birmingham, 540
Birquelle, 487
biscuit, 123, 233, 234, 255, 267
bishop, 149
biskit, 406
Bismarck, 529, 537
bit, 580
bitch, 301, 302
bit of a lad, 569
bitten, 428, 429, 444
bitter, 244
Bittinger, 484
bizar, 401
Bizjak, 489
bj, 490
Bjerstjerne, 510
Björnson Björnstjerne, 510
Black, 482, 485, 489
Blackbear, 514
blackbird, 124
black-coated, 239
blacked, 247
black-eye, 12
Blackfoot, 485
black-hand, 222
black-ink, 255
blackleg, 239
black-stripe, 149
black treacle, 235
-blad, 491
Bladder, 159, 584
blah, 185, 557
blame, to, 199
blamed, 375
Blancamano, 493
blanch, 335
blanche, 214
Blanco, 493
bland, 337
blankety, 316
blarneyfest, 218
blasphemious, 353
blast, 182, 184, 315
blasting-engineer, 290
blather, 338
Blaustein, 500
Blauvelt, 481
bleachers, 191
bleater, 587
Bleba, 521
bled, 429

bleed, to, 429
bleeding, 316
blessed-event, 561
blew, 429, 440
blighty, 573
blimp, 573
blind, 36; -baggage, 147; -pig, 149; -tiger, 100
blintzes, 217
blizzard, 144, 219, 231, 568
Bloch, 482
Block, 482
block, 12, 239, 247, 554, 557
blockhead, 563
Block Island, 533
block of flats, 233, 247
block of service-flats, 233
blond, 411, 412
blonde, 411, 412
blood, 312, 382
blood count, to, 197
blood disease, 307
blooded, 120
bloodfest, 218
blood-poison, 304
bloody, 311, 314, 316
Bloom, 482
Blooma, 522
Bloomer, 523
bloomer, 144
Bloomingdale, 498
blotter, 243
blotto, 573
blow, 315, 602
blow, to, 118, 429, 440, 566, 581
blowed, 429, 440
blow in, to, 227
blown, 429, 440
blow-out, 144
blow smoke, to, 583
blud, 382
blue, 231, 345
Blue Ball, 536
blue-blazer, 149
blue-grass, 114
Blue Hen's Chicken, 552
Bluehill, 539
Blue Jay, 537
blue-law, 150
bluf, 401, 403
bluff, 3, 57, 115, 231
bluff, to, 231, 609
Blum, 482, 484

Blumenthal, 498
blummie, 109
blurb, 557
blustiferous, 568
blut, 312
blutarm, 312
blutwurst, 155
bo, 170, 581; bo-, 491
B. O., 586
boar, 302, 308
board, 349
boarded, 604
board-school, 241
boat, 182
bob, to, 373
bobateria, 177, 179
bobatorium, 179
bobby, 243
Bobo, 505
bobolink, 12
Bob Ruly, 533
bob-sled, 115
boche, 295
bock-beer, 112, 155
bodacious, 359
boddy, 397
body, 397; -snatcher, 577
boedel, 109
bog, 115, 246
bogie, 147
bogue, 214
Boguehomme, 547
bogus, 108, 120, 231, 373, 538
Bohdan, 511
Bohdanka, 511
bohee, 295
boheme, to, 192
bohick, 295
bohoe, 295
bohunk, 263, 295
boid, 350, 367
boil, 346
Boileau, 495
boiled, 568; -dinner, 247; -shirt, 144
boiler, 585
Bois Boulogne, 348
Boiseite, 549
boko, 260
Bolander, 491
boll-weevil-expert, 291
bologna, 391
boloney, 391, 263, 560, 572
bolt, to, 148

bolter, 148
bolts, 119
bom, 402
Boman, 491
bomb, 580
bonanza, 152
Bonaparte, 478
Bon Cœur, 481
bond, 244
bonds, 244
bone-dry, 565
bone-head, 187, 563, 564
bone-orchard, 577
bones, 566
bonnet, 236
Bonne Terre, 542
Bon Pas, 482
Bon Secour, 539
Bons Enfants, 547
boob, 37, 170, 263
boobarian, 560
boobariat, 560
booberati, 560
booboisie, 560
boobomaniac, 560
boobuli, 560
boocoo, 573
boocoop, 573
boodle, 108, 231
boodle, to, 148
boodler, 148
boogie, 296
Boohum, 524
book-concern, 150
bookdom, 178
Booker, 485
bookfest, 218
booking-clerk, 238
booking-office, 147
bookseller's shop, 99
bookstore, 12, 99
boom, 167, 227, 565, 602
boom, to, 93, 141, 167, 227
boomer, 142, 582, 583
boom-town, 142
Boomy, 524
boor, 614
boost, 171
boost, to, 35, 141, 231, 567
booster, 47, 263, 565
boot, 122, 158, 233, 235,
    266, 344, 391
bootchkey, 295
bootee, 12
bootery, 176, 266
bootician, 179, 288

Bootjack, 524
bootlace, 235
boot-legger, 149, 288, 565
boot-maker, 122, 266
boots, 85, 247
boot-shop, 122, 266
booze, 244, 566; -fest, 218;
    -foundry, 564; -hister,
    346
boozer, 244
boozery, 176
Boozeville, 536
borax-house, 218
Borbély, 496
Bordeaux, 348
Borecký, 512
bored, 349
boredom, 178
boric-boracic, 415
boro, 402, 403, 539
borracho, 153
borrow, to, 433
bosch, 532
bosom, 302
boss, 24, 69, 98, 108, 231,
    372, 570, 609
boss, to, 609
boss around, to, 262
boss-rule, 148
Boston, 527, 528
Boston Common, 115
Bostonia, 529, 548
bother, 315
bottle, 587, 603
bottom, to, 15
bottom, 359; -dollar, 144;
    -land, 99, 115; -round,
    236
bottoms, 115
Bouchevaldre, 487
Boughman, 479
bought, 429
boughten, 425, 429, 438,
    442
boulevard, 546, 547
bouncer, 142, 149, 236, 245
bound, 428
bound'ry, 353
Bourbon, 547
bourbon, 263
bourgeois, 250
bout, 182
bower, 157
Bowers, 483
Bowery, 533
bowl, 368

bowler, 234, 239
bowling-alley, 236
bowls, 248
Bowman, 479, 483, 491
bowsprit, 105
Bowzar, 524
box-canyon, 152
box-car, 146, 238
box-engineer, 290
Boyd, 367
boyologist, 179
bozart, 411
Bozo, 497
bozo, 564, 585
Bozoian, 497
bracelet, 335
braces, 85, 235, 239, 391
bracken, 115
brains, 583
brain-trust, 186
brainy, 143
brake, 429
brake-van, 238
brakie, 572
branch, 115, 334, 336, 337
brand-new, 352
brandy-champarelle, 149
brandy-crusta, 149
brang, 429
Brasby, 523
brash, 143
brassière, 347
brass-mounted, 137
brass-pounder, 583
Braswell, 516
Braun, 477, 483
Braunstein, 477, 499
brave, 108
bravo, 108
bread-basket, 566
breadery, 176
breadstuffs, 12, 35, 120,
    122
break, 235
break, to, 429
breakaway, 587
break away, to, 609
breakbone, 563
breakfast, 240
breast, 302, 303, 308, 309
bred, 381, 401, 403
Bredevelt, 485
breeze, to, 16, 578
breezer, 579
brekfast, 401
brekfest, 403

brekker, 568
Bremen, 530
bresh, 360
brest, 381
brethren, 353, 614
breve, 250
brevier, 250
brevis, 250
Brian, 487
briar, 392, 393
briars, 580
bribd, 402
brick, 603
brickstein, 159
Bridgewater, 479
brief a barrister, to, 246
brief-case, 246
brier, 393
brigadier, 283
brigghity, 110
Brigham, 516
brile, 346
Brill, 482
brilliant, 250
bring, to, 429
brioche, 214
briqué, 214
brisbanality, 175
Bristol, 527, 528
broad, 305, 577
broad-bean, 260
broadcast, to, 197, 439
broadcasted, 439
broad-gauge man, 147
Broadway, 546
Brodie, 578
broil, 346
broiled, 234
broiler, 240
broke, 422, 429, 565
broken, 428, 429
broker, 244
bromid, 401
Bromide, 536
bromide, 227
bromo-seltzer, 172
bronc, 152, 170
bronchitis, 341
bronco, 152
bronichal, 353
Bronislawa, 510
Brookfreed, 485
Brooklyn, 532; -ite, 549
broom, 344
brother, 280, 614; -act, 562

brought, 429
Brown, 477, 478, 483, 486, 498, 514
brown, 247; -skin, 296
Bruce, 492
Brühl, 482
brung, 423, 429, 437
brush off a hat, to, 251
brush your hat off, 198
brusk, 394
Bruss, 492
bryanize, to, 193
Bryant, 516
Bryn Jenkins, 546
Bryn Jones, 529
b. s., 209
bt, 401
Bubble, 536
Bucher, 485
buchershelf, 159
buchta, 216
Buchwalter, 487
Buck, 520
buck, 302, 308, 582
buck, to, 263
buckaroo, 152
bucket, 243; -shot, 228
Buckeye, 101, 552
buckeye, 12
Buck moon, 106
buck-private, 573
buckra, 98, 112, 113
buckshot, 308
buck the tiger, to, 143
buckwheat, 85; -cake, 12
Bud, 519
budge, to, 126
Buena, 543
Buerckel, 487
Buffalo, 529, 536; -nian, 549
buffalo, 296
Buffalo Creek, 536
buffer, 238
buffet, 292, 347
bug, 12, 86, 233, 310, 577
bugaboo, 144
Bug-eater, 552
bug-eye, 117
bugger, 314
buggy, 583
bug-house, 186
Bugtown, 554
build, to, 429
builder-upper, 586
building, 414

building-lot, 121
build-up, 576
built, 384, 429, 438
bull, 286, 301, 302, 308, 309, 361, 577, 585; -fist, 218, 581; -frog, 114, 308; -snake, 12
Bulldog, 536
bulldoze, to, 141, 142, 263
bulldozing, 148
Bull Head, 514
Bull Run, 535
bullsh, 378
Bulltown, 537
bully, 229
bullyrag, to, 232
Bulow, 410
Bülow, 410
Bulpitt, 505
bum, 92, 155, 156, 170, 263, 306, 310, 581; -bum, 500
bum, to, 156
bum-bailiff, 310
bum food, 156
bummelei, 156
bummelig, 156
bummelleben, 156
bummeln, 156
bummelzug, 156
bummer, 93, 156
bummery, 156
bumming-place, 156
bummler, 156
bump, 184
bump, to, 564, 586
bump a block, 261
bumped off, to be, 40
bumper, 147, 238
bump off, to, 578
Bumpus, 482
bum's-rush, 156
bum steer, 156
bunco, 92; -steerer, 37
buncombe, 92, 144, 148, 225
-bund, 219
bundling, 12
bung-starter, 149, 236, 244
bunk, 92, 170; -shooter, 263
Bunker, 481
bunker, 562
bunkum, 558, 572
Bunnie, 552
bunt, to, 191

Buonaparte, 479
burden, 389
bureau, 12, 100, 108, 254
bureaucracy, 406
bureau-of-information, 238
burg, 263, 539
burgh, 539
Burgh de Walter, 479
burglarize, to, 93
burgle, to, 141, 192
burial-abbey, 288
buried, to be, 581
Burl, 522
burlesk, 406
burly, 128
burn, to, 429, 581
Burnett, 503
Burning Bear, 536
burnt, 429, 536
buro, 403
burocracy, 406
burp, to, 309, 564
burro, 152; -load, 152; -trail, 152; -train, 152; -weed, 152
Burroughs, 499
burst, 429, 439, 602
burthen, 389
Burton, 498
Burtyce, 521
bury deep, to, 465
bury the hatchet, 106, 232
bush, 108, 532; -fighting, 108; -league, 108; -leaguer, 191; -ranger, 108; -town, 108; -whacker, 108
bushel, 462
busher, 108
bushwah, 301
business-block, 247
business-suit, 235
bust, 92, 102, 150, 185, 350, 422, 439
bust, to, 429
busted, 429, 439
buster, 102
bust-head, 429, 568
Busyjack, 489
but, 203
butch, to, 192
Butcher, 496
butcher, 344; -shop, 587
Butrus, 513

Butt, 499
butt, to, 198
butte, 151
Butte Creek, 535
butterine, 86
butter-krust, 407
Buttermilk, 505
butter-muslin, 234
butter no parsnips, to, 565
butter-nut, 114
butt in, to, 198
buttinski, 103, 222
buttle, to, 192
buttonwood, 12
but what, 454
buy, to, 429
buz, 401, 403
Buzzard, 552
buzzard, 587
buzz-saw, 144
B. V. D., 208
by God, 316
by gosh, 316
by gum, 316
by Jove, 313
by-law, 243
Byrd, 367
by 'r Lady, 312
Byron, 516
by way of being, 256
c, 383, 386, 394, 401, 402, 404
cab, 169, 343
cabaret, 347
cabeca, 216
Cabinet, 245
cablegram, 171
caboodle, 231
caboose, 146, 238
Cabot, 498
cach, 400
cache, 98, 108, 182
cacodemonize, to, 117
cacogen, 175
cactuses, 413
caddy, 579
-cade, 180
cadet, 283
Cadogen, 503
Caesar, 523
café, 177, 292, 347, 409
cafeteria, 176, 221, 228
cag, 383, 384
cage, 583
cahoots, 263
Caillé, 481

Cain, 498
Cairo, 541
Caitlin, 513
cake-eater, 561
cakery, 176
caketeria, 177
cake-walk, 145
Cal, 183
calaboose, 98, 152, 263
calabozo, 152
Calais, 348
calamity-howler, 145
calculate, to, 24, 99
cald, 401, 403
Caldeno, 538
calendar, 246
Calexico, 537
calf-slobber, 583
caliber, 394
calibre, 383
California, 349
call, to, 191, 198, 613
call down, to, 198
called to the bar, to be, 246
Callowhill, 503
calm, 334, 335, 338, 371
calox, 173
calumet, 106
calv, 461
calvary, 353
Calvert, 540
calves, 335
Calvin, 512, 517
Cam, 522
Cambria, 530
Cambridge, 527
Camdenite, 549
came, 430
camelcade, 179
camerado, 75
Cameron, 486
camino, 153
camouflage, 347
Camp, 503
campaign, 228
camp-meeting, 116, 150
campo santo, 153
campus, 144, 263
can, 228, 243, 334, 339, 420, 446, 581
can, to, 199, 263
Canaan, 535
canary, 587
canary's tusks, 561
canch, 361

can cha, 446
cand, 402
candidacy, 30, 148, 245
candidate, 283
candidature, 245
candour, 395
c. & s., 209
candy, 41, 234; -shop, 266; -store, 234; -studio, 292
candyteria, 177
cane-brake, 116
canitist, 179
canned, 568; -goods, 234; -music, 186
cannibal, 112
cannon, 236, 578
canoe, 3, 57, 112, 155
canon, 248, 279
cañon, 411
canoodle, to, 142
can-opener, 234
can't, 334, 336, 446
Cantabrigian, 550
can't come it, 99
Canton, 537
can't you, 446
canuck, 151, 295
canvas-back, 114
canyon, 57, 152, 231, 411, 543
Cap, 523
cap, 170, 614
Cape May, 533
capitalize, to, 101
capitan, 153
capitol, 11
Capone, 494
capote Anglaise, 296
captain, 243, 273, 274, 583
cap the climax, to, 142
car, 85, 182, 247, 335
caracter, 401
Caranguejo, 495
carborundum, 172, 173
carburetor, 559
card, 101
Cardozo, 501
care, 339
careless, 466
carencro, 214
Caress, 537
care-taker, 235, 247
caribou, 104, 105
Carl, 506, 510
Carlo, 509

Carlotta, 509
Carlson, 492
carnal connection, 303
carniceria, 177
carnival, 145; of crime, 145
Carol, 506
Carolinas, 526
carom, 236
caroussel, 236
Carpenter, 484, 485, 498
carpet-bagger, 144, 148, 227, 228, 558
carriage, 85; -paid, 238, 240; -rug, 237
carrid, 401, 403
carrier, 147
carriole, 108
Carroll of Carrollton, 504
carry-all, 108, 117, 582
carry on, to, 265
cars, 147
cart, 334
Carthage, 530
Carthagenian, 551
car-toad, 583
carton, 347
cartoon, 347
cart-wheel, 564
carv, 401
car-washery, 176
carwhacker, 583
casa, 152
Casalegno, 493
Casbergue, 487
cascaret, 173
case, 287
case, to, 578
casement-window-engineer, 290
case work, 292
Casey, 487, 510
cashateria, 177
cash in, to, 191
Casitas Springs, 534
casket, 287; -coach, 287
casketeria, 177
Cassels, 503
Cassia, 503
cast, to, 429, 439
casted, 429, 439
casting-couch, 587
Castle, 485
castrate, to, 302
Castro, 494
Cataline, 509

catalog, 391, 399, 400, 402, 403, 406
catalogue, 406
Catalpa, 522
catalpa, 104, 105
catapult, 239
catarrh, 360
catawba, 106
cat-bird, 114
cat-boat, 86, 116, 117
cat-burglar, 243
catcal, 380
catch, 339, 400
catch, to, 429
catched, 429
Catchpole, 505
catcht, 339
catch you up, to, 251
catch up, to, 251
caterpillar, 336
caterpillar-engineer, 289
Catfish, 536
catfish, 114
Cathill, 505
Cathleen, 513
Catholic, 249
catnip, 246
Cato, 523
Cato Sabo, 524
cats, 257
Catskill, 532
cat's pajamas, 561
catsup, 391
cattle, 368
catty-cornered, 128
caucauasu, 107
caucus, 57, 98, 102, 107, 147, 225
caucusdom, 225
caucuser, 225
caught, 339, 429
cauliflower-ear, 562
cause-list, 246
cavalieress, 101
Cavannah, 524
cave in, to, 99, 558
cawcawaassough, 107
cayuse, 150
C.B., 183
C.C.C., 209
cedarblade, 491
cede, 401
cecil, 516, 518, 519
Cecil Manor, 546
Cedar Bayou, 535
Cedric, 518

ceed, 401
cellarette, 178
cellarman, 243
cellophane, 172
celotex, 173
Cement, 536
Cenék, 511
census, to, 196
cent, 116
centenary, 325
center, 393, 402, 539
Centerville, 537
centre, 383
centurion, 398
cereal, 227
cerebras, 413
ceremony, 325
Cerné, 489
Cerro, 543
certain, 6, 339
certainly, 253, 467
Cerviček, 486
cesspool, 128
ch, 335, 382, 384, 401, 404
chafer, 304
chaff, 336
chafing-dish, 227
chained, 375
chain-gang, 144
chain-store, 229, 234
chair, 302, 339, 614; -car, 147, 238; -warmer, 62, 145, 186
chairman, 244
chaise, 382
Chalene, 521
Challman, 491
chamber, 335
chambers, 247
chamois, 343, 347
chamois, to, 194
Champ, 522
champ, 169, 346
champeen, 346
champion, 346
chancellor, 241
Chancie, 522
chanct, 360
Chandler, 498
change, to, 302
change cars, to, 147
channel, 246
chant, 334, 337
chaparejos, 152
chaparral, 98, 152
chapel, 249, 268, 287

chaperon, 126
chaps, 152, 263
chapter, 284
char, 128, 266
char-a-banc, 237
character, 376, 382
charade, 338
chargé, 410
charged, 234
charge-sheet, 243
Charity, 516
Charles, 506, 507, 510, 512, 515, 516, 520, 527
Charleston, 497, 591
Charley, 510
charley-horse, 191
Charlie, 513
Charline, 521
Charlotte, 507, 529
Chartres, 547
charwoman, 128, 266
chase, 115
chase one's self, to, 609
chaser, 150
Chatahospee, 539
chauf, to, 192
Chauffe, 487
chauffeur, 347
Chauncey, 512, 516
chautauqua, 221
chaw, 161, 570
Cheapside, 546
cheap-skate, 187
check, 159, 389, 391, 604
check, to, 198
check against, to, 198
check-book, 244
checkers, 236
check in, to, 198
checkinqumin, 105
check out, to, 198
check over, 198
check-room, 238
check up, to, 198, 229
check with, to, 198
chee, 462
cheek, 375
cheer, 339
cheerio, 265, 269, 573
cheese, 462; -cloth, 234
cheese it, 562
Cheesewright, 505
chef, 347
cheka, 209
chelly, 375
chemist, 234, 385, 401

chemist's-shop, 234
Chemquasabamticook, 539
cheque, 390, 391, 392; -book, 244
chequered, 392
Cherubim, 516
cheskey, 295
chest, 340, 346
Chester, 508, 510, 515, 516
chest of drawers, 254
chevalier, 382, 384
Chevy Chase, 115
chewing-gum, 231
chew the rag, to, 198, 573, 609
chianti, 222
Chiariglione, 493
Chicago, 528; -an, 548; -rilla, 552, 561
chick, 375
chicken, 240, 569
chickenburger, 220
chicken-yard, 234
chiclet, 173
chico, 153
chicory, 260
chief, 182; -constable, 243; -lithographer, 289; of police, 243; of the ushers, 289
chiffon, 347
chigger, 152
chigoe, 152
chigre, 152
Chilberg, 490
chilblained, 558
children, 353, 614
childs, 614
child-welfare, 588
chile, 152
chile con carne, 221
Chilgren, 491
Chilson, 512
Chilstrand, 491
chimbley, 353
chimist, 385
chimly, 22
chimny, 402
China jack, 373
Chinberg, 490
chinch, 128, 152, 233
chinche, 152
Chindbloom, 490
Chinee, 111, 461

chink, 295
chink, to, 141
chinkapin, 104, 105
Chinlund, 490
chin-music, 187
chip in, to, 191, 609
chipped beef, 144
chippy, 305
chiquito, 153
chiropodist, 288
chiropract, to, 196
chiropractic, 263
chiropractor, 179
chirotonsor, 288
chisel, to, 567
chist, 346
chit, 376
chlorid, 394
Chloride, 536
chloride, 604
chlorine, 341
Chmielewski, 489
chocolate, 112, 152
chocolateria, 177
choir, 612, 614
cholic, 382
Cholmondeley, 503, 605
chomp, to, 346
choo-choo, 240
choose, to, 429
Chopper, 488
chops, 236
chop-suey, 162, 263; -joint, 162
chore, 128, 234, 266
chorine, 180
chortle, 171
chorus, 382
chose, 429
chosen, 429
Chotau, 495
Choto, 495
Chouteau, 495
chow, 162, 376, 573
chowder, 108
chow-mein, 162
chowmeinery, 176
Christ, 305, 318
Christiaanse, 485
Christiania, 530
Christians, 485
Christides, 486
Christie, 486
Christkind'l, 156
Christkindlein, 156
Christopher-Columbus-

Who-Discovered-America, 523
Christos, 512
Chrome, 536
chromo, 169
Chronos, 486
chrysanthe'em, 353
chuck, 236, 582
chucker-out, 236
Chumly, 503
chump, 129
chump-bone chops, 236
chunky, 120
church, 249, 489
churchman, 249
chute, 98, 151
Cicognani, 494
cider, 389
cigaret, 401, 403
cigarette, 325; -butt, 234; -end, 234
Cilstrom, 490
cinch, 37, 152, 565
cinch, to, 152
cincho, 152
cinder-cruncher, 583
Cinderella, 537
cinema, 95, 237
cipher, 390, 396
circuit-rider, 150
circus, 547; -catch, 191; -play, 562
cite, to, 199
cited as correspondent, to be, 310
citified, 141
citizenize, to, 140
cits, 573
City, 244, 292
city, 539
City editor, 244
City man, 244
city ordinance, 243
city-stock, 244
civilizee, 75
civil-servant, 243
civvies, 573
ck, 386
claim, to, 199, 210
claim-agent, 239
claim-jumper, 144
clam-baker, 247
clamburger, 220
Clam-catcher, 552
clam-chowder, 247
clam-jamphrie, 568

clamorous, 395
clamour, 395
clang, 430
clangorous, 395
clangour, 395
clapboard, 99
clap-boarded, 116
clapperdogeon, 577
Clarence, 507
Clarene, 521
Clark, 520
Clary, 360
clas, 401
clash, 182, 184
clasp, 334, 335, 336
class, 241, 336, 368; -day, 242
classic, 211
classification-yard, 239
classy, 93, 464
clatter, 577
Claude, 518, 524
clawhammer, 86, 144, 167
cleaneteria, 177
cleanlily, 467
cleanly, 340, 467
clean up, 37, 183
clearance, to, 195
clearing, 115
clear the track, to, 147
Clem, 519
Clement, 519
Clendolia, 524
clergyman, 249
clerk, 85, 86, 123, 255
clerk, to, 118
Cleveland, 516, 529
clever, 6, 24, 25, 99, 101, 128
click, to, 560
cliff, 115
Clifford, 516
clift, 360
climb, to, 430, 436
climbed, 436
Cline, 483
cling, to, 430
cling-stone, 114
Clinton, 537
clipped, 438
clipping, 239
clipt, 438
cloak-room, 238
clockologist, 179
clock-watcher, 187
clodhopper, 128

cloister, 288
clomb, 416, 430, 436
clorid, 401
close, 352
close-call, 227, 570
closed season, 236
close season, 236
closet, 310
close-up, 227
closure 394
clothes-peg, 234
clothes-pin, 234
clothing-engineer, 290
clothing store, 27
cloture, 394
clôture, 394
cloud-burst, 144
clove, 109
Clove Valley, 532
clown, 577, 583; -wagon, 583
Clown Alley, 584
club, 243; -car, 147; -sandwich, 247
clue, 393
clumb, 430, 441
clumsy, 558
clung, 430
cmear, 443
c'n, 445
C.O., 573
coal-oil, 234
coal-operator, 256
coal-owner, 256
Coal Run, 536
coast, to, 141
coatee, 141
coax, to, 126
Coba, 521
cocain, 411
cocaine, 411
cock, 85, 235, 301, 304, 308
cockarouse, 107
cockchafer, 304
cockerel, 235
Cockey, 485
cock-eyed, 308, 568
cockroach, 112, 296, 301, 304
cocksure, 126, 308
cocktail, 149, 155, 604
cocktail-room, 292
cocotte, 305
C.O.D., 205, 208
codfish, 93, 143

Cody, 537
co-ed, 86, 170, 263
Coelo, 521
Coenties, 533
Coeur d'Alene, 541
cof, 403
coffee, 604; -engineer, 290
coffin-nail, 186
coffin-varnish, 568
coffin-warehouse, 27
Cogenhoe, 503
cohanize, to, 193
Cohen, 477, 478, 487, 498
Cohn, 498
cohoss, 119
coiner, 243
coive, 367
Coke, 485
coke, 170
cold-deck, 191
cold-feet, 227, 573
Cold moon, 106
cold-slaw, 411
cold-snap, 100, 115, 144, 231, 570
Cold Spring, 536
Coldwater, 536
Coleman, 499, 513
cole-slaw, 108, 263, 411
Colgate, 516
Colice, 521
collar-button, 234
collar-stud, 234
collateral, 145, 231
collecker, 568
collecting-stage, 260
college, 580; -engineer, 291; -widow, 186
collegiate, 581
Collenberg, 483
collide, to, 141, 231
collide head-on, to, 147
Colonel, 552
colonel, 273, 274, 283, 612
coloniarch, 16
colony, 293
color, 402
Colorado, 339, 543
colored, 231, 300
colorful, 229
colorific, 395
colorous, 395
colour, 395
colourable, 396

coloured, 396
Columbard, 548
Columbia Maypole, 522
Columbian, 551
Columbus, 517, 519
columnist, 178
Colwich, 537
com, 402
comb, 402
Comba, 524
combe, 115
combinations, 236
combine, 231
combust, to, 192
come, 422; -back, 183, 186, 227, 565; -down, 144, 227; -on, 565, 576; -onter, 150
come, to, 423, 430, 436, 604
comed, 436
come in collision, to, 231
come out at the little end of the horn, to, 100, 143, 198
come to stay, to, 227
come up, to, 434
comisario, 153
command, 334
commencement, 242; -engineer, 290
commissioner, 283
committee, 245
common, 115
common-loafer, 156
communicable disease, 306
community-chest, 588
commutation, 31; -ticket, 146
commute, to, 147, 192
commuter, 147, 238
company, 245, 344, 414; -lawyer, 246
comparativ, 403
compensate, 325
com(p)fort, 439
complected, 120
complex, 210, 211
compromit, to, 7, 118, 119
Compton, 516
con, 170, 582, 583
conant, 376
conbobberation, 568
concededly, 167

concentrate, to, 325
Concepcion, 535
concertize, to, 141
conch, 378
conciet, 402, 403
condensery, 176
Conder, 524
condit, 402
conduct, to, 99
conductor, 85, 146, 239, 263, 273
conductorette, 178
cone, 303
confab, 183
confessional-address, 220
confirmand, 220
confiscate, 325
conflagrative, 22, 119
Congress, 11
congressional, 98, 119
conjure, 344
conk, 576
con-man, 263
Conn, 498
connexion, 390, 392
conniption, 144, 263
Conola, 522
conscious, 211
conservatory, 227
considerable, 25
consignment-note, 238
consistent, 211
consociational, 98, 140
consols, 244
constable, 243, 344
Constantine, 512
Constantinopoulos, 485
constituency, 120, 245
constitution, 614
contact, to, 194
contact-manager, 288
container-engineer, 290
contested election, 245
controled, 406
controlled, 406
controversialist, 165
conventionitis, 179
convocation, 248
coo, 602
Cook, 485, 488, 496
cook, to, 580
cook-book, 234
cook coffee, to, 215
cookery-book, 234
cookey, 108
cookie, 234

cooking-stove, 234
cook-stove, 234
cooler, 149, 580
coon, 153, 169, 170, 264, 296
Coons, 482, 483
coop, 344
Cooper, 481, 485
cooper, 344
cooter, 113
cootie, 573
cop, 40, 243
c.o.p., 209
cop a mope, to, 581
copious, 128
Copoulos, 486
copper-bellied, 137
copper-head, 114
Coraopolis, 530
corbigeau, 214
cord, 247
cord, to, 118
cord-wood, 128
Corey, 494, 496
Corlaers's Hook, 532
corn, 7, 12, 42, 85, 106, 122, 234; -belt, 144, 239; -brake, 122; -broom, 122; -cake, 122; -cob, 122; -crib, 115, 122; -cutter, 122; -dodger, 115, 122; -factor, 245; -fed, 122; -flour, 234; -fodder, 122; -fritter, 122; -grater, 122; -hook, 122; -husk, 122; -juice, 122, 149, 568; -knife, 122; -market, 256; -meal, 122, 234; -pone, 122; -shuck, 122; -snake, 122; -stalk, 122; -starch, 122, 234
corned-beef, 352
corned willie, 573
corner, 544
corner, to, 141, 231
corner-loafer, 156, 256
Cornhill, 546
Cornielsen, 481
Corn Laws, 122
Corn moon, 106
Cornstalk, 537
corp, 461
corporation, 244; -lawyer, 246; -profits, 244

corpse, 287; -maker, 137; -reviver, 149
corral, 92, 152
corral, to, 152
Correia, 494
correspondence-engineer, 290
corridor, 238
corset, 301
Cortlandt, 532
corus, 401
cos, 260
cosma, 413
cosmetician, 179, 288
Cosmopolis, 530
cosmos, 413
cost, to, 440
Costanza, 509
coster, 234; -monger, 234
Costilla, 543
cosy, 393
cotched, 429
Cotica, 524
cotilion, 406
cotillion, 406
Cotton, 499
cotton, 234; -belt, 239; -wood, 234
Cottonwood, 529
cottonwood, 536
Cottonwood Crossing, 554
couch, 254
Coughlin, 504
cough up, to, 227
coulda, 443, 444
coulee, 151
council, 245
Council Bluffs, 535
councillor, 243
council-school, 241, 243
counterfeiter, 243
counterfoils, 244
county, 414; -farm, 293; -home, 293
coupé, 347
coupla, 443, 471, 570
Courey, 496
court, 386, 547
courtesan, 305
courthouse, 539
Courtney, 512
Coury, 496
cove, 536
cover, 346
cow, 364; -beast, 361;

-boy, 152; -brute, 306, 361; -cage, 583; -catcher, 96, 146; college, 187; -creature, 301, 302; -critter, 302; -hand, 152; -juice, 582; -puncher, 152
Cowan, 498
cowcumber, 129
Cowhide, 536
cowhide, to, 114
Cow-Tail, 536
Cox, 308, 485
Coyne, 498
coyote, 150, 536
cozy, 393
crab, to, 263
crab-cocktail, 247
crabfest, 218
Crabtree, 495
Cracker, 552
cracker, 7, 101, 122, 123, 234, 267
crackerjack, 264
crack up, to, 143
Craig, 478
cranberry-bog, 115
crane-navvy, 239
crank, 145, 231
crap, 584
crape, 409
craps, 86, 264
crash, 182, 184
crash, to, 578, 581, 602
crass, 16
Crawfish, 536
crawfish, to, 142, 148
Crawthumper, 552
crayfish, 105
crazy-bone, 239
crazy-quilt, 116, 145
Crček, 489
cream-cracker, 235
creamery, 176
creature, 341
Credilla, 522
credit, 242
Creed, 522
creek, 7, 12, 70, 115, 121, 341, 609
creep, to, 430
Crenshawe, 503
creole, 112
creosote, 155
crep, 352, 430, 437
crêpe, 409

crescent, 547
Crespigny, 503
creton, 401
crevasse, 98, 151
crew, 430
crib, 583
cricket, 248
crickthatch, 119
Crile, 483
crime, 603
criminal, 293; -assault, 304; -engineer, 290; -operation, 304
Crippiny, 503
crisco, 173
crise, to, 192
crispette, 173
Crist, 512
Cristsylf, 459
criteria, 412
criterions, 413
critic, 380
critikin, 118
crix, 586
croaker, 577
cronic, 401
Cronkhite, 483
crook, 167, 227, 565
crookdom, 178
crook the elbow, to, 150
crope, 430
crossed, 398
crossing-plate, 96, 146
cross, purposes, 128, 231
crossroads, 539
crosswordpuzzleitis, 179
crotchet, 250
croud, 384
crow, to, 430
crowd, 30, 383, 384
crowd out, to, 227
crowed, 430
crower, 308
crown, 116
crucified, 398
cruller, 108
crum, 402, 406
crumb, 406
crummy, 582, 583
crypt, 248
cuanto, 376
cub, 227
Cuba, 349
Cubéan, 353
cucaracha, 112
cuckoo, 562

Cueller, 487
Cuffee, 524
Cuffey, 524
Cuffy, 523, 524
cultus, 150
Cump, 517
cunning, 257
cupiding, 561
curate, 248, 249
curator, 325
curb, 393
curb, to, 199, 394
curet, 411
curette, 411
curio, 169
curled, 561
curricula, 412
curriculas, 413
Curry, 494
curse, 316
curse, to, 430
curse out, to, 229
Curtis, 486
Curtiss, 499
curv, 403
curve, 367
Curzon, 497
Cush, 524
cushion, 583
cuspidor, 216
cuss, 74, 169, 170, 231, 316, 350; -word, 167
cuss, to, 430
cussed, 430
cussedness, 145
cuss out, to, 430
Custer, 480
customable, 119
customize, to, 193
custom-made, 234
cut, 182, 227, 261
cut, to, 199, 430, 440, 580
cut across lots, to, 121
cut a swath, to, 142
cute, 120, 226
cutex, 173
cuticura, 173
cut no figure, to, 95
cut no ice, to, 232, 565
cut-off, 144
cut one's eye-teeth, to, 568
cut out, to, 38
cut paper-dolls, to, 562
cutting, 239
Cy, 252

cyar, 364
cyclery, 176
Cyclone, 537
cyclone, 231
cyder, 389
cymbi, 113
cypher, 389
Cyril, 518
cystoscope, to, 197
Czar, 537
czar, 390
Czeslaw, 510
d, 335, 348, 352, 360, 368, 375, 397, 401, 438, 447
da, 113
dachshund, 155, 347
da-da, 113
daffy, 464
dago, 86, 110, 231, 294, 295, 305; -red, 222
dahlia, 155
Daisette, 522
Dakoming, 537
Dakota, 526
dalite, 407
Dalsemer, 500
Dalsheimer, 500
Dame's Quarter, 537
damfino, 316
damn, 205, 313, 318, 464
damnation, 316, 317
damndest, 316
damned, 317, 464
damphool, 316
Dan, 509, 519
dance, 329, 335, 336, 337, 338
dance, to, 581
dance-hall, 227, 581
dance marathon, 180
dancethon, 180
dancingest, 463
D. & D., 208
dandy, 257
danger, 24
Daniel, 506, 509, 511, 515
Daniel of St. Thomas, 518
Daniels, 490
Danielson, 489
Dănila, 509
Daniliwsky, 490
dansant, 409
dansant-engineer, 290
Danylchenko, 489
Danylchuk, 489
Danylshyn, 489

dar, 339
Darby, 503
dare, 375
dare, to, 430
dared, 430
darken one's doors, to, 100, 119
dark-horse, 148
Darky, 520
darky, 120
Darlene, 521
darn, 316, 317
darned, 317
darnfoolski, 222
daSilva, 501
das'n't, 430
dast, 430
dat, 367
data, 338, 412
Dauphine, 547
Dauud, 513
davenport, 254
Davenporter, 549
David, 506, 510, 513, 515
Davidovitch, 498
Davis, 477, 498, 499
dawter, 381
day-coach, 147
daylight time, 234
dayyan, 217
D-Cady, 517
D. D., 273, 281
de-, 194
deacon, to, 140
dead as a door-nail, 570
dead-beat, 37, 144, 167
deader'n, 464
dead-head, 228
dead-head, to, 147
dead pan, 587
deaf, 340
deal, 182
deal, to, 430
dealt, 430
dean, 242, 248, 274, 279, 289; of women, 241
Deane, 507
dear, 311
death-knell, 587
debamboozle, to, 194
Debaun, 495
debenture, 244
De Bon, 495
debt, 383
debunk, to, 174, 194, 199, 226

debunking, 174
debut, to, 192
début, 347, 409
débutante, 409
debutramp, 561
decalog, 400
deCasseres, 501
deceit, 380
deceived, 310
decent, 303, 308
deciev, 402, 403
deck, 144, 236
decoy, 325
ded, 403
deed, to, 7, 117
deep, 368, 465
Deering, 482
defect, 325
defence, 383, 394
defense, 386, 394
defensive, 394
defi, 169
deficit, 325
definit, 399, 401, 403
deft, 128
DeGrasse, 514
degree-day, 242
degrees of frost, 246
Degroff, 539
dehorning-engineer, 290
deign, 380
Dejean, 481
dejelly, to, 194
De La Haye, 481
Delaware, 525, 530
Delaware Water Gap, 535
delayd, 403
Delhi, 540
de l'Hôtel, 482
delicate condition, 304
delicatessen, 155
delicatessens, 412
delinquent, 293
deliveress, 75
deliver the goods, to, 227
dell, 115
Delmar, 538
Del-Mar, 537
Delmarva, 538
Delmer, 523
delouse, to, 194
Delphia, 521
Delsey, 524
demagogue, to, 192, 196
demean, to, 121, 165
Demetrios, 512

Demikof, 478
deminition bow-wows, 317
demisemiquaver, 250
demmed, 317
demolition-engineer, 289
Demon Rum, 244
demonstrate, 325
Demopolis, 530
demoralize, to, 118
Demos, 512
De Moss, 512
Demosthenes, 512
dendanthropology, 117
Denis, 481
Dennis, 505
Denny, 481
dénouement, 409
Denva, 521
Deodolphus, 524
depart, 335
deposit-slip, 244
depot, 147, 151, 409
dépôt, 409
deputize, to, 7, 118
deputy-pro-chancellor, 241
derange, to, 118
Derby, 503
derby, 234, 239
Dermen, 497
Dermenjian, 497
Dermott, 479
derned, 317
derrière, 307
DeRue, 522
desave, 161
Desbrosses, 547
Des Champs, 495
deserv, 401
Deshong, 481
desk, 150, 254
Des Moines, 541
desperado, 152
dessert, 247
destitution, 15
destructor, 234
det, 383, 401, 403
detainer, 583
determin, 401, 403
determine, 383, 384
detour, 236, 325
dettor, 401
develop, 391
develope, 391
De Vere, 479

device, 394
devil, 318
devil-dog, 574
devilinsky, 222
devilled-crab, 247
devotee, 412
dewax, to, 194
Dewey, 512, 516
DeWitt, 506
diagnosticate, to, 197
diagram, 402
diagramme, 394
dialog, 394
dialogicians, 179
diamond, 250, 341, 583
diamond-cracker, 583
Diarmuid, 479
diarrhea, 411
diarrhœa, 411
diary, 341
dick, 577
dicker, to, 118
dickey-seat, 237
dicta, 412
dictograph, 173
did, 430, 442
diddle, to, 22
did I say no?, 217
didn't, 352
Diego, 110
diener, 220
dierne, 317
diet-kitchen-engineer, 290
die with one's boots on, to, 142
diff, 170
different, 466
different than, 472
dig, to, 430, 436
diggings, 98, 145
dilatory, 24
Dillehay, 481
diminute, to, 75
din, 128
dinah, 577
dindon farouche, 214
dindon sauvage, 214
diner, 170
dinge, 296
dinger, 583
dingus, 176, 210, 211, 263
dinky, 464
dinner, 240
dinner-bell, 97
dino, 582

dioxygen, 173
dip, 368, 576
diphtheria, 352
diphthong, 352
Dipucci, 497
directly, 251
director, 242
directory-engineer, 290
direct primaries, 245
dirt, 165, 310, 580
dirty, 467
Dirty Face, 514
disagreeable, 268
discipline, 384
discommode, to, 168
disdain, 380
disembarked, 604
dishpan, 234
disme, 116
disorderly house, 304
display-ad, 170
dissenter, 248, 249
distaff, 386
distributing, 376
district, 245, 247
ditch, to, 227
div, 430
dive, 37, 149
dive, to, 430
dived, 430
divide, 115
division, 245
divorcée, 409, 412
divot, 562
Divver, 479
divvy, 191
divvy, to, 148, 192
Dixie, 101
dixième, 116
do, to, 306, 430, 446, 566, 604
do a land-office business, to, 142
do a tailspin, to, 198
Doc, 520
doc, 170
docile, 341
docket, 145
dock-walloper, 263
dock-yard, 239
doctor, 271, 289
doctorine, 180
doctrin, 406
doctrine, 406
Dodge City, 529
dodge the issue, to, 142

do don't, 99
does, 24
doesn't, 446
dogdom, 178
dog-eater, 373
doggery, 145, 149
doggone, 316, 317
dog-house, 583
dognaper, 180
dog on it, 317
do-gooder, 187
dog-robber, 573
dog-weary, 564
Dohme, 484
do it all, to, 581
dokus, 217
dol, 401
dole, 430, 437
Doley, 523
dollar, 116, 155
Dollarhide, 505
dollars to doughnuts, 259
Dollarville, 536
doll up, to, 264
Dolly, 520
Dolor, 522
dolour, 395
-dom, 109, 178
dominie, 109
Dominus, 281
don, 183, 242
donate, to, 121, 165, 231
donation-party, 150
Don Carlos, 516
done, 422, 430, 441, 442
donee, 180
donivorous, 118
donkey, 302
donky, 402
don't, 445, 446, 471
donut, 402
doodad, 176, 211
-doodle, 176
Doolittle, 482
door, 614
Dope, 582
dope, 38, 95, 108, 229, 565, 609; -fiend, 232
dope, to, 55
dope out, 264
dopester, 178
D. O. R. A., 209
Doran, 503
dorg, 350
dorm, 170

Dorothy, 507, 511
dorp, 109, 532
Dorpian, 550
do the book, to, 578, 581
Dotterer, 484
Dötterer, 484
doubld, 403
double-cross, 565
double-header, 191
double pica, 250
double team, 122
doubt, 397
Doug, 183
dough, 45
doughboy, 573, 575
doughface, 74
doughnutery, 176
Douglas, 482, 516
do up brown, to, 143
dout, 397, 401, 403
dove, 430, 437
Dow, 516
down, 115
down-and-out, 93, 143
down-East, 246
downhil, 380
down-town, 143, 246
down-train, 247
doxologize, to, 96, 140
dozen, 462
Dozine, 524
Dr., 272, 280
draft, 334, 382, 394
draftee, 180
drag, 582
drag, to, 430
drain, 339
drains, 235
drama, 337
drank, 422, 425, 430, 440, 442
draper's-shop, 234
drapes, 170
draught, 382
draughts, 236
draw, 70, 120, 170
draw, to, 430
draw a bead, to, 119
draw a bead on, to, 232
draw-bridge, 70, 120
drawed, 430
drawers, 234, 239
drawing-pin, 239
drawing-room, 266
drawing-room-car, 101
dreadful, 99, 210

dream, to, 430
dreampt, 438
dreamt, 392
dreen, 339
dremp, 430
drempt, 430, 439
dres, 403
dress-circle, 228
dress in, to, 580
Dretha, 522
drew, 430
Drewry, 503
drill, to, 578
drillery, 176
drill-hall, 239
drily, 392, 393
drink, to, 430, 440
drinked, 430
drinkery, 176
Drinkwater, 495
driv, 416, 431
drive, 182, 546
drive, to, 431
driver, 260
drive urself, 407
drove, 431, 437
drown, to, 431
drown'd, 438
drownded, 161, 431, 438
drowned, 431
drug, 430
druggist, 231, 234
drug-store, 231, 234, 263
drugteria, 177
drummer, 37, 583
drunk, 430, 440
druv, 423, 431
dry, 86, 191, 565
dry-cleaning-engineer, 290
dry-goods, 122, 123
dry-goods store, 27, 234
drygoodsteria, 177
dryly, 393, 396
Drytown, 534
dub, 37, 565
Dubois, 495
Duchesne, 539
Duck, 537
duck, 149, 564, 569
ducker, 579
dude, 180
Dudelant, 482
dude-wrangler, 180
dudine, 180
duds, 567

du-du, 113
due, 345
dug, 430
dug-out, 144, 231
duke, 345
duket, 584
dul, 401
dum, 402
dumb, 109, 112, 158, 374
dumb Dora, 561
dumbell, 561
dumbfound, 171
dumbfounded, 126
dumb John, 573
dumb-waiter, 86, 254
Dumitrue, 509
dumm, 109
dummy, 580
dump, to, 118
Duncan, 516
Dunkard, 250
Dunke, 524
dunski, 222
duo, 183
Dupriel, 522
Durhamite, 549
Düring, 482
Durstine, 499
dust-bin, 233
dust-cart, 233
dust-engineer, 290
dustman, 233
Dusty, 520
dutchie, 295
Dutch oven, 260
dutiable, 119, 120
Dutrow, 484
Duttera, 484
Dutterer, 484
duty, 345
Duyvel, 533
Dvořák, 487
dwelling-engineer, 290
dwindle, to, 564
Dykehouse, 485
Dÿkhuis, 485
dynamo, 236
dynasty, 341
dysentery, 376
Džán, 512
Džaník, 512
Džim, 512
Džimik, 512
e, 339, 340, 341, 346, 347,
    359, 368, 375, 384, 389,
    393, 394, 401, 405, 438,

451, 469, 484; -e, 464,
    549
ea, 381, 401
each way, 248
eagle, 116
Eagle Pass, 535
Eammarell, 525
eankke, 110
ear, 603
Earl, 517
earlier'n, 464
earnest, 367
Earthly, 525
earth-wire, 236
Earvila, 524
eastbound, 247
East End, 247
easy, 465
easy-mark, 565, 576
eat, 404, 424
eat, to, 431
eat crow, to, 148, 198
eaten, 431
eatery, 176
eatfest, 218
eat out of my hand, to,
    95
Ecker-R, 496
eclaircise, to, 75
éclaircissement, 75
éclat, 409
eco, 401
ecology, 155
écrevisse, 105
ed, 401, 402; -ed, 377, 435,
    464
-ede, 438
Edelstein, 501
Edelweiss, 522
Eden, 183
Edgar, 506
edict, 183
Edina, 522
Edith, 506
editor, 289
editorial, 165
Edward, 506, 507, 515, 519
Edwin, 506, 515
Edyth, 520
ee, 381, 412; -ee, 180, 549
eel, 600; -grass, 114
-een, 491
-eer, 180
effuse, to, 75
eg, 401, 403
egad, 315

egg, 340, 614
egg-plant, 114, 246
eggs, 614
egofest, 218
egoist, 340
ei, 402, 484
Eibhlin, 513
eighth note, 250
Eileen, 513
einen bummeln machen,
    156
Einstein, 501
Eisenach, 484
either, 6, 341, 472
el, 86
elastic, 334
Eldarema, 521
Eldeese, 524
Eldorado, 534, 539
eldorado, 152
electioneer, to, 228
electragist, 178, 284, 287
electric-sign-engineer,
    290
electrize, to, 192
electrocute, to, 192
electrolier, 171
Eleroy, 538
elevator, 57, 120, 234, 239,
    254; -boy, 234
Elias, 506
Elihu, 515
Elijah, 515, 519
élite, 409
Elizabeth, 506, 507, 509,
    511, 519, 520, 529
Elk, 529, 536
Elkdom, 178
Ellen, 510
Elliott, 507
Ellis, 499, 507
Ellsworth, 512
ellum, 129, 353
Elly, 510
Elmer, 510, 515, 516, 517
elocute, to, 192
Elpasoan, 548
Elseroad, 483
Elserode, 483
Elserote, 483
Elsinore, 534
Elsroad, 483
Elsrode, 483
Eltzroth, 483
Ely, 508
Elzie, 523

Em, 519
em, 452
Emanuel, 508
Emavida, 522
embalm, 335
embalmed-beef, 174
embalming-fluid, 582
embalming surgeon, 287
emerald, 250
Emersonthusiast, 570
emfasis, 402
Emil, 513
Emily, 507
Emjo, 518
Emma, 509, 519
Emmanuel, 506
emote, to, 192
emperor, 395
Empire, 552
empire, 346
employd, 401
employé, 409
employée, 412
emporiums, 413
-en, 193
enceinte, 304
enceinte sow, 305
enclose, 390
encumbrance, 390
endeavour, 395
endive, 260
endorse, 390
endorse, to, 141
Eneatha, 521
enervate, 325
Engberg, 490
Enghien, 547
engin, 403
engine, 347
engineer, 227, 228, 604, 605
engineer, to, 93, 141, 231
engineer of good taste, 289
engineman, 291
Englewoodite, 549
English, 250, 296
engulf, 391
engulph, 391
Eno, 499
Enoch, 511
enquire, 390, 392, 393
Enroughty, 503
Ensenada, 534
ensure, to, 393
ent, 446; -ent, 192

enter a claim, to, 142
enthuse, to, 141, 165, 192, 232
enthusiasm, 126
entire, 325
entrance-hall, 237
enuf, 402, 403
envoy, 183
eolian, 394
eower, 449
eowrum, 449
Episcopalian, 249
epoc, 401
epoch, 340
Epstein, 499
equestrian-director, 584
equipment-engineer, 290
er, 353, 367, 396, 399, 402, 411; -er, 192, 463, 549, 568
eraser, 239
Erdmann, 484
Erez Israel, 299
Erie Canal, 525
Erik, 510
Erin go bragh, 160
Ernest, 507
Ernst, 510
erosion-expert, 291
errant, 360
errata, 338
error, 395
-ers, 346
erster, 367
eruptiveness, 101
-ery, 176, 325
Esbjörn, 490
Esbyorn, 490
escaped, 604
Eschscholtzia, 522
Esco, 522
escritoire, 254
Eselkopf, 501
eskate, 375
esleep, 375
esophagus, 391, 411
espace, 375
espantoon, 243
Esq., 278
-est, 463
estampida, 152
estate-agent, 239
estator, 286
Estelle, 507
Estha, 522
Estherina, 522

esthetic, 388, 401
estudent, 375
et, 431
eternal, 316, 317, 339, 379
eternal triangle, 570
Ethel, 507
ether, 155, 390
etiology, 411
etiquet, 391
-ette, 178
étude, 347
eu, 484
Euclid, 525
Eulalia, 525
Euliel, 522
eunuch, 305
European-plan, 86
Eusona, 522
Eva Belle, 520
evangelizationeer, 118
Eve, 535
Evelyn, 518, 520
evensong, 268
eventuate, to, 7, 118, 232
Everett, 516
everything, 352, 353
every time, 611
evincive, 120
evolution, 339
ex-, 274
exactly, 253
exam, 183
examin, 403
examind, 403
example, 334, 336
excede, 401
Excellentia Reverendissima, 282
excess, 325
exchange, 292
exciting, 211
exculpate, 325
excursionist, 231
excurt, to, 141
excuse me, 267
executive-session, 148
ex-ex-seventh, 241
exfluncticate, to, 145
exflunctify, to, 568
expect, to, 24, 99
expenditure, 118
experience, to, 168
experience-meeting, 150
expert, 291
expertize, to, 193
explosion, 602

export-engineer, 291
exposé, 409, 411
express, to, 147
express-car, 146
expressman, 146
express-office, 146
express post, 238
exquisite, 325
ex-seventh, 241
exterior, 380, 395
exterminating engineer, 284, 290
extra, 126
extraordinary, 324, 328, 353
ey, 402
eye, 577
eye-opener, 149
E.Z., 209
ez, 365
Ezekiel, 515
Ezra, 515
f, 335, 375, 383, 386, 402
face-cloth, 236
faced, 402
face the music, to, 119
facile, 341
fact, 402
faculty, 242, 268
fade away, to, 609
fade out, to, 264
fag, 573
faggot, 392
fail, 614
failed, 375
failure to compensate, 293
fair, 466
Fairfield, 480
fairway, 562
fairy, 305
Faith, 516
fake, 565, 609
faker, 86
fall, 33, 42, 62, 100, 128
fall, to, 431, 440, 578
fall down, to, 227
fallen, 428, 431, 440
Fallentimber, 539
fallen woman, 304
fall for, to, 227, 229, 565
fallopian, 411
Falloppian, 411
Fall Riverite, 549
fambly, 353
family welfare, 292

fan, 191, 227, 565; -club, 586
fancy, 334
fandom, 178
Fanestil, 484
fanlight, 236
fantan, 162
fantom, 402, 406
far, 335, 336
farina, 341
Farinholt, 503
farmateria, 177
farmerette, 178
farther, 349
farzino, 472
fast, 336
faster'n, 464
fast-freight, 146
fat-cat, 186
Fate, 525
father, 280, 334, 349, 371
Father of Waters, 150
Fats, 520
fattigmand, 215
faucet, 235
fault, 397
faut, 397
Fava, 522
faveur, 384
favor, 383, 384, 386, 388, 390
favorit, 403
favorite-son, 148
favour, 383, 388, 395
favourite, 396
F.D.R., 183
Fearhake, 484
feaselick, 110
feather, 383, 384
feature, to, 37, 227
featurize, to, 193
feaze, to, 141
February, 379
Feb'uary, 353
fed, 431
fed-up, 269
feed, to, 431
feed-plant-engineer, 290
feel, to, 431, 439
feeled, 439
feel good, to, 254
feet, 612
Feil, 484
Feivel, 506
Felicity, 547
Felix, 507

fell, 115, 431, 440
fella, 353, 425
feller, 425
fellow, 254
fellow countrymen, 6
fellowship, 98
fellowship, to, 128, 150
felonious attack, 304
felt, 431, 439
female, 184, 303, 304
fen, 115
fence, 386
fences, 148
fender, 236
F.E.R.A., 209
Feramorz, 516
Ferguson, 499
Fernall, 503
Ferreira, 494
ferry, 536
fertile, 341
fertilizer, 292
fervour, 395
-fest, 218
festschrift, 220
fetch, to, 431
fetched, 431
fete, 183
fether, 384
feuillage, 75
few, 374
ffarington, 504
Ffebrewarie, 379
ffinch, 504
ffoulkes, 504
ffrench, 504
F.F.V., 208
f.h.b., 209
fiancée, 347, 409, 412
fiat, 173
fib, 126
fiber, 388, 402
fictioneer, 180
fiction-engineer, 290
Fielder, 498
Fieldhouse, 485
fiend, 182
fierce, 466
54° 40', 518
fight, to, 431
fight-fight, 373
fightingest, 463
figure, 345
figure, to, 572
fil, 403
fild, 402, 403

filed, 402
filibuster, 148, 231
filing-cabinet, 228
Filipino, 375
Filipowicz, 488
fill, to, 30
fillet, 236, 240
filling-station, 227, 582
fill the bill, to, 142, 558
fillum, 353
filmdom, 178
film-engineer, 290
filosofy, 406
filthy, 467
fin, 578
financial editor, 244
financial-engineer, 290
find, 352
find, to, 431
Findlay, 479
fine, 71, 352, 466
fine, to, 431
finger, 150
finger, to, 578
finif, 578
Finis, 522
finish up, to, 198
finite, 405
Finkelstein, 499
Finly, 516
Fionnlagh, 479
fir, 397
fire, 397; -assessor, 239;
    -brigade, 243; -bug, 145,
    183, 243; -call, 243; -de-
    partment, 243; -dog, 27;
    -eater, 62, 563; -raiser,
    243; -water, 106
fire, to, 147, 199, 227
fire-alarm box, 243
fireboy, 583
fireman, 228
fireworks, 564
firr, 397
first, 346, 367, 605
first broom, 587
first floor, 235, 238
first joint, 302
first speed, 237
first standard, 241
first storey, 238
first-year-man, 242
fish, 580; -dealer, 234;
    -monger, 234; -plate,
    147; -slice, 260
Fisher, 513

Fishpaugh, 482
Fishpaw, 482
fisic, 402
fit, 423, 431
Fits-U, 209
five-and-ten, 234
fivebled, 25
five minutes of three,
    159
five-o'clock tea, 155
fix, 231
fix, to, 26, 197, 210, 253
fixt, 403
fizz, 149
fizzle, 565
fizzle, to, 119
fizzle out, to, 142, 232
flag, to, 147
flagman, 146
flag-stop, 238
flang, 431
flap, 586
flap-jack, 128
flapper, 266, 569, 586
flapperdom, 178
flare up, to, 99
flat, 233; -boat, 145; -car,
    146, 582; -foot, 563;
    -footed, 93, 143; -joint,
    584
flatten out, to, 578
flavorous, 395
flavour, 395
flaw, 328, 349
flay, 184
flay, to, 199
flea, 375
flea's eyebrows, 561
flee, 184
flem, 383, 402
flesh-peddler, 587
fletcherize, to, 193
flew, 432
flimflam, 557
flimsy, 126, 583
fling, 184
fling, to, 431
flip-flop, 47, 185, 263
flippant, 126
flirtation, 126
flit, 184
flivver, 263
Flo, 519
Floarea, 509
floater, 148
flong, 261

flooey, 263
flooie, 184
flookum, 584
floor, 231, 328, 349
floor-covering-engineer,
    290
floorwalker, 234
floozy, 176, 263, 305
flop, to, 162
flophouse, 162
Flora, 509
Floramay, 521
Florea, 509
Florence, 507, 509, 518
Florentine, 551
Florida, 526
flour and feed store, 27
flow, to, 432
flowed, 432
flowerdom, 178
Flower moon, 106
Floyd, 510
flu, 170
flume, 37, 108
flummuck, to, 568
flung, 431
flunk out, to, 99
flurry, 145, 231
Flushing, 532
fly, 109, 532
fly, to, 432
fly a kite, to, 581
flyer, 239, 565
Flynn, 493
fly off the handle, to, 119,
    558
fly-time, 101, 102
fo, 401
F.O.B., 208
foes, 401
fog, 343
Fogelsong, 484
foist, 367, 368
fold up, to, 585
followd, 403
folly, 119
fonetic, 406
fonograf, 403, 406
Fonseca, 501
Fontaine, 481
food, 344
foofff, 561
fool-proof, 228
foot, 462; -hill, 115; -path,
    235, 247; -wash, 150;
    -wear, 227

foots, 170
fop, 126
foppish, 564
forbid, to, 432
force, 101
Ford, 483
fordize, to, 193
fore, 562
forego, 394
Foreman, 483
Forest, 492
forestal, 380
for ever, 350
forgather, 392
forget, to, 432
Forgetto, 505
forgo, 392
forgot, 432
forgotten, 428, 432
fork, 101, 115, 536
for keeps, 95, 232, 609
fork over, to, 99
form, 241, 268
former, 274
formulæ, 412
fornication, 303
For Rent, 266
Forrest, 492
forsake, to, 432
forsaken, 428, 432
forsook, 432
forte, 585
forth and back, 215
fortnight, 250
Fort Riley, 529
forty-rod, 149, 568
forward, 204
forwards, 204, 468
fosfate, 406
fotch, 431
foto, 406
fotograf, 402, 403, 406
Foucher, 547
fought, 431
found, 431
Fountain, 481
fourbled, 25
four-flusher, 187, 191
Fourth of July, 577
fowl-run, 234
Fox, 499, 552
fox-fire, 128
fox-grape, 115
fox-trot, 155
foyer, 237
fragile, 341

frame, to, 263, 264
frame-house, 57, 116, 234, 263
frame-up, 227, 565
frame up, to, 564
franchize, 402
Francis, 513, 515, 519
Francisco, 508, 509
Frank, 505, 507, 508, 509, 513, 515, 519, 520
frankfurt, 220
frankfurter, 155, 186, 220
Franklinton, 529
Franz, 505
Franzosen, 296
frat, 170, 242
fraternal-order, 239
Frates, 494
frau, 347
Frazier's Bottom, 535
frazzled, 568
F.R.C.S., 272
Fred, 515, 519
Frederick, 507, 515, 520, 524
Fredericktonian, 550
Freedman, 483
free-lunch, 85
freez, 401
freeze, to, 432
freeze on to, to, 142, 565
freeze-out, 86, 167, 232
freeze the hub, to, 583
freight, 238; -car, 146; -train, 609
freinschaft, 159
Freitas, 494
Fremont, 484
Frémont, 484
French, 296
French-bean, 235
French letter, 296
French Lick, 535
frend, 381
fresh, 158, 572
fresher, 242
freshet, 122
freshman, 242
Fresser, 501
fretful, 564
Friday, 496
fried, 568
Friedmann, 483
friendly-society, 239
frier, 240

frijol, 152
frijole, 152
Frisco, 543
frisk, to, 566
Fritz, 110, 506, 519
friz, 432
frizzgig, 118
Frog, 573
frog, 96, 146, 294
froggie, 294
Frogtown, 554
frolick, 383, 386
frolicksome, 386
from hell to breakfast, 314
from here, 468
from the hoofs up, 259
from there, 468
from where, 468
frontier, 324
front-lot, 121
front-room, 579
Front Royal, 537
froze, 432
frozen, 432
fruit-dealer, 234
fruiterer, 234
fruiterer's, 234
fruiteria, 177
fruit-seller, 234
fruit-store, 234
fry, to, 581
fudge, 317
fuhrer, 411
führer, 411
Führmann, 483
fulfill, 348
full-house, 191
full professor, 242
fumigating-engineer, 290
fun, 126
function, to, 210
funds, 244
funeral-car, 287
funeral-director, 287
funeral-home, 287
funeralize, to, 140
funk-hole, 573
funny, 464
funny-bone, 239
Funny Louis, 533
funster, 178
fur, 359
furlo, 402, 403
furnished-roomateria, 292
furnishing-engineer, 290

furnitor, 179
furniture-engineer, 290
Furth, 483
further, 372
furtherest, 463
fuse, 389, 394
fust, 346
fuze, 389
g, 348, 352, 368, 377, 389, 402, 405, 484
G.A., 206
gabblefest, 218
gabfest, 218
gadget, 211
gaffer, 584
gag, 394, 586; -rule, 148
gage, 394, 411
gaiety, 392
gaily, 467
Gainsborough, 500
gal, 346
Galgenvogel, 501
Gallagher, 504
Gallipolis, 530
Gallo, 493
gallon, 462
Galloway, 493
galoot, 144
galoshes, 235
Galway, 582
gambling, 126
game-chicken, 302
gandy-dancer, 582, 584
gang, to, 564
gangster, 178
gangway, 236
ganov, 578
ganze, 250
ganz gut, 157
gaol, 383, 389, 390, 392, 393
gaoler, 389
gape, 335
G.A.R., 208
Garabedian, 497
garage, 215, 338
garantee, 402
garbage, 233, 582; -incinerator, 234
Garcia, 494, 543
gard, 399, 402
garden, 547, 583
garden-lot, 121
gargle, 359
garmenteria, 176
Garnett, 479

Garnette, 521
garter, 234, 309; -snake, 114
gas, 169, 170, 183, 236, 334, 559, 564, 566, 585
gasoline, 236, 256
gassed, 199
gastly, 402
gat, 259
gate, 583
gate-money, 191
gather, 338
gauge, 411
gauz, 401
gave, 432, 440
gavel, to, 195
gavot, 401
Gawd, 305
Gawd-a-mighty, 308
gayety, 394
Gay-pay-oo, 209
gay Quaker, 100
gazer, 579
gazet, 401, 403
gazooney, 582
G.B., 208
G.b.F., 209
gear-lever, 236
gear-shift, 236
Geary, 542
gebummelt, 156
gee, 257
geechy, 113
gee-gee, 240
geek, 584
gee-whiz, 158, 316
Geez, 305
gefilte-fisch, 217
geflop, 146
Geisdorff, 514
gelastics, 117
Gelbfisch, 500
Geldschrank, 501
gelt, 578
gem, 183
gemütlich, 157
gemütlichkeit, 409
general, 274, 283, 340, 379, 583
general expert, 292
generally, 467
generator, 236
gentil, 411
Gentle Judge, 525
gentleman, 69, 294; -author, 294; -clerk, 294;

-cow, 301; -player, 294; -rider, 294
gentlemanly, 120
gentlewoman, 294
gent'man, 352
genuin, 403
genuine, 347
genuinely, 406
genuinly, 406
Geoghan, 504
George, 486, 494, 505, 507, 509, 510, 512, 513, 515, 520, 524
Georgiou, 486
Georgious, 486
Gerard, 503
Gerasimopoulos, 485
Gerled, 538
gerrymander, 148, 171, 228
Gersteinian, 175
Gertrude, 507, 510
Gervaise, 481
ges, 402
geschwister, 460
gesplash, 146
gesture, 210, 211
gesture, to, 195
gesundheit, 157, 347
get, 217, 340
get, to, 150, 197, 210, 432, 604
get ahead of, to, 142, 197, 604
get a move on, to, 95, 227
getaway, 197, 263
get away with, to, 227, 264, 563
get away with it, to, 197
get back at, to, 197
get behind, to, 197
get busy, to, 227
get by, to, 197, 565, 604
get going, to, 197, 604
gether, 360
get it in the neck, to, 609
get off, to, 197, 604
get on, to, 604
get one's goat, to, 572
get on to, to, 198
get on well, to, 251
get over, to, 604
get religion, to, 197, 604
get-rich-quick, 466
get solid, to, 197
get solid with, to, 142

get sore, to, 197, 609
get the bulge on, to, 142, 197
get the deadwood on, to, 142
get the drop, to, 142
get the drop on, to, 197
get the hang of, to, 99, 232
get there, to, 197
get the works, to, 581
getting, 428
get together, to, 197
get wise, to, 197, 604, 609
Geurdon, 523
gewitter, 602
geyser, 236
gh, 402
Gheorghe, 509
ghost, 587
Giacomo, 509
Giannopoulos, 485
gibe, 252
Gid, 519
gide, 402
Gideon, 519
gift-shop, 266
gigolo, 215
Gila Monster Route, 582
gild, 402
Gillespie, 503
Gillgren, 491
gillotin, 384
Gilsum, 538
gin, 169, 416, 432; -fix, 149; -fizz, 149
gink, 564
Gins, 500
Ginsbern, 500
Ginsbourgh, 500
Ginsburgh, 500
Ginsbury, 500
Ginzberg, 500
Ginzbourg, 500
ginzo, 295
Giovanni, 509
gipsy, 392, 402
giraf, 401
giraffe, to, 568
Girardean, 550
Girl, 505
girl, 346, 367
girl-mad, 561
girt, 438
Giuliana, 509
Giuseppe, 509

giv, 381, 384, 399, 401, 403
give, 383, 384, 416, 422, 432, 440
give, to, 198, 432, 440, 447, 604
give-away, 565
give hell, to, 314
give him the works, to, 564
given, 432, 440
given-name, 129
give out, to, 198
give suck, to, 303
give the once-over, to, 578
give tittie, to, 309
Gizzard, 536
glad-hand, 186
gladiola, 413
gladiolus, 413
glad-rags, 564
Gladstone, 499
Gladys, 512
Gladyška, 512
glands, 307
glas, 401
Glasby, 503
glass, 243, 337, 368
Glazypool, 533
glebe, 248
glee, 126
Glenice, 521
Glenola, 521
glick, 159
glide, 602
glide, to, 432
glode, 432
Gloria, 183
Glover, 516
Gluck, 482
Glück, 482
glug, 184
G.M., 206
gm, 402
go, to, 198, 432, 604
go-aheadativeness, 96
go astray, to, 303
goatee, 145
Goatleg, 505
go a-whoring, to, 303
gob, 573, 574, 583
go back, to, 198
go back on, to, 142, 167, 198, 232
gobbie, 574
gobble, 574

Gobbler's Knob, 554
go big, to, 198
God, 305, 312, 318, 343, 397
god, 413
goddam, 315, 316
God-damned, 316
goddspell, 397
Godfrey, 507
go for, to, 143
go gandering, to, 578
go-getter, 96, 565
go-ghetto, 561
go gunning for, to, 95
go haywire, to, 198
go hostile, to, 378
goil, 350, 367
goingest, 463
going some, 95, 254
going strong, 609
go it blind, to, 142, 232
G.o.k., 209
goldarn, 316
goldarned, 316
Goldberg, 487
gold-brick, 227
golden-slipper, 149
Goldfield, 536
Goldfish, 500
gold-fish, 573
gold-mine, 566
Goldstein, 499, 500, 501
Goldstone, 500
Goldwyn, 500
Goldye, 520
golf-engineer, 290
golfer, 579
golfitis, 179
golly, 316
goloshes, 235
Golson, 500
Golston, 500
G.O.M., 183, 208
Gomeria, 522
Gomez, 494
gon, 401
Gonadia, 525
gonads, 307
gondola, 146
gondole, to, 192
gone, 401, 432
gone coon, 100
goner, 117, 231
gonorrhæal, 411
gonorrhea, 304, 306
gonorrheal, 411

gonov, 584
gonta, 471
Gonzalez, 494
goober, 113
good, 253
good-afternoon, 252
good and, 227
good and hard, 254
good and tired, 254
good-bye, 252, 414
good-day, 252
good egg, 257
good-form, 269
good mixer, 47
good night, 414, 566
good scout, 109
good-sized, 352
goods-train, 86, 609
goods-waggon, 147
good time, 580
goof, 96, 263, 562, 577
goo-goo, 296
gook, 296
goom, 360
go one better, to, 232
go on the bum, to, 156
go on the stump, to, 232
go on the warpath, to, 119
go on well, to, 251
goose, 295, 583
goose, to, 197
gooseberry it, to, 582
Goose Bill, 536
Goose Hill, 553
go over big, to, 262
go over the wall, to, 581
gopher, 108
gorilla, 263, 560
gorn, 351
gosh, 316
go slo, to, 407
go slow, 466
gospel, 397
gospel-shark, 187
Gossett, 481
gossipfest, 218
gost, 402
go stir-bug, to, 581
got, 51, 251, 432, 604
got away, 604
Gotham, 101
go the limit, to, 562
go the whole hog, to, 137, 143, 232, 373, 568
go through, to, 143, 167
go to bed, to, 302

got off, 604
go-to-meeting, 143, 150
got on, 604
got over, 604
Gott, 535
gotten, 100, 251, 257, 428, 432
got up, 604
goul, 402
goulash, 263
Gould, 498
go under, to, 232
go up Salt River, to, 148
gover'ment, 353
Government, 245
governmental, 231
government bonds, 244
governor, 243, 266, 395
govrenment, 353
goy, 217, 580
g.p., 209
grab, to, 148
grab-bag, 145, 239
grabber, 583
grab-joint, 584
grad, 170
grade, 15, 241
grade-crossing, 239
grade-school, 241
graduate, 243
graduate, to, 196
graft, 37, 191, 228, 337
Graham, 516
grain-broker, 245
grain-market, 256
gram, 391, 394, 401, 403
Gramercy, 532
grammar-school, 241
gramme, 391, 393
gramophone, 235
grand, 99, 210, 557
Grande Ronde, 534
grandificent, 175
grand-marshal, to, 195
grandstand-play, 191
Granger, 503
Grant, 498
grant, 337, 335
Granuloma, 525
grasp, 337
grass, 334, 336, 350, 366
grass-cutter, 562
gratis, 338
Gray, 520
gray, 394
grease, to, 566

grease-ball, 295, 582
grease-joint, 584
greaser, 101, 296
great God, 316
great primer, 250
greats, 243
great Scott, 316
Great War, 248
Great White Father, 150
Great White Way, 546
greef, 381
Greek, 296
Green, 482, 486, 490, 492
green, 99
Greene, 513
greenhorn, 128, 231
Greensboroite, 550
Greensburger, 550
Greenwich, 540
greev, 381
Gregory, 511
-gren, 491
grewsome, 391
grey, 392
Grieg, 478
Griffith, 503
Griffiths, 503
grill, to, 572
grilled, 234
grilly, 109
grind, to, 586
grip-sack, 145
gris-gris, 214
Grisha, 510
Grizzy, 524
groceries, 234
grocerteria, 177
grocery, 176
groceryteria, 177
grog, 155
groggery, 176
Grön, 490
Grondahl, 490
groom, 344
groop, 384
grope, to, 432
grope around, to, 432
gros-bec, 214
Grosscup, 483
Grosskopf, 483
grotesk, 384
grotesque, 384
ground floor, 238
ground-hog, 100, 114, 246
grounds, 462

ground-wire, 236
group, 383, 384
grove, 536, 539
grow, to, 432
growed, 432
growler, 243
grrr, 184
grub, 566
grub-stake, 145, 167
gruesome, 393
Grün, 482
grunt, 587
Grzegdrz, 510, 511
guard, 85, 147, 239, 266, 273
guardeen, 346
guardian, 346
Guarinot, 479
gubernatorial, 165, 231
gue, 402
Guela, 524
Guerci, 494
guess, to, 22, 24, 99, 100, 102, 128
guest, to, 586
guffer, 113
Guglielminetti, 494
gu-gu, 295
Guilherme, 509
guillotin, 384
guillotine, 384
guinea, 295
Guinness-Bourg, 500
Guinsburg, 500
Guinzburg, 500
guitar, 360
Guizot, 481
gulch, 144, 231
gullibility, 22
gully, 144
gum, 235
gumbo, 113, 246
Gummeson, 492
gump, 582
gum-shoe, 144
gum-shoe, to, 95
gun, 578, 583
gun-mob, 578
gun-moll, 259, 578
Gunnar, 510
guntzel, 582, 584
Gus, 508, 512
gusher, 86
Gussie, 519
Gustaf, 510
gut, 582

Guthrian, 549
Gutmann, 484
guts, 305, 309
guv, 432
Guy, 515
guy, 39, 254, 564
guy, to, 167, 254
guyascutis, 145
guy-rope, 254
gyarden, 364
gyirls, 364
gym, 170
gyp, to, 577, 581
gypsy, 394, 577
gypsydom, 178
Gyulay, 496
h, 270, 327, 348, 351, 377, 401, 402, 469
ha, 460
Habella, 524
haberdashery, 254
haberteria, 177
Habib, 513
habitan, 75
habit-disease, 293
hablaing, 376
hacienda, 98, 153
hack, 580, 583
had, 432
hadda, 443
hadda bit, 444
Haddad, 477, 496
hadden, 432, 442
hadn't oughter, 445
had ought, 420
Hadwen, 522
hæm, 411
hæmophilia, 411
hæmorrhage, 411
Haerlen, 481
Haffner, 514
hafta, 443
Hagerstonian, 550
Hagerstown, 529; -er, 550
Hahti, 492
haidang, 109
haima, 411
hainous, 383, 384
Hakomäki, 492
Hal, 519
halbe, 250
Halcyon, 537
half, 335, 379
half an hour, 251
half-breed, 231

half-brother to the cholera, 137
halfe, 379
half hour, 251
half note, 250
half past ten, 251
half-pint, 243
Halfway, 505
halitosis, 307, 309
hall, 414
hallelujah, 338
ham, 170
Hämäläinen, 492
Hamburg, 530
hamburger, 155, 220
Hamlin, 492
hammer, 336
hammer-gang, 584
Hammerstein, 499
hammock, 112
Hampar, 497
Hampartzoomian, 497
Hampton, 516
hand, 343
Handbag, 524
hand-car, 146
handcuff, 560
hand down a decision, to, 246
hand him a lemon, to, 198, 563
hand it to him, to, 563
handle without gloves, to, 142
hand-me-down, 101, 239
hand-out, 564
hand-pick, to, 227
hand-shaker, 573
handsome, 336
handy, 120
hang, to, 432
hangar, 215
hang-bird, 100
hanged, 432
hang-out, 186, 582
Hank, 519
Hanks, 482
hankstelo, 577
Hanna, 513
Hanska, 488
hant, 360
haole, 373
happify, to, 119
happy, 465
happy hunting-grounds, 150

har, 339
Haralampos, 512
Harald, 510
harang, 402
harangue, 360
harass, 324
harbor, 391
harbour, 391
hard, 336, 349, 464, 465, 466
hard-boiled, 561
hard-cider, 86, 149, 244
Hardened Artery, 561
hard hat, 234
hard liquor, 244
hardly, 335, 466, 467
Hard-Scrabble, 553
hardshell, 143, 150
hard-shell Baptist, 250
hard stuff, 577
Hard-Times Square, 561
hardware, 234
hare, 123, 246
hari-kari, 149
harken, 406
Harland, 481
Harlem, 532
harlot, 305, 309
harm, 334
harmonica, 120
harmonicon, 120
harmonika, 120
Harold, 506, 507, 515
harp, 295
Harper, 498
Harris, 496, 499
Harrison, 498
Harry, 507, 510, 511, 512, 513, 515, 519
Hart, 490
hart, 401, 600
Harte, 499
Hartford City, 529
harth, 401
Hartikainen, 492
Hartman, 492
Harvey, 507, 515
Harwick, 499
has, 375
has-been, 92
hash, 260
hashery, 176
hash-slinger, 187
has not, 469
hass, 375
Hassie, 521

Hastings, 508
hatateria, 177
hatatorium, 179
Hatch, 497
Hatetoleaveit, 546
hat-shop, 266
hatta, 443
hattery, 176
Hattie, 519
Hatton, 516
Hatzakordzian, 497
haul, to, 122, 124
haunch, 236
haunt, 344
hausfrau, 155
hav, 399, 401, 403
have, 251, 425, 441, 471
have, to, 432, 442, 443
have an ax to grind, to, 143
have got, 257, 443
have gotten, 257
have money in the stocks, to, 244
have not, 445
haven't, 377, 445
have the brokers (or bailiffs) in, to, 244
have the floor, to, 142
have the goods, to, 565
Havre de Grace, 542
haw, 349
hawker, 234
Hawthorne, 503
hay-barrack, 108
haycock, 301
Hayseed Center, 554
haystack, 301
H-bone, 236
he, 448, 451, 458, 461
head, 183, 243, 383, 384; -cheese, 86; -electrician, 289; -guy, 254; -master, 241, 268; -mistress, 241
headache, 560
head-guy, 254
headlights, 582
headlineitis, 179
headliner, 236
healthatorium, 179
healtheteria, 177
healthful, 203
health-mobile, 180
healthy, 203
he am, 363

he-and-she, 460
heap big chief, 150
hear, to, 432
hear, hear!, 252
hearing, 350
hearken, 406
hearse, 287, 406, 583
heat, 580
heat, to, 432
heaten, 432
heaten, to, 432
heath, 115
heave, to, 432
Heber, 516
he-biddy, 302
Hebrew, 249, 297, 298, 525; -comedian, 297; -holidays, 297; -rabbi, 297
Hector, 523
hed, 381, 383, 384, 401, 403
Hedison, 497
Heditzian, 497
Hedvig, 510
heeler, 167
heer, 460
heerd, 432
hefer, 406
heft, to, 122, 124, 129
hefty, 124, 464
heheheh, 561
Heid, 483
heifer, 406
height, 353
heighth, 161
heights, 546
-heim, 500
-heimer, 219, 500
heinie, 110, 295
heinous, 383, 384
Heinrich, 505, 511
Heintz, 483
Heinz, 511
heir, 351
hekka, 373
held, 433
Helen, 507, 509, 511
Helena, 511
Helentzi, 522
Helga, 506
hell, 205, 305, 313, 318, 377
hell and high water, 314
hell and red niggers, 314
hell and scissors, 314

hell around, to, 314
hell-bender, 314
hell-bent, 314
hell-bent for election, 314
hell-box, 144
hellcat, 305
hellenium, 171
hell-fired, 316
hell-for-leather, 314
Hell-For-Sartain, 536
Hell-Gate, 532
helliferocious, 568
hellion, 140, 314
hellishing, 314
hell-raiser, 314
hell-roaring, 140, 314
hell-robber, 150
hell to pay, 314
helluva, 316
Helm, 490
Helma, 510
help, 69, 98, 101, 228, 292
help, to, 433
helped, 433
help make, to, 229
helpt, 402
Help Wanted, 228
helt, 360, 433, 438
helter-skelter, 126
helth, 403
hem, 411, 452, 460
he-man, 96
hemidemisemiquaver, 250
hemlock, 124
Hen, 519
Hence, 519
hence, 467, 468
Henderson, 519
Hendricksen, 481
hendy, 365
hen-party, 86
Henrik, 510
Henriola, 522
Henry, 505, 507, 510, 515, 519
heo, 448
heom, 445
heora, 448
he-or-she, 460
her, 448, 451, 454, 455, 456
Herald, 516
heraus mit ihm, 157
herb, 351, 375
Herbert, 507

Herchheimer, 479
here, 448, 467, 600
her ear, 350
here'bouts, 468
heren, 448
Her Excellency, 277
Herkimer, 479
Herman, 513
Hermosa Beach, 534
hern, 432, 448, 456
hernia, 307
heroic, 351
herring choker, 296
Herrmann, 505
herse, 406
herun, 448
hes, 460
he's, 461
hesh, 175, 460
hesped, 217
het, 432
het up, 432
heurack, 159
hev, 360, 365
hex, 159
hex-doctor, 159
hez, 460
hi, 406
hiccup, 402
hick, 263, 566, 576
hickory, 104
hid, 433
hidden, 428, 433
hide, to, 433
hide-out, 580
hie, 448
high-ball, 149, 236, 583
high-binder, 162, 263
high-boot, 233
high-brow, 186, 227, 230, 232
high-brown, 296
highfalutin, 143, 231
Highfield, 491
high-hat, 560
Highland, 536
Highlandtown, 553
high-liner, 583
high-school, 241
high-steppingest, 463
high steward, 242
Highstone, 485
High street, 547
high-tone, 464
high-toned, 464
Highwater, 524

high-yellow, 296
hi-jack, to, 578
hike, 151, 656
Hill, 492
hill, to, 16
hill-side, 99
him, 448, 451, 454, 455, 456, 459
him-and-her, 460
himer, 460; -himer, 500
Himself, 525
himself, 459
Hines, 483
hir, 460
Hiram, 515
hired-girl, 116, 266
hired-man, 116
hire-purchase system, 235
hire system, 235
his, 383, 448, 461
His Eminence, 282
hiser, 460
His Excellency, 275, 277, 282
His Grace, 282
His Highness, 275
His Honor, 277
His Lordship, 279, 282
hisn, 22, 359, 448, 451
his-or-her, 460
hisself, 459
hist, to, 161, 346, 433, 578
histed, 433
historic, 351
hist'ry, 353
His Worship, 279
hit, 360
hit, to, 199, 433, 440
hit-and-run, 585
Hitchcock, 308
hitched, 38, 609
Hite, 483
hither, 467, 468
hit the bricks, to, 581
hit the ceiling, to, 198
hit the grit, to, 583
hit the pipe, to, 564
hiz, 383
hj, 490
Hjalmar, 510
Hjelm, 490
Hjort, 490
ho, 401
hoacky, 206
hoar, 349
hoarding, 86, 95, 235, 266

Hobbes, 488
Hobbs, 488
hobo, 37, 188, 191, 565, 581
Hoboken, 553
Hobson, 489
Hobza, 488
Hoch, 482
hoch, 157
hock, 240, 402
hockey, 406
hocky, 406
Hodge, 252
Hoeber, 480
hoe-cake, 102, 114, 115
hoed, 401
hoek, 532
hofbräu, 347, 409
Hoffman, 487
hog, 582, 583
hog, to, 93, 95
Hogan, 514
hogan, 151
hog-expert, 291
Hog-Eye, 554
Högfelt, 491
hoggish, 466
hoghead, 582, 583
Hog Heaven, 554
hog-wallow, 102, 114
Hohokus, 553
hoist, 346
hoist, to, 433
hoisting-engineer, 346
Hoke, 482, 522
hokum, 188, 189, 191
hola, 376
hold, 352
hold, to, 433, 438
hold on, 158
hold on, to, 99
hold out, to, 191
hold-up, 37, 167, 227, 232
hold up, to, 557
hold with, to, 215
hole, 119, 580
Holger, 510
Holič, 486
holiday, 237
holiday, to, 195
holla, to, 142
hölle, 602
holler, 353
holler, to, 142, 433
hollered, 433
holloa, to, 142

holloe, to, 142
hollow, 115
hollow, to, 142
hollow ware, 27
Holm, 510
holmendods, 577
Holmgrain, 491
holo, to, 142
holow, to, 142
holsum, 406
holt, 352
holy catfish, 514
holy gee, 316
holy Jesus, 316
Holy Joe, 573
holy jumping Jesus, 316
holy orders, 249
holy-roller, 250
ho-made, 406
hombre, 152, 153
homely, 86, 128, 251
Homer, 515, 517
homer, 191
Homera, 522
home-run, 191
homesickness, 155
home-spun, 128, 231
home-stretch, 144
homicidious, 16
hominy, 100, 105
Homo boobiens, 560
Homo boobus, 560
homologize, to, 119
homosexuality, 311
hon, 170
Hon., the, 266, 275, 277, 278, 279
hon. agent, 278
hon. and gallant member, 294
hon. and learned member, 294
honest, 351
honeyfogle, to, 142
honeyteria, 177
hon. gentleman, 275
honky-tonk, 263, 564
hon. lady, 294
hon. member, 276, 294
honneur, 384
Honolulu, 541
honor, 351, 383, 384, 386, 390, 402
honorarium, 396
honorary, 278, 395, 396
honoree, 180

honorific, 396
honors, 268
honour, 383, 395, 396
honourable, 396
honours, 242
Hoober, 480
hooch, 149, 221, 263
hoochfest, 218
hood, 236, 237
hoodlum, 37, 167
hoodoo, 113
hoof, 344
hoof, to, 585
Hoofer, 480
hoofer, 586
Hoogsteen, 485
hooiberg, 108
hook, 108, 109, 115, 532
Hook Mountain, 532
hoop, 344
hoopla, 584
hoosegow, 221, 557, 558
Hoosier, 101, 552, 553, 570
hoosier, 580
hootch, 263
hoov, 461
Hoover, 480
hooverize, to, 193
hooves, 344
hop, 162, 183, 343
Hope, 511, 516
hop-head, 186
hop-pillow, 162
Hopson, 489
Hořčička, 488
Horicon, 532
hornswoggle, to, 142, 145, 568
horror, 389, 395
horse-engineer, 290
horse of another color, 101
horse-opera, 587
horse's caboose, 301
horse-sense, 144, 227
horse's neck, 149
Horsethief, 536
Horton, 503
Horvath, 496, 507
hose, 302
hospice, 301
hospital, 351
hospitalization-engineer, 290
hospitalize, to, 193

hospital nurse, 240
hoss, 129, 350, 523
host, to, 195
hostil, 401, 403
hostile, 341
hostler, 351, 393
hot, 252; -air, 227; -box, 147; -cake, 231; -dog, 186; -dog-engineer, 290; -mamma, 305; -seat, 581; -spot, 186; -squat, 581; -stuff, 582; -tamale, 152
Hot Coffee, 536
hotel, 351
hotelette, 292
Hot moon, 106
hot patootie, 259
hotter'n, 464
hour, 351
house, 247, 414
house, to, 194
house and lot, 121
household-engineer, 290
housekeep, to, 192
house-lot, 121
Houseman, 485
house-master, 268
house of detention, 293
house of ill repute, 304
house of questionable repute, 304
house of refuge, 292
housing-expert, 291
Houston, 540
Hovanesian, 497
hove, 432
Hover, 480
how, 25
Howard, 516
Howarth, 496
How did you get that way?, 566
How'd you like to be the ice-man?, 566
Howland, 499
Hoyt, 492
Hrdlička, 488
Hřebec, 486
Hryhory, 511
Hub, 553
hub, 98
hubbub, 564
Huber, 480
Hubsy, 488
huckleberry, 114

huckster, 234
Hudson-pup, 579
Huerlin, 490
huero, 153
hug, 447
Huisman, 485
Hulda, 506
human-engineer, 290
humble, 351
humbug, 99, 126, 373
humgig, 118
humility, 351
humor, 351
humorous, 395
humour, 395
hump, 585
hun, 183, 295
hunderd, 353
hunderder, 398
hundred and twenty-eighth note, 250
hung, 432
Hungarian cuisine, 299
hunger, 374
hungry, 374
hunker, 99
hunkie, 295
hunkydory, 145
Hunter, 513
hunting, 236, 252
Hunting moon, 106
hupmobile, 173
Hurayz, 496
Hurbick, 486
hurl, 184
hurrah, 360
hurricane, 231
hurry up, 198
hurry up, to, 198
-hurst, 546
hurt, 320
hurt, to, 433, 440
hurtle, 184
hurtleberry, 114
hush-money, 566
hussy, 309
hustle, to, 128, 227
hustler, 231
hut, 583
huzzy, 305
hw, 351
hyak, 151
hyar, 360
Hyde, 483
hygiologist, 179
-hym, 500

Hyman, 508
Hynek, 511
hyperfirmatious, 145
hyphenated-American, 173
i, 339, 340, 341, 346, 353, 368, 377, 382, 389, 401, 402, 405, 451, 469; -i, 548
I, 447, 455, 458
-ia, 548
iad, 451
-ian, 548
Iantha, 522
-iat, 180
ice, 577; -berg, 557; -box, 580; -cream soda, 85, 228; -engineer, 290; -house, 579; -tong doctors, 579; -water, 165
Icel, 521
Icsylf, 459
Icy Victorious, 522
Idahoan, 548
ide, 401
idea, 325
idea-engineer, 290
idealer, 463
idolatries, 303
I don't think, 566
ie, 381, 402
Ignač, 511
Ignacio, 508, 509
Ignát, 511
Ignatius, 511
Ignês, 509
ignoramus, 339
I is, 363
Ila, 522
iland, 384, 406
ile, 346, 401
Ill, 505
ill, 62, 127, 251
illegitimate child, 293
illegitimate mother, 293
ill-gotten, 432
Illinois, 541
I'll say so, 566
illustrate, 325
illy, 15, 467
Ilmari, 510
Iloah, 522
imagin, 403
imagine, 384
imkeeled, 16
immabloodymaterial, 316

immigrate, to, 118
imperturbe, to, 75
imprecriptible, 118
improper assault, 311
impurities, 303
Inabeth, 522
in a certain condition, 311
in-and-in, 576
in back of, 252
in bad, 202
Inc., 244
inch, 462
incidence, 462
incident, 6, 462
inclement, 325
incog, 558
incohonee, 106
income-engineer, 290
incommunicado, 221
incorporated, 244
indegoddampendent, 315
Indiana, 526
Indian corn, 122, 234
Indian-file, 106
Indian-giver, 106
Indianians, 548
Indian meal, 234
Indian-Summer, 106, 229
india-rubber, 239
indices, 412
indifferent, 465
indignation-meeting, 231
individual, 184
indorsation, 390
indorsee, 118, 390
indorser, 118
indorst, 402, 403
induced, 345
ine, 401
-ine, 180, 347
in embryo, 303
inexhaustiveness, 166
inexpressibles, 302, 303
Inez, 514
infanticipating, 561
infantorium, 179
infants'-school, 235, 241
infinit, 399, 403
infirmary, 293
inflexion, 392
influent, 120
influential, 120, 223
infract, to, 118
-ing, 192, 315, 348, 352
Ingeborg, 510
Ingerval, 510

-ingwell, 315
in husband trouble, 561
initial-sack, 562
initiative and referen-
    dum, 245
injunct, to, 167
ink-slinger, 101
inland, 239
inland revenue, 239
inn, 123
inner-mission, 220
inning, 248
innovate, to, 192
-ino, 176
inquire, 390
inquiry, 325; -office, 238
insane, 325, 360; -asylum,
    293
insect, 310
insignia, 412
insignias, 413
inspector, 243
instal, 392, 393
install, 393
instalment-plan, 235
instead, 340, 384
insted, 384, 403
instruct a barrister, to,
    246
instructor, 242
insubordination, 118
insurance-adjuster, 239
insure, to, 393
insurge, to, 192
insurrecto, 221
intelligentlemen, 561
intelligentsia, 462
interduce, 353
interest, 328
interesting   condition,
    304
interfere with, to, 311
interiour, 380
intermission, 237
intern, 411
intern, to, 194
internal revenue, 239
interne, 411
interstitial glands, 307
interval, 235, 237
interval-land, 99
interview, to, 192
in the belly, 303
intransigeant, 409
intransigent, 409
int'res', 353

intuition, 614
inure, to, 75
invalid-coach, 288
invite, 129
invoist, 403
involv, 401
in writing, 252
Ioan, 509
Iodine, 524
iodine, 341
Ionescu, 494
Iowa, 526, 541
I.Q., 588
Irby, 522
ire, to, 199
Irene, 507, 520
Irish turkey, 583
iron-horse, 147
iron-jawed, 137
Ironmonger, 503
ironmonger, 85
ironmongery, 234
iron out, to, 227
Ironroad, 514
Irving, 506, 507
is, 375, 427
Isaac, 506, 507
Isaiah, 515
-isation, 389
I say!, 252
ise, 401
-ise, 389
Isennock, 484
is going to, 201
ish ka bibble, 217
I should worry, 217
Isidor, 506
island, 383, 384, 406, 605
isle, 183
is not, 428, 445
isn't, 445
isolate, 341
Isom, 524
Isophene, 522
isquontersquash, 105
Israel, 506
Israelite, 298
iss, 375
issue, 352
-ist, 178
-ista, 221
is to go, 201
I swan, 259
Iszatso, 546
it, 448
Italian, 296, 299

ite, 401; -ite, 178, 549
itemize, to, 93, 141, 167, 232
it gets me, 197
Ithamer, 522
-itis, 178, 179, 347
it is me, 51, 422, 455, 457, 458
it is to laugh, 159
it listens well, 220
its, 448
itself, 459
it's her, 455
it's him, 455
it's me, 51, 422, 455, 457, 458
it's up to you, 191
it's us, 455
Itzik, 506
Ivan, 511, 513
Ivanhoe, 537
Ivason, 523
ive, 401
I.X.L., 209
Izabel, 509
ize, 402; -ize, 192
j, 375, 404
Jaakko, 493, 510
jabon, 373
Jace, 519
Jack, 498, 507, 509, 510
jack, 302, 308, 585
jackass, 302
Jackass Flat, 536
Jack Johnson, 573
jack-pot, 191
jack-rabbit, 167
Jackson, 489, 493, 498, 514, 517, 529
Jacob, 498, 506
Jacobovitch, 498
Jacobovsky, 498
Jacobson, 498
Jacques, 507, 508
jag, 150
Jaggers, 569
jail, 292, 293, 383, 386, 389, 390, 393, 396
jailer, 389
Jaimé, 508
Jake, 498
Jakša, 489
Jakšič, 489
jam, 167
jambalaya, 214
jam-buster, 583

James, 505, 506, 507, 511, 513, 515, 524, 527, 531
Jameson, 486
Jamestown, 527
Jamestown weed, 114
Jamgotvhain, 497
Jamison, 497
jamoca, 580
Jan, 511
jan, to, 192, 196
janders, 360
Jane, 506
janit, to, 196
janitor, to, 196, 235
Janke, 110
Jansen, 477, 481
Jap, 183
japalac, 172, 173
Japanee, 461
Japan jack, 373
Jap Chief, 183
jardinière, 347
Jared, 516
Jaroscz, 488
Jarvi, 492
Järvi, 493
Jarvis, 481, 493
Jasha, 508
Jason, 519
jaundice, 335, 344, 346
jawbone, 573
jawfest, 218
Jayhawk, 552
jay-walker, 186, 227
jazz, 155, 188, 189, 191, 604
jeans, 128, 263
jedge, 346
Jedlička, 488
Jedlicker, 488
Jeff, 519
Jefferson, 498, 513, 515, 517, 519, 529
jell, to, 93, 191
jelly, 375
Jem, 519
Jeneal, 522
Jennie, 507
Jennings, 513, 516
Jens, 510
jeopard, to, 165
jeopardize, to, 121, 141, 165
jeopardy, 126
jerked-beef, 112
jerk-water, 146, 582

Jerome, 507, 520
Jerris, 488
Jerry, 573
jerry, 583
Jerseyman, 552
Jesse - James - and - Frank, 523
jest, 346
Jesus, 305, 313, 316, 318, 508
Jesús, 509
Jesus Christ, 308, 316
Jesus H. Christ, 316
Jesus H. Particular Christ, 316
Jew, 249, 297, 298, 305
jew, to, 122, 124, 297, 299
jew down, to, 297
jeweler, 383, 388
jeweller, 383
jewellery, 391, 392
jewelry, 391
Jewish boy, 299
Jewish cooking, 299
Jewish religion, 299
jibe, to, 252
jick, 216
jickie, 216
jig, 296
jigabo, 296
jigaboo, 296
jigger, 152, 211
jig-saw, 167
jig's up, 101
jilt, 126
Jim, 508, 512, 513
jiminy, 316
Jim-Jam, 536
Jimmie, 512
Jimson weed, 114, 115
jine, 161, 346
jiner, 346
jinerll, 379
Jingo, 537
jint, 136
jist, 346
jit, 169, 296
jitney, 86, 93, 188, 189, 191, 263
João, 509
Job, 535
Jobber, 488
jobbernoll, 577
job-holder, 243
jocker, 582
jockey, 155, 587

jockungage, 577
Joe, 508, 509, 519
Joey, 584
Johann, 505
Johannes, 482
Johannsen, 483
Johannson, 477, 491, 492
John, 482, 505, 506, 508, 509, 510, 511, 512, 513, 515, 516, 524, 573
John-Collins, 85, 149
Johnnie, 512
Johnny-cake, 115
Johnny-jump-up, 115
Johnson, 477, 478, 483, 485, 492, 497, 514
Johnstown, 529
join, 346
joiner, 85
joint, 167, 235, 576, 584
joist, 346
joke-smith, 565
Joki, 492
jolly, 253, 264, 270
Jonas, 506
Jonase, 479
Jonathan, 302
Jones, 477, 478, 479, 494, 498, 514
Jones Gulch, 535
Jones of William, 504
Jonsson, 491
jonteel, 411
Joosh, 561
Jordan, 494, 535
Jordão, 494
Jorge, 494, 508
jornada, 153
José, 508, 509
Joseph, 506, 509, 513, 515
Josephine, 507
Josh, 515, 519
Joshua, 515
joss, 162
josshouse, 162
journalese, 570
joyfulest, 420
joy-ridden, 439
joy-ride, 62, 186, 227, 565
joy-ride, to, 439
joy-rided, 439
joy-rider, 579
joy-rode, 439
Juan, 508
Juba, 524
juba, 113

Judean, 298
judge, 257, 274, 279, 346
judgement, 389
judgmatical, 120
judgment, 392
jug, 235, 566
Juhana, 510
julep, 85
Jules, 507
Julina, 524
Julius, 507, 508, 510
July, 496
jump, to, 142, 232
jumper, 145
jumping-off place, 145
Jump-Off, 536
jump on with both feet, to, 143
jump the rails, to, 147
junction, 539
June-bug, 114
Jung, 483
jungle, 582
jungle-buzzard, 582
Junior, 520
junior, 242
junior school, 241
junk, 229, 235
junker, 579
junta, 221
Jupiter, 523
Jurjus, 512
Jussi, 510
just, 253, 346
just how many?, 253
just in time, 253
just lovely, 253
just what do you mean?, 253
juve, 586
juvenile, 184
juzgado, 221
k, 368, 375, 382, 383, 394, 406, 484
Kaarlo, 510
Kaatersill Clove, 532
Kabotchnick, 499
kaddish, 217
Kaduggan, 503
kafateria, 177
Kahler, 484
kaif, 177, 347
kake, 407
Kalamazoo, 528, 553
kalfeteria, 177
Kállay, 496

Kalle, 510
Kalomeris, 479
Kaltenberg, 483
Kamariotis, 486
Kamp Takitezy, 546
kanaapie, 110
Kanorado, 537
Kansas Citian, 548
Kansas Nebraska, 517
kant-leek, 407
kar, 407
Kara, 497
karacter, 382
Karageozian, 497
Karen, 506, 510
Karfunkel, 501
Karin, 510
Karl, 510
Karlsson, 491, 492
katchina, 151
Katel, 524
Kathryn, 520
Katie, 509
katy-did, 114
Katzenberger, 487
Katzenellenbogen, 485
katzenjammer, 155
Kauchee, 524
kaukau, 373
Kay, 507
Kayla, 496
Kayler, 496
kayo, 210, 562
Kazimierz, 510
K.C., 246
Keams Canyon, 535
Kearny, 542
kedge, 24
kee, 381
keek, 296
Keeley, 483
keen-kutter, 407
keep, to, 433, 604
keep a stiff upper lip, to, 142, 232
keep one's eye peeled, to, 232
keep tab, to, 142
keer, 339
keg, 340, 383, 384
Keller, 487
Kelly, 478, 493, 496
Kemp, 483
Kempf, 483
Kenesaw Mountain, 517
Kenjockety, 514

Kennebec, 528
Kenneth, 512
Keokuk, 553
kep, 352, 433
kept, 433
ker-, 146; -bang, 146;
-bim, 146; -chunk, 146;
-flop, 146; -flummux,
146; -plunk, 146; -slam,
146; -slap, 146; -souse,
146; -splash, 146;
-swash, 146; -swosh,
146; -thump, 146;
-whut, 483
kerb, 390, 394
kerbstone, 394
kerbstone broker, 390
Kerekes, 496
Kerngood, 483
Kerngut, 483
Kershaw, 503
Kerttu, 510
Kester, 483
ketch, 161, 339, 429
ketcht, 339
ketchup, 391
kettle, 346, 368
key, 112, 115
keyless-watch, 96, 235,
239
key-man, 227
Keystone, 552
Key West, 535
Khachadoorian, 497
Khouri, 496
Khoury, 496
Khuri, 496
ki, 113, 490; -ki, 296
kibitzer, 217, 578
kibosh, 263, 573
kick, 142, 227
kick, to, 141
kicker, 142
kick in, to, 198
kick the bucket, to, 142
kick up hell, to, 314
kidding, 37
Kiercereau, 495
kife, to, 585
kike, 295, 305
kiki, 296
Kilander, 491
Kilberg, 490
Kilgren, 490
kill, 109, 532
killfish, 109

kill-joy, 187, 564
Kill van Kull, 532
kilogram, 390, 391
kilometer, 325
Kilpatrick, 501
Kilström, 490
kilt, 360
kilter, 129
kin, 339
kinda, 443, 471
Kindberg, 490
Kindbloom, 490
kindergarten, 112, 155,
235
Kinderhook, 532
Kindlund, 490
kindness, 348
King, 485, 498
king-pin, 583
King's Counsel, 246
king snipe, 583
King Solomon, 525
kinker, 584
kinky, 120
Kirk, 485
Kirkeslager, 485
Kirstein, 499
Kish, 496
kishkes, 217
Kiss, 496
kissingest, 463
kitchen-cabinet, 228
kitchenette, 178
kitchen-fender, 256
kittenship, 118
kittl, 217
kittle, 346
kitty, 191
kiva, 151
kiver, 22, 129, 346
Kizirboghosian, 497
Kjellman, 490
Kjellstrand, 490
klainzaric, 109
klassy, 407
kleen, 407
kleenex, 173
Klein, 483, 499
Klicklighter, 505
Kline, 483
kloof, 532
klothes, 407
kn, 484
Knapp, 493
kneel, to, 433, 439
kneeled, 433, 439

knelt, 433, 439
knew, 433, 437
knew not, 469
knickebein, 85
knicker, 170
knife, to, 148
knob, 115
knocked-up, 309, 310
knock into a cocked hat,
to, 143
knockout-drops, 609
knock out of the box, to,
191
Knoebel, 484
know, to, 433
knowed, 424, 433, 436, 437
know him like a book, to,
142
know-nothing, 102
know the ropes, to, 142
Knoxville, 529
Knut, 510
Knutson, 492
Koch, 485
kodak, 172, 173, 559; -er,
173; -fiend, 173
kodak, to, 173
Koesegi, 496
Koester, 482
Koevesh, 496
Kohler of Kohler, 504
Koith, 522
kokshut, 151
kolach, 216
kolic, 382
kollege-kut, 407
komusta kayo, 376
König, 484, 485
Koning, 485
Kookno, 503
Koorey, 496
korus, 382
Korzienowski, 489
kosher, 216, 217, 299, 347,
578
Koski, 492
kosy, 407
Köszegy, 496
kotex, 172, 173
Kouba, 488
Kovács, 477, 496
Kovár, 477
Kovář, 486
Köves, 496
Kowalczyk, 477, 488
kowtow, to, 162

Krankheit, 483
Krantz, 484
Krauswood, 529
kraut, 295
Krawiec, 488
kreem, 406
Kreil, 483
Krejčí, 487
Krisking'l, 156
Kriss Kringle, 156
Kriton, 486
kruller, 98
kruxingiol, 214
Kuba, 488
Kubíček, 512
Kucharz, 488
Kuehle, 483
Kühn, 500
Kühne, 484
Kuhns, 483
Kuiper, 481, 485
kuleana, 373
kümmel, 157
Kuntz, 482, 483
Kurtz, 484, 485
Küssemich, 501
Küster, 480
Kutiš, 486
kutlery, 407
-kvist, 491
kwality, 407
-ky, 296
Kyle, 481
L, 208
l, 348, 352, 375, 377, 402;
    -l, 380
lab, 373
Labelle, 533
labor, 390, 397, 402
laboratory, 325, 373
laborer, 239
laborious, 395
Laboris, 500
La Borwit, 500
Labouiss, 500
labour, 395, 397
labourer, 396
Labovitz, 500
lace-engineer, 290
lachrymal, 411
lackey, 393
lacquey, 392, 393
lacrimal, 394, 411
La Crosse, 539
Lacygné, 533
ladder, 235

ladened, 193
ladies' championship, 293
ladies' international, 293
ladies' room, 414
ladies' round, 293
ladies' wear, 293
ladrone, 221
lady, 69, 284, 293, 302;
    -actor, 293; -champion,
    293; -doctor, 293;
    -golfer, 293; -inspector,
    293; -secretary, 293;
    -superintendent, 294
læt, 465
laf, 381, 402, 403
Lafayette, 337, 519, 529,
    533, 542
Lafe, 519
lag, 215
lager, 112, 368
lager-beer, 155
lagged, to be, 581
lagniappe, 151, 214
Lagrange, 533
Lähteenmäki, 492
Laib, 484
laid, 433
lain, 433
Laine, 492
La Junta, 543
Lake, 492, 493
Lake George, 532
lallapalooza, 160, 175
lam, 402
lam, to, 579
Laman, 516
La Mar, 516
lamb, 582
lame-duck, 92, 148, 187
laminated - wood - engi-
    neer, 290
Lamiza, 522
Lamoine, 533
Lamonte, 533
lamp, to, 263
lanai, 377
Lancastrian, 550
Lance, 493
landläufer, 156
land-office, 116
landscape-architect, 288
landscape-gardener, 288
land-slide, 115, 148
Landsschaffshausen, 497
Lane, 479, 492
lane, 547

Lang, 483, 484
Langestraet, 480
Lantz, 484
Lanza, 493
Lapáček, 487
La Pache, 487
lap-robe, 237
Laramie, 541
larcensy, 353
Larch, 495
L'Archevêque, 495
(la) reata, 152
larf, 351
lariat, 152
LaRivière, 495
lark, 124
larn, 339
Larraby, 495
La Rue, 495, 516
La Salle, 520
Las Palomas, 534
lass, 334
lasso, 152
lasso, to, 152
last, 334
last waltz, 581
late, 465, 467
lately, 467
Lath, 522
lather, 338
Latrina, 521
laud, 249, 328
laudanum, 155
Laudenschläger, 483
Laudenslager, 483
Laudensläger, 483
laugh, 334, 336, 366
laughingest, 463
laugh in your sleeve, to,
    563
laugh like a hyena over a
    dead nigger, to, 137
laugh that off, to, 560
La Una, 521
launch, 344
laundry, 344
laurel, 124
Lauria, 493
Lauten, 484
Lautenberger, 483
Lautenschläger, 483
Lautenschleger, 483
L'Auvergne, 482
lava, 338
Lavake, 482
lavandera, 376

Lavar, 516
lavatory, 373
Lavaun, 521
La Verne, 512, 516
law, 577
law-abiding, 120
lawn, 349
Lawrence, 494, 507, 509, 511
lay, 420
lay, to, 309, 433, 439
lay off, to, 40
lay-reader, 249
Lazarre, 507
lazo, 152
ld, 438
lead, to, 433, 437
leader, 228
leader of the orchestra, 289
leads, 238
Leadville, 536
leag, 402
leakingest, 463
lean, to, 433, 439
leaned, 439
leap, to, 433, 439
leapt, 392
learn, 339
learn, to, 433, 435, 440
learnéd, 438
leather, 406
leather and finding store, 27
Leatherhead, 552
leather-neck, 187, 263, 570, 573, 574
leave, to, 433, 440
Lebenschweiler, 485
leberwurst, 155, 220
LeBlanc, 495
lecturer, 242
led, 433, 437
Lee, 492, 498, 506, 507, 508, 513, 517
Leebakken, 492
leech, 272
leery, 464
Le Esta, 522
Leetha, 522
leetle, 346
lefse, 215
left, 433, 440
left at the post, to be, 142
Left Hand, 537
left-luggage room, 238

leg, 302, 308, 309, 340
legal holiday, 237
légion d'honneur, 409
legion of honor, 409
legislate, to, 118, 119, 120, 191
Lehi, 516
Lehman, 500
Lehn, 480
Lehnert, 479
Leider, 514
Leilabeth, 521
Leipzig, 530
Lejitta, 522
Lekander, 491
Lem, 523
Le Maine, 479
Lemon, 525
lend, 439
lend, to, 433, 439
length, 360
lengthy, 15, 100, 119, 120, 223
leniency, 121, 165
lens-hog, 587
lent, 433, 438, 439
Leon, 506
Leonard, 479, 508
Leonhard, 479
Leonhardt, 479
leopard, 383, 384
Leora, 522
lep, 161, 433, 437
leperd, 384
lepero, 153
lepper, 269
lernt, 433
Les, 507
les, 352, 401, 402
Leser, 484
Leslie, 512, 516
Lester, 506, 507
let, to, 433, 440, 604
let George do it, 572
let-George-do-it-itis, 179
lether, 406
Let her go, Gallegher, 566
Letitia, 519
let it slide, to, 143
Letizia, 509
let on, to, 99
let's, 352
letter-box, 235
letter-carrier, 85, 235, 238, 266

letters, 238
Leuvenmark, 490
Levay, 498
levee, 98, 151
level-crossing, 260
leveler, 389
leveller, 389
Levene, 498
l'Evêque, 482
lever, 340
Levering, 480
Leveson-Gower, 503
Levey, 498
Levie, 498
LeVie, 498
Levien, 498
Levin, 498
Levine, 498
Levitt, 498
Levoy, 498
Levvy, 498
Levy, 477, 498, 500
lewdness, 303
lewd woman, 303
Lewis, 494, 499, 505
Lewy, 498
ley fuga, 221
L.G., 183
Li, 513
Liam, 513
liar, 306
libertad, 75
Liberty, 537
liberty-cabbage, 155
libretti, 412
lib'ry, 353
-lic, 464
-lice, 464
license, 394, 462
licensed trade, 243
licensed victualler, 243
Liceta, 524
Lichtenstein, 498
Lichtman, 498
lickety-split, 114
lick to a frazzle, to, 95
lid, 368
lie, to, 433, 439
Liebel, 506
Liebering, 480
lied, 433
lieutenant, 243, 345
lieutenant-colonel, 283
lieutenant-commissioner, 283
lifebelt, 252

lifeboat, 252
lifeguard, 252
life-preserver, 252
lift, 234, 239, 368
liftman, 234
Lige, 519
light, to, 198, 433
lightning-bug, 114
lightning-rod, 100
light out, to, 142, 167, 198
Liisa, 510
like, 420, 424, 425, 458, 472
likeable, 389
like a snowbird in hell, 314
like greased lightning, 563
like hell, 314
likely, 99, 100, 128
Liliecrona, 491
lilj, 490
Lilja, 510
Liljedáhl, 491
Liljegren, 491
Liljeqvist, 491
Lillian, 510, 520
Lillquist, 491
Lilydahl, 491
Lilygren, 491
Lilymary, 521
Lilyquist, 491
lim, 402
lima-bean, 260
limb, 302, 304
limberger, 295
lime-juicer, 295
lime-tree, 115
limey, 55, 295
limited, 147
limited liability company, 244
Limmer, 524
Limus, 524
Lina, 509
Lincoln, 480, 498, 508, 517
Lindbergh, 491
linden, 115
line, 147
linen-draper, 85
Lingo, 525
lingon, 215
lingreese, 216
Linkhorn, 480
Lionel, 507
lip, 566, 576
liqueur, 347
Lisi, 510

Lister, 516
listerine, 172, 173
lit, 368, 433
lite, 406
literat, 75
literature, 352
lithographic-engineer, 289
Little, 493
little, 346
Little Giant, 101
Little Mary, 310
Little Snoring, 537
liturgy, 249
Litvinoff, 499
liv, 399, 401, 403
livd, 403
lived, 368
live-oak, 100, 114
liver, 463
livercheese, 220
liverwurst, 155
live-wire, 37
living, 248
living-room, 219, 235, 266
Livingston, 499
Lizard, 552
Lizzie, 509, 510, 519
lj, 491
Ljung, 491
Ljungdahl, 491
ll, 401; -ll, 380
LL.D., 273
Llewelyn, 508
Lloyd, 516
(l)m, 335
load, 586
loaden, to, 193
loaf, 156
loaf, to, 156
loafer, 99, 155
loafing-place, 156
loan, 439; -office, 292; -shark, 186
loan, to, 128, 195, 433
loaned, 433
lobby, 237
lobby, to, 148, 232
lobby-display, to, 195
lobbyist, 254
Lobe, 484
Lobenstein, 498
Lobenstine, 498
locate, to, 7, 31, 118, 119, 120, 165, 191, 232
loch, 544

locker, 368
locoed, 153
loco foco, 99
locomobile, 173
locomotive, 149
loco-weed, 152
locum tenens, 248
locust, 100, 115, 536
lodger, 235
Loeb, 484
Loeser, 484
log-cabin, 57, 115
log-house, 115
logroll, to, 114
log-rolling, 227, 228
lohengrined, 561
Lom, 519
Lomoe, 492
Lömoe, 492
London, 527, 528
Lonesomehurst, 546
Lone Star, 552
Lone Wolf, 514
Long, 483
longa, 250
long-distance, 235
long-haul, 239
long-horn, 582
long primer, 250
long sauce, 100
Longstreet, 480
Lonnquist, 490
Lony, 523
look, 159
loom, to, 199
loop-hole, 128
Loose Creek, 533
loosen, to, 433
loosened, 433
Looson-Gor, 503
loot, 169
Lopes, 495
Lopez, 494, 495
Lord, 272, 305, 318, 349
lord, 328
lorn, 349
los, 401
Los Angeles, 542
lose, to, 433
lose out, to, 198
Los Gatan, 549
loss, 603
lost, 433
lot, 98, 121
Lotawana, 522
loud, 465

Loudenslager, 483
Louis, 505, 506, 515, 524
Louisvillain, 552
Louisville, 529, 541
Louisvillian, 550
lounge, 243; -lizard, 187, 263, 569, 572; -suit, 235
Lourenço, 494, 509
louse, 305; -cage, 583
lousy, 566
Louvenia, 524
lov'd, 438
love, 308, 406
loved, 438
lovefest, 218
love her up, to, 308
lovely, 257
love-nest, 186, 570
Lovern, 482
low-brow, 186
low-down, 102, 231
Lowe, 482
Löwe, 482
Lowell, 498
Lowery, 493
low-flung, 143
Low Freight, 533
low-gear, 237
low-life, 564
lowly, 467
lozenger, 353
Ltd., 244
lubritorium, 179
lucer, 402
Lüchow, 482
Lucien, 508
Lucille, 507
lucky-dip, 239
lucre, 386
Lucybelle, 521
Luda, 522
Ludie, 524
Ludwig, 505, 507
luggage, 85, 233, 254; -shop, 266; -van, 147
Luiz, 494
Luke, 506
Lum, 523
lumber, 7, 12, 57, 122, 123; -jack, 123; -man, 123; -room, 123; -yard, 123
lump, 582
lump o' lead, 578
lunatickest, 463
lunch, 240
lunch-counter, 239

luncheon, 171
lunchery, 176
luncheteria, 177
Lundquist, 514
Lunette, 521
lunger, 563
lure, to, 199
lustre, 383
lutfisk, 215
Luther, 512, 513, 515, 517, 525, 535
lux, 172
lv, 335, 401
-ly, 464, 465, 466, 467
lynch, to, 141, 231, 232
lynching-bee, 142
lynch-law, 98
Lynner, 549
Lyons, 499
lysol, 173
M., 348
m, 375
ma, 170, 284
Mabel, 512, 513
mac, 235
Macá, 486, 488
MacEochagain, 504
machete, 221
Macheyovsky, 489
machine, 148, 227, 382, 384
machine-shop, 123
MacIlleathiain, 479
Mack, 490
Mackey, 492
mackinaw, 105
mackintosh, 235
Mackis, 512
MacMahon, 489
MacSuihhne, 504
Macy, 486, 498
mad, 12, 143
madam, 305
Madame, 283, 503
Madames, 412
Madames of the Sacred Heart, 412
mad as a hornet, as, 144
mad as a March hare, as, 144
mad-dog, 144
made, 433
made-to-measure, 234
mad-house, 144
Madison, 537
Mae, 507, 520

ma femme, 75
mafia, 222
Magazine, 525
magazine, 325
Magdalene, 510
Maggie, 509
Maggio, 493
magnisonant, 118
Magnus, 510
Mahala, 522
Mahmoud, 513
Máhoney, 504
Mahonri, 516
maid, 266
maiden, 308
Maija, 510
mail, 238, 256; -bag, 238; -box, 238; -car, 238; -carrier, 238; -clerk, 147; -order, 238; -man, 238; -matter, 238; -train, 238; -van, 238
Main street, 547
maiz, 122, 384
maize, 3, 106, 122, 234, 384
major, 242, 274, 283
makai-ewa, 377
make, to, 433, 604
make a get away, to, 198
make a kick, to, 143
make good, to, 227, 229
make out, to, 229
make the fur fly, to, 142
make the grade, to, 565
make tracks, to, 142
make whoopee, to, 561
Maki, 492
Mäki, 492
Makláry, 496
Makohon, 489
malafee, 113
malaise, 409
Malcolm, 497, 507
malease, 409
male-cow, 301
male-hog, 302
Malen, 523
male-sheep, 302
mama, 585
mama-san, 373
Mamie, 519
Mamie Taylor, 149
mamma, 325
managing director, 244
mañana, 221

man-and-woman it, to, 561
mangelwurzel, 246
mangle, 261
Manhattan, 532
manhattanize, to, 193
manicure, 178
manicurist, 178
manifest, 582
manitee, 106
Mann, 484
männerchor, 157, 347
Manney, 479
Manoel, 509
mansions, 247, 414
Månsson, 491
Manuel, 508, 509
map, to, 199
marathon, 180
March, 493
march, 614
marcy, 339, 340
Mar-Del, 537
mare, 302
Mareda, 524
Marenisco, 538
Marg, 519
Margaret, 509, 519, 520
Margarida, 509
Margorilla, 524
Maria, 509
María, 508
Marian, 509
Mariano, 509
Marie, 511, 513
Marilyn, 511, 512
Marin, 509
Marinaccio, 493
Marinace, 493
Marion, 537
Marjette, 521
Marjoribanks, 503
Mark, 506, 507
marketeria, 177
marketing-expert, 291
Marks, 494
Marlborough, 503
Marques, 494
marriage-certificate, 235
marriage-lines, 235
marrid, 402
marsh, 246, 339
Marshall, 515, 517
Marshbanks, 503
Marston, 487
mart, 183

Marth, 519
Martha, 519
Martin, 494, 507, 509
martin, 536
Martinez, 514
Martini-cocktail, 85
Martins, 494
Marttinen, 479
marvelous, 388
Marvin, 507, 516
Mary, 183, 506, 507, 509, 510, 513, 519
Maryland, 540
Marysville, 529
Masculine, 505
ma'sh, 246, 350
masheen, 382, 384
Mason, 486, 498
mass, 249, 334
massa, 271
masseur, 347
massive, 334
mass-meeting, 98, 144, 148, 231
Masten, 487
master, 241, 242, 268, 281, 334, 583; -maniac, 583; -mind, 583; of ceremonies, 586; of properties, 289
masterpiece, 155
Master(s), 485
masticate, 334
mastiff, 386
mat, 261, 614
match, to, 256
mater, 338
Matha, 524
Mathias, 507
Mathushek, 487
Matilda, 519
matinée, 409
matins, 268
Matoka, 524
Matoušek, 487
matrimonial-engineer, 290
Matrimony, 536
mat-roller, 261
matron, 289
Mattagomonsis, 531
Mattawamkeag, 531
matter, 336, 349
Matthew, 506, 510
Matthews, 487
Matti, 510

mattins, 249
mattress-engineer, 289
Matuscheck, 487
matzoth, 216, 217
Mauch Chunk, 532
mauka, 377
Mauna Loa, 522
Maurice, 503
Maury, 516
mauvaises terres, 108
Mauwauwaming, 532
maverick, 144, 188, 189
maw, 328, 349
Mawlbra, 503
Max, 507
Maximilian, 507
Maxwell, 507
may, 420
Maybeth, 521
Maynard, 497
mayorality, 353
mazuma, 216, 217, 263
mazzaltov, 217
mb, 402
McClautz, 489
McCleary, 496
McCoy, 580
McDonald, 514
McKaba, 496
McKeesport, 529
McLane, 479
McLoud, 487
McShane, 477
McSweeney, 504
M.D., 272
me, 447, 454, 455, 456, 457, 458; -me, 390, 391
meal, to, 196
Mealy, 524
mean, 25, 384, 466
mean, to, 433
measure up, to, 256
measure up to the standard, to, 229
meat, 373, 614
mecanic, 401
mecca, 183
media, 412
mediæval, 393
medic, 170
medical lady, 272
medical man, 272
medical woman, 272
medicine-man, 106
medieval, 391, 401
mediocer, 402

Meek, 523
meen, 381, 384
meeou, 184
meet, to, 433
megaphonia, 175
Meier, 500
Meilach, 498
Meilachson, 498
Meister, 485
melancholy, 267, 325
mêlée, 409
Melkonian, 497
Melrose Abbey, 522
melt, to, 436
melted, 436
Melvin, 508, 516
member, 242
memo, 170
memorandum-book, 247
memorial-park, 288
Memphian, 549
mendery, 176
Mendes, 506
menhaden, 104, 105
ment, 381, 433
mental-hygiene, 588
menu, 347
merchantor, 179
Mercy, 516
mercy, 339, 340
merged, 561
Merl, 522
Merrimac, 527
mes, 401
mesa, 152, 153
mescal, 152
Mesdames, 412
Meshach, 515
meshuggah, 216, 217, 580
meshummad, 217
mesquite, 152
mess, 346
Messiah, 524
Messieurs, 412
Messrs., 282
Mészáros, 496
met, 433
metals, 147
metaphor, 395
Metella, 522
meteorological-office, 239
meter, 402
Methodist, 462
Methodist New Con-
    nexion, 249
meticulous, 211

Metsa, 492
Meyer, 477
mezzo-brow, 186
Miamian, 548
Michael, 507, 511, 512, 518
Michaelis, 483
Michaels, 483
Michal, 511
Michayil, 510
Michel, 498
Michigan, 532; -der, 552
michigouen, 106
mick, 295
middle-aisled, 561
middle-aisle it, to, 259
Middlemarch, 537
middle-neck, 236
middle-rump, 236
Middletown, 536
midsommarfest, 215
Miechyslawa, 510
Mielnik, 488
might, 99
mightily, 467
mighty, 467
Miguel, 514
Mihai, 509
mijn, 379
Mike, 509, 510, 511, 512, 513
Mikha'il, 512
Miklavec, 489
Mikuláš, 511
mil, 403
Mila, 524
Milavič, 489
Mildred, 510, 519
mile, 462
mileage, 120, 147, 231, 389
mileage-book, 147
Miles, 524
Miley, 524
militaire, 75
militia-armory, 239
milk-churn, 260
milk-engineer, 290
mill, 116
Millar, 477
millenial, 16
Miller, 477, 478, 484, 485, 486, 488, 494, 520
milliard, 255
Millicent, 519
Millie, 519
milligram, 391
Millin, 499

millinteria, 177
mills, 539
Milton, 505, 506, 515, 516
min, 449
Minas, 524
mince, 260
mince-pie, 578
Minda, 524
mind-set, 588
mine, 379, 447, 449
Miner, 482
minerals, 86, 149, 237
minestrone, 222
Mingo, 524
minim, 250
minima, 250
minion, 250
minion-nonpareil, 250
minister, 245, 249
ministry, 245
Minnesota, 526
minni, 353
minnow, 353
minor-leaguer, 191
minster, 248
minum, 449
mirage, 338
Miriam, 507
Mirnada, 521
Mirrle, 522
mirror, 395
mis, 401
Mis', 124
mischievious, 353
mischievous, 325
misdemeanour, 396
miserable, 465
Misha, 508
misogynist, 341
mistaken, to, 193
Miss, 124
missil, 406
missile, 406
missionary, 24
missionate, to, 98, 140, 150
mission-festival, 220
mission-stiff, 582
Mississippi, 526, 528
Missouri, 525, 532, 541
Missouri Compromise, 517
misstep, 231
Missus, 412
Mister, 273, 274, 280, 412
mistook, 442

Mitchell, 490, 498, 507, 512
mit-joint, 584
MiXail, 490
mixer, 227
mixologist, 179
mizzen-brow, 186
Mlle., 348
Mlynář, 486
mob, 126, 169, 182, 368, 558
-mobile, 180
mobile police, 226
mobster, 178
moccasin, 101, 102, 105
mocho, 153
model, to, 194
moderately, 253
Modjeska, 489
Modjeski, 489
modren, 353
Modrzejewski, 489
mods, 243
Moe, 507
mohel, 217
Mohr, 477
Möhr, 477
Moiseyev, 498
Moishe, 506
moke, 296
molasses, 62, 128, 235, 462
mold, 386, 402
moldering, 388
mollagausauger, 568
Möller, 477
Mollie, 519
mollusc, 390
mollusk, 394
molt, 436
momentum, to, 194
momzer, 218
monarc, 401
monarchy, 401
monastery, 325
Monat, 482
mon cher, 75
Monday-man, 585
moneybund, 219
money-to-burn, 227
moniker, 582
Monimea, 524
monitor, 268
monkey-doodle, 176
monkey-house, 583
monkey with, to, 232
monkey-wrench, 235

monolog, 394
monologuist, 178
Monongahela, 526
monoxide, to, 196
Monroe, 506
monsignori, 412
monsignors, 412
Montagu-Stuart-Wortley-Mackenzie, 502
Montana, 339
Montereyan, 549
Monte Vista, 534
Montréalais, 550
Montrealer, 549
Monumental City, 101, 553
mony, 402; -mony, 325
Mood, 524
moom-pitcher, 561
moonshine, 576
Moor, 477
moor, 115
Mooradian, 497
Moore, 477, 497
Moosa, 524
moose, 104, 536
moosu, 104
Mop, 582
mop, 368
Morais, 494
moral, 341
Móran, 504
Morariu, 494
Mord, 522
More, 477
more, 328, 349, 463, 538
more better, 420, 463
more looser'n, 464
more queerer, 463
more ultra, 463
more uniquer, 463
more worse, 463
Morgan, 499
morgen, 110
Morgenthau, 500
morgue, 563
Mork, 490
Mormon, 57
moron, 174, 570
Moroni, 516
moronize, to, 193
morphician, 289
morphine, 155
morphology, 155
Morris, 494, 506
mortgage-shark, 144

mortician, 86, 178, 284, 287
Mortimer, 507
Morton, 506, 507
moscheto, 112
Moscowite, 549
mose, 104
Moses, 506, 507, 513, 535
Mosetta, 522
mosey, to, 152
Mosie, 507
moslem, 409
Mosnička, 486
mosquito, 112
moss-back, 116, 145
most, 463, 468
most Almighty God, 463
Most Hon., 277
most principal, 463
Most Rev., 282
mote, 347
Motel, 506
mother, 349
motorcade, 179
motor-car, 233, 247
motoritis, 179
motortorium, 179
mototeria, 177
mought, 347
mould, 386, 390, 393
mouldering, 388
moult, 393
mound mainstay, 570
mountain-dew, 568
mountainious, 353
Mountbatten, 500
Mount Ohio, 530
mourners' bench, 150, 250
moustache, 392, 393
mouth-organ, 120
mouthpiece, 576
moveable, 380
movey-star, 108
movie, 95, 169, 170, 187; -cathedral, 188, 292; -filling-station, 188; -house, 237; -mosque, 188; -parlor, 188; -synagogue, 188
moviedom, 178
mow, to, 433
mowed, 433
mown, 433
moyder a skoyt, to, 263
Mozingo, 524

mozo, 153
M.P., 573
Mr., 275, 278, 281, 413
Mráček, 487
Mr. Chief Justice, 279
Mr. Justice, 279
Mrs., 124
Mrs. ex-Senator, 274
Mrs. Major, 283
Mrs. Professor, 274
Mt. Rainier, 532
Muccia, 494
much, 110, 374
mucilage, 235
mud, 582; -guard, 236;
 -hen, 114; -scow, 116;
 -show, 585; -splasher,
 573
mudhop, 583
Mueller, 484
muffler, 237
mug-joint, 584
mugquomp, 106
mugwump, 106, 107, 148,
 231
Mühler, 477
Muir, 477
Mulcahy, 504
mule-skinner, 167
muletress, 168
Muller, 484
Müller, 477
mulligan, 582
multiple-shop, 234
Mummy, 269
muncheon, 171
Munger, 503
municipial, 353
munnawhattecug, 105
Munsing Underwear, 525
Muqabba'a, 496
Murdena, 522
Murphy, 477, 478, 504,
 520
murphy, 566
Murray, 507, 508
mus, 104
Musallem, 496
muscato, 112
muscle in, to, 198, 580
mush, 116
music, 380, 603
music hall, 237
muskeito, 112
musketa, 112
muskmelon, 360

Muskogeean, 549
Muskrat, 552
muskrat, 114, 360
muslim, 409
musqueto, 112
muss, 99, 128, 346
muss, to, 142
must, 443
musta, 443
mustache, 325, 394
mustang, 152
mutt, 169
mutual, 168
mutual-society, 239
my, 447, 449
my dear, 311
My Lady's Manor, 537
Mylonas, 485
My Lord, 279
Myra, 507
Myron, 511
Myroslava, 511
myself, 459
Myšička, 488
Myška, 488
my word, 269
n, 335, 375, 397, 405, 425,
 445, 451; -n, 549; ñ,
 543
na, 469
nab, to, 199
nabisco, 172, 173
nabor, 383, 406
naborhood, 406
Nadia, 511
næfth, 469
naht, 469
naïve, 410
naïveté, 409, 410
name, to, 199
nameable, 101
nance, 305
Naneta, 524
nanitch, 150
-naper, 180
naphtha, 352, 407, 408
Napoli, 493
Nappy, 520
narcissis, 413
narcissuses, 413
narrator, 325
narrow, 359
nary, 129, 470
Nash, 490
Nassau, 533
nasty, 268, 464, 467

Nat, 519
nat, 469
Nathan, 506, 512
Nathaniel, 506
nation, 614
nativ, 403
natur, 345
nature-faker, 174
naturelogues, 171
naught, 393
naughty, 467
Nauwagesic, 514
naval-yard, 239
Navilla, 522
navvy, 239
navy-yard, 239
Nazarene, 524
Nazary, 503
na zdar, 216
Nazi, 183, 209
Nazro, 525
nch, 446
nd, 438
ne, 469
near, 93, 384, 466
near-, 180, 181; -accident,
 103, 181; -antique, 181;
 -beer, 181; -champion,
 181; -finish, 181;
 -leather, 181; -mahog-
 any, 181; -porcelain,
 181; -seal, 181; -silk,
 181; -silver, 181
nearby, 229
Neary, 496
neat, 466
Nebraska, 532
necessarily, 267
necessary, 325
neck, 115
neck, to, 199, 309, 564,
 565
necktie, 235
née, 347
Needa, 521
needle, to, 580
needless, 401
neer, 381, 384
negative, to, 118, 232
neger, 385
négligé, 287, 347
negligée, 409
Negolia, 524
Negress, 300
Negro, 299, 385
ne-hæfth, 469

neighbour, 383, 395
neither, 341, 472
neither don't, 471
Nell, 511
Nelly, 511
Nelson, 477
neolin, 173
N.E.P., 209
nephew, 352
Nephi, 516, 518
nerts, 226, 309, 572
nerve, 367
nervous, 126
nerz, 367
ne singan, 469
-ness, 178
nestes, 360
net, 390, 396
net, to, 199
nether-garments, 302
netop, 106
nett, 389, 390
Neuta, 522
Nevada, 339
New, 529
New Amsterdam, 532
Newberlin, 539
New Boston, 528
Newbranch, 491
New Dorp, 532
Newer, 487
Newhouse, 485
ne-wiste, 469
Newlake, 492
New London, 528
Newman, 485, 487, 499
Newmann, 485
ne-wolde, 469
New Orleans, 531, 541
Newport, 528
Newport News, 537
newspaperdom, 178
newspaper men, 228
Newt, 519
New Thought, to, 196
Newton, 492, 519
New York, 532; -er, 549
Ney, 499
ng, 348
N.G., 92, 205, 208
'ngombo, 113
Niagara, 527, 531
Nias, 523
nib, 239
nice, 71, 210, 464, 557
Nicholas, 486, 511, 515

nichts kommt heraus, 157
Nick, 511
Nicolo, 509
Niemi, 492
Nieuwhuis, 485
nifty, 581
nigger, 296, 299, 305
night-rider, 102
nigmenog, 577
Nikolaou, 486
Nils, 510
nine-pins, 237, 248
Nineveh, 530
nip, 35
nipple, 303
Nira, 209
nit, 157
nite, 406
niter, 394
nitsky, 157
nix, 157, 573
nix come erous, 157
nixie, 157
nixy, 157
N.M., 206
no, 469
no-account, 114, 117
Noble, 484
nobody home, 561
no-end, 269
no flies on, 232
no-how, 114, 117, 470
noise, 367
noive, 367
no kerry, 376
nolde, 469
Nolte, 487
nominated, 245
non-committal, 143, 231
non-committalism, 143
non-committally, 143
nonconformist, 248, 249
nonconformist consci-
ence, 250
none, 451, 469, 471
Non Intervention, 536
nonpareil, 250
Noodle, 536
noodle, 112, 155
noodle-hook, 359
nook, 344
nope, 229, 354
Nopie, 522
no place, 204
Norfolk-Howard, 310
Norlina, 537

Norman, 507
Norse, 183
Norsworthy, 503
North, 529
north and south, 578
North Clove, 532
north-east corner, 247
Norwich, 540
nose-paint, 568
no-siree, 161
no slouch, 232
Nosodak, 537
not, 343, 445, 446, 469
notaseme, 407
notch, 115
note, 233
note-case, 239
not has, 469
nothin' doin', 95
nothing, 469, 470
nothing doing, 227
notice, to, 7
notify, to, 6, 122
notions, 254
not my funeral, 232
not nothing, 424
no(t)-one, 451
Notre Dame, 525
not so hot, 585
not to sing, 469
no two ways about it, 99,
232
nought, 392, 393
nourish, to, 303
Novák, 487
novel, 343
noways, 468
nowheres, 22
nowheres else, 204
N.R.A., 209
nt, 446; n't, 445
nucleuses, 412
nuf sed, 407
null, to, 199
number-dummy, 583
Number Four, 536
number-grabber, 583
numbers, 222
Nunes, 495
Nunez, 495
Nurse, 240
nurse, 240
nurse, to, 303
nurse a constituency, to,
245
nursery, 235

nursery-school, 235
nursing-home, 240, 266
nursing sister, 240
nut, 263, 557
nuts, 301, 566
nut-splitter, 583
nut-sundae, 228
nuttery, 176
nutty, 464
ny, 543
nyam, 113
Nygren, 491
Nyiri, 496
nyste, 469
Nyzovych, 490
o, 343, 344, 346, 401, 402, 484, 490; -o, 548; ö, 490; ò, 382
Oakhurst, 534
Oarly, 522
oatmeal, 235
Oberkuchen, 484
Oberkugen, 484
obflisticate, to, 568
obituarize, to, 194
objurgate, to, 325
O'Black, 489
obleek, 382
obligate, to, 40, 99, 118, 231
obligation, 614
obligoddamnation, 316
oblique, 382
Oblong, 536
O'Brien, 487
obscene, 309
obstetricate, to, 197
obtained, 604
O.C., 573
occlusion, 15
oceanography, 155
ocelot, 106
Očenášek, 487
ock, 402
Octavia, 519
od, 403
odditorium, 179
odd jobs, 234
odds and ends, 235
-ode, 438
Oder, 522
odeur, 384
odor, 384
odorous, 395
odour, 395
odsblood, 315

oe, 401, 484
Oehler, 484
Oehm, 483
œsophagus, 411
of, 443, 471
ofay, 214, 296
offal, 128
offence, 394
offense, 386, 388, 394
offensive, 394
off from, 471
office-holder, 95, 101, 102, 243
officerette, 178
office-seeker, 148
off'n, 471
off of, 471
offset, 98
of late, 467
often, 348
-ogist, 178, 179
Ogpu, 209
O'Green, 489
Ogrin, 489
oh, 404, 490
Oha, 522
Ohanesian, 497
O'Hare, 487
Ohio, 526
Ohiowa, 537
Ohler, 484
Ohman, 490
oh, oh!, 252
Ohslund, 490
oh-yeah, 40, 566
oi, 345, 367, 368
oil, 346
Oil City, 536
oiled, 568
oil-plan, 237
oinest, 367
oi-yoi, 217
O.K., 92, 205, 226, 230, 466, 565
okay, 207, 208
okeh, 206
Okerberg, 490
okey, 207
Oklahoman, 548
okra, 113
Olabelle, 521
Olaf, 510
old, 352
old-boy, 243
old dear, 269
Old Dominion, 552

Old Hickory, 101
oldsmobile, 173
ole, 352
-olis, 549
-olitan, 549
Ollie, 522, 523
Olof, 510
Olouise, 521
Olseen, 491
Olsen, 510
Olsie, 521
Olson, 491, 510
Olsson, 491, 492
Omahog, 552
OMaolcathaigh, 504
Ombra, 521
omelet, 390
ommigenous, 75
omnibus-bill, 101, 148
OMurchadha, 504
on, 343; -on, 548
on a bust, 429
on an avenue, 247
on a street, 247
once, 352, 353
once-over, 263
oncet, 161
one, 451, 464, 612
one-he, 203
one-horse, 117
100% American, 174
onery, 95, 161, 353
onesome, 562
one-step, 155
on fire, 561
on his legs, to be, 245
Onlak, 489
onliest, 463
onnozel, 109
Ono, 534
Onola, 522
on point duty, 243
onry, 353
on the bench, 191
on the bum, 156
on the fence, 143, 148, 228
on the job, 265
on the merge, 561
on the Q.T., 208
on the side, 227
on the verge, 561
ontil, 360
on time, 232, 238
on to his curves, 191
Onza, 521
oo, 344, 345, 383

oof, 184
oona, 113
ooze, 404, 602
opassom, 104
open up, to, 165, 198
operate, to, 31, 196
operating-room, 287
operative, 325
Opferkuchen, 484
opinion, to, 25
opossum, 100, 104
oppose, to, 117, 120
opposit, 403
opuses, 413
Oquossoc, 531
-or, 178, 179, 192, 285, 383, 384, 386, 389, 390, 395
Oral, 522
Orange, 505
orangeade, 173
orate, to, 192
orator, 242
oratory, 24
Orba, 521
Orcellia, 524
orchestra, 237
ordinary, 353
orf, 350
organization, 225
organlog, 171
Oriel, 522
oriole, 124
-orium, 178, 179
Orleenian, 548
ornate, 128
orphanest, 463
orse, 377
orta, 471
orter, 350
Orvetta, 521
-ory, 325
Osborn, 490
Oscar, 507, 510
Osey, 522
O'Shaunnessy, 487
Oshkosh, 553
Osie, 522
oslerize, to, 193
ossified, 568
ostent, 75
ostermoor, 564
ostler, 393
OSuilleohhain, 504
O'Sullivan, 504
otchock, 105

Otella, 521
other, 349
O'Tracy, 487
Otřáska, 487
O'Tresaigh, 504
otter, 536
Otto, 505, 506
ou, 402
ouch, 158
ough, 402
oughta, 445
oughten, 445
oughter, 445
oughtna, 445
ought not, 445
ought to, 445
our, 402, 447, 456
-our, 380, 381, 383, 386, 390, 392, 393, 394, 395, 396, 397, 399
ouren, 448
ourn, 425, 447, 456
oust, to, 199
outa, 443, 471
outfit, 573
out for the coin, 559
Outhouse, 505
out-house, 62, 231
outlandishest, 463
out of wedlock, 293
out of window, 251
outstander, 586
outstanding, 210, 211, 220, 588
outstandingly, 211
Oven, 489
Oven Fork, 536
over all, 350
Overflow, 524
overhall, 353
overhead-expenses, 86
over his signature, 165, 252
overseas, 239
overshoes, 235
over the left, 566
over the top, 573
ow, 353, 382, 383, 484
-ow, 437
Owens, 489
Owl Wahneeta, 514
own, 459
oyster, 367; -stew, 247; -supper, 144, 247
p, 354, 368, 439, 493
pa, 170

Paatalo, 492
paccan, 105
pack, 236
package, 235
package-engineer, 290
packing, 261
packing-engineer, 290
Pacoman, 538
pact, 182
Paddy, 511
Padraic, 513
padre, 152, 573
pad-room, 584
pageant-engineer, 290
Pagger-Wagger, 569
pahea oe, 377
paid, 433, 436
paint-engineer, 290
painting-engineer, 290
paint-maintenance-engineer, 290
paint the town red, to, 142
pair, 462
pajama-engineer, 290
pajamas, 391
pajamboree, 175
pal, 573
palace, 414
palace-car, 147
pale, 99
pale-face, 106, 231
palm, 334, 338
Palmer, 520
Palmetto, 552
palmolive, 173
Palo Altan, 549
palooka, 259, 560
Pamo, 524
pan, to, 196
panaderia, 177
Panagiotopoulos, 485
Panagoitis, 512
pandering, 311
panel-house, 102
pan-fish, 115
panhandle, 86
panhandler, 263, 582
Pannebacker, 480
pan out, to, 142
pansy, 305
pantaloons, 302
pantáta, 216
pantatorium, 179
panther-sweat, 568
pantorium, 179

pantry, 336
pants, 234, 239
papa, 325, 335, 579
papaios, 105
Pape, 493
paper, 584
paper bleu, 214
paper-hanger, 577, 579
paper tut, 159
papoose, 105, 106
Papp, 496
Pappachristides, 485
Pappadakis, 485
Pappadimitracoupoulos, 485, 486
Pappageorgiou, 486
Pappapolychronopoulos, 486
Pappas, 485, 486
Pappatheodorokomoun-doronicolucopoulos, 486
pappekak, 145
par, 562
paraffin, 234
paralize, 402
parcel, 235, 350
pard, 170
parfait, 411
parfay, 411
park, 334, 414
park, to, 195, 227
Parker, 516
Parker Notch, 535
Park 'N Dine, 210
Park Rowgue, 561
parley, 182
parlor, 266, 583
parlor-car, 147
parlour, 243, 395
Parry, 489
parson, 249, 280
part, 349
partiolist, 75
partridge, 7, 122, 123
party, 184
pas, 401
paseo, 153, 376
pash, 169, 561, 581, 586
pass, 335, 336
pass, to, 198, 227
passage, 547
passageway, 102
Passaicite, 549
pass-degree, 242
passel, 350

passenger-coach, 147
pass out, to, 198
past, 337
pastor, to, 140, 150
pastorium, 150, 179
pasture-lot, 121
Pat, 110, 519
Patapsco, 527
Patapsco Neck, 535
patent, to, 338
patent-engineer, 290
path, 247, 267, 334, 335, 336, 366
pathetiker, 463
patio, 152, 153
Patlow, 492
Pătrascu, 494
patriarch, 614
Patricius, 511
Patrick, 505, 511, 513
patrioteer, 180
patriotism, 339
patrolman, 86, 102
patroon, 108
patter, 169
Patterson, 494
Patuxent, 528
pau, 377
paugh, 482
Paul, 507, 515
pauperdom, 178
pavement, 33, 42, 235, 247
paw, 349
pawn-shop, 292
paw-paw, 104, 105, 536
pay, to, 433
Paya, 524
pay dirt, 100, 102, 145
paying-in-slip, 244
pay-off, 576
pay-roll, 239
peacharino, 176
P.D.Q., 92, 205, 208
Peabody, 482
peach-pit, 108
Peadar, 513
pea-nut, 114
pearl, 250, 367
pearline, 173
peart, 143
Peazzoni, 514
pebeco, 173
pecan, 104, 105
peck, 462
peculiar members, 303
ped, 436

pedagog, 400
pediatric-engineer, 290
Pedlar, 520
Pedro, 508, 509
peedoodles, 568
peek, 382
peek, to, 252
peek-a-boo, 252
Peekskill, 532
peep, to, 439
pee-pee, 265
peeve, to, 192
Pee Wee, 523
peg, 340
Peggy, 519
Peijariniemi, 492
Pekin, 525
pell-mell, 126
Pelto, 493
pemmican, 105
pen, 169
penalize, 340
penepne, 113
penitent-form, 250
penitentiary, 293
penitent-seat, 250
Pen-Mar, 537
pennant-winner, 191
penny, 101, 116, 267; -ante, 191, 267; -arcade, 267; -bank, 267; bill, 116; -in-the-slot, 267
Penn Yan, 537
Pennypacker, 480
pennyroyal, 346
pennyr'yal, 346
Penobscot, 527
pen-point, 239
Pentapang, 527
Péntek, 496
peon, 152
peonage, 152
people, 603
Peoria, 582
pep, 169, 170, 227, 263, 565
Pepper, 482
pepsin, 155
peptomint, 173
perambulator, 233, 256
perc, to, 192
Percival, 516, 519
Percy, 502, 516, 518
per-diem, 148
Peregrine, 516
Pereira, 494

Perey, 489
Pérez, 494
perfect, 367
perfectest, 463
perfectly, 372
perform an abortion, to, 311
permanent-way, 147
Pernella, 524
Perry, 494
Pershin, 480
Pershing, 480
persimmon, 100, 104, 105, 231, 246
person, 184
personal, 256
persuasion-engineer, 290
Perth Amboy, 537
pesach, 217
pesky, 129, 231
Pet, 522
pet, to, 309
Pete, 508, 510, 512
Pete-in-the-Field, 492
Pete-in-the-Street, 492
Peter, 509, 513
peter out, to, 142
Peters, 490, 494
Peterson, 477, 489, 497
Petersson, 492
Petit, 481
Petoskey, 514
Petr, 511
petrol, 236, 256
Petrusiw, 490
Petrussylf, 459
Petryshak, 489
Petryshyn, 489
Pfannenstiel, 484
Pfau, 479
Pfeffer, 482
Pfeil, 484
Pfoersching, 480
Pfüger, 484
pfui, 220
Pfund, 485
ph, 383, 402
phalanx, 338
phantom, 383, 406
phenix, 394
phenomena, 412
phenomenons, 413
Ph.D., 272
phffft, 561
phial, 389, 390
Phi-Beta-Kappa-itis, 179

Phil, 519
Philadelphia, 522, 528; -n, 548
philanthropy, 292
Philip, 488, 506, 507
Phillips, 488
phizz, 260
Phlegar, 484
phlegm, 383; -cutter, 149
phlizz, 260
Phoenician, 551
phœnix, 394
phone, 169, 170, 228
phone, to, 191
phoney, 187
phonograph, 235, 604
phooey, 220
photo, 169, 170, 183, 558
photo, to, 199
photographic-engineer, 290
photoplay, 187
Phronie, 519
phthisic, 605
physician, 272
physick, 383, 386
piano, 338, 347
pianola, 172
pianologues, 171
Pibaudière, 481
pica, 250
picayune, 151
Piccolo, 493
pick a crow with, to, 568
pickaninny, 112, 372
Picketwire, 533
pick on, to, 227
Pictorial Review, 525
picture, 328, 352
picture-gallery, 584
picture-house, 237
picturize, to, 193
pie, 122, 235
piece, 308
piece-of-eight, 116
pie-counter, 148
pie-eyed, 568
Pierce, 507
pietje-kamaakal, 109
Pietroluongo, 494
Pietrus, 488
Pietruszka, 488
pifflicated, 568
Pig, 505
Pig Eye, 536
pigmy, 390, 392

pike, 169, 170
Pikler, 498
Pilipino, 375
pillar-box, 235
piller, 353
pimp, 309
pinch-hitter, 191
pinder, 113
pineapple, 580
pine-knot, 115
pin for home, to, 583
pin-head, 186
pinkster, 109
pint, 237, 243
pinto, 152, 153
Piotr, 510
pipe-of-peace, 106
pippin, 263
pique, 382
pisen, 346
Pism, 525
pismire, 302
piss, 308
pissoir, 304
pistarine, 116
pit, 108
pitcher, 235
pitchfork, to, 373
pitch-pine, 114
pitilacker, 175
Pitkäjärvi, 492
Pittsburgh, 529, 539
Pittsburgher, 549
Pittsburgh Landing, 529
pivotal, 231
placate, to, 118, 230
place, 123, 248
Placenta, 525
placer, 152
plaguy, 99
plain, 536
plaintiff, 386
planing-machine, 101
plank, 148
plank down, to, 142
planning-expert, 291
plant food, 292
Plant moon, 106
plastered, 568
plastic, 334
plate, 235
platform, 148, 228
platinum, 604
play ball, to, 191
playdom, 178
played-out, 143, 231

play golf some, to, 254
play hell, to, 314
play possum, to, 143, 198, 232
play-room, 235
plaza, 152, 547
plea, 183, 375
plead, to, 433, 437
pleadings, 246
pleasd, 403
plebe, 170
pled, 433, 437
plesure, 403
plop, 184
plough, 96, 146, 383, 390, 393
plow, 381, 383, 386
plug along, to, 609
plumb, 143, 232
plumb, to, 192
plumb crazy, 143
plump, 143
plunder, 99, 101, 159
plunderbund, 219
plunge, 184
Plunkett-Ernle-Erle-Drax, 502
pluralist, 248
plus, 210, 211
plute, 169, 263
Plymouth Brethren, 249
Plymouth Rock, 527
pneumony, 360
poche, 158
pochen, 157
pochspiel, 157
pocketbook, 247
pocket-diary, 247
počkij, 216
poco, 152
podiatrist, 288
Podlesnik, 489
Podunk, 553, 554
Poe, 479
Po-ell, 503
poem, 341
Poh, 479
pohickery, 105
poifect, 367
poil, 367
Poincaré, 410
point, 242, 250
pointer, 227
Point Loma, 534
points, 147
poison, 346

poison-ivy, 246
Poke, 523
poke, 577
poker, 157, 591
Poker City, 536; Flat, 535
poke-weed, 114
polack, 296
pole, 368
police, 360, 604
policy, 222
politeness, 374
politician, 30, 245
Polk, 493
Polly, 519
poly, 577
pomp, 343
Pompey, 523
poncho, 152
pond, 115, 121
pone, 100, 105
pontiff, 386
Pontius Pilate, 578
pony up, to, 191, 562
pooldoo, 214
pool-room, 237
poorhouse, 243
poorlaw institution, 243
poorly, 467
poozly, 110
pop, 149, 170
pop-corn, 85, 115, 122, 229
Pope, 493
poppycock, 47, 144, 565
poque, 158
porch-climber, 243
pore, 349
pork-barrel, 148
porpoise, 383, 384
porque, 376
porridge, 116, 235
Portage, 535, 542
portage, 108, 151
porte-cochère, 409
porter, 235, 247
porterhouse, 231, 236
portière, 347, 409
Port Tobacco, 527, 537
Portugee, 111, 461
positiv, 403
Positive Wassermann, 525
Pospíšil, 512
possum, 104, 169, 170; -belly, 583
Possum Hollow, 554

post, 238, 256, 283
post-bag, 238
posterior, 380
postes, 360
post-free, 238
postilion, 393
postillion, 392, 393
postman, 85, 235, 238, 266
Post No Bills, 239
postpaid, 238
postum, 172, 173
pot, 191
potato, 603; -bug, 114
potecary, 22
Poteet, 481
potlach, 150
potman, 236, 243
Potomac, 527
Potowanmeac, 527
Potunk, 553
Poughkeepsian, 549, 550
Poulos, 485, 486
Pound, 485
pound, 250, 462
pounding, 150
povidla, 216
Powell, 503
powerful, 99
powerize, to, 193
powerphobe, 570
Powhatan, 531
powwow, 105, 231
pox upon it, a, 317
practical, 336
practice, 393
practis, 401, 403
practise, 394
practise, to, 393
prairie, 57, 108, 151, 536; -dog, 151; -hen, 151; -schooner, 145
Prairie du Chien, 536
praline, 214
pram, 233
pre-, 181
prebendary, 248
precinct, 148
precisely, 253
predicate, to, 141
prefect, 268
preferd, 403
pregnant, 301, 310, 311
prelim, 170, 562
prélude, 347
première, 347

premiss, 392
Prentiss, 516
prepaid, 238
preparation-room, 287
preparatory, 325
prepare a body, to, 287
prepare a patient, to, 287
prep school, 240
pres, 401
prescriptive, 118
presentation, 248
Preserved, 516
president, 11, 242, 244, 289
presidentiad, 75
presidential, 98, 119, 120, 165, 231
presidio, 152
prespiration, 353
press-agent, to, 195
press engineer, 291
pressmen, 228
press-representative, 289
Preston, 498
pretty, 340
pretty boy, 584
pretzel, 112, 295
Preussen, 296
preventable disease, 306
preventorium, 179
previous, 231
pre-Volstead, 181
pre-war, 181, 183
priceless, 269
prickly-heat, 116
Priest, 496
prig, 126
primarily, 324
primary, 148
primary school, 241
primate, 248
Prince, 485
Prince-Albert, 37
Princell, 492
Princess Anne, 537
Princeton, 528, 530
Princilla, 524
principal, 241, 242
Prins, 485
printery, 176
printing-engineer, 290
printorium, 179
Priscilla, 512
prise, to, 252
private, 256
private-bar, 243

prize, to, 252
probably, 376
probate a will, to, 246
probationary captain, 283; lieutenant, 283
probe, 182, 185
pro'bition, 353
prob'ly, 353
procede, 401
pro-chancellor, 241
proctor, 242
produce a certain state, to, 311
prof, 170
professor, 100, 242, 272
professoriat, 180
progenitor, 395
program, 389, 390, 396, 400, 401, 403, 406
programme, 239, 390, 393, 394
progress, to, 7, 15, 24, 117, 120
project, 588
prolog, 400, 403
prom, 170
promenade, 338
promis, 403
promotion-engineer, 291
promulgate, 325
promulge, to, 75
pronto, 152
proof, 344
proov, 381, 383
propaganda, 101, 196
proper, 465
prophecy, 394
Prophet, 524
proposal, 239
proposition, 31, 210, 227
props, 289
prosaic, 380
prosit, 157
prostitute, 293, 303, 305, 311
protectograph, 173
protégé, 347, 409
protest, to, 195
Protestant Episcopal Church, 249
protozoa, 155
proud, 465
prove, 382, 383
prove, to, 433
prove a will, to, 246
proved, 433

proven, 433
pro-vice-chancellor, 242
provost, 242
prowler, 582
Prudence, 516
Prujín, 487
prushun, 582
pry, to, 252
psychological-engineer, 290
psychology, 155
psycho-neurosis, 293
psychopathic hospital, 293
psychopathic personality, 293
pub, 237, 243
public, 383
public-bar, 243
public comfort station, 304
public company, 244
public elementary school, 241
public-house, 237, 243
publicist, 288
publicity, 227
publick, 383
public relations counsel, 288
public school, 240
public-servant, 96, 243
publishment, 98, 141
puckerstopple, to, 568
Puckey-Huddle, 554
pudding, 155
puff-puff, 240
puffy, 558
pug, 169
puka, 377
Puke, 552
puke, 309
Pulkka, 493
Pulkkinen, 493
pull, 148, 227, 565
pull hard, to, 465
Pullman, 147, 238
pull the pin, to, 583
pull up stakes, to, 142, 232
pull wool over his eyes, to, 142
pulmotor, 171
pulque, 152
pumpernickel, 155
Pumpkin Hollow, 554

pun, 169
punch-drunk, 562
punctuate, 352
pung, 117
pungy, 116, 117
punk, 305, 562, 573, 580, 582
punt, 248
pup, 580
pur, 403
Púrcell, 504
purp, 350
purse, 247
push, 609
push, to, 199
push-cart, 235
pushed, 438
pusher, 583
pushover, 560
pusht, 438
pussyfoot, to, 255
pussy-footer, 174
put, to, 198, 440, 604
put a bug in his ear, to, 142
put across, to, 227
putchamin, 105
put down, to, 234
put it across, to, 191
put it over, to, 191
put it through, to, 232
put one across, to, 191
put one over, to, 191
put on the spot, to, 580
put over, to, 198, 227, 611
put the skids under, to, 198
puzzledom, 178
pygmy, 390, 394
pyjama, 389
pyjamas, 391
pyrex, 173
Q, 582
q, 404
Q-room, 208
Qua, 524
quack, 184
Quaco, 524
quadril, 403
quadroon, 112
quahaug, 98, 106
quake, 183
Quaker City, 553
quality, 335
Quamana, 524

Quamina, 524
quandary, 126
quanity, 352
quantity, 335
quarrel, 341, 343
quarter, 255
quarter-days, 255
quarter hour, 251
quartern-loaf, 255
quarter note, 250
quarter of an hour, 251
quarter of nine, 250
quarter to nine, 250
quartet, 401, 403
quartette, 393
Quash, 524
quash, 335
quash, to, 199
Quashey, 524
quasihemidemisemiquaver, 250
quaver, 250
Quay, 524
Quebecer, 549
Québecois, 550
Queener, 569
queer the pitch, to, 260
Quentin, 513
-quest, 491
questionize, to, 141
quick, 420, 465, 466
Quico, 524
quien sabe?, 152
Quincyan, 549
quinine, 341
-quist, 491
quit, 433
quit, to, 199, 433
quite, 251
quitter, 37, 227
quiz, 30, 182
Quod, 524
Quomana, 524
quotes, 170
-qvist, 491
qw, 404
r, 335, 340, 348, 349, 350, 369, 375, 383, 600
rabbit, 123
Rabbit Ridge, 554
rabble-rouser, 186
Rabinovitch, 498
raccoon, 104
race-course, 237; -track, 237
Rachel, 507

racket, 565, 566, 580
racketeer, to, 195, 565, 580
radio, 226, 338, 559, 604
radiodor, 561
radioitis, 179
radiorator, 175
radioteria, 177
radiotrician, 288
radish, 339
Rae, 507
Rafael, 509
raft, 336
rag, 377, 584
ragamuffin, 128
rahaugcum, 104
rahrah-boy, 186
railroad, 57, 165, 239
railroad, to, 147, 195
railroading, 96
railroad-man, 147
railway, 239, 267
railway-carriage, 247
railway man, 228
railway-rug, 147
Raimund, 505
raincoat, 235
raise, to, 7, 30, 101, 434
raise Cain, to, 232
raised, 434, 436
rake-off, 62, 572
Raleigh, 541
Raleighite, 549
rally, 227
Ralph, 507, 509, 520
ram, 184, 302, 308
rambler, 219
rambler-society, 219
rambunctious, 47, 145, 175, 568
rambustious, 568
ran, 434, 440, 442
Rance, 519
ranch, 152, 231
ranch, to, 152
rancher, 152
ranchero, 98
ranch-house, 152
ranchman, 152
rancho, 98, 152
rancorous, 395
rancour, 395
Rand, 499
Randolph, 507, 516, 529
Randolph of Roanoke, 504

Ranft, 484
rang, 434
range, 145
Ranhojič, 488
ranker, 270
Ransom, 519
rap, to, 199
rape, 311
rapids, 115, 151
rapport, 75
rare, 346
rarowcun, 104
raspberry, 192
rat, 576
ratepayer, 235, 243
rates, 235, 243
rather, 336, 337, 371
rathskeller, 155, 412
Rat Lake, 536
Raton, 543
ratskeller, 112, 347
rattle, to, 227
rattled, 231
rattler, 169, 582
Rattles, 505
raugroughcum, 104
Raven's Eye, 537
ravioli, 222
raw, 349
ray, 246
Raymond, 505, 510, 515
razor-back, 114, 584
razz, to, 192
Razzle-Dazzle, 536
r.b., 209
rd, 438
re, 383, 399, 402, 411; -re, 386, 390, 393
reach-me-down, 239
reaction, 210, 588
Reada, 524
reader, 242
read for holy orders, to, 249
Readingite, 550
read the law, to, 240
ready, to, 195, 586
ready-made, 293
ready-tailored, 293
ready-to-put-on, 293
ready-to-wear, 293
real, 341, 466, 467
real-estate, 165; -agent, 85; -man, 285
real good, 467
reality, 353

really, 466, 467
really true, 467
realm, 384
real McCoy, 580
real nice, 467
real smart, 467
realtor, 179, 239, 284, 286
realtress, 287
rear, 346
Rebecca, 507
rebel, 582
rebound, 325
rebuilt, 293
recall, 245
receipt, 380
reception-clerk, 239
receptionist, 178
recess, 235, 325
reciet, 403
Reckawackes, 527
reckon, 259
reckon, to, 24, 99
recluse, 325
recognize, 447
recognize, to, 433
reconditioned, 293
reco'nize, 352
recontre, 409
recovered, 604
recreation-engineer, 290
Rector, 523
rector, 241, 242, 249
red, 403; -ball, 582; -cap, 573; -eye, 149, 568; -lead, 582
Redheffer, 505
Red Kettle, 514
red-light district, 304
reducathon, 180
reed-bird, 114
reefer, 582
reel, 235
ref, 580
reflection, 393
reflexion, 392, 393
reformatory, 292, 293
reform school, 292
refresher, 246
régime, 409
Reginald, 518
registered nurse, 240
regius, 242
regular, 148, 465
regular guy, 254
rehabilitation, 292
Reichman, 498

Reifschneider, 499
Reifsnider, 499
Reifsnyder, 499
Reiger, 481
Reilly, 499
Reindollar, 485
Reino, 510
Reiter, 499
relapse, 360
release, 191
releasement, 98, 141
reliable, 120, 121, 165, 168, 223, 224, 231
relief, 292
religion, 150
relm, 381, 384
reminisce, to, 192
remove, 268
rench, 161
rench, to, 434
renched, 434
rencounter, 409
rendezvous, 409
Renee, 507
Reno-vated, 561
rense, to, 434
rent, 438
reo, 173
repeater, 148
répertoire, 409
repertory, 409
reposing-room, 287
repossessed, 293
reptile, 341
requirement, 98
requisite, 383, 384
research, 325
resinol, 173
resolute, to, 141, 192
resolv, 403
respectablize, to, 193
respiratory, 325
restatorium, 179
restaurant, 292
restauranteria, 176
resteteria, 176
restorium, 179
rest-room, 308
résumé, 409
resurrect, to, 93, 141, 165
retainer, 246
Retha, 521
retiracy, 141
retire, to, 302
retiring-room, 304
retoric, 402

return, to, 245
Reuben, 515
reumatism, 402
reune, to, 192
reunion, to, 195
Reuss, 482
Rev. 268, 279, 281
Reverend, 280
Reverendissimus, 283
reviev, 403
revievd, 403
revolving-table, 254
Revs., 282
rh, 402
Rheinthaler, 485
Rhine wine, 240
Rhine-wine-cup, 85
Rhode Islander, 550
rhyme, 391
rib, 236
Riccardo, 509
Richard, 507, 509, 515
Richards, 499
Richman, 498
Richmond, 528; -er, 549; -ite, 549
rickey, 149
rid, 434
ridden, 428, 434
ride, to, 434
riffle, 115
rig, 377
right, 93, 253
right along, 253
right away, 25, 253
right good, 253
Right Hon., 276, 277
Right Honourable, 273
right now, 253
righto, 230, 265, 573
right off, 253
right often, 253
right-of-way, 147
right on time, 253
Right Rev., 282
right smart, 253
right there, 253
right well, 253
Right Worshipful, 279
rigor, 396
rigor mortis, 396
rigorous, 395
rigour, 395
Riker, 481
rile, 346, 422
rile, to, 434

riled, 434
rime, 391, 402
Rindkopf, 501
ring, 148
ring, to, 434
ringmaster, 583
ringster, 178
ripping, 264, 557
ripsniptiously, 568
rise, to, 245, 434
rised, 436
rising generation, 184
riss, 434
riter, 404
rithm, 402
ritschi, 159
ritualism, 349
ritzy, 464
River, 492
riveted, 389
rivetted, 389
riz, 416, 434
rize, 402
ro, 401
roach, 301, 304
road, 247, 547
road-agent, 37
road diversion, 236
road-louse, 186
roadster, 237
road-sweeper, 239
Roanoke, 532
Roanza, 524
roar, 349, 602
roast, 235
roast-beef, 155
roasting-ear, 115
rob, 343
robbed, 614
Robbins, 498
robd, 402
robed, 614
Robert, 506, 515
robustious, 568
Rochesterian, 549
rock, 7, 99, 101, 122, 123, 343
Rockaway, 527
Rockefeller, 483
rock-pile, 123
Rocky Mounter, 549
rod, 343
rode, 422, 434, 442
rodeo, 221, 558
rodéo, 347
Rodriguez, 514

rog, 402
Roger, 515
Rogers, 498
Roggenfelder, 483
Rogowsky, 498
rogue, 402
rohlík, 215
roil, 346
roil, to, 434
role, 409
rôle, 409
roll, 401
roller-coaster, 142, 237
rolling-country, 115
Rolyat, 538
romaine, 260
Roman, 551
Roman Catholic, 249
romance, 325
Rome, 530
Romiette, 521
Rondinone, 493
Rondy, 493
röntgenogram, 347
rood, 344
roof, 344
roof-garden, 583
rook, 344
rookie, 573
room, 344
room, to, 118, 196
room-clerk, 239
roomer, 235
rooming-house, 292
room-mate, 263
roorback, 148
Roos, 485, 491
Roosevelt, 480, 537
rooster, 85, 235, 302, 304, 308, 344; -swain, 301
root, 328, 344
root, to, 191
rooter, 191
rooves, 344
rope in, to, 142
Ros, 491
Rose, 485, 498, 499, 507
rose, 434, 436
Rosecrans, 480
Rosella, 521
Rosenbau, 480, 500
Rosenblum, 480
Rosenfeldt, 480
Rosenkrantz, 480
Rosenthal, 480
Rosenvelt, 480

rosinback, 584
Ross, 498
Rossacampo, 480
rot-gut, 566
Roth, 484
rôtisserie, 215
rotten, 309
Rotten Row, 105
rotter, 269
rough, 202, 383, 399
Rough-and-Ready, 536
rough cider, 244
rough-house, 92, 227
rough-neck, 144, 187
round-trip, 147
round-up, 145, 227
'rous mit 'im, 157
roustabout, 144, 263
route, 328
route de roi, 105
row, 126, 183, 247, 547
rowdy, 145, 231, 565
royal supreme knight commander, 289
Royalty, 505
Royce, 482
R.Ú., 209
rubarb, 402
rubberneck, 37, 62, 186, 220, 227, 557
rubberneck-wagon, 237
rubbers, 235
rubbish, 235
rube, 37, 170, 252
Rubinstein, 499
Ruby, 518
ruby, 250; -nonpariel, 250
ruddy, 316
Rudolph, 505, 506
Rue, 495
ruf, 383, 399, 402, 403
Ruiz, 494, 514
rule, to, 199
rum, 244; -dealer, 244; -dumb, 158, 244; -evil, 244; -hound, 244; -trade, 244
rumble-seat, 237
rum-dealer, 244
rumour, 395
rump, 236
run, 115, 147, 235, 350, 422
run, to, 148, 198, 232, 423, 434

runabout, 236
run for office, to, 245
rung, 434, 437, 441
run in, to, 198
run into the ground, to, 142
runner-bean, 260
run slow, 202
rupture, 307
rurale, 221
rush, 242
Russ, 183
russet, 247
Russian, 296
rutabaga, 246
ruther, 359
Ruven, 506
ruz, 436
rv, 401
s, 335, 353, 375, 383, 386, 389, 394, 447, 448, 449, 484, 503
S.A., 208, 560
saace, 22
Saarikoski, 492
Sabany, 524
Sabbaday, 169
sabe, 152
Sabinoso, 534
Sacco, 494
sachem, 105, 106
sack, 101
sack-suit, 235
Sacramentan, 549
Sacramento, 535, 543
sacred-ox, 583
Sadie, 507
Sadye, 520
safe, 466
safen, to, 193
sagamore, 98, 106
Sage, 494
Sagebrush Center, 554
Saguache, 543
said, 404, 434, 614
Saint George, 496
Saint-Maure, 479
Saint Peter, 496
saints, 318
sala, 153
salad-basket, 260
salat, 360
salery, 360
sales-engineer, 291
saleslady, 294
salesman, 288

sales-promotion-engineer, 291
saleswoman, 294
Sali, 510
Salida, 543
Salinan, 549
sallat, 359
Sällström, 490
Sally, 507
Sally Ann, 582
Sallyrose, 521
Salmon, 498
salmon, 337
Salomon, 498
saloon, 85, 149, 219, 237, 243; -bar, 243; -car, 237; -corner men, 256; -keeper, 150, 243
salt-lick, 116
saltwater-taffy, 37
salve, 335, 582
Sam, 519
Sambo, 524
sambuke, 151
samp, 106
sample-room, 86, 149, 292
Samuel, 506, 507, 515
San Anselmo, 534
San Antonio, 541
sanatoria, 412
San Bernardino, 543
Sanchez, 494
sand, 167, 580
sand-bag, to, 227
Sanders, 506
San Diegan, 549
Sandusky, 525
Sandy, 110, 295
Sandy Hook, 532, 535
sanemagogna, 317
San Franciscan, 549
San Francisco, 543
sang, 434, 442
Sanger, 482
Sänger, 482
sängerfest, 112, 157, 218
sanguinary, 316
sanitary-engineer, 289
sanitize, to, 193
San Jacinto, 543
San José, 542; -an, 549
sank, 434
San Luis, 543
San Matean, 549
San Patricio, 534
San Pedro, 543

Santa Clara, 542
Santa Claus, 108
Santa Cruzan, 549
Santa Fe, 542
Santa Margarita, 534
Santa Monica, 543
Santiago, 508
Sant Klaas, 108
sap, 169, 566; -head, 263
sapolio, 173
Sara, 507
Sarah, 507
sarge, 170
sarsaparilla, 112
sartain, 360
sartin, 339
sarve, 339
Sasha, 508
sass, 161, 339
sass, to, 434
sassafras, 112
sassed, 434
sassy, 360, 379
sat, 434, 439
satisfaction, 336
Saturday, 336
Satyra, 522
sauce, 328, 335, 339, 349
sauce, to, 434
saucy, 339
sauer-braten, 155, 411
sauer-kraut, 98, 112, 155, 219, 411
Saugonian, 550
Sault Ste. Marie, 542
Saumagen, 501
Sauny, 524
savagerous, 137, 141
Savannah, 525
savant, 75
saviour, 394, 395
savory, 395
savour, 395
saw, 349, 378, 420, 423, 434, 442
Sawney, 524
saw wood, to, 119, 198
Say!, 252
say, to, 434
say a mouthful, to, 257
says, 447
's blood, 312
's bloud, 312
sc, 402
scab, 37, 239
sca'cely, 350

scalawag, 145, 175, 231
Scaler, 488
scallywag, 231
scally-wampus, 145, 176
scalp, to, 117
scandihoovian, 296
scandinoovian, 296
scant, 128
scarce, 339, 466
scarcely, 466, 467
scarfeteria, 177
scarf-pin, 235
scary, 93, 143
scatter, 349
Scellato, 493
scenarioize, to, 193
scent-spray, 233
sch, 484
Schaefer, 485
Schaf, 487
schedule, 352; -time, 227
Schenectadian, 550
schepel, 110
scherzo, 347
schicker, 217
schiksa, 217
schlacht, 602
Schlachtfeld, 498
Schlegel, 484
Schleigh, 499
schlepper, 217
Schlesinger, 500
Schluter, 484
Schmetterling, 501
Schmidt, 477, 482
schmierkäse, 411
schmiessed, 218
schmus, 217
Schnäbele, 482
Schneider, 484, 487, 493, 501
schnitzel, 155
schnookel, 218
schochet, 217
Schoen, 484
scholard, 22
scholom aleichim, 217
Scholtz, 483
Schön, 484, 500
school, 293
schoolmarm, 231, 350
schooner, 116, 149, 243, 372
schout, 109
Schrader, 483
Schroeder, 483

Schugren, 490
schul, 217
Schultz, 483
Schumacher, 485, 487
schützenfest, 157
Schuyler, 481, 498, 516
Schuylkill, 532
Schwab, 483
Schwaben, 296
Schwartz, 477, 485, 495
Schweiszhund, 501
schweizer, 155, 347
scientist, 559
scimetar, 390
scimitar, 390
scissor-bill, 582
scoffings, 582
scofflaw, 174
scolar, 401
Scomp, 495
scone, 233
scool, 401
scoon, to, 116
scooner, 116, 117
scoop, 583
scoot, to, 142, 232
scoovy, 296
score, to, 199
scout, 109
scow, 16, 108
scowegian, 296
scowoogian, 296
scrag-end, 236
scram, to, 560, 581
scrap, 231
scrape, 145
scratcher, 579
scratch-pad, 239
screw, 580, 581
screw-spanner, 235
scribbling-block, 239
scrimp, to, 129, 252
scrubwoman, 266
scrumdifferous, 145
scrumptious, 145
Scrymsoure-Steuart-Fothringham, 503
scule, 110
sculp, to, 192
se, 451
sea-board, 99
Seac, 524
sea-food, 247
Seagren, 490
sealed, 561
Seaman, 496

seamstress, 340
Sean, 513
Sears, 482
Seashore, 491
sea-shore, 99
seaside, 236
season-ticket-holder, 238
seat, 302
seater, 119
Seattleite, 549
Sebes, 496
secesh, 170
sech, 346
secondary-school, 241
second floor, 235, 238
second-hand, 293
second-year-man, 242
secretary, 267
secret disease, 304
section, 247
sedan, 237
seduced, 302, 310
see, 375, 442
see, to, 191, 434
seed, 434
see'd, 416
seed-ox, 302
seen, 420, 423, 434, 436, 441, 442
see the elephant, to, 142
see the light, to, 227
segankw, 104
segongw, 104
Segren, 490
seidel, 157, 243, 347
Selby, 501
selectman, 98, 116
self, 459
Sellstrom, 490
semester, 220, 242
semi-, 180, 181; -annual, 181; -breve, 250; -brevis, 250; -centennial, 181; -national, 181; -occasional, 96, 143, 181; -open-air, 181; -panic, 181; -quaver, 250; -wild, 181
semidemisemiquaver, 250
semiminima, 250
seminar, 220
Senate, 57
senator, 395
sende, 438
senery, 402
senile, 341

senior, 242
senior-prom, 242
señor, 152, 409
señorita, 152, 376
sensual, 352
sent, 438
sent down, to be, 243
sente, 438
sented, 402
Seosmh, 513
septer, 402
Seraphim, 516
Serb, 183
sergeant, 243
Seril, 522
serious, 466
serious charge, 304
serv, 403
servant, 228, 292
serve, 339
service, 210, 211
service, to, 192, 194
servile, 341
Servisk, 486
set, to, 199, 434, 439, 613
set-back, 167
settled, to be, 581
Seumas, 513
Sevčík, 512
Seventh Day Adventist, 250
sew, 383, 384
Sewell, 481, 496
Sewer, 504
sewerage, 235
sex glands, 307
sexual, 305
Seymour, 479, 506, 507, 516
sez, 434, 447
sez you, 222, 226
sh, 375, 382, 384
shabby, 126
shack, 37, 231, 582
shackle, to, 194
shackles, 582
shadchan, 216
shade, 375
shadow-boxing, 562
Shadrach, 515
shafts, 561
Shain, 500
shake, to, 434, 440
shake down, to, 578
shaken, 428, 434, 440
Shakespeare, 537

shal, 401, 403
shall, 24, 199, 200, 201, 420, 425, 445
sham, 126; -battle, 239; -fight, 239
shammy, to, 194
Shampoo, 495
Sham'un, 496
Shane, 484, 500
Shannon, 496
sha'n't, 445
shanty, 151, 231, 583; -man, 151; -town, 151
shanty, to, 151
Shanty Irish, 151
Shapiro, 500
share, 244; -holder, 244
shark, 582
Sharlot, 520
Sharon, 535
shavatorium, 179
shaveteria, 176
Shawangunk, 540
Shawnee-cake, 115
shaze, 382
she, 375, 448, 451, 458
Shean, 500
she-cow, 361
shed, 375, 579
Shedlicker, 488
sheenie, 295
sheep-dip-expert, 291
sheeps, 419
sheer-crapper, 359
Sheila, 513
shell, 243
Shellat, 493
shellbone, 236
shell-road, 116
Shepherd, 485
Sheppard, 485
Sher, 498
Sherman, 498, 508
sherry-cobbler, 149
Sherwood, 503
shet, 346, 434
shevaleer, 382, 384
Shevchynsky, 489
shew, to, 391
shillelah, 160
Shiltz, 483
shily, 392, 393
shim, 460
shin, to, 118
shine, 296
shine, to, 434

shined, 247, 434
shingle, 116; -engineer, 290
shingles, 238
shinola, 173
Shin Pond, 536
shin up, to, 232
ship's-boat, 252
shipt, 402, 403
shirker, 372
Shirley, 506, 520
shirt, 302
shis, 460
shoat, 100, 128
shock-absorber, 237
shoe, 7, 12, 122, 158, 235, 247, 266, 391; -fixery, 176; -lace, 235; -rebuilder, 288; -string, 235; -studio, 292
shoe, to, 434, 439
shoed, 434
Shoemaker, 485
shoes, 85
shoeteria, 176
shofle, 218
Shogren, 490
sholder, 402
shoo-fly, 566
shook, 434
shooting, 236, 252
shootingest, 463
shoot the chutes, to, 198
shoot up in the burg, 40
shop, 122, 123, 265, 292; -walker, 234; -worn, 293
shoppe, 266
shopper, 266
shopping, 266
shore, 360; -dinner, 247
Short, 485
shortcake, 261
short-haul, 239
Shortie, 520
shot, 237
shot-gun, 144
Shoto, 495
should, 25, 445
should not ought, 445
shouldn't, 444
should of, 471
should ought, 424, 445
should've, 471
Shoultz, 483
shout, to, 150

show, to, 198, 248, 391, 434
show a yellow streak, to, 198
show business, 585
showdown, 30, 62, 191
Show Me, 552
shown, 434
show up, to, 198
shriek, 602
Shrinedom, 178
shrub, 149
shruffle, 119
Shuard, 503
shuck, 434, 440
shuffle, 126
shunt, 147
shur-on, 407
shut, 346, 359
shut, to, 434
shut-out, 562
shut out, to be, 191
shutted, 434
shuyster, 158, 229
Shy Beaver, 536
shyly, 393
shyster, 74, 86, 158, 178, 231
si, 451
siad, 451
siblings, 460
sich, 360
Sicilian, 299
sick, 12, 62, 70, 127, 251; -bed, 251; -kidneys, 251; -leave, 251; -nerves, 251; -room, 251; -teeth, 251
side-hill, 99
side-lot, 121
side-step, to, 227, 562
side-stepper, 37
side-swipe, 147
side-track, to, 147, 167, 227
side-walk, 33, 42, 116, 235, 247
sideways, 204, 468
Sidney, 479, 506, 507
sience, 402
sierra, 152
Sierraville, 534
siesta, 152
siffer, 159
Sighle, 513
sight-seeing-car, 237

signature, to, 195
signd, 403
sign-engineer, 290
Sigrid, 510
sig-sog, 375
silencer, 237
Silla, 524
Sillinger, 503
Silva, 494
silvan, 402
Silver, 494
Silverberg, 501
silver-fizz, 85
Silvernail, 485
Silvers, 490
silverside, 236
silverware, 235
Silvestr, 511
Silvig, 493
Silvy, 493
Silwerovitch, 490
Siminowicz, 489
Simmons, 489
simonize, to, 193
simp, 169
Simpson, 514
simultaneous, 341
sinagog, 402, 403
sing, to, 434, 469
singan, 469
Singer, 482
singfest, 218
single, 585
singlet, 236, 239
single-track mind, 147
Sing-Sing, 532
sing-sing, 106
Sinjin, 503
sink, to, 434
sinker, 564
siphon, 389
Sir, 272, 273, 281
siren, 390
sirloin, 236
sissors, 402
sissy, 309
sit, 447
sit, to, 245, 422, 439
Sit 'N Eat, 210
sitting member, 245
sitting-room, 235
sit up and take notice, to, 227
Six, 537
Sixkiller, 514
six-shooter, 231

sixteenth note, 250
sixth form, 241
sixty-fourth note, 250
size up, to, 232
Sjörgren, 490
Sjöstrand, 491
Skála, 488
skan, 434
Skaneateles, 553
skate, 246, 375
skedaddle, 561
skedaddle, to, 145
skedannumi, 146
skeerce, 339
skeert, 360
skeet, 170
skeeter, 170
skeptic, 389, 394
-ski, 222
skibby, 295
skiddoo, 561
Skidoo, 534
skilful, 406
skilley, 580
skillful, 388, 406
skimp, to, 252
skin, 149
skin, to, 434
Skintown, 554
skipper, 583
skirt, 563, 576
skittle-alley, 236, 248
skittles, 248
skookum, 150
Skull Run, 537
skun, 434, 437
skunk, 104, 296
Skunk Center, 554
Skunktown, 536
-sky, 222
sky-scraper, 186, 228
Slabtown, 554
slacker, 565
slæpan, 437
slæpte, 437
Slagel, 484
slam, 184
slam the pill, to, 562
slander, 335
slang, 434, 555; -whanger, 99, 568
slash, 184
slate, 167, 183
Slättengren, 490
Slaughter, 525
Slazenger, 500

sled, 235
sledge, 235
sleek, 341
sleep, 375
sleep, to, 93, 196, 434, 437
sleep-engineer, 289
sleeper, 170
sleep good, to, 254
Sleepy Eye, 536
sleigh, 108
slenderize, to, 193
slep, 352, 434, 437
slept, 434, 438
Slessinger, 500
Slettengren, 490
sleuth, 86
slew, to, 252
slew-foot, 252
slick, 24, 231, 341
slick up, to, 129
slid, 434
slide, 373
slide, to, 434
slightly-second, 293
slily, 392
Slim, 520
slim, 143; -attendance, 143; -chance, 143; -support, 143
sliness, 380
sling, 149; -shot, 239
sling, to, 434
slip, 120
slipova, 407
slipper, 122
sliver, 341
slo, 407
slops, 582
slough, to, 585
slow, 466
slowly, 466
sluck, 109
slug-fest, 218, 562
slum, 573, 580, 582, 584
slumber-robe, 288; -room, 287; -shirt, 288
slumgullion, 145
slum-joint, 579
slung, 434
slush, 602
slut, 305
Sluter, 484
sly, 373
sly, to, 373
slyly, 380

Smackover, 533
smale, 379
small, 143, 379; -pearl, 250; -pica, 250; -potatoes, 100, 145, 373
smart, 99
smartski, 222
smash, 149, 184, 602
smearcase, 108, 112
smearkase, 411
Smed, 477
smell, 303
smell, to, 435
smell like a wet dog, to, 136
smelt, 435
smidgen, 361
smilefest, 218
smited, 436
Smith, 477, 478, 482, 486, 488, 489, 493, 494, 496, 498, 513, 514, 520; -Barry, 502; -dale, 546; of F, 504; -vale, 529
smithereens, 160
Smithson, 502
Smitty, 520
smog, 266
smoke, 296, 583; -eater, 563; -fest, 218
smoker, 169, 170
smoketeria, 177
smote, 436
smoulder, to, 126
Smudge, 520
Snabely, 482
snack-bar, 239
snag, 183, 231
Snailwell, 537
snake, 583; -fence, 145
snake's hips, 561
snap, 170
snappy, 464, 565
Snavely, 482
sneak, to, 435
sneez, 401
sneezd, 402
snew, 437
snicker, 129
snipe, 583
snitz, 157
snively, 482
snoop, to, 108
snooser, 296
snoot, 346, 570
snoozer, 583

snot, to, 309
snout, 346
snow, to, 437
snowball, 296
Snow moon, 106
snow-plow, 115
snow under, to, 227
snozzled, 568
snuck, 435
snug, 243
Snyder, 484, 493, 514
soap-box, 227
soar, 349
Soares, 495
s.o.b., 305, 316, 317
sobfest, 218
sob-sister, 186
sob-stuff, 232
soc, to, 216
Social Circle, 536
social disease, 304, 306
social-engineer, 290, 291
socialize, to, 588
Sociamelia, 524
society-engineer, 290
socio-religious-engineer, 290
sockdolager, 145, 176, 568
socko, 184
sock-suspenders, 234
socony, 172
soda-biscuit, 235
soda-cracker, 235
soda-fountain, 228
sodalicious, 175
sodateria, 177
soda-water, 149
Soderstrom, 490
Sodom, 535
soe, 383, 384
soft, 465
soft-drinks, 149, 237
soft-pedal, to, 227
soi, 460
soirée, 409
sokol, 216
Sol, 519
sol, 402
soldier, 283
Soldiers Delight, 537
soli, 412
Solicitor, 524
solicitor, 245, 255
solid, 120
Solis Cohen, 501, 502
Solmson, 498

Solomon, 498, 506
solon, 183
so-long, 219
solos, 412
somber, 388
sombrero, 152
some, 254; -girl, 254; -place, 204, 407; -pumpkins, 100
someone else's, 461
someone's else, 461
some(p)thing, 439
something else again, 217
someway, 407
somewheres, 468
somewheres else, 204
son, 460; -son, 491, 493
Sonia, 508
son-in-laws, 461
Sonntag, 485
son-of-a- ——, 305
son-of-a-bitch, 305, 313, 317
son-of-a-gun, 316, 317
Sons, 505
sons-in-law, 461
Soo, 542
soogan, 582
soon, 344
soot, 344, 383, 384
Sophia, 507
sophimore, 116
sophomore, 116, 242
Sophronia, 519
soprani, 412
sopranos, 412
sore, 349
sorry, 267
sorta, 443, 471
S.O.S., to, 196
So's your old man, 566
sot, 416, 434
sothers, 175
soul, 402
Soulé, 481
sound, 246
Soup Line, 582
sour, 149
source, 328, 349
soured, 561
South, 529
south-paw, 562
soveran, 384
sovereign, 384
sow, 302; -belly, 304; -bosom, 304

sowegian, 296
sox, 406, 407
spa, 338
space, 375
space-saving-engineer, 290
spade, 296
spade, to, 16
spaghetteria, 177
spaghetti, 222
span, 108, 435
Spånberg, 490
spanner, 86
sparking-plug, 237
spark-plug, 237
Sparta, 530
Spartan, 551
spats, 169
speak, to, 435, 613
speakeasy, 160, 565
speakie, 187
speak loud, to, 465
spearmint, 173
spec, 170
special, to, 197
special delivery, 238
speciality, 415
specialty, 415; -shop, 266
specie, 111, 461
species, 461
specific blood-poison, 304; stomach, 307; ulcer, 307
speck, 109
spectroscope, 155
sped, 440
speech-day, 243
Speed, 496, 523
speed, to, 199, 435, 439
speedathon, 180
speed-cop, 92, 226
speeded, 435, 440
speeder, 439
speeding, 439
speed-limit, 439
speed-mania, 439
speed-maniac, 439
speedster, 178
speed-way, 227, 546
speek, 381
spell, to, 435
spellbind, to, 186
spellbinder, 167, 186
spelling-bee, 116
spelt, 435
Spencer, 516

spera, 376
spick, 296
spider, 27, 579
spiel, 577, 578
spiggoty, 296
spigot, 235
spike, 184
spile, 346
spile for a fight, to, 136
spill, to, 435
spill the beans, to, 198
spilt, 435
spin, to, 435
spindliest, 463
spirit lamp, 233
spirits, 244
spit, 309
spit, to, 435, 440
spitzbub, 157
splash, 602
splendiferous, 176
splendour, 395
split a ticket, to, 148
splurge, 142, 231
splurge, to, 141, 232
spoil, 346
spoil, to, 435
spoils-system, 148
spoilt, 435
Spokane, 542
spoke, 435
spondulix, 145
spong, 119
Spongberg, 490
spooffest, 218
spook, 35, 108, 231, 344
spool, 235
spoon, 344
sport, 155
sportdom, 178
sporting-goods, 237
sporting house, 304
sportive, 564
sports-requisites, 237
spot, to, 585
sprang, 435
spread, to, 439
spread-eagle, 144
spreaded, 439
spread oneself, to, 142, 232
spring, to, 435, 581
Springfield, 537
sprung, 435
spruts, 215
spry, 99

Spud, 520
spuke, 98
spun, 435
spunk, 567
spur, to, 199
spurious, 558
Spuyten, 533
squabery, 176
squalid, 343
squander, 343
squantersquash, 105
squarehead, 295, 296
square-meal, 145
square the beef, to, 556
squash, 104, 105, 169
squat, to, 118, 121, 581
squatter, 98, 121, 231
squaw, 105
squawk, 171
squaw-man, 150
squeak, 602
squealer, 562
Squedunk, 553
Squire, 278
Squirrel, 524
squirrel-whiskey, 149, 568
squunck, 104
ss, 401
stable-horse, 308
Stacros, 512
stadhuis, 109
staf, 406
staff, 242, 268, 335, 406
stage, 99
stage-manager, 289
stagger-soup, 568
stag-party, 144
Stäheli, 482
staircase, 235
stairs, 235, 462
stairway, 235
Staley, 482, 483
stalk, 349
stall, to, 263
stallion, 301, 302, 308
stall off, to, 562
stalls, 237
stalwart, 167
stamp, 334, 338
stampede, 152, 231
stamping-ground, 116
stamps, 346
stance, 562
stand, to, 245
standard, 241
standchen, 409

ständchen, 409
stand for, to, 227, 229
Standing Bear, 514
Standingdeer, 514
stand pat, to, 191
stand-patter, 187
standpoint, 120, 121, 158, 165, 231
standpunkt, 121
stang, 435
Stănilă, 494
Stanislaw, 510
stank, 435
Stanley, 494, 506, 510, 516
Stanton, 494
star, to, 199
stardom, 178
starry, 350
start, 349
start in, to, 198, 229
start off, to, 198
start out, to, 198, 229
statehouse, 109
statement, 118
Staten, 532
station, 147, 539; -agent, 238; -master, 238
statistics, 155
status, 338
statutory offense, 304
staunch, 335, 392
Staunton, 541
stave off, to, 99
stay, 373, 374
staylit, 407
stay put, 198, 227
St. Cyr, 482
St. Denis, 479
steady, 340, 383, 384, 397, 466
steal, to, 435
steamboat, 57
steam-roller, 186, 196
steam-shovel, 239
-steam, 499
stean, 499
steddy, 384, 397
steering-committee, 148
Stehli, 483
Stein, 499
stein, 155, 237, 243; -stein, 499, 507
Steinmetz, 484
Steinway, 482
St. Elmo, 537
stem-winder, 96, 235, 239

stench, to, 196
Stenny, 486
steno, 169
stenog, 169
Stephen, 510, 512, 513
-ster, 178
Stern, 499
stern, 372
Steve, 510, 512
Stevens, 514
stew, 260, 345
steward, 245
stewed, 568
stick, 149
stick, to, 579
sticker, 229
Stick No Bills, 239
stick up, to, 558
sticky-back, 229
stiff, 563
stiff upper lip, 565
stile, 384
still better, 463
Stilton cheese, 261
Stimits, 484
stimulis, 413
stimulus-response-bond, 588
-stine, 499
sting, to, 435
Sting Tail, 514
stingy, 126
stink, 303, 309
stink, to, 435
stinkibus, 149
Stiobhan, 513
St. John, 496, 503
St. Joseph, 535; -ite, 549
St. Lawrence, 531
St. Leger, 503
St. Louis, 531, 541
stock, 128, 244
stockbroker, 244
stockholder, 244
Stockholm, 530
stocking, 378; -feet, 145
stockings, 302, 308
stocks, 244
Stock Yards, 536
stockyards, 462
stoker, 583
Stolar, 498
stole, 435, 437, 442
stomac, 401
stomach, 302, 310
stomps, 346

stonden, 442
stone, 99, 250, 308
stone-fence, 149
stones, 303
stone-wall, 149
stood, 442
stoop, 98, 108
stop, 602
stop-over, to, 147, 198
store, 7, 122, 123, 266, 292; -clothes, 145; -used, 293
stores, 234
storey, 390, 392
stork, 349
storked, 561
Storm, 492
storm, 578, 585, 602
story, 390
Stout, 537
St. Patrick, 535
St. Paul, 528, 531, 535
straddle, to, 148
straddling, 143
strafe, to, 573
straight, 149, 605
straight-ticket, 148
strap, 346
strap-hanger, 228
strata, 338, 412
stratas, 413
stratosphere, 559
Strauss, 500
Streed, 491
street, 544; -cleaner, 239; -railway, 239
Streeter, 489
strength, 360
strenuous, 558; -life, 174
stricken out, 246
Strid, 491
strife, 578
strike, to, 435
strike it rich, to, 142
strike oil, to, 167
strike out, to, 191
striker, 30, 573
string, 247; -bean, 235, 260
strings, 583
strip, to, 586
stripe, 585
Stritar, 489
Stromberg, 490
strong-arm-squad, 243
strop, 346
struck, 435
struck out, 246

struggld, 402
strychnine, 341
St. Therese, 543
stube, 219, 292
stubs, 244
stuccoed, 568
Studebaker, 485
Studebecker, 485
student, 375
Studie, 579
studio, 292
study for the ministry, to, 249
study law, to, 240
study medicine, to, 240
stuf, 403
stump, to, 35, 93, 118, 228
stumped, 114
Stumptown, 537
stung, 435
stunk, 435
stunt, 159, 232
stuntfest, 218
Sturgeon moon, 106
Stuyvesant, 481
stye, 389
style, 384
style, to, 93, 194
subpena, 401
subsidize, 118
subsist, to, 196
succede, 401
successor, 395
succotash, 98, 100, 105
such, 346
Suciu, 494
Suck, 505
sucker, 37, 263, 556, 562, 576, 584
Sucker Branch, 535
suddint, 360
Sue, 507
suffragan, 248
Sug, 519
sugar, 585
sugar-basin, 235
sugar-bowl, 235
suicide, to, 167
suitatorium, 179
Suke, 519
Sukey, 519
sulfite, 394
sulfur, 402
Sullivan, 477, 500
Summer time, 234

Summit, 536
summon, 461
summons, 461
sump, 237
sundae, 86, 188, 190, 191
Sunday, 485
sunflower, 536
sung, 434, 441
sunk, 434
supawn, 106
super-, 180, 181, 464;
-American, 181; -cabi-
net, 181; -criminal, 181;
-film, 181; -gang, 181;
-highway, 181; -love,
181; -perfect, 181;
-production, 181
supergobosnoptious, 145
supergobsloptious, 176
super-highway, 181
superintendent, 243, 288
superior, 395
supernaculum, 577
supper, 240
surallikus, 109
sure, 93, 103, 202, 262,
465, 467
sure-fire, 262
surely, 467
surface-protection-engi-
neer, 290
survey, 325, 588
Susan, 519
Susanville, 534
suspectful, 175
suspenders, 85, 145, 235,
239, 391
suspicion, to, 25
Susquehanna, 528
susy, 359
sut, 383, 384
Sutter, 542
Suva, 488
suveran, 384
Svec, 487
Sven, 510
Svensson, 491
Swaffham, 537
swagger, 269
swaller, 353
swallow, 124
swam, 435
swamp, 246, 343
Swampskeeter, 552
swan, 343
Swanell, 522

swang, 435
swanga, 113
swank, 269, 568
Swanson, 492
swap, to, 126
Swashing Creek, 533
swatfest, 218
sweat, 309
sweat, to, 435
Swede, 240
sweep, to, 435
sweepstakes, 155
sweet, 247, 602; -corn,
240; -potato, 114, 246;
-shop, 234
sweets, 41, 234
swell, 557
swell, to, 435
swelled, 438
Swensson, 492
swep, 435, 437
swerve, to, 252
Swiler, 485
swim, to, 435
swimmingly, 126
swim-suit, 233
swing, to, 435
switch, 146; -engine, 146;
-man, 146; -yard, 146
switch, to, 147
switchback-railway, 237
swole, 435, 438
swollen, 435
Swope, 483
sword, 349
's wounds, 312
swum, 435, 441
swung, 435
sycamore, 536
Sydney, 508
Sylvester, 511, 519
Sylvia, 507, 509
Syphax, 524
syphilis, 304, 306
Sýr, 487
Syracuse, 530
syren, 389
Syringia, 522
syrup, 235
Szabó, 496
Szemán, 496
Szentgyörgyi, 496
Szentpétery, 496
Sztefan, 510
Szüle, 496
t, 335, 348, 352, 353, 360,

368, 375, 389, 401, 402,
447, 493, 600; -t, 438
Taaffe, 478
Taavetti, 510
tab, 229
table, to, 7, 117
taboobery, 175
Tacoma, 532; -n, 549
tactic, 111, 461
tactics, 461
Tadpole, 552
taffy, 235
Taft, 478
Tahoma, 532
tail, 308
take, to, 435, 604
take a back seat, to, 142
take a bath, to, 252
take a lunar, to, 250
take for a ride, to, 558,
580
taken, 428, 435
take on, to, 99
take silk, to, 246
take the cake, to, 232
take the first turning, to,
253
take to the woods, to, 119
talented, 70, 98, 120, 223
Taliaferro, 503
talk, 183
talkfest, 218
talkie, 170, 187
talk-talk, 373
talk through your hat, to,
563
tall, 614
Tallahassee, 528
tallest, 420
tallow-pot, 583
Talmadge, 524
Talvi, 492
tamal, 152
tamale, 152
tamber, 409
Tamer, 524
tamer, 584
tammany, 106
tan, 247
tangle-foot, 167
tango, 155
tank, 582
tanked, 568
tank-town, 147
Taos, 541
Taoseño, 550

tap, 235
tapioca, 112
tap-room, 243, 292
Tarheel, 552
tariff reform, 245
Tarkington, 513
tarn, 115
tarnal, 316, 317, 339
tarnation, 35, 316, 317
tart, 235, 305
tassel, 334
tasty, 93, 96
Tatiyopa, 514
taught, 349, 435
Taunton, 541
taut, 349
tavern, 123, 292
Tavia, 519
taw, 349
tay, 161
Taylor, 488, 496, 497, 499, 520, 529
taxed-paid, 194
taxes, 235
taxi, 374
taxi, to, 192
taximeter, 155
taxpaid, 194
taxpay, to, 194
taxpayer, 235
T.B., 208, 536
-te, 438
tea, 240; -cake, 233; -shop, 266
teach, to, 435, 440
team, 7, 122
tear, to, 435
tear-bucket, 587
teat, 303, 309
tech, 346
technical - publicity - engineer, 291
tecnical, 401
Tecumseh, 517
Ted, 519
Teddy, 519
tee off, to, 562
teeth, 612
teetotal, 161
teetotaler, 145
tegua, 151
tel, 401, 403
telefone, 402, 403
telegraf, 402, 403
telegram, 147, 604
telegramme, 394

telegraph-blank, 247
telegrapher, 165, 324
telegraph-form, 247
telegraphic communication, 147
telegraphic dispatch, 147
teleology, 155
telephone, 591, 604
telescoped, 228
tell, to, 435
tell'd, 435
tell it to a judge, to, 561
Telluride, 536
Tell your troubles to a policeman, 566
Temba, 524
temporarily, 324
Tenah, 524
tend, to, 435
tended, 435
tender, 239
tender-foot, 145, 231
tenderloin, 236, 240
Ten Eyck, 481
Tennessee Iron and Coal, 525
Tennyson, 513
ten-pins, 237, 248
tent, 435
ten thirty, 251
tepee, 106
tequila, 152
Tera, 523
Terence, 505
Terjesen, 492
terminal, 147
Terra, 494
Terra Amarilla, 534
terrace, 547
terrapin, 104, 105, 246
Terre Haute, 541
Terry, 494
Tertzagian, 497
testicles, 307
tête, 214, 557
tête-a-tête, 409
Texarkana, 537
Texhoma, 537
Texico, 537
textil, 403
th, 335, 353, 367, 375, 382, 404
-thal, 499, 500
Thalberg, 500
Thalheimer, 500
Thames, 540

than, 458, 464, 472
thanx, 406
that, 367, 452, 453, 454
that-a way, 471
that-ere, 452
thatn, 451, 454
that'n, 471
that-one, 451
that-there, 451, 452
that way, 561
-thau, 499
theatre, 325, 383, 388, 402
The Dalles, 537
thé dansant, 409
thee, 450, 454
the Hon., 275, 277, 278, 279
their, 448, 456, 460
theirn, 448, 456, 461
theirs, 448
theirself, 419, 459
theirselves, 459
the limit, 227, 230
them, 420, 424, 448, 451, 452, 454, 455, 456
them-ere, 452
them'ere, 471
Themicoud, 479
them'n, 452
themselves, 459, 460
them-there, 451, 452
them-two, 449
thence, 468
Theodore, 507, 519
Theotiste, 522
there, 24, 375, 420, 467
Thermopolis, 530
thermos, 173
thés-dansants, 412
these, 451, 452
these-here, 451, 452
thesen, 451
These States, 75
these-yur, 452
thet, 365
they, 424, 448, 451
they is, 363
thief, 584
thin, 375
think, to, 435
thinnen, to, 193
third, 367
third-degree, 243, 264, 577
thirty-second note, 250
this, 452
this-and-that-way, 561

this-a way, 471
this-here, 424, 451, 452
thish-yur, 452
thisn, 451
this'n, 464
this-one, 451
thither, 468
tho, 399, 400, 402, 403, 406
thoid, 350, 367, 368
Thomas, 493, 506, 509, 515
Thompson, 439, 488
thon, 460
-thon, 180
thon's, 460
thoro, 400, 402, 403, 406
thorofare, 400, 403
thoroly, 400, 403
Thoroughgood, 479
Thorrel, 522
those, 451, 452, 460
thosen, 451
those-there, 451, 452
thou, 449, 450
thought, 435
thrash, 346
thread, 383, 384
threat, 384
thred, 384
Three Churches, 537
Three Fingers, 536
three-of-a-kind, 191
three-sheet, to, 585
threesome, 562
three - strikes - and - out, 191
Threetops, 539
thresh, 346
thret, 384
threw, 422, 435, 440
thro, 406
through, 605
throw, to, 435, 440
throw a rock, to, 123
throw a scare into, to, 198
throwed, 435, 440
thrown, 435
thru, 399, 400, 402, 403, 404, 406
thrung, 435
thruout, 400, 403
Thugut, 478
thum, 384, 402
thumb, 383, 384
thumb-tack, 239
thunder, 602
Thunichgut, 478

thunk, 435
Thurgod, 479
thusly, 467
Thusnelda, 522
ticket, 101; -agent, 238; -chopper, 239; -office, 147; -scalper, 145, 147
tickler, 145
tickrum-juckrum, 577
tiddy-bit, 361
tie, 147, 235
tie-pin, 235
tie-up, 239
Tildy, 519
tiles, 238
till, 160
till hell freezes over, 314
tillicum, 150
Tilman, 516
timbre, 409
tin, 228, 238, 375
tin-hat, 573
tinhorn, 263
tinker, 236
tin-key, 234
tinner, 236
tin-opener, 234
tinsmith, 236
tipe, 402
tiptoe, to, 192
tire, 389, 390, 394; -engineer, 290
tiro, 390
Tish, 519
tiswin, 151
tit, 309
tit for tat, 578
tithe, 248
title-holder, 562
tiz, 173
to, 401, 471
to a frazzle, 167
tobacco, 112, 152, 604
toboggan, 105
tocking, 378
to-day, 414
Todenacker, 479
toffee, 235
toggery, 266
to go big, 202
toilet, 304, 389, 391, 394
toilette, 389
Tola, 516
told, 352, 438
tole, 352, 435, 438
To Let, 266

Tolliver, 503
Tom, 512, 513, 519
tom, 402
tomahawk, 105, 372
tomahawk, to, 117
Tom-and-Jerry, 149
Tomas, 508
Tomáš, 511
Tomasini, 493
Tomaso, 509
Tomaszewski, 488
tomato, 112, 152, 334, 337
tomb, 402
tombé, 151
Tombstone, 536
Tom Collins, 149
tommy-rot, 564
to-morrow, 414, 605
tomtomery, 175
tongue, 383, 384, 399
tonguey, 129
tong, 162; -war, 162
to-night, 414
tonked, 260
tonsil-paint, 568
tonsorial-artist, 288; -studio, 292
tony, 96, 145, 464
took, 435
tooken, 442
toor, 382
Toothacher, 479
Toothpick, 552
toot sweet, 573
top, 237; -hole, 269; -kick, 573; -liner, 236; -round, 236; -side, 236
Topekan, 549
topped, to be, 581
topping, 269, 557
toppings, 583
topsy-turvy, 126
tore, 349, 435
Torial, 525
torn, 435
tornado, 152, 231, 339, 347
Torontonian, 549
torope, 105
torpedo, 580
torpor, 389, 395
tort, 349
tortilla, 152
tortillia, 152
tosh, 269
tote, to, 99, 119, 232
touch, 346

touchy, 126
tough, 609
tough guy, 39
toune, 379
tour, 382
tourist, 155
tovôdoun, 113
towards, 204, 468
towerman, 146
town, 379, 539
town-loafer, 156
Toycen, 492
T.R., 183
track, 238
track-walker, 146
Tracy, 504, 507
trade off, to, 232
tradesmen's-entrance, 266
traffic, 269, 406; -block-
  ade, 239; -division, 243
trafic, 406
Trailing Arbutus, 521
train-boy, 147
trained-, 291
trained nurse, 240
trainer, 584
trait, 328, 348
tram-car, 247
tramp, 347, 581
Trampleasure, 503
tramway, 239
transom, 236
transportation, 31
trap, 260
trapee, 461
trapeze, 461
trapezist, 178
trash, 128
träumerei, 347
traveld, 403
traveldom, 178
traveler, 383, 388, 399
Travelers' moon, 106
traveling, 388
traveling salesman, 305
traveller, 383, 388, 389,
  399
travelogue, 171
tray, 328
treacle, 62, 235
treasurer, 289
treated good, to be, 254
treatment, 293
tree-surgeon, 288
trefa, 217
tremendious, 353

trewe, 465
trez beans, 573
Triantafyllou, 485
tribunal, 325, 341
trick, 585
trigger-man, 580
trim, to, 562
Trinidad, 535
tripos, 243
tripper, 147
triscuit, 173
troble, 400
trocha, 221
Trojan, 551
trollop, 305
tromp, to, 346
Trosley, 503
Trotsky, 499
Trotterscliffe, 503
troubld, 403
trouble, 400, 578
Troy, 530
Trpaslik, 488
truck, 147
truckologist, 179
true, 345
true-blue, 143
true inwardness, 232
trufit, 407
trun, 435
truncheon, 243
trunk, 235
trunk-call, 86
trunk-line, 239
trust-buster, 429, 565
try, 170
try a case, to, 246
try and, 165
try out, to, 198, 227, 229
tsar, 390
tub, to, 269
tube, 266
tuck, 435
tuckhoe, 106
Tucson, 542; -ian, 548
Tuesday, 345
tuf, 381, 402, 403
Tug, 520
Tuisku, 492
tummy, 265, 310
tumour, 395
tumtum, 150
tung, 383, 384, 399, 402
Tunicotto, 478
tupelo, 106
turbot, 246

turfdom, 178
Turk, 183, 295
turkey, 582, 585
turkey-gobbler, 114
turn, to, 198
turn at the first corner,
  to, 253
turn down, to, 198, 227,
  565, 609
turnfest, 218
turn him in, to, 581
turnip, 240
turnpike, 57, 99
turn up missing, to, 198
turnverein, 112, 157
turtle, 126
tut, 159
tuxedo, 173
T.V.A., 209
twang, 126
twelv, 401, 403
twelve-month, 250
twenty-three, 561
Twila, 521
twine, 247
Twisleton - Wykeham -
  Fiennes, 502
twist and twirl, 578
Twitty, 505
two-fer, 143
two-seater, 237
twosome, 562
two-step, 582
two-time loser, 580
typewrite, to, 192
typo, 170
tyre, 389, 390
Tyson, 492
U, 170
u, 344, 359, 360, 383, 386,
  393, 394, 395, 396, 399,
  402, 441; ü, 482
Uarda, 522
Uberto, 509
ue, 402
ugly, 99
uh-huh, 561
Uhler, 484
U Kan Kom In, 546
uke, 585
ulk, 184
ultimatum, 339
umbrella, 603
umpire, 346
Unable-to-Fornicate, 514
uncle, 579

under-brush, 115
under-cut, 236, 240
undergraduate, 242
underground - railroad, 147
underhanded, 165
underlay a cut, to, 261
underpinned, 120
underpinning, 128
undershirt, 236, 239
Undershirt Hill, 536
under-the-weather, 143, 232
Underwood, 489
Unéaukara, 527
Uneeda, 537
uneeda, 172, 209, 407
Uneedme, 209
union-suit, 236
uniquer, 463
Unisian, 548
unit, 116
Unitedstatesian, 548
Universal, 99
university, 292
university-man, 243
unjustest, 463
unloosen, 464
unloosen, to, 433
unmarried mother, 293
unmentionables, 303
unmixed, 379
Uno, 534
unrivaledest, 168
unrol, 380
Unsijärvi, 492
Unsuntabunt, 531
untaxpaid, 194
unwhisperables, 303
unworthy, 465
up, 402
up, to be, 245
up against, 227
up against a tough proposition, 227
up-lift, 62
up-line, 247
Upperco, 484
uppish, 567
Uprchl, 488
up-state, 93, 246
Upthegrove, 505
up to, 227
up to time, 238
uptown, 246
up-train, 247

U-Put-It-On, 209
Uretha, 522
U-Rub-It-In, 209
us, 447, 455, 458
us-all, 378
used, 293
used to be, 447
used to could, 99
usen't, 471
use'to, 471
ush, to, 192
Usher, 516
usher, 241, 245
us is, 363
us-two, 449
usually, 467
us-uns, 450
Utahna, 522
Utensil, 525
Utica, 530
utilize, to, 16
v, 375, 377, 401
vacation, to, 195, 237
vacationize, to, 193
Vaccarelli, 493
vaccine, 341
Václav, 511
vag, 402
vagrate, to, 16
vague, 402
Väinö, 510
Valaria, 522
Valdez, 494
Valentino, 578
valeteria, 177
Vališ, 486
vallje, 119
vally, 402
valorous, 395
valour, 395
valspar, 173
vamoose, 152
vamos, 152
vamose, 152
vamose, to, 232
vamp, 169
vamp, to, 192, 565
van, 169, 481
Van Arsdale, 481
Van Buren, 481
Vanderbilt, 498
Van de Veer, 481
Vandiver, 481
vanilla, 349
Vannersdale, 481
Van Rensselaer, 481

Vanzetti, 494
vaporize, 395
vapour, 395
vaquero, 75, 152
variate, to, 99
variety, 237
Varlow, 522
vase, 337
vaseline, 172, 559
vase-line, 591
Vashti, 524
Vatslaw, 510
vaud, 237
vaude, 237
vaudevil, 401, 403
vaudeville, 237, 347, 411; -theatre, 237
Vavřinec, 511
vegetable, 376
vegetable-slice, 260
Veilchenduft, 501
Veldhuis, 485
Vella, 521
Velvalee, 522
Venables, 503
Venables-Vernon, 502
veneer, 155
venereal disease, 306
Venice, 530
Venton Orlaydo, 524
Ventura, 542
veranda, 393
verandah, 392, 393
verb, 375
verdrübt, 150
vereins, 412
verger, 248
veribest, 407
Verl, 522
Verla, 522
Verlie, 521
Vernon, 507
Versailles, 542
Versey, 522
vertebrae, 347
Vertie Ven, 524
Very Rev., 282, 283
Ves, 519
Vespasien, 304
vest, 236, 239, 377
vestry, 245
veteran, 255
Veverka, 512
vial, 389, 390
vicar, 220, 248, 249
vice-chancellor, 241

vice disease, 306
vice-president, 289
Victor, 507
victrola, 172
vie, to, 199
Viereck, 484
viertel, 250
vigilante, 152
vigorous, 395
vigour, 395
Vilda, 522
Villenol, 487
Vincent, 509, 511
Vincenzo, 509
Vinegar Bend, 56
violet, 341
Viol-Inn, 546
Virgil, 512
virgin, 305, 308
Virginia City, 530
virtue, 352
virtuosi, 412
virtuosos, 412
virtuous, 306
visa, 410
visé, 410
vision-engineer, 290
visit, 377
Vista, 521
Vitolo, 494
vivil, 173
Vivinne, 522
Vladimir, 511
Vladislaw, 510
Vlastimil, 511
vlei, 532
Vlk, 486
vly, 532
vnmixt, 379
vodvil, 411
Vogelgesang, 484, 485
void, to, 199
Vojtěch, 511
Vola, 521
Volodymyr, 511
Volz, 514
vomick, 360
voodoo, 113
vote, 245
Votruba, 487
vous tout, 450
voyageur, 108
Vrba, 512
Vunies, 525
vurry, 257
w, 351, 377, 404, 469

wa, 343
Waddell, 504
waffle, 108
Wagenaar, 485
Wagensbach, 487
wage-sheet, 239
waggon, 383, 390, 392
Wagner, 484, 485, 489
wagon, 85, 158, 383, 386, 389, 390, 396
Waguespack, 487
waikiki, 377
Waiter, 488
Waitr, 488
Waitzel, 522
Waive, 521
wake, to, 435
Walden Pond, 535
Waldo, 479
Waldow, 479
walk, 547
walkathon, 180
walk'd, 438
Walker, 514
walkfest, 218
walk the hospitals, to, 240
walk the ties, to, 147
walk through a fence like a falling tree through cobwebs, 137
walk tiptoe, to, 192
Wall, 516
Wallabout, 532
Wallace, 486, 510
Walla Walla, 537
Waller, 499
wallet, 247
Wall Street broker, 244
walnut, 124
Walter, 507, 510, 511, 515
waltz, 155
waltz, to, 194
wam, 184
wampum, 100, 106
wampum-keeper, 106
wan, 436, 440
wander, 343
wanderlust, 219; -club, 219; -er, 219; -ing, 219
wangle, to, 265
want, 343
wan't, 446
want-ad, 170
war, 344
warant, 406
warden, 242, 243

warder, 243
War Eagle, 537
Warfield, 498
warm, 252
warm(p)th, 439
warm-slaw, 108
Warner, 482
Wärner, 482
war-paint, 106
war-path, 106
Warrah, 524
warrant, 406
Warren, 516, 537
Warsaw, 530
was, 427
Wascott, 538
Wash, 519
wash, 343, 344
wash-basin, 231, 236
wash-bowl, 236
wash-hand-basin, 231
wash-hand-stand, 231, 236
Washington, 515, 517, 519, 529, 537
Washingtonian, 552
washing-up bowl, 234
wash-rag, 236
wash-room, 304
wash-stand, 85, 231, 236
Wasil, 511
wassermann, to, 192, 197
waste-basket, to, 195, 236
waste-paper basket, 236
watch, 343, 344
watch-crystal, 239
watch-glass, 239
water, 343, 344, 349; -closet, 304, 310; -gap, 115; -heater, 236; -pitcher, 85; -shed, 115; wagon, 92
water, to, 228
Watkins Gully, 535
Watt, 553
Wauskakamick, 514
Wave, 522
way, 256, 547
way-bill, 146
way-car, 583
Wayman, 483
Wayne, 510, 512
Wayne Junction, 529
way-station, 238
W.C., 210, 304
we, 447, 455
weakly, 467

weal, 351
weald, 115
wear, to, 436
Weasel, 552
weasle-word, 174
weather, 351, 603; -bu-
reau, 239
Weaver, 485
Weber, 485
Web-feet, 552
wedding-engineer, 289
Weeda, 521
week-end, to, 195
Weems, 503
weep, to, 436, 437
Weigand(t), 499
weight, 237
Weil, 499
Weinberg, 499
weinstube, 219
weir, 248
Weisberg, 502
Weiss, 479, 485
wel, 383, 403
welded, 561
well, 103, 383
wellest, 463
well-heeled, 143
Wellington, 233, 513
well-posted, 143
Wemyss, 503
wen, 351
wench, 305
went, 424, 432, 442
weop, 437
wep, 436, 437
wepte, 437
wer, 401
were, 401, 428
Werkman, 485
Werner, 484
Wes, 511
Weshinawatok, 514
Wesley, 511, 513, 516, 517,
535
Wesley chapel, 210
Wesleyville, 535
West, 529
west, 377
westbound, 247
West End, 247
Westphal, 483
Westphal, 483
wet, 86, 191, 565
wet, to, 436
wether, 403

we-two, 449
we-uns, 450
Weymann, 483
wh, 351
Wham, 504, 536
whang-doodle, 176
whap, 98, 184
whar, 339
what, 335, 343, 452, 454
what-all, 450
whatdyecallem, 564
what'ell, 316
what price, 265
what the hell, 316
wheatena, 173
wheatlet, 173
wheat-pit, 144
wheel, 351
Wheeler, 496
wheel-horse, 148
Wheelingite, 549
Whelp, 552
when, 351
whence, 468
where, 24, 351, 467
Where am I at?, 258
where'bouts, 468
Where did you get that
hat?, 566
Where do you get that
stuff?, 566
whether, 351
Whetstone, 523
which, 452, 454
whichn, 454
which one, 454
while, 119, 351
While-U-Wait, 209
whiskers, 579
whiskey, 393, 394; -and-
soda, 149, 236; -daisy,
149; -sour, 85
White, 485, 489, 493, 495,
499
white-collar, 239
white-face, 584
Whitehand, 493
Whitehill, 502
white-lion, 85
White Mountains, 532
Whiteneck, 479
white-plush, 149
White Sox, 407
White Thunder, 514
Whitetree, 514
white wagon, 556

whitewash, 101
whitewash, to, 118
white-wings, 186
whither, 351, 468
whittle, to, 128
whizz-bang, 573, 579
who, 201, 422, 452, 453,
454, 461, 600
who-all, 450
whole, 600
whole kit and boodle, 109
whole note, 250
whole-souled, 143, 231
whom, 201, 202, 453, 454,
459
whoopee, 560
whooptician, 179
whore, 303, 305, 309, 310,
349
whoredom, 303
whortleberry, 114
whose, 452, 453
whosen, 452, 453
Wichita, 541
wick, 532
wid, 465
wide, 465
Wide Mouth, 537
wie geht's, 157
wiener, 155
wienerwurst, 112, 155
wienie, 155, 186
wierd, 402
wife, 302, 578
wig, 169
wigwam, 100, 105
wijk, 532
wikiwiki, 373
wil, 401, 403
Wilbur, 524
Wilburn, 516
wilcut, 407
Wild, 523
Wildeman, 561
wile, 351
Wilfred, 518
Wilhelm, 505
Wilkes-Barré, 537
will, 25, 199, 200, 201, 420,
445, 519
Will-A., 517
William, 505, 507, 509,
511, 513, 515, 516, 519,
520
Williams, 477
Williamsburg, 529

Willis, 507
Wilson, 477, 498, 520
wilt, to, 98, 128
wimmen, 383, 384
win, 248, 416, 436, 447
win, to, 436, 440
Winar, 488
wind, to, 198
windfall, 101
window-cleaning-engi-
  neer, 290
window-shade, 236
windscreen, 237
windshield, 237
wind up, to, 198
Windy City, 553
wing, 236
wing-ding, 579
wing her, to, 583
Winiarecki, 488
winned, 440
Winnipegger, 549
Winnipiseogee, 540
win out, to, 227
Winston-Salem, 537
Winter, 492
winterize, to, 193
wipe out, to, 578
wireless, 226, 559
wire-puller, 30, 167, 228
Wirt, 480
Wise, 479, 499
wise-crack, 263
wise-cracker, 585
wise-guy, 576
wiseheimer, 219
wisenheimer, 263
wise up, to, 263
wish, 352
wish, to, 436
wished, 436
wisht, 399, 403, 436
wisit, 377
Wistaria, 522
wit, 367
with, 367
wither, 351
without hardly, 470
witness-box, 246
witness-stand, 229, 246
Witt, 502
Wittenacht, 479
Wittkofsky, 502
wize, 402
W J, 517
w.k., 209

wo, 383, 401
wobble, to, 126
wobbly, 188, 190, 191, 581
woe, 383
woik, 367
woke, 435, 442
woken, 435
wold, 115
Wolf, 486, 490
wolf, 582
Wolfgang, 505
Wolfsohn, 498
woman, 303
womanishest, 463
woman of a certain class,
  311
womb, 303
women, 383, 384
women's ice hockey,
  293
women's singles, 293
women's wear, 293
won, 436, 437, 440
wonderful, 464, 465
won't, 377
woodchuck, 105
wooden-house, 234
Woodhouse, 493
Woodrow, 512
Woods, 495
woods, 462
woodscolt, 308
woof, 344
woop-woop, 378
woozy, 568
wop, 45, 295
Worcester, 540
wore, 436
work, 367
workhouse, 243
Workman, 485
World War, 248
worm-fence, 145, 166
Worm moon, 106
worse, 463
worser, 420, 463
worshiper, 388
Wörth, 480
worth-while, 229
woud, 404
would, 25
woulda, 443, 471
would not, 469
wouldn't, 425, 471
would of, 471
would've, 471

Would you for fifty
  cents?, 566
wow, 184, 185, 564, 586
Wowk, 490
wowser, 265, 378
wrang, 436
wrangler, 221, 243
wrapping-engineer, 290
wrassle, 346
wrecketeria, 177
wrecking-crew, 146
wren, 209
wrestle, 346
wring, to, 436
write, to, 436, 613
writing-table, 254
written, 436, 442, 613
wrongd, 402
wrote, 424, 436, 442, 613
wroten, 442
wrung, 436
wust, 109
Wyoming, 526, 532
wytopitlock, 531
x, 404
XLent, 209
x-ray, to, 197, 559
Y, 170
y, 341, 345, 360, 364, 389,
  394, 401, 402, 404, 446,
  469; -y, 467, 548
yabo, 373
yacht, 397
yah, 353
y'all, 363, 449, 450
yam, 113, 246
Yank, 111
yank, to, 99, 111
Yankee, 110, 295
Yankel, 506
Yankelevitch, 498
yarb, 129, 351
yard, 547, 585
yawp, 75
ye, 454
yeah, 353
year, 379
yeare, 379
yearn, 406
yeggman, 263
yellow, 247
yellow-belly, 295, 562
Yellow Dog, 536
Yellow Robe, 514
yen, to, 162, 263
Yengees, 110

yentzer, 578
yep, 229, 353
yerba, 152
Yerma, 516
yern, 406
yes, 353
yes, to, 195
yes-indeedy, 161
yes-man, 563
Yes, we have no bananas, 561
yet, 340
Yetive, 522
yhar, 360
yid, 295, 305
yip, 577
yo, 360
yodel, 157
yok-a-mi, 162
yom kippur, 216
Yonaha, 524
Yonkers, 533; -ite, 549
York, 527; -er, 549
Yorktown, 529
Yosel, 506
yot, 397
you, 447, 450, 451, 454
you-all, 363, 449
you betcha, 258
y'ought, 450
you is, 363, 427
Young, 483, 491
Youngdahl, 491
young-horse, 580

young person, 184
Youngreen, 491
young-un, 309
your, 447, 449
youre, 449
youren, 449
youres, 449
you're telling me, 572
Your Honor, 279
yourn, 447
yours, 449
yous, 447, 451
You said a mouthful, 566
you said it, 561
you-three, 449
you-two, 449
you-uns, 450
you was, 428
you were, 428
Yrgö, 510
Ysobel, 520
yu, 403
Yuhudi, 298
Yukkanatche, 514
yurp, 184
z, 375, 389, 394, 401, 510
Zaba, 488
Zach, 519
Zachariah, 519
Záchod, 487
Zajíc, 487
Zampariello, 493
Zannis, 521
zarape, 152, 153

Zděný, 486
zeal, 384
ZeBarney, 518
zeber, 385
zebra, 385
Zebulon, 515
Zechariah, 515
zed, 352
zee, 352
zeel, 381, 384
Zelény, 486
Zhinchak, 489
zig-zag, 375
Zilpah, 522
Zilvernagel, 485
Zimmermann, 485
Zion, 524
Zirst, 503
zombie, 587
zone, 239
Zooa, 524
zook, 577
Zotas, 522
zounds, 312, 317
zowie, 184, 564
Zulu, 296
Zurhorst, 503
Zwartefoote, 485
zwei, 157
zwei bier, 157
zwieback, 112, 155
zwok, 109
Zymole, 512

INDEX

Aarkawa, S., 88
Aasen, Ivar, 89 n
Abbott, Lyle, 180 n
Abbreviations, 92, 204, 205, 209, 414, 542 n
Abramson, S. H., 551 n, 691 n
Absolon, William, 488 n, 512
Académie Française, 63 n, 89, 192, 572 n
Academy, projects for an American, 7, 49
Acadians, speech of, 638, 639
Accent, 324 ff, 503
Ackerman, Carl W., 172 n
Acta Apostolicæ Sedis, 282 n
Actors, speech of, 267, 331, 340
Adamic, Louis, 489, 667
Adams, Charles Francis, 276 n
Adams, Franklin P., 269
Adams, James Truslow, 124 n, 569 n
Adams, Joe, 490
Adams, John, 7, 49, 108, 119, 132, 147
Adams, John Quincy, 14, 49, 118
Addison, Joseph, 71, 126, 137, 438 n, 455, 472
Ade, George, 72, 257, 424, 560
Adjectives, 119, 143, 203, 459, 463 ff, 601
Adverbs, 253, 464 ff
Advisory Committee on Spoken English, 329
Afrikaans, 622
Agar, Herbert, 44
Ager, Cecelia, 210 n

Agricultural History, 122 n
Ahrend, Evelyn R., 371 n
Aiken, Janet R., 337 n, 405 n, 422 n, 471, 598 n, 605 n, 606 n, 613
Aikman, Duncan, 551 n
Ain't-less Week, 51
Alabama Christian Advocate, 281 n
Alabama, 428 n; given-names in, 522, 523; place-names, 536; speech of, 257, 362
Albany *Evening Journal*, 147 n
Aldington, Richard, 46
Alexander, Caleb, 385
Alexander, Donald M., 407 n
Alexander, Henry, 333 n, 366 n, 367, 416 n, 428 n, 429 n, 435 n
Alford, Henry, 27, 140, 184
Alger, John G., 84
Allard, Harry, 551 n
Alldredge, D. C., 551 n
Allen, Crombie, 604 n
Allen, Frances Anne, 343 n
Allen, Henry Ware, 551 n
Allen, Hervey, 30 n
Allen, W. H., 159
Allsop, Thomas, 28
Allvine, Glendon, 586
Alter, Nicholas M., 496 n, 682 n
Amador, Manuel E., 605 n
Amend, Ottilie, 586 n
Ament, William S., 261 n
American Academy of

Arts and Letters, 63, 66, 67, 331
American Academy of Arts and Sciences, 49
American Academy of Languages and Belles Lettres, 49
American Association for the Study of the Feeble-minded, 175
American Church Monthly, 537 n
American Council of Learned Societies, 55, 58, 59, 483 n
American Dialect Society, 52 ff, 58, 356
American Dictionary of the English Language, Webster's, 9, 134, 135, 151
American difficulties with English, 260, 269 ff
American Hebrew and Jewish Tribune, 298, 602 n
American Journal of Philology, 364 n, 601 n, 617 n, 637 n, 638 n
American-Language Legion, 83
American Law Review, 577 n
American Literature, Sydney Smith on, 13 n; sales of in 1806, 17; rise of, 134 ff
American Literature, 54 n, 261 n
American Literature Group, Modern Language Association, 54 n
American Magazine, 10 n

American Medical Association Style Book, 411 n

American Mercury, 57 n, 77, 88 n, 149 n, 176 n, 183 n, 210 n, 211 n, 218 n, 288 n, 296 n, 323 n, 329 n, 343 n, 350 n, 362 n, 363 n, 369 n, 443 n, 449 n, 463 n, 477 n, 481 n, 488 n, 524 n, 562 n, 577 n, 578 n, 582 n, 584 n, 586 n, 591 n, 594 n, 598 n, 605 n, 610 n, 634 n, 640 n, 643 n, 644 n, 650 n, 651 n, 655 n, 656 n, 662 n, 667 n

American movies and talkies in England, 37 ff, 221, 225, 233

American Museum, 11 n

American National Language Magazine, 83

American Philological Association, 399

American Philological Journal, 52

American Review of History and Politics, 21

American Roumanian News, 494 n, 509 n, 653

American Speech, 10 n, 12 n, 16 n, 29 n, 33 n, 36 n, 42 n, 51 n, 52, 54, 59, 72 n, 75 n, 79 n, 115 n, 137 n, 146 n, 148 n, 150 n, 153 n, 155 n, 157 n, 159 n, 171 n, 172 n, 176, 177, 178 n, 179 n, 180 n, 181 n, 183 n, 185 n, 187 n, 188, 190 n, 193 n, 194 n, 195 n, 196 n, 197 n, 199 n, 203 n, 211, 215 n, 216 n, 218 n, 219 n, 237 n, 239 n, 257 n, 258 n, 261, 263, 272 n, 274 n, 282 n, 287, 292 n, 296 n, 303 n, 305 n, 308, 309 n, 312 n, 313, 320 n, 321, 322 n, 325 n, 327 n, 332 n, 333 n, 334 n, 349 n, 350 n, 352 n, 353 n, 354 n, 359 n, 360 n, 361 n, 362 n, 363 n, 364 n, 365 n, 366 n, 367 n, 369 n, 370 n, 371 n, 372 n, 375 n, 378 n, 405 n, 407 n, 410 n, 416 n, 422 n, 426 n, 430 n, 431 n, 432 n, 441 n, 443 n, 444 n, 446 n, 449 n, 450 n, 453 n, 455 n, 463 n, 464 n, 466 n, 467 n, 478 n, 480 n, 486 n, 488 n, 489 n, 490 n, 495 n, 500 n, 503 n, 505 n, 511 n, 512 n, 514 n, 518 n, 521 n, 522 n, 523 n, 524 n, 525 n, 526 n, 527 n, 530 n, 531 n, 532 n, 537 n, 541 n, 543 n, 546 n, 549 n, 552 n, 553 n, 554 n, 555 n, 556 n, 561 n, 562 n, 568 n, 569 n, 571 n, 572 n, 573 n, 577 n, 579 n, 581 n, 584 n, 585 n, 586 n, 587 n, 588 n, 589 n, 591 n, 596 n, 605 n, 606 n, 607 n, 612 n, 613 n, 618 n, 625 n, 627 n, 636 n, 640 n, 644 n, 655 n, 685 n, 697 n

Americanism, first use of term, 6; definitions of, 62, 97 ff, 332; characters of, 90 ff, 94

Americophil Englishmen, 44 ff

Amerikan Suometar, 676

Ames, Nathaniel, 116

Anbury, Thomas, 110

Anderson, A. H., 627 n, 631 n

Anderson, Maxwell, 265

Anderson, Thomas, 38

Andreen, Gustav, 624

Andrews, Charlton, 325 n

Angel, Anne, 562 n

Anglic, 405

Anglin, Margaret, 331

Anglistische Forschungen, 521 n, 538 n

Anglo-American Trade, 262 n

Anglomania, 20, 28, 50, 64, 67, 68, 95, 131, 164, 264, 265 ff, 331, 349, 387, 391, 414 n, 502

Annual Review, 14, 15

Anti-Jacobin Review, 16 n, 19, 23

Anti-Semitism, 213, 497 n

Appalachia, speech of, 129, 358 ff, 429 n, 431 n, 435 n, 467 n, 470, 519, 521, 523

Arabic language, 593; in America, 683 ff

Arakawa, Sawbay, 591, 692 n

Arbuthnot, John, 431 n

Arcadian Magazine, 370 n

Archaisms, 124 ff, 126, 144, 161, 168, 169, 232, 617

Archer, William, 45

Archiv für das Studium der neueren Sprachen und Literaturen, 86, 555 n, 641 n

Argentina, English in, 590, 604 n

Argot, 556, 575 ff

Arizona place-names, 536, 542, 543

Arkansas, 428 n; place-names in, 533, 535, 536, 537, 538, 541; speech of, 357, 360 n

Arliss, George, 331

Armenian immigrants, 693; language in America, 693; surnames, 495, 496, 497

Armfield, Blanche Britt, 523 n

Armfield, H. T., 129

Armistead, George, 479

Army Medical Corps, 306

Army slang, 573 ff

Aron, Albert W., 620, 621

Article, definite, 161, 251, 279, 600; indefinite, 351

Asbury, Herbert, 478 n, 576 n
Ashkenazim, 502, 506
Ashleigh, Charles, 581 n
Associated Advertising, 170 n
Associated Press, 38, 256 n, 266 n
Association for the Advancement of Colored People, 299
Association of Electragists International, 287
Astor, John Jacob, 206
Atcherley, Mary H., 694
Atherton, H. E., 321 n
Atkins, Morris Fletcher, 551 n
Atlanta *Constitution,* 548
Atlanta *Journal,* 548
Atlantic Monthly, 61, 73, 204, 254, 304, 322 n, 332 n, 340 n, 349 n, 361 n, 363 n, 393, 409, 531 n, 607 n
Atlantica, 641 n
Atlantis, 512, 685, 686
Atlas linguistique de la France, 89 n
Audubon, J. J., 134
Austen, Jane, 431 n
Austin, Mary, 153 n
Australian English, 108, 277, 316, 378 n, 576, 578; spelling, 396
Austro-Hungarian immigrants, 213
Authors' and Printers' Dictionary, 389 ff
Autocar, 259 n
Automobile terms, 236
Avery, Elizabeth, 320 n
Axley, Lowry, 361 n, 449 n
Ayer's Directory of Newspapers and Periodicals, 693 n
Ayres, Harry Morgan, 321, 371, 372
Ayres, Leonard P., 603

Babbitt, E. H., 53, 170 n, 367, 569 n, 590 n
Bache, Richard Meade, 337 n

Back-formation, 92, 111, 168 ff, 183, 191
Baddour, S., 685 n
Baedeker's United States, 86
Baer, Arthur (Bugs), 560
Bailey, John, 34 n
Bailey, Joseph G., 71
Baker, Anna R., 262 n
Baker, Ernest A., 390 n
Balassa, József, 682 n
Baldwin, Joseph G., 72
Baldwin, Stanley, 228
Balfour, Earl of, 32, 33 n, 408
Ballard, Marshall, 541 n, 551 n
Ballard, P. B., 198 n, 322 n, 460 n, 605 n
Baltimore *Evening Sun,* 51 n, 146 n, 149 n, 185 n, 260 n, 288 n, 396 n, 410, 537 n, 560 n, 658 n
Baltimore *Post,* 198 n
Baltimore *Sun,* 485 n
Banche, Henry, 89
Bancroft, Aaron, 15, 386
Bancroft, George, 135
Banking terms, 244
Baptist and Commoner, 338 n, 462 n
Baptists, 280, 309, 462, 467 n, 524
Baradinsky, Herman, 551 n
Barbey, J. E., 551 n
Barde, Alexandre, 639
Bardsley, Charles W., 516 n
Barker, E. O., 214 n
Barker, Howard F., 477, 478, 479, 480, 481 n, 483, 503 n, 518 n, 581 n
Barkley, Dorothy, 588 n
Barlow, Joel, 15, 16
Barnes, Matthew, 412 n
Barnes, Walter, 565 n
Barnes, W. C., 543 n
Barnett, A. G., 378 n
Barr, Robert T., 392 n
Barrère, Albert, 571
Barrows, Sarah T., 344
Barry, Jerome B., 375 n
Barry, Phillips, 177
Bartlett, John H., 195 n

Bartlett, J. R., his glossary, 36, 61, 86, 98, 101, 139, 140, 157 n, 167, 301, 339 n, 430 n, 431 n, 434 n, 435 n, 442, 539 n
Bartosz, Adam, 674
Baruch, Sylvan, 293 n
Baseball terms, 562 n
Basic English, 603 ff
Basshe, Emjo, 518
Baten, Anderson M., 572 n
Batie, Russell V., 584 n
Beath, P. R., 587 n
Beck, N. B., 373 n, 695 n
Beck, T. Romeyn, 35 n
Beckman, Robert, 625 n, 626, 627 n
Bede, the Venerable, 29
Beecher, Henry Ward, 140
Beirne, Francis E., 183 n
Belfast Printing Trades Employers' Association, 389
Belgion, Montgomery, 263 n
Bell System Technical Journal, 200 n
Bellamann, Henry, 173 n
Belloc, Hilaire, 322, 343
Benchley, Robert, 305 n
Bencze, John, 682 n
Bendall, F. W. D., 39
Bennett, Arnold, 257
Bennett, James O'Donnell, 406 n
Bennett, John, 113 n
Bense, J. F., 111 n
Bentham, Jeremy, 21, 119, 223
Bentley, Harold W., 153 n, 534, 651 n
Berg, Ruben G:son, 624 n
Berger, V., 530 n, 624 n
Bergman, B. A., 442 n
Bergmann, Karl, 574 n
Bergström, G. A., 172 n
Bernstein, Herbert B., 449 n, 588 n
Better-Speech Week, 51
Betts, E. A., 424 n
Bevans, C. A., 322 n
Beverley, Robert, 115
Bevier, Thyra Jane, 444 n
Beyer, H. Otley, 375 n

Bible, 42 n, 106, 127, 202 n, 303, 308 n, 398 n, 429 n, 436, 448, 465, 515, 535, 572, 601
Bible Belt, 309, 522
Biblical names, 515
Bicknell, Frank M., 256
Bierce, Ambrose, 67, 556 n
Billboard, 366 n
Birmingham (Eng.) *Gazette*, 230 n
Birss, John Howard, 553 n
Bishop, W. W., 574 n
Bissell, Clifford H., 391 n
Bjarnason, J. M., 633
Black, Harry C., 552 n, 560 n
Blackshirt, 38 n
Blackwood's Magazine, 18 n, 23
Blaine, James G., 107
Blair, Hugh, 97 n
Blanco, Enrique, 613
Blandford, F. G., 332
Blanton, Thomas L., 462 n
Blashfield, Mrs. E. H., 63
Blauvelt, Hiram D., 569 n
Blends, 171, 173, 317, 537
Blinn, Holbrook, 331
Bliven, Bruce, 257
Bloch, Israel, 551 n
Bloom, Margaret, 370 n
Bloomfield, Leonard, 58 n, 310
Blum, August, 619 n
Blumenfeld, D. L., 262 n
Blumenfeld, R. D., 31
Boas, Louis A., 549 n
Boas, F. S., 34 n
Boggs, Ralph S., 327 n
Bohannon, James A., 208
Bolgar, E. H., 682 n
Bolingbroke, Henry, 126
Bonaparte, L.-L., 320
Bone, James, 294 n
Bontz, Mable E., 551 n
Book of Common Prayer, 204
Bookman, 31, 40, 77 n, 173 n, 584 n, 586 n
Books, sales of in America, 17–19
Boot, H. E., 202 n

Booth, Alfred C., 551 n
Booth, Ernest, 577 n, 578, 579
Borchard, D., 86
Bosson, Olaf E., 575 n
Boston area, speech of, 333, 334, 335 ff, 344, 349, 601; surnames in, 477, 478
Boston *Atlas*, 205
Boston Brahmins, 131, 139
Boston *Evening Globe*, 499 n
Boston *Herald*, 554
Boston *Journal*, 186 n
Boston *Transcript*, 205
Boston *Traveler*, 187 n
Boston University, 401
Botkin, B. A., 361 n
Boucher, Jonathan, 34, 35 n, 120, 169, 313, 324 n, 354
Boulenger, Marcel, 149 n
Boulevardier, 226 n
Bowen, Ray P., 87
Bowker, R. R., 171 n
Bowman, LeRoy E., 588 n
Boxing argot, 562
Boy Scouts, 231
Boyd, Ernest, 41, 77, 78, 504, 513 n, 560 n
Boyd, Stephen G., 527 n
Boynton, H. W., 31
Bozart, 411
Brackbill, Hervey, 588 n
Bradley, Helen Merrill, 550 n
Bradley, Henry, 46 n, 272, 390, 400, 408, 448 n, 556, 559 n, 563
Brailsford, H. N., 40, 45
Brain Trust, 291, 305
Braley, Berton, 259 n
Branco, A. S., 652 n
Bratter, C. A., 87
Brauer, Dora Lee, 172 n
Brazil, Portuguese in, 653
Bready, M. McIlvaine, 175
Brevoort, Henry, 17
Bridges, Robert, 32 n, 46, 328, 329, 349, 390, 405, 408
Brighouse, Harold, 228, 229 n

Bright, James W., 32 n, 53 n
Brisbane, Arthur, 175
Bristed, C. A., 69 ff, 79, 140, 158
Briticisms in the United States, 202, 264 ff
British Academy, 329
British Board of Trade, 391
British Broadcasting Corporation, 48, 529
British Critic, 14, 15, 119
Broadway Journal, 552
Broadway slang, 560 ff
Broderick, Henry, 551 n
Brodhead, L. W., 538 n
Brody, Alter, 369 n
Bronson, L. K., 551 n
Brooke, Rupert, 258
Brooklyn, surnames in, 478 n
Brooks, Cleanth, Jr., 362, 363 n
Brooks, J. G., 20 n, 302 n
Brophy, John, 314, 519 n, 574 n
Brown, Bertram H., 363 n, 449 n
Brown, C. B., 17
Brown, Frederick W., 591 n, 692 n
Brown, George William, 593 n
Brown, Irving, 490 n
Browne, C. F. (Artemus Ward), 71, 224, 429 n, 430 n, 434 n, 442
Browne, Thomas, 140 n
Brownell, W. C., 63 n
Bryant, W. C., 17, 120, 134, 135, 138, 184, 280, 342 n, 386
Brythonic Celtic, 682
Buchwald, Nathaniel, 636 n
Buck, Gene, 560
Buckner, Mary Dale, 587 n
Buffalo, Poles in, 675
Bug, Joshua, 310 n
Bulgarian surnames, 489
Bulletin of the University of Arizona, 648 n
Bulletin of the University

of South Carolina, 113 n, 363 n

Bulwer-Lytton, Edward, 225

Burgess, Gelett, 173 n, 560

Burham, Josephine M., 178 n, 179 n

Burke, Edmund, 459, 558

Burnham, Josephine M., 370 n

Burns, E. L. M., 551 n, 637 n

Burr, Aaron, 130, 148

Burton, Richard, 77, 169 n, 303

Burwell, M. A., 370 n

Butcher, Jesse S., 332 n

Butler, Joseph, 465

Butler, Kate L., 174

Butler, Mrs. Nicholas Murray, 207 n

Butte (Mont.) *Standard*, 208 n

Buxbaum, Katherine, 370 n, 521, 522

Byington, Steven T., 172 n, 183 n

Byrantios, D. K., 685

Byron, Arthur, 331

Byron, Lord, 17

B.-Z. am Mittag, 483 n

Cable, George W., 639

Cahan, Abraham, 498 n, 506, 635 n, 636

Cain, James M., 264 323 n

Cairns, W. B., 14 ff, 16 n, 17, 18 n, 19, 23

California, 576; place-names in, 534, 535, 536, 542

Callahan, Patrick H., 273 n, 551 n

Callender, Harold, 599 n

Callender, N. R., 551 n

Cambridge History of American Literature, 20 n, 71, 114 n, 126 n, 220 n, 224 n, 636 n, 639 n; of English Literature, 391, 413

Cambridge, R. O., 4

Campbell, George, 50 n, 97 n

Campbell, John C., 361 n

Campbell, J. L., 682

Campbell, Mrs. Patrick, 311

Campbell - Bannerman, Henry, 183 n

Campora, Vincenzo, 642

Camps, names of, 546

Canada, English in, 277, 338, 396, 609; French, 544 n, 636 ff; Gaelic, 682; spelling, 396

Canadian Geographical Society, 396

Canadian Historical Association, 396

Canadian Journal, 371 n

Canal Zone, speech of, 548, 649

Canby, H. S., 34 n, 46 n

Canning, George, 120

Canonge, Placide, 639

Çant, 556, 575 ff

Capek, Thomas, 295 n

Capitalization, 413 ff

Capone, Al, 494

Carlisle Indian School, 513

Carlsmith, Carl S., 695 n

Carlson, Gabriel, 626

Carlyle, Thomas, 178, 322 n

Carnegie, Andrew, 400

Carnegie Corporation, 55 n, 58, 421 n

Carnegie Foundation for the Advancement of Teaching, 421 n

Carnival argot, 584

Carpenter, Charles, 361 n, 584 n

Carpenter, William H., 109 n

Carr, H. J., 205

Carr, J. W., 53, 360 n

Carroll, Lewis, 171

Carroll, T. W., 316 n

Carroll of Carrollton, Charles, 504

Carruthers, C. H., 58 n

Carter, C. W., 200 n

Carter, Virginia, 569 n

Cassell's New English Dictionary, 390, 391, 408

Cate, Garth, 180 n

Catholic World, 406 n

Cautela, Guiseppe, 494 n, 644 n

Cellini, Benvenuto, 296 n

Central Conference of American Rabbis, 499

Century, 361 n

Century Dictionary, 151

Čermak, Anton J., 658

Česko-Ameriký Kalendář, 511 n

Chadbourn, Charles N., 285

Chamberlain, A. F., 638 n

Chang Shih-chao, 690

Chao Yüan-jên, 691

Chapin, Sylva, 637

Chapman, Maristan, 360, 361

Charters, W. W., 418, 419, 421, 425, 445, 447, 455, 458, 460, 463, 465, 468

Chaucer, Geoffrey, 128, 232, 296 n, 436, 465, 469, 608

Chautauqua, 221; argot of, 585 n

Cheke, John, 379, 397

Cherry, Donald L., 538 n, 551 n

Chesebrough, Robert A., 172 n

Chester, Joseph L., 366

Chesterfield, Lord, 413

Chesterton, Cecil, 43

Chesterton, G. K., 185, 254, 256, 563

Chicago *Daily News*, 587 n

Chicago *Evening Post*, 620

Chicago *Herald and Examiner*, 192 n, 562 n

Chicago *Inter-Ocean*, 186, 562 n

Chicago *Radio Weekly*, 332

Chicago *Record-Herald*, 562 n

Chicago, surnames in, 477

Chicago *Tribune*, 84, 263, 288, 406, 414, 620

Child, Francis J., 53, 399

Chin, A. Kaiming, 691 n

China Critic, 691 n

China, English in, 590, 597, 598
Chinese Christian Student, 513, 691 n
Chinese given-names, 513; immigrants, 691; language, 591; in America, 688 ff; loan-words from, 162, 373, 574
Chinook language, 150
Chitimacha language, 417 n
Chopin, Kate, 639
Christian Disciple, 140
Christian Index, 281 n
Christian Science Monitor, 377, 518 n
Christian World, 571
Churchill, William, 372 n
Ciarlantini, Franco, 641 n
Cincinnati *Enquirer*, 208 n
Cincinnati, surnames in, 477
Cincinnati *Volksblatt*, 620
Cinema, 262 n
Cinematograph Films Act (English), 37 n, 38 n
Circus argot, 584
Citizens, names applied to, 548 ff
Civil War, 67, 72, 111, 164 ff, 212, 274, 287 n, 346, 502, 576
Clapin, Sylva, 106 n, 111 n
Clark, C. H. (Max Adeler), 224
Clark College, 401
Clark, E. L., 551 n
Clark, G. N., 111 n
Clark, John Spencer, 76 n
Clark, J. W., 587 n
Clarke, Hewson, 575
Clarke, R. M., Jr., 569 n
Clarke, W. E. C., 378 n
Clarke, Tom, 277 n
Classical Journal, 412 n
Claxton, P. P., 296 n
Clemenceau, Georges, 597
Clemens, S. L. (Mark Twain), 13, 54 n, 67, 71, 72, 137, 167, 168, 224, 251, 327, 351 n,

411 n, 424, 429 n, 430 n, 442, 446 n, 447, 561 n, 567, 602 n, 614
Cleveland *Plain Dealer*, 205 n
Climate, effects of, 323
Clipped words, 168 ff, 183
Clive, C. J., 240
Clough, Wilson O., 551 n, 589 n
Coates, Foster, 315
Cobb, Collier, 364 n
Cobb, Lyman, 60, 336, 385, 386, 387
Cockney English, 270, 327, 337, 352, 417, 426, 578
Coelho, Arthur R., 216 n, 653 n
Coffin, Harold, 691 n
Cohan, George M., 111
Coit, J. Milnor, 268
Coke, Edward, 450
Colburn, Dorothy, 588 n
Colby, Elbridge, 573 n
Colby, Frank Moore, 196 n
Cole, Hilda, 587 n
Coleridge, S. T., 28, 165, 223, 431 n, 472
College Entrance Examination Board, 455 n
College slang, 170, 559, 568 ff
Collier's, 577 n
Collins, F. Howard, 389 n
Collinson, W. E., 232, 426 n, 574 n
Collitz, Hermann, 531 n
Collitz, Klara H., 171 n, 464 n
Colonialism, 164
Colorado place-names, 537, 539, 542
Columbia, 322 n
Columbia Broadcasting System, 332
Columbia University, 446
Columbus, 642 n
Columbus (Ga.) *Ledger*, 300
Combs, Josiah, 53, 332, 358, 435 n, 467 n, 470, 519
Comfort, Anne W., 589 n

Comic-strip, influence of, 184
Common speech, American, 416 ff
Commonweal, 195 n, 283 n, 288 n, 491 n
Commonwealth Fund, 34 n
Compendions Dictionary of the English Language, Webster's, 9 n
Compounds, 114, 115, 144, 186
Compton, Nellie Jane, 588 n
Comstock Postal Act, 304
Conant, Louise, 218 n
Concise Oxford Dictionary, 123 n, 222, 224, 230, 231, 251, 253, 263, 325, 388, 389, 390, 391, 409
Condon, E. A., 426 n
Coneys, J. A., 551 n
Congo French, 639
Congrés de la Langue Française au Canada, 638 n
Congress, Continental, 4, 5, 8, 79
Congress, debates in, 139, 141, 201, 294, 300
Congressional Globe, 139, 518
Congressional Record, 142 n, 143, 194 n, 195 n, 198, 203, 203 n, 204 n, 210 n, 213 n, 275 n, 279, 291, 407, 410, 460 n, 462 n, 470, 481 n
Congreve, William, 431 n
Conkle, E. P., 584 n
Connecticut, 434 n; place-names, 530 n, 540; speech of, 368
Connecticut Code of 1650, 121 n
Conrad, Joseph, 455 n, 489
Conrad, Mrs. Joseph, 260
Consonants in American, 348 ff
Constantine, Arthur, 650 n
Contemporary Review, 188

Converse, Charles Crozat, 460 n
Conway, Jack, 560
Conway, Kerry, 331
Cooke, Alistair, 48, 232, 255
Coolidge, Calvin, 183 n
Coolidge, Grace, 407 n
Cooper, J. F., 16, 17, 21, 67, 68, 134, 135, 138, 330, 355, 369
Copland, Robert, 575
Cornell, Robert H., 170 n
Corry, Harry, 551 n
Costa, J. Da Providéncia, 595 n
Couleer, E. Merton, 140 n
Council of English, 33
Counter-words, 210
Cournos, John, 606
Cox, Harold, 608 n
Coxe, A. Cleveland, 121 n, 223, 387
Craigie, W. A., 34 n, 55 ff, 127 n, 129, 151, 219, 223, 228 n, 358 n
Crane, W. W., 544
Crawford, Nelson Antrim, 304 n
Creegan, J. S., 551 n
Creighton, Robert E., 562 n
Creole French, 638, 639
Crespigny, Claude de, 607
Criminal argot and cant, 556, 576 ff
Critical Review, 14
Croatian immigrants, 667
Crocker, Lionel, 591 n
Crockett, David, 187, 568
Croessmann, Harley K., 177, 346 n, 551 n, 573 n
Crofton, H. T., 696 n
Croker, J. W., 455 n
Croucher, E. J., 588 n
Crowley, Leo T., 276 n
Crowninshield, Gerald, 367 n
Cuba, Spanish in, 650
Cummins, John William, 551 n
Cunningham, Vincent, 283 n
Curculakis, T. D., 486 n, 512 n, 687 n

Curme, George O., 319 n, 422 n, 432 n, 461, 471
Curtiss, William H., 173 n
Cushing Company, J. S., 392
Custer, George A., 480
Cyrillic alphabet, 489
Czech given-names, 511; immigrants, 659; language in America, 655 ff; loan-words from, 216; surnames, 477, 486 ff
Czecho-Slovak Student Life, 216 n, 295 n, 448 n, 655 n

Dabney, Virginius, 551 n
Daggett, Windsor P., 366 n
Dai Nippon Hogen Chidzu, 89 n
Daily Svornost, 659 n
d'Amboise, Georges, 572 n
Dana, Charles A., 184
Dana, R. H., Jr., 156, 312, 566
Daniel, Samuel, 614
Daniels, Thomas, 205
Danish immigrants, 628; language, 600, 601; in America, 627 ff; surnames, 477, 492
d'Annunzio, Gabriele, 601
Dano-Norwegian language, 627 ff
Darbinian, R., 497 n, 693
D'Arcy, William C., 170 n
Darwin, Charles, 399
Daudet, Alphonse, 76
Dauncey, Enid C., 210 n
Dauzet, Albert, 574 n
Davenport-ffoulkes, Trevor, 504 n
Davidson, Eugene, 551 n
Davidson, George, 530 n
Davidson, L. J., 587 n, 589 n
Davies, Constance, 333 n
Davis, A. K., Jr., 365 n
Davis, Chester C., 276 n
Davis, Elmer, 288 n
Davis, Elrick B., 36 n, 573 n

Davis, H. L., 150 n, 522 n
Davis, Phillip, 178 n
Davy, Humphrey, 390 n
Dayton, O., Daily News, 146 n, 275 n
Dealey, James Q., 551 n
Dearborn Independent, 221 n
Decatur (Ill.) Review, 260
Dechelette, François, 574 n
Declaration of Independence, 5, 413
de Courmont, Felix, 639
Dedham Records, 379
de Filleneufve, Le Blanc, 639
Defoe, Daniel, 71, 472
deFord, Miriam Allen, 542 n, 546 n, 552 n
de Gourmont, Rémy, 640
Deiler, J. Hanno, 487 n
de Kruif, Paul, 485 n, 624 n
de La Grasserie, Raoul, 557 n
Delaney, Frank, 276 n
Delano, Frederic A., 276 n
Delaware place-names, 537, 538; speech of, 357
Delineator, 410 n, 569 n
Delmarva, 538
Delta Kappa Epislon Quarterly, 569 n
Democratic Review, 387 n
de Montigny, Louvigny, 495 n, 637, 638 n
Denby Herald, 39 n
Denmark, English in, 590, 594
Dennis, C. T., 609 n
Denver Rocky Mountain News, 450 n, 553 n
Department of Commerce, 262
DeQuincey, Thomas, 472
Derby, George H., 71
de Roquigny, Jacques, 639
Derrick, Paul E., 262 n
Dessewffy, A., 682 n
Detroit Jewish Chronicle, 480 n
Deutsche Grammophon Gesellschaft, 320

Dewey, Godfrey, 406
Dewey, John, 95
Dewey, Melvil, 196 n
Dialect Notes, 3 n, 12 n, 20 n, 29 n, 35 n, 36 n, 52, 53, 54, 55 n, 59, 109 n, 110 n, 145 n, 153 n, 159 n, 170 n, 173 n, 176 n, 180 n, 185 n, 187 n, 204 n, 209 n, 214 n, 217 n, 219 n, 222 n, 267, 295 n, 302 n, 303 n, 309 n, 313 n, 318 n, 336 n, 350 n, 352 n, 354 n, 356, 358 n, 359 n, 360 n, 361 n, 362 n, 363 n, 364 n, 366 n, 367 n, 370 n, 371 n, 407 n, 429 n, 430 n, 432 n, 434 n, 435 n, 462 n, 464 n, 467 n, 470 n, 495 n, 569 n, 577 n, 581 n, 584 n, 588 n, 619 n, 621 n, 627 n, 629 n, 631 n, 638 n
Dialects, American, 90, 416
Dickens, Charles, 71, 223, 252, 271, 361, 417, 431 n, 561 n, 575 n
Dickinson, Lowes, 227
Dictionaries of Americanisms, 34 ff, 97 ff
Dictionary of American Biography, 29, 40
Dictionary of American English on Historical Principles, 55 ff, 102, 167
Dillon, Philip, R., 330
Dilnot, Frank, 45
Dilnot, George, 576 n
Diminutives, 519
Dionne, N. E., 637
Disparagement, terms of, 187
Disraeli, Benjamin, 225, 460
Dobbins, T. J., 172 n
Dobson, Austin, 408
Dodge, David B., 316, 414 n
Dodson, Edwin C., 418 n
Doe, Jane, 502 n
Domizio, Carlo di, 85 n

Dondore, Dorothy, 137 n
Donlevy's Irish Catechism, 161 n
Doolittle, James, 551 n
Dorf, A. Th., 86 n
Dorgan, T. A., 186 n, 560, 561
Dorrance, W. A., 640 n
Dothan (Ala.) *Eagle*, 548
Downing, Mortimer, 190
Doyle, Arthur Conan, 257
Doyle, Jack, 561 n
Drachmann, Holger, 601
Drennan, C. M., 378 n
Dresen, M. H., 180 n
Drinking terms, 149, 243, 568
Drinkwater, John, 271
Dryden, John, 126
Dudek, J. B., 216 n, 295 n, 487, 488, 511, 512, 551 n, 655, 657, 659
Dugué, Oscar, 639
Duke, Alba W., 449 n
Dumont-Wilden, M., 548
Dunglison, Robley, 35, 36 n
Dunlap, Fayette, 495 n
Dunlap, Maurice P., 376 n
Dunlap, William, 10 n
Dunn, Jacob P., 548 n
Dunne, F. P., 96
Durham (N. C.) *Sun*, 300
Dutch immigrants, 623; language in America, 621 ff; loan-words from, 108 ff, 532, 637; place-names, 532, 547; surnames, 477, 479, 481, 485, 487 n
Dutch philologians on American, 87
Dwight, Thomas, 22
Dwight, Timothy, 21, 68, 354
Dykstra, B. D., 623 n
Dyson, Verne, 690 n

Eames, Hamilton, 262 n, 263 n
Earthquake, Billy, 136
East and West, 633 n
East Midland dialect, 608

Easthampton Records, 434 n
Eastman, George, 172 n
Ecclesiastical Review, 589 n
Ecclesiastical terms, 140, 150, 248, 273, 279
Ecker-Rácz, L. Lázzló, 496
Eclectic Review, 14, 16 n
Eden, Anthony, 183 n
Edgerton, William B., 362 n
Edilbach, Gerold, 575
Edinburgh Master Printers' Association, 389
Edinburgh Review, 13 n, 14, 15, 16, 16 n, 126 n, 165
Edinburgh *Scotsman*, 682 n
Editor and Publisher, 169 n, 288 n
Edmont, E., 89 n
Educator-Journal, 418 n
Egan, Pierce, 562 n, 575
Eggleston, Edward, 370 n
Ehrensperger, Edward C., 282 n
Eichenauer, Charles F., 551 n
Einarsson, Stefán, 631, 632
Electric Congress, 559
Elementary English Review, 424 n
Elementary School Journal, 426 n
Eliot, John, 105, 106
Eliot, Thomas Dawes, 292
Elliott, A. Marshall, 53 n, 637, 638 n
Elliott, John, 385
Ellis, Alexander J., 320, 333 n, 398, 455 n
Ellis, Havelock, 296 n
Elwin, A. L., his glossary, 36, 99
Embalmers' Monthly, 287
Emerson, O. F., 53, 367 n, 455 n
Emerson, R. W., 135, 138, 556 n
Emerson College, 401
Encyclopaedia Britan-

nica, 43, 158, 556 n, 559 n, 659 n

Engineering News-Record, 289

England, George A., 366 n, 371 n

English, 94 n, 155 n, 202 n, 211 n, 254, 311 n, 355, 390 n, 460 n, 597 n, 606 n

English as a world language, 590 ff

English Association, 329

English Dialect Dictionary, 166 n, 363

English difficulties with American, 256 ff

English Journal, 52, 56, 63 n, 66, 169 n, 200 n, 332 n, 423 n, 432 n, 433 n, 447 n, 521 n, 591 n

English opposition to Americanisms, 3 ff, 12 ff, 165, 268, 388

English place-names, 535 n, 540 n

English Place-Name Society, 527 n

English Review, 47

English slang, 567, 568, 574 n, 576

English Studies, 309 n

English travelers in America, 23 ff

Englishe Studien, 362 n

Entzler, Beverly, 525 n

Ernst, C. W., 56 n

Erskine, John, 322

Ervine, St. John, 251, 269, 270, 348 n, 353, 455 n

Esnault, Gaston, 574 n

Esperanto, 605, 606, 607

Espinosa, Aurelio M., 89 n, 647, 648, 650 n

Essex place-names in New England, 129

Estienne, Henri, 572 n

Estonia, English in, 590, 594

Etheredge, George, 455

Ethridge, George B., 460

Étude, 190 n

Euphemisms, 127, 251, 284 ff, 316

European Magazine & London Review, 14, 16 n, 23, 224

Evans, Lewis, 4

Evans, Mary S., 371 n

Evans, Medford, 362 n

Evelyn, John, 431 n

Everett, Edward, 21, 67, 80, 135

Everett, William, 107

Everyman, 582 n

Ewen, C. L'Estrange, 501, 502 n, 518 n

Expletives, 311 ff, 316

Fairfield, Edmund Burke, 480

Fairweather, John, 190 n

Far East, English in, 591, 597, 609, 611

Farley, James A., 275

Farm Journal, 193

Farmer, J. S., 36, 99, 101, 157 n, 204, 224, 294 n, 295 n, 314, 539 n, 570

Farrand, M. L., 569 n

Farrar, F. W., 426

Faulkner, W. G., 37

Faust, A. B., 480 n, 483 n

Fay, E. Stewart, 545

Feather, William, 261

Fechner, Robert, 276 n

Federal Reserve Act, 266

Feeger, L. M., 551 n

Feipel, Louis, 352 n, 531

Ferguson, Katherine, 550 n

Ferguson, Miriam, 284 n

Ferrazzano, Carlo, 641

Fessenden, T. G., 431 n

Field, Eugene, 260 n

Fields, Raymond, 551 n

Figaro Hebdomadaire, 149 n

Film Fun, 188 n

Film records of pronunciation, 321

Final-G Week, 51

Finerty, James J., 577 n

Finglish, 676 ff

Finland, English in, 594

Finley, John H., 290

Finley, Ruth E., 303 n

Finnish given-names, 510; immigrants, 675; language in America, 675; surnames, 492

First Catholic Slovak Union, 661

Fishberg, Maurice, 497 n

Fischer, W., 449 n

Fischer, Walther, 86, 641 n

Fishbein, Morris, 196 n, 197 n, 307, 443 n, 500

Fisher, Bud, 169 n

Fisher, Sydney George, 125 n

Fiske, John, 75, 76

Fithian, Philip Vickers, 365 n

Fitzgerald, H. A., 486 n

Fitzgerald, J. A., 426 n

Flaten, Nils, 627, 629, 630

Flemish language, 622

Flesch, H., 501

Fletcher, John, 454

Fleur de Lis, 649 n

Flint, James, 301

Flom, George T., 53, 492 n, 627, 628, 629, 630

Flügel, Felix, 86

Flynt, Josiah, 188

Folk etymology, 105

Folk-Say, 588 n

Follin, Maynard D., 618 n

Foote, William J., 517 n

Forbes, John D., 206 n

Forbes-Robertson, Johnston, 329

Ford, Michael A., 271 n

Foreign observers, 85 ff

Foreign Quarterly, 28

Foreign-born in America, 212

Fortier, Edward J., 639 n

Forum, 175, 223 n

Fosdick, H. E., 30

Foster, J. A. B., 265 n

Foster, R. F., 158

Fountain, J. H., 583 n

Fowler, H. W., 47 n, 197, 200, 202 n, 203, 204, 210, 263, 282, 342, 394 n, 431 n

Fowler, H. W. and F. G., 33 n, 42, 200, 224, 263, 388, 394 n, 455 n, 459, 460, 470 n

Fowler, Kenneth A., 549 n

Fowler, W. C., 60, 98, 139, 140
Fox, Charles Edwin, 197 n
Fox, Charles James, 348
Fox, John W., 358 n
France, Anatole, 601
Francis, Alexander, 94 n
Francis, J. Dwight, 238 n
Franklin, Benjamin, 4 n, 7, 11, 112, 117, 120, 124, 125, 126, 131, 335, 340, 380, 381, 383, 397, 398
Fraser, Edward, 574 n
Fraser, John Foster, 47, 48
Frazier, W. L., 551 n
Freeman, 368 n
Freeman, Edward A., 274
Freeman, Merrill P., 530 n
Freeman, Pearl, 226 n
French-Canadian immigrants, 476
French language, 590, 591, 593, 594, 595, 596, 597 n, 601, 602 n; in America, 63 n, 636 ff; in Canada, 599; loan-words from, 108, 151, 214, 382, 384, 395, 412, 572; place-names, 533, 535, 536, 539, 542, 543, 547; slang, 574 n; surnames, 479, 481, 495
French, N. R., 200 n
Frey, Carroll H., 569 n
Fries, C. C., 201 n
Frisbie, W. A., 286 n
Frith, Walter, 257
Frost, Robert, 75
Fuller, Torrey, 551 n
Fullerton, Hugh, 562 n
Funk, W. J., 560
Furdek, 661
Furnivall, F. I., 400
Furst, Hubert, 226 n
Fwnetik Orthqgrafi, 404

Gable, J. Harris, 586 n
Gaelic, influence of, 161, 451 n; language in America, 682, 683; surnames, 504 n
Gaelic-speaking immigrants, 682
Gaffney, Wilbur, 461 n

Galsworthy, John, 257, 259, 260
Galt, John, 206 n
Gandhi, Mahatma, 593 n
Garay, Narcisco, 649 n
Garland, Hamlin, 67 n, 151 n
Garrick, David, 340
Gayerré, Charles E. A., 640
Geddes, James Jr., 638 n
Geeza, Vladimir, 490 n, 511 n, 667 n
Geikie, A. S., 371 n
Geller, David, 218 n
General Education Board, 56, 58
Genthe, Arnold, 555 n
Gentleman's Magazine, 14, 18
Geographic Board of Canada, 533 n
George I, 343
George, W. L., 255, 288
Georgia, 429 n, 430 n
Georgia place-names, 536; speech of, 3, 257, 362, 363 n
Gepp, Edward, 129, 366
Gerard, W. R., 106 n
German gipsies in Pennsylvania, 696
German given-names, 505; immigrants, 213, 214, 476, 616, 619; language, 590, 592, 593, 594, 595, 596, 597 n, 600, 601, 602 n, 614; in America, 616 ff, 653; loan-words from, 109, 146, 154, 158, 176, 217, 370, 575, 578, 637; place-names, 543; slang, 574 n; surnames, 477, 479, 480, 482 ff
German philologians on American, 85 ff
German-American Annals, 370 n, 487 n
Germany, English in, 590
Gibbons, John, 574 n
Gibbs, Henry J., 38 n
Giddings, Franklin H., 175
Gideon Society, 196 n
Gifford, William, 19, 79

Gilbert, W. S., 141 n, 316
Gill, Alexander, 3
Gillette, J. M., 426 n
Gillieron, J., 89 n
Gipsies, 489, 575
Gipsy language, 696
Given-names, 505 ff
Givens, Charles G., 577 n
G. K.'s *Weekly*, 185 n
Gladstone, W. E., 183 n, 208, 223
Glasgow (Scotland) *Record*, 296 n
Glass, Montague, 369 n
Gleason, James, 263, 560
Glossaries of Americanisms, 34 ff, 97 ff, 262
Goddard, Harold, 254 n
Goddard, Henry H., 174
Godwin, Murray, 78
Goethe, J. W., 601
Goffin, R. C., 378 n, 450 n, 597
Goidelic Celtic, 682
Goldberg, Isaac, 179 n
Goldberg, Rube, 560
Golding-Bird, Cyril, 226 n
Goldsmith, Oliver, 71
Goldstein, Fanny, 499 n
Goldstrom, John, 627 n
Golf argot, 562
Gollancz, Israel, 34 n
Gonzalez, Ambrose E., 113 n, 363 n
Goodmane, W. F., 302
Goodrich, Chauncey A., 411 n
Goodspeed, Edgar J., 42 n
Gordon, George, 127 n
Gordon, William, 107
Gosse, Edmund, 408
Gould, E. S., 27 n, 121, 164, 165, 203, 204, 280, 342, 387
Government Printing Office, 393, 400
Gower, John, 128
Grafton, Samuel, 551 n
Graham, William, 32
Grammar, vulgar American, 416 ff
Grammar-books, 319
Grandgent, C. H., 32 n, 53, 58 n, 161, 336, 337, 350 n, 366, 400

Grand Rapids (Mich.) *Evening Express,* 218 n

Graves, Robert, 314

Greek immigrants, 688; language, 79; in America, 685 ff; loan-words from, 382, 411, 412; surnames, 485

Greeley, Horace, 387, 412

Green, B. W., 365 n, 503 n

Greene, Robert, 454

Greenough, J. B., 309 n

Greet, W. C., 54, 320 n, 321, 361, 362, 363, 364, 365 n

Gregg, Darrell L., 321 n

Greig, J. Y. T., 43, 46 n, 66 n, 94 n, 186 n, 231, 328, 330, 453 n, 610

Grieg, Edvard, 478

Grigaitis, Pius, 673 n

Grigson, Geoffrey, 43

Grimm, Jakob, 599

Griswold, Rufus Wilmot, 136

Grose, Francis, 562 n, 567, 575

Gross, Milt, 369 n, 560

Groton School, 268, 279, 520 n

Grover, John S., 196 n

Grumbine, Lee L., 370 n

Gumbo, French, 639

Guiler, W. S., 424 n

Gullah dialect, 113

Gustafson, Walter, 627 n

Hackett, Roger C., 265 n

Hagan, J. Foster, 286

Haines, Henry H., 525 n

Haines, Mahlon N., 551 n

Hairenik, 497 n, 693

Hakluyt's Voyages, 112

Haldeman, S. S., 399, 483 n, 617 n

Hale, Edward E., 153 n, 532 n

Hale, Sarah Josepha, 303

Haliburton, Thomas C., 71, 140, 301, 429 n

Hall, Basil, 25, 27

Hall, B. H., 569 n

Hall, Fitzedward, 61, 166, 168 n, 472

Hall, Henry, 230

Hall, Joseph, 281

Hall, Julian, 548 n, 551 n

Hall, Prescott E., 124, 154 n

Halliwell-Phillips, J. O., 36, 128

Halpine, Charles G., 71

Hamilton, Alexander, 119, 130, 131 n

Hamilton, Dr. Alexander, 274, 313

Hamilton, Marian, 588 n

Hamilton, Thomas, 18, 23, 24, 27

Hammond, J. L., 30

Hampden, Walter, 331

Handbook of Simplified Spelling, 401

Hanemann, H. W., 306 n, 587

Hanes, Mrs. F. M., 550 n

Haney, John L., 325 n

Hanley, Miles L., 58, 336 n, 379 n, 500 n, 552 n

Hansen, Marcus L., 58 n

Hanson, Charles L., 272 n

Hanson, Frank, 623 n

Hanson, Harry, 260

Hapgood, Norman, 276 n

Harap, Henry, 423 n, 432 n, 433 n, 447 n

Harbaugh, Heinrich, 617, 618

Harberton, Viscount, 407 n

Harding, Warren Gamaliel, 203

Hardy, Thomas, 408

Harper, Francis, 364 n

Harper, Robert S., 584 n

Harper, W. R., 53 n

Harper's Magazine, 62, 76 n, 77 n, 193, 316 n, 602 n

Harris, Rachel S., 366 n

Hart, Horace, 389, 390 n

Hart, James D., 567 n

Harte, Bret, 96, 167, 168, 257

Hartford *Courant,* 525 n

Hartford Town Votes, 379

Hartford Wits, 71

Hartogensis, B. H., 218 n

Harvard University, 93 n, 125, 281 n, 387, 401

Harvey, B. T., 588 n

Haugen, Einas, 89 n

Hausen, T. Josephine, 370 n

Hawaii, English in, 694

Hawaiian language, 693 ff

Hawkins, Lewis, 305 n

Hawthorne, Nathaniel, 43, 125, 134, 287 n

Hay, John, 72

Hayden, Marie Gladys, 187 n

Hays, Mrs. B. K., 462 n

Hays, H. M., 619

Hazlitt, William, 558

Hazard, Ebenezer, 10 n

Headline vocabulary, 181 ff, 199

Healey, Ellis, 230 n

Healy, Jack, 588 n

Hearn, Lafcadio, 639

Hearst, William R., 184

Hebrew language, 79; loan-words from, 189

Heck, Henry J., 237 n, 464 n, 537 n, 562 n

Hecker, E. A., 265

Heckewelder, John Gottlieb Ernestus, 110

Heckstall-Smith, Brooke, 226 n

Heil, J. A., 366 n

Heimskringla, 633

Hellyer, C. R., 577 n

Hemingway, Ernest, 43

Hempl, George, 53, 350 n

Hench, Atcheson L., 180 n, 181 n, 482 n

Henderson, Leon, 194

Henley, W. E., 570

Henry, John, 131 n

Herold, A. L., 20 n

Herrick, Robert, 206 n

Herrig, Ludwig, 86

Herry, Edward, 587 n

Herschel, William, 223

Herzberg, Max J., 175 n

Heshin, H., 216 n

Hess, Charles E., 554

Hess, Irving C., 551 n

Hewart, Lord, 294 n

Hewlett, Maurice, 408

Heyne, Paul, 86

Hicklin, Maurice, 183 n, 199 n

Hiemenga, John J., 485 n, 624 n

Higginson, T. W., 366

Hildreth, Richard, 124 n

Hill, A. A., 365 n

Hills, E. C., 176, 178 n, 179 n, 185 n, 318 n, 445, 446, 450 n, 464, 636

Hillyard, Anna Branson, 258

Hindi language, 591, 593

Hindustani language, 597

Hinke, W. J., 482 n

Hinton, Eugene M., 424 n

Hirsch, Heinrich Reinhold, 620 n

Hispania, 592 n, 647 n

Hitti, Philip K., 496, 684

Hoar, G. F., 366

Hoboes' argot, 581 ff

Hodgin, Cyrus W., 530 n

Hoffman, Josiah O., 10 n

Hogan, Julia, 229

Hogue, Richard W., 190 n

Holbrook, Stewart H., 582 n, 587 n

Holladay, Lois, 606 n

Holland, J. G., 429 n

Holland, Lady, 120 n

Hollister, Howard K., 368 n

Hollywood, 39, 181, 195 n, 210 n, 267, 301, 305, 331, 567, 650, 658 n

Holmes, Burton, 171 n

Holmes, O. W., 71, 336, 565

Holmes, Urban T., 524

Holter, Thorvald E., 215 n

Holy Name Society, 313

Holzinges, John J., 369 n

Honorifics, 124, 266 n, 268, 271 ff, 289

Hood, Thomas, 71

Hoops, Johannes, 54, 86

Hoover, Herbert C., 480

Hoover, Theodore J., 291 n

Hopkins, Harry L., 276 n

Hopwood, David, 378 n

Hornberger, Theodore, 237 n

Horne, A. R., 617 n

Hornung, E. W., 256

Horwill, H. W., 181, 226, 249, 255, 274 n, 546

Hospital terms, 240

Hotten, J. C., 571

Household terms, 233 ff

Household Words, 575 n

Housman, Laurence, 455 n

Howard, Ebenezer, 546

Howard, Leon, 12 n, 16 n, 75 n

Howe, E. W., 337

Howe, Will D., 71

Howell, Clark, 276 n

Howells, W. D., 75, 76, 143 n, 168, 327

Hrdlička, Aleš, 488 n

Hsiao, Y. E., 691 n

Hu Shih, 688

Hughes, Charles Evans, 203

Hughes, Rupert, 77

Hugo, Victor, 556 n

Hujer, Oldrich, 659 n

Hulbert, J. R., 57

Hume, David, 465

Hummel, Arthur W., 688

Humphreys, David, 35, 339 n, 432 n, 472, 567

Hungarian immigrants, 680; language, 602 n; in America, 653, 680 ff; surnames, 477, 495, 496

Huntington Records, 434 n

Hutchinson, A. S. M., 455 n

Hurwitz, Maximilian, 297 n

Hutchinson, Thomas, 122

Huxley, T. H., 273, 470

Hyder, Clyde K., 551 n

Hygeia, 287 n, 307 n, 588 n

Hyman, Carolina Penna, 551 n

Hyne, C. J. Cutcliffe, 256

Icelandic immigrants, 633; language in America, 631 ff

Ichikawa, Sanki, 87, 88, 591, 692 n

Idaho, given-names in, 522

Idiom Neutral, 605

Illinois place-names, 536, 538, 541; speech of, 357

Immigration Acts of 1921 and 1924, 212

Immigration to the United States, 212 ff

Imperial Dictionary, 431 n

Improved Order of Red Men, 106 n

Independent, 258 n

Index Expurgatorius, W. C. Bryant's, 120, 184, 280; E. S. Gould's, 165; of Hollywood, 305

India, English in, 597

Indian languages, loanwords from, 104 ff, 110, 150, 189, 207, 221, 622; given-names, 513; place-names, 526, 527, 529, 531, 532, 539, 540, 541, 542

Indiana Magazine of History, 553 n

Indiana, speech of, 357, 472

Indianapolis *News*, 548 n

Industrial Worker, 175

Industrialisti, 493 n, 510 n

Infinitive, split, 203

Infixes, 315

Inge, W. R., 269 n, 312, 602

Ingersoll, C. J., 21

Ingleman, Anna A., 359 n

Innes, Guy, 378 n

Intensives, 162, 210

Interlingua, 605, 606

International Conference on English, 32 ff

International Convention for the Amendment of English Orthography, 399

International Correspondence Schools, 321 n

International Phonetic Alphabet, 320

International Telecommunication Convention, 207

International Y.M.C.A. College, 401

Intonation, 322

Iowa, given-names in, 521; place-names, 537, 538, 541
Iret, 605 n
Irish English, 72, 345, 436
Irish given-names, 505, 513, 518; immigrants, 476; influence on American, 154, 160, 200 n, 252, 346, 451 n; surnames, 477, 479, 504
Irish Statesman, 78
Irish World, 412 n
Irving, Washington, 16, 21, 67, 71, 110, 134, 135, 138, 149, 386, 526, 532
Irwin, Godfrey, 576 n, 581 n
Isenberg, Meyer, 125 n
Istochin, James R., 660
Italian given-names, 509; immigrants, 213, 214, 476, 646; language, 318, 590, 591, 593; in America, 640 ff; loan-words from, 222, 575; surnames, 493 ff
Ives, George B., 201 n, 352 n, 393 n
Ivey, Louise S., 669 n
I.W.W., 175, 190, 581

Jackson, Andrew, 132, 207
Jackson, Herbert Spencer, 177
Jackson, Louis E., 577 n
Jacobs, Joseph, 502 n
Jacobson, Eli B., 88n, 594 n
Jacobson, J. N., 83
James, A. Lloyd, 34 n, 329 n
James, Earle K., 591 n
James, Henry, 43, 67, 138, 204, 349
Japan, American in, 87; English in, 590, 597, 598
Japanese, literature on Americanisms in, 87
Japanese immigrants, 692; language, 591, 593; in America, 691 ff; loanwords from, 188, 373
Jednota, 661
Jefferson, Thomas, 11, 14,

17, 20, 116, 118, 119, 120, 125 n, 130, 131, 132, 147, 224, 381, 413
Jeffrey, Francis, 126 n
Jenifer, Daniel of St. Thomas, 518
Jerome, Jerome K., 564, 575 n
Jerrold, Douglas, 71
Jersey Dutch, 622
Jespersen, Otto, 87, 93, 94 n, 169 n, 202 n, 446 n, 455 n, 461 n, 563, 593 n, 597 n, 599, 600, 601, 602, 605, 606 n, 613 n
Jewish Daily Forward, 633
Jewish Encyclopedia, 507 n
Jewish given-names, 506 ff; immigrants, 213, 214, 295, 368, 476, 633 ff, 675; surnames, 477, 487 n, 497 ff
Jews in New York, 368
Joesten, Joachin, 296 n
Johns Hopkins Alumni Magazine, 531 n
John O'London's Weekly, 573
Johnson, Gerald W., 551 n
Johnson, Guy B., 363 n
Johnson, Harriet Lane, 479
Johnson, H. P., 362 n
Johnson, Hugh S., 567
Johnson, James Weldon, 296 n, 300, 363 n
Johnson, Magnus, 83
Johnson, Philander, 551 n
Johnson, R. U., 32 n, 33 n, 34 n, 63 n
Johnson, Samuel, 4, 9 n, 52, 93, 126, 137, 198 n, 350, 380, 381, 383, 384, 431 n
Johnson, Samuel, Jr., 385
Johnson, Spud, 550
Johnson, William E. (Pussyfoot), 255
Johnston, Harry, 171 n
Joke-towns, 553
Jones, Alice M., 426 n
Jones, Daniel, 202 n, 319 n, 323, 327, 329, 334 n

Jones, Grover, 584 n
Jones, Hugh, 49
Jones, J. J., 407 n
Jones, Lloyd, 34 n
Jonson, Ben, 97 n, 428 n, 558
Jopson, N. B., 659 n
Jordan, David Starr, 503
Jornal Portugues, 495 n, 509 n, 652
Journal of American Folk-Lore, 106 n
Journal of American Insurance, 579 n
Journal of Applied Psychology, 426 n
Journal of Engineering Education, 291 n
Journal of English and Germanic Philology, 52
Journal of the American Medical Association, 196, 307, 394 n, 411, 500, 562 n
Joyce, P. W., 160, 200 n, 249 n, 436, 451 n
Judd, Charles H., 421 n
Judd, Henry P., 373 n, 695 n
Juiliter, Mrs. Pieter, 544 n
Júlíus, N. Kristján, 633
Junco, Edith del, 593 n

Kamitsch, G., 86
Kane, Elisha, K., 363 n, 576, 578, 579
K'ang Yu-wei, 690
Kansas, 428 n; place-names in, 537, 541
Kansas City, 418
Kansas Magazine, 304 n
Kaplan, Albert, 217 n
Karpf, Fritz, 86, 322 n
Kartzke, Georg, 86
Katibah, H. I., 497 n, 513 n, 684
Katzenelenbogen, Uriah, 672 n
Kay, Leon L., 221 n
Keating, Isabelle, 316 n
Keeley, Mary Paxton, 573 n
Kellman, Frank A., 206 n
Kelly, Loudon, 450 n
Kelly, Obediah, 206

Kelly, Paul, 493
Kelly, R. S., 162 n
Kelty, Paul R., 551 n
Kemeny, George, 682 n
Kendall, Amos, 207
Kennedy, A. G., 54, 333 n, 360, 363 n, 365 n, 366 n, 370 n, 371 n, 378 n, 398 n, 405 n, 502 n, 527 n, 571 n, 612
Kennedy, John P., 135
Kennedy, W. S., 73 n
Kennell, Margaret, 514 n
Kent, Hugh, 586 n
Kent, James, 134
Kentucky, given-names in, 523; place-names, 535, 536, 539, 541; speech of, 257, 360, 361 n
Kenyon, John S., 58 n, 320 n, 326 n, 327, 334 n, 349, 350 n, 540 n
Ker, Edmund T., 527 n
Ker, W. P., 308
Kidds, H. Kendall, 236 n
Kiernan, James M. 186 n
Killheffer, Marie, 366 n
Killian, J. R., Jr., 179 n
Kimber, Edward, 274
King, Don, 180 n
King, Grace Elizabeth, 639
King, Lincoln, 460 n
Kingsley, Walter J., 189, 190
Kipling, Rudyard, 256, 544, 560 n
Kirkconnell, Walter, 601, 602
Kirkconnell, Watson, 663 n
Kirkpatrick, Helen P., 663 n
Kittredge, George L., 53 n, 309 n
Klaeber, Fr., 555 n
Klein, Nicholas, 581 n
Kleiser, Grenville, 120 n
Klimowicz, Paul, 675 n
Klondike gold-rush, 221
Knapp, Samuel Lorenzo, 134, 164 n
Knickerbocker Magazine, 156, 432 n

Knight, Sarah Kemple, 434 n
Knight's Journal, Mme., 428 n
Knights of Columbus, 297
Knights Templar, 273
Knortz, Karl, 86
Know Nothing movement, 476 n
Knox, Adrian, 396
Knox, Alfred, 32
Kober, Arthur, 369 n
Koenig, Walter, Jr., 200 n
Köhler, Friedrich, 86
Kohler of Kohler, 504
Kökeritz, Helge, 333 n
Koo, Vi-Kyuin Welling-ton, 513
Kormor, Hugo, 682 n
Kormos, Hugo, 496 n
Kostalek, J. A., 551 n
Krapp, George Philip, 8 n, 34 n, 43, 55 n, 58 n, 71, 109, 110 n, 116 n, 119 n, 121, 129, 187 n, 211, 317, 323, 332, 333, 334, 335 n, 336, 338, 340, 344, 345, 350, 356, 358 n, 362, 363, 365, 382, 398 n, 406, 428 n, 432 n, 444 n, 453, 455, 553, 562, 567, 568, 608 n, 612
Kretchman, H. F., 541 n
Krieger, W. M., 298 n
Kristensen, Evald, 86 n
Kron, R., 85
Krug, Elsie Clark, 691 n
Krumpelmann, John T., 292 n
Kuethe, J. Louis, 569 n
Kuhns, L. Oscar, 483 n
Kuiper, B. K., 485 n, 624 n
Kurath, Hans, 55, 58, 356, 356 n

Lacher, J. H. A., 296 n, 480 n, 494 n
Laffoon, Ruby, 273 n, 518
Lake, Charles Stewart, 551 n
Lamb, Charles, 71
Lambert, Claude, 574 n
Lambert, M. B., 544 n, 616 n
Lamont, T. W., 34 n
Landor, W. S., 16, 390

Landsmaal, Norwegian, 89 n
Lane, George S., 639, 640
Lane, James W., 491 n
Langdon, William M., 694
Langenfelt, Gösta, 333 n
Langereis, H. H. D., 624 n
Language, 52, 159 n, 316 n, 417 n, 593 n, 636 n, 639 n, 647 n
Language Monographs, 620 n
Lanigan, George T., 425
Lanusse, Armand, 640
Larabee, H. A., 84
Lardner, Ring, 352 n, 424, 425, 429 n, 430 n, 431 n, 432 n, 433 n, 434 n, 436 n, 443 n, 445, 447, 455, 457, 458, 460, 465, 468, 469, 560
Larousse's Grand Dictionnaire Universal, 548
Larsen, Thorleif, 334 n, 339, 343, 347
Latham, H. S., 392 n
Latil, Alexandre, 639
Latin, words from, 412, 413
Latin-America, English in, 591, 595 ff, 611; Spanish and Portuguese in, 89, 647, 649 ff
Law terms, 240, 278
Lawrence, F. W., 530 n
Laws to establish the American language, 81 ff
Learned, M. D., 617 n
Lederer, L. G., 198 n
Lee, F. B., 370 n
Lee, Gretchen, 585
Leech, Esther Gladys, 526 n
Leechman, Douglas, 150 n
Legal terms, 246
Lehman, Herbert H., 500 n
Leland, C. G. (Hans Breitmann), 72, 220, 224, 571, 696 n
Lemaître, Charles, 639
LeMesurier, H. G., 263, 264
Lemoine, Henry, 18

L'Enfant, Pierre-Charles, 546
Leonard, John M., 83
Leonard, S. A., 200 n, 203, 428 n, 430 n, 431 n, 432 n, 433 n, 434 n, 453 n
Leplae, Hortense, 624 n
Lepouzé, Constant, 639
Levering, Joshua, 480
Lewis, J. H., 198 n
Lewis, R. G., 211 n
Lewis, Sinclair, 67, 263, 285, 286, 546, 575 n
Lewis, Wyndham, 46, 47, 264, 329 n, 330, 407 n
Liang Chi-chao, 690
Liberty, 196 n, 561 n
Libraries in America, 18
Lienan, F. W., 195 n
Life and Letters, 48, 329 n
Lighthall, W. D., 371 n
Lilien, Ernest, 673, 675 n
Lim-boon Keng, 597
Lin Yutang, 691 n
Lincoln, Abraham, 157 n, 480
Lincoln's Gettysburg Address in Anglic, 405; in Panamane, 605 n
Lindbergh, Charles A., 491
Lindsay, Charles, 587 n
Lindsay, Dorothy N., 589 n
Lindsay, Vachel, 75, 77
Linguistic Atlas of the United States, 55 ff, 89, 321, 356
Linguistic Society of America, 58
Lins, James C., 617 n
Linthicum, Richard, 95 n
Lippincott's Magazine, 483 n, 544 n
Listener, 48 n, 232 n
Literary Digest, 44 n, 189 n, 190 n, 401, 560, 562 n
Literary Digest International Book Review, 66 n, 611 n, 614 n
Literary Magazine and British Review, 16 n
Lithuanian immigrants,

669; language in America, 669 ff
Little English, 605 n
Little Review, 407 n
Liu Fu, 691
Living Age, 210 n, 409, 558 n
Livingston, Arthur, 41, 544 n, 640, 641, 643, 644 n, 645 n, 646
Lloyd-George, David, 183 n, 597
Loane, George G., 210 n
Locke, D. R. (Petroleum V. Nasby), 71, 224
Locke, William J., 227
Lodge, H. C., 20 n, 20, 21, 131, 164 n, 203
Logan, George, 49
Lögberg, 633
Lomax, John A., 560 n
Lomoe, Wallace, 492 n, 631 n
London Association of Correctors of the Press, 389
London *Athenæum*, 258, 388
London *Daily Chronicle*, 171 n
London *Daily Express*, 31, 39, 230 n, 310
London *Daily Herald*, 40
London *Daily Mail*, 37, 234 n, 348 n
London *Daily News*, 38, 229 n, 572 n, 576 n
London *Daily Telegraph*, 174 n, 206 n, 207 n, 226 n, 229, 293
London *Evening Standard*, 47, 141 n, 269 n, 353 n
London *Jewish Daily Post*, 501 n
London *Mercury*, 311 n
London *Morning Post*, 43, 186 n, 222 n, 572 n
London *Nation*, 41, 189, 390 n, 476 n, 595 n
London *New Statesman*, 33, 44, 229 n
London, *New Witness*, 43
London *News Chronicle*, 39, 229 n
London *Observer*, 251 n

London *Review*, 470
London Saturday Review, 66 n, 225, 253 n, 269, 388
London *Sketch*, 240
London *Spectator*, 34, 230, 255 n, 269, 354 n, 571, 595 n, 608
London *Sunday Chronicle*, 315 n
London *Sunday Graphic*, 48 n
London *Sunday Times*, 190 n, 504 n
London *Times*, 29, 33, 43, 44, 94 n, 194 n, 200, 210 n, 229 n, 230 n, 249, 260, 262 n, 282, 293, 329, 384 n, 388, 389, 390 n, 409 n, 413, 527 n, 556, 595 n
Long, Frank D., 611 n
Long, Percy W., 53, 55 n, 209 n
Long, Theodore, 516 n
Longfellow, H. W., 135, 138
Longstreet, Augustus B., 71, 72
Longstreet, James, 480
Lontos, Sotirios S., 485, 512, 685, 686, 687 n
Loomis, C. P., 588 n
Loos, Anita, 500 n
Lopez, Vincent, 190
López-Penha, A. Z., 650
Lopushansky, Joseph and Michael, 587 n
Lord's Prayer, 404
Lorimer, George Horace, 181
Los Angeles *Examiner*, 457 n
Los Angeles *Times*, 304
Lossing, B. J., 131
Lostutter, Melvin, 551 n
Louisiana, 434 n; French of, 113, 214 n, 638 ff; place-names in 533, 536, 537, 541, 542; speech of, 638, 639; surnames in, 487 n
Louisiana Purchase, 111, 133 n
Louisiana State University Bulletin, 362 n

Louisiana State University Studies, 362 n, 638 n
Louisville *Herald-Post*, 206 n
Louisville *Times*, 561 n
Louis-Jaray, Gabriel, 548
Lounsbury, T. R., 61 ff, 69, 93 n, 101, 387, 400, 438, 452, 454, 608 n
Lovell, Charles J., 216 n, 495 n, 509 n
Low, Sidney, 36, 37
Lowell, Amy, 63, 201 n, 430 n
Lowell, J. R., 53 n, 71, 75, 119, 127, 155, 365, 366 n, 424, 429 n, 430 n, 431 n, 432 n, 435 n
Lower, J. L., 32 n, 34 n
Lowie, Robert H., 171 n
Loyalists, American, 130, 141 n
Lubbock, John, 399
Lüchow, August, 482 n
Lüdeke, H., 87
Ludlow, Louis, 219 n
Lund, Lenora, 525 n
Lussan, A., 639
Luther, Martin, 575
Lutoslawski, Wincenty, 87
Lyell, Charles, 118
Lyell, Thomas R. G., 570
Lyman, Johnny, 560
Lynch, Charles, 141 n
Lynchburg (Va.) *News*, 141 n
Lynching, 141 n
Lynd, Robert, 558

Maar, Charles, 530 n
Macaulay, Rose, 257
Macaulay, T. B., 120 n, 165, 223, 558
Macaulay, T. C., 606 n
MacChesney, Nathan William, 286
Macdonald, J. A., 206 n, 511 n
Macleish, Archibald, 43
Macmillan Company, 392
Macready, George, 525 n
Macy, Randolph B., 303
Madariaga, Salvador de, 602

Madden, Henry, 522 n
Madden, Henry Miller, 496 n
Madison, James, 11 n
Magyar Herald, 496 n
Mahoney, Jeremiah T., 276 n
Maine, 432 n; place-names in, 536, 539; speech of, 357
Malone, Kemp, 33, 52 n, 54, 322 n, 386 n, 443 n
Mally, J. W., 669 n
Manchester *Guardian*, 30, 228 n, 229 n, 586 n
Manchester *Guardian Weekly*, 78, 571 n
Manchester *Sunday Chronicle*, 38
Manchon, J., 555 n
Manly, J. M., 32 n, 53, 56 n, 551 n
March, F. A., 53 n, 399, 400
March, James E., 493
Marcy, William L., 79
Marines, U. S., 574
Marlowe, Christopher, 454
Marlowe, Julia, 331
Marquardt, Frederic S., 572 n
Marquis, Don, 63
Marriott, John A. R., 597
Marryat, Frederick, 25, 26, 248 n, 302, 330 n, 431 n, 481
Marsh, Edward, 258
Marsh, G. P., 60, 201, 324, 355
Marshall, Archibald, 227, 311, 351
Marshall, John, 14, 15, 118, 119, 134
Marston, John, 558
Martin, J. V., 332
Martin, Maria Ewing, 530 n
Martland, Harrison S., 562 n
Marx, Julius H., 585
Maryland Archives, 115
Maryland, given-names in, 522; place-names,

535, 536, 537, 538, 539, 540, 541, 542; speech of, 357; surnames, 483 n
Masefield, John, 227
Mason, C. P., 495 n
Mason, John M., 49
Massachusetts, 428 n; place-names in, 541; speech of, 366
Massachusetts Tech, 401
Master Printers' and Allied Trades' Association of London, 389
Masters, Edgar Lee, 63, 75, 157 n, 201 n
Mather, Cotton, 112, 126
Mather, George H., 238 n
Mather, Increase, 115
Mathews, M. M., 5 n, 8 n, 9 n, 35 n, 57, 118 n, 339 n, 354 n, 364 n, 568 n
Matthews, Albert, 109
Matthews, Brander, 63 n, 65, 66, 67, 169 n, 173, 174, 185 n, 388, 410, 558, 565, 566, 611
Matthews, Cornelius, 156
Matthison, Edith Wynne, 331
Matthison, Harriet E., 551 n
Maugham, W. Somerset, 431 n
Maurer, David W., 577 n, 579 n, 584 n, 587 n
Maurois André, 547
Mausser, O., 574 n
Maverick, George M., 189
Maverick, Maury, 116 n, 121 n, 551 n
Mawer, Allen, 527 n
Maxfield, E. K., 369, 432 n, 450 n
McAndrew, William, 272
McArthur, Lewis A., 151 n, 526, 534 n
McCartney, Eugene S., 574 n
McClintock, Theodore, 155 n
McClure's Magazine, 472 n
McCormick, Washington Jay, 81

McCullagh, Joseph S., 218 n
McDermott, John Francis, 495
McDevitt, William, 404
McDowell, Tremaine, 72 n, 363 n
McIver, M. E., 290 n
McKinsey, Folger, 551 n
McKinstry, H. E., 591 n, 650 n
McKnight, George H., 117 n, 126 n, 127 n, 167, 309 n, 312, 379 n, 387 n, 398 n, 455 n, 556, 563, 564 n, 569 n, 608 n
McLaughlin, Henry A., 392
McLaughlin, W. A., 295 n
McLay, W. S. W., 371 n
McLellan, Howard, 577 n
McMasters, J. B., 19
McPhee, M. C., 569 n
McTee, A. R., 588 n
McWilliams, Carey, 135 n
Mead, Leon, 173 n
Meanings, changed, 121 ff, 144
Mearns, Hugh, 472 n
Measures, names of, 255
Meats, names of cuts of, 236 n
Medary, Samuel, 205
Medical Press, 40 n
Medical terms, 411
Meekins, Lynn W., 38 n
Meeks, J. L., 551 n
Meine, F. J., 137 n
Melbourne *Herald,* 378 n
Mellen, Ida M., 546 n, 589 n
Mellis, John C., 226 n
Mellon, Andrew W., 80
Meloney, William Brown, 116 n
Melville, A. H., 557 n
Melville, Herman, 43, 54 n, 261 n
Mencken, H. L., 32, 450 n, 505 n, 602 n, 613, 614
Menner, R. J., 322, 332 n, 349, 367 n, 416 n, 421, 423, 428 n, 429 n, 430 n, 431 n, 432 n, 433 n,

434 n, 435 n, 440, 441, 442, 446, 453
Mercier, Alfred, 639
Meredith, Mamie, 137 n, 178 n, 272 n, 303 n, 505 n, 531 n, 537 n
Merry, P. B., 208 n
Merryweather, L. W., 313, 581 n
Mesick, J. L., 20 n
Methodists, 280, 309, 524
Metoula-Sprachführer, 85
Mexicans, 212 n
Mexican War, 534
Mexico, Spanish in, 650, 651
Meyer, A. W., 159
Meyer, Herman H. B., 266 n
Meysenberg, Hermann U., 86
Michigan place-names, 533, 536, 538, 542
Middle English, 345, 427, 454, 457 n, 465, 469; pronunciation, 397
Migliaacio, Edoardo (Farfariello), 641
Milburn, George, 188, 584 n, 588 n
Miller, Charles, 587 n
Miller, Daniel, 617 n
Miller, Edith, 419 n
Miller, Edmund E., 42 n
Miller, Edwin L., 211 n
Miller, Jessie I., 550 n
Milne, A. A., 455 n
Millner, Isaac A., 633 n
Milton, John, 117, 126, 128, 436, 459, 558
Mindi language, 622
Minneapolis *Daily News,* 286 n
Minneapolis Real Estate Board, 285
Minneapolis *Star,* 162 n
Minneapolis, surnames in, 477, 491
Minnesota place-names, 536, 538, 543
Mississippi place-names, 536, 537 n; speech of, 257
Missouri, 428 n; place-names in, 526, 533, 541,

542; speech of, 357, 360 n
Missouri Alumnus, 370 n
Missouri Historical Review, 526 n
Mitchel, John Purroy, 291
Mitchell, Anna C., 190 n
Mitchell, E. P., 185
Mitchell, Samuel L., 10 n
Mitteilungen der Akademie zur wissenschaftlichen Erforschung, 483 n
Mizner, Wilson, 560
Modern Language Association, 52 n, 55 n, 58, 431 n, 638 n
Modern Language Notes, 52, 172 n, 180 n, 638 n
Modern Philology, 52, 109 n, 172 n, 358 n
Modjeska, Helena, 489
Modjeski, Ralph, 489
Moen, N. T., 83
Moffat, Donald, 525 n
Moffett, H. Y., 200 n, 203
Moffett, W. A., 196 n
Molière, J. B., 572 n
Mondell, Frank W., 474
Money, names of, 116
Monkhouse, Allan, 571
Monroe, B. S., 366
Monroe (Mich.) *Evening News,* 304 n
Montaigne, Michel de, 96, 572 n
Montana place-names, 535, 536
Montesquieu, Charles, 126
Montgomery (Ala.) *Advertiser,* 300
Monthly Magazine and American Review, 11
Monthly Mirror, 15
Monthly Review, 14, 16 n
Montreal *Petit Journal,* 533 n
Moon, G. Washington, 27 n, 166
Moore, Francis, 3
Moore, H. E., 47
Moore, John M., 281 n
Moore, Thomas, 19
Morávek, S., 661

Moravesky, E., 663 n
More, Paul Elmer, 63 n
More, Thomas, 465
Morehouse, Harry Gwynn, 472 n
Morfill, W. R., 138
Morgan, B. Q., 199 n
Mori, Masatoshi Gensen, 692 n
Morison, S. E., 278 n, 281 n, 481 n
Morley, Christopher, 391 n
Mormons, 140, 589 n; their names, 516
Morris, Gouverneur, 116, 118
Morrison, Estelle Rees, 449 n
Morrison, Hugh, 494 n, 509 n, 649 n
Morse, John T., 125 n
Morse, Marion L., 197 n
Morse, W. R., 569 n
Mortimer, Raymond, 41
Morton, James F., 460 n
Morton, John, 479
Moscow (Idaho) *Star-Mirror*, 549
Motherwell, Hiram, 586 n
Moton, R. R., 300
Movie argot, 585; influence of, 37 ff, 221, 225, 233
Muir, P. H., 238 n
Muirhead's London, 86
Mulcaster, Richard, 590, 614
Mullen, Kate, 370 n
Müller, F. Max, 364 n, 426, 593 n
Müller, Leo, 169 n
Munroe, Helen C., 371 n
Murfree, Mary N. (Charles Egbert Craddock), 358 n
Murray, Gilbert, 408
Murray, James A. H., 389, 399
Murray, Lindley, 93 n, 380
Murry, J. Middleton, 42 n, 455 n
Musical terms, 250
Musser, Benjamin, 589 n

Mutschmann, Heinrich, 86, 87
Myers, Walter E., 173 n

Nadanyi, Paul, 682 n
Národné Noviny, 661
Nasal twang, 323, 330
Nashe, Thomas, 117
Nathan, Matthew, 277 n
National Advisory Council on Radio in Education, 307
National Association of Real Estate Boards, 285, 286
National Broadcasting Company, 332
National Council of Teachers of English, 51, 66, 428 n, 430 n, 431 n, 433 n, 453 n, 455 n
National Education Association, 400, 403
National Fertilizer Association, 292
National Geographic Magazine, 530 n
National Institute of Arts and Letters, 475
National Selected Morticians, 287
National Slovak Society, 661
Natural objects, names of, 114, 123, 246
Nautical terms, 116
Nautilus, 196 n
Navas, J., 321 n
Neal, John, 21, 429 n, 567 n
Nebraska place-names, 536, 537, 538, 541; speech of, 461
Negative, double, 468 ff
Nègre, 639
Negro American, 71, 212, 271, 316, 429 n, 431 n, 461; French, 639; given-names, 523 ff; surnames, 478
Negro languages, loan-words from, 112, 189
Neher, H. L., 426 n
Nelson, Herbert U., 286
Nelson, V. F., 579 n

Nesom, W. E., 449 n
Nevins, Allan, 20, 26 n, 275 n, 302
New England, speech of, 58, 71, 124, 132, 335, 336, 357 ff, 365, 366, 428 n, 431 n, 434 n
New England Magazine, 577 n
New England Palladium, 11
New Hampshire place-names, 538; speech of, 357
New Hampshire Spy, 569 n
New Haven Records, 434 n
New International Encyclopedia, 90, 196 n, 279
New Jersey Archives, 120
New Jersey, Dutch in, 622; place-names, 533; speech of, 257, 368, 369
New Life, 490 n, 511 n, 667 n
New London Monthly Magazine, 68
New Masses, 368
New Mexico *Historical Review*, 151 n, 153 n, 371 n
New Mexico place-names, 537, 541, 542, 543
New Orleans, speech of, 409; surnames in, 477
New Republic, 95n, 257 n, 286, 368
New York, 428 n; place-names in, 530, 532, 535, 536, 537, 539, 540; speech of, 257; surnames, 487 n
New York *Age*, 296 n
New York *American*, 206 n, 305, 410, 450 n, 588 n
New York City, surnames in, 477, 478
New York *Evening Post*, 42 n, 75 n, 190, 217 n, 305, 342 n, 387

New York *Evening Sun,* 188 n
New York *Galaxy,* 165 n, 199 n
New York *Graphic,* 560 n
New York *Herald,* 472
New York *Herald Tribune,* 180 n, 186 n, 269, 305, 331 n, 517 n
New York *Mirror,* 561 n
New York *Nation,* 190 n, 203, 259 n, 322 n, 364, 461 n, 515 n
New York *News,* 415 n
New York *Staats-Zeitung,* 620
New York *Sun,* 184, 185, 190 n, 305, 404, 473, 587 n, 638 n
New York *Telegraph,* 305
New York *Times,* 65, 178 n, 196, 271 n, 297, 299, 305, 307, 311, 325 n, 413, 421 n, 426 n, 471 n, 478 n, 500 n, 586 n, 589 n, 599 n
New York *Tribune,* 306, 387
New York *World,* 189 n, 260 n, 315, 370 n, 650 n
New York *World-Telegram,* 196 n, 208 n, 305
New Yorker, 186 n, 220 n, 290 n, 292 n, 305 n, 369 n, 425 n, 457 n
Newbolt, Henry, 32 n, 34 n
Newell, R. H., (Orpheus C. Kerr), 531
Newlin, Claude M., 365 n, 370 n
Newman, John, 472
News of the World, 226 n, 260 n, 310
Newspaper style, 137, 211; terms, 181 ff, 199
Newton, Simon, 515 n, 519
Niagara Falls, 136, 527, 531
Nice, Margaret Morse, 426 n
Nichols, E. J., 588 n

Nichols, Thomas L., 137
Nicholson, George A., 178 n
Nicholson, Meredith, 472
Nicknames, 519 n, 552
Nieland, Dirk, 623, 624 n
Niles' Register, 148, 226
Nippon Romazikwai, 692
Nisonen, Professor, 676
Nock, S. A., 86
Nöel-Armfield, H. T., 366
Non-English languages in the United States, 616 ff
Norman Conquest, 607
Norris, Charles G., 407 n
Norris, George W., 210 n
North American Review, 17, 21, 23, 67, 68, 75, 80, 119, 269 n, 337 n
North Carolina, given-names in, 524; place-names, 536, 537, 538, 541; speech of, 257, 462
North Dakota place-names, 537
Northrup, C. S., 53, 588 n
Norton, Charles Ledyard, 147
Norwalk records, 121
Norway, English in, 594
Norwegian immigrants, 476, 628; language in America, 627 ff; surnames, 492
Norwich (Eng.) Eastern *Evening News,* 229 n
Notes and Queries, 180 n, 391, 692 n
Nouns, 459, 461 ff, 566, 603
Novial, 605, 606
Novoye Russkaye Slovo, 663 n
Noyes, Theodore W., 551 n
Nugent, William Henry, 149 n, 562 n
Nyland, W. A., 624 n

Oberndorf, C. P., 497 n
O'Brien, Seumas, 407 n

O'Connor, Johnny, 560
O'Day, J. Christopher, 551 n
O'Donnell, Jack, 306 n, 587
O'Flaherty, Hal, 263
Ogden, C. K., 545, 590 n, 591 n, 592 n, 593 n, 596 n, 598 n, 603, 604, 605, 689 n
Ohio, 428 n; place-names in, 542; speech of, 357
Ohio Statesman, 205
O Independente, 495 n, 509 n, 652
Oklahoma place-names, 537
Ólafsson, Jón, 632 n
Old English, 427, 428 n, 437, 438, 448, 459, 464, 465, 469
Oliphant, S. Grant, 484
Oliver, Robert E., 581 n
O'London, John, 39 n
Onions, C. T., 229, 571
Onomatopeia, 183, 184, 199
Oppenheimer, Reuben, 589 n
Opportunity, 378 n
Orbeck, Anders, 333 n, 366
Oregon Geographic Board, 534
Oregon Historical Quarterly, 526 n
Oregon place-names, 526, 534, 538, 539
Ormin, 397
Orosz, Anthony J., 682 n
O'Rourke, L. J., 53 n, 421
Osborn, Chase S., 480 n
Oscillograph records of American speech, 321
Osgood, C. G., 32 n
Osgood, Henry Osborne, 190 n
Osler, William, 193
O'Toole, Richard F., 591 n, 651 n
Ottawa *Journal,* 371
Our Army, 573 n
Outdoor Life, 237 n
Outlook, 256 n
Overman, Lee S., 192 n
Owens, Bess Alice, 361 n

Owens, Hamilton, 185
Oxford Dictionary, 6 n, 22 n, 29, 30 n, 36 n, 55, 56, 57, 104, 108 n, 112, 118, 120 n, 140 n, 141 n, 142 n, 143 n, 145 n, 146, 150 n, 152, 155, 157, 158, 166, 167, 171 n, 185, 186 n, 187, 189, 190, 195 n, 206, 207 n, 210 n, 211 n, 216, 218 n, 219, 223 n, 225, 229, 252, 286, 295 n, 296 n, 297, 308 n, 342, 345 n, 389, 429 n, 467 n, 555, 567 n, 572
Oxford English, 328, 608, 609, 611; slang, 568
Oxford (N. C.) *Public Ledger*, 462 n
Ozark dialect, 308, 428 n, 430 n, 450 n, 462, 463, 469

Pacific Coast, given-names on, 522
Padín, José, 596 n
Page, Walter Hines, 95, 444 n
Paget, Ed. O., 86
Pall Mall Gazette, 193 n, 297
Palmer, H. E., 319 n, 332
Palmer, M. H., 222 n
Panama, Spanish in, 640
Panamane, 605 n
Papers of the Michigan Academy of Science, Arts and Letters, 574 n
Paradise of the Pacific, 694
Paris *Figaro*, 548
Paris *Herald*, 330 n
Park, Robert E., 620 n
Parmenter, C. E., 321 n, 322 n, 371 n
Parran, Thomas, Jr., 307
Parry, Albert, 587 n
Parton, James, 133
Partridge, Eric, 265 n, 314, 378 n, 519 n, 569 n, 570, 574 n, 575, 576
Parts of speech, interchange of, 92, 117, 374
Pascoli, Giovanni, 641, 642

Passing Show, 611 n
Passy, P. E., 320
Pater, Walter, 388
Patriarchs Militant, 273
Pattee, F. L., 91 n
Paulding, J. K., 16, 17, 19, 20 n, 21, 22, 23, 68, 71, 139
Pawlik, Martin, 86
Payne, L. W., Jr., 53
Peacock, T. L., 17
Pearce, T. M., 151 n, 153 n
Peck, J. M., 35, 36 n
Pedagogical Seminary, 557 n
Pedagogues, their influence, 51 ff, 211, 220, 326, 331, 332, 417, 454, 458, 472, 473; their language, 588
Peebles, Bernard M., 179 n
Peel, Robert, 576
Pemberton, Alfred, 261
Pemberton, Max, 256
Pendleton, Paul E., 361 n
Pennsylvania, 428 n, 616 ff
Pennsylvania-Dutch, see Pennsylvania-German
Pennsylvania German, 129, 154, 155, 159, 214, 544 n, 616 ff, 649
Pennsylvania Journal and Weekly Advertiser, 5
Pennsylvania place-names, 530, 536, 537, 539; speech of, 257; surnames in, 482 ff, 487 n.
Pennypacker, Samuel W., 480, 616
Penzl, Herbert, 366 n
Pep, 306 n
Pérennes, P., 639
Perkins, Anne E., 196 n, 366 n
Perry, Bliss, 63 n, 125, 204 n
Pershing, J. J., 480
Peters, R. R., 551 n
Petersburg, Va., *Progress-Index*, 446
Peterson, Mary B., 569 n
Pettus, W. W., 691 n

Pfeiler, W. K., 85
Philadelphia, 305 n, 335, 457 n, 530; surnames in, 477
Philadelphia *Evening Bulletin*, 197 n
Philadelphia *North American*, 401
Philadelphia *Public Ledger*, 305
Philippine Constitution, 376, 596
Philippines, English in, 596; languages of, 375
Phillips, Ze Barney T., 518
Philologians, their lack of interest in American, 52, 59
Philological Society of England, 399
Philological Quarterly, 172 n
Philological Society of New York, 10 n
Phipson, Evacustes, 267, 337
Phonetic alphabets, 320
Phonetic Society, 399
Phonograph records of American speech, 321
Phonographic Journal, 399
Pickering, John, 17, 35, 50, 97, 107, 143, 354
Pickering, Timothy, 381
Pickford, Mary, 183 n
Pidgin English, 597
Piers Plowman, 128, 195 n, 572
Pike, Ruth Schad, 505 n
Pingry, Carl, 569 n
Pinkney, William, 120
Pirandello, Luigi, 40, 41
Pitman, Isaac, 398, 399
Pittsburgh *Courier*, 219 n, 300, 524
Place-names, 129, 525 ff
Plimpton, E. A., 553
Plural, formation of, 412, 600, 612
Plymouth town records, 116
Pocket Oxford Dictionary, 263

Poe, Edgar Allan, 43, 138, 163, 175, 479
Poetry, 46
Polack, W. G., 200 n, 338 n
Police terms, 243
Polish given-names, 510; immigrants, 213, 214, 675; language in America, 673 *ff*; surnames, 477, 488
Political terms, 139, 147, 245, 284, 589 n
Pollock, F. Walker, 239 n
Polyglott Kuntze, 85
Pomeroy, Samuel C., 136
Pond, F. R., 588 n
Pontiac (Mich.) *Daily Press*, 486
Pooley, Robert C., 200 n, 417 n, 467 n, 468 n, 472
Pope, Alexander, 126, 303, 431 n
Pope, T. Michael, 254 n
Popular Science, 290 n
Port Folio, 11
Portland, Ore., *Journal*, 196 n
Portland *Oregonian*, 193, 587 n
Portmanteau words, 171
Portsmouth, R. I., Records, 379
Portugal, English in, 590, 595
Portuguese given-names, 509; immigrants, 653; language, 591, 593; in America, 652 *ff*; loan-words from, 216; surnames, 494
Pory, John, 114
Post, Anita C., 648, 649
Post, Emily, 278 n, 311
Post, Hermann, 217 n
Postoffice terms, 238
Pound, Ezra, 42 n, 461 n
Pound, Louise, 34 n, 53 *ff*, 57, 75 n, 169 n, 172 n, 173, 176, 180 n, 195 n, 210 n, 211 n, 219 n, 222 n, 274 n, 317, 332, 343, 350 n, 353, 407 n, 410, 412, 413, 461, 462, 463, 464 n,

505, 521, 538 n, 554, 562 n
Pound, Olivia, 211 n
Powell, J. W., 171 n
Power, C. Oliver, 551 n
Power, H. Darcy, 404
Power, William, 296 n
Practical Phonetics Group, Modern Language Association, 320
Prance, C. R., 388 n
Prefixes, 180 *ff*
Prendergast, Joseph M., 543 n
Prenner, Manuel, 568 n
Prepositions, 203
Present-Day English Group, Modern Language Association, 52 n, 321, 385
President of the United States, 275, 275 n
Prime, Sylvester, 364 n
Prince, J. Dyneley, 110 n, 378 n, 621, 622
Pringle, Henry F., 186 n
Printers' terms, 250
Prior, Matthew, 455
Prison argot, 580, 581
Proceedings of the American Philological Association, 370 n
Proceedings of the New York Historical Society, 526 n
Proceedings of the Pennsylvania German Society, 616 n, 617 n
Profanity, 308, 311 *ff*, 316
Professional Engineer, 290 n
Prohibition, 174 n, 219, 255, 292, 480
Prokosch, Eduard, 58 n
Pronouns, 201, 374, 378, 419 *ff*, 446 *ff*, 603
Pronunciation, American, 329 *ff*, 385, 611
Pronunciation, English, 329 *ff*
Protestant Episcopal Church, 268, 273, 280
Providence, R. I., *Journal*, 522 n
Psychoanalytic Review, 497 n

Psychological Clinic, 426 n
Psychological Corporation, 421 n
Public Health Reports, 279 n
Public Printer, 393
Public School English, 327, 330, 608, 611
Publications of the Historical Society of New Mexico, 647 n
Publications of the Modern Language Association, 49 n, 52 n, 64 n, 89 n, 201 n, 333 n, 359 n, 364 n, 381 n, 467 n, 519 n, 571 n
Publications of the Texas Folk-Lore Society, 588 n
Puerto Rico, English in, 595; Spanish, 649
Pulitzer, Joseph, 184, 315
Pullman Company, 147 n
Pullman News, 584 n
Pulvermacher, N., 507 n
Punch, 224 n, 259
Punctuation, 414, 415 n
Purchas's Pilgrimage, 105, 431 n
Pure, Simon, 41
Puritans, 114, 313, 333, 515, 516 n
Purvey, John, 448
Pusey, E. B., 223
Putnam, Ruth, 530 n

Quakers, 450 n, 589 n
Quarterly Journal of Speech, 363 n, 367 n
Quarterly Journal of Speech Education, 591 n, 692 n
Quarterly Journal of the New York State Historical Association, 530 n
Quarterly Review, 16, 19, 21, 22, 23, 78, 79, 118 n, 354 n, 574
Queen's Quarterly, 366 n
Quil, Grace Yee, 691 n
Quil, Rosalie Yee, 691 n
Quiller-Couch, Arthur, 94, 227, 408

Quinn, Philip G., 551 n
Quintilian, 97 n

Racketeers' argot, 579
Radio, 48, 306, 325 n, 329, 332, 347, 499
Radiographs, speech, 322
Radioland, 306 n, 587 n
Railroad Men's Maga-zine, 583 n
Railroad terms, 96, 146, 238, 247, 582, 583
Raleigh (N. C.) *News*, 300
Raleigh, Walter, 46 n, 408 n
Ramsay, David, 17
Ramsay, Robert L., 526 n
Ramsaye, Terry, 187 n
Ramus, Petrus, 455 n
Randolph, Vance, 308, 359, 360, 428 n, 430 n, 450 n, 462, 463, 469, 569 n
Randolph of Roanoke, John, 504
Ransom, J. C., 43
Rantamaki, John E., 676
Ratcliffe, S. K., 229
Rauch, E., 617 n, 618
Read, Allen Walker, 3 n., 10 n, 20 n, 29 n, 35 n, 49 n, 53, 57, 64 n, 79 n, 122 n, 181, 219, 274 n, 302 n, 303 n, 308, 313 n, 354 n, 370 n, 381 n, 385 n, 526, 527 n, 541 n
Read, William A., 53, 58 n, 352 n, 362 n, 528 n, 638, 639, 640
Real Academia Españo-la de la Lengua, 89
Realtors' Bulletin, 286
Received Standard Eng-lish, 327
Reed, Margaret, 353 n
Rees, John E., 530 n
Reflex, 502 n
Reid, Louise, 588 n
Reid, Thomas R., Jr., 378 n
Reinecke, John E., 372 n, 375 n, 691 n
Remény, Joseph, 496 n, 544 n, 682 n

Reves, H. F., 556 n
Review of Reviews, 376 n
Revolution, American, 4 ff, 130, 131, 274
Revue de Dialectologie Romane, 647
Revue Philosophique, 557 n
Revyuk, Emil, 489 n, 511 n, 664
Rhode Island, given-names in, 522; speech of, 357
Rice, Wallace, 431 n, 432 n, 443 n, 455 n, 466 n
Richardson, C. B. W., 588 n
Richardson, Samuel, 460, 472
Richmond *Christian Ad-vocate*, 281 n
Richmond *Examiner*, 298 n
Richmond *Times-Dis-patch*, 450 n
Ridderhof, Corneil, 287 n
Riedel, E., 214 n
Riegel, Jean E., 550 n
Rinaldi, Adelina, 646 n
Ritchie, Eleanor L., 543 n
Rittenberg, Louis, 602 n
Ritter, O., 555
Rivard, Adjutor, 544 n
Riverside Press, 292
Roback, A. A., 636 n
Roberts, A. J., 83
Roberts, Owen J., 194 n
Roberts, Willa, 196 n, 313 n
Robertson, Ben, 691 n
Robertson, D. M., 63 n
Robertson, Stuart, 257 n, 398 n
Robins, E. L., 292
Robinson, Andrew, 117
Rocha, João R, 495 n, 509 n, 652
Rockefeller Foundation, 58
Rockwell, Harold E., 182, 562 n
Rogers, Will, 425 n, 455, 471
Rollins, H. E., 522 n

Romanic Review, 544 n, 640
Rooney, Alicia L., 551 n
Roosevelt, Franklin D., 183 n, 186 n, 275 n, 480 n, 567
Roosevelt, Theodore, 107, 174, 183 n, 400, 403, 430 n
Rose, Howard N., 570 n
Rosecrans, W. S., 480
Ross, A. C., 551 n
Ross, Hal J., 180 n
Ross, Nellie Taylor, 284
Rossi, Adolfo, 640 n, 644 n
Rotary International, 211, 604 n
Rouquette, Adrien, 639
Rouquette, Dominique, 639
Rousseau, J. J., 126
Routh, James, 214 n
Royal Academy of Dra-matic Art, 329
Royal American Maga-zine, 8
Royal Commission on Venereal Diseases, 271 n
Royal Society of Canada, 396
Royal Society of Litera-ture, 329
Royall, Anne, 369
Rubinstein, Anton, 499
Rumania, English in, 590
Rumanian given-names, 509; immigrants, 653; language in America, 653 ff; surnames, 494
Runyon, Damon, 560
Ruppenthal, J. C., 217 n, 370 n, 484
Rush, Benjamin, 11
Ruskin, John, 460
Ruskowski, Carl J., 551 n
Russell, G. Oscar, 58 n, 322
Russell, J. A., 569 n
Russell, William, 337
Russia, American in, 88; English in, 594, 611
Russian given-names, 510; immigrants, 213, 663; language, 590, 592, 600,

602 n, 603; in America, 662 ff; loan-words from, 222; surnames, 489

Ruszkiewicz, A. E., 674 n

Rutter, H. F., 234 n, 238 n

Ryan, Frank, 82

Sacred Congregation of Rites, 282

Sadilek, Exha Akins, 146 n

Saerprent, 627 n

Sage, Evan T., 530 n

Saineau, Lazar, 574 n

Saint-Céran, Tullius, 639

Saintsbury, George, 408, 565

Salvation Army terms, 250, 283

Samolar, Charlie, 581 n

San Francisco *Chronicle*, 353 n, 463 n

San Francisco *News*, 462 n

San Francisco, surnames in, 478

San José *Mercury-Herald*, 288 n

Sandburg, Carl, 63, 74, 201 n, 263, 556 n

Sanstedt, Knut, 607

Sarafian, K. A., 497 n

Sargent, Epes W., 586 n

Sargent, John S., 67 n

Sargent, Porter E., 268 n

Sato, H., 692 n

Saturday Evening Post, 424 n, 577 n

Saturday Review of Literature, 4 n, 41, 47, 79 n, 391 n

Saul, Vernon W., 581 n

Savage, Howard J., 569 n

Savannah *News*, 267 n

Sayce, A. H., 97, 319, 340 n, 398 n, 399, 437, 455 n, 471

Scandinavia, English in, 594

Scandinavian given-names, 509; immigrants, 213; place-names, 543; surnames, 490 ff

Scandinavian Studies and Notes, 492 n

Schele de Vere, Maximilien, 36, 99, 106 n, 108, 158, 442, 481, 482 n, 533

Schiavo, Giovanni, 646 n

Schilles, Paul S., 421 n

Schlieder, Karl von, 109 n

Schoch, Alfred D., 85

Schöer, Arnold, 87

Schonemann, A. C. E., 588 n

Schönemann, Friedrich, 87

School and Society, 426 n

School Journal, 272 n

School Review, 332 n

School terms, 240 ff

Schoolcraft, H. R., 134, 526

Schoolmarm, see Pedagogues

Schuette, Oswald F., 186 n

Schultz, J. R., 219 n, 313 n, 585 n

Schultz, W. E., 569 n

Schuyler, George S., 300

Schwery, Edgard, 593 n

Science, 426 n

Scientific Monthly, 265 n, 426 n

Scotch, loan-words from, 117

Scot's Magazine, 17

Scott, C. P., 30

Scott, F. N., 4 n, 32 n, 34 n, 64, 65, 66, 322

Scott, Walter, 17, 18 n

Scottish Gaelic, 682, 683

Scribner's Magazine, 45, 228 n, 588 n

Scripps Northwest League, 306

Scripture, E. W., 321

Seaman, H. W., 233 n, 252, 260, 315, 323 n, 329 n, 609

Seaman, Owen, 259

Seashore, C. H., 491

Sebastian, Hugh, 569 n

Sechrist, Frank K., 557, 563

Sedgwick, Anne Douglas, 455 n

Seeley, J. R., 124 n

Sélincourt, Basil de, 95 n, 394 n, 610

Senn, Alfred, 512 n, 669, 670, 673 n

Senykoff, Sergei, 489 n, 663 n

Sephardic Jews, 501, 506

Serbian immigrants, 667; surnames, 489

Serbo-Croat language in America, 667 ff

Sewall, Samuel, 123 n, 429 n

Sex Hygiene Movement, 306

Seybert, Adam, 13 n

Seymour, Charlie, 562 n

Shakespeare, William, 93, 125 n, 126, 127 n, 128, 232, 299, 303, 312, 379, 383, 431 n, 436, 450, 454, 465, 470, 557 n, 572, 608

Shanklin, Edwin M., 551 n

Shanks, Edward, 46, 47

Shaw, G. B., 34 n, 40 n, 311, 329, 390, 610

Shaw, Henry Irving, 174

Shaw, H. W. (Josh Billings), 71, 442

Sheldon, E. S., 53

Shelley, P. B., 17, 432 n

Shenton, Herbert Newhard, 591 n, 596, 606

Shepherd, William G., 579 n

Sheridan, Thomas, 335

Sherman, L. Y., 192 n, 194 n

Sherman, Stuart Pratt, 305

Sherman, W. T., 517

Sherwood, Adiel, 364 n, 429 n, 430 n

Shewmake, Edwin F., 365 n

Shidler, John A., 569 n

Shipman, S. S., 592 n

Shoemaker, Henry W., 697 n

Shoemaker, William H., 592 n

Shorey, Paul, 63 n, 227, 559

Short, O. D., 553 n

Shorter, Clement K., 269

Sidmouth (England) *Observer*, 206 n

Sidney, F. H., 581 n, 584 n
Sidney, Philip, 459
Siegfried, André, 548
Sigourney, Lydia H., 134, 528 n
Silberer, Abraham, 497 n
Silveira, Peter L. C., 495 n, 509 n
Silverman, Sime, 560, 586 n
Simley, Anne, 629
Simmons, George H., 196 n, 197 n
Simplified Spelling Board, 400, 406
Simplified Spelling Leag, 400 n
Simplified spelling movement, 397 ff
Simpson, J. H., 517 n
Sims, J. G., Jr., 551 n
Sinclair, May, 455 n
Sizer, Miriam M., 521 n, 523
Skeat, W. W., 90 n, 399, 400
Skelton, Reginald, 415 n
Slang, 29, 555 ff
Slavonic Review, 663 n
Sloane, W. M., 63 n
Slovak languages in America, 659 ff
Slovenské Pohľady, 661
Smart, B. C., 696 n
Smith, Alfred E., 183 n, 338, 368, 560
Smith, C. Alphonso, 72 n, 449 n
Smith, Charles M., 85 n
Smith, Clay, 190 n
Smith College, 401
Smith, Edward Conrad, 589 n
Smith, E. Peshine, 147 n
Smith, Esther, 522 n
Smith, John, 3, 104, 105, 107, 112
Smith, Joseph C., 569 n
Smith, L. Pearsall, 46 n, 65, 155 n, 159, 178, 204, 329, 408, 409 n, 422 n
Smith, Maurice G., 577 n
Smith, Rebecca W., 364 n
Smith, Reed, 113 n, 363 n
Smith, Seba (Major Jack Downing), 71, 207

Smith, Sydney, 13 n, 19, 28, 225
Smith, Thomas, 398
Smith, William C., 372 n
Smithsonian Institution, 106 n
Sobel, B., 586 n
Social Hygiene Bulletin, 306 n
Social Register, 522
Société des Parlers de France, 89
Société du Parler Français au Canada, 638 n
Society for Pure English, 46, 408
Society for the History of the Germans in Maryland, 483 n
Söderblom, Nathan, 491
Sokolsky, George, 501 n
Soldiers' terms, 265
Solis Cohen, Solomon, 298, 502
Sonkin, Robert, 369 n
Soujanen, Reino W., 510 n
South, speech of the, 334, 337, 347
South African English, 108; Dutch, 622
South Atlantic Quarterly, 113 n
South Carolina place-names, 539, 541
South Carolina, speech of, 364 n, 365
South Dakota place-names, 537
South Holland language, 622
Southern English, 41, 327 ff
Southern given-names, 520
Southey, Robert, 16, 19, 22, 117, 223
Southport *Visiter*, 329
Southwest Review, 129 n, 135 n, 567 n
Spaeth, Sigmund, 425 n, 457 n
Spanish given-names, 508; language, 509, 590, 591, 592, 593, 602 n, 603; in America, 647 ff; loan-

words from, 111 ff, 150, 152, 177, 220, 370, 376, 377, 558; place-names, 534, 539, 542, 547; surnames, 494
Spanish-American War, 184, 220
Spanish-speaking immigrants, 651
Spear, J. W., 551 n
Spectator, 380, 438 n, 465
Speech tunes, 322, 362, 369
Spelling, 379 ff, 400, 603, 605, 612
Spelling-pronunciation, 324, 339, 340, 346, 352, 540
Spelling Reform Association, 399
Spenser, Edmund, 590
S.P.E. Tracts, 46 n, 56 n, 64 n, 111 n, 127 n, 138 n, 151 n, 155 n, 197 n, 203 n, 223 n, 228 n, 272 n, 282, 328, 358 n, 378 n, 390 n, 408 n, 409 n, 410 n, 412 n, 450 n, 597 n, 666 n
Spies, Heinrich, 87
Spiller, R. E., 130 n
Sporting terms, 236, 248, 252, 562, 651, 652
Sprachatlas des Deutschen Reiches, 89 n
Sprachführer, 85
Squire, J. C., 34 n, 42 n
Stabell, Otto, 551 n
Stahlberg, John A., 491 n, 626, 627 n
Stallings, Laurence, 265
Stanculescu, George, 494 n, 509 n, 653, 654
Standard Dictionary, 144 n, 297, 411 n, 560
Standardization of English, 126
Stanley, Johnny, 560
Stanley, Marion E., 524 n
Stars and Stripes, 574 n
State Government, 276 n
Steadman, J. M., Jr., 177 n, 211 n, 309, 310 n, 359 n
Stebbins, Henry E., 38 n
Steel and Garnet, 569 n

Steele, Richard, 71, 126, 472, 569
Stefánsson, Vilhjálmar, 631, 632
Stein, Gertrude, 175 n
Stein, Kurt M., 620
Stenton, F. M., 527 n
Stephanchev, Stephen, 669 n
Stephanovsky, Peter, 663 n
Stephen, Leslie, 470
Stephens, Henry, 461 n
Stephens, James, 455 n
Stephenson, George M., 492, 624
Stephenson, R. M., 262 n
Sterling, T. S., 242 n
Stevens, Harry Mozely, 186 n
Stevens, James, 587 n
Stevenson, R. L., 194 n, 229, 470, 525
Stewart, Chalmers K., 587 n
Stewart, George R., Jr., 548, 549
Stewer, Jan, 226 n
Still, James A., 521 n, 522
Stinchcomb, James, 691 n
Stinchfield, Sara M., 426 n
St. Louis *Globe-Democrat*, 218 n
St. Louis *Republic*, 189
St. Louis *Westliche Post*, 620 n
Stockbridge, Frank Parker, 651 n
Stock-exchange terms, 244
Stockholm, English in, 594
Stone, Walter C., 332
Storer, Edward, 41
Storfer, A. J., 208 n
Stork, Willis, 562 n
Story, W. W., 17
Stowe, Harriet Beecher, 363 n
St. Paul *Dispatch*, 215 n
St. Paul, surnames in, 477
St. Paul's School, 268
Strachey, Charles, 44
Strachey, William, 104

Stradonitz, Stephen Kekule von, 483 n
Strakosch, Edgar, 187
Stranger, R., 587 n
Straumann, Heinrich, 184 n
Street names, 544 ff
Streeter, Edward, 425 n
Stretch-forms, 176
Stribling, T. S., 271
Strong, W. D., 371 n
Struble, George G., 370 n, 375 n, 376 n
Stuart, Charles, 291 n
Stuart, J. E. B., 287 n
Studi Baltici, 512 n, 669 n
Studia Neophilologica, 333 n
Studies in English Literature, 692 n
Sturtevant, E. H., 53, 58
Style, American, 42
Style book of Detroit *News*, 414 n; of Scripps-Howard papers, 415; of New York *Herald Tribune*, 415 n; or Chicago *Tribune*, 415 n; of New York *News*, 415 n
Style manual of the Government Printing Office, 393
Su Chen Ho, 691 n
Suburbs, names of, 546
Suffixes, 176 ff, 218, 219, 221, 222
Sullivan, A. E., 174 n, 226 n
Sullivan, Joseph M., 577 n
Sunday, William A., 485 n
Sunderland *Echo*, 228 n
Sunnanfari, 632 n
Suojanen, Reino W., 493 n, 676 n
Supreme Court of the United States, 203
Supreme Court Reporter, 131 n, 194 n, 203 n
Surgery, Gynecology and Obstetrics, 40 n
Surnames, 474 ff; as given-names, 516
Survey, 293 n
Sutherland, George, 131 n

Svoboda, 489 n, 511 n
Swadesh, Morris, 417 n
Swaen, A. E. H., 532 n
Swann, Nancy Lee, 691 n
Swanson, Gloria, 183 n
Swanson, Roy W., 215 n, 490, 491, 530 n, 543 n
Swearing, 311 ff, 316
Sweden, English in, 607
Swedish immigrants, 476, 627; language, 594; in America, 624 ff; loan-words from, 215; surnames, 477, 490 ff
Swedish-American Historical Bulletin, 530 n, 543 n
Sweet, Henry, 333 n, 399, 438, 448 n, 452, 455 n, 456, 458, 469
Swem, E. G., 116 n, 365 n
Swenson, Elaine, 604 n, 605 n
Swenson English, 605 n
Swift, Jonathan, 126, 169 n, 459, 558, 569
Sydney *Evening News*, 378 n
Sylcauga, Ala., *News*, 522 n
Symonds, Percival M., 424 n
Syrian given-names, 512; immigrants, 683; surnames, 477, 495, 496
Syrian World, 497 n, 513 n, 684
Sze, Sao-ke Alfred, 513

Taft, W. H., 403
Talkies, influence of, 38 ff
Tall talk, 136 ff
Tallichet, H., 153 n
Talman, Charles Fitzhugh, 409
Tammany Hall, 106 n, 148
Tank Corps, 202
Taos *Valley News*, 550
Tatler, 169 n
Taylor, Bayard, 135, 219
Taylor, Jay L. B., 360 n, 430 n
Taylor, William, 223
Taylor, W. O., 188
T-Bone Slim, 175

Teachers College Record, 424 n

Teachers of English, their number, 53 n

"Ten Nights in a Barroom," 139

Tennessee, 428 n; given-names in, 521; place-names, 536, 544; speech of, 257, 360, 462

Tennyson, Alfred, 399, 431 n

Testut, Charles, 639

Texas, given-names in, 522; place-names, 530 n, 536, 537, 540, 541; speech of, 357, 361

Thackeray, W. M., 431 n, 472

Theater terms, 236, 585

Thomas, C. K., 367 n, 368 n, 369 n

Thomas, E. H., 150 n

Thomas, Jameson, 39

Thomas, Rowland, 551 n

Thompson, Alexander M., 598 n

Thompson, Blanche Jennings, 406 n

Thompson, Herbert M., 595

Thompson, William F., 137 n

Thompson, William H., 83, 272

Thorndike, A. H., 52 n

Thorndike, E. L., 170 n, 421 n

Thornton, R. H., 12, 14, 36, 37 n, 54 n, 100, 104, 105, 108 n, 112, 113, 115 n, 119 n, 128, 136, 139, 142, 143, 144 n, 146, 148, 149, 150, 151, 156, 157 n, 158, 167, 171 n, 204, 205, 252, 254, 295 n, 296 n, 301, 316, 352, 431 n, 516, 570

Thugut, Franz Maria von, 478

Tibbals, Kate W., 450 n, 589 n

Ticknor, George, 135

Tidewater gentry, 139

Time, 230 n, 280

Time and Tide, 230 n

Tinker, Edward Laroque, 639 n

Tobin, Edward J., 455 n

Tojo, M., 89 n

Tokimasa, Aiko, 372 n, 375 n

Toland, Leigh, 551 n

Tomita, G., 88

Tooke, John Horne, 466

Toronto *Saturday Night*, 517 n

Toronto *Week*, 371 n

Town Topics, 157

Townsend, E. W., 367 n

Trager, Geo. L., 334 n 543 n

Tramps' argot, 581 ff

Transactions of the Albany Institute, 35 n

Translations into American, 40 ff

Traubel, Horace, 73

Tressler, J. C., 63 n, 66

Treviño, S. N., 321 n, 322, 371 n

Triad, 378 n, 397

Trollope, Frances, 301, 330

Trollope, Anthony, 224

Trumbull, J. H., 107, 399

Tsung-tse Yeh, 591, 689

Tucker, Gilbert M., 101, 128 n, 269, 295 n, 316, 395, 540 n

Tucker, R. Whitney, 159 n

Tucker, Thomas G., 228 n

Tugwell, Rexford G., 276 n

Tully, Jim, 151 n

Turano, Anthony M., 640 n, 643, 644, 645 n

Turkey, English in, 590, 595

Turnbull, John, 111

Turner, Frederick J., 154 n

Tyler, Royall, 365

Tysell, Helen Trace, 185 n, 426 n, 443 n

Tyson, F. H., 277 n

Uhström, W. P., 555 n

Ukrainian given-names, 511; immigrants, 663;

language in America, 663 ff

Ulmer, J. R., 573 n

Uncle Remus's Magazine, 449 n

Uncle Shylock, 28

"Uncle Tom's Cabin," 135, 139

Underworld argot, 576 ff

Ungdomsvännen, 624 n

Unitedstatish, 77

University of Chicago Linguistic Studies in Germanic, 178 n

University of Missouri Bulletin, 419 n

University of Missouri Studies, 640 n

University of North Carolina Magazine, 364 n

University of Texas, 522 n

University of Virginia, 93 n, 272

University terms, 241 ff

Untermeyer, Louis, 74, 75 n

Urbana, O., *Citizen*, 205

U. S. Geographic Board, 414, 489 n, 517 n, 526, 529, 531, 533, 535, 537, 538, 539, 542, 553, 653 n, 662 n

U. S. Official Postoffice Guide, 157 n, 526, 528

U. S. Public Health Service, 411

U. S. State Department, 410

Vachell, Horace Annesley, 572

Vallée, Rudy, 306 n, 466

Valley German, 619

Van Andel, Henry J. G., 485 n, 623

Van Buren, Martin, 148

Van den Bark, Melvin, 370 n, 587 n

Van Dam, B. A. P., 312

Van Doren, Carl, 91 n

van Dyke, Henry, 63 n, 64, 65, 67

van Hinte, J., 623 n

Van Hoven, Harry, 586 n
Van Lancker, J. L., 624 n
Van Patten, Nathan, 363 n
Van Riemsdyck, D. J., 624 n
Van Stantvoord, George, 263
Vancouver *Sun*, 206 n
Vanity Fair, 269, 560 n, 586 n, 588 n
Vapaa, Ivar, 493 n, 510 n, 680 n
Variety, 193, 195 n, 210 n, 237 n, 282 n, 298 n, 307 n, 407, 500 n, 560, 577 n, 586 n
Vasché, Joseph B., 543
Vassar College, 303
Vaughn, Herbert H., 640 n, 644 n
Verband Deutscher Amateurphotographen-Vereine, 172 n
Verb-phrases, 197 ff
Verbs, 114, 117 ff, 140 ff, 191 ff, 231, 250, 252, 374, 419 ff, 427 ff, 558, 566, 603, 613
Verger, V., 627 n
Vestur-íslenska, 631, 632, 649
Vieni, Rosina, 642
Vigne, G. T., 26
Viking, Valdemar, 627 n, 630 n
Virginia, 428 n, 619; given-names in, 521, 523, 524; place-names, 536, 538, 539, 541; speech of, 78, 337, 360, 365, 471, 503, 619
Virginia Literary Museum, 36 n
Vizetelly, Frank H., 171 n, 188, 189, 332, 426 n, 593
Vocabularies, estimates of, 426, 603
Vogue-words, 210, 465
Voice, American, 322
Voight-Goldsmith, Frau, 86
Volapük, 605
Voltaire, 126, 413
Vossische Zeitung, 208 n

Vowels, 320, 328, 330, 334 ff, 601, 612
Vulgate, American, 138, 416 ff

Wachtel, C. H., 675 n
Waddel, Moses, 140 n
Wade, Thomas, 691
Wagstaff, W. B., 34 n
Wald, Lillian D., 487 n
Waldo, John, 11 n, 17
Walker, Francis C., 334 n
Walker, John, 339, 343, 345, 347, 349 n
Wallace, Edgar, 257
Wallasey, chief constable of, 39
Waller, Edmund, 293
Wallis, Johannis, 201 n
Walsh, Robert, Jr., 21
Walsh, Thomas J., 192 n
Walwoja, 493 n, 510 n
Wansey, Henry, 18
War Cry, 283 n
War of 1812, 16, 67, 131, 330, 567, 639
Ward, Harry F., 461 n
Ward, Mrs. Humphrey, 227
Ward, Ned, 313
Ware, J. R., 141 n, 146
Warnock, Elsie L., 145 n, 176 n
Washburn, Lennie, 562 n
Washington, George, 118, 130, 381
Washington, Martha, 284
Washington *Post*, 460 n
Washington *Star*, 496 n
Washington State place-names, 538, 542
Wasmuth, Hanes-Werner, 575 n
Wasson, Mildred, 258
Watson, George, 57
Watson, H. B. Marriott, 257
Watson, J. A., 229
Watson, John B., 178 n
Weather Bureau, 266
Webster, Daniel, 139
Webster, John, 454
Webster, Noah, 7, 9, 10, 12, 14, 25, 43, 52, 60, 93 n, 97 n, 109, 110, 118, 124, 131 n, 134, 135, 140,

151, 165, 269 n, 302 n, 303, 324 n, 335, 339 n, 340, 341, 345, 347, 352, 369, 379 ff, 399 ff, 417 n, 428 n, 429 n, 431 n, 432 n, 470 n
Webster's New International Dictionary, 113, 123 n, 145 n, 151, 156, 170 n, 175, 178 n, 187, 188, 189, 191, 193, 206, 216, 219, 225, 296 n, 297, 308 n, 320 n, 324 n, 342, 392 n, 393, 394 n, 407, 408 n, 411 n, 414 n, 460 n, 555
Webster's Spelling Book, 383, 385
Weekley, Ernest, 43, 126 n, 145 n, 156, 188, 197, 232, 545 n, 546, 547, 555, 607
Weeks, A. L., 415 n
Weeks, John W., 198 n
Wefald, Knud, 276 n
Weil, Maurice K., 547 n
Weinbaum, Mark, 663 n
Weiss, George, Jr., 620 n
Wellesley College, 401
Wells, H. B., 489 n, 636 n, 662
Wells, H. G., 256
Welsh Language in America, 682; surnames, 504
Wendell, Barrett, 134, 426, 455 n
Wentworth, Harold, 172 n
Wentworth, John, 8
Werner, W. L., 180 n, 561 n, 588 n
Weseen, Maurice H., 570
Wesley, John, 3, 384
West, Michael, 606 n
West, M. P., 604 n
West, Rebecca, 41
West, S. George, 595 n
West Saxon dialect, 607
West Virginia place-names, 535, 536, 537; speech of, 360, 361 n
West Virginia Review, 361 n
Westendorff, Karl, 575 n

Western American, 137, 327 n, 333, 356 ff, 366, 370 n

Western emigration, 133

Western Union Telegraph Company, 157 n, 195 n, 316 n, 414 n

Western Recorder, 338 n

Westernisms, 133, 137, 153, 224

Westminster Gazette, 36, 45, 258

Westminster (Md.) *Democratic Advance*, 484 n

Westricher dialect, 616, 617

Whaley, Marcellus S., 363 n

Wharton, Morton Bryan, 179 n

Whately, Roger, 306 n, 586

Wheatley, Katherine E., 362 n

Wheeler, B. I., 53 n

Wheeler, Kettredge, 183 n

Wheeler, William Morton, 265 n

Whewell, William, 559

Whibley, Charles, 31

Whicher, Mrs. Frances M., 71

Whicher, George F., 224

White, Charles, 186 n

White, Frederick, 237 n

White, Percy W., 584 n, 586 n

White, R. G., 61, 62, 101, 118, 121, 158, 164, 165, 168 n, 199, 204, 268, 280, 297, 303 n, 304, 320, 323, 342, 345, 398 n, 540, 612

White, Walter, 141 n

White, Wilfrid, 206 n

Whitehead, Henry S., 378 n

Whitman, Walt, 54 n, 67, 73, 74, 75, 137, 147 n, 156, 167, 175, 327, 363, 410, 526, 531 n, 552, 556 n

Whitney, W. D., 53 n, 60,

164, 342, 399, 455 n, 559, 563

Who's Who, 503 n

Who's Who in America, 475, 488 n, 503 n, 504, 515, 519

Who's Who in Engineering, 291 n

Wignall, Ernest, 238 n

Wilde, Oscar, 363

Wiley, H. A., 574

Wilkins, John, 398

Willebrandt, Mabel Walker, 284

Williams, Guy, 587 n

Williams, R. O., 135, 253

Williams, Talcott, 196 n

Williams, Whiting, 270

Wilson, A. J., 245 n

Wilson, Charles M., 361 n

Wilson, Edmund, Jr., 265

Wilson, G. M., 418 n

Wilson, George P., 362 n

Wilson, J. Dover, 34 n

Wilson, W. A., 306

Wilson, Woodrow, his use of Americanisms, 40, 95, 207, 460, 597

Wimberly, Lowry Charles, 148 n, 589 n

Winchell, Walter, 552 n, 560, 561 n, 586

Winer, Earl L. and Samuel G., 507 n

Wingfield, Frederick S., 404

Winslow, Thyra Samter, 282 n

Wirt, William, 480

Wisconsin place-names, 533, 536, 537, 538, 542; speech of, 627

Wise, C. M., 362 n, 363 n

Wise, H. P., 188

Wise, Isaac M., 297 n

Witherspoon, John, 4 ff, 60, 64, 143, 169, 354, 428 n, 431 n, 434 n, 442, 452 n, 567

Withington, Frederick B., 373 n, 694

Withington, Robert, 172 n, 312 n

Witman, Fred, 587 n

Wittmann, Elisabeth, 85, 170 n, 192

Witwer, H. C., 425 n

Wolfe, George, 634 n

Wolfe, Humbert, 230 n

Wolverton, Charles, 188, 584 n

Woman's Home Companion, 262 n

Wood, Francis A., 145 n, 172 n

Wood, William, 104

Woodhouse, Henry, 493

Woodridge, William, 385

Woodward, William E., 174

Woofter, Carey, 361 n

Woolf, Virginia, 47

Worcester, J. E., 60, 93 n, 336, 386, 387

Word-Lore, 588 n

Word Study, 175 n

World Almanac, 230 n, 478 n, 515 n, 552 n, 593 n

World War, 67, 84, 91, 180, 183, 209, 219, 225, 248, 254, 300, 499, 573, 574

World's Work, 587 n, 590 n

Wright, Almroth, 273

Wright, Joseph, 363

Wright, Sewell Peaslee, 262 n

Writer's Digest, 262 n, 584 n

Writer's Monthly, 366 n

Writers, their attitude toward Americanisms, 67 ff

Wundt, Wilhelm, 426

Wycliffe, John, 128, 448

Wyld, H. C., 311 n, 326, 327, 333 n, 350, 441 n

Wyoming place-names, 541; speech of, 457 n

Yale Review, 173 n, 198, 639 n

Yale University, 281 n, 345

Yankee dialect, 71, 365

Yankee-Dutch, 623, 649

"Yankee in England, The," 35
Yartin, Joseph, 496 n, 682 n
Yeaman, M. V. P., 211 n
Yeats, W. B., 200
Yen, W. W., 591
Yiddish language in America, 633 ff, 653; loan-words from, 42, 189, 214, 216, 386, 369, 578, 580
Y.M.C.A., 84

Yonkers *Herald Statesman*, 549 n
Young, Arthur A., 691 n
Young, Ella Flagg, 460 n
Yugo-Slavic surnames, 489
Yule, Emma Sarepta, 375 n, 596 n

Zachrisson, R. E., 333 n, 405, 607 n
Zallio, A. G., 640 n
Zandvoort, R. W., 611

Zarathustra, 642 n
Zeisberg, Carl, 471
Zeta Beta Tau fraternity, 499, 499 n, 507
Zeta Beta Tau Quarterly, 507
Zettel, Rose, 659 n
Zetterstrand, E. A., 624 n
Zhitlowsky, Ch., 634
Zipf, George Kingsley, 472

A Note on the Type in which this Book is Set

This book was set on the linotype in Janson, a recutting made direct from the type cast from matrices (*now in possession of the Stempel foundry, Frankfurt am Main*) made by Anton Janson some time between 1660 and 1687.

Of Janson's origin nothing is known. He may have been a relative of Justus Janson, a printer of Danish birth who practised in Leipzig from 1614 to 1635. Some time between 1657 and 1668 Anton Janson, a punch-cutter and type-founder, bought from the Leipzig printer Johann Erich Hahn the type-foundry which had formerly been a part of the printing house of M. Friedrich Lankisch. Janson's types were first shown in a specimen sheet issued at Leipzig about 1675. Janson's successor, and perhaps his son-in-law, Johann Karl Edling, issued a specimen sheet of Janson types in 1689. His heirs sold the Janson matrices in Holland to Wolffgang Dietrich Erhardt, of Leipzig.

Composed, printed and bound by The Plimpton Press, Norwood, Mass. Paper made by S. D. Warren Co., Boston. Designed by W. A. DWIGGINS.

β